GUN TRADER'S GUIDE

19th Edition—Completely Revised and Updated

STOEGER PUBLISHING COMPANY

COVER DESIGN AND PHOTOGRAPHS: Ray Wells

FRONT COVER: The two beauties pictured on the front cover were both produced in the late-1800s in Connecticut. The rifle at left is the Winchester Model 1873 Deluxe, 1st Model. In 44-40 caliber, it is silver plated and profusely engraved, with additional engraving on the hammer, lever, magazine-retaining bands, and the end of the tubular magazine. It is the only known rifle with engraving on the magazine and was produced in 1877 by the Winchester Repeating Arms Company of New Haven. The Colt Single Action Army Revolver at right is a 45 caliber with 7 1/2-inch barrel and smooth walnut grips. It was manufactured in 1873, by the Colt Patent Fire Arms Company of Hartford.

Published by:
Stoeger Publishing Company
5 Mansard Court
Wayne, New Jersey 07470

International Standard Book Number: 0-88317-193-7
Library of Congress Catalog Card No.: 85-641040

Manufactured in the United States of America

In the United States, distributed to the book trade and to the sporting goods trade by:
Stoeger Industries
5 Mansard Court
Wayne, New Jersey 07470
201-872-9500 Fax: 201-872-2230

In Canada, distributed to the book trade and to the sporting goods trade by:
Stoeger Canada Ltd.
1801 Wentworth Street, Unit 16
Whitby, Ontario, L1N 8R6, Canada

INTRODUCTION

Firearms comprise a unique position in our culture. In terms of design, they span a wide range—from the blackpowder fowlers of centuries ago to the sleek stainless steel pistols of the present. In terms of function, few human-contrived devices can boast such a working range, for many of the firearms that were produced at or before the turn of this century are still in use today—and are still doing what they were intended to do.

The status of firearms in our society—as hunting tools, as implements for competitive Olympic sports, as components of a valuable collection, or as weapons of war and self-defense—has created a booming market. Trading at gun shows and used-gun shops is healthy because most buyers are very aware that firearms are a lifetime investment, which usually increases in value over time.

Why is it necessary and important to know the value of firearms? Aside from wanting to know how much to charge for a firearm you want to sell, or how much to pay for one you wish to buy, we humans seem to need to know the value of our personal belongings in order to assess their relative worth, to determine how much they should be insured for and to whom they should be entrusted for safe keeping. This is especially true of older firearms that cannot be referenced via the usual commercial outlets.

We have all heard stories of someone finding an old letter in an attic. Upon checking the value of the unusual stamp on it, the owners were astounded to discover that it was worth tens of thousands of dollars. A gun, too, can be a valuable treasure that had been stashed away in some covert alcove and all but forgotten. How do you determine whether it is an old wallhanger or a valuable collector's item? Faced with this question, a person quickly realizes that it is a lot more difficult to obtain reliable resources to assess the value of a firearm than the value of a rare postage stamp.

With the gun, other questions arise: How does its current condition affect its price? Is it likely that the firearm will increase even more in value over, say, the next five years? These and a multitude of other questions are answered in this current edition of GUN TRADER'S GUIDE, a publication whose usefulness approaches that of the firearms themselves. In terms of longevity, GUN TRADER'S GUIDE has been in print for more than 40 years, serving gun dealers, collectors, gunsmiths, law-enforcement agencies, forensics experts, military personnel, museum curators, auctioneers, insurance adjusters and appraisers, the general shooting public, and shooting writers and editors. In short, it is The Wall Street Journal of the firearms industry, accepted and consulted by everyone involved with firearms.

The format of GUN TRADER'S GUIDE is simple and straightforward. It lists thousands of firearms that have been manufactured in the United States and abroad since about 1900. Most entries include complete specifications: model number or name, caliber/gauge, barrel length, overall length, weight, distinguishing features, variations, plus the dates of manufacture (when they can be accurately determined). Over 2,600 illustrative photos and drawings accompany the text to help the reader with identifications and comparisons.

GUN TRADER'S GUIDE is revised annually to ensure that its wealth of information is the most up to date available. The highlight for many users is the current price of used guns. This feature is essential in determining the value of that "old treasure" you may have found stashed away. Prices are based on the national average, obtained by conferring with hundreds of different gun dealers and not by some formula, which could be way off the mark. The values that are listed accurately reflect the prices being charged nationwide at the time of publication. In other words, the prices are what they *actually* are—not what someone *thinks* they should be.

ORGANIZATION OF LISTINGS

In the early editions of GUN TRADER'S GUIDE, firearms were frequently organized chronologically by date of production within manufacturers' listings. Firearms aficionados know that many gun-making companies used the date that a particular model was introduced as the model number. For example, the Colt U.S. Model 1911 semiautomatic pistol was introduced in 1911; the French Model 1936 military rifle was introduced in 1936; and the Remington Model 32 shotgun debuted in 1932. However, during the first quarter of this century, gunmakers began assigning names and numbers that did not relate to the year a gun was introduced. And as the models and their variations multiplied through the years, it became increasingly difficult to track them by date—especially for the less experienced shooting enthusiasts.

To overcome any confusion and to provide information most accurately, GUN TRADER'S GUIDE was dramatically reorganized to simplify use for the reader. In today's edition, guns are:

- Grouped by category first: Handguns, Rifles and Shotguns.
- They are then arranged alphabetically by name of manufacturer. Or, in the case of some military weapons, by country.
- Within each manufacturer's entries, *Model Numbers* appear first in consecutive numerical order (Model 58, Model 66, Model 629), followed by *Model Names* in alphabetical order (Single Action Army, Target, Woodsmaster).
- In addition, the large handgun manufacturers, such as Colt, Smith & Wesson, etc., are broken down further into separate groupings of PISTOLS and REVOLVERS. The index in the back of the book parallels these refinements, so you can find with ease the page on which any gun appears.

In researching data for firearms, we have found through the years that not all the information is obtainable. Some manufacturers' records may have been lost, or just not kept up accurately. The result is that some listings may not be complete, and production dates, for example, may be approximate. We apologize for any inconvenience this may cause you as users of GUN TRADER'S GUIDE, but we encourage you to communicate with us at the Stoeger offices and send in any clues you may come across, especially in relation to older, out-of-production models.

CAUTION TO READERS: To comply with new Federal regulations, all manufacturers who produce firearms that are intended for disposition to the general public and that are designed to accept large-capacity ammunition feeding devices are required to redesign those models to limit their capacities to 10 rounds or less, or discontinue production or importation. This amendment to the Gun Control Act prohibits the manufacture, transfer or possession of all such devices manufactured after October 13, 1994. The "grandfather" clause of this amendment exempts all such devices lawfully possessed at the time the legislation became law. These "pre-ban" arms (those manufactured before October 13, 1994) may therefore be bought, sold or traded without any additional restrictions imposed by this law.

All "post-ban" feeding devices must meet the new requirements. *For purposes of this book:* Models previously designed to accept high-capacity feeding devices will be listed at their original specifications and capacities if only the feeding device was modified to reduce that capacity.

Regarding shotguns, the general public should be aware that shotgun barrels must be 18 inches or longer. A 14-inch shotgun barrel is illegal, except for use by military and law-enforcement personnel. A special permit from the Bureau of Alcohol, Tobacco and Firearms is required for all others.

ACKNOWLEDGMENTS

The Publisher wishes to express special thanks to the numerous collectors, dealers, manufacturers, shooting editors and others whose suggestions and advice always contribute to making this a better book.

A big thank you is extended, in particular, to the firearms firms and distributors—their public relations and product personnel, and all the research people the Stoeger editors work with throughout the year—we are especially grateful to all of you for your assistance and cooperation in compiling information for GUN TRADER'S GUIDE and for allowing us to reproduce photographs and illustrations of your firearms. Previous permission was obtained from Triple K Manufacturing Co. to use pistol illustrations from their catalog (indicated by * throughout this edition). Finally, thank you to all the dedicated readers who take the time to write in with comments, suggestions and queries about various firearms. We appreciate them all.

HOW TO USE THIS GUIDE

When a gun enthusiast is ready to buy or sell a used gun, he inevitably turns to GUN TRADER'S GUIDE. He opens the book, then silently asks two questions: "How much will I be able to get (or expect to pay) for a particular gun?" and, "How was that price obtained?" This chapter strives to answer those questions so that all readers will understand the information in this book and know how to use it most effectively.

First, be aware that the prices contained in this book are "retail"; that is, the price the consumer may expect to pay for a similar item. However, many variables must be considered when buying or selling any gun. In general, scarcity, demand, geographical location, the buyer's position and the gun's condition will govern the selling price of a particular gun. Sentiment also enters into the value of an individual's gun, but cannot be logically cataloged.

To illustrate how the price of a particular gun may fluctuate, let's take the popular Winchester Model 94 and see what its value might be.

In general, the Model 1894 (94) is a lever action, solid-frame repeater. Round or octagon barrels of 26 inches were standard when the rifle was first introduced in 1894. However, half-octagon barrels were available for a slight increase in price. A full-length magazine, holding nine shots, was standard. Weight ran about 7¾ pounds.

Fancy grade versions in all Model 94 calibers were available with 26-inch round, octagon or half-octagon nickel-steel barrels. This grade used a checkered fancy walnut pistol-grip stock and forearm, and was available with either shotgun or rifle-type buttplates.

In addition, Winchester turned out this model in carbine-style with a saddle ring in the side of the receiver. The carbine had a 20-inch round barrel and full- or half-magazine. Some carbines were supplied with standard grade barrels, while others were made of nickel steel.

In later years, the rifle version was dropped and only the carbine remained. Eventually, the saddle ring was eliminated from this model and the carbine buttstock was replaced with a shotgun-type buttstock and shortened forend. After World War II, the finish on Winchester Model 94 carbines changed to strictly hot-caustic bluing; thus, pre-war models usually demand a premium over post-war models.

Then in 1964, beginning with serial number 2,700,000, the action on Winchester Model 94s was redesigned for easier manufacturing. Many collectors and firearms enthusiasts considered the change inferior to former models. Whether this is true or not is not the issue; the main reason for a price increase of pre-1964 models was that they were no longer available. This put them immediately in the "scarce" class and made them desirable to collectors.

Shortly after the 1964 transition, Winchester started producing Model 94 commemoratives in an almost endless number-further adding to the confusion on prices. If this were not enough, the Winchester Company was sold in the 1980s and the name changed to U.S. Repeating Arms Co. This firm still manufactured the Model 94 in both standard carbine and Big Bore, and later introduced its "Angle-Eject" model to allow for the mounting of telescopic sights directly over the action.

With the above facts in mind, let's see how to use GUN TRADER'S GUIDE to find out the approximate value of a particular Winchester Model 94. Let's say that you recently inherited a rifle that has the inscription "Winchester Model 94" on the barrel. You turn to the rifle section of this book and look under the W's until you find "Winchester." The Contents pages will also tell you that Winchester Rifles begin on page 379. Since the listings in GUN TRADER'S GUIDE are arranged within each manufacturer's entry first by Model Numbers in consecutive numerical order (followed by Model Names in alphabetical order), you brief through the pages until you come to "Model 94." If you prefer to use the Index at the back of the book, it will quickly tell you that Winchester Model 94 Carbines and Rifles begin on page 396. At first glance, you realize there are two pages of Model 94 listings, not including the commemoratives. Which of these is yours?

The first step is to try to match the appearance of your model with an illustration in the book. They may all look similar at first, but paying careful attention to detail will soon weed out the models that don't apply. You look at your gun and see that the buttplate is kind of curved, or crescent-shaped. Matching up the appearance leads you to the "Winchester Model 94 Lever Action Rifle."

You think you have your model, but, to be sure, you read through the specifications and see that the barrel on the rifle was 26 inches long—either round, octagonal or half-octagonal. Upon measuring, you find that yours is approximately 26 inches long, maybe a trifle under, and it is obviously round. (Please note that the guns are not always shown in proportion to one another; that is, a carbine might not appear shorter than a rifle.)

Your rifle is marked ".38-55"—the caliber designation. Since the caliber offerings include 38-55, you are further convinced. You read on to find that this rifle was manufactured from 1894 to 1937. After this date, only the shorter-barreled carbine was offered by Winchester and only in calibers 30-30, 32 Special and 25-35.

At this point you know you have a Winchester Model 94 rifle manufactured before World War II. You read the value as $1295 and decide to take the rifle to your local dealer and collect your money. Here are some of the scenarios you may encounter:

1. If the rifle is in excellent condition—that is, if it contains at least 95 percent of its original finish on both the metal and wood and has a perfect bore—then the gun does have a retail value of $1295. However, the dealer is in business to make some profit. If he pays you $1295 for the gun, he will have to charge more than this when he sells it. If more is charged than the fair market value, then either the gun will not sell, or someone will pay more than the gun is worth. Therefore, an honest dealer will have to offer you less than the retail price for the gun to make a fair profit. However, the exact amount will vary. For example, if this dealer already has a dozen or so of the same model on his shelf and they have been slow moving, his offer will probably be low. On the other hand, if the dealer does not have any of this model in stock, but knows several collectors who want it, chances are the dealer may raise his offer.

2. Perhaps you overlooked the rifle's condition. Although the gun apparently functions flawlessly, not much of the original bluing is left. Rather, there are several shiny bright spots mixed with a brown patina finish over the remaining metal. You also notice that much of the original varnish on the wood has disappeared. Consequently, your rifle is not in "excellent" condition, and you will have to settle for less than the value shown in this book.

3. So your Winchester Model 94 rifle looks nearly new, just out of the box, and the rifle works perfectly. Therefore, you are convinced that the dealer is going to pay you full value, less a reasonable profit of between 25% and 35%. When the dealer offers you about half of what you expected, you are shocked! Perhaps you were not aware that the gun had recently been refinished, and although the finish looks new to you, you did not notice the rounding of the formerly sharp edges on the receiver, or the slight funneling of some screw holes—all of which are a dead giveaway that the rifle had at one time been refinished. Therefore, your rifle has less than "book" value.

Now if you are somewhat of an expert and know for certain that your rifle has never been refinished or otherwise tampered with, and there is still at least 95% of its original finish left, and you believe you have a firearm that is worth full book value, a dealer will still offer you from 25% to 35% less; perhaps even less if he is overstocked with this model.

Another alternative is to advertise in a local newspaper, selling the firearm directly to a private individual. However, this approach may prove both frustrating and expensive. In addition, there are federal and local restrictions on the sale of firearms. Chances are, the next time you have a firearm to sell, you will be more than happy to sell to a dealer, letting him make his fair share of profit.

CONDITION

The condition of a firearm is a big factor in determining its value. In some rare collector models, a jump from one condition to another can mean a value difference of several thousand dollars. Therefore, you must be able to determine condition before you can accurately evaluate firearms. Several sets of standards are available, with the National Rifle Association Standards of Condition of Modern Firearms probably being the most popular. However, in recent years, condition has been specified by percentage of original finish remaining on the firearm-both on the wood and metal. Let's see how these standards stack up against each other.

NRA STANDARDS OF CONDITION OF MODERN FIREARMS

- **New:** Not previously sold at retail, in same condition as current factory production
- **New, Discontinued:** Same as *New*, but discontinued model
- **Perfect:** In new condition in every respect; sometimes referred to as *mint*
- **Excellent:** New condition, used very little, no noticeable marring of wood or metal, bluing perfect (except at muzzle or sharp edges)
- **Very Good:** In perfect working condition, no appreciable wear on working surfaces, no corrosion or pitting, only minor surface dents or scratches
- **Good:** In safe working condition, minor wear on working surfaces, no broken parts, no corrosion or pitting that will interfere with proper functioning
- **Fair:** In safe working condition, but well worn, perhaps requiring replacement of minor parts or adjustments that should be indicated in advertisement; no rust, but may have corrosion pits that do not render the gun unsafe or inoperable
- **Poor:** Badly worn, rusty and battered, perhaps requiring major adjustment or repairs to place in operating condition

When a collector firearm has been expertly refinished to "excellent" condition, a rule of thumb is to deduct 50% from the value indicated in this book; if poorly done, deduct 90%.

For the purpose of assigning comparative values as a basis for trading, firearms listed in this book are assumed to be in "excellent" condition, with 95% or better remaining overall finish, no noticeable marring of wood or metal, and bores excellent with no pits. To the novice, this means a practically new gun, almost as though you had removed it from the factory carton. The trained eye, however, will know the difference between "new or mint" condition, and "excellent."

From the above paragraph, any other defects, regardless of how minor, lower the value from those listed in this book. For example, if more than 5% of the original finish is gone and there are minor surface dents or scratches—regardless of how small— the gun is no longer in "excellent" condition; rather, it takes on the condition of "very good," provided the gun is in perfect working order. Even in this state,

other than for the minor defects, the gun will still look relatively new to the uninitiated gun buyer.

If the gun is in perfect working condition—functions properly, does not jam and is accurate—but has minor wear on working surfaces, perhaps some bad scratches on the wood or metal, etc., then the gun takes on the condition of "good," one grade below "very good," according to the NRA Standards. Again, the price in this book for that particular firearm must be lowered more to obtain its true value.

The two remaining NRA conditions fall under the headings of "fair" and "poor," respectively.

Previous editions of GUN TRADER'S GUIDE gave multiplication factors to use for firearms in other than "excellent" condition. While these factors are still listed below, please be aware that they are not infallible. They are only one means of establishing a value.

TABLE OF MULTIPLICATION FACTORS FOR GUNS IN OTHER THAN EXCELLENT CONDITION

For guns in other than "excellent" condition, multiply the price in this book for the model in question by the following appropriate factors:

Condition	Multiplication Factor
• Mint or New	1.25
• Excellent	1.00
• Very Good	0.85
• Good	0.68
• Fair	0.35
• Poor	0.15

The above examples present some of the factors that influence firearms values. There are countless others, and the brief examples given here are meant to provide you with only a basic understanding of the process. Remember, the word "Guide" in GUN TRADER'S GUIDE should be taken literally. It is a *guide* only, not *gospel*. We sincerely hope, however, that it is helpful when you do decide to buy or sell a used firearm.

> **NOTE:** All prices shown in this book are for guns in excellent condition (almost new) and the prices are retail (what a dealer would normally charge for them). A dealer will seldom pay the full value shown in this book. If a gun is in any condition other than excellent, the price in this book must be multiplied by the appropriate factor to obtain a true value of the gun in question.

CONTENTS

RIFLES
Section II

SHOTGUNS
Section III

HANDGUNS
Section I

ACCU-TEK
Chino, California

Accu-Tek AT-9mm

ACTION ARMS
Philadelphia, Pennsylvania

See also listings under CZ Pistols. Action Arms stopped importing firearms in 1994.

**Action Arms AT-84
Double Action Pistol**

Accu-Tek Model AT-9 DAO Auto Pistol
Caliber: 9mm Parabellum. 8-shot magazine. Double action only. 3.2-inch barrel. 6.25 inches overall. Weight: 28 oz. Sights: fixed blade front; adjustable rear w/3-dot system. Firing-pin block with no external safety. Stainless or black over stainless finish. Checkered black nylon grips. Announced 1992, but introduced 1995.
Satin Stainless Model **$195**
Matte Black Stainless **200**

Accu-Tek Model AT-25 Auto Pistol
Similar to Model AT-380, except for caliber 25 ACP with 7-shot magazine. Made from 1991 to date.
Lightweight w/Aluminum Frame **$115**
Bright Stainless (Discontinued 1991) **120**
Satin Stainless **115**
Matte Black Stainless **120**

Accu-Tek Model AT-32 Auto Pistol
Similar to Model AT-380, except in 32 ACP. Made from 1990 to date.
Lightweight w/Aluminum Frame (Disc. 1991) . . . . **$ 95**
Satin Stainless Model **129**
Matte Black Stainless **135**

Accu-Tek Model AT-40 DAO Auto Pistol
Same as Model AT-9 DAO, except chambered for 40 S&W, with 7-shot magazine. Announced 1992, but introduced 1995.
Satin Stainless Model **$200**
Matte Black Stainless **205**

Accu-Tek Model AT-380 Auto Pistol
Caliber: 380 ACP. 5-shot magazine. 2.75-inch barrel. 5.6 inches overall. Weight: 20 oz. External hammer with slide safety. Grooved black composition grips. Alloy frame. Stainless finish; satin and matte black introduced 1992. Made from 1990 to date.
Standard Alloy Frame (Disc. 1992) **$130**
Satin Stainless Model **135**
Matte Black Stainless **140**

Accu-Tek Model HC-380SS Auto Pistol **$170**
Caliber: 380 ACP. 13-shot magazine. 2.75-inch barrel. 6 inches overall. Weight: 28 oz. External hammer with slide safety. Checkered black composition grips. Stainless finish. Made from 1993 to date.

Action Arms AT-84 Selective DA Auto Pistol . . . **$395**
Caliber: 9mm Parabellum. 15-shot magazine. 4³/4-inch barrel. 8 inches overall. Weight: 35 oz. Fixed front sight; drift adjustable rear. Checkered walnut stocks. Blued finish. Made in Switzerland 1987–89.

Action Arms AT-88 Selective DA Auto Pistol . . . **$400**
Similar to Model AT-84, except available in both 9mm (15-shot) or 41 Action Express (10-shot) with cocked and locked capabilities. Imported 1987–89.

ADVANTAGE ARMS
St. Paul, Minnesota

**Advantage Arms
Model 422**

Advantage Arms Model 422 DA Derringer **$225**
Hammerless, top-break, 4-barrel derringer w/rotating firing pin. Caliber: 22 LR. 2$1/2$-inch barrels. 4$1/2$ inches overall. Weight: 15 oz. Smooth walnut grips. Blued, nickel or PDQ matte black finish. Made 1983–87.

═ S. A. ALKARTASUNA FABRICA DE ARMAS ═
Guernica, Spain

Alkartasuna Ruby

Alkartasuna Ruby Automatic Pistol **$250**
Caliber: 32 Automatic (7.65mm). 9-shot magazine. 3$5/8$-inch barrel. 6$3/8$ inches overall. Weight: about 34 oz. Fixed sights. Blued finish. Checkered wood or hard rubber stocks. Made 1917–1922. *Note:* Mfd. by a number of Spanish firms, the Ruby was a secondary standard service pistol of the French Army in World Wars I and II. Specimens made by Alkartasuna bear the "Alkar" trademark.

═══ AMERICAN ARMS ═══
Kansas City, Missouri

American Arms CX-22

American Arms CX-22 DA Automatic Pistol
Similar to Model PX-22, except with 3.33-inch barrel. 8-shot magazine. 6.5 inches overall. Weight: 22 oz. Made from 1990 to date.
Standard w/Chrome Slide (Disc. 1990) **$130**
Classic Model **125**

American Arms EP-380

American Arms EP-380 DA Automatic Pistol **$320**
Caliber: 380 Automatic. 7-shot magazine. 3.5-inch barrel. 6.5 inches overall. Weight: 25 oz. Fixed front sight; square-notch adjustable rear. Stainless finish. Checkered wood stocks. Made 1989–1991.

American Arms Escort DAO Auto Pistol **$220**
Caliber: 380 Automatic (7.65mm). 7-shot magazine. 3$3/8$-inch barrel. 6$1/8$ inches overall. Thin profile ($13/16$ inches wide). Weight: 19 oz. Fixed low-profile sights. Soft polymer grips. Satin stainless steel finish.

American Arms P-98

American Arms P-98 DA Automatic Pistol **$145**
Caliber: 22 LR. 8-shot magazine. 5-inch barrel. 8$1/4$ inches overall. Weight: 25 oz. Fixed front sight; square-notch adj. rear. Blued finish. Serrated black polymer stocks.

American Arms PK-22

American Arms PK-22 DA Automatic Pistol $145
Caliber: 22 LR. 8-shot magazine. 3.33-inch barrel. 6.33 inches overall. Weight: 22 oz. Fixed front sight; V-notch rear. Blued finish. Checkered black polymer stocks. Made from 1989 to date.

American Arms PX-22

American Arms PX-22 DA Automatic Pistol $135
Caliber: 22 LR. 7-shot magazine. 2.75-inch barrel. 5.33 inches overall. Weight: 15 oz. Fixed front sight; V-notch rear. Blued finish. Checkered black polymer stocks. Made from 1989 to date.

American Arms PX-25 DA Automatic Pistol $140
Same general specifications as the Model PX-22, except chambered for 25 ACP. Made from 1991 to date.

American Arms Regulator

American Arms Regulator Single Action Revolver
Calibers: 357 Mag., 44-40, 45 Long Colt. 6-shot cylinder. 4.75- and 7.5-inch barrel. Blade front sight, fixed rear sight. Brass trigger guard/backstrap Standard model. Case-hardened steel Deluxe model. Made from 1992 to date.
Standard Model **$215**
Standard Combo Set
   (45 LC/45 ACP & 44-40/44 Spec.) **250**
Deluxe Model **240**
Deluxe Combo Set
   (45 LC/45 ACP & 44-40/44 Spec.) **275**

American Arms Sabre

American Arms Sabre DA Automatic Pistol
Calibers: 9mm Luger, 40 S&W. 8-shot magazine in 9mm, 9-shot in 40 S&W. 3.75-inch barrel. 6.9 inches overall. Weight: 26 oz. Fixed blade front sight; square notch adjustable rear. Black polymer stocks. Blued or stainless finish. Advertised 1991–92, but not imported.
Blued Finish **$295**
Stainless Steel **310**

American Arms Spectre DA Automatic Pistol
Calibers: 9mm Luger, 40 S&W, 45 ACP. 30-shot magazine. 6-inch barrel. 13.75 inches overall. Weight: 4.5 pounds. Adjustable post front sight; fixed U-notch rear. Matte black finish. Imported by American Arms 1990–93 (previously imported by F.I.E.).
9mm **$295**
40 S&W (Discontinued 1991) **320**
45 ACP (1992–93) **350**

American Arms Woodmaster

American Arms Woodmaster SA Auto Pistol $140
Caliber: 22 LR. 10-shot magazine. 5.875-inch barrel. 10.5 inches overall. Weight: 31 oz. Fixed front sight; square-notch adj. rear. Blued finish. Checkered wood stocks. Discontinued 1989.

HANDGUNS

AMERICAN DERRINGER CORPORATION
Waco, Texas

American Derringer Model 1

American Derringer Model 1, Stainless
Single-action pocket pistol. 2-shot capacity. Barrel: 3 inches. 4.82 inches overall. Weight: 15 oz. Automatic barrel selection. Satin or high-polished stainless steel. Rosewood grips. Made from 1985 to date.

45 Colt, 44-40 Win., 44 Special	$265
45 Colt or 2½" .410, .410 × 2½" or 45 Colt	230
45 Win. Mag.	195
45-70, 44 Mag., 41 Mag., 30-30 Win., 223 Rem.	225
357 Max.	190
357 Mag.	185
38 Special, 32 Mag., 22 LR, 22 Rim. Mag.	165
38 Super, 380 Auto, 9mm Luger, 30 Luger	175

American Derringer Model 2 Steel "Pen" Pistol
Calibers: 22 LR, 25 Auto, 32 Auto (7.65mm). Single shot. 2-inch barrel. 5.6 inches overall (4.2 inches in pistol format). Weight: 5 oz. Stainless finish. Made 1993–94.

22 Long Rifle	$195
25 Auto	205
32 Auto	225

American Derringer Model 3

American Derringer Model 3 Stainless Steel $75
Single Shot. Caliber: 38 Special. Barrel: 2½ inches. 4.9 inches overall. Weight: 8.5 oz. Rosewood grips. Made from 1984 to date.

American Derringer Model 4 Double Derringer
Calibers: 357 Mag., 357 Max., 44 Mag., 45 LC, 45 ACP (upper barrel) and 3-inch .410 shotshell (lower barrel). Barrel: 4.1 inches. 6 inches overall. Weight: 16½ oz. Stag horn grips. Stainless steel. Made from 1984 to date.

357 Mag., 357 Max.	$255
44 Mag.	320
45 LC, 45 ACP	315

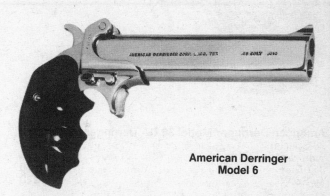

American Derringer Model 6

American Derringer Model 6
Caliber: 22 Mag., 357 Mag., 45 LC, 45 ACP or 45 LC/.410 O/U. Barrel: 6 inches. 8.2 inches overall. Weight: 1 lb. 6 oz. Satin or high-polished stainless steel with rosewood grips. Made from 1986 to date.

22 Magnum	$195
357, 45 ACP, 45 LC	225
45 LC/.410 O/U	275

American Derringer Model 7
Same general specifications as the Model 1, except high-strength aircraft aluminum is used to replace some of the stainless steel parts, which reduces its weight to 7½ oz. Made from 1986 to date.

22 Long Rifle, 22 Mag.	$145
38 Special, 32 Mag., 32 S&W Long	135
38 S&W, 380 Auto	130

American Derringer Model 10
Same general specifications as the Model 7, except chambered for 45 ACP or 45 Long Colt.

45 ACP	$165
45 Long Colt	180

American Derringer Model 11 .... $135
Same general specifications as Model 7, except chambered for .38 Special only, and weighs 11 oz. Made 1980 to date.

American Derringer 25 Automatic Pistol
Calibers: 25 ACP or 250 Mag. Barrel: 2.1 inches. 4.4 inches overall. Weight: 15½ oz. Smooth rosewood grips. Blued or stainless finish. Made from 1984 to date.

25 ACP Blue	$350
25 ACP Stainless	310
250 Mag. Stainless	395

American Derringer Model 38 Double Action Derringer
Hammerless, double action, double barrel (over/under). Calibers: 38 Special, 9mm Luger, 357 Mag., 40 S&W. 3-inch barrel. Weight: 14.5 oz. Made from 1990 to date.

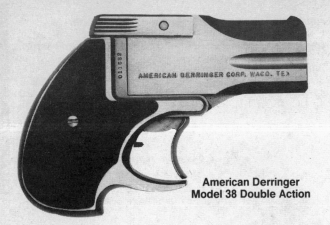

American Derringer
Model 38 Double Action

American Derringer
Semmerling LM-4

American Derringer Model 38 DA Derringer (cont.)

38 Special **$155**
9mm Luger **175**
357 Mag. **210**
40 S&W **220**

American Derringer Alaskan Survival Model **$250**
Same general specifications as the Model 4, except upper barrel comes in 45-70 or 3-inch .410 and 45 Colt lower barrel. Made from 1985 to date.

American Derringer Cop DA Derringer **$235**
Hammerless, double action, four-barrel derringer. Caliber: 357 Mag. 3.15-inch barrel. 5.5 inches overall. Weight: 16 oz. Stainless steel with rosewood grips. Made 1990–95.

American Derringer Semmerling LM-4
Manually operated repeater. Calibers: 45 ACP or 9mm. 5-shot (45 ACP) or 7-shot magazine (9mm). 3.6-inch barrel. 5.2 inches overall. Weight: 24 oz. Made from 1986 to date. Limited availability.
Blued Finish **$2395**
Stainless Steel **2150**

American Derringer Texas Commemorative
Same general specifications as Model 1, except with solid brass frame, stainless barrels and rosewood grips. Calibers: 38 Special, 44-40 Win. or 45 Colt. Made 1991 to date.
38 Special **$175**
44-40 or 45 Colt **250**

American Derringer
Lady Derringer

═══ AMERICAN FIREARMS MFG. CO., INC. ═══
San Antonio, Texas

American 25 Auto Pistol
Caliber: 25 Auto. 8-shot magazine. 2.1-inch barrel. 4.4 inches overall. Weight: 14½ oz. Fixed sights. Stainless or blued ordnance steel. Smooth walnut stocks. Made 1966–1974.
Stainless Steel Model **$170**
Blued Steel Model **135**

American Derringer Lady Derringer
Same general specifications as Model 1, except with custom-tuned action fitted with scrimshawed synthetic ivory grips. Calibers: 32 H&R Mag., 32 Special, 38 Special (additional calibers on request). Deluxe Grade engraved and highly polished with French fitted jewelry box. Made from 1991 to date.
Lady Derringer **$175**
Deluxe Engraved **560**

American Derringer Mini-Cop DA Derringer **$195**
Same general specifications as the American Derringer Cop, except chambered for 22 Magnum. Made 1990–95.

American 380 Automatic

American 380 Auto Pistol $350
Stainless steel. Caliber: 380 Auto. 8-shot magazine. 3½-inch barrel. 5½ inches overall. Weight: 20 oz. Smooth walnut stocks. Made 1972–74.

AMT (ARCADIA MACHINE & TOOL)
Irwindale, California

AMT 45 ACP Hardballer
Caliber: 45 ACP. 7-shot magazine. 5-inch barrel. 8½ inches overall. Weight: 39 oz. Millett adjustable sights. Serrated matte slide rib. Wraparound Neoprene grips. Made from about 1979 to date.
Hardballer Model (Standard) **$375**
Hardballer Long Slide (w/7-inch bbl./slide, 46 oz.,
   intro. about 1980) **395**

AMT 1911 Government Model Auto Pistol
Caliber: 45 ACP. 7-shot magazine. 5-inch barrel. 8½ inches overall. Weight: 38 ounces. Fixed sights. Made from 1979 to date.
Standard Model **$295**
Stainless (Disc. 1991) **375**

AMT Automag II

AMT Automag II Automatic Pistol $225
Caliber: 22 WMR. 9-shot magazine. Barrel lengths: 3⅜-, 4½-, 6-inch. Weight: 32 oz. Fully adjustable Millett sights. Stainless finish. Smooth black composition stocks. Made from 1986 to date.

AMT Automag III Automatic Pistol $275
Calibers: 30 M1 and 9mm Win. 8-shot magazine. 6⅜-inch barrel. 10½ inches overall. Weight: 43 ounces. Millett adjustable sights. Stainless finish. Carbon fiber grips. Made from 1989 to date.

AMT Automag IV Automatic Pistol $425
Calibers: 10mm Mag., 45 Win. Mag. 7-shot magazine. 6½- or 8⅝-inch barrel. 10½ inches overall. Weight 46 oz. Millett adjustable sights. Stainless finish. Carbon fiber grips. Made from 1990 to date.

AMT Automag V Automatic Pistol $675
Caliber: 50 A.E. 5-shot magazine. 7-inch barrel. 10½ inches overall. Weight: 46 oz. Custom adjustable sights. Stainless finish. Carbon fiber grips. Made 1994 to date.

AMT Backup

AMT Backup Automatic Pistol
Calibers: 22 LR, 380 ACP. 8-shot (22 LR) or 5-shot (380 ACP) magazine. 2½-inch barrel. 5 inches overall. Weight: 18 oz. Open sights. Carbon fiber or walnut grips. Stainless steel finish.
22 LR (Discontinued 1987) **$185**
380 ACP (Discontinued 1993) **175**

AMT Backup II Automatic Pistol $180
Caliber: 380 ACP. 5-shot magazine. 2½-inch barrel. 5 inches overall. Weight: 18 oz. Open sights. Carbon fiber grips. Stainless steel finish. *Note:* This model was introduced in 1993 as a continuation of the original 380 Backup w/traditional double-action function.

AMT Backup DAO

AMT Backup DAO Auto Pistol
Calibers: 380 ACP, 38 Super, 9mm Luger, 40 S&W, 45 ACP. 6-shot (380, 38 Super, 9mm) or 5-shot (40 S&W, 45 ACP) magazine. Double action only. Barrel: 2½-inch (380 ACP) or 3-inch. Overall length: 5 inches (380 ACP) or 5.75 inches. Weight: 18 oz. (380 ACP) or 23 oz. Open fixed sights. Carbon fiber grips. Stainless steel finish. Made from 1992 to date.
380 ACP **$219**
38 Super, 9mm, 40 S&W, 45 ACP (Intro. 1995) . . **300**

AMT Bulls Eye Target Model

AMT Skipper Auto Pistol

AMT Bulls Eye Target Model **$290**
Caliber: 40 S&W. 8-shot magazine. 5-inch barrel. 8¹/₂ inches overall. Weight: 38 oz. Millet adjustable sights. Wide adjustable trigger. Wraparound Neoprene grips. Made 1990–92.

AMT Javelina **$435**
Caliber: 10mm. 8-shot magazine. 7-inch barrel. 10¹/₂ inches overall. Weight: 48 oz. Long grip safety, beveled magazine well, wide adj. trigger. Millet adj. sights. Wraparound Neoprene grips. Stainless finish. Made 1991–93.

AMT Lightning Auto Pistol
Caliber: 22 LR. 10-shot magazine. 5-, 6¹/₂-, 8¹/₂-, 10-inch barrels. 10³/₄ inches overall w/6¹/₂-inch barrel. Weight: 45 oz. w/6¹/₂-inch barrel. Millett adj. sights. Checkered rubber grips. Stainless finish. Made 1984–87.
Standard Model **$185**
Bull's-Eye Model **275**

AMT On Duty Auto Pistol

AMT On Duty Double Action Pistol
Calibers: 40 S&W, 9mm Luger, 45 ACP. 15-shot (9mm), 13-shot (40 S&W) or 9-shot (45 ACP) magazine. 4¹/₂-inch barrel. 7³/₄ inches overall. Weight: 32 oz. Hard anodized aluminum frame. Stainless steel slide and barrel. Carbon fiber grips. Made 1991–94.
9mm or 40 S&W **$325**
45 ACP **380**

AMT Skipper Auto Pistol **$295**
Calibers: 40 S&W and 45 ACP. 7-shot magazine. 4¹/₄-inch barrel. 7¹/₂ inches overall. Weight: 33 oz. Millet adj. sights. Walnut grips. Matte finish stainless steel. Made 1990–92.

ANSCHUTZ PISTOLS
Ulm, Germany
Mfd. by J.G. Anschutz GmbH Jagd und Sportwaffenfabrik

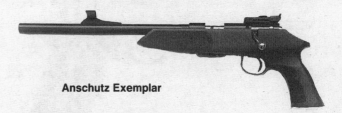

Anschutz Exemplar

Anschutz Exemplar Bolt Action Pistol
Calibers: 22 LR, 22 Magnum, 22 Hornet. 5-shot clip. 10- or 14-inch barrel. 19 inches overall (w/10-inch bbl.). Weight: 3¹/₃ lbs. Match 64 action. Slide safety. Hooded ramp post front sight; adjustable open notched rear. European walnut contoured grip. Made from 1990 to date.
22 LR with 10-inch bbl. **$300**
22 LR with 14-inch bbl. **345**

Anschutz Exemplar Hornet

Anschutz Exemplar Hornet **$595**
Same general specifications as the standard Exemplar Pistol, except a centerfire version with Match 54 action, wing safety, tapped and grooved for scope mounting. Made from 1990 to date.

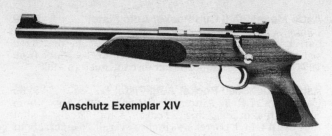

Anschutz Exemplar XIV

Anschutz Exemplar XIV **$325**
Same general specifications as the standard Exemplar Bolt
Action Pistol, except with 14-inch barrel, weight 4.15 lbs.
Made from 1990 to date.

ASTRA PISTOLS
Guernica, Spain
Manufactured by Unceta y Compania

Astra Model 41 Double Action Revolver **$200**
Same general specifications as Model 44, except in 41 Mag.
Discontinued 1985.

Astra Model 44 Revolver

Astra Model 44 Double Action Revolver
Similar to Astra 357, except chambered for 44 Magnum.
Barrels: 6-, 8¹/₂-inch. 11¹/₂ inches overall with 6-inch bar-
rel. Weight: 44 oz. with 6-inch barrel. Blued or stainless
finish. Made 1980–1993.
Blued Finish (Discontinued 1987) **$225**
Stainless Finish (Discontinued 1993) **275**

Astra Model 45 Double Action Revolver **$220**
Similar to Astra 357, except chambered for 45 Colt or 45
ACP. Barrels: 6- or 8¹/₂-inch. 11¹/₂ inches overall w/6-
inch bbl. Weight: 44 oz. w/6-inch bbl. Made 1980–87.

Astra Model 200 Firecat

Astra Model 200 Firecat Vest Pocket Auto Pistol $175
Caliber: 25 Automatic (6.35mm). 6-shot magazine. 2¹/₄-
inch barrel. 4³/₈ inches overall. Weight: 11³/₄ oz. Fixed
sights. Blued finish. Plastic stocks. Made from 1920 to
date; U.S. importation discontinued in 1968.

Astra 357, 3-inch barrel

Astra 357 Double Action Revolver **$190**
Caliber: 357 Magnum. 6-shot cylinder. Barrels: 3-, 4-, 6-,
8¹/₂-inch. 11¹/₄ inches overall w/6-inch bbl. Weight: 42 oz.
w/6-inch bbl. Ramp front sight, adjustable rear sight.
Blued finish. Checkered wood stocks. Made 1972–1988.

Astra Model 400

Astra Model 400 Auto Pistol **$275**
Caliber: 9mm Bayard Long (38 ACP, 9mm Browning
Long, 9mm Glisenti, 9mm Luger and 9mm Steyr cartridges
may be used interchangeably in this pistol because of its
chamber design). 9-shot magazine. 6-inch barrel. 10 inches
overall. Weight: 35 oz. Fixed sights. Blued finish. Plastic
stocks. Made 1921–1945. *Note:* This pistol, as well as Astra
Models 600 and 3000, is a modification of the FN Browning Model 1910.

Astra Model 600

Astra Model 600 Mil./Police Type Auto Pistol . . . **$300**
Calibers: 32 Automatic (7.65mm), 9mm Luger. Magazine:
10- (32 cal.) or 8-shot (9mm). 5¹/₄-inch barrel. 8 inches
overall. Weight: about 33 oz. Fixed sights. Blued finish.
Checkered wood or plastic stocks. Made 1944–45.

Astra Model 800 Condor

Astra Model 800 Condor Military Auto Pistol $925
Similar to Models 400 and 600, except has an external hammer. Caliber: 9mm Luger. 8-shot magazine. 5¼-inch barrel. 8¼ inches overall. Weight: 32½ oz. Fixed sights. Blued finish. Plastic stocks. Made 1958–1965.

Astra Model 2000 Camper

Astra Model 2000 Camper Automatic Pistol $255
Same as Model 2000 Cub, except chambered for 22 Short only, has 4-inch barrel; overall length, 6¼ inches; weight, 11½ oz. Made 1955–1960.

Astra Model 2000 Cub

Astra Model 3000

Astra Model 2000 Cub Pocket Auto Pistol $190
Calibers: 22 Short, 25 Auto. 6-shot magazine. 2¼-inch barrel. 4½ inches overall. Weight: about 11 oz. Fixed sights. Blued or chromed finish. Plastic stocks. Made from 1954 to date; U.S. importation discontinued in 1968.

Astra Model 3000 Pocket Auto Pistol $265
Calibers: 22 LR, 32 Automatic (7.65mm), 380 Auto (9mm Short). 10-shot magazine (22 cal.), 7-shot (32 cal.), 6-shot (380 cal.). 4-inch barrel. 6⅜ inches overall. Weight: about 22 oz. Fixed sights. Blued finish. Plastic stocks. Made 1947–1956.

Astra Model 4000 Falcon

Astra Model 4000 Falcon Auto Pistol $350
Similar to Model 3000, except has an external hammer. Calibers: 22 LR, 32 Automatic (7.65mm), 380 Auto (9mm Short). 10-shot magazine (22 LR), 8-shot (32 Auto), 7-shot (380 Auto). 3⅔-inch barrel. 6½ inches overall. Weight: 20 oz. (22 cal.) or 24¾ oz. (32 and 380). Fixed sights. Blued finish. Plastic stocks. Made 1956–1971.

Astra Model A-60 DA Automatic Pistol $275
Similar to the Constable, except in 380 only, with 13-shot magazine and slide-mounted ambidextrous safety. Blued finish only. Made 1980–1991.

Astra Model A-70 Compact Auto Pistol
Calibers: 9mm Parabellum, 40 S&W. 8-shot (9mm) or 7-shot (40 S&W) magazine. 3.5-inch barrel. 6.5 inches overall. Blued, nickel or stainless finish. Weight: 29.3 oz. Made from 1992 to date.

Blued Finish	**$245**
Nickel Finish	275
Stainless Finish	295

Astra Model A-75 Decocker Auto Pistol
Similar to the Model 70, except in 9mm, 40 S&W and 45 ACP with decocking system and contoured pebble-textured grips. Made from 1993 to date.

Blued Finish, 9mm or 40 S&W	**$295**
Nickel Finish, 9mm or 40 S&W	325
Stainless, 9mm or 40 S&W	360
Blued Finish, 45 ACP	325
Nickel Finish, 45 ACP	350
Stainless, 45 ACP	395

Astra Model A-75 Ultralight $385
Similar to the standard Model 75, except 9mm only with 24-oz. alloy frame. Made from 1994 to date.

Astra Model A-80

Astra Model A-90

Astra Model A-80 Auto Pistol $280
Calibers: 9mm Parabellum, 38 Super, 45 ACP. 15-shot magazine or 9-shot (45 ACP). Barrel: 3³/₄ inches. 7 inches overall. Weight: 36 oz. Made 1982–89.

Astra Model A-90 DA Automatic Pistol $295
Calibers: 9mm Parabellum, 45 ACP. 15-shot (9mm) or 9-shot (45 ACP) magazine. 3.75-inch barrel. 7 inches overall. Weight: about 40 oz. Fixed sights. Blued finish. Checkered plastic stocks. Made 1985–1990.

Astra Model A-100 Double Action Auto Pistol
Same general specifications as the Model A-90, except selective double action chambered for 9mm Luger, 40 S&W or 45 ACP. Made in 1991.
Blued Finish $295

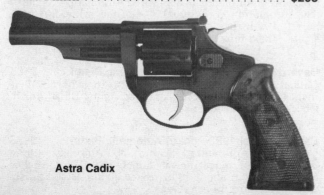

Astra Cadix

Astra Model A-100 DA Auto Pistol (cont.)
Nickel Finish $330
For Night Sights, **add** 100

Astra Cadix Double Action Revolver $150
Calibers: 22 LR, 38 Special. 9-shot (22 LR) or 5-shot (38 cal.) cylinder. Barrels: 4- or 6-inch. Weight: about 27 oz. w/6-inch barrel. Ramp front sight, adjustable rear sight. Blued finish. Plastic stocks. Made 1960–68.

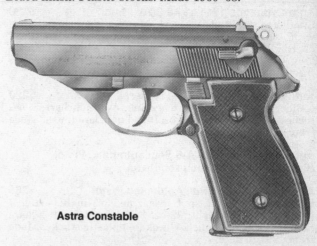

Astra Constable

Astra Constable Double Action Auto Pistol
Calibers: 22 LR, 32 Automatic (7.65mm), 380 Auto (9mm Short). Magazine capacity: 10-shot (22 LR), 8-shot (32), 7-shot (380). 3¹/₂-inch barrel. 6¹/₂ inches overall. Weight: about 24 oz. Blade front sight, windage adjustable rear. Blued, chrome or stainless finish. Made 1965–1992.
Blued or Chrome Finish $235
Stainless Finish 285

Astra Terminator Double Action Revolver
Same general specifications as Model 44, except with 2¹/₂-inch shrouded barrel. Discontinued 1989.
Blued or Chrome Finish $225
Stainless Finish 275

═══ AUTO-ORDNANCE CORPORATION ═══
West Hurley, New York

**Auto-Ordnance 1911A1
Gov't. Automatic Pistol**

Auto-Ordnance 1911A1 Government Auto Pistol

Calibers: 9mm Para., 38 Super, 10mm, 45 ACP. 9-shot (9mm, 38 Super) or 7-shot (10mm, 45 ACP) magazine. 5-inch barrel. 8½ inches overall. Weight: 39 oz. Fixed blade front sight; rear adjustable. Blued finish. Checkered plastic stocks. (*See* photo, preceding page.)

45 ACP Caliber **$265**
9mm, 10mm, 38 Super **305**

Auto-Ordnance 1911A1 40 S&W Pistol $320

Similar to the Model 1911A1, except has 4½-inch barrel with 7¾-inch overall length. 8-shot magazine. Weight: 37 oz. Blade front and adjustable rear sights with 3-dot system. Checkered black rubber wraparound grips. Made from 1991 to date.

Auto-Ordnance 1911 "The General" $290

Caliber: 45 ACP. 7-shot magazine. 4½-inch barrel. 7¾ inches overall. Weight: 37 oz. Blued nonglare finish. Made from 1992 to date.

Auto-Ordnance 1927 A-5 Semiautomatic Pistol

See listing under Thompson Pistol.

Auto-Ordnance Pit Bull Automatic Pistol $285

Caliber: 45 ACP. 7-shot magazine. 3½-inch barrel. 7 inches overall. Weight: 32 oz. Fixed front sight; square notch rear. Blued finish. Checkered plastic stocks. Made from 1991 to date.

Auto-Ordnance ZG-51

Auto-Ordnance ZG-51 Government Auto Pistol . . $290

Caliber: 45 ACP. 7-shot magazine. 3½-inch barrel. 7¼ inches overall. Weight: 36 oz. Fixed blade front sight; drift adjustable rear. Blued finish. Checkered plastic stocks. Made 1989–1990.

═══ BAUER FIREARMS CORPORATION ═══
Fraser, Michigan

Bauer 25 Automatic Pistol $125

Stainless steel. Caliber: 25 Automatic. 6-shot magazine. 2⅛-inch barrel. 4 inches overall. Weight: 10 oz. Fixed

Bauer 25 Automatic

Bauer 25 Automatic Pistol (cont.)

sights. Checkered walnut or simulated pearl stocks. Made 1972–1984.

═══ BAYARD PISTOLS ═══
Herstal, Belgium
Mfd. by Anciens Etablissements Pieper

Bayard Model 1908*

Bayard Model 1908 Pocket Automatic Pistol . . . $175

Calibers: 25 Automatic (6.35mm), 32 Automatic (7.65mm), 380 Automatic (9mm Short). 6-shot magazine. 2¼-inch barrel. 4⅞ inches overall. Weight: about 16 oz. Fixed sights. Blued finish. Hard rubber stocks.

Bayard Model 1923 Pocket Automatic Pistol . . . $165

Caliber: 25 Automatic (6.35mm). 2⅛-inch barrel. 4⁵⁄₁₆ inches overall. Weight: 12 oz. Fixed sights. Blued finish. Checkered hard rubber stocks.

Bayard Model 1923 Pocket Automatic Pistol . . . $185

Calibers: 32 Automatic (7.65mm), 380 Automatic (9mm Short). 6-shot magazine. 3⁵⁄₁₆-inch barrel. 5½ inches overall. Weight: about 19 oz. Fixed sights. Blued finish. Checkered hard rubber stocks.

Bayard Model 1930

Bayard Model 1930 Pocket 25 Automatic Pistol ... **$190**
This is a modification of the Model 1923, which it closely resembles.

BEEMAN PRECISION ARMS, INC.
Santa Rosa, California

Beeman P08 Automatic Pistol

Beeman Mini P08 Automatic Pistol **$265**
Caliber: Same general specifications as P08, except shorter 3½-inch barrel, 7.4 inches overall and weight of 20 oz. Imported 1986–1991.

Beeman P08 Automatic Pistol **$270**
Caliber: 22 LR. 10-shot magazine. 3.8-inch barrel. 7.8 inches overall. Weight: 25 oz. Fixed sights. Blued finish. Checkered hardwood grips. Imported 1986–1991.

Beeman SP Deluxe Metallic Silhouette
Caliber: 22 LR. Single shot. Barrel: 6, 8, 10 or 15 inches. Adjustable rear sight; receiver ground for scope mount. Walnut target grips w/adj. palm rest. Made 1985–86.
With 8-or 10-inch bbl. **$195**
With 12-inch bbl. 215
With 15-inch bbl. 235

Beeman/FAS 601 Semiautomatic
Caliber: 22 Short. 9¼-inch sight radius. Weight: about 41 oz. Top loading magazine. Ventilated with gas vents. Adjustable, removable trigger.
Right **$650**
Left 675

Beeman/FAS 602 Semiautomatic
Caliber: 22 LR. 8½-inch sight radius. Weight: 40 oz.
Right **$620**
Left 650

Beeman/Hämmerli Model 150
Free Pistol

Beeman/Hämmerli Model 150 Free Pistol **$1300**
Caliber: 22 LR. Free-floating precision barrel w/low axis relative to hand. Martini-type locking action w/side-mounted locking lever. Sight radius 14.8 inches. Micrometer rear sight adjustable for windage and elevation. Select walnut grip with handrest. Made from 1990 to date.

Beeman/Hämmerli Model 152 Electronic Pistol
Same general specifications as Model 150, except with electronic trigger.
Right Hand **$1400**
Left Hand 1450

Beeman/Hämmerli Model 208S Target Pistol .. **$1095**
Caliber: 22 LR. 8-shot magazine. 6-inch barrel. 10.2 inches overall. Weight: 37.3 oz. Micrometer rear sight, ramp front sight. Blued finish. Stippled walnut stocks with adjustable heel plate. Imported from 1990 to date.

Beeman/Hämmerli Model 212

Beeman/Hämmerli Model 212 Hunter Pistol **$925**
Caliber: 22 LR. 8-shot magazine. 5-inch barrel. 8.6 inches overall. Weight: 31 oz. Blade front sight, square notched rear. Blued finish. Checkered walnut stocks. Imported from 1990 to date.

Beeman/Hämmerli Model 215 Target Pistol **$910**
Same general specifications as Model 208S, except with fewer deluxe features. Imported from 1990 to date.

Beeman/Hämmerli Model 232 Rapid Fire Pistol . **$995**
Caliber: 22 Short. 6-shot magazine. 5.2-inch barrel. 10.5 inches overall. Weight: 44 oz. Fully adjustable target sights. Blued finish. Stippled walnut wraparound target stocks. Imported from 1990 to date.

Beeman/Hämmerli Model 280 Sport Pistol

Beeman/Hämmerli Model 280 Sport Pistol **$1095**
Calibers: 22 LR, 32 S&W. 5-shot (32 S&W) or 6-shot (22LR) clip. 4^1/$_2$-inch barrel. Weight: 35 to 39 oz. Handrest grip. Made from 1990 to date.

Beeman/Korth Revolver

Beeman/Korth Revolver **$2195**
Calibers: 357 Mag. or 22 LR with interchangeable combo cylinders of 357 Mag./9mm Para or 22 LR/22 WMR. Barrel: 6-inch target; 3-, 4-inch combat. Walnut grips. Discontinued 1993.

Beeman/Korth Semiauto Pistol

Beeman/Korth Semiauto Pistol **$1895**
Calibers: 30 Luger, 9mm Para. 14-shot magazine. 4- or 5-inch barrel. All-steel construction; recoil-operated. Adjustable rear sight. Imported from 1990 to date.

Beeman/Unique 32U Rapid Fire Pistol
Caliber: 32 S&W Long (wadcutter). 5.9-inch barrel. Weight: 40 oz. Blade front, adj. rear target sights. Trigger

Beeman/Unique 32U Rapid Fire Pistol (cont.)
adjustable for weight and position. Blued finish. Stippled handrest grips. Imported from 1990 to date.
Right-Hand Model . . . . **$ 970**
Left-Hand Model **1025**

Beeman/Unique DES/69-U

Beeman/Unique DES/69-U Target Pistol
Caliber: 22 LR. 5-shot magazine. 5.9-inch barrel. Trigger adjusts for position and pull weight. Comes with 250 gm counterweight. Weight: about 36 oz. Adjustable grips. Imported 1990–93.
Right-Hand Model **$950**
Left-Hand Model **975**

Beeman/Unique 2000-U Target Pistol

Beeman/Unique 2000-U Match Pistol
Caliber: 22 Short. Designed for rapid fire. Weight: 2.7 lbs. Special light alloy frame, solid steel slide and shock absorber. Five vents for recoil reduction. Handrest grip. Imported 1990–93.
Right-Hand Model **$695**
Left-Hand Model **750**

=== **BEHOLLA PISTOL** ===
Suhl, Germany
Mfd. by both Becker and Holländer and Stenda-Werke GmbH

Beholla Pocket Automatic Pistol **$175**
Caliber: 32 Automatic (7.65mm). 7-shot magazine. 2.9-inch barrel. 5^1/$_2$ inches overall. Weight: 22 oz. Fixed sights. Blued finish. Serrated wood or hard rubber stocks. Made by Becker and Holländer 1915–1920, by Stenda-Werke circa 1920–25. *Note:* Essentially the same pistol was manufactured concurrently with the Stenda version as the "Leonhardt" by H. M. Gering and as the "Menta" by August Menz.

Beholla Pocket Pistol*

Beretta Model 70

BERETTA USA CORP.
Accokeek, Maryland

Beretta pistols are manufactured by Fabbrica D'Armi Pietro Beretta S.p.A. in the Gardone Valtrompia (Brescia), Italy. This prestigious firm has been in business for over 300 years. Since the late 1970s, many of the models sold in the U.S. have been made at the Accokeek (MD) plant.

Beretta Model 20 Double Action Auto Pistol **$135**
Caliber: 25 ACP. 8-shot magazine. 2.5-inch barrel. 4.9 inches overall. Weight: 10.9 oz. Plastic or walnut grips. Fixed sights. Made 1984–85.

Beretta Model 21

Beretta Model 21 Double Action Auto Pistol
Calibers: 22 LR and 25 ACP. 7-shot (22 LR) or 8-shot (25 ACP) magazine. 2¹/₂-inch barrel. 4.9 inches overall. Weight: about 12 oz. Blade front sight; V-notch rear. Walnut grips. Made from 1985 to date.
Blued Finish **$155**
Nickel Finish (22 LR only) **200**
Model 21EL Engraved Model **205**

Beretta Model 70 Automatic Pistol **$195**
Improved version of Model 1935. Steel or lightweight alloy. Calibers: 32 Auto (7.65mm), 380 Auto (9mm Short). 8-shot (32) or 7-shot (380) magazine. 3¹/₂-inch barrel. 6¹/₂ inches overall. Weight: steel, 22¹/₄ oz.; alloy, 16 oz. Fixed

Beretta Model 70 Automatic Pistol (cont.)
sights. Blued finish. Checkered plastic stocks. Made 1959–1985. *Note:* Formerly marketed in U.S. as "Puma" (alloy model in 32) and "Cougar" (steel model in 380).

Beretta Model 70S **$215**
Similar to Model 70T, except chambered for 22 Auto and 380 Auto. Longer barrel guide, safety lever blocking hammer; front and rear sight blade fixed on breechblock. Weight: 1 lb. 7 oz. Made 1977–1985.

Beretta Model 70T

Beretta Model 70T Automatic Pistol **$250**
Similar to Model 70. Caliber: 32 Automatic (7.65mm). 9-shot magazine. 6-inch barrel. 9¹/₂ inches overall. Weight: 19 oz. Adjustable rear sight, blade front sight. Blued finish. Checkered plastic stocks. Introduced in 1959. Discont.

Beretta Model 71

Beretta Model 71 Automatic Pistol **$225**
Same general specifications as alloy Model 70. Caliber: 22
LR. 6-inch barrel. 8-round magazine. Adjustable rear sight.
Medium frame. Single action. Made 1959–1989. *Note:*
Formerly marketed in U.S. as the "Jaguar Plinker." (*See*
photo, preceding page.)

Beretta Model 72

Beretta Model 72 . . . . **$220**
Same as Model 71, except has 6-inch barrel, weighs 18 oz.
Made from 1959 to date. *Note:* Formerly marketed in U.S.
as "Jaguar Plinker." Discontinued.

Beretta Model 76

Beretta Model 76 Auto Target Pistol
Caliber: 22 LR. 10-shot magazine. 6-inch barrel. 8.8 inches
overall. Weight: 33 oz. Adjustable rear sight, front sight
with interchangeable blades. Blued finish. Checkered
plastic or wood grips (Model 76W). Made 1966–1985. *Note:*
Formerly marketed in the U.S. as the "Sable."
Model 76 w/Plastic Grips **$295**
Model 76W w/Wood Grips 315

Beretta Model 81

Beretta Model 81 Double Action Auto Pistol **$250**
Caliber: 32 Automatic (7.65mm). 12-shot magazine. 3.8-
inch barrel. 6.8 inches overall. Weight: 23.5 oz. Fixed
sights. Blued finish. Plastic stocks. Made principally for
the European market 1975–1984, with similar variations
to the Model 84.

Beretta Model 84 Double Action Auto Pistol **$345**
Same as Model 81, except made in caliber 380 Automatic
with 13-shot magazine. 3.82-inch barrel. 6.8 inches overall.
Weight: 23 oz. Fixed front and rear sights. Made from
1975 to about 1982.

**Beretta Model 84B
Double Action Pistol**

Beretta Model 84B DA Auto Pistol **$325**
Improved version of Model 84 with strengthened frame
and slide, and firing-pin block safety added. Ambidextrous,
reversible magazine release. Blued or nickel finish.
Checkered black plastic or wood grips. Other specifications
same. Made about 1982–84.

Beretta Model 84BB Double Action Auto Pistol
Improved version of Model 84B, with further strengthened
slide, frame and recoil spring. Caliber: 380 ACP. 13-shot
magazine. Barrel: 3.82 inches. 6.8 inches overall. Weight:
23 oz. Checkered black plastic or wood grips. Blued or
nickel finish. Fixed sights. Made c. 1984 to date.
Blued Finish **$350**
Blued w/Wood Grips 375
Nickel Finish 390

**Beretta Model 85BB
Double Action Pistol**

Beretta Model 85 Double Action Auto Pistol $295

This is basically the same gun as the Model 84 and has seen a similar evolution. However, this 8-shot version has no ambidextrous magazine release, has a slightly narrower grip and weighs 21.8 oz. It was introduced a little later than the Model 84.

Beretta Model 85B DA Auto Pistol $315

Improved version of the Model 85. Made about 1982–85.

Beretta Model 85BB Double Action Pistol

Improved version of the Model 85B, with strenthened frame and slide. Caliber: 380 ACP. 8-shot magazine. 3.82-inch barrel. 6.8 inches overall. Weight: 21.8 oz. Blued or nickel finish. Checkered black plastic or wood grips. Made from 1985 to date.

Blued Finish w/Plastic Grips	**$325**
Blued Finish w/Wood Grips	**345**
Nickel Finish	**360**

Beretta Model 85F Double Action Pistol

Similar to the Model 85BB, except has re-contoured trigger guard and manual ambidextrous safety with decocking device. Made in 1990.

Blued Finish w/Plastic Grips	**$335**
Blued Finish w/Wood Grips	**350**
Nickel Finish w/Wood Grips	**385**

Beretta Model 86

Beretta Model 86 Double Action Auto Pistol $355

Caliber: 380 Auto. 8-shot magazine. 4.33-inch, tip-up barrel. 7.33 inches overall. Weight: 23 oz. Made 1986–89. (Reintroduced 1990 in the Cheetah Series.)

Beretta Model 87BB

Beretta Model 87BB Auto Pistol

Similar to the Model 85, except in 22 LR with 8-shot magazine and optional extended 6-inch barrel (in single action). Overall length: 6.8 inches; 8.9 w/6-inch bbl. Weight: 20.8 oz.; 23 oz. w/6-inch bbl. Checkered wood grips. Made from 1977 to date.

Blued Finish (Double Action)	**$340**
Long Barrel (Single Action)	**350**

Beretta Model 89 Target Automatic Pistol $475

Caliber: 22 LR. 8-shot magazine. 6-inch barrel. 9.5 inches overall. Weight: 41 oz. Adjustable target sights. Blued finish. Target-style walnut stocks. Made 1990 to date.

Beretta Model 90

Beretta Model 90 Double Action Auto Pistol $220

Caliber: 32 Auto (7.65mm). 8-shot magazine. $3^5/_8$-inch barrel. $6^5/_8$ inches overall. Weight: $19^1/_2$ oz. Fixed sights. Blued finish. Checkered plastic grips. Made 1969–1975.

Beretta Model 92

Beretta Model 92 Double Action Auto Pistol $395

Caliber: 9mm Luger. 15-shot magazine. 4.9-inch barrel. 8.5 inches overall. Weight: 33.5 oz. Fixed sights. Blued finish. Plastic stocks. Made from 1976 to date.

Beretta Model 92D Double Action Auto Pistol

Same general specifications as Model 92F, except DA only with bobbed hammer and 3-Dot Sight.

Model 92D	**$420**
Model 92D w/Triticon Sight...................	**470**

Beretta Model 92F Compact DA Auto $395

Caliber: 9mm Parabellum. 12-shot magazine. 4.3-inch barrel. 7.8 inches overall. Weight: 31.5 oz. Wood grips. Square-notched bar rear sight; blade front sight, integral with slide. Made from 1986 to date.

Beretta Model 92F Double Action Auto Pistol

Same general specifications as Model 92, except with slide-mounted safety and repositioned magazine release. Replaced Model 92SB. Blued or stainless finish. Made from 1985 to date.

Blued Finish **$410**
Stainless Finish **495**

Beretta Model 92F-EL Double Action Auto Pistol

Deluxe version of Model 92F with gold trim and logo inlay. Deluxe walnut stocks.

Model 92F-EL Gold **$595**
Model 92F-EL Stainless **930**

Beretta Model 92SB Double Action Auto Pistol . . **$395**

Same general specifications as standard Model 92, except has slide-mounted safety and repositioned magazine release. Discontinued 1985.

Beretta Model 318 (1934)*

Beretta Model 92 SB-F

Beretta Model 92 SB-F DA Auto Pistol **$415**

Caliber: 9mm Parabellum. 15-shot magazine. Barrel: 4.9 inches. 8 1/2 inches overall. Weight: 34 oz. Plastic or wood grips. Square-notched bar rear sight; blade front sight, integral with slide. This model, also called **Model 92S-1**, the standard-issue sidearm for the U.S. Armed Forces. Made from 1985 to date.

Beretta Model 96 Double Action Auto Pistol

Same general specifications as Model 92F, except in 40 S&W. 10-shot magazine (9-shot in Compact Model).

Model 96 Standard **$425**
Model 96 Centurion (Compact) **435**
Model 96 D (DA only) **420**
Model 96 w/Triticon Sights **485**

Beretta Model 101 . . . . **$215**

Same as Model 70T, except caliber 22 LR, has 10-shot magazine. Introduced in 1959. Discontinued.

Beretta Model 318 (1934) Auto Pistol **$255**

Caliber: 25 Automatic (6.35mm). 8-shot magazine. 2 1/2-inch barrel. 4 1/2 inches overall. Weight: 14 oz. Fixed sights. Blued finish. Plastic stocks. Made 1934–c. 1939.

Beretta Model 949 Olimpionico Auto Pistol **$525**

Calibers: 22 Short, 22 LR. 5-shot magazine. 8 3/4-inch barrel. 12 1/2 inches overall. Weight: 38 oz. Target sights. Adjustable barrel weight. Muzzle brake. Checkered walnut stocks with thumbrest. Made 1959–1964.

Beretta Model 949 Olimpionico

Beretta Model 950B

Beretta Model 950B Auto Pistol **$125**

Same general specifications as Model 950CC, except caliber 25 Auto, has 7-shot magazine. Made from 1959 to date. *Note:* Formerly marketed in the U.S. as "Jetfire."

Beretta Model 950 BS Single Action Semiautomatic

Calibers: 25 ACP or 22 Short. Magazine capacity: 7 rounds (22 short); 8 rounds (25 ACP). 2 1/2- or 4-inch barrel. 4 1/2 inches overall (2 1/2-inch bbl.) Weight: about 10 oz. Blade front sight; V-notch in rear. Checkered black plastic grips. Made from 1987 to date.

Blued Finish **$125**
Nickel Finish **160**
With 4-inch bbl. (22 short) **140**
Model 950 EL gold-etched version **210**

**Beretta Model 950 BS
22 Short**

Beretta Model 951 (1951)

Beretta Model 951 (1951) Military (cont.)
Egyptian and Israeli models usually command a premium. Formerly marketed in the U.S. as the "Brigadier."

Beretta Model 950CC

Beretta Model 950CC Auto Pistol **$125**
Caliber: 22 Short. 6-shot magazine. Hinged, 2³/₈-inch barrel. 4³/₄ inches overall. Weight: 11 oz. Fixed sights. Blued finish. Plastic stocks. Made from 1959 to date. *Note:* Formerly marketed in the U.S. as "Minx M2."

Beretta Model 1915

Beretta Model 1915 Auto Pistol **$285**
Calibers: 9mm Glisenti and 32 ACP (7.65mm). 8-shot magazine. 4-inch barrel. 6.7 inches overall (9mm), 5.7 inches (32 ACP). Weight: 30 oz. (9mm), 20 oz. (32 ACP). Fixed sights. Blued finish. Wood grips. Made 1915–1922. An improved postwar 1915/1919 version in caliber 32 ACP was later offered for sale in 1922 as the Model 1922.

Beretta Model 950CC Special

Beretta Model 950CC Special Auto Pistol **$130**
Same general specifications as Model 950CC Auto, except has 4-inch barrel. Made from 1959 to date. *Note:* Formerly marketed in the U.S. as "Minx M4."

Beretta Model 951 (1951) Military Auto Pistol . . . **$245**
Caliber: 9mm Luger. 8-shot magazine. 4¹/₂-inch barrel. 8 inches overall. Weight: 31 oz. Fixed sights. Blued finish. Plastic stocks. Made from 1952 to date. *Note:* This is the standard pistol of the Italian Armed Forces; also used by Egyptian and Israeli armies and by the police in Nigeria

Beretta Model 1923

Beretta Model 1923 Auto Pistol $565
Caliber: 9mm Glisenti (Luger). 8-shot magazine. 4-inch barrel. 6½ inches overall. Weight: 30 oz. Fixed sights. Blued finish. Plastic stocks. Made 1923–c. 1936. (*See photo, preceding page.*)

Beretta Model 1934

Beretta Model 1934 Auto Pistol
Caliber: 380 Automatic (9mm Short). 7-shot magazine. 3⅜-inch barrel. 5⅞ inches overall. Weight: 24 oz. Fixed sights. Blued finish. Plastic stocks. Official pistol of the Italian Armed Forces. Wartime pieces not as well made and finished as commercial models. Made 1934–1959.
Commercial Model **$265**
War Model **325**

Beretta Model 1935

Beretta Model 1935 Auto Pistol
Caliber: 32 ACP (7.65mm). 8-shot magazine. 3½-inch barrel. 5¾ inches overall. Weight: 24 oz. Fixed sights. Blued finish. Plastic stocks. A roughly finished version of this pistol was produced during WW II. Made 1935–1959.
Commercial Model **$245**
War Model **225**

══ VINCENZO BERNARDELLI, S.P.A. ══
Gardone V. T. (Brescia), Italy

Bernardelli Model 60 Pocket Automatic Pistol . . **$190**
Calibers: 22 LR, 32 Auto (7.65mm), 380 Auto (9mm Short). 8-shot magazine (22 and 32), 7-shot (380). 3½-inch barrel. 6½ inches overall. Weight: about 25 oz. Fixed sights. Blued finish. Bakelite stocks. Made 1959–1990.

Bernardelli Model 60

Bernardelli Model 68 Automatic Pistol $120
Caliber: 6.35. 5- and 8-shot magazine. 2⅛-inch barrel. 4⅛ inches overall. Weight: 10 oz. Fixed sights. Blued or chrome finish. Bakelite or pearl stocks. This model, like its smaller bore 22-counterpart, was known as the "Baby" Bernardelli.

Bernardelli Model 69 Automatic Target Pistol . . . $395
Caliber: 22 LR. 10-shot magazine. 5.9-inch barrel. 9 inches overall. Weight: 2.2 lbs. Fully adjustable target sights. Blued finish. Stippled right- or left-hand wrap-around walnut grips. Made from 1987 to date. *Note:* This was previously Model 100.

Bernardelli Model 80

Bernardelli Model 80 Automatic Pistol **$165**
Calibers: 22 LR, 32 ACP (7.65mm), 380 Auto (9mm Short). Magazine capacity: 10-shot (22), 8-shot (32), 7-shot (380). 3½-inch barrel. 6½ inches overall. Weight: 25.6 oz. Adjustable rear sight, white dot front sight. Blued finish. Plastic thumbrest stocks. *Note:* Model 80 is a modification of Model 60 designed to conform with U.S. import regulations. Made 1968–1988.

Bernardelli Model 90 Sport Target **$175**
Same as Model 80, except has 6-inch barrel, is 9 inches overall, weighs 26.8 oz. Made 1968–1990.

Bernardelli Model 90

Bernardelli P018 Compact Model **$395**
Slightly smaller version of the Model P018 standard DA automatic, except has 14-shot magazine and 4-inch barrel. 7.68 inches overall. Weight: 33 oz. Walnut grips only. Imported 1987–1991.

**Bernardelli P018 DA
Auto Pistol**

Bernardelli Model 100

Bernardelli P018 Double Action Automatic Pistol
Caliber: 9mm Parabellum. 16-shot magazine. 4³/₄-inch barrel. 8¹/₂ inches overall. Weight: 36 oz. Fixed combat sights. Blued finish. Checkered plastic or walnut stocks. Imported 1987–1991.
With Plastic Grips **$370**
With Walnut Grips **380**

Bernardelli Model 100 Target Automatic Pistol . . **$315**
Caliber: 22 LR. 10-shot magazine. 5.9-inch barrel. 9 inches overall. Weight: 37³/₄ oz. Adj. rear sight, interchangeable front sights. Blued finish. Checkered walnut thumbrest stocks. Made 1969–1986: *Note:* Formerly Model 69.

Bernardelli Sporter

Bernardelli "Baby"

Bernardelli Sporter Automatic Pistol **$245**
Caliber: 22 LR. 8-shot magazine. Barrel lengths: 6-, 8-, and 10-inch. 13 inches overall with 10-inch barrel. Weight: about 30 oz. with 10-inch barrel. Target sights. Blued finish. Walnut stocks. Made 1949–1968.

Bernardelli "Baby" Automatic Pistol **$175**
Calibers: 22 Short, 22 Long. 5-shot magazine. 2¹/₈-inch barrel. 4¹/₈ inches overall. Weight: 9 oz. Fixed sights. Blued finish. Bakelite stocks. Made 1949–1968.

Bernardelli Model P010 Automatic Pistol **$405**
Caliber: 22 LR. 5- and 10-shot magazine. 5.9-inch barrel with 7.5-inch sight radius. Weight: 40.0 oz. Interchangeable front sight; adjustable rear. Blued finish. Textured walnut stocks. Discontinued 1990.

Bernardelli Vest Pocket

Bernardelli Vest Pocket Automatic Pistol $185

Caliber: 25 Auto (6.35mm). 5- or 8-shot magazine. 2$\frac{1}{8}$-inch barrel. 4$\frac{1}{8}$ inches overall. Weight: 9 oz. Fixed sights. Blued finish. Bakelite stocks. Made 1945–1968. (*See* photo, preceding page.)

BERSA PISTOLS
Imported from Argentina by Eagle Imports

Bersa firearms have been imported by other distributors, including Interarms and Outdoor Sports Headquarters.

Bersa Model 23

Bersa Model 23 Double Action Auto Pistol

Caliber: 22 LR. 10-shot magazine. 4-inch barrel. Fixed front sight; square-notch adj. rear. Blued or satin nickel finish. Textured wood stocks. Imported 1989 to date.
Blued Finish **$175**
Satin Nickel **200**

Bersa Model 83

Bersa Model 83 Double Action Auto Pistol

Caliber: 380 ACP. 7-shot magazine. 3$\frac{1}{2}$-inch barrel. Front blade sight integral on slide; square-notch rear adjustable for windage. Blued or satin nickel finish. Custom wood stocks. Imported 1990 to date.
Blued Finish **$170**
Satin Nickel **205**

Bersa Model 85

Bersa Model 85 Double Action Auto Pistol

Same general specifications as Model 83, except 13-shot magazine. Imported 1990 to date.
Blued Finish **$230**
Satin Nickel **275**

Bersa Model 86 Double Action Auto Pistol

Same general specifications as Model 85, except available in matte blue finish and with neoprene grips.
Matte Blue Finish **$235**
Nickel Finish **265**

Bersa Model 97

Bersa Model 97 Auto Pistol $275

Caliber: 380 ACP. 7-shot magazine. 3$\frac{1}{2}$-inch barrel. 6$\frac{1}{2}$ inches overall. Weight: 28 oz. Introduced 1982; disc.

Bersa Model 223

Same general specifications as Model 383, except in 22 LR w/10-round magazine capacity. Discontinued 1987.
Double Action **$165**
Single Action **150**

Bersa Model 224

Caliber: 22 LR. 10-shot magazine. 4-inch barrel. Weight: 26 oz. Front blade sight; square-notched rear adj. for windage. Blued finish. Checkered nylon or custom wood grips. Made from 1984; SA discontinued 1986.
Double Action **$170**
Single Action **165**

Bersa Model 226

Same general specifications as Model 224, but with 6-inch barrel. Discontinued.
Double Action **$170**
Single Action **160**

Bersa Model 383 Auto Pistol
Caliber: 380 Auto. 7-shot magazine. 3½-inch barrel. Front blade sight integral on slide; square-notched rear sight adjustable for windage. Custom wood grips on double action; nylon grips on single action. Blued or satin nickel finish. Made from 1984; SA discontinued 1989.

Double Action	**$145**
Single Action	**125**
Satin Nickel	**155**

Bersa Model 622

Bersa Model 622 Auto Pistol $125
Caliber: 22 LR. 7-shot magazine. 4- or 6-inch barrel. 7 or 9 inches overall. Weight: 2¼ pounds. Blade front sight; square-notch rear adj. for windage. Blued finish. Nylon grips. Made 1982–87.

Bersa Model 644

Bersa Model 644 Auto Pistol $135
Caliber: 22 LR. 10-shot magazine. 3.5-inch barrel. Weight: 26½ oz. 6½ inches overall. Adjustable rear sight, blade front. Contoured black nylon grips. Made 1980–88.

Bersa Thunder 9 Pistol

Bersa Thunder 9 Auto Pistol
Caliber: 9mm Parabellum. 15-shot magazine. 4-inch barrel. 7⅜ inches overall. Weight: 30 oz. Blade front sight, adjustable rear w/3-dot system. Ambidextrous safety and decocking devise. Checkered black polymer grips. Matte blue, satin nickel or Duo-Tone finish. Made from 1993 to date.

Blued Finish	**$295**
Satin Nickel Finish	**340**
Duo-Tone Finish	**310**

Bersa Thunder 380 DA Auto Pistol
Caliber: 380 ACP. 7-shot magazine. 3½-inch barrel. 6.6 inches overall. Weight: 25.75 oz. Fixed sights. Black rubber grips. Blued, satin nickel or Duo-Tone finish. Made 1995 to date.

Blued Finish	**$160**
Satin Nickel Finish	**190**
Duo-Tone Finish	**175**

BRNO PISTOLS

Manufactured in Czechoslovakia

See listings under CZ Pistols.

BRONCO PISTOL
Eibar, Spain
Manufactured by Echave y Arizmendi

Bronco Model 1918*

Bronco Model 1918 Pocket Automatic Pistol ... $115
Caliber: 32 ACP (7.65mm). 6-shot magazine. 2½-inch barrel. 5 inches overall. Weight: 20 oz. Fixed sights. Blued finish. Hard rubber stocks. Made circa 1918–1925.

BROWNING PISTOLS
Morgan, Utah

The following Browning pistols have been manufactured by Fabrique Nationale d'Armes de Guerre (now Fabrique Nationale Herstal) of Herstal, Belgium; by Arms Technology Inc. of Salt Lake City; and by J. P. Sauer & Sohn of Eckernförde, W. Germany. (*See also* FN Browning and J.P. Sauer & Sohn listings.)

Browning 9mm Gold Classic

Browning 9mm Classic
Same general specifications as 9mm Auto (Hi-Power), except for high-grade engraving, finely checkered walnut grips with double border, and limited to 5000 production. Gold Classic limited to 500 production. Made 1985–86.
Gold Classic **$1595**
Standard Classic   850

**Browning 25 Automatic
Standard Model**

Browning 25 Automatic Pistol
Same general specifications as FN Browning Baby (*see* separate listing). Standard Model, blued finish, hard rubber grips. Lightweight Model, nickel-plated, Nacrolac pearl grips. Renaissance Engraved Model, nickel-plated, Nacrolac pearl grips. Made by FN 1955–1969.
Standard Model **$260**
Lightweight Model   355
Renaissance Model   695

**Browning 380 Automatic
Standard Model (1955-Type)**

Browning 380 Automatic Pistol, 1955 Type
Same general specifications as FN Browning 380 Pocket Auto. Standard Model, Renaissance Engraved Model, as furnished in 25 Automatic. Made by FN 1955–1969.
Standard Model **$325**
Renaissance Model   895

**Browning 380 Automatic
Standard Model (1971-Type)**

Browning 380 Automatic Pistol, 1971 Type
Same as 380 Automatic, 1955 Type, except has longer slide, $4^{7}/_{16}$-inch barrel, is $7^{1}/_{16}$ inches overall, weighs 23 oz. Rear sight adjustable for windage and elevation, plastic thumbrest stocks. Made 1971–75.
Standard Model **$275**
Renaissance Model   795

Browning BDA Automatic

Browning BDA Double Action Automatic Pistol . . **$375**
Similar to SIG-Sauer P220. Calibers: 9mm Luger, 38 Super Auto, 45 Auto. 9-shot magazine (9mm and 38), 7-shot (45 cal). 4.4-inch barrel. 7.8 inches overall. Weight: 29.3 oz. Fixed sights. Blued finish. Plastic stocks. Made from 1977–79 by J. P. Sauer.

**Browning BDA-380
Nickel**

Browning BDA-380 Double Action Automatic Pistol
Caliber: 380 Auto. 13-shot magazine. Barrel length: $3^{13}/_{16}$ inches. $6^{3}/_{4}$ inches overall. Weight: 23 oz. Fixed blade front sight, square notch drift adjustable rear sight. Made from 1982 to date.
Blued finish **$335**
Nickel finish   350

**Browning BDM 9mm
Double Action**

**Browning Buck Mark 22
Silhouette**

Browning BDM 9mm DA Automatic Pistol **$395**
Caliber: 9mm Luger. 15-shot magazine. 4.73-inch barrel.
7.85 inches overall. Weight: 31 oz. Low-profile removable
blade front sight and windage-adjustable rear sight w/3-
Dot system. Matte blue finish. Features selectable shooting mode. Made from 1991 to date.

Browning Buck Mark 22 Automatic Pistol **$155**
Caliber: 22 LR. 10-shot magazine. Barrel: 5½ inches. 9½
inches overall. Weight: 32 oz. Black molded grips. Adjustable rear sight. Made from 1985 to date.

Browning Buck Mark 22 Field Auto **$165**
Same general specifications as the standard Buck Mark
22, except with hoodless ramp-style front and low-profile
rear sights. Contoured walnut grips. Made 1991 to date.

**Browning Buck Mark
Micro 22**

Browning Buck Mark 22 Micro
Same general specifications as standard Buck Mark 22,
except with 4-inch barrel. 8 inches overall. Weight: 32 oz.
Molded composite grips. Ramp front sight; Pro Target
rear sight. Made from 1992 to date.
Blued Finish **$145**
Nickel finish **180**

Browning Buck Mark 22 Plus **$175**
Same general specifications as standard Buck Mark 22,
except for black molded, impregnated hardwood grips.
Made from 1987 to date.

Browning Buck Mark 22 Silhouette **$255**
Same general specifications as standard Buck Mark 22,
except for 9⅞-inch barrel, 53-oz. weight, target sights
mounted on full-length scope base, and laminated hardwood grips and forend. Made from 1987 to date.

Browning Buck Mark 22 Target 5.5 . . . . **$235**
Same general specifications as Buck Mark 22, except 5½-
inch barrel, 35½-oz. weight and target sights mounted on
full-length scope base. Made from 1989 to date.

Browning Buck Mark 22 Target 5.5 (Gold) **$255**
Caliber: 22 LR. 10-shot magazine. 5½-inch barrel. 9⅝
inches overall. Weight: 35 oz. Hooded blade front sight;
adjustable rear sight. Contoured walnut grips. Made from
1991 to date.

Browning Buck Mark 22 Unlimited Silhouette . . . **$295**
Same general specifications as standard Buck Mark 22
Silhouette, except with 14-inch barrel. 18¹¹⁄₁₆ inches
overall. Weight: 64 oz. Interchangeable post front sight
and Pro Target rear. Nickel finish. Made 1992 to date.

Browning Buck Mark 22 Varmint Auto Pistol **$225**
Same general specifications as standard Buck Mark 22,
except for 9⅞-inch barrel, 48-oz. weight, no sights, full-
length scope base, and laminated hardwood grips. Made
from 1987 to date.

**Browning Challenger
Standard Model**

**Browning Challenger
Gold Model**

Browning Challenger Renaissance Model

Browning Challenger Automatic Pistol

Caliber: 22 LR. 10-shot magazine. Barrel lengths: 4 1/2- and 6 3/4-inch. 11 7/16 inches overall w/6 3/4-inch bbl. Weight: 38 oz. w/6 3/4-inch bbl. Removable blade front sight, screw adjustable rear. Standard finish, blue; also furnished gold-inlaid (Gold Model) and engraved and chrome-plated (Renaissance Model). Checkered walnut stocks; finely figured and carved stocks on Gold and Renaissance Models. Standard made by FN 1962–1975, higher grades intro. in 1971; discontinued. (*See* photos, preceding page.)

Standard Model . . . . $ 275
Gold Model 950
Renaissance Model 1095

Browning Challenger II

Browning Challenger III

Browning Challenger III Sporter 22

Browning Challenger II Automatic Pistol $185
Same general specifications as Challenger Standard Model with 6 3/4-inch barrel, changed grip angle and impregnated hardwood stocks. Original Challenger design modified for lower production costs. Made by ATI 1976–1983.

Browning Challenger III Automatic Pistol $180
Same general description as Challenger II, except has 5 1/2-inch bull barrel, alloy frame and new sight system. Weight: 35 oz. Made 1982–84. **Sporter Model** w/6 3/4-inch barrel made 1984–86.

Browning 9mm Hi-Power Ambidextrous Safety

Browning Hi-Power 9mm Ambidextrous Safety . . $345
Same general specifications as standard 9mm Hi-Power (*see* below), except with matte blued finish and ambidextrous safety. Made from 1987 to date.

Browning Hi-Power SA w/Contour Molded Grips

Browning 9mm Hi-Power Standard Model (Fixed Sights, Walnut Grips)

Browning Hi-Power 9mm Automatic Pistol

Same general specifications as FN Browning Model 1935 (*see* separate listing). DA or SA. 13-shot. Barrel: about 5 inches. 7³/₄ inches overall. Weight: 32 oz. Fixed sights; also available with rear sight adjustable for windage and elevation and ramp front sight. Standard Model, blued finish, checkered walnut or contour-molded stocks. Renaissance Engraved Model, chrome-plated, Nacrolac pearl stocks. Made by FN from 1955 to date.

Standard Model, fixed sights **$335**
Standard Model, adjustable sights **375**
Renaissance Model, fixed sights **795**
Renaissance Model, adjustable sights **850**

Browning Hi-Power 40 S&W Auto Pistol **$395**

Similar to the standard 9mm Hi-Power, except in caliber 40 S&W with 10-shot magazine. 4⁵/₈-inch barrel. 7³/₄ inches overall. Weight: 35 oz. Matte blued finish. Molded Polyamide grips. Made from 1993 to date.

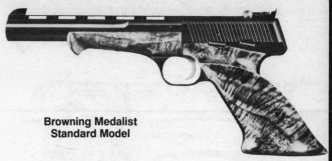

**Browning Medalist
Standard Model**

**Browning Medalist
Renaissance Model**

Browning HP Practical

Browning HP Practical Hi-Power Automatic Pistol

Similar to the standard Hi-Power, except has silver-chromed frame and blued slide with Commander-style hammer. Made from 1991 to date.

With Fixed Sights **$395**
With Adjustable Sights **445**

Browning Medalist Automatic Target Pistol

Caliber: 22 LR. 10-shot magazine. 6³/₄-inch barrel w/vent rib. 11¹⁵/₁₆ inches overall. Weight: 46 oz. Removable blade front sight, click-adjustable micrometer rear. Standard finish, blue; also furnished gold-inlaid (Gold Model) and engraved and chrome-plated (Renaissance Model). Checkered walnut stocks with thumbrest (for right- or left-handed shooter); finely figured and carved stocks on Gold and Renaissance Models. Made by FN 1962–1975; higher grades introduced in 1971.

Standard Model . . . . **$ 595**
Gold Model **1200**
Renaissance Model **1650**

Browning International Medalist

Browning International Medalist Automatic Target Pistol **$575**

Modification of Medalist to conform with International Shooting Union rules; has 5.9-inch barrel, smaller grip, no forearm. Weight: 42 oz. Made 1970–73.

Browning Nomad

Browning Nomad Automatic Pistol **$265**

Caliber: 22 LR. 10-shot magazine. Barrel lengths: 4¹/₂- and 6³/₄-inch. 8¹⁵/₁₆ inches overall w/4¹/₂-inch bbl. Weight: 34 oz. (4¹/₂-inch bbl.). Removable blade front sight, screw adjustable rear. Blued finish. Plastic stocks. Made by FN 1962–1974.

Browning Renaissance 9mm, 25 Auto and 380 Auto (1955) Engraved Models, Cased Set **$3595**

One pistol of each of the three models in a special walnut carrying case; all chrome-plated with Nacrolac pearl stocks. Made by FN 1955–1969.

BUDISCHOWSKY PISTOL
Mt. Clemens, Michigan
Mfd. by Norton Armament Corporation

Budischowsky TP-70

Budischowsky TP-70 Double Action Automatic Pistol
Calibers: 22 LR, 25 Auto. 6-shot magazine. 2.6-inch barrel. 4.65 inches overall. Weight: 12.3 oz. Fixed sights. Stainless steel. Plastic stocks. Made 1973–77.
22 Long Rifle **$375**
25 Automatic **275**

CALICO LIGHT WEAPONS SYSTEMS
Bakersfield, California

Calico Model 110 Auto Pistol **$300**
Caliber: 22 LR. 100-shot magazine. 6-inch barrel. 17.9 inches overall. Weight: 3³/₄ lbs. Sights: adjustable post front; fixed U-notch rear. Black finish aluminum frame. Molded composition grip. Made 1986–1994.

Calico Model M-950 Auto Pistol **$395**
Caliber: 9mm Parabellum. 50- or 100-shot magazine. 7¹/₂-inch barrel. 14 inches overall. Weight: 2¹/₄ lbs. Sights: adjustable post front; fixed U-notch rear. Glass-filled polymer grip. Made 1989–1994.

CHARTER ARMS CORPORATION
Stratford, Connecticut

AUTOMATIC PISTOLS

NOTE: For ease in finding a particular Charter Arms handgun, the listings are divided into two groupings: Automatic Pistols (below) and Revolvers, which follows. For a complete listing of Charter Arms handguns, please refer to the Index.

Charter Arms Model 40 Automatic Pistol **$235**
Caliber: 22 RF. 8-shot magazine. 3.3-inch barrel. 6.3 inches overall. Weight: 21¹/₂ oz. Fixed sights. Checkered walnut grips. Stainless steel finish. Made 1985–86.

Charter Arms Model 79K Automatic Pistol **$295**
Calibers: 380 or 32 Auto. 7-shot magazine. 3.6-inch barrel. 6.5 inches overall. Weight: 24¹/₂ oz. Fixed sights. Checkered walnut grips. Stainless steel finish. Made 1985–86.

Charter Arms Explorer II

**Charter Arms Explorer II
Silvertone w/Optional Barrels**

Charter Arms Explorer II Semiauto Survival Pistol
Caliber: 22 RF. 8-shot magazine. 6-, 8- or 10-inch barrel. 13¹/₂ inches overall w/6-inch barrel. Weight: 28 oz. Finishes: black, heat cured, semigloss textured enamel or silvertone anticorrosion. Discontinued 1987.
Standard Model **$75**
Silvertone (w/optional 6- and 10-inch bbls.) **85**

REVOLVERS

NOTE: The following section contains only Charter Arms Revolvers. Pistols may be found in the preceding section. For a complete listing of Charter Arms handguns, please refer to the Index.

Charter Arms Bonnie

Charter Arms Clyde

Charter Arms Bonnie and Clyde Set $395

Matching pair of shrouded 2½-inch barrel revolvers, chambered for 32 Magnum and 38 Special. Blued finish with scrolled name on barrels.

Charter Arms Bulldog 44

Charter Arms Bulldog 44 Double Action Revolver

Caliber: 44 Special. 5-shot cylinder. 2½-inch bull or 3-inch unshrouded barrel. 7½ inches overall (w/3-inch bbl.). Weight: 19 oz. (3-inch bbl.) Fixed sights. Blued, electroless nickel or stainless finish. Checkered walnut or neoprene grips. Made 1973–91; reintroduced 1994.

Blued Finish w/2½") bull bbl.	$190
Blued Finish w/3" bbl. (Disc. 1988)	195
Nickel Finish	215
Stainless Finish	225

Charter Arms Bulldog 357

Charter Arms Bulldog 357 DA Revolver $165

Caliber: 357 Magnum. 5-shot cylinder. 6-inch barrel. 11 inches overall. Weight: 25 oz. Fixed sights. Blued finish. Square, checkered walnut grips. Intro. 1977; discontinued.

Charter Arms Bulldog New Police DA Revolver

Same general specifications as Bulldog Police, except chambered for 44 Special. 5-shot cylinder. 2½- or 3½-inch barrel. Made 1990–92.

Blued Finish	$180
Stainless Finish (2½-inch barrel only)	220

**Charter Arms Police Bulldog
Old Model**

**Charter Arms Police Bulldog
New Model**

**Charter Arms Police Bulldog
32 H&R Magnum**

Charter Arms Bulldog Police Double Action Revolver

Caliber: 38 Special or 32 H&R Magnum. 6-shot cylinder. 4-inch barrel. 8½ inches overall. Weight: 20½ oz. Adjustable rear sight, ramp front. Blued or stainless finish. Square checkered walnut grips. Made from 1976 to date. Shroud dropped on new model.

Blued Finish	$160
Stainless Finish	195
32 H&R Magnum (Discontinued 1992)	210

Charter Arms Bulldog Pug Double Action Revolver

Caliber: 44 Special. 5-shot cylinder. 2½-inch barrel. 7¼ inches overall. Weight: 20 oz. Blued or stainless finish. Fixed ramp front sight; fixed square-notch rear. Checkered

Charter Arms Bulldog Pug

Charter Arms Bulldog Pug DA (cont.)
neoprene or walnut grips. Made from 1988 to date.
Blued Finish **$195**
Stainless Finish **220**

Charter Arms Bulldog Target

Charter Arms Bulldog Target DA Revolver
Calibers: 357 Magnum, 44 Special (latter introduced in 1977). 4-inch barrel. 8$1/2$ inches overall. Weight: in 357, 20$1/2$ oz. Adjustable rear sight, ramp front. Blued finish. Square checkered walnut grips. Made 1976–1992.
Blued Finish **$175**
Stainless Steel **225**

Charter Arms Bulldog Tracker

Charter Arms Bulldog Tracker DA Revolver **$165**
Caliber: 357 Mag. 5-shot cylinder. 2$1/2$-, 4- or 6-inch barrel. 11 inches overall w/6-inch barrel. Weight: 21 oz., 2$1/2$-

Charter Arms Bulldog Tracker DA (cont.)
inch barrel. Adjustable rear sight, ramp front. Checkered walnut grips. Blued finish. 4- and 6-inch barrels discontinued 1986.

Charter Arms Off-Duty Double Action Revolver
Calibers: 22 LR or 38 Special. 6-shot (22 LR) or 5-shot (38 Spec.) cylinder. 2-inch barrel. 6$1/4$ inches overall. Weight: 16 oz. Fixed rear sight, Patridge-type front sight. Plain walnut grips. Matte black, electroless nickel or stainless steel finish.
Matte Black Finish **$130**
Electroless Nickel **185**
Stainless Steel **175**

**Charter Arms Pathfinder
Old Model**

**Charter Arms Pathfinder
New Model**

**Charter Arms Pathfinder
Stainless**

Charter Arms Pathfinder Double Action Revolver
Calibers: 22 LR, 22 WMR. 6-shot cylinder. Barrel lengths: 2-, 3-, 6-inch. 7$1/8$ inches overall w/3-inch barrel and regular stocks. Weight: 18$1/2$ oz. w/3-inch barrel. Adjustable rear sight, ramp front. Blued or stainless finish. Plain walnut regular, checkered Bulldog or square buttstocks. Made from 1970 to date. *Note:* Originally designated "Pocket Target," name was changed in 1971 to "Pathfinder." Grips changed in 1984. Disc. 1993.
Blued Finish **$145**
Stainless Finish **175**

Charter Arms Pitbull Double Action Revolver

Calibers: 9mm, 357 Magnum, 38 Special. 5-shot cylinder. 2½-, 3½- or 4-inch barrel. 7 inches overall w/2½-inch barrel. Weight: 21½ to 25 oz. All stainless steel frame. Fixed ramp front sight; fixed square-notch rear. Checkered neoprene grips. Blued or stainless finish. Made 1989–1993.

Blued Finish **$175**
Stainless Finish **195**

Charter Arms Undercover Pocket Police (cont.)

Blued Finish **$150**
Stainless Steel **165**

**Charter Arms Undercover Police
38 Special, Blued**

**Charter Arms Undercover
Stainless**

Charter Arms Undercover Double Action Revolver

Caliber: 38 Special. 5-shot cylinder. Barrel lengths: 2-, 3-, 4-inch. 6¼ inches overall w/2-inch barrel and regular grips. Weight: 16 oz. w/2-inch barrel. Fixed sights. Plain walnut, checkered Bulldog or square buttstocks. Made 1965–1994.

Blued or Nickel-plated Finish **$155**
Stainless Finish **175**

**Charter Arms Undercover Police
32 H&R Magnum**

Charter Arms Undercover Police DA Revolver

Same general specifications as standard Undercover, except has 6-shot cylinder.

38 Special, Blued **$165**
38 Special, Stainless **185**
32 H&R Magnum **150**

**Charter Arms Undercover
32 S&W Long**

Charter Arms Undercoverette

Charter Arms Undercover 32 H&R Magnum or S&W Long

Same general specifications as standard Undercover, except chambered for 32 H&R Magnum or 32 S&W Long, has 6-shot cylinder and 2½" barrel.

32 H&R Magnum (Blued) **$140**
32 H&R Magnum (Stainless) **180**
32 S&W Long (Blued) Disc. 1989 . . . . **125**

Charter Arms Undercover Pocket Police DA

Same general specifications as standard Undercover, except has 6-shot cylinder and pocket-type hammer. Blued or stainless steel finish.

Charter Arms Undercoverette DA Revolver **$135**

Same as Undercover model with 2-inch barrel, except caliber 32 S&W Long, 6-shot cylinder, blued finish only; weighs 16½ oz. Made 1972–1983.

COLT MANUFACTURING CO., INC.
Hartford, Connecticut

Previously Colt Industries, Firearms Division. Production of some Colt handguns spans the period from before World War II to the postwar years. Values shown for these models are for earlier production. Those manufactured c. 1946 and later generally are less desirable to collectors, and values are approximately 30 percent lower.

AUTOMATIC PISTOLS

NOTE: For ease in finding a particular firearm, Colt handguns are grouped into three sections: Automatic Pistols (below), Single Shot Pistols and Deringers (page 50), and Revolvers (page 51). For a complete listing, please refer to the Index.

Colt Model 1900 38 Automatic Pistol **$4595**
Caliber: 38 ACP (*modern high-velocity cartridges should not be used in this pistol*). 7-shot magazine. 6-inch barrel. 9 inches overall. Weight: 35 oz. Fixed sights. Blued finish. Plain walnut stocks. Sharp-spur hammer. Combination rear sight and safety. Made 1900–1903.

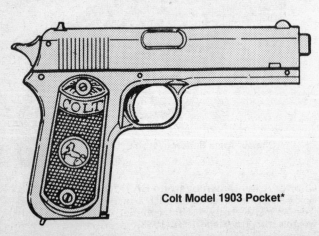

Colt Model 1902 Military

Colt Model 1902 Military 38 Automatic Pistol . . **$1295**
Caliber: 38 ACP (*modern high-velocity cartridges should not be used in this pistol*). 8-shot magazine. 6-inch barrel. 9 inches overall. Weight: 37 oz. Fixed sights, knife-blade and V-notch. Blued finish. Checkered hard rubber stocks. Round back hammer, changed to spur type in 1908. No safety. Made 1902–1929.

Colt Model 1903 Pocket*

Colt Model 1902 Sporting 38 Automatic Pistol . **$1650**
Caliber: 38 ACP (*modern high-velocity cartridges should not be used in this pistol*). 7-shot magazine. 6-inch barrel. 9 inches overall. Weight: 35 oz. Fixed sights, knife-blade and V-notch. Blued finish. Checkered hard rubber stocks. Round back hammer. No safety. Made 1902–1908.

Colt Model 1903 Pocket 38 Automatic Pistol . . . **$725**
Caliber: 38 ACP (*modern high-velocity cartridges should not be used in this pistol*). Similar to Model 1902 Sporting 38, but with 4 1/2-inch barrel. 7 1/2 inches overall. Weight: 31 oz. Fixed sights, knife-blade and V-notch. Blued finish. Checkered hard rubber stocks. Round back hammer, changed to spur type in 1908. No safety. Made 1903–1929.

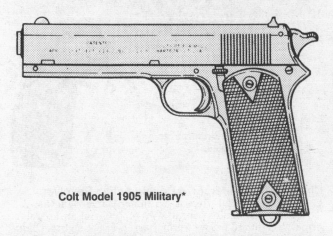

Colt Model 1905 Military*

Colt Model 1905 Military 45 Automatic Pistol . . . **$995**
Caliber: 45 Automatic. 7-shot magazine. 5-inch barrel. 8 inches overall. Weight: 32 1/2 oz. Fixed sights, knife-blade and V-notch. Blued finish. Checkered walnut stocks. Similar to Model 1902 38 Auto Pistol. Made 1905–1911.

Colt M1991A1

Colt Model M1991A1 Semiauto Pistol
Reissue of Model 1911A1 (*see* Government Model 45) with a continuation of the original serial number range from 1945. Caliber: 45 ACP. 7-shot magazine. 5-inch barrel. 8 1/2 inches overall. Weight: 39 oz. Fixed blade front sight; square notch rear. Parkerized finish. Black composition stocks. Made from 1991 to date. (Commander and Compact variations introduced 1993).
Standard Model **$350**
Commander w/4 1/2-inch bbl. 355
Compact w/3 1/2-inch bbl. (6-shot) 360

Colt Ace Automatic

Colt Ace Automatic Pistol **$1025**
Caliber: 22 LR (regular or high speed). 10-shot magazine. Built on the same frame as the Government Model 45 Auto, with same safety features, etc. Hand-honed action, target barrel, adjustable rear sight. 4³/₄-inch barrel. 8¹/₄ inches overall. Weight: 38 oz. Made 1930–1940.

**Colt All American
Model 2000**

Colt All American Model 2000 DA Pistol **$365**
Caliber: 9mm Luger. 15-shot magazine. Semiautomatic. 4¹/₂-inch barrel. 7¹/₂ inches overall. Weight: 29 oz. Fixed blade front sight; square notch rear w/3-dot system. Blued slide with polymer receiver. Made 1992–94.

Colt Cadet 22

Colt Cadet 22 Automatic Pistol **$160**
Caliber: 22 LR. 11-shot magazine. 4¹/₂-inch vent-rib barrel. 8⁵/₈ inches overall. Weight: 48 oz. Sights: blade front; dovetailed rear. Stainless steel. Textured black polymer grips with Colt medallion. Made from 1993 to date.

Colt Challenger Automatic Pistol **$295**
Same basic design as Woodsman Target, Third Issue, but lacks some of the refinements. Fixed sights. Magazine catch on butt as in old Woodsman. Does not stay open on last shot. Lacks magazine safety. 4¹/₂- or 6-inch barrel. 9 to 10¹/₂ inches overall. Weight: 30 oz., 4¹/₂-inch bbl.; 31¹/₂ oz., 6-inch bbl. Blued finish. Checkered plastic stocks. Made 1950–55.

Colt Combat Commander

Colt Combat Commander Automatic Pistol **$425**
Same as Lightweight Commander, except has steel frame, available in blued, nickel-plated or stainless steel finish. Weighs 36 oz. Made from 1970 to date.

Colt Commander Lightweight

Colt Commander Lightweight Automatic Pistol . . **$435**
Same basic design as Government Model, but shorter and lighter in weight; receiver and mainspring housing are forged from a special lightweight metal, "Coltalloy." Calibers: 45 Auto, 38 Super Auto, 9mm Luger. 7-shot magazine in 45 cal., 9-shot in 38 Auto and 9mm Luger. 4¹/₄-inch barrel. 8 inches overall. Weight: 26¹/₂ oz. Fixed sights. Round spur hammer. Improved safety lock. Blued finish. Checkered plastic or walnut stocks. Made 1951 to date.

Colt Conversion Unit—22-45 . . . . **$2095**
Converts Service Ace 22 to National Match 45 Auto. Unit consists of match-grade slide assembly and barrel, bushing, recoil spring, recoil spring guide and plug, magazine and slide stop. Made 1938–1942.

Colt Conversion Unit—45-22 . . . . **$325**
Converts Government Model 45 Auto to a 22 LR target pistol. Unit consists of slide assembly, barrel, floating

Colt Conversion Unit—45-22 (cont.)

chamber (as in Service Ace), bushing, ejector, recoil spring, recoil spring guide and plug, magazine and slide stop. Made from 1938 to date. *Note:* Now designated "22 Conversion Unit," postwar model of this unit is also adaptable to the Super 38 pistols.

Colt Delta Elite Semiauto Pistol

Caliber: 10 mm. 5-inch barrel. 8½ inches overall. 8-round cylinder. Weight: 38 oz., empty. Checkered rubber combat grips with Delta medallion. 3-dot, high-profile front and rear combat sights. Blued or stainless finish.

Blued Finish **$495**
Stainless Finish **625**

**Colt Delta Gold Cup
Stainless**

Colt Delta Gold Cup Semiauto Pistol

Same general specifications as Delta Elite, except weighs 39 oz. with 6¾-inch sight radius. Adjustable rear sight. Made 1989 to date.

Blued Finish **$550**
Stainless Steel Finish **625**

Colt Gold Cup Mark III National Match **$725**
Similar to Gold Cup National Match 45 Auto, except chambered for 38 Special mid-range. 5-shot magazine. Made 1961–1974.

Colt Gold Cup National Match 45

Colt Gold Cup National Match 45 Auto **$625**
Match version of Government Model 45 Auto with same general specifications, except: match grade barrel with new design bushing, flat mainspring housing, long wide trigger with adjustable stop, hand-fitted slide with improved ejection port, adjustable rear sight, target front sight, checkered walnut grips with gold medallions. Weight: 37 oz. Made 1957–1970.

**Colt Government Model 45
Commercial, M1911A1-Type**

Colt Government Model 45 Automatic Pistol

U.S. Models 1911 and 1911A1. Caliber: 45 Auto. 7-shot magazine. 5-inch barrel. 8½ inches overall. Weight: 39 oz. Fixed sights. Blued finish on Commercial Model, Parkerized or similar finish on most military pistols. Checkered walnut stocks (early production), plastic grips (later production). Checkered, arched mainspring housing and longer grip safety spur adopted in 1923 (on M1911A1). Made 1911–1970. Letter "C" precedes or follows serial number on Commercial Model 45s.

Note: During both World Wars, Colt licensed other firms to make these pistols under government contract: Ithaca Gun Co., North American Arms Co. Ltd. (Canada), Remington-Rand Co., Remington-UMC, Singer Sewing Machine Co., and Union Switch & Signal Co.; M1911 also produced at Springfield Armory.

U.S. Model 1911
  Colt manufacture . . . . **$ 950**
  North American manufacture **9095**
  Remington-UMC manufacture **1550**
  Springfield manufacture **1095**
  Commercial Model M1911 Type **1200**
U.S. Model 1911A1
  Singer manufacture **9425**
  Colt, Ithaca, Remington-Rand, Union Switch
    manufacture **695**
  Commercial Model, M1911A1 Type **650**

Colt Huntsman

Colt Huntsman **$285**
Same specifications as the Challenger. Made 1955–1976.

Colt Match Target Auto Pistol, Second Issue . . . **$595**
Same basic design as Woodsman Target, Third Issue. Caliber: 22 LR (reg. or high speed). 10-shot magazine. 6-inch flat-sided heavy barrel. 10½ inches overall. Weight: 40 oz. Click adjustable rear sight, ramp front. Blued finish. Checkered plastic or walnut grips. Made 1948–1976.

Colt Match Target, Second Issue

Colt Match Target "4½" Automatic Pistol **$550**
Same as Match Target, 2nd Issue, except w/4½-inch bbl.
9 inches overall. Weight: 36 oz. Made 1950–1976.

Colt MK II/Series '90 Double Eagle Combat Commander **$475**
Calibers: 40 S&W, 45 ACP. 7-shot magazine. 4¼-inch
barrel. 7¾ inches overall. Weight: 36 oz. Fixed blade front
sight; square notch rear. Checkered Xenoy® grips.
Stainless finish. Made from 1992 to date.

**Colt MKII/Series '90
Double Eagle 10mm**

Colt MK II/Series '90 Double Eagle DA Semiauto Pistol
Calibers: 38 Super, 9mm, 40 S&W, 10mm, 45 ACP. 7-shot
magazine. 5-inch barrel. 8½ inches overall. Weight: 39
oz. Fixed or Accro™ adjustable sights. Matte stainless
finish. Checkered Xenoy grips. Made from 1991 to date.
38 Super, 9mm, 40 S&W (Fixed Sights) **$450**
45 ACP (Adjustable Sights) 475
45 ACP (Fixed Sights) 455
10mm (Adjustable Sights) 470
10mm (Fixed Sights) 450

Colt MK IV/Series '70 Combat Commander
Same general specifications as the Lightweight Comman-
der, except made from 1970–1983.
Blued Finish **$365**
Nickel Finish 375
Stainless 415

**Colt MK IV/Series '70 Gold Cup National Match 45
Auto** **$595**
Match version of MK IV/Series '70 Government Model.
Caliber: 45 Auto only. Flat mainspring housing. Accurizor
barrel and bushing. Solid rib, Colt-Elliason adj. rear sight,
undercut front sight. Adj. trigger, target hammer. 8¾
inches overall. Weight: 38½ oz. Blued finish. Checkered
walnut stocks. Made 1970–1984.

**Colt MK IV/Series '70
Gold Cup National Match 45**

**Colt MK IV/Series '70
Government Model 45**

Colt MK IV/Series '70 Gov't. 45 Auto Pistol **$450**
Calibers: 45 Auto, 38 Super Auto, 9mm Luger. 7-shot
magazine in 45, 9-shot in 38 and 9mm. 5-inch barrel. 8⅜
inches overall. Weight: 38 oz., 45; 39 oz., 38 and 9mm.
Fixed rear sight and ramp front sight. Blued or nickel-
plated finish. Checkered walnut stocks. Made 1970–1984.

**Colt MK IV/Series '80
380 Govt., Bright Nickel**

Colt MK IV/Series '80 380 Automatic Pistol
Caliber: 380 ACP. 3.29-inch barrel. 6.15 inches overall.
Weight: 21.8 oz. Composition grips. Fixed sights. Made
from 1984 to date.

Colt MK IV/Series '80 380 Automatic (cont.)

Blued Finish	$250
Bright Nickel	295
Satin Nickel	275
Stainless Finish	325
Pocketlite (Blued, 14.75 oz.)	305

**Colt MK IV/Series '80
Combat Commander**

**Colt MK IV/Series '80
Government Model, Matte Stainless**

Colt MK IV/Series '80 Combat Commander
Updated version of the MK IV/Series '70 with same general specifications. Blued or stainless steel with "pebbled" black neoprene wraparound grips.

Blued Finish	$415
Stainless Finish	460

Colt MK IV/Series '80 Combat Elite
Same general specifications as MK IV/Series '80 Combat Commander, except with Elite enhancements. Calibers: 38 Super, 40 S&W, 45 ACP. Stainless frame with blued steel slide. Accro™ adjustable sights and beavertail grip safety. Made from 1992 to date.

38 Super, 45 ACP	$495
40 S&W	485

**Colt MK IV/Series '80
Gold Cup National Match**

Colt MK IV/Series '80 Gold Cup National Match
Same general specifications as Match '70 version, except with additional finishes and "pebbled" wraparound neoprene grips.

Blued Finish	$550
Bright Blue Finish	575
Stainless Finish	595

Colt MK IV/Series '80 Government Model
Same general specifications as Government Model Series '70, except also chambered in 40 S&W, with "pebbled" wraparound neoprene grips; blue or stainless finish.

Blued Finish	$425
Bright Blue Finish	450
Bright Stainless Finish	510
Matte Stainless Finish	495

Colt MK IV/Series '80 Lightweight Commander . $475
Updated version of the MK IV/Series '70 with same general specifications.

Colt MK IV/Series '80 Mustang 380 Automatic
Caliber: 380 ACP. 5-round magazine. 2³/₄-inch barrel. 5.5 inches overall. Weight: 18¹/₂ oz. Black composition grips. Currently in production.

Blued Finish	$275
Nickel Finish	305
Stainless Finish	295

**Colt MK IV/Series '80
Mustang Plus II**

Colt MK IV/Series '80 Mustang Plus II
Caliber: 380 ACP. 7-round magazine. 2³/₄-inch barrel. 5.5 inches overall. Weight: 20 oz. Blued finish with checkered, black composition grips, full-length as the 380 Government Model. Made from 1988 to date.

Blued Finish	$265
Stainless Finish	295

Colt MK IV/Series '80 Mustang Pocketlite
Same general specifications as the Mustang 380 Automatic, except weighs only 12¹/₂ oz. with aluminum alloy

**Colt Woodsman Sport Model
Second Issue**

**Colt Woodsman Target
Third Issue**

Colt Woodsman Sport Model Automatic Pistol, Second Issue $500

Same as Woodsman Target, 3rd Issue, but with 4½-inch barrel. 9 inches overall. Weight: 30 oz. Made 1948–1976.

**Colt Woodsman Target
First Issue**

Colt Woodsman Target Model Automatic, First Issue $495

Caliber: 22 LR (reg. velocity). 10-shot magazine. 6½-inch barrel. 10½ inches overall. Weight: 28 oz. Adjustable sights. Blued finish. Checkered walnut stocks. Made 1915–1932. *Note:* The mainspring housing of this model is not strong enough to permit safe use of high-speed cartridges. Change to a new heat-treated mainspring housing was made at pistol No. 83,790. Many of the old models were converted by installation of new housings. The new housing may be distinguished from the earlier type by the checkering in the curve under the breech; new housing is grooved straight across, while the old type bears a diagonally checkered oval.

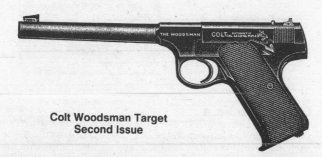

**Colt Woodsman Target
Second Issue**

Colt Woodsman Target Model Automatic, Second Issue $425

Caliber: 22 LR (reg. or high speed). Same as original model, except has heavier barrel and high-speed mainspring housing. *See* note under Woodsman, First Issue. Weight: 29 oz. Made 1932–1948.

Colt Woodsman Target Model Automatic, Third Issue $375

Same basic design as previous Woodsman pistols, but with longer grip, magazine catch on left side, larger thumb safety, slide stop, slide stays open on last shot, magazine disconnector, thumbrest stocks. Caliber: 22 LR (reg. or high speed). 10-shot magazine. 6-inch barrel. 10½ inches overall. Weight: 32 oz. Click adjustable rear sight, ramp front sight. Blued finish. Checkered plastic or walnut stocks. Made 1948–1976.

**Colt WWI Commemorative
Deluxe Grade, Meuse Argonne**

**Colt WW I Commemorative
Standard, Second Battle of the Marne**

Colt World War I 50th Anniversary Commemorative Series 45 Auto

Limited production replica of Model 1911 45 Auto engraved with battle scenes, commemorating Battles at Chateau Thierry, Belleau Wood, Second Battle of the Marne, Meuse Argonne. In special presentation display cases. Production: 7,400 standard model, 75 deluxe, 25 special deluxe grade. Match numbered sets offered. Made

Colt WW I 50th Anniversary Commem. (cont.)

in 1967, 1968, 1969. Values indicated are for commemoratives in new condition.

Standard Grade	$ 595
Deluxe Grade	1350
Special Deluxe Grade	2600

**Colt WW II Commemorative
European Theater**

**Colt WW II Commemorative
Pacific Theater**

Colt World War II Commemorative 45 Auto $695

Limited production replica of Model 1911A1 45 Auto engraved with respective names of locations where historic engagements occurred during WW II, as well as specific issue and theater identification. European model has oak leaf motif on slide; palm leaf design frames the Pacific issue. Cased. 11,500 of each model were produced. Made in 1970. Value listed is for gun in new condition.

SINGLE SHOT PISTOLS AND DERINGERS

NOTE: For ease in finding a particular firearm, Colt handguns are grouped into three sections: Automatic Pistols (which precedes this one), this section, and Revolvers, which follows. For a complete listing, please refer to the Index.

Colt Camp Perry, First Issue

Colt Camp Perry Model Single Shot Pistol, First Issue $995

Built on Officers' Model frame. Caliber: 22 LR (embedded head chamber for high-speed cartridges after 1930). 10-inch barrel. 13¾ inches overall. Weight: 34½ oz. Adjustable target sights. Hand-finished action. Blued finish. Checkered walnut stocks. Made 1926–1934.

Colt Camp Perry, Second Issue

Colt Camp Perry Model, Second Issue $915

Same general specifications as First Issue, except has shorter hammer fall and 8-inch barrel. 12 inches overall. Weight: 34 oz. Made 1934–1941 (about 440 produced).

**Colt
Civil War Centennial
(Cased Pair)**

Colt Civil War Centennial Model Pistol

Single-shot replica, ⅞ scale, of Colt Model 1860 Army Revolver. Caliber: 22 Short. 6-inch barrel. Weight: 22 oz. Blued finish with gold-plated frame, grip frame, and trigger guard, walnut grips. Cased. 24,114 were produced. Made in 1961.

Single Pistol	$150
Pair with consecutive serial numbers	350

**Colt Deringer No. 4
(Cased Pair)**

Colt Deringer No. 4

Replica of Deringer No. 3 (1872). Single shot with side-swing barrel. Caliber: 22 Short. 2½-inch barrel. 4¹⁵/₁₆ inches overall. Weight: 7¾ oz. Fixed sights. Gold-finished frame, blued barrel, walnut grips; also nickel-plated with simulated ivory grips. Cased. Made 1959–1963.

Single Pistol	$125
Pair with consecutive serial numbers	250

Colt Deringer No. 4 Commemorative Models

Limited production version of 22 Deringer issued, with appropriate inscription, to commemorate historical events.

Colt Deringer No. 4 Commemorative Models (cont.)

1961 Issue
Geneseo, Illinois, 125th Anniversary
(104 produced) **$625**

1962 Issue
Fort McPherson, Nebraska, Centennial
(300 produced) **$375**

Colt Lord and Lady Deringers
Same as Deringer No. 4. Lord model is blued with gold-plated frame and walnut stocks. Lady model is gold-plated with simulated pearl stocks. Furnished in cased pairs. Made 1970–72.
Lord Deringer, pair in case **$200**
Lady Deringer, pair in case **200**
Lord and Lady Deringers, one each, in case **200**

Colt Rock Island Arsenal Centennial Pistol **$250**
Limited production (550 pieces) version of Civil War Centennial Model single shot 22 pistol, made exclusively for Cherry's Sporting Goods, Geneseo, Illinois, to commemorate the centennial of the Rock Island Arsenal in Illinois. Cased. Made in 1962.

REVOLVERS

NOTE: This section of Colt handguns contains only revolvers. For automatic pistols or single shot pistols and deringers, please see the two sections that precede this. For a complete listing, please refer to the Index.

Colt Agent, First Issue

Colt Agent, Second Issue

Colt Agent Double Action Revolver, First Issue . . **$295**
Same as Cobra, First Issue, except has short-grip frame, 38 Special only, weighs 14 oz. Made 1962–1973.

Colt Agent DA Revolver, Second Issue **$250**
Same as Cobra, Second Issue, except has short service stocks, 6⅝ inches overall, weighs 16 oz. Made 1973–1981.

Colt Anaconda Double Action Revolver
Calibers: 44 Mag., 45 Colt. Barrel lengths: 4, 6 or 8 inches. 11⅝ inches overall w/6-inch bbl. Weight: 53 oz. w/6-inch

Colt Anaconda

Colt Anaconda DA Revolver (cont.)
bbl. Adjustable white outline rear sight, red insert ramp-style front. Matte stainless finish. Black neoprene combat grips with finger grooves. Made from 1992 to date.
44 Magnum **$415**
45 Colt (6-inch bbl. only) **425**

Colt Army Special Double Action Revolver **$395**
41-caliber frame. Calibers: 32-20, 38 Special (41 Colt). 6-shot cylinder, right revolution. Barrel lengths: 4-, 4½-, 5- and 6-inch. 9¼ inches overall w/4-inch bbl. Weight: 32 oz. w/4-inch bbl. Fixed sights. Blued or nickel-plated finish. Hard rubber stocks. Made 1908–1927. *Note:* This model has a somewhat heavier frame than the New Navy, which it replaced. Serial numbers begin with 300,000. The heavy 38 Special High Velocity loads should not be used in 38 Special arms of this model.

Colt Bankers' Special

Colt Bankers' Special Double Action Revolver
This is the Police Positive with a 2-inch barrel, otherwise specifications same as that model; rounded butt introduced in 1933. Calibers: 22 LR (embedded head-cylinder for high speed cartridges introduced 1933), 38 New Police. 6½ inches overall. Weight: 23 oz. (22 LR); 19 oz. (38). Made 1926–1940.
38 Caliber . . . . **$ 575**
22 Caliber **1195**

Colt Bisley

Colt Bisley Model Single Action Revolver
Variation of the Single Action Army, developed for target shooting; grips, trigger and hammer changed. Calibers: general specifications same as Single Action Army. Target

Colt Bisley Model SA Revolver (cont.)

Model made w/flat-topped frame and target sights. Made 1894–1915.

Standard Model **$3795**
Target Model **6350**

Colt Buntline Scout

Colt Buntline Scout **$350**

Same as Frontier Scout, except has 9¹/₂-inch barrel. Made from 1959–1971.

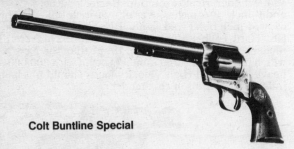

Colt Buntline Special

Colt Buntline Special 45 . . . . **$695**

Same as standard Single Action Army, except has 12-inch barrel, caliber 45 Long Colt. Made 1957–1975.

**Colt Cobra, Round Butt
First Issue**

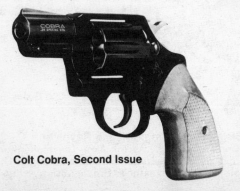

Colt Cobra, Second Issue

Colt Cobra DA Revolver, Round Butt

First Issue **$325**

Lightweight Detective Special with same general specifications as that model, except with Colt-alloy frame. 2-inch barrel. Calibers: 38 Special, 38 New Police, 32 New Police. Weight: 15 oz., 38 cal. Blued finish. Checkered plastic or walnut stocks. Made 1951–1973.

Colt Cobra DA Revolver, Second Issue **$285**

Lightweight version of Detective Special, Second Issue; has aluminum alloy frame. 16¹/₂ oz. Made 1973–1981.

Colt Cobra DA Revolver Square Butt **$295**

Lightweight Police Positive Special with same general specifications, except has Colt-alloy frame. 4-inch barrel. Calibers: 38 Special, 38 New Police, 32 New Police. Weight: 17 oz. in 38 caliber. Blued finish. Checkered plastic or walnut stocks. Made 1951–1973.

Colt Commando Special

Colt Commando Special DA Revolver **$295**

Caliber: 38 Special. 6-shot cylinder. 2-inch barrel; 6⁷/₈ inches overall. Weight: 21¹/₂ oz. Fixed sights. Low-luster blue finish. Made 1982–86.

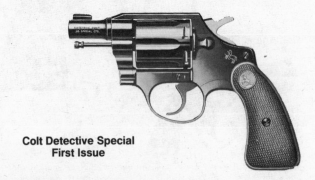

**Colt Detective Special
First Issue**

Colt Detective Special DA Revolver,

First Issue **$450**

This is the Police Positive Special with 2-inch barrel, otherwise specifications same as that model; rounded butt intro. 1933. Originally supplied in 38 Special only; also made in calibers 32 New Police, 38 New Police. Weight: 17 oz. (38 cal.) 6³/₄ inches overall. Made 1926–1972.

Colt Detective Special DA Revolver, 2nd Issue

"D" frame, shrouded ejector rod. Caliber: 38 Special. 6-shot cylinder. 2-inch barrel. 6⁷/₈ inches overall. Weight:

Colt Detective Special, Second Issue

Colt Detective Special DA, 2nd Issue (cont.)

21 1/2 oz. Fixed rear sight, ramp front. Blued or nickel-plated finish. Checkered walnut wraparound stocks. Made 1972–1984. Reintroduced in 1993 with checkered black composition grips.

Second Issue **$295**
Reissue **325**

Colt Diamondback

Colt Diamondback Double Action Revolver $325

"D" frame, shrouded ejector rod. Calibers: 22 LR, 38 Special. 6-shot cylinder. Barrels: 2 1/2-, 4-inch; vent rib. 9 inches overall w/4-inch bbl. Weight: w/4-inch bbl., 22 cal., 31 3/4 oz.; 38 cal., 28 1/2 oz. Adjustable rear sight, ramp front. Blued or nickel finish. Checkered walnut stocks. Made 1966–1984.

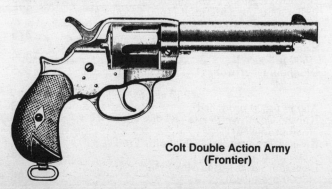

**Colt Double Action Army
(Frontier)**

Colt Double Action Army Revolver $2250

Also called Double Action Frontier. Similar in appearance to the smaller Lightning Model, but has heavier frame of different shape, round disc on left side of frame, lanyard loop in butt. Calibers: 38-40, 44-40, 45 Colt. 6-shot cylinder. Barrel lengths: 3 1/2- and 4-inch without ejector; 4 3/4-, 5 1/2- and 7 1/2-inch with ejector. 12 1/2 inches overall with 7 1/2-inch bbl. Weight: 45 cal. with 7 1/2-inch bbl., 39 oz. Fixed sights. Hard rubber bird'shead grips. Blued or nickel finish. Made 1878–1905.

Colt Frontier Scout

Colt Frontier Scout Revolver

Single Action Army replica, 7/8 scale. Calibers: 22 Short, Long, LR; 22 WMR (interchangeable cylinder available.) 6-shot cylinder. 4 3/4-inch barrel. 9 15/16 inches overall. Weight: 24 oz. Fixed sights. Plastic stocks. Originally made with bright alloy frame; since 1959 with steel frame, blued finish, also in all nickel finish with wood stocks. Made 1958–1971.

Blued Finish, plastic stocks **$295**
Nickel Finish, wood stocks **315**
Extra interchangeable cylinder **35**

Colt Frontier Scout Revolver Commemorative Models

Limited production versions of Frontier Scout issued, with appropriate inscription, to commemorate historical events. Cased. *Note:* Values indicated are for commemoratives in new condition.

1961 Issues
Kansas Statehood Centennial (6201 produced) ... **$350**
Pony Express Centennial (1007 produced) **460**

1962 Issues
Columbus, Ohio, Sesquicentennial
(200 produced) .... **$ 575**
Fort Findlay, Ohio, Sesquicentennial
(130 produced) **710**
Fort Findlay Cased Pair, 22 Long Rifle and
22 Magnum (20 produced) **2950**
New Mexico Golden Anniversary
(1000 produced) **395**
West Virginia Statehood Centennial
(3452 produced) **365**

1963 Issues
Arizona Territorial Centennial (5355 produced) . **$365**
Battle of Gettysburg Centennial
(1019 produced) **375**
Carolina Charter Tercentenary (300 produced) .. **395**
Fort Stephenson, Ohio, Sesquicentennial
(200 produced) **575**

Colt Frontier Scout Commemoratives (cont.)

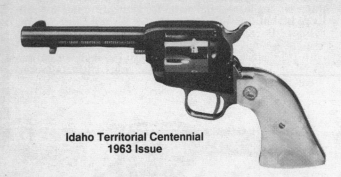

**Idaho Territorial Centennial
1963 Issue**

1963 Issues (cont.)

General John Hunt Morgan Indiana Raid
(100 produced) **$675**
Idaho Territorial Centennial (902 produced) **395**

**General Hood Centennial
1964 Issue**

**Montana Territory Centennial
1964 Issue**

1964 Issues

California Gold Rush (500 produced) **$375**
Chamizal Treaty (450 produced) **410**
General Hood Centennial (1503 produced) **385**
Montana Territorial Centennial
(2300 produced) **375**
Nevada "Battle Born" (981 produced) **375**
Nevada Statehood Centennial (3984 produced) . . . **375**
New Jersey Tercentenary (1001 produced) **365**
St. Louis Bicentennial (802 produced) **375**
Wyoming Diamond Jubilee (2357 produced) **375**

Colt Frontier Scout Commemoratives (cont.)

**New Jersey Tercentenary
1964 Issue**

1965 Issues

Appomattox Centennial (1001 produced) **$375**
Forty-Niner Miner (500 produced) **375**
General Meade Campaign (1197 produced) **365**
Kansas Cowtown Series—Wichita
(500 produced) **365**
Old Fort Des Moines Reconstruction
(700 produced) **375**
Oregon Trail (1995 produced) **365**
St. Augustine Quadricentennial (500 produced) . . . **375**

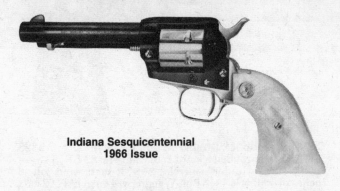

**Indiana Sesquicentennial
1966 Issue**

1966 Issues

Colorado Gold Rush (1350 produced) **$375**
Dakota Territory (1000 produced) **375**
Indiana Sesquicentennial (1500 produced) **375**
Kansas Cowtown Series—Abilene
(500 produced) **375**
Kansas Cowtown Series—Dodge City
(500 produced) **365**
Oklahoma Territory (1343 produced) **365**

1967 Issues

Alamo (4500 produced) **$365**
Kansas Cowtown Series—Coffeyville
(500 produced) **365**
Kansas Trail Series—Chisholm Trail
(500 produced) **365**
Lawman Series—Bat Masterson
(3000 produced) **385**

Colt Frontier Scout Commoratives (cont.)

1968 Issues

Kansas Trail Series—Santa Fe Trail
(501 produced) **$365**
Kansas Trail Series—Pawnee Trail
(501 produced) **365**
Lawman Series—Pat Garrett (3000 produced) ... **385**
Nebraska Centennial (7001 produced) **350**

**Golden Spike Centennial
1969 Issue**

1969 Issues

Alabama Sesquicentennial (3001 produced) **$365**
Arkansas Territory Sesquicentennial
(3500 produced) **365**
California Bicentennial (5000 produced) **350**
General Nathan Bedford Forrest
(3000 produced) **365**
Golden Spike (11,000 produced) **350**
Kansas Trail Series—Shawnee Trail
(501 produced) **365**
Lawman Series—Wild Bill Hickock
(3000 produced) **375**

1970 Issues

Kansas Fort Series—Fort Larned
(500 produced) **$365**
Kansas Fort Series—Fort Hays (500 produced) .. **365**
Kansas Fort Series—Fort Riley (500 produced) .. **365**
Lawman Series—Wyatt Earp (3000 produced) ... **475**
Maine Sesquicentennial (3000 produced) **350**
Missouri Sesquicentennial (3000 produced) **365**

1971 Issues

Kansas Fort Series—Fort Scott (500 produced) .. **$365**

1972 Issues

Florida Territory Sesquicentennial
(2001 produced) **$365**

1973 Issues

Arizona Ranger (3001 produced) **$350**

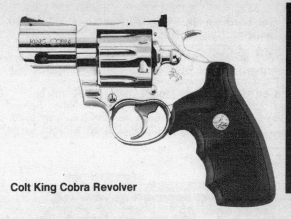

Colt King Cobra Revolver

Colt King Cobra Revolver
Caliber: 357 Mag. Barrel lengths: 2¹/₂-, 4-, 6- or 8-inch. 9 inches overall w/4-inch barrel. Weight: 42 oz., average. Matte stainless steel finish. Black neoprene combat grips. Made from 1986 to date. 2¹/₂-inch barrel, and "Ultimate" bright or blued finish made 1988–1992.
Matte Stainless **$325**
Ultimate Bright Stainless **350**
Blued **295**

Colt Lawman MK III

Colt Lawman MK III Double Action Revolver $200
"J" frame, shrouded ejector rod on 2-inch barrel only. Caliber: 357 Magnum. 6-shot cylinder. Barrel lengths: 2-, 4-inch. 9³/₈ inches overall with 4-inch barrel. Weight: with 4-inch bbl., 35 oz. Fixed rear sight, ramp front. Service trigger and hammer or target trigger and wide-spur hammer. Blued or nickel-plated finish. Checkered walnut service or target stocks. Made 1969–1982.

Colt Lawman MK V

Colt Lawman MK V DA Revolver **$225**
Similar to Trooper MK V. Caliber: 357 Mag. 6-shot cylinder.
2- or 4-inch barrel; 9³/₈ inches overall w/4-inch barrel.
Weight: 35 oz. w/4-inch barrel. Fixed sights. Checkered walnut grips. Made 1983–85. (*See* photo, preceding page.)

Colt Marine Corps Model (1905) DA Revolver . . . **$1925**
General specifications same as New Navy, Second Issue,
except this has round butt, was supplied only in 38 caliber
(38 Short & Long Colt, 38 Special) with 6-inch barrel. Made
1905–1909.

Colt Metropolitan MK III

Colt Metropolitan MK III DA Revolver **$235**
Same as Official Police MK III, except has 4-inch barrel,
service or target stocks; weighs 36 oz. Made 1969–1972.

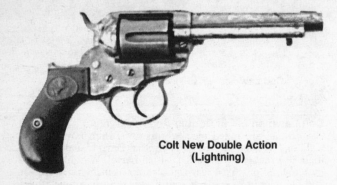

Colt New Double Action
(Lightning)

Colt New Double Action Central Fire Revolver . . . **$1250**
Also called Lightning Model. Calibers: 38 and 41 Centerfire.
6-shot cylinder. Barrel lengths: 2¹/₂-, 3¹/₂-, 4¹/₂- and 6-inch
without ejector, 4¹/₂- and 6-inch w/ejector. 8¹/₂ inches overall
w/3¹/₂-inch barrel. Weight: 38 cal. w/3¹/₂-inch bbl., 23 oz.
Fixed sights. Blued or nickel finish. Hard rubber bird'shead
grips. Made 1877–1909.

Colt New Frontier Buntline Special
Second Generation

Colt New Frontier Buntline Special
Same as New Frontier Single Action Army, except has 12-inch barrel.
Second Generation (1962–1975) **$995**
Third Generation (1976–1992) **695**

Colt New Frontier SA Army
Second Generation

Colt New Frontier Single Action Army Revolver
Same as Single Action Army, except has flat-top frame,
adjustable target rear sight, ramp front sight, smooth walnut grips. 5¹/₂- or 7¹/₂-inch barrel. Calibers: 357 Magnum,
44 Special, 45 Colt. Made 1961–1992.
Second Generation (1961–75) **$1295**
Third Generation (1976–92) **650**

Colt New Frontier 22

Colt New Frontier Single Action 22 Revolver . . . **$260**
Same as Peacemaker 22, except has flat-top frame, adjustable rear sight, ramp front sight. Made 1971–76.

Colt New Navy

Colt New Navy DA, First Issue **$925**
Also called New Army. Calibers: 38 Short & Long Colt, 41
Short & Long Colt. 6-shot cylinder, left revolution. Barrel
lengths: 3-, 4¹/₂- and 6-inch. 11¹/₄ inches overall w/6-inch

Colt New Navy DA, First Issue (cont.)

bbl. Weight: 32 oz., 6-inch bbl. Fixed sights, knife-blade and V-notch. Blued or nickel-plated finish. Walnut or hard rubber grips. Made 1889–1894. *Note:* This model, which was adopted by both the Army and Navy, was Colt's first revolver of the solid frame, swing-out cylinder type. It lacks the cylinder-locking notches found on later models made on this 41 frame; ratchet on the back of the cylinder is held in place by a double projection on the hand.

Colt New Navy DA, Second Issue $725

Also called New Army. General specifications same as First Issue, except has double cylinder notches and double locking bolt. Calibers: 38 Special added in 1904 and 32-20 in 1905. Made 1892–1907. *Note:* The heavy 38 Special High Velocity loads should not be used in 38 Special arms of this model.

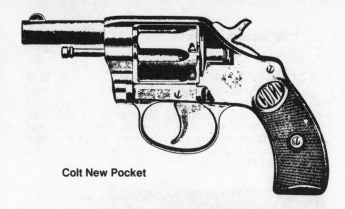

Colt New Pocket

Colt New Pocket Double Action Revolver $395

Caliber: 32 Short & Long Colt. 6-shot cylinder. Barrel lengths: 2½-, 3½- and 6-inch. 7½ inches overall with 3½-inch barrel. Weight: 16 oz., 3½-inch bbl. Fixed sights, knife-blade and V-notch. Blued or nickel finish. Rubber stocks. Made 1893–1905.

Colt New Police Double Action Revolver $325

Built on New Pocket frame, but with larger grip. Calibers: 32 Colt New Police, 32 Short & Long Colt. Barrel lengths: 2½-, 4- and 6-inch. 8½ inches overall w/4-inch barrel. Weight: 17 oz., 4-inch bbl. Fixed sights: knife-blade, V-notch. Blued or nickel finish. Rubber stocks. Made 1896–1905.

Colt New Police Target DA Revolver $595

Target version of the New Police with same general specifications. Target sights. 6-inch barrel. Blued finish only. Made 1896–1905.

Colt New Service

Colt New Service Double Action Revolver

Calibers: 38 Special, 357 Magnum (intro. 1936), 38-40, 44-40, 44 Russian, 44 Special, 45 Auto, 45 Colt, 450 Eley, 455 Eley, 476 Eley. 6-shot cylinder. Barrel lengths: 4-, 5- and 6-inch in 38 Special and 357 Magnum; 4½-, 5½- and 7½-inch in other calibers. 9¾ inches overall w/4½-inch bbl. Weight: 39 oz., 45 cal. w/4½-inch bbl. Fixed sights. Blued or nickel finish. Checkered walnut stocks. Made 1898–1942. *Note:* More than 500,000 of this model in caliber 45 Auto (designated "Model 1917 Revolver") were purchased by the U.S. Gov't. during WW I. These arms were later sold as surplus to National Rifle Association members through the Director of Civilian Marksmanship. Price was $16.15 plus packing charge. Supply exhausted during the early 1930s.

Commercial Model	**$950**
Magnum	**695**
1917 Army	**795**

Colt New Service Target

Colt New Service Target $1195

Target version of the New Service; general specifications same as that model. Calibers: originally chambered for 44 Russian, 450 Eley, 455 Eley and 476 Eley; later models in 44 Special, 45 Colt and 45 Auto. Barrel lengths: 6- and 7½-inch. 12¾ inches overall with 7½-inch bbl. Adjustable target sights. Hand-finished action. Blued finish. Checkered walnut stocks. Made 1900–1940.

Colt Officers' Model Match

Colt Officers' Model Match $395

Same general design as Officers' Model revolvers. Has tapered heavy barrel, wide hammer spur, Accro™ rear sight, ramp front sight, large target stocks of checkered walnut. Calibers: 22 LR, 38 Special. 6-inch barrel. 11¼ inches overall. Weight: 43 oz., 22 cal.; 39 oz., 38 cal. Blued finish. Made 1953–1970.

Colt Officers' Model Special $495

Target arm replacing Officers' Model, Second Issue; basically the same as that model, but with heavier, non-tapered barrel, redesigned hammer, ramp front sight and

Colt Officers' Model Special (cont.)

"Coltmaster" rear sight adj. for windage and elevation. Calibers: 22 LR, 38 Special. 6-inch barrel. 11¼ inches overall. Weight: 39 oz., 38 cal.; 43 oz., 22 cal. Blued finish. Checkered plastic stocks. Made 1949–1953.

Colt Officers' Model Target DA Revolver, First Issue $995

Caliber: 38 Special. 6-inch barrel. Hand-finished action. Adjustable target sights. Checkered walnut stocks. General specifications same as New Navy, Second Issue. Made 1904–1908.

**Colt Officers' Model Target
Second Issue**

Colt Officers' Model Target, Second Issue $750

Calibers: 22 LR (intro. 1930, embedded head-cylinder for high-speed cartridges after 1932), 32 Police Positive (made 1932–1942), 38 Special. 6-shot cylinder. Barrel lengths: 4-, 4½-, 5-, 6- and 7½-inch in 38 Special; 6-inch only in 22 LR and 32 PP. 11¼ inches overall w/6-inch bbl. (38 Special). Adjustable target sights. Blued finish. Checkered walnut stocks. Hand-finished action. General features same as Army Special and Official Police of same date. Made 1908–1949 (with exceptions noted).

Colt Official Police

Colt Official Police Double Action Revolver

Calibers: 22 LR (intro. 1930, embedded head-cylinder for high-speed cartridges after 1932), 32-20 (discontinued 1942), 38 Special, 41 Long Colt (discontinued 1930). 6-shot cylinder. Barrel lengths: 4-, 5-, and 6-inch; 2-inch and 6-inch heavy barrel in 38 Special only, 22 LR w/4- and 6-inch barrels only. 11¼ inches overall. Weight: 36 oz. w/standard 6-inch bbl. in 38 Special. Fixed sights. Blued or nickel-plated finish. Checkered walnut stocks on all revolvers of this model, except some of postwar production had checkered plastic stocks. Made 1927–1969. *Note:* This model is a refined version of the Army Special, which it replaced in 1928 at about serial number 520,000. The Commando 38 Special was a wartime adaptation of the Official Police made to Government specifications. Commando can be identified by its sandblasted blued fin-

Colt Official Police DA Revolver (cont.)

ish; serial numbers start with number 1 (1942).
Commercial Model **$395**
Commando Model **350**

Colt Official Police MK III

Colt Official Police MK III DA Revolver $170

"J" frame, without shrouded ejector rod. Caliber: 38 Special. 6-shot cylinder. Barrel lengths: 4-, 5-, 6-inch. 9¼ inches overall with 4-inch bbl. Weight: 34 oz. w/4-inch bbl. Fixed rear sight, ramp front. Service trigger and hammer or target trigger and wide-spur hammer. Blued or nickel-plated finish. Checkered walnut service stocks. Made 1969–1975.

Colt Peacekeeper

Colt Peacekeeper Double Action Revolver $265

Caliber: 357 Mag. 6-shot cylinder. 4- and 6-inch barrels; 11⅛ inches overall with 6-inch barrel. Weight: 46 oz. with 6-inch barrel. Adjustable white outline rear sight; red insert ramp-style front. Non-reflective matte blued finish. Made 1985–89.

**Colt Peacemaker 22
Second Amendment Commemorative**

Colt Peacemaker 22 Second Amendment Commemorative $350

Peacemaker 22 Single Action Revolver with 7½-inch barrel. Nickel-plated frame, barrel, ejector rod assembly,

Colt Peacemaker 22 Second Amendment (cont.)

hammer and trigger; blued cylinder, backstrap and trigger guard. Black pearlite stocks. Barrel inscribed "The Right to Keep and Bear Arms." Presentation case. Limited edition of 3000 issued in 1977. Value is for revolver in new condition.

Colt Peacemaker 22

Colt Peacemaker 22 Single Action Revolver $250

Calibers: 22 LR and 22 WMR. Furnished with cylinder for each caliber. 6-shot. Barrel: 4³⁄₈-, 6- or 7¹⁄₂-inch. 11¹⁄₄ inches overall w/6-inch bbl. Weight: 30¹⁄₂ oz. w/6-inch bbl. Fixed sights. Black composite stocks. Made 1971–76.

Colt Pocket Positive

Colt Pocket Positive Double Action Revolver ... $375

General specifications same as New Pocket, except this model has positive lock feature (see Police Positive). Calibers: 32 Short & Long Colt (discontinued 1914), 32 Colt New Police (32 S&W Short & Long). Fixed sights, flat top and square notch. Made 1905–1940.

Colt Police Positive, First Issue

Colt Police Positive DA, First Issue $345

Improved version of the New Police with the "Positive Lock," which prevents the firing pin from coming in contact with the cartridge except when the trigger is

Colt Police Positive DA, First Issue (cont.)

pulled. Calibers: 32 Short & Long Colt (discontinued 1915), 32 Colt New Police (32 S&W Short & Long), 38 New Police (38 S&W). 6-shot cylinder. Barrel lengths: 2¹⁄₂- (32 cal. only), 4-, 5- and 6-inch. 8¹⁄₂ inches overall w/4-inch bbl. Weight: 20 oz. w/4-inch bbl. Fixed sights. Blued or nickel finish. Rubber or checkered walnut stocks. Made 1905–1947.

Colt Police Positive, Second Issue

Colt Police Positive DA, Second Issue $285

Same as Detective Special, Second Issue, except has 4-inch barrel, is 9 inches overall, weighs 26¹⁄₂ oz. Introduced in 1977. *Note:* Original Police Positive (First Issue) has a shorter frame, is not chambered for 38 Special.

Colt Police Positive Special

Colt Police Positive Special DA Revolver $315

Based on the Police Positive with frame lengthened to permit longer cylinder. Calibers: 32-20 (discontinued 1942), 38 Special, 32 New Police and 38 New Police (introduced 1946). 6-shot cylinder. Barrel lengths: 4- (only length in current production), 5- and 6-inch. 8³⁄₄ inches overall w/4-inch bbl. Weight: 23 oz. (38 Special) w/4-inch bbl. Fixed sights. Checkered stocks of hard rubber, plastic or walnut. Made 1907–1973.

Colt Police Positive Target

Colt Police Positive Target DA Revolver **$595**
Target version of the Police Positive. Calibers: 22 LR (introduced 1910, embedded head-cylinder for high-speed cartridges after 1932), 22 WRF (intro. 1910, disc. 1935), 32 Short & Long Colt (disc. 1915), 32 New Police (32 S&W Short & Long). 6-inch barrel. Blued finish only. 10 1/2 inches overall. Weight: 26 oz. in 22 cal. Adjustable target sights. Checkered walnut stocks. Made 1905–1940. (*See* photo, preceding page.)

Colt Shooting Master

Colt Python—Early Model

Colt Shooting Master Double Action Revolver . . **$950**
Deluxe target arm based on the New Service model. Calibers: originally made only in 38 Special; 44 Special, 45 Auto and 45 Colt added in 1933, 357 Magnum in 1936. 6-inch barrel. 11 1/4 inches overall. Weight: 44 oz., 38 cal. Adj. target sights. Hand-finished action. Blued finish. Checkered walnut stocks. Rounded butt. Made 1932–1941.

Colt Single Action Army

**Colt Python Matte
Stainless**

Colt Python Double Action Revolver
"I" frame, shrouded ejector rod. Calibers: 357 Magnum, 38 Special. 6-shot cylinder. Barrels: 2 1/2-, 4-, 6-, 8-inch; vent rib. 11 1/4 inches overall w/6-inch bbl. Weight: 44 oz. w/6-inch bbl. Adjustable rear sight, ramp front. Blued, nickel-plated or stainless finish. Checkered walnut target stocks. Made from 1955 to date. Ultimate stainless finish made from 1985 to date.

Blued Finish	**$395**
Royal Blue Finish	445
Nickel Finish	385
Stainless Finish	525

Colt Sheriff's Model 45
Limited edition of replica of Storekeeper's Model in caliber 45 Colt, made exclusively for Centennial Arms Corp., Chicago, Illinois. Numbered from "1SM." Blued finish with casehardened frame or nickel-plated. Walnut stocks. 478 were produced in blue, 25 in nickel. Made in 1961.

Blued Finish	**$1595**
Nickel Finish	4250

Colt Single Action Army Revolver
Also called Frontier Six-Shooter and Peacemaker. Calibers: 22 Rimfire (Short, Long, LR), 22 WRF, 32 Rimfire, 32 Colt, 32 S&W, 32-20, 38 Colt, 38 S&W, 38 Special, 357 Magnum, 38-40, 41 Colt, 44 Rimfire, 44 Russian, 44 Special, 44-40, 45 Colt, 45 Auto, 450 Boxer, 450 Eley, 455 Eley, 476 Eley. 6-shot cylinder. Barrel lengths: 4 3/4, 5 1/2 and 7 1/2 inches with ejector; 3 and 4 inches w/o ejector. 10 1/4 inches overall w/4 3/4-inch barrel. Weight: 36 oz., 45 cal. w/4 3/4-inch barrel. Fixed sights. Also made in Target Model with flat top-strap and target sights. Blued finish with casehardened frame or nickel-plated. One-piece smooth walnut or checkered black rubber stocks.

S.A. Army Revolvers with serial numbers above 165,000 (circa 1896) are adapted to smokeless powder; cylinder pin screw was changed to spring catch at about the same time. Made 1873–1942; production resumed in 1955 with serial number 1001SA. Current calibers: 357 Magnum, 44 Special, 45 Long Colt.

Frontier Six-Shooter, 44-40	**$4550**
Storekeeper's Model, 3-inch/4-inch barrel, no ejector	4595
Target Model, flat top-strap, target sights	9850
U.S. Artillery Model, 45 Colt, 5 1/2-inch bbl.	6595
U.S. Cavalry Model, 45, 7 1/2-inch bbl.	8995

*(Above values apply only to original models, not to similar
S.A.A. revolvers of recent manufacture.)*

Standard Model, pre-1942	**$2950**
Standard Model (1955–1982)	1595
Standard Model (Reissued 1992)	795

Colt Single Action Army—125th Anniversary . . $1050

Limited production deluxe version of Single Action Army issued in commemoration of Colt's 125th Anniversary. Caliber: 45 Long Colt. 7½-inch barrel. Gold-plated frame, trigger, hammer, cylinder pin, ejector rod tip, and stock medallion. Presentation case with anniversary medallion. Serial numbers from "50AM." 7368 were made in 1961.

Colt Single Action Army Commemorative Models

Limited production versions of Single Action Army 45 issued, with appropriate inscription to commemorate historical events. Cased. *Note:* Values indicated are for commemorative revolvers in new condition.

1963 Issues

Arizona Territorial Centennial (1280 produced)	$1125
West Virginia Statehood Centennial (600 produced)	1100

1964 Issues

Chamizal Treaty (50 produced)	$1325
Colonel Sam Colt Sesquicentennial Presentation (4750 produced)	1100
Deluxe Presentation (200 produced)	2150
Special Deluxe Presentation (50 produced)	3200
Montana Territorial Centennial (851 produced)	1125
Nevada "Battle Born" (100 produced)	1425
Nevada Statehood Centennial (1877 produced)	1100
New Jersey Tercentenary (250 produced)	1125
Pony Express Presentation (1004 produced)	1200
St. Louis Bicentennial (450 produced)	1100
Wyatt Earp Buntline (150 produced)	1995

1965 Issues

Appomattox Centennial (500 produced)	$1100
Old Fort Des Moines Reconstruction (200 produced)	1125

1966 Issues

Abercrombie & Fitch Trailblazer—Chicago (100 produced)	$1125
Abercrombie & Fitch Trailblazer—New York (200 produced)	1125
Abercrombie & Fitch Trailblazer—San Francisco (100 produced)	1125
California Gold Rush (130 produced)	1325
General Meade (200 produced)	1100
Pony Express Four Square (4 guns)	4950

1967 Issues

Alamo (1000 produced)	$1100
Lawman Series—Bat Masterson (500 produced)	1325

1968 Issues

Lawman Series—Pat Garrett (500 produced)	$1150

1969 Issues

Lawman Series—Wild Bill Hickok (500 produced)	$1125

1970 Issues

Lawman Series—Wyatt Earp (501 produced)	$1950
Missouri Sesquicentennial (501 produced)	1050
Texas Ranger (1000 produced)	2000

Colt Single Action Army Commemoratives (cont.)

1971 Issues

NRA Centennial, 357 or 45 (5001 produced)	$1125

Peacemaker Centennial 45
1975 Issue

Peacemaker Centennial 44-40
1975 Issue

1975 Issues

Peacemaker Centennial 45 (1501 produced)	$1150
Peacemaker Centennial 44-40 (1501 produced)	1225
Peacemaker Centennial Cased Pair (501 produced)	2500

1979 Issues

Ned Buntline 45 (3000 produced)	$895

Colt Three-Fifty-Seven Double Action Revolver

Heavy frame. Caliber: 357 Magnum. 6-shot cylinder. 4- or 6-inch barrel. Quick-draw ramp front sight, Accro™ rear sight. Blued finish. Checkered walnut stocks. 9¼ or 11¼ inches overall. Weight: 36 oz., 4-inch bbl.; 39 oz., 6-inch bbl. Made 1953–1961.

With standard hammer and service stocks	$325
With wide-spur hammer and target stocks	375

Colt Trooper

Colt Trooper Double Action Revolver

Same specifications as Officers' Model Match, except has 4-inch barrel with quick-draw ramp front sight, weighs 34 oz. in 38 caliber. Made 1953–1969. (*See* photo, preceding page.)

Standard Hammer/Service Stocks **$275**
Wide-spur Hammer/Target Stocks **315**

Colt Trooper MK III

Colt U.S. Bicentennial Commemorative Set

Colt Trooper MK III Double Action Revolver **$225**

"J" frame, shrouded ejector rod. Calibers: 22 LR, 22 Magnum, 38 Special, 357 Magnum. 6-shot cylinder. Barrel lengths: 4-, 6-inch. 9½ inches overall w/4-inch bbl. Weight: 39 oz. w/4-inch bbl. Adjustable rear sight, ramp front. Target trigger and hammer. Blued or nickel-plated finish. Checkered walnut target stocks. Made 1969–1978.

Colt Trooper MK IV Double Action Revolver **$265**

Same general specifications as Trooper MK III with action modifications. Introduced in 1978; discontinued.

Colt U.S. Bicentennial Commemorative Set **$2100**

Replica Colt 3rd Model Dragoon Revolver with accessories, Colt Single Action Army Revolver, and Colt Python Revolver. Matching roll-engraved unfluted cylinders, blued finish, and rosewood stocks with Great Seal of the United States silver medallion. Dragoon revolver has silver grip frame. Serial numbers 0001 to 1776; all revolvers in set have same number. Deluxe drawer-style presentation case of walnut, with book compartment containing a reproduction of "Armsmear." Issued in 1976. Value is for revolvers in new condition.

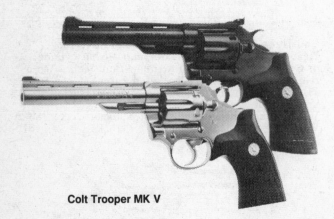

Colt Trooper MK V

Colt Viper

Colt Trooper MK V Revolver **$260**

Re-engineered Mark III for smoother, faster action. Caliber: 357 Magnum. 6-shot cylinder. Barrel lengths: 4-, 6-, 8-inch w/vent rib. Adjustable rear sight, ramp front, red insert. Checkered walnut stocks. Made 1982–86.

Colt Viper Double Action Revolver **$295**

Same as Cobra, Second Issue, except has 4-inch barrel, is 9 inches overall, weighs 20 oz. Made 1977–1984.

COONAN ARMS, INC.
St. Paul, Minnesota

Coonan Arms Model 357

Coonan Arms Model 357 Magnum Auto Pistol
Caliber: 357 Mag. 7-round magazine. 5- or 6-inch barrel. 8.3 inches overall (w/5-inch bbl.). Weight: 42 oz. Front ramp interchangeable sight; fixed rear sight, adjustable for windage. Black walnut grips.

Model A Std. Grade w/o Grip Safety (Disc. 1991)	**$775**
Model B Competition Grade	**810**
Model B Std. Grade w/5-inch Bbl.	**550**
Model B Std. Grade w/6-inch Bbl.	**575**

Coonan Arms 357 Magnum Cadet Compact $550
Similar to the standard 357 Magnum Model, except with 3.9-inch barrel. 6-shot magazine and compact frame. Weight: 39 oz. 7.8 inches overall. Made from 1993 to date.

CZ PISTOLS
Uhersky Brod (formerly Strakonice), Czechoslovakia
Mfd. by Ceska Zbrojovka-Nardoni Podnik (formerly Böhmische Waffenfabrik A. G.)

Currently manufactured models are imported by Magnum Research, Inc.; prior to 1994 were imported by Action Arms. Vintage importation is by Century International Arms.

CZ Model 27 Automatic Pistol

CZ Model 27 Auto Pistol $395
Caliber: 32 Automatic (7.65mm). 8-shot magazine. 4-inch barrel. 6 inches overall. Weight: 23½ oz. Fixed sights. Blued finish. Plastic stocks. Made 1927–1951. *Note:* After the German occupation, March 1939, Models 27 and 38 were marked with manufacturer code "fnh." Designation of Model 38 was changed to "Pistole 39(t)."

CZ Model 38 DA Auto Pistol

CZ Model 38 Double Action Auto Pistol $325
Caliber: 380 Automatic (9mm). 9-shot magazine. 3¾-inch barrel. 7 inches overall. Weight: 26 oz. Fixed sights. Blued finish. Plastic stocks. Made 1939–1945.

CZ Model 52 SA Auto Pistol $125
Roller-locking breech system. Caliber: 7.62mm. 8-shot magazine. 4.7-inch barrel. 8.1 inches overall. Weight: 31 oz. Fixed sights. Blued finish. Grooved composition grips.

CZ 75 DA Auto Pistol

CZ 75 Double Action Automatic Pistol
Caliber: 9mm Parabellum. 15-shot magazine. 4¾-inch barrel. 8 inches overall. Weight: 35 oz. Fixed sights. Blued or black polymer finish. Checkered wood or high-impact plastic stocks.

Black Polymer Finish	**$365**
High-Polish Blued Finish	**395**
Matte Blue Finish	**375**

CZ 82 Double Action Auto Pistol $250
Similar to the standard CZ 83 Model, except chambered in 9×18 Makarov.

CZ 83 Double Action Automatic Pistol $295
Calibers: 32 ACP, 380 ACP. 15-shot (32 ACP) or 13-shot (380 ACP) magazine. 3¾-inch barrel. 6¾ inches overall. Weight: 26½ oz. Fixed sights. Blued finish. Checkered black plastic stocks.

CZ 85 Automatic DA Pistol

Same as CZ 75, except with ambidextrous slide release and safety. Calibers: 9mm Parabellum, 7.65mm. Made from 1986 to date.
Black Polymer Finish **$395**
High-Polish Blued Finish **450**
Matte Blued Finish **425**

CZ 85 Combat DA Automatic Pistol

CZ 85 Combat DA Automatic Pistol

Similar to the standard CZ 85 Model, except with 13-shot magazine, combat-style hammer, fully adjustable rear sight and walnut grips.
Black Polymer Finish **$400**
High-Polish Blued Finish **465**
Matte Blued Finish **440**

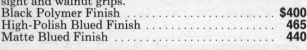

CZ Model 1945 Pocket Auto

CZ Model 1945 DA Pocket Auto Pistol $195

Caliber: 25 Auto (6.35mm). 8-shot magazine. 2½-inch barrel. 5 inches overall. Weight: 15 oz. Fixed sights. Blued finish. Plastic stocks. Introduced 1945; discontinued.

CZ Duo Pocket Auto

CZ Duo Pocket Auto Pistol $195

Caliber: 25 Automatic (6.35mm). 6-shot magazine. 2⅛-inch barrel. 4½ inches overall. Weight: 14½ oz. Fixed sights. Blued or nickel finish. Plastic stocks. Made 1926 to c. 1960.

CZ New Model .006

CZ New Model .006 Double Action Auto Pistol . . $395

Caliber: 32 Automatic (7.65mm). 8-shot magazine. 3⅛-inch barrel. 6½ inches overall. Weight: 24 oz. Fixed sights. Blued finish. Plastic stocks. Introduced 1951. Discont. *Note:* Official designation of this pistol, used by the Czech National Police, is "VZ50." "New Model .006" is export designation.

DAEWOO PISTOLS
Seoul, Korea
Mfd. by Daewoo Precision Industries Ltd.

Daewoo Model DH40

Daewoo DH40 Auto Pistol $295

Caliber: 40 S&W. 12-shot magazine. 4.25-inch barrel. 7 inches overall. Weight: 28 oz. Sights: blade front; dovetailed rear w/3-dot system. Blued finish. Checkered composition grips. DH/DP series feature a patented "fastfire" action with 5–6 lb. trigger pull. Made from 1994 to date.

Daewoo DH380 Auto Pistol $285

Caliber: 380 ACP. 3.8 barrel; 6.7 inches overall. Weight: 24 oz. Sights: blade front; dovetailed rear. Blued finish. Checkered composition grips. Made from 1994 to date.

Daewoo Model DP51

Dakota Model 1875 Outlaw

Daewoo DP51 Auto Pistol **$275**
Caliber: 9mm Parabellum. 13-shot magazine. 4.1-inch barrel. 7.5 inches overall. Weight: 28 oz. Blade front and square-notch rear sights. Matte black finish. Checkered composition grips. Made from 1991 to date.

Dakota Model 1875 Outlaw SA Revolver **$325**
Calibers: 45 Long Colt, 357 Mag., 44-40. 7¹/₂-inch barrel. Casehardened frame, blued finish. Walnut grips. This is an exact replica of the Remington #3 revolver produced 1875–1889.

Daewoo Model DP52

Dakota Model 1890 Remington Police

Daewoo DP52 Auto Pistol **$235**
Caliber: 22 LR. 10-shot magazine. 3.8-inch barrel. 6.7 inches overall. Weight: 23 oz. Sights: blade front; dovetailed rear w/3-dot system. Blued finish. Checkered wood grips. Made from 1994 to date.

Dakota Model 1890 Remington Police
Calibers: 357 Mag., 44-40, 45 Long Colt. 5³/₄-inch barrel. Blue or nickel finish. Exact replica of Colt original with lanyard ring.
Standard Model **$355**
Nickel Model **420**
Engraved Model **465**

DAKOTA/E.M.F. CO.
Santa Ana, California

Dakota Model 1873

Dakota Bisley SA Revolver

Dakota Model 1873 Single Action Revolver
Calibers: 22 LR, 22 Mag., 357 Mag., 45 Long Colt, 30 M1 carbine, 38-40, 32-20, 44-40. Barrel lengths: 3¹/₂, 4³/₄, 5¹/₂, 7¹/₂ inches. Blue or nickel finish. Engraved models avail.
Standard Model **$295**
With Extra Cylinder **425**

Dakota Bisley Single Action Revolver
Calibers: 44-40, 45 Long Colt, 357 Mag. 5¹/₂- or 7¹/₂-inch barrel. Discontinued 1992; reintroduced 1994.
Standard Model **$245**
Target Model **295**

**Dakota Hartford Single Action
Scroll Engraved**

Dakota Hartford Single Action Revolver
Calibers: 22 LR, 32-20, 357 Mag., 38-40, 44-40, 44 Special, 45 Long Colt. These are exact replicas of the original Colts, with steel backstraps, trigger guards and forged frames. Blued or nickel finish.

Standard Model **$340**
Engraved Model 495
Hartford Artillery, U.S. Cavalry Models 310

Dakota Sheriff's Model SA Revolver $280
Calibers: 32-20, 357 Mag., 38-40, 44 Special, 44-40, 45 LC. 3½-inch barrel. Reintroduced 1994.

Dakota Target Revolver

Dakota Target Single Action Revolver $295
Calibers: 45 Long Colt, 357 Mag., 22 LR. 5½- or 7½-inch barrel. Polished, blued finish, casehardened frame. Walnut grips. Ramp front, blade target sight, adj. rear sight.

DAVIS INDUSTRIES, INC.
Chino, California

Davis Model D Derringer
Single-action double derringer. Calibers: 22 LR, 22 Mag., 25 ACP, 32 Auto, 32 H&R Mag., 9mm, 38 Special. 2-shot capacity. 2.4-inch or 2.75-inch barrel. 4 inches overall (2.4-inch bbl.). Weight: 9 to 11½ oz. Laminated wood grips. Black Teflon or chrome finish. Made from 1987 to date.

22 LR or 25 ACP **$50**
22 Mag., 32 H&R Mag., 38 Spec. 65
32 Auto 70
9mm Parabellum 75

Davis Model P-32

Davis Model P-380

Davis Model P-32 .... $70
Caliber: 32 Auto. 6-round magazine. 2.8-inch barrel. 5.4 inches overall. Weight: 22 oz. Black teflon or chrome finish. Laminated wood grips. Made from 1987 to date.

Davis Model P-380 .... $70
Caliber: 380 Auto. 5-shot magazine. 2.8-inch barrel. 5.4 inches overall. Weight: 22 oz. Black teflon or chrome finish. Made from 1990 to date.

DESERT INDUSTRIES, INC.
Las Vegas, Nevada

Desert Industries Double Deuce DA Pistol $285
Caliber: 22 LR. 6-shot magazine. 2½-inch barrel. 5½ inches overall. Weight: 15 oz. Matte-finish stainless steel. Rosewood grips.

Desert Industries Two-Bit Special Pistol $295
Similar to the Double Deuce Model, except chambered in 25 ACP with 5-shot magazine.

Desert Industries War Eagle DA Pistol $495
Calibers: 9mm Parabellum, 10mm, 40 S&W, 45 ACP. Magazine: 14-shot, 9mm/40 S&W; 13-shot, 10mm; and 12-shot, 45 ACP. 4-inch barrel. 7.5 inches overall. Weight: 35.5 oz. Fixed sights. Matte-finish stainless steel. Rosewood grips. Made from 1986 to date.

(NEW) DETONICS MFG. CORP.
Phoenix, Arizona
(Formerly Detonics Firearms Industries, Bellevue, WA)

Detonics Combat Master

Detonics Combat Master
Calibers: 45 ACP, 451 Detonics Mag. 6-round magazine. 3½-inch barrel. 6¾ inches overall. Combat-type with fixed or adjustable sights. Checkered walnut stock. Stainless steel construction. Discontinued 1992.

MK I Matte Stainless, Fixed Sights	$425
MK I Stainless Steel Finish	400
MK IV Polished Blue, Adj. Sights, Disc.	415
MK V Matte Stainless, Fixed Sights, Disc.	530
MK VI Polished Stainless, Adj. Sights	560
MK VI in 451 Magnum	825
MK VII Matte Stainless Steel, No Sights	750
MK VII in 451 Magnum	995

Detonics Pocket 9 .... $350
Calibers: 9mm Parabellum, 380. 6-round magazine. 3-inch barrel. 5⅞ inches overall. Fixed sights. Double- and single-action trigger mechanism. Discontinued 1986.

Detonics Scoremaster

Detonics Scoremaster $825
Calibers: 45 ACP, 451 Detonics Mag. 7-round magazine. 5- or 6-inch heavyweight match barrel. 8¾ inches overall. Weight: 47 oz. Stainless steel construction, self-centering barrel system. Discontinued 1992.

Detonics Service Master $525
Caliber: 45 ACP. 7-round magazine. 4¼-inch barrel. Weight: 39 oz. Interchangeable front sight, millett rear sight. Discontinued 1986.

Detonics Service Master II $625
Same general specifications as standard Service Master, except comes in polished stainless steel with self-centering barrel system. Discontinued 1992.

DREYSE PISTOLS
Sommerda, Germany
Mfd. by Rheinische Metallwaren und Maschinenfabrik ("Rheinmetall")

Dreyse Model 1907*

Dreyse Model 1907 Automatic Pistol $200
Caliber: 32 Auto (7.65mm). 8-shot magazine. 3½-inch barrel. 6¼ inches overall. Weight: about 24 oz. Fixed sights. Blued finish. Hard rubber stocks. Made 1907–c. 1914.

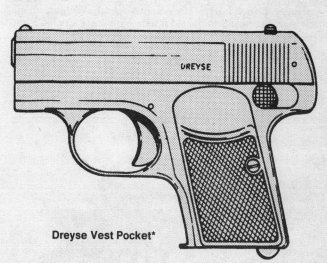

Dreyse Vest Pocket*

Dreyse Vest Pocket Automatic Pistol $185
Conventional Browning type. Caliber: 25 Auto (6.35mm). 6-shot magazine. 2-inch barrel. 4½ inches overall. Weight: about 14 oz. Fixed sights. Blued finish. Hard rubber stocks. Made from c. 1909–1914.

DWM PISTOL
Berlin, Germany
Mfd. by Deutsche Waffen-und-Munitionsfabriken

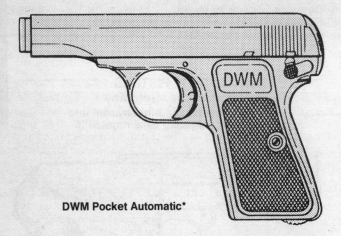

DWM Pocket Automatic*

DWM Pocket Automatic Pistol **$595**
Similar to the FN Browning Model 1910. Caliber: 32 Automatic (7.65mm). 3½-inch barrel. 6 inches overall. Weight: about 21 oz. Blued finish. Hard rubber stocks. Made from c. 1921–1931.

ENFIELD REVOLVER
Enfield Lock, Middlesex, England
Manufactured by Royal Small Arms Factory

Enfield (British Service) No. 2 MK 1 Revolver . . . **$195**
Webley pattern. Hinged frame. Double action. Caliber: 380 British Service (38 S&W w/200-grain bullet). 6-shot cylinder. 5-inch barrel. 10½ inches overall. Weight: about 27½ oz. Fixed sights. Blued finish. Vulcanite stocks. First issued in 1932, this was the standard revolver of the British Army in WW II. Now obsolete. *Note:* This model also produced w/spurless hammer as No. 2 Mk 1* and Mk 1**

ERMA-WERKE
Dachau, Germany

**Erma Model ER-772
Match Revolver**

Erma Model ER-772 Match Revolver **$795**
Caliber: 22 LR. 6-shot cylinder. 6-inch barrel. 12 inches overall. Weight: 47¼ oz. Adjustable micrometer rear sight and front sight blade. Adjustable trigger. Interchangeable walnut sporter or match grips. Polished blue finish. Made from 1991 to date.

Erma Model ER-773 Match Revolver **$750**
Same general specifications as Model 772, except chambered for 32 S&W. Made from 1991 to date.

Erma Model ER-777 Match Revolver **$725**
Caliber: 357 Magnum. 6-shot cylinder. 4- or 5½-inch barrel. 9.7 to 11.3 inches overall. Weight: 43.7 oz. w/5½-inch bbl. Micrometer adjustable rear sight. Checkered walnut sporter or match-style grip (interchangeable). Made from 1991 to date.

**Erma Model ESP-85A
Competition Pistol**

Erma Model ESP-85A Competition Pistol
Calibers: 22 LR and 32 S&W Wadcutter. 8- or 5-shot magazine. 6-inch barrel. 10 inches overall. Weight: 40 oz. Adjustable rear sight; blade front sight. Checkered walnut grip with thumbrest. Made from 1991 to date.

Match Model	**$835**
Chrome Match	**895**
Sporting Model	**815**
Conversion Unit 22 LR	**795**
Conversion Unit 32 S&W	**815**

Erma-Werke Model KGP68

Erma-Werke Model KGP68 Automatic Pistol **$270**
Luger type. Calibers: 32 Auto (7.65mm), 380 Auto (9mm Short). 6-shot magazine in 32, 5-shot in 380. 4-inch barrel. 7⅜ inches overall. Weight: 22½ oz. Fixed sights. Blued finish. Checkered walnut stocks. Made from 1968 to date.

Erma-Werke Model KGP69

Erma-Werke Model KGP69 Automatic Pistol **$265**
Luger type. Caliber: 22 LR. 8-shot magazine. 4-inch barrel.
7³/₄ inches overall. Weight: 29 oz. Fixed sights. Blued finish. Checkered walnut stocks. Made from 1969 to date.

EUROPEAN AMERICAN ARMORY
Hialeah, Florida

See also listings under Astra Pistols.

European American Armory Model 380 DA Auto Pistol
Similar to the standard European Model, except double
action and chambered in 380 only. Made 1992 to date.
Blued Finish **$125**
Chrome **135**
Ladies Model **160**

**European American Armory
Big Bore Bounty Hunter**

**European American Armory Big Bore Bounty Hunter
Single Action Revolver**
Calibers: 357 Mag., 41 Mag., 44-40, 44 Mag., 45 Colt. Bar-
rel lengths: 4⁵/₈, 5¹/₂, 7¹/₂ inches. Blade front and grooved
topstrap rear sights. Blued or chrome finish with color-
casehardened or gold-plated frame. Smooth walnut grips.
Made from 1992 to date.
Blued Finish **$195**
Blued w/Color-Casehardened Frame **215**
Blued w/Gold-Plated Frame **235**
Chrome Finish **240**

European American Armory Bounty Hunter SA Revolver
Calibers: 22 LR, 22 WRF. Barrel lengths: 4³/₄, 6 or 9
inches. Blade front and dovetailed rear sights. Blued finish
or blue with gold-plated frame. European hardwood grips.
Made from 1991 to date.

European American Armory Bounty Hunter (cont.)
Blued Finish (4³/₄-inch bbl.) .... **$ 90**
Blued 22 LR/22 WRF Combo (4³/₄-inch bbl.) **100**
Blued 22 LR/22 WRF Combo (6-inch bbl.) **110**
Blued 22 LR/22 WRF Combo (9-inch bbl.) **115**
For Gold-Plated Frame, **add** **10%**

European American Armory EA22 Target **$275**
Caliber: 22 LR. 12-shot magazine. 6-inch barrel. 9.10
inches overall. Weight: 40 oz. Ramp front sight, fully adjustable rear. Blued finish. Checkered walnut grips with
thumbrest.

European American Armory European Model Auto Pistol
Calibers: 32 ACP, 380 ACP. 7-shot magazine. 3.85-inch
barrel. 7³/₈ inches overall. Weight: 26 oz. Blade front sight,
rear sight drift-adjustable for windage. Blued or chrome
finish. European hardwood grips.
Blued Finish SA **$115**
Chrome SA **135**
Ladies Model SA **165**
Blued Finish DA only; Disc. 1995 .... **160**

European American Armory FAB 92 Auto Pistol
Similar to the Witness Model, except chambered in 9mm
only with slide-mounted safety and no cock-and-lock pro-
vision.
FAB 92 Standard **$255**
FAB 92 Compact **245**

European American Armory Standard Grade Revolver
Calibers: 22 LR, 22 WRF, 32 H&R Mag., 38 Special. 2-,
4- or 6-inch barrel. Blade front sight, fixed or adjustable
rear. Blued finish. European hardwood grips with finger
grooves. Made from 1991 to date.
22 LR (4-inch bbl.) **$135**
22 LR (6-inch bbl.) **140**
22 LR Combo (4-inch bbl.) **195**
22 LR Combo (6-inch bbl.) **205**
32 H&R, 38 Special (2-inch bbl.) **140**
38 Special (4-inch) **150**

European American Armory Tactical Grade Revolver
Similar to the Standard Model, except chambered in 38
Special only. 2- or 4-inch barrel. Fixed sights. Available
with compensator. Made from 1991 to date.
Tactical Revolver **$175**
Tactical Revolver w/Compensator **265**

**European American Armory
Windicator**

European American Armory Windicator Target Revolver **$295**
Calibers: 22 LR, 38 Special, 357 Magnum. 8-shot cylinder in 22 LR; 6-shot in 38 Special/357 Magnum. 6-inch barrel w/barrel weights. 11.8 inches overall. Weight: 50.2 oz. Interchangeable blade front sight, fully adjustable rear. Walnut competition-style grips. Made from 1991 to date. (*See* photo preceding page.)

**European American Armory
Witness**

European American Armory Witness DA Auto Pistol
Similar to the Brno CZ-75 with a cocked-and-locked system. Double or single action. Calibers: 9mm Parabellum, 38 Super, 38 S&W, 10mm, 41 AE and 45 ACP. 16-shot magazine in 9mm; 12-shot in 38 Super/40 S&W; 10-shot in 10mm/45 ACP. 4.75-inch barrel. 8.10 inches overall. Weight: 35.33 oz. Blade front sight, rear sight adjustable for windage with 3-dot sighting system. Blued, satin chrome, blue/chrome or stainless finish. Checkered rubber grips. Made from 1991 to date.

9mm Blue	**$280**
9mm Chrome or Blue/Chrome	**290**
9mm Stainless	**335**
38 Super and 40 S&W Blued	**295**
38 Super and 40 S&W Chrome or Blue/Chrome	**315**
38 Super and 40 S&W Stainless	**345**
10mm, 41 AE and 45 ACP Blued	**365**
10mm, 41 AE and 45 ACP Chrome or Blue/ Chrome	**380**
10mm, 41 AE and 45 ACP Stainless	**425**

European American Armory Witness Subcompact DA Auto Pistol
Calibers: 9mm Para., 40 S&W, 41 AE, 45 ACP. 13-shot magazine in 9mm; 9-shot in 40 S&W. 3.66-inch barrel. 7.25 inches overall. Weight: 30 oz. Blade front sight, rear sight adj. for windage. Blued, satin chrome or blue/chrome finish.

9mm Blue	**$270**
9mm Chrome or Blue/Chrome	**295**
40 S&W Blue	**295**
40 S&W Chrome or Blue/Chrome	**325**
41 AE Blue	**350**
41 AE Chrome or Blue/Chrome	**375**
45 ACP Blue	**360**
45 ACP Chrome or Blue/Chrome	**385**

European American Armory Witness Target Pistol
Similar to standard Witness Model, except fitted with 2- or 3-port compensator, competition frame and S/A target trigger. Calibers: 9mm Parabellum, 9×21, 40 S&W, 10mm and 45 ACP. 5.25-inch match barrel. 10.5 inches overall.

European American Armory Witness Target (cont.)
Weight: 38 oz. Square post front sight, fully adjustable rear or drilled and tapped for scope. Blued or hard chrome finish. Low-profile competition grips.

Silver Team (Blued w/2-Port Compensator)	**$ 650**
Gold Team (Chrome w/3-Port Compensator)	**1295**

FEATHER INDUSTRIES, INC.
Boulder, Colorado

**Feather Guardian
Angel Derringer**

Feather Guardian Angel Derringer
Double-action over/under derringer with interchangeable, drop-in loading blocks. Calibers: 22 LR, 22 WMR, 9mm, 38 Spec. 2-shot capacity. 2-inch barrel. 5 inches overall. Weight: 12 oz. Stainless steel. Checkered black grips. Made from 1988 to date.

22 LR, 22 WMR	**$75**
9mm, 38 Special (Disc. 1989)	**80**

FEG (FEGYVERGYAN) PISTOLS
Budapest, Soroksariut, Hungary

Currently imported by KBI, Inc. and Century International Arms (previously by Interarms).

FEG Model GKK-9 Auto Pistol **$245**
Improved version of the double-action FEG Model MBK. Caliber: 9mm Parabellum. 14-shot magazine. 4-inch barrel. 7.4 inches overall. Weight: 34 oz. Blade front sight; rear sight adj. for windage. Checkered wood grips. Blued finish. Imported 1992–93.

FEG Model GKK-45 Auto Pistol
Improved version of the double-action FEG Model MBK. Caliber: 45 ACP. 8-shot magazine. 4.1-inch barrel. 7.75 inches overall. Weight: 36 oz. Blade front sight; rear sight adj. for windage w/3-Dot system. Checkered walnut grips. Blued or chrome finish.

Blued Model (Discontinued 1994)	**$245**
Chrome Model	**265**

FEG Model MBK-9HP Auto Pistol **$255**
Similar to the double-action Browning Hi-Power. Caliber: 9mm Parabellum. 14-shot magazine. 4.6-inch barrel. 8 inches overall. Weight: 36 oz. Blade front sight; rear sight adj. for windage. Checkered wood grips. Blued finish. Imported 1992–93.

**FEG Model PJK-9HP
Auto Pistol**

FEG Model PJK-9HP Auto Pistol
Similar to the single-action Browning Hi-Power. Caliber: 9mm Parabellum. 13-shot magazine. 4.75-inch barrel. 8 inches overall. Weight: 21 oz. Blade front sight; rear sight adj. for windage w/3-Dot system. Checkered walnut or rubber grips. Blued or chrome finish.
Blued Model **$235**
Chrome Model **285**

FEG Model PSP-25 Auto Pistol
Similar to the Browning 25. Caliber: 25 ACP. 6-shot magazine. 2.1-inch barrel. 4.1 inches overall. Weight: 9.5 oz. Fixed sights. Checkered composition grips. Blued or chrome finish.
Blued Model **$175**
Chrome Model **215**

FEG Model SMC-22 Auto Pistol **$195**
Same general specifications as FEG Model SMC-380, except in 22 LR. 8-shot magazine. 3.5-inch barrel. 6.1 inches overall. Weight: 18.5 oz. Blade front sight; rear sight adj. for windage. Checkered composition grips w/thumbrest. Blued finish.

FEG Model SMC-380 Auto Pistol **$195**
Similar to the Walther double-action PPK with alloy frame. Caliber: 380 ACP. 6-shot magazine. 3.5-inch barrel. 6.1 inches overall. Weight: 18.5 oz. Blade front sight; rear sight adj. for windage. Checkered composition grips w/thumbrest. Blued finish. Imported 1993 to date.

FEG Model SMC-918 Auto Pistol **$195**
Same general specifications as FEG Model SMC-380, except chambered in 9×18mm Makarov. Imported 1994 to date.

FIALA OUTFITTERS, INC.
New York, New York

Fiala Repeating Pistol **$395**
Despite its appearance, which closely resembles that of the early Colt Woodsman and High-Standard, this arm is not an automatic pistol. It is hand-operated by moving the slide to eject, cock and load. Caliber: 22 LR. 10-shot magazine. Barrel lengths: 3-, 7½- and 20-inch. 11¼ inches overall w/7½-inch bbl. Weight: 31 oz. w/7½-inch bbl. Target sights. Blued finish. Plain wood stocks. Shoulder stock was originally supplied for use with 20-inch barrel. Made 1920–23. Value shown is for pistol with one barrel and no shoulder stock.

F.I.E. CORPORATION
Hialeah, Florida

The F.I.E. Corporation became QFI (Quality Firearms Corp.) of Opa Locka, Fl., about 1990, when most of F.I.E.'s models were discontinued.

F.I.E. Model A27BW

F.I.E. Model A27BW "The Best" Semiauto **$95**
Caliber: 25 ACP. 6-round magazine. 2½-inch barrel. 6¾ inches overall. Weight: 13 oz. Fixed sights. Checkered walnut stock. Discontinued 1990.

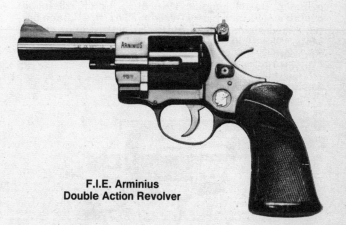

**F.I.E. Arminius
Double Action Revolver**

F.I.E. Arminius Double Action Revolver
Calibers: 22 LR; 22 combo w/interchangeable cylinder; 32 S&W, 38 Special, 357 Magnum. 6, 7 or 8 rounds depending on caliber. Swingout cylinder. Barrel lengths: 2-, 3-, 4-, 6-inch. Vent rib on calibers other than 22. 11 inches overall w/6-inch barrel. Weight: 26 to 30 oz. Fixed or micro-adjustable sights. Checkered plastic or walnut stocks. Blued finish. Made in Germany; discontinued.
22 LR . . . . **$ 95**
22 Combo **95**
32 S&W **100**
38 Special **105**
357 Magnum **150**

F.I.E. Buffalo Scout Single Action Revolver
Calibers: 22 LR, 22 WRF; 22 combo w/interchangeable cylinder. 4³/₄-inch barrel. 10 inches overall. Weight: 32 oz. Adjustable sights. Blued or chrome finish. Smooth walnut or black checkered nylon grips. Made in Italy.

Blued Standard	$ 50
Blued Convertible	100
Chrome Standard	65
Chrome Convertible	110

F.I.E. Hombre Single Action Revolver $160
Calibers: 357 Magnum, 44 Magnum, 45 Colt. 6-shot cylinder. Barrel lengths: 6 or 7¹/₂ inches. 11 inches overall w/6-inch barrel. Weight: 45 oz. w/6-inch barrel. Fixed sights. Blued barrel with color-casehardened receiver. Smooth walnut stocks. Made 1979–1990.

F.I.E. Little Ranger Single Action Revolver
Same as the Texas Ranger, except with 3¹/₄-inch barrel and bird's-head grips. Made 1986–1990.

Standard	$80
Convertible	95

F.I.E. Super Titan II
Caliber: 32 ACP or 380 ACP. 3¹/₄-inch barrel. Weight: 28 oz. Blued or chrome finish. Discontinued 1990.

32 ACP in Blue	$130
32 ACP in Chrome	145
380 ACP in Blue	160
380 ACP in Chrome	175

F.I.E. Texas Ranger Single Action Revolver
Calibers: 22 LR, 22 WRF; 22 combo w/interchangeable cylinder. Barrel lengths: 4³/₄-, 6¹/₂-, 9-inch. 10 inches overall w/4³/₄-inch barrel. Weight: 32 oz. w/4³/₄-inch barrel. Fixed sights. Blued finish. Smooth walnut stocks. Made 1983–1990.

Standard	$65
Convertible	95

F.I.E. Titan II

F.I.E. Titan II Semiautomatic
Calibers: 22 LR, 32 ACP, 380 ACP. 10-round magazine. Integral tapered post front sight, windage-adjustable rear sight. European walnut grips. Blued or chrome finish. Discontinued 1990.

22 LR in Blue	$ 95
32 ACP in Blue	145
32 ACP in Chrome	175
380 ACP in Blue	165
380 ACP in Chrome	185

**F.I.E. Model TZ75
Satin Chrome**

F.I.E. Model TZ75 DA Semiautomatic
Double action. Caliber: 9mm. 15-round magazine. 4¹/₂-inch barrel. 8¹/₄ inches overall. Weight: 35 oz. Ramp front sight, windage-adjustable rear sight. European walnut or black rubber grips. Discontinued 1989.

Blued Finish	$295
Satin Chrome	325

F.I.E. Yellow Rose Single Action Revolver
Same general specifications as the Buffalo Scout, except in 22 combo w/interchangeable cylinder and plated in 24 karat gold. Limited Edition with scrimshawed ivory polymer grips and American walnut presentation case. Made 1987–1990.

Yellow Rose 22 Combo	$100
Yellow Rose Ltd. Edition	250

F.I.E. Titan Tiger

F.I.E. Titan Tiger Double Action Revolver $100
Caliber: 38 Special. 6-shot cylinder. 2- or 4-inch barrel. 8¹/₄ inches overall w/4-inch barrel. Weight: 30 oz. w/4-inch barrel. Fixed sights. Blued finish. Checkered plastic or walnut stocks. Made in the U.S. Discontinued 1990.

FIREARMS INTERNATIONAL CORP.
Washington, D.C.

Firearms International Model D

Firearms International Regent

Firearms Int'l. Model D Automatic Pistol **$165**
Caliber: 380 Automatic. 6-shot magazine. 3¹/₈-inch barrel. 6¹/₈ inches overall. Weight: 19¹/₂ oz. Blade front sight, windage-adjustable rear sight. Blued, chromed, or military finish. Checkered walnut stocks. Made 1974–77.

Firearms Int'l. Regent Double Action Revolver . . . **$80**
Calibers: 22 LR, 32 S&W Long. 8-shot cylinder (22 LR), 7-shot (32). Barrels: 3-, 4-, 6-inch (22 LR); 2¹/₂-, 4-inch (32). Weight: with 4-inch barrel, 28 oz. Fixed sights. Blue finish. Plastic stocks. Made 1966–1972.

FN BROWNING PISTOLS
Liege, Belgium
Mfd. by Fabrique Nationale Herstal

See also Browning Pistols.

FN Browning 6.35mm

FN Browning 6.35mm Pocket Auto Pistol **$315**
Same specifications as Colt Pocket Model 25 Automatic.

FN Browning Model 1900*

FN Browning Model 1900 Pocket Auto Pistol . . . **$325**
Caliber: 32 Automatic (7.65mm). 7-shot magazine. 4-inch barrel. 6³/₄ inches overall. Weight: 22 oz. Fixed sights. Blued finish. Hard rubber stocks. Made 1899–1910.

FN Browning Model 1903 Military Auto Pistol . . . **$390**
Caliber: 9mm Browning Long. 7-shot magazine. 5-inch barrel. 8 inches overall. Weight: 32 oz. Fixed sights. Blued finish. Hard rubber stocks. *Note:* Aside from size, this pistol is of the same basic design as the Colt Pocket 32 and 380 Automatic pistols. Made 1903–1939.

FN Browning Model 1910

FN Browning Model 1910 Pocket Auto Pistol . . . **$500**
Calibers: 32 Auto (7.65mm), 380 Auto (9mm). 7-shot magazine (32 cal.), 6-shot (380 cal.). 3¹/₂-inch barrel. 6 inches overall. Weight: 20¹/₂ oz. Fixed sights. Blued finish. Hard rubber stocks. Made 1910–1922.

FN Browning Model 1922

FN Browning Model 1922 Police/Military Auto .. $255

Calibers: 32 Auto (7.65mm), 380 Auto (9mm). 9-shot magazine (32 cal.), 8-shot (380 cal.). 4½-inch barrel. 7 inches overall. Weight: 25 oz. Fixed sights. Blued finish. Hard rubber stocks. Made 1922–1959. (*See* photo, preceding page.)

FN Browning Model 1935 Hi-Power

FN Browning Model 1935 Military Hi-Power Pistol

Variation of the Browning-Colt 45 Auto design. Caliber: 9mm Luger. 13-shot magazine. 4⅝-inch barrel. 7¾ inches overall. Weight: about 35 oz. Adjustable rear sight and fixed front, or both fixed. Blued finish (Canadian manufacture Parkerized). Checkered walnut or plastic stocks. *Note:* Above specifications in general apply to both the original FN production and the pistols made by John Inglis Company of Canada for the Chinese Government. A smaller version, with shorter barrel and slide and 10-shot magazine, was made by FN for the Belgian and Rumanian Governments about 1937–1940. Both types were made at the FN plant during the German Occupation of Belgium.

With adjustable rear sight **$625**
FN manufacture, with fixed rear sight **545**
Inglis manufacture, with fixed rear sight **630**

FN Browning Baby

FN Browning Baby Auto Pistol $325

Caliber: 25 Automatic (6.35mm). 6-shot magazine. 2⅛-inch barrel. 4 inches overall. Weight: 10 oz. Fixed sights. Blued finish. Hard rubber stocks. Made 1931–1983.

FOREHAND & WADSWORTH
Worcester, Massachusetts

Forehand & Wadsworth Revolvers

See listings of comparable Harrington & Richardson and Iver Johnson revolvers for values.

LE FRANCAIS PISTOLS
St. Etienne, France
Produced by Manufacture Francaise d'Armes et Cycles

Le Francais Army Model Automatic Pistol $995

Similar in operation to the Le Francais 25 Automatics. Caliber: 9mm Browning Long. 8-shot magazine. 5-inch barrel. 7¾ inches overall. Weight: about 34 oz. Fixed sights. Blued finish. Checkered walnut stocks. Made from 1928–1938.

Le Francais Policeman*

Le Francais Policeman Model Automatic Pistol . $695

DA. Hinged barrel. Caliber: 25 Automatic (6.35mm). 7-shot magazine. 3½-inch barrel. 6 inches overall. Weight: about 12 oz. Fixed sights. Blued finish. Hard rubber stocks. Intro. 1914; discontinued.

Le Francais Staff Officer*

Le Francais Staff Officer Model Automatic Pistol .. $225

Caliber: 25 Automatic. Similar to the "Policeman" Model, except does not have cocking-piece head, barrel is about an inch shorter and weight is an oz. less. Intro. 1914; disc.

FREEDOM ARMS
Freedom, Wyoming

Freedom Arms Model FA-44 SA Revolver
Similar to Model 454 Casull, except chambered in 44 Mag. Made from 1988 to date.

Field Grade	$ 725
Premier Grade	765
Silhouette Class (w/10-inch bbl.)	695
Silhouette Pac (10-inch bbl., access.)	750
For Fixed Sights, **deduct**	95

Freedom Arms Model FA-45 SA Revolver
Similar to Model 454 Casull, except chambered in 45 Long Colt. Made 1988–1990.

Field Grade	$695
Premier Grade	750
For Fixed Sights, **deduct**	95

**Freedom Arms Model FA-252
Silhouette Class**

Freedom Arms Model FA-252 SA Revolver
Calibers: 22 LR w/optional 22 Mag. cylinder. Barrel lengths: 5^1/$_8$ and 7^1/$_2$ (Varmint Class); 10 inches (Silhouette Class). Adjustable express or competition silhouette sights. Brushed or matte stainless finish. Black micarta (Silhouette) or black and green laminated hardwood grips (Varmint). Made from 1991 to date.

Silhouette Class	$ 895
Silhouette Class w/extra 22 Mag. cyl.	1125
Varmint Class	850
Varmint Class w/extra 22 Mag. cyl.	1095

**Freedom Arms Model FA-353
Field Grade**

Freedom Arms Model FA-353 SA Revolver
Caliber: 357 Mag. Barrel lengths: 4³/4, 6, 7¹/2 or 9 inches. Removable blade front sight; adjustable rear sight. Brushed or matte stainless finish. Pachmayr Presentation or impregnated hardwood grips.

Field Grade	$ 725
Premier Grade	765
Silhouette Class (w/9-inch bbl.)	695

**Freedom Arms
Model FA-454 Casull**

Freedom Arms Model FA-454AS Revolver
Caliber: 454 Casull (w/optional 45 ACP, 45 LC, 45 Win. Mag. cylinders). 5-shot cylinder. Barrel lengths: 4³/4, 6, 7¹/2 or 10 inches. Adjustable express or competition silhouette sights. Pachmayr presentation or impregnated hardwood grips. Brushed or matte stainless steel finish.

Field Grade	$ 730
Premier Grade	775
Silhouette Class (w/10-inch bbl.)	735
For Fixed Sights, **deduct**	95
For Extra Cylinder, **add**	250

Freedom Arms Model FA-454FS Revolver $950
Same general specifications as Model FA-454AS, except with fixed sight.

**Freedom Arms FA-454GAS
Field Grade**

Freedom Arms Model FA-454GAS Revolver $895
Field Grade version of Model FA-454AS, except not made w/12-inch barrel. Matte stainless finish, Pachmayr presentation grips. Adj. sights; fixed sight on 4³/4-inch bbl.

Freedom Arms Model FA-555 Revolver
Similar to Model 454 Casull, except chambered in 50 AE. Made 1994 to date.

Field Grade	$715
Premier Grade	765

Freedom Arms Model FA-BG-22LR
Mini-Revolver $120
Caliber: 22 LR. 3-inch tapered barrel. Partial high-gloss stainless steel finish. Discontinued 1987.

Freedom Arms Model FA-BG-22M
Mini-Revolver $135
Same general specifications as model FA-BG-22LR, except in caliber 22 WMR.

Freedom Arms Model FA-BG-22P
Mini-Revolver $120
Same general specifications as Model FA-BG-22LR, except in 22 percussion. Discontinued 1987.

Freedom Arms Model FA-L-22LR Mini-Revolver . . $85
Caliber: 22 LR. 1³/₄-inch contoured barrel. Partial high-gloss stainless steel finish. Bird's-head-type grips. Discontinued 1987.

Freedom Arms Model FA-L-22M Mini-Revolver . $120
Same general specifications as Model FA-L-22LR, except in caliber 22 WMR. Discontinued 1987.

Freedom Arms Model FA-L-22P Mini-Revolver . . . $95
Same general specifications as Model FA-L-22LR, except in 22 percussion. Discontinued 1987.

**Freedom Arms
Model FA-S-22LR**

Freedom Arms Model FA-S-22LR Mini-Revolver $110
Caliber: 22 LR. 1-inch contoured barrel. Partial high-gloss stainless steel finish. Discontinued.

Freedom Arms Model FA-S-22M Mini-Revolver . $120
Same general specifications as Model FA-S-22LR, except in caliber 22 WMR. Discontinued.

Freedom Arms Model FA-S-22P Mini-Revolver . . . $95
Same general specifications as Model FA-S-22LR, except in percussion. Discontinued.

FRENCH MILITARY PISTOLS
Cholet, France
Mfd. originally by Société Alsacienne de Constructions Mécaniques (S.A.C.M.); currently made by Manufacture d'Armes Automatiques, Lotissement Industriel des Pontots, Bayonne

French Model 1935A

French Model 1935A Automatic Pistol $225
Caliber: 7.65mm Long. 8-shot magazine. 4.3-inch barrel. 7.6 inches overall. Weight: 26 oz. Two-lug locking system similar to the Colt U.S. M1911A1. Fixed sights. Blued finish. Checkered stocks. Made 1935–1945. *Note:* This pistol was used by French troops during WW II and in Indo-China 1945–1954.

French Model 1935S Automatic Pistol $250
Similar to Model 1935A, except shorter (4.1-inch barrel and 7.4 inches overall) and heavier (28 oz.). Single-step lug locking system.

French Model 1950 Automatic Pistol $250
Caliber: 9mm Parabellum. 9-shot magazine. 4.4-inch barrel. 7.6 inches overall. Weight: 30 oz. Fixed sights; tapered post front and U-notched rear. Similar in design and function to the U.S. 45 service automatic, except no barrel bushing.

French Model MAB F1 Automatic Pistol $550
Similar to Model MAB P-15, except with 6-inch barrel and 9.6 inches overall. Adjustable target-style sights. Parkerized finish.

French Model MAB P-8 Automatic Pistol $375
Similar to Model MAB P-15, except with 8-shot magazine.

French Model MAB P-15 Automatic Pistol $465
Caliber: 9mm Parabellum. 9-shot magazine. 4.5-inch barrel. 7.9 inches overall. Weight: 38 oz. Fixed sights; tapered post front and U-notched rear.

FROMMER PISTOLS
Budapest, Hungary
Mfd. by Fémáru-Fegyver-és Gépgyár R.T.

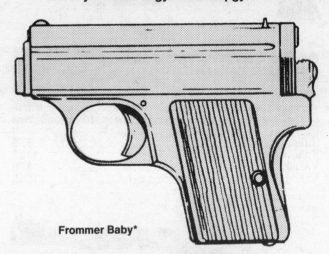

Frommer Baby*

Frommer Baby Pocket Automatic Pistol $175
Similar to Stop model, except has 2-inch barrel, is about 4³/₄ inches overall, weighs about 17¹/₂ oz. Magazine capacity is one round less. Introduced shortly after WW I.

Frommer Liliput Pocket Automatic Pistol $195
Caliber: 25 Automatic (6.35mm). 6-shot magazine. 2.14-inch barrel. 4.33 inches overall. Weight: 10¹/₂ oz. Fixed sights. Blued finish. Hard rubber stocks. Made during early 1920s. *Note:* Although similar in appearance to the Stop and Baby, this pistol is blowback operated.

Frommer Stop Pocket Automatic Pistol $165
Locked-breech action, outside hammer. Calibers: 32 Automatic (7.65mm), 380 Auto (9mm short). 7-shot (32 cal.) or 6-shot (380 cal.) magazine. 3⁷/₈-inch barrel. 6¹/₂ inches overall. Weight: about 21 oz. Fixed sights. Blued finish. Hard rubber stocks. Made 1912–1920.

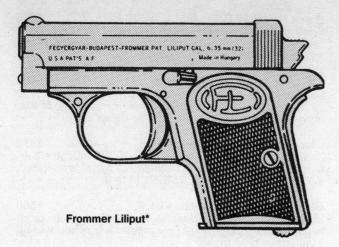

Frommer Liliput*

Frommer Stop Pocket Auto*

GALESI PISTOLS
Collebeato (Brescia), Italy
Mfd. by Industria Armi Galesi

Galesi Model 6*

Galesi Model 6 Pocket Automatic Pistol **$125**
Calibers: 22 Long, 25 Automatic (6.35mm). 6-shot magazine. 2¹/₄-inch barrel. 4³/₈ inches overall. Weight: about 11 oz. Fixed sights. Blued finish. Plastic stocks. Made from 1930 to date.

Galesi Model 9*

Galesi Model 9 Pocket Automatic Pistol
Calibers: 22 LR, 32 Auto (7.65mm), 380 Auto (9mm Short). 8-shot magazine. 3¹/₄-inch barrel. 5⁷/₈ inches overall. Weight: about 21 oz. Fixed sights. Blued finish. Plastic stocks. Made from 1930 to date. *Note:* Specifications vary; those shown are for 32 Automatic of common type.
22 Long Rifle or 380 Automatic **$160**
32 Automatic **150**

GLISENTI PISTOL
Carcina (Brescia), Italy
Mfd. by Societa Siderurgica Glisenti

Glisenti Model 1910

Glisenti Model 1910 Italian Service Automatic . . **$495**
Caliber: 9mm, Glisenti. 7-shot magazine. 4-inch barrel. 8¹/₂ inches overall. Weight: about 32 oz. Fixed sights. Blued finish. Checkered wood. Hard rubber or plastic stocks. Adopted 1910 and used through WW II.

GLOCK, INC.
Smyrna, Georgia

Glock Model 17 DA Automatic Pistol **$385**
Caliber: 9mm Parabellum. 17-shot magazine. 4¹/₂-inch barrel. 7.2 inches overall. Weight: about 22 oz., empty. Hi-tech polymer frame and receiver; steel barrel, slide and springs. Fixed or adjustable rear sights. Matte, nonglare finish. Made of only 33 components, including 3 internal

Glock Model 17

Glock Model 17 DA Automatic Pistol (cont.)

safety devices. This gun received the "Best Pistol Award of Merit" in 1987 by the American Firearms Industry. Made in Austria from 1983 to date.

Glock Model 17L Competition $535
Same general specifications as Model 17, except weighs 23.35 oz. with 6-inch barrel; 8.85 inches overall. Currently manufactured.

Glock Model 19 Compact

Glock Model 20

Glock Model 19 Compact $395
Same general specifications as Model 17, except smaller version with 4-inch barrel, 6.85 inches overall and 21-oz. weight. Made from 1988 to date.

Glock Model 20 DA Auto Pistol $475
Caliber: 10mm. 15-shot. Hammerless. 4.6-inch barrel. 7.59 inches overall. Weight: 26.3 oz. Fixed or adj. sights. Matte, nonglare finish. Made from 1991 to date.

Glock Model 21 Automatic Pistol $470
Same general specifications as Model 17, except chambered in 45 ACP. 13-shot magazine. 7.59 inches overall. Weight: 25.2 oz. Made from 1991 to date.

Glock Model 22 Automatic Pistol $360
Same general specifications as Model 17, except chambered for 40 S&W. 15-shot magazine. 7.4 inches overall. Made from 1992 to date.

Glock Model 23 Automatic Pistol $395
Same general specifications as Model 19, except chambered for 40 S&W. 13-shot magazine. 6.97 inches overall. Made from 1992 to date.

Glock Model 24 Automatic Pistol $465
Same general specifications as Model 17L, except chambered for 40 S&W. Made from 1994 to date.

Glock Desert Storm Commemorative $750
Same general specifications as Model 17, except "Operation Desert Storm, January 16–February 27, 1991" engraved on side of slide with list of coalition forces. Limited issue of 1,000 guns. Made in 1991.

GREAT WESTERN ARMS CO.
North Hollywood, California

Great Western Double Barrel Derringer $195
Replica of Remington Double Derringer. Caliber: 38 S&W. Double barrels (superposed), 3-inch. Overall length: 5 inches. Fixed sights. Blued finish. Checkered black plastic grips. Made 1953–1962.

Great Western Single Action

Great Western Single Action Frontier Revolver . $575
Replica of the Colt Single Action Army Revolver. Calibers: 22 LR, 357 Magnum, 38 Special, 44 Special, 44 Magnum, 45 Colt. 6-shot cylinder. Barrel lengths: 4³/₄-, 5¹/₂- and 7¹/₂-inch. Weight: 40 oz., 22 cal. w/5¹/₂-inch bbl. Overall length: 11¹/₈ inches w/5¹/₂-inch bbl. Fixed sights. Blued finish. Imitation stag grips. Made 1951–1962. *Note:* Value shown is for improved late model revolvers; early Great

Great Western SA Frontier (cont.)

Westerns are variable in quality and should be evaluated accordingly. It should also be noted that, beginning about July 1956, these revolvers were offered in kit form; values of guns assembled from these kits will, in general, be lower than for factory-completed weapons.

GRENDEL, INC.
Rockledge, Florida

Grendel Model P-12

Grendel Model P-12 DA Automatic Pistol

Caliber: 380 ACP. 11-shot Zytel magazine. 3-inch barrel. 5.3 inches overall. Weight: 13 oz. Fixed sights. Polymer DuPont ST-800 grip. Made from 1991 to date.

Standard Model $125
Electroless Nickel 145

Grendel Model P-30

Grendel Model P-30 Automatic Pistol

Caliber: 22 WMR. 30-shot magazine. 5-or 8-inch barrel. 8.5 inches overall with 5-inch bbl. Weight: 21 oz. Blade front sight; fixed rear sight. Made from 1991 to date.

With 5-inch Barrel $165
With 8-inch Barrel 185

Grendel Model P-31 Automatic Pistol $235

Caliber: 22 WMR. 30-shot Zytel magazine. 11-inch barrel. 17.3 inches overall. Weight: 48 oz. Adjustable blade front sight; fixed rear sight. Checkered black polymer DuPont ST-800 grip and forend. Made from 1991 to date.

H&R 1871, INC.
Gardner, Massachusetts
See listings under Harrington & Richardson, Inc.

HÄMMERLI AG JAGD-UND SPORTWAFFENFABRIK
Lenzburg, Switzerland

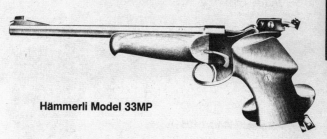

Hämmerli Model 33MP

Hämmerli Model 33MP Free Pistol $800

System Martini single-shot action, set trigger. Caliber: 22 LR. 11½-inch octagon barrel. 16½ inches overall. Weight: 46 oz. Micrometer rear sight, interchangeable front sights. Blued finish. Walnut grips, forearm. Made 1933–1949.

Hämmerli Model 100 Free Pistol

Same general specifications as Model 33MP. Improved action and sights, redesigned stock. Standard model has plain stocks and forearm; deluxe model has carved stocks and forearm. Made 1950–56.

Standard Model $635
Deluxe Model 725

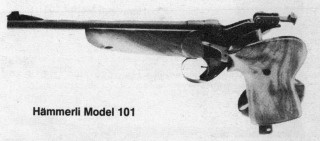

Hämmerli Model 101

Hämmerli Model 101 . . . . $615

Similar to Model 100, except has heavy round barrel with matte finish, improved action and sights, adjustable stocks. Weight: about 49 oz. Made 1956–1960.

Hämmerli Model 102 Deluxe

Hämmerli Model 102

Same as Model 101, except barrel has highly polished blued finish. Deluxe model (illustrated) has carved stocks and forearm. Made 1956–1960.

Standard Model $615
Deluxe Model 730

Hämmerli Model 103 . . . . $625
Same as Model 101, except has lighter octagon barrel (as in Model 100) with highly polished blued finish, stocks and forearm of select French walnut. Weight: about 46 oz. Made 1956–1960.

Hämmerli Model 104 . . . . $575
Similar to Model 102, except has lighter round barrel, improved action, redesigned stocks and forearm. Weight: 46 oz. Made 1961–65.

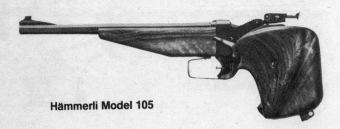

Hämmerli Model 105

Hämmerli Model 105 . . . . $690
Similar to Model 103, except has improved action, redesigned stocks and forearm. Made 1961–65.

Hämmerli Model 106

Hämmerli Model 106 . . . . $595
Similar to Model 104, except has improved trigger and stocks. Made 1966–1971.

Hämmerli Model 107 Deluxe

Hämmerli Model 107
Similar to Model 105, except has improved trigger and stock. Deluxe model (illustrated) has engraved receiver and barrel, carved stocks and forearm. Made 1966–1971.
Standard Model **$675**
Deluxe Model **900**

Hämmerli Model 120 Heavy Barrel
Same as Models 120-1 and 120-2, except has 5.7-inch heavy barrel. Weight: 41 oz. Available with standard or adjustable stocks. Made from 1972 to date.
With standard stocks . . . . **$ 415**
With adjustable stocks **440**

Hämmerli Model 120 Heavy Barrel Adjustable Stocks

Hämmerli Model 120-1

Hämmerli Model 120-1 Single Shot Free Pistol . . **$375**
Side lever-operated bolt action. Adjustable single-stage or two-stage trigger. Caliber: 22 LR. 9.999-inch barrel. 14³/4 inches overall. Weight: 44 oz. Micrometer rear sight, front sight on high ramp. Blued finish barrel and receiver, lever and grip frame anodized aluminum. Checkered walnut thumbrest stocks. Made from 1972 to date.

Hämmerli Model 120-2 . . . . **$395**
Same as Model 120-1, except has hand-contoured stocks with adjustable palm rest (available for right or left hand). Made from 1972 to date.

Hämmerli Model 150 Free Pistol

Hämmerli Models 150/151 Free Pistol
Improved Martini-type action with lateral-action cocking lever. Set trigger adjustable for weight, length and angle of pull. Caliber: 22 LR. 11.3-inch round barrel, free-floating. 15.4 inches overall. Weight: 43 oz. (w/extra weights, 49¹/2 oz.). Micrometer rear sight, front sight on high ramp. Blued finish. Select walnut forearm and stocks w/adj. palm shelf. Made 1972–1993.
Model 150 (Disc. 1989) **$1395**
Model 151 (Disc. 1993) **1425**

Hämmerli Model 160 Free Pistol

Hämmerli Models 160/162 Free Pistols

Caliber: 22 LR. Single shot. 11⁵/₁₆-inch barrel. 17¹/₂ inches overall. Weight: 46.9 oz. Sights: interchangeable front blade; fully adjustable match rear. Match-style stippled walnut stocks w/adj. palm shelf. Made from 1993 to date.

Model 160 w/Mechanical Set Trigger **$1125**
Model 162 w/Electronic Trigger **1295**

Hämmerli Model 208

Hämmerli Model 208 Standard Auto Pistol $1195

Caliber: 22 LR. 8-shot magazine. 5.9-inch barrel. 10 inches overall. Weight: 35 oz. (barrel weight adds 3 oz.). Micrometer rear sight, ramp front. Blued finish. Checkered walnut stocks w/adjustable heel plate. Made 1966–1988.

Hämmerli Model 211 .... $1095

Same as Model 208, except has standard thumbrest stocks. Made from 1966 to date.

Hämmerli Model 212 Hunter's Pistol $925

Caliber: 22 LR. 4⁷/₈-inch barrel. 8¹/₂ inches overall. Weight: 31 oz. Fully adjustable sights. Blued finish. Checkered walnut stocks. Made 1984–1990.

Hämmerli Model 230-1 Rapid Fire Auto Pistol ... $595

Caliber: 22 Short. 5-shot magazine. 6.3-inch barrel. 11.6 inches overall. Weight: 44 oz. Micrometer rear sight, post front. Blued finish. Smooth walnut thumbrest stocks. Made 1970–1983.

Hämmerli Model 230-2

Hämmerli Model 230-2 .... $625

Same as Model 230-1, except has checkered walnut stocks with adjustable heel plate. Made 1970–1983.

Hämmerli Model 232 Rapid Fire Auto Pistol $995

Caliber: 22 LR. 5-shot magazine. 5.2-inch barrel. 10³/₈ inches overall. Weight: 44 oz. Fully adjustable target sights. Blued finish. Stippled walnut wraparound target stocks. Made from 1984 to date.

**Hämmerli Model 232
Rapid Fire Pistol**

Hämmerli Model 280 Target Pistol

Carbon-reinforced synthetic frame and barrel housing. Calibers: 22 LR, 32 S&W Long WC. 6-shot (22 LR) or 5-shot (32 S&W) magazine. 4¹/₂-inch barrel w/interchangeable metal or carbon fiber counterweights. 11⁷/₈ inches overall. Weight: 39 oz. Micro-adjustable match sights w/interchangeable elements.

22 Long Rifle .... **$ 895**
32 S&W Long WC **1095**

Hämmerli International Model 206

Hämmerli International Model 206 Auto Pistol .. $525

Calibers: 22 Short, 22 LR. 6-shot (22 Short) or 8-shot (22 LR) magazine. 7¹/₁₆-inch barrel w/muzzle brake. 12¹/₂ inches overall. Weight: 33 oz. (22 Short); 39 oz. (22 LR), (supplementary weights add 5 and 8 oz.). Micrometer rear sight, ramp front. Blued finish. Standard thumbrest stocks. Made 1962–69.

Hämmerli International Model 207

Hämmerli International Model 207 .... $550

Same as Model 206, except has stocks with adjustable heel plate, weighs 2 oz. more. Made 1962–69.

Hämmerli International Model 209 Auto Pistol .. $650

Caliber: 22 Short. 5-shot mag. 4³/₄-inch barrel w/muzzle brake and gas-escape holes. 11 inches overall. Weight: 39 oz. (interchangeable front weight adds 4 oz.). Micrometer rear sight, post front. Blued finish. Standard thumbrest stocks of checkered walnut. Made 1966–1970.

Hämmerli International Model 210

Hämmerli International Model 210 . . . . $675
Same as Model 209, except has stocks with adjustable heel plate; is 0.8-inch longer and weighs 1 ounce more. Made 1966–1970.

Hämmerli Virginian

Hämmerli Virginian Single Action Revolver $495
Similar to Colt Single Action Army, except has base pin safety system (SWISSAFE). Calibers: 357 Magnum, 45 Colt. 6-shot cylinder. Barrels: 4⅝-, 5½-, 7½-inch. 11 inches overall w/5½-inch bbl. Weight: 40 oz. w/5½-inch bbl. Fixed sights. Blued barrel and cylinder, casehardened frame, chrome-plated grip frame and trigger guard. One-piece smooth walnut stock. Made 1973–76 for Interarms, Alexandria, Va.

Hämmerli-Walther Olympia Model 200 1952-Type

Hämmerli-Walther Olympia Model 200 Automatic Pistol, 1952-Type $575
Similar to 1936 Walther Olympia Funfkampf Model. Calibers: 22 Short, 22 LR. 6-shot (22 Short) or 10-shot (22 LR) magazine. 7.5-inch barrel. 10.7 inches overall. Weight: 27.7 oz. (22 Short; light alloy breechblock); 30.3 oz. (22 LR); supplementary weights provided. Adjustable target sights. Blued finish. Checkered walnut thumbrest stocks. Made 1952–58.

Hämmerli-Walther Olympia Model 200 1958-Type, Standard Stocks

Hämmerli-Walther Olympia Model 200, 1958-Type $600
Same as Model 200, 1952 Type, except has muzzle brake, 8-shot magazine (22 LR). 11.6 inches overall. Weight: 30 oz. (22 Short); 33 oz. (22 LR) Made 1958–1963.

Hämmerli-Walther Olympia Model 201 . . . . $590
Same as Model 200, 1952 Type, except has 9½-inch barrel. Made 1955–57.

Hämmerli-Walther Olympia Model 202 . . . . $600
Same as Model 201, except has stocks with adjustable heel plate. Made from 1955–57.

Hämmerli-Walther Olympia Model 203, 1958-Type

Hämmerli-Walther Olympia Model 203
Same as corresponding Model 200 (1955-Type lacks muzzle brake), except has stocks with adjustable heel plate. Made 1955–1963.
1955-Type $595
1958-Type 615

Hämmerli-Walther Olympia Model 204
American Model. Same as corresponding Model 200 (1956-Type lacks muzzle brake), except in 22 LR only, has slide stop and micrometer rear sight. Made 1956–1963.
1956-Type $695
1958-Type 645

Hämmerli-Walther Olympia Model 205

Hämmerli-Walther Olympia Model 205

American Model. Same as Model 204, except has stocks with adjustable heel plate. Made 1956–1963.

1956-Type **$750**
1958-Type **675**

SIG-Hämmerli Model P240

SIG-Hämmerli Model P240 Automatic Pistol

Caliber: 38 Special (wadcutter). 5-shot magazine. 6-inch barrel. 10 inches overall. Weight: 41 oz. Micrometer rear sight, post front. Blued finish. Smooth walnut thumbrest stocks. Accessory 22 LR conversion unit available. Made from 1975 to date.

Model P240 .... **$1095**
22 Conversion Unit **500**

SIG-Hämmerli Model P240 Target Auto Pistol .. **$2595**

Same general specifications as Model P240 Automatic, except with fully adjustable target sights and stippled walnut wraparound target stocks. Weight: 49 oz.

═══ HARRINGTON & RICHARDSON, INC. ═══
Gardner, Massachusetts
Now H&R 1871, Inc., Gardner, Mass.

Formerly Harrington & Richardson Arms Co. of Worcester, Mass. One of the oldest and most distinguished manufacturers of handguns, rifles and shotguns, H&R had suspended operations in 1986; it was purchased by New England Firearms in the early 1990s.

H&R Self-Loading 25*

AUTOMATIC/SINGLE SHOT PISTOLS

NOTE: For ease in finding a particular firearm, H&R handguns are grouped into Automatic/Single Shot Pistols, followed by Revolvers. For a complete listing, please refer to the Index.

Harrington & Richardson Self-Loading 25 Pistol .. **$325**

Modified Webley & Scott design. Caliber: 25 Auto. 6-shot magazine. 2-inch barrel. 4½ inches overall. Weight: 12 oz. Fixed sights. Blued finish. Black hard rubber stocks. Discontinued prior to 1942.

H&R Self-Loading 32*

Harrington & Richardson Self-Loading 32 Pistol .. **$315**

Modified Webley & Scott design. Caliber: 32 Auto. 8-shot magazine. 3½-inch barrel. 6½ inches overall. Weight: about 20 oz. Fixed sights. Blued finish. Black hard rubber stocks. Discontinued prior to 1942.

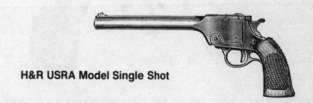

H&R USRA Model Single Shot

Harrington & Richardson USRA Model Single Shot Target Pistol **$395**

Hinged frame. Caliber: 22 LR. Barrel lengths: 7-, 8- and 10-inch. Weight: 31 oz. with 10-inch bbl. Adj. target sights. Blued finish. Checkered walnut stocks. Made 1928–1941.

REVOLVERS

NOTE: This section contains only H&R Revolvers. Pistols may be found in the preceding section. For a complete listing of H&R handguns, please refer to the Index.

H&R Model 4 (1904)
Double Action Revolver

Harrington & Richardson Model 4 (1904) DA **$75**
Solid frame. Calibers: 32 S&W Long, 38 S&W. 6-shot cylinder (32 cal.), 5-shot (38 cal.). Barrel lengths: 2¹/₂-, 4¹/₂- and 6-inch. Weight: about 16 oz., 32 cal. Fixed sights. Blued or nickel finish. Hard rubber stocks. Discontinued prior to 1942. (*See* illustration, preceding page.)

H&R Model 5

Harrington & Richardson Model 5 (1905) DA **$80**
Solid frame. Caliber: 32 S&W. 5-shot cylinder. Barrel lengths: 2¹/₂-, 4¹/₂- and 6-inch. Weight: about 11 oz. Fixed sights. Blued or nickel finish. Hard rubber stocks. Discontinued prior to 1942.

H&R Model 6

Harrington & Richardson Model 6 (1906) DA **$85**
Solid frame. Caliber: 22 LR. 7-shot cylinder. Barrel lengths: 2¹/₂-, 4¹/₂- and 6-inch. Weight: about 10 oz. Fixed sights. Blued or nickel finish. Hard rubber stocks. Discontinued prior to 1942.

H&R 22 Special

Harrington & Richardson 22 Special DA **$140**
Heavy hinged frame. Calibers: 22 LR, 22 W.R.F. 9-shot cylinder. 6-inch barrel. Weight: 23 oz. Fixed sights, front gold-plated. Blued finish. Checkered walnut stocks. Recessed safety cylinder on later models for high-speed ammunition. Discontinued prior to 1942.

H&R Model 199 Sportsman

Harrington & Richardson Model 199 Sportsman SA Revolver **$155**
Hinged frame. Caliber: 22 LR. 9-shot cylinder. 6-inch barrel. 11 inches overall. Weight: 30 oz. Adjustable target sights. Blued finish. Checkered walnut stocks. Discontinued 1951.

Harrington & Richardson Model 504 DA **$145**
Caliber: 32 H&R Magnum. 5-shot cylinder. 4- or 6-inch barrel, square butt; 3- or 4-inch barrel, round butt. Made 1984–1986.

Harrington & Richardson Model 532 DA **$85**
Caliber: 32 H&R Magnum. 5-shot cylinder. 2¹/₂- or 4-inch barrel. Weight: approx. 20 and 25 oz. respectively. Fixed sights. American walnut grips. Lustre blue finish. Made 1984–86.

Harrington & Richardson Model 586 DA **$140**
Caliber: 32 H&R Magnum. 5-shot cylinder. Barrel lengths: 4¹/₂, 5¹/₂, 7¹/₂, 10 inches. Weight: 30 oz. average. Adjustable rear sight, blade front. Walnut finished hardwood grips. Made 1984–86.

Harrington & Richardson Model 603 Target **$115**
Similar to Model 903, except in 22 WMR 6-shot capacity with unfluted cylinder. Made 1980–83.

Harrington & Richardson Model 604 Target **$135**
Similar to Model 603, except with 6-inch bull barrel. Weight: 38 oz. Made 1980–83.

H&R Model 622

Harrington & Richardson Model 622/623 DA **$85**
Solid frame. Caliber: 22 Short, Long, LR. 6-shot cylinder. Barrel lengths: 2¹/₂-, 4-, 6-inch. Weight: 26 oz. w/4-inch bbl. Fixed sights. Blued finish. Plastic stocks. Made 1957–1986. *Note:* **Model 623** is same, except chrome or nickel finish.

Harrington & Richardson Model 632/633 Guardsman Double Action Revolver **$90**
Solid frame. Caliber: 32 S&W Long. 6-shot cylinder. Barrel lengths: 2¹/₂- or 4-inch. Weight: 19 oz. w/2¹/₂-inch barrel.

H&R Model 632 Guardsman

Harrington & Richardson 632/633 Guardsman (cont.)
Fixed sights. Blued or chrome finish. Checkered Tenite
stocks (round butt on 2½-inch, square butt on 4-inch). Made
1953–1986. *Note:* **Model 633** is the same, except for chrome
or nickel finish.

H&R Model 649

H&R Model 650, Nickel Finish

Harrington & Richardson Model 649/650 DA **$115**
Solid frame. Side loading and ejection. Convertible model
with two 6-shot cylinders. Calibers: 22 LR, 22 WMR. 5½-
inch barrel. Weight: 32 oz. Adjustable rear sight, blade
front. Blued finish. One-piece, Western-style walnut stock.
Made 1976–1986. *Note:* **Model 650** is same, except nickel
finish.

H&R Model 666

Harrington & Richardson Model 666 DA **$90**
Solid frame. Convertible model with two 6-shot cylinders.
Calibers: 22 LR, 22 WMR. 6-inch barrel. Weight: 28 oz.
Fixed sights. Blued finish. Plastic stocks. Made 1976–78.

H&R Model 676

Harrington & Richardson Model 676 DA **$120**
Solid frame. Side loading and ejection. Convertible model
with two 6-shot cylinders. Calibers: 22 LR, 22 WMR.
Barrel lengths: 4½-, 5½-, 7½-, 12-inch. Weight: 32 oz.
w/5½-inch bbl. Adjustable rear sight, blade front. Blued
finish, color-casehardened frame. One-piece, Western-
style walnut stock. Made 1976–1980.

H&R Model 686

Harrington & Richardson Model 686 DA **$145**
Caliber: 22 LR and 22 WMR. Barrels: 4½-, 5½-, 7½-,
10- and 12-inches. 6-shot magazine. Adjustable rear sight,
ramp and blade front. Blued, color-casehardened frame.
Weight: 31 oz. w/4½-inch bbl. Made 1980–86.

H&R Model 733, Nickel Finish

Harrington & Richardson Model 732/733 DA **$90**
Solid frame, swing-out 6-shot cylinder. Calibers: 32 S&W,
32 S&W Long. Barrel lengths: 2½-, 4-inch. Weight: 26
oz.w/4-inch bbl. Fixed sights (windage adjustable rear on
4-inch bbl. model). Blue finish. Plastic stocks. Made 1958–
1986. *Note:* **Model 733** is same, except nickel finish.

Harrington & Richardson Model 826 DA **$110**
Caliber: 22 WMR. 6-shot magazine. 3-inch bull barrel.
Ramp and blade front sight, adjustable rear. American
walnut grips. Weight: 28 oz. Made 1981–83.

H&R Model 830, Nickel Finish

H&R Model 904

Harrington & Richardson Model 829/830 DA
Same as Model 826, except in 22 LR caliber. 9-shot capacity. Made 1981–83.
Model 829, Blued **$115**
Model 830, Nickel **120**

Harrington & Richardson Model 832/833 DA
Same as Model 826, except in 32 S&W Long. Blued or nickel finish. Made 1981–83.
Model 832, Blued **$125**
Model 833, Nickel **130**

Harrington & Richardson Model 904 Target $130
Similar to Model 903, except 4- and 6-inch bull barrels. 4-inch barrel weighs 32 oz. Made 1980–86.

H&R Model 900

H&R Model 905

Harrington & Richardson Model 900/901 DA $75
Solid frame, snap-out cylinder. Calibers: 22 Short, Long, LR. 9-shot cylinder. Barrel lengths: 2½-, 4-, 6-inch. Weight: 26 oz. w/6-inch bbl. Fixed sights. Blued finish. Blade Cycolac stocks. Made 1962–1973. *Note:* **Model 901** (discontinued in 1963) is the same, except has chrome finish and white Tenite stocks.

Harrington & Richardson Model 905 Target $135
Same as Model 904, except with 4-inch barrel only. Nickel finish. Made 1981–83.

H&R Model 922, First Issue

H&R Model 903

Harrington & Richardson Model 903 Target $125
Caliber: 22 LR. 9-shot capacity. SA/DA. 6-inch target-weight flat-side barrel. Swing-out cylinder. Weight: 35 oz. Blade front sight, adjustable rear. American walnut grips. Made 1980–83.

H&R Model 922, Second Issue

Harrington & Richardson Model 922 DA Revolver, First Issue **$150**
Solid frame. Caliber: 22 LR. 9-shot cylinder. Barrel: early model, 10-inch, octagon; later production, 6-inch, round. Weight: 26 oz. w/6-inch bbl. Fixed sights. Blued finish. Checkered walnut stocks. Safety cylinder on later models. Discontinued prior to 1942.

Harrington & Richardson Model 922/923 DA Revolver, Second Issue **$75**
Solid frame. Caliber: 22 LR. 9-shot cylinder. Barrel lengths: 2½-, 4-, 6-inch. Weight: 24 oz. w/4-inch bbl. Fixed sights. Blued finish. Plastic stocks. Made 1950–1986. *Note:* Second Issue Model 922 has a different frame from that of the First Issue. **Model 923** is same as Model 922, Second Issue, except for nickel finish.

H&R Model 929

H&R Model 925

Harrington & Richardson Model 925 Defender . . **$115**
DA. Hinged frame. Caliber: 38 S&W. 5-shot cylinder. 2½-inch barrel. Weight: 22 oz. Adjustable rear sight, fixed front. Blued finish. One-piece wraparound grip. Made 1964–1978.

H&R Model 926

Harrington & Richardson Model 926 DA **$115**
Hinged frame. Calibers: 22 LR, 38 S&W. 9-shot (22 LR) or 5-shot (38) cylinder. 4-inch barrel. Weight: 31 oz. Adjustable rear sight, fixed front. Blued finish. Checkered walnut stocks. Made 1968–1978.

Harrington & Richardson Model 929/930 Sidekick DA Revolver **$85**
Caliber: 22 LR. Solid frame, swing-out 9-shot cylinder. Barrel lengths: 2½-, 4-, 6-inch. Weight: 24 oz. w/4-inch

Harrington & Richardson 929/930 Sidekick (cont.)
bbl. Fixed sights. Blued finish. Checkered plastic stocks. Made 1956–1986. *Note:* **Model 930** is same, except nickel finish.

H&R Model 939

Harrington & Richardson Model 939/940 Ultra Sidekick DA Revolver **$110**
Solid frame, swing-out 9-shot cylinder. Safety lock. Calibers: 22 Short, Long, LR. Flat-side 6-inch barrel w/ vent rib. Weight: 33 oz. Adjustable rear sight, ramp front. Blued finish. Checkered walnut stocks. Made 1958–1986; reintroduced by H&R 1871 in 1992. *Note:* **Model 940** is same, except has round barrel.

H&R Model 949

H&R Model 950

Harrington & Richardson Model 949/950 Forty-Niner DA Revolver **$110**
Solid frame. Side loading and ejection. Calibers: 22 Short, Long, LR. 9-shot cylinder. 5½-inch barrel. Weight: 31 oz. Adjustable rear sight, blade front. Blue or nickel finish. One-piece, Western-style walnut grip. Made 1960–1986; reintroduced by H&R 1871 in 1992. *Note:* **Model 950** is same, except nickel finish. (*See* photos, preceding page.)

Harrington & Richardson Model 976 DA **$90**
Same as Model 949, except has color-casehardened frame, 7½-inch barrel, weighs 36 oz. Intro. 1977; discontinued.

**H&R Model 999 Sportsman
First Issue**

Harrington & Richardson Model 999 Sportsman DA Revolver, First Issue **$165**
Hinged frame. Calibers: 22 LR, 22 WRF. Same specifications as Model 199 Sportsman Single Action. Discontinued before 1942.

Harrington & Richardson Model 999 Sportsman DA Revolver, Second Issue **$175**
Hinged frame. Caliber: 22 LR. 9-shot cylinder. 6-inch barrel w/vent rib. Weight: 30 oz. Adjustable sights. Blued finish. Checkered walnut stocks. Made 1950–1986.

**H&R New Model 999
Sportsman Double Action**

Harrington & Richardson (New) Model 999 Sportsman DA Revolver **$170**
Hinged frame. Caliber: 22 Short, Long, LR. 9-shot cylinder. 6-inch barrel w/vent rib. Weight: 30 oz. Sights: Blade front adjustable for elevation; square-notched rear adjustable for windage. Blued finish. Checkered hardwood stocks. Reintroduced by H&R 1871 in 1992.

Harrington & Richardson American DA **$75**
Solid frame. Calibers: 32 S&W Long, 38 S&W. 6-shot (32 cal.) or 5-shot (38 cal.) cylinder. Barrel lengths: 2½-, 4½- and 6-inch. Weight: about 16 oz. Fixed sights. Blued or nickel finish. Hard rubber stocks. Discont. prior to 1942.

Harrington & Richardson Automatic Ejecting DA Revolver **$145**
Hinged frame. Calibers: 32 S&W Long, 38 S&W. 6-shot cylinder (32 cal.), 5-shot (38 cal.). Barrel lengths: 3¼-,

H&R Automatic Ejecting

Harrington & Richardson Auto Ejecting DA (cont.)
4-, 5- and 6-inch. Weight: about 16 oz., 32 cal.; 15 oz., 38 cal. Fixed sights. Blued or nickel finish. Black hard rubber stocks. Discontinued prior to 1942.

H&R Bobby

Harrington & Richardson Bobby DA **$250**
Hinged frame. Calibers: 32 S&W, 38 S&W. 6-shot cylinder (32 cal.), 5-shot (38 cal.). 4-inch barrel. 9 inches overall. Weight: 23 oz. Fixed sights. Blued finish. Checkered walnut stocks. Discontinued 1946. *Note:* Originally designed and produced for use by London's bobbies.

H&R Defender 38

Harrington & Richardson Defender 38 DA **$105**
Hinged frame. Based on the Sportsman design. Caliber: 38 S&W. Barrel lengths: 4- and 6-inch. 9 inches overall w/4-inch barrel. Weight: 25 oz., 4-inch bbl. Fixed sights. Blued finish. Black plastic stocks. Discontinued 1946. *Note:* This model was manufactured during WW II as an arm for plant guards, auxiliary police, etc.

Harrington & Richardson Expert Model DA **$150**
Same specifications as 22 Special, except has 10-inch barrel. Weight: 28 oz. Discontinued prior to 1942.

Harrington & Richardson Hammerless DA, Large Frame **$105**
Hinged frame. Calibers: 32 S&W Long, 38 S&W. 6-shot cylinder (32 cal.), 5-shot (38 cal.). Barrel lengths: 3¼-, 4-,

Harrington & Richardson Hammerless DA, Lg. (cont.)
and 6-inch. Weight: about 17 oz. Fixed sights. Blued or nickel finish. Hard rubber stocks. Discont. prior to 1942.

**H&R Hammerless
Small Frame**

Harrington & Richardson Hammerless DA, Small Frame **$105**
Hinged frame. Calibers: 22 LR, 32 S&W. 7-shot (22 cal.), 5-shot (32 cal.) cylinder. Barrel lengths: 2-, 3-, 4-, 5- and 6-inch. Weight: about 13 oz. Fixed sights. Blued or nickel finish. Hard rubber stocks. Discont. prior to 1942.

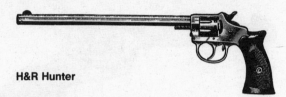

H&R Hunter

Harrington & Richardson Hunter Model DA **$105**
Solid frame. Caliber: 22 LR. 9-shot cylinder. 10-inch octagon barrel. Weight: 26 oz. Fixed sights. Blued finish. Checkered walnut stocks. Safety cylinder on later models. *Note:* An earlier Hunter Model was built on the smaller 7-shot frame. Discontinued prior to 1942.

H&R New Defender

H&R Premier

Harrington & Richardson New Defender DA **$195**
Hinged frame. Caliber: 22 LR. 9-shot cylinder. 2-inch barrel. 6¼ inches overall. Weight: 23 oz. Adjustable sights. Blued finish. Checkered walnut stocks, round butt. *Note:* Basically, this is the Sportsman DA with a short barrel. Discontinued prior to 1942.

Harrington & Richardson Premier DA **$90**
Small hinged frame. Calibers: 22 LR, 32 S&W. 7-shot (22 LR) or 5-shot (32) cylinder. Barrel lengths: 2-, 3-, 4-, 5- and 6-inch. Weight: 13 oz. (22 LR); 12 oz. (32). Fixed sights. Blued or nickel finish. Black hard rubber stocks. Discontinued prior to 1942.

Harrington & Richardson Model STR 022 Blank Revolver **$65**
Caliber: 22 RF blanks. 9-shot cylinder. 2½-inch barrel. Weight: 19 oz. Satin blue finish.

Harrington & Richardson Model STR 032 Blank Revolver **$75**
Same general specifications as STR 022 except chambered for 32 S&W blank cartridges.

H&R Target Model

Harrington & Richardson Target Model DA **$130**
Small hinged frame. Calibers: 22 LR, 22 W.R.F. 7-shot cylinder. 6-inch barrel. Weight: 16 oz. Fixed sights. Blued finish. Checkered walnut stocks. Discont. prior to 1942.

H&R Trapper

Harrington & Richardson Trapper Model DA **$115**
Solid frame. Caliber: 22 LR. 7-shot cylinder. 6-inch octagon barrel. Weight: 12¼ oz. Fixed sights. Blued finish. Checkered walnut stocks. Safety cylinder on later models. Discontinued prior to 1942.

H&R Ultra Sportsman

Harrington & Richardson Ultra Sportsman **$185**
SA. Hinged frame. Caliber: 22 LR. 9-shot cylinder. 6-inch barrel. Weight: 30 oz. Adjustable target sights. Blued finish. Checkered walnut stocks. This model has short action, wide hammer spur; cylinder is length of a 22 LR cartridge. Discont. prior to 1942. (*See* illustration, preceding page.)

H&R Vest Pocket

Harrington & Richardson Vest Pocket DA **$75**
Solid frame. Spurless hammer. Calibers: 22 Rimfire, 32 S&W. 7-shot (22 cal.) or 5-shot (32 cal.) cylinder. 1¹/₈-inch barrel. Weight: about 9 oz. Blued or nickel finish. Hard rubber stocks. Discontinued prior to 1942.

H&R Young America

Harrington & Richardson Young America DA **$75**
Solid frame. Calibers: 22 Long, 32 S&W. 7-shot (22 cal.) or 5-shot (32 cal.) cylinder. Barrel lengths: 2-, 4¹/₂- and 6-inch. Weight: about 9 oz. Fixed sights. Blued or nickel finish. Hard rubber stocks. Discont. prior to 1942.

=== **HARTFORD ARMS & EQUIPMENT CO.** ===
Hartford, Connecticut

Hartford pistols were the forebears of the original High Standard line, since High Standard Mfg. Corp. acquired Hartford Arms & Equipment Co. in 1932. The High Standard Model B is essentially the same as the Hartford Automatic.

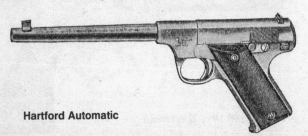

Hartford Automatic

Hartford Automatic Target Pistol **$525**
Caliber: 22 LR. 10-shot magazine. 6³/₄-inch barrel. 10³/₄ inches overall. Weight: 31 oz. Target sights. Blued finish. Black rubber stocks. This arm closely resembles the early Colt Woodsman and High Standard pistols. Made 1929–1930.

Hartford Repeating Pistol **$400**
Same general design as the automatic pistol of this manufacture, but this model is a hand-operated repeating pistol on the order of the Fiala. Made 1929–1930.

Hartford Single Shot Target Pistol **$425**
Similar in appearance to the Hartford Automatic. Caliber: 22 LR. 6³/₄-inch barrel. 10³/₄ inches overall. Weight: 38 oz. Target sights. Mottled frame and slide, blued barrel. Black rubber or walnut stocks. Made 1929–1930.

=== **HAWES FIREARMS** ===
Van Nuys, California

Hawes Deputy Denver Marshal

Hawes Deputy Denver Marshal
Same as Deputy Marshal SA, except has brass frame.
22 LR (plastic grips) **$75**
Combination, 22 LR/22 WMR (plastic) **85**
Extra for walnut stocks **5**

Hawes Deputy Marshal

Hawes Deputy Marshal Single Action Revolver
Calibers: 22 LR; also 22 WMR in two-cylinder combination. 6-shot cylinder. 5¹/₂-inch barrel. 11 inches overall. Weight: 34 oz. Adjustable rear sight, blade front. Blued finish. Plastic or walnut grips. Made from 1973 to date.
22 Long Rifle (plastic grips) **$70**
Combination, 22 LR/22 WMR (plastic) **75**
Extra for walnut stocks **5**

Hawes Deputy Montana Marshal

Hawes Deputy Montana Marshal
Same as Deputy Marshal, except has brass grip frame, walnut grips only.
22 Long Rifle **$75**
Combination, 22 LR/22 WMR **95**

Hawes Deputy Silver City Marshal

Hawes Deputy Silver City Marshal
Same as Deputy Marshal, except has chrome-plated frame, brass grip frame, blued cylinder and barrel.
22 Long Rifle (plastic grips) **$70**
Combination, 22 LR/22 WMR (plastic) **90**
Extra for walnut grips **5**

Hawes Deputy Texas Marshal

Hawes Favorite

Hawes Deputy Texas Marshal
Same as Deputy Marshal, except has chrome finish.
22 Long Rifle (plastic grips) **$70**
Combination, 22 LR/22 WMR (plastic) **85**
Extra for walnut grips **5**

Hawes Favorite Single Shot Target Pistol **$130**
Replica of Stevens No. 35. Tip-up action. Caliber: 22 LR. 8-inch barrel. 12 inches overall. Weight: 24 oz. Target sights. Chrome-plated frame. Blued barrel. Plastic or rosewood grips (add $5). Made 1968–1976.

Hawes Sauer Chief Marshal

Hawes Sauer Chief Marshal SA Target Revolver
Same as Western Marshal, except has adjustable rear sight and front sight, oversized rosewood grips. Not made in 22 caliber.
357 Magnum or 45 Colt **$200**
44 Magnum **225**
Combination, 357 Magnum and 9mm Luger,
   45 Colt and 45 Auto **250**
Combination, 44 Magnum and 44-40 . . . . **245**

Hawes Sauer Federal Marshal

Hawes Sauer Federal Marshal
Same as Western Marshal, except has color-casehardened frame, brass grip frame, one-piece walnut grip. Not made in 22 caliber.
357 Magnum or 45 Colt **$200**
44 Magnum **230**
Combination, 357 Magnum and 9mm Luger,
   45 Colt and 45 Auto **250**
Combination, 44 Magnum and 44-40 . . . . **245**

Hawes Sauer Montana Marshal
Same as Western Marshal, except has brass grip frame. 22 caliber discontinued.
357 Magnum or 45 Colt **$200**
44 Magnum **225**
Combination, 357 Magnum and 9mm Luger,
   45 Colt and 45 Auto **240**

Hawes Sauer Montana Marshal

Hawes Sauer Western Marshal

Hawes Sauer Montana Marshal (cont.)
Combination, 44 Magnum and 44-40 . . . . $250
22 LR   195
Combination, 22 LR and 22 WMR   210

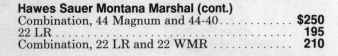

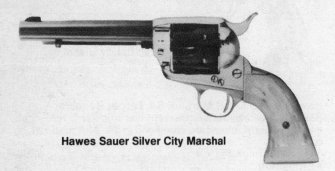

Hawes Sauer Silver City Marshal

Hawes Sauer Western Marshal 22

Hawes Sauer Silver City Marshal
Same as Western Marshal, except has nickel-plated frame, brass grip frame, blued cylinder and barrel, pearlite grips.
44 Magnum $240
Combination, 357 Magnum and 9mm Luger,
   45 Colt and 45 Auto 225
Combination, 44 Magnum and 44-40 260

Hawes Sauer Western Marshal Single Action Revolver
Calibers: 22 LR (discont.), 357 Magnum, 44 Magnum, 45 Auto. Also in two-cylinder combinations: 22 WMR (discont.), 9mm Luger, 44-40, 45 Auto. 6-shot cylinder. Barrel lengths: 5 1/2-inch (discont.), 6-inch. 11 3/4 inches overall w/6-inch bbl. Weight: 46 oz. Fixed sights. Blued finish. Originally furnished with simulated stag plastic stocks; recent production has smooth rosewood stocks. Made 1968 to date by J. P. Sauer & Sohn, Eckernforde, Germany.
357 Magnum or 45 Colt $200
44 Magnum 230
Combination, 357 Magnum and 9mm Luger,
   45 Colt and 45 Auto 225
Combination, 44 Magnum and 44-40 240
22 Long Rifle 195
Combination, 22 LR and 22 WMR 210

Hawes Sauer Texas Marshal

Hawes Sauer Texas Marshal
Same as Western Marshal, except nickel-plated, has pearlite grips. 22 caliber discontinued.
357 Magnum or 45 Colt $225
44 Magnum 240
Combination, 357 Magnum and 9mm Luger,
   45 Colt and 45 Auto 260
Combination, 44 Magnum and 44-40 275
22 Long Rifle 195
Combination, 22 LR and 22 WMR 230

HECKLER & KOCH
Oberndorf/Neckar, West Germany, and Chantilly, Virginia

Heckler & Koch Model HK4 DA Auto Pistol
Calibers: 380 Automatic (9mm Short); also 22 LR, 25 Automatic (6.35mm), 32 Automatic (7.65mm) with conversion kits. 7-shot magazine in 380; 8-shot in other calibers. 3 11/32-inch barrel. 6 3/16 inches overall. Weight: 18 oz. Fixed sights. Blued finish. Plastic stock. Discontinued 1984.
380 Automatic $295
380 Automatic with 22 conversion unit 425
380 Automatic with 22, 25, 32 conversion units . . . 695

Heckler & Koch Model P7K3 DA Auto Pistol
Caliber: 380 ACP. 8-round magazine. 3.8 inch-barrel. 6.3 inches overall. Weight: about 26 oz. Adjustable rear sight. Made from 1988 to date.
P7K3 in 380 Cal. $750
22 LR Conversion Kit 495

Heckler & Koch HK4

**Heckler & Koch
Model P7K3**

Heckler & Koch P7M8

Heckler & Koch Model P7M8 . . . . **$750**
Caliber: 9mm. 8-shot magazine. 4.13-inch barrel. 6.73 inches overall. Weight: 29.9 oz. Matte black finish. Adjustable rear sight. Made 1985 to date.

Heckler & Koch Model P7M10
Caliber: 40 S&W. 9-shot magazine. 4.2-inch barrel. 6.9 inches overall. Weight: 43 oz. Sights: fixed front blade; adjustable rear w/3-dot system. Made from 1992 to date.
Blued Finish **$895**
Nickel Finish **950**

Heckler & Koch P7M13

Heckler & Koch Model P7M13 . . . . **$850**
Caliber: 9mm. 13-shot magazine. 4.13-inch barrel. 6.65 inches overall. Weight: 34.42 oz. Matte black finish. Adjustable rear sight. Made 1985–89.

Heckler & Koch Model P7 (PSP)

Heckler & Koch Model P7(PSP) Auto Pistol **$895**
Caliber: 9mm Parabellum/Luger. 8-shot magazine. DA. 4.13-inch barrel. 6.54 inches overall. Weight: about 33.5 oz. Blue finish. Made 1983–85.

Heckler & Koch Model P9S DA Automatic Pistol
Calibers: 9mm Luger, 45 Automatic. 9-shot (9mm) or 7-shot (45 Auto) magazine. 4-inch barrel. 7⅝ inches overall. Weight: 32 ounces. Fixed sights. Blued finish. Plastic grips. Discontinued 1986. (*See* photo, next page.)
9mm **$650**
45 Automatic **695**

Heckler & Koch Model P9S 45

**Heckler & Koch Model P9S
9mm Target**

Heckler & Koch Model P9S 9mm Target **$995**
Same as standard Model P9S 9mm, except has adjustable
trigger, trigger stop, adjustable rear sight.

Heckler & Koch Model P9S 9mm Competition Kit

Heckler & Koch Model P9S 9mm Target Competition Kit
Same as Model P9S 9mm Target, except comes with extra
5 1/2-inch barrel and barrel weight. Also available with
walnut competition stock.
With Standard stock **$850**
With Competition stock **950**

Heckler & Koch Model SP89 . . . . **$2100**
Semiautomatic, recoil-operated, delayed roller-locked bolt
system. Caliber: 9mm Luger. 15-shot magazine. 4.5-inch
barrel. 13 inches overall. Weight: 68 oz. Hooded front
sight; adj. rotary-aperture rear. Made from 1989 to date.

Heckler & Koch Model USP Auto Pistol
Polymer integral grip/frame design with recoil reduction
system. Calibers: 9mm Parabellum, 40 S&W. 15-shot
(9mm) or 13-shot (40 S&W) magazine. 4 3/4-inch barrel.
6 7/8 inches overall. Weight: 28 oz. Sights: blade front; adjustable rear w/3-dot system. Matte black finish. Stippled
black polymer grip. Available in SA/DA or DAO. Made
from 1993 to date.
Right-Hand Model **$550**
Left-Hand Model **575**

Heckler & Koch Model VP'70Z

Heckler & Koch Model VP'70Z Auto Pistol **$325**
Caliber: 9mm Luger. 18-shot magazine. DA. 4 1/2-inch barrel. 8 inches overall. Weight: 32 1/2 oz. Fixed sights. Blued
slide, plastic receiver and stock. Discontinued 1986.

═══════ **HELWAN PISTOL** ═══════
See Interarms.

═══════ **HERITAGE MANUFACTURING** ═══════
Opa Locka, Florida

Heritage Model HA25 Auto Pistol
Caliber: 25 ACP. 6-shot magazine. 2 1/2-inch barrel. 4 5/8
inches overall. Weight: 12 oz. Fixed sights. Blued or
chrome finish. Made from 1993 to date.
Blued **$60**
Chrome **70**

Heritage Rough Rider

Heritage Rough Rider SA Revolver
Calibers: 22 LR, 22 WRF. 6-shot cylinder. Barrel lengths: 3, 4³/₄, 6¹/₂, 9 inches. Weight: 31–38 oz. Sights: blade front; fixed rear. High-polished blued finish with gold accents. Smooth walnut grips. Made from 1993 to date.
22 Long Rifle . . . . **$ 75**
22 WRF **100**

Heritage Sentry DA

Heritage Sentry DA Revolver
Caliber: 38 Special. 6-shot cylinder. 2- or 4-inch barrel. 6¹/₄ inches overall w/2-inch bbl. Sights: ramp front; fixed rear. Blued or chrome finish. Checkered plastic grips. Made from 1993 to date.
Blued . . . . **$ 95**
Chrome **100**

═══ HI-POINT FIREARMS ═══
Mansfield, Ohio

Hi-Point JS Series 9mm

Hi-Point Model JS-9mm Auto Pistol **$100**
Caliber: 9mm Parabellum. 8-shot magazine. 4³/₄-inch barrel. 7³/₄ inches overall. Weight: 42 oz. Fixed low-profile sights. Matte black finish. Checkered plastic grips.

Hi-Point Model JS-9mm Compact Pistol **$90**
Similar to standard JS-9, except with 3¹/₂-inch barrel.

Hi-Point Model JS-40 Auto Pistol **$115**
Similar to Model JS-9mm, except in caliber 40 S&W.

Hi-Point Model JS-45 Auto Pistol **$115**
Similar to Model JS-9mm, except in caliber 45 ACP with 7-shot magazine.

═══ J. C. HIGGINS HANDGUNS ═══
See Sears, Roebuck & Company.

═══ HIGH STANDARD SPORTING FIREARMS ═══
East Hartford, Connecticut
Formerly High Standard Mfg. Co., Hamden, Connecticut

A long-standing producer of sporting arms, High Standard discontinued its operations in 1984. *See* new High Standard models under separate entry that follows.

AUTOMATIC PISTOLS

> **NOTE:** For ease in finding a particular firearm, High Standard handguns are grouped into three sections: Automatic Pistols (below), Derringers, and Revolvers, which follow. For a complete listing, please refer to the Index.

High Standard Model A

High Standard Model A Automatic Pistol **$495**
Hammerless. Caliber: 22 LR. 10-shot magazine. Barrel lengths: 4¹/₂, 6³/₄ inch. 11¹/₂ inches overall w/6³/₄-inch bbl. Weight: 36 oz. w/6³/₄-inch bbl. Adjustable target sights. Blued finish. Checkered walnut stocks. Made 1938–1942.

High Standard Model B

High Standard Model B Automatic Pistol $435
Original Standard pistol. Hammerless. Caliber: 22 LR. 10-shot magazine. Barrel lengths: 4½-, 6¾-inch. 10¾ inches overall w/6¾-inch bbl. Weight: 33 oz. w/6¾-inch bbl. Fixed sights. Blued finish. Hard rubber stocks. Made 1932–1942. (*See* illustration, preceding page.)

High Standard Model C Automatic Pistol $525
Same as Model B, except in 22 Short. Made 1935–1942.

High Standard Model D

High Standard Model D Automatic Pistol $495
Same general specifications as Model A, but heavier barrel. Weight: 40 oz. w/6¾-inch barrel. Made 1937–1942.

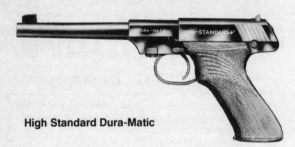

High Standard Dura-Matic

High Standard Dura-Matic Automatic Pistol $275
Takedown. Caliber: 22 LR. 10-shot magazine. Barrels: 4½- or 6½-inch, interchangeable. 10⅞ inches overall w/6½-inch bbl. Weight: 35 oz. w/6½-inch bbl. Fixed sights. Blued finish. Checkered grips. Made 1952–1970.

High Standard Model E

High Standard Model E Automatic Pistol $695
Same general specifications as Model A, but with extra heavy barrel and thumbrest stocks. Weight: 42 oz. w/6¾-inch bbl. Made 1937–1942.

High Standard Field-King Automatic Pistol
Same general specifications as Sport-King, but with heavier barrel and target sights. Late model 6¾-inch barrels have recoil stabilizer feature. Weight: 43 oz. w/6¾-inch barrel. Made 1951–58.

With One Barrel $395
With Both Barrels 435

High Standard Flite-King Automatic Pistol—First Model
Same general specifications as Sport-King, except in caliber 22 Short with aluminum alloy frame and slide; weighs 26 oz. w/6½-inch bbl. Made 1953–58.

With One Barrel $325
With Both Barrels 365

High Standard Flite-King Automatic Pistol Second Model $295
Same as Sport-King—Second Model, except caliber 22 Short and weighs 2 oz. lighter. Made 1958–1966.

High Standard Model G-380

High Standard Model G-380 Automatic Pistol . . . $495
Lever takedown. Visible hammer. Thumb safety. Caliber: 380 Automatic. 6-shot magazine. 5-inch barrel. Weight: 40 oz. Fixed sights. Blued finish. Checkered plastic stocks. Made 1943–1950.

High Standard Model G-B

High Standard Model G-B Automatic Pistol
Lever takedown. Hammerless. Interchangeable barrels. Caliber: 22 LR. 10-shot magazine. Barrel lengths: 4½-, 6¾-inch. 10¾ inches overall w/6¾-inch bbl. Weight: 36 oz. w/6¾-inch bbl. Fixed sights. Blued finish. Checkered plastic stocks. Made 1948–1951.

With One Barrel $425
With Both Barrels 460

High Standard Model G-D Automatic Pistol
Lever takedown. Hammerless. Interchangeable barrels. Caliber: 22 LR. 10-shot magazine. Barrel lengths: 4½-, 6¾-inch. 11½ inches overall w/6¾-inch bbl. Weight: 41 oz. w/6¾-inch bbl. Target sights. Blued finish. Checkered walnut stocks. Made 1948–1951.

With One Barrel $525
With Both Barrels 585

High Standard Model G-E Automatic Pistol
Same general specifications as Model G-D, but with extra heavy barrel and thumbrest stocks. Weight: 44 oz. w/6¾-inch barrel. Made 1949–1951.

High Standard Model G-E

High Standard Model G-E Automatic Pistol (cont.)
With One Barrel **$750**
With Both Barrels **835**

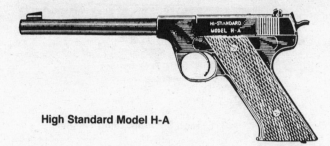

High Standard Model H-A

High Standard Model H-A Automatic Pistol **$550**
Same as Model A, but with visible hammer, no thumb safety. Made 1939–1942.

High Standard Model H-B

High Standard Model H-B Automatic Pistol **$415**
Same as Model B, but with visible hammer, no thumb safety. Made 1940–42.

High Standard Model H-D Automatic Pistol **$795**
Same as Model D, but with visible hammer, no thumb safety. Made 1939–1942.

High Standard Model H-DM Automatic Pistol . . . **$395**
Also called H-D Military. Same as Model H-D, but with thumb safety. Made 1941–1951.

High Standard Model H-E

High Standard Model H-E Automatic Pistol **$1150**
Same as Model E, but with visible hammer, no thumb safety. Made 1939–1942.

High Standard Olympic, First Model

High Standard Olympic Automatic—First Model
Same general specifications as Model G-E, but in 22 Short with light alloy slide. Made 1950–51.
With one barrel **$395**
With both barrels **465**

High Standard Olympic, Second Model

High Standard Olympic Automatic—Second Model
Same general specifications as Supermatic, but in 22 Short with light alloy slide. Weight: 39 oz. w/6³/₄-inch barrel. Made 1951–58.
With one barrel **$525**
With both barrels **600**

High Standard Olympic Automatic Pistol
Third Model **$615**
Same as Supermatic Trophy with bull barrel, except in caliber 22 Short. Made 1963–66.

High Standard Olympic Commemorative
Limited edition of Supermatic Trophy Military issued to commemorate the only American-made rimfire target pistol ever to win an Olympic Gold Medal. Highly engraved with Olympic rings inlaid in gold. Deluxe presentation case. Two versions issued: in 1972 (22 LR) and 1980 (22 Short). *Note:* Value shown is for pistol in new, unfired condition.
1972 Issue **$3495**
1980 Issue **1250**

High Standard Olympic I.S.U. **$695**
Same as Supermatic Citation, except caliber 22 Short, 6³/₄- and 8-inch tapered barrels with stabilizer, detachable

High Standard Olympic I.S.U.

High Standard Plinker

High Standard Olympic I.S.U. (cont.)
weights. Made from 1958 to date; 8-inch barrel discontinued in 1964.

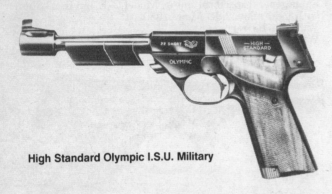

High Standard Olympic I.S.U. Military

High Standard Sharpshooter

High Standard Olympic I.S.U. Military **$725**
Same as Olympic I.S.U., except has military grip and bracket rear sight. Introduced in 1965. Discontinued.

High Standard Sharpshooter Automatic Pistol . . **$350**
Takedown. Hammerless. Caliber: 22 LR. 10-shot magazine. 5½-inch bull barrel. 9 inches overall. Weight: 42 oz. Micrometer rear sight, blade front sight. Blued finish. Plastic stocks. Made 1971–1983.

High Standard Olympic Military

High Standard Sport-King First Model

High Standard Olympic Military **$625**
Same as Olympic—Third Model, except has military grip and bracket rear sight. Made in 1965.

High Standard Plinker **$295**
Similar to Dura-Matic with same general specifications. Made 1971–73.

High Standard Sport-King Automatic—First Model
Takedown. Hammerless. Interchangeable barrels. Caliber: 22 LR. 10-shot magazine. Barrel lengths: 4½-, 6¾-inch. 11½ inches overall w/6¾-inch bbl. Weight: 39 oz. w/6¾-inch bbl. Fixed sights. Blued finish. Checkered plastic thumbrest stocks. Made 1951–58. *Note:* 1951–54 production has lever takedown as in "G" series; later version illustrated has push-button takedown.
With One Barrel **$295**
With Both Barrels **375**

**High Standard Sport-King
Second Model**

High Standard Sport-King Automatic Pistol
Second Model **$250**
Caliber: 22 LR. 10-shot magazine. Barrels: 4¹/₂- or 6³/₄-inch, interchangeable. 11¹/₄ inches overall w/6³/₄-inch bbl. Weight: 42 oz. w/6³/₄-inch bbl. Fixed sights. Blued finish. Checkered grips. Made 1958–1970.

**High Standard Sport-King
Third Model**

High Standard Sport-King Automatic Pistol
Third Model **$265**
Similar to Sport-King—Second Model, with same general specifications. Blued or nickel finish. Introduced in 1974. Discontinued.

High Standard Sport-King Lightweight
Same as standard Sport-King, except has forged aluminum alloy frame, weighs 30 oz. with 6³/₄-inch barrel. Made 1954–1965.
With One Barrel **$350**
With Both Barrels **425**

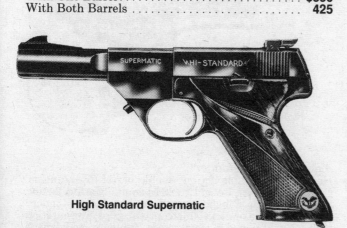

High Standard Supermatic

High Standard Supermatic Automatic Pistol
Takedown. Hammerless. Interchangeable barrels. Caliber: 22 LR. 10-shot magazine. Barrel lengths: 4¹/₂-, 6³/₄-inch. Late model 6³/₄-inch barrels have recoil stabilizer feature. Weight: 43 oz. w/6³/₄-inch bbl. 11¹/₂ inches overall w/6³/₄-

High Standard Supermatic Automatic Pistol (cont.)
inch bbl. Target sights. Elevated serrated rib between sights. Adjustable barrel weights add 2 or 3 oz. Blued finish. Checkered plastic thumbrest stocks. Made 1951–58.
With One Barrel **$395**
With Both Barrels **445**

**High Standard Supermatic Citation
Bull Barrel**

High Standard Supermatic Citation
Same as Supermatic Tournament, except 6³/₄-, 8-, 10-inch tapered barrels with stabilizer and two removable weights. Also furnished with Tournament's 5¹/₂-inch bull barrel, adjustable trigger pull, recoil-proof click-adjustable rear sight (barrel-mounted on 8- and 10-inch barrels), checkered walnut thumbrest grips on bull barrel model. Currently mfd. with only bull barrel. Made 1958 to date.
With bull barrel **$510**
With tapered barrel **550**

**High Standard Supermatic Citation
Military Fluted Barrel**

High Standard Supermatic Citation Military
Same as Supermatic Citation, except has military grip and bracket rear sight, barrels as in Supermatic Trophy. Made from 1965 to date.
With Bull Barrel **$450**
With Fluted Barrel **500**

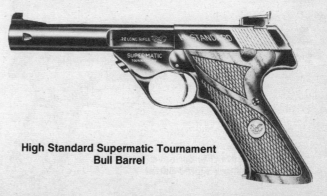

**High Standard Supermatic Tournament
Bull Barrel**

High Standard Supermatic Tournament **$425**

Takedown. Caliber: 22 LR. 10-shot magazine. Barrels (interchangeable): 5½-inch bull, 6¾-inch heavy tapered, notched and drilled for stabilizer and weights. 10 inches overall w/5½-inch bbl. Weight: 44 oz. w/5½-inch bbl. Click adjustable rear sight, undercut ramp front. Blued finish. Checkered grips. Made 1958–1966. (*See* photo, preceding page.)

**High Standard
Supermatic Tournament Military
Tapered Barrel**

High Standard Supermatic Tournament Military
. . . . **$425**

Same as Supermatic Tournament, except has military grip. Made 1965–1971.

**High Standard Supermatic Trophy
Bull Barrel**

High Standard Supermatic Trophy

Same as Supermatic Citation, except 5½-inch bull barrel or 7¼-inch fluted barrel with detachable stabilizer and weights, extra magazine. High-luster blued finish, checkered walnut thumbrest grips. Made 1963–66.

With Bull Barrel **$575**
With Fluted Barrel **615**

**High Standard Supermatic Trophy
Military Fluted Barrel**

High Standard Supermatic Trophy Military

Same as Supermatic Trophy, except has military grip and bracket rear sight. Made 1965–1984.

With Bull Barrel **$550**
With Fluted Barrel **600**

**High Standard Victor
Solid Rib Barrel**

High Standard Victor Automatic Pistol **$525**

Takedown. Caliber: 22 LR. 10-shot magazine. Barrels: 4½-inch solid or vent rib, 5½-inch vent rib; interchangeable. 9¾ inches overall w/5½-inch bbl. Weight: 52 oz. kw/5½-inch bbl. Rib-mounted target sights. Blued finish. Checkered walnut thumbrest stocks. Standard or military grip configuration. Made from 1972 to date (standard-grip model, 1974–75).

DERRINGER

> **NOTE:** High Standard Automatic Pistols can be found in the preceding section, while Revolvers immediately follow this Derringer listing.

High Standard Derringer

High Standard Derringer

Hammerless, double action, double barrel (over/under). Calibers: 22 Short, Long, LR; 22 Magnum Rimfire. 2-shot. 3½-inch barrels. 5 inches overall. Weight: 11 oz. Standard model has blued or nickel finish, plastic grips; presentation model is gold-plated in walnut case. Standard model made from 1963 (22 S-L-LR) and 1964 (22 MRF) to date; gold model, 1965–1983.

Gold Presentation, one derringer **$350**
Gold Presentation, matched pair, consecutive
   numbers **595**
Standard Model **185**

REVOLVERS

NOTE: Only High Standard Revolvers can be found in this section. For Automatic Pistols and Derringers, see the preceding sections. For a complete listing of High Standard handguns, please refer to the Index.

High Standard Camp Gun

High Standard Camp Gun **$200**
Same as Sentinel Mark I/Mark IV, except has 6-inch barrel, adjustable rear sight, target-style checkered walnut stocks. Caliber: 22 LR or 22 WMR. Made 1976–1983.

High Standard Double-Nine Double Action Revolver—Aluminum Frame **$215**
Western-style version of Sentinel. Blued or nickel finish with simulated ivory, ebony or stag grips. 5½-inch barrel. 11 inches overall. Weight: 27¼ oz. Made 1959–1971.

High Standard Double-Nine Deluxe **$225**
Same as Double-Nine—Steel Frame, except has adjustable target rear sight. Introduced in 1971. Discontinued.

**High Standard Double-Nine—
Steel Frame**

High Standard Double-Nine—Steel Frame **$250**
Similar to Double-Nine—Aluminum Frame, with same general specifications, except has extra cylinder for 22 WMR, walnut stocks. Introduced in 1971. Discont.

High Standard Durango

High Standard Durango **$190**
Similar to Double-Nine—Steel Frame, except 22 LR only, available with 4½- and 5½-inch barrels. Made 1971–73.

High Standard High Sierra

High Standard High Sierra Double Action Revolver
Similar to Double-Nine—Steel Frame, except has 7-inch octagon barrel, gold-plated grip frame; fixed or adjustable sights. Made 1973–1983.
With fixed sights **$190**
With adjustable sights **250**

High Standard Hombre **$195**
Similar to Double-Nine—Steel Frame, except 22 LR only, lacks single-action type ejector rod and tube, has 4½-inch barrel. Made 1971–73.

High Standard Kit Gun

High Standard Kit Gun Double Action Revolver . **$175**
Solid frame, swing-out cylinder. Caliber: 22 LR. 9-shot cylinder. 4-inch barrel. 9 inches overall. Weight: 19 oz. Adjustable rear sight, ramp front. Blued finish. Checkered walnut stocks. Made 1970–73.

**High Standard Longhorn
Aluminum Frame**

High Standard Longhorn—Aluminum Frame
Similar to Double-Nine—Aluminum Frame. Longhorn hammer spur. Blued finish 4½-inch barrel with simulated

High Standard Longhorn—Aluminum Frame (cont.)

pearl grips; 5½-inch, simulated stag grips; 9½-inch, walnut grips. Latter model made 1960–1971; others made 1961–66.

With 4½- or 5½-inch barrel **$160**
With 9½-inch barrel **225**

High Standard Longhorn—Steel Frame

High Standard Longhorn—Steel Frame

Similar to Double-Nine—Steel Frame, except has 9½-inch barrel; available with fixed or adjustable sights. Made 1971–1983.

With Fixed Sights **$175**
With Adjustable Sights **295**

High Standard Natchez

High Standard Natchez **$120**

Similar to Double-Nine—Aluminum Frame, except 4½-inch barrel (10 inches overall, weighs 25¼ oz.), blued finish, simulated ivory bird's head grips. Made 1961–66.

High Standard Posse

High Standard Posse **$130**

Similar to Double-Nine—Aluminum Frame, except 3½-inch barrel (9 inches overall, weighs 23¼ oz.), blued finish, brass-grip frame and trigger guard, walnut grips. Made 1961–66.

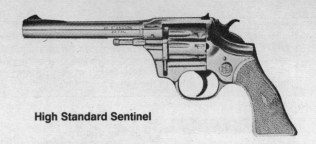

High Standard Sentinel

High Standard Sentinel DA Revolver **$300**

Solid frame, swing-out cylinder. Caliber: 22 LR. 9-shot cylinder. Barrels: 3-, 4- or 6-inch. 9 inches overall w/4-inch bbl. Weight: 19 oz. w/4-inch bbl. Fixed sights. Aluminum frame. Blued or nickel finish. Checkered grips. Made 1955–56.

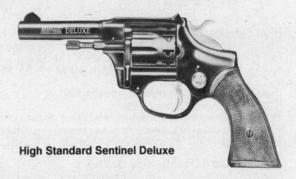

High Standard Sentinel Deluxe

High Standard Sentinel Deluxe **$250**

Same as Sentinel, except 4- or 6-inch barrels only; has wide trigger, movable rear sight, two-piece square-butt grips. Made 1957–1974. *Note:* Designated Sentinel after 1971.

High Standard Sentinel Imperial **$235**

Same as Sentinel, except has onyx-black or nickel finish, two-piece checkered walnut grips, ramp front sight. Made 1962–65.

High Standard Sentinel I

High Standard Sentinel I Double Action Revolver

Steel frame. Caliber: 22 LR. 9-shot cylinder. Barrel lengths: 2-, 3-, 4-inch. 6⅞ inches overall w/2-inch bbl. Weight: 21½ oz. w/2-inch bbl. Ramp front sight, fixed or adjustable rear. Blued or nickel finish. Smooth walnut stocks. Made 1974–1983.

With fixed sights **$245**
With adjustable sights **265**

HANDGUNS

High Standard Sentinel Mark II

High Standard Sentinel Mark III

High Standard Sentinel Mark II DA Revolver $295
Caliber: 357 Magnum. 6-shot cylinder. Barrel lengths: 2¹/₂-, 4-, 6-inch. 9 inches overall with 4-inch bbl. Weight: 38 oz. w/4-inch bbl. Fixed sights. Blued finish. Walnut service or combat-style stocks. Made 1974–76.

High Standard Sentinel Mark III $300
Same as Sentinel Mark II, except has ramp front and adjustable rear sights. Made 1974–76.

High Standard Sentinel Mark IV
Same as Sentinel Mark I, except in caliber 22 WMR. Made 1974–1983.
With fixed sights $250
With adjustable sights 275

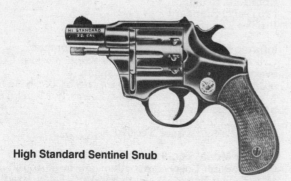

High Standard Sentinel Snub

High Standard Sentinel Snub $180
Same as Sentinel Deluxe, except with 2³/₈-inch barrel (7¹/₄ inches overall, weighs 15 oz.), checkered bird's-head-type grips. Made 1957–1974.

HIGH STANDARD MFG. CO., INC.
Houston, Texas
Distributed from Hartford, Connecticut

High Standard 10X Automatic Pistol $550
Caliber: 22 LR. 10-shot magazine. 5¹/₂-inch barrel. 9¹/₂ inches overall. Weight: 45 oz. Checkered walnut grips. Blued finish. Made from 1994 to date.

High Standard Citation MS Auto Pistol $315
Similar to the Supermatic Citation, except has 10-inch barrel. 14 inches overall. Weight: 49 oz. Made from 1994 to date.

High Standard Olympic I.S.U. Automatic Pistol
Caliber: 22 Short. 10-shot magazine. 6³/₄-inch fluted barrel. 10³/₄ inches overall. Weight: 45 oz. Frame-mounted, micro-adjustable rear sight; undercut ramp front sight. Checkered walnut grips. Made from 1994 to date.
Olympic I.S.U. Model $405
Olympic I.S.U. Military Model 315

High Standard Sport King Auto Pistol $240
Caliber: 22 LR. 10-shot magazine. 4¹/₂- or 6³/₄-inch barrel. 8¹/₂ or 10³/₄ inches overall. Weight: 44 oz. (4¹/₂-inch bbl.); 46 oz. (6³/₄-inch bbl.). Fixed sights, slide mounted. Checkered walnut grips. Parkerized finish. Made from 1994 to date.

High Standard Supermatic Citation Auto Pistol
Caliber: 22 LR. 10-shot magazine. 5¹/₂- or 7³/₄-inch barrel. 9¹/₂ or 11³/₄ inches overall. Weight: 44 oz. (5¹/₂-inch bbl.); 46 oz. (7³/₄-inch bbl.). Frame-mounted, micro-adjustable rear sight; undercut ramp front sight. Blued or Parkerized finish. Made from 1994 to date.
Supermatic Citation Model $285
22 Short Conversion 250

High Standard Supermatic Tournament $275
Caliber: 22 LR. 10-shot magazine. Barrel length: 4¹/₂, 5¹/₂ or 6³/₄ inches. Overall length: 8¹/₂, 9¹/₂ or 10³/₄ inches. Weight: 43, 44 or 45 oz. depending on bbl. length. Slide-mounted, micro-adjustable rear sight; undercut ramp front sight. Checkered walnut grips. Parkerized finish. Made from 1994 to date.

High Standard Supermatic Trophy
Caliber: 22 LR. 10-shot magazine. 5¹/₂ or 7¹/₄-inch barrel. 9¹/₂ or 11¹/₄ inches overall. Weight: 44 oz. (5¹/₂-inch bbl.) or 46 oz. (7¹/₄-inch bbl.). Slide-mounted, micro-adjustable rear sight; undercut ramp front sight. Checkered walnut grips w/thumbrest. Blued or Parkerized finish. Made from 1994 to date.
Supermatic Trophy $325
22 Short Conversion 250

High Standard Victor Automatic
Caliber: 22 LR. 10-shot magazine. 4¹/₂- or 5¹/₂-inch barrel. 8¹/₂ or 9¹/₂ inches overall. Weight: 45 oz. (4¹/₂-inch bbl.); 46 oz. (5¹/₂-inch bbl.). Barrel-mounted rib w/micro-adjustable rear sight; post front sight. Checkered walnut grips. Blued or Parkerized finish. Made from 1994 to date.
Victor Model $325
22 Short Conversion 265

NOTE: After June 1, 1995 all High Standard pistols were drilled and tapped to accept scope mounts.

HOPKINS & ALLEN ARMS CO.
Norwich, Connecticut

Hopkins & Allen Revolvers
See listings of comparable Harrington & Richardson and Iver Johnson models for values.

INTERARMS
Alexandria, Virginia

See also Bersa Pistol.

Interarms/Helwan Brigadier

Interarms/Helwan Brigadier Auto Pistol **$165**
Caliber: 9mm Parabellum. 8-shot magazine. 4¹/₂-inch barrel. 8 inches overall. Weight: 32 oz. Sights: blade front; dovetailed rear. Blued finish. Grooved plastic grips.

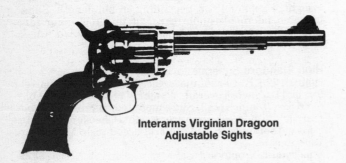

Interarms Virginian Dragoon
Adjustable Sights

Interarms Virginian Dragoon Single Action Revolver
Calibers: 357 Magnum, 44 Magnum, 45 Colt. 6-shot cylinder. Barrels: 5- (not available in 44 Magnum), 6-, 7¹/₂-, 8³/₈-inch (latter only in 44 Magnum w/adjustable sights). 11⁷/₈ inches overall w/6-inch bbl. Weight: 48 oz. w/6-inch bbl. Fixed sights or micrometer rear and ramp front sights. Blued finish with color-casetreated frame. Smooth walnut stocks. SWISSAFE base pin safety system. Manufactured by Interarms Industries Inc., Midland, VA. 1977–1984.
Standard Dragoon **$250**
Engraved Dragoon **475**
Deputy Model **250**

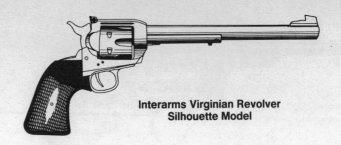

Interarms Virginian Revolver
Silhouette Model

Interarms Virginian Revolver Silhouette Model . . **$375**
Same general specifications as regular model except designed in stainless steel with untapered bull barrel lengths of 7¹/₂, 8³/₈ and 10¹/₂ inches. Made 1985–86.

Interarms Virginian Single Action Revolver **$295**
See listing under Hämmerli (manufacturer).

INTRATEC U.S.A. INC.
Miami, Florida

Intratec Category 9 DAO Semiautomatic **$185**
Blowback action w/polymer frame. Caliber: 9mm Parabellum. 8-shot magazine. 3-inch barrel. 7.7 inches overall. Weight: 18 oz. Textured black polymer grips. Matte black finish. Made from 1993 to date.

Intratec Category 40 DAO Semiautomatic **$205**
Locking-breech action w/polymer frame. Caliber: 40 S&W. 7-shot magazine. 3.25-inch barrel. 8 inches overall. Weight: 21 oz. Textured black polymer grips. Matte black finish. Made from 1994 to date.

Intratec Category 45 DAO Semiautomatic **$215**
Locking-breech action w/polymer frame. Caliber: 45 ACP. 6-shot magazine. 3.25-inch barrel. 8 inches overall. Weight: 21 oz. Textured black polymer grips. Matte black finish. Made from 1994 to date.

Intratec Model ProTec 22 DA Semiautomatic
Caliber: 25 ACP. 10-shot magazine. 2.5-inch barrel. 5 inches overall. Weight: 14 oz. Wraparound composition grips. Black Teflon, satin grey or Tec-Kote finish. Made from 1992 to date.
ProTec 22 Standard **$65**
ProTec 22 w/Satin or Tec-Kote **70**

Intratec Model ProTec 25 DA Semiautomatic
Caliber: 25 ACP. 8-shot magazine. 2.5-inch barrel. 5 inches overall. Weight: 14 oz. Fixed sights. Wraparound composition grips. Black Teflon, satin grey or Tec-Kote finish. Made from 1991 to date. *Note:* Formerly Model Tec-25; name changed about 1995.
ProTec 25 Standard **$70**
ProTec 25 w/Satin or Tec-Kote **75**

Intratec Model Tec-9 Semiautomatic
Caliber: 9mm Luger/Parabellum. 20- or 36-round magazine. 5-inch barrel. Weight: 50-51 oz. Open fixed front sight, adjustable rear. Military nonglare blued or stainless finish.
Tec-9 w/Blued Finish **$245**
Tec-9 w/Electroless Nickel Finish **275**
Tec 9S w/Stainless Finish **295**

Intratec Model Tec-9M Semiautomatic

Same specifications as Model Tec-9, except has 3-inch barrel without shroud and 20-round magazine. Blued or stainless finish.

Tec-9M w/Blued Finish	**$225**
Tec-9MS w/Stainless Finish	**280**

Intratec Model Tec-22T Semiautomatic

Caliber: 22 LR. 10/22-type 30-shot magazine. 4-inch barrel. 11³/₁₆ inches overall. Weight: 30 oz. Protected post front sight; adjustable rear sight. Matte black or Tec-Kote finish. Made from 1989 to date.

Tec-22T Standard	**$155**
Tec-22TK Tec-Kote	**175**

Intratec Model Tec Double Derringer $90

Calibers: 22 WRF, 32 H&R Mag., 38 Special. 2-shot capacity. 3-inch barrel. 4⁵/₈ inches overall. Weight: 13 oz. Fixed sights. Matte black finish.

JAPANESE MILITARY PISTOLS
Tokyo, Japan
Manufactured by Government Plant

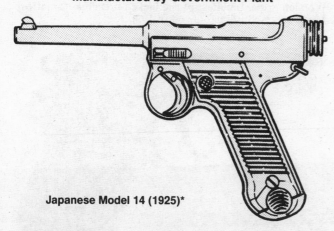

Japanese Model 14 (1925)*

Japanese Model 14 (1925) Automatic Pistol $475

Modification of the Nambu Model 1914, changes chiefly intended to simplify mass production. Standard round trigger guard or oversized guard for use with gloves. Caliber: 8mm Nambu. 8-shot magazine. 4³/₄-inch barrel. 9 inches overall. Weight: about 29 oz. Fixed sights. Blued finish. Grooved wood stocks. Introduced 1925; mfd. through WW II.

Japanese Model 94

Japanese Model 94 (1934) Automatic Pistol $220

Poorly design and constructed, this pistol can be fired merely by applying pressure on the sear, which is exposed on the left side. Caliber: 8mm Nambu. 6-shot magazine. 3¹/₈-inch barrel. 7¹/₈ inches overall. Weight: about 27 oz. Fixed sights. Blued finish. Hard rubber or wood stocks. Introduced in 1934, principally for export to Latin American countries, production continued thru WW II.

Japanese Nambu Model 1914 Automatic Pistol . $460

Original Japanese service pistol, resembles Luger in appearance and Glisenti in operation. Caliber: 8mm Nambu. 7-shot magazine. 4¹/₂-inch barrel. 9 inches overall. Weight: about 30 oz. Fixed front sight, adjustable rear sight. Blued finish. Checkered wood stocks. Made 1914–1925.

JENNINGS FIREARMS INC.
Irvine, California

Jennings Model J Auto Pistol

Calibers: 22 LR, 25 ACP. 6-shot magazine. 2¹/₂-inch barrel. About 5 inches overall. Weight: 13 oz. Fixed sights. Chrome, satin nickel or black Teflon finish. Walnut, grooved black Cycolac or resin-impregnated wood grips. Made from 1981 to date.

Model J-22	**$65**
Model J-25	**50**

Jennings Model M38 Bryco Auto Pistol $90

Calibers: 32 ACP, 380 ACP. 6-shot magazine. 2¹³/₁₆-inch barrel. 5⁵/₁₆ inches overall. Weight: 15 oz. Fixed sights. Chrome, satin nickel or black Teflon finish. Walnut, grooved black Cycolac or resin-impregnated wood grips. Made from 1988 to date.

Jennings Model M48 Bryco Auto Pistol $100

Calibers: 380 ACP, 9mm. 7-shot magazine. 4-inch barrel. 6¹¹/₁₆ inches overall. Weight: 20 oz. Fixed sights. Chrome, satin nickel or black Teflon finish. Smooth wood or black Teflon grips. Made from 1989 to date.

Jennings Model M58 Bryco Auto Pistol $110

Caliber: 380 ACP. 13-shot magazine. 3³/₄-inch barrel. 5¹/₂ inches overall. Weight: 30 oz. Fixed sights. Chrome, satin nickel, blued or black Teflon finish. Smooth wood or black Teflon grips. Made from 1993 to date.

Jennings Model M59 Bryco Auto Pistol $120

Caliber: 9mm Parabellum. 13-shot magazine. 4-inch barrel. 6¹/₂ inches overall. Weight: 33 oz. Fixed sights. Chrome, satin nickel, blued or black Teflon finish. Smooth wood or black Teflon grips. Made from 1994 to date.

IVER JOHNSON'S ARMS, INC.
Jacksonville, Arkansas

Operation of this company dates back to 1871, when Iver Johnson and Martin Bye partnered to manufacture metallic cartridge revolvers. Johnson became the sole owner and changed the name to Iver Johnson's Arms & Cycle Works, which it was known as for almost 100 years. Modern management shortened the name, and after several owner changes, the firm was moved from Massachusetts, its original base, to Jacksonville, Arkansas. In 1987, the American Military Arms Corporation (AMAC) acquired the operation, which subsequently ceased in 1993.

AUTOMATIC PISTOLS

NOTE: For ease in finding a particular firearm, Iver Johnson handguns are divided into two sections: Automatic Pistols (below) and Revolvers, which follows. For the complete handgun listing, please refer to the Index.

Iver Johnson Pony

Iver Johnson 9mm DA Automatic

Iver Johnson 9mm Double Action Automatic ... **$295**
Caliber: 9mm. 6-round magazine. 3-inch barrel. 6.5 inches overall. Weight: 26 oz. Sights: blade front; adjustable rear. Smooth hardwood grip. Blued or matte blued finish. Introduced in 1986.

Iver Johnson Compact 25 ACP **$150**
Bernardelli V/P design. Caliber: 25 ACP. 5-shot magazine. 2^1/$_8$-inch barrel. 4^1/$_8$ inches overall. Weight: 9.3 oz. Fixed sights. Checkered composition grips. Blued slide, matte blue frame and color casehardened trigger. Made from 1991 to date.

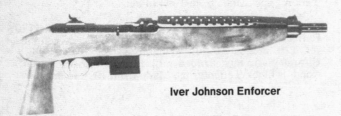

Iver Johnson Enforcer

Iver Johnson Enforcer **$345**
Caliber: 30. 5-, 15-, or 30-round magazine. Semiautomatic. 9^1/$_2$ inch barrel. Weight: 5^1/$_2$ pounds. Adjustable sights. Walnut stock. Made mid-1980s to date.

Iver Johnson PP30 Super Enforcer Automatic ... **$375**
Caliber: 30 US Carbine. 15- or 30-shot magazine. 9^1/$_2$-inch barrel. 17 inches overall. Weight: 4 pounds. Adjustable peer rear sight, blade front. American walnut stock. Made 1984–86.

Iver Johnson Pony Automatic Pistol **$250**
Caliber: 380 Auto. 6-shot magazine. 3.1-inch barrel. 6.1 inches overall. Weight: 20 oz. Blue, matte or nickel finish. Wooden grips. Smallest of the locked breech automatics. Made 1982–88; reintroduced in 1990.

Iver Johnson Model TP

Iver Johnson Model TP DA Automatic **$155**
Calibers: 22 LR, 25 ACP. 7-shot magazine. 2.85-inch barrel. 5.39 inches overall. Blue finish. Weight: 14.46 oz. Introduced in 1982. Discontinued.

Iver Johnson Model TP22 DA Pocket Pistol **$150**
Double-action automatic. Caliber: 22 LR. 7-round magazine. 3-inch barrel. 5^1/$_2$ inches overall. Weight: 12 oz. Black plastic grips and blued finish. Discontinued 1990.

Iver Johnson Model TP25 Pocket Pistol **$115**
Same general specifications as the Model TP22, except made in 25 ACP caliber. Discontinued.

Iver Johnson Trailsman Automatic Pistol
Caliber: 22 LR. 10-shot magazine. 4^1/$_2$- or 6-inch barrel. 8^3/$_4$ inches overall w/4^1/$_2$-inch bbl. Weight: 46 oz. Fixed target-type sights. Checkered composition grips. Made 1984–1990.
Standard Model **$175**
Deluxe Model **195**

REVOLVERS

NOTE: Only Iver Johnson Revolvers can be found in the section below. For Pistols, please see the preceding pages. For a complete listing, please refer to the Index.

Iver Johnson Model 55A

Iver Johnson Model 55A Target DA Revolver . . . **$115**
Solid frame. Caliber: 22 LR. 8-shot cylinder. Barrel lengths: 4½-, 6-inch. 10¾ inches overall (6-inch bbl.). Weight: 30½ oz. (6-inch bbl.). Fixed sights. Blued finish. Walnut stocks. *Note:* Original model designation was 55, changed to 55A when loading gate was added in 1961. Made 1955–1977.

Iver Johnson Model 57A Target

Iver Johnson Model 57A Target DA Revolver . . . **$135**
Solid frame. Caliber: 22 LR. 8-shot cylinder. Barrel lengths: 4½-, 6-inch. 10¾ inches overall (6-inch bbl.). Weight: 30½ oz., 6-inch bbl. Adjustable sights. Blued finish. Walnut stocks. *Note:* Original model designation was 57, changed to 57A when loading gate was added in 1961. Made 1956–1975.

Iver Johnson Model 66 Trailsman

Iver Johnson Model 66 Trailsman DA Revolver . . **$95**
Hinged frame. Rebounding hammer. Caliber: 22 LR. 8-shot cylinder. 6-inch barrel. 11 inches overall. Weight: 34 oz. Adjustable sights. Blued finish. Walnut stocks. Made 1958–1975.

Iver Johnson Model 67 Viking

Iver Johnson Model 67 Viking DA Revolver **$110**
Hinged frame. Caliber: 22 LR. 8-shot cylinder. Barrel lengths: 4½- and 6-inch. 11 inches overall w/6-inch bbl. Weight: 34 oz. w/6-inch bbl. Adjustable sights. Walnut stocks w/thumbrest. Made 1964–1975.

**Iver Johnson
Model 67S Viking Snub**

Iver Johnson Model 67S Viking Snub Revolver . . **$125**
DA. Hinged frame. Calibers: 22 LR, 32 S&W Short and Long, 38 S&W. 8-shot cylinder in 22; 5-shot in 32 and 38 calibers. 2¾-inch barrel. Weight: 25 oz. Adjustable sights. Tenite grips. Made 1964–1975.

**Iver Johnson Model 1900
Double Action Revolver**

Iver Johnson Model 1900 DA Revolver **$110**
Solid frame. Calibers: 22 LR, 32 S&W, 32 S&W Long, 38 S&W. 7-shot cylinder (22 cal.), 6-shot (32 S&W), 5-shot (32 S&W Long, 38 S&W). Barrel lengths: 2½-, 4½- and 6-inch. Weight: 12 oz., 32 S&W w/2½-inch bbl. Fixed sights. Blued or nickel finish. Hard rubber stocks. Made 1900–1947.

Iver Johnson Model 1900 Target DA Revolver . . **$150**
Solid frame. Caliber: 22 LR. 7-shot cylinder. Barrel lengths: 6- and 9½-inch. Fixed sights. Blued finish.

Iver Johnson Model 1900 Target DA (cont.)

Checkered walnut stocks. This earlier model does not have counterbored chambers as in the Target Sealed 8. Made 1925–1942.

Iver Johnson American Bulldog

Iver Johnson American Bulldog Double Action Revolver

Solid frame. Calibers: 22 LR, 22 WMR, 38 Special. 6-shot cylinder in 22, 5-shot in 38. Barrel lengths: 2¹/₂-, 4-inch. 9 inches overall w/4-inch bbl. Weight: 30 oz. w/4-inch bbl. Adjustable sights. Blued or nickel finish. Plastic stocks. Made 1974–76.

38 Special	$145
Other calibers	125

Iver Johnson Armsworth Model 855 SA $135

Hinged frame. Caliber: 22 LR. 8-shot cylinder. 6-inch barrel. 10³/₄ inches overall. Weight: 30 oz. Adjustable sights. Blued finish. Checkered walnut one-piece grip. Adjustable finger rest. Made 1955–57.

Iver Johnson Cadet Double Action Revolver $125

Solid frame. Calibers: 22 LR, 22 WMR, 32 S&W Long, 38 S&W, 38 Special. 6- or 8-shot cylinder in 22, 5-shot in other calibers. 2¹/₂-inch barrel. 7 inches overall. Weight: 22 oz. Fixed sights. Blued finish; nickel finish also available in 32 and 38 Special models. Plastic stocks. *Note:* Loading gate added in 1961; 22 cylinder capacity changed from 8 to 6 rounds in 1975. Made 1955–1977.

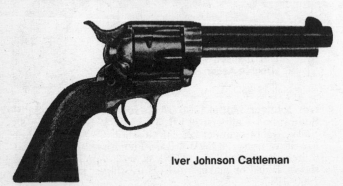

Iver Johnson Cattleman

NOTE: For engraved Cattleman revolvers, add **$450** to values indicated.

Iver Johnson Cattleman Single Action Revolver

Calibers: 357 Magnum, 44 Magnum, 45 Colt. 6-shot cylinder. Barrel lengths: 4³/₄-, 5¹/₂- (not available in 44), 6- (44 only), 7¹/₄-inch. Weight: about 41 oz. Fixed sights. Blued barrel and cylinder, color-casehardened frame, brass grip frame. One-piece walnut stock. Made by Aldo Uberti, Brescia, Italy, 1973–78.

44 Magnum	$250
Other calibers	195

Iver Johnson Cattleman Buckhorn

Iver Johnson Cattleman Buckhorn SA Revolver

Same as standard Cattleman, except has adjustable rear and ramp front sights. Barrels: 4³/₄- (44 only), 5³/₄- (not available in 44), 6- (44 only), 7¹/₂-, 12-inch. Weight: almost 44 oz. Made 1973–78.

357 Magnum or 45 Colt, 12-inch barrel	$300
357 Magnum or 45 Colt, other barrels	330
44 Magnum, 12-inch barrel	300
44 Magnum, other barrels	330

Iver Johnson Cattleman Buntline

Iver Johnson Cattleman Buntline SA Revolver

Same as Cattleman Buckhorn, except has 18-inch barrel, walnut shoulder stock with brass fittings. Weight: about 56 oz. Made 1973–78.

44 Magnum	$385
Other calibers	345

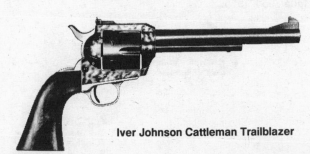

Iver Johnson Cattleman Trailblazer

Iver Johnson Cattleman Trailblazer $155

Similar to Cattleman Buckhorn, except 22 caliber; has interchangeable 22 LR and 22 WMR cylinders, 5¹/₂- or 6¹/₂-inch barrel. Weight: about 40 oz. Made 1973–78.

Iver Johnson Champion

Iver Johnson Champion 22 Target SA **$185**
Hinged frame. Caliber: 22 LR. 8-shot cylinder. Single action. Counterbored chambers as in Sealed 8 models. 6-inch barrel. 10³/₄ inches overall. Weight: 28 oz. Adjustable target sights. Blued finish. Checkered walnut stocks, adjustable finger rest. Made 1938–1948.

Iver Johnson Deluxe Target

Iver Johnson Deluxe Target **$160**
Same as Sportsman, except has adjustable sights. Made 1975–76.

Iver Johnson Protector Sealed 8

Iver Johnson Protector Sealed 8 DA Revolver . . **$150**
Hinged frame. Caliber: 22 LR. 8-shot cylinder. 2¹/₂-inch barrel. 7¹/₄ inches overall. Weight: 20 oz. Fixed sights. Blued finish. Checkered walnut stocks. Made 1933–1949.

Iver Johnson Rookie

Iver Johnson Rookie Double Action Revolver **$95**
Solid frame. Caliber: 38 Special. 5-shot cylinder. 4-inch barrel. 9-inches overall. Weight: 30 oz. Fixed sights. Blued or nickel finish. Plastic stocks. Made 1975–77.

Iver Johnson Safety Hammer

Iver Johnson Safety Hammer DA Revolver **$115**
Hinged frame. Calibers: 22 LR, 32 S&W, 32 S&W Long, 38 S&W. 7-shot cylinder (22 cal.), 6-shot (32 S&W Long), 5-shot (32 S&W, 38 S&W). Barrel lengths: 2, 3, 3¹/₄, 4, 5 or 6 inches. Weight with 4-inch bbl.: 15 oz., 22, 32 S&W; 19¹/₂ oz., 32 S&W Long; 19 oz., 38 S&W. Fixed sights. Blued or nickel finish. Hard rubber stocks, round butt; square butt, rubber and walnut stocks available. *Note:* 32 S&W Long and 38 S&W models built on heavy frame. Made 1892–1950.

Iver Johnson Safety Hammerless

Iver Johnson Safety Hammerless DA Revolver . . **$125**
Hinged frame. Calibers: 22 LR, 32 S&W, 32 S&W Long, 38 S&W. 7-shot cylinder (22 cal.), 6-shot (32 S&W Long), 5-shot (32 S&W, 38 S&W). Barrel lengths: 2, 3, 3¹/₄, 4, 5 or 6 inches. Weight with 4-inch bbl.: 15 oz., 22, 32 S&W; 20¹/₂ oz., 32 S&W Long; 20 oz., 38 S&W. Fixed sights. Blued or nickel finish. Hard rubber stocks, round butt. Square butt, rubber and walnut stocks available. *Note:* 32 S&W Long & 38 S&W models built on heavy frame. Made 1895–1950.

Iver Johnson Sidewinder DA Revolver **$130**
Solid frame. Caliber: 22 LR. 6- or 8-shot cylinder. Barrel lengths: 4³/₄-, 6-inch. 11¹/₄ inches overall w/6-inch bbl. Weight: 31 oz. w/6-inch bbl. Fixed sights. Blued or nickel finish w/plastic "staghorn" stocks; also color-casehardened frame with walnut stocks. *Note:* Cylinder capacity changed from 8 to 6 rounds in 1975. Intro. 1961; disc.

Iver Johnson Sidewinder "S" $145
Same as Sidewinder, except has interchangeable cylinders in 22 LR and 22 WMR, adjustable sights. Introduced 1974; discontinued.

Iver Johnson Sportsman DA Revolver $95
Solid frame. Caliber: 22 LR. 6-shot cylinder. Barrel lengths: 4³/₄-, 6-inch. 10³/₄ inches overall w/6-inch bbl. Weight: 30¹/₂ oz. w/6-inch bbl. Fixed sights. Blued finish. Plastic stocks. Made 1974–76.

Iver Johnson Supershot 9-Shot DA Revolver . . . $135
Same as Supershot Sealed 8, except has nine non-counterbored chambers. Made 1929–1949.

Iver Johnson Supershot 22 DA Revolver $95
Hinged frame. Caliber: 22 LR. 7-shot cylinder. 6-inch barrel. Fixed sights. Blued finish. Checkered walnut stocks. This earlier model does not have counterbored chambers as in the Supershot Sealed 8. Made 1929–1949.

Iver Johnson Supershot Model 844 DA $225
Hinged frame. Caliber: 22 LR. 8-shot cylinder. Barrel lengths: 4¹/₂- or 6-inch. 9¹/₄ inches overall w/4¹/₂-inch bbl. Weight: 27 oz. w/4¹/₂-inch bbl. Adjustable sights. Blued finish. Checkered walnut one-piece grip. Made 1955–56.

Iver Johnson Supershot Sealed 8

Iver Johnson Supershot Sealed 8 DA Revolver . $165
Hinged frame. Caliber: 22 LR. 8-shot cylinder. 6-inch barrel. 10³/₄ inches overall. Weight: 24 oz. Adjustable target sights. Blued finish. Checkered walnut stocks. Postwar model does not have adjustable finger rest as earlier version. Made 1931–1957.

Iver Johnson Swing Out

Iver Johnson Swing Out Double Action Revolver
Calibers: 22 LR, 22 WMR, 32 S&W Long, 38 Special. 6-shot cylinder in 22, 5-shot in 32 and 38. Barrels: plain, 2-, 3-, 4-inch; vent rib, 4-, 6-inch. 8³/₄ inches overall w/4-inch bbl. Fixed or adjustable sights. Blued or nickel finish.

Iver Johnson Swing Out DA Revolver (cont.)
Walnut stocks. Made in 1977.
W/Plain Barrel, Fixed Sights $125
W/Ventilated Rib, Adjustable Sights **175**

Iver Johnson Target 9-Shot DA Revolver $135
Same as Target Sealed 8, except has nine non-counterbored chambers. Made 1929–1946.

Iver Johnson Target Sealed 8

Iver Johnson Target Sealed 8 DA Revolver $145
Solid frame. Caliber: 22 LR. 8-shot cylinder. Barrel lengths: 6- and 10-inch. 10³/₄ inches overall w/6-inch barrel. Weight: 24 oz. w/6-inch bbl. Fixed sights. Blued finish. Checkered walnut stocks. Made 1931–1957.

Iver Johnson Trigger-Cocking

Iver Johnson Trigger-Cocking SA Target $165
Hinged frame. First pull on trigger cocks hammer, second pull releases hammer. Caliber: 22 LR. 8-shot cylinder, counterbored chambers. 6-inch barrel. 10³/₄ inches overall. Weight: 24 oz. Adjustable target sights. Blued finish. Checkered walnut stocks. Made 1940–47.

KAHR ARMS
Blauvelt, New York

Kahr K9 9mm

Kahr Model K9 DA Auto Pistol **$450**
Caliber: 9mm Parabellum. 8-shot magazine. 3½-inch barrel. 6 inches overall. Weight: 24 oz. Fixed sights. Blued finish. Wraparound smooth hardwood grips. Made from 1994 to date.

LAHTI PISTOLS
Mfd. by Husqvarna Vapenfabriks A. B. Huskvarna, Sweden, and Valtion Kivaar Tedhas ("VKT") Jyväskyla, Finland

Lahti, Swedish Model

Lahti Automatic Pistol
Caliber: 9mm Luger. 8-shot magazine. 4¾-inch barrel. Weight: about 46 oz. Fixed sights. Blued finish. Plastic stocks. Specifications given are those of the Swedish Model 40 but also apply in general to the Finnish Model L-35, which differs only slightly. A considerable number of Swedish Lahti pistols were imported and sold in the U.S.; the Finnish Model, somewhat better made, is a rather rare pistol. Finnish Model L-35 adopted 1935; Swedish Model 40 adopted 1940; mfd. thru 1944.
Finnish Model **$1100**
Swedish Model **450**

L.A.R. MANUFACTURING, INC.
West Jordan, Utah

**L.A.R. Mark I
Grizzly Win. Mag.**

L.A.R. Mark I Grizzly Win. Mag. Automatic Pistol
Calibers: 357 Mag., 45 ACP, 45 Win. Mag. 7-shot magazine. 6½-inch barrel. 10½ inches overall. Weight: 48 oz. Fully adjustable sights. Checkered rubber combat-style grips. Blued finish. Made from 1983 to date. 8-inch and 10-inch barrels made from 1987 to date.
357 Mag. (6½" barrel) **$650**
45 Win. Mag.(6½" barrel) **615**
8-inch barrel **900**
10-inch barrel **995**

L.A.R. Mark IV Grizzly Automatic Pistol **$695**
Same general specifications as the L.A.R. Mark I, except chambered for 44 Magnum; has 5.5- or 6.5-inch barrel, beavertail grip safety, matte blue finish. Made from 1991 to date.

L.A.R. Mark V Auto Pistol **$775**
Similar to the Mark I, except chambered in 50 Action Express. 6-shot magazine. 5.4- or 6.5-inch barrel. 10.6 inches overall w/5.4-inch bbl. Weight: 56 oz. Checkered walnut grips. Made from 1993 to date.

LIGNOSE PISTOLS
Suhl, Germany
Aktien-Gesellschaft "Lignose" Abteilung

The following Lignose pistols were manufactured from 1920 to the mid-1930s. They were also marketed under the Bergmann name.

Lignose Model 2 Pocket Auto Pistol **$150**
Conventional Browning type. Same general specifications as Einhand Model 2A, but lacks the one-hand operation.

Lignose Einhand Model 2A*

Lignose Einhand Model 3A

Lignose Einhand Model 2A Pocket Auto Pistol . . **$215**
As the name implies, this pistol is designed for one-hand operation; pressure on a "trigger" at the front of the guard

Lignose Einhand Model 2A Pocket Pistol (cont.)
retracts the slide. Caliber: 25 Automatic (6.35mm). 6-shot
magazine. 2-inch barrel. 4³/₄ inches overall. Weight: about
14 oz. Blued finish. Hard rubber stocks.

Lignose Einhand Model 3A Pocket Auto Pistol . . **$225**
Same as the Model 2A except has longer grip, 9-shot magazine, weighs about 16 oz. (*See* illus., preceding page.)

LLAMA HANDGUNS
Mfd. by Gabilondo y Cia, Vitoria, Spain
Imported by S.G.S., Wanamassa, New Jersey

AUTOMATIC PISTOLS

> **NOTE:** For ease in finding a particular Llama handgun, the
> listings are divided into two groupings: Automatic Pistols
> (below) and Revolvers, which follows. For a complete listing
> of Llama handguns, please refer to the Index.

Llama Model IIIA

Llama Model IIIA Automatic Pistol **$230**
Caliber: 380 Auto. 7-shot magazine. 3¹¹/₁₆-inch barrel. 6¹/₂
inches overall. Weight: 23 oz. Adjustable target sights.
Blued finish. Plastic stocks. Intro. 1951; discontinued.

Llama Model IIIA Deluxe
Blue Engraved

Llama Models IIIA, XA, XV Deluxe
Same as standard Model IIIA, XA and XV, except w/en-
graved chrome or blued finish and simulated pearl stocks.

Llama Model IIIA Deluxe
Chrome Engraved

Llama Models IIIA, XA, XV Deluxe (cont.)
Discontinued 1984.
Chrome-engraved Finish **$250**
Blue-engraved Finish **200**

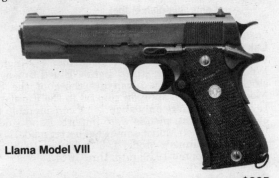

Llama Model VIII

Llama Model VIII Automatic Pistol **$295**
Caliber: 38 Super. 9-shot magazine. 5-inch barrel. 8¹/₂
inches overall. Weight: 40 oz. Fixed sights. Blued finish.
Wood stocks. Introduced in 1952; discontinued.

Llama Models VIII, IXA, XI Deluxe
Same as standard Models VIII, IXA and XI, except fin-
ish—chrome engraved or blue engraved—and simulated
pearl stocks. Discontinued 1984.
Chrome-engraved Finish **$325**
Blue-engraved Finish **350**

Llama Model IXA Automatic Pistol **$275**
Same as Model VIII, except caliber 45 Automatic, 7-shot
magazine.

Llama Model XA Automatic Pistol **$200**
Same as Model IIIA, except caliber 32 Automatic, 8-shot
magazine.

Llama Model XI

Llama Model XI Automatic Pistol **$250**
Same as Model VIII, except caliber 9mm Luger.

Llama Model XV Automatic Pistol **$220**
Same as Model XA, except caliber 22 LR.

Llama Models BE-IIIA, BE-XA, BE-XV **$250**
Same as Models IIIA, XA and XV, except with blue-engraved finish. Made 1977–1984.

Llama Models BE-VIII, BE-IXA, BE-XI Deluxe . . . **$320**
Same as Models VIII, IXA and XI, except with blue-engraved finish. Made 1977–1984.

Llama Models C-IIIA, C-XA, C-XV **$335**
Same as Models IIIA, XA and XV, except in satin-chrome.

Llama Model C-XI

Llama Models C-VIII, C-IXA, C-XI **$350**
Same as Models VIII, IXA and XI, except in satin-chrome.

Llama Model CE-IIIA

Llama Models CE-IIIA, CE-XA, CE-XV **$385**
Same as Models IIIA, XA and XV, except w/chrome-engraved finish. Made 1977–1984.

Llama Models CE-VIII, CE-IXA, CE-XI **$400**
Same as Models VIII, IXA and XI, w/except chrome-engraved finish. Made 1977–1984.

Llama Compact Frame Auto Pistol **$355**
Calibers: 9mm Para., 38 Super, 45 Auto. 7-, 8- or 9-shot. 5-inch barrel. 7⅞ inches overall. Weight: 34 oz. Blued, satin-chrome or Duo-Tone finishes. Made 1990 to date; Duo-Tone discontinued 1993.

Llama Duo-Tone Automatic Large Frame

Llama Duo-Tone Large Frame Auto Pistol **$295**
Caliber: 45 ACP. 7-shot magazine. 5-inch barrel. 8.5 inches overall. Weight: 36 oz. Adj. rear sight. Blued finished with satin chrome. Polymer black grips. Made 1990–93.

Llama Duo-Tone Automatic Small Frame

Llama Duo-Tone Small Frame Auto Pistol **$285**
Calibers: 22 LR, 32 and 380 Auto. 7- or 8-shot magazine. 3¹¹⁄₁₆-inch barrel. 6½ inches overall. Weight: 23 oz. Square-notch rear sight; Patridge-type front. Blued finish with chrome. Made 1990–93.

Llama Model G-IIIA Deluxe **$895**
Same as Model IIIA, except is gold-damascened w/simulated pearl stocks. Discontinued 1982.

Llama Large-Frame 45

Llama Large-Frame Automatic Pistol (IXA)

Caliber: 45 Auto. 7-shot magazine. 5-inch barrel. Weight: 2 lbs. 8 oz. Adjustable rear sight, Patridge-type front. Walnut grips; teakwood on satin chrome model; later models with polymer grips. Made from 1984 to date. (*See photo, preceding page.*)

Blued Finish	**$300**
Satin Chrome Finish	**310**

Llama M-82 9mm Double Action Automatic

Llama M-82 DA Automatic Pistol $525

Caliber: 9mm Parabellum. 15-shot magazine. 4¼-inch barrel. 8 inches overall. Weight: 39 oz. Drift adjustable rear sight. Matte blue finish. Matte black polymer grips. Made 1988–1993.

Llama M-87 Comp Pistol $825

Caliber: 9mm Parabellum. 15-shot magazine. 5.5-inch barrel. 9½ inches overall. Weight: 40 oz. Low-profile combat sights. Satin nickel finish. Matte black grip panels. Built-in ported compensator to minimize recoil and muzzle rise. Made 1989–1993.

Llama Omni

Llama Omni 9mm Double Action Automatic $350

Same general specifications as 45 Omni, except chambered for 9mm w/13-shot magazine. Discontinued 1986.

Llama Omni 45 Double Action Automatic Pistol . $375

Caliber: 45 Auto. 7-shot magazine. 4¼-inch barrel. 7¾ inches overall. Weight: 40 oz. Adjustable rear sight, ramp front. Highly polished deep blue finish. Made 1984–86.

Llama Single Action Automatic Pistol $345

Calibers: 38 Super, 9mm, 45 Auto. 9-shot magazine (7-shot for 45 Auto). 5-inch barrel. 8½ inches overall. Weight: 2 lbs. 8 oz. Introduced in 1981.

Llama Small-Frame Automatic

Llama Small-Frame Automatic Pistol

Calibers: 380 Auto (9mm); 7-shot magazine; 22 RF (8-shot magazine). 3¹¹⁄₁₆-inch barrel. Weight: 23 oz. Adjustable rear sight, Patridge-type front. Blued or satin-chrome finish.

Blued Finish	**$225**
Satin-Chrome Finish	**295**

REVOLVERS

> **NOTE:** This section contains only Llama Revolvers. Pistols may be found on the preceding pages. For a complete listing of Llama handguns, please refer to the Index.

Llama Comanche I

Llama Comanche I Double Action Revolver $180

Same gen. specifications as Martial 22. Made 1977–1983.

Llama Comanche II $195

Same gen. specifications as Martial 38. Made 1977–1983.

Llama Comanche III Double Action Revolver ... $250

Caliber: 357 Magnum. 6-shot cylinder. 4-inch barrel. 9¼ inches overall. Weight: 36 oz. Adjustable rear sight, ramp front. Blued finish. Checkered walnut stocks. Made from 1975 to date. *Note:* Prior to 1977, this model was designated "Comanche."

Llama Comanche III Chrome

Llama Comanche III Chrome $295

Same gen. specifications as Comanche III, except has satin chrome finish, 4- or 6-inch barrels. Made 1979 to date.

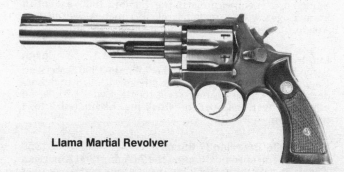

Llama Martial Revolver

Llama Martial Double Action Revolver $215

Calibers: 22 LR, 38 Special. 6-shot cylinder. Barrel lengths: 4-inch (38 Special only), 6-inch. 11¼ inches overall w/6-inch barrel. Weight: about 36 oz. w/6-inch barrel. Target sights. Blued finish. Checkered walnut stocks. Made 1969–1976.

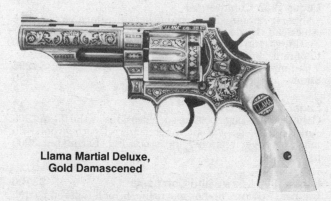

Llama Martial Deluxe, Gold Damascened

Llama Martial Double Action Deluxe

Same as standard Martial, except finish—satin chrome, chrome engraved, blue engraved, gold damascened; has simulated pearl stocks. Discontinued 1978.

Llama Martial Double Action Deluxe (cont.)

Satin-chrome Finish	$ 275
Chrome-engraved Finish	325
Blue-engraved Finish	300
Gold-damascened Finish	1500

Llama Super Comanche IV

Llama Super Comanche IV DA Revolver $295

Caliber: 44 Magnum. 6-shot cylinder. 6-inch barrel. 11¾ inches overall. Weight: 3 lbs. 2 oz. Sights: adjustable rear, ramp front. Polished deep blue finish. Checkered walnut grips. Made from 1980 to date.

Llama Super Comanche V DA Revolver $275

Caliber: 357 Mag. 6-shot cylinder. 4-, 6- or 8½-inch barrel. Weight: 3 pounds. Sights: click-adjustable rear, ramped blade front.

LUGER PISTOLS
GERMANY and SWITZERLAND

Mfd. by Deutsche Waffen und Munitionsfabriken (DWM), Berlin, Germany; also by Königlich Gewehrfabrik Erfurt, Heinrich Krieghoff Waffenfabrik, Mauser-Werke, Simson & Co., Vickers Ltd., Waffenfabrik, Bern.

See also Mauser and Stoeger handgun listings.

**Luger 1900
U.S. Army Pistol**

Luger 1900 American Eagle $2400

Caliber: 7.65mm. 8-shot magazine. Thin, 4¾-inch long, tapered barrel. 9½ inches overall . Weight: 32 oz. Fixed rear sight, dovetailed front sight. Grip safety. Checkered walnut grips. Early-style toggle, narrow trigger, wide guard, no stock lug. American Eagle over chamber. Estimated 8000 production.

Luger 1900 Commercial **$1550**
Same specifications as Luger 1900 American Eagle, except DWM on early-style toggle, no chamber markings. Estimated 8000 production.

Luger 1900 Swiss **$2100**
Same specifications as Luger 1900 American Eagle, except Swiss cross in sunburst over chamber. Estimated 9000 production.

Luger 1902 American Eagle **$4500**
Caliber: 9mm Luger. 8-shot magazine. 4-inch, heavy tapered barrel. 8³/₄ inches overall. Weight: 30 oz. Fixed rear sight, dovetailed front sight. Grip safety. Checkered walnut stocks. American Eagle over chamber, DWM on early-style toggle, narrow trigger, wide guard, no stock lug. Estimated 700 production.

Luger 1902 Carbine **$6300**
Caliber: 7.65mm. 8-shot magazine. 11³/₄-inch tapered barrel. 16¹/₂ inches overall. Weight: 46 oz. Adjustable 4-position rear sight, long ramp front sight. Grip safety. Checkered walnut stocks and forearm. DWM on early-style toggle, narrow trigger, wide guard, no chamber markings, stock lug. Estimated 3200 production.

Luger 1902 Cartridge Counter **$9300**
Caliber: 9mm Luger. 8-shot magazine. Heavy, tapered 4-inch barrel. 8³/₄ inches overall. Weight: 30 oz. Fixed rear sight, dovetailed front sight. Grip safety. Checkered walnut stocks. DWM on dished toggle with lock, American Eagle over chamber when marked; no stock lug. Estimated production unknown.

Luger 1902 Commercial **$4550**
Same basic specifications as Luger 1902 Cartridge Counter, except DWM on early-style toggle, narrow trigger, wide guard, no chamber markings, no stock lug. Estimated 400 production.

Luger 1903 American Eagle **$5500**
Same basic specifications as Luger 1902 Cartridge Counter, except American Eagle over chamber, DWM on early-style toggle, narrow trigger, wide guard, no stock lug. Estimated 700 production.

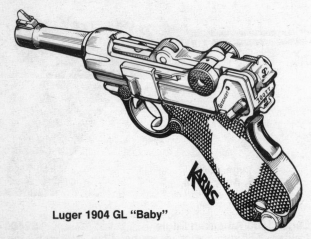
Luger 1904 GL "Baby"

Luger 1904 GL "Baby" **$150,000**
Caliber: 9mm Luger. 7-shot magazine. 3¹/₄-inch barrel. 7³/₄ inches overall. Weight: approx. 20 oz. Serial number 10077B. "GL" marked on rear of toggle. Georg Luger's personal sidearm. Only one made in 1904.

Luger 1904 Naval (Reworked) **$6500**
Caliber: 9mm Luger. 8-shot magazine. Barrel length altered to 4 inches. 8³/₄ inches overall. Weight: 30 oz. Adjustable two-position rear sight, dovetailed front sight. Thumb lever safety. Checkered walnut stocks. Heavy tapered barrel. DWM on new-style toggle with lock, 1902 over chamber. With or without grip safety and stock lug. Estimated 800 production.

Luger 1906 (11.35) **$45,000**
Caliber: 45 ACP. 6-shot magazine. 5-inch barrel. 9³/₄ inches overall. Weight: 36 oz. Fixed rear sight, dovetailed front sight. Grip safety. Checkered walnut stocks. GL monogram on rear toggle link, larger frame with altered trigger guard and trigger, no proofs, no markings over chamber. No stock lug. Estimated production 2.

Luger 1906 American Eagle (7.65) **$1495**
Caliber: 7.65mm. 8-shot magazine. Thin, 4³/₄-inch, tapered barrel. 9¹/₂ inches overall. Weight: 32 oz. Fixed rear sight, dovetailed front sight. Grip safety. Checkered walnut stocks. DWM on new-style toggle, American Eagle over chamber; no stock lug. Estimated 8000 production.

Luger 1906 American Eagle (9mm) **$2400**
Same basic specifications as the 7.65mm 1906, except in 9mm Luger with 4-inch barrel, 8³/₄ inches overall and weight of 30 ounces. Estimated 3500 production.

Luger 1906 Bern (7.65mm) **$750**
Same basic specifications as the 7.65mm 1906 American Eagle, except checkered walnut stocks with 3/8-inch borders, Swiss Cross on new-style toggle, Swiss proofs, no markings over chamber, no stock lug. Estimated 17,874 production.

Luger 1906 Brazilian (7.65mm) **$1350**
Same general specifications as the 7.65mm 1906 American Eagle, except with Brazilian proofs, no markings over chamber, no stock lug. Estimated 4500 production.

Luger 1906 Brazilian (9mm) **$1625**
Same basic specifications as the 9mm 1906 American Eagle, except with Brazilian proofs, no markings over chamber, no stock lug. Estimated production unknown.

Luger 1906 Commercial
Calibers: 7.65mm, 9mm. Same specifications as the 1906 American Eagle versions, above, except no chamber markings, no stock lug. Estimated production: 6000 (7.65mm); 3500 (9mm).
7.65mm **$1295**
9mm **1450**

Luger 1906 Dutch **$1425**
Caliber: 9mm Luger. Same specifications as the 9mm 1906 American Eagle, except tapered barrel with proofs, no markings over chamber, no stock lug. Estimated 3000 production.

Luger 1906 Loewe and Company **$3100**
Caliber: 7.65mm. 8-shot magazine. 6-inch tapered barrel. 10³/₄ inches overall. Weight: 35 oz. Adjustable two-position rear sight, dovetailed front sight. Grip safety. Checkered walnut stocks. Loewe & Company over chamber, Naval proofs, DWM on new-style toggle, no stock lug. Estimated production unknown.

Luger 1906 Naval **$2600**
Caliber: 9mm Luger. 8-shot magazine. 6-inch tapered barrel. 10³/₄ inches overall. Weight: 35 oz. Adjustable two-position rear sight, dovetailed front sight. Grip safety and thumb safety with lower marking (1st issue), higher marking (2nd issue). Checkered walnut stocks. No chamber markings, DWM on new-style toggle without lock; with stock lug. Estimated production: 8000 (1st issue); 12,000 (2nd issue).

Luger 1906 Naval Commercial **$2850**
Same basic specifications as the 1906 Naval, except lower marking on thumb safety, no chamber markings, DWM on new-style toggle, with stock lug and commercial proofs. Estimated 3000 production.

Luger 1906 Portuguese Army **$995**
Same specifications as the 7.65mm 1906 American Eagle, except with Portuguese proofs, crown and crest over chamber; no stock lug. Estimated 3500 production.

Luger 1906 Portuguese Naval **$7500**
Same specifications as the 9mm 1906 American Eagle, except with Portuguese proofs, crown and anchor over chamber; no stock lug. Estimated production unknown.

Luger 1906 Russian **$9500**
Same general specifications as the 9mm 1906 American Eagle, except thumb safety has markings concealed in up position, DWM on new-style toggle, DWM barrel proofs, crossed rifles over chamber. Est. prod. unknown.

Luger 1906 Swiss **$2200**
Same general specifications as the 7.65mm 1906 American Eagle Luger, except Swiss Cross in sunburst over chamber, no stock lug. Estimated 10,300 production.

Luger 1906 Swiss (Rework) **$3000**
Same basic specifications as the 7.65mm 1906 Swiss, except in barrel lengths of 3⁵/₈, 4 and 4³/₄ inches, overall length 8³/₈ inches and up, weight 32 oz. and up. DWM on new-style toggle, barrel with serial number and proof marks, Swiss Cross in sunburst or shield over chamber, no stock lug. Estimated production unknown.

Luger 1906 Swiss Police **$2400**
Same general specifications as the 7.65mm 1906 Swiss, except DWM on new-style toggle, Swiss Cross in matted field over chamber, no stock lug. Estimated 10,300 production.

Luger 1908 Bulgarian **$2145**
Caliber: 9mm Luger. 8-shot magazine. 4-inch tapered barrel. 8³/₄ inches overall. Weight: 30 oz. Fixed rear sight, dovetailed front sight. Thumb safety with lower marking concealed. Checkered walnut stocks. DWM chamber marking, no proofs, crown over shield on new-style toggle, lanyard loop, no stock lug. Estimated production unknown.

Luger 1908 Commercial **$995**
Same basic specifications as the 1908 Bulgarian, except higher marking on thumb safety. No chamber markings, commercial proofs, DWM on new-style toggle; no stock lug. Estimated 4000 production.

Luger 1908 Erfurt Military **$995**
Caliber: 9mm Luger. 8-shot magazine. 4-inch tapered barrel. 8³/₄ inches overall. Weight: 30 oz. Fixed rear sight, dovetailed front sight. Thumb safety with higher marking

Luger 1908 Erfurt Military (cont.)
concealed. Checkered walnut stocks. Serial number and proof marks on barrel, crown and Erfurt on new-style toggle, dated chamber; no stock lug. Estimated production unknown.

Luger 1908 Military
Same general specifications as the 9mm 1908 Erfurt Military Luger, except *1st and 2nd Issue* have thumb safety with higher marking concealed, serial number on barrel, no chamber markings, proofs on frame, DWM on new-style toggle; no stock lug. Estimated production: 10,000 (1st issue); 5000 (2nd issue). *3rd Issue* has serial number and proof marks on barrel, dates over chamber, DWM on new-style toggle; no stock lug. Estimated 3000 production.

1st Issue	**$1200**
2nd Issue	1400
3rd Issue	995

Luger 1908 Naval **$2895**
Same basic specifications as the 9mm 1908 Military Lugers, except with 6-inch barrel, adjustable two-position rear sight, no chamber markings, DWM on new-style toggle; with stock lug. Estimated 26,000 production.

Luger 1908 Naval (Commercial) **$3750**
Same specifications as the 1908 Naval Luger, except no chamber markings or date. Commercial proofs, DWM on new-style toggle; with stock lug. Est. 1900 produced.

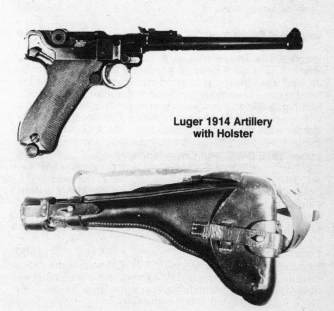

**Luger 1914 Artillery
with Holster**

Luger 1914 Erfurt Artillery **$1550**
Caliber: 9mm Luger. 8-shot magazine. 8-inch tapered barrel. 12³/₄ inches overall. Weight: 40 oz. Artillery rear sight, dovetailed front sight. Thumb safety with higher marking concealed. Checkered walnut stocks. Serial number and proof marks on barrel, crown and Erfurt on new-style toggle, dated chamber, with stock lug. Estimated production unknown.

Luger 1914 Erfurt Military **$795**
Same specifications as the 1914 Erfurt Artillery, except with 4-inch barrel and corresponding length, weight, etc., and fixed rear sight. Estimated 3000 production.

Luger 1914 Naval **$2195**
Same specifications as 9mm 1914 Lugers, except has 6-inch barrel with corresponding length and weight, and adjustable two-position rear sight. Dated chamber, DWM on new-style toggle; with stock lug. Est. 40,000 produced.

Luger 1914-1918 DWM Artillery **$1175**
Caliber: 9mm Luger. 8-shot magazine. 8-inch tapered barrel. 12³/₄ inches overall. Weight: 40 oz. Artillery rear sight, dovetailed front sight. Thumb safety with higher marking concealed. Checkered walnut stocks. Serial number and proof marks on barrel, DWM on new-style toggle, dated chamber; with stock lug. Estimated 3000 production.

Luger 1914-1918 DWM Military **$850**
Same specifications as the 9mm 1914-1918 DWM Artillery, except with 4-inch tapered barrel and corresponding length, weight, etc., and fixed rear sight. Estimated production unknown.

Luger 1920 Carbine
Caliber: 7.65mm. 8-shot magazine. 11³/₄-inch tapered barrel. 15³/₄ inches overall. Weight: 44 oz. Four-position rear sight, long ramp front sight. Grip (or thumb) safety. Checkered walnut stocks and forearm. Serial numbers and proof marks on barrel, no chamber markings, various proofs, DWM on new-style toggle; with stock lug. Estimated production unknown.
Carbine With Forearm **$7500**
Carbine Less Forearm 3500

Luger 1920 Commercial **$610**
Calibers: 7.65mm, 9mm Luger. 8-shot magazine. Barrel lengths: 3⁵/₈, 3³/₄, 4, 4³/₄, 6, 8, 10, 12, 16, 18, 20 inches; tapered. Overall length: 8³/₈ to 24³/₄ inches. Weight: 30 oz. and up. Varying rear sight configurations, dovetailed front sight. Thumb safety. Checkered walnut stocks. Serial numbers and proof marks on barrel, no chamber markings, various proofs, DWM or crown over Erfurt on new-style toggle; with stock lug. Est. production not documented.

Luger 1920 DWM and Erfurt Military **$795**
Caliber: 9mm Luger. 8-shot magazine. 4-inch tapered barrel. 8³/₄ inches overall. Weight: 30 oz. Fixed rear sight, dovetailed front sight. Thumb safety. Checkered walnut stocks. Serial numbers and proof marks on barrel, dated chamber, various proofs, DWM or crown over Erfurt on new-style toggle; with stock lug. Est. 3000 production.

Luger 1920 Police **$900**
Same specifications as 9mm 1920 DWM with some dated chambers, various proofs, DWM or crown over Erfurt on new-style toggle, identifying marks on grip frame; with stock lug. Estimated 3000 production.

Luger 1923 Commerical **$695**
Calibers: 7.65mm and 9mm Luger. 8-shot magazine. Barrel lengths: 3⁵/₈, 3³/₄, 4, 6, 8, 12 and 16 inches; tapered. Overall length: 8³/₈ inches and up. Weight: 30 oz. and up. Various rear sight configurations, dovetailed front sight. Thumb lever safety. Checkered walnut stocks. DWM on new-style toggle, serial number and proofs on barrel, no chamber markings, with stock lug. Estimated 15,000 production.

Luger 1923 Dutch Commerical **$2000**
Same basic specifications as 1923 Commercial Luger, with same caliber offerings, but only 3⁵/₈- or 4-inch barrel. Fixed rear sight, thumb lever safety with arrow markings. Estimated production unknown.

Luger 1923 Krieghoff Commercial **$1950**
Same specifications as 1923 Commercial Luger, with same caliber offerings but barrel lengths of 3⁵/₈, 4, 6, and 8 inches. "K" marked on new-style toggle; serial number, proofs and Germany on barrel; no chamber markings; with stock lug. Estimated production unknown.

Luger 1923 Safe and Loaded **$1100**
Same caliber offerings, barrel lengths and specifications as the 1923 Commercial, except thumb lever safety with safe markings. Other markings the same; with stock lug. Estimated 10,000 production.

Luger 1923 Stoeger

Luger 1923 Stoeger **$2900**
Same general specifications as the 1923 Commercial Luger, with the same caliber offerings and barrel lengths of 3³/₄, 4, 6, and 8 inches. Thumb lever safety. DWM on new-style toggle, serial number and/or proof marks on barrel, American Eagle over chamber usually; no stock lug. Estimated production unknown.

Luger 1926 "Baby" Prototype **$85,000**
Calibers: 7.65mm Browning and 9mm Browning (short). 5-shot magazine. 2¹⁵/₁₆ inches overall. About 6¹/₄ inches overall. Small-sized frame and toggle assembly. Prototype for a Luger "pocket pistol," but never manufactured commercially. Checkered walnut grips, slotted for safety. Only four known to exist, but possibly as many as a dozen could have been made.

Luger 1929 Swiss **$1350**
Caliber: 7.65mm. 8-shot magazine. 4³/₄-inch tapered barrel. 9¹/₂ inches overall. Weight: 32 oz. Fixed rear sight, dovetailed front sight. Long grip safety and thumb lever with S markings. Stepped receiver and straight grip frame. Checkered plastic stocks. Swiss Cross in shield on new-style toggle, serial numbers and proofs on barrel, no markings over chamber; no stock lug. Est. 1900 prod.

**Luger 1934 Krieghoff Commercial
(Side Frame)** **$6995**
Caliber: 7.65mm and 9mm Luger. 8-shot magazine. Barrel lengths: 4, 6, and 8 inches. Overall length: 8³/₄ inch and up. Weight: 30 oz. and up. Various rear sight configurations, dovetailed front sight. Thumb lever safety. Checkered brown plastic stocks. Anchor with H K Krieghoff Suhl on new-style toggle, no chamber markings, tapered barrel with serial number and proofs; with stock lug. Estimated 1700 production.

Luger 1934 Krieghoff S
Caliber: 9mm Luger. 8-shot magazine. 4-inch tapered barrel. 8³/₄ inches overall. Weight: 30 oz. Fixed rear sight, dovetailed front sight. Thumb lever safety. Anchor with

Luger 1934 Krieghoff S (cont.)
H K Krieghoff Suhl on new-style toggle, S dated chamber, barrel proofs; stock lug. *Early Model:* Checkered walnut or plastic stocks. Estimated 2500 production. *Late Model:* Checkered brown plastic stocks. Est. 1200 production.
Early Model **$1850**
Late Model **1750**

Luger 1934 byf **$895**
Caliber: 9mm Luger. 8-shot magazine. 4-inch tapered barrel. 8¾ inches overall. Weight: 30 oz. Fixed rear sight, dovetailed front sight. Thumb lever safety. Checkered walnut or plastic stocks. byf on new-style toggle, serial number and proofs on barrel, 41-42 dated chamber; stock lug. Estimated 3000 production.

Luger 1934 Mauser 42 .... **$1500**
Caliber: 9mm Luger. 8-shot magazine. 4-inch tapered barrel. 8¾ inches overall. Weight: 30 oz. Fixed rear sight, dovetailed front sight. Thumb lever safety. Checkered walnut or plastic stocks. 42 on new-style toggle, serial number and proofs on barrel, 1939-40 dated chamber markings; stock lug. Estimated 3000 production.

Luger 1934 Mauser 42 (Dated) **$2300**
Same specifications as Luger 1934 Mauser 42, above, except 41 dated chamber markings; stock lug. Estimated production unknown.

Luger 1934 Mauser Banner (Military) **$1595**
Same specifications as Luger 1934 Mauser 42, except Mauser in banner on new-style toggle, tapered barrel with serial number and proofs usually, dated chamber markings; stock lug. Estimated production unknown.

Luger 1934 Mauser Commercial **$2800**
Same specifications as Luger 1934 Mauser 42, except checkered walnut stocks. Mauser in banner on new-style toggle, tapered barrel with serial number and proofs usually, no chamber markings; stock lug. Estimated production unknown.

Luger 1934 Mauser Dutch **$1395**
Same specifications as Luger 1934 Mauser 42, except checkered walnut stocks. Mauser in banner on new-style toggle, tapered barrel with caliber, 1940 dated chamber markings; stock lug. Estimated production unknown.

Luger 1934 Mauser Latvian **$3000**
Caliber: 7.65mm. 8-shot magazine. 4-inch tapered barrel. 8¾ inches overall. Weight: 30 oz. Fixed, square-notched rear sight, dovetailed Patridge front sight. Thumb lever safety. Checkered walnut stocks. Mauser in banner on new-style toggle, 1937 dated chamber markings; stock lug. Estimated production unknown.

Luger 1934 Mauser (Oberndorf) **$2100**
Same specifications as Luger 1934 Mauser 42, except checkered walnut stocks. Oberndorf 1934 on new-style toggle, tapered barrel with proofs and caliber, Mauser in banner over chamber; stock lug. Est. 6000 produced.

Luger 1934 Simson-S Toggle **$1800**
Same specifications as Luger 1934 Mauser 42, except checkered walnut stocks. S on new-style toggle, tapered barrel with serial number and proofs, no chamber markings; stock lug. Estimated 10,000 production.

Luger 42 Mauser Banner **$1350**
Same specifications as Luger 1934 Mauser 42, except weight 32 oz.; Mauser in banner on new-style toggle, tapered barrel with serial number and proofs usually, dated chamber markings; stock lug. Estimated production unknown.

Luger Abercrombie and Fitch **$4795**
Calibers: 7.65mm and 9mm Luger. 8-shot magazine. 4¾-inch tapered barrel. 9½ inches overall. Weight: 32 oz. Fixed rear sight, dovetailed front sight. Grip safety. Checkered walnut stocks. DWM on new-style toggle, Abercrombie & Fitch markings on barrel, Swiss Cross in sunburst over chamber; no stock lug. Est. 100 production.

Luger Dutch Royal Air Force **$1150**
Caliber: 9mm Luger. 8-shot magazine. 4-inch tapered barrel. 8¾ inches overall. Weight: 30 oz. Fixed rear sight, dovetailed front sight. Grip safety and thumb safety with markings and arrow. Checkered walnut stocks. DWM on new-style toggle, barrel dated with serial number and proofs, no markings over chamber, no stock lug. Estimated 4000 production.

Luger DWM (G Date) **$825**
Caliber: 9mm Luger. 8-shot magazine. 4-inch tapered barrel. 8¾ inches overall. Weight: 30 oz. Fixed rear sight, dovetailed front sight. Thumb lever safety. Checkered walnut stocks. DWM on new-style toggle, serial number and proofs on barrel, G (1935 date) over chamber; with stock lug. Estimated production unknown.

Luger DWM and Erfurt **$895**
Caliber: 9mm Luger. 8-shot magazine. Barrel length: 4 or 6 inches, tapered. Overall length: 8¾, 10¾ inches. Weight: 30 or 38 oz. Fixed rear sight, dovetailed front sight. Thumb safety. Checkered walnut stocks. Serial numbers and proof marks on barrel, double dated chamber, various proofs, DWM or crown over Erfurt on new-style toggle; with stock lug. Estimated production unknown.

Luger Krieghoff 36 .... **$2150**
Caliber: 9mm Luger. 8-shot magazine. 4-inch tapered barrel. 8¾ inches overall. Weight: 30 oz. Fixed rear sight, dovetailed front sight. Thumb lever safety. Checkered brown plastic stocks. Anchor with H K Krieghoff Suhl on new-style toggle, 36 dated chamber, serial number and proofs on barrel; stock lug. Estimated 700 production.

Luger Krieghoff—Dated 1936-1945 .... **$1950**
Same specifications as Luger Krieghoff 36, except 1936-1945 dated chamber, barrel proofs. Est. 8600 production.

Luger Krieghoff (Grip Safety) **$3625**
Same specifications as Luger Krieghoff 36, except grip safety and thumb lever safety. No chamber markings, tapered barrel with serial number, proofs and caliber; no stock lug. Estimated production unknown.

Luger Mauser Banner (Grip Safety) **$2800**
Caliber: 7.65mm. 8-shot magazine. 4¾-inch tapered barrel. 9½ inches overall. Weight: 30 oz. Fixed rear sight, dovetailed front sight. Grip safety and thumb lever safety. Checkered walnut stocks. Mauser in banner on new-style toggle, serial number and proofs on barrel, 1939 dated chamber markings; no stock lug. Estimated production unknown.

Luger Mauser Banner 42 (Dated) **$1295**
Caliber: 9mm Luger. 8-shot magazine. 4-inch tapered barrel. 8³/₄ inches overall. Weight: 30 oz. Fixed rear sight, dovetailed front sight. Thumb lever safety. Checkered walnut or plastic stocks. Mauser in banner on new-style toggle, serial number and proofs on barrel usually, 42 dated chamber markings; stock lug. Est. production unknown.

Luger Mauser Banner (Swiss Proof) **$1800**
Same specifications as Luger Mauser Banner 42, above, except checkered walnut stocks and 1939 dated chamber.

Luger Mauser Freise **$3000**
Same specifications as Mauser Banner 42, except checkered walnut stocks, tapered barrel with proofs on sight block and Freise above chamber. Estimated production unknown.

**German Luger S/42
Dated 1936**

Luger S/42
Caliber: 9mm Luger. 8-shot magazine. 4-inch tapered barrel. 8³/₄ inches overall. Weight: 30 oz. Fixed rear sight, dovetailed front sight. Thumb lever safety. Checkered walnut stocks. S/42 on new-style toggle, serial number and proofs on barrel; stock lug. *Dated Model:* has dated chamber; estimated 3000 production. *G Date:* has G (1935 date) over chamber; estimated 3000 production. *K Date:* has K (1934 date) over chamber; prod. figures unknown.
Dated Model . . . . **$ 895**
G Date Model **825**
K Date Model **1895**

Luger Russian Commercial **$2000**
Caliber: 7.65mm. 8-shot magazine. 3⁵/₈-inch tapered barrel. 8³/₈ inches overall. Weight: 30 oz. Fixed rear sight, dovetailed front sight. Thumb lever safety. Checkered walnut stocks. DWM on new-style toggle, Russian proofs on barrel, no chamber markings; with stock lug. Estimated production unknown.

Luger Simson and Company **$1295**
Calibers: 7.65mm and 9mm Luger. 8-shot magazine. Weight: 32 oz. Fixed rear sight, dovetailed front sight. Thumb lever safety. Checkered walnut stocks. Simson & Company Suhl on new-style toggle, serial number and proofs on barrel, date over chamber usually; with stock lug. Estimated 10,000 production.

Luger Vickers-Dutch **$2450**
Caliber: 9mm Luger. 8-shot magazine. 4-inch tapered barrel. 8³/₄ inches overall. Weight: 30 oz. Fixed rear sight, dovetailed front sight. Grip safety and thumb lever with arrow markings. Checkered walnut stocks (coarse). Vickers LTD on new-style toggle, no chamber markings, dated barrel; no stock lug. Estimated 10,000 production.

LUNA FREE PISTOL
Zella-Mehlis, Germany
Originally mfd. by Ernst Friedr. Büchel and later by Udo Anschütz

Luna Model 300 Free Pistol

Luna Model 300 Free Pistol **$1150**
Single shot. System Aydt action. Set trigger. Caliber: 22 LR. 11-inch barrel. Weight: 40 oz. Target sights. Blued finish. Checkered and carved walnut stock and forearm; improved design with adjustable hand base on later models of Udo Anschütz manufacture. Made prior to WW II.

M.A.C./DEFENSE SYSTEMS INTL.
Marietta, Georgia

M.A.C. Ingram Model 10A1S

M.A.C. Ingram Model 10A1S Semiautomatic **$795**
Caliber: 9mm or 45 ACP. 30- or 32-round magazine. 5³/₄-inch barrel. 10¹/₂ inches overall. Weight: 6¹/₄ pounds. Front protected post sight, fixed aperture rear sight. Manually operated Garand-type safety in trigger guard. Based on Military Armament Corporation's Ingram 10 design.

MAGNUM RESEARCH INC.
Minneapolis, Minnesota

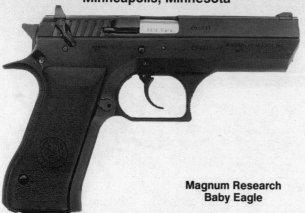

**Magnum Research
Baby Eagle**

Magnum Research Baby Eagle Semiautomatic . **$425**
DA. Calibers: 9mm, 40 S&W, 41 AE. 15-shot magazine (9mm), 9-shot magazine (40 S&W), 10-shot magazine (41 AE). 4.75-inch barrel. 8.15 inches overall. Weight: 35.4 oz. Combat sights. Matte blued finish.

**Magnum Research
Desert Eagle**

Magnum Research Desert Eagle Semiautomatic
Calibers: 357 Mag., 41 Mag., 44 Mag., 50 Action Express (AE). 8- or 9-shot magazine. Gas-operated. Barrel lengths: 6 (standard), 10 and 14 inches; polygonal. 10.6 inches overall w/6-inch barrel. Weight (w/6-inch bbl.): 357 Mag.—52 oz. w/alum. alloy frame, 62 oz. w/steel frame; 41/44 Mag.–56 oz. w/alloy; 67 oz. w/steel. Fixed or adjustable combat sights. Combat-type trigger guard. Finish: Military black oxide, nickel, chrome, stainless or blued. Wraparound rubber stocks. Made by Israel Military Industries from 1984 to date.
357 Standard (steel) or Alloy (6-inch bbl.)	**$595**
357 Stainless Steel (6-inch bbl.)	675
41 Mag. Standard (steel) or Alloy (6-inch bbl.)	650
41 Mag. Stainless Steel (6-inch bbl.)	725
44 Mag. Standard (steel) or Alloy (6-inch bbl.)	625
44 Mag. Stainless Steel (6-inch bbl.)	695
50 AE Magnum Standard	950
Add for 10-inch Barrel	100
Add for 14-inch Barrel	125

**Magnum Research Mountain Eagle
Semiautomatic** . **$175**
Caliber: 22 LR. 15-shot polycarbonate resin magazine. 6.5-inch injection-molded polymer and steel barrel. 10.6 inches overall. Weight: 21 oz. Sights: ramp blade front; adjustable rear. Injection-molded, checkered and textured grip. Matte black finish. Made from 1992 to date.

**Magnum Research
Mountain Eagle**

**Magnum Reasearch
Lone Eagle**

Magnum Research SSP-91 Lone Eagle Pistol
Single-shot action with interchangeable rotating breech-barrel assembly. Calibers: 22 LR, 22 Mag., 22 Hornet, 22-250, 223 Rem., 243 Rem., 6mm BR, 7mm-08, 7mm BR, 30-06, 30-30, 308 Win., 35 Rem., 357 Mag., 44 Mag., 444 Marlin. 14-inch interchangeable barrel assembly. 15 inches overall. Weight: 4½ lbs.
SSP-91 S/S Pistol (Complete)	**$255**
14-inch Barrel Assembly	190
Stock Assembly	65

MAUSER PISTOLS
Oberndorf, Germany
Waffenfabrik Mauser of Mauser-Werke A.G.

Mauser Model 80-SA

Mauser Model 80-SA Automatic . **$330**
Caliber: 9mm Para. 13-shot magazine. 4.66-inch barrel. 8 inches overall. Weight: about 31.5 oz. Blued finish. Hardwood grips. Made 1991–94.

Mauser Model 90-DA

Mauser Model 90-DA Automatic **$375**
Caliber: 9mm Para. 14-shot magazine. 4.66-inch barrel. 8 inches overall. Weight: 35 oz. Blued finish. Hardwood grips. Made 1991–94.

Mauser Model 90 DAC Compact **$385**
Caliber: 9mm Para. 14-shot magazine. 4.13-inch barrel. 7.4 inches overall. Weight: 33¼ oz. Blued finish. Hardwood grips. Made 1991–94.

Mauser Model 1898 Military

Mauser Model 1898 Military Auto Pistol **$2595**
Caliber: 7.63mm Mauser; also chambered for 9mm Mauser and 9mm Luger; the latter is identified by a large red "9" in the stocks. Box magazine, 10-shot. 5¼-inch barrel. 12 inches overall. Weight: 45 oz. Adjustable rear sight. Blued finish. Walnut stocks. Made 1898–1945. *Note:* Specialist collectors recognize a number of variations at higher values. Price here is for more common type.

Mauser Model HSc

Mauser Model HSc Double Action Auto Pistol . . **$450**
Calibers: 32 Auto (7.65mm), 380 Auto (9mm Short). 8-shot (32) or 7-shot (380) magazine. 3.4-inch barrel. 6.4 inches overall. Weight: 23.6 oz. Fixed sights. Blued or nickel finish. Checkered walnut stocks. Made 1938–1945; from 1968 to date.

Mauser Luger Lange Pistole 08

Mauser Luger Lange Pistole 08 . . . . **$1995**
Caliber: 9mm Para. 8-inch barrel. Checkered grips. Blued finish. Accessorized w/walnut shoulder stock, front sight tool, spare magazine, leather case. Currently in production. Commemorative version made in limited quantities w/ ivory grips and 14-carat gold monogram plate.

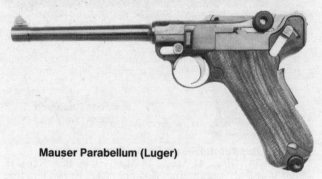

Mauser Parabellum (Luger)

Mauser Parabellum (Luger) Auto Pistol **$1000**
Current commercial model. Swiss pattern with grip safety. Calibers: 7.65mm Luger, 9mm Luger. 8-shot magazine. Barrel lengths: 4-, 6-inch. 8¾ inches overall w/4-inch bbl. Weight: 30 oz. w/4-inch bbl. Fixed sights. Blued finish. Checkered walnut stocks. Made from 1970 to date. *Note:* Pistols of this model sold in the U.S. have the American Eagle stamped on the receiver.

Mauser Pocket Model 1910 Auto Pistol **$345**
Caliber: 25 Auto (6.35mm). 9-shot magazine. 3.1-inch barrel. 5.4 inches overall. Weight: 15 oz. Fixed sights. Blued finish. Checkered walnut or hard rubber stocks. Made 1910–1934.

Mauser Pocket Model 1914 Automatic **$325**
Similar to Pocket Model 1910. Caliber: 32 Auto (7.65mm). 8-shot magazine. 3.4-inch bbl. 6 inches overall. Weight: 21 oz. Fixed sights. Blued finish. Checkered walnut or hard rubber stocks. Made 1914–1934.

Mauser Pocket Model 1934 . . . . **$365**
Similar to Pocket Models 1910 and 1914 in the respective calibers. Chief difference is in the more streamlined one-piece stocks. Made 1934–c. 1939.

Mauser WTP Model I

Mauser WTP Model I Auto Pistol **$395**
"Westentaschen-Pistole" (Vest Pocket Pistol). Caliber:
25 Automatic (6.35mm). 6-shot magazine. 2½-inch barrel.
4½ inches overall. Weight: 11½ oz. Blued finish. Hard
rubber stocks. Made c. 1922–1937.

Mauser WTP Model II

Mauser WTP Model II Auto Pistol **$550**
Similar to Model I, but smaller and lighter. Caliber: 25
Automatic (6.35mm). 6-shot magazine. 2-inch barrel. 4
inches overall. Weight: 9½ oz. Blued finish. Hard rubber
stocks. Made 1938–1940.

MITCHELL ARMS, INC.
Santa Ana, California

Mitchell Arms Model 1911 Gold Signature
Caliber: 45 ACP. 8-shot magazine. 5-inch barrel. 8.75
inches overall. Weight: 39 oz. Interchangeable blade front
sight; drift adjustable combat or fully adjustable rear.
Smooth or checkered walnut grips. Blued or stainless fin-
ish. Made from 1994 to date.
Blued Model w/Fixed Sights **$365**
Blued Model w/Adj. Sights **400**
Stainless Model w/Fixed Sights **390**
Stainless Model w/Adj. Sights **425**

Mitchell Arms Alpha Model
Dual action w/interchangeable trigger modules. Caliber:
45 ACP. 8-shot magazine. 5-inch barrel. 8.75 inches over-
all. Weight: 39 oz. Interchangeable blade front sight; drift
adjustable rear. Smooth or checkered walnut grips. Blued
or stainless finish. Made from 1994 to date.
Blued Model w/Fixed Sights **$495**
Blued Model w/Adj. Sights **550**
Stainless Model w/Fixed Sights **540**
Stainless Model w/Adj. Sights **575**

Mitchell Arms American Eagle Pistol **$495**
Stainless-steel re-creation of the American Eagle Parabellum auto pistol. Caliber: 9mm Parabellum. 7-shot
magazine. 4-inch barrel. 9.6 inches overall. Weight: 26.6
oz. Blade front sight, fixed rear. Stainless finish. Checkered walnut grips. Discontinued 1994.

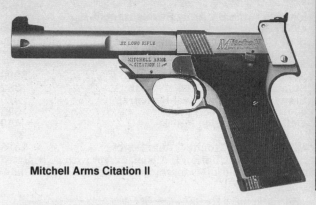

Mitchell Arms Citation II

Mitchell Arms Citation II Auto Pistol **$295**
Re-creation of the High Standard Supermatic Citation
Military. Caliber: 22 LR. 10-shot magazine. 5.5-inch bull
barrel or 7.25 fluted barrel. 9.75 inches overall (5.5-inch
bbl.). Weight: 44.5 oz. Ramp front sight, slide-mounted
micro-adj. rear. Satin blue or stainless finish. Checkered
walnut grips w/thumbrest. Made from 1992 to date.

Mitchell Arms Olympic I.S.U. Auto Pistol **$435**
Similar to the Citation II Model, except chambered in 22
Short. 6.75-inch round tapered barrel with stabilizer and
removable counterweights. Made from 1992 to date.

Mitchell Arms Sharpshooter II

Mitchell Arms Sharpshooter II Auto Pistol **$275**
Re-creation of the High Standard Sharpshooter. Caliber:
22 LR. 10-shot magazine. 5-inch bull barrel. 10.25 inches
overall. Weight: 42 oz. Ramp front sight, slide-mounted
micro-adj. rear. Satin blue or stainless finish. Checkered
walnut grips w/thumbrest. Made from 1992 to date.

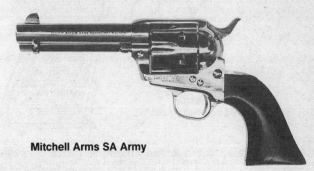

Mitchell Arms SA Army

Mitchell Arms Single Action Army Revolver
Calibers: 357 Mag., 44 Mag., 45 Colt/45 ACP. 6-shot cylinder. Barrel lengths: 4¾, 5½, 7½ inches. Weight: 40–

Mitchell Arms SA Army Revolver (cont.)

43 oz. Sights: blade front; grooved topstrap or adjustable rear. Blued or nickel finish w/color-casehardened frame. Brass or steel backstrap/trigger guard. Smooth one-piece walnut grips.

Standard Model w/Blued Finish **$295**
Standard Model w/Nickel Finish **350**
Standard Model w/Steel Backstrap **420**
45 Combo w/Blued Finish **395**
45 Combo w/Nickel Finish **450**

Mitchell Arms Trophy II Auto Pistol **$325**

Similar to the Citation II Model, except with gold-plated trigger and gold-filled markings. Made from 1992 to date.

Mitchell Arms Victor II

Mitchell Arms Victor II Auto Pistol **$395**

Re-creation of the High Standard Victor with full-length vent rib. Caliber: 22 LR. 10-shot magazine. 4.5- or 5.5-inch barrel. 9.75 inches overall (5.5-inch bbl.). Weight: 52 oz.(5.5-inch bbl.) Rib-mounted target sights. Satin blue or stainless finish. Checkered walnut grips w/thumbrest.

MKE PISTOL
Ankara, Turkey
Mfd. by Makina ve Kimya Endüstrisi Kurumu

MKE Kirikkale
Double Action Automatic*

MKE Kirikkale Double Action Automatic Pistol .. **$295**

Similar to Walther PP. Calibers: 32 Auto (7.65mm), 380 Auto (9mm Short). 7-shot magazine. 3.9-inch barrel. 6.7 inches overall. Weight: 24 oz. Fixed sights. Blued finish. Checkered plastic stocks. Made 1948 to date. *Note:* This is a Turkish Army standard service pistol.

MOA CORPORATION
Dayton, Ohio

MOA Maximum Pistol

MOA Maximum Single Shot Pistol **$475**

Calibers: 22 Hornet to 358 Win. 10- or 14-inch Douglas barrel. Weight: 3 lbs. 13 oz.–4 lbs. 3 oz. Smooth walnut grips. Currently in production.

MOA Maximum Carbine Pistol **$495**

Similar to Maximum Pistol, but with 18-inch barrel. Currently in production.

O.F. MOSSBERG & SONS, INC.
New Haven, Connecticut

Mossberg "Brownie" DA Derringer **$325**

Hammerless, top-break, four-barrel derringer w/rotating firing pin. Caliber: 22 LR. 2½-inch barrels. 4½ inches overall. Weight: 15 oz. Blued finish. Serrated wood grips. Made 1919–1932.

NAVY ARMS COMPANY
Ridgefield, New Jersey

Navy Arms Model 1873 Single Action Revolver

Calibers: 44-40, 45 Colt. 6-shot cylinder. Barrel lengths: 3, 4¾, 5½, 7½ inches. 10¾ inches overall (5½-inch bbl.). Weight: 36 oz. Sights: blade front; grooved topstrap rear. Blued w/color-casehardened frame or nickel finish. Smooth walnut grips. Made from 1991 to date.

Blued Finish w/Brass Backstrap **$295**
U.S. Artillery Model w/5-inch bbl. **395**
U.S. Cavalry Model w/7-inch bbl. **400**

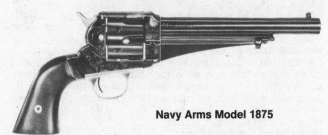

Navy Arms Model 1875

Navy Arms Model 1875 Schofield Revolver

Replica of S&W Model 3. Top-break single-action w/auto ejector. Calibers: 44-40 or 45 LC. 6-shot cylinder. 5- or 7-inch barrel. 10¾ or 12¾ inches overall. Weight: 39 oz. Blade front sight; square-notched rear. Polished blued finish. Smooth walnut stocks. Made 1994 to date.

Cavalry Model (7-inch bbl.) **$515**
Wells Fargo Model (5-inch bbl.) **495**

Navy Arms Model 1875 Single Action Revolver . $295
Replica of Remington Model 1875. Calibers: 357 Magnum, 44-40, 45 Colt. 6-shot cylinder. 7 1/2-inch barrel. 13 1/2 inches overall. Weight: about 48 oz. Fixed sights. Blued or nickel finish. Smooth walnut stocks. Made in Italy c. 1955–1980. *Note:* Originally marketed in the U.S. as Replica Arms Model 1875; that firm was acquired by Navy Arms Co.

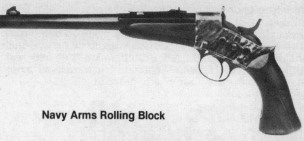

Navy Arms Rolling Block

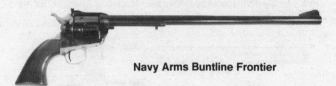

Navy Arms Buntline Frontier

Navy Arms Buntline Frontier $375
Same as Target Frontier, except has detachable shoulder stock and 16 1/2-inch barrel. Calibers: 357 Magnum and 45 Colt only. Made 1975–79.

Navy Arms Rolling Block Single Shot Pistol $180
Calibers: 22 LR, 22 Hornet, 357 Magnum. 8-inch barrel. 12 inches overall. Weight: about 40 oz. Adjustable sights. Blued barrel, color-casehardened frame, brass trigger guard. Smooth walnut stock/forearm. Made 1965–1980.

Navy Arms TT-Olympia Pistol $225
Reproduction of the Walther Olympia Target Pistol. Caliber: 22 LR. 4.6-inch barrel. 8 inches overall. Weight: 28 oz. Blade front sight, adjustable rear. Blued finish. Checkered hardwood grips. Made from 1992 to date.

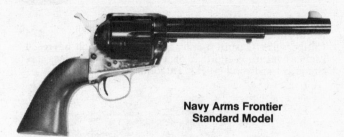

**Navy Arms Frontier
Standard Model**

NEW ENGLAND FIREARMS
Gardner, Massachusetts

Navy Arms Frontier SA Revolver $230
Calibers: 22 LR, 22 WMR, 357 Mag., 45 Colt. 6-shot cylinder. Barrel lengths: 4 1/2-, 5 1/2-, 7 1/2-inch. 10 1/4 inches overall w/4 1/2-inch bbl. Weight: about 36 oz. w/4 1/2-inch bbl. Fixed sights. Blued barrel and cylinder, color-casehardened frame, brass grip frame. One-piece smooth walnut stock. Made 1975–79.

**New England Firearms
Model R73**

**Navy Arms Frontier
Target Model**

New England Firearms Model R73 Revolver $125
Caliber: 32 H&R Mag. 5-shot cylinder. 2 1/2- or 4-inch barrel. 8 1/2 inches overall w/4-inch bbl. Weight: 26 oz. w/4-inch bbl. Fixed or adjustable sights. Blued or nickel finish. Walnut-finish hardwood stocks. Made from 1988 to date.

New England Firearms Model R92 Revolver $110
Same general specifications as Model R73, except chambered for 22 LR. 9-shot cylinder. Weight: 28 oz. with 4-inch barrel.

Navy Arms Frontier Target Model $250
Same as Standard Frontier, except has adjustable rear sight and ramp front sight. Made 1975–79.

Navy Arms Luger (Standard) Automatic $165
Caliber: 22 LR, standard or high velocity. 10-shot magazine. Barrel: 4.5 inches. 8.9 inches overall. Weight: 1 lb. 13 1/2 oz. Square blade front sight w/square notch, stationary rear sight. Walnut checkered grips. Non-reflecting black finish. Discontinued 1983.

**New England Firearms
Ultra (Nickel)**

New England Firearms Ultra Revolver **$130**
Calibers: 22 LR, 22 WRF. 9-shot cylinder in 22 LR, 6-shot cylinder in 22 WRF. 4- or 6-inch ribbed bull barrel. 10⅝ inches overall w/6-inch bbl. Weight: 36 oz. w/6-inch bbl. Blade front sight; adjustable square-notched rear. Blued or nickel finish. Walnut-finish hardwood grips. Made 1989 to date. (*See* photo, preceding page.)

**New England Firearms
Lady Ultra**

New England Firearms Lady Ultra Revolver **$150**
Same basic specifications as the Ultra, except in 32 H&R Mag. w/5-shot cylinder and 3-inch ribbed bull barrel. 7½ inches overall. Weight: 31 oz. Made from 1992 to date.

NORTH AMERICAN ARMS
Spanish Fork, Utah

North American Arms Model 22LR

North American Arms Model 22LR **$125**
Same as Model 22S, except chambered for 22 LR, is 3⅞ inches overall, weighs 4½ oz. Made 1976 to date.

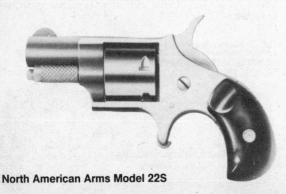

North American Arms Model 22S

**North American Arms Model 22S Mini
Revolver** **$155**
SA. Caliber: 22 Short. 5-shot cylinder. 1⅛-inch barrel. 3½ inches overall. Weight: 4 oz. Fixed sights. Stainless steel. Plastic stocks. Made from 1975 to date.

North American Arms 450 Magnum Express . . . **$850**
SA. Calibers: 450 Magnum Express, 45 Win. Mag. 7½-inch barrel. Matte stainless steel finish. Cased. Discontinued 1986.

North American Arms Model 454C

North American Arms Model 454C SA **$745**
Caliber: 454 Casull. 5-shot cylinder. 7½-inch barrel. 14 inches overall. Weight: 50 oz. Fixed sights. Stainless steel. Smooth hardwood stocks. Introduced 1977.

**North American Arms
Black Widow**

**North American Arms
Mini-Master**

North American Arms Black Widow Revolver
SA. Calibers: 22 LR, 22 WMR. 5-shot cylinder. 2-inch heavy vent barrel. 5⅞ inches overall. Weight: 8.8 oz. Fixed or adjustable sights. Full-size black rubber grips. Stainless steel brush finish. Made from 1990 to date.

North American Arms Black Widow (cont.)
Adjustable Sight Model **$210**
Adjustable Sight Combo Model **220**
Fixed Sight Model **195**
Fixed Sight Combo Model..................... **200**

North American Arms Mini-Master Revolver
SA. Calibers: 22 LR, 22 WMR. 5-shot cylinder. 4-inch heavy vent-rib barrel. 7³/₄ inches overall. Weight: 10³/₄ inches. Fixed or adjustable sights. Black rubber grips. Stainless steel brush finish. Made from 1990 to date.
Adjustable Sight Model **$205**
Adjustable Sight Combo Model **250**
Fixed Sight Model **210**
Fixed Sight Combo Model..................... **245**

NORWEGIAN MILITARY PISTOLS
Mfd. by Kongsberg Vaapenfabrikk, the government arsenal at Kongsberg, Norway

Norwegian Model 1914

Norwegian Model 1914 Automatic Pistol **$325**
Similar to Colt Model 1911 45 Automatic with same general specifications, except has lengthened slide stop. Made 1919–1946.

Norwegian Model 1912 is same except has conventional slide stop. Since only 500 were made, this is a very rare collector's item.

ORTGIES PISTOLS
Erfurt, Germany
Manufactured by Deutsche Werke A.G.

Ortgies Pocket Pistol

Ortgies Pocket Automatic Pistol **$235**
Calibers: 32 Automatic (7.65mm), 380 Automatic (9mm). 7-shot magazine (380 cal.), 8-shot (32 cal.). 3¹/₄-inch barrel. 6¹/₂ inches overall. Weight: 22 oz. Fixed sights. Blued finish. Plain walnut stocks. Made in 1920s.

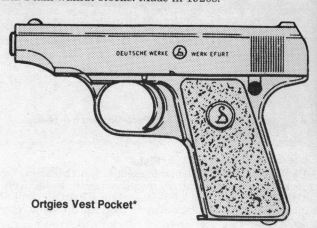

Ortgies Vest Pocket*

Ortgies Vest Pocket Automatic Pistol **$225**
Caliber: 25 Automatic (6.35mm). 6-shot magazine. 2³/₄-inch barrel. 5³/₁₆ inches overall. Weight: 13¹/₂ oz. Fixed sights. Blued finish. Plain walnut stocks. Made in 1920s.

PARA-ORDNANCE MFG., INC.
Scarborough, Ontario, Canada

Para-Ordnance P•12

Para-Ordnance P•12 Compact Auto Pistol
Caliber: 45 ACP. 11-shot magazine. 3.5-inch barrel. 7 inches overall. Weight: 24 oz. (alloy frame). Blade front sight, adjustable rear w/ 3-Dot system. Textured composition grips. Matte black alloy or steel finish. Made from 1990 to date.
Model P1245 (Alloy) **$465**
Model P1245C (Steel) **515**

Para-Ordnance P•13 Auto Pistol
Same general specifications as Model P-12, except with 12-shot magazine. 4.5-inch barrel. 8 inches overall. Weight: 25 oz. (alloy frame). Blade front sight, adjustable rear w/ 3-dot system. Textured composition grips. Matte black alloy or steel finish. Made from 1990 to date.
Model P1345 (Alloy) **$455**
Model P1345C (Steel) **500**

Para-Ordnance P•14-45

Para-Ordnance P•14 Auto Pistol

Caliber: 45 ACP. 13-shot magazine. 5-inch barrel. 8.5 inches overall. Weight: 28 oz. alloy frame. Blade front sight, adjustable rear w/ 3-dot system. Textured composition grips. Matte black alloy or steel finish. Made from 1990 to date.
Model P1445 (Alloy) **$450**
Model P1445C (Steel) **495**

PLAINFIELD MACHINE COMPANY
Dunellen, New Jersey

The operation of this firm was discontinued about 1982.

Plainfield Model 71

Plainfield Model 72

Plainfield Model 71 Automatic Pistol

Calibers: 22 LR, 25 Automatic; conversion kit available. 10-shot magazine in 22, 8-shot in 25. 2½-inch barrel. 5⅛ inches overall. Weight: 25 oz. Fixed sights. Stainless steel frame/slide. Checkered walnut stocks. Made 1970–1982.
22 LR or 25 Auto only **$135**
With Conversion Kit **150**

Plainfield Model 72

Same as Model 71, except has aluminum slide, 3½-inch barrel, is 6 inches overall. Made 1970–1982.
22 LR or 25 Auto only **$140**
With Conversion Kit **160**

RADOM PISTOL
Radom, Poland
Manufactured by the Polish Arsenal

Radom P-35 Automatic

Radom P-35 Automatic Pistol

Variation of the Colt Government Model 45 Auto. Caliber: 9mm Luger. 8-shot magazine. 4¾-inch barrel. 7¾ inches overall. Weight: 29 oz. Fixed sights. Blued finish. Plastic stocks. Made 1935 thru WW II.
Polish Model w/Slide Lock & Eagle Logo **$1295**
Nazi Model w/Nazi Proofmarks, no Slide Lock .. **495**

RECORD-MATCH PISTOLS
Zella-Mehlis, Germany
Manufactured by Udo Anschütz

Record-Match Model 200

Record-Match Model 200 Free Pistol **$895**
Basically the same as Model 210 except plainer, with different stock design and conventional set trigger, spur trigger guard. Made prior to WW II.

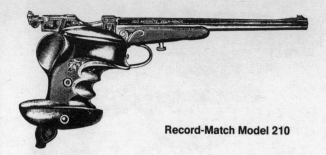

Record-Match Model 210

Remington Model 95 Double Derringer Engraved Model

Record-Match Model 210 Free Pistol **$1295**
System Martini action, set trigger with button release. Caliber: 22 LR. Single shot. 11-inch barrel. Weight: 46 oz. Target sights, micrometer rear. Blued finish. Carved and checkered walnut stock and forearm, adjustable hand base. Also made with dural action (Model 210A); weight of this model, 35 oz. Made prior to WW II.

REISING ARMS CO.
Hartford, Connecticut

Reising Target Automatic*

Reising Target Automatic Pistol **$375**
Hinged frame. Outside hammer. Caliber: 22 LR. 12-shot magazine. 6¹/₂-inch barrel. Fixed sights. Blued finish. Hard rubber stocks. Made 1921–24.

REMINGTON ARMS COMPANY
Ilion, New York

Remington Model 51

Remington Model 51 Automatic Pistol **$525**
Calibers: 32 Auto, 380 Auto. 7-shot magazine. 3¹/₂-inch barrel. 6⁵/₈ inches overall. Weight: 21 oz. Fixed sights. Blued finish. Hard rubber stocks. Made 1918–1934.

Remington Model 95 Double Derringer
SA. Caliber: 41 Short Rimfire. 3-inch double barrels (superposed). 4⁷/₈ inches overall. Early models have long hammer spur and two-armed extractor; later production have short hammer spur and sliding extractor (a few have no extractor). Fixed sights: front blade integral with barrels, rear groove. Finish: all blued, blued w/nickel-plated frame, fully nickel-plated; also with factory engraving. Grips: walnut, checkered hard rubber, pearl, ivory. Weight: 11 oz. Made 1866–1935. Approximately 150,000 were manufactured. *Note:* During the 70 years of its production, serial numbering of this model was repeated two or three times. Therefore, aside from hammer and extractor differences between the earlier and later models, the best clue to the age of a Double Derringer is the stamping of the company's name on the top of the barrel or side rib. Prior to 1888, derringers were stamped "E. Remington & Sons"; 1888–1910, "Remington Arms Co."; 1910–1935, "Remington Arms-U.M.C. Co."
Plain Model **$1000**
Factory-engraved Model with ivory or pearl
  grips **1895**

Remington New Model Single Shot Target Pistol **$1650**
Also called Model 1901 Target. Rolling-block action. Calibers: 22 Short, 22 LR, 44 S&W Russian. 10-inch barrel, half-octagon. 14 inches overall. Weight: 45 oz. (22 cal.). Target sights. Blued finish. Checkered walnut grips and forearm. Made 1901–1909.

Remington Model XP-100 Custom Pistol

Remington Model XP-100 Custom, Heavy Barrel

Remington Model XP-100 Custom Pistol **$695**
Bolt-action, single-shot, long-range pistol. Calibers: 223 Rem., 7mm-08 or 35 Rem. 14¹/₂-inch barrel, standard contour or heavy. Weight: about 4¹/₄ pounds. Currently in production.

Remington Model XP-100 Silhouette

Remington Model XP-100 Silhouette **$375**
Same general specifications as Model XP-100, except chambered for 7mm BR Rem., 14³/₄-inch barrel and weighs 4¹/₈ pounds.

Remington Model XP-100 Single Shot Pistol **$280**
Bolt action. Caliber: 221 Rem. "Fire Ball." 10¹/₂-inch vent-rib barrel. 16³/₄ inches overall. Weight: 3³/₄ pounds. Adjustable rear sight, blade front; receiver drilled and tapped for scope mounts. Blued finish. One-piece brown nylon stock. Made 1963–1988.

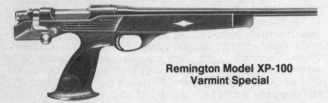

Remington Model XP-100 Varmint Special

Remington Model XP-100 Varmint Special **$295**
Bolt-action, single-shot, long-range pistol. Calibers: 223 Rem., 7mm BR. 14¹/₂-inch barrel. 21¹/₄ inches overall. Weight: about 4¹/₄ pounds. One-piece Du Pont nylon stock with universal grips. Discontinued 1991.

Remington Model XP-100R KS Custom Repeater

Remington Model XP-100R KS Custom Repeater **$545**
Same general specifications as Model XP-100 Custom, except chambered for 22-250, 223 Rem., 250 Savage, 7mm-08 Rem., 308 Win., 35 Rem. and 350 Rem. Mag. Kevlar-reinforced synthetic stock with blind magazine and sling swivel studs. Made from 1990 to date.

Remington XP-22R Rimfire Repeater **$300**
Bolt-action clip repeater built on Model 541-style action. Caliber: 22 Short, Long, LR. 5-shot magazine. 14¹/₂-inch barrel. Weight: 4¹/₄ pounds. Rem. synthetic stock. Made 1991–92.

RG REVOLVERS
Miami, Florida

RG Model 23
SA/DA. 6-shot magazine, swing-out cylinder. Caliber: 22 LR. 1³/₄- and 3³/₈-inch barrels. Overall length: 5¹/₈ and 7¹/₂ inches. Weight 16–17 oz. Fixed sights. Blued or nickel

RG Model 23

RG Model 23 (cont.)
finish. Discontinued.
Blued Finish **$75**
Nickel Finish **80**

RG Model 38S

RG Model 38S
SA/DA. 6-shot magazine, swing-out cylinder. Caliber: 38 Special. 3- and 4-inch barrels. Overall length: 8¹/₄ and 9¹/₄ inches. Weight: 32–34 oz. Windage-adjustable rear sight. Blued finish. Discontinued.
With Plastic Grips **$100**
With Wood Grips **110**

ROSSI REVOLVERS
Sáo Leopoldo, Brazil
Manufactured by Amadeo Rossi S.A.

Rossi Model 31 Double Action Revolver **$100**
Caliber: 38 Special. 5-shot cylinder. 4-inch barrel. Weight: 20 oz. Blue or nickel finish. Discontinued 1985.

Rossi Model 51 Double Action Revolver **$125**
Caliber: 22 LR. 6-shot cylinder. 6-inch barrel. Weight: 28 oz. Blued finish.

Rossi Model 68 .... **$135**
Caliber: 38 Special. 5-round magazine. 2- or 3-inch barrel. Overall length: 6¹/₂ and 7¹/₂ inches. Weight: 21–23 oz. Blued finish. Nickel finish available with 3-inch barrel.

Rossi Model 84 Double Action Revolver **$175**
Caliber: 38 Special. 6-shot. 3-inch barrel. 8 inches overall. Weight: 27¹/₂ oz. Stainless steel finish. Made 1984–86.

Rossi Model 84 Revolver

Rossi Model 85 Double Action Revolver **$190**
Same as Model 84 except has ventilated rib.

Rossi Model 88 Double Action Revolver **$185**
Caliber: 38 Special. 5-shot cylinder. 2- or 3-inch barrel.
Weight: 21 oz. Stainless steel finish.

Rossi Model 88/2 Double Action Revolver **$200**
Caliber: 38 Special. 5-shot cylinder. 2- or 3-inch barrel.
6½ inches overall. Weight: 21 oz. Stainless steel finish.
Made 1985–87.

Rossi Model 89 Revolver

Rossi Model 89 Double Action Revolver **$150**
Caliber: 32 S&W. 6-shot cylinder. 3-inch barrel. 7½ inches
overall. Weight: 17 oz. Stainless steel finish. Disc. 1986.

Rossi Model 94 Double Action Revolver **$165**
Caliber: 38 Special. 6-shot cylinder. 3-inch barrel. 8 inches
overall. Weight: 29 oz. Discontinued 1986.

Rossi Model 95 Revolver **$165**
Caliber: 38 Special. 6-round magazine. 3-inch barrel. 8
inches overall. Weight: 27½ oz. Ventilated rib. Blued finish. Discontinued 1986.

Rossi Model 511 DA Revolver **$145**
Similar to the Model 51, except in stainless steel. Made
1986–1990.

Rossi Model 515 Double Action Revolver
Calibers: 22 LR, 22 WRF. 6-shot cylinder. 4-inch barrel.
9 inches overall. Weight: 30 oz. Red ramp front sight;
adjustable square-notched rear. Stainless finish. Checkered hardwood stocks. Made 1992–93.
Model 515 (22 LR) **$175**
Model 515M (22 WRF) **185**

Rossi Model 518 DA Revolver **$175**
Similar to the Model 515, except in caliber 22 LR. Made
1993 to date.

Rossi Model 720 Double Action Revolver **$205**
Caliber: 44 Special. 5-shot cylinder. 3-inch barrel. 8 inches
overall. Weight: 27.5 oz. Red ramp front sight; adjustable
square-notched rear. Stainless finish. Checkered neoprene
combat-style stocks. Made from 1992 to date.

Rossi Model 841 Revolver

Rossi Model 841 Double Action Revolver **$190**
Same general specifications as Model 84, except has 4-inch
barrel (9 inches overall), weighs 30 oz. Made 1985–86.

Rossi Model 851 Double Action Revolver **$175**
Same general specifications as Model 85, except with 3-
or 4-inch barrel. 8 inches overall w/3-inch bbl. Weight:
27.5 oz. w/3-inch bbl. Red ramp front sight; adjustable
square-notched rear. Stainless finish. Checkered hardwood
stocks. Made from 1991 to date.

Rossi Model 941 Double Action Revolver **$150**
Caliber: 38 Special. 6-shot cylinder. 4-inch barrel. 9 inches
overall. Weight: 30 oz. Blue finish. Made 1985–86.

Rossi Model 951 Double Action Revolver **$185**
Same general specifications as Model 941 except has ventilated rib.

Rossi Model 971

Rossi Model 971 Double Action Revolver
Caliber: 357 Magnum. 6-shot cylinder. 2½-, 4- or 6-inch
barrel. 9 inches overall w/4-inch bbl. Weight: 36 oz. w/4-
inch bbl. Blade front sight; adjustable square-notched rear.
Blued or stainless finish. Checkered hardwood stocks.
Made from 1990 to date.
Blued Finish **$200**
Stainless Finish **235**

Rossi Double Action Revolver

Rossi Double Action Revolver **$120**
Calibers: 22 LR, 32 S&W Long, 38 Special. 5-shot (38) or 6-shot cylinder (other calibers). Barrel lengths: 3-, 6-inch. Weight: 22 oz. w/3-inch bbl. Sights: adjustable rear, ramp front. Blued or nickel finish. Wood or plastic stocks. Made 1965–1991.

Rossi Sportsman's 22

Rossi Sportsman's 22 . . . . **$180**
Caliber: 22 LR. 6-round magazine. 4-inch barrel. 9 inches overall. Weight: 30 oz. Stainless steel finish. Disc. 1991.

RUBY PISTOL
Manufactured by Gabilondo y Urresti, Eibar, Spain, and others

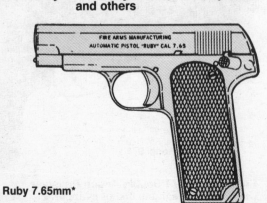

Ruby 7.65mm*

Ruby 7.65mm Automatic Pistol **$175**
Secondary standard service pistol of the French Army in World Wars I and II. Essentially the same as the Alkartasuna (*see* separate listing). Other manufacturers: Ar-

Ruby 7.65mm Automatic Pistol (cont.)
menia Elgoibarresa y Cia., Eceolaza y Vicinai y Cia., Hijos de Angel Echeverria y Cia., Bruno Salaverria y Cia., Zulaika y Cia., all of Eibar, Spain; Gabilondo y Cia., Elgoibar, Spain; Ruby Arms Company, Guernica, Spain. Made 1914–1922.

RUGER HANDGUNS
Southport, Connecticut
Manufactured by Sturm, Ruger & Co.

Rugers made in 1976 are designated "Liberty" in honor of the U.S. Bicentennial and bring a premium of approximately 25 percent in value over regular models.

AUTOMATIC/SINGLE SHOT PISTOLS

NOTE: For ease in finding a particular Ruger handgun, the listings are divided into two groupings: Automatic/Single Shot Pistols (below) and Revolvers, which follows. For a complete listing, please refer to the Index.

Ruger Hawkeye

Ruger Hawkeye Single Shot Pistol **$1050**
SA. Cylinder replaced by rotating breechblock; chamber is in barrel. Caliber: 256 Magnum. 8$^{1/2}$-inch barrel. 14$^{1/2}$ inches overall. Weight: 45 oz. Blued finish. Click adjustable rear sight, ramp front sight. Smooth walnut stocks. Made 1963–65.

Ruger Mark I Target

Ruger Mark I Target Model Automatic Pistol
Caliber: 22 LR. 9-shot magazine. Barrels: 5$^{1/4}$- or 6$^{7/8}$-inch heavy tapered, 5$^{1/2}$-inch untapered bull barrel. 10$^{7/8}$ inches overall w/6$^{6/8}$-inch bbl. Weight: 42 oz. w/5$^{1/2}$- or 6$^{7/8}$-inch bbl. Sights: adjustable rear, under-cut target front. Blued finish. Hard rubber stocks or checkered walnut thumbrest stocks (add $10 to value for latter). Made 1951–1981.
Standard **$180**
With Red Medallion **495**

**Ruger Mark II Stainless
22 Long Rifle**

Ruger Mark II Automatic Pistol

Caliber: 22 LR, standard or high velocity. 4³/₄- or 6-inch tapered barrel. 10-shot magazine. 8⁵/₁₆ w/4³/₄-inch bbl. Weight: 36 oz. Fixed front sight; square notch rear. Blued or stainless finish. Made 1982 to date.

Blued **$165**
Stainless **215**
Bright Stainless (Ltd. prod. 5,000 in 1982) **350**

Ruger 22/45 Zytel Frame

Ruger Mark II 22/45 Automatic Pistol

Same general specifications as Ruger Mark II 22 LR, except with stainless receiver and barrel in three lengths: 4³/₄-inch tapered w/fixed sights, 5¹/₄-inch tapered w/adj. sights and 5¹/₂-inch bull. Fitted with Zytel grip frame of the same design as the Model 1911 45 ACP.

Model KP4 . . . . **$165**
Model KP512, KP514 . . . . **210**

Ruger Mark II Bull Barrel

Ruger Mark II Bull Barrel Automatic Pistol

Same as standard Mark II, except for bull barrel (5¹/₂- or 10-inch). Weight: about 2³/₄ pounds.

Ruger Mark II Bull Barrel Automatic (cont.)

Blued Finish **$195**
Stainless Model, intro. 1985 . . . . **250**

**Ruger Mark II Government
Target Automatic**

Ruger Mark II Government Target Auto Pistol

Civilian version of the Mark II used by U.S. Armed Forces. Caliber: 22 LR rimfire. 10-shot magazine. 6⁷/₈-inch bull barrel. 11¹/₈ inches overall. Weight: 44 oz., empty. Made from 1986 to date.

Blued **$230**
Stainless Steel **275**
Slab Side Bull Barrel **290**

**Ruger Mark II Target Model
22 LR Stainless**

Ruger Mark II Target Pistol

Same as standard Mark II, except has 6⁷/₈-inch tapered barrel. Made from 1982 to date.

Blued Finish **$200**
Stainless Steel Finish **255**

**Ruger P-85
Double Action Pistol**

Ruger Model P-85 Automatic Pistol

Caliber: 9mm. DA, recoil-operated. 15-shot capacity. 4¹/₂-inch barrel. 7.84 inches overall. Weight: 32 oz. Fixed rear

Ruger Model P-85 Automatic Pistol (cont.)

sight, square-post front. Available with decocking levers, ambidextrous safety or in DA only. Blued or stainless finish. Made 1987 to date.

Blued Finish **$270**
Stainless Steel Finish **290**

Ruger Model P-89 Automatic Pistol

Caliber: 9mm. DA with slide-mounted safety levers. 15-shot magazine. 4.5-inch barrel. 7.84 inches overall. Weight: 32 oz. Square post front sight, adjustable rear with 3-dot system. Blued or stainless steel finish. Grooved black Xenoy grips. Made from 1986 to date; stainless introduced in 1990.

P-89 Blued **$265**
P-89 Stainless **290**

Ruger Model P-89 DAC

Ruger Model P-89 DAC/DAO Auto Pistols

Similar to the standard Model P-89, except the P-89 DAC has ambidextrous decocking levers. The P-89 DAO operates in double-action-only mode, has stainless finish only and was introduced in 1991.

P-89 DAC Blued **$260**
P-89 DAC Stainless **305**
P-89 DAO Stainless **295**

Ruger Model P-90 Double Action Automatic Pistol

Caliber: 45 ACP. 7-shot magazine. 4 1/2-inch barrel. 7 7/8 inches overall. Weight: 33 1/2 oz. Square post front sight; adj. square-notched rear w/3-dot system. Grooved black Xenoy composition stocks. Stainless finish. DAC model has ambidextrous decocking levers. Made 1991 to date.

Model P-90 Standard **$315**
Model P-90 DAC (Decockers) **320**

Ruger Model P-91 Double Action Automatic Pistol

Same general specifications as the Model P-90, except chambered for 40 S&W with 12-shot double-column magazine. Made from 1992 to date.

Model P-91 Standard **$315**
Model P-91 DAC (Decockers) **320**
Model P-91 DAO (Double Action Only) **325**

Ruger Model P-93 Compact Auto Pistol

Similar to the standard Model P-89, except with 3.9-inch barrel (7.3 inches overall) and weighs 31 oz. Stainless steel finish. Made from 1993 to date.

Model P-93 DAC (Decocker) (Disc. 1994) **$345**
Model P-93 DAO (Double Action Only) **340**

Ruger Model P-94 Automatic Pistol

Similar to the Model P-91, except with 4.25-inch barrel. Calibers: 9mm or 40 S&W. Stainless steel finish. Made from 1994 to date.

Model P-94 DAC (Decocker) **$340**
Model P-94 DAO (Double Action Only) **335**

Ruger Standard Automatic Pistol

Ruger Standard Model Automatic Pistol

Caliber: 22 LR. 9-shot magazine. 4 3/4- or 6-inch barrel. 8 3/4 inches overall w/4 3/4-inch bbl. Weight: 36 oz. w/4 3/4-inch bbl. Fixed sights. Blued finish. Hard rubber or checkered walnut stocks. Made from 1949 to date. *Note:* In 1951, after the death of Alexander Sturm, the color of the eagle on the stock medallion was changed from red to black as a memorial. Known as the "Red Eagle Automatic," this early type is now a collector's item. Discontinued 1981.

With Red Eagle Medallion **$495**
With Black Eagle Medallion **145**
Extra for Walnut Stocks **15**

REVOLVERS

NOTE: This section contains only Ruger Revolvers. Automatic and Single Shot Pistols may be found on the preceding pages. For a complete listing of Ruger handguns, please refer to the Index.

Ruger Bearcat (Old Model)

Ruger Bearcat SA (Old Model) $295

Aluminum frame. Caliber: 22 LR. 6-shot cylinder. 4-inch barrel. 8 7/8 inches overall. Weight: 17 oz. Fixed sights. Blued finish. Smooth walnut stocks. Made 1958–1973.

Ruger Bisley, Large Frame

Ruger Blackhawk 44

Ruger Bisley SA Revolver, Large Frame $265
Calibers: 357 Mag., 41 Mag., 44 Mag., 45 Long Colt. 7¹/₂-inch barrel. 13 inches overall. Weight: 48 oz. Non-fluted or fluted cylinder, no engraving. Sights: adjustable rear, ramp front. Blued satin finish. Made from 1986 to date.

Ruger Blackhawk SA 44 Mag. Revolver (cont.)
Standard **$395**
Flat Top **625**

Ruger Bisley, Small Frame

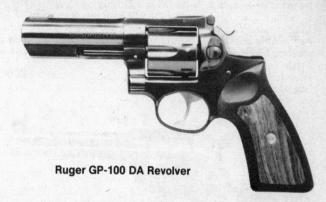

Ruger GP-100 DA Revolver

Ruger Bisley Single-Six Revolver, Small Frame . $220
Calibers: 22 LR and 32 Mag. 6-shot cylinder. 6¹/₂-inch barrel. 11¹/₂ inches overall. Weight: 41 oz. Sights: fixed rear, blade front. Made from 1986 to date.

Ruger GP-100 Double Action Revolver
Caliber: 357 Magnum. 4-inch heavy barrel, or 6-inch standard or heavy barrel. Overall length: 9³/₈ or 11³/₈ inches. Cushioned grip panels. Made from 1986 to date.
Blued Finish **$240**
Stainless Steel Finish **280**

Ruger Blackhawk Single Action Convertible $295
Same as Blackhawk, except has extra cylinder. Caliber combinations: 357 Magnum and 9mm Luger, 45 Colt and 45 Automatic. Made 1967–1972.

Ruger New Bearcat SA Revolver
Similar to the Super Bearcat, except with longer frame. Calibers: 22 LR and 22 WMR (extra cylinder). Blued or high-gloss stainless finish. Smooth walnut grips w/Ruger logo. Made 1994 to date.
Blued Finish **$185**
Stainless Steel Finish **215**

Ruger Blackhawk

Ruger New Model Blackhawk Convertible $245
Same as New Model Blackhawk, except has extra cylinder; blued finish only. Caliber combinations: 357 Magnum and 9mm Luger, 45 Colt and 45 Automatic. 45 Colt and 45 Automatic discontinued 1983.

Ruger Blackhawk Single Action Revolver $245
Calibers: 30 Carbine, 357 Magnum, 41 Magnum, 45 Colt. 6-shot cylinder. Barrel lengths: 4⁵/₈-inch (357, 41, 45 caliber), 6¹/₂-inch (357, 41 caliber), 7¹/₂-inch (30, 45 caliber). 10¹/₈ inches overall (357 Mag. w/4⁵/₈-inch bbl.). Weight: 38 oz. (357 w/4⁵/₈-inch bbl.). Sights: adjustable rear, ramp front. Blued finish. Checkered hard rubber or smooth walnut stocks. Made 1956–1973.

Ruger Blackhawk SA 44 Magnum Revolver
SA with heavy frame and cylinder. Caliber: 44 Magnum. 6-shot cylinder. 6¹/₂-inch barrel. 12¹/₈ inches overall. Weight: 40 oz. Adjustable rear sight, ramp front. Blued finish. Smooth walnut stocks. Made 1956–1973.

Ruger New Model Blackhawk

Ruger New Model Blackhawk SA Revolver
Interlocked mechanism. Calibers: 30 Carbine, 357 Mag., 41 Mag., 45 Long Colt. 6-shot cylinder. Barrel

Ruger New Model Blackhawk
Stainless, 357 Magnum

Ruger New Model Super
Single-Six Convertible

Ruger New Model Blackhawk SA (cont.)

lengths: 4⁵/₈-inch; 5¹/₂-inch (45 LC only); 6¹/₂-inch (357, 41 Mag.); 7¹/₂-inch (30, 45 LC). 10³/₈ inches overall in 357 Mag. w/4⁵/₈-inch bbl. Weight: 40 oz. (357 w/4⁵/₈-inch bbl.). Adjustable rear sight, ramp front. Finish: Blued, stainless steel or high-gloss stainless steel. Smooth walnut stocks. Made from 1973 to date.

Blued Finish	**$200**
Stainless Steel	**275**

Ruger New Model Super Single-Six Convertible Revolver

SA with interlocked mechanism. Calibers: 22 LR and 22 WMR. Interchangeable 6-shot cylinders. Barrel lengths: 4⁵/₈, 5¹/₂, 6¹/₂, 9¹/₂ inches. 10¹³/₁₆ inches overall w/4⁵/₈-inch bbl. Weight: 33 oz. w/4⁵/₈-inch bbl. Adjustable rear sight, ramp front. Blued finish or stainless steel; latter only with 5¹/₂- or 6¹/₂-inch bbl. Smooth walnut stocks. Made from 1972 to date.

Blued Finish	**$185**
Stainless Steel	**235**

Ruger New Model Single-Six SSM
32 Magnum

Ruger Police Service-Six
Stainless Steel

Ruger New Model Single-Six SSM Revolver $180

Same general specifications as standard Single-Six, except chambered for 32 H&R Magnum cartridge. Barrel length: 4⁵/₈, 5¹/₂, 6¹/₂ or 9¹/₂ inches.

Ruger Police Service-Six

Same general specifications as Speed-Six, except has square butt. Stainless steel models and 9mm Luger caliber available with only 4-inch barrel. Made 1971–1988.

38 Special, Blued Finish	**$175**
38 Special, Stainless Steel	**185**
357 Magnum or 9mm Luger, Blued Finish	**190**
357 Magnum, Stainless Steel	**215**

Ruger New Model
Super Blackhawk

Ruger Redhawk Alloy Steel
Blued

Ruger New Model Super Blackhawk SA Revolver

Interlocked mechanism. Caliber: 44 Magnum. 6-shot cylinder. 5¹/₂-inch, 7¹/₂-inch and 10¹/₂-inch bull barrel. 13³/₈ inches overall. Weight: 48 oz. Adjustable rear sight, ramp front. Blued and stainless steel finish. Smooth walnut stocks. Made from 1973 to date. 5¹/₂-inch barrel made from 1987 to date.

Blued Finish	**$245**
Stainless Steel	**285**

Ruger Redhawk Double Action Revolver

Calibers: 357 Mag., 41 Mag., 44 Mag. 6-shot cylinder. 5¹/₂- and 7¹/₂-inch barrel. 11 and 13 inches overall, respectively. Weight: about 52 oz. Adjustable rear sight, interchangeable front sights. Stainless finish. Made 1979 to date; 357 Mag. discontinued 1986. Alloy steel model with blued finish introduced in 1986 in 41 Mag. and 44 Mag. calibers.

Blued Finish	**$285**
Stainless Steel	**335**

Ruger Redhawk w/Integral Scope Mounting System

Ruger Redhawk Stainless DA Scope-Ring Revolver $365
Same general specifications as standard Redhawk, except chambered for 44 Mag. only, and has integral scope mounting system.

Ruger Security-Six

Ruger Security-Six Double Action Revolver
Caliber: 357 Magnum; handles 38 Special. 6-shot cylinder. Barrel lengths: 2³/₄-, 4-, 6-inch. 9¹/₄ inches overall w/4-inch bbl. Weight: 33¹/₂ oz. w/4-inch bbl. Adjustable rear sight, ramp front. Blued finish or stainless steel. Square butt. Checkered walnut stocks. Made 1971–1985.
Blued Finish $195
Stainless Steel 225

Ruger Single-Six

Ruger Single-Six Single Action Revolver
Calibers: 22 LR, 22 WMR. 6-shot cylinder. Barrel lengths: 4⁵/₈, 5¹/₂, 6¹/₂, 9¹/₂ inches. 10⁷/₈ inches overall w/5¹/₂-inch bbl. Weight: about 35 oz. Fixed sights. Blued finish. Checkered hard rubber or smooth walnut grips. Made 1953–1973. *Note:* Pre-1956 model with flat loading gate

Ruger Single-Six SA Revolver (cont.)
is worth about twice as much as later version.
Standard $195
Convertible (w/2 cylinders, 22 LR/22 WMR) 215

Ruger Single-Six Lightweight

Ruger Single-Six—Lightweight $250
Same general specifications as Single-Six, except has 4⁵/₈-inch barrel, lightweight alloy cylinder and frame, 10 inches overall length, weighs 23 oz. Made in 1956.

Ruger SP101 Double Action

Ruger SP101 Double Action Revolver
Calibers: 22 LR, 32 Mag., 9mm, 38 Special+P, 357 Mag. 5- or 6-shot cylinder. 2¹/₄-, 3¹/₁₆- or 4-inch barrel. Weight: 25–34 oz. Stainless steel finish. Cushioned grips. Made from 1988 to date.
Standard Model $260
DAO Model (DA only, spurless hammer) 265

Ruger Speed-Six

Ruger Speed-Six Double Action Revolver
Calibers: 38 Special, 357 Magnum, 9mm Luger. 6-shot cylinder. Barrel lengths: 2³/₄-, 4-inch; 9mm available only

Ruger Speed-Six DA Revolver (cont.)

with 2³/₄-inch bbl. 7³/₄ inches overall w/2³/₄-inch bbl. Weight: 31 oz. w/2³/₄-inch bbl. Fixed sights. Blued or stainless steel finish; latter available in 38 Special w/2³/₄-inch bbl., 357 Magnum and 9mm with either barrel. Round butt. Checkered walnut stocks. Made 1973–1987.

38 Special, Blued Finish	**$150**
38 Special, Stainless Steel	**180**
357 Magnum or 9mm Luger, Blued Finish	**215**
357 Magnum or 9mm Luger, Stainless Steel	**245**

Ruger Super Bearcat

Ruger Super Bearcat $300

Same general specifications as Bearcat (Old Model), except has steel frame. Weight: 25 oz. Made 1971–73.

Ruger Super Blackhawk

Ruger Super Blackhawk SA Revolver $250

Caliber: 44 Magnum. 6-shot cylinder. 7¹/₂-inch barrel. 13³/₈ inches overall. Weight: 48 oz. Click adjustable rear sight, ramp front. Blued finish. Steel or brass grip frame. Smooth walnut stocks. Made 1959–1973.

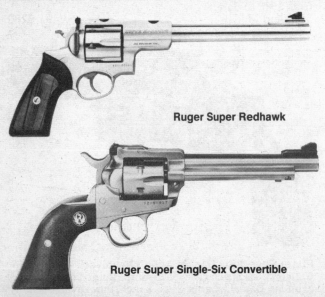

Ruger Super Redhawk

Ruger Super Single-Six Convertible

Ruger Super Redhawk Revolver $375

Caliber: 44 Magnum. 7¹/₂- or 9¹/₂-inch barrel. 13 or 15 inches overall. Weight: 53–58 oz. Cushioned grips. Satin polished stainless steel finish. Made from 1987 to date.

Ruger Super Single-Six Convertible Revolver

Same general specifications as Single-Six, except has ramp front, click-adj. rear sights with protective ribs integral with frame; 5¹/₂- or 6¹/₂-inch bbl. only; two interchangeable cylinders, 22 LR and 22 WMR. Made from 1973 to date.

Blued	**$185**
Stainless Steel	**235**

Ruger Vaquero

Ruger Vaquero SA Revolver

Calibers: 44-40, 44 Magnum, 45 Colt. 6-shot cylinder. Barrel lengths: 4⁵/₈, 5¹/₂, 7¹/₂ inches. 13⁵/₈ inches overall (7¹/₂-inch bbl.). Weight: 41 oz. (7¹/₂-inch bbl.). Sights: blade front; grooved topstrap rear. Blued with color-casehardened frame or polished stainless finish. Smooth rosewood grips w/Ruger medallion. Made 1993 to date.

Blued w/Color-casehardened Frame	**$265**
Stainless Finish	**265**

══ RUSSIAN SERVICE PISTOLS ══
Mfd. by Government plants at Tula and elsewhere

Tokarev-type pistols have also been made in Hungary, Poland, Yugoslavia, People's Republic of China, N. Korea.

Russian Tokarev

Russian Model 30 Tokarev Service Automatic . . $350

Modified Colt-Browning type. Caliber: 7.62mm Russian Automatic (also uses 7.63mm Mauser Automatic cartridge). 8-shot magazine. 4¹/₂-inch barrel. 7³/₄ inches overall. Weight: about 29 oz. Fixed sights. Made 1930–

HANDGUNS

Russian Model 30 Tokarev Service Auto (cont.)
mid-1950s. *Note:* A slightly modified version with improved locking system and different disconnector was adopted in 1933.

Russian Model PM Makarov Auto Pistol $135
Double-action, blowback design. Caliber: 9mm Makarov. 8-shot magazine. 3.8-inch barrel. 6.4 inches overall. Weight: 26 oz. Blade front sight; square-notched rear. Checkered composition grips.

SAKO HANDGUNS
Riihimaki, Finland
Manufactured by Oy Sako Ab

Sako 22-32 Olympic Pistol

Sako 22-32 Olympic Pistol
Calibers: 22 LR, 22 Short, 32 S&W Long. 5-round magazine. Barrels: 6 or 8.85 (22 Short) inches. Weight: about 46 oz. (22 LR); 44 oz. (22 Short); 48 oz. (32). Steel frame. ABS plastic, anatomically designed grip. Non-reflecting matte black upper surface and chromium-plated slide. Equipped w/carrying case and tool set. Made 1983–89.
Sako 22-32 Single Pistol **$1045**
Sako Triace, triple-barrel set w/wooden grip **1840**

SAUER HANDGUNS
Mfd. through WW II by J. P. Sauer & Sohn, Suhl, Germany. Now mfd. by J. P. Sauer & Sohn, GmbH, Eckernförde, Germany

See also listings under SIG-Sauer.

Sauer Model 1913*

Sauer Model 1913 Pocket Automatic Pistol $260
Caliber: 32 Automatic (7.65mm). 7-shot magazine. 3-inch barrel. 5⅞ inches overall. Weight: 22 oz. Fixed sights. Blue finish. Black hard rubber stocks. Made 1913–1930.

Sauer Model 1930

Sauer Model H

Sauer Model 1930 Pocket Automatic Pistol $295
Authority Model (Behorden Modell). Successor to Model 1913, has improved grip and safety. Caliber: 32 Auto (7.65mm). 7-shot magazine. 3-inch barrel. 5¾ inches overall. Weight: 22 oz. Fixed sights. Blued finish. Black hard rubber stocks. Made 1930–38. *Note:* Some pistols made with indicator pin showing when cocked. Also mfd. with dural slide and receiver; this type weighs about ⅓ less than the standard model.

Sauer Model H Double Action Automatic Pistol . $395
Calibers: 25 Auto (6.35mm), 32 Auto (7.65mm), 380 Auto (9mm). Specifications shown are for 32 Auto model. 7-shot magazine. 3¼-inch barrel. 6¼ inches overall. Weight: 20 oz. Fixed sights. Blued finish. Black plastic stocks. Also made in dural model weighing about ⅓ less. Made 1938–1945. *Note:* This pistol, designated Model 38, was mfd. during WW II for military use. Wartime models are inferior to earlier production, as some lack safety lever.

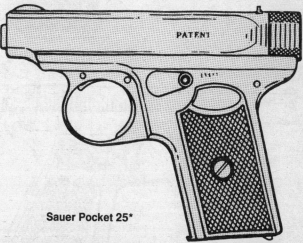

Sauer Pocket 25*

Sauer Pocket 25 Automatic Pistol $295
Smaller version of Model 1913, issued about same time as 32 caliber model. Caliber: 25 Auto (6.35mm). 7-shot

Sauer Pocket 25 Automatic Pistol (cont.)
magazine. 2¹/₂-inch barrel. 4¹/₄ inches overall. Weight: 14¹/₂ oz. Fixed sights. Blued finish. Black hard rubber stocks. Made 1913–1930.

Sauer Single Action Revolvers
See listings under Hawes.

SAVAGE ARMS CO.
Utica, New York

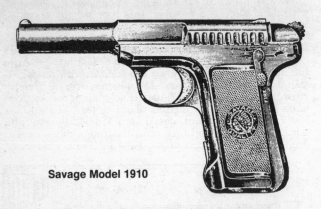

Savage Model 101

Savage Model 101 SA Single Shot Pistol **$150**
Barrel integral with swing-out cylinder. Caliber: 22 Short, Long, LR. 5¹/₂-inch barrel. Weight: 20 oz. Blade front sight, slotted rear, adjustable for windage. Blued finish. Grips of compressed, impregnated wood. Made 1960–68.

Savage Model 1910

Savage Model 1917*

Savage Model 1910 Automatic Pistol **$195**
Calibers: 32 Auto, 380 Auto. 10-shot magazine (32 cal.), 9-shot (380 cal.). 3³/₄-inch barrel (32 cal.), 4¹/₂-inch (380 cal.). 6¹/₂ inches overall (32 cal.), 7 inch (380 cal.). Weight: about 23 oz. Fixed sights. Blued finish. Hard rubber stocks. Made in hammerless type with grip safety or with exposed hammer spur. Made 1910–17.

Savage Model 1917 Automatic Pistol **$325**
Same specifications as 1910 Model, except has spur-type hammer and redesigned heavier grip. Made 1917–1928.

SEARS, ROEBUCK & COMPANY
Chicago, Illinois

Sears/J.C. Higgins Model 80 Auto Pistol **$150**
Caliber: 22 LR. 10-shot magazine. 4¹/₂- or 6¹/₂-inch interchangeable barrel. 10⁷/₈ inches overall w/6¹/₂-inch bbl. Weight: 41 oz. w/6¹/₂-inch bbl. Fixed Patridge sights. Blued finish. Checkered stocks with thumbrest.

Sears/J.C. Higgins Model 88 DA Revolver **$90**
Caliber: 22 LR. 9-shot cylinder. 4- or 6-inch barrel. 9¹/₂ inches w/4-inch bbl. Weight: 23 oz. w/4-inch bbl. Fixed sights. Blued or nickel finish. Checkered plastic stocks.

Sears/J.C. Higgins Ranger DA Revolver **$105**
Caliber: 22 LR. 9-shot cylinder. 5¹/₂-inch barrel. 10³/₄ inches overall. Weight: 28 oz. Fixed sights. Blued or chrome finish. Checkered plastic stocks.

SECURITY INDUSTRIES OF AMERICA
Little Ferry, New Jersey

Security Model PM357

Security Model PM357 Double Action Revolver . **$195**
Caliber: 357 Magnum. 5-shot cylinder. 2¹/₂-inch barrel. 7¹/₂ inches overall. Weight: 21 oz. Fixed sights. Stainless steel. Walnut stocks. Introduced 1975; discontinued.

Security Model PPM357 DA Revolver **$180**
Caliber: 357 Magnum. 5-shot cylinder. 2-inch barrel. 6¹/₈ inches overall. Weight: 18 oz. Fixed sights. Stainless steel. Walnut stocks. Made from 1976 to date. *Note:* Spurless hammer (illustrated) discontinued in 1977; replaced with conventional hammer of other Security revolvers.

Security Model PPM357

Security Model PSS38

Security Model PSS38 Double Action Revolver . . **$165**
Caliber: 38 Special. 5-shot cylinder. 2-inch barrel. 6 1/2 inches overall. Weight: 18 oz. Fixed sights. Stainless steel. Walnut stocks. Intro. 1973. Discontinued.

R. F. SEDGLEY, INC.
Philadelphia, Pennsylvania

Sedgley Baby Hammerless Ejector Revolver . . . **$395**
DA. Solid frame. Folding trigger. Caliber: 22 Long. 6-shot cylinder. 4 inches overall. Weight: 6 oz. Fixed sights. Blued or nickel finish. Rubber stocks. Made c. 1930–39.

SHERIDAN PRODUCTS, INC.
Racine, Wisconsin

Sheridan Knocabout

Sheridan Knocabout Single Shot Pistol **$145**
Tip-up type. Caliber: 22 LR, Long, Short. 5-inch barrel. 6 3/4 inches overall. Weight: 24 oz. Fixed sights. Checkered plastic stocks. Blue finish. Made 1953–1960.

SIG PISTOLS
Neuhausen am Rheinfall, Switzerland
Mfd. by SIG Schweizerische Industrie-Gesellschaft

See also listings under SIG-Sauer.

SIG Model P210-1

SIG Model P210-1 Automatic Pistol **$1495**
Calibers: 22 LR, 7.65mm Luger, 9mm Luger. 8-shot magazine. 4 3/4-inch barrel. 8 1/2 inches overall. Weight: 33 oz. (22 cal.); 35 oz. (7.65mm, 9mm). Fixed sights. Polished blued finish. Checkered wood stocks. Made 1949–1986.

SIG Model P210-2 . . . . **$1195**
Same as Model P210-1, except has sandblasted finish, plastic stocks; not avail. in 22 LR. Discontinued 1987.

SIG Model P210-5 Target Pistol **$1495**
Same as Model P210-2, except has 6-inch barrel, micrometer adjustable rear sight, target front sight, adjustable trigger stop. 9.7 inches overall. Weight: about 38.3 oz. Discontinued.

SIG Model P210-6

SIG Model P210-6 Target Pistol **$1450**
Same as Model P210-2, except has micrometer adjustable rear sight, target front sight, adjustable trigger stop. Weight: about 37 oz. Discontinued 1987.

SIG P210 22 Conversion Unit **$595**
Converts P210 pistol to 22 LR. Consists of barrel with
recoil spring, slide and magazine.

SIG-Hämmerli Model P240 Automatic Pistol . . . **$1095**
For data, *see* listing under Hämmerli. Discont. 1986.

SIG-SAUER HANDGUNS
Mfd. by J. P. Sauer & Sohn of West Germany, SIG of Switzerland, and other manufacturers

SIG-Sauer Model P220

SIG-Sauer Model P220 DA Automatic Pistol **$545**
Calibers: 9mm Luger, 38 Super, 45 Automatic. 7-shot in
45, 9-shot in other calibers. 4.4-inch barrel. 8 inches over-
all. Weight: 9mm, 26.5 oz. Fixed sights. Blued finish.
Checkered plastic stocks. Made from 1976 to date. *Note:*
Also sold in U.S. as Browning BDA.

SIG-Sauer Model P225

SIG-Sauer Model P225 DA Automatic **$560**
Caliber: 9mm Parabellum. 8-shot magazine. 3.85-inch
barrel. 7 inches overall. Weight: 26.1 oz. Blue finish.

SIG-Sauer Model P226 DA Automatic **$565**
Caliber: 9mm Parabellum. 15-shot magazine. 4.4-inch
barrel. 7³/₄ inches overall. Weight: 26.5 oz. Blue finish.
Made from 1985 to date.

SIG-Sauer Model P228 DA Automatic
Same general specifications as Model P226, except with
3.86-inch barrel. 7¹/₈ inches overall. Blued or K-Kote finish. Made from 1990 to date.

SIG-Sauer Model P228 DA Automatic (cont.)
Blued Finish **$525**
K-Kote Finish 570
For Siglite Nite Sights, **add** 80

Sig-Sauer Model P229 DA Automatic
Same general specifications as Model P226, except cham-
bered in 40 S&W with 12-shot magazine. 3.86-inch barrel.
7¹/₈ inches overall. Weight: 30.5 oz. Blued finish. Made
from 1991 to date.
Blued Finish **$625**
Blued Finish DAO (double action only) 600
For Siglite Nite Sights, **add** 80

SIG-Sauer Model P230

SIG-Sauer Model P230 DA Automatic Pistol
Calibers: 22 LR, 32 Automatic (7.65mm), 380 Automatic
(9mm Short), 9mm Police. 10-shot magazine in 22, 8-shot
in 32, 7-shot in 9mm. 3.6-inch barrel. 6.6 inches overall.
Weight: 32 Auto, 18.2 oz. Fixed sights. Blued or stainless
finish. Plastic stocks. Made from 1976 to date.
Blued Finish **$350**
Stainless Finish 395

SMITH & WESSON, INC.
Springfield, Massachusetts

AUTOMATIC/SINGLE SHOT PISTOLS

> **NOTE:** For ease in locating a particular S&W handgun, the
> listings are divided into two groupings: Automatic/Single
> Shot Pistols (below) and Revolvers (page 148). For a com-
> plete handgun listing, please refer to the Index.

S&W 32 Automatic

Smith & Wesson 32 Automatic Pistol **$1850**
Caliber: 32 Automatic. Same general specifications as 35
caliber model, but barrel is fastened to the receiver instead
of hinged. Made 1924–1937.

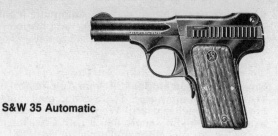

S&W 35 Automatic

Smith & Wesson 35 Automatic Pistol **$675**
Caliber: 35 S&W Automatic. 7-shot magazine. 3¹/₂-inch barrel (hinged to frame). 6¹/₂ inches overall. Weight: 25 oz. Fixed sights. Blued or nickel finish. Plain walnut stocks. Made 1913–1921.

S&W Model 39

Smith & Wesson Model 39 9mm DA Auto Pistol
Caliber: 9mm Luger. 8-shot magazine. 4-inch barrel. Overall length: 7⁷/₁₆ inches. Weight: 26¹/₂ oz. Click adjustable rear sight, ramp front. Blued or nickel finish. Checkered walnut stocks. Made 1954–1982. *Note:* Between 1954 and 1966, 927 pistols of this model were made w/ steel instead of alloy frames.
With Steel Frame **$825**
With Alloy Frame **315**

S&W Model 41

Smith & Wesson Model 41 22 Automatic Pistol . **$545**
Caliber: 22 LR, 22 Short (not interchangeably). 10-shot magazine. Barrel lengths: 5-, 5¹/₂-, 7³/₈-inch; latter has detachable muzzle brake. 12 inches overall (7³/₈-inch bbl.). Weight: 43¹/₂ oz. (7³/₈-inch bbl.). Click adj. rear sight, undercut Patridge front. Blued finish. Checkered walnut stocks w/thumbrest. Made from 1957 to date.

S&W Model 46

Smith & Wesson Model 46 22 Automatic Pistol . **$425**
Caliber: 22 LR. 10-shot magazine. Barrel lengths: 5, 5¹/₂, 7 inches. 10⁹/₁₆ inches overall (7-inch bbl.). Weight: 42 oz. (7-inch bbl.). Click adjustable rear sight, undercut Patridge front. Blue finish. Molded nylon stocks w/thumbrest. Only 4,000 produced. Made 1957–1966.

S&W Model 52

Smith & Wesson Model 52 38 Master Auto **$750**
Caliber: 38 Special (midrange wadcutter only). 5-shot magazine. 5-inch barrel. Overall length: 8⁵/₈ inches. Weight: 41 oz. Micrometer click rear sight, Patridge front, on ramp base. Blued finish. Checkered walnut stocks. Made 1961–1994.

S&W Model 59

Smith & Wesson Model 59 9mm DA Auto **$325**
Similar specifications as Model 39, except has 14-shot magazine, checkered nylon stocks. Made 1971–1981.

S&W Model 61

Smith & Wesson Model 61 Escort Pocket Automatic Pistol $225
Caliber: 22 LR. 5-shot magazine. 2¹/₈-inch barrel. 4¹³/₁₆ inches overall. Weight: 14 oz. Fixed sights. Blued or nickel finish. Checkered plastic stocks. Made 1970–74.

Smith & Wesson Model 411 Auto Pistol $350
Similar to S&W Model 915, except in caliber 40 S&W. 11-shot magazine. Made from 1994 to date.

S&W Model 422

S&W Model 439

Smith & Wesson Model 422 SA Auto Pistol
Caliber: 22 LR. 10-shot magazine. 4¹/₂- or 6-inch barrel. 7¹/₂ inches overall w/4¹/₂-inch bbl. Weight: 22–23¹/₂ oz.

Smith & Wesson Model 422 SA Automatic (cont.)
Fixed or adjustable sights. Checkered plastic or walnut grips. Blued finish. Made from 1987 to date.
Standard Model $150
Target Model   190

Smith & Wesson Model 439 9mm Automatic . . . $295
DA. Caliber: 9mm Luger. Two 8-round magazines. 4-inch barrel. 7⁷/₁₆ inches overll. Weight: 30 oz. Serrated ramp square front sight, square notch rear. Checkered walnut grips. Blue or nickel finish. Discontinued 1988.

S&W Model 459

Smith & Wesson Model 459 DA Automatic
Caliber: 9mm Luger. Two 14-round magazines. 4-inch barrel. 7⁷/₁₆ inches overall. Weight: 28 oz. Blued or nickel finish. Discontinued 1988.
Standard Model $325
FBI Model   550

S&W Model 469

Smith & Wesson Model 469 9mm Automatic . . . $335
DA. Caliber: 9mm Luger. Two 12-round magazines. 3¹/₂-inch barrel. 6⁷/₈ inches overall. Weight: 26 oz. Yellow ramp front sight, dovetail mounted square notch rear. Sandblasted blue finish. Optional ambidextrous safety. Discontinued 1988.

Smith & Wesson Model 622 SA Auto Pistol
Same general specifications as Model 422, except with stainless finish. Made from 1990 to date.
Standard Model $175
Target Model   220

S&W Model 639

Smith & Wesson Model 639 Automatic **$330**
Caliber: 9mm Luger Parabellum. Two 12-round magazines. 3½-inch barrel. 6.9 inches overall. Weight: 26 oz. Nonglare blued finish. Discontinued 1988.

S&W Model 645

Smith & Wesson Model 645 DA Automatic **$370**
Caliber: 45 ACP. 8-shot. 5-inch barrel. Overall length: 8½ inches. Weight: Approx. 38 oz. Red ramp front, fixed rear sights. Stainless. Made 1986–88.

S&W Model 659 Stainless

Smith & Wesson Model 659 9mm Automatic . . . **$335**
DA. Similar to S&W Model 459, except weight is 39½ oz. and finish is satin stainless steel. Discontinued 1988.

Smith & Wesson Model 669 Automatic **$300**
Caliber: 9mm. 12-shot magazine. Barrel: 3½ inches. 6.9 inches overall. Weight: 26 oz. Serrated ramp front sight with red bar, fixed rear. Nonglare stainless-steel finish. Made 1986–88.

**S&W Model 745
Automatic Pistol**

Smith & Wesson Model 745 Automatic Pistol
Caliber: 45 ACP. 8-shot magazine. 5-inch barrel. 8⅝ inches overall. Weight: 38¾ oz. Fixed sights. Blued slide, stainless frame. Checkered walnut grips. Similar to the model 645, but w/o DA capability. Made 1987–1990.
With Standard Competition Features **$450**
IPSC Commemorative (first 5,000) **545**

Smith & Wesson Model 909/910 Auto Pistols
Caliber: 9mm Parabellum. 9-shot (Model 909) or 10-shot (Model 910) magazine. 4-inch barrel. 7⅜ inches overall. Weight: 28 oz. Post front sight; fixed rear. Delrin straight backstrap grips. Blued steel slide with alloy frame. Made 1994 to date.
Model 909 . . . . **$270**
Model 910 . . . . **285**

S&W Model 915

Smith & Wesson Model 915 Auto Pistol **$295**
DA. Caliber: 9mm Luger. 15-shot magazine. 4-inch barrel. 7½ inches overall. Weight: 28½ oz. Post front sight, fixed square-notched rear w/3-dot system. Xenoy wraparound grip. Blued steel slide and alloy frame. Made 1992–94.

S&W Model 1026

Smith & Wesson Model 1000 Series DA Auto

Caliber: 10mm. 9-shot magazine. 4¼- or 5-inch barrel. 7⅞ or 8⅝ inches overall. Weight: about 38 oz. Post front sight, adjustable or fixed square-notched rear w/3-dot system. One-piece Xenoy® wraparound grips. Stainless slide and frame. Made 1990–94.

Model 1006 (Fixed Sights, 5″ bbl.) **$445**
Model 1006 (Adj. Sights, 5″ bbl.) **475**
Model 1026 (Fixed Sights, 5″ bbl.,
  Decocking Lever) **475**
Model 1066 (Fixed Sights, 4¼″ bbl.) **450**
Model 1076 (Fixed Sights, 4¼″ bbl., Frame-
  mounted Decocking Lever, Straight Backstrap) . . **465**
Model 1076 (same as above w/Tritium Night
  Sight) **495**
Model 1086 (same as Model 1076 in DA only) **450**

Smith & Wesson Model 2206 SA Automatic Pistol

Similar to Model 422, except w/stainless-steel slide and frame, weighs 35–39 oz., has Patridge front sight on adj. sight model; post w/white dot on fixed sight model, plastic grips.

Standard Model **$200**
Target Model **245**

Smith & Wesson Model 2213 Sportsman Auto . . **$190**

Caliber: 22 LR. 8-shot magazine. 3-inch barrel. 6⅛ inches overall. Weight: 18 oz. Patridge front sight, fixed square-notched rear w/3-Dot system. Black synthetic molded grips. Stainless steel slide w/alloy frame. Made 1992 to date.

Smith & Wesson Model 2214 Sportsman Auto . . **$185**

Same general specifications as Model 2214, except with blued slide and matte black alloy frame. Made from 1990 to date.

S&W Model 3906

Smith & Wesson Model 3904/3906 DA Auto Pistol

Caliber: 9mm. 8-shot magazine. 4-inch barrel. 7½ inches overall. Weight: 25½ oz. (Model 3904); 34 oz. (Model 3906). Fixed or adj. sights. Delrin one-piece wraparound, checkered grips. Alloy frame w/blued carbon steel slide (Model 3904) or satin stainless (Model 3906). Made 1989–1991.

Model 3904 w/Adjustable Sights **$365**
Model 3904 w/Fixed Sights **325**
Model 3904 w/Novak LC Sight **360**
Model 3906 w/Adjustable Sights **410**
Model 3906 w/Novak LC Sight **400**

S&W Model 3914

Smith & Wesson Model 3913/3914 DA Automatic

Caliber: 9mm Parabellum (Luger). 8-shot magazine. 3½-inch barrel. 6⅞ inches overall. Weight: 25 oz. Post front sight; fixed or adjustable square-notched rear. One-piece Xenoy® wraparound grips w/straight backstrap. Alloy frame with stainless or blued slide. Made 1990 to date.

Model 3913 Stainless **$395**
Model 3913LS Lady Smith Stainless w/contoured
  Trigger Guard **410**
Model 3914 Blued **370**

Smith & Wesson Model 3953/3954 DA Auto Pistol

Same general specifications as Model 3913/3914, except double action only. Made from 1991 to date.

Model 3953 Stainless, Double Action Only **$395**
Model 3954 Blued, Double Action Only **350**

S&W Model 4046

Smith & Wesson Model 4000 Series DA Auto

Caliber: 40 S&W. 11-shot magazine. 4-inch barrel. 7⁷/₈ inches overall. Weight: 28–30 oz. (alloy frame); 36 oz. (stainless frame). Post front sight; adjustable or fixed square-notched rear w/2 white dots. Straight backstrap. One-piece Xenoy® wraparound grips. Blued or stainless finish. Made between 1990/1992 to date.

Model 4003 Stainless w/Alloy Frame	**$475**
Model 4004 Blued w/Alloy Frame	450
Model 4006 Stainless Frame, Fixed Sights	395
Model 4006 Stainless Frame, Adj. Sights	495
Model 4026 w/Decocking Lever (disc. 1994)	535
Model 4043 DA only, Stainless w/Alloy Frame	465
Model 4044 DA only, Blued w/Alloy Frame	440
Model 4046 DA only, Stainless Frame, Fixed Sights	400
Model 4046 DA only, Stainless Frame, Tritium Night Sight	565

Smith & Wesson Model 4013/4014 DA Automatic

Caliber: 40 S&W. 8-shot capacity. 3¹/₂-inch barrel. 7 inches overall. Weight: 26 oz. Post front sight; fixed Novak LC rear w/3-dot system. One-piece Xenoy® wraparound grips. Stainless or blued slide w/alloy frame. Made 1991 to date.

Model 4013 w/Stainless Slide	**$455**
Model 4014 w/Blued Slide	435

Smith & Wesson Model 4053/4054 DA Auto Pistol

Same general specifications as Model 4013/4014, except double action only. Alloy frame fitted with blued steel slide. Made from 1991 to date.

Model 4053 DA only w/Stainless Slide	**$455**
Model 4054 DA only w/Blued Slide	395

S&W Model 4506
With Fixed Sights

Smith & Wesson Model 4500 Series DA Automatic

Caliber: 45 ACP. 7-shot magazine (Model 4516); 8-shot magazine (Model 4506). Barrel lengths: 3³/₄, 4¹/₄ or 5 inches. 7¹/₈ to 8⁵/₈ inches overall. Weight: 34¹/₂ to 38¹/₂ oz. Post front sight; fixed Novak LC rear w/2-Dot system or adj. One-piece Xenoy® wraparound grips. Satin stainless finish. Made from 1990 to date.

Model 4506 w/Fixed Sights, 5-inch bbl.	**$435**
Model 4506 w/Novak LC Sight, 5-inch bbl.	445
Model 4516 w/3³/₄-inch bbl.	475
Model 4526 w/5-inch bbl., Alloy Frame, Decocking Lever, Fixed Sights	425
Model 4536 w/Anodized frame, Decocking Lever	415
Model 4556 w/3³/₄-inch bbl., DA only, Alloy Frame	395

Smith & Wesson Model 4500 Series (cont.)

Model 4566 4¹/₄-inch bbl., Ambidextrous Safety, Fixed Sights	**$425**
Model 4576 w/4¹/₄-inch bbl., Decocking Lever	485
Model 4586 w/4¹/₄-inch bbl., DA only	495

S&W Model 5904
9mm Double Action

Smith & Wesson Model 5900 Series DA Automatic

Caliber: 9mm. 15-shot magazine. 4-inch barrel. 7¹/₂ inches overall. Weight: 26–38 oz. Fixed or adjustable sights. One-piece Xenoy® wraparound grips. Alloy frame w/stainless-steel slide (Model 5903) or blued slide (Model 5904); stainless-steel frame and slide (Model 5906). Made from 1989/1990 to date.

Model 5903 w/Adjustable Sights	**$435**
Model 5903 w/Novak LC Rear Sight	425
Model 5904 w/Adjustable Sights	430
Model 5904 w/Novak LC Rear Sight	405
Model 5905 w/Adjustable Sights	430
Model 5905 w/Novak LC Rear Sight	405
Model 5906 w/Adjustable Sights	440
Model 5906 w/Novak LC Rear Sight	405
Model 5906 w/Tritium Night Sight	550
Model 5924 Anodized frame, Blued Slide	385
Model 5926 Stainless frame, Decocking Lever	450
Model 5943 Alloy Frame/Stainless Slide, DA only	440
Model 5944 Alloy Frame/Blued Slide, DA only	395
Model 5946 Stainless Frame/Slide, DA only	445

S&W Model 6906
With Tritium Night Sight

Smith & Wesson Model 6900 Compact Series

Double action. Caliber: 9mm. 12-shot magazine. 3½-inch barrel. 6⅞ inches overall. Weight: 26½ oz. Ambidextrous safety. Post front sight; fixed Novak LC rear w/3-Dot system. Alloy frame w/blued carbon steel slide (Model 6904) or stainless steel slide (Model 6906). Made from 1989 to date. (*See* photo, preceding page.)

Model 6904	**$385**
Model 6906 w/Fixed Sights	425
Model 6906 w/Tritium Night Sight	495
Model 6926 Same as Model 6906 w/Decocking Lever	375
Model 6944 Same as Model 6904 in DA only	395
Model 6946 Same as Model 6906 in DA only, Fixed Sights	425
Model 6946 w/Tritium Night Sight	495

**S&W Model 1891
Single Shot Pistol**

Smith & Wesson Model 1891 Single Shot Target Pistol, First Model

Hinged frame. Calibers: 22 LR, 32 S&W, 38 S&W. Barrel lengths: 6-, 8- and 10-inch. Approx. 13½ inches overall w/10-inch bbl. Weight: about 25 oz. Target sights, barrel catch rear adj. for windage and elevation. Blued finish. Square butt, hard rubber stocks. Made 1893–1905. *Note:* This model was available also as a combination arm w/ accessory 38 revolver barrel and cylinder enabling conversion to a pocket revolver. It has the frame of the 38 SA Revolver Model 1891 w/side flanges, hand and cylinder stop slots.

Single-shot Pistol, 22 LR	**$ 495**
Single-shot Pistol, 32 S&W or 38 S&W	895
Combination Set, Revolver and Single-shot Barrel	1350

Smith & Wesson Model 1891 Single Shot Target Pistol, Second Model $550

Basically the same as the First Model, except side flanges, hand and stop slots eliminated, cannot be converted to revolver, redesigned rear sight. Caliber: 22 LR only. 10-inch barrel only. Made 1905–1909.

Smith & Wesson Perfected Single Shot Target Pistol

Also called Olympic Model. Similar to 1891 Single Shot Second Model, except has double-action lockwork. Caliber: 22 LR only. 10-inch barrel. Checkered walnut stocks, extended square butt target type. Made 1909–1923. *Note:* In 1920 and thereafter, this model was made w/barrels having bore diameter of .223 instead of .226 and tight, short chambering. The first group of these pistols was produced for the U.S. Olympic Team of 1920, thus the designation Olympic Model.

Pre-1920 Type	**$495**
Olympic Model	675

Smith & Wesson Sigma Series

Double action only. Calibers: 9mm Parabellum or 40 S&W. 10-, 15- or 17-shot magazine. 4½-inch barrel. 7⅜ inches overall. Weight: 26 oz. Fixed sights w/3-Dot system or optional Tritium sights. Integral polymer grip and frame. Made 1994 to date.

Model SW9F	**$365**
Model SW40F	375
For Tritium Night Sight, **add**	115

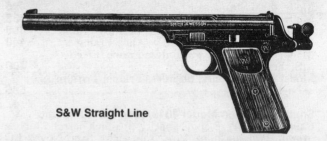

S&W Straight Line

Smith & Wesson Straight Line Single Shot Target Pistol $1095

Frame shaped like that of an automatic pistol, barrel swings to the left on pivot for extracting and loading, straight line trigger and hammer movement. Caliber: 22 LR. 10-inch barrel. 11¼ inches overall. Weight: 34 oz. Target sights. Blued finish. Smooth walnut stocks. Supplied in metal case with screwdriver and cleaning rod. Made 1925–1936.

REVOLVERS

> **NOTE:** This section contains only S&W Revolvers. Pistols, both automatic and single shot, may be found on the preceding pages. For a complete listing of S&W handguns, please refer to the Index.

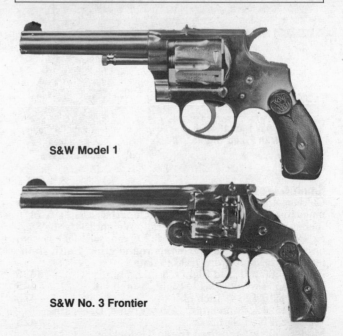

S&W Model 1

S&W No. 3 Frontier

Smith & Wesson Model 1 Hand Ejector DA $360

First Model. Forerunner of the current 32 Hand Ejector and Regulation Police models, this was the first S&W

Smith & Wesson Model 1 Hand Ejector DA (cont.)
revolver of the solid-frame, swing-out cylinder type. Top
strap of this model is longer than those of later models,
and it lacks the usual S&W cylinder latch. Caliber: 32
S&W Long. Barrel lengths: 3¼-, 4¼-, and 6-inch. Fixed
sights. Blued or nickel finish. Round butt, hard rubber
stocks. Made 1896–1903.

Smith & Wesson No. 3 SA Frontier **$1595**
Caliber: 44-40 Winchester. Barrel lengths: 4-, 5- and 6½-
inch. Fixed or target sights. Blued or nickel finish. Round,
hard rubber or checkered walnut grips. Made 1885–1908.

Smith & Wesson No. 3 SA (New Model) **$1350**
Hinged frame. 6-shot cylinder. Caliber: 44 S&W Russian.
Barrel lengths: 4-, 5-, 6-, 6½-, 7½- and 8-inch. Fixed or
target sights. Blued or nickel finish. Round, hard rubber
or checkered walnut grips. Made 1878–1908. *Note:* Value
shown is for standard model. Specialist collectors recognize numerous variations with a range of higher values.

Smith & Wesson No. 3 SA Target **$1750**
Hinged frame. 6-shot cylinder. Calibers: 32/44 S&W, 38/
44 S&W Gallery & Target. 6½-inch barrel only. Fixed or
target sights. Blued or nickel finish. Round, hard rubber
or checkered walnut grips. Made 1887–1910.

**S&W Model 10 M&P
Model of 1905**

S&W Model 10, Round Butt

Smith & Wesson Model 10 38 Military & Police DA
Also called Hand Ejector Model of 1902, Hand Ejector
Model of 1905, Model K. Manufactured substantially in
its present form since 1902, this model has undergone
numerous changes, most of them minor. Round or square-
butt models, the latter introduced in 1904. Caliber: 38
Special. 6-shot cylinder. Barrel lengths: 2- (introduced
1933), 4-, 5-, 6- and 6½-inch (latter discontinued 1915),
also 4-inch heavy barrel (introduced 1957). 11⅛ inches
overall in square-butt model w/6-inch barrel. Round-butt
model is ¼-inch shorter, weighs about ½ oz. less. Fixed
sights. Blued or nickel finish. Checkered walnut stocks,
hard rubber available in round-butt style. Current Model
10 has short action. Made 1902 to date. *Note:* S&W Victory
Model, wartime version of the M & P 38, was produced
for the U.S. Government from 1940 to the end of the war.
A similar revolver, designated 38/200 British Service Revolver, was produced for the British Government during
the same period. These arms have either brush-polished

Smith & Wesson Model 10 38 M&P (cont.)
or sandblast blued finish; most have plain, smooth walnut
stocks and lanyard swivels.

Model of 1902 (1902–1905)	**$450**
Model of 1905 (1905–1940)	395
38/200 British Service (1940–45)	350
Victory Model (1942–45)	295
Model of 1944 (1945–48)	165
Model 10 (1948–date)	170

S&W Model 10, Heavy Barrel

**Smith & Wesson Model 10 38 Military & Police
Heavy Barrel** **$185**
Same as standard Model 10, except has heavy 4-inch
barrel, weighs 34 oz. Made from 1957 to date.

S&W Model 12

Smith & Wesson Model 12 38 M&P Airweight . . . **$215**
Same as standard Military & Police, except has light alloy
frame, furnished with 2- or 4-inch barrel only, weighs 18
oz. (with 2-inch barrel). Made 1952–1986.

Smith & Wesson Model 13 357 Military/Police . . **$190**
Same as Model 10 38 Military & Police Heavy Barrel,
except chambered for 357 Magnum and 38 Special with
3- or 4-inch barrel. Made 1974 to date.

S&W Model 13, Heavy Barrel

Smith & Wesson Model 13 (Heavy Barrel) DA . . **$205**
Calibers: 357 Mag.; 38 S&W Special. 6-shot cylinder. Barrel lengths: 3 and 4 inches. 9¼ inches overall. Weight: 34 oz. Square notch rear sight, ramp front. (*See* photo, preceding page.)

S&W Model 14 Single Action

Smith & Wesson Models 14 (K38) and 16 (K32) Masterpiece Revolvers
Calibers: 22 LR, 22 Magnum Rimfire, 32 S&W Long, 38 Special. 6-shot cylinder. DA/SA. Barrel lengths: 4- (22 MRF only), 6-, 8⅜-inch (latter not available in K32). 11⅛ inches overall (6-inch bbl.). Weight: 38½ oz. w/6-inch bbl. Click adjustable rear sight, Patridge front. Blued finish. Checkered walnut stocks. Made 1947 to date. (Model 16 discontinued 1974, with only 3,630 produced; reissued 1990–93.)

Model 14 (K-38, Double Action)	**$225**
Model 14 (K-38, Single Action, 6-inch bbl.)	**250**
Model 14 (K-38, Single Action, 8⅜-inch bbl.)	**265**
Model 16 (K-32, Double Action)	**235**

S&W Model 15 Double Action

Smith & Wesson Models 15 (38) and 18 (22) Combat Masterpiece Double Action Revolvers
Same as K-22 and K-38 Masterpiece but with 2- (38) or 4-inch barrel and Baughman quick-draw front sight. 9⅛ inches overall with 4-inch bbl. Weight: 34 oz. (38 cal.). Introduced 1950; Model 18 discontinued 1985.

Model 15	**$235**
Model 18	**255**

S&W Model 17 K-22 Masterpiece

Smith & Wesson Model 17 K-22 Masterpiece . . . **$245**
Caliber: 22 LR. 6-shot cylinder. DA. Barrel lengths: 4, 6 or 8⅜ inches. 11⅛ inches overall w/6-inch bbl. Weight: 38½ oz. w/6-inch bbl. Patridge-type front sight; S&W micrometer click rear. Checkered walnut Service grips w/ S&W monogram. S&W blued finish. Made 1947 to date.

S&W Model 19 Round Butt

S&W Model 19

Smith & Wesson Model 19 357 Combat Magnum Double Action Revolver **$245**
Caliber: 357 Magnum. 6-shot cylinder. Barrel lengths: 2½ (round butt), 4, 6 inches. 9½ inches overall (4-inch bbl.). Weight: 35 oz. (4-inch bbl.). Click adj. rear sight, ramp front. Blued or nickel finish. Target stocks of checkered Goncalo Alves. Made from 1956 to date.

S&W Model 20

Smith & Wesson Model 20 38/44 Heavy Duty DA
Caliber: 38 Special. 6-shot cylinder. Barrel lengths: 4, 5 and 6½ inches. 10⅜ inches overall w/5-inch bbl. Weight: 40 oz. w/5-inch bbl. Fixed sights. Blued or nickel finish. Checkered walnut stocks. Short action after 1948. Made 1930–1967.

Pre-World War II	**$595**
Postwar	**250**

S&W Model 21

S&W 22/32 Target

Smith & Wesson Model 21 1950 44 Military Double Action Revolver $1295
Postwar version of the 1926 Model 44 Military with same general specifications, except redesigned hammer. Made 1950–1967.

Smith & Wesson 22/32 Target DA (cont.)
ceived 292 pieces. These are the true "Bekeart Model" revolvers worth about double the value shown for the standard 22/32 Target.

S&W Model 22

S&W Model 23

Smith & Wesson Model 22 1950 Army DA $995
Postwar version of the 1917 Army w/same general specifications, except redesigned hammer. Made 1950–1967.

Smith & Wesson Model 23 38/44 Outdoorsman Double Action Revolver
Target version of the 38/44 Heavy Duty. 6½-inch barrel only. Weight: 41¾ oz. Target sights, micrometer-click rear on postwar models. Blued finish only. 1950 model has ribbed barrel, redesigned hammer. Made 1930–1967.
Prewar $595
Postwar 465

S&W 22/32 Kit Gun

S&W Model 24

Smith & Wesson 22/32 Kit Gun $495
Same as 22/32 Target, except has 4-inch barrel, round grips, 8 inches overall, weighs 21 oz. Made 1935–1953.

Smith & Wesson 22/32 Target DA Revolver $695
Also known as the Bekeart Model. Design based upon "32 Hand Ejector." Caliber: 22 LR (recessed head cylinder for high-speed cartridges introduced 1935). 6-shot cylinder. 6-inch barrel. 10½ inches overall. Weight: 23 oz. Adjustable target sights. Blued finish. Checkered walnut stocks. Made 1911–1953. *Note:* In 1911, San Francisco gun dealer Phil Bekeart, who suggested this model, re-

Smith & Wesson Model 24 1950 44 Target DA Revolver $565
Postwar version of the 1926 Model 44 Target w/same specifications, except has redesigned hammer, ribbed barrel, micrometer click rear sight. Made 1950–1967.

Smith & Wesson Model 25 1950 45 Target DA Revolver $355
Same as 1950 Model 44 Target but chambered for 45 Automatic cartridge. Made 1950 to date.

S&W Model 27

S&W Model 30

Smith & Wesson Model 27 357 Magnum DA
Caliber: 357 S&W Magnum. 6-shot cylinder. Barrel lengths: 3½-, 5-, 6-, 6½- and 8⅜-inch. 11⅜ inches overall w/6-inch bbl. Weight: 44 oz. w/6-inch bbl. Adjustable target sights, Baughman quick-draw ramp front sight on 3½-inch barrel. Blued or nickel finish. Checkered walnut stocks. Made 1935 to date. *Note:* Until 1938, the 357 Magnum was custom made in any barrel length from 3½-inch to 8¾-inch; each of these revolvers was accompanied by a registration certificate and has its registration number stamped on the inside of the yoke. Postwar Magnums have a redesigned hammer with shortened fall and the new S&W micrometer click rear sight.
Prewar Registered Model	$825
Prewar Model without Registration Number	495
Current Model with 8⅜-inch Barrel	325
Current Model, other barrel lengths	285

S&W Model 28

Smith & Wesson Model 28 Highway Patrolman Double Action Revolver $225
Caliber: 357 Magnum. 6-shot cylinder. Barrel lengths: 4- or 6-inch. 11¼ inches overall w/6-inch bbl. Weight: 44 oz. w/6-inch bbl. Adjustable rear sight, ramp front. Blued finish. Checkered walnut stocks, Magna or target type. Made 1954–1986.

Smith & Wesson Model 29 44 Magnum DA Revolver
Caliber: 44 Magnum. 6-shot cylinder. Barrel lengths: 4-, 6½-, 8⅜-inch. 11⅞ inches overall (6½-inch bbl.). Weight: 47 oz., 6½-inch bbl. Click adjustable rear sight, ramp front. Blued or nickel finish. Checkered Goncalo Alves target stocks. Made 1956–1991.
With 8⅜-inch barrel	$335
Other barrel lengths	300

Smith & Wesson Model 30 32 Hand Ejector Double Action Revolver $225
Caliber: 32 S&W Long. 6-shot cylinder. Barrel lengths: 2- (introduced 1949), 3-, 4- and 6-inch. 8 inches overall

Smith & Wesson Model 30 32 Hand Ejector DA (cont.)
w/4-inch bbl. Weight: 18 oz. w/4-inch bbl. Fixed sights. Blued or nickel finish. Round, checkered walnut or hard rubber stocks. Made 1903–1976. Numerous changes, mostly minor, as in M & P model.

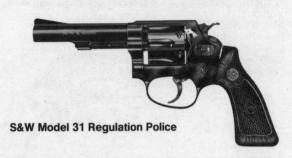

S&W Model 31 Regulation Police

Smith & Wesson Models 31 & 33 Regulation Police Double Action Revolver $200
Same basic type as 32 Hand Ejector, except has square buttstocks. Calibers: 32 S&W Long (Model 31), 38 S&W (Model 33). 6-shot cylinder in 32 caliber, 5-shot in 38 caliber. Barrel lengths: 2- (introduced 1949), 3-, 4- and 6-inch in 32 cal.; 4-inch only in 38 cal. 8½ inches overall w/4-inch bbl. Weight: 18 oz., 38 cal. w/4-inch barrel; 32 cal., ¾-oz. heavier. Fixed sights. Blued or nickel finish. Checkered walnut stocks. Made from 1917. Model 33 discontinued in 1974; Model 31 discontinued in 1992.

S&W Model 32 Double Action

Smith & Wesson 32 Double Action Revolver ... $195
Hinged frame. Caliber: 32 S&W. 5-shot cylinder. Barrel lengths: 3-, 3½- and 6-inch. Fixed sights. Blued or nickel finish. Hard rubber stocks. Made 1880–1919. *Note:* Value shown applies generally to the several varieties. Exception is the rare first issue of 1880 (identified by squared sideplate and serial no. 1 to 30) valued at **$2,000.**

Smith & Wesson Model 32 Terrier DA $225
Caliber: 38 S&W. 5-shot cylinder. 2-inch barrel. 6¼ inches overall. Weight: 17 oz. Fixed sights. Blued or nickel finish. Checkered walnut or hard rubber stocks. Built on 32 Hand Ejector frame. Made 1936–1974.

Smith & Wesson 32-20 Military & Police DA

Same as M & P 38, except chambered for 32-20 Winchester cartridge. First introduced in the 1899 model, M & P Revolvers were produced in this caliber until about 1940. Values same as for corresponding M & P 38 models.

S&W Model 34

Smith & Wesson Model 34 1953 22/32 Kit Gun . . $225

Same general specifications as previous 22/32 Kit Gun, except with 2-inch or 4-inch barrel and round or square buttstocks, blue or nickel finish. Made 1953–1991.

S&W Model 35

Smith & Wesson Model 35 1953 22/32 Target . . $275

Same general specifications as previous model 22/32 Target, except has micrometer-click rear sight, Magna-type target stocks, weighs 25 oz. Made 1953–1974.

S&W Model 36 Chiefs Special

Smith & Wesson Model 36 Chiefs Special DA . . $215

Based on 32 Hand Ejector with frame lengthened to permit longer cylinder for 38 Special cartridge. Caliber: 38 Special. 5-shot cylinder. Barrel lengths: 2- or 3-inch. 6½ inches overall w/2-inch bbl. Weight: 19 oz. Fixed sights. Blued or nickel finish. Checkered walnut stocks, round or square butt. Made 1952–1991.

Smith & Wesson Model 37 Airweight Chiefs Special $205

Same general specifications as standard Chiefs Special, except has light alloy frame, weighs 12½ oz. with 2-inch bbl., blued finish only. Made 1954 to date.

Smith & Wesson Model 38 Airweight DA $225

Caliber: 38 Special. 5-shot cylinder. Barrel length: 2 or 4 inches. 6⅞ inches (2-inch barrel) overall. Weight: 18 oz. Square notch rear sight, ramp front sight.

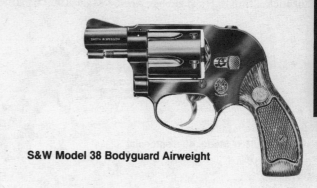

S&W Model 38 Bodyguard Airweight

Smith & Wesson Model 38 Bodyguard Airweight Double Action Revolver $220

"Shrouded" hammer. Light alloy frame. Caliber: 38 Special. 5-shot cylinder. 2-inch barrel. 6⅜ inches overall. Weight: 14½ oz. Fixed sights. Blued or nickel finish. Checkered walnut stocks. Made 1955 to date.

Smith & Wesson 38 Double Action Revolver . . . $850

Hinged frame. Caliber: 38 S&W. 5-shot cylinder. Barrel lengths: 4-, 4¼-, 5-, 6-, 8- and 10-inch. Fixed sights. Blued or nickel finish. Hard rubber stocks. Made 1880–1911. *Note:* Value shown applies generally to the several varieties. Exceptions are the first issue of 1880 (identified by squared sideplate and serial no. 1 to 4,000) and the 8- and 10-inch barrel models of the third issue (1884–1895).

Smith & Wesson Model 38 Hand Ejector DA $670

Military & Police—First Model. Resembles Colt New Navy in general appearance, lacks barrel lug and locking bolt common to all later S&W hand ejector models. Caliber: 38 Long Colt. 6-shot cylinder. Barrel lengths: 4-, 5-, 6- and 6½-inch. 11½ inches overall w/6½-inch bbl. Fixed sights. Blued or nickel finish. Round, checkered walnut or hard rubber stocks. Made 1899–1902.

S&W 38 M&P Target

Smith & Wesson 38 Military & Police Target DA

Target version of the Military & Police with standard features of that model. Caliber: 38 Special. 6-inch barrel. Weight: 32¼ oz. Adj. target sights. Blued finish. Checkered walnut stocks. Made 1899–1940. For values, add **$75** to those shown for corresponding M&P 38 models.

Smith & Wesson Model 38 Perfected DA **$550**
Hinged frame. Similar to earlier 38 Double Action Model,
but heavier frame, side latch as in solid-frame models,
improved lockwork. Caliber: 38 S&W. 5-shot cylinder.
Barrel lengths: 3¼-, 4-, 5- and 6-inch. Fixed sights. Blued
or nickel finish. Hard rubber stocks. Made 1909–1920.

S&W Model 40 Centennial

**Smith & Wesson Model 40 Centennial Double
Action Hammerless Revolver** **$350**
Similar to Chiefs Special, but has Safety Hammerless-
type mechanism with grip safety. 2-inch barrel. Weight:
19 oz. Made 1953–1974.

**Smith & Wesson Model 42 Centennial
Airweight** **$395**
Same as standard Centennial model, except has light alloy
frame, weighs 13 oz. Made 1954–1974.

S&W Model 43

**Smith & Wesson Model 43 1955 22/32 Kit Gun
Airweight** **$395**
Same as Model 34 Kit Gun, except has light alloy frame,
furnished with 3½-inch barrel only, weighs 14¼ oz.,
square buttstock. Made 1954–1974.

Smith & Wesson Model 44 1926 Military DA Revolver
Basically the same as the early New Century model, having
the extractor rod casing but lacking the "Triple Lock"
feature. Caliber: 44 S&W Special. 6-shot cylinder. Barrel
lengths: 4, 5 and 6½ inches. 11¾ inches overall w/6½-
inch bbl. Weight: 39½ oz., 6½-inch bbl. Fixed sights.
Blued or nickel finish. Checkered walnut stocks. Made
1926–1941.
Standard Model . . . . **$ 695**
Target Model w/6½-inch bbl., Target Sights,
   Blued **1095**

Smith & Wesson 44 Double Action Revolver
Also called Wesson Favorite (lightweight model), Frontier
(caliber 44-40). Hinged frame. 6-shot cylinder. Calibers:
44 S&W Russian, 38-40, 44-40. Barrel lengths: 4-, 5-, 6-
and 6½-inch. Weight: 37½ oz. w/6½-inch bbl. Fixed

Smith & Wesson 44 DA (cont.)
sights. Blued or nickel finish. Hard rubber stocks. Made
1881–1913; Frontier discontinued 1910.
Standard Model, 44 Russian . . . . **$ 850**
Standard Model, 38-40 . . . . **1995**
Frontier Model **1350**
Favorite Model **3595**

S&W 44 Hand Ejector, Second Model

**Smith & Wesson 44 Hand Ejector, Second
Model DA Revolver** **$595**
Basically the same as New Century, except crane lock
("Triple Lock" feature) and extractor rod casing
eliminated. Calibers: 44 S&W Special, 44-40 Win., 45 Colt.
Barrel lengths: 4-, 5-, 6½- and 7½-inch. 11¾ inches
overall w/6½-inch bbl. Weight: 38 oz. w/6½-inch bbl.
Fixed sights. Blued or nickel finish. Checkered walnut
stocks. Made 1915–1937.

**Smith & Wesson Model 48 (K-22) Masterpiece
M.R.F. DA Revolver** **$250**
Caliber: 22 Mag. and 22 RF. 6-shot cylinder. Barrel
lengths: 4 and 6 inches. 11⅛ inches overall. Weight: 39
oz. Adjustable rear sight, ramp front.

Smith & Wesson Model 49 Bodyguard **$245**
Same as Model 38 Bodyguard Airweight, except has steel
frame, weighs 20½ oz. Made 1959 to date.

S&W Model 51

S&W Model 53

Smith & Wesson Model 51 1960 22/32 Kit Gun . . **$375**
Same as Model 34 Kit Gun, except chambered for 22 WMR; has 3½-inch barrel, weighs 24 oz. Made 1960–74.

Smith & Wesson Model 53 22 Magnum DA **$595**
Caliber: 22 Rem. Jet C.F. Magnum. 6-shot cylinder (inserts permit use of 22 Short, Long, or LR cartridges). Barrel lengths: 4-, 6-, 8⅜-inches. 11¼ inches w/6-inch bbl. Weight: 40 oz. w/6-inch bbl. Micrometer-click rear sight, ramp front. Checkered walnut stocks. Made 1960–1974.

Smith & Wesson Model 57 41 Magnum DA Revolver
Caliber: 41 Magnum. 6-shot cylinder. Barrel lengths: 4-, 6-, 8⅜-inches. Weight: with 6-inch barrel, 40 oz. Micrometer click rear sight, ramp front. Target stocks of checkered Goncalo Alves. Made 1964 to date.
With 8⅜-inch barrel **$355**
Other barrel lengths **295**

S&W Model 58 41 M&P

Smith & Wesson Model 58 41 Military & Police Double Action Revolver **$325**
Caliber: 41 Magnum. 6-shot cylinder. 4-inch barrel. 9¼ inches overall. Weight: 41 oz. Fixed sights. Checkered walnut stocks. Intro. 1964; discontinued.

S&W Model 60 Lady Smith

Smith & Wesson Model 60 Stainless DA **$250**
Caliber: 38 Special. 5-shot cylinder. Barrel length: 2 or 3 inches (Lady Smith Model). 6½ or 7½ inches overall. Weight: 19 oz. Square notch rear sight, ramp front. Satin finish stainless steel. Made 1965 to date.

Smith & Wesson Model 63 (1977) Kit Gun DA . . **$235**
Caliber: 22 LR. 6-shot cylinder. 4-inch barrel. 6½ inches overall. Weight: 24½ oz. Adj. rear sight, ramp front.

Smith & Wesson Model 64 38 M&P Stainless . . . **$195**
Same as standard Model 10, except satin-finished stainless steel; square butt w/4-inch heavy barrel or round butt w/ 2-inch barrel. Made 1970 to date.

S&W Model 65 357 M&P

Smith & Wesson Model 65 357 Military/Police Stainless **$200**
Same as Model 13, except satin-finished stainless steel. Made 1974 to date.

S&W Model 66 357 Combat Magnum

Smith & Wesson Model 66 357 Combat Magnum Stainless **$250**
Same as Model 19, except satin-finished stainless steel. Made 1971 to date.

S&W Model 67 Combat Masterpiece

Smith & Wesson Model 67 38 Combat Masterpiece Stainless **$215**
Same as Model 15, except satin-finished stainless steel; available only with 4-inch barrel. Made 1972–1988.

**S&W 125th Anniversary
Commemorative, Deluxe Edition**

Smith & Wesson 125th Anniversary Commemorative

Issued to celebrate the 125th anniversary of the 1852 partnership of Horace Smith and Daniel Baird Wesson. Standard Edition is Model 25 revolver, caliber 45 Colt, with 6½-inch barrel, bright blued finish, gold-filled barrel roll mark "Smith & Wesson 125th Anniversary," sideplate marked with gold-filled Anniversary seal, smooth Goncalo Alves stocks, in presentation case with nickel silver Anniversary medallion and book, *125 Years with Smith & Wesson,* by Roy Jinks. Deluxe Edition is same, except revolver is Class A engraved with gold-filled seal on sideplate, ivory stocks; Anniversary medallion is sterling silver and book is leather bound; limited to 50 units. Total issue is 10,000 units, of which 50 are Deluxe Edition and two are a Custom Deluxe Edition not for sale. Made in 1977. Values are for revolvers in new condition.

Standard Edition .... **$ 595**
Deluxe Edition **1600**

Smith & Wesson Model 547 DA Revolver **$250**

Caliber: 9mm. 6-shot cylinder. Barrel length: 3 or 4 inches. 7⁵/₁₆ inches overall. Weight: 32 oz. Square notch rear sight, ramp front. Discontinued 1986.

Smith & Wesson Models 581 Revolver

Caliber: 357 Magnum. Barrel: 4 inches. Weight: 34 oz. Serrated ramp front sight, square notch rear. Checkered walnut grips.

Blued Finish **$195**
Nickel Finish **225**

**S&W Model 586
Distinguished Combat Magnum**

Smith & Wesson Model 586 Distinguished Combat Magnum **$265**

Caliber: 357 Magnum. 6-shot. Barrel lengths: 4, 6 and 8³/₈ inches. Overall length: 9¾ inches w/4-inch bbl.; 13¹³/₁₆ inches w/8³/₈-inch bbl. Weight: 42, 46, 53 oz., respectively. Red ramp front sight, micrometer-click adjustable rear. Checkered grip. S&W blue or nickel finish.

Smith & Wesson Model 610 DA Revolver **$385**

Similar to Model 625, except in caliber 10mm. Magnaclassic grips.

Smith & Wesson Model 617 Double Action Revolver

Similar to Model 17, except in stainless. Made 1992–93.
Semi-Target Model with 4- or 6-inch bbl. **$275**
Target Model with 6-inch bbl. **295**
Target Model with 8³/₈-inch bbl. **315**

Smith & Wesson Model 624 Double Action Revolver

Same general specifications as Model 24, except satin-finished stainless steel. Limited production of 10,000 made in 1985 only.
Standard Model **$375**
Semi-target Model **315**
Target Model **395**

S&W Model 625

Smith & Wesson Model 625 DA Revolver **$355**

Same general specifications as Model 25, except 3-, 4- or 5-inch barrel, round-butt Pachmayr grips and satin stainless steel finish. Made from 1989 to date.

Smith & Wesson Model 627 DA Revolver **$345**

Same general specifications as Model 27, except satin stainless steel finish. Made 1989–1991.

S&W Model 629

Smith & Wesson Model 629 Double Action Revolver

Same as Model 29 in 44 Magnum, except in stainless. Classic made from 1990 to date.
Model 629 (4- and 6-inch bbl.) **$365**
Model 629 (8³/₈-inch bbl.) **385**
Model 629 Classic (5- and 6½-inch bbl.) **395**
Model 629 Classic (8³/₈-inch bbl.) **415**

Smith & Wesson Model 631 Double Action Revolver
Similar to Model 31, except chambered for 32 H&R Mag.
Goncalo Alves combat grips. Made 1991–92.
Fixed Sights, 2-inch bbl. **$250**
Adjustable Sights, 4-inch bbl. **275**

Smith & Wesson Model 632 Centennial DA **$295**
Same general specifications as Model 640, except chambered for 32 H&R Mag. 2-inch barrel. Weight: 15½ oz.
Stainless slide with alloy frame. Santoprene combat grips.
Made in 1991.

Smith & Wesson Model 640 Centennial DA **$325**
Caliber: 38 Special. 5-shot cylinder. 2- or 3-inch barrel.
6⁵⁄₁₆ inches overall. Weight: 20–22 oz. Fixed sights. Stainless finish. Smooth hardwood service stocks. Made 1990 to date.

**S&W Model 642
Centennial Airweight**

**Smith & Wesson Model 642 Centennial
Airweight Double Action Revolver** **$315**
Same general specifications as Model 640, except with 2-inch barrel only; weight of 15.8 oz. with stainless steel/
aluminum alloy frame and finish. Santoprene combat grips. Made 1990–93.

Smith & Wesson Model 648 DA Revolver **$295**
Same general specifications as Models 17/617, except in stainless and chambered for 22 Magnum. Made 1992–93.

Smith & Wesson Model 649 Bodyguard DA **$250**
Caliber: 38 Special. 5-shot cylinder. Barrel length: 2 inches.
6¼ inches overall. Weight: 20 oz. Square notch rear sight, ramp front. Stainless frame and finish.

Smith & Wesson Model 650 Revolver **$275**
Caliber: 22 Mag. 6-shot cylinder. 3-inch barrel. 7 inches overall. Weight: 23½ oz. Serrated ramp front sight, fixed square notch rear. Round butt, checkered walnut monogrammed stocks. Stainless steel finish. Made 1983–85.

Smith & Wesson Model 651 Stainless DA **$265**
Caliber: 22 Mag. Rimfire. 6-shot cylinder. Barrel length: 3 and 4 inches. 7 and 8⁵⁄₈ inches, respectively, overall.
Weight: 24½ oz. Adjustable rear sight, ramp front.

Smith & Wesson Model 657 Revolver
Caliber: 41 Mag. 6-shot cylinder. Barrel: 4, 6 or 8.4 inches.
9.6, 11.4, and 13.9 inches overall. Weight: 44.2, 48 and 52.5 oz. Serrated black ramp front sight on ramp base;
click rear, adjustable for windage and elevation. Satin-finished stainless steel.
With 4- or 6-inch barrel **$295**
With 8.4-inch barrel **340**

S&W Model 681

Smith & Wesson Model 681 .... **$215**
Same as S&W Model 581, except in stainless finish only.

Smith & Wesson Model 686 .... **$275**
Same as S&W Model 586 Distinguished Combat Magnum,
except in stainless finish w/additional 2½-inch barrel.

Smith & Wesson Model 940 Centennial DA **$285**
Same general specifications as Model 640, except chambered for 9mm. 2- or 3-inch barrel. Weight: 23 oz. w/2-inch bbl. Santoprene combat grips. Made 1991 to date.

Smith & Wesson Model 1891 Single Action Revolver
Hinged frame. Caliber: 38 S&W. 5-shot cylinder. Barrel lengths: 3¼-, 4-, 5- and 6-inch. Fixed sights. Blued or nickel finish. Hard rubber stocks. Made 1891–1911. *Note:*
Until 1906, an accessory single-shot target barrel (*see*
Model 1891 Single Shot Target Pistol) was available for this revolver.
Revolver only .... **$ 895**
Set with 22 single-shot barrel **1295**

Smith & Wesson 1917 Army Double Action Revolver
Caliber: 45 Automatic, using 3-cartridge half-moon clip;
45 Auto Rim, without clip. 6-shot cylinder. 5½-inch barrel.
10³⁄₄ inches overall. Weight: 36¼ oz. Fixed sights. Blued finish (blue-black finish on commercial model, brush polish on military). Checkered walnut stocks (commercial model, smooth on military). Made under U.S. Government contract 1917–19; produced commercially 1919–1941.
Note: About 175,000 of these revolvers were produced during WWI. The DCM sold these to NRA members during the 1930s at $16.15 each.
Commercial Model **$395**
Military Model **375**

Smith & Wesson K-22 Masterpiece DA **$895**
Improved version of K-22 Outdoorsman with same specifications but with micrometer-click rear sight, short action and antibacklash trigger. Manufactured in 1940.

S&W K-22 Outdoorsman

**S&W Ladysmith
Second Model**

**S&W Ladysmith
Third Model**

Smith & Wesson K-22 Outdoorsman DA $475
Design based on the 38 Military & Police Target. Caliber: 22 LR. 6-shot cylinder barrel. 11⅛ inches overall. Weight: 35 oz. Adjustable target sights. Blued finish. Checkered walnut stock. Made 1931–1940.

Smith & Wesson K32 and K38 Heavy Masterpiece Double Action Revolvers
Same as K32 and K38 Masterpiece, but with heavy barrel. Weight: 38½ oz. Made 1950–53. *Note:* All K32 and K38 revolvers made after September 1953 have heavy barrels and the "Heavy Masterpiece" designation was discontinued. Values for Heavy Masterpiece models are the same as shown for Models 14 and 16. (*See* separate listing).

Smith & Wesson K-32 Target DA Revolver $995
Same as 38 Military & Police Target, except chambered for 32 S&W Long cartridge, slightly heavier barrel. Weight: 34 oz. Only 98 produced. Made 1938–1940.

Smith & Wesson Ladysmith (cont.)
ficulty of manufacture and high frequency of repairs.

First Model	**$1195**
Second Model	**1025**
Third Model, fixed sights, 3- or 3½-inch barrel	**995**
Third Model, fixed sights, 2¼- or 6-inch barrel . . .	**1150**
Third Model, adjustable sights, 6-inch barrel	**1195**

Smith & Wesson New Century Model Hand Ejector Double Action Revolver $895
Also called "Triple Lock" because of its third cylinder lock at the crane. 6-shot cylinder. Calibers: 44 S&W Special, 450 Eley, 455 Mark II. Barrel lengths: 4-, 5-, 6½- and 7½-inch. Weight: 39 oz. w/6½-inch bbl. Fixed sights. Blued or nickel finish. Checkered walnut stocks. Made 1907–1915.

**S&W Ladysmith
First Model**

Smith & Wesson Ladysmith (Model M Hand Ejector) Double Action Revolver
Caliber: 22 LR. 7-shot cylinder. Barrel lengths: 2¼-, 3-, 3½- and 6-inch (Third Model only). Approximately 7 inches overall w/3½-inch bbl. Weight: about 9½ oz. Fixed sights, adjustable target sights available on Third Model. Blued or nickel finish. Round butt, hard rubber stocks on First and Second Model; checkered walnut or hard rubber square buttstocks on Third Model. First Model—1902 to 1906: cylinder locking bolt operated by button on left side of frame, no barrel lug and front locking bolt. Second Model—1906 to 1911: rear cylinder latch eliminated, has barrel lug, forward cylinder lock with draw-bolt fastening. Third Model—1911 to 1921: same as Second Model except has square buttstocks, target sights and 6-inch barrel available. *Note:* Legend has it that a straight-laced D.B. Wesson ordered discontinuance of the Ladysmith when he learned of the little revolver's reputed popularity with ladies of the evening. The story, which undoubtedly has enhanced the appeal of this model to collectors, is not true: Wesson Ladysmith was discontinued because of dif-

S&W Regulation Police Target

Smith & Wesson Regulation Police Target DA . . $325
Target version of the Regulation Police with standard features of that model. Caliber: 32 S&W Long. 6-inch barrel. 10¼ inches overall. Weight: 20 oz. Adjustable target sights. Blued finish. Checkered walnut stocks. Made about 1917–1940.

Smith & Wesson Safety Hammerless Revolver . . $595
Also called New Departure Double Action. Hinged frame. Calibers: 32 S&W, 38 S&W. 5-shot cylinder. Barrel lengths: 32 cal.—2-, 3- and 3½-inch; 38 cal.—2-, 3¼-, 4-, 5- and 6-inch. Length overall: 6¾ inches, 32 cal. w/3-inch bbl.; 7½ inches, 38 cal. w/3¼-inch bbl. Weight: 14¼ oz., 32 cal. w/3-inch bbl.; 18¼ oz., 38 cal. w/3¼-inch bbl. Fixed

S&W Safety Hammerless

Smith & Wesson Safety Hammerless (cont.)
sights. Blued or nickel finish. Hard rubber stocks. 32 cal. made 1888–1937; 38 cal. 1887–1941. Various minor changes.

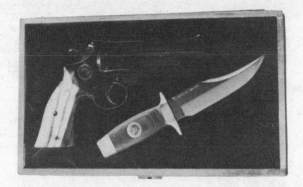

S&W Texas Ranger Commemorative

Smith & Wesson Texas Ranger Commem. $895
Issued to honor the 150th anniversary of the Texas Rangers. Model 19 357 Combat Magnum with 4-inch barrel, sideplate stamped with Texas Ranger Commemorative Seal, smooth Goncalo Alves stocks. Special Bowie knife. In presentation case. 8,000 sets made in 1973. Value is for set in new cond.

SPRINGFIELD, INC.
Colona, Illinois
(Formerly Springfield Armory of Geneseo, Ill.)

**Springfield Armory
Model 1911-A1 Auto Pistol**

Springfield Armory 1911-A1 Automatic Pistol
Calibers: 9mm Parabellum, 38 Super, 40 S&W, 45 ACP. 7-, 8- or 10-shot magazine. 5-inch barrel. 8½ inches overall. Weight: 36 oz. Fixed combat sights. Blued or parkerized finish. Checkered walnut stocks. *Note:* This is an exact duplicate of the Colt M1911A1 that was used by the U.S. Armed Forces for many years.
Blued Finish **$395**
Parkerized Finish **350**

Springfield Armory Bobcat

Springfield Armory Bobcat Automatic Pistol **$340**
Caliber: 380 ACP. 13-shot magazine. 3.5-inch barrel. 6.6 inches overall. Weight: 21.95 oz. Blade front sight; rear adjustable for windage. Textured composition grip. Matte blue finish. Made 1991–93.

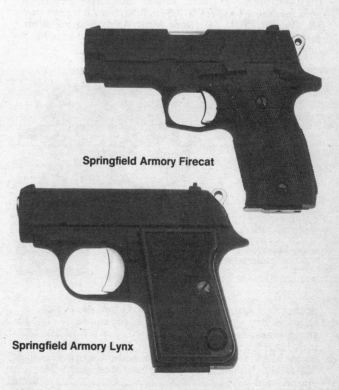

Springfield Armory Firecat

Springfield Armory Lynx

Springfield Armory Firecat Automatic Pistol
Calibers: 9mm, 40 S&W. 8-shot magazine (9mm); 7-shot magazine (40 S&W). 3.5-inch barrel. 6.5 inches overall. Weight: 25.75 oz. Fixed sights with 3-Dot system. Check-

Springfield Armory Firecat Automatic (cont.)

ered walnut grip. Matte blue finish. Made 1991–93.

9mm	**$370**
40 S&W	**390**

Springfield Armory Lynx Automatic Pistol **$190**

Caliber: 25 ACP. 7-shot magazine. 2.25-inch barrel. 4.45 inches overall. Weight: 10.55 oz. Blade front sight; rear adjustable for windage with 3-Dot system. Checkered composition grip. Matte blued finish. Made 1991–93. (*See* photo, preceding page.)

Springfield Armory Panther

Springfield Armory Panther Automatic Pistol . . . **$455**

Calibers: 9mm, 40 S&W. 15-shot magazine (9mm); 11-shot magazine (40 S&W). 3.8-inch barrel. 7.5 inches overall. Weight: 28.95 oz. Blade front sight; rear adjustable for windage w/3-dot system. Checkered walnut grip. Matte blue finish. Made 1991–93.

**Springfield Armory
Model P9**

Springfield Armory Model P9 DA Automatic Pistol

Calibers: 9mm, 40 S&W, 45 ACP. Magazine capacity: 15-shot (9mm); 11-shot (40 S&W); 10-shot (45 ACP). 4.75-inch barrel. 8 inches overall. Weight: 32 oz. Fixed sights with 3-Dot system. Checkered walnut grip. Finishes: Matte blue, Parkerized or stainless. Made 1990–94.

9mm Blued	**$395**
9mm Parkerized	**415**
9mm Stainless	**425**
40 S&W or 45 ACP Blued	**410**
40 S&W or 45 ACP Parkerized	**400**
40 S&W or 45 ACP Stainless	**450**

Springfield Armory Model P9 Ultra LPS Pistol

Same general specifications as Model P9, except with dual port compensator system, extended safety and magazine release.

9mm Bi-Tone	**$515**
9mm Stainless	**525**
40 S&W Bi-Tone	**535**
40 S&W Stainless	**540**
45 ACP Bi-Tone	**545**
45 ACP Stainless	**550**

STAR PISTOLS
Eibar, Spain
Star, Bonifacio Echeverria, S.A.

Star Model 30M

Star Model 30M Double Action Auto Pistol **$335**

Caliber: 9mm Parabellum. 15-shot magazine. 4³/₈-inch barrel. 8 inches overall. Weight: 40 oz. Steel frame with combat features. Adjustable sights. Checkered composition stocks. Blued finish. Made 1984–1991.

Star Model 30PK

Star Model 30PK Double Action Auto Pistol **$320**

Same gen. specifications as Star Model 30M, except 3.8-inch barrel, 30-oz. weight and alloy frame. Made 1984–89.

Star Model 31P Double Action Auto Pistol
Same general specifications as Model 30M, except removable backstrap houses complete firing mechanism. Weight: 39.4 oz. Made 1990 to date.
Blued Finish **$275**
Starvel Finish **375**

Star Model 31PK Double Action Auto Pistol **$285**
Same general specifications as Model 31P, except with alloy frame. Weight: 30 oz. Made 1990 to date.

Star Model A Automatic Pistol **$205**
Modification of the Colt Government Model 45 Auto, which it closely resembles; lacks grip safety. Caliber: 38 Super. 8-shot magazine. 5-inch barrel. 8-inches overall. Weight: 35 oz. Fixed sights. Blued finish. Checkered stocks. Made 1934 to date. No longer imported.

Star Model AS

Star Models AS, BS, PS **$285**
Same as Models A, B and P, except have magazine safety. Made in 1975.

Star Model B **$225**
Same as Model A, except in 9mm Luger. Made 1934–1975.

Star Model BKM **$230**
Similar to Model BM, except has aluminum frame and weight 25.6 oz. Made 1976–1992.

Star Model BKS

Star Model BKS Starlight Automatic Pistol **$225**
Light alloy frame. Caliber: 9mm Luger. 8-shot magazine. 4¼-inch bbl. 7 inches overall. Weight: 25 oz. Fixed sights. Blued or chrome finish. Plastic grips. Made 1970–1981.

Star Model BM Automatic Pistol
Caliber: 9mm. 8-shot magazine. 3.9-inch barrel. 6.95 inches overall. Weight: 34.5 oz. Fixed sights. Checkered walnut stocks. Blued or Starvel finish. Made 1976–1992.
Blued Finish **$225**
Starvel Finish **250**

Star Model CO Pocket Automatic Pistol **$175**
Caliber: 25 Automatic (6.35mm). 2¾-inch barrel. 4½ inches overall. Weight: 13 oz. Fixed sights. Blued finish. Plastic stocks. Made 1941–1957.

Star Model CU Starlet*

Star Model CU Starlet Pocket Automatic Pistol . **$180**
Light alloy frame. Caliber: 25 Automatic (6.35mm). 8-shot magazine. 2⅜-inch barrel. 4¾ inches overall. Weight: 10½ oz. Fixed sights. Blued or chrome-plated slide; frame anodized in black, blue, green, gray or gold. Plastic stocks. Made 1957 to date. U.S. importation discont. 1968.

Star Model F Automatic

Star Model F Automatic Pistol **$150**
Caliber: 22 LR. 10-shot magazine. 4½-inch barrel. 7¼ inches overall. Weight: 25 oz. Fixed sights. Blued finish. Plastic stocks. Made 1942–1967.

Star Model F Olympic Rapid-Fire **$275**
Caliber: 22 Short. 9-shot magazine. 7-inch barrel. 11¹¹⁄₁₆ inches overall. Weight: 52 oz. with weights. Adjustable target sight. Adjustable 3-piece barrel weight. Aluminum alloy slide. Muzzle brake. Plastic stocks. Made 1942–1967.

Star Model FM

Star Model FM **$165**
Similar to Model FR, except has heavier frame with web
in front of trigger guard, 4¼-inch heavy barrel; weighs 32
oz. Made 1972–1991.

Star Model FR **$170**
Similar to Model F with same general specifications, but
restyled, has slide stop and adjustable rear sight. Made
1967–1972.

Star Model FRS

Star Model FRS **$160**
Same as Model FR, except has 6-inch barrel, weighs 28
oz.; also available in chrome finish. Made 1967–1991.

Star Model FS

Star Model FS **$175**
Same as regular Model F, but with 6-inch barrel and adjustable sights. Weight: 27 oz. Made 1942–1967.

Star Model H*

Star Model H **$175**
Same as Model HN except caliber 32 Automatic (7.65mm).
7-shot magazine. Weight: 20 oz. Made 1934–1941.

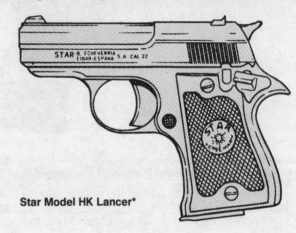

Star Model HK Lancer*

Star Model HK Lancer Automatic Pistol **$210**
Similar to Starfire with same general specifications, except
caliber 22 LR. Made 1955–1968.

Star Model HN Automatic Pistol **$155**
Caliber: 380 Automatic (9mm Short). 6-shot magazine.
2¾-inch barrel. 5⁹/₁₆ inches overall. Weight: 20 oz. Fixed
sights. Blued finish. Plastic stocks. Made 1934–1941.

Star Model I*

Star Model I Automatic Pistol **$170**
Caliber: 32 Automatic (7.65mm). 9-shot magazine. 4¹³/₁₆-inch barrel. 7½ inches overall. Weight: 24 oz. Fixed sights. Blued finish. Plastic stocks. Made 1934–36.

Star Model IN **$175**
Same as Model I, except caliber 380 Automatic (9mm Short), 8-shot magazine, weighs 24½ oz. Made 1934–36.

Star Model PD

Star Model M Military

Star Model S

Star Model M Military Automatic Pistol **$295**
Modification of the Colt Government Model 45 Auto, which it closely resembles; lacks grip safety. Calibers: 9mm Bergmann, 38 Super, 9mm Luger. 8-shot magazine, except 7-shot in 45 caliber. 5-inch barrel. 8½ inches overall. Weight: 36 oz. Fixed sights. Blued finish. Checkered stocks. Made 1934–39.

Star Models M40, M43, M45 Firestar Auto Pistols
Calibers: 9mm, 40 S&W, 45 ACP. 7-shot magazine (9mm); 6-shot (other calibers). 3.4-inch barrel. 6.5 inches overall. Weight: 30.35 oz. Blade front sight, adjustable rear w/3 Dot system. Checkered rubber grips. Blued or Starvel finish. Made 1990 to date.
M40 Blued (40 S&W) **$255**
M40 Starvel (40 S&W) 285
M43 Blued (9mm) 250
M43 Starvel (9mm) 275
M45 Blued (45 ACP) 295
M45 Starvel (45 ACP) 325

Star Megastar Automatic Pistol
Calibers: 10mm, 45 ACP. 12-shot magazine. 4.6-inch barrel. 8.44 inches overall. Weight: 47.6 oz. Sights: blade front; adjustable rear. Checkered composition grip. Finishes: Blued or Starvel. Made from 1992 to date.
Blued Finish, 10mm or 45 ACP **$365**
Starvel Finish, 10mm or 45 ACP 395

Star Model P **$290**
Same as Model A, except caliber 45 Automatic; has 7-shot magazine. Made 1934–1975.

Star Model PD Automatic Pistol
Caliber: 45 Automatic. 6-shot magazine. 3¾-inch barrel. 7 inches overall. Weight: 25 oz. Adjustable rear sight, ramp front. Blued or Starvel finish. Checkered walnut stocks. Made 1975–1992.
Blued Finish **$245**
Starvel Finish 270

Star Model S **$160**
Same as Model SI except caliber 380 Automatic (9mm), 7-shot magazine, weighs 19 oz. Made 1941–1965.

Star Model SI

Star Model SI Automatic Pistol **$185**
Reduced-size modification of the Colt Government Model 45 Auto; lacks grip safety. Caliber: 32 Automatic (7.65mm). 8-shot magazine. 4-inch barrel. 6½ inches overall. Weight: 20 oz. Fixed sights. Blued finish. Plastic stocks. Made 1941–1965.

Star Starfire Automatic Pistol **$295**
Light alloy frame. Caliber: 380 Automatic (9mm Short). 7-shot magazine. 3⅛-inch barrel. 5½ inches overall. Weight: 14½ oz. Fixed sights. Blued or chrome-plated slide; frame anodized in black, blue, green, gray or gold. Plastic stocks. Made 1957 to date. U.S. importation discont. 1968.

Star Models Super A, Super B, Super P **$230**
Same as Models A, B and P, except with improvements described under Super Star. Made c. 1946–1989/1990.

Star Models Super SI, Super S **$235**
Same general specifications as the regular Model SI and S, except with improvements described under Super Star. Made c. 1946–1972.

Star Model Super SM

Star Model Super SM **$230**
Similar to Model Super S, except has adjustable rear sight, wood stocks. Made 1973–1981.

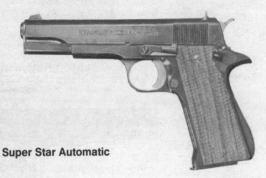

Super Star Automatic

Super Star Automatic Pistol **$285**
Improved version of the Model M with same general specifications; has disarming bolt permitting easier takedown, indicator of cartridge in chamber, magazine safety, takedown magazine, improved sights with luminous spots for aiming in darkness. Calibers: 38 Super, 9mm Luger. This is the standard service pistol of the Spanish Armed Forces, adopted 1946.

Super Star Target Model **$495**
Same as regular Super Star, except with adjustable target rear sight. Discontinued.

STENDA-WERKE PISTOL
Suhl, Germany

Stenda Pocket Automatic Pistol **$230**
Essentially the same as the Beholla; *see* listing of that pistol for specifications. Made c. 1920–25. *Note:* This pistol may be marked "Beholla" along w/the Stenda name and address.

STERLING ARMS CORPORATION
Gasport, New York

Sterling Model 283

Sterling Model 283 Target 300 Auto Pistol **$135**
Caliber: 22 LR. 10-shot magazine. Barrel lengths: 4½-, 6-, 8-inch. 9 inches overall with 4½-inch bbl. Weight: with 4½-inch bbl., 36 oz. Adjustable sights. Blued finish. Plastic stocks. Made 1970–71.

Sterling Model 284

Sterling Model 284 Target 300L **$150**
Same as Model 283, except has 4½- or 6-inch "Luger"-type barrel. Made 1970–71.

Sterling Model 285

Sterling Model 285 Husky **$150**
Same as Model 283, except has fixed sights, 4½-inch barrel only. Made 1970–71.

NOTE: Total production of Models 283, 284, 285 and 286 was 2700 pieces.

Sterling Model 286

Sterling Model 400

Sterling Model 286 Trapper $145
Same as Model 284, except w/fixed sights. Made 1970–71.

Sterling Model 287 PPL-380 Automatic Pistol $90
Caliber: 380 Automatic. 6-shot magazine. 1-inch barrel.
5³/₈ inches overall. Weight: 22¹/₂ oz. Fixed sights. Blued
finish. Plastic stocks. Made 1971–72.

Sterling Model 400S $235
Same as Model 400, except stainless steel. Made 1977–
1983.

Sterling Model 300

Sterling Model 450

Sterling Model 300 Automatic Pistol $115
Caliber: 25 Automatic. 6-shot magazine. 2¹/₃-inch barrel.
4¹/₂ inches overall. Weight: 13 oz. Fixed sights. Blued or
nickel finish. Plastic stocks. Made 1972–1983.

Sterling Model 300S $105
Same as Model 300, except in stainless steel. Made 1976–
1983.

Sterling Model 302 . . . . $115
Same as Model 300, except in 22 LR. Made 1973–1983.

Sterling Model 302S $125
Same as Model 302, except in stainless steel. Made 1976–
1983.

Sterling Model 400 DA Automatic Pistol $195
Caliber: 380 Automatic. 7-shot magazine. 3¹/₂-inch barrel.
6¹/₂ inches overall. Weight: 24 oz. Adjustable rear sight.
Blued or nickel finish. Checkered walnut stocks. Made
1975–1983.

Sterling Model PPL-22

Sterling Model 450 DA Auto Pistol **$295**
Caliber: 45 Automatic. 8-shot magazine. 4-inch barrel. 7½ inches overall. Weight: 36 oz. Adjustable rear sight. Blued finish. Smooth walnut stocks. Made 1977–1983. (*See* photo, preceding page.)

Sterling Model PPL-22 Automatic Pistol **$150**
Caliber: 22 LR. 10-shot magazine. 1-inch barrel. 5½ inches overall. Weight: about 24 oz. Fixed sights. Blued finish. Wood stocks. *Note:* Only 382 made 1970–71. (*See* photo, preceding page.)

J. STEVENS ARMS & TOOL CO.
Chicopee Falls, Mass.

This firm was established in Civil War days by Joshua Stevens, for whom the company was named. In 1936 it became a subsidiary of Savage Arms.

Stevens No. 10

Stevens No. 10 Single Shot Target Pistol **$225**
Caliber: 22 LR. 8-inch barrel. 11½ inches overall. Weight: 37 oz. Target sights. Blued finish. Hard rubber stocks. In external appearance this arm resembles an automatic pistol; it has a tip-up action. Made 1919–1939.

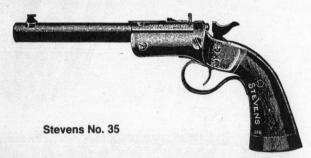

Stevens No. 35

Stevens No. 35 Offhand Model Single Shot Target Pistol **$340**
Tip-up action. Caliber: 22 LR. Barrel lengths: 6, 8, 10, 12¼ inches. Weight: 24 oz. with 6-inch bbl. Target sights. Blued finish. Walnut stocks. *Note:* This pistol is similar to the earlier "Gould" model. No. 35 was also supplied chambered for .410 shotshell. Made 1907–1939.

STEYR PISTOLS
Steyr, Austria

Steyr GB Semiautomatic Pistol **$465**
Caliber: 9mm Parabellum. 18-round magazine. 5.4-inch barrel. 8.9 inches overall. Weight: 2.9 pounds. Post front

Steyr GB Semiautomatic

Steyr GB Semiautomatic Pistol (cont.)
sight; fixed, notched rear. Double, gas-delayed, blow-back action. Made 1981–88.

Steyr-Hahn M12

Steyr-Hahn M12 Automatic Pistol **$445**
Caliber: 9mm Steyr. 8-shot fixed magazine, charger loaded. 5.1-inch barrel. 8.5 inches overall. Weight: 35 oz. Fixed sights. Blued finish. Checkered wood stocks. Made 1911–19. Adopted by the Austro-Hungarian Army in 1912. *Note:* Confiscated by the Germans in 1938, an estimated 250,000 of these pistols were converted to 9mm Luger and stamped with an identifying "08" on the left side of the slide. Mfd. by Osterreichische Waffenfabrik-Gesellschaft.

STOEGER LUGERS
Formerly mfd. by Stoeger Industries, So. Hackensack, N.J.; then Classic Arms, Union City, N.J.

See also Luger and Mauser handgun listings.

Stoeger American Eagle Luger
Caliber: 9mm Parabellum. 7-shot magazine. 4- or 6-inch barrel. 8¼ inches (w/4-inch bbl.) or 10¼ inches (w/6-inch bbl.) overall. Weight: 30 or 32 oz. Checkered walnut grips. Stainless steel frame. Made from 1994 to date.
P-08 Model (4-inch bbl.) **$515**
Navy Model (6-inch bbl.) **525**

Stoeger Standard Luger

Stoeger Standard Luger 22 Automatic Pistol . . . $150
Caliber: 22 LR. 10-shot magazine. Barrels: 4$^{1/2}$, 5$^{1/2}$ inches. 8$^{7/8}$ inches overall w/4$^{1/2}$-inch bbl. Weight: 29$^{1/2}$ oz. w/ 4$^{1/2}$-inch bbl. Fixed sights. Black finish. Smooth wood stocks. Made 1969–1986.

Stoeger Steel Frame Luger 22 Auto Pistol $165
Caliber: 22 LR. 10-shot magazine. 4$^{1/2}$-inch barrel. 8$^{7/8}$ inches overall. Blued finish. Checkered wood stocks. Features one-piece solidly forged and machined steel frame. Made 1980–86.

Stoeger Target Luger 22 Automatic Pistol $195
Same as Standard Luger 22, except has target sights. 9$^{3/8}$ inches overall with 4$^{1/2}$-inch bbl. Checkered wood stocks. Made 1975–1986.

TARGA PISTOLS
Italy
Manufactured by Armi Tanfoglio Guiseppe

Targa Model GT26S Automatic Pistol $45
Caliber: 25 ACP. 6-shot magazine. 2$^{1/2}$-inch barrel. 4$^{5/8}$ inches overall. Weight: 15 oz. Fixed sights. Checkered composition stocks. Blued or chrome finish. Disc. 1990.

Targa Model GT32 Automatic Pistol
Caliber: 32 ACP. 6-shot magazine. 4$^{7/8}$-inch barrel. 7$^{3/8}$ inches overall. Weight: 26 oz. Fixed sights. Checkered composition or walnut stocks. Blued or chrome finish.
Blued finish **$95**
Chrome finish **100**

Targa Model GT 380XE

Targa Model GT380 Automatic Pistol
Same as the Targa GT32, except chambered for 380 ACP.
Blued finish **$110**
Chrome finish **115**

Targa Model GT380XE Automatic Pistol **$135**
Caliber: 380 ACP. 11-shot magazine. 3$^{3/4}$-inch barrel. 7$^{3/8}$ inches overall. Weight: 28 oz. Fixed sights. Blued or satin nickel finish. Smooth wooden stocks. Made 1980–1990.

FORJAS TAURUS S.A.
Porto Alegre, Brazil

Taurus Model 44 Double Action Revolver
Caliber: 44 Mag. 6-shot cylinder. 4-, 6$^{1/2}$ or 8$^{3/8}$-inch barrel. Weight: 44.75 oz. (4-inch bbl.), 52.5 or 57.25 oz. Brazilian hardwood grips. Blued or stainless steel finish. Made 1994 to date.
Blued Finish (4-inch bbl.) **$275**
Blued Finish (6- or 8$^{3/8}$-inch bbl.) **295**
Stainless (4-inch bbl.) **315**
Stainless (6- or 8$^{3/8}$-inch bbl.) **335**

**Taurus Model 65
Satin Nickel**

Taurus Model 65 Double Action Revolver
Caliber: 357 Magnum. 6-shot cylinder. 3- or 4-inch barrel. Weight: 32 oz. Front ramp sight, square notch rear. Checkered walnut target stock. Royal blue or satin nickel finish. Currently in production.
Blued **$175**
Satin Nickel **225**

Taurus Model 66

Taurus Model 66 Double Action Revolver
Calibers: 357 Magnum, 38 Special. 6-shot cylinder. Barrels: 3, 4 and 6 inches. Weight: 35 oz. Serrated ramp front

Taurus Model 66 DA Revolver (cont.)

sight; rear click adjustable. Checkered walnut grips. Royal blue or nickel finish. Currently in production.

Blued **$185**
Stainless **235**

Taurus Model 73 Double Action Revolver **$145**

Caliber: 32 Long. 6-shot cylinder. 3-inch heavy barrel. Weight: 20 oz. Checkered grips. Blued or satin finish. Discontinued 1993.

Taurus Model 74

Taurus Model 74 Target Grade DA Revolver . . . **$135**

Caliber: 32 S&W Long. 6-shot cylinder. 3-inch barrel. $8^{1}/_{4}$ inches overall. Weight: 20 oz. Adjustable rear sight, ramp front. Blued or nickel finish. Checkered walnut stocks. Made 1971–1990.

Taurus Model 80

Taurus Model 82

Taurus Model 80 Double Action Revolver

Caliber: 38 Special. 6-shot cylinder. Barrel lengths: 3, 4 inches. $9^{1}/_{4}$ inches overall with 4-inch bbl. Weight: with 4-inch bbl., 30 oz. Fixed sights. Blued or nickel finish.

Taurus Model 80 DA Revolver (cont.)

Checkered walnut stocks. Made 1971 to date.

Blued **$140**
Stainless **175**

Taurus Model 82 Heavy Barrel **$145**

Same as Model 80, except has heavy barrel. Weight: with 4-inch bbl., 33 oz. Made 1971 to date.

Taurus Model 83

Taurus Model 83 Heavy Barrel Target Grade

Same as Model 84, except has heavy barrel, weighs $34^{1}/_{2}$ oz. Made 1977 to date.

Blued **$145**
Stainless **175**

Taurus Model 84

Taurus Model 84 Target Grade Revolver **$185**

Caliber: 38 Special. 6-shot cylinder. 4-inch barrel. $9^{1}/_{4}$ inches overall. Weight: 31 oz. Adjustable rear sight, ramp front. Blued or nickel finish. Checkered walnut stocks. Made 1971–1989.

Taurus Model 85

Taurus Model 85 Double Action Revolver
Caliber: 38 Special. 5-shot cylinder. Barrel. 2- or 3-inch Weight: 21 oz. Fixed sights. Checkered walnut grips. Blued, satin nickel or stainless-steel finish. Currently in production.
Blued or Satin Nickel **$165**
Stainless Steel **195**

Taurus Model 86

Taurus Model 86 Target Master DA Revolver . . . **$175**
Caliber: 38 Special. 6-shot cylinder. 6-inch barrel. 11¼ inches overall. Weight: 34 oz. Adjustable rear sight, Patridge-type front. Blued finish. Checkered walnut grips. Made 1971 to date.

Taurus Model 94 Target Grade
Same as Model 74, except caliber 22 LR, with 9-shot cylinder. 3- or 4-inch barrel. Weight: 25 oz. Blued or stainless finish. Made 1971 to date.
Blued Finish **$165**
Stainless Finish **195**

Taurus Model 96 Target Master **$190**
Same as Model 86, except in 22 LR. Made 1971 to date.

Taurus Model 431 Double Action Revolver
Caliber: 44 Spec. 5-shot cylinder. 3- or 4-inch solid-rib barrel with ejector shroud. Weight: 35 oz.with 4-inch bbl. Serrated ramp front sight, notched topstrap rear. Blued or stainless finish. Made 1992 to date.
Blued Finish **$165**
Stainless Finish **205**

Taurus Model 441 Double Action Revolver
Similar to the Model 431, except w/6-inch barrel and fully adj. target sights. Weight: 40 oz. Made 1991 to date.
Blued Finish **$175**
Stainless Finish **225**

Taurus Model 669VR

Taurus Model 669/669VR Double Action Revolver
Caliber: 357 Mag. 6-shot cylinder. 4- or 6-inch solid-rib barrel with ejector shroud; Model 669VR has vent-rib barrel. Weight: 37 oz. with 4-inch bbl. Serrated ramp front sight, micro-adjustable rear. Royal blue or stainless finish.

Taurus Model 669/669VR DA (cont.)
Checkered Brazilian hardwood grips. Model 669 made 1989 to date; Model 669VR from 1990.
Model 669 Blued **$185**
Model 669 Stainless **235**
Model 669VR Blued **200**
Model 669VR Stainless **245**

Taurus Model 689 Double Action Revolver
Current designation of Model 669VR with vent rib. Blued or stainless finish. Made from 1990 to date.
Blued Finish **$205**
Stainless Finish **250**

Taurus Model 741/761 Double Action Revolver
Caliber: 32 H&R Mag. 6-shot cylinder. 3- or 4-inch solid-rib barrel with ejector shroud. Weight: 20 oz. with 3-inch bbl. Serrated ramp front sight, micro-adjustable rear. Blued or stainless finish. Checkered Brazilian hardwood grips. Made 1991 to date.
Model 741 Blued **$175**
Model 741 Stainless **265**
Model 761 (6-inch bbl., blued, 34 oz.) **225**

Taurus Model 941 Target Revolver
Caliber: 22 Magnum. 8-shot cylinder. Solid-rib barrel with ejector shroud. Micro-adjustable rear sight. Brazilian hardwood grips. Blued or stainless finish.
Blued Finish **$200**
Stainless Finish **240**

Taurus Model PT 22

Taurus Model PT 22/25 DA Auto Pistol **$135**
Caliber: 22 LR. 9-shot magazine 2.75-inch barrel. Weight: 12.3 oz. Fixed open sights. Brazilian hardwood grips. Blued finish. Made 1991 to date. **Model PT 25** has same general specs/price as Model PT 22, except in 25 ACP.

Taurus Model PT 58

Taurus Model PT 58 Semiautomatic Pistol

Caliber: 380 ACP. 12-shot magazine. 4-inch barrel. 7.2 inches overall. Weight: 30 oz. Blade front sight; rear adj. for windage w/3-dot sighting system. Blued, satin nickel or stainless finish. Made 1988 to date. (*See* photo, preceding page.)

Blued Finish	$275
Satin Nickel Finish	285
Stainless Finish	325

Taurus Model PT 92AF

Taurus Model PT 92AF Semiautomatic Pistol

Caliber: 9mm Parabellum. 15-round magazine. Double action. Barrel: about 5 inches. 8½ inches overall. Weight: 34 oz. Blade front sight, notched bar rear. Smooth Brazilian walnut grips. Blued, satin nickel or stainless finish. Made 1991 to date.

Blued Finish	$305
Satin Nickel Finish	345
Stainless Finish	370

Taurus Model PT 92AFC Compact Pistol

Same general specifications as Model PT-92AF, except with 13-shot magazine. 4.25-inch barrel. 7.5 inches overall. Weight: 31 oz. Made 1991 to date.

Blued Finish	$315
Satin Nickel Finish	345
Stainless Finish	370

Taurus Model PT 99AF

Taurus Model PT 99AF Semiautomatic Pistol ... $295

Same general specifications as Model PT 92AF, except rear sight is adjustable for elevation and windage, and finish is blued or satin nickel. Discontinued 1993.

Taurus Model PT 100 DA Automatic Pistol

Caliber: 40 S&W. 11-shot magazine. 5-inch barrel. Weight: 34 oz. Fixed front sight; adj. rear w/3-Dot system. Smooth

Taurus Model PT 100 DA Automatic (cont.)

hardwood grips. Blued, satin nickel or stainless finish. Made 1991 to date.

Blued Finish	$300
Satin Nickel Finish	335
Stainless Finish	350

Taurus Model PT 101 DA Automatic Pistol

Same general specifications as Model 100, except w/micrometer click adj. sights.

Blued	$330
Satin Nickel	365
Stainless	375

Taurus Model PT 908

Taurus Model PT 908 Semiautomatic Pistol

Caliber: 9mm Parabellum. 8-shot magazine. 3.8-inch barrel. 7 inches overall. Weight: 30 oz. Sights: drift-adjustable front; combat rear w/3-dot system. Blued, satin nickel or stainless finish. Made from 1993 to date.

Blued Finish	$295
Satin Nickel Finish	325
Stainless Finish	355

TEXAS ARMS
Waco, Texas

**Texas Arms
Defender Derringer**

Texas Arms Defender Derringer $215

Calibers: 9mm, 357 Mag., 44 Mag., 45 ACP, 45 Colt/.410. 3-inch barrel. 5 inches overall. Weight: 21 oz. Sights: blade front; fixed rear. Matte gun-metal grey finish. Smooth grips. Made from 1993 to date.

TEXAS LONGHORN ARMS
Richmond, Texas

Texas Longhorn Arms Keith No. 5 Single Action Revolver **$730**
Caliber: 44 Magnum. 6-shot. 5½-inch barrel. 11 inches overall. Weight: 44 oz. Adjustable rear sight, blade front. One-piece deluxe walnut stock. Blued finish. Intro. 1987.

Texas Longhorn Arms Sesquicentennial Single Action Revolver **$1875**
Same as South Texas Army Limited Edition, except engraved and nickel-plated with one-piece ivory stock. Introduced in 1986.

Texas Longhorn Arms Single Action Revolver Cased Set
Set contains one each of the Texas Longhorn Single Actions. Each chambered in the same caliber and with the same serial number. Introduced in 1984.
Standard Set **$4300**
Engraved Set 5700

Texas Longhorn Arms South Texas Army Limited Edition Single Action Revolver **$1195**
Calibers: all popular centerfire pistol calibers. 6-shot cylinder. 4¾-inch barrel. 10¼ inches overall. Weight: 40 oz. Fixed sights. Color casehardened frame. One-piece deluxe walnut stocks. Blued barrel. Introduced in 1984.

Texas Longhorn Arms Texas Border Special Single Action Revolver **$1195**
Same as South Texas Army Limited Edition, except with 3½-inch barrel and bird's-head grips. Introduced in 1984.

Texas Longhorn Arms West Texas Flat Top Target Single Action Revolver **$1195**
Same as South Texas Army Limited Edition, except with choice of barrel lengths from 7½ to 15 inches. Same special features with flat-top style frame and adjustable rear sight. Introduced in 1984.

THOMPSON PISTOL
West Hurley, New York
Mfd. by Auto-Ordnance Corporation

Thompson Model 27A-5 w/Drum Magazine

Thompson Model 27A-5 Semiautomatic Pistol
Similar to Thompson Model 1928A submachine gun, except has no provision for automatic firing, does not have detachable buttstock. Caliber: 45 Auto. 20-shot detachable box magazine (5-, 15- and 30-shot box magazines, 39-shot drum also avail.). 13-inch finned barrel. 26 inches overall.

Thompson Model 27A-5 Semiauto Pistol (cont.)
Weight: about 6¾ pounds. Adj. rear sight, blade front. Blued finish. Walnut grips. Made 1977–1994.
With box magazine . . . . **$ 995**
With drum magazine (as illustrated) 1195

THOMPSON/CENTER ARMS
Rochester, New Hampshire

Thompson/Center Contender Standard Model, 1967-Type

Thompson/Center Contender Vent-Rib Model

Thompson/Center Contender Single Shot Pistol
Break frame, underlever action. Calibers: (rimfire) 22 LR, 22 WMR, 5mm RRM; (standard centerfire), 218 Bee, 22 Hornet, 22 Rem. Jet, 221 Fireball, 222 Rem., 25-35, 256 Win. Mag., 30 M1 Carbine, 30-30, 38 Auto, 38 Special, 357 Mag./Hot Shot, 9mm Luger, 45 Auto, 45 Colt, 44 Magnum/Hot Shot; (wildcat centerfire) 17 Ackley Bee, 17 Bumblebee, 17 Hornet, 17 K Hornet, 17 Mach IV, 17-222, 17-223, 22 K Hornet, 30 Herrett, 357 Herrett, 357-4 B&D. Interchangeable barrels: 8¾- or 10-inch standard octagon (357 Mag., 44 Mag. and 45 Colt available with detachable choke for use with Hot Shot cartridges); 10-inch with ventilated rib and detachable internal choke tube for Hot Shots, 357 and 44 Magnum only; 10-inch bull barrel, 30 or 357 Herrett only. 13½ inches overall with 10-inch bbl. Weight: with standard 10-inch bbl., about 43 oz. Adj. rear sight, ramp front; vent-rib model has folding rear sight, adjustable front; bull barrel available with or w/o sights; Lobo 1½ X scope and mount (add $40 to value). Blued finish. Receiver photoengraved. Checkered walnut thumbrest stock and forearm (pre-1972 model has different stock with silver grip cap). Made 1967 to date, with the following revisions and variations.
Standard Model **$210**
Ventilated-Rib Model 240
Bull Barrel Model, with sights 245
Bull Barrel Model, without sights 215
Extra standard barrel 85
Extra ventilated rib or bull barrel 90

Thompson/Center Contender—Bull Barrel **$250**
Caliber offerings of the bull barrel version expanded in 1973, with another bump in 1978, making it the Contender

**Thompson/Center Contender
Early Bull Barrel Model w/Scope**

**Thompson/Center Contender
Bull Barrel—New Model**

Thompson/Center Contender—Bull Barrel (cont.)

model with the widest range of caliber options: 22 LR, 22 Win. Mag., 22 Hornet, 223 Rem., 7mm T.C.U., 7×30 Waters, 30 M1 Carbine, 30-30 Win., 32 H&R Mag., 32-20 Win., 357 Rem. Max., 357 Mag., 10mm Auto, 44 Magnum, 445 Super Magnum. 10-inch heavy barrel. Patridge-style iron sights. Contoured Competitor™ grip. Blued finish.

Thompson/Center Contender—Internal Choke Model

Originally made in 1968–69 with octagonal barrel, this Internal Choke version in 45 Colt/.410 caliber only was reintroduced in 1986 with 10-inch bull barrel. Vent rib also available. Iron sights: fixed rear, bead front. Detachable choke screws into muzzle. Blued finish. Contoured American black walnut Competitor™ Grip, also introduced in 1986, has nonslip rubber insert permanently bonded to back of grip.

With Bull Barrel **$280**
With Vent Rib **325**

**Thompson Center Contender
Octagon Barrel**

Thompson/Center Contender—Octagon Barrel $245

The original Contender design, this octagonal barrel version began to see the discontinuance of caliber offerings in 1980, so that now it is available in 22 LR only. 10-inch octagonal barrel. Patridge-style iron sights. Contoured Competitor™ Grip. Blued finish.

Thompson/Center Contender—Stainless

Similar to the standard Contender Models, except stainless steel with blued sights. Black Rynite forearm and ambidextrous finger-groove grip. Made from 1993 to date.
Standard SS Model (10-inch bbl.) **$315**
SS Super 14 . . . . **325**
SS Super 16 . . . . **335**

**Thompson/Center
Contender Super 14**

Thompson/Center Contender Super 14 . . . . $275

Calibers: 22 LR, 222 Rem., 223 Rem., 6mm T.C.U., 6.5mm T.C.U., 7mm T.C.U., 7×30 Waters, 30 Herrett, 30-30 Win., 357 Herrett, 357 Rem. Max., 35 Rem., 10mm Auto, 44 Mag., 445 Super Mag. 14-inch bull barrel. 18 inches overall. Weight: 56 oz. Patridge-style ramp front sight, adjustable target rear. Blued finish. Made 1978 to date.

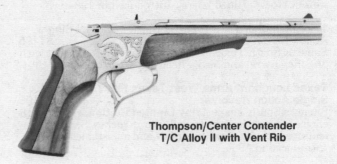

**Thompson/Center Contender
T/C Alloy II with Vent Rib**

Thompson/Center Contender TC Alloy II

Calibers: 22 LR, 223 Rem., 357 Magnum, 357 Rem. Max., 44 Magnum, 7mm T.C.U., 30-30 Win.; 45 Colt/.410 with internal choke; 35 Rem. and 7×30 Waters (14-inch bbl.). 10- or 14-inch bull barrel or 10-inch vent-rib barrel (w/ internal choke). All metal parts permanently electroplated with T/C Alloy II, which is harder than stainless steel, ensuring smoother action, 30 percent longer barrel life. Other design specifications the same as late model Contenders. Made 1986–89.

T/C Alloy II 10-inch Bull Barrel **$305**
T/C Alloy II Vent-rib Barrel w/Choke **340**
T/C Alloy II Super 14 . . . . **350**

==
UNIQUE PISTOLS
Hendaye, France
Mfd. by Manufacture d'Armes des Pyrénées Francaises
==

Unique Model B/cf Automatic Pistol $185

Calibers: 32 Auto (7.65mm), 380 Auto (9mm Short). 9-shot (32) or 8-shot (380) magazine. 4-inch barrel. 6.6

Unique Model B/cf

Unique Model B/cf Automatic (cont.)
inches overall. Weight: 24.3 oz. Blued finish. Plain or thumbrest plastic stocks. Intro. 1954; discontinued.

Unique Model D2 . . . . **$235**
Same as Model D6, except has 4¼-inch barrel, 7½ inches overall, weighs 24½ oz. Made 1954 to date.

Unique Model D6

Unique Model D6 Automatic Pistol **$215**
Caliber: 22 LR. 10-shot magazine. 6-inch bbl. 9¼ inches overall. Weight: about 26 oz. Adjustable sights. Blued finish. Plain or thumbrest plastic stocks. Introduced in 1954; discontinued.

Unique Model DES/69

Unique Model DES/69 Standard Match **$875**
Caliber: 22 LR. 5-shot magazine. 5.9-inch barrel. 10.6 inches overall. Weight: 35 oz. (barrel weight adds about

Unique Model DES/69 Standard Match (cont.)
9 oz.). Click adjustable rear sight, ramp front. Blued finish. Checkered walnut thumbrest stocks w/adj. handrest. Made 1969 to date.

Unique Model DES/VO

Unique Model DES/VO Rapid Fire Match
Automatic Pistol **$710**
Caliber: 22 Short. 5-shot magazine. 5.9-inch barrel. 10.4 inches overall. Weight: 43 oz. Click adjustable rear sight, blade front. Checkered walnut thumbrest stocks w/adj. handrest. Trigger adjustable for length of pull. Made from 1974 to date.

Unique Kriegsmodell

Unique Model L

Unique Kriegsmodell Automatic Pistol **$225**
Caliber: 32 Automatic (7.65mm). 9-shot magazine. 3.2-inch barrel. 5.8 inches overall. Weight: 26.5 oz. Fixed sights. Blued finish. Plastic stocks. Mfd. during German occupation of France 1940–45. *Note:* Bears the German military acceptance marks and may have stocks marked "7.65m/m 9 SCHUSS." (*See* photo, preceding page.)

Unique Model L Automatic Pistol **$215**
Calibers: 22 LR, 32 Auto (7.65mm), 380 Auto (9mm Short). 10-shot magazine in 22, 7 in 32, 6 in 380. 3.3-inch barrel. 5.8 inches overall. Weight: about 16½ oz. (380) w/light alloy frame; 23 oz. with steel frame. Fixed sights. Blued finish. Plastic stocks. Introduced 1955; discontinued. (*See* photo, preceding page.)

Unique Model Mikros

Unique Model Mikros Pocket Automatic Pistol . . **$150**
Calibers: 22 Short, 25 Auto (6.35mm). 6-shot magazine. 2¼-inch barrel. 4⁷/₁₆ inches overall. Weight: 9½ oz. w/light alloy frame; 12½ oz. w/steel frame. Fixed sights. Blued finish. Plastic stocks. Intro. 1957; discontinued.

Unique Model Rr

Unique Model Rr 51 Police Automatic **$165**
Postwar commercial version of WW II Kriegsmodell with same general specifications. Intro. 1951; discontinued.

UNITED STATES ARMS CORPORATION
Riverhead, New York

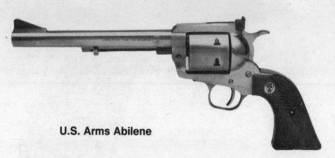

U.S. Arms Abilene

U.S. Arms Abilene Single Action Revolver
Safety Bar action. Calibers: 357 Magnum, 41 Magnum, 44 Magnum, 45 Colt; also 9mm Luger and 357 convertible model with two cylinders. 6-shot cylinder. Barrel lengths: 4⅝-, 5½-, 6½-inch; 7½- and 8½-inch in 44 Magnum only. Weight: about 48 oz. Adjustable rear sight, ramp front. Blued finish or stainless steel. Smooth walnut stocks. Made 1976 to date.
44 Magnum, blued finish **$250**
44 Magnum, stainless steel **275**
Other calibers, blued finish **225**
357 Magnum, stainless steel **240**
Convertible, 357 Mag./9mm Luger, blued finish . . **215**

UNIVERSAL FIREARMS CORPORATION
Hialeah, Florida

This company was purchased by Iver Johnson's Arms in the mid-1980s, when the Enforcer listed below was discontinued. An improved version was issued under the Iver Johnson name (*see* separate listing).

Universal Enforcer

Universal Enforcer Semiautomatic Pistol **$275**
M-1 Carbine-type action. Caliber: 30 Carbine. 5-, 15- or 30-shot clip magazine. 10¼-inch barrel. 17¾ inches overall. Weight: 4½ pounds w/30-shot magazine. Adj. rear sight, blade front. Blued finish. Walnut stock with pistol grip and handguard. Made 1964–1983.

HANDGUNS

UZI PISTOLS
Mfd. by Israel Military Industries, Israel

Uzi 9mm Semiautomatic

Uzi Semiautomatic Pistol **$950**
Caliber: 9mm Parabellum. 20-round magazine. 4¹/₂-inch barrel. About 9¹/₂ inches overall. Weight: 3.8 pounds. Front post-type sight; rear open-type, both adjustable. Disc.

WALTHER PISTOLS
Manufactured by German, French and Swiss firms

The following Walther pistols were made before and during World War II by Waffenfabrik Walther, Zella-Mehlis (Thür.), Germany.

Walther Model 1*

Walther Model 1 Automatic Pistol **$375**
Caliber: 25 Auto (6.35mm). 6-shot. 2.1-inch barrel. 4.4 inches overall. Weight: 12.8 oz. Fixed sights. Blued finish. Checkered hard rubber stocks. Intro. 1908.

Walther Model 2

Walther Model 2 Automatic Pistol **$395**
Caliber: 25 Auto (6.35mm). 6-shot magazine. 2.1-inch barrel. 4.2 inches overall. Weight: 9.8 oz. Fixed sights. Blued finish. Checkered hard rubber stocks. Intro. 1909.

Walther Model 3 Automatic Pistol **$1050**
Caliber: 32 Auto (7.65mm). 6-shot magazine. 2.6-inch barrel. 5 inches overall. Weight: 16.6 oz. Fixed sights. Blued finish. Checkered hard rubber stocks. Intro. 1910.

Walther Model 4

Walther Model 4 Automatic Pistol **$265**
Caliber: 32 Automatic (7.65mm). 8-shot magazine. 3.5-inch barrel. 5.9 inches overall. Weight: 18.6 oz. Fixed sights. Blued finish. Checkered hard rubber stocks. Made 1910–1918.

Walther Model 5

Walther Model 5 Automatic Pistol $290
Improved version of Model 2 with same general specifications, distinguished chiefly by better workmanship and appearance. Introduced 1913. (*See* photo, preceding page.)

Walther Model 6

Walther Model 6 Automatic Pistol $2450
Caliber: 9mm Luger. 8-shot magazine. 4³/₄-inch barrel. 8¹/₄ inches overall. Weight: 34 oz. Fixed sights. Blued finish. Checkered hard rubber stocks. Made 1915–1917. *Note:* Since the powerful 9mm Luger cartridge is too much for the simple blow-back system of this pistol, firing is not recommended.

Walther Model 7

Walther Model 7 Automatic Pistol $425
Caliber: 25 Auto. (6.35mm). 8-shot magazine. 3-inch barrel. 5.3 inches overall. Weight: 11.8 oz. Fixed sights. Blued finish. Checkered hard rubber stocks. Made 1917–1918.

Walther Model 8 Automatic Pistol $345
Caliber: 25 Auto. (6.35mm). 8-shot magazine. 2⁷/₈-inch barrel. 5¹/₈ inches overall. Weight: 12³/₈ oz. Fixed sights. Blued finish. Checkered plastic stocks. Made 1920–1945.

Walther Model 8 Lightweight Automatic Pistol . . $390
Same as standard Model 8 except about 25 percent lighter due to use of aluminum alloys.

Walther Model 8

Walther Model 9

Walther Model 9 Vest Pocket Automatic Pistol . . $365
Caliber: 25 Automatic (6.35mm). 6-shot magazine. 2-inch barrel. 3¹⁵/₁₆ inches overall. Weight: 9 oz. Fixed sights. Blue finish. Checkered plastic stocks. Made 1921–1945.

Walther Model HP

Walther Model HP Double Action Automatic . . . $1050
Prewar commercial version of the P38. "HP" is abbreviation of "Heeres Pistole" (Army Pistol). Caliber: 9mm Luger. 8-shot magazine. 5-inch barrel. 8³/₈ inches overall. Weight: about 34¹/₂ oz. Fixed sights. Blued finish. Checkered wood or plastic stocks. The Model HP is distinguished by its fine material and workmanship. Made 1937–1944.

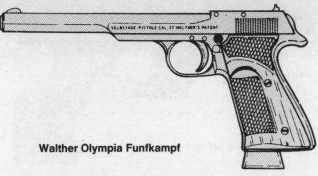

Walther Olympia Funfkampf

Walther Model PP (Prewar)

Walther Olympia Funfkampf Model Automatic . . **$895**
Caliber: 22 LR. 10-shot magazine. 9.6-inch barrel. 13 inches overall. Weight: 33 oz., less weight. Set of 4 detachable weights. Adjustable target sights. Blued finish. Checkered stocks. Introduced 1936.

Walther Olympia Hunting Model Automatic **$695**
Same general specifications as Olympia Sport Model, but with 4-inch barrel. Weight: 28½ oz.

Walther Olympia Rapid Fire Model Automatic . . **$795**
Caliber: 22 Short. 6-shot magazine. 7.4-inch barrel. 10.7 inches overall. Weight: without 12⅜ oz. detachable muzzle weight, 27½ oz. Adjustable target sights. Blued finish. Checkered stocks. Made about 1936–1940.

Walther Olympia Sport Model Automatic **$995**
Caliber: 22 LR. 10-shot magazine. 7.4-inch barrel. 10.7 inches overall. Weight: 30½ oz., less weight. Adjustable target sights. Blued finish. Checkered stocks. Set of four detachable weights was supplied at extra cost. Made about 1936–1940.

Walther Model PP DA Automatic Pistol (cont.)
overall. Weight: 23 oz. Fixed sights. Blued finish. Checkered plastic stocks. *Note:* Wartime models are inferior in quality to prewar commercial pistols. Made 1929–1945.
22 caliber, Commercial Model **$595**
25 caliber, Commercial Model 795
32 and 380 caliber, Commercial Model 810
Wartime Model 400

Walther Model PP Lightweight
Same as standard Model PP, except about 25 percent lighter due to use of aluminum alloys. Values 50 percent higher.

Walther Model PP 7.65mm Presentation **$1400**
Made of soft aluminum alloy in green-gold color, these pistols were not intended to be fired.

Walther Model P38 (WW II)

Walther Model PPK (WW II)

Walther P38 Military DA Automatic **$625**
Modification of the Model HP adopted as an official German Service arm in 1938 and produced throughout WW II by Walther (code "ac"), Mauser (code "byf") and a few other manufacturers. General specifications same as Model HP, but with a vast difference in quality, the P38 being a mass-produced military pistol; some of the late wartime models were very roughly finished and tolerances were quite loose.

Walther Model PP DA Automatic Pistol
Polizeipistole (Police Pistol). Calibers: 22 LR (5.6mm), 25 Auto (6.35mm), 32 Auto (7.65mm), 380 Auto (9mm). 8-shot magazine, 7-shot in 380. 3⅞-inch barrel. 6⁵/₁₆ inches

Walther Model PPK DA Automatic Pistol
Polizeipistole Kriminal (Detective Pistol). Calibers: 22 LR (5.6mm), 25 Auto (6.35mm), 32 Auto (7.65mm), 380 Auto (9mm). 7-shot magazine, 6-shot in 380. 3¼-inch barrel. 5⅞ inches overall. Weight: 19 oz. Fixed sights. Blued finish. Checkered plastic stocks. *Note:* Wartime models are inferior in workmanship to prewar commercial pistols. Made 1931–1945.
25, commercial model . . . . **$ 795**
32, commercial model 475
22 LR & 380 1500

Walther Model PPK Lightweight
Same as standard Model PPK, except about 25 percent lighter due to aluminum alloys. Values 50 percent higher.

Walther Model PPK 7.65mm Presentation **$1095**
Made of soft aluminum alloy in green-gold color, these pistols were not intended to be fired.

Walther Self-Loading Sport

Walther Model OSP

Walther Self-Loading Sport Pistol **$610**
Caliber: 22 LR. 10-shot magazine. Barrel lengths: 6- and 9-inch. 9⅞ inches overall with 6-inch barrel. Target sights. Blued finish. One-piece, wood or plastic stocks, checkered. Introduced in 1932.

> **NOTE:** The following Walther pistols were or are now mfd. by Carl Walther Waffenfabrik, Ulm/Donau, Germany.

Walther Model GSP, 22 LR

**Walther Model GSP
32 S&W Long Wadcutter**

Walther Model GSP Target Automatic Pistol
Calibers: 22 LR, 32 S&W Long Wadcutter. 5-shot magazine. 4.5-inch barrel. 11.8 inches overall. Weights: 44.8 oz., 22 cal.; 49.4 oz., 32 cal. Adj. target sights. Black finish. Walnut thumbrest stocks w/adj. handrest. Made 1969–1994.
22 Long Rifle. . . . . **$ 995**
32 S&W Long Wadcutter **1250**
Conversion unit, 22 Short or 22 LR extra **1000**

Walther Model OSP Rapid Fire Target Pistol . . . **$950**
Caliber: 22 Short. 5-shot magazine. 4.5-inch barrel. 11.8 inches overall. Weight: 42.3 oz. Adj. target sights. Black finish. Walnut thumbrest stocks w/adj. handrest. 22 LR conversion unit available (add $275). Made 1968–1994.

Walther Model P 1 DA Automatic **$445**
Postwar military P38 (*See* current listing below) used by the German Armed forces and officially adopted as P 1 in 1963. Slide marked "P 1 Cal. (or Kal.) 9mm." Phased out c. 1980. Some P 1's assembled by Manurhin in France 1963–late 1970s.

Walther Model P4

Walther Model P4 (P38-IV) DA Pistol **$465**
Similar to P38, except has an uncocking device instead of a manual safety. Caliber: 9mm Luger only. 4.3-inch barrel. 7.9 inches overall. Other general specifications same as for current model P38. Made 1974–1982.

Walther Model P5 Double Action Pistol **$595**
Alloy frame with frame-mounted decocking levers. Caliber: 9mm Parabellum. 8-shot magazine. 3.5-inch barrel. 7 inches overall. Weight: 28 oz. Blued finish. Checkered walnut or synthetic grips. Made from 1988 to date.

Walther Model P5 Compact Pistol **$595**
Similar to Model P5, except with 3.1-inch barrel. Weight: 26 oz. Made 1988 to date.

Walther Model P38 Double Action Automatic
Postwar commercial version of the P38 with light alloy frame. Calibers: 22 LR, 7.65mm Luger, 9mm Luger. 8-shot magazine. Barrel lengths: 5.1 inches (22 LR); 4.9 inches (7.65mm, 9mm). 8.5 inches overall. Weight: 28.2 oz. Fixed sights. Nonreflective black finish. Checkered plastic stocks. Made 1957 to date.

Walther Model P38 (Current)

Walther Model P38 DA (cont.)
22 Long Rifle	**$575**
9mm, 7.65mm	**445**

Walther Model P38 Deluxe Engraved Pistol
Elaborately engraved. Available in blued, chrome-, silver- or gold-plated finish.
Blued finish	**$1150**
Chrome-plated	**1110**
Silver-plated	**1195**
Gold-plated	**1495**

Walther Model P38K

Walther Model P38K $595
Short-barreled version of current P38, the "K" standing for *kurz* (short). Same general specifications as standard model, except 2.8-inch barrel, 6.3 inches overall, weighs 27.2 oz., front sight is slide mounted. Caliber: 9mm Luger only. Made 1974–1980.

**Walther Model P88
9mm Double Action**

Walther Model P88 Double Action Automatic ... $795
Caliber: 9mm Luger. 15-shot magazine. 4-inch barrel. 7.38 inches overall. Weight: 31.5 oz. Blade front sight; adjustable rear. Checkered black composition grip. Ambidextrous decocking levers. Blued finish. Made 1987 to date.

Walther Model P88 DA Compact $895
Similar to the standard P88 Model, except with 13-shot magazine. 3.8-inch barrel. 7.1 inches overall. Weight: 29 oz. Blued finish.

Walther Model PP (Current)

Walther Model PP Double Action Automatic Pistol
Calibers: 22 LR, 32 Auto (7.65mm), 380 Auto (9mm Short). 8-shot magazine in 22 and 32, 7-shot in 380. 3.9-inch barrel. 6.7 inches overall. Weight: 32 cal., 23.3 oz. Fixed sights. Blued finish. Checkered plastic stocks. Made 1963 to date.
22 Long Rifle	**$355**
Other calibers	**325**

Walther Model PP-Super

Walther Model PP-Super DA Pistol $495
Caliber: 9×18mm. 7-shot magazine. 3.6-inch barrel. 6.9 inches overall. Weight: 30 oz. Fixed sights. Blued finish. Checkered plastic stocks. Made 1974–1981.

Walther Model PPK DA Automatic Pistol
Steel or dural frame. Calibers: 22 LR, 32 Auto (7.65mm), 380 Auto (9mm Short); latter caliber not available in model with dural frame. 3.3-inch barrel. 6.1 inches overall. Weight (32 caliber): with steel frame, 20.8 oz.; with dural frame, 16.6 oz. Fixed sights. Blued finish. Checkered plas-

Walther Model PPK (Current)

Walther Model TPH

Walther Model PPK DA Automatic (cont.)

tic grips. German-made 1963 to date; U.S. importation discontinued in 1968. U.S. version made by Interarms since 1986, incl. a stainless steel model.

22 Long Rifle	**$650**
Other calibers	**595**

Walther Model PPK/S

Walther Model PPK/S Double Action Automatic Pistol

Designed to meet the requirements of the U.S. Gun Control Act of 1968, this model has the frame of the PP and the shorter slide and barrel of the PPK. Overall length: 6.1 inches. Weight: 23 oz. Other specifications same as standard PPK, except steel frame only. German-made 1971 to date. U.S. version made by Interarms 1979 to date.

22 Long Rifle	**$315**
Other calibers	**295**

Walther Models PP, PPK, PPK/S Deluxe Engraved

These elaborately engraved models are available in blued finish, chrome-, silver- or gold-plated.

Blued finish	**$ 875**
Chrome-plated	**995**
Silver-plated	**1000**
Gold-plated	**1145**
Add for 22 Long Rifle	**50**

Walther Model TPH DA Pocket Pistol $450

Light alloy frame. Calibers: 22 LR, 25 ACP (6.35mm). 6-shot magazine. 2¼-inch barrel. 5³/₈ inches overall. Weight:

Walther Model TPH DA Pocket Pistol (cont.)

14 oz. Fixed sights. Blued finish. Checkered plastic stocks. Made 1968 to date. *Note:* Few Walther-made models reached the U.S. because of import restrictions; a U.S.-made version has been mfd. by Interarms since 1986.

> **NOTE:** The following Mark IIs have been made in France since 1950 by Manufacture de Machines du Haut-Rhin (MANURHIN) at Mulhouse-Bourtzwiller. The designation "Mark II" is used here to distinguish between these and the prewar models. Early (1950–54) production bears MANURHIN trademark on slide and grips. Later models are marked "Walther Mark II." U.S. importation disc. 1968.

Walther Mark II Model PP Auto Pistol $410
Same general specifications as prewar Model PP.

Walther Mark II Model PPK Auto Pistol $475
Same general specifications as prewar Model PPK.

Walther Mark II Model PPK Lightweight $510
Same as standard PPK except has dural receiver. Calibers: 22 LR and 32 Auto.

> **NOTE:** The Walther Olympia Model pistols were manufactured 1952–1963 by Hämmerli AG Jagd-und Sportwaffenfabrik, Lenzburg, Switzerland, and marketed as "Hämmerli-Walther." *See* Hämmerli listings for specific data.

Hämmerli-Walther Olympia Model 200 Auto
Pistol, 1952 Type $575
Similar to 1936 Walther Olympia Funfkampf Model.

Hämmerli-Walther Olympia Model 200,

1958 Type	**$600**
Hämmerli-Walther Olympia Model 201	**$590**
Hämmerli-Walther Olympia Model 202	**$600**

Hämmerli-Walther Olympia Model 203

1955 Type	**$595**
1958 Type	**615**

Hämmerli-Walther Olympia American Model 204

1956 Type	**$695**
1958 Type	**645**

Hämmerli-Walther Olympia American Model 205

1956 Type	**$750**
1958 Type	**675**

WARNER PISTOL
Norwich, Connecticut
Warner Arms Corp. (or Davis-Warner Arms Co.)

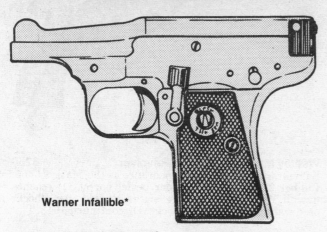

Warner Infallible*

Warner Infallible Pocket Automatic Pistol **$275**
Caliber: 32 Automatic. 7-shot magazine. 3-inch barrel. 6½ inches overall. Weight: about 24 oz. Fixed sights. Blued finish. Hard rubber stocks. Made 1917–19.

WEBLEY & SCOTT LTD.
London and Birmingham, England

Webley 9mm M&P

Webley 9mm Military & Police Auto Pistol **$795**
Caliber: 9mm Browning Long. 8-shot magazine. 8 inches overall. Weight: 32 oz. Fixed sights. Blued finish. Checkered vulcanite stocks. Made 1909–1930.

Webley 25 Hammer

Webley 25 Hammer Model Automatic Pistol . . . **$225**
Caliber: 25 Automatic. 6-shot magazine. Overall length: 4¾ inches. Weight: 11¾ oz. No sights. Blued finish. Checkered vulcanite stocks. Made 1906–1940.

Webley 25 Hammerless

Webley 25 Hammerless Model Auto Pistol **$220**
Caliber: 25 Automatic. 6-shot magazine. Overall length: 4¼ inches. Weight: 9¾ oz. Fixed sights. Blued finish. Checkered vulcanite stocks. Made 1909–1940.

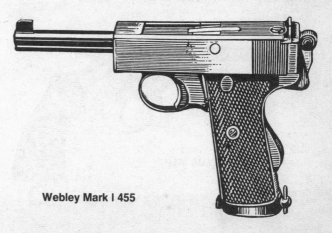

Webley Mark I 455

Webley Mark I 455 Automatic Pistol **$995**
Caliber: 455 Webley Automatic. 7-shot magazine. 5-inch barrel. 8½ inches overall. Weight: about 39 oz. Fixed sights. Blued finish. Checkered vulcanite stocks. Made 1913–1931. Reissued during WWII. Total production about 9,300. *Note:* **Mark I No. 2** is same pistol with adjustable rear sight and modified manual safety.

Webley Mark III

Webley Mark III 38 Military & Police Revolver . . . **$295**
Hinged frame. DA. Caliber: 38 S&W. 6-shot cylinder. Barrel lengths: 3- and 4-inch. 9½ inches overall w/4-inch bbl. Weight: 21 oz. w/4-inch bbl. Fixed sights. Blued finish. Checkered walnut or vulcanite stocks. Made 1897–1945.

Webley Mark IV 22 LR

Webley Mark VI 22

Webley Mark IV 22 Caliber Target Revolver **$345**
Same frame and general appearance as Mark IV 38. Caliber: 22 LR. 6-shot cylinder. 6-inch barrel. 10¹/₈ inches overall. Weight: 34 oz. Target sights. Blued finish. Checkered stocks. Discontinued. 1945.

Webley Mark VI 22 Target Revolver **$250**
Same frame and general appearance as the Mark VI 455. Caliber: 22 LR. 6-shot cylinder. 6-inch barrel. 11¹/₄ inches overall. Weight: 40 oz. Target sights. Blued finish. Checkered walnut or vulcanite stocks. Discontinued 1945.

Webley Mark IV 38 M&P

Webley Metropolitan Police

Webley Mark IV 38 Military & Police Revolver . . **$250**
Hinged frame. DA. Caliber: 38 S&W. 6-shot cylinder. Barrel lengths: 3-, 4- and 5-inch. 9¹/₈ inches overall w/5-inch bbl. Weight: 27 oz. w/5-inch bbl. Fixed sights. Blued finish. Checkered stocks. Made 1929–c. 1957.

Webley Metropolitan Police Automatic Pistol . . . **$675**
Calibers: 32 Auto, 380 Auto. 8-shot (32) or 7-shot (380) magazine. 3¹/₂-inch barrel. 6¹/₄ inches overall. Weight: 20 oz. Fixed sights. Blued finish. Checkered vulcanite stocks. Made 1906–1940 (32); 1908–1920 (380).

Webley Mark VI No. 1 455

Webley RIC Model

Webley Mark VI No. 1 British Service Revolver . . **$275**
DA. Hinged frame. Caliber: 455 Webley. 6-shot cylinder. Barrel lengths: 4-, 6- and 7¹/₂-inch. 11¹/₄ inches overall w/6-inch bbl. Weight: 38 oz. w/6-inch bbl. Fixed sights. Blued finish. Checkered walnut or vulcanite stocks. Made 1915–1947.

Webley RIC Model Revolver **$275**
Royal Irish Constabulary or Bulldog Model. Double action. Solid frame. Caliber: 455 Webley. 5-shot cylinder. 2¹/₄-inch barrel. Weight: 21 oz. Fixed sights. Blued finish. Checkered walnut or vulcanite stocks. Discontinued.

Webley "Semiautomatic" Single Shot Pistol.... $250

Similar in appearance to the Webley Metropolitan Police Automatic, this pistol is "semiautomatic" in the sense that the fired case is extracted and ejected and the hammer cocked as in a blow-back automatic pistol; it is loaded singly and the slide manually operated in loading. Caliber: 22 Long. Barrel lengths: 4½- and 9-inch. 10¾ inches overall w/9-inch bbl. Weight: 24 oz. w/9-inch bbl. Adj. sights. Blued finish. Checkered vulcanite stocks. Made 1911–1927.

Webley Single Shot Target

Webley Single Shot Target Pistol $250

Hinged frame. Caliber: 22 LR. 10-inch barrel. 15 inches overall. Weight: 37 oz. Fixed sights on earlier models, current production has adjustable rear sight. Blued finish. Checkered walnut or vulcanite stocks. Made 1909 to date.

Webley-Fosbery Automatic Revolver

Webley-Fosbery Automatic Revolver $2500

Hinged frame. Recoil action revolves cylinder and cocks hammer. Caliber: 455 Webley. 6-shot cylinder. 6-inch barrel. 12 inches overall. Weight: 42 oz. Fixed sights. Blued finish. Checkered walnut stocks. Made 1901–1939. *Note:* A few were produced in caliber 38 Colt Auto with an 8-shot cylinder; this is a very rare collector's item.

═══ WESSON FIREARMS CO., INC. ═══
Palmer, Massachusetts
Formerly Dan Wesson Arms, Inc.

Dan Wesson Model 8 Service

Same general specifications as Model 14, except caliber 38 Special. Made 1971–75. Values same as for Model 14.

Dan Wesson Model 8-2 Service

Same general specifications as Model 14-2, except caliber 38 Special. Made 1975 to date. Values same as for Model 14-2.

Dan Wesson Model 9 Target

Same as Model 15, except caliber 38 Special. Made 1971–75. Values same as for Model 15.

Dan Wesson Model 9-2 Target

Same as Model 15-2, except caliber 38 Special. Made 1975 to date. Values same as for Model 15-2.

Dan Wesson Model 9-2H Heavy Barrel

Same as Model 15-2H, except caliber 38 Special. Made 1975 to date. Values same as for Model 15-2H. Discontinued 1983.

Dan Wesson Model 9-2HV Vent-Rib Heavy Barrel

Same as Model 15-2HV, except caliber 38 Special. Made 1975 to date. Values same as for Model 15-2HV.

Dan Wesson Model 9-2V Ventilated Rib

Same as Model 15-2V, except caliber 38 Special. Made 1975 to date. Values same as for Model 15-2H.

Dan Wesson Model 11

Dan Wesson Model 11 Service Double Action Revolver

Caliber: 357 Magnum. 6-shot cylinder. Barrel lengths: 2½-, 4-, 6-inch; interchangeable barrel assemblies. 9 inches overall w/4-inch bbl. Weight: 38 oz. w/4-inch bbl. Fixed sights. Blued finish. Interchangeable stocks. Made 1970–71. *Note:* The Model 11 has an external barrel nut.

With one barrel assembly and stock **$175**
Extra barrel assembly **50**
Extra stock **25**

Dan Wesson Model 12

Dan Wesson Model 12 Target

Same general specifications as Model 11, except has adjustable sights. Made 1970–71.

With one-barrel assembly and stock **$195**
Extra barrel assembly **50**
Extra stock **25**

Dan Wesson Model 14

Dan Wesson Model 14 Service Double Action Revolver

Caliber: 357 Magnum. 6-shot cylinder. Barrel lengths: 2¼-, 3¾-, 5¾-inch; interchangeable barrel assemblies. 9 inches overall w/3¾-inch bbl. Weight: 36 oz. w/3¾-inch bbl. Fixed sights. Blued or nickel finish. Interchangeable stocks. Made 1971–75. *Note:* Model 14 has recessed barrel nut.

With one-barrel assembly and stock	**$200**
Extra barrel assembly	50
Extra stock	25

Dan Wesson Model 14-2

Dan Wesson Model 14-2 Service DA Revolver

Caliber: 357 Magnum. 6-shot cylinder. Barrel lengths: 2½-, 4-, 6-, 8-inch; interchangeable barrel assemblies. 9¼ inches overall w/4-inch bbl. Weight: 34 oz. w/4-inch. Fixed sights. Blued finish. Interchangeable stocks. Made 1975 to date. *Note:* Model 14-2 has recessed barrel nut.

W/one-barrel assembly (8″) and stock	**$190**
W/one-barrel assembly (other lengths) and stock . . .	175
Extra barrel assembly, 8″	65
Extra barrel assembly, other lengths	50
Extra stock	25

Dan Wesson Model 15

Dan Wesson Model 15 Target

Same general specifications as Model 14, except has adjustable sights. Made 1971–75.

With one-barrel assembly and stock	**$210**
Extra barrel assembly	50
Extra stock	25

Dan Wesson Model 15-2

Dan Wesson Model 15-2 Target

Same general specifications as Model 14-2, except has adjustable rear sight and interchangeable blade front; also avail. with 10-, 12- and 15-inch barrels. Made 1975 to date.

With one-barrel assembly (8″) and stock	**$240**
With one-barrel assembly (10″) and stock	245
With one-barrel assembly (12″)/stock. Disc.	250
With one-barrel assembly (15″)/stock. Disc.	270
With one-barrel assembly (other lengths)/stock . .	190
Extra barrel assembly (8″)	75
Extra barrel assembly (10″)	95
Extra barrel assembly (12″). Discontinued.	100
Extra barrel assembly (15″). Discontinued.	115
Extra barrel assembly (other lengths)	50
Extra stock	20

Dan Wesson Model 15-2H Interchangeable Heavy Barrel Assemblies

Dan Wesson Model 15-2H Heavy Barrel

Same as Model 15-2, except has heavy barrel assembly; weight, with 4-inch barrel, 38 oz. Made 1975–1983.

With one-barrel assembly (8″) and stock	**$240**
With one-barrel assembly (10″) and stock	245
With one-barrel assembly (12″) and stock	265
With one-barrel assembly (15″) and stock	295
With one-barrel assembly (other lengths)/stock . .	250
Extra barrel assembly (8″)	80
Extra barrel assembly (10″)	100
Extra barrel assembly (12″)	110
Extra barrel assembly (15″)	125
Extra barrel assembly (other lengths)	60
Extra stock	20

Dan Wesson Model 15-2HV Vent-Rib Heavy Barrel

Same as Model 15-2, except has vent-rib heavy barrel assembly; weighs 37 oz. w/4-inch bbl. Made 1975 to date.

Dan Wesson Model 15-2HV VR Heavy Barrel (cont.)

With one-barrel assembly (8") and stock	$265
With one-barrel assembly (10") and stock	280
With one-barrel assembly (12") and stock	295
With one-barrel assembly (15") and stock	325
With one-barrel assembly (other lengths) and stock	260
Extra barrel assembly (8")	90
Extra barrel assembly (10")	110
Extra barrel assembly (12")	125
Extra barrel assembly (15")	140
Extra barrel assembly (other lengths)	70
Extra stock	20

Dan Wesson Model 15-2V Ventilated Rib

Same as Model 15-2, except has vent-rib barrel assembly, weighs 35 oz. w/4-inch barrel. Made 1975 to date. Values same as for 15-2H.

Dan Wesson Hunter Pacs

Dan Wesson Hunter Pacs are offered in all Magnum calibers and include heavy vent 8-inch shroud barrel revolver, Burris scope mounts, barrel changing tool in a case.

HP22M-V	$515
HP22M-2	475
HP722M-V	565
HP722M-2	525
HP32-V	515
HP32-2	455
HP732-V	550
HP732-2	515
HP15-V	515
HP15-2	475
HP715-V	555
HP715-2	515
HP41-V	450
HP741-V	595
HP741-2	515
HP44-V	585
HP44-2	515
HP744-V	645
HP744-2	625
HP40-V	395
HP40-2	565
HP740-V	675
HP740-2	625
HP375-V	375
HP375-2	565
HP45-V	495

WHITNEY FIREARMS COMPANY
Hartford, Connecticut

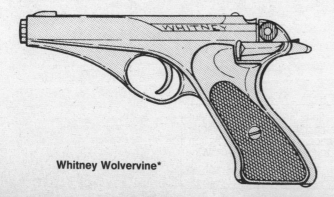

Whitney Wolvervine*

Whitney Wolverine Automatic Pistol $325

Dural frame/shell contains all operating components. Caliber: 22 LR. 10-shot magazine. 4⅝-inch barrel. 9 inches overall. Weight: 23 oz. Patridge-type sights. Blue or nickel finish. Plastic stocks. Made 1955–1962.

WICHITA ARMS
Wichita, Kansas

Wichita Classic Pistol

Caliber: Chambered to order. Bolt-action, single shot. 11¼-inch octagonal barrel. 18 inches overall. Weight: 78 oz. Open micro sights. Custom-grade checkered walnut stock. Blued finish. Made 1980 to date.

Standard	$2195
Presentation Grade (engraved)	3595

Wichita Hunter Pistol $450

Bolt-action, single shot. Calibers: 22 LR, 22 WRF, 7mm Super Mag., 7-30 Waters, 30-30 Win., 32 H&R Mag., 357 Mag., 357 Super Mag. 10½-inch barrel. 16½ inches overall. Weight: 60 oz. No sights (scope mount only). Stainless-steel finish. Walnut stock. Made 1983 to date.

Wichita International Pistol

Wichita International Pistol $490

Top-break, single-shot. SA. Calibers: 7-30 Waters, 7mm Super Mag., 7R (30-30 Win. necked to 7mm), 30-30 Win., 357 Mag., 357 Super Mag., 32 H&R Mag., 22 Mag. RF, 22 LR. 10- and 14-inch barrel (10½" for centerfire calibers). Weight: 50–71 oz. Patridge front sight; adjustable rear. Walnut forend and grips.

Wichita MK-40 Silhouette Pistol $800

Calibers: 22-250, 7mm IHMSA, 308 Win. Bolt-action, single shot. 13-inch barrel. 19½ inches overall. Weight: 72 oz. Wichita Multi-Range sight system. Aluminum receiver with blued barrel. Gray fiberthane glass stock. Made 1981 to date.

**Wichita Silhouette Pistol
w/Center Grip**

Wichita Silhouette Pistol $800

Calibers: 22-250, 7mm IHMSA, 308 Win. Bolt-action, single shot. 14¹⁵/₁₆-inch barrel. 21³/₈ inches overall. Weight: 72 oz. Wichita Multi-Range sight system. Blued finish. Walnut or gray fiberthane glass stock. Walnut center or rear grip. Made 1979 to date.

WILKINSON ARMS
Parma, Idaho

Wilkinson Linda

Wilkinson Sherry

Wilkinson Linda Semiautomatic Pistol **$275**
Caliber: 9mm Luger Parabellum. 31-shot magazine. 8¼-inch barrel. 12¼ inches overall. Weight: 77 oz., empty. Rear peep sight with blade front. Blued finish. Checkered composition stocks.

Wilkinson Sherry Semiautomatic Pistol **$135**
Caliber: 22 LR. 8-shot magazine. 2⅛-inch barrel. 4⅜ inches overall. Weight: 9¼ oz., empty. Crossbolt safety. Fixed sights. Blued or blue-gold finish. Checkered composition stocks. Made 1985 to date.

NOTE: The following abbreviations are used throughout the Handgun Section: *adj.* = adjustable; *avail.* = available; *bbl.* = barrel; *DA* = Double Action; *DAO* = Double Action Only; *LR* = Long Rifle; *SA* = Single Action; *WMR* = Winchester Magnum Rimfire.

RIFLES

Section II

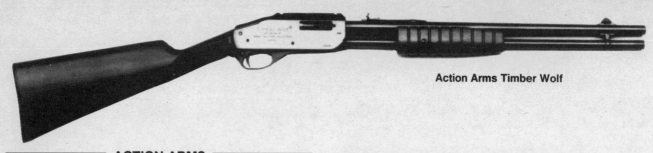

Action Arms Timber Wolf

ACTION ARMS
Philadelphia, Pennsylvania

Action Arms Model B Sporter Semiautomatic Carbine **$525**
Similar to the Uzi Carbine (*see* separate listing), except with thumbhole stock. Caliber: 9mm Parabellum. 10-shot magazine. 16-inch barrel. Weight: 8¾ pounds. Post front sight; adjustable rear. Imported 1993–94.

Action Arms Timber Wolfe Repeating Rifle
Calibers: 357 Magnum, 38 Special, 44 Magnum. Slide action. Tubular magazine holds 10 (357 Mag./38 Spec.) or 8 shots (44 Mag.). 18½-inch barrel. 36½ inches overall. Weight: 5½ pounds. Fixed blade front sight; adj. rear. Receiver w/integral scope mount. Checkered walnut stock. Imported 1989–1994.
Blued Model **$225**
Chrome Model **295**

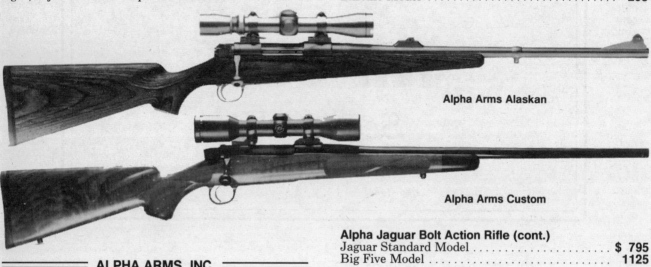

Alpha Arms Alaskan

Alpha Arms Custom

Alpha Jaguar Bolt Action Rifle (cont.)
Jaguar Standard Model . . . . **$ 795**
Big Five Model **1125**

ALPHA ARMS, INC.
Dallas, Texas

Alpha Alaskan Bolt Action Rifle **$1095**
Same as Custom model, except w/stainless-steel barrel and receiver and all other parts coated with Nitex; sling swivel stud attached to barrel. Left-hand model available. Made 1984–89.

Alpha Custom Bolt Action Rifle **$1025**
Calibers: 17 Rem. thru 338 Win. Mag. Three action lengths w/three-lug locking system and 60-degree bolt rotation. 20- to 24-inch barrel; round or octagonal. Weight: 6 to 7¼ pounds. No sights. Pistol-grip stock of presentation-grade California claro walnut; hand-rubbed oil finish. Custom inletted sling swivel stud attached to forend. Ebony forend tip. Left-hand models avail. Made 1984–89.

Alpha Grand Slam Bolt Action Rifle **$925**
Same as Custom model, except w/Alphawood (fiberglass and wood) classic-style stock featuring Niedner-style grip cap. Weight: 6½ lbs. Left-hand models. Made 1984–89.

Alpha Jaguar Bolt Action Rifle
Same as Custom Rifle, except designed on Mauser-style action w/claw extractor. Calibers: up to 338 Win. Mag. (Standard); 338 thru 458 Win. Mag. (Big Five). Made 1984–88.

AMT (ARCADIA MACHINE & TOOL)
Irwindale, California

AMT Challenger Edition Autoloading Target Rifle **$595**
Similar to the Small Game Hunter, except with McMillan target fiberglass stock. Caliber: 22 LR. 10-shot magazine. 16.5-, 18-, 20- or 22-inch bull barrel. Drilled and tapped for scope mount; no sights. Stainless steel finish. Made 1994 to date.

AMT Lightning

AMT Lightning 25/22 Autoloading Rifle **$170**
Caliber: 22 LR. 25-shot magazine. 18-inch tapered or bull barrel. Weight: 6 pounds. 37 inches overall. Sights: adj. rear; ramp front. Folding stainless-steel stock with matte finish. Made 1984–1994.

AMT Small Game Hunter II

AMT Lightning Small Game Hunter **$175**
Similar to the AMT 25/22, except with conventional matte
black fiberglass/nylon stock. 10-shot rotary magazine. 22-
inch barrel. 40½ inches overall. Weight: 6 pounds.
Grooved for scope; no sights. Made 1987–1994.

AMT Lightning Small Game Hunter II **$180**
Similar to the original Small Game Hunter, except with
free-floated 22-inch heavy target barrel. Weight: 6³/₄
pounds. Made 1992–93.

AMT Magnum Hunter Auto Rifle **$290**
Similar to the Lightning Small Game Hunter II Model,
except chambered in 22 WRF with 22-inch match-grade
barrel. Made from 1993 to date.

ANSCHUTZ RIFLES
Ulm, Germany
Mfd. by J.G. Anschutz GmbH Jagd und Sportwaffenfabrik

Anschutz Models 1407 ISU, 1408-ED, 1411, 1413, 1418,
1432, 1433, 1518 and 1533 were marketed in the U.S. by
Savage Arms. Further, Anschutz Models 1403, 1416,
1422D, 1441, 1516 and 1522D were sold as Savage/An-
schutz with Savage model designations. (*See also* listings
under Savage Arms.) Precision Sales Int'l., Inc. of Westfield,
Mass., is now the U.S. distributor for all Anschutz rifles.

Anschutz Model 54.18MS **$925**
Bolt action, single shot. Caliber: 22 LR. 22-inch barrel.
European hardwood stock w/cheekpiece. Forend and
Wundhammer swell pistol grip stipple checkered. Receiver
grooved, drilled and tapped for scope blocks. Weight: 8³/₈
pounds. Made 1982 to date.

Anschutz Model 54.18MS-REP Repeating Rifle
Same as the Model 54.18MS, except with repeating action
and 5-shot magazine. 22- to 30-inch barrel. 41–49 inches
overall. Avg. Weight: 7 lbs. 12 oz. Hardwood or synthetic
gray thumbhole stock. Made 1989 to date.
Standard MS-REP Model **$1095**
MS-REP Deluxe w/Fibergrain Stock **1295**

Anschutz Model 64MS Bolt Action Single Shot Rifle
Bolt action, single shot. Caliber: 22 LR. 21¼-inch barrel.
European hardwood silhouette-style stock w/cheekpiece.
Forend base and Wundhammer swell pistol grip stipple
checkered. Adj. two-stage trigger. Receiver grooved, drilled
and tapped for scope blocks. Weight: 8 pounds. Made
1982–1990.
Standard or Featherweight **$550**
Left-hand Model **585**

Anschutz Model 520/61 Semiautomatic **$225**
Caliber: 22 LR. 10-shot magazine. 24-inch barrel. Sights:
folding leaf rear; hooded ramp front. Receiver grooved for
scope mounting. Rotary-style safety. Monte Carlo stock
and beavertail forend, checkered. Weight: 6½ pounds.
Imported 1982–83.

Anschutz Model 525 Autoloading Rifle **$365**
Caliber: 22 LR. 10-shot magazine. 24-inch barrel. 43 inches
overall. Weight: 6½ pounds. Adj. folding rear sight; hooded
ramp front. Checkered European hardwood Monte Carlo-
style buttstock and beavertail forend. Sling swivel studs.
Imported since 1982.

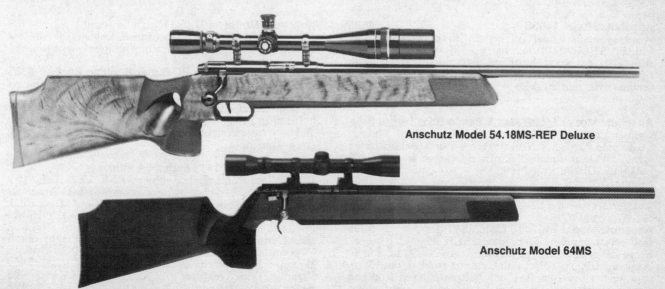

Anschutz Model 54.18MS-REP Deluxe

Anschutz Model 64MS

Anschutz Model 1403B

Anschutz Model 1407

Anschutz Model 1408-ED

Anschutz Model 1411

Anschutz Model 1403B **$695**
A lighter weight model designed for Biathlon competition. Caliber: 22 LR. 21½-inch barrel. Adj. two-stage trigger. Adj. grooved wood buttplate, stipple-checkered deep thumbrest flute and straight pistol grip. Weight: about 9 pounds with sights. Made 1982–1992.

Anschutz Model 1403D Match Single Shot Target Rifle
Caliber: 22 LR. 25-inch barrel. 43 inches overall. Weight: 8.6 pounds. No sights, receiver grooved for Anschutz target sights. Walnut finished hardwood target stock w/adj. buttplate. Discontinued 1992.
Standard Model **$505**
W/Match Sights **695**

Anschutz Model 1407 ISU Match 54 Rifle **$395**
Bolt action, single shot. Caliber: 22 LR. 26⅞-inch barrel. Scope bases. Receiver grooved for Anschutz sights. Single-stage adj. trigger. Select walnut target stock w/deep forearm for position shooting, adj. buttplate, hand stop and swivel. Model 1407-L has left-hand stock. Weight: about

Anschutz Model 1407 ISU Match 54 (cont.)
10 pounds. Made 1970, discontinued. Value is for rifle less sights; add $65 for Anschutz International sight set.

Anschutz Model 1408-ED Super Running Boar . . . **$395**
Bolt action, single shot. Caliber: 22 LR. 23½-inch barrel w/sliding weights. No metallic sights. Receiver drilled and tapped for scope bases. Single-stage adj. trigger. Oversize bolt knob. Select walnut stock w/thumbhole, adj. comb and buttplate. Weight: about 9½ pounds. Introduced 1976; discontinued.

Anschutz Model 1411 Match 54 Rifle
Bolt action, single shot. Caliber: 22 LR. 27½-inch extra heavy barrel. Scope bases. Receiver grooved for Anschutz sights. Single-stage adj. trigger. Select walnut target stock w/cheekpiece (adj. in 1973 and later production), full pistol grip, beavertail forearm, adj. buttplate, hand stop and swivel. Model 1411-L has left-hand stock. Weight: about 11 pounds. Discontinued.
W/non-adjustable cheekpiece **$450**
W/adjustable cheekpiece **495**
Extra for Anschutz International sight set **125**

Anschutz Model 1413 Super Match 54 Rifle

Freestyle international target rifle w/specifications similar to those of Model 1411, except has special stock with thumbhole, adj. pistol grip, adj. cheekpiece in 1973 and later production, adj. hook buttplate, adj. palmrest. Model 1413-L has left-hand stock. Weight: about 15½ pounds. Discontinued.

W/non-adjustable cheekpiece	**$795**
W/adjustable cheekpiece	**825**
Extra for Anschutz International sight set	**125**

Anschutz Model 1416D $375

Bolt-action sporter. Caliber: 22 LR. 22½-inch barrel. Sights: folding leaf rear; hooded ramp front. Receiver grooved for scope mounting. Select European stock w/ cheekpiece, skip-checkered pistol grip and forearm. Weight: 6 pounds. Made 1982 to date.

Anschutz Model 1416D Classic/Custom Sporters

Same as Model 1416D, except w/American classic-style stock (Classic) or modified European-style stock w/Monte Carlo rollover cheekpiece and schnabel forend (Custom). Weight: 5½ pounds. (Classic); 6 pounds. (Custom). Made 1986 to date.

Model 1416D Classic	**$450**
Model 1416D Classic, "True" Left-Hand	**465**
Model 1416D Custom	**425**
Model 1416D Fiberglass (1991–92)	**425**

Anschutz Model 1418 Bolt Action Sporter $375

Caliber: 22 LR. 5- or 10-shot magazine. 19¾-inch barrel. Sights: folding leaf rear; hooded ramp front. Receiver grooved for scope mounting. Select walnut stock, Mannlicher type, w/cheekpiece, pistol grip and forearm skip checkered. Weight: 5½ pounds. Intro. 1976; discontinued.

Anschutz Model 1418D Bolt Action Sporter $650

Caliber: 22 LR. 5- or 10-shot magazine. 19¾-inch barrel. European walnut Monte Carlo stock, Mannlicher type, w/cheekpiece, pistol grip and forend skip-line checkered, buffalo horn schnabel tip. Weight: 5½ pounds. Made from 1982 to date.

Anschutz Model 1422D Classic/Custom Rifle

Bolt-action sporter. Caliber: 22 LR. 5-shot removable straight-feed clip magazine. 24-inch barrel. Sights: folding leaf rear; hooded ramp front. Select European walnut stock, classic type (Classic); Monte Carlo w/hand-carved rollover cheekpiece (Custom). Weight: 7¼ lbs. (Classic); 6½ lbs. (Custom). Made 1982–89.

Model 1422D Classic	**$550**
Model 1422D Custom	**595**

Anschutz Model 1427B Biathlon Rifle $1095

Bolt-action clip repeater. Caliber: 22 LR. 21½-inch barrel. Two-stage trigger w/wing-type safety. Hardwood stock

RIFLES

Anschutz Model 1413

Anschutz Model 1416D

Anschutz Model 1418

Anschutz Model 1422D Classic

Anschutz Model 1427B Biathlon (cont.)

w/deep fluting, pistol grip and deep forestock with adj. hand stop rail. Weight: about 9 pounds w/sights. Made from 1982 to date.

Anschutz Model 1430D Match **$525**

Improved version of Model 64S. Bolt action, single shot. Caliber: 22 LR. 26-inch medium heavy barrel. Walnut Monte Carlo stock w/cheekpiece, adj. buttplate, deep midstock tapered to forend. Pistol grip and contoured thumb groove w/stipple checkering. Single-stage adj. trigger. Weight: 8³/₈ pounds. Made 1982–83.

Anschutz Model 1432 Bolt Action Sporter **$895**

Caliber: 22 Hornet. 5-shot box magazine. 24-inch barrel. Sights: folding leaf rear; hooded ramp front. Receiver grooved for scope mounting. Select walnut stock w/Monte Carlo comb and cheekpiece, pistol grip and forearm skip checkered. Weight: 6³/₄ pounds. Made 1974–1989.

Anschutz Model 1432D Classic/Custom Rifle

Bolt-action sporter similar to Model 1422D, except chambered for 22 Hornet. 4-shot magazine. 23¹/₂-inch barrel. Weight: 7³/₄ lbs. (Classic); 6¹/₂ lbs. (Custom). Classic stock on Classic model; fancy-grade Monte Carlo w/hand-carved rollover cheekpiece (Custom). Made 1982–89.

Model 1432D Classic **$895**
Model 1432D Custom **920**

Anschutz Model 1433 Bolt Action Sporter **$760**

Caliber: 22 Hornet. 5-shot box magazine. 19³/₄-inch barrel. Sights: folding leaf rear; hooded ramp front. Receiver grooved for scope mounting. Single-stage or double-set trigger. Select walnut Mannlicher stock; cheekpiece, pistol grip and forearm skip checkered. Weight: 6¹/₂ pounds. Made 1976–1986.

Anschutz Model 1449 Sporter **$185**

Bolt-action sporter version of Model 2000. Caliber: 22 LR. 5-shot box magazine. 16¹/₄-inch barrel. Weight: 3¹/₂

Anschutz Model 1427B

Anschutz Model 1430D Match

Anschutz Model 1432 Sporter

Anschutz Model 1432D Classic

Anschutz Model 1433

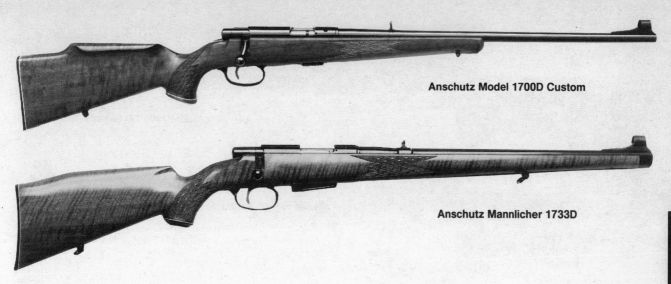

Anschutz Model 1700D Custom

Anschutz Mannlicher 1733D

Anschutz Model 1449 Sporter (cont.)
pounds. Hooded ramp front sight, adjustable rear. Walnut-finished hardwood stock. Made 1989–1992.

Anschutz Model 1450B Target Rifle **$395**
Biathlon rifle developed on the 2000 Series action. 19¹/₂-inch barrel. Weight: 5¹/₂ pounds. Adjustable buttplate. Target sights. Imported 1993–94.

Anschutz Model 1516D Bolt Action Sporter **$460**
Same as Model 1416D, except chambered for 22 Magnum RF. Made from 1982 to date.

Anschutz Model 1516D Classic/Custom Rifle
Same as Model 1516D, except w/American classic-style stock (Classic) or modified European-style stock w/Monte Carlo rollover cheekpiece and schnabel forend (Custom). Weight: 5¹/₂ lbs. (Classic); 6 lbs. (Custom). Made from 1986 to date.
Model 1516D Classic **$520**
Model 1516D Custom **525**

Anschutz Models 1518/1518D Sporting Rifle
Same as Model 1418, except chambered for 22 Magnum RF, 4-shot box magazine. Model 1518 introduced 1976; discontinued. Model 1518D has full Mannlicher-type stock; made from 1982 to date.
Model 1518 . . . . **$515**
Model 1518D **650**

Anschutz Model 1522D Classic/Custom Rifle
Same as Model 1422D, except chambered for 22 Magnum RF, 4-shot magazine. Weight: 6¹/₂ pounds. Classic stock on Classic Model; fancy-grade Monte Carlo stock w/hand-carved rollover cheekpiece (Custom). Made 1982–89.
Model 1522D Classic **$775**
Model 1522D Custom **720**

Anschutz Model 1532D Classic/Custom Rifle
Same as Model 1432D, except chambered for 222 Rem. 3-shot mag. Weight: 6¹/₂ lbs. (Custom). Classic stock on Classic Model; fancy-grade Monte Carlo stock w/hand-carved rollover cheekpiece (Custom). Made 1982–89.
Model 1532D Classic **$625**
Model 1532D Custom **795**

Anschutz Model 1533 . . . . **$750**
Same as Model 1433 except chambered for 222 Rem. 3-shot box magazine. Introduced 1976; discontinued.

Anschutz Model 1700 Series Bolt Action Repeater
Match 54 Sporter. Calibers: 22 LR, 22 Magnum, 22 Hornet, 222 Rem. Removable straight-feed clip magazine. 24-inch barrel. 43 inches overall. Weight: 7¹/₂ pounds. Folding leaf rear sight; hooded ramp front. Select European walnut stock w/cheekpiece and schnabel forend tip. Made from 1989 to date.
Standard Model 1700 Bavarian—RF calibers . . . **$ 820**
Standard Model 1700 Bavarian—CF calibers . . . **985**
Model 1700D Classic (Classic stock, 6³/₄ lbs.)
  Rimfire calibers **845**
Model 1700D Classic—Centerfire calibers **975**
Model 1700D Custom (Select walnut stock w/roll-
  over cheekpiece) Rimfire calibers **825**
Model 1700D Custom—Centerfire calibers **995**
Model 1700D Graphite Custom (McMillian graphite-
  reinforced stock, 22″ bbl., intro. 1991) **865**
Model 1700 FWT Featherweight (6¹/₂ lbs.)
  Rimfire calibers **885**
Model 1700 FWT—Centerfire calibers **1025**

Anschutz Model 1733D Mannlicher **$995**
Same as the Model 1700D, except with 19-inch barrel and Mannlicher-style stock. 39 inches overall. Weight: 6¹/₄ pounds. Made 1993 to date.

Anschutz Model 1803D Match Single Shot Target Rifle
Caliber: 22 LR 25¹/₂-inch barrel. 43³/₄ inches overall. Weight: 8¹/₂ pounds. No sights, receiver grooved, drilled and tapped for scope mounts. Blonde or walnut-finished hardwood stock with adj. cheekpiece, stippled grip and forend. Left-hand version. Imported 1987–1992.
Right-hand Model **$675**
Left-hand Model. **750**

Anschutz Model 1807 ISU Standard Match **$825**
Bolt action, single shot. Caliber: 22 LR. 26-inch barrel. Improved Super Match 54 action. Two-stage match trigger. Removable cheekpiece, adj. buttplate, thumbpiece and forestock w/stipple checkered. Weight: 10 pounds. Imported 1982–88.

Anschutz Model 1808 ED Super

Anschutz Model 1813 Super Match

Anschutz Model 1913

Anschutz Model 1808ED Super-Running Target
Bolt action, single shot. Caliber: 22 LR. 23^1/$_2$-inch barrel w/sliding weights. Improved Super Match 54 action. Heavy beavertail forend, adj. cheekpiece and buttplate. Adj. single-stage trigger. Weight: 9^1/$_4$ pounds. Made from 1982 to date.

Right-Hand Model . . . . $ 995
Left-Hand Model 1035

Anschutz Model 1810 Super Match II $1295
A less detailed version of the Super Match 1813 Model. Tapered forend w/deep receiver area. Select European hardwood stock. Weight: about 13^1/$_2$ pounds. Imported 1982–88.

Anschutz Model 1811 Prone Match $995
Bolt action, single shot. Caliber: 22 LR. 27^1/$_4$-inch barrel. Improved Super Match 54 action. Select European hardwood stock w/beavertail forend, adj. cheekpiece, and deep thumb flute. Thumb groove and pistol grip w/stipple checkering. Adj. buttplate. Weight: about 11^1/$_2$ pounds. Imported 1982–88.

Anschutz Model 1813 Super Match $1250
Bolt action, single shot. Caliber: 22 LR. 27^1/$_4$-inch barrel. Improved Super Match 54 action w/light firing pin, one-point adj. trigger. European walnut thumbhole stock, adj. palmrest, forend and pistol grip stipple checkered. Adj. cheekpiece and hook buttplate. Weight: 15^1/$_4$ pounds. Imported 1982–88.

Anschutz Model 1827 Biathlon Rifle
Bolt action. Caliber: 22 LR. 21^1/$_2$-inch barrel. 42^1/$_2$ inches overall. Weight: 8^1/$_2$ pounds w/sights. 6827 Sight Set w/ snow caps; 10-click adj. Slide safety. European walnut stock w/cheekpiece, stippled pistol grip and forearm. Discontinued 1989.

Anschutz Model 1827 Biathlon Rifle (cont.)
Model 1827B w/Super Match 54 action $1350
Model 1827BT w/Fortner straight-pull bolt
   Right-hand 2595
   Left-hand 2895

Anschutz Model 1907 International Match Rifle
Same general specifications Model 1913, except w/26-inch barrel. 44^1/$_2$ inches overall. Weight: 11 pounds. Designed for ISU 3-position competition. Fitted w/vented blonde finished stock.

Right-hand Model $1095
Left-hand Model 1225

Anschutz Model 1910 International Super Match Rifle
Same general specifications Model 1913, except w/less-detailed hardwood stock w/tapered forend. Weight: 13^1/$_2$ pounds.

Right-hand Model $1695
Left-hand Model 1845

Anschutz Model 1911 Prone Match Rifle
Same general specifications Model 1913, except w/specialized prone match hardwood stock w/beavertail forend. Weight: 11^1/$_2$ pounds.

Right-hand Model $1295
Left-hand Model 1395

Anschutz Model 1913 Super Match Rifle
Bolt action, single-shot Super Match. Caliber: 22 LR. 27^1/$_4$-inch barrel. Weight: 15.2 pounds. Adj. two-stage trigger. Vented International thumbhole stock w/adj. cheekpiece, hand and palmrest; fitted w/10-way butthook. Made 1982 to date.

Right-hand Model $1825
Left-hand Model 1895

Anschutz Model 2007 Special

Anschutz Achiever

Anschutz Model BR-50
Bench Rest Rifle

Anschutz Mark 2000

Anschutz Model 2007 ISU Standard Rifle **$1595**
Bolt action, single shot. Caliber: 22 LR. 19³/₄-inch barrel.
43¹/₂ to 44¹/₂ inches overall. Weight: 10.8 pounds. Two-stage trigger. Standard ISU stock w/adj. cheekpiece. Made from 1992 to date.

Anschutz Model 2013 Super Match Rifle **$2595**
Bolt action, single shot. Caliber: 22 LR. 19³/₄-inch barrel.
43 to 45¹/₂ inches overall. Weight: 12¹/₂ pounds. Two-stage trigger. International thumbhole stock w/adj. cheekpiece, hand and palmrest; fitted w/10-way butthook. Made from 1992 to date.

Anschutz Achiever Bolt Action Rifle **$245**
Caliber: 22 LR. 5-shot magazine. Mark 2000-type repeating action. 19¹/₂-inch barrel. 36¹/₄ inches overall. Weight: 5 pounds. Adj. open rear sight; hooded ramp front. Plain European hardwood target-style stock w/vented forend and adj. buttplate. Imported since 1987.

Anschutz Achiever ST-Super Target **$350**
Same as the Achiever, except single shot with 22-inch barrel and adjustable stock. 38³/₄ inches overall. Weight: 6¹/₂ pounds. Target sights. Imported since 1994.

Anschutz Model BR-50 Bench Rest Rifle **$1495**
Single shot. Caliber: 22 LR. 19³/₄-inch barrel (23 inches w/muzzle weight). 37³/₄–42¹/₂ inches overall. Weight: 11 pounds. Grooved receiver; no sights. Walnut-finished hardwood or synthetic benchrest stock w/adj. cheekpiece. Made 1994 to date.

Anschutz Kadett Bolt Action Repeating Rifle ... **$190**
Caliber: 22 LR. 5-shot detachable box magazine. 22-inch barrel. 40 inches overall. Weight: 5¹/₂ pounds. Adj. folding leaf rear sight; hooded ramp front. Checkered European hardwood stock w/walnut finish. Imported 1987–88.

Anschutz Mark 2000 Match **$275**
Takedown. Bolt action, single shot. Caliber: 22 LR. 26-inch heavy barrel. Walnut stock w/deep-fluted thumb groove, Wundhammer swell pistol grip, beavertail-style forend. Adj. buttplate, single-stage adj. trigger. Weight: 8¹/₂ pounds. Imported 1982–89.

ARMALITE INC.
Costa Mesa, California

Armalite AR-7 Explorer Survival Rifle **$100**
Takedown. Semiautomatic. Caliber: 22 LR. 8-shot box magazine. 16-inch cast aluminum barrel with steel liner. Sights: peep rear; blade front. Brown plastic stock, re-

Armalite AR-7 Explorer Survival Rifle

Armalite AR-7 Explorer Custom

Armalite AR-180

Armalite AR-7 Explorer Survival Rifle (cont.)
cessed to stow barrel, action, and magazine. Weight: 2³/₄ pounds. Will float stowed or assembled. Made 1959–1973 by Armalite; 1974–1990 by Charter Arms; now manufactured by Survival Arms, Cocoa, FL.

Armalite AR-7 Explorer Custom Rifle $130
Same as AR-7 Survival Rifle, except has deluxe walnut stock w/cheekpiece and pistol grip. Weight: 3¹/₂ pounds. Made 1964–1970.

Armalite AR-180 Semiautomatic Rifle $995
Commercial version of full automatic AR-18 Combat Rifle. Gas-operated semiautomatic. Caliber: 223 Rem. (5.56mm). 5-, 20-, 30-round magazines. 18¹/₄-inch barrel w/flash hider/muzzle brake. Sights: flip-up "L" type rear, adj. for windage; post front, adj. for elevation. Accessory 3× scope and mount (add $60 to value). Folding buttstock of black nylon, rubber buttplate, pistol grip, heat-dissipating fi-

Armalite AR-180 Semiautomatic Rifle (cont.)
berglass forend (hand guard), swivels, sling. 38 inches overall, 28³/₄ inches folded. Weight: 6¹/₂ pounds. *Note:* Made by Armalite Inc. 1969–1972; manufactured for Armalite by Howa Machinery Ltd., Nagoya, Japan, 1972–73; by Sterling Armament Co. Ltd., Dagenham, Essex, England, 1976 to date. Importation discontinued due to federal restrictions.

ARMI JAGER
Turin, Italy

Armi Jager AP-74 Commando $185
Similar to standard AP-74, but styled to resemble original version of Uzi 9mm submachine gun w/wood buttstock; lacks carrying handle and flash suppressor, has different type front sight mount and guards, wood stock, pistol grip and forearm. Introduced 1976; discontinued.

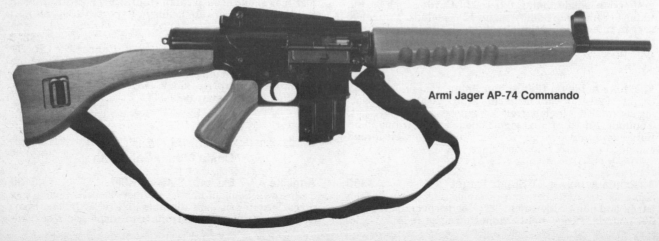

Armi Jager AP-74 Commando

Armi Jager Model AP-74

Armi Jager AP-74 Semiautomatic Rifle
Styled after U.S. M16 military rifle. Calibers: 22 LR, 32 Auto (pistol cartridge). Detachable clip magazine; capacity: 14 rounds 22 LR, 9 rounds 32 ACP. 20-inch barrel with flash suppressor. Weight: about 6½ pounds. M16 type sights. Stock, pistol grip and forearm of black plastic, swivels and sling. Introduced 1974; discontinued.
22 LR **$225**
32 Automatic **250**

Armi Jager AP-74 with Wood Stock
Same as standard AP-74, except has wood stock, pistol grip and forearm, weighs about 7 pounds. Discontinued.
22 LR **$250**
32 Automatic **285**

ARMSCOR (Arms Corp.)
Manila, Philippines
Imported until 1991 by Armscor Precision, San Mateo, CA; currently imported by Ruko Products, Inc., Buffalo, NY

Armscor Model 20 Auto Rifle
Caliber: 22 LR. 15-shot magazine. 21-inch barrel. 39¾ inches overall. Weight: 6½ pounds. Sights: hooded front; adjustable rear. Checkered or plain walnut-finished mahogany stock. Blued finish. Imported 1990–91. Reinstated by Ruko in the M series.
Model 20 (Checkered Stock) **$110**
Model 20C (Carbine-style Stock) **105**
Model 20P (Plain Stock) **90**

Armscor Model 1600 Auto Rifle
Caliber: 22 LR. 15-shot magazine. 19½-inch barrel. 38 inches overall. Weight: 6 pounds. Sights: post front; aperture rear. Plain mahogany stock. Matte black finish. Imported 1987-91. Reinstated by Ruko in the M series.
Standard Model **$150**
Retractable Stock Model **160**

Armscor Model AK22 Auto Rifle
Caliber: 22 LR. 15- or 30-shot magazine. 18½-inch barrel. 36 inches overall. Weight: 7 pounds. Sights: post front; adjustable rear. Plain mahogany stock. Matte black finish. Imported 1987–1991.
Standard Model **$225**
Folding Stock Model **275**

Armscor/Ruko Model M14 Bolt Action Rifle
Caliber: 22 LR. 10-shot magazine. 23-inch barrel. Weight: 6¼ pounds. Open sights. Walnut-finished mahogany stock. Imported 1991 to date.
M14P Standard Model **$80**
M14D Deluxe Model (Checkered Stock) **90**

Armscor/Ruko Model M1400 Bolt Action Rifle
Similar to the Model 14P, except has checkered stock w/ schnabel forend. Weight: 6 pounds. Imported 1991–92.
M1400LW (Lightweight) **$165**
M1400SC (Super Classic) **195**

Armscor/Ruko Model M1500 Bolt Action Rifle
Caliber: 22 Mag. 5-shot magazine. 21½-inch barrel. Weight: 6½ pounds. Open sights. Checkered mahogany stock. Imported 1991 to date.
M1500 (Standard) **$165**
M1500LW (Euro-style Walnut Stock, Disc. 1992) **165**
M1500SC (Monte Carlo Stock) **195**

Armscor/Ruko Model M1600 Auto Rifle **$145**
Similar to the Model 1600 Standard, except chambered for 22 Mag. 5-shot magazine. 21½-inch barrel. Weight: 6½ pounds. Open sights. Checkered mahogany stock. Imported 1991 to date.

Armscor/Ruko Model M2000 Auto Rifle
Similar to the Model 20P, except with checkered mahogany stock and adjustable sights. Imported 1991 to date.
M2000 (Standard) .... **$ 85**
M2000SC (Checkered Walnut Stock) **175**

A-SQUARE COMPANY INC.
Bedford, Kentucky

A-Square Caesar Bolt Action Rifle
Custom rifle built on the Remington 700 receiver. Calibers: Same as Hannibal, Groups I, II and III. 20- to 26-inch barrel. Weight: 8½ to 11 pounds. Express 3-leaf rear sight, ramp front. Synthetic or classic Claro oil-finished walnut stock w/flush detachable swivels and Coil-Check recoil system. Three-way adj. target trigger; 3-position safety. Right- or left-hand. Made 1984 to date.
Synthetic Stock Model **$1950**
Walnut Stock Model **1825**

A-Square Genghis Khan Bolt Action Rifle
Custom varmint rifle developed on the Winchester 70 receiver; fitted w/heavy tapered barrel and coil-check stock. Calibers: 22-250 Rem., 243 Win., 25-06 Rem., 6mm Rem. Weight: 8–8½ pounds. Made 1994 to date.
Synthetic Stock Model **$1750**
Walnut Stock Model **1625**

A-Square Hamilcar Bolt Action Rifle
Similar to the Hannibal Model except lighter. Calibers: 25-06, 257 Wby., 6.5×55 Swedish, 270 Wby., 7×57, 7mm Rem., 7mm STW, 7mm Wby., 280 Rem., 30-06, 300 Win., 300 Wby., 338-06, 9.3×62. Weight: 8–8½ pounds. Made

RIFLES

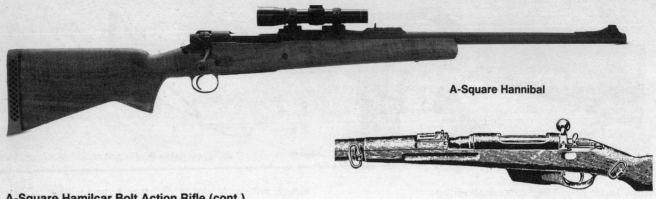

A-Square Hannibal

Austrian Model 95 Rifle

A-Square Hamilcar Bolt Action Rifle (cont.)
1994 to date.
Synthetic Stock Model **$1950**
Walnut Stock Model **1825**

A-Square Hannibal Bolt Action Rifle
Custom rifle built on reinforced P-17 Enfield receiver. Calibers: *Group I:* 30-06; *Group II:* 7mm Rem. Mag., 300 Win. Mag., 416 Taylor, 425 Express, 458 Win. Mag.; *Group III:* 300 H&H, 300 Wby. Mag., 8mm Rem. Mag., 340 Wby. Mag., 375 H&H, 375 Wby. Mag., 404 Jeffery, 416 Hoffman, 416 Rem Mag., 450 Ackley, 458 Lott; *Group IV:* 338 A-Square Mag., 375 A-Square Mag., 378 Wby. Mag., 416 Rigby, 416 Wby. Mag., 460 Short Square Mag., 500 A-Square Mag. 20- to 26-inch barrel. Weight: 9 to 11 3/4 pounds. Express 3-leaf rear sight, ramp front. Classic Claro oil-finished walnut stock, or synthetic stock w/flush detachable swivels and Coil-Check recoil system. Adj. trigger with 2-position safety. Made 1983 to date.
Synthetic Stock Model **$1950**
Walnut Stock Model **1825**

AUSTRIAN MILITARY RIFLES
Steyr, Austria
Manufactured at Steyr Armory

Austrian Model 90 Steyr-Mannlicher Carbine ... **$140**
Same general specifications as Model 95 Rifle, except has 19 1/2-inch barrel, weighs about 7 pounds.

Austrian Model 95 Steyr-Mannlicher Service Rifle **$130**
Straight-pull bolt action. Caliber: 8×50R Mannlicher (many of these rifles were altered during World War II to use the 7.9mm German service ammunition). 5-shot Mannlicher-type box magazine. 30-inch barrel. Weight:

Austrian Model 95 Steyr-Mannlicher Service (cont.)
about 8 1/2 pounds. Sights: blade front; rear adj. for elevation. Military-type full stock.

AUTO-ORDNANCE CORPORATION
West Hurley, New York

Auto-Ordnance Thompson Model 22-27A-3 .... **$395**
Small-bore version of Deluxe Model 27A-1. Same general specifications, except caliber 22 LR, has lightweight alloy receiver, weighs about 6 1/2 pounds; magazines include 5-, 20-, 30- and 50-shot box types, 80-shot drum. Introduced 1977.

Auto-Ordnance Thompson Model 27A-1 Deluxe
Same as Standard Mod. 27A-1, except has finned barrel w/compensator, adj. rear sight, pistol-grip forestock. Caliber: 10mm or 45 ACP. Weight: about 11 1/2 pounds. Made 1976 to date.
45 ACP.................................... **$995**
10mm (Made 1991–93) **950**
50-Round Drum Magazine, **add** **250**
100-Round Drum Magazine, **add** **450**
Violin Carrying Case, **add** **100**

Auto-Ordnance Thompson Model 27A-1 Standard Semiauto Carbine **$875**
Similar to Thompson submachine gun ("Tommy Gun"), except has no provision for automatic firing. Caliber: 45 Automatic. 20-shot detachable box magazine (5-, 15- and 30-shot box magazines, 39-shot drum also available). 16-

**Auto-Ordnance
Thompson Model 27A-1 Deluxe**

**Auto-Ordnance
Thompson Model 27A-1 Standard**

RIFLES

Auto-Ordnance Thompson Model 27A-1 Std. (cont.)
inch plain barrel. Weight: about 14 pounds. Sights: aperture rear; blade front. Walnut buttstock, pistol grip and grooved forearm, sling swivels. Made 1976–1986.

Auto-Ordnance Thompson 27A-1C Lightweight Carbine **$895**
Similar to the Model 27A-1, except with lightweight alloy receiver. Weight: 9¼ pounds. Made 1984 to date.

Auto-Ordnance Thompson M1 Semiautomatic Carbine **$950**
Similar to the Model 27A-1, except in M-1 configuration w/side cocking lever and horizontal forearm. Weight: 11½ pounds. Made 1986 to date.

BARRETT FIREARMS MFG., INC.
Murfreesboro, Tennessee

Barrett Model 82 A-1 Semiautomatic Rifle **$5095**
Caliber: 50 BMG. 10-shot detachable box magazine. 29-inch recoiling barrel with muzzlebrake. 57 inches overall. Weight: 28½ lbs. Open iron sights and 10x scope. Composition stock with Sorbothane recoil pad and self-leveling bipod. Blued finish. Made 1985 to date.

Barrett Model 90 Bolt Action Rifle **$2995**
Caliber: 50 BMG. 5-shot magazine. 29-inch match barrel. 45 inches overall. Weight: 22 pounds. Composition stock with retractable bipod. Made 1990 to date.

BEEMAN PRECISION ARMS, INC.
Santa Rosa, California
Since 1993 all European firearms imported by Beeman have been distributed by Beeman Outdoor Sports, Div. Roberts Precision Arms, Inc., Santa Rosa, CA

Beeman/Weihrauch HW Models 60J and 60J-ST Bolt Action Rifles
Calibers: 22 LR (60J-ST), 222 Rem. (60J). 22⁴/₅-inch barrel. 41.7 inches overall. Weight: 6½ lbs. Sights: hooded blade front; open adjustable rear. Blued finish. Checkered walnut stock with cheekpiece. Made 1988–1994.
Model 60J **$495**
Model 60J-ST **440**

Beeman/Weihrauch HW Model 60M Small Bore Rifle **$450**
Caliber: 22 LR. Single shot. 26⁴/₅-inch barrel. 45.7 inches overall. Weight: 10⁴/₅ lbs. Adjustable trigger with push-

Beeman/Weihrauch HW Model 60M Small Bore (cont.)
button safety. Sights: hooded blade front on ramp, precision aperture rear. Target-style stock with stippled forearm and pistol grip. Blued finish. Made 1988–1994.

Beeman/Weihrauch HW Model 660 Match Rifle . **$595**
Caliber: 22 LR. 26-inch barrel. 45.3 inches overall. Weight: 10.7 pounds. Adjustable match trigger. Sights: globe front; precision aperture rear. Match-style walnut stock with adjustable cheekpiece and buttplate. Made 1988–1994.

Beeman/Feinwerkbau Model 2600 Target Rifle
Caliber: 22 LR. Single shot. 26.3-inch barrel. 43.7 inches overall. Weight: 10³/₅ lbs. Match trigger with fingertip weight adjustment dial. Sights: globe front; micrometer match aperture rear. Laminated hardwood stock with adjustable cheekpiece. Made 1988–1994.
Standard Model (left-hand) **$1195**
Standard Model (right-hand) **995**
Free Rifle Model (left-hand) **1595**
Free Rifle Model (right-hand) **1450**

BELGIAN MILITARY RIFLES
Mfd. by Fabrique Nationale D'Armes de Guerre, Herstal, Belgium; Fabrique D'Armes de L'Etat, Luttich, Belgium

Hopkins & Allen Arms Co. of Norwich, Conn., as well as contractors in Birmingham, England, also produced these arms during World War I.

Belgian Model 1889 Mauser Military Rifle **$125**
Caliber: 7.65mm Belgian Service (7.65mm Mauser). 5-shot projecting box magazine. 30³/₄-inch barrel w/jacket. Weight: about 8½ pounds. Adj. rear sight, blade front. Straight-grip military stock. This and the carbine version were the principal weapons of the Belgian Army at the start of WWII. Made 1889 to c.1935.

Belgian Model 1916 Mauser Carbine **$180**
Same as Model 1889 Rifle, except has 20³/₄-inch barrel, weighs about 8 pounds and has minor differences in the rear sight graduations, lower band closer to the muzzle and swivel plate found on side of buttstock.

Belgian Model 1935 Mauser Military Rifle **$215**
Same general specifications as F.N. Model 1924; minor differences. Caliber: 7.65mm Belgian Service. Mfd. by Fabrique Nationale D'Armes de Guerre.

Belgian Model 1936 Mauser Military Rifle **$185**
An adaptation of the Model 1889 w/German M/98-type bolt, Belgian M/89 protruding box magazine. Caliber: 7.65mm Belgian Service. Mfd. by Fabrique Nationale D'Armes de Guerre.

**Benton & Brown
Model 93**

BENTON & BROWN FIREARMS, INC.
Fort Worth, Texas

Benton & Brown Model 93 Bolt Action Rifle
Similar to the Blaser Model R84 (the B&B rifle is built on the Blaser action, *see* separate listing) w/an interchangeable barrel system. Calibers: 243 Win., 6mm Rem., 25-06, 257 Wby., 264 Win., 270 Win., 280 Rem., 7mm

Benton & Brown Model 93 (cont.)
Rem Mag., 30-06, 308, 300 Wby., 300 Win. Mag., 338 Win., 375 H&H. 22- or 24-inch barrel. 41 or 43 inches overall. Barrel-mounted scope rings and one-piece base; no sights. Two-piece walnut or fiberglass stock. Made 1993 to date.

Walnut Stock Model	**$1295**
Fiberglass Stock Model	1195
Extra Barrel Assembly, **add**	425
Extra Bolt Assembly, **add**	400

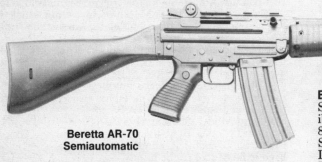

**Beretta AR-70
Semiautomatic**

BERETTA U.S.A. CORP.
Accokeek, Maryland
**Manufactured by Fabbrica D'Armi Pietro Beretta
S.p.A. in the Gardone Valtrompia (Brescia), Italy**

Beretta 455 SxS Express Double Rifle
Sidelock action with removable sideplates. Calibers: 375 H&H, 458 Win. Mag., 470 NE, 500 NE (3 inches), 416 Rigby. Barrels: $23^1/_2$ or $25^1/_2$-inch. Weight: 11 lbs. Double triggers. Sights: blade front; V-notch folding leaf rear. Checkered European walnut forearm and buttstock with recoil pad. Color casehardened receiver with blued barrels. Made 1990 to date.

Model 455	**$27,000**
Model 455EELL	35,250

Beretta 500 Bolt Action Sporter
Centerfire bolt-action rifle w/a Sako AI short action. Calibers: 222 Rem., 223 Rem. 5-shot magazine. $23^5/_8$-inch barrel. Weight: $6^1/_2$ pounds. No sights. Tapered dovetailed receiver. European walnut stock. Discontinued.

Standard	**$ 465**
DL Model	1095
Engraved	1195

Beretta 501 Bolt Action Sporter
Same as Model 500, except w/Sako AII medium action. Calibers: 243 Win., 308 Win. Weight: $7^1/_2$ pounds. Disc.

Standard	**$ 495**
Standard w/Iron Sights	515
DL Model	1125
Engraved	1225

Beretta 502 Bolt Action Sporter
Same as Model 500, except w/Sako AIII long action. Calibers: 270 Win., 7mm Rem. Mag., 30.06, 375 H&H. Weight: $8^1/_2$ pounds. Discontinued.

Standard	**$ 530**
DL Model	1200
Engraved	1325

Beretta AR-70 Semiautomatic Rifle $995
Caliber: 223 Rem. (5.56mm). 30-shot magazine. $17^3/_4$-inch barrel. Weight: $8^1/_4$ pounds. Sights: rear peep adj. for windage and elevation; blade front. High-impact synthetic buttstock. Made 1984 to date. No longer imported.

Beretta Small Bore Sporting Carbine $240
Semiautomatic w/bolt handle raised, conventional bolt-action repeater w/handle in lowered position. Caliber: 22 LR. 4-, 8-, or 20-shot magazines. $20^1/_2$-inch barrel. Sights: 3-leaf folding rear; patridge front. Stock w/checkered pistol grip, sling swivels. Weight: $5^1/_2$ pounds.

Beretta Express SSO O/U Double Rifle
Sidelock. Calibers: 375 H&H, 458 Win. Mag., 9.3×74R. Barrels: $25^1/_2$-inch. Weight: 11 pounds. Double triggers. Sights: blade front, V-notch folding leaf rear. Checkered European walnut forearm with recoil pad. Color receiver with blued barrels. Made 1990 to date.

Model SS06	**$14,950**
Model SS06 Gold	17,000

BLASER USA, INC.
Fort Worth, Texas
Mfd. by Blaser Jagdwaffen GmbH, Germany

Blaser Model R84 Bolt Action Rifle
Calibers: 22-250, 243, 6mm Rem., 25-06, 270, 280 Rem., 30-06; 257 Wby. Mag., 264 Win. Mag., 7mm Rem Mag., 300 Win. Mag., 300 Wby. Mag., 338 Win. Mag., 375 H&H. Interchangeable barrels w/standard or Magnum bolt assemblies. Barrel length: 23 inches (standard); 24 inches

Blaser Model R 84 Bolt Action

Blaser Model R84 Bolt Action Rifle (cont.)
(Magnum). 41 to 42 inches overall. Weight: 7 to 7¼ pounds. No sights. Barrel-mounted scope system. Two-piece Turkish walnut stock w/solid black recoil pad. Imported 1989–1994.

Right-hand Model	**$1690**
Left-hand Model	1725
Extra Barrel Assembly	430

Blaser Model R93 Bolt Action Rifle
Similar to the Model R84, except restyled action w/straight-pull bolt. Additional chamberings: 6.5×55, 7×57, 308, 416 Rem. Optional open sights. Imported 1994 to date.

Standard Model	**$1725**
Safari Model (375 H&H, 416 Rem.)	1795
Extra Barrel Assembly, **add**	430

British S.M.L.E. No. 1 Mark III

British No. 3 Mark I

BRITISH MILITARY RIFLES
Mfd. at Royal Small Arms Factory, Enfield Lock, Middlesex, England, as well as private contractors

British Army Rifle No. 1 Mark III* **$165**
Short Magazine Lee-Enfield (S.M.L.E.). Bolt action. Caliber: 303 British Service. 10-shot box magazine. 25¼-inch barrel. Weight: about 8¾ pounds. Sights: adjustable rear; blade front w/guards. Two-piece, full-length military stock. *Note:* The earlier Mark III (approved 1907) is virtually the same as the Mark III* (adopted 1918) except for sights and different magazine cut-off that was eliminated on the latter.

British Army Rifle No. 3 Mark I* (Pattern '14) . . . **$170**
Modified Mauser-type bolt action. Except for caliber, 303 British Service, and long-range sights, this rifle is the same as U.S. Model 1917 Enfield. *See* listing of the latter for general specifications.

British Army Rifle No. 4 Mark I* **$150**
Post-World War I modification of the S.M.L.E. intended to simplify mass production. General specifications same as Rifle No. 1 Mark III* except weighs 9¼ pounds, has aperture rear sight, minor differences in construction.

British Army Light Rifle No. 4 Mark I* **$130**
Modification of the S.M.L.E. Caliber: 303 British Service. 10-shot box magazine. 23-inch barrel. Weight: about 6¾ pounds. Sights: micrometer click rear peep; blade front. One-piece military-type stock w/recoil pad. Made during WWII.

British Army Rifle No. 5 Mark I* **$175**
Jungle Carbine. Modification of the S.M.L.E. similar to Light Rifle No. 4 Mark I* except has 20½-inch barrel w/flash hider, carbine-type stock. Made during WWII, originally designed for use in the Pacific Theater.

BRNO SPORTING RIFLES
Brno, Czechoslovakia
Manufactured by Ceska Zbrojovka

See also CZ Rifles.

Brno Model I Bolt Action Sporting Rifle **$495**
Caliber: 22 LR. 5-shot detachable magazine. 22¾-inch barrel. Weight: about 6 pounds. Sights: three-leaf open rear; hooded ramp front. Sporting stock w/checkered pistol grip, swivels. Discontinued.

RIFLES

Brno Model II

Brno Model 21H

Brno Model 22F

Brno Hornet

Brno Model II **$525**
Same as Model I except w/deluxe grade stock. Discont.

Brno Model 21H Bolt Action Sporting Rifle **$585**
Mauser-type action. Calibers: 6.5×57mm, 7×57mm,
8×57mm. 5-shot box magazine. 20¹/₂-inch barrel. Double-
set trigger. Weight: about 6³/₄ pounds. Sights: two-leaf
open rear; hooded ramp front. Half-length sporting stock
w/cheekpiece, checkered pistol grip and forearm, swivels.
Discontinued.

Brno Model 22F **$795**
Same as Model 21H except has full-length Mannlicher-
type stock, weighs about 6 lbs 14 oz. Discontinued.

Brno Hornet Bolt Action Sporting Rifle **$725**
Miniature Mauser action. Caliber: 22 Hornet. 5-shot detachable box magazine. 23-inch barrel. Double set trigger.
Weight: about 6¹/₄ pounds. Sights: three-leaf open rear;
hooded ramp front. Sporting stock w/checkered pistol grip
and forearm, swivels. Discontinued. *Note:* This was also
marketed in the U.S. as "Z-B Mauser Varmint Rifle."

Brno ZKB 680 Bolt Action Rifle **$350**
Calibers: 22 Hornet, 222 Rem. 5-shot detachable box
magazine. 23¹/₂-inch barrel. Weight: 5³/₄ lbs. Double-set
triggers. Adj. open rear sight, hooded ramp front. Walnut
stock. No longer imported.

BROWN PRECISION COMPANY
Los Molinos, California

Brown Precision Model 7 Super Light Sporter . . **$795**
Lightweight sporter built on a Remington Model 7 bar-
reled action w/18-inch factory barrel. Weight: 5¹/₄ pounds.
Kevlar stock. Made 1984–1992.

Brown Precision High Country Bolt Action Sporter
Custom sporting rifles built on Blaser, Remington 700,
Ruger 77 and Winchester 70 actions. Calibers: 243 Win.,
25-06, 270 Win., 7mm Rem. Mag., 308 Win., 30-06. 5-shot
magazine (4-shot in 7mm Mag.). 22- or 24-inch barrel.
Weight: about 6¹/₂ pounds. Fiberglass stock w/recoil pad,
sling swivels. No sights. Made 1975 to date.
Standard High Country . . . . **$ 850**
Custom High Country **1395**
Left-Hand Action, **add** **100**

Brown Precision High Country

Brown Precision High Country Youth

**Brown Precision
Pro-Hunter Elite**

**Brown Precision
Tactical Elite**

Brown Precision High Country Sporter (cont.)
Stainless Barrel, **add** . . . . $ 100
70, 77 or Blaser Actions, **add** 125
70 SG Action, **add** 300

Brown Precision High Country Youth Rifle $850
Similar to the standard Model 7 Super Light, except with
Kevlar or graphite stock scaled-down to youth dimensions.
Calibers: 223, 243, 6mm, 7mm-08, 308. Made 1992 to date.

Brown Precision Pro-Hunter Bolt Action Rifle
Custom sporting rifle built on Remingtom 700 or Winchester 70 SG action, fitted with match-grade Shilen barrel
chambered in customer's choice of caliber. Matte blued,
electroless nickel or Teflon finish. Express-style rear sight,
hooded ramp front. Synthetic stock. Made 1989 to date
Standard Pro-Hunter **$1495**
Pro-Hunter Elite (1993 to date) 2350
Left-Hand Action, **add** 100

Brown Precision Pro-Varminter Bolt Action Rifle
Custom varminter built on a Remington 700 or 40X action
fitted w/Shilen stainless steel benchrest barrel. Varmint
or benchrest-style stock. Made 1993 to date.
Standard Pro-Varminter **$1150**
Pro-Hunter w/Rem 40X Action 1595
Left-Hand Action, **add** 100

Brown Precision Selective Target Model $825
Tactical law-enforcement rifle built on a Remington 700V
action. Caliber: 308 Win. 20-, 22- or 24-inch barrel. Synthetic stock. Made 1989–1992.

Brown Precision Tactical Elite Rifle $1550
Similar to the Selective Target Model, except fitted w/
select match-grade Shilen benchrest heavy stainless barrel. Calibers: 223, 308, 300 Win. Mag. Black or camo Kev-
lar/graphite composite fiberglass stock w/adj. buttplate.
Non-reflective black Teflon metal finish. Made 1993 to
date.

═══ BROWNING RIFLES ═══
Morgan, Utah

Mfd. for Browning by Fabrique Nationale d'Armes de
Guerre (now Fabrique Nationale Herstal), Herstal, Belgium;
Miroku Firearms Mfg. Co., Tokyo, Japan; Oy Sako Ab,
Riihimaki, Finland

Browning 22 Automatic Rifle, Grade I
Similar to discontinued Remington Model 241A. Autoloading. Takedown. Calibers: 22 LR, 22 Short (not interchangeably). Tubular magazine in buttstock holds 11 LR,
16 Short. Barrel lengths: 19$\frac{1}{4}$-inch (22 LR), 22$\frac{1}{4}$-inch
(22 Short). Weight: about 4$\frac{3}{4}$ lbs. (22 LR); 5 lbs. (Short).
Receiver scroll engraved. Open rear sight, bead front.

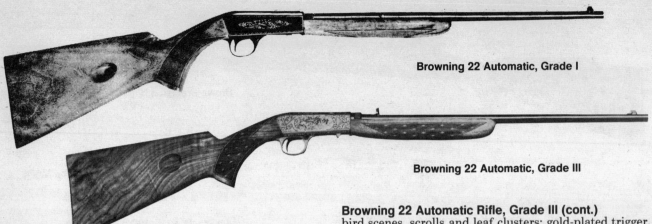

Browning 22 Automatic, Grade I

Browning 22 Automatic, Grade III

Browning 22 Automatic Rifle, Grade I (cont.)
Checkered pistol-grip buttstock, semibeavertail forearm. Made 1965–1972 by FN; 1972 to date by Miroku. *Note:* Illustrations are of rifles manufactured by FN.
FN manufacture **$350**
Miroku manufacture **250**

Browning 22 Automatic Rifle, Grade II
Same as Grade I, except satin chrome-plated receiver engraved w/small game animal scenes, gold-plated trigger, select walnut stock and forearm. 22 LR only. Made 1972–1984.
FN manufacture **$550**
Miroku manufacture **295**

Browning 22 Automatic Rifle, Grade III
Same as Grade I, except satin chrome-plated receiver elaborately hand-carved and engraved w/dog and game-

Browning 22 Auto Grade VI

Browning 22 Automatic Rifle, Grade III (cont.)
bird scenes, scrolls and leaf clusters: gold-plated trigger, extra-fancy walnut stock and forearm, skip-checkered. 22 LR only. Made 1972–1984.
FN manufacture **$1350**
Miroku manufacture **560**

Browning 22 Automatic, Grade VI **$495**
Same general specifications as standard 22 Automatic, except for engraving, high-grade stock with checkering and glossy finish. Made 1986 to date.

Browning Model 52 Bolt Action Rifle **$425**
Limited Edition of the Winchester Model 52C Sporter. Caliber: 22 LR. 5-shot magazine. 24-inch barrel. Weight: 7 pounds. Micro-Motion trigger. No sights. Checkered select walnut stock w/rosewood forend and metal grip cap. Blued finish. Only 5000 made in 1991.

Browning Model 53 Lever Action Rifle **$450**
Limited Edition of the Winchester Model 53. Caliber: 32-20. 7-shot tubular half-magazine. 22-inch barrel. Weight: 6½ pounds. Adj. rear sight, bead front. Select walnut checkered pistol-grip stock w/high-gloss finish. Classic-style forearm. Blued finish. Only 5000 made in 1990.

Browning Model 65 Grade I Lever Action Rifle . . **$475**
Caliber: 218 Bee. 7-shot tubular half-magazine. 24-inch barrel. Weight: 6¾ pounds. Sights: adj. buckhorn-style rear; hooded bead front. Select walnut pistol-grip stock w/high-gloss finish. Semibeavertail forearm. Limited edition made in 1989 only.

Browning Model 52 Limited Edition

Browning Model 53 Limited Edition

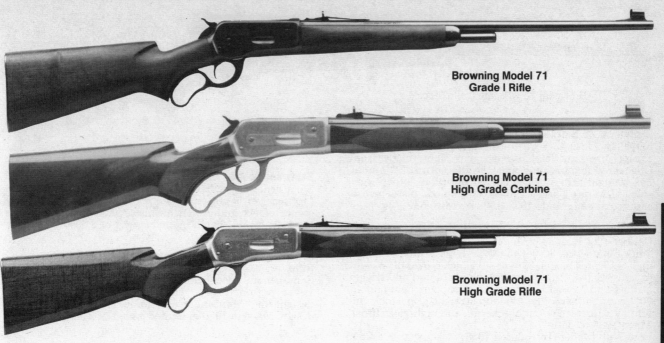

Browning Model 71
Grade I Rifle

Browning Model 71
High Grade Carbine

Browning Model 71
High Grade Rifle

RIFLES

Browning Model 65 High Grade Rifle **$795**
Same general specifications as Model 65 Grade I, except
w/engraving and gold-plated animals on grayed receiver.
Cut-checkering on pistol grip and forearm. Limited edition
made in 1989 only.

Browning Model 71 Grade I Carbine **$425**
Same general specifications as Model 71 Grade I Rifle,
except carbine has 20-inch round barrel. Disc. 1989.

Browning Model 71 Grade I Lever Action Rifle . . . **$430**
Caliber: 348 Win. 4-shot magazine. 24-inch round barrel.
Weight: 8 lbs. 2 oz. Open buckhorn sights. Select walnut
straight grip stock with satin finish. Classic-style forearm,
flat metal buttplate. Made 1986–89.

Browning Model 71 High Grade Carbine **$650**
Same general specifications as Model 71 High Grade Rifle,
except carbine has 20-inch round barrel. Disc. 1989.

Browning Model 71 High Grade Rifle **$675**
Caliber: 348 Win. 4-shot magazine. 24-inch round barrel.
Weight: 8 lbs. 2 oz. Engraved receiver. Open buckhorn
sights. Select walnut checkered pistol-grip stock w/high-
gloss finish. Classic-style forearm, flat metal buttplate.
Made 1987 only.

Browning 78 Bicentennial

Browning 78 Bicentennial Set **$2200**
Special Model 78 45-70 w/same specifications as standard
type, except sides of receiver engraved w/bison and eagle,
scroll engraving on top of receiver, lever, both ends of
barrel and buttplate; high-grade walnut stock and forearm.
Accompanied by an engraved hunting knife and stainless-
steel commemorative medallion, all in an alder wood presentation case. Each item in set has matching serial number beginning with "1776" and ending with numbers 1 to
1,000. Edition limited to 1,000 sets. Made in 1976. Value
is for set in new condition.

Browning 78 Single Shot Rifle **$475**
Falling-block lever action similar to Winchester 1885 High
Wall S.S. Calibers: 22-250, 6mm Rem., 243 Win., 25-06,
7mm Rem. Mag., 30-06, 45-70 Govt. 26-inch octagon or
heavy round barrel; 24-inch octagon bull barrel on 45-70
model. Weight: w/octagon barrel, about 7¾ lbs.; w/round

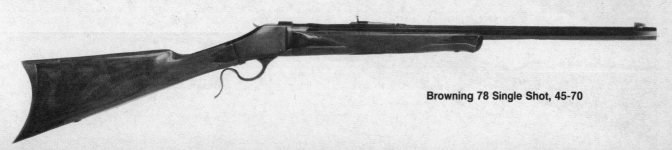

Browning 78 Single Shot, 45-70

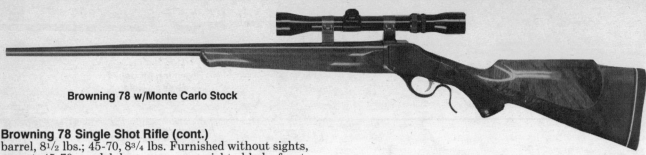

Browning 78 w/Monte Carlo Stock

Browning 78 Single Shot Rifle (cont.)

barrel, 8½ lbs.; 45-70, 8¾ lbs. Furnished without sights, except 45-70 model has open rear sight, blade front. Checkered fancy walnut stock and forearm. 45-70 model has straight-grip stock w/curved buttplate; others have stock w/Monte Carlo comb and cheekpiece, pistol grip w/cap, recoil pad. Made 1973–1983 by Miroku.

Browning Model 1885 Single Shot Rifle

Calibers: 22 Hornet, 223, 243, (Low Wall); 22-250, 270, 7mm Rem. Mag., 30-06, 45 Govt. (High Wall). 24- or 28-inch octagonal barrel. 39½ or 43½ inches overall. Weight: 6¼ to 8¾ lbs. Blued receiver. Gold-colored adj. trigger. Drilled and tapped for scope mounts, open sights on 45-70 Govt. caliber only. Walnut straight-grip stock and schnabel forearm w/cut checkering and high-gloss finish. Made 1985 to date.

Low Wall Model (Introduced 1995) **$515**
High Wall Model **525**

Browning Model 1886 Grade I Lever Action Rifle . . **$625**

Caliber: 45-70 Govt. 8-round magazine. 26-inch octagonal barrel. 45 inches overall. Weight: 9 lbs. 5 oz. Deep blued finish on receiver. Open buckhorn sights. Straight-grip walnut stock. Classic-style forearm. Metal buttplate. Satin finish. Made in 1986 in limited issue 1 of 7,000 by Miroku.

Browning Model 1886 High Grade Lever Action . . **$1095**

Same general specifications as the Model 1886 Grade I, except receiver is grayed steel embellished with scroll; game scenes of elk and American bison engraving. High-gloss stock. Made in 1986 in limited issue 1 of 3,000 by Miroku.

Browning Model 1886 Montana Centennial Rifle **$1125**

Same general specifications as the Model 1886 High Grade Lever Action, except has specially engraved receiver designating Montana Centennial; also different stock design. Made in 1986 in limited issue 1 of 2,000 by Miroku.

Browning Model 1895 Grade I Lever Action Rifle **$495**

Caliber: 30-06, 30-40 Krag. 4-shot magazine. 24-inch round barrel. 42 inches overall. Weight: 8 pounds. French walnut stock and schnabel forend. Sights: rear buckhorn; gold bead on elevated ramp front. Made in 1984 in limited issue 1 of 6,000. The 30-40 Krag caliber made in 1985 in limited issue 1 of 2,000. Mfd. by Miroku.

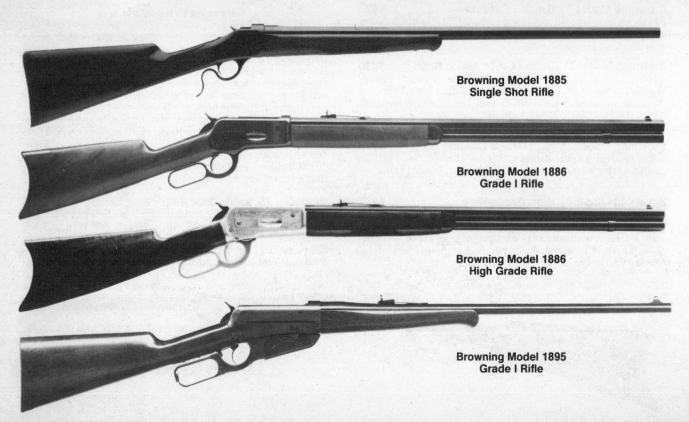

Browning Model 1885 Single Shot Rifle

Browning Model 1886 Grade I Rifle

Browning Model 1886 High Grade Rifle

Browning Model 1895 Grade I Rifle

**Browning Model 1895
High Grade Rifle**

Browning Model 1895 High Grade Lever Action Rifle **$875**

Same general specifications as Model 1895 Grade I except engraved receiver and Grade III French walnut stock and forend with fine checkering. Made in 1985 in limited issue 1 of 1,000 by Miroku.

Browning Model A-Bolt 22 Rifle

Calibers: 22 LR, 22 Magnum. 5- and 15-shot magazines. 22-inch round barrel. 40¼ inches overall. Weight: 5 lbs. 9 oz. Gold-colored adj. trigger. Laminated walnut stock with checkering. Rosewood forend grip cap; pistol grip. With or without sights. Ramp front and adj. folding leaf rear on open sight model. 22 LR made 1985 to date; 22 Magnum, 1990 to date.

Grade I 22 LR **$235**
Grade I 22 Magnum **285**
Deluxe Grade Gold Medallion **350**

Browning Model A-Bolt Euro-Bolt Rifle

Same general specifications as Model A-Bolt Hunter Rifle, except has checkered satin-finished walnut stock w/continental-style cheekpiece, palm-swell grip, schnabel forend. Mannlicher-style spoon bolt handle and recontoured bolt shroud. Calibers: 270, 30-06 and 7mm Mag. only. Weight: 6¾ lbs. Made 1993 to date.

Euro-Bolt Model **$475**
Euro-Bolt Model II **495**
BOSS Option, **add** **90**

Browning Model A-Bolt Hunter Grade Rifle

Calibers: 22 Hornet, 22-250, 223, 243, 257 Roberts, 7mm-08, 308, (short action) 25-06, 270, 280, 30-06, 7mm Rem., 300 Win. Mag., 338 Win. 4-shot magazine (Std.), 3-shot (Mag.). 22-inch barrel (Std.); 24-inch (Mag.). Weight: 7½ lbs. (Std.); 8½ lbs. (Mag.). Open sights optional. Classic-style walnut stock. Produced in two action lengths w/nine locking lugs, fluted bolt w/60 degree rotation. Mfd. by Miroku since 1985. An improved variation w/anti-binding bolt and redesigned trigger system (A-Bolt II) was introduced in 1993.

Hunter **$340**
Hunter II **350**
BOSS Option, **add** **90**
Open Sights, **add** **50**

Browning Model A-Bolt Medallion Grade Rifle

Same as Hunter Grade, except w/high-gloss deluxe stock, rosewood grip cap and forend, high-luster blued finish. Also in 375 H&H. w/open sights. Left Hand Models in 270, 30-06, 7mm Rem. Mag.

Big Horn Sheep Ltd. Ed. (600 made 1986,
  270 Win.) **$895**
Gold Medallion Deluxe Grade **525**
Gold Medallion II Deluxe Grade **540**
Medallion, Standard Grade **415**
Medallion II, Standard Grade **425**
Medallion, 375 H&H **575**
Medallion II, 375 H&H **595**
Micro Medallion **425**
Micro Medallion II **430**
Pronghorn Antelope Ltd. Ed. (500 made 1987,
  243 Win.) **850**
BOSS Option, **add** **90**
Open Sights, **add** **50**

Browning Model A-Bolt Stalker Rifle

Same general specifications as Model A-Bolt Hunter Rifle, except w/checkered graphite-fiberglass composite stock and matte blued or stainless metal. Nonglare matte finish on all exposed metal surfaces. 3 models: Camo Stalker orig. w/multi-colored laminated wood stock, matte blued metal; Composite Stalker w/graphite-fiberglass stock, matte blued metal; Stainless Stalker w/composite stock,

RIFLES

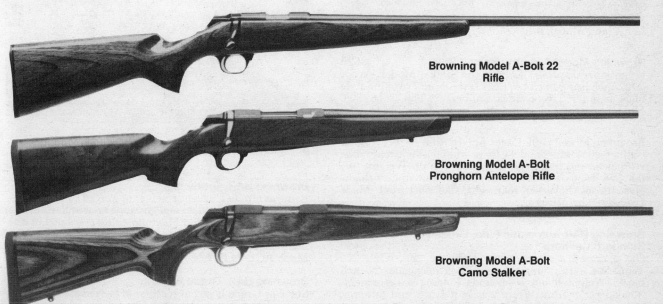

**Browning Model A-Bolt 22
Rifle**

**Browning Model A-Bolt
Pronghorn Antelope Rifle**

**Browning Model A-Bolt
Camo Stalker**

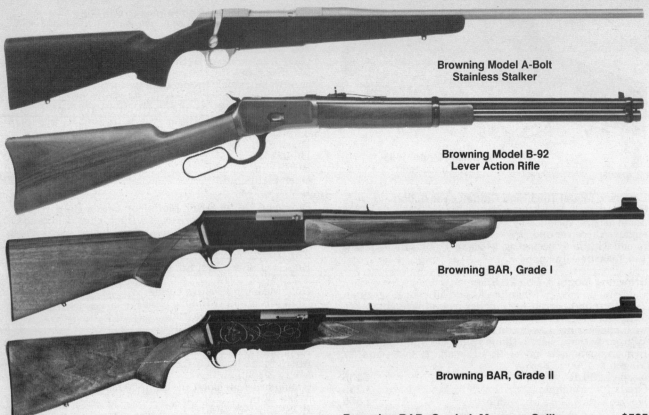

**Browning Model A-Bolt
Stainless Stalker**

**Browning Model B-92
Lever Action Rifle**

Browning BAR, Grade I

Browning BAR, Grade II

Browning Model A-Bolt Stalker Rifle (cont.)
stainless metal. Made 1987 to date.
Camo Stalker (orig. Laminated Stock) **$425**
Composite Stalker **430**
Composite Stalker II **450**
Stainless Stalker. **515**
Stainless Stalker II **530**
Stainless Stalker, 375 H&H **600**
BOSS Option, **add** **90**
Left-Hand Model, **add** **30**

Browning Model A-Bolt Varmint II Rifle **$525**
Same general specifications as the Stalker Model, except
w/22-inch heavy barrel w/BOSS system and varmint-style
black laminated wood stock. Calibers: 22-250, 223 or 308.
No sights. Bright blued or satin finish. Made 1994 to date.

Browning Model B-92 Lever Action Rifle **$315**
Calibers: 357 Mag. and 44 Rem. Mag. 11-shot magazine.
20-inch round barrel. 37$^1/_2$ inches overall. Weight: 5$^1/_2$
lbs. to 6 lbs. 6 oz. Seasoned French walnut stock w/high-
gloss finish. Cloverleaf rear sight; steel post front. Made
1979–1989 by Miroku.

**Browning BAR Automatic Rifle, Grade I,
Standard Calibers** **$450**
Gas-operated semiautomatic. Calibers: 243 Win., 270
Win., 308 Win., 30-06. 4-round box magazine. 22-inch
barrel. Weight: about 7$^1/_2$ pounds. Folding leaf rear sight,
hooded ramp front. French walnut stock and forearm,
checkered, QD swivels. Made 1967 to date by FN.

Browning BAR, Grade I, Magnum Calibers **$525**
Same as BAR in standard calibers, except chambered for
7mm Rem. Mag., 300 Win. Mag.; has 3-round box magazine, 24-inch barrel, recoil pad. Weight: about 8$^1/_2$ pounds.
Made 1969 to date by FN.

Browning BAR, Grade II
Same as Grade I, except receiver engraved w/big-game
heads (deer and antelope on standard-caliber rifles, ram
and grizzly on Magnum-caliber) and scrollwork, higher
grade wood. Made 1967–1974 by FN.
Standard calibers **$595**
Magnum calibers **640**

Browning BAR, Grade III

Browning BAR, Grade III **$995**
Same as Grade I, except receiver of grayed steel engraved
w/big-game heads (deer and antelope on standard-caliber
rifles, moose and elk on Magnum-caliber) framed in fine-
line scrollwork, gold-plated trigger, stock and forearm of
highly figured French walnut, hand-checkered and carved.
Made 1971–74 by FN.

Browning BAR, Grade IV **$1350**
Same as Grade I, except receiver of grayed steel engraved
w/full detailed rendition of running deer and antelope on

Browning BAR, Grade IV

Browning BAR, Grade V

Browning BAR, Grade IV (cont.)
standard-caliber rifles, moose and elk on Magnum-caliber, gold-plated trigger, stock and forearm of highly figured French walnut, hand checkered and carved. Made 1971–1986 by FN.

Browning BAR, Grade V $2600
Same as Grade I, except receiver w/complete big-game scenes executed by a master engraver and inlaid with 18K gold (deer and antelope on standard-caliber rifles,

Browning BAR, Grade V (cont.)
moose and elk on Magnum caliber), gold-plated trigger, stock and forearm of finest French walnut, intricately hand-checkered and carved. Made 1971–74 by FN.

Browning Model BAR Mark II Semiautomatic Rifle
Same general specifications as standard BAR Model, except has redesigned gas and buffer systems, new bolt release lever, removable trigger assembly and engraved receiver. Made 1993 to date.
Standard Calibers **$495**
Magnum Calibers **550**
BOSS Option, **add** **90**
Open Sights, **add** **15**

Browning BAR-22 Automatic Rifle
Semiautomatic. Caliber: 22 LR. Tubular magazine holds 15 rounds. 20¼-inch barrel. Weight: 6¼ pounds. Sights: folding-leaf rear; gold bead front on ramp. Receiver grooved for scope mounting. French walnut pistol-grip stock and forearm, checkered. Made 1977–1981.
BAR-22, Standard Version **$235**
BAR-22, 1982 Version 6 lbs. (Made 1982–84) **215**

Browning BBR Lightning Bolt Action Rifle **$795**
Bolt-action rifle with short throw bolt of 60 degrees. Calibers: 25-06 Rem., 270 Win., 30-06, 7mm Rem. Mag., 300 Win. Mag. 24-inch barrel. Weight: 8 pounds. Made 1979–1984.

Browning BL-22 Lever Action Repeating Rifle
Short-throw lever action. Caliber: 22 LR, Long, Short. Tubular magazine holds 15 LR, 17 Long, 22 Short. 20-inch barrel. Weight: 5 pounds. Sights: folding leaf rear; bead front. Receiver grooved for scope mounting. Walnut

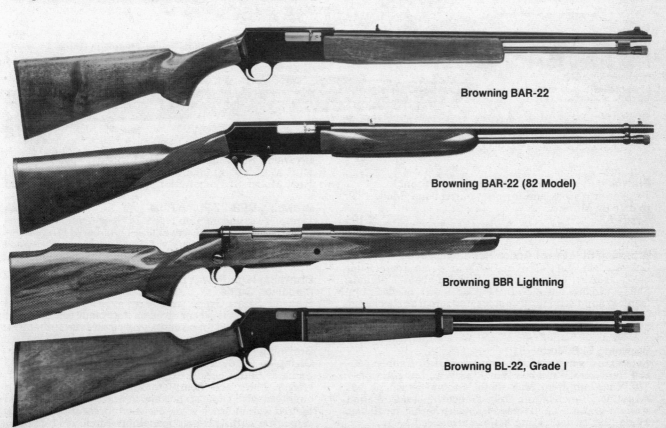

Browning BAR-22

Browning BAR-22 (82 Model)

Browning BBR Lightning

Browning BL-22, Grade I

Browning BL-22, Grade II

Browning BLR

Browning BLR Model '81

Browning BPR-22

Browning High-Power, Medallion Grade

Browning High-Power, Olympian Grade

Browning BL-22 Lever Action Repeater (cont.)
straight-grip stock and forearm, barrel band. Made 1970 to date by Miroku.

Grade I	**$185**
Grade II w/Scroll Engraving	**225**

Browning BLR Lever Action Repeating Rifle $325
Calibers: 243 Win., 308 Win., 358 Win. 4-round detachable box magazine. 20-inch barrel. Weight: about 7 pounds. Sights: windage and elevation adj. open rear; hooded ramp front. Walnut straight-grip stock and forearm, checkered, barrel band, recoil pad. Made 1971 by FN, 1972 to date by Miroku.

Browning BLR Model '81
Redesigned version of the Browning BLR. Calibers: 22-250 Rem., 243 Win., 308 Win., 358 Win; Long Action—270 Win., 7mm Rem. Mag., 30-06. 4-round detachable box magazine. 20-inch barrel. Weight: about 7 pounds. Walnut straight-grip stock and forearm, cut checkering, recoil pad. Made 1982 to date; Long Action introduced 1991.

Browning BLR Model '81 (cont.)

BLR Model '81 Standard	**$350**
BLR Model '81 Long Action	**395**

Browning BPR-22 Pump Rifle $195
Hammerless slide-action repeater. Specifications same as for BAR-22, except also available chambered for 22 Magnum RF; magazine capacity, 11 rounds. Made 1977–1982 by Miroku.

Browning High-Power Bolt Action Rifle, Medallion Grade $1150
Same as Safari Grade, except receiver and barrel scroll engraved, ram's head engraved on floorplate; select walnut stock w/rosewood forearm tip, grip cap. Made 1961–1974.

Browning High-Power Bolt Action Rifle, Olympian Grade $2395
Same as Safari Grade, except barrel engraved; receiver, trigger guard and floorplate satin chrome-plated and engraved with game scenes appropriate to caliber; finest figured walnut stock with rosewood forearm tip and grip cap, latter with 18K-gold medallion. Made 1961–1974.

RIFLES

Browning High-Power, Safari Grade
Medium Action, Heavy Barrel

Browning High-Power, Safari Grade
Short Action, Heavy Barrel

Browning High-Power, Safari Grade
Standard Action

Browning "T-Bolt" T-1

Browning "T-Bolt" T-2

**Browning High-Power Bolt Action Rifle,
Safari Grade, Medium Action** **$695**
Same as Standard, except medium action. Calibers: 22/
250, 243 Win., 264 Win. Mag., 284 Win. Mag., 308 Win.
Barrel: 22-inch lightweight barrel; 22/250 and 243 also
available w/24-inch heavy barrel. Weight: 6 lbs. 12 oz. w/
lightweight barrel; 7 lbs. 13 oz. w/heavy barrel. Made 1963–
1974 by Sako.

**Browning High-Power Bolt Action Rifle,
Safari Grade, Short Action** **$725**
Same as Standard, except short action. Calibers: 222 Rem.,
222 Rem. Mag. 22-inch lightweight or 24-inch heavy
barrel. No sights. Weight: 6 lbs. 2 oz. w/lightweight barrel;
7$1/2$ lbs. w/heavy barrel. Made 1963–1974 by Sako.

**Browning High-Power Bolt Action Rifle,
Safari Grade, Standard Action** **$895**
Mauser-type action. Calibers: 270 Win., 30-06, 7mm Rem.
Mag., 300 H&H Mag., 300 Win. Mag., 308 Norma Mag.,
338 Win. Mag., 375 H&H Mag., 458 Win. Mag. Cartridge
capacity: 6 rounds in 270, 30-06; 4 in Magnum calibers.

Browning High-Power Rifle, Safari Std. (cont.)
Barrel length: 22 in., 270, 30-06; 24 in., Magnum calibers.
Weight: 7 lbs. 2 oz., 270, 30-06; 8$1/4$ lbs., Mag. calibers.
Folding leaf rear sight, hooded ramp front. Checkered
stock w/pistol grip, Monte Carlo cheekpiece, QD swivels;
recoil pad on Magnum models. Made 1959–1974 by FN.

Browning "T-Bolt" T-1 22 Repeating Rifle **$325**
Straight-pull bolt action. Caliber: 22 LR. 5-shot clip magazine. 24-inch barrel. Sights: peep rear; blade/ramp front.
Plain walnut stock w/pistol grip. Weight: 6 lbs. Also left-
hand model. Made 1965–1974 by FN.

Browning "T-Bolt" T-2 . . . . **$365**
Same as T-1, except fancy-figured walnut stock, check-
ered. Discontinued 1974.

F.N. Browning Semiautomatic Rifle **$2500**
Same as F.N. FAL Semiautomatic Rifle. *See* listing of
that rifle for specifications. Sold by Browning for a brief
period c. 1960.

BSA Model 12/15 Martini

BSA No. 13 Martini

BSA Model 15 Martini

BSA CF-2 Stutzen Rifle

BSA GUNS LTD.
Birmingham, England

Importation of BSA rifles was discontinued in 1989.

BSA No. 12 Martini Single Shot Target Rifle **$285**
Caliber: 22 LR. 29-inch barrel. Weight: about 8 3/4 pounds. Parker-Hale Model 7 rear sight and Model 2 front sight. Straight-grip stock, checkered forearm. *Note:* This model was also available with open sights or with BSA No. 30 and 20 sights. Made before WWII.

BSA Model 12/15 Martini Heavy **$325**
Same as Standard Model 12/15 except has extra heavy barrel, weighs about 11 pounds.

BSA Model 12/15 Martini Single Shot Target Rifle **$330**
Caliber: 22 LR. 29-inch barrel. Weight: about 9 pounds. Parker-Hale No. PH-7A rear sight and No. FS-22 front sight. Target stock w/high comb and cheekpiece, beavertail forearm. *Note:* This is a post-WWII model; however, a similar rifle, the BSA-Parker Model 12/15, was produced c. 1938.

BSA No. 13 Martini Single Shot Target Rifle **$275**
Caliber: 22 LR. Lighter version of the No. 12 w/same general specifications, except has 25-inch barrel, weighs 6 1/2 pounds. Made before WWII.

BSA No. 13 Sporting Rifle
Same as No. 13 Target except fitted w/Parker-Hale "Sportarget" rear sight and bead front sight. Also available

BSA No. 13 Sporting Rifle (cont.)
in 22 Hornet. Made before WW II.
22 Long Rifle **$275**
22 Hornet **340**

BSA Model 15 Martini Single Shot Target Rifle .. **$325**
Caliber: 22 LR. 29-inch barrel. Weight: about 9 1/2 pounds. BSA No. 30 rear sight and No. 20 front sight. Target stock w/cheekpiece and pistol grip, long semibeavertail forearm. Made before WWII.

BSA Centurion Model Match Rifle **$435**
Same general specifications as Model 15 except has "Centurion" match barrel, 1 1/2-inch groups at 100 yards guaranteed. Made before WWII.

BSA CF-2 Bolt Action Hunting Rifle **$295**
Mauser-type action. Calibers: 7mm Rem. Mag., 300 Win. Mag. 3-shot magazine. 23.6-inch barrel. Weight: 8 pounds. Sights: adjustable rear; hooded ramp front. Checkered walnut stock w/Monte Carlo comb, rollover cheekpiece, rosewood forend tip, recoil pad, sling swivels. Made 1975–1987. *Note:* Also marketed in the U.S.A. as Ithaca-BSA CF-2. *See* Ithaca listings for that photo.

BSA CF-2 Stutzen Rifle **$375**
Calibers: 222 Rem., 22/250, 243 Win., 270 Win., 308 Win., 30-06. 4-round capacity (5 in 222 Rem.). 20.6-inch barrel. 41 1/2 inches (approx.) overall length. Weight: 7 1/2 to 8 lbs. Williams front and rear sights. Hand-finished European walnut stock. Monte Carlo cheekpiece and Wundhammer palmswell. Double-set triggers. Discontinued 1987.

BSA CFT Target Rifle

BSA Martini-International ISU Match

BSA Martini-International Mark V

BSA Martini-International MK III

BSA CFT Target Rifle **$650**
Single shot, bolt action. Caliber: 7.62mm. 26½-inch barrel. About 47½ inches overall. Weight: 11 pounds, incl. accessories. Barrel and action weight: 6 lbs. 12 oz. Discontinued 1987.

BSA Majestic Deluxe Featherweight Bolt Action Hunting Rifle
Mauser-type action. Calibers: 243 Win., 270 Win., 308 Win., 30-06, 458 Win. Mag. 4-shot magazine. 22-inch barrel with BESA recoil reducer. Weight: 6¼ lbs.; 8¾ lbs. in 458. Folding leaf rear sight, hooded ramp front. Checkered European-style walnut stock w/cheekpiece, pistol grip, schnabel forend, swivels, recoil pad. Made 1959–1965.
458 Win. Mag. caliber **$425**
Other calibers **265**

BSA Majestic Deluxe Standard Weight **$295**
Same as Featherweight Model, except heavier barrel without recoil reducer. Calibers: 22 Hornet, 222 Rem., 243 Win., 7×57mm, 308 Win., 30-06. Weight: 7¼ to 7¾ pounds. Discontinued.

BSA Martini-International ISU Match Rifle **$695**
Similar to MK III, but modified to meet International Shooting Union "Standard Rifle" specifications. 28-inch standard weight barrel. Weight: 10¾ pounds. Redesigned stock and forearm; latter attached to barrel with "V" section alloy strut. Introduced 1968, discontinued.

BSA Martini-International Mark V Match Rifle . . . **$495**
Same as ISU model, except has heavier barrel. Weight: 12¼ pounds. Introduced 1976, discontinued.

**BSA Martini-International Match Rifle
Single Shot Heavy Pattern** **$395**
Caliber: 22 LR. 29-inch heavy barrel. Weight: about 14 pounds. Parker-Hale "International" front and rear sights. Target stock w/full cheekpiece and pistol grip, broad beavertail forearm, handstop, swivels. Right- or left-hand models. Mfd. 1950–53.

**BSA Martini-International Match Rifle—
Light Pattern** **$390**
Same general specifications as Heavy Pattern, except has 26-inch lighter weight barrel. Weight: about 11 pounds. Discontinued.

BSA Martini-International MK II Match Rifle **$435**
Same general specifications as original model. Heavy and Light Pattern. Improved trigger mechanism and ejection system. Redesigned stock and forearm. Made 1953–59.

BSA Martini-International MK III Match Rifle **$495**
Same general specifications as MK II Heavy Pattern. Longer action frame with I-section alloy strut to which forearm is attached; barrel is fully floating. Redesigned stock and forearm. Made 1959–1967.

BSA Monarch Deluxe Varmint

BSA Monarch Deluxe Bolt Action Hunting Rifle . **$325**
Same as Majestic Deluxe Standard Weight Model, except
has redesigned stock of U.S. style with contrasting hardwood forend tip and grip cap. Calibers: 222 Rem., 243
Win., 270 Win., 7mm Rem. Mag., 308 Win., 30-06. 22-
inch barrel. Weight: 7 to 7¼ pounds. Made 1965–1974.

BSA Monarch Deluxe Varmint Rifle **$335**
Same as Monarch Deluxe, except has 24-inch heavy barrel
and weighs 9 pounds. Calibers: 222 Rem., 243 Win.

CALICO LIGHT WEAPONS SYSTEMS
Bakersville, California

Calico Model M-900 Semiautomatic Carbine . . . **$495**
Caliber: 9mm Parabellum. 50- or 100-shot magazine. 16.1-
inch barrel. 28.5 inches overall. Weight: 3.7 pounds. Post
front sight adjustable for windage and elevation, fixed
notch rear. Collapsible steel buttstock and glass-filled
polymer grip. Matte black finish. Made 1989–1994.

Calico Model M-951 Tactical Carbine
Similar to the Model 900, except with long compensator
and adjustable forward grip. Made 1990–94.
Model 951 . . . . **$495**
Model 951-S **505**

CANADIAN MILITARY RIFLES
Quebec, Canada
Manufactured by Ross Rifle Co.

**Canadian Model 1907 Mark II Ross Military
Rifle** **$185**
Straight-pull bolt action. Caliber: 303 British. 5-shot box
magazine. 28-inch barrel. Weight: about 8½ pounds.
Sights: adj. rear; blade front. Military-type full stock. *Note:*
The Ross was originally issued as a Canadian service rifle
in 1907. There were several variations; it was the official
weapon at the start of WWI, but has been obsolete for
many years. For Ross sporting rifle, *see* listing under Ross
Rifle Co.

CHARTER ARMS CORPORATION
Stratford, Connecticut

**Charter AR-7 Explorer
(Disassembled and Stowed in Stock)**

Charter AR-7 Explorer Survival Rifle **$125**
Same as Armalite AR-7, except has black, instead of
brown, "wood grain" plastic stock. *See* listing of that rifle
for specifications. Made 1973–1990.

CHIPMUNK MANUFACTURING INC.
Medford, Oregon

Succeeded by Oregon Arms Co.

Chipmunk Bolt Action Single Shot Rifle
Calibers: 22 LR or 22 WMR. Barrel: 16⅛ inches. Weight:
about 2½ pounds. Sights: peep rear; ramp front. Plain
American walnut stock. Made 1982 to date.
Standard Model (Discontinued 1987) **$105**
Camouflage Model **125**
Deluxe Grade **150**

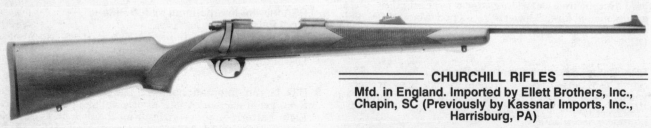

Churchill Highlander

CHURCHILL RIFLES
Mfd. in England. Imported by Ellett Brothers, Inc.,
Chapin, SC (Previously by Kassnar Imports, Inc.,
Harrisburg, PA)

Churchill Highlander Bolt Action Rifle **$350**
Calibers: 243 Win., 25-06 Rem., 270 Win., 308 Win., 30-
06, 7mm Rem. Mag., 300 Win. Mag. 4-shot magazine
(standard); 3-shot (magnum). Barrel length: 22-inch
(standard); 24-inch (magnum). 42½ to 44½ inches overall.
Weight: 7½ pounds. Adj. rear sight, blade front. Checkered
European walnut pistol-grip stock. Imported 1986–1991.

Churchill "One of One Thousand"

Churchill Regent

Churchill "One of One Thousand" Rifle $1195
Made for Interarms to commemorate that firm's 20th anniversary. Mauser-type action. Calibers: 270, 7mm Rem. Mag., 308, 30-06, 300 Win. Mag., 375 H&H Mag., 458 Win. Mag. 5-shot magazine (3-shot in Magnum calibers). 24-inch barrel. Weight: about 8 pounds. Classic-style French walnut stock with cheekpiece, black forend tip, checkered pistol grip and forearm, swivel-mounted recoil

Churchill "One of One Thousand" Rifle (cont.)
pad w/cartridge trap, pistol-grip cap w/trap for extra front sight, barrel-mounted sling swivel. Limited issue of 1,000 rifles made in 1973.

Churchill Regent Bolt Action Rifle $425
Calibers: 243 Win., 25-06 Rem., 270 Win., 308 Win., 30-06, 7mm Rem. Mag. 4-shot magazine. 22-inch round barrel. 42.5 inches overall. Weight: 7.5 pounds. Ramp front sight w/gold bead; adj. rear. Hand-checkered Monte Carlo-style stock of select European walnut; recoil pad. Made 1986–1990.

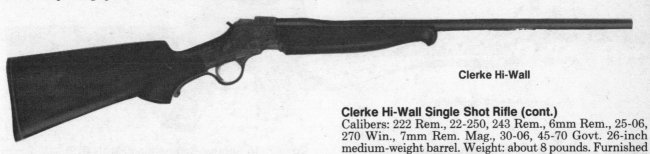

Clerke Hi-Wall

CLERKE RECREATION PRODUCTS
Santa Monica, California

Clerke Hi-Wall Single Shot Rifle $220
Falling-block lever action similar to Winchester 1885 High Wall S.S. Color casehardened investment-cast receiver.

Clerke Hi-Wall Single Shot Rifle (cont.)
Calibers: 222 Rem., 22-250, 243 Rem., 6mm Rem., 25-06, 270 Win., 7mm Rem. Mag., 30-06, 45-70 Govt. 26-inch medium-weight barrel. Weight: about 8 pounds. Furnished without sights. Checkered walnut pistol-grip stock and schnabel forearm. Made 1972–74.

Clerke Deluxe Hi-Wall $275
Same as standard model, except has adj. trigger, half-octagon barrel, select wood, stock w/cheekpiece and recoil pad. Made 1972–74.

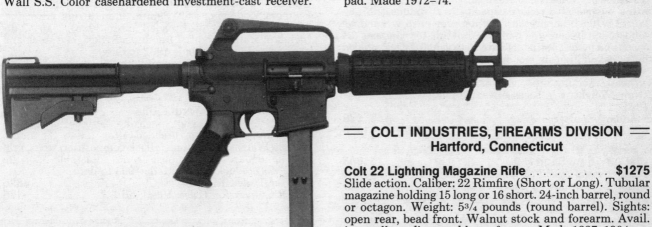

Colt AR-15 9mm Carbine

COLT INDUSTRIES, FIREARMS DIVISION
Hartford, Connecticut

Colt 22 Lightning Magazine Rifle $1275
Slide action. Caliber: 22 Rimfire (Short or Long). Tubular magazine holding 15 long or 16 short. 24-inch barrel, round or octagon. Weight: $5\frac{3}{4}$ pounds (round barrel). Sights: open rear, bead front. Walnut stock and forearm. Avail. in small, medium and large frames. Made 1887–1904.

Colt AR-15 Compact 9mm Carbine $1025
Semiautomatic. Caliber: 9mm NATO. 20-round detachable magazine. Barrel: 16-inch round. Weight: 6.3 pounds.

RIFLES

Colt AR-15 Sporter

Colt AR-15 w/Adjustable Stock

Colt AR-15 A2 Sporter II

Colt AR-15 Compact 9mm Carbine (cont.)
Adj. rear and front sights. Adj. buttstock. Ribbed round handguard. Made 1985–86.

Colt AR-15 Semiautomatic Sporter
Commercial version of U.S. M16 rifle. Gas-operated. Takedown. Caliber: 223 Rem. (5.56mm). 20-round magazine w/spacer to reduce capacity to 5 rounds. 20-inch barrel w/flash suppressor. Sights: rear peep w/windage adjustment in carrying handle; front adj. for windage. 3× scope and mount optional (add $70 to value). Black molded buttstock of high-impact synthetic material, rubber buttplate. Barrel surrounded by handguards of black fiberglass w/heat-reflecting inner shield. Swivels, black web sling strap. Weight: w/o accessories, 6.3 pounds. Made 1964–1994.
Standard Sporter . . . . **$ 975**
w/Adj. Stock, Redesigned Forearm (Disc. 1988) . . **1150**

Colt AR-15 A2 Sporter II **$1095**
Same general specifications as standard AR-15 Sporter except heavier barrel, improved pistol grip, weight of 7½ pounds and optional 3× or 4× scope. Made 1985–89.

Colt AR-15 Sporter Competition HBAR Rifle **$850**
Similar to the AR-15 Sporter Target Model, except with integral Weaver-type mounting system on a flat-top receiver. 20-inch barrel with counter-bored muzzle and 1:9″ rifling twist. Made 1991 to date.

Colt AR-15 Sporter Competition HBAR (RS) Rifle **$1275**
Similar to the AR-15 Sporter Competition HBAR Model, except "Range Selected" for accuracy with 3×9 rubber-clad scope with mount. Carrying handle with iron sights. Made 1992–94.

Colt AR-15 Sporter Match Target Lightweight
Calibers: 223 Rem., 7.62×39mm, 9mm. 5-shot magazine. 16-inch barrel (non-threaded after 1994). 34½–35½ inches overall. Weight: 7.1 pounds. Redesigned stock and shorter handguard. Made 1991 to date.
Standard LW Sporter (except 9mm) **$750**
Standard LW Sporter, 9mm **585**
22 LR Conversion (Disc. 1994), **add** **175**

Colt AR-15 Sporter Target Rifle
Caliber: 223 Rem. 5-shot magazine. 20-inch barrel with flash suppressor (non-threaded after 1994). 39 inches overall. Weight: 7½ pounds. Black composition stock, grip and handguard. Sights: post front; adjustable aperture rear. Matte black finish. Made 1993 to date.
Sporter Target Rifle **$825**
22 LR Conversion (Disc. 1994), **add** **175**

> **NOTE:** On Colt AR-15 Sporter models currently produced (i.e., Competition HBAR, Sporter Match Target Lightweight, and Sporter Target Rifle, **add $200** to pre-ban models made prior to 10-13-94.

Colt Lightning Carbine
Same as Lightning Magazine Rifle, except has 12-shot magazine, 20-inch barrel, weighs 6 1/4 pounds.
Carbine **$2595**
Baby Carbine (5 1/2 pounds) **3795**

Colt Lightning Magazine Rifle **$1395**
Slide action. Calibers: 32-20, 38-40, 44-40. 15-shot tubular magazine. 26-inch barrel, round or octagon. Weight: 6 3/4 pounds (round barrel). Sights: open rear; bead or blade front. Walnut stock and forearm. Made 1884–1902.

Colt Stagecoach 22 Autoloader **$265**
Same as Colteer 22 Autoloader, except has engraved receiver, saddle ring, 16 1/2-inch barrel. Weight: 4 lbs. 10 oz. Made 1965–1975.

Colteer 1-22 Single Shot Bolt Action Rifle **$220**
Caliber: 22 LR, Long, Short. 20- or 22-inch barrel. Sights: open rear; ramp front. Pistol-grip stock w/Monte Carlo comb. Weight: about 5 pounds. Made 1957–1967.

Colteer 22 Autoloader **$230**
Caliber: 22 LR. 15-round tubular magazine. 19 3/8-inch barrel. Sights: open rear; hooded ramp front. Straight-

Colteer 22 Autoloader (cont.)
grip stock, Western carbine-style forearm with barrel band. Weight: about 4 3/4 pounds. Made 1964–1975.

Coltsman Custom Bolt Action Sporting Rifle **$425**
FN Mauser action, side safety, engraved floorplate. Calibers: 30-06, 300 H&H Mag. 5-shot box magazine. 24-inch barrel, ramp front sight. Fancy walnut stock, Monte Carlo comb, cheekpiece, pistol grip, checkered, QD swivels. Weight: about 7 1/4 pounds. Made 1957–1961. Value shown is for rifle, as furnished by manufacturer, w/o rear sight.

Coltsman Deluxe Rifle **$650**
FN Mauser action. Same as Custom model except plain floorplate, plainer wood and checkering. Made 1957–1961. Value shown is for rifle, as furnished by manufacturer, without rear sight.

Coltsman Models of 1957 Rifles
Sako Medium action. Calibers: 243, 308. Weight: about 6 3/4 pounds. Other specifications similar to those of models w/FN actions. Made 1957–1961.
Custom **$575**
Deluxe **450**
Standard **395**

RIFLES

Colt Stagecoach

Colteer 1-22

Colteer 22 Autoloader

Coltsman Deluxe

Coltsman 1957 Standard

Coltsman 1961 Custom

Coltsman 1961 Standard

Coltsman Model of 1961, Custom Rifle **$460**
Sako action. Calibers: 222, 222 Mag., 223, 243, 264, 270, 308, 30-06, 300 H&H. 23-, 24-inch barrel. Sights: folding leaf rear; hooded ramp front. Fancy French walnut stock w/Monte Carlo comb, rosewood forend tip and grip cap, skip checkering, recoil pad, sling swivels. Weight: 6½ to 7½ pounds. Made 1963–65.

Coltsman Model of 1961, Standard Rifle **$395**
Same as Custom model, except plainer, American walnut stock. Made 1963–65.

Coltsman Standard Rifle **$395**
FN Mauser action. Same as Deluxe model, except in 243, 30-06, 308, 300 Mag. and stock w/o cheekpiece, barrel length 22 inches. Made 1957–1961. Value shown is for rifle, as furnished by manufacturer, w/o rear sight.

> **NOTE:** The following Colt-Sauer rifles are manufactured for Colt by J. P. Sauer & Sohn, Eckernförde, Germany.

Colt-Sauer Drillings
See Colt shotgun listings.

Colt-Sauer Grand African **$1200**
Same specifications as standard model, except caliber 458 Win. Mag., weighs 9½ pounds. Sights: adj. leaf rear; hooded ramp front. Magnum-style stock of Bubinga. Made 1973–1985.

Colt-Sauer Grand Alaskan **$1195**
Same specifications as standard model, except caliber 375 H&H, weighs 8½ pounds. Sights: adj. leaf rear; hooded ramp front. Magnum-style stock of walnut.

Colt-Sauer Magnum **$965**
Same specifications as standard model, except calibers 7mm Rem. Mag., 300 Win. Mag., 300 Weatherby. Weight: 8½ pounds. Made 1973–1985.

Colt-Sauer Short Action **$895**
Same specifications as standard model, except calibers 22-250, 243 Win., 308 Win. Weight: 7½ lbs.; 8¼ lbs. (22-250). Made 1973–1988.

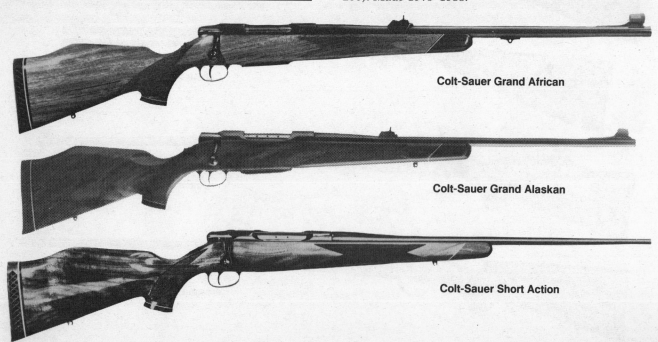

Colt-Sauer Grand African

Colt-Sauer Grand Alaskan

Colt-Sauer Short Action

Colt-Sauer Standard Sporter

Commando Mark III

Commando Mark 9

Commando Mark 45

Colt-Sauer Sporting Rifle, Standard Model **$925**
Sauer 80 nonrotating bolt-action. Calibers: 25-06, 270 Win., 30-06. 3-round detachable box magazine. 24-inch

Colt-Sauer Sporting Rifle, Standard (cont.)
barrel. Weight: 7¾ lbs.; 8½ lbs. (25-06). Furnished w/o sights. American walnut stock w/Monte Carlo cheekpiece, checkered pistol grip and forearm, rosewood forend tip and pistol-grip cap, recoil pad. Made 1973–1988.

COMMANDO CARBINES
Knoxville, Tennessee
Manufactured by Volunteer Enterprises, Inc.

Commando Mark III Semiautomatic Carbine
Blow-back action, fires from closed bolt. Caliber: 45 ACP. 15- or 30-shot magazine. 16½-inch barrel w/cooling sleeve and muzzle brake. Weight: 8 pounds. Sights: peep rear; blade front. "Tommy Gun" style stock and forearm or grip. Made 1969–1976.
With Horizontal Forearm **$325**
With Vertical Foregrip **415**

Commando Mark 9
Same specifications as Mark III and Mark 45, except caliber 9mm Luger. Made 1976–1981.
With Horizontal Forearm **$360**
With Vertical Foregrip **375**

Commando Mark 45
Same specifications as Mark III. Has redesigned trigger housing and magazine. 5-, 15-, 30- and 90-shot magazines available. Made 1976–1988.
With Horizontal Forearm **$375**
With Vertical Foregrip **425**

CONTINENTAL RIFLES

Manufactured in Belgium for Continental Arms Corp., New York, N.Y.

Continental Double Rifle **$4750**
Calibers: 270, 303 Sav., 30-40, 348 Win., 30-06, 375 H&H, 400 Jeffrey, 465, 470, 475 No. 2, 500, 600. Side-by-side. Anson-Deeley reinforced boxlock action w/triple bolting lever-work. Two triggers. Nonautomatic safety. 24- or 26-inch barrels. Sights: express rear; bead front. Checkered cheekpiece stock and forend. Weight: from 7 pounds, depending on caliber.

COOPER ARMS

Stevensville, Montana

Cooper Arms Model 21
Similar to the Model 36CF, except in calibers 17 Rem., 17 Mach IV, 221 Fireball, 222, 223, 6×45, 6×47. 24-inch stainless or chrome-moly barrel. 43½ inches overall. Weight: 8¾ pounds. Made 1994 to date.
Benchrest **$950**
Varmint Extreme **795**

Cooper Arms Model 36CF Bolt Action Rifle
Calibers: 17 CCM, 22 CCM, 22 Hornet. 4-shot magazine. 23¾-inch barrel. 42½ inches overall. Weight: 7 pounds. Walnut or synthetic stock. Made 1992–94.
Marksman **$595**
Sportsman **475**
Classic Grade **795**
Custom Grade **725**
Custom Classic Grade **825**

Cooper Arms Model 36RF Bolt Action Rifle
Similar to the Model 36CF, except in caliber 22 LR. 5-shot magazine. Weight: 6½–7 pounds. Made 1992 to date.
BR-50 (22-inch stainless bbl.) **$795**
Custom Grade **725**
Custom Classic Grade **825**
Featherweight **775**

Cooper Arms Model 38 Sporter
Similar to the Model 36CF, except in calibers 17 CCM or 22 CCM w/3-shot magazine. Weight: 8 pounds. Made 1992–93.
Sporter Standard **$595**
Classic Grade **675**
Custom Grade **775**
Custom Classic Grade **850**

CZ Model ZKK 600

CZ ZKM 527

CZ RIFLES

Strankonice, Czechoslovakia
(Currently Uhersky Brod and Brno, Czecho.)
Mfd. by Ceska Zbrojovka-Nardoni Podnik
(formerly Bohmische Waffenfabrik A.G.)

See also listings under Brno Sporting Rifles and Springfield, Inc.

CZ ZKK 600 Bolt Action Rifle
Calibers: 270 Win., 7×57, 7×64, 30-06. 5-shot magazine. 23½-inch barrel. Weight: 7½ pounds. Adj. folding-leaf rear sight, hooded ramp front. Pistol-grip walnut stock. Imported 1990 to date.
Standard Model **$475**
Deluxe Model **525**

CZ ZKK 601 Bolt Action Rifle
Similar to Model ZKK 600, except w/short action in calibers 223 Rem., 243 Win., 308 Win. 43 inches overall. Weight: 6 lbs. 13 oz. Checkered walnut pistol-grip stock w/Monte Carlo cheekpiece. Imported 1990 to date.
Standard Model **$395**
Deluxe Model **425**

CZ ZKK 602 Bolt Action Rifle
Similar to Model ZKK 600, except w/Magnum action in calibers 300 Win. Mag., 8×68S, 375 H&H, 458 Win. Mag. 25-inch barrel. 45.5 inches overall. Weight: 9¼ pounds. Imported 1990 to date.
Standard Model **$550**
Deluxe Model **625**

CZ ZKM 452 Bolt Action Repeating Rifle **$190**
Caliber: 22 LR. 5- or 10-shot magazine. 25-inch barrel. 43½ inches overall. Weight: 6 pounds. Adj. rear sight, hooded bead front. Checkered oil-finished beechwood stock. Currently imported.

CZ ZKM 527 Bolt Action Rifle
Calibers: 22 Hornet, 222 Rem. 223 Rem. 5-shot magazine. 23½-inch barrel. 42½ inches overall. Weight: 6¾ pounds.

CZ ZKM 527 Bolt Action Rifle (cont.)

Adj. rear sight, hooded ramp front. Grooved receiver. Adj. double-set triggers. Synthetic or walnut stock w/Monte Carlo.

Synthetic Stock Model **$450**
Walnut Stock Model **490**

CZ ZKM 537 Sporter Bolt Action Rifle

Calibers: 270 Win., 308 Win., 30-06. $23\frac{1}{2}$-inch barrel. $44\frac{3}{4}$ inches overall. Weight: $7\frac{1}{2}$ pounds. Adj. folding leaf rear sight, hooded ramp front. Shrouded bolt and grooved. Synthetic or checkered walnut stock. Imported 1992 to date.

Synthetic Stock Model **$450**
Walnut Stock Model **500**

CZECHOSLOVAKIAN MILITARY RIFLES
Brno, Czechoslovakia
Manufactured by Ceska Zbrojovka

Czech Model 1924 (VZ24) Mauser Military Rifle ... **$185**

Basically the same as the German Kar., 98k and F.N. (Belgian Model 1924.) Caliber: 7.9mm Mauser. 5-shot box magazine. $23\frac{1}{4}$-inch barrel. Weight: about $8\frac{1}{2}$ pounds. Sights: adj. rear; blade front w/guards. Military stock of Belgian-type, full handguard. Mfd. 1924 thru WWII. Many of these rifles were made for export. As produced during the German occupation, this model was known as Gewehr 24t.

Czech Model 1933 (VZ33) Mauser Military
Carbine **$220**

Modification of the German M/98 action with smaller receiver ring. Caliber: 7.9mm Mauser. $19\frac{1}{4}$-inch barrel. Weight: about $7\frac{1}{2}$ pounds. Sights: adj. rear; blade front

Czech Model 1933 Mauser Mil. Carbine (cont.)

w/guards. Military-type full stock. Mfd. 1933 thru WWII; a similar model, produced during the German occupation, was designated Gew. 33/40.

DAISY RIFLES
Rogers, Arkansas

Daisy V/L rifles carry the first and only commercial caseless cartridge system. These rifles are expected to appreciate considerably in future years. The cartridge, no longer made, is also a collector's item.

Daisy V/L Collector's Kit **$295**

Presentation-grade rifle w/gold plate inscribed w/owner's name and gun serial number mounted on the stock. Also includes a special gun case, pair of brass gun cradles for wall-hanging, 300 rounds of 22 V/L ammunition and a certificate signed by Daisy president Cass S. Hough. Approx. 1,000 manufactured 1968–69.

Daisy V/L Presentation Grade **$265**

Same specifications as standard model, except w/walnut stock. Approx. 4,000 manufactured 1968–69.

Daisy V/L Standard Rifle **$175**

Single shot, under-lever action. Caliber: 22 V/L (caseless cartridge; propellant ignited by jet of hot air). 18-inch barrel. Weight: 5 pounds. Sights: adj. open rear; ramp w/ blade front. Wood-grained Lustran stock (foam-filled). Approx. 19,000 manufactured 1968–69.

RIFLES

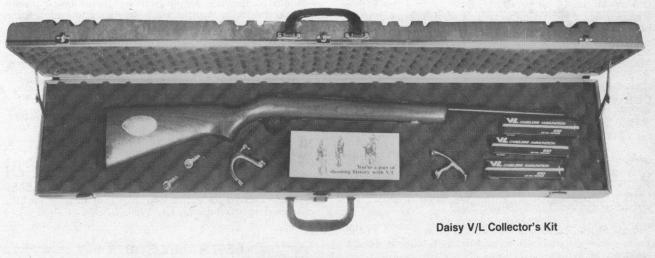

Daisy V/L Collector's Kit

Daisy V/L Standard

Dakota Model 10 Single Shot

Dakota 22 LR Sporter

Dakota Model 76 Classic Grade

DAKOTA ARMS, INC.
Sturgis, South Dakota

Dakota Model 10 Single Shot Rifle **$1675**
Chambered for most commercially loaded calibers. 23-inch barrel. 39 1/2 inches overall. Weight: 5 1/2 pounds. Top tang safety. No sights. Checkered pistol-grip buttstock and semibeavertail forearm, QD swivels, rubber recoil pad. Made 1992 to date.

Dakota 22 Bolt Action Sporter Rifle **$875**
Calibers: 22 LR, 22 Hornet. 5-shot magazine. 22-inch barrel. Weight: 6 1/2 pounds. Adjustable trigger. Checkered classic-style Clara or English walnut stock w/black recoil pad. Made 1992 to date.

Dakota Model 76 African Bolt Action Rifle **$2795**
Same general specifications as Model 76 Safari. Calibers: 404 Jeffery, 416 Rigby, 416 Dakota, 450 Dakota. 24-inch barrel. Weight: 8 pounds. Checkered select walnut stock w/two crossbolts. Made 1989 to date.

Dakota Model 76 Alpine Bolt Action Rifle **$1450**
Same general specifications as Model 76 Classic, except short action w/blind magazine. Calibers: 22-250, 243, 6mm Rem., 250-3000, 7mm-08, 308. 21-inch barrel. Weight: 7 1/2 pounds. Made 1989 to date.

Dakota Model 76 Classic Bolt Action Rifle **$1550**
Calibers: 257 Roberts, 270 Win., 280 Rem., 30-06, 7mm Rem. Mag., 300 Win. Mag., 338 Win. Mag., 375 H&H Mag., 458 Win. Mag. 21- or 23-inch barrel. Weight: 7 1/2 pounds. Receiver drilled and tapped for sights. Adj. trigger. Classic-style checkered walnut stock w/steel grip cap and solid recoil pad. Right- and left-hand models. Made 1988 to date.

Dakota Model 76 Safari Bolt Action Rifle **$2295**
Calibers: 300 Win. Mag., 338 Win. Mag., 375 H&H Mag., 458 Win. Mag. 23-inch barrel w/barrel band swivel. Weight: 8 1/2 pounds. Ramp front sight; standing leaf rear. Checkered fancy walnut stock w/ebony forend tip and solid recoil pad. Made 1988 to date.

CHARLES DALY RIFLE
Made by Franz Jaeger & Co., Suhl, Germany

Distributed in the U.S. by Outdoor Sports Headquarters, Inc., Dayton, Ohio.

Charles Daly Hammerless Drilling
See listing under Charles Daly shotguns.

Charles Daly Hornet Rifle **$850**
Same as Herold Rifle. *See* listing of that rifle for specifications. Imported during the 1930s.

DESERT INDUSTRIES, INC.
Las Vegas, Nevada
Formerly Steel City Arms, Pittsburg, PA

Desert Industries G-90 Single Shot Rifle **$390**
Falling-block action. Calibers: 22-250, 220 Swift 223, 243, 6mm, 257 Roberts, 25-06, 270 Win., 270 Wby., 280, 7×57, 7mm Rem. Mag., 30-06, 300 Win. Mag., 300 Wby., 338 Win. Mag., 375 H&H, 45-70, 458 Win. Mag. 20-, 22-, 24-, or 26-inch barrel in light, medium or heavy configuration. Weight: 7 1/2 lbs. Checkered walnut stock. Blued finish. Made 1990 to date.

EAGLE ARMS INC.
Coal Valley, Illinois

Eagle Arms Model EA-15 Semiautomatic Rifle
Caliber: 223 Rem. (5.56mm). 30-shot magazine. 20-inch barrel. 39 inches overall. Winged post front sight; fully adj. rear. Weight: 7 pounds. Fixed black composition stock w/pistol-grip and barrel-shroud handguard. Black anodized receiver w/E2-style forward-assist mechanism. Made 1989 to date.
EA-15 Standard **$895**
EA-15 E2 H-Bar (20″ heavy barrel, 8¾ lbs.) **950**

Eagle Arms Model EA-15 Carbine
Same general specifications as EA-15 Standard, except w/16-inch barrel and collapsible buttstock. Weight: 5¾ pounds (E1); 6¼ pounds (E2 w/heavy bbl. & NM sights). Made 1989 to date.
E1 Carbine **$925**
E2 Carbine **975**

Eagle Arms Model EA-15 Golden Eagle Match Rifle **$1025**
Same general specifications as EA-15 Standard, except w/E2-style National Match sights. 20-inch Douglas Heavy Match barrel. NM trigger and bolt-carrier group. Weight: 12¾ pounds. Made 1991 to date.

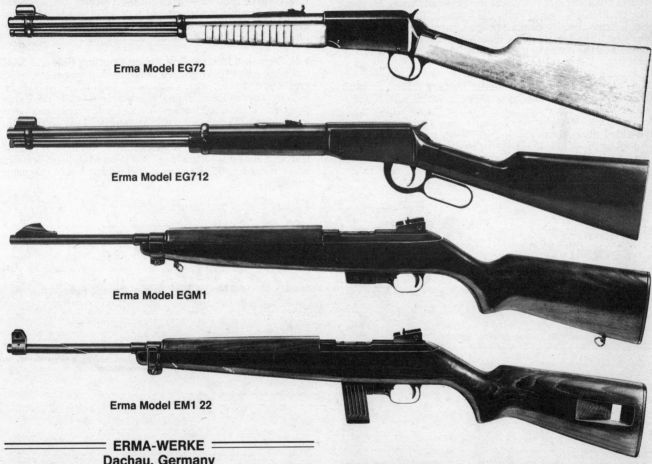

Erma Model EG72

Erma Model EG712

Erma Model EGM1

Erma Model EM1 22

ERMA-WERKE
Dachau, Germany

Erma EG72 Pump Action Repeater **$115**
Visible hammer. Caliber: 22 LR. 15-shot magazine. 18½-inch barrel. Weight: about 5¼ pounds. Sights: open rear; hooded ramp front. Receiver grooved for scope mounting. Straight-grip stock, grooved slide handle. Made 1970–76.

Erma Model EG73 . . . . **$215**
Same as Model EG712, except chambered for 22 WMR, has 12-shot tubular magazine, 19.3-inch barrel. Made 1973 to date.

Erma Model EG712 Lever Action Repeating Carbine **$200**
Styled after Winchester Model 94. Caliber: 22 LR, Long, Short. Tubular magazine holds 15 LR, 17 Long, 21 Short. 18½-inch barrel. Weight: about 5½ pounds. Sights: open

Erma Model EG712 Lever Action (cont.)
rear; hooded ramp front. Receiver grooved for scope mounting. Western carbine-style stock and forearm w/ barrel band. Made 1976 to date. *Note:* A similar carbine of Erma manufacture is marketed in the U.S. as Ithaca Model 72 Saddlegun.

Erma Model EGM1 . . . . **$205**
Same as Model EM1, except has unslotted buttstock, ramp front sight, 5-shot magazine standard. Introduced 1970; discontinued.

Erma Model EM1 22 Semiautomatic Carbine . . . **$245**
Styled after U.S. Carbine Cal. 30 M1. Caliber: 22 LR. 10- or 15-round magazine. 18-inch barrel. Weight: about 5½ pounds. Carbine-type sights. Receiver grooved for scope mounting. Military stock/handguard. Intro. 1966; disc.

RIFLES

FABRIQUE NATIONALE HERSTAL
Herstal, Belgium
Formerly Fabrique Nationale d'Armes de Guerre

F.N. Models 1924, 1934/30 and 1930 Mauser Military Rifles **$275**
Basically the same as the German Kar. 98k. Straight bolt handle. Calibers: 7mm, 7.65mm and 7.9mm Mauser. 5-shot box magazine. 23½-inch barrel. Weight: about 8½ pounds. Sights: adj. rear; blade front. Military stock of M/98 pattern w/slight modification. Model differences are minor. Also produced in a short carbine model with 17¼-inch barrel. *Note:* These rifles were manufactured under contract for Abyssinia, Argentina, Belgium, Bolivia, Brazil, Chile, China, Colombia, Ecuador, Iran, Luxembourg, Mexico, Peru, Turkey, Uruguay and Yugoslavia. Such arms usually bear the coat of arms of the country for which they were made, together with the contractor's name and the date of manufacture. Also sold commercially and exported to all parts of the world.

F.N. Model 1949 Semiautomatic Military Rifle ... **$450**
Gas-operated. Calibers: 7mm, 7.65mm, 7.92mm, 30M2 (30-06). 10-round box magazine, clip fed or loaded singly. 23.2-inch barrel. Weight: 9½ pounds. Sights: tangent rear; shielded post front. Pistol-grip stock, handguard. *Note:* Adopted in cal. 30 by Belgium in 1949; also by Belgian Congo, Brazil, Colombia, Luxembourg, and Netherlands East Indies; Venezuela bought this rifle in 7mm, Egypt in 7.92mm. Approx. 160,000 were made.

F.N. Model 1950 Mauser Military Rifle **$295**
Same as previous F.N. models of Kar. 98k type, except chambered for 30-06.

F.N. Deluxe Mauser Bolt Action Sporting Rifle .. **$550**
American calibers: 220 Swift, 243 Win., 244 Rem., 250/3000, 257 Roberts, 270 Win., 7mm, 300 Sav., 308 Win., 30-06. *European calibers:* 7×57, 8×57JS, 8×60S, 9.3×62, 9.5×57, 10.75×68mm. 5-shot box magazine. 24-inch barrel. Weight: about 7½ lbs.; in 270, 8¼ lbs. American model is standard w/hooded ramp front sight and Tri-Range rear; Continental model has two-leaf rear. Checkered stock w/cheekpiece, pistol grip, swivels. Made 1947–1963.

F.N. Deluxe Mauser—Presentation Grade **$995**
Same as regular model, except has select grade stock; engraving on receiver, trigger guard, floorplate and barrel breech. Discontinued 1963.

F.N. Supreme Mauser Bolt Action Sporting Rifle .. **$540**
Calibers: 243, 270, 7mm, 308, 30-06. 4-shot magazine in 243 and 308; 5-shot in other calibers. 22-inch barrel in 308; 24-inch in other calibers. Sights: hooded ramp front; Tri-Range peep rear. Checkered stock w/Monte Carlo cheekpiece, pistol grip, swivels. Weight: about 7¾ pounds. Made 1957–1975.

F.N. Supreme Magnum Mauser **$595**
Calibers: 264 Mag., 7mm Mag., 300 Win. Mag. Specifications same as for standard-caliber model except 3-shot magazine capacity.

FN Model 1949 Semiautomatic Rifle

FN Model 1950 Mauser

FN Deluxe Mauser

FN Supreme Mauser

F.N.-FAL Semiautomatic Rifle

F.N.-FAL Semiautomatic Rifle **$1795**
Same as the standard FAL military rifle except w/o provision for automatic firing. Gas-operated. Caliber: 7.62mm NATO (.308 Win.). 10- or 20-round box magazine. 25½-inch barrel (including flash hider). Weight: about 9 pounds. Sights: post front; aperture rear. Wood buttstock, pistol grip, forearm/handguard; carrying handle, sling swivels. Made 1950 to date.

== **FEATHER INDUSTRIES, INC.** ==
Boulder, Colorado

Feather Model AT-9 Semiautomatic Rifle
Caliber: 9mm Parabellum. 25-shot magazine. 17-inch barrel. 35 inches overall (extended). Hooded post front

Feather Model AT-9 Semiautomatic Rifle (cont.)
sight; adj. aperture rear. Weight: 5 pounds. Telescoping wire stock w/composition pistol-grip and barrel-shroud handguard. Matte black finish. Made 1988 to date.
Model AT-9 . . . . **$410**
Model F-9 (AT-9 w/Fixed Polymer Stock) **450**

Feather Model AT-22
Caliber: 22 LR. 20-shot magazine. 17-inch barrel. 35 inches overall (extended). Hooded post front sight; adj. aperture rear. Weight: 3¼ pounds. Telescoping wire stock w/composition pistol-grip and barrel-shroud handguard. Matte black finish.
Model AT-22 . . . . **$185**
Model F-22 (AT-22 w/Fixed Polymer Stock) **195**

RIFLES

Finnish Lion Champion

Finnish Lion Match

== **FINNISH LION RIFLES** ==
Jyväskylä, Finland
Manufactured by Valmet Oy, Tourula Works

Finnish Lion Champion Free Rifle **$475**
Bolt action, single shot. Double-set trigger. Caliber: 22 LR. 28¾-inch heavy barrel. Weight: about 16 pounds. Sights: extension rear peep; aperture front. Walnut free-rifle stock w/full pistol grip, thumbhole, beavertail forearm, hook buttplate, palmrest, hand stop, swivel. Made 1965–1972.

Finnish Lion Standard ISU Target Rifle **$295**
Bolt action, single shot. Caliber: 22 LR. 27½-inch barrel. Weight: about 10½ pounds. Sights: extension rear peep; aperture front. Walnut target stock w/full pistol grip, checkered beavertail forearm, adj. buttplate, sling swivel. Made 1966–1977.

Finnish Lion Match Rifle **$410**
Bolt action, single shot. Caliber: 22 LR. 28¾-inch heavy barrel. Weight: about 14½ pounds. Sights: extension rear peep; aperture front. Walnut free-rifle stock w/full pistol grip, thumbhole, beavertail forearm, hook buttplate, palmrest, hand stop, swivel. Made 1937–1972.

Finnish Lion Standard Target

Finnish Lion Standard Target Rifle
Bolt action. Single shot. Caliber: 22 LR. 27½-inch barrel. 44½ inches overall. Weight: 10½ pounds. No sights; mi-

Finnish Lion Standard Target Rifle (cont.)
crometer rear and globe front International-style sights available. Select walnut stock in target configuration. Currently in production.
Standard Model **$550**
Thumbhole Stock Model **625**

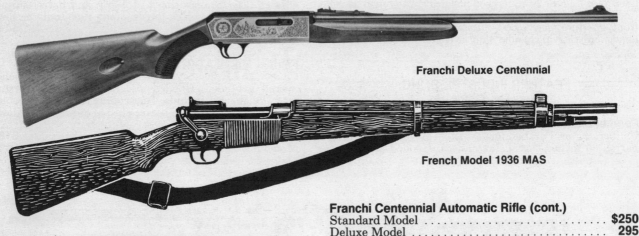

Franchi Deluxe Centennial

French Model 1936 MAS

Franchi Centennial Automatic Rifle (cont.)
Standard Model **$250**
Deluxe Model **295**

=== **LUIGI FRANCHI, S.P.A.** ===
Brescia, Italy

Franchi Centennial Automatic Rifle
Commemorates Franchi's 100th anniversary (1868–1968). Centennial seal engraved on receiver. Semiautomatic. Takedown. Caliber: 22 LR. 11-shot magazine in buttstock. 21-inch barrel. Weight: 5⅛ pounds. Sights: open rear; goldbead front, on ramp. Checkered walnut stock and forend. Deluxe model has fully engraved receiver, premium grade wood. Made 1968.

=== **FRENCH MILITARY RIFLE** ===
Saint Etienne, France

French Model 1936 MAS Military Rifle **$100**
Bolt action. Caliber: 7.5mm MAS. 5-shot box magazine. 22½-inch barrel. Weight: about 8¼ pounds. Sights: adj. rear; blade front. Two-piece military-type stock. Bayonet carried in forend tube. Made 1936–1940 by Manufacture Francaise d'Armes et de Cycles de St. Etienne (MAS).

Galil Model 223 AR Semiautomatic Rifle

=== **GALIL RIFLES** ===
Manufactured by Israel Military Industries, Israel

Galil AR Semiautomatic Rifle
Calibers: 308 Win. (7.62 NATO), 223 Rem. (5.56mm). 25-shot (308) or 35-shot (223) magazine. 16-inch (223) or 18½-inch (308) barrel w/flash suppressor. Weight: 9½ pounds. Folding aperture rear sight, post front. Folding metal stock w/carrying handle. Imported early 1980s.
Model 223 AR **$1295**
Model 308 AR **1350**

Galil Sporter Semiautomatic Rifle **$995**
Same general specifications as AR Model, except w/hardwood thumbhole stock and 5-shot magazine. Weight: 8½ pounds. Made 1991–94.

Garcia Bronco 22

GARCIA CORPORATION
Teaneck, New Jersey

Garcia Bronco 22 Single Shot Rifle $85
Swing-out action. Takedown. Caliber: 22 LR, Long, Short. 16½-inch barrel. Weight: 3 pounds. Sights: open rear; blade front. One-piece stock and receiver, crackle finish. Introduced 1967; discontinued.

GERMAN MILITARY RIFLES
Mfd. by Ludwig Loewe & Co., Berlin, other contractors and by German arsenals and various plants under German Government control.

German Model 24T (Gew. 24T) Mauser Rifle . . . $295
Same general specifications as the Czech Model 24 (VZ24) Mauser Rifle w/minor modifications, has laminated wood stock. Weight: about 9¼ pounds. Made in Czechoslovakia during German occupation; adopted 1940.

German Model 29/40 (Gew. 29/40) Mauser Rifle . . $195
Same general specifications as Kar. 98K, with minor differences. Made in Poland during German occupation; adopted 1940.

German Model 33/40 (Gew. 33/40) Mauser Rifle . . $550
Same general specifications as the Czech Model 33 (VZ33) Mauser Carbine with minor modifications, has laminated wood stock as found in war-time Model 98K carbines. Made in Czechoslovakia during German occupation; adopted 1940.

German Models 41 and 41-W (Gew. 41, Gew. 41-W) Semiautomatic Military Rifles $1150
Gas-operated, muzzle cone system. Caliber: 7.9mm Mauser. 10-shot box magazine. 22½-inch barrel. Weight: about 10¾ pounds. Sights: adj. leaf rear; blade front. Mili-

German Models 41 and 41-W (cont.)
tary-type stock w/semi-pistol grip, plastic handguard. *Note:* Model 41 lacks bolt release found on Model 41-W; otherwise, the models are the same. A Walther design, these early models were mfd. in that firm's Zella-Mehlis plant. Made c.1941–43.

German Model 43 (Gew. 43, Kar. 43) Semiauto Military Rifles $900
Gas-operated, barrel vented as in Russian Tokarev. Caliber: 7.9mm Mauser. 10-shot detachable box magazine. 22- or 24-inch barrel. Weight: about 9 pounds. Sights: adj. rear; hooded front. Military-type stock w/semipistol grip, wooden handguard. *Note:* These rifles are alike except for minor details, have characteristic late WWII mfg. short cuts: cast receiver and bolt cover, stamped steel parts, etc. Gew. 43 may have either 22- or 24-inch barrel; the former length was standardized in late 1944, when weapon designation was changed to "Kar. 43." Made 1943–45.

German Model 1888 (Gew. 88) Mauser-Mannlicher Service Rifle $165
Bolt action, straight handle. Caliber: 7.9mm Mauser (8×57mm). 5-shot Mannlicher box magazine. 29-inch barrel with jacket. Weight: about 8½ pounds. Fixed front sight, adjustable rear. Military-type full stock. Mfd. by Ludwig Loewe & Co., Haenel, Schilling and other contractors.

German Kar. 88

German Model 1888 (Kar. 88) Mauser-Mannlicher Carbine $165
Same general specifications as Gew. 88, except w/18-inch barrel, w/o jacket, flat turned-down bolt handle, weighs about 6¾ pounds. Mfd. by Ludwig Loewe & Co., Haenel, Schilling and other contractors.

German Gew. 33/40

German Gew. 43

RIFLES

German Gew. 98

German Kar. 98K

German Model 1898 (Gew. 98) Mauser Military Rifle $225

Bolt action, straight handle. Caliber: 7.9mm Mauser (8×57mm). 5-shot box magazine. 29-inch steeped barrel. Weight: 9 pounds. Sights: blade front; adj. rear. Military-type full stock w/rounded bottom pistol grip. Adopted 1898.

NOTE: German Mauser Military Rifles (Gew. 98, Kar. 98) were made before and during WWI at the government arsenals at Amberg, Brunn, Danzig, Erfurt and Spandau; they were also manufactured by contractors such as Haenel, Loewe, Mauser, Schilling and Steyr. These rifles bear the Imperial Crown, maker's name and date of manufacture on the receiver ring. Post-WWI Kar. 98B bears maker's name and date. During WWII as well as the years immediately before (probably from c. 1935), a letter or number code was used to indicate maker. This code and date of manufacture will be found stamped on the receiver ring of rifles of this period. German Service Mausers also bear the model number (Gew. 98, Kar. 98K, G. 33/40, etc.) on the left side of the receiver. An exception is Model VK98, which usually bears no identifying marks. Gew. is abbreviation for *gewehr* (rifle), Kar. for *karabiner* (carbine).

German Model 1898A (Kar. 98A) Mauser Carbine $225

Same general specifications as Model 1898 (Gew. 98) Rifle, except has turned-down bolt handle, smaller receiver ring, light 23½-inch straight taper barrel, front sight guards, sling is attached to left side of stock, weighs 8 pounds. *Note:* Some of these carbines are marked "Kar. 98"; the true Kar. 98 is the earlier original M/98 carbine with 17-inch barrel and is rarely encountered.

German Model 1898B (Kar. 98B) Mauser Carbine $235

Same general specifications as Model 1898 (Gew. 98) Rifle, except has turned-down bolt handle and sling attached to left side of stock. This is post-WWI model.

German Model 1898K (Kar. 98K) Mauser Carbine $225

Same general specifications as Model 1898 (Gew. 98) Rifle, except has turned-down bolt handle, 23½-inch barrel, may have hooded front sight, sling is attached to left side of stock, weighs about 8½ pounds. Adopted in 1935, this was the standard German Service rifle of WWII. *Note:* Late-war models had stamped sheet steel trigger guards and many of the Model 98K carbines made during WWII had laminated wood stocks; these weigh about ½ to ¾ pound more than the previous Model 98K. Value shown is for earlier type.

German Model VK 98 People's Rifle ("Volksgewehr") $150

Kar. 98K-type action. Caliber: 7.9mm. Single shot or repeater (latter w/rough hole-in-the-stock 5-shot "magazine" or fitted w/10-shot clip of German Model 43 semiauto rifle). 20.9-inch barrel. Weight: 7 pounds. Fixed V-notch rear sight dovetailed into front receiver ring; front blade welded to barrel. Crude, unfinished, half-length stock w/o buttplate. Last ditch weapon made in 1945 for issue to German civilians. *Note:* Of value only as a military arms collector's item, this hastily made rifle should be regarded as *unsafe* to shoot.

══ GÉVARM RIFLE ══
Saint Etienne, France
Manufactured by Gévelot

Gévarm E-1 Autoloading Rifle $160

Caliber: 22 LR. 8-shot clip magazine. 19½-inch barrel. Sights: open rear; post front. Pistol-grip stock and forearm of French walnut.

Gévarm E-1

Golden Eagle Model 7000

GOLDEN EAGLE RIFLES
Houston, Texas
Mfd. by Nikko Firearms Ltd., Tochigi, Japan

Golden Eagle Model 7000 Grade I African **$575**
Same as standard model, except calibers 375 H&H Mag. and 458 Win. Mag., 2-shot magazine in 458, weighs 8¾ lbs. in 375 and 10½ lbs. in 458, furnished with sights. Introduced 1976; discontinued.

Golden Eagle Model 7000 Grade I Big Game . . . **$525**
Bolt action. Calibers: 22-250, 243 Win., 25-06, 270 Win., 270 Weatherby Mag., 7mm Rem. Mag., 30-06, 300 Weath. Mag., 300 Win. Mag., 338 Win. Mag. Magazine capacity: 4 rounds in 22-250, 3 rounds in other calibers. 24- or 26-inch barrel (26-inch only in 338). Weight: 7 lbs., 22-250; 8¾ lbs., other calibers. Furnished w/o sights. Fancy American walnut stock, skip checkered, contrasting wood forend tip and grip cap w/gold eagle head, recoil pad. Introduced 1976; discontinued.

GREIFELT & CO.
Suhl, Germany

Greifelt Sport Model 22 Hornet Bolt Action Rifle . **$1495**
Caliber: 22 Hornet. 5-shot box magazine. 22-inch Krupp steel barrel. Weight: 6 pounds. Sights: two-leaf rear; ramp front. Walnut stock, checkered pistol grip and forearm. Made before WWII.

CARL GUSTAF RIFLES
Eskilstuna, Sweden
Mfd. by Carl Gustafs Stads Gevärsfaktori

Carl Gustaf Model 2000 Bolt Action Rifle
Calibers: 243, 6.5×55, 7×64, 270, 308 Win., 30-06, 7mm Rem. Mag., 300 Win. Mag. 3-shot magazine. 24-inch barrel. 44 inches overall. Weight: 7½ pounds. Receiver drilled and tapped. Hooded ramp front sight; open rear. Adj. trigger. Checkered European walnut stock w/Monte Carlo cheekpiece and Wundhammer palmswell grip. Made 1991 to date.
Model 2000 w/o Sights **$1195**
Model 2000 with Sights 1250

Carl Gustaf Deluxe **$550**
Same specifications as Monte Carlo Standard. Calibers: 6.5×55, 308 Win., 30-06, 9.3×62. 4-shot magazine in 9.3×62. Jeweled bolt. Engraved floorplate and trigger guard. Deluxe French walnut stock w/rosewood forend tip. Made 1970–77.

Carl Gustaf Grand Prix Single Shot Target Rifle . . **$475**
Special bolt action with "world's shortest lock time." Single-stage trigger adjusts down to 18 oz. Caliber: 22 LR. 26¾-inch heavy barrel w/adj. trim weight. Weight: 9¾ lbs. Furnished w/o sights. Target-type Monte Carlo stock of French walnut, adj. cork buttplate. Made 1970 to date.

RIFLES

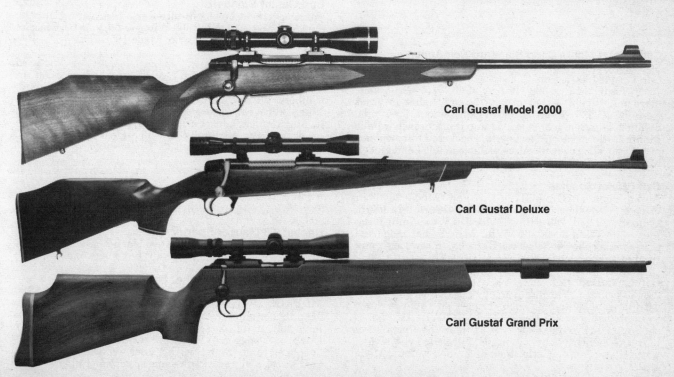

Carl Gustaf Model 2000

Carl Gustaf Deluxe

Carl Gustaf Grand Prix

Carl Gustaf Monte Carlo Standard

Carl Gustaf Special

Carl Gustaf Sporter

Carl Gustaf Trofé

Carl Gustaf Monte Carlo Standard Bolt Action
Sporting Rifle **$350**
Carl Gustaf 1900 action. Calibers: 6.5×55, 7×64, 270 Win.,
7mm Rem. Mag., 308 Win., 30-06, 9.3×62. 5-shot
magazine, except 4-shot in 9.3×62 and 3-shot in 7mm
Rem. Mag. 23¹/₂-inch barrel. Weight: about 7 pounds.
Sights: folding leaf rear; hooded ramp front. French walnut
Monte Carlo stock w/cheekpiece, checkered forearm and
pistol grip, sling swivels. Also available in left-hand model.
Made 1970–77.

Carl Gustaf Special **$395**
Also designated "Grade II" in U.S. and "Model 9000" in
Canada. Same specifications as Monte Carlo Standard.
Calibers: 22-250, 243 Win., 25-06, 270 Win., 7mm Rem.
Mag., 308 Win., 30-06, 300 Win. Mag. 3-shot magazine
in Magnum calibers. Select wood stock w/rosewood forend
tip. Left-hand model avail. Made 1970–77.

Carl Gustaf Sporter **$475**
Also designated "Varmint-Target" in U.S. Fast bolt action
with large bakelite bolt knob. Trigger pull adjusts down
to 18 oz. Calibers: 222 Rem., 22-250, 243 Win., 6.5×55. 5-
shot magazine, except 6-shot in 222 Rem. 26³/₄-inch heavy
barrel. Weight: about 9¹/₂ pounds. Furnished w/o sights.
Target-type Monte Carlo stock of French walnut. Made
1970 to date.

Carl Gustaf Standard **$425**
Same specifications as Monte Carlo Standard. Calibers:
6.5×55, 7×64, 270 Win., 308 Win., 30-06, 9.3×62. Classic-
style stock w/o Monte Carlo. Made 1970–77.

Carl Gustaf Trofé **$595**
Also designated "Grade III" in U.S. and "Model 8000" in
Canada. Same specifications as Monte Carlo Standard.
Calibers: 22-250, 25-06, 6.5×55, 270 Win., 7mm Rem.
Mag., 308 Win., 30-06, 300 Win. Mag. 3-shot magazine
in Magnum calibers. Furnished w/o sights. Fancy wood
stock w/rosewood forend tip, high-gloss lacquer finish.
Made 1970–77.

C.G. HAENEL
Suhl, Germany

Haenel '88 Mauser Sporter **$395**
Same general specifications as Haenel Mauser-Mannlicher, except has Mauser 5-shot box magazine.

Haenel Mauser-Mannlicher Bolt Action
Sporting Rifle **$350**
Mauser M/88-type action. Calibers: 7×57, 8×57, 9×57mm.
Mannlicher clip-loading box magazine, 5-shot. 22- or 24-
inch half or full octagon barrel with raised matted rib.
Double-set trigger. Weight: 7¹/₂ pounds. Sights: leaf-type
open rear; ramp front. Sporting stock w/cheekpiece, check-
ered pistol grip, raised side-panels, schnabel tip, swivels.

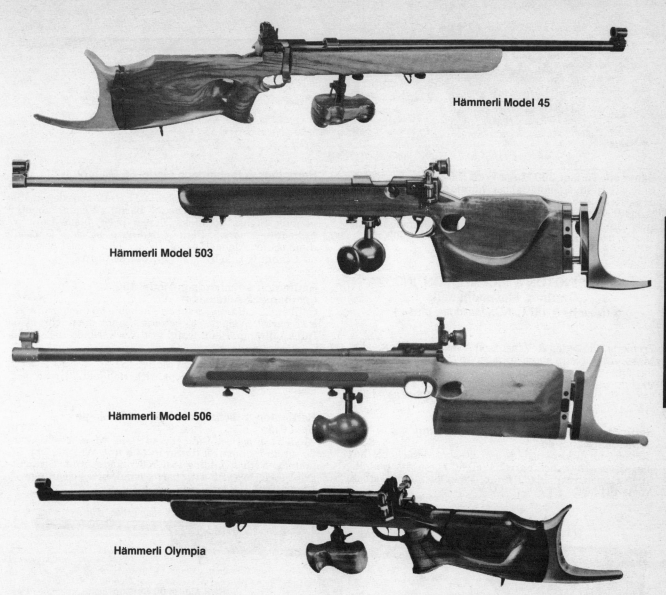

Hämmerli Model 45

Hämmerli Model 503

Hämmerli Model 506

Hämmerli Olympia

HÄMMERLI AG JAGD-UND SPORTWAFFENFABRIK
Lenzburg, Switzerland

Hämmerli Model 45 Smallbore Bolt Action Single Shot Match Rifle **$525**
Calibers: 22 LR, 22 Extra Long. 27½-inch heavy barrel. Weight: about 15½ pounds. Sights: micrometer peep rear; globe front. Free-rifle stock w/cheekpiece, full pistol grip, thumbhole, beavertail forearm, palmrest, Swiss-type butt-plate, swivels. Made 1945–1957.

Hämmerli Model 54 Smallbore Match Rifle **$495**
Bolt action, single shot. Caliber: 22 LR. 27½-inch heavy barrel. Weight: about 15 pounds. Sights: micrometer peep rear; globe front. Free- rifle stock w/cheekpiece, thumbhole, adj. hook buttplate, palmrest, swivel. Made 1954–57.

Hämmerli Model 503 Free Rifle **$475**
Bolt action, single shot. Caliber: 22 LR. 27½-inch heavy barrel. Weight: about 15½ pounds. Sights: micrometer peep

Hämmerli Model 503 Free Rifle (cont.)
rear; globe front. Free-rifle stock w/cheekpiece, thumbhole, adj. hook buttplate, palmrest, swivel. Made 1957–1962.

Hämmerli Model 506 Smallbore Match Rifle **$515**
Bolt action, single shot. Caliber: 22 LR. 26¾-inch heavy barrel. Weight: about 16½ pounds. Sights: micrometer peep rear; globe front. Free-rifle stock w/cheekpiece, thumbhole, adj. hook buttplate, palmrest, swivel. Made 1963–66.

Hämmerli Model Olympia 300 Meter Bolt Action Single Shot Free Rifle **$625**
Calibers: 30-06, 300 H&H Magnum for U.S.A.; ordinarily produced in 7.5mm, other calibers available on special order. 29½-inch heavy barrel. Double-pull or double-set trigger. Sights: micrometer peep rear; globe front. Free-rifle stock w/cheekpiece, full pistol grip, thumbhole, beavertail for-end, palmrest, Swiss-type buttplate, swivels. Made 1945–1959.

Hämmerli-Tanner 300M

Hämmerli-Tanner 300 Meter Free Rifle **$795**
Bolt action, single shot. Caliber: 7.5mm standard, available in most popular centerfire calibers. 29½-inch heavy barrel. Weight: about 16¾ pounds. Sights: micrometer peep rear; globe front. Free-rifle stock w/cheekpiece, thumbhole, adj. hook buttplate, palmrest, swivel. Introduced 1962; disc.

HARRINGTON & RICHARDSON, INC.
Gardner, Massachusetts
(Now H&R 1871, INC., Gardner, Mass.)

Formerly Harrington & Richardson Arms Co. of Worcester, Mass. After a long and distinguished career in gunmaking this firm suspended operation in 1986. However, in 1992, the firm was bought by New England Firearms of Gardner, Mass. Some models are mfd. under that banner as well as H&R 1871, Inc.

Harrington & Richardson Model 60 Reising Semiautomatic Rifle **$350**
Caliber: 45 Automatic. 12- and 20-shot detachable box magazines. 18¼-inch barrel. Weight: about 7½ pounds. Sights: open rear; blade front. Plain pistol-grip stock. Made 1944–46.

Harrington & Richardson Model 65 Military Autoloading Rifle **$255**
Also called "General." Caliber: 22 LR. 10-shot detachable box magazine. 23-inch heavy barrel. Weight: about 9 pounds. Sights: Redfield 70 rear peep; blade front w/ protecting "ears." Plain pistol-grip stock, "Garand" dimensions. Made 1944–46. *Note:* This model was used as a training rifle by the U.S. Marine Corps.

Harrington & Richardson Model 150 Leatherneck Autoloader **$110**
Caliber: 22 LR only. 5-shot detachable box magazine. 22-inch barrel. Weight: 7¼ pounds. Sights: open rear; blade front, on ramp. Plain pistol-grip stock. Made 1949–1953.

Harrington & Richardson Model 151 . . . . **$125**
Same as Model 150 except with Redfield 70 rear peep sight.

Harrington & Richardson Model 155 Single Shot Rifle **$110**
Model 158 action. Calibers: 44 Rem. Mag., 45-70 Govt. 24- or 28-inch barrel (latter in 44 only). Weight: 7 or 7½ pounds. Sights: folding leaf rear; blade front. Straight-grip stock, forearm with barrel band, brass cleaning rod. Made 1972–1982.

H&R Model 60 Reising

H&R Model 65

H&R Model 155

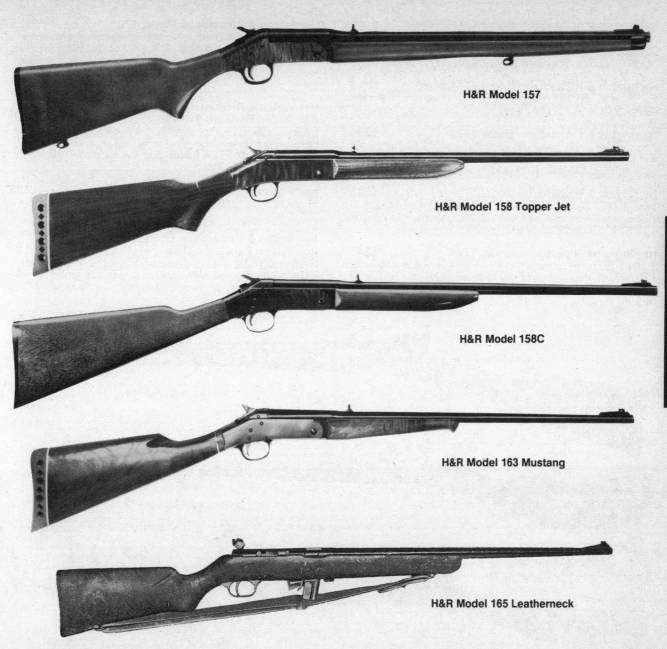

H&R Model 157

H&R Model 158 Topper Jet

H&R Model 158C

H&R Model 163 Mustang

H&R Model 165 Leatherneck

RIFLES

Harrington & Richardson Model 157 Single Shot Rifle **$100**
Model 158 action. Calibers: 22 WMR, 22 Hornet, 30-30. 22-inch barrel. Weight: 6¼ pounds. Sights: folding leaf rear; blade front. Pistol-grip stock, full-length forearm, swivels. Made 1976–1986.

Harrington & Richardson Model 158 Topper Jet Single Shot Combination Rifle
Shotgun-type action w/visible hammer, side lever, auto ejector. Caliber: 22 Rem. Jet. 22-inch barrel (interchanges with 30-30, .410 ga., 20 ga. barrels). Weight: 5 pounds. Sights: Lyman folding adj. open rear; ramp front. Plain pistol-grip stock and forearm, recoil pad. Made 1963–67.
Rifle only **$120**
Interchangeable barrel—30-30, shotgun **35**

Harrington & Richardson Model 158C **$145**
Same as Model 158 Topper Jet, except calibers 22 Hornet, 30-30, 357 Mag., 357 Max., 44 Mag. Straight-grip stock. Made 1963–1986.

Harrington & Richardson Model 163 Mustang Single Shot Rifle **$110**
Same as Model 158 Topper except has gold-plated hammer and trigger, straight-grip stock and contoured forearm. Made 1964–67.

Harrington & Richardson Model 165 Leatherneck Autoloader **$125**
Caliber: 22 LR. 10-shot detachable box magazine. 23-inch barrel. Weight: about 7½ pounds. Sights: Redfield 70 rear peep; blade front, on ramp. Plain pistol-grip stock, swivels, web sling. Made 1945–1961.

Harrington & Richardson Model 171 . . . . **$280**
Model 1873 Springfield Cavalry Carbine replica. Caliber: 45-70. 22-inch barrel. Weight: 7 pounds. Sights: leaf rear; blade front. Plain walnut stock. Made 1972–1981.

Harrington & Richardson Model 171 Deluxe **$315**
Same as Model 171, except engraved action and different sights. Made 1972–1986.

Harrington & Richardson Model 172 . . . . **$995**
Same as Model 171 Deluxe, except silver-plated, has fancy walnut stock, checkered, with grip adapter; tang-mounted aperture sight. Made 1972–1986.

Harrington & Richardson Model 173 . . . . **$325**
Model 1873 Springfield Officer's Model replica, same as 100th Anniversary Commemorative, except w/o plaque on stock. Made 1972–1986.

Harrington & Richardson Model 174 . . . . **$340**
Little Big Horn Commemorative Carbine. Same as Model 171 Deluxe, except has tang-mounted aperture sight, grip adapter. Made 1972–1984. Value is for carbine in new, unfired condition.

Harrington & Richardson Model 178 . . . . **$325**
Model 1873 Springfield Infantry Rifle replica. Caliber: 45-70. 32-inch barrel. Weight: 8 lbs. 10 oz. Sights: leaf rear; blade front. Full-length stock with barrel bands, swivels, ramrod. Made 1973–1986.

**Harrington & Richardson Model 250 Sportster
Bolt Action Repeating Rifle** **$80**
Caliber: 22 LR. 5-shot detachable box magazine. 23-inch barrel. Weight: about 6½ pounds. Sights: open rear; blade front, on ramp. Plain pistol-grip stock. Made 1948–1961.

Harrington & Richardson Model 251 . . . . **$85**
Same as Model 250 except has Lyman 55H rear sight.

**Harrington & Richardson Model 265 "Reg'lar"
Bolt Action Repeating Rifle** **$80**
Caliber: 22 LR. 10-shot detachable box magazine. 22-inch barrel. Weight: about 6½ pounds. Sights: Lyman 55 rear peep; blade front, on ramp. Plain pistol-grip stock. Made 1946–49.

H&R Model 171

H&R Model 172

H&R Model 173

H&R Model 174
Little Big Horn Commemorative Carbine

H&R Model 265 "Reg'lar"

H&R Model 301 Carbine

H&R Model 317 Ultra Wildcat

H&R Model 317P

H&R Model 330 Hunter's Rifle

H&R Model 333

RIFLES

Harrington & Richardson Model 300 Ultra Bolt Action Rifle **$395**
Mauser-type action. Calibers: 22-250, 243 Win., 270 Win., 30-06, 308 Win., 7mm Rem. Mag., 300 Win. Mag. 3-round magazine in 7mm and 300 Mag. calibers, 5-round in others. 22- or 24-inch barrel. Sights: open rear; ramp front. Checkered stock w/rollover cheekpiece and full pistol grip, contrasting wood forearm tip and pistol grip, rubber buttplate, swivels. Weight: 7¼ pounds. Made 1965–1982.

Harrington & Richardson Model 301 Carbine . . . **$380**
Same as Model 300, except has 18-inch barrel, Mannlicher-style stock, weighs 7¼ pounds; not available in caliber 22-250. Made 1967–1982.

Harrington & Richardson Model 317 Ultra Wildcat Bolt Action Rifle **$495**
Sako short action. Calibers: 17 Rem., 17/223 (handload), 222 Rem., 223 Rem. 6-round magazine. 20-inch barrel.

Harrington & Richardson Model 317 (cont.)
No sights, receiver dovetailed for scope mounts. Checkered stock w/cheekpiece and full pistol grip, contrasting wood forearm tip and pistol-grip cap, rubber buttplate. Weight: 5¼ pounds. Made 1968–1976.

Harrington & Richardson Model 317P Presentation Grade **$595**
Same as Model 317, except has select grade fancy walnut stock with basketweave carving on forearm and pistol grip. Made 1968–1976.

Harrington & Richardson Model 330 Hunter's Rifle **$295**
Similar to Model 300, but w/plainer stock. Calibers: 243 Win., 270 Win., 30-06, 308 Win., 7mm Rem. Mag., 300 Win. Mag. Weight: about 7⅛ pounds. Made 1967–1972.

Harrington & Richardson Model 333 . . . . **$230**
Plainer version of Model 300 with uncheckered walnut-finished hardwood stock. Calibers: 7mm Rem. Mag. and 30-06. 22-inch barrel. Weight: 7¼ pounds. No sights. Made in 1974.

Harrington & Richardson Model 340 . . . . **$295**
Mauser-type action. Calibers: 243 Win., 308 Win., 270 Win., 30-06, 7×57mm. 22-inch barrel. Weight: 7 1/4 pounds. Hand-checkered, American walnut stock. Made 1982–84.

Harrington & Richardson Model 360 Ultra Automatic Rifle **$325**
Gas-operated semiautomatic. Calibers: 243 Win., 308 Win. 3-round detachable box magazine. 22-inch barrel. Sights: open rear; ramp front. Checkered stock with rollover cheekpiece, full pistol grip, contrasting wood forearm tip and pistol-grip cap, rubber buttplate, sling swivels. Weight: 7 1/2 pounds. Introduced 1965; discontinued 1978. (*Note:* Originally designated Model 308, changed to 360 in 1967).

Harrington & Richardson Model 361 . . . . **$355**
Same as Model 360, except has full rollover cheekpiece for right- or left-hand shooters. Made 1970–73.

Harrington & Richardson Model 365 Ace Bolt Action Single Shot Rifle **$100**
Caliber: 22 LR. 22-inch barrel. Weight: about 6 1/2 pounds. Sights: Lyman 55 rear peep; blade front, on ramp. Plain pistol-grip stock. Made 1946–47.

Harrington & Richardson Model 370 Ultra Medalist **$395**
Varmint and target rifle based on Model 300. Calibers: 22-250, 243 Win., 6mm Rem. 5-round magazine. 24-inch varmint weight barrel. No sights. Target-style stock with semibeavertail forearm. Weight: 9 1/2 pounds. Made 1968–1973.

Harrington & Richardson Model 422 Slide Action Repeater **$125**
Caliber: 22 LR, Long, Short. Tubular magazine holds 21 Short, 17 Long, 15 LR. 24-inch barrel. Weight: about 6 pounds. Sights: open rear; ramp front. Plain pistol-grip stock, grooved slide handle. Made 1956–58.

Harrington & Richardson Model 450 . . . . **$130**
Same as Model 451, except w/o front and rear sights.

Harrington & Richardson Model 451 Medalist Bolt Action Target Rifle **$155**
Caliber: 22 LR. 5-shot detachable box magazine. 26-inch barrel. Weight: about 10 1/2 pounds. Sights: Lyman 524F extension rear; Lyman 77 front, scope bases. Target stock w/full pistol grip and forearm, swivels and sling. Made 1948–1961.

Harrington & Richardson Model 465 Targeteer Special Bolt Action Repeater **$145**
Caliber: 22 LR. 10-shot detachable box magazine. 25-inch barrel. Weight: about 9 pounds. Sights: Lyman 57 rear peep; blade front, on ramp. Plain pistol-grip stock, swivels, web sling strap. Made 1946–47.

Harrington & Richardson Model 700 Autoloader . . **$175**
Caliber: 22 WMR. 5-shot magazine. 22-inch barrel. Weight: about 6 1/2 pounds. Sights: folding leaf rear; blade front, on

H&R Model 340

H&R Model 360 Ultra Automatic

H&R Model 370 Ultra Medalist

H&R Model 465 Targeteer

H&R Model 700

H&R Model 700 Deluxe

H&R Model 750 Pioneer

H&R "New" Model 750

H&R Model 755 Sahara

Harrington & Richardson Model 700 Autoloader (cont.)
ramp. Monte Carlo-style stock of American walnut. Introduced 1977; discontinued.

Harrington & Richardson Model 700 Deluxe **$275**
Same as Model 700 Standard except has select custom polished and blued finish, select walnut stock, hand checkering, and no iron sights. Fitted with H&R Model 432 4× scope. Made 1980–86.

Harrington & Richardson Model 750 Pioneer Bolt Action Single Shot Rifle **$90**
Caliber: 22 LR, Long, Short. 22- or 24-inch barrel. Weight: about 5 pounds. Sights: open rear; bead front. Plain pistol-grip stock. Made 1954–1981; redesigned 1982; discont. 1985.

Harrington & Richardson Model 751 Single Shot Rifle **$75**
Same as Model 750, except has Mannlicher-style stock. Made 1971.

Harrington & Richardson Model 755 Sahara Single Shot Rifle **$75**
Blow-back action, automatic ejection. Caliber: 22 LR, Long, Short. 18-inch barrel. Weight: 4 pounds. Sights: open rear; military-type front. Mannlicher-style stock. Made 1963–1971.

Harrington & Richardson Model 760 Single Shot **$80**
Same as Model 755, except has conventional sporter stock. Made 1965–1970.

Harrington & Richardson Model 765 Pioneer Bolt Action Single Shot Rifle **$60**
Caliber: 22 LR, Long, Short. 24-inch barrel. Weight: about 5 pounds. Sights: open rear; hooded bead front. Plain pistol-grip stock. Made 1948–1954.

H&R Model 866

H&R Model 1873
100th Anniversary Springfield Replica

H&R Model 5200

H&R Ultra Varmint

Harrington & Richardson Model 800 Lynx Autoloading Rifle **$110**
Caliber: 22 LR. 5- or 10-shot clip magazine. 22-inch barrel. Open sights. Weight: 6 pounds. Plain pistol-grip stock. Made 1958–1960.

Harrington & Richardson Model 852 Fieldsman Bolt Action Repeater **$90**
Caliber: 22 LR, Long, Short. Tubular magazine holds 21 Short, 17 Long, 15 LR. 24-inch barrel. Weight: about 5½ pounds. Sights: open rear; bead front. Plain pistol-grip stock. Made 1952–53.

Harrington & Richardson Model 865 Plainsman Bolt Action Repeater **$85**
Caliber: 22 LR, Long, Short. 5-shot detachable box magazine. 22- or 24-inch barrel. Weight: about 5¼ pounds. Sights: open rear; bead front. Plain pistol-grip stock. Made 1949–1986.

Harrington & Richardson Model 866 Bolt Action Repeater **$85**
Same as Model 865, except has Mannlicher-style stock. Made 1971.

Harrington & Richardson Model 1873 100th Anniversary (1871–1971) Commemorative Officer's Springfield Replica **$595**
Model 1873 "trap door" single-shot action. Engraved breech block, receiver, hammer, lock, band and buttplate. Caliber: 45-70. 26-inch barrel. Sights: peep rear; blade front. Checkered walnut stock w/anniversary plaque. Ramrod. Weight: about 8 pounds. 10,000 made 1971. Value is for rifle in new, unfired condition.

Harrington & Richardson Model 5200 Sporter . . . **$475**
Turn-bolt repeater. Caliber: 22 LR. 24-inch barrel. Classic-style American walnut stock. Adj. trigger. Sights: peep receiver; hooded ramp front. Weight: 6½ pounds. Discontinued 1983.

Harrington & Richardson Model 5200 Match Rifle **$425**
Same action as 5200 Sporter. Caliber: 22 LR. 28-inch target weight barrel. Target stock of American walnut. Weight: 11 pounds. Made 1982–86.

Harrington & Richardson Custer Memorial Issue
Limited Edition Model 1873 Springfield Carbine replica, richly engraved and inlaid with gold, fancy walnut stock, in mahogany display case. Made 1973. Value is for carbine in new, unfired condition.
Officers' Model, limited to 25 pieces **$3500**
Enlisted Men's Model, limited to 243 pieces **2250**

Harrington & Richardson Targeteer Jr. Bolt Action Rifle **$110**
Caliber: 22 LR 5-shot detachable box magazine. 20-inch barrel. Weight: about 7 pounds. Sights: Redfield 70 rear peep; Lyman 17A front. Target stock, junior size with pistol grip, swivels and sling. Made 1948–1951.

Harrington & Richardson Ultra Single Shot Rifle
Side-lever single shot. Calibers: 22-250 Rem., 223 Rem., 25-06 Rem., 308 Win. 22- to 26-inch barrel. Weight: 7–8 pounds. Curly maple or laminated stock. Barrel-mounted scope mount; no sights. Made 1993 to date.
Ultra Hunter (25-06, 308) **$150**
Ultra Varmint **190**

HARRIS GUNWORKS
Phoenix, Arizona
See McMillan Gun Works

HECKLER & KOCH, GMBH
Oberndorf/Neckar, Germany

Heckler & Koch Model 911 Semiauto Rifle **$1025**
Caliber: 308 (7.62mm). 5-shot magazine. 19.7-inch bull barrel. 42^2/$_5$ inches overall. Sights: hooded post front; adjustable aperture rear. Weight: 11 pounds. Kevlar reinforced fiberglass thumbhole-stock.

Heckler & Koch Model HK91 A-2 Semiauto **$1995**
Delayed roller-locked blow-back action. Caliber: 7.62mm × 51 NATO (308 Win.). 5- or 20-round box magazine. 19-inch barrel. Weight: w/o magazine, 9.37 pounds. Sights: "V" and aperture rear; post front. Plastic buttstock and forearm. No longer imported.

Heckler & Koch Model HK91 A-3 .... **$2350**
Same as Model HK91 A-2, except has retractable metal buttstock, weighs 10.56 pounds. Currently manufactured.

Heckler & Koch Model HK93 Semiautomatic
Delayed roller-locked blow-back action. Caliber: 5.56mm × 45 (223 Rem.). 5- or 20-round magazine. 16.13-inch barrel. Weight: w/o magazine, 7.6 pounds. Sights: "V" and aperture rear; post front. Plastic buttstock and forearm. Currently manufactured.
HK93, A-2 .... **$1895**
HK93, A-3 with retractable stock **2450**

Heckler & Koch Model HK94 Semiautomatic Carbine
Caliber: 9mm Para. 15-shot magazine. 16-inch barrel. Weight: 6^3/$_4$ pounds. Aperture rear sight, front post. Plastic buttstock and forend or retractable metal stock. Made 1983 to date.
HK94-A2 w/Standard Stock **$2295**
HK94-A3 w/Retractable Stock **2595**

RIFLES

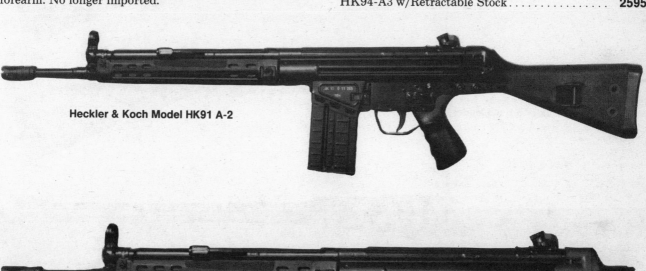
Heckler & Koch Model HK91 A-2

Heckler & Koch Model HK91 A-3

Heckler & Koch Model HK93 A-2

Heckler & Koch Model HK300

Heckler & Koch Model HK630

Heckler & Koch Model HK770

Heckler & Koch Model KH940

Heckler & Koch Model HK300 Semiautomatic . . . **$525**
Caliber: 22 WMR. 5- or 15-round box magazine. 19.7-inch barrel. Weight: about 5¾ pounds. Sights: V-notch rear; ramp front. European walnut stock w/cheekpiece, checkered forearm and pistol grip. No longer imported.

Heckler & Koch Model HK630 Semiautomatic . . . **$650**
Caliber: 223 Rem. 4- or 10-round magazine. Overall length: 42 inches. Weight: 7 pounds. Sights: open rear; ramp front. European walnut stock w/Monte Carlo cheekpiece. Made 1983–1990.

Heckler & Koch Model HK770 Semiautomatic . . . **$795**
Caliber: 308 Win. 3- or 10-round magazine. Overall length: 44½ inches. Weight: 8 pounds. Sights: open rear; ramp front. European walnut stock w/Monte Carlo cheekpiece. Made 1983–1990.

Heckler & Koch Model HK940 Semiautomatic . . . **$875**
Caliber: 30-06 Springfield. 3- or 10-round magazine. Overall length: 47 inches. Weight: 8.8 pounds. Sights: open rear; ramp front. European walnut stock w/Monte Carlo cheekpiece. Made 1983–1990.

Heckler & Koch Model HK PSG-1 Marksman's Rifle . . . **$7500**
Caliber: 308 (7.62mm). 5- and 20-shot magazine. 25.6-inch barrel. 47½ inches overall. Hensoldt 6×42 telescopic sight. Weight: 17.8 pounds. Matte black composition stock w/ pistol grip. Made 1988 to date.

Heckler & Koch Model SR-9 Semiauto Rifle . . . **$1750**
Caliber: 308 (7.62mm). 5-shot magazine. 19.7-inch bull barrel. 42.4 inches overall. Hooded post front sight; adj. aperture rear. Weight: 11 pounds. Kevlar reinforced fiberglass thumbhole-stock w/wood grain finish.

Heckler & Koch Model SR-9 Target Rifle . . . **$1895**
Same general specifications as standard SR-9, except w/ PSG-1 trigger group and adj. buttstock. Made 1992–94.

HERCULES RIFLES
See listings under "W" for Montgomery Ward.

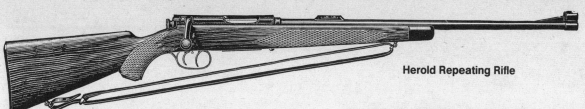

Herold Repeating Rifle

HEROLD RIFLE
Suhl, Germany
Made by Franz Jaeger & Company

Herold Bolt Action Repeating Sporting Rifle **$850**
"Herold-Repetierbüchse." Miniature Mauser-type action with unique 5-shot box magazine on hinged floorplate. Double-set triggers. Caliber: 22 Hornet. 24-inch barrel. Sights: leaf rear; ramp front. Weight: about 7¾ pounds. Fancy checkered stock. Made before WWII. *Note:* These rifles were imported by Charles Daly and A.F. Stoeger Inc. of New York City and sold under their own names.

HEYM AMERICA, INC.
Fort Wayne, Indiana

Currently imported by Heckler & Koch, Sterling, VA.

Heym Model 55B O/U Double Rifle
Kersten boxlock action with double cross bolt and cocking indicators. Calibers: 308 Win., 30-06, 375 H&H, 458 Win. Mag., 470 N.E. 25-inch barrel. 42 inches overall. Weight: 8¼ pounds. Sights: fixed V-type rear; front ramp with silver bead. Engraved receiver with optional sidelocks, interchangeable barrels and claw mounts. Checkered European walnut stock. Imported from Germany.

Model 55 (boxlock)	**$8250**
Model 55 (sidelock)	**9550**
Add for extra rifle barrels	**4500**
Add for extra shotgun barrels	**2500**

Heym Model 88B Double Rifle
Modified Anson & Deeley boxlock action with standing sears, double underlocking lugs and Greener extension w/crossbolt. Calibers: 8×57 JRS, 9.3×74R, 30-06, 375 H&H, 458 Win. Mag., 470 Nitro Express, 500 Nitro Express. Weight: 8 to 10 pounds. Top tang safety and cocking indicators. Double triggers with front set. Fixed or 3-leaf

Heym Model 88B Double Rifle (cont.)
express rear sight; front ramp w/silver bead. Engraved receiver w/optional sidelocks. Checkered French walnut stock. Imported from Germany.

Model 88B Boxlock	**from $ 8,775**
Model 88B/SS Sidelock	**from 11,500**
Model 88B Safari (Magnum)	**11,950**

Heym Express Bolt Action Rifle
Same general specifications as Model SR-20 Safari, except w/modified Magnum Mauser action. Checkered AAA-grade European walnut stock w/cheekpiece, solid rubber recoil pad, rosewood forend tip and grip cap. Calibers: 338 Lapua Magnum, 375 H&H, 378 Wby. Mag., 416 Rigby, 450 Ackley, 460 Wby. Mag., 500 A-Square, 500 Nitro Express, 600 Nitro Express. Made 1989 to date.

Standard Express Magnum	**$4150**
600 Nitro Express	**7950**
Add for Left-hand Models	**600**

Heym SR-20 Bolt Action Rifle
Calibers: 243 Win., 270 Win., 308 Win., 30-06, 7mm Rem. Mag., 300 Win. Mag., 375 H&H. 5-shot (standard) or 3-shot (Magnum) magazine. Barrel length: 20½-inch (SR-20L); 24-inch (SR-20N); 26-inch (SR-20G). Weight: 7¾ pounds. Adj. rear sight, blade front. Checkered French walnut stock in Monte Carlo style (N&G Series) or full Mannlicher (L Series). Imported from Germany. Discontinued 1992.

SR-20L	**$1050**
SR-20N	**1195**
SR-20G	**1395**

Heym SR-20 Classic Bolt Action Rifles
Same as SR-20, except w/22-250 and 338 Win. Mag., plus metric calibers on request. 24-inch (standard) or 25-inch (Magnum) barrel. Checkered French walnut stock. Left-hand models. Imported from Germany since 1985; Sporter version from 1989–1993.

Classic (Standard)	**$1395**
Classic (Magnum)	**1525**

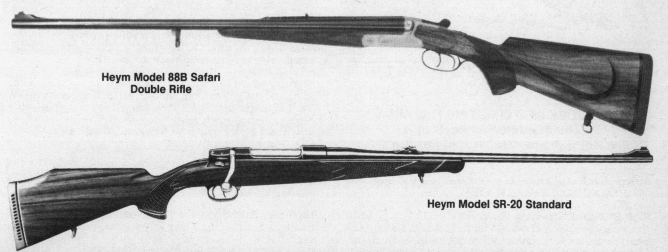

Heym Model 88B Safari Double Rifle

Heym Model SR-20 Standard

Heym Model SR-20 Trophy Series

Heym SR-20 Classic Bolt Action Rifles (cont.)
Left-hand Models, **add** . . . . $ 300
Classic Sporter (Std. w/22-inch bbl.) 1595
Classic Sporter (Mag. w/24-inch bbl.) 1650

Heym SR-20 Alpine, Safari and Trophy Series
Same general specifications as Model SR-20 Classic
Sporter, except **Alpine Series** has 20-inch barrel, Mann-
licher stock, chambered in standard calibers only; **Safari
Series** has 24-inch barrel, 3-leaf express sights and mag-

Heym SR-20 Alpine, Safari and Trophy Series (cont.)
num action in calibers 375 H&H, 404 Jeffrey, 425 Express,
458 Win. Mag.; **Trophy Series** has Krupp-Special tapered
octagon barrel with quarter rib and open sights, standard
and Magnum calibers. All imported from Germany 1989–
1993.
Alpine Series $1450
Safari Series 1525
Trophy Series (Standard Calibers) 1595
Trophy Series (Magnum Calibers) 1625

High Standard Flite-King Pump

High Standard Hi-Power Deluxe

High Standard Hi-Power Field

High Standard Sport-King Auto Carbine

=== **J.C. HIGGINS RIFLES** ===
See Sears, Roebuck & Company.

=== **HIGH STANDARD SPORTING FIREARMS** ===
East Hartford, Connecticut
Formerly High Standard Mfg. Co., Hamden, CT

A long-standing producer of sporting arms, High Standard
discontinued its operations in 1984.

High Standard Flite-King Pump Rifle $110
Hammerless slide action. Caliber: 22 LR, 22 Long, 22
Short. Tubular mag. holds 17 LR, 19 Long, or 24 Short.
24-inch barrel. Weight: 5½ pounds. Sights: Patridge rear;

High Standard Flite-King Pump Rifle (cont.)
bead front. Monte Carlo stock w/pistol grip, serrated
semibeavertail forearm. Made 1962–1975.

High Standard Hi-Power Deluxe Rifle $285
Mauser-type bolt action, sliding safety. Calibers: 270, 30-
06. 4-shot magazine. 22-inch barrel. Weight: 7 pounds.
Sights: folding open rear; ramp front. Walnut stock w/
checkered pistol grip and forearm, Monte Carlo comb,
QD swivels. Made 1962–66.

High Standard Hi-Power Field Bolt Action Rifle . $225
Same as Hi-Power Deluxe, except has plain field style
stock. Made 1962–66.

High Standard Sport-King Autoloading Carbine . $135
Same as Sport-King Field Autoloader, except has 18¼-
inch barrel, Western-style straight-grip stock w/barrel
band, sling and swivels. Made 1964–1973.

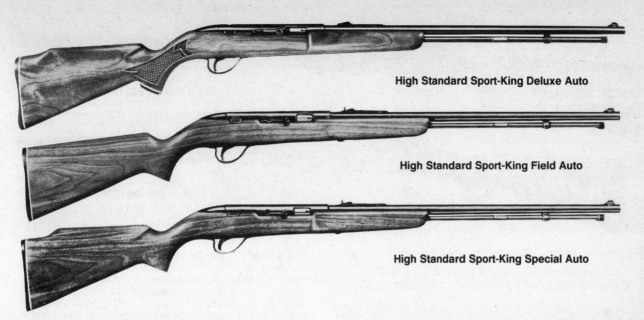

High Standard Sport-King Deluxe Auto

High Standard Sport-King Field Auto

High Standard Sport-King Special Auto

High Standard Sport-King Deluxe Autoloader . . . **$155**
Same as Sport-King Special Autoloader, except has checkered stock. Made 1966–1975.

High Standard Sport-King Field Autoloader **$100**
Calibers: 22 LR, 22 Long, 22 Short (high speed). Tubular magazine holds 15 LR, 17 Long, or 21 Short. $22\frac{1}{4}$-inch barrel. Weight: $5\frac{1}{2}$ pounds. Sights: open rear; beaded post front. Plain pistol-grip stock. Made 1960–66.

High Standard Sport-King Special Autoloader . . **$125**
Same as Sport-King Field, except stock has Monte Carlo comb and semibeavertail forearm. Made 1960–66.

HOLLAND & HOLLAND, LTD.
London, England

**Holland & Holland No. 2 Model Hammerless
Ejector Double Rifle** **$12,500**
Same general specifications as Royal Model, except plainer finish. Discontinued 1960.

Holland & Holland Best Quality Magazine Rifle . . **$6850**
Mauser or Enfield action. Calibers: 240 Apex, 300 H&H Magnum, 375 H&H Magnum. 4-shot box magazine. 24-inch barrel. Weight: about $7\frac{1}{4}$ lbs., 240 Apex; $8\frac{1}{4}$ lbs., 300 Mag. and 375 Mag. Sights: folding leaf rear; hooded ramp front. Detachable French walnut stock w/cheekpiece, checkered pistol grip and forearm, swivels. Currently mfd. Specifications given are those of the present model; however, in general they apply also to prewar models.

Holland & Holland Deluxe Magazine Rifle **$5950**
Same specifications as Best Quality, except has exhibition grade stock and special engraving. Currently mfd.

Holland & Holland Royal Deluxe Double Rifle . . . **$37,500**
Formerly designated "Modele Deluxe." Same specifications as Royal Model, except has exhibition grade stock and special engraving. Currently mfd.

**Holland & Holland Royal Hammerless Ejector
Double Rifle** **$29,750**
Sidelock. Calibers: 240 Apex, 7mm H&H Mag., 300 H&H Mag., 300 Win. Mag., 30-06, 375 H&H Mag., 458 Win. Mag., 465 H&H Mag. 24- to 28-inch barrels. Weight: from $7\frac{1}{2}$ pounds. Sights: folding leaf rear; ramp front. Cheekpiece stock of select French walnut, checkered pistol grip and forearm. Currently mfd. Same general specifications apply to prewar model.

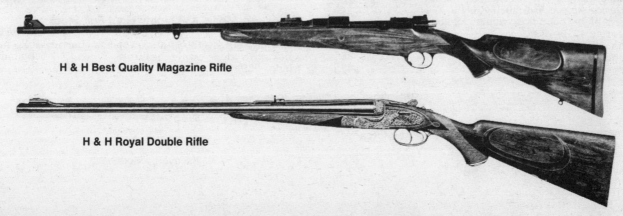

H & H Best Quality Magazine Rifle

H & H Royal Double Rifle

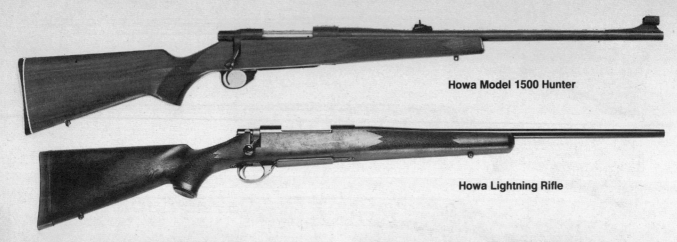

Howa Model 1500 Hunter

Howa Lightning Rifle

HOWA MACHINERY LTD.
Shinkawa-Chonear, Nagoya 452, Japan
Currently imported by Interarms, Alexandria, VA

See also Mossberg (1500), Smith & Wesson (1500 & 1700) and Weatherby (Vanguard).

Howa Model 1500 Hunter
Similar to the Trophy Model, except w/standard walnut stock. No Monte Carlo cheekpiece or grip cap. Imported 1988–89.
Standard Calibers **$300**
Magnum Calibers **325**

Howa Model 1500 Lightning Bolt Action Rifle
Similar to the Hunter Model, except fitted with black Bell & Carlson Carbelite stock with checkered grip and forend. Weight: 7¹/₂ pounds. Imported 1988–89.
Standard Calibers **$330**
Magnum Calibers **355**

Howa Model 1500 Realtree Camo Rifle **$375**
Similar to the Trophy Model, except fitted with Camo Bell & Carlson Carbelite stock with checkered grip and forend. Weight: 8 pounds. Stock, action and barrel finished in Realtree camo. Available in standard calibers only. Imported 1993 to date.

Howa Model 1500 Trophy/Varmint Bolt Action Rifle
Calibers: 22-250, 223, 243 Win., 270 Win., 308 Win., 30-06, 7mm Mag., 300 Win. Mag., 338 Win. Mag. 22-inch barrel (standard); 24-inch barrel (Magnum). 42¹/₂ inches overall (standard). Weight: 7¹/₂ pounds. Adj. rear sight; hooded ramp front. Checkered walnut stock w/Monte Carlo cheekpiece. **Varmint Model** has 24-inch heavy barrel, weight of 9¹/₂ pounds in calibers 22-250, 223 and 308 only. Imported 1979–1993.
Trophy Standard **$340**
Trophy Magnum **365**
Varmint (Parkerized Finish) **425**

Howa Model Lightning Bolt Action Rifle
Calibers: 22-250, 223, 243, 270, 7mm Rem. Mag., 30-06, 308, 300 Win. Mag., 338 Win. Mag. 3-shot magazine (Mag.). Barrel length: 22-inch (Std.); 24-inch (Mag.). 42- to 44-inches overall. Weight: 7¹/₂–7³/₄ pounds. Receiver drilled and tapped for scope mount; no sights. Checkered synthetic polymer stock. Imported 1993 to date.
Standard Calibers **$300**
Magnum Calibers **325**
Woodgrain Stock, **add** **35**

HUNGARIAN MILITARY RIFLES
Budapest, Hungary
Manufactured at Government Arsenal

Hungarian Model 1935M Mannlicher Military
Rifle **$200**
Caliber: 8×52mm Hungarian. Bolt action, straight handle. 5-shot projecting box magazine. 24-inch barrel. Weight: about 9 pounds. Adj. leaf rear sight, hooded front blade. Two-piece military-type stock. Made 1935–1940.

Hungarian Model 1943M (German Gew. 98/40)
Mannlicher Military Rifle **$240**
Modification, during German occupation, of the Model 1935M. Caliber: 7.9mm Mauser. Turned-down bolt handle and Mauser M/98-type box magazine; other differences are minor. Made 1940 to end of war in Europe.

HUSQVARNA VAPENFABRIK A.B.
Huskvarna, Sweden

Husqvarna Model 456 Lightweight Full-Stock
Sporter **$415**
Same as Series 4000/4100 except has sporting-style full stock with slope-away cheekrest. Weight: 6¹/₂ pounds. Made 1959–1970.

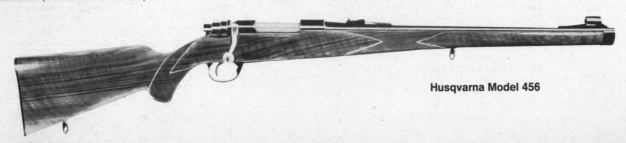

Husqvarna Model 456

Husqvarna 1100 Deluxe

Husqvarna 1951 Hi-Power

Husqvarna 3000 Crown Grade

Husqvarna 4100 Lightweight

Husqvarna 6000 Imperial Custom

Husqvarna Series 1000 Super Grade **$425**
Same as 1951 Hi-Power, except has European walnut
sporter stock w/Monte Carlo comb and cheekpiece. Made
1952–56.

**Husqvarna Series 1100 Deluxe Model Hi-Power
Bolt Action Sporting Rifles** **$435**
Same as 1951 Hi-Power, except has "jeweled" bolt, European
walnut stock. Made 1952–56.

Husqvarna 1950 Hi-Power Sporting Rifle **$275**
Mauser-type bolt action. Calibers: 220 Swift, 270 Win.,
30-06 (*see* note below), 5-shot box magazine. 23¾-inch
barrel. Weight: about 7¾ pounds. Sights: open rear;
hooded ramp front. Sporting stock of Arctic beech, checkered pistol grip and forearm, swivels. *Note:* Husqvarna
sporters were first introduced in the U.S. about 1948; earlier models were also available in calibers 6.5×55, 8×57
and 9.3×57. Made 1946–1951.

Husqvarna 1951 Hi-Power Rifle **$345**
Same as 1950 Hi-Power, except has high-comb stock, low
safety.

Husqvarna Series 3000 Crown Grade **$430**
Same as Series 3100, except has Monte Carlo comb stock.

Husqvarna Series 3100 Crown Grade **$450**
HVA improved Mauser action. Calibers: 243, 270, 7mm,
30-06, 308 Win. 5-shot box magazine. 23¾-inch barrel.
Weight: 7¼ pounds. Sights: open rear; hooded ramp front.
European walnut stock, checkered, cheekpiece, pistol-grip
cap, black foretip, swivels. Made 1954–1972.

Husqvarna Series 4000 Lightweight Rifle **$450**
Same as Series 4100, except has no rear sight and has
Monte Carlo comb stock.

Husqvarna Series 4100 Lightweight Rifle **$425**
HVA improved Mauser action. Calibers: 243, 270, 7mm,
30-06, 308 Win. 5-shot box magazine. 20½-inch barrel.
Weight: about 6¼ pounds. Sights: open rear; hooded ramp
front. Lightweight walnut stock w/cheekpiece, pistol grip,
schnabel foretip, checkered, swivels. Made 1954–1972.

**Husqvarna Series 6000 Imperial Custom
Grade** **$595**
Same as Series 3100, except fancy-grade stock, 3-leaf
folding rear sight, adj. trigger. Calibers: 243, 270, 7mm
Rem. Mag., 308, 30-06. Made 1968–1970.

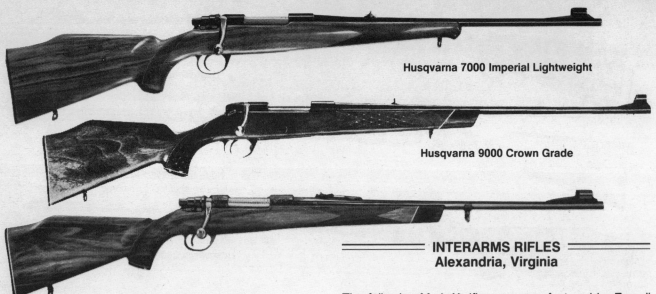

Husqvarna 7000 Imperial Lightweight

Husqvarna 9000 Crown Grade

Husqvarna P-3000 Presentation Grade

Husqvarna Series 7000 Imperial Monte Carlo Lightweight **$550**
Same as Series 4000 Lightweight, except fancy-grade stock, 3-leaf folding rear sight, adj. trigger. Calibers: 243, 270, 308, 30-06. Made 1968–1970.

Husqvarna Model 8000 Imperial Grade Rifle **$550**
Same as Model 9000, except has jeweled bolt, engraved floorplate, deluxe French walnut stock, no sights. Made 1971–72.

Husqvarna Model 9000 Crown Grade Rifle **$395**
New design Husqvarna bolt action. Adj. trigger. Calibers: 270, 7mm Rem. Mag., 30-06, 300 Win. Mag. 5-shot box magazine, hinged floorplate. 23³/₄-inch barrel. Sights: folding leaf rear; hooded ramp front. Checkered walnut stock w/Monte Carlo cheekpiece, rosewood forearm tip and pistol-grip cap. Weight: 7 lbs. 3 oz. Made 1971–72.

Husqvarna Series P-3000 Presentation Rifle . . . **$695**
Same as Crown Grade Series 3000, except w/selected stock, engraved action, adj. trigger. Calibers: 243, 270, 7mm Rem. Mag., 30-06. Made 1968–1970.

INTERARMS RIFLES
Alexandria, Virginia

The following Mark X rifles are manufactured by Zavodi Crvena Zastava, Belgrade, Yugoslavia.

Interarms Mark X Alaskan **$410**
Same specifications as Mark X Sporter, except calibers 375 H&H Mag. and 458 Win. Mag., 3-round magazine, weighs 8¹/₄ pounds, has stock with recoil-absorbing cross bolt and heavy duty recoil pad. Made 1976–1984.

Interarms Mark X Bolt Action Sporter Series
Mauser-type action. Calibers: 22-250, 243, 25-06, 270, 7×57, 7mm Rem. Mag., 308, 30-06, 300 Win. Mag. 5-shot magazine (3-shot in Magnum calibers). 24-inch barrel. Weight: 7¹/₂ pounds. Sights: adj. leaf rear; ramp front, with hood. Classic-style stock of European walnut w/ Monte Carlo comb and cheekpiece, checkered pistol grip and forearm, black forend tip, QD swivels. Made 1972 to date.
American Field Model, Std. (Rubber recoil Pad) . . **$465**
American Field, Magnum (Rubber recoil Pad) . . . **495**
Mark X Standard Model **295**

Interarms Mark X Cavalier **$325**
Same specifications as Mark X Sporter, except has contemporary-style stock with rollover cheekpiece, rosewood forend tip/grip cap, recoil pad. Introduced 1974; disc.

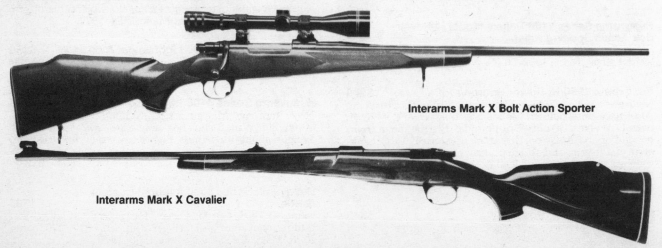

Interarms Mark X Bolt Action Sporter

Interarms Mark X Cavalier

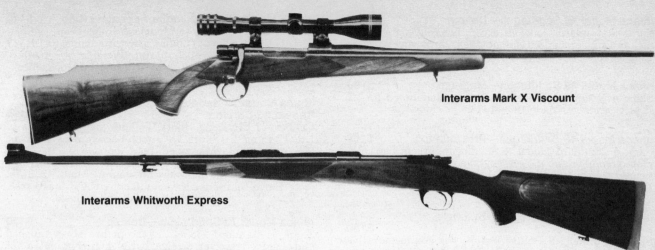

Interarms Mark X Viscount

Interarms Whitworth Express

RIFLES

Interarms Mark X Continental Mannlicher Style Carbine **$385**

Same specifications as Mark X Sporter, except straight European-style comb stock w/sculptured cheekpiece. Precise double-set triggers and classic "butter-knife" bolt handle. French checkering. Weight: about 7¼ pounds. Discontinued.

Interarms Mark X Marquis Mannlicher Style Carbine **$395**

Same specifications as Mark X Sporter, except has 20-inch barrel, full-length Mannlicher-type stock with metal forend/muzzle cap. Calibers: 270, 7×57, 308, 30-06. Made 1976 to date.

Interarms Mini-Mark X Bolt Action Rifle **$325**

Miniature M98 Mauser action. Caliber: 223 Rem. 5-shot magazine. 20-inch barrel. 39¾ inches overall. Weight: 6¼

Interarms Mini-Mark X Bolt Action Rifle (cont.)

pounds. Adj. rear sight, hooded ramp front. Checkered hardwood stock. Imported 1987 to date.

Interarms Mark X Viscount **$335**

Same specifications as Mark X Sporter, except has plainer field grade stock. Made 1974–1987.

Interarms Whitworth Express Rifle, African Series **$495**

Mauser-type bolt action. Calibers: 375 H&H Mag., 458 Win. Mag. 3-shot magazine. 24-inch barrel. Weight: about 8 pounds. Sights: 3-leaf express open rear; ramp front, with hood. English-style stock of European walnut, w/ cheekpiece, black forend tip, checkered pistol grip and forearm, recoil pad, QD swivels. Made 1974 to date by Whitworth Rifle Co., England.

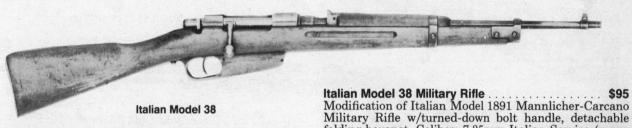

Italian Model 38

══ ITALIAN MILITARY RIFLES ══
Manufactured by Government plants at Brescia, Gardone, Terni and Turin, Italy

Italian Model 38 Military Rifle **$95**

Modification of Italian Model 1891 Mannlicher-Carcano Military Rifle w/turned-down bolt handle, detachable folding bayonet. Caliber: 7.35mm Italian Service (many arms of this model were later converted to the old 6.5mm caliber). 6-shot box magazine. 21¼-inch barrel. Weight: about 7½ pounds. Sights: adj. rear; blade front. Military straight-grip stock. Adopted 1938.

Ithaca Model 49 Deluxe

══ ITHACA GUN COMPANY, INC. ══
King Ferry (formerly Ithaca), New York

Ithaca Model 49 Saddlegun Lever Action Single Shot Rifle **$80**

Martini-type action. Hand-operated rebounding hammer. Caliber: 22 LR, Long, Short. 18-inch barrel. Open sights. Western carbine-style stock. Weight: 5½ pounds. Made 1961–1978.

Ithaca Model 49 Saddlegun—Deluxe **$95**
Same as standard Model 49, except has gold-plated hammer and trigger, figured walnut stock, sling swivels. Made 1962–1975.

Ithaca Model 49 Saddlegun—Magnum **$100**
Same as standard Model 49, except chambered for 22 WMR cartridge. Made 1962–1978.

Ithaca Model 49 Saddlegun—Presentation **$160**
Same as standard Model 49 Saddlegun, except has gold-plated hammer and trigger, engraved receiver, full fancy-figured walnut stock w/gold nameplate. Available in 22 LR or 22 WMR. Made 1962–1974.

**Ithaca Model 49 Saddlegun—St. Louis
Bicentennial** **$180**
Same as Model 49 Deluxe, except has commemorative inscription. 200 made in 1964. Value is for rifle in new, unfired condition.

Ithaca Model 49 Youth Saddlegun **$85**
Same as standard Model 49, except shorter stock for young shooters. Made 1961–1978.

Ithaca Model 49R Saddlegun Repeating Rifle . . . **$140**
Similar in appearance to Model 49 Single Shot. Caliber: 22 LR, Long, Short. Tubular magazine holds 15 LR, 17 Long, 21 Short. 20-inch barrel. Weight: 5½ pounds. Sights: open rear; bead front. Western-style stock, checkered grip. Made 1968–1971.

**Ithaca Model 72 Saddlegun Lever Action
Repeating Carbine** **$195**
Caliber: 22 LR, Long, Short. Tubular magazine holds 15 LR, 17 Long, 21 Short. 18½-inch barrel. Weight: about 5½ pounds. Soghts: open rear; hooded ramp front. Receiver grooved for scope mounting. Western carbine stock and forearm of American walnut. Made 1973–78. *Note:* Barrel and action are manufactured by Erma-Werke, Dachau, W. Germany; wood installed by Ithaca.

Ithaca Model 72 Saddlegun—Deluxe **$180**
Same as standard Model 72, except has silver-finished and engraved receiver, octagon barrel, higher grade walnut stock and forearm. Made 1974–76.

Ithaca Model 72 Saddlegun—Magnum **$175**
Same as standard Model 72, except chambered for 22 WMR, has 11-shot tubular magazine, 18½-inch barrel. Made 1975–78.

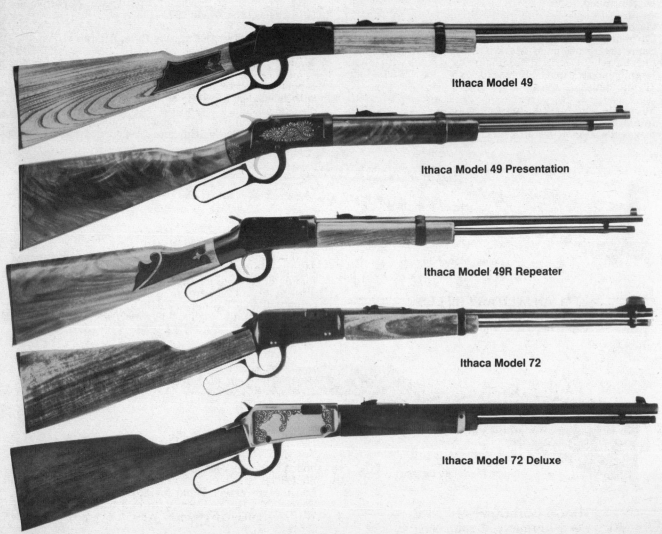

Ithaca Model 49

Ithaca Model 49 Presentation

Ithaca Model 49R Repeater

Ithaca Model 72

Ithaca Model 72 Deluxe

RIFLES

Ithaca Model LSA-55 Bolt Action

Ithaca Model LSA-55 Deluxe

Ithaca Model LSA-65 Standard

Ithaca Model X5-T

Ithaca Model X-15

Ithaca Model LSA-55 Bolt Action Standard Grade Repeating Rifle **$375**
Mauser-type action. Calibers: 222 Rem., 22-250, 6mm Rem., 243 Win., 308 Win. 3-shot detachable clip magazine. 22-inch barrel. Weight: 6½ pounds. Sights: folding leaf rear; hooded ramp front. Checkered walnut stock w/Monte Carlo cheekpiece, detachable swivels. Made 1969–1977. Mfd. by Oy Tikkakoski AB, Tikkakoski, Finland.

Ithaca Model LSA-55 Deluxe **$405**
Same as Model LSA-55 Standard Grade, except has roll-over cheekpiece, rosewood grip-cap and forend tip, skip checkering, high-luster blue, no iron sights, scope mount standard equipment. Made 1969–1977.

Ithaca Model LSA-55 Heavy Barrel **$400**
Same as Model LSA-55, except calibers 222 Rem. and 22-250 only; has 23-inch heavy barrel, no sights, special stock with beavertail forearm, weighs about 8½ pounds. Made 1974–77.

Ithaca Model LSA-65 Bolt Action Standard Grade **$370**
Same as Model LSA-55 Standard Grade, except calibers 25-06, 270, 30-06; 4-shot magazine, 23-inch barrel, weighs 7 pounds. Made 1969–1977.

Ithaca Model LSA-65 Deluxe **$410**
Same as Model LSA-65 Standard Grade, except has special features of Model LSA-55 Deluxe. Made 1969–1977.

Ithaca Model X5-C Lightning Autoloader Clip Repeating Rifle **$105**
Takedown. Caliber: 22 LR. 7-shot clip magazine. 22-inch barrel. Weight: 6 pounds. Sights: open rear; Raybar front. Pistol-grip stock, grooved forearm. Made 1958–1964.

Ithaca Model X5-T Lightning Autoloader Tubular Repeating Rifle **$115**
Same as Model X5-C except has 16-shot tubular magazine, stock with plain forearm. Made 1959–1963.

Ithaca Model X-15 Lightning Autoloader **$110**
Same general specifications as Model X5-C, except forearm is not grooved. Made 1964–67.

Ithaca-BSA CF-2

Ithaca-BSA CF-2 Bolt Action Repeating Rifle ... **$325**
Mauser-type action. Calibers: 7mm Rem. Mag., 300 Win.
Mag. 3-shot magazine. 23.6-inch barrel. Weight: 8 pounds.

Ithaca-BSA CF-2 Bolt Action Repeater (cont.)
Sights: adj. rear; hooded ramp front. Checkered walnut
stock w/Monte Carlo comb, rollover cheekpiece, rosewood
forend tip, recoil pad, sling swivels. Made 1976–77. Mfd.
by BSA Guns Ltd., Birmingham, England.

Japanese Model 38

Japanese Model 99

JAPANESE MILITARY RIFLES
Tokyo, Japan
Manufactured by Government Plant

Japanese Model 38 Arisaka Carbine **$130**
Same general specifications as Model 38 Rifle, except has
19-inch barrel, heavy folding bayonet, weighs about 7¼
pounds.

Japanese Model 38 Arisaka Service Rifle **$135**
Mauser-type bolt action. Caliber: 6.5mm Japanese. 5-shot
box magazine. Barrel lengths: 25³⁄₈ and 31¼ inches.
Weight: about 9¼ pounds w/long barrel. Sights: fixed
front; adj. rear. Military-type full stock. Adopted in 1905,
the 38th year of the Meiji reign; hence, the designation
"Model 38."

Japanese Model 44 Cavalry Carbine **$195**
Same general specifications as Model 38 Rifle except has
19-inch barrel, heavy folding bayonet, weighs about 8½
pounds. Adopted in 1911, the 44th year of the Meiji reign;
hence, the designation "Model 44."

Japanese Model 99 Service Rifle **$165**
Modified Model 38. Caliber: 7.7mm Japanese. 5-shot box
magazine. 25³⁄₄-inch barrel. Weight: about 8³⁄₄ pounds.
Sights: fixed front; adj. aperture rear; anti-aircraft sighting
bars on some early models; fixed rear sight on some late
WWII rifles. Military-type full stock, may have bipod.
Takedown paratroop model was also made during WWII.
Adopted in 1939, Japanese year 2599 from which the designation "Model 99" is taken. *Note:* The last Model 99
rifles made were of poor quality; some have cast steel receivers. Value shown is for earlier type.

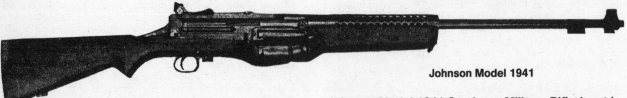

Johnson Model 1941

JOHNSON AUTOMATICS, INC.
Providence, Rhode Island

Johnson Model 1941 Semiauto Military Rifle .. **$1295**
Short-recoil-operated. Removable, air-cooled, 22-inch
barrel. Calibers: 30-06, 7mm Mauser. 10-shot rotary magazine. Two-piece, wood stock, pistol grip; perforated metal

Johnson Model 1941 Semiauto Military Rifle (cont.)
radiator sleeve over rear half of barrel. Sights: receiver
peep; protected post front. Weight: 9½ pounds. *Note:* The
Johnson M/1941 was adopted by the Netherlands Government in 1940–41 and the major portion of the production of this rifle, 1941–43, was on Dutch orders. A quantity
was also bought by the U.S. Government for use by Marine
Corps parachute troops (1943) and for Lend Lease. All
these rifles were caliber 30-06; the 7mm Johnson rifles
were made for a South American government.

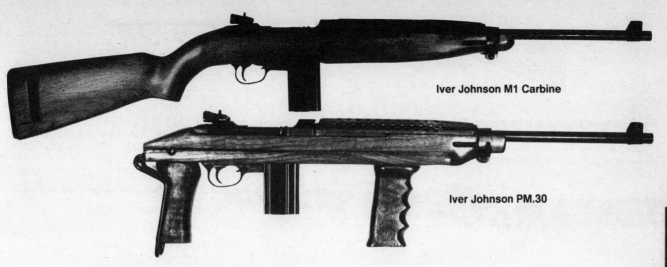

Iver Johnson M1 Carbine

Iver Johnson PM.30

IVER JOHNSON'S ARMS, INC.
Jacksonville, Arkansas
Formerly of Fitchburg, Massachusetts, and Middlesex, New Jersey

Iver Johnson Model 5100A1 Bolt Action Rifle . . **$3850**
Single-shot long-range rifle with removable bolt for breech loading. Caliber: 50BMG. Flutted 29-inch barrel with muzzle break. 51½ inches overall. Adj. composition stock w/folding bipod. Scope rings; no sights.

Iver Johnson Li'l Champ Bolt Action Rifle **$75**
Caliber: 22 S, L, LR. Single shot. 16¼-inch barrel. 32½ inches overall. Weight: 3¼ pounds. Adjustable rear sight, blade front. Synthetic composition stock. Made 1986–88.

Iver Johnson Model M-1 Semiautomatic Carbine
Similar to U.S. M-1 Carbine. Calibers: 9mm Parabellum, 30 U.S. Carbine. 15- or 30-shot magazine. 18-inch barrel. 35½ inches overall. Weight: 6½ pounds. Sights: blade front, with guards; adj. peep rear. Walnut, hardwood or collapsible wire stock. Parkerized finish.
Model M-1 (30 cal. w/hardwood) **$265**
Model M-1 (30 cal. w/walnut) 290
Model M-1 (30 cal. w/wire) 350

Iver Johnson Model M-1 Carbine (cont.)
Model M-1 (9mm w/hardwood) **$345**
Model M-1 (9mm w/walnut) 365
Model M-1 (9mm w/wire) 395

Iver Johnson Model PM.30 Semiautomatic Carbine **$270**
Similar to U.S. Carbine, Cal. .30 M1. 18-inch barrel. Weight: about 5½ pounds. 15- or 30-round detachable magazine. Both hardwood and walnut stock.

Iver Johnson Model SC30FS Semiautomatic Carbine **$295**
Similar to Survival Carbine except has folding stock. Made 1983 to date.

Iver Johnson Survival Semiautomatic Carbine . . **$325**
Similar to Model PM.30 except in stainless steel w/high-impact plastic, one-piece stock. Made 1983 to date. W/ folding high-impact plastic stock add $35.

Iver Johnson Trailblazer Semiauto Rifle **$135**
Caliber: 22 LR. 18-inch barrel. Weight: 5½ pounds. Sights: open rear; blade front. Hardwood stock. Made 1983–85.

Iver Johnson Model SC30FS

Iver Johnson Survival Carbine

Iver Johnson Trailblazer

RIFLES

Iver Johnson Model 2X

Iver Johnson Model X Bolt Action Rifle $110
Takedown. Single shot. Caliber: 22 Short, Long and LR. 22-inch barrel. Weight: about 4 pounds. Sights: open rear; blade front. Pistol-grip stock w/knob forend tip. Made 1928–1932.

Iver Johnson Model XX (2X) Bolt Action $115
Improved version of the Model X, has heavier 24-inch barrel, larger stock (w/o knob tip), weighs about 4½ pounds. Made 1932–1955.

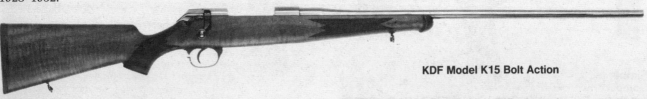

KDF Model K15 Bolt Action

K.D.F. INC.
Sequin, Texas

KDF Model K15 Bolt Action Rifle
Calibers: (Standard) 22-250, 243 Win., 6mm Rem., 25-06, 270 Win., 280 Rem., 7mm Mag., 30-06; (Magnum) 300 Wby., 300 Win., 338 Win., 340 Wby., 375 H&H, 411 KFD,

KDF Model K15 Bolt Action Rifle (cont.)
416 Rem., 458 Win. 4-shot magazine (standard), 3-shot (magnum). 22-inch (standard) or 24-inch (magnum) barrel. 44½ to 46½ inches overall. Weight: 8 pounds. Sights optional. Kevlar composite or checkered walnut stock in classic, European or thumbhole-style.

Standard Model	**$1150**
Magnum Model	**1350**

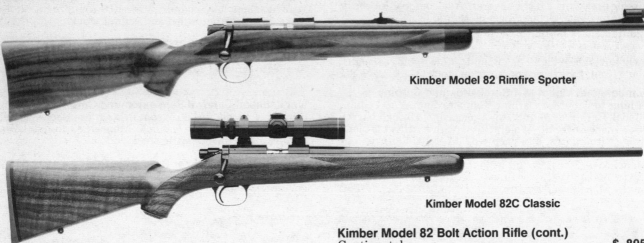

Kimber Model 82 Rimfire Sporter

Kimber Model 82C Classic

KIMBER OF AMERICA, INC.
Clackamas, Oregon
(Formerly Kimber of Oregon, Inc., Colton, OR)

Kimber Model 82 Bolt Action Rifle
Small action based on the Kimber "A" Model 82 rimfire receiver with twin rear locking lugs. Calibers: 22 LR, 22 WRF, 22 Hornet, 218 Bee, 25-20. 5- or 10-shot magazine (22 LR); 5-shot magazine (22WRF); 3-shot magazine (22 Hornet). 218 Bee and 25-20 are single shot. 18- to 25-inch barrel. 37⅝ to 42½ inches overall. Weight: 6 lbs. (Light Sporter); 6½ lbs. (Sporter); 7½ lbs. (Varmint); 10¾ lbs. (Target). Right- and left-hand actions are available in distinctive stock styles.

Cascade (discontinued 1987)	**$ 640**
Classic (discontinued 1988)	**595**

Kimber Model 82 Bolt Action Rifle (cont.)

Continental	**$ 895**
Custom Classic (discontinued 1988)	**685**
Mini Classic	**475**
Super America	**875**
Super Continental	**1100**
1990 Classifications	
All-American Match	**650**
Deluxe Grade (discontinued 1990)	**925**
Hunter (Laminated Stock)	**635**
Super America	**825**
Target (Government Match)	**495**

Kimber Model 82C Classic Bolt Action Rifle
Caliber: 22 LR. 4-shot or 10-shot magazine. 21-inch air-gauged barrel. 40½ inches overall. Weight: 6½ pounds. Receiver drilled and tapped for Warne scope mounts; no sights. Single-set trigger. Checkered Claro walnut stock w/red buttpad and polished steel grip cap. Reintroduced 1993.

Classic Model	**$575**
Left-Hand Model, **add**	**75**

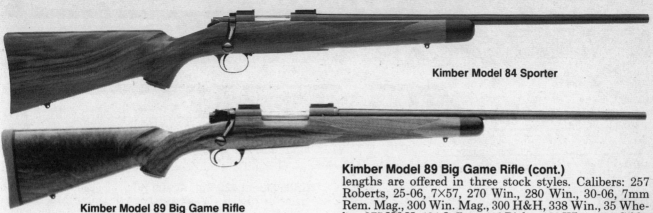

Kimber Model 84 Sporter

Kimber Model 89 Big Game Rifle

Kimber Model 84 Bolt Action Rifle

Compact medium action based on a "scaled down" Mauser-type receiver, designed to accept small base centerfire cartridges. Calibers: 17 Rem., 221 Fireball, 222 Rem., 223 Rem. 5-shot magazine. Same general barrel and stock specifications as Model 82.

Classic (discontinued 1988)...................	$ 650
Continental	895
Custom Classic (Discontinued 1988)	850
Super America (Discontinued 1988)	975
Super Continental (Discontinued 1988)	1125
1990 Classifications	
Deluxe Grade (Discontinued 1990)	895
Hunter/Sporter (Laminated Stock)	725
Super America (discontinued 1991)	995
Super Varmint (discontinued 1991)	1025
Ultra Varmint (discontinued 1991)	950

Kimber Model 89 Big Game Rifle

A large action combining the best features of the pre-64 Model 70 Winchester and the Mauser 98. Three action

Kimber Model 89 Big Game Rifle (cont.)

lengths are offered in three stock styles. Calibers: 257 Roberts, 25-06, 7×57, 270 Win., 280 Win., 30-06, 7mm Rem. Mag., 300 Win. Mag., 300 H&H, 338 Win., 35 Whelen, 375 H&H, 404 Jeffrey, 416 Rigby, 460 Wby., 505 Gibbs (308 cartridge family to follow). 5-shot magazine (standard calibers); 3-shot magazine (Magnum calibers). 22- to 24-inch barrel. 42 to 44 inches overall. Weight: 7½ to 10½ lbs. Model 89 African features express sights on contoured quarter rib, banded front sight. Barrel-mounted recoil lug w/integral receiver lug and twin recoil crosspins in stock.

BGR Long Action Classic (disc. 1988)	$ 795
Custom Classic (discontinued 1988)	950
Super America	1095
1990 Classifications	
Deluxe Grade	
Featherweight	1295
Medium	1325
375 H&H	1350
Hunter Grade (Laminated Stock)	
270 and 30-06	925
375 H&H	1150
Super America	
Featherweight	1495
Medium	1570
375 H&H	2000
African—All calibers	3395

Krico Model 311

KRICO RIFLES
Stuttgart-Hedelfingen, Germany
Mfd. by Sportwaffenfabrik Kriegeskorte GmbH

Krico rifles currently imported are available thru Beeman Precision Arms, Inc., Santa Rosa, CA.

Krico Model 311 Small Bore Rifle

Bolt action. Caliber: 22 LR. 5- or 10-shot clip magazine. 22-inch barrel. Weight: about 6 pounds. Single- or double-set trigger. Sights: open rear; hooded ramp front; available with factory-fitted Kaps 2½× scope. Checkered stock w/ cheekpiece, pistol grip and swivels.

Krico Model 311 Small Bore Rifle (cont.)

W/Scope Sight	$325
W/Iron Sights Only	280

Krico Model 260 Semiautomatic Rifle $465

Caliber: 22 LR. 10-shot magazine. 20-inch barrel. 38.9 inches overall. Weight: 6.6 pounds. Hooded blade front sight; adj. rear. Grooved receiver. Beech stock. Blued finish. Imported 1991 to date.

Krico Model 300 Bolt Action Rifle

Calibers: 22 LR, 22 WMR, 22 Hornet. 19.6-inch barrel (22 LR), 23.6-inch (22 Hornet). 38½ inches overall. Weight: 6.3 pounds. Double-set triggers. Sights: ramped blade front; adjustable open rear. Checkered walnut-finished hardwood stock. Blued finish. Made 1993 to date.

Model 300 Standard...........................	$525
Model 300 Deluxe	560
Model 300 SA (Monte-Carlo walnut stock)	565
Model 300 Stutzen (full-length walnut stock)	620

RIFLES

Krico Model 320 Sporter

Krico Model 340
Metallic Silhouette Rifle

Krico Model 320 Bolt Action Sporter **$550**
Caliber: 22 LR. 5-shot detachable box magazine. 19½-inch barrel. 38½ inches overall. Weight: 6 pounds. Adj. rear sight, blade ramp front. Checkered European walnut Mannlicher-style stock w/low comb and cheekpiece. Single or double-set triggers. Discontinued 1989.

Krico Model 340 Metallic Silhouette Bolt Action Rifle **$595**
Caliber: 22 LR. 5-shot magazine. 21-inch heavy, bull barrel. 39½ inches overall. Weight: 7½ pounds. No sights. Grooved receiver for scope mounts. European walnut stock in off-hand match-style configuration. Match or double-set triggers. Imported 1983–86.

Krico Model 360S Biathlon Rifle **$1025**
Caliber: 22 LR. Five 5-shot magazines. 21¼-inch barrel with snow cap. 40½ inches overall. Weight: 9¼ pounds. Straight-pull action. Match trigger with 17½ oz. pull. Sights: globe front; adjustable match peep rear. Biathlon-style walnut stock with high comb and adjustable buttplate. Made 1991 to date.

Krico Model 360 S2 Biathlon Rifle **$950**
Similar to the Model 360S, except with pistol-grip activated action. Biathlon-style walnut stock with black epoxy finish. Made 1991 to date.

Krico Model 400 Bolt Action Rifle **$710**
Caliber: 22 Hornet. 5-shot detachable box magazine. 23½-inch barrel. Weight: 6¾ pounds. Adj. open rear sight, ramp front. European walnut stock. Discontinued 1990.

Krico Model 420 Bolt Action Rifle **$695**
Same as Model 400, except has full-length Mannlicher-style stock and double-set triggers. Scope optional, extra. Discontinued 1989.

Krico Model 440 S Bolt Action Rifle **$650**
Caliber: 22 Hornet. Detachable box magazine. 20-inch barrel. 36½ inches overall. Weight: 7½ pounds. No sights. French walnut stock w/ventilated forend. Discont. 1988.

Krico Model 500 Match Rifle **$3000**
Caliber: 22 LR. Single shot. 23.6-inch barrel. 42 inches overall. Weight: 9.4 pounds. Kricotronic electronic ignition system. Sights: globe front; match micrometer aperture rear. Match-style European walnut stock w/adj. butt.

Krico Model 600 Bolt Action Rifle **$995**
Same general specifications as Model 700, except with short action. Calibers: 17 Rem., 222, 223, 22-250, 243, 5.6×50 Mag. and 308.

Krico Model 620 Bolt Action Rifle **$895**
Same as Model 600, except has short action chambered 308 Win. only and full-length Mannlicher-style stock with schnabel forend tip. 20¾-inch barrel. Weight: 6½ pounds. No longer imported.

Krico Model 640 Super Sniper Bolt Action Repeating Rifle **$1095**
Calibers: 223 Rem., 308 Win. 3-shot magazine. 26-inch barrel. 44¾ inches overall. Weight: 9½ pounds. No sights, drilled and tapped for scope mounts. Single or double-set triggers. Select walnut stock with adjustable cheekpiece and recoil pad. Discontinued 1989.

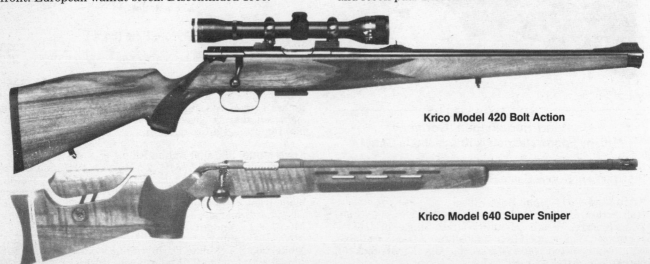

Krico Model 420 Bolt Action

Krico Model 640 Super Sniper

Krico Bolt Action Sporting Rifle

Krico Model 640 Varmint Rifle **$695**
Caliber: 222 Rem. 4-shot magazine. 23³/₄-inch barrel.
Weight: 9¹/₂ pounds. No sights. European walnut stock.
No longer imported.

Krico Model 700 Bolt Action Rifle
Calibers: 17 Rem., 222, 222 Rem. Mag., 223, 22-250, 5.6×50
Mag., 243, 5.6×57 RSW, 6×62, 6.5×55, 6.5×57, 6.5×68,
270 Win., 7×64, 7.5 Swiss, 7mm Mag., 30-06, 300 Win.,
8×68S, 9.3×64. 24-inch (standard) or 26-inch (magnum)
barrel. 44 inches overall (standard). Weight: 7¹/₂ pounds.
Adj. rear sight; hooded ramp front. Checkered European-
style walnut stock w/Bavarian cheekpiece and rosewood
schnabel forend tip. Imported 1983 to date.
Model 700 . . . . **$ 750**
Model 700 Deluxe **850**
Model 700 Deluxe S **1120**
Model 700 Stutzen **970**

Krico Model 720 Bolt Action Rifle
Same general specifications as Model 700, except in cal-
ibers 270 Win. and 30-06 with full-length Mannlicher-
style stock and schnabel forend tip. 20³/₄-inch barrel.
Weight: 6³/₄ pounds. Discontinued importing 1990.
Sporter Model . . . . **$ 950**
Ltd. Edition **1695**

Krico Bolt Action Sporting Rifle **$535**
Miniature Mauser action. Single- or double-set trigger.
Calibers: 22 Hornet, 222 Rem. 4-shot clip magazine. 22-,
24- or 26-inch barrel. Weight: about 6¹/₄ pounds. Sights:
open rear; hooded ramp front. Checkered stock w/cheek-
piece, pistol grip, black forend tip, sling swivels. Made
1956–1962.

Krico Carbine **$450**
Same as Krico Sporting Rifle, except has 20- or 22-inch
barrel, full-length Mannlicher-type stock.

Krico Special Varmint Rifle **$525**
Same as Krico Rifle, except has heavy barrel, no sights,
weighs about 7¹/₄ pounds. Caliber: 222 Rem. only.

RIFLES

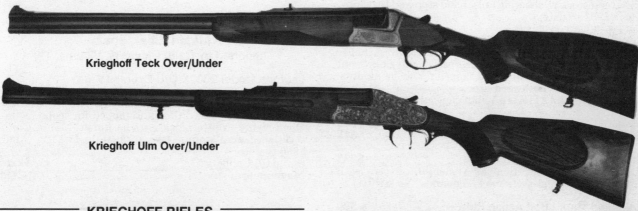

Krieghoff Teck Over/Under

Krieghoff Ulm Over/Under

=== **KRIEGHOFF RIFLES** ===
Ulm (Donau), Germany
Mfd. by H. Krieghoff Jagd und Sportwaffenfabrik

See also combination guns under Krieghoff shotgun listings.

Krieghoff Teck Over/Under Rifle
Kersten action, double crossbolt, double underlugs. Boxlock. Calibers: 7×57r5, 7×64, 7×65r5, 30-30, 308 Win.,
30-06, 300 Win. Mag., 9.3×74r5, 375 H&H Mag., 458 Win.
Mag. 25-inch barrels. Weight: 8 to 9¹/₂ pounds. Sights:
express rear; ramp front. Checkered walnut stock and
forearm. Made 1967 to date.

Krieghoff Teck Over/Under Rifle (cont.)
Standard calibers **$4925**
375 H&H Mag. (disc. 1988), 458 Win. Mag. **5850**

Krieghoff Ulm Over/Under Rifle **$7950**
Same general specifications as Teck model, except has
sidelocks with leaf arabesque engraving. Made 1963 to
date.

Krieghoff ULM-Primus Over/Under Rifle **$9750**
Deluxe version of Ulm model, has detachable sidelocks,
higher grade engraving and stock wood. Made 1963 to
date.

=== **LAKEFIELD ARMS LTD.** ===
Ontario, Canada

Lakefield Model 64B Semiautomatic Rifle **$120**
Caliber: 22 LR. 10-shot magazine. 20-inch barrel. Weight:
5¹/₂ pounds. 40 inches overall. Bead front sight, adjustable

Lakefield Model 64B

Lakefield Model 92S

Lakefield Mark I

Lakefield Mark II Bolt Action Rifle (cont.)
Mark II Standard .... $ 95
Mark II Youth (19-inch barrel) 95
Mark II Left-hand 105

L.A.R. MANUFACTURING, INC.
West Jordan, Utah

L.A.R. Big Boar Competitor Bolt Action Rifle ... **$1595**
Single shot, bull-pup action. Caliber: 50 BMG. 36-inch
barrel. 45½ inches overall. Weight: 28.4 pounds. Made
1994 to date.

LAURONA RIFLES
Mfd.in Eibar, Spain
Imported by Galaxy Imports, Victoria, TX

Laurona Model 2000X O/U Express Rifle
Calibers: 30-06, 8×57 JRS, 8×75 JR, 375 H&H, 9.3×74R
5-shot magazine. 24-inch separated barrels. Weight: 8½
pounds. Quarter rib drilled and tapped for scope mount.
Open sights. Matte black chrome finish. Monte Carlo-
style checkered walnut buttstock; tulip forearm. Made
1993 to date.
Standard Calibers $2250
Magnum Calibers 2795

LUNA RIFLE
Mehlis, Germany
Manufactured by Ernst Friedr. Büchel

Luna Single Shot Target Rifle **$895**
Falling block action. Calibers: 22 LR, 22 Hornet. 29-inch
barrel. Weight: about 8¼ pounds. Sights: micrometer peep
rear tang; open rear; ramp front. Cheekpiece stock w/full
pistol grip, semibeavertail forearm, checkered, swivels.
Made before WWII.

Lakefield Model 64B Semiautomatic (cont.)
rear. Grooved receiver for scope mounts. Checkered walnut-finished hardwood stock with Monte Carlo. Made
1990 to date.

Lakefield Model 90B Bolt Action Target Rifle ... **$350**
Caliber: 22 LR. 5-shot magazine. 21-inch barrel w/snow
cap. 39⅝ inches overall. Weight: 8¼ pounds. Adj. receiver
peep sight; globe front w/inserts. Receiver drilled and
tapped for scope mounts. Biathlon-style natural finished
hardwood stock w/shooting rails, hand stop and butthook.
Made 1991 to date.

Lakefield Model 91T/91TR Bolt Action Target Rifle
Calibers: 22 Short, Long, LR. 25-inch barrel. 43⅝ inches
overall. Weight: 8 pounds. Adj. rear peep sight; globe front
w/inserts. Receiver drilled and tapped for scope mounts.
Walnut finished hardwood stock w/shooting rails and
hand stop. **Model 91TR** is a 5-shot clip-fed repeater. Made
1991 to date.
Model 91T Single Shot **$295**
Model 91TR Repeater (22 LR only) 315

Lakefield Model 92S Target Rifle **$275**
Same general specifications as Model 90B, except with
conventional target-style stock. 8 pounds. No sights.

Lakefield Mark I Bolt Action Rifle **$90**
Calibers: 22 Short, Long, LR. Single-shot. 20½-inch barrel
(19-inch Youth Model); available in smoothbore. Weight:
5½ pounds. 39½ inches overall. Bead front sight; adj.
rear. Grooved receiver for scope mounts. Checkered walnut-finished hardwood stock w/Monte Carlo and pistol
grip. Blued finish. Made 1990 to date.

Lakefield Mark II Bolt Action Rifle
Same general specifications as the Mark I, except in the
repeater version with 10-shot clip magazine in 22 LR only.

Luna Single Shot Target Rifle

**Magnum Research
Mountain Eagle Bolt Action Rifle**

MAGNUM RESEARCH, INC.
Minneapolis, Minnesota

**Magnum Research Mountain Eagle Bolt Action
Rifle** **$1150**
Calibers: 270 Win., 280 Rem., 7mm Rem. Mag., 30-06, 300
Win. Mag., 338 Win. Mag. 5-shot (Std.) or 4-shot (Mag.).
24-inch barrel. 44 inches overall. Weight: 7³/₄ pounds.
Receiver drilled and tapped for scope mount; no sights.
Blued finish. Fiberglass composite stock. 1000 made 1994.

MANNLICHER SPORTING RIFLES
Steyr, Austria
Manufactured by Steyr-Daimler-Puch, A.-G.

In 1967, Steyr-Daimler-Puch introduced a series of sporting
rifles with a bolt action that is a departure from the Mannlicher-Schoenauer system of earlier models. In the latter,
the action is locked by lugs symmetrically arranged behind
the bolt head as well as by placing the bolt handle ahead
of the right flank of the receiver, the rear section of which
is open on top for backward movement of the bolt handle.
The current action, made in four lengths to accommodate
different ranges of cartridges, has a closed-top receiver;
the bolt locking lugs are located toward the rear of the bolt
(behind the magazine), and the Mannlicher-Schoenauer rotary magazine has been redesigned as a detachable box
type of Makrolon.

Mannlicher Model L Carbine **$995**
Same general specifications as Model SL Carbine, except
has type "L" action, weighs about 6.2 pounds. Calibers
same as for Model L Rifle. Made 1968 to date.

Mannlicher Model L Rifle **$1050**
Same general specifications as Model SL Rifle, except has
type "L" action, weighs about 6.3 pounds. Calibers: 22-
250, 5.6×57 (discontinued 1991), 243 Win., 6mm Rem.,
308 Win. Made 1968 to date.

Mannlicher Model L Varmint Rifle **$1065**
Same general specifications as Model SL Varmint Rifle,
except has type "L" action. Calibers: 22-250, 243 Win.,
308 Win. Made 1969 to date.

Mannlicher Model Luxus Bolt Action Rifle
Same general specifications as Models L and M, except
with 3-shot detachable box magazine and single-set trigger. Full or half-stock with low-luster oil or high-gloss
lacquer finish.
Full stock **$1325**
Half stock **1295**

Mannlicher Model M Carbine
Same general specifications as Model SL Carbine, except
has type "M" action, stock w/recoil pad, weighs about 6.8
pounds. Made 1969 to date. Left-hand version w/addi-
tional 6.5×55 and 9.3×62 calibers introduced in 1977.
Right-hand Carbine **$1000**
Left-hand Carbine **1250**

RIFLES

Mannlicher Model L Carbine

Mannlicher Model L Rifle

Mannlicher Model M Carbine

Mannlicher Model M Professional

Mannlicher Model M Rifle

Mannlicher Model M Left-hand Rifle

Mannlicher Model SL Carbine

Mannlicher Model SL Rifle
Double-Set Trigger

Mannlicher Model M Professional Rifle **$1025**
Same as standard Model M Rifle, except has synthetic
(Cycolac) stock, weighs about 7½ pounds. Calibers:
6.5×55, 6.5×57, 270 Win., 7×57, 7×64, 7.5 Swiss, 30-06,
8×57JS, 9.3×62. Introduced 1977.

Mannlicher Model M Rifle
Same general specifications as Model SL Rifle, except w/
type "M" action, stock w/forend tip and recoil pad; weighs
about 6.9 pounds. Calibers: 6.5×57, 270 Win., 7×57, 7×64,
30-06, 8×57JS, 9.3×62. Made 1969 to date. Left-hand
version also in calibers 6.5 × 55 and 7.5 Swiss intr. 1977.
Right-hand Rifle . . . . **$ 895**
Left-hand Rifle **1250**

Mannlicher Model S Rifle **$995**
Same general specifications as Model SL Rifle, except has
type "S" action, 4-round magazine, 25⅝-inch barrel, stock
with forend tip and recoil pad, weighs about 8.4 pounds.
Calibers: 6.5×68, 257 Weatherby Mag., 264 Win. Mag.,
7mm Rem. Mag., 300 Win. Mag., 300 H&H Mag., 308
Norma Mag., 8×68S, 338 Win. Mag., 9.3×64, 37 H&H
Mag. Made 1970 to date.

Mannlicher Model SL Carbine **$995**
Same general specifications as Model SL Rifle, except has
20-inch barrel and full-length stock, weighs about 6
pounds. Made 1968 to date.

Mannlicher Model SL Rifle **$960**
Steyr-Mannlicher SL bolt action. Calibers: 222 Rem., 222
Rem. Mag., 223 Rem. 5-shot rotary magazine, detachable.

Mannlicher Model SL Rifle
Single-Set Trigger

Mannlicher Model SSG
Match Target Rifle

> **NOTE:** Certain Mannlicher-Schoenauer models were produced before WWII. Manufacture of sporting rifles and carbines was resumed at the Steyr-Daimler-Puch plant in Austria in 1950 during which time the Model 1950 rifles and carbines were introduced.

Mannlicher Model SL Rifle (cont.)

$23^5/8$-inch barrel. Weight: about 6 pounds. Single- or double-set trigger (mechanisms interchangeable). Sights: open rear; hooded ramp front. Half stock of European walnut w/Monte Carlo comb and cheekpiece, skip-checkered forearm and pistol grip, rubber buttpad, QD swivels. Made 1967 to date.

Mannlicher Model SL Varmint Rifle $995

Same general specifications as Model SL Rifle, except caliber 222 Rem. only, has $25^5/8$-inch heavy barrel, no sights, weighs about 7.92 pounds. Made 1969 to date.

Mannlicher Model SSG Match Target Rifle

Type "L" action. Caliber: 308 Win. (7.62×51 NATO). 5- or 10-round magazine, single-shot plug. $25^1/2$-inch heavy barrel. Weight: $10^1/4$ pounds. Single trigger. Sights: micrometer peep rear; globe front. Target stock, European walnut or synthetic, with full pistol grip, wide forearm w/ swivel rail, adj. rubber buttplate. Made 1969 to date.
W/walnut stock **$1495**
W/synthetic stock **1240**

Mannlicher Model S/T Rifle $1050

Same as Model S Rifle, except has heavy $25^5/8$-inch barrel, weighs about 9 pounds. Calibers: 9.3×64, 375 H&H Mag., 458 Win. Mag. Option of $23^5/8$-inch barrel in latter caliber. Made 1975 to date.

Mannlicher-Schoenauer Model 1903 Bolt Action Sporting Carbine $925

Caliber: 6.5×53mm (referred to in some European gun catalogs as 6.7×53mm, following the Austrian practice of designating calibers by bullet diameter). 5-shot rotary magazine. 450mm (17.7-inch) barrel. Weight: about $6^1/2$ pounds. Double-set trigger. Sights: two-leaf rear; ramp front. Full-length sporting stock w/cheekpiece, pistol grip, trap buttplate, swivels. Pre-WWII.

Mannlicher-Schoenauer Model 1905 Carbine . . . $825

Same as Model 1903, except caliber 9×56mm and has 19.7-inch barrel, weighs about $6^3/4$ pounds. Pre-WWII.

Mannlicher-Schoenauer Model 1908 Carbine . . . $850

Same as Model 1905, except calibers 7×57mm and 8×56mm. Pre-WWII.

Mannlicher-Schoenauer Model 1910 Carbine . . . $995

Same as Model 1905, except in 9.5×57mm. Pre-WWII.

Mannlicher-Schoenauer Model 1924 Carbine . . . $895

Same as Model 1905, except caliber 30-06 (7.62×63mm). Pre-WWII.

Mannlicher-Schoenauer Model 1903
Sporting Carbine

Mannlicher-Schoenauer
Model 1905 Carbine

Mannlicher-Schoenauer Model 1950 Bolt Action Sporting Rifle **$795**
Calibers: 257 Roberts, 270 Win., 30-06. 5-shot rotary magazine. 24-inch barrel. Weight: about 7¼ pounds. Single trigger or double-set trigger. Redesigned low bolt handle, shot-gun-type safety. Sights: folding leaf open rear; hooded ramp front. Improved half-length stock w/cheekpiece, pistol grip, checkered, ebony forend tip, swivels. Made 1950–52.

Mannlicher-Schoenauer Model 1950 Carbine . . . **$750**
Same general specifications as Model 1950 Rifle except has 20-inch barrel, full-length stock, weighs about 7 pounds. Made 1950–52.

Mannlicher-Schoenauer Model 1950 6.5 Carbine **$725**
Same as other Model 1950 Carbines except caliber 6.5×53mm, has 18¼-inch barrel, weighs 6¾ pounds. Made 1950–52.

Mannlicher-Schoenauer Model 1952 Improved Carbine **$895**
Same as Model 1950 Carbine except has swept-back bolt handle, redesigned stock. Calibers: 257, 270, 7mm, 30-06. Made 1952–56.

Mannlicher-Schoenauer Model 1952 Improved 6.5 Carbine **$825**
Same as Model 1952 Carbine except caliber 6.5×53mm, has 18¼-inch barrel. Made 1952–56.

Mannlicher-Schoenauer Model 1952 Improved Sporting Rifle **$675**
Same as Model 1950 except has swept-back bolt handle, redesigned stock. Calibers: 257, 270, 30-06, 9.3×62mm. Made 1952–56.

Mannlicher-Schoenauer Model 1956 Custom Carbine **$795**
Same general specifications as Models 1950 and 1952 Carbines, except has redesigned stock with high comb. Calibers: 243, 6.5mm, 257, 270, 7mm, 30-06, 308. Made 1956–1960.

Mannlicher-Schoenauer Model 1956 Custom Sporting Rifle **$650**
Same general specifications as Models 1950 and 1952 except 22-inch barrel, redesigned stock with high comb. Calibers: 243 and 30-06. Made 1956–1960.

Mannlicher-Schoenauer Carbine, Model 1961-MCA **$650**
Same as Model 1956 Carbine, except has universal Monte Carlo design stock. Calibers: 243 Win., 6.5mm, 270, 308, 30-06. Made 1961–1971.

Mannlicher-Schoenauer Rifle, Model 1961-MCA . . **$725**
Same as Model 1956 Rifle, except has universal Monte Carlo design stock. Calibers: 243, 270, 30-06. Made 1961–1971.

Mannlicher-Schoenauer
Model 1950 Rifle

Mannlicher-Schoenauer
Model 1950 Carbine

Mannlicher-Schoenauer
Model 1952 Carbine

Mannlicher-Schoenauer
Model 1956 Rifle

Mannlicher-Schoenauer
Model 1961-MCA Carbine

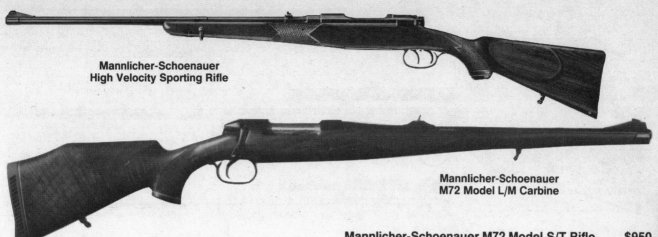

**Mannlicher-Schoenauer
High Velocity Sporting Rifle**

**Mannlicher-Schoenauer
M72 Model L/M Carbine**

**Mannlicher-Schoenauer High Velocity Bolt
Action Sporting Rifle** **$1200**
Calibers: 7×64 Brenneke, 30-06 (7.62×63), 8×60 Magnum,
9.3×62, 10.75×68mm. 23.6-inch barrel. Weight: about 7½
pounds. Sights: British-style 3-leaf open rear; ramp front.
Half-length sporting stock w/cheek-piece, pistol grip,
checkered, trap buttplate, swivels. Also produced in takedown
model. Pre-WWII.

**Mannlicher-Schoenauer M72 Model L/M
Carbine** **$795**
Same general specifications as M72 Model L/M Rifle,
except has 20-inch barrel and full-length stock, weighs
about 7.2 pounds. Made 1972 to date.

Mannlicher-Schoenauer M72 Model L/M Rifle . . **$875**
M72 bolt action, type L/M receiver, front-locking bolt,
internal rotary magazine (5-round). Calibers: 22-250,
5.6×57, 6mm Rem., 243 Win., 6.5×57, 270 Win., 7×57,
7×64, 308 Win., 30-06. 23⅝-inch barrel. Weight: about
7.3 pounds. Single- or double-set trigger (mechanisms interchangeable). Sights: open rear; hooded ramp front. Half
stock of European walnut, checkered forearm and pistol
grip, Monte Carlo cheekpiece, rosewood forend tip, recoil
pad, QD swivels. Made 1972 to date.

Mannlicher-Schoenauer M72 Model S Rifle **$825**
Same general specifications as M72 Model L/M Rifle, except has Magnum action, 4-round magazine, 25⅝-inch
barrel, weighs about 8.6 pounds. Calibers: 6.5×68, 7mm
Rem. Mag., 8×68S, 9.3×64, 375 H&H Mag. Made 1972
to date.

Mannlicher-Schoenauer M72 Model S/T Rifle . . . **$950**
Same as M72 Model S Rifle, except has heavy 25⅝-inch
barrel, weighs about 9.3 pounds. Calibers: 300 Win. Mag.,
9.3×64, 375 H&H Mag., 458 Win. Mag. Option of 23⅝-
inch barrel in latter caliber. Made 1975 to date.

MARLIN FIREARMS CO.
North Haven, Connecticut

Marlin Model 9 Semiautomatic Carbine
Calibers: 9mm Parabellum. 12-shot magazine. 16.5-inch
barrel. 35½ inches overall. Weight: 6¾ pounds. Manual
bolt hold-open. Sights: hooded post front; adj. open rear.
Walnut-finished hardwood stock w/rubber buttpad. Blued
or nickel-Teflon finish. Made 1985 to date.
Model 9 . . . . **$245**
Model 9N (Nickel-Teflon) **295**

Marlin Model 15Y/15YN
Bolt-action, single-shot "Little Buckaroo" rifle. Caliber:
22 Short, Long or LR. 16¼-inch barrel. Weight: 4¼
pounds. Thumb safety. Ramp front sight, adj. open rear.
One-piece walnut Monte Carlo stock w/full pistol grip.
Made 1984–88. Reintroduced in 1989 as Model 15YN.
Model 15Y . . . . **$ 90**
Model 15YN **100**

Marlin Model 18 Baby Slide Action Repeater . . . **$225**
Exposed hammer. Solid frame. Caliber: 22 LR, Long,
Short. Tubular magazine holds 14 Short. 20-inch barrel,

**Marlin Model 9
9mm Carbine**

**Marlin Model 15Y
"Little Buckaroo"**

Marlin Model 20

Marlin Model 25 Bolt Action Rifle

Marlin Model 25M w/Scope

Marlin Model 25MB
Midget Magnum

Marlin Model 18 Baby Slide Action (cont.)
round or octagon. Weight: 3³/₄ pounds. Sights: 0pen rear; bead front. Plain straight-grip stock and slide handle. Made 1906–1909.

Marlin Model 20 Slide Action Repeating Rifle . . . $240
Exposed hammer. Takedown. Caliber: 22 LR, Long, Short. Tubular magazine: half-length holds 15 Short, 12 Long, 10 LR; full-length holds 25 Short, 20 Long, 18 LR. 24-inch octagon barrel. Weight: about 5 pounds. Sights: open rear; bead front. Plain straight-grip stock, grooved slide handle. Made 1907–1922. *Note:* After 1920 was designated "Model 20-S."

Marlin Model 25 Bolt Action Rifle $105
Caliber: 22 Short, Long or LR. 7-shot clip. 22-inch barrel. Weight: 5¹/₂ pounds. Ramp front sight, adj. open rear. One-piece walnut Monte Carlo stock w/full pistol grip. Mar-Shield finish. Made 1984–88.

Marlin Model 25 Slide Action Repeater $255
Exposed hammer. Takedown. Caliber: 22 Short (also handles 22 CB Caps). Tubular magazine holds 15 Short. 23-inch barrel. Weight: about 4 pounds. Sights: open rear; beaded front. Plain straight-grip stock and slide handle. Made 1909–1910.

Marlin Model 25M Bolt Action W/Scope $120
Caliber: 22 WMR. 7-shot clip. 22-inch barrel. Weight: 6 pounds. Ramp front sight w/brass bead, adj. open rear. Walnut-finished stock w/Monte Carlo styling and full pistol grip. Sling swivels. Made 1986–88.

Marlin Model 25MB Midget Magnum $115
Bolt action. Caliber: 22 WMR. 7-shot capacity. 16¹/₄-inch barrel. Weight: 4³/₄ pounds. Walnut-finished Monte Carlo-

Marlin Model 25MB Midget Magnum (cont.)
style stock w/full pistol grip and abbreviated forend. Sights: ramp front w/brass bead, adj. open rear. Thumb safety. Made 1986–88.

Marlin Model 25MN/25N Bolt Action Rifle
Caliber: 22 WMR (Model 25MN) or 22 LR (Model 25N). 7-shot clip magazine. 22-inch barrel. 41 inches overall. Weight: 5¹/₂ to 6 pounds. Adj. open rear sight, ramp front; receiver grooved for scope mounts. One piece walnut-finished hardwood Monte Carlo stock w/pistol grip. Made 1989 to date.
Marlin Model 25MN $125
Marlin Model 25N 115

Marlin Model 27 Slide Action Repeating Rifle . . . $245
Exposed hammer. Takedown. Calibers: 25-20, 32-20. ²/₃ magazine (tubular) holds 7 shots. 24-inch octagon barrel. Weight: about 5³/₄ pounds. Sights: open rear; bead front. Plain straight-grip stock, grooved slide handle. Made 1910–1916.

Marlin Model 27

Marlin Model 27S **$250**
Same as Model 27, except has round barrel, also chambered for 25 Stevens R.F. Made 1920–1932.

Marlin Model 29 Slide Action Repeater **$260**
Similar to Model 20, has 23-inch round barrel, half magazine only, weighs about 5¾ pounds. **Model 37** is same type except has 24-inch barrel and full magazine. Made 1913–1916.

Marlin Model 30AS Lever Action **$195**
Caliber: 30/30 Win. 6-shot tubular magazine. 20-inch barrel with Micro-Groove rifling. 38¼ inches overall. Weight: 7 pounds. Brass bead front sight, adj. rear. Solid top receiver, offset hammer spur for scope use. Walnut-finished hardwood stock w/pistol grip. Mar-Shield finish. Made 1984 to date.

Marlin Model 32 Slide Action Repeater **$265**
Hammerless. Takedown. Caliber: 22 LR, Long, Short. ⅔ tubular magazine holds 15 Short, 12 Long, 10 LR; full magazine, 25 Short, 20 Long, 18 LR. 24-inch octagon barrel. Weight: about 5½ pounds. Sights: open rear; bead front. Plain pistol-grip stock, grooved slide handle. Made 1914–1915.

Marlin Model 36 Lever Action Repeating Carbine **$285**
Calibers: 30-30, 32 Special. 6-shot tubular magazine. 20-inch barrel. Weight: about 6½ pounds. Sights: Open rear;

Marlin Model 36 Lever Action Carbine (cont.)
bead front. Pistol-grip stock, semibeavertail forearm w/ carbine barrel band. Made 1936–1948. *Note:* In 1936, this was designated "Model 1936."

Marlin Model 36 Sporting Carbine **$295**
Same as Model 36A rifle except has 20-inch barrel, weighs 6¼ pounds.

Marlin Model 36A/36A-DL Lever Action Repeating Rifle
Same as Model 36 Carbine, except has ⅔ magazine holding 5 cartridges, 24-inch barrel, weighs 6¾ pounds, has hooded front sight, semibeavertail forearm. Model 36A-DL has deluxe checkered stock, swivels and sling. Made 1938–1948.
Model 36A Standard **$210**
Model 36A-DL (Deluxe) **280**

Marlin Model 38 Slide Action Repeating Rifle ... **$245**
Hammerless. Takedown. Caliber: 22 LR, Long, Short. ⅔ magazine (tubular) holds 15 Short, 12 Long, 10 LR. 24-inch octagon barrel. Weight: about 5½ pounds. Sights: open rear; bead front. Plain pistol-grip stock, grooved slide handle. Made 1920–1930.

Marlin Model 39 Carbine **$180**
Same as Model 39M, except has lightweight barrel, ¾ magazine (capacity: 18 Short, 14 Long, 12 LR), slimmer forearm. Weight: 5¼ pounds. Made 1963–67.

RIFLES

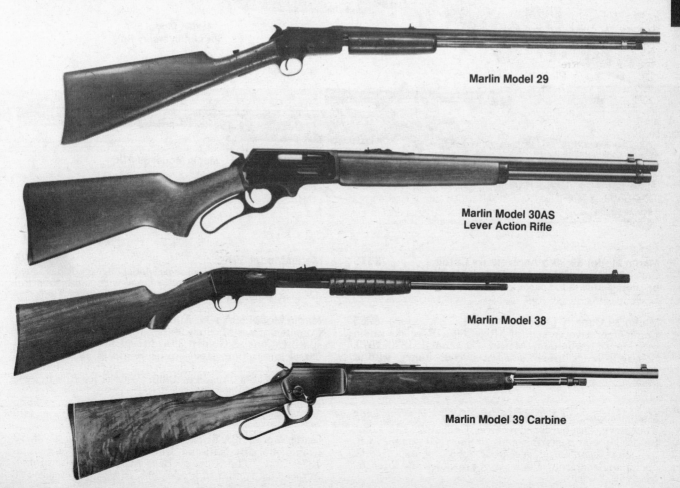

Marlin Model 29

Marlin Model 30AS
Lever Action Rifle

Marlin Model 38

Marlin Model 39 Carbine

Marlin Model 39
90th Anniversary Carbine

Marlin 39 Century Ltd.

Marlin Model 39 Rifle

Marlin Model 39A
90th Anniversary Rifle

Marlin Model 39-ADL

Marlin Model 39 90th Anniversary Carbine **$575**
Carbine version of 90th Anniversary Model 39A. 500 made
in 1960. Value is for carbine in new, unfired condition.

Marlin 39 Century Ltd. **$265**
Commemorative version of Model 39A. Receiver inlaid
with brass medallion, Marlin Centennial 1870–1970.
Square lever. 20-inch octagon barrel. Fancy walnut
straight-grip stock and forearm; brass forend cap, buttplate, nameplate in buttstock. 35,388 made in 1970.

Marlin Model 39 Lever Action Repeater **$695**
Takedown. Casehardened receiver. Caliber: 22 LR, Long,
Short. Tubular magazine holds 25 Short, 20 Long, 18 LR.
24-inch octagon barrel. Weight: about 5¾ pounds. Sights:
open rear; bead front. Plain pistol-grip stock and forearm.
Made 1922–1938.

Marlin Model 39A **$395**
General specifications same as Model 39, except has blued
receiver, round barrel, heavier stock with semibeavertail
forearm, weighs about 6½ pounds. Made 1938–1960.

Marlin Model 39A 90th Anniversary Rifle
Commemorates Marlin's 90th anniversary. Same general
specifications as Golden 39A, except has chrome-plated
barrel and action, stock and forearm of select walnut,
finely checkered, carved figure of a squirrel on right side
of buttstock. 500 made in 1960. Value is for rifle in new,
unfired condition.
Model 39A 90th Anniversary Rifle **$525**
Model 39-ADL (Blued Bbl./Action, 1960–63) **200**

Marlin Model 39A Article II Rifle **$250**
Commemorates National Rifle Association Centennial
1871–1971. "The Right to Bear Arms" medallion inlaid
in receiver. Similar to Model 39A. Magazine capacity: 26

Marlin Model 39A Article II Rifle (cont.)
Short, 21 Long, 19 LR. 24-inch octagon barrel. Fancy walnut pistol-grip stock and forearm; brass forend cap, buttplate. 6,244 made in 1971.

Marlin Golden 39A/39AS Rifle
Same as Model 39A, except has gold-plated trigger, hooded ramp front sight, sling swivels. Made 1960–1987 (39A); Model 39AS currently manufactured.
Golden 39A **$195**
Golden 39AS (W/Hammer Block Safety) **215**

Marlin Model 39A "Mountie" Lever Action Repeating Rifle **$210**
Same as Model 39A, except has lighter, straight-grip stock, slimmer forearm. Weight: 6¼ pounds. Made 1953–1960.

Marlin Model 39A Octagon **$450**
Same as Golden 39A, except has octagon barrel, plain bead front sight, slimmer stock and forearm, no pistol-grip cap or swivels. Made 1973.

Marlin Model 39D **$195**
Same as Model 39M, except has pistol-grip stock, forearm with barrel band. Made 1970–74.

Marlin 39M Article II Carbine **$225**
Same as 39A Article II Rifle, except has straight-grip buttstock, square lever, 20-inch octagon barrel, reduced magazine capacity. 3,824 made in 1971.

Marlin Golden 39M
Calibers: 22 Short, Long and LR. Tubular magazine holds 21 Short, 16 Long or 15 LR cartridges. 20-inch barrel. 36 inches overall. Weight: about 6 pounds. Gold-plated trig-

RIFLES

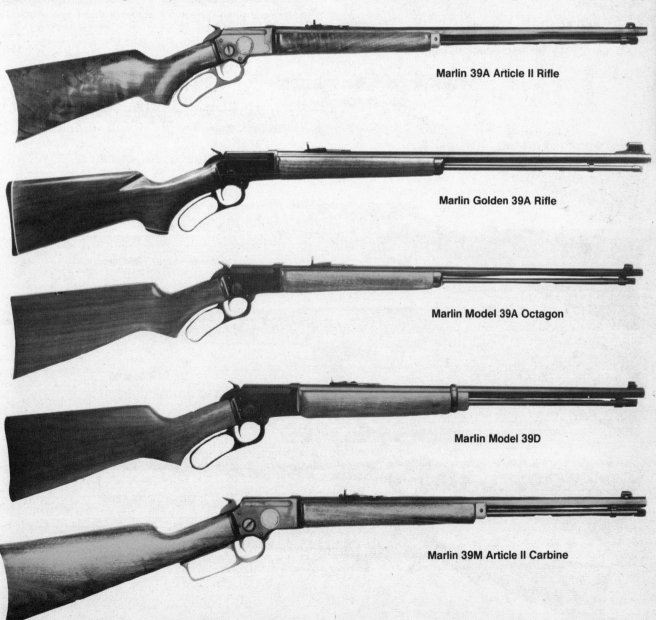

Marlin 39A Article II Rifle

Marlin Golden 39A Rifle

Marlin Model 39A Octagon

Marlin Model 39D

Marlin 39M Article II Carbine

Marlin Golden 39M (cont.)

ger. Hooded ramp front sight, adjustable folding semi-buckhorn rear. Two-piece, straight-grip American black walnut stock. Sling swivels. Mar-Shield finish. Made 1960–1987.

Golden 39M **$190**
Model 39M Octagon (octagonal barrel, plain bead
   front sight, no swivels, made 1973) **$250**

Marlin Model 39M "Mountie" Carbine **$220**

Same as Model 39A "Mountie" Rifle, except has 20-inch barrel and reduced magazine capacity: 21 Short, 16 Long, 15 LR. Weight: 6 pounds. Made 1954–1960.

Marlin Model 39TDS Carbine **$260**

Same general specifications as Model 39M, except take-down style with 16½-inch barrel and reduced magazine capacity. 32⅝ inches overall. Weight: 5¼ pounds. Made 1988 to date.

Marlin Model 45 . . . . **$250**

Semiautomatic action. Caliber: 45 Auto. 7-shot clip. 16½-inch barrel. 35½ inches overall. Weight: 6¾ pounds.

Marlin Model 45 (cont.)

Manual bolt hold-open. Sights: ramp front sight w/brass bead, adj. folding rear. Receiver drilled and tapped for scope mount. Walnut-finished hardwood stock. Made 1986 to date.

Marlin Model 49/49DL Autoloading Rifle

Same as Model 99C, except has two-piece stock, checkered after 1970. Made 1968–1971. **Model 49DL** has scrollwork on sides of receiver, checkered stock and forearm; made 1971–78.

Model 49 . . . . **$120**
Model 49DL **130**

Marlin Model 50/50E Autoloading Rifle

Takedown. Caliber: 22 LR. 6-shot detachable box magazine. 22-inch barrel. Weight: about 6 pounds. Sights: open rear; bead front; **Model 50E** has peep rear sight, hooded front. Plain pistol-grip stock, forearm with finger grooves. Made 1931–34.

Model 50 . . . . **$130**
Model 50E **150**

Marlin Golden 39M Rifle

Marlin Model 39M Octagon

Marlin Model 45

Marlin Model 49DL

Marlin Model 50

Marlin Model 56

Marlin Model 57

Marlin Model 60SS

Marlin Model 62

Marlin Model 70HC

Marlin Model 56 Levermatic Rifle **$140**
Same as Model 57 except clip-loading. Magazine holds
eight rounds. Weight: about 5¾ pounds. Made 1955–1964.

Marlin Model 57 Levermatic Rifle **$155**
Lever action. Caliber: 22 LR, 22 Long, 22 Short. Tubular
magazine holds 19 LR, 21 Long, 27 Short. 22-inch barrel.
Weight: about 6¼ pounds. Sights: open rear; hooded ramp
front. Monte Carlo-style stock with pistol grip. Made
1959–1965.

Marlin Model 57M Levermatic **$190**
Same as Model 57, except chambered for 22 WMR cartridge, has 24-inch barrel, 15-shot magazine. Made 1960–
69.

Marlin Model 60 Semiautomatic Rifle **$105**
Caliber: 22 LR. 14-shot tubular magazine. 22-inch barrel.
40½ inches overall. Weight: 5½ pounds. Grooved receiver.
Ramp front sight; adj. open rear. Anodized receiver w/
blued barrel. Monte Carlo-style walnut-finished hardwood
stock w/Mar-Shield® finish. Made 1981 to date. *Note:*
Marketed 1960–1980 under the Glenfield promotion logo.

Marlin Model 60SS Semiautomatic Rifle **$155**
Same general specifications as the Model 60, except w/
stainless barrel and magazine tube; laminated black/gray
Maine birch stock w/nickel-plated swivel studs. Made
1993 to date.

Marlin Model 62 Levermatic Rifle **$250**
Lever action. Calibers: 256 Magnum, 30 Carbine. 4-shot
clip magazine. 23-inch barrel. Weight: 7 pounds. Sights:
open rear; hooded ramp front. Monte Carlo-style stock
w/pistol grip, swivels and sling. Made in 256 Magnum
1963–66; in 30 Carbine 1966–69.

Marlin Model 65 Bolt Action Single Shot Rifle . . . **$115**
Takedown. Caliber: 22 LR, Long, Short. 24-inch barrel.
Weight: about 5 pounds. Sights: open rear; bead front.
Plain pistol-grip stock with grooved forearm. Made 1932–
38. **Model 65E** is same as Model 65, except has rear peep
sight and hooded front sight.

Marlin Model 70HC Semiautomatic **$100**
Caliber: 22 LR. 7- and 15-shot magazine. 18-inch barrel.
Weight: 5½ pounds. 36¾ inches overall. Ramp front sight,
adj. open rear. Grooved receiver for scope mounts. Walnut-
finished hardwood stock w/Monte Carlo and pistol grip.

Marlin Model 70P
"Papoose"

Marlin Model 75C
Semiautomatic

Marlin Model 80C

Marlin Model 80DL

Marlin Model 70P Semiautomatic **$120**
"Papoose" takedown. Caliber: 22 LR. 7-shot clip. 16¼-
inch barrel. 35¼ inches overall. Weight: 3¾ pounds.
Sights: ramp front; adj. open rear. Side ejection, manual
bolt hold-open. Cross-bolt safety. Walnut-finished hardwood stock w/abbreviated forend, pistol grip. Made 1984
to date.

Marlin Model 75C Semiautomatic **$125**
Caliber: 22 LR. 13-shot tubular magazine. 18-inch barrel.
36½ inches overall. Weight: 5 pounds. Side ejection.
Cross-bolt safety. Sights: ramp front; adj. open rear. Monte
Carlo-style walnut-finished hardwood stock w/pistol grip.
Made 1975 to date.

Marlin Model 80 Bolt Action Repeating Rifle
Takedown. Caliber: 22 LR, Long, Short. 8-shot detachable
box magazine. 24-inch barrel. Weight: about 6 pounds.
Sights: open rear; bead front. Plain pistol-grip stock. Made
1934–39. **Model 80E,** w/peep rear sight; hooded front,
made 1934–1940.

Marlin Model 80 Bolt Action Repeater (cont.)
Model 80 Standard **$110**
Model 80E **105**

Marlin Model 80C/80DL Bolt Action Repeater
Improved version of Model 80. **Model 80C** has bead front
sight, semibeavertail forearm; made 1940–1970. **Model
80DL** has peep rear sight; hooded front, swivels; made
1940–1965.
Model 80C **$100**
Model 80DL **105**

Marlin Model 81/81E Bolt Action Repeater
Takedown. Caliber: 22 LR, Long, Short. Tubular magazine
holds 24 Short, 20 Long, 18 LR. 24-inch barrel. Weight:
about 6¼ pounds. Sights: open rear; bead front. Plain
pistol-grip stock. Made 1937–1940. **Model 81E** has peep
rear sight; hooded front.
Model 81 . . . . **$120**
Model 81E **140**

Marlin Model 81DL

Marlin Model 88-C

Marlin Model 89-C

Marlin Model 93 Carbine

Marlin Model 81C/81DL Bolt Action Repeater
Improved version of Model 81 with same general specifications. **Model 81C** has bead front sight, semibeavertail forearm; made 1940–1970. **Model 81DL** has peep rear sight; hooded front, swivels; discontinued 1965.
Model 81C **$120**
Model 81DL **130**

Marlin Model 88-C/88-DL Autoloading Rifle
Takedown. Caliber: 22 LR. Tubular magazine in buttstock holds 14 cartridges. 24-inch barrel. Weight: about 6¾ pounds. Sights: open rear; hooded front. Plain pistol-grip stock. Made 1947–1956. **Model 88-DL** has receiver peep sight, checkered stock and sling swivels; made 1953–56.
Model 88-C **$125**
Model 88-DL **125**

Marlin Model 89-C/89-DL Autoloading Rifle
Clip magazine version of Model 88-C. 7-shot clip (12-shot in later models); other specifications same. Made 1950–1961. **Model 89-DL** has receiver peep sight, sling swivels.
Model 89-C **$125**
Model 89-DL **160**

Marlin Model 92 Lever Action Repeating Rifle . . **$895**
Calibers: 22 Short, Long, LR; 32 Short, Long (rimfire or centerfire by changing firing pin). Tubular magazines: holding 25 Short, 20 Long, 18 LR (22); 17 Short, 14 Long (32); 16-inch barrel model has shorter magazine holding 15 Short, 12 Long, 10 LR. Barrel lengths: 16 (22 cal. only), 24, 26, 28 inches. Weight: with 24-inch bbl., about 5½ pounds. Sights: open rear; blade front. Plain straight-grip stock and forearm. Made 1892–1916. *Note:* Originally designated "Model 1892."

Marlin Model 93/93SC Carbine
Same as Standard Model 93 Rifle, except in calibers 30-30 and 32 Special only. **Model 93** has 7-shot magazine, 20-inch round barrel, carbine sights, weighs about 6¾ pounds. **Model 93SC** has ⅔ magazine holding 5 shots, weighs 6½ pounds.
Model 93 Carbine **$875**
Model 93SC Sporting Carbine **750**

Marlin Model 93 Lever Action Repeating Rifle . . **$795**
Solid frame or takedown. Calibers: 25-36 Marlin, 30-30, 32 Special, 32-40, 38-55. Tubular magazine holds 10 car-

Marlin Model 93 Rifle

Marlin Model 98

Marlin Model 99DL

Marlin Model 100

Marlin Model 93 Lever Action Rifle (cont.)

tridges. 26-inch round or octagon barrel standard; also made with 28-, 30- and 32-inch barrels. Weight: about 7¼ pounds. Sights: open rear; bead front. Plain straight-grip stock and forearm. Made 1893–1936. *Note:* Before 1915 designated "Model 1893."

Marlin Model 93 Musket $1100
Same as Standard Model 93, except has 30-inch barrel, angular bayonet, ramrod under barrel, musket stock, full-length military-style forearm. Weight: 8 pounds. Made 1893–1915.

Marlin Model 94 Lever Action Repeating Rifle . . $895
Solid frame or takedown. Calibers: 25-20, 32-20, 38-40, 44-40. 10-shot tubular magazine. 24-inch round or octagon barrel. Weight: about 7 pounds. Sights open rear; bead front. Plain straight-grip stock and forearm (also available with pistol-grip stock). Made 1894–1934. *Note:* Before 1906 designated "Model 1894."

Marlin Model 97 Lever Action Repeating Rifle . . $925
Takedown. Caliber: 22 LR, Long, Short. Tubular magazine; full length holds 25 Short, 20 Long, 18 LR; half length holds 16 Short, 12 Long and 10 LR. Barrel lengths: 16, 24, 26, 28 inches. Weight: about 6 pounds. Sights: open rear; bead front. Plain straight-grip stock and forearm (also avail. w/pistol-grip stock). Made 1897–1922. *Note:* Before 1905 designated "Model 1897."

Marlin Model 98 Autoloading Rifle $150
Solid frame. Caliber: 22 LR. Tubular magazine holds 15 cartridges. 22-inch barrel. Weight: about 6¾ pounds. Sights: open rear; hooded ramp front. Monte Carlo stock w/cheekpiece. Made 1950–1961.

Marlin Model 99 Autoloading Rifle $165
Caliber: 22 LR. Tubular magazine holds 18 cartridges. 22-inch barrel. Weight: about 5½ pounds. Sights: open rear; hooded ramp front. Plain pistol-grip stock. Made 1959–1961.

Marlin Model 99C $170
Same as Model 99 except has gold-plated trigger, receiver grooved for tip-off scope mounts, Monte Carlo stock (checkered in later production). Made 1962–1978.

Marlin Model 99DL $200
Same as Model 99 except has gold-plated trigger, jeweled breech bolt, Monte Carlo stock w/pistol grip, swivels and sling. Made 1960–65.

Marlin Model 99M1 Carbine $210
Same as Model 99C except styled after U.S. 30M1 Carbine; 9-shot tubular magazine, 18-inch barrel. Sights: open rear; military-style ramp front; carbine stock w/handguard and barrel band, sling swivels. Weight: 4½ pounds. Made 1966–1979.

Marlin Model 100 Bolt Action Single Shot Rifle . . $100
Takedown. Caliber: 22 LR, Long, Short. 24-inch barrel. Weight: about 4½ pounds. Sights: open rear; bead front. Plain pistol-grip stock. Made 1936–1960.

Marlin Model 122

Marlin Model 336 Marauder

Marlin Model 336 Sporting Carbine

Marlin Model 336 Zane Grey Century

Marlin Model 100SB **$175**
Same as Model 100 except smoothbore for use with 22 shot cartridges, shotgun sight. Made 1936–1941.

Marlin Model 100 Tom Mix Special **$500**
Same as Model 100 except has peep rear sight; hooded front; sling. Made 1936–1946.

Marlin Model 101 . . . . **$105**
Improved version of Model 100 with same general specifications except has stock with beavertail forearm, weighs about 5 pounds. Introduced 1951; discontinued.

Marlin Model 101DL **$130**
Same as Model 101 except has peep rear sight; hooded front, swivels. Discontinued.

Marlin Model 122 Single Shot Junior Target Rifle **$105**
Bolt action. Caliber: 22 LR, 22 Long, 22 Short. 22-inch barrel. Weight: about 5 pounds. Sights; open rear; hooded ramp front. Monte Carlo stock w/pistol grip, swivels, sling. Made 1961–65.

Marlin Model 322 Bolt Action Varmint Rifle **$365**
Sako short Mauser action. Caliber: 222 Rem. 3-shot clip magazine. 24-inch medium weight barrel. Checkered stock. Sights: two-position peep rear; hooded ramp front. Weight: about 7½ pounds. Made 1954–57.

Marlin Model 336 Marauder **$315**
Same as Model 336 Texan Carbine except has 16¼-inch barrel, weighs about 6¼ pounds. Made 1963–64.

Marlin Model 336 Micro Groove Zipper **$525**
General specifications same as Model 336 Sporting Carbine, except caliber 219 Zipper. Made 1955–1961.

Marlin Model 336 Octagon **$255**
Same as Model 336T, except chambered for 30-30 only, has 22-inch octagon barrel. Made 1973.

Marlin Model 336 Sporting Carbine **$225**
Same as Model 336A rifle, except has 20-inch barrel, weighs 6¼ pounds. Made 1948–1963.

Marlin Model 336 Zane Grey Century **$325**
Similar to Model 336A, except has 22-inch octagonal barrel, caliber 30-30; Zane Grey Centennial 1872–1972 medallion inlaid in receiver; select walnut stock with classic pistol grip and forearm; brass buttplate, forend cap. Weight: 7 pounds. 10,000 produced (numbered ZG1 through ZG10,000). Made 1972.

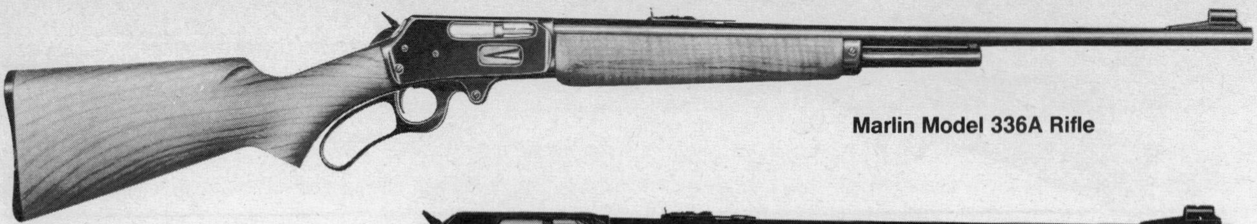

Marlin Model 336A Rifle

Marlin Model 336A-DL

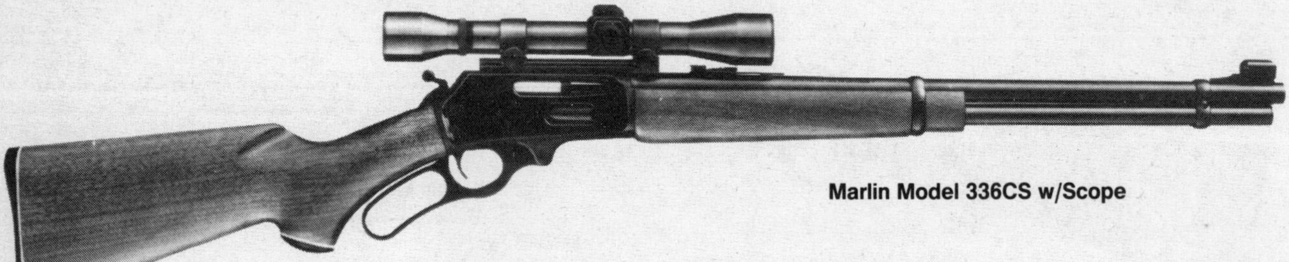

Marlin Model 336CS w/Scope

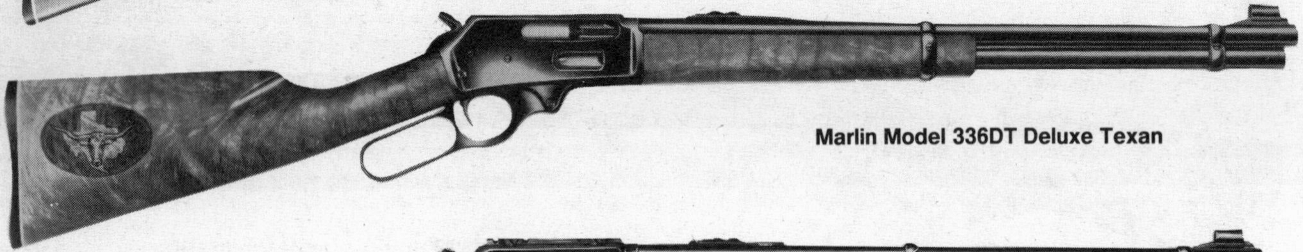

Marlin Model 336DT Deluxe Texan

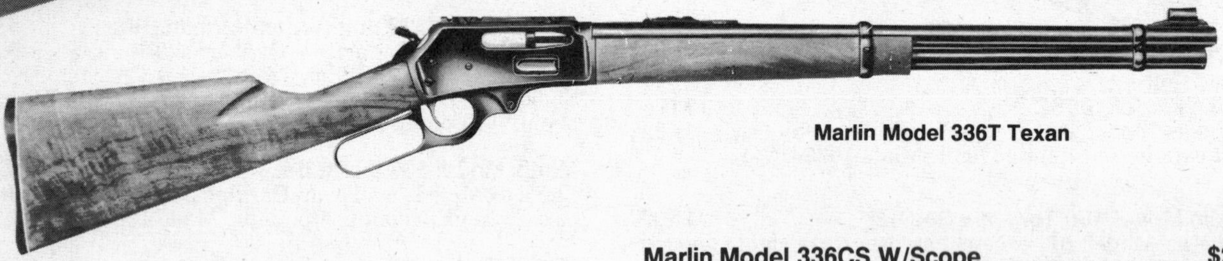

Marlin Model 336T Texan

Marlin Model 336A Lever Action Rifle **$220**
Improved version of Model 36A Rifle with same general
specifications, has improved action with round breech bolt.
Calibers: 30-30, 32 Special (discontinued 1963), 35 Rem.
(introduced 1952). Made 1948–1963; reintroduced 1973,
discontinued 1980.

Marlin Model 336A-DL **$385**
Same as Model 336A Rifle except has deluxe checkered
stock and forearm, swivels and sling. Made 1948–1963.

Marlin Model 336C Lever Action Carbine **$225**
Improved version of Model 36 Carbine with same general
specifications, has improved action with round breech bolt.
Made 1948–1983. *Note:* Cal. 35 Rem. introduced 1953. Cal.
32 Win. Spl. discontinued 1963.

Marlin Model 336CS W/Scope **$295**
Lever action with hammer block safety. Caliber: 30/30
Win. or 35 Rem. 6-shot tubular magazine. 20-inch barrel
with Micro-Groove rifling. $38\frac{1}{2}$ inches overall. Weight: 7
pounds. Ramp front sight, adj. semibuckhorn folding rear.
Solid top receiver for scope mount or receiver sight; offset
hammer spur for scope use. American black walnut stock
w/pistol grip, fluted comb. Mar-Shield finish. Made 1984
to date.

Marlin Model 336DT Deluxe Texan **$275**
Same as Model 336T, except has select walnut stock and
forearm, hand-carved longhorn steer and map of Texas
on buttstock. Made 1962–64.

Marlin Model 336T Texan Carbine **$200**
Same as Model 336 Carbine, except has straight-grip stock
and is not available in caliber 32 Special. Made 1953–
1983. Caliber 44 Magnum made 1963–67.

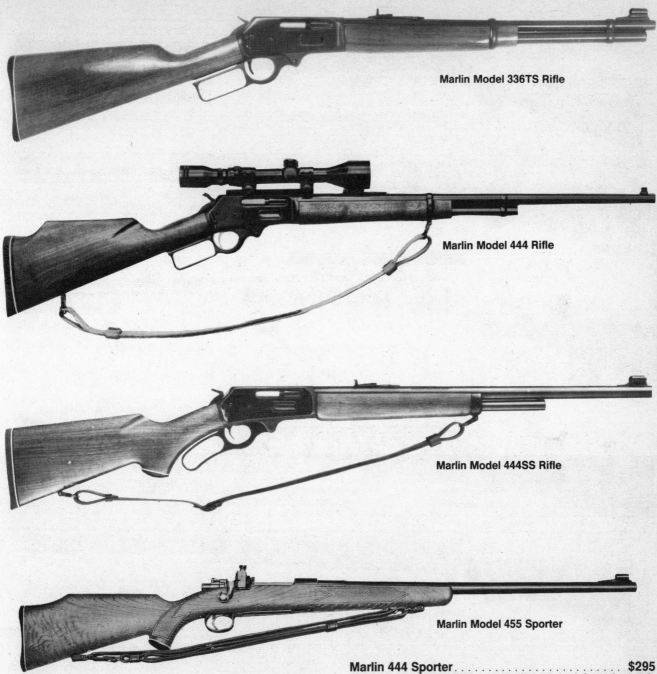

Marlin Model 336TS Rifle

Marlin Model 444 Rifle

Marlin Model 444SS Rifle

Marlin Model 455 Sporter

RIFLES

Marlin Model 336TS **$225**
Lever action with hammer block safety. Caliber: 30/30
Win. 6-shot tubular magazine. 18½-inch Micro-Groove
barrel. 37 inches overall. Weight: 6½ pounds. Ramp front
sight, adjustable semibuckhorn folding rear. Straight-grip
American black walnut stock. Made 1983–87.

Marlin Model 444 Lever Action Repeating Rifle . **$255**
Action similar to Model 336. Caliber: 444 Marlin. 4-shot
tubular magazine. 24-inch barrel. Weight: 7½ pounds.
Sights: open rear; hooded ramp front. Monte Carlo stock
w/straight grip, recoil pad. Carbine-style forearm w/barrel
band. Swivels, sling. Made 1965–1971.

Marlin 444 Sporter **$295**
Same as Model 444 Rifle, except has 22-inch barrel, pistol-
grip stock and forearm as on Model 336A, recoil pad, QD
swivels and sling. Made 1972–1983.

Marlin Model 444SS **$305**
Same general specifications as Model 444, except has
hammer safety. Made 1984 to date.

Marlin Model 455 Bolt Action Sporter **$325**
FN Mauser action with Sako trigger. Calibers: 270,
30-06, 308. 5-shot box magazine. 24-inch medium weight
stainless-steel barrel. Monte Carlo stock w/cheekpiece,
checkered pistol grip and forearm. Lyman 48 receiver
sight; hooded ramp front. Weight: about 8½ pounds. Made
1957–59.

Marlin Model 780

Marlin Model 781

Marlin Model 783

Marlin Model 882L

Marlin Model 883N

Marlin Model 780 Bolt Action Repeater Series

Caliber: 22 LR, Long, Short. 7-shot clip magazine. 22-inch barrel. Weight: 5½ to 6 pounds. Sights: open rear; hooded ramp front. Receiver grooved for scope mounting. Monte Carlo stock w/checkered pistol grip and forearm. Made 1971–1988.

Model 780 Standard	$ 95
Model 781 (w/tubular magazine holding 17 LR, 19 Long, 25 Short)	95
Model 782 (22 WMR, w/swivels, sling)	120
Model 783 (w/12-shot tubular magazine)	125

Marlin Model 880 Bolt Action Repeater Series

Caliber: 22 rimfire. 7-shot magazine. 22-inch barrel. 41 inches overall. Weight: 5½ to 6 pounds. Hooded ramp front sight; adj. folding rear. Grooved receiver for scope

Marlin Model 880 Bolt Action Repeater Series (cont.)

mounts. Checkered Monte Carlo-style walnut stock w/ QD studs and rubber recoil pad. Made 1989 to date.

Model 880 (22 LR)	**$130**
Model 881 (w/Tubular Magazine of 17 LR, 19 Long or 25 Short)	**135**
Model 882 (22 WMR)	**140**
Model 882L (w/Laminated Hardwood Stock)	**150**
Model 883 (22 WMR w/12-shot Tubular Magazine)	**145**
Model 883N (w/Nickel-Teflon Finish)	**165**
Model 883SS (Stainless w/Laminated Stock)	**175**

Marlin Model 922 Magnum Self-Loading Rifle $245

Similar to the Model 9, except chambered for 22 WMR. 7-shot magazine. 20½-inch barrel. 39¾ inches overall. Weight: 6½ pounds. American black walnut stock with Monte Carlo. Blued finish. Made 1993 to date.

Marlin Model 980 22 Magnum **$125**
Bolt action. Caliber: 22 WMR. 8-shot clip magazine. 24-inch barrel. Weight: about 6 pounds. Sights: open rear; hooded ramp front. Monte Carlo stock, swivels, sling. Made 1962–1970.

Marlin Model 989 Autoloading Rifle **$100**
Caliber: 22 LR. 7-shot clip magazine. 22-inch barrel. Weight: about 5½ pounds. Sights: open rear; hooded ramp front. Monte Carlo walnut stock w/pistol grip. Made 1962–66.

Marlin Model 989M2 Carbine **$110**
Same as Model 99M1, except clip-loading, 7-shot magazine. Made 1966–1979.

Marlin Model 990 Semiautomatic
Caliber: 22 LR. 17-shot tubular magazine. 22-inch barrel. 40¾ inches overall. Weight: about 5½ pounds. Side ejection. Cross-bolt safety. Ramp front sight w/brass bead; adj. semibuckhorn folding rear. Receiver grooved for scope mount. Monte Carlo-style American black walnut stock w/checkered pistol grip and forend. Made 1979–1987.
Model 990 Semiautomatic **$110**
Model 990L (w/14 Rounds, Laminated hardwood
   stock, QD studs, Black recoil pad; 1992 to date)   **135**

Marlin Model 995 Semiautomatic **$130**
Caliber: 22 LR. 7-shot clip magazine. 18-inch barrel. 36¾ inches overall. Weight: about 5 pounds. Cross-bolt safety. Sights: ramp front w/brass bead; adj. folding semibuckhorn rear. Monte Carlo-style American black walnut stock w/checkered pistol grip and forend. Made 1979 to date.

RIFLES

Marlin Model 980

Marlin Model 989

Marlin Model 989M2

Marlin Model 990
Semiautomatic

Marlin Model 990L
(Laminated Stock)

Marlin Model 995
Semiautomatic

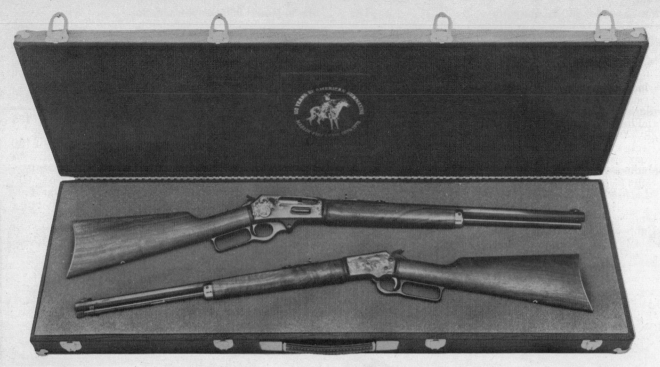

Marlin 1870–1970 Centennial Matched Pair, Models 336 and 39 .... **$1495**
Presentation grade rifles in luggage-style case. Matching serial numbers. Fancy walnut straight-grip buttstock and forearm, brass buttplate and forend cap. Engraved receiver w/inlaid medallion; square lever. 20-inch octagon barrel.

Marlin 1870–1970 Centennial Matched Pair, Models 336 and 39 (cont.)
Model 336: 30-30, 7-shot, 7 pounds. **Model 39:** 22 Short, Long, LR; tubular magazine holds 21 Short, 16 Long, 15 LR. 1,000 sets produced. Made 1970. Value is for rifles in new, unfired condition.

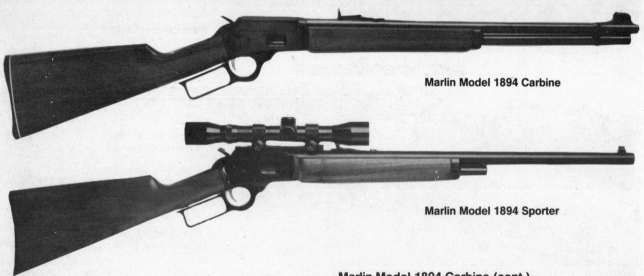

Marlin Model 1894 Carbine

Marlin Model 1894 Sporter

Marlin Model 1892 Lever Action Rifle
See Marlin Model 92.

Marlin Model 1893 Lever Action Rifle
See Marlin Model 93.

Marlin Model 1894 Carbine
Replica of original Model 94. Caliber: 44 Rem. 10-shot magazine. 20-inch round barrel. Weight: 6 pounds. Sights:

Marlin Model 1894 Carbine (cont.)
open rear; ramp front. Straight-grip stock. Made 1969–1984.
Standard Model 1894 Carbine **$285**
Model 1894 Octagon (w/Octagon barrel, bead front
  sight; made 1973) **275**
Model 1894 Sporter (w/22-inch barrel, 6-shot
  magazine; made 1973 .... **310**

Marlin Model 1894 Lever Action Rifle
See Marlin Model 94.

Marlin 1894CL Classic **$285**
Calibers: 218 Bee, 25-20 Win., 32-20 Win. 6-shot tubular magazine. 22-inch barrel. 38³/₄ inches overall. Weight: 6¹/₄ pounds. Adjustable semi-buckhorn folding rear sight, brass bead front. Receiver tapped for scope mounts. Straight-grip American black walnut stock with Mar-Shield® finish. Made 1988 to date.

Marlin Model 1894CS Lever Action **$275**
Caliber: 357 Magnum, 38 Special. 9-shot tubular magazine. 18¹/₂-inch barrel. 36 inches overall. Weight: 6 pounds. Side ejection. Hammer block safety. Square finger lever. Bead front sight, adj. semibuckhorn folding rear. Offset hammer spur for scope use. Two-piece straight-grip American black walnut stock w/white buttplate spacer. Mar-Shield® finish. Made 1984 to date.

Marlin Model 1894M Lever Action **$215**
Caliber: 22 WMR. 11-shot tubular magazine. 20-inch barrel. Weight: 6¹/₄ pounds. Sights: ramp front w/brass bead

Marlin Model 1894M Lever Action (cont.)
and Wide-Scan hood; adj. semibuckhorn folding rear. Offset hammer spur for scope use. Straight-grip American black walnut stock w/white buttplate spacer. Squared finger lever. Made 1986–88.

Marlin Model 1894S Lever Action **$275**
Calibers: 41 Mag., 44 Rem. Mag., 44 S&W Special, 45 Colt. 10-shot tubular magazine. 20-inch barrel. 37¹/₂ inches overall. Weight: 6 pounds. Sights and stock same as Model 1894M. Made 1984 to date.

Marlin Model 1895 45-70 Repeater **$275**
Model 336-type action. Caliber: 45-70 Government. 4-shot magazine. 22-inch barrel. Weight: about 7 pounds. Sights: open rear; bead front. Straight-grip stock, forearm w/metal end cap, QD swivels, leather sling. Made 1972–79.

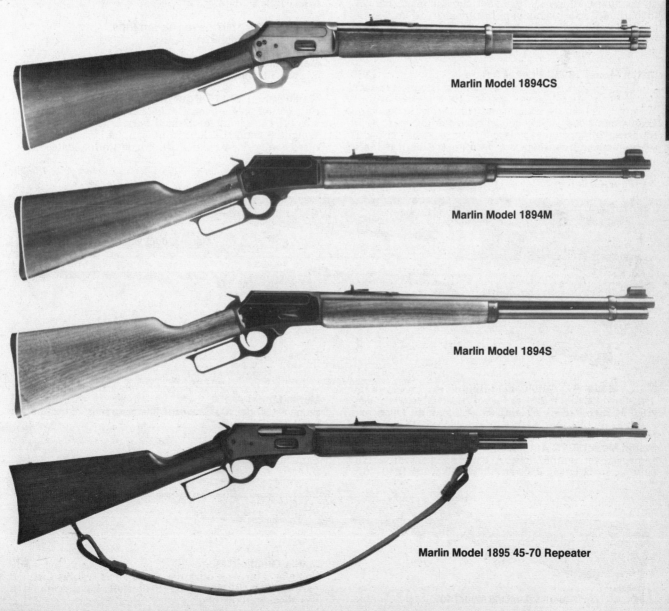

Marlin Model 1894CS

Marlin Model 1894M

Marlin Model 1894S

Marlin Model 1895 45-70 Repeater

Marlin Model 1895

Marlin Model 1895SS

Marlin Model 1895 Lever Action Repeater **$1295**
Solid frame or takedown. Calibers: 33 WCF, 38-56, 40-65, 40-70, 40-82, 45-70. 9-shot tubular magazine. 24-inch round or octagon barrel standard (other lengths available). Weight: about 8 pounds. Sights: open rear; bead front. Plain stock and forearm (also available w/pistol-grip stock). Made 1895–1915.

Marlin Model 1895SS Lever Action **$295**
Caliber: 45/70 Govt. 4-shot tubular magazine. 22-inch barrel with Micro-Groove rifling. 40½ inches overall. Weight: 7½ pounds. Ramp front sight w/brass bead and Wide-Scan hood; adj. semibuckhorn folding rear. Solid top receiver tapped for scope mount or receiver sight. Off-set hammer spur for scope use. Two-piece American black

Marlin Model 1895SS Lever Action (cont.)
walnut stock w/fluted comb, pistol grip, sling swivels. Made 1984 to date.

Marlin Model 1897 Lever Action Rifle
See Marlin Model 97.

Marlin Model 1936 Lever Action Carbine
See Marlin Model 36.

Marlin Model 2000 Target Rifle **$425**
Bolt-action single-shot. Caliber: 22 LR. Optional 5-shot adapter kit available. 22-inch barrel. 41 inches overall. Weight: 8 pounds. Globe front sight, adj. peep rear. Textured composite Kevlar stock. Made 1991 to date.

Marlin Model 2000

Marlin Model A-1 Autoloader

Marlin Model A-1 Autoloading Rifle **$150**
Takedown. Caliber: 22 LR. 6-shot detachable box magazine. 24-inch barrel. Weight: about 6 pounds. Open rear sight. Plain pistol-grip stock. Made 1935–1946.

Marlin Model A-1C Autoloading Rifle **$160**
Improved version of Model A-1 w/same general specifications, stock w/semibeavertail forend. Made 1940–46.

Marlin Model A-1DL **$195**
Same as Model A-1C, except has peep rear sight; hooded front, swivels.

Marlin Model A-1E **$175**
Same as Model A-1, except has peep rear sight; hooded front.

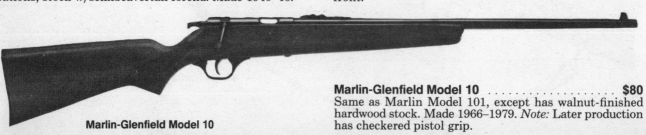

Marlin-Glenfield Model 10

Marlin-Glenfield Model 10 .... **$80**
Same as Marlin Model 101, except has walnut-finished hardwood stock. Made 1966–1979. *Note:* Later production has checkered pistol grip.

Marlin-Glenfield Model 20 . . . . $80
Same as Marlin Model 80/780, except has bead front sight, walnut-finished hardwood stock. Made 1966 to date. *Note:* Recent production has checkered pistol grip.

Marlin-Glenfield Model 30 . . . . $165
Same as Marlin Model 336C, except chambered for 30-30 only, has 4-shot magazine, plainer stock and forearm of walnut-finished hardwood. Made 1966–68.

Marlin-Glenfield Model 30A $175
Same as Marlin Model 336C, except chambered for 30-30 only, has checkered stock of walnut-finished hardwood. Made 1969 to date.

Marlin-Glenfield Model 36G $225
Same as Marlin Model 336C, except chambered for 30-30 only, has 5-shot magazine, plainer stock. Made 1960–65.

Marlin-Glenfield Model 60 . . . . $70
Same as Marlin Model 99C, except has walnut-finished hardwood stock. Made 1960–1980.

Marlin-Glenfield Model 70 . . . . $75
Same as Marlin Model 989M2, except has walnut-finished hardwood stock, no handguard. Made 1966–69.

RIFLES

Marlin-Glenfield Model 20

Marlin-Glenfield Model 30A

Marlin-Glenfield Model 60

Marlin-Glenfield Model 70

Marlin-Glenfield Model 80G

Marlin-Glenfield Model 80G $80
Same as Marlin Model 80C, except has plainer stock, bead front sight. Made 1960–65.

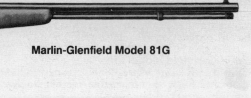

Marlin-Glenfield Model 81G

Marlin-Glenfield Model 81G **$80**
Same as Marlin Model 81C, except has plainer stock, bead
front sight. Made 1960–65.

Marlin-Glenfield Model 99G **$80**
Same as Marlin Model 99C, except has plainer stock, bead
front sight. Made 1960–65.

Marlin-Glenfield Model 101G **$70**
Same as Marlin Model 101, except has plainer stock. Made
1960–65.

Marlin-Glenfield Model 989G Autoloading Rifle . . **$70**
Same as Marlin Model 989, except has plain stock, bead
front sight. Made 1962–64.

MAUSER SPORTING RIFLES
Oberndorf am Neckar, Germany
Manufactured by Mauser-Werke GmbH

Before the end of WWI, the name of the Mauser firm was
"Waffenfabrik Mauser A.-G." Shortly after WWI, it was
changed to "Mauser-Werke A.-G." This may be used as
a general clue to the age of genuine Original-Mauser sporting rifles made before WWII, because all bear either of these
firm names as well as the "Mauser" banner trademark.

The first four rifles listed were manufactured before WWI.
Those that follow were produced between World Wars I
and II. The early Mauser models can generally be identified
by the pistol grip, which is rounded instead of capped, and
the M/98 military-type magazine floorplate and catch; the
later models have hinged magazine floorplate with lever or
button release.

PRE-WORLD WAR I MODELS

Mauser Bolt Action Sporting Carbine **$795**
Calibers: 6.5×54, 6.5×58, 7×57, 8×57, 957mm. 19³/₄-inch
barrel. Weight: about 7 pounds. Full-stocked to muzzle.
Other specifications same as for standard rifle.

Mauser Bolt Action Sporting Rifle **$650**
Calibers: 6.5×55, 6.5×58, 7×57, 8×57, 9×57, 9.3×62,
10.75×68. 5-shot box magazine, 23¹/₂-inch barrel. Weight:
7 to 7¹/₂ pounds. Double-set trigger. Sights: tangent curve
rear; ramp front. Pistol-grip stock, forearm w/schnabel
tip, swivels.

**Mauser Bolt Action Sporting Rifle, Military
Type** **$495**
So called because of "stepped" M/98-type barrel, military
front sight and double-pull trigger. Calibers: 7×57, 8×57,
9×57mm. Other specifications same as for standard rifle.

Mauser Bolt Action Sporting Rifle, Short Model . **$650**
Calibers: 6.5×54, 8×51mm. 19³/₄-inch barrel. Weight:
about 6¹/₄ pounds. Other specifications same as for standard rifle.

PRE-WORLD WAR II MODELS

**Mauser Model DSM34 Bolt Action Single Shot
Sporting Rifle** **$375**
Also called "Sport-model." Caliber: 22 LR. 26-inch barrel.
Weight: about 7³/₄ pounds. Sights: tangent curve open
rear; barleycorn front. M/98 military-type stock, swivels.
Intro. c. 1935.

**Mauser Model EL320 Bolt Action Single Shot
Sporting Rifle** **$345**
Caliber: 22 LR. 23¹/₂-inch barrel. Weight: about 4¹/₄
pounds. Sights: adj. open rear; bead front. Sporting stock
w/checkered pistol grip, swivels.

**Mauser Model EN310 Bolt Action Single Shot
Sporting Rifle** **$325**
Caliber: 22 LR. ("22 Lang für Büchsen.") 19³/₄-inch barrel.
Weight: about 4 pounds. Sights: fixed open rear; blade
front. Plain pistol-grip stock.

**Mauser Model ES340 Bolt Action Single Shot
Target Rifle** **$350**
Caliber: 22 LR. 25¹/₂-inch barrel. Weight: about 6¹/₂
pounds. Sights: tangent curve rear; ramp front. Sporting
stock w/checkered pistol grip and grooved forearm,
swivels.

**Mauser Model ES340B Bolt Action Single Shot
Target Rifle** **$375**
Caliber: 22 LR. 26³/₄-inch barrel. Weight: about 8 pounds.
Sights: tangent curve open rear; ramp front. Plain pistol-
grip stock, swivels.

> **NOTE:** The "B" series of Mauser 22 rifles (Model ES340B,
> MS350B, etc.) were improved versions of their correspond-
> ing models and were introduced about 1935.

Mauser Model ES340B

Mauser Model MM410B

Mauser Model MS350B

Mauser Model MS420B

Mauser Standard Model

Mauser Model ES350 Bolt Action Single Shot Target Rifle **$495**
"Meistershaftsbüchse" (Championship Rifle). Caliber: 22 LR. 27 1/2-inch barrel. Weight: about 7 3/4 pounds. Sights: open micrometer rear; ramp front. Target stock w/ checkered pistol grip and forearm, grip cap, swivels.

Mauser Model ES350B Bolt Action Single Shot Target Rifle **$445**
Same general specifications as Model MS350B except single shot, weighs about 8 1/4 pounds.

Mauser Model KKW Bolt Action Single Shot Target Rifle **$395**
Caliber: 22 LR. 26-inch barrel. Weight: about 8 3/4 pounds. Sights: tangent curve open rear; barleycorn front. M/98 military-type stock, swivels. *Note:* This rifle has an improved design Mauser 22 action w/separate nonrotating bolt head. In addition to being produced for commercial sale, this model was used as a training rifle by the German armed forces; it was also made by Walther and Gustloff. Introduced just before WWII.

Mauser Model M410 Bolt Action Repeating Sporting Rifle **$425**
Caliber: 22 LR. 5-shot detachable box magazine. 23 1/2-inch barrel. Weight: about 5 pounds. Sights: tangent curve open rear; ramp front. Sporting stock w/checkered pistol grip, swivels.

Mauser Model MM410B Bolt Action Repeating Sporting Rifle **$695**
Caliber: 22 LR. 5-shot detachable box magazine. 23 1/2-inch barrel. Weight: about 6 1/4 pounds. Sights: tangent

Mauser Model MM410B Bolt Action Sporter (cont.)
curve open rear; ramp front. Lightweight sporting stock w/checkered pistol grip, swivels.

Mauser Model MS350B, Bolt Action Repeating Target Rifle **$675**
Caliber: 22 LR. 5-shot detachable box magazine. Receiver and barrel grooved for detachable rear sight or scope. 26 3/4-inch barrel. Weight: about 8 1/2 pounds. Sights: micrometer open rear; ramp front. Target stock w/checkered pistol grip and forearm, grip cap, sling swivels.

Mauser Model MS420 Bolt Action Repeating Sporting Rifle **$695**
Caliber: 22 LR. 5-shot detachable box magazine. 25 1/2-inch barrel. Weight: about 6 1/2 pounds. Sights: tangent curve open rear; ramp front. Sporting stock w/checkered pistol grip, grooved forearm swivels.

Mauser Model MS420B Bolt Action Repeating Target Rifle **$625**
Caliber: 22 LR. 5-shot detachable box magazine. 26 3/4-inch barrel. Weight: about 8 pounds. Sights: tangent curve open rear; ramp front. Target stock w/checkered pistol grip, grooved forearm, swivels.

Mauser Standard Model Rifle **$475**
Refined version of the German Service Kar. 98k. Straight bolt handle. Calibers: 7mm Mauser (7×57mm), 7.9mm Mauser (8×57mm). 5-shot box magazine. 23 1/2-inch barrel. Weight: about 8 1/2 pounds. Sights: blade front; adj. rear. Walnut stock of M/98 military-type. *Note:* These rifles were made for commercial sale and are of the high quality found in the Oberndorf Mauser sporters. They bear the Mauser trademark on the receiver ring.

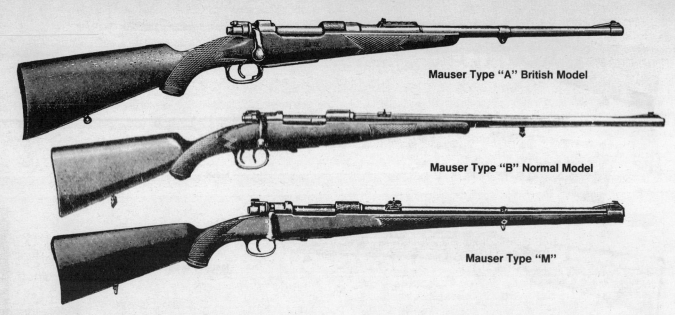

Mauser Type "A" British Model

Mauser Type "B" Normal Model

Mauser Type "M"

Mauser Type "A" Bolt Action Sporting Rifle . . . $1195
Special British Model. Calibers: 7×57, 30-06 (7.62×63), 8×60, 9×57, 9.3×62mm. 5-shot box magazine. 23½-inch round barrel. Weight: about 7¼ pounds. Military-type single trigger. Sights: express rear; hooded ramp front. Circassian walnut sporting stock w/checkered pistol grip and forearm, with or w/o cheekpiece, buffalo horn forend tip and grip cap, detachable swivels. Variations: octagon barrel, double-set trigger, shotgun-type safety, folding peep rear sight, tangent curve rear sight, three-leaf rear sight.

Mauser Type "A" Bolt Action Sporting Rifle, Magnum Model $1250
Same general specifications as standard Type "A," except has Magnum action, weighs 7½ to 8½ pounds. Calibers: 280 Ross, 318 Westley Richards Express, 10.75×68mm, 404 Nitro Express.

Mauser Type "A" Bolt Action Sporting Rifle, Short Model $1050
Same as standard Type "A," except has short action, 21½-inch round barrel, weighs about 6 pounds. Calibers: 250-3000, 6.5×54, 8×51mm.

Mauser Type "B" Bolt Action Sporting Rifle $950
Normal Model. Calibers: 7×57, 30-06 (7.62×63), 8×57, 8×60, 9×57, 9.3×62, 10.75×68mm. 5-shot box magazine. 23½-inch round barrel. Weight: about 7¼ pounds. Double-set trigger. Sights: three-leaf rear; ramp front. Fine walnut stock w/checkered pistol grip, schnabel forend tip, cheekpiece, grip cap, swivels. Variations: octagon or half-octagon barrel, military-type single trigger, shotgun-type trigger, shotgun-type safety, folding peep rear sight, tangent curve rear sight, telescopic sight.

Mauser Type "K" Bolt Action Sporting Rifle . . . $1595
Light Short Model. Same specifications as Normal Type "B" model except has short action, 21½-inch round barrel, weighs about 6 lbs. Calibers: 250-3000, 6.5×54, 8×51mm.

Mauser Type "M" Bolt Action Sporting Carbine $895
Calibers: 6.5×54, 7×57, 30-06 (7.62×63), 8×51, 8×60, 9×57mm. 5-shot box magazine. 19¾-inch round barrel. Weight: 6 to 6¾ pounds. Double-set trigger, flat bolt handle. Sights: three-leaf rear; ramp front. Stocked to muzzle, cheekpiece, checkered pistol grip and forearm, grip cap, steel forend cap, swivels. Variations: military-type single trigger, shotgun-type trigger, shotgun-type safety, tangent curve rear sight, telescopic sight.

Mauser Type "S" Bolt Action Sporting Carbine . $925
Calibers: 6.5×54, 7×57, 8×51, 8×60, 9×57mm. 5-shot box magazine. 19¾-inch round barrel. Weight: about 6 to 6¾ pounds. Double-set trigger. Sights: three-leaf rear; ramp front. Stocked to muzzle, schnabel forend tip, cheekpiece, checkered pistol grip w/cap, swivels. Variations: same as listed for Normal Model Type "B."

POST-WORLD WAR II MODELS

NOTE: Production of original Mauser sporting rifles (66 Series) resumed at the Oberndorf plant in 1965 by Mauser-Jagdwaffen GmbH, now Mauser-Werke Oberndorf GmbH. The Series 2000-3000-4000 rifles, however, were made for Mauser by Friedrich Wilhelm Heym Gewehrfabrik, Muennerstadt, West Germany.

Mauser Model 66S Standard

Mauser Model 66S Bolt Action Standard Sporting Rifle
Telescopic short action. Barrels interchangeable within caliber group. Single- or double-set trigger (interchangeable). Calibers: 243 Win., 6.5×57, 270 Win., 7×64, 308

Mauser Model 66S Deluxe

Mauser Model 66SP Super Match Target Rifle

Mauser Model 66ST Carbine

Mauser Model 66S Bolt Action Standard Sporter (cont.)

Win., 30-06. 3-round magazine. 23.6-inch barrel (25.6-inch in 7×64). Weight: about 7.3 pounds (7.5 pounds in 7×64). Sights: adj. open rear; hooded ramp front. Select European walnut stock, Monte Carlo w/cheekpiece, rosewood forend tip and pistol-grip cap, skip checkering, recoil pad, sling swivels. Made 1965 to date; export to U.S. discontinued 1974. *Note:* U.S. designation, 1971–73, was "Model 660."
With one barrel **$1195**
Extra barrel assembly **500**

Mauser Model 66S Deluxe Sporter

On special order, Model 66S rifles and carbines are available with elaborate engraving, gold and silver inlays and carved stocks of the finest select walnut. Added value is upward of **$1000.**

Mauser Model 66S Ultra

Same general specifications as Model 66S Standard, except has 20.9-inch barrel, weighs about 6.8 pounds.
With one barrel **$1295**
Extra barrel assembly **500**

Mauser Model 66SG Big Game

Same general specifications as Model 66S Standard, except has 25.6-inch barrel, weighs about 9.3 pounds. Calibers: 375 H&H Mag., 458 Win. Mag. *Note:* U.S. designation, 1971–73, was "Model 660 Safari."
With one barrel **$1450**
Extra barrel assembly **550**

Mauser Model 66SH High Performance

Same general specifications as Model 66S Standard, except has 25.6-inch barrel, weighs about 7.5 pounds (9.3 pounds in 9.3×64). Calibers: 6.5×68, 7mm Rem. Mag., 7mm S.E.v. Hofe, 300 Win. Mag., 8×68S, 9.3×64.
With one barrel **$1050**
Extra barrel assembly **500**

Mauser Model 66SP Super Match Bolt Action
Target Rifle **$2550**

Telescopic short action. Adjustable single-stage trigger. Caliber: 308 Win. (chambering for other cartridges available on special order). 3-shot magazine. 27.6-inch heavy barrel with muzzle brake, dovetail rib for special scope mount. Weight: about 12 pounds. Target stock with wide and deep forearm, full pistol grip, thumbhole, adjustable cheekpiece, adjustable rubber buttplate.

Mauser Model 66ST Carbine

Same general specifications as Model 66S Standard, except has 20.9-inch barrel, full-length stock, weighs about 7 pounds.
With one barrel **$1095**
Extra barrel assembly **500**

Mauser Model 83 Bolt Action Rifle **$1895**

Centerfire single-shot, bolt-action rifle for 300-meter competition. Caliber: 308 Win. 25½-inch fluted barrel. Weight: 10½ pounds. Adj. micrometer rear sight, globe front. Fully adj. competition stock. Discontinued 1988.

Mauser Model 99

Mauser Model 201

Mauser Model 3000

Mauser Model 4000

Mauser Model 99 Classic Bolt Action Rifle
Calibers: 243 Win., 25-06, 270 Win., 30-06, 308 Win., 257 Wby., 270 Wby., 7mm Rem. Mag., 300 Win., 300 Wby., 375 H&H. 4-shot magazine (standard), 3-shot (Magnum). Barrel: 24-inch (standard) or 26-inch (Magnum). 44 inches overall (standard). Weight: 8 pounds. No sights. Checkered European walnut stock with rosewood grip cap available in Classic and Monte Carlo styles with High-Luster or oil finish. Discontinued importing 1994.

Standard Classic or Monte Carlo (Oil Finish) . . .	$ 895
Magnum Classic or Monte Carlo (Oil Finish) . . .	945
Standard Classic or Monte Carlo (H-L Finish) . . .	925
Magnum Classic or Monte Carlo (H-L Finish) . .	995

Mauser Model 107 Bolt Action Rifle $275
Caliber: 22 LR. Mag. 5-shot magazine. 21¹/₂-inch barrel. 40 inches overall. Weight: 5 pounds. Receiver drilled and tapped for rail scope mounts. Hooded front sight, adjustable rear. Discontinued importing 1994.

Mauser Model 201/201 Luxus Bolt Action Rifle
Calibers: 22 LR, 22 Win. Mag. 5-shot magazine. 21-inch barrel. 40 inches overall. Weight: 6¹/₂ pounds. Receiver drilled and tapped for scope mounts. Sights optional. Checkered walnut-stained beech stock with Monte Carlo. **Model 201 Luxus** has checkered European walnut stock, QD swivels, rosewood forend and rubber recoil pad. Made 1989 to date. Discontinued importing 1994.

Mauser Model 201/201 Luxus (cont.)
Model 201 Standard	$450
Model 201 Magnum	495
Model 201 Luxus Standard	575
Model 201 Luxus Magnum	625

Mauser Model 2000 Bolt Action Sporting Rifle . . $295
Modified Mauser-type action. Calibers: 270 Win., 308 Win., 30-06. 5-shot magazine. 24-inch barrel. Weight: about 7¹/₂ pounds. Sights: folding leaf rear; hooded ramp front. Checkered walnut stock w/Monte Carlo comb and cheekpiece, forend tip, sling swivels. Made 1969–1971. *Note:* Model 2000 is similar in appearance to Model 3000.

Mauser Model 3000 Bolt Action Sporting Rifle . . $445
Modified Mauser-type action. Calibers: 243 Win., 270 Win., 308 Win., 30-06. 5-shot magazine. 22-inch barrel. Weight: about 7 pounds. No sights. Select European walnut stock, Monte Carlo style w/cheekpiece, rosewood forend tip and pistol-grip cap, skip checkering, recoil pad, sling swivels. Made 1971–74.

Mauser Model 3000 Magnum $495
Same general specifications as standard Model 3000, except has 3-shot magazine, 26-inch barrel, weighs about 8 pounds. Calibers: 7mm Rem. Mag., 300 Win. Mag., 375 H&H Mag.

Mauser Model 4000 Varmint Rifle $395
Same general specifications as standard Model 3000, except w/smaller action, folding leaf rear sight; hooded ramp front, rubber buttplate instead of recoil pad, weighs about 6³/₄ pounds. Calibers: 222 Rem., 223 Rem.

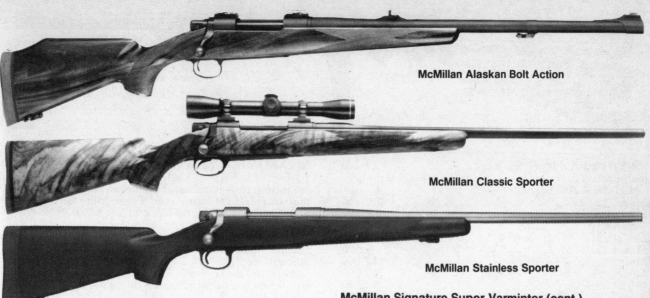

McMillan Alaskan Bolt Action

McMillan Classic Sporter

McMillan Stainless Sporter

RIFLES

McMILLAN GUN WORKS
Phoenix, Arizona
Now owned by Harris Gunworks

McMillan Signature Alaskan Bolt Action Rifle . . **$2450**
Same general specifications as Classic Sporter, except with match-grade barrel. Rings and mounts. Sights: single-leaf rear; barrel band front. Checkered Monte Carlo stock w/ palmswell and solid recoil pad. Electroless nickel finish. Calibers: *LA (long)*—270 Win., 280 Rem., 30-06; *MA (Magnum)*—7mm Rem. Mag., 300 Win. Mag., 300 Wby. Mag., 340 Wby. Mag., 358 Win., 375 H&H Mag. Made 1989 to date.

McMillan Signature Classic Sporter
The "prototype" for McMillan's Signature Series, this bolt-action is available in three lengths: *SA (standard/ short)*—22-250, 243 Win., 6mm Rem., 6mm BR, 7mm BR, 7mm-08, 284, 308, 350 Rem Mag.; *LA (long)*—25-06, 270 Win., 280 Rem.; *MA (Magnum)*—7mm STW, 7mm Rem. Mag., 300 Win. Mag., 300 Wby. Mag., 300 H&H Mag., 338 Win. Mag., 340 Wby. Mag., 375 H&H Mag., 416 Rem. Mag.

Four-shot or 3-shot (Magnum) magazine. Barrel lengths: 22, 24 or 26 inches. Weight: 7 pounds (short action). No sights; rings and bases provided. McMillan fiberglass stock, Fibergrain or wood stock optional. Stainless, matte black or black chrome sulfide finish. Available in right- and left-hand models. Made 1987 to date. Stainless introduced 1990. **Talon Sporter,** introduced 1991, has pre-64 Model 70-style action for dangerous game.
Classic Sporter Standard **$1695**
Classic Sporter Stainless 1750
Talon Sporter 1795

McMillan Signature Mountain Rifle **$1675**
Same general specifications as Classic Sporter, except w/ titanium action and graphite-reinforced fiberglass stock. Weight: 5½ pounds. Calibers: 270 Win., 280 Rem., 30-06, 7mm Mag., 300 Win. Mag. Made 1989 to date.

McMillan Signature Super Varminter **$1495**
Same general specifications as Classic Sporter, except w/ heavy, contoured barrel, adj. trigger, fiberglass stock and

McMillan Signature Super Varminter (cont.)
field bipod. Calibers: 223, 22-250, 220 Swift, 243 Win., 6mm Rem., 25-06, 7mm-08, 308 Win., 350 Rem. Mag. Made 1989 to date.

McMillan Talon Safari Rifle
Same general specifications as Classic Sporter, except w/ McMillan Safari-grade action, match-grade barrel and "Safari" fiberglass stock. Calibers: *Magnum*—300 H&H Mag., 300 Win Mag., 300 Wby. Mag., 338 Win. Mag., 340 Wby. Mag., 375 H&H Mag., 404 Jeffrey, 416 Rem. Mag., 458 Win.; *Super Magnum*—300 Phoenix, 338 Lapua, 378 Wby. Mag., 416 Rigby, 416 Wby. Mag., 460 Wby Mag. Matte black finish. Made 1989 to date.
Safari Magnum **$2450**
Safari Super Magnum 2995

GEBRÜDER MERKEL
Suhl, Germany

For Merkel combination guns and drillings, *see* listings under Merkel shotguns.

Merkel O/U Rifle Model 221

Merkel Over/Under Rifles ("Bock-Doppelbüchsen")
Calibers: 5.6×35 Vierling, 6.5×58r5, 7×57r5, 8×57JR, 8×60R Magnum, 9.3×53r5, 9.3×72r5, 9.3×74r5, 10.3×60R as well as most of the British calibers for African and Indian big game. Various barrel lengths, weights. In general, specifications correspond to those of Merkel over/ under shotguns. Values of these over/under rifles (in calibers for which ammunition is obtainable) are about the same as those of comparable shotgun models. Currently

**Mitchell Model 15/22
Carbine**

Merkel Over/Under Rifles (cont.)
manufactured. For more specific data, *see* Merkel shotgun
models indicated below.

Model 220	$ 6,250
Model 220E	7,295
Model 221	5,950
Model 221E	7,850
Model 320	6,500
Model 320E	12,000
Model 321	13,250
Model 321E	14,000
Model 322	14,500
Model 323	15,500
Model 324	17,500

MEXICAN MILITARY RIFLE
Mfd. by Government Arsenal, Mexico, D.F.

Mexican Model 1936 Mauser Military Rifle **$175**
Same as the German Kar. 98k with minor variations, has
U.S. M/1903 Springfield-type knurled cocking piece.

MITCHELL ARMS. INC.
Santa Ana, California

Mitchell Model 15/22 Semiautomatic
High Standard-style action. Caliber: 22 LR. 15-shot mag-
azine (10-shot after 10/13/94). 20$\frac{1}{2}$-inch barrel. 37$\frac{1}{2}$
inches overall. Weight: 6$\frac{1}{4}$ pounds. Ramp front sight; adj.
open rear. Blued finish. Mahogany stock; Monte Carlo-
style American walnut stock on Deluxe Model. Made 1994
to date.

Model 15/22 SP (Special) w/plastic buttplate	$ 70
Model 15/22 Carbine	105
Model 15/22D Deluxe	125

Mitchell Model 9300 Series Bolt Action Rifle
Calibers: 22 LR, 22 Mag. 5- or 10-shot magazine. 22$\frac{1}{2}$-
inch barrel. 40$\frac{3}{4}$ inches overall. Weight: 6$\frac{1}{2}$ pounds.
Beaded ramp front sight; adj. open rear. Blued finish.
American walnut stock. Made 1994–95.

9301 (22 LR, Checkered, Rosewood Caps)	$185
9302 (22 Mag., Checkered, Rosewood Caps)	195
9303 (22 LR, Plain Stock)	145
9304 (22 Mag., Checkered Stock, No Rosewood Caps)	155
9305 (22 LR, Special Stock)	125

Mitchell AK-22 Semiautomatic Rifle **$245**
Replica of the AK-47 rifle. Calibers: 22 LR, 22 WMR.
20-shot magazine (22 LR), 10-shot (22 WMR). 18-inch
barrel. 36 inches overall. Weight: 6$\frac{1}{2}$ lbs. Sights: post
front; open adj. rear. European walnut stock and forend.
Matte black finish. Made 1985–1994.

Mitchell CAR-15 22 Semiautomatic Rifle **$250**
Replica of the AR-15 CAR rifle. Caliber: 22 LR. 15-shot
magazine. 16$\frac{1}{4}$-inch barrel. 32 inches overall. Sights: adj.
post front; adj. aperture rear. Telescoping buttstock and
ventilated forend. Matte black finish. Made 1990–94.

Mitchell Galil 22 Semiautomatic Rifle **$250**
Replica of the Israeli Galil rifle. Calibers: 22 LR, 22 WMR.
20-shot magazine (22 LR), 10-shot (22 WMR). 18-inch
barrel. 36 inches overall. Weight: 6$\frac{1}{2}$ lbs. Sights: adj. post
front; rear adj. for windage. Folding metal stock with European walnut grip and forend. Matte black finish. Made
1987–1993.

Mitchell M-16A 22 Semiautomatic Rifle **$245**
Replica of the AR-15 rifle. Caliber: 22 LR. 15-shot mag-
azine. 20$\frac{1}{2}$-inch barrel. 38$\frac{1}{2}$ inches overall. Weight: 7
pounds. Sights: adj. post front; adj. aperture rear. Black
composition stock and forend. Matte black finish. Made
1990–94.

Mitchell MAS 22 Semiautomatic Rifle **$255**
Replica of the French MAS bullpup rifle. Caliber: 22 LR.
20-shot magazine. 18-inch barrel. 28 inches overall.
Weight: 7$\frac{1}{2}$ pounds. Sights: adj. post front; folding aperture rear. European walnut buttstock and forend. Matte
black finish. Made 1987–1993.

Mitchell PPS Semiautomatic Rifle
Caliber: 22 LR. 20-shot magazine, 50-shot drum. 16$\frac{1}{2}$-
inch barrel. 33$\frac{1}{2}$ inches overall. Weight: 5$\frac{1}{2}$ pounds.
Sights: blade front; adjustable rear. European walnut stock
with ventilated barrel shroud. Matte black finish. Made
1989–1994.

Model PPS (20-shot)	$270
Model PPS/50 (50-shot drum)	350

O.F. MOSSBERG & SONS, INC.
North Haven, Connecticut

Mossberg Model 10 Bolt Action Single Shot Rifle . **$105**
Takedown. Caliber: 22 LR, Long, Short. 22-inch barrel.
Weight: about 4 pounds. Sights: open rear; bead front.
Plain pistol-grip stock w/swivels, sling. Made 1933–35.

Mossberg Model 14 Bolt Action Single Shot Rifle . **$110**
Takedown. Caliber: 22 LR, Long, Short. 24-inch barrel.
Weight: about 5$\frac{1}{4}$ pounds. Sights: peep rear; hooded ramp
front. Plain pistol-grip stock with semibeavertail forearm,
1$\frac{1}{4}$-inch swivels. Made 1934–35.

Mossberg Model 20 Bolt Action Single Shot Rifle . **$115**
Takedown. Caliber: 22 LR, Long, Short. 24-inch barrel.
Weight: about 4$\frac{1}{2}$ pounds. Sights: open rear; bead front.
Plain pistol-grip stock and forearm with finger grooves,
sling and swivels. Made 1933–35.

Mossberg Model 26B

Mossberg Model 35

Mossberg Model L42A

Mossberg Model 42B

RIFLES

Mossberg Model 25/25A Bolt Action Single Shot Rifle
Takedown. Caliber: 22 LR, Long, Short. 24-inch barrel. Weight: about 5 pounds. Sights: peep rear; hooded ramp front. Plain pistol-grip stock w/semibeavertail forearm. 1¼-inch swivels. Made 1935–36.
Model 25 .... **$100**
Model 25A (Improved Model 25, 1936-38) **125**

Mossberg Model 26B/26C Bolt Action Single Shot
Takedown. Caliber: 22 LR, Long, Short. 26-inch barrel. Weight: about 5½ pounds. Sights: Rear, micrometer click peep or open; hooded ramp front. Plain pistol-grip stock, swivels. Made 1938–1941.
Model 26B **$125**
Model 26C (No rear sight/swivels) **100**

Mossberg Model 30 Bolt Action Single Shot Rifle . **$100**
Takedown. Caliber: 22 LR, Long, Short. 24-inch barrel. Weight: about 4½ pounds. Sights: peep rear; bead front, on hooded ramp. Plain pistol-grip stock, forearm with finger grooves. Made 1933–35.

Mossberg Model 34 Bolt Action Single Shot Rifle . **$110**
Takedown. Caliber: 22 LR, Long, Short. 24-inch barrel. Weight: 5½ pounds. Sights: peep rear; hooded ramp front. Plain pistol-grip stock w/semibeavertail forearm, 1¼-inch swivels. Made 1934–35.

Mossberg Model 35 Target Grade Bolt Action Single Shot Rifle . **$220**
Caliber: 22 LR. 26-inch heavy barrel. Weight: about 8¼ pounds. Sights: micrometer click rear peep; hooded ramp front. Large target stock w/full pistol grip, cheekpiece, full beavertail forearm, 1¼-inch swivels. Made 1935–37.

Mossberg Model 35A Bolt Action Single Shot Rifle . **$225**
Caliber: 22 LR. 26-inch heavy barrel. Weight: about 8¼ pounds. Sights: micrometer click peep rear; hooded front. Target stock w/cheekpiece, full pistol grip and forearm, 1¼-inch sling swivels. Made 1937–38.

Mossberg Model 35A-LS **$235**
Same as Model 35A but with Lyman 57 rear sight, 17A front.

Mossberg Model 35B **$200**
Same specifications as Model 44B, except single shot. Made 1938–1940.

Mossberg Model 40 Bolt Action Repeater **$95**
Same specifications as Model 30, except has a tubular magazine (holds 16 LR) and weighs about 5 pounds. Made 1933–35.

Mossberg Model 42 Bolt Action Repeater **$100**
Takedown. Caliber: 22 LR, Long, Short. 7-shot detachable box magazine. 24-inch barrel. Weight: about 5 pounds. Sights: receiver peep, open rear; hooded ramp front. Pistol-grip stock. 1¼-inch swivels. Made 1935–37.

Mossberg Model 42A/L42A Bolt Action Repeaters
Takedown. Caliber: 22 LR, Long, Short. 7-shot detachable box magazine. 24-inch barrel. Weight: about 5 pounds. Sights: receiver peep, open rear; ramp front. Plain pistol-grip stock. Made 1937–38.
Model L42A, made 1937–1941, has left-hand action.
Model 42A **$115**
Model L42A **150**

Mossberg Model 42B/42C Bolt Action Repeaters
Takedown. Caliber: 22 LR, Long, Short. 5-shot detachable box magazine. 24-inch barrel. Weight: about 6 pounds.

Mossberg Model 42C

Mossberg Model L43

Mossberg Model 43B

Mossberg Model 44B

Mossberg Model 44US

Mossberg Model 42B/42C Repeaters (cont.)

Sights: micrometer click receiver peep, open rear; hooded ramp front. Plain pistol-grip stock, swivels. Made 1938–1941.

Model 42B **$100**
Model 42C (No rear peep sight) **95**

Mossberg Model 42M Bolt Action Repeater $145

Caliber: 22 LR, Long, Short. 7-shot detachable box magazine. 23-inch barrel. Weight: about 6¾ pounds. Sights: microclick receiver peep, open rear; hooded ramp front. Two-piece Mannlicher-type stock w/cheekpiece and pistol grip, swivels. Made 1940–1950.

Mossberg Model 43/L43 Bolt Action Repeaters . . $215

Speedlock, adj. trigger pull. Caliber: 22 LR. 7-shot detachable box magazine. 26-inch heavy barrel. Weight: about 8¼ pounds. Sights: Lyman 57 rear; selective aperture front. Target stock w/cheekpiece, full pistol grip, beavertail forearm, adj. front swivel. Made 1937–38. **Model L43** is same as Model 43 except has left-hand action.

Mossberg Model 43B $225

Same as Model 44B, except with Lyman 57 receiver sight and 17A front sight. Made 1938–39.

Mossberg Model 44 Bolt Action Repeater $135

Takedown. Caliber: 22 LR, Long, Short. Tubular magazine holds 16 LR. 24-inch barrel. Weight: 6 pounds. Sights: peep rear; hooded ramp front. Plain pistol-grip stock w/ semibeavertail forearm, 1¼-inch swivels. Made 1934–35. *Note:* Do not confuse this rifle with the later Models 44B and 44US, which are clip repeaters.

Mossberg Model 44B Bolt Action Target Rifle . . $200

Caliber: 22 LR. 7-shot detachable box magazine. 26-inch heavy barrel. Weight: about 8 pounds. Sights: micrometer click receiver peep; hooded front sight. Target stock w/ full pistol grip, cheekpiece, beavertail forearm, adj. swivel. Made 1938–1941.

Mossberg Model 44US Bolt Action Repeater . . . $185

Caliber: 22 LR. 7-shot detachable box magazine. 26-inch heavy barrel. Weight: about 8½ pounds. Sights: micrometer click receiver peep; hooded front. Target stock, swivels. Made 1943–48. *Note:* This model was used as a training rifle by the U.S. Armed Forces during WWII.

Mossberg Model 45 Bolt Action Repeater $140

Takedown. Caliber: 22 LR, Long, Short. Tubular magazine holds 15 LR, 18 Long, 22 Short. 24-inch barrel. Weight:

Mossberg Model 45

Mossberg Model L45A

Mossberg Model 45B

Mossberg Model 46

Mossberg Model 45 Bolt Action Repeater (cont.)
about 6³/₄ pounds. Sights: rear peep; hooded ramp front. Plain pistol-grip stock, 1¹/₄-inch swivels. Made 1935–37.

Mossberg Model 45A, L45A, 45AC Bolt Action Repeaters
Takedown. Caliber: 22 LR, Long, Short. Tubular magazine holds 15 LR, 18 Long, 22 Short. 24-inch barrel. Weight: about 6³/₄ pounds. Sights: receiver peep, open rear; hooded ramp front. Plain pistol-grip stock, 1¹/₄-inch swivels. Made 1937–38.
Model 45A **$130**
Model L45A (Left-Hand Action) **175**
Model 45AC (No receiver peep sight) **115**

Mossberg Model 45B/45C Bolt Action Repeaters
Takedown. Caliber: 22 LR, Long, Short. Tubular magazine holds 15 LR, 18 Long, 22 Short. 24-inch barrel. Weight: about 6¹/₄ pounds. Open rear sight, hooded front. Plain pistol-grip stock, swivels. Made 1938–1940.
Model 45B **$125**
Model 45C (No sights, made 1935–37) **110**

Mossberg Model 46 Bolt Action Repeater **$140**
Takedown. Caliber: 22 LR, Long, Short. Tubular magazine holds 15 LR, 18 Long, 22 Short. 26-inch barrel. Weight:

Mossberg Model 46 Bolt Action Repeater (cont.)
7¹/₂ pounds. Sights: micrometer click rear peep; hooded ramp front. Pistol-grip stock w/cheekpiece, full beavertail forearm, 1¹/₄-inch swivels. Made 1935–37.

Mossberg Model 46A, 46A-LS, L46A-LS Bolt Action Repeaters
Takedown. Caliber: 22 LR, Long, Short. Tubular magazine holds 15 LR, 18 Long, 22 Short. 26-inch barrel. Weight: about 7¹/₄ pounds. Sights: micrometer click receiver peep, open rear; hooded ramp front. Pistol-grip stock w/cheekpiece and beavertail forearm, quick-detachable swivels. Made 1937–38.
Model 46A **$135**
Model 46A-LS (w/Lyman 57 Receiver Sight) **180**
Model L46A-LS (Left-hand Action) **245**

Mossberg Model 46B Bolt Action Repeater **$115**
Takedown. Caliber: 22 LR, Long, Short. Tubular magazine holds 15 LR, 18 Long, 22 Short. 26-inch barrel. Weight: about 7 pounds. Sights: micrometer click receiver peep, open rear; hooded front. Plain pistol-grip stock w/cheekpiece, swivels. *Note:* Postwar version of this model has full magazine holding 20 LR, 23 Long, 30 Short. Made 1938–1950.

Mossberg Model L46A-LS

Mossberg Model 46B

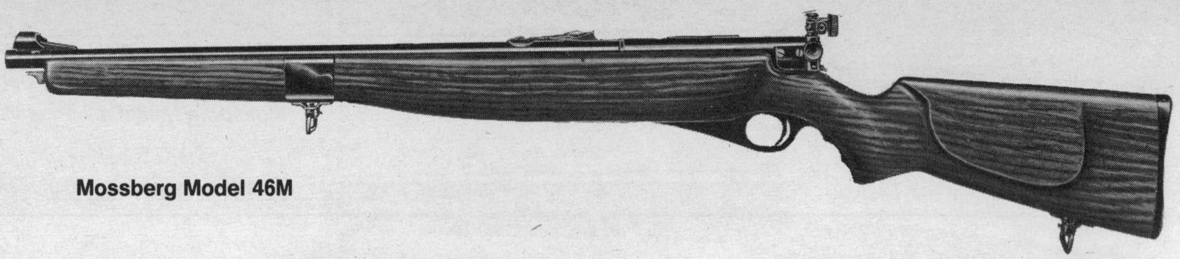

Mossberg Model 46M

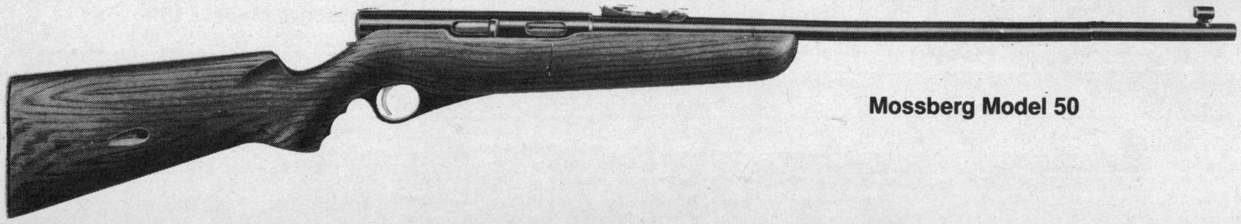

Mossberg Model 50

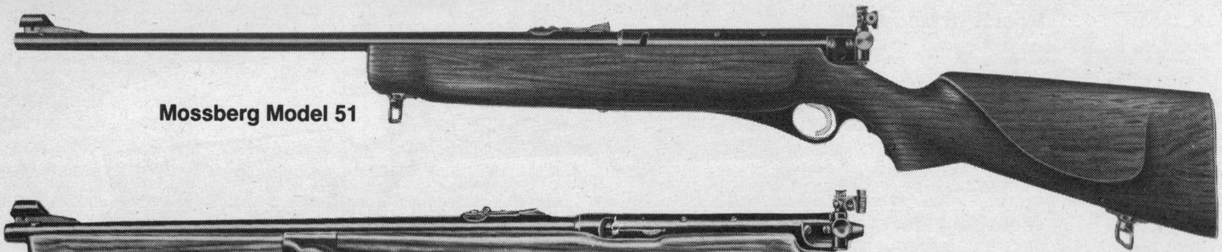

Mossberg Model 51

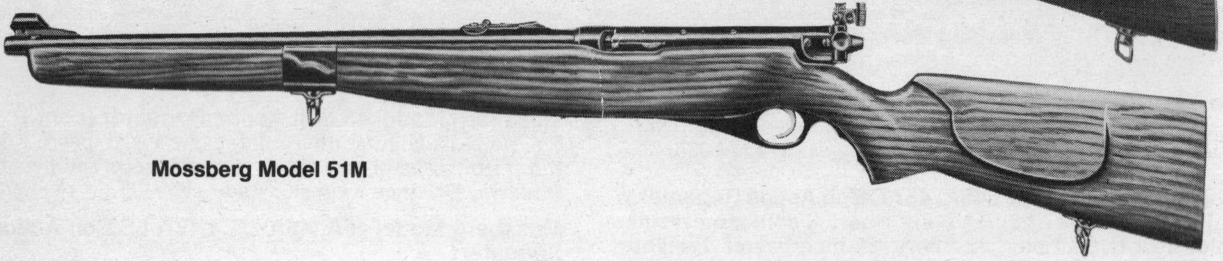

Mossberg Model 51M

Mossberg Model 46BT **$155**
Same as Model 46B, except has heavier barrel and stock,
weighs 7³/₄ pounds. Made 1938–39.

Mossberg Model 46C **$115**
Same as Model 46 except has a heavier barrel and stock
than that model, weighs 8¹/₂ pounds. Made 1936–37.

Mossberg Model 46M Bolt Action Repeater **$140**
Caliber: 22 LR, Long, Short. Tubular magazine holds 22
Short, 18 Long, 15 LR. 23-inch barrel. Weight: about 7
pounds. Sights: microclick receiver peep, open rear; hooded
ramp front. Two-piece Mannlicher-type stock w/cheek-
piece and pistol grip, swivels. Made 1940–1952.

Mossberg Model 50 Autoloading Rifle **$135**
Same as Model 51, except has plain stock w/o beavertail,
cheekpiece, swivels or receiver peep sight. Made 1939–
1942.

Mossberg Model 51 Autoloading Rifle **$150**
Takedown. Caliber: 22 LR. 15-shot tubular magazine in
buttstock. 24-inch barrel. Weight: about 7¹/₄ pounds.
Sights: micrometer click receiver peep, open rear; hooded
ramp front. Cheekpiece stock w/full pistol grip and beavertail forearm, swivels. Made 1939 only.

Mossberg Model 51M Autoloading Rifle **$155**
Caliber: 22 LR. 15-shot tubular magazine. 20-inch barrel.
Weight: about 7 pounds. Sights: microclick receiver peep,
open rear; hooded ramp front. Two-piece Mannlicher-type
stock w/pistol grip and cheekpiece, swivels. Made 1939–
1946.

Mossberg Model 140B Sporter-Target Rifle **$140**
Same as Model 140K, except has peep rear sight, hooded
ramp front sight. Made 1957–58.

Mossberg Model 140K Bolt Action Repeater . . . **$120**
Caliber: 22 LR, 22 Long, 22 Short. 7-shot clip magazine.
24¹/₂-inch barrel. Weight: 5³/₄ pounds. Sights: open rear;

Mossberg Model 140B

Mossberg Model 140K

Mossberg Model 144LS

Mossberg Model 146B

Mossberg Model 140K Bolt Action Repeater (cont.)
bead front. Monte Carlo stock w/cheekpiece and pistol grip, sling swivels. Made 1955–58.

Mossberg Model 142-A Bolt Action Repeating Carbine $150
Caliber: 22 Short, Long, LR. 7-shot detachable box magazine. 18-inch barrel. Weight: about 6 pounds. Sights: peep rear; military-type front. Monte Carlo stock w/pistol grip, hinged forearm pulls down to form hand grip, sling swivels mounted on left side of stock. Made 1949–1957.

Mossberg Model 142K $100
Same as Model 142, except has open rear sight. Made 1953–57.

Mossberg Model 144 Bolt Action Target Rifle . . . $190
Caliber: 22 LR. 7-shot detachable box magazine. 26-inch heavy barrel. Weight: about 8 pounds. Sights: microclick receiver peep; hooded front. Pistol-grip target stock w/ beavertail forearm, adj. hand stop, swivels. Made 1949–1954. *Note:* This model designation was resumed c.1973 for previous Model 144LS. *See* listing below. Disc. 1985.

Mossberg Model 144LS $225
Same as Model 144 except has Lyman 57MS or Mossberg S331 receiver sight and Lyman 17A front sight. Made 1954 to date. *Note:* This model since c.1973 has been marketed as Model 144.

Mossberg Model 146B Bolt Action Repeater . . . $140
Takedown. Caliber: 22 LR, Long, Short. Tubular magazine holds 30 Short, 23 Long, 20 LR. 26-inch barrel. Weight: about 7 pounds. Sights: micrometer click rear peep, open rear; hooded front. Plain stock with pistol grip, Monte Carlo comb and cheekpiece, knob forend tip, swivels. Made 1949–1954.

Mossberg Model 151K $130
Same as Model 151M except has 24-inch barrel, weighs about 6 pounds, w/o peep sight, plain stock w/Monte Carlo comb and cheekpiece, pistol-grip knob, forend tip, w/o swivels. Made 1950–51.

Mossberg Model 151M Autoloading Rifle $155
Improved version of Model 51M with same general specifications, complete action is instantly removable without use of tools. Made 1946–1958.

Mossberg Model 151K

Mossberg Model 151M

Mossberg Model 152

Mossberg Model 320B

Mossberg Model 320K

Mossberg Model 333

Mossberg Model 340B

Mossberg Model 340K

Mossberg Model 152 Autoloading Carbine **$150**
Caliber: 22 LR. 7-shot detachable box magazine. 18-inch barrel. Weight: about 5 pounds. Sights: peep rear; military-type front. Monte Carlo stock w/pistol grip, hinged fore-arm pulls down to form hand grip, sling mounted on swivels on left side of stock. Made 1948–1957.

Mossberg Model 152K **$120**
Same as Model 152, except w/open instead of peep rear sight. Made 1950–57.

Mossberg Model 320B Boy Scout Target Rifle . . **$125**
Same as Model 340K, except single shot w/auto. safety. Made 1960–1971.

**Mossberg Model 320K Hammerless Bolt Action
Single Shot** **$100**
Same as Model 346K except single shot, has drop-in loading platform, automatic safety. Weight: about 5³⁄4 pounds. Made 1958–1960.

Mossberg Model 321B **$115**
Same as Model 321K, except has receiver peep sight. Made 1972–75.

Mossberg Model 321K Bolt Action Single Shot . . **$120**
Same as Model 341, except single shot. Made 1972–1980.

Mossberg Model 333 Autoloading Carbine **$130**
Caliber: 22 LR. 15-shot tubular magazine. 20-inch barrel. Weight: about 6¹⁄4 pounds. Sights: open rear; ramp front. Monte Carlo stock w/checkered pistol grip and forearm, barrel band, swivels. Made 1972–73.

Mossberg Model 340B Target Sporter **$135**
Same as Model 340K, except has peep rear sight, hooded ramp front sight. Made 1958–1981.

**Mossberg Model 340K Hammerless Bolt
Action Repeater** **$130**
Same as Model 346K, except clip type, 7-shot magazine. Made 1958–1971.

Mossberg Model 341

Mossberg Model 342K Carbine

Mossberg Model 346B

Mossberg Model 346K

Mossberg Model 350K Clip

Mossberg Model 351K Sporter

Mossberg Model 340M **$195**
Same as Model 340K, except has 18¹/₂-inch barrel, Mannlicher-style stock with swivels and sling. Weight: 5¹/₄
pounds. Made 1970–71.

Mossberg Model 341 Bolt Action Repeater **$95**
Caliber: 22 Short, Long, LR. 7-shot clip magazine. 24-
inch barrel. Weight: 6¹/₂ pounds. Sights: open rear; ramp
front. Monte Carlo stock w/checkered pistol grip and
forearm, sling swivels. Made 1972 to date.

**Mossberg Model 342K Hammerless Bolt
Action Carbine** **$100**
Same as Model 340K, except has 18-inch barrel, stock has
no cheekpiece, extension forend is hinged, pulls down to
form hand grip; sling swivels and web strap on left side
of stock. Weight: about 5 pounds. Made 1958–1974.

Mossberg Model 346B **$130**
Same as Model 346K, except has peep rear sight, hooded
ramp front sight. Made 1958–1967.

**Mossberg Model 346K Hammerless Bolt
Action Repeater** **$115**
Caliber: 22 Short, Long, LR. Tubular magazine holds 25
Short, 20 Long, 18 LR. 24-inch barrel. Weight: about 6¹/₂
pounds. Sights: open rear; bead front. Walnut stock w/
Monte Carlo comb, cheekpiece, pistol grip, sling swivels.
Made 1958–1971.

**Mossberg Model 350K Autoloading Rifle—Clip
Type** **$105**
Caliber: 22 Short (high speed), Long, LR. 7-shot clip
magazine. 23¹/₂-inch barrel. Weight: about 6 pounds.
Sights: open rear; bead front. Monte Carlo stock w/pistol
grip. Made 1958–1971.

Mossberg Model 351C Automatic Carbine **$135**
Same as Model 351K, except has 18¹/₂-inch barrel, West-
ern carbine-style stock w/barrel band and sling swivels.
Weight: 5¹/₂ pounds. Made 1965–1971.

Mossberg Model 351K Automatic Sporter **$125**
Caliber: 22 LR. 15-shot tubular magazine in buttstock.
24-inch barrel. Weight: about 6 pounds. Sights: open rear;
bead front. Monte Carlo stock w/pistol grip. Made 1960–
1971.

Mossberg Model 352K Carbine

Mossberg Model 353 Carbine

Mossberg Model 377 Plinkster

Mossberg Model 380

Mossberg Model 400

Mossberg Model 402

Mossberg Model 352K Autoloading Carbine **$115**
Caliber: 22 Short, Long, LR. 7-shot clip magazine. 18-inch barrel. Weight: about 5 pounds. Sights: open rear; bead front. Monte Carlo stock w/pistol grip; extension forend of Tenite is hinged, pulls down to form hand grip; sling swivels, web strap. Made 1958–1971.

Mossberg Model 353 Autoloading Carbine **$125**
Caliber: 22 LR. 7-shot clip magazine. 18-inch barrel. Weight: about 5 pounds. Sights: open rear; ramp front. Monte Carlo stock w/checkered pistol grip and forearm; black Tenite extension forend pulls down to form hand grip. Made 1972–1985.

Mossberg Model 377 Plinkster Autoloader **$145**
Caliber: 22 LR. 15-shot tubular magazine. 20-inch barrel. Weight: about 6¼ pounds. 4X scope sight. Thumbhole

Mossberg Model 377 Plinkster Autoloader (cont.)
stock with rollover cheekpiece, Monte Carlo comb, checkered forearm; molded of modified polystyrene foam in walnut finish; sling swivel studs. Introduced 1977.

Mossberg Model 380 Semiautomatic Rifle **$120**
Caliber: 22 LR. 15-shot buttstock magazine. 20-inch barrel. Weight: 5½ pounds. Sights: open rear; bead front. Made 1980–85.

Mossberg Model 400 Palomino Lever Action Rifle **$175**
Hammerless. Caliber: 22 Short, Long, LR. Tubular magazine holds 20 Short, 17 Long, 15 LR. 24-inch barrel. Weight: about 5½ pounds. Sights: open rear; bead front. Monte Carlo stock w/checkered pistol grip; beavertail forearm. Made 1959–1964.

Mossberg Model 402 Palomino Carbine **$180**
Same as Model 400, except has 18½-inch (1961–64) or 20-inch barrel (1964–71), forearm with barrel band, swiv-

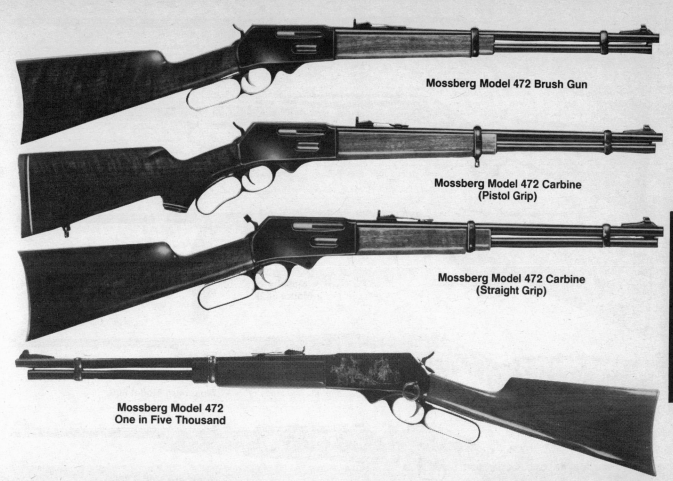

Mossberg Model 472 Brush Gun

Mossberg Model 472 Carbine
(Pistol Grip)

Mossberg Model 472 Carbine
(Straight Grip)

Mossberg Model 472
One in Five Thousand

Mossberg Model 402 Palomino Carbine (cont.)
els; magazine holds two less rounds. Weight: about 4³/₄ pounds. Made 1961–1971.

Mossberg Model 430 Automatic Rifle $115
Caliber: 22 LR. 18-shot tubular magazine. 24-inch barrel. Weight: about 6¹/₄ pounds. Sights: open rear; bead front. Monte Carlo stock w/checkered pistol grip; checkered forearm. Made 1970–71.

Mossberg Model 432 Western-Style Auto Carbine $110
Same as Model 430 except has plain straight-grip carbine-type stock and forearm, barrel band, sling swivels. Magazine capacity: 15 cartridges. Weight: about 6 pounds. Made 1970–71.

Mossberg Model 472 Brush Gun $175
Same as Model 472 Carbine with straight-grip stock, except has 18-inch barrel, weighs about 6¹/₂ pounds. Caliber: 30-30. Magazine capacity: 5 rounds. Made 1974–76.

Mossberg Model 472 Lever Action Carbine $195
Calibers: 30-30, 35 Rem. centerfire. 6-shot tubular magazine. 20-inch barrel. Weight: 6³/₄ to 7 pounds. Sights: open rear; ramp front. Pistol-grip or straight-grip stock, forearm w/barrel band; sling swivels on pistol-grip model, saddle ring on straight-grip model. Made 1972–79.

Mossberg Model 472 One in Five Thousand $325
Same as Model 472 Brush Gun, except has Indian scenes etched on receiver; brass buttplate, saddle ring and barrel bands, gold-plated trigger; bright blued finish; select walnut stock and forearm. Limited edition of 5,000; serial numbered 1 to 5,000. Made in 1974.

Mossberg Model 472 Rifle $165
Same as Model 472 Carbine with pistol-grip stock, except has 24-inch barrel, 5-shot magazine, weighs about 7 pounds. Made 1974–76.

Mossberg Model 620K $110
Same as Model 640K, except single shot. Made 1960–64.

Mossberg Model 640K

Mossberg Model 640K Chuckster Hammerless Bolt Action Rifle $125
Caliber: 22 WMR. 5-shot detachable clip magazine. 24-inch barrel. Weight: about 6 pounds. Sights: open rear;

Mossberg Model 640KS

Mossberg Model 640M

Mossberg Model 642K

Mossberg Model 800

Mossberg Model 800D

Mossberg Model 800M

Mossberg Model 640K Chuckster (cont.)

bead front. Monte Carlo stock w/cheekpiece, pistol grip, sling swivels. Made 1959–1984.

Mossberg Model 640KS $130

Deluxe version of Model 640K, has select walnut stock, hand checkering; gold-plated front sight, rear sight elevator, and trigger. Made 1960–64.

Mossberg Model 640M $195

Similar to Model 640K, except chambered for 22 WMR; has 20-inch barrel, Mannlicher-style stock w/Monte Carlo comb and cheekpiece, swivels. Made 1967–1973.

Mossberg Model 642K $175

Same as Model 640K, except has 18½-inch barrel, forearm with black Tenite extension that pulls down to form hand grip. Made 1961–64.

Mossberg Model 800 Bolt Action Centerfire
Rifle $175

Calibers: 222 Rem., 22-250, 243 Win., 308 Win. 4-shot magazine, 3-shot in 222. 22-inch barrel. Weight: about 7½ pounds. Sights: folding leaf rear; ramp front. Monte Carlo stock w/cheekpiece, checkered pistol grip and forearm, sling swivels. Made 1967–1979.

Mossberg Model 800D Super Grade $295

Deluxe version of Model 800; has stock w/rollover comb and cheekpiece, rosewood forend tip and pistol-grip cap. Weight: about 6¾ pounds. Not chambered for 222 Rem. Made 1970–73.

Mossberg Model 800M $265

Same as Model 800, except has flat bolt handle, 20-inch barrel, Mannlicher-style stock. Weight: 6½ pounds. Calibers: 22-250, 243 Win., 308 Win. Made 1969–1972.

Mossberg Model 810

RIFLES

Mossberg Model 800VT Varmint/Target $235
Similar to Model 800, except has 24-inch heavy barrel, no sights. Weight: about 9½ pounds. Calibers: 222 Rem., 22-250, 243 Win. Made 1968–1979.

Mossberg Model 810 Bolt Action Centerfire Rifle
Calibers: 270 Win., 30-06, 7mm Rem. Mag., 338 Win. Mag. Detachable box magazine (1970–75) or internal magazine with hinged floorplate (1972 to date). Capacity: 4-shot in 270 and 30-06, 3-shot in Magnums. 22-inch barrel in 270 and 30-06, 24-inch in Magnums. Weight: 7½ to 8 pounds. Sights: leaf rear; ramp front. Stock w/Monte Carlo comb and cheekpiece, checkered pistol grip and forearm, grip cap, sling swivels. Made 1970–79.
Standard calibers $260
Magnum calibers   295

Mossberg Model 1500 Mountaineer Grade I Centerfire Rifle $245
Calibers: 223, 243, 270, 30-06, 7mm Mag. 22-inch or 24-inch (7mm Mag.) barrel. Weight: 7 lbs. 10 oz. Hardwood

Mossberg Model 1500 Mountaineer Grade I (cont.)
walnut finished checkered stock. Sights: hooded ramp front w/gold bead; fully adj. rear. Drilled and tapped for scope mounts. Sling swivel studs. Made 1987–88.

Mossberg Model 1500 Varmint Bolt Action Rifle
Same as Model 1500 Grade I, except with 22-inch heavy barrel. Chambered in 222, 22-250, 223 only. High-luster blued finish or Parkerized satin finished stock. Imported from Japan 1982 to date.
High-Luster Blue $300
Parkerized Satin Finish   340

Mossberg Model 1700LS Classic Hunter Bolt Action Rifle $355
Same as Model 1500 Grade I, except w/checkered classic-style stock and schnabel forend. Chambered in 243, 270, 30-06 only. Imported from Japan 1983 to date.

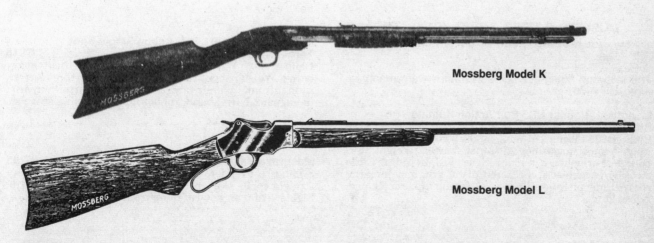

Mossberg Model K

Mossberg Model L

Mossberg Model B Bolt Action Rifle $125
Takedown. Caliber: 22 LR, Long, Short. Single shot. 22-inch barrel. Sights: open rear; bead front. Plain pistol-grip stock. Made 1930–32.

Mossberg Model K Slide Action Repeater $215
Hammerless. Takedown. Caliber: 22 LR, Long, Short. Tubular magazine holds 20 Short, 16 Long, 14 LR. 22-inch barrel. Weight: about 5 pounds. Sights: open rear; bead front. Plain straight-grip stock, grooved slide handle. Made 1922–1931.

Mossberg Models L42A, L43, L45A, L46A-LS
See Models 42A, 43, 45A and 46A-LS respectively; "L" refers to left-hand version of those rifles.

Mossberg Model L Single Shot Rifle $325
Martini-type falling-block lever action. Takedown. Caliber: 22 LR, Long, Short. 24-inch barrel. Weight: about 5 pounds. Sights: open rear; bead front. Plain pistol-grip stock and forearm. Made 1929–1932.

Mossberg Model M Slide Action Repeater $210
Specifications same as for Model K except has 24-inch octagon barrel, pistol-grip stock, weighs about 5½ pounds. Made 1928–1931.

Mossberg Model R Bolt Action Repeater $205
Takedown. Caliber: 22 LR, Long, Short. Tubular magazine. 24-inch barrel. Sights: open rear; bead front. Plain pistol-grip stock. Made 1930–32.

Musgrave Premier NR5

Musgrave RSA NR1

Musgrave Valiant NR6

MUSGRAVE MFRS. & DIST. (PTY) LTD.
Bloemfontein, South Africa

The following Musgrave bolt-action rifles were manufactured 1971–76.

Musgrave Premier NR5 Bolt Action Hunting Rifle $350
Calibers: 243 Win., 270 Win., 30-06, 308 Win., 7mm Rem. Mag. 5-shot magazine. 25$1/2$-inch barrel. Weight: 8$1/4$ pounds. Furnished w/o sights. Select walnut Monte Carlo stock w/cheekpiece, checkered pistol grip and forearm, contrasting pistol-grip cap and forend tip, recoil pad, swivel studs.

Musgrave RSA NR1 Bolt Action Single Shot Target Rifle $345
Caliber: 308 Win. (7.62mm NATO). 26.4-inch heavy barrel. Weight: about 10 pounds. Sights: aperture receiver; tunnel front. Walnut target stock w/beavertail forearm, handguard, barrel band, rubber buttplate, sling swivels.

Musgrave Valiant NR6 Hunting Rifle $295
Similar to Premier, except has 24-inch barrel; stock w/ straight comb, skip checkering, no grip cap or forend tip. Sights: leaf rear; hooded ramp front. Weight: 7$3/4$ pounds.

Musketeer Mauser

MUSKETEER RIFLES
Washington, D.C.
Mfd. by Firearms International Corp.

Musketeer Mauser Sporter $315
FN Mauser bolt action. Calibers: 243, 25-06, 270, 264 Mag., 308, 30-06, 7mm Mag., 300 Win. Mag. Magazine holds 5 standard, 3 Magnum cartridges. 24-inch barrel. Weight: about 7$1/4$ pounds. No sights. Monte Carlo stock w/checkered pistol grip and forearm, swivels. Made 1963–1972.

Navy Arms 45-70 Mauser Rifle

Navy Arms Model 1873 Carbine

Navy Arms 1874 Sharps
Cavalry Carbine

Navy Arms 1874 Sharps
Sniper Rifle

NAVY ARMS CO.
Martinsburg, WV (formerly Ridgefield, NJ)

Navy Arms 45-70 Mauser Carbine **$175**
Same as 45-70 Mauser Rifle, except has 18-inch barrel,
straight-grip stock with low comb, weighs about 7¹/₂
pounds. Discontinued.

Navy Arms 45-70 Mauser Rifle **$160**
Siamese Mauser bolt action. Caliber: 45-70 Gov't. 3-round
magazine. 24- or 26-inch barrel. Weight: about 8¹/₂ pounds
with 26-inch barrel. Sights: open rear; ramp front. Checkered stock w/Monte Carlo comb. Intro. 1973; discontinued.

Navy Arms 1873 Carbine **$535**
Similar to Model 1873 Rifle, except has blued receiver,
10-shot magazine, 19-inch round barrel, carbine-style
forearm w/barrel band, weighs about 6³/₄ pounds. Discontinued. Reissued in 1991 in 44-40 or 45 Colt.

Navy Arms Model 1873 Lever Action Rifle **$560**
Replica of Winchester Model 1873. Casehardened receiver.
Calibers: 22 LR, 357 Magnum, 44-40. 15-shot magazine.
24-inch octagon barrel. Weight: about 8 pounds. Sights:
open rear; blade front. Straight-grip stock, forearm w/end
cap. Discontinued. Reissued in 1991 in 44-40 or 45 Colt
with 12-shot magazine. Discontinued 1994.

Navy Arms 1873 Trapper's Model **$600**
Same as Model 1873 Carbine, except has 16¹/₂-inch barrel,
8-shot magazine, weighs about 6¹/₄ pounds. Discontinued.

Navy Arms 1874 Sharps Cavalry Carbine **$495**
Replica of Sharps 1874 Cavalry Carbine. Similar to the
Sniper Model, except w/22-inch barrel and carbine stock.
Caliber: 45-70. Imported 1994 to date.

Navy Arms 1874 Sharps Sniper Rifle
Replica of Sharps 1874 Sharpshooter's Rifle. Caliber: 45-
70. Falling breech, single shot. 30-inch barrel. 46³/₄ inches
overall. Weight: 8¹/₂ pounds. Double-set triggers. Color
casehardened receiver. Blade front sight; rear sight w/
elevation leaf. Polished blued barrel. Military three-band
stock w/patch box. Imported 1994 to date.
Infantry Model (Single Trigger) **$615**
Sniper Model (DST) **675**

Navy Arms Engraved Models
Yellowboy and Model 1873 rifles and carbines are available
in deluxe models with select walnut stocks and forearms
and engraving in three grades. Grade "A" has delicate
scrollwork in limited areas. Grade "B" is more elaborate
with about 40 percent coverage. Grade "C" has highest
grade engraving. Add to value:
Grade "A" **$100**
Grade "B" **135**
Grade "C" **350**

Navy Arms Martini Target Rifle **$340**
Martini single-shot action. Calibers: 444 Marlin, 45-70.
26- or 30-inch half-octagon or full-octagon barrel. Weight:
about 9 pounds with 26-inch barrel. Sights: Creedmore
tang peep, open middle, blade front. Stock w/cheekpiece

Navy Arms Martini Target Rifle

Navy Arms Revolving Carbine

Navy Arms Rolling Block Baby Carbine

Navy Arms Rolling Block Buffalo Rifle

Navy Arms Martini Target Rifle (cont.)
and pistol grip, forearm with schnabel tip, both checkered. Introduced 1972; discontinued.

Navy Arms Revolving Carbine **$435**
Action resembles that of Remington Model 1875 Revolver. Casehardened frame. Calibers: 357 Magnum, 44-40, 45 Colt. 6-shot cylinder. 20-inch barrel. Weight: about 5 pounds. Sights: open rear; blade front. Straight-grip stock, brass trigger guard and buttplate. Intro. 1968; discont.

Navy Arms Rolling Block Baby Carbine **$195**
Replica of small Remington Rolling Block single-shot action. Casehardened frame, brass trigger guard. Calibers: 22 LR, 22 Hornet, 357 Magnum, 44-40. 20-inch octagon or 22-inch round barrel. Weight: about 5 pounds. Sights: open rear; blade front. Straight-grip stock, plain forearm, brass buttplate. Made 1968–1981.

Navy Arms Rolling Block Buffalo Carbine **$275**
Same as Buffalo Rifle, except has 18-inch barrel, weighs about 10 pounds.

Navy Arms Rolling Block Buffalo Rifle **$285**
Replica Remington Rolling Block single-shot action. Casehardened frame, brass trigger guard. Calibers: 444 Marlin, 45-70, 50-70. 26- or 30-inch heavy half-octagon or full-octagon barrel. Weight: 11 to 12 pounds. Sights: open rear; blade front. Straight-grip stock w/brass buttplate, forearm w/brass barrel band. Made 1971 to date.

Navy Arms Rolling Block Creedmoor Rifle **$495**
Same as Buffalo Rifle, except calibers 45-70 and 50-70 only, 28- or 30-inch heavy half-octagon or full-octagon barrel, Creedmoor tang peep sight.

Navy Arms Yellowboy Carbine **$425**
Similar to Yellowboy Rifle, except has 19-inch barrel, 10-shot magazine (14-shot in 22 Long Rifle), carbine-style forearm. Weight: about 6¾ pounds. Discontinued. Reissued 1991 in 44-40 only.

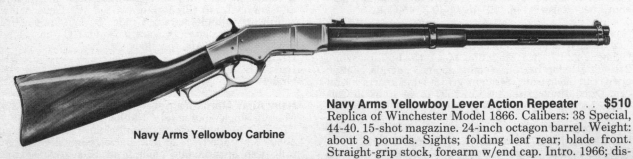

Navy Arms Yellowboy Carbine

Navy Arms Yellowboy Lever Action Repeater . . **$510**
Replica of Winchester Model 1866. Calibers: 38 Special, 44-40. 15-shot magazine. 24-inch octagon barrel. Weight: about 8 pounds. Sights; folding leaf rear; blade front. Straight-grip stock, forearm w/end cap. Intro. 1966; dis-

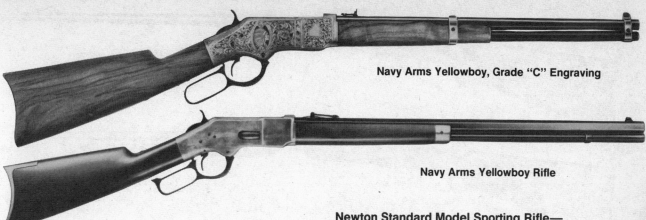

Navy Arms Yellowboy, Grade "C" Engraving

Navy Arms Yellowboy Rifle

RIFLES

Navy Arms Yellowboy Lever Action Repeater (cont.)
continued. Reissued 1991 in 44-40 only w/12-shot magazine and adj. ladder-style rear sight.

Navy Arms Yellowboy Trapper's Model **$540**
Same as Yellowboy Carbine, except has 16½-inch barrel, magazine holds two fewer rounds, weighs about 6¼ pounds. Discontinued.

=== **NEW ENGLAND FIREARMS** ===
Gardner, Massachusetts

New England Firearms Handi-Rifle
Single-shot, break-open action with side-lever release. Calibers: 22 Hornet, 22-250, 223, 243, 270, 30-30, 30-06, 45-70. 22-inch barrel. Weight: 7 pounds. Sights: ramp front; folding rear. Drilled and tapped for scope mounts. Walnut-finished hardwood stock. Blued finish. Made 1989 to date.
22-250, 243, 270 and 30-06 . . . . **$150**
22 Hornet, 223, 30-30 and 45-70 . . . . **140**

=== **NEWTON SPORTING RIFLES** ===
Buffalo, New York
Mfd. by Newton Arms Co., Charles Newton Rifles Corp. and Buffalo Newton Rifle Co.

Buffalo Newton Sporting Rifle **$695**
Same general specifications as Standard Model—Second Type. Made c. 1922–32 by Buffalo Newton Rifle Co.

Newton-Mauser Sporting Rifle **$675**
Mauser (Oberndorf) action. Caliber: 256 Newton. 5-shot box magazine, hinged floorplate. Double-set triggers. 24-inch barrel. Open rear sight, ramp front sight. Sporting stock with checkered pistol grip. Weight: about 7 pounds. Made c. 1914 by Newton Arms Co.

Newton Standard Model Sporting Rifle—
First Type **$795**
Newton bolt action, interrupted screw-type breech-locking mechanism, double-set triggers. Calibers: 22, 256, 280, 30, 33, 35 Newton; 30-06. 24-inch barrel. Sights: open rear or cocking-piece peep; ramp front. Checkered pistol-grip stock. Weight: 7 to 8 pounds, depending on caliber. Made c. 1916–1918 by Newton Arms Co.

Newton Standard Model Sporting Rifle—
Second Type **$735**
Newton bolt action, improved design; distinguished by reversed-set trigger and 1917-Enfield-type bolt handle. Calibers: 256, 30, 35 Newton; 30-06. 5-shot box magazine. 24-inch barrel. Sights: open rear; ramp front. Checkered pistol-grip stock. Weight: 7¾ to 8¼ pounds. Made c. 1921 by Charles Newton Rifle Corp.

=== **NIKKO FIREARMS LTD.** ===
Tochiga, Japan
See **listings under Golden Eagle Rifles.**

=== **NOBLE MFG. CO.** ===
Haydenville, Massachusetts

Noble Model 10 Bolt Action Single Shot Rifle **$65**
Caliber: 22 LR, Long, Short. 24-inch barrel. Plain pistol-grip stock. Sights: open rear; bead front. Weight: about 4 pounds. Made 1955–58.

Noble Model 20 Bolt Action Single Shot Rifle **$65**
Manually cocked. Caliber: 22 LR, Long, Short. 22-inch barrel. Weight: about 5 pounds. Sights: open rear; bead front. Walnut stock w/pistol grip. Made 1958–1963.

Noble Model 33 Slide Action Repeater **$70**
Hammerless. Caliber: 22 LR, Long, Short. Tubular magazine holds 21 Short, 17 Long, 15 LR. 24-inch barrel.

Noble Model 10

Noble Model 222

Noble Model 236

Noble Model 275

Noble Model 33 Slide Action Repeater (cont.)
Weight: 6 pounds. Sights: open rear; bead front. Tenite
stock and slide handle. Made 1949–1953.

Noble Model 33A **$65**
Same general specifications as Model 33 except has wood
stock and slide handle. Made 1953–55.

Noble Model 222 Bolt Action Single Shot Rifle . . . **$75**
Manually cocked. Caliber: 22 LR, Long, Short. Barrel integral w/receiver. Overall length: 38 inches. Weight: about
5 pounds. Sights: interchangeable V-notch and peep rear;
ramp front. Scope mounting base. Pistol-grip stock. Made
1958–1971.

Noble Model 236 Slide Action Repeating Rifle . . . **$85**
Hammerless. Caliber: 22 Short, Long, LR. Tubular mag-
azine holds 21 Short, 17 Long, 15 LR. 24-inch barrel.
Weight: about 5½ pounds. Sights: open rear; ramp front.
Pistol-grip stock, grooved slide handle. Made 1951 to date.

Noble Model 275 Lever Action Rifle **$100**
Hammerless. Caliber: 22 Short, Long, LR. Tubular mag-
azine holds 21 Short, 17 Long, 15 LR. 24-inch barrel.
Weight: about 5½ pounds. Sights: open rear; ramp front.
Stock w/semipistol grip. Made 1958–1971.

PARKER-HALE LIMITED
Birmingham, England

Parker-Hale Model 81 African **$625**
Same general specifications as Model 81 Classic, except
in caliber 375 H&H only. Sights: African express rear;
hooded blade front. Barrel-band swivel. All-steel trigger
guard. Checkered European walnut stock w/pistol grip
and recoil pad. Engraved receiver. Imported since 1986.

**Parker-Hale Model 81 Classic Bolt Action
Rifle** **$495**
Calibers: 22-250, 243 Win., 270 Win., 6mm Rem., 6.5×55,
7×57, 7×64, 308 Win., 30-06, 300 Win. Mag., 7mm Rem.
Mag. 4-shot magazine. 24-inch barrel. Weight: 7¾ pounds.
Sights: adj. open rear; hooded ramp front. Checkered
pistol-grip stock of European walnut. Imported since 1984.

Parker-Hale Model 85 Sniper Rifle **$1325**
Caliber: 308 Win. 10- or 20-shot M-14-type magazine.
24¼-inch barrel. 45 inches overall. Weight: 12½ pounds.
Blade front sight, folding aperture rear. McMillan fiberglass stock w/detachable bipod. Made 1992 to date.

**Parker-Hale Model 87 Bolt Action Repeating
Target Rifle** **$950**
Calibers: 243 Win., 6.5×55, 308 Win., 30-06 Springfield,
300 Win. Mag. 5-shot detachable box magazine. 26-inch
barrel. 45 inches overall. Weight: 10 pounds. No sights;
grooved for target-style scope mounts. Stippled walnut
stock w/adj. buttplate. Sling swivel studs. Parkerized
finish. Folding bipod.

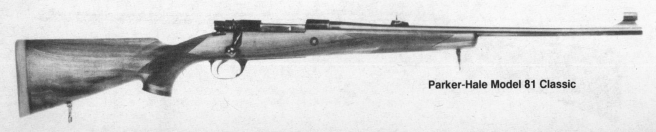

Parker-Hale Model 81 Classic

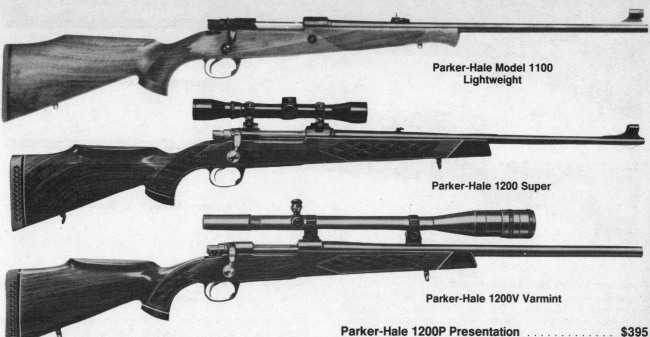

Parker-Hale Model 1100 Lightweight

Parker-Hale 1200 Super

Parker-Hale 1200V Varmint

Parker-Hale Model 1000 Standard Rifle **$295**
Calibers: 22-250, 243 Win., 270 Win., 6mm Rem., 308 Win., 30-06. 4-shot magazine. Bolt action. 22-inch or 24-inch (22-250) barrel. 43 inches overall. 7¼ pounds. Checkered walnut Monte Carlo-style stock with satin finish. Imported 1984–88.

Parker-Hale Model 1100 Lightweight Bolt Action Rifle **$365**
Same general specifications as the Model 1000 Standard, except w/22-inch lightweight profile barrel, hollow bolt handle, alloy trigger guard and floorplate, 6½ pounds, schnabel forend. Imported since 1984.

Parker-Hale Model 1100M African Magnum Rifle **$595**
Same as Model 1000 Standard, except w/24-inch barrel in calibers 404 Jeffery, 458 Win. Mag. Weight: 9½ pounds. Sights: adj. rear; hooded post front. Imported since 1984.

Parker-Hale Model 1200 Super Clip Bolt Action Rifle **$425**
Same as Model 1200 Super, except w/detachable box magazine in calibers 243 Win., 6mm Rem., 270 Win., 30-06 and 308 Win., 300 Win. Mag., 7mm Rem. Mag. Imported from England since 1984.

Parker-Hale 1200 Super Bolt Action Sporting Rifle **$395**
Mauser-type bolt action. Calibers: 22-250, 243 Win., 6mm Rem., 25-06, 270 Win., 30-06, 308 Win. 4-shot magazine. 24-inch barrel. Weight: 7¼ pounds. Sights: folding open rear; hooded ramp front. European walnut stock w/ rollover Monte Carlo cheekpiece, rosewood forend tip and pistol-grip cap, skip checkering, recoil pad, sling swivels. Made 1968 to date.

Parker-Hale 1200 Super Magnum **$495**
Same general specifications as 1200 Super, except calibers 7mm Rem. Mag. and 300 Win. Mag., 3-shot magazine.

Parker-Hale 1200P Presentation **$395**
Same general specifications as 1200 Super, except has scroll-engraved action, trigger guard and floorplate, no sights. QD swivels. Calibers: 243 Win. and 30-06. Made 1969–1975.

Parker-Hale 1200V Varmint **$385**
Same general specifications as 1200 Super, except has 24-inch heavy barrel, no sights, weighs 9½ pounds. Calibers: 22-250, 6mm Rem., 25-06, 243 Win. Made 1969 to date.

Parker-Hale Model 1300C Scout **$465**
Calibers: 243, 308 Win. 10-round magazine. 20-inch barrel w/muzzle brake. 41 inches overall. Weight: 8½ pounds. No sights, drilled and tapped for scope. Checkered laminated birch stock w/QD swivels. Made 1992 to date.

Parker-Hale Model 2100 Midland Bolt Action Rifle **$275**
Calibers: 22-250, 243 Win., 6mm Rem., 270 Win., 6.5×55, 7×57, 7×64, 308 Win., 30-06. 4-shot box magazine. 22-inch or 24-inch (22-250) barrel. 43 inches overall. Weight: 7 pounds. Sights: adj. folding rear; hooded ramp front. Checkered European walnut Monte Carlo stock w/pistol grip. Imported since 1984.

Parker-Hale Model 2700 Lightweight **$295**
Same general specifications as Model 2100 Midland, except w/tapered lightweight barrel and aluminum trigger guard. Weight: 6½ pounds. Made 1992 to date.

Parker-Hale Model 2800 Midland **$290**
Same general specifications as Model 2100, except w/ laminated birch stock. Made 1992 to date.

PEDERSEN CUSTOM GUNS
North Haven, Connecticut
Division of O.F. Mossberg & Sons, Inc.

Pedersen Model 3000 Grade I Bolt Action Rifle . **$795**
Richly engraved with silver inlays, full-fancy American black walnut stock. Mossberg Model 810 action. Calibers: 270 Win., 30-06, 7mm Rem. Mag., 338 Win. Mag. 3-shot

Pedersen Model 3000 Grade I

Pedersen Model 3000 Grade III

Pedersen Model 3000 Grade I (cont.)

magazine, hinged floorplate. 22-inch barrel in 270 and 30-06, 24-inch in Magnums. Weight: 7 to 8 pounds. Sights: open rear; hooded ramp front. Monte Carlo stock w/roll-over cheekpiece, wraparound hand checkering on pistol grip and forearm, rosewood pistol-grip cap and forend tip, recoil pad or steel buttplate with trap, detachable swivels. Made 1973–75.

Pedersen Model 3000 Grade II $595
Same as Model 3000 Grade I, except less elaborate engraving, no inlays, fancy grade walnut stock with recoil pad. Made 1973–75.

Pedersen Model 3000 Grade III $495
Same as Model 3000 Grade I, except no engraving or inlays, select grade walnut stock w/recoil pad. Made 1973–74.

Pedersen Model 4700 Custom Deluxe Lever Action Rifle $195
Mossberg Model 472 action. Calibers: 30-30, 35 Rem. 5-shot tubular magazine. 24-inch barrel. Weight: 7½ pounds. Sights: open rear; hooded ramp front. Hand-finished black walnut stock and beavertail forearm, barrel band swivels. Made 1975.

J.C. PENNEY CO., INC.
Dallas, Texas

Firearms sold under the J.C. Penney label were mfd. by Marlin, High Standard, Stevens, Savage and Springfield.

J.C. Penney Model 2025 Bolt Action Repeater . . . $50
Takedown. Caliber: 22 RF. 8-shot detachable box magazine. 24-inch barrel. Weight: about 6 pounds. Sights: open rear; bead front. Plain pistol-grip stock. Mfd. by Marlin.

J.C. Penney Model 2035 Bolt Action Repeater . . . $50
Takedown. Caliber: 22 RF. 8-shot detachable box magazine. 24-inch barrel. Weight: about 6 pounds. Sights: open rear; bead front. Plain pistol-grip stock. Mfd. by Marlin.

J.C. Penney Model 2935 Lever Action Rifle $145
Same general specifications as Marlin Model 336.

J.C. Penney Model 6400 Bolt Action Centerfire Rifle $120
Same general specifications as Savage Model 340.

J.C. Penney Model 6660 Autoloading Rifle $75
Caliber: 22 RF. Tubular magazine. 22-inch barrel. Weight: about 5½ pounds. Sights: open rear; hooded ramp front. Plain pistol-grip stock. Mfd. by Marlin.

Plainfield M-1 Carbine

PLAINFIELD MACHINE COMPANY
Dunellen, New Jersey

Plainfield M-1 Carbine $150
Same as U.S. Carbine, Cal. 30, M-1, except also available in caliber 5.7mm (22 with necked-down 30 Carbine cartridge case). Current production has ventilated metal handguard and barrel band w/o bayonet lug; earlier models have standard military-type fittings. Made 1960–1977.

**Plainfield M-1 Carbine
Commando Model**

**Plainfield M-1 Carbine
Military Sporter**

Plainfielder M-1 Deluxe Sporter

Plainfield M-1 Carbine, Commando Model **$175**
Same as M-1 Carbine, except has paratrooper-type stock w/telescoping wire shoulderpiece. Made 1960–1977.

Plainfield M-1 Carbine, Military Sporter **$150**
Same as M-1 Carbine, except has unslotted buttstock and wood handguard. Made 1960–1977.

Plainfielder M-1 Deluxe Sporter **$175**
Same as M-1 Carbine, except has Monte Carlo sporting stock. Made 1960–1973.

=== **POLISH MILITARY RIFLES** ===
Manufactured by Government Arsenals at Radom and Warsaw, Poland

**Polish Model 1898 (Karabin 98, K98) Mauser
Military Carbine** **$175**
Same, except for minor details, as the German Kar. 98a. First manufactured during early 1920s.

**Polish Model 1898 (Karabin 98, WZ98A) Mauser
Military Rifle** **$110**
Same, except for minor details, as the German Gew. 98 used in WWI. Manufacture began c. 1921.

**Polish Model 1929 (Karabin 29, WZ29) Mauser
Military Rifle** **$175**
Same, except for minor details, as the Czech Model 24. Mfd. 1929 thru WWII. A similar model produced during German occupation was designated Gew. 29/40.

=== **WILLIAM POWELL & SON LTD.** ===
Birmingham, England

Powell Double-Barrel Rifle **$25,000**
Boxlock. Made to order in any caliber during the time that the rifle was manufactured. Barrels: Made to order in any legal length, but 26 inches recommended. Highest grade French walnut buttstock and forearm with fine checkering. Metal is elaborately engraved. Imported by Stoeger about 1938–1951.

=== **JAMES PURDEY & SONS LTD.** ===
London, England

Purdey Double Rifle **$32,500**
Sidelock action, hammerless, ejectors. Calibers: 375 Flanged Magnum Nitro Express, 500/465 Nitro Express, 470 Nitro Express, 577 Nitro Express. 25½-inch barrels (25-inch in 375). Weight: 9½ to 12¾ pounds. Sights: folding leaf rear; ramp front. Cheekpiece stock, checkered

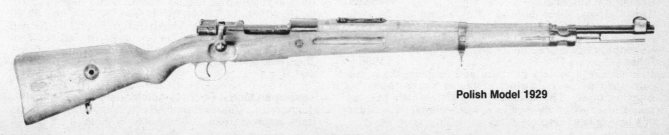

Polish Model 1929

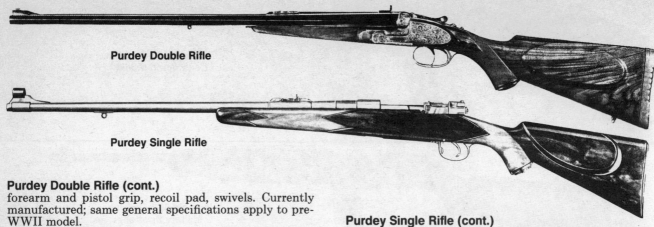

Purdey Double Rifle

Purdey Single Rifle

Purdey Double Rifle (cont.)
forearm and pistol grip, recoil pad, swivels. Currently manufactured; same general specifications apply to pre-WWII model.

Purdey Single Rifle $4500
Mauser-type bolt action. Calibers: 7×57, 300 H&H Magnum, 375 H&H Magnum, 10.75×73. 3-shot magazine. 24-

Purdey Single Rifle (cont.)
inch barrel. Weight: 7½ to 8¾ pounds. Sights: folding leaf rear; hooded ramp front. Cheekpiece stock, checkered forearm and pistol grip, swivels. Currently manufactured; same general specifications apply to pre-WWII model.

Remington No. 2

Remington No. 3

Remington Model Four

REMINGTON ARMS COMPANY
Ilion, New York

Remington No. 2 Sporting Rifle
Single-shot, rolling-block action. Calibers: 22, 25, 32, 38, 44 rimfire or centerfire. Barrel lengths: 24, 26, 28 or 30 inches. Weight: 5 to 6 pounds. Sights: open rear; bead front. Straight-grip sporting stock and knobtip forearm of walnut. Made 1873–1910.
Calibers: 22, 25, 32 . . . . $550
Calibers: 38, 44 650

Remington Model 2C $595
Target Grade. Same as Model 12A, except has 24-inch octagon barrel, pistol-grip stock.

Remington No. 3 Creedmoor and Schuetzen Rifles . . . . $5000+
Produced in a variety of styles and calibers, these are collector's items and bring far higher prices than the sporting types. The Schuetzen Special, which has an under-lever action, is especially rare—perhaps less than 100 having been made.

Remington No. 3 High Power Rifle
Single shot. Hepburn falling-block action w/side lever. Calibers: 30/30, 30/40, 32 Special, 32/40, 38/55, 38/72 (high-power cartridges). Barrel lengths: 26-, 28-, 30-inch. Weight: about 8 pounds. Open sporting sights. Checkered pistol-grip stock and forearm. Made 1893–1907.
Calibers: 30/30, 30/40, 32 Special, 32/40 . . . . $1425
Calibers: 38/55, 38/72 1750

Remington No. 3 Sporting Rifle $1050
Single shot. Hepburn falling-block action w/side lever. Calibers: 22 WCF, 22 Extra Long, 25/20 Stevens, 25/21 Stevens, 25/25 Stevens, 32 WCF, 32/40 Ballard & Marlin, 32/40 Rem., 38 WCF, 38/40 Rem., 38/50 Rem., 38/55 Ballard & Marlin, 40/60 Ballard & Marlin, 40/60 WCF, 40/65 Rem. Straight, 40/82 WCF, 45/70 Gov., 45/90 WCF; also was supplied on special order in bottle-necked 40/50, 40/70, 40/90, 44/77, 44/90, 44/105, 50/70 Gov., 50/90 Sharps Straight. Barrel lengths: 26-inch (22, 25, 32 cal. only), 28-inch, 30-inch; half-octagon or full-octagon. Weight: 8 to 10 pounds. Sights: open rear; blade front. Checkered pistol-grip stock and forearm. Made 1880 to c. 1911.

Remington Model Four (4) Autoloading Rifle
Hammerless. Calibers: 6mm Rem., 243 Win., 270 Win., 7mm Express Rem., 30-06, 308 Win. 22-inch barrel.

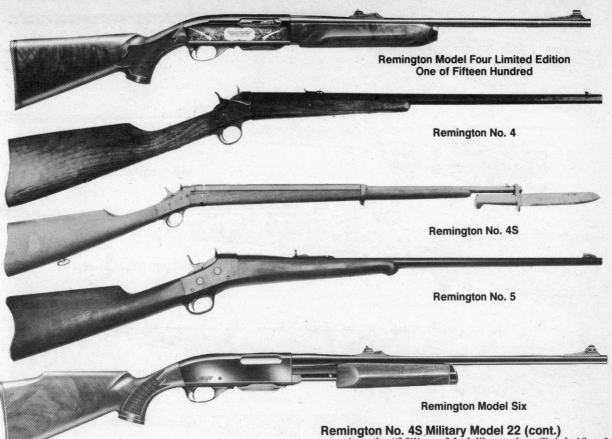

**Remington Model Four Limited Edition
One of Fifteen Hundred**

Remington No. 4

Remington No. 4S

Remington No. 5

Remington Model Six

Remington Model Four (4) Autoloader (cont.)
Weight: 7½ pounds. Sights: open rear; bead front, on ramp. Monte Carlo checkered stock and forearm. Made 1981–88.

Standard	$ 325
Peerless Grade (Engr. receiver)	1250
Premier Grade (Engr. receiver, gold inlay)	3500

Remington Model Four Diamond Anniversary Ltd. Edition
Same as Model Four Standard, except has engraved receiver w/inscription, checkered high-grade walnut stock and forend. Only 1,500 produced. Made 1981 only.

Standard Grade	$ 895
Peerless Grade	1720
Premier Grade	3540
Premier Gold Grade	5250

Remington No. 4 Single Shot Rifle $425
Rolling-block action. Solid frame or takedown. Calibers: 22 Short and Long, 22 LR, 25 Stevens R.F., 32 Short and Long R.F. 22½-inch octagon barrel, 24-inch available in 32 caliber only. Weight: about 4½ pounds. Sights: open rear; blade front. Plain walnut stock and forearm. Made 1890–1933.

Remington No. 4S Military Model 22 Single Shot Rifle $795
Rolling-block action. Calibers: 22 Short only, 22 LR only. 28-inch barrel. Weight: about 5 pounds. Sights: military-type rear; blade front. Military-type stock w/handguard, stacking swivel, sling. Has a bayonet stud on the barrel; bayonet and scabbard were regularly supplied. *Note:* At

Remington No. 4S Military Model 22 (cont.)
one time the "Military Model" was the official rifle of the Boy Scouts of America and was called the "Boy Scout Rifle." Made 1913–1933.

Remington No. 5 Special Rifle
Single shot. Rolling-block action. Calibers: 7mm Mauser, 30-30, 30-40 Krag, 303 British, 32-40, 32 Special, 38-55 (high-power cartridges). Barrel lengths: 24, 26 and 28 inches. Weight: about 7 pounds. Open sporting sights. Plain straight-grip stock and forearm. Made 1902–1918. *Note:* Models 1897 and 1902 Military Rifles, intended for the export market, are almost identical with the No. 5 except for 30-inch barrel, full military stock and weight (about 8½ pounds); a carbine was also supplied. The military rifles were produced in caliber 8mm Lebel for France, 7.62mm Russian for Russia and 7mm Mauser for the Central and South American government trade. At one time, Remington also offered these military models to retail buyers.

Sporting Model	$395
Military Model	250

Remington Model Six (6) Peerless Grade $1235
Same as Model Six Standard, except has engraved receiver. Made 1981–88.

Remington Model Six (6) Premier Grade $3500
Same as Model Six Standard, except has engraved receiver with gold inlay. Made 1981–88.

Remington Model Six (6) Slide Action Repeater .. $325
Hammerless. Calibers: 6mm Rem., 243 Win., 270 Win., 7mm Express Rem., 30-06, 308 Win. 22-inch barrel. Weight: 7½ pounds. Checkered Monte Carlo stock and forearm. Made 1981–88.

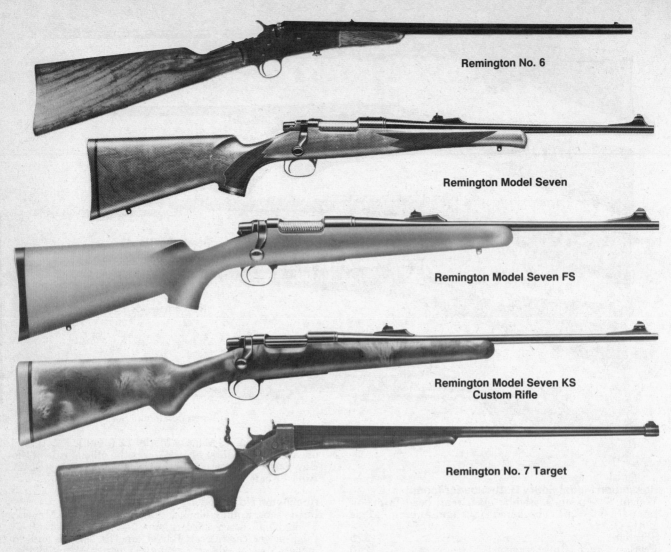

Remington No. 6

Remington Model Seven

Remington Model Seven FS

Remington Model Seven KS
Custom Rifle

Remington No. 7 Target

Remington No. 6 Takedown Rifle **$310**
Single shot. Rolling-block action. Calibers: 22 Short, 22
Long, 22 LR, 32 Short/Long RF. 20-inch barrel. Weight:
avg. 4 pounds. Sights: open front and rear; tang peep.
Plain straight-grip stock, forearm. Made 1901–1933.

Remington Model Seven (7) CF Bolt Action Rifle
Calibers: 17 Rem., 222 Rem., 223 Rem., 243 Win., 6mm
Rem., 7mm-08 Rem., 308 Win. Magazine capacity: 5-shot
in 17 Rem., 222 Rem., 223 Rem., 4-shot in other calibers.
18½-inch barrel. Weight: 6¼ pounds. Walnut stock,
checkering, and recoil pad. Made 1983 to date. 223 Rem.
added in 1984.
Standard calibers except 17 Rem. **$395**
Caliber 17 Rem. **415**

Remington Model Seven (7) FS Rifle **$385**
Calibers: 243, 7mm-08 Rem., 308 Win. 18½-inch barrel.
37½ inches overall. Weight: 5¼ pounds. Hand layup fiberglass stock, reinforced with DuPont Kevlar at points
of bedding and stress. Made 1987–1990.

Remington Model Seven (7) KS Rifle **$620**
Calibers: 223 Rem., 7mm-08, 308, 35 Rem. and 350 Rem.
Mag. 20-inch barrel. Custom made in Remington's Custom
shop with Kevlar stock. Made 1987 to date.

Remington Model Seven (7) MS Custom Rifle . . **$695**
Similar to the standard Model 7, except fitted with a lam-
inated full Mannlicher-style stock. Weight: 6¾ pounds.
Calibers: 222 Rem., 22-250, 243, 6mm Rem., 7mm-08, 308,
350 Rem. Additional calibers available on special order.
Made 1993 to date.

Remington Model Seven (7) SS Rifle **$375**
Same as Model 7, except 20-inch stainless barrel, receiver
and bolt; black synthetic stock. Calibers: 243, 7mm-08 or
308. Made 1994 to date.

Remington Model Seven (7) Youth Rifle **$300**
Similar to the standard Model 7, except fitted with hardwood stock with a 12³/₁₆-inch pull. Calibers: 243, 6mm,
7mm-08 only. Made 1993 to date.

Remington No. 7 Target and Sporting Rifle **$695**
Single shot. Rolling-block Army Pistol frame. Calibers:
22 Short, 22 LR, 25 Stevens R.F. (other calibers as available in No. 2 Rifle were supplied on special order). Half-
octagon barrels: 24-, 26-, 28-inch. Weight: about 6 pounds.
Sights: Lyman combination rear; Beach combination
front. Fancy walnut stock and forearm; Swiss buttplate
available as an extra. Made 1903–1911.

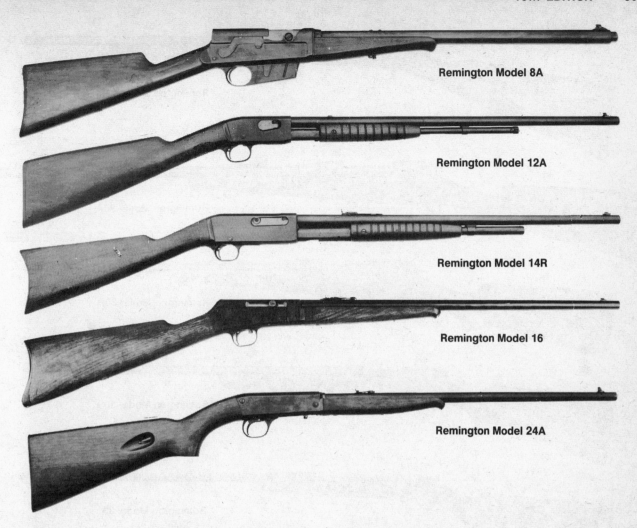

Remington Model 8A

Remington Model 12A

Remington Model 14R

Remington Model 16

Remington Model 24A

RIFLES

Remington Model 8A Autoloading Rifle **$395**
Standard Grade. Takedown. Calibers: 25, 30, 32 and 35
Rem. Five-shot, clip-loaded magazine. 22-inch barrel.
Weight: 7¾ pounds. Sights: open rear; bead front. Plain
straight-grip stock and forearm of walnut. Made 1906–
1936.

**Remington Model 12A, 12B, 12C, 12CS Slide Action
Repeaters**
Standard Grade. Hammerless. Takedown. Caliber: 22
Short, Long or LR. Tubular magazine holds 15 Short, 12
Long or 10 LR cartridges. 22- or 24-inch round or octag-
onal barrel. Open rear sight, bead front. Plain, half-pistol-
grip stock and grooved slide handle of walnut. Made 1912–
1935.
Model 12A **$295**
Model 12B (22 Short only w/octagon bbl.) **310**
Model 12C (w/24-inch octagon bbl.) **335**
Model 12CS (22 WRF w/24-inch octagon bbl.) . . . **295**

**Remington Model 14A High Power Slide Action
Repeating Rifle** **$350**
Standard Grade. Hammerless. Takedown. Calibers: 25,
30, 32 and 35 Rem. 5-shot tubular magazine. 22-inch
barrel. Weight: about 6¾ pounds. Sights: open rear; bead
front. Plain, half-pistol-grip stock and grooved slide
handle of walnut. Made 1912–1935.

Remington Model 14R Carbine **$375**
Same as Model 14A except has 18½-inch barrel, straight-
grip stock, weighs about 6 pounds.

Remington Model 14½ Carbine **$695**
Same as Model 14½ Rifle, except has 9-shot magazine,
18½-inch barrel.

Remington Model 14½ Rifle **$725**
Similar to Model 14A, except calibers 38/40 and 44/40,
11-shot full magazine, 22½-inch barrel. Made 1912 to
early 1920s.

Remington Model 16 Autoloading Rifle **$225**
Takedown. Closely resembles the Winchester Model 03.
Calibers: 22 Short, 22 LR, 22 Rem. Auto. 15-shot tubular
magazine in buttstock. 22-inch barrel. Weight: 5¾ pounds.
Sights: open rear; bead front. Plain straight-grip stock
and forearm. Made 1914–1928. *Note:* In 1918 this model
was discontinued in all calibers except 22 Rem. Auto;
specifications given are for that.

Remington Model 24A Autoloading Rifle **$250**
Standard Grade. Takedown. Calibers: 22 Short only, 22
LR only. Tubular magazine in buttstock, holds 15 Short
or 10 LR. 21-inch barrel. Weight: about 5 pounds. Sights:
open rear; bead front. Plain walnut stock and forearm.
Made 1922–1935.

Remington Model 25R

Remington Model 30A

Remington Model 30R

Remington Model 30S

Remington Model 33

Remington Model 25A Slide Action Repeater ... **$325**
Standard Grade. Hammerless. Takedown. Calibers:
25/20, 32/20. 10-shot tubular magazine. 24-inch barrel.
Weight: about 5½ pounds. Sights: open rear; bead front.
Plain, pistol-grip stock, grooved slide handle. Made 1923–1936.

Remington Model 25R Carbine **$395**
Same as Model 25A, except has 18-inch barrel. 6-shot
magazine, straight-grip stock, weighs about 4½ pounds.

**Remington Model 30A Bolt Action Express
Rifle** **$395**
Standard Grade. Modified M/1917 Enfield Action.
Calibers: 25, 30, 32 and 35 Rem., 7mm Mauser, 30-06. 5-
shot box magazine. 22-inch barrel. Weight: about 7¼
pounds. Sights: open rear; bead front. Walnut stock w/
checkered pistol grip and forearm. Made 1921–1940. *Note:*
Early Model 30s had a slender forend with schnabel tip,
military-type double-pull trigger, 24-inch barrel.

Remington Model 30R Carbine **$495**
Same as Model 30A, except has 20-inch barrel, plain stock,
weighs about 7 pounds.

Remington Model 30S Sporting Rifle **$575**
Special Grade. Same action as Model 30A. Calibers: 257
Roberts, 7mm Mauser, 30-06. 5-shot box magazine. 24-
inch barrel. Weight: about 8 pounds. Lyman #48 Receiver
sight, bead front sight. Special high comb stock with long,
full forearm, checkered. Made 1930–1940.

**Remington Model 33 Bolt Action Single Shot
Rifle** **$120**
Takedown. Caliber: 22 Short, Long, LR. 24-inch barrel.
Weight: about 4½ pounds. Sights: open rear; bead front.
Plain, pistol-grip stock, forearm with grasping grooves.
Made 1931–36.

Remington Model 33 NRA Junior Target Rifle ... **$150**
Same as Model 33 Standard, except has Lyman peep rear
sight, Patridge-type front sight, ⅞-inch sling and swivels,
weighs about 5 pounds.

Remington Model 34

Remington Model 37 (1937)

Remington Model 37 (1940)

Remington Model 40X Standard Rimfire

Remington Model 40-XB Centerfire

RIFLES

Remington Model 34 Bolt Action Repeater **$135**
Takedown. Caliber: 22 Short, Long, LR. Tubular magazine holds 22 Short, 17 Long or 15 LR. 24-inch barrel. Weight: 5¼ pounds. Sights: open rear; bead front. Plain, pistol-grip stock, forearm w/grasping grooves. Made 1932–36.

Remington Model 34 NRA Target Rifle **$195**
Same as Model 34 Standard, except has Lyman peep rear sight, Patridge-type front sight, ⅞-inch sling and swivels, weighs about 5¾ pounds.

**Remington Model 37 Rangemaster Bolt Action
Target Rifle (I)**
Model of 1937. Caliber: 22 LR. 5-shot box magazine, single shot adapter also supplied as standard equipment. 28-inch heavy barrel. Weight: about 12 pounds. Remington front and rear sights, scope bases. Target stock, swivels, sling. *Note:* Original 1937 model had a stock with outside barrel band similar in appearance to that of the old-style Winchester Model 52; forearm design was modified and barrel band eliminated in 1938. Made 1937–1940.
With factory sights. **$395**
Without sights **345**

**Remington Model 37 Rangemaster Bolt Action
Target Rifle (II)**
Model of 1940. Same as Model of 1937, except has "Miracle" trigger mechanism and Randle design stock with high comb, full pistol grip and wide beavertail forend. Made 1940–1954.

Remington Model 37 Rangemaster Target (II) (cont.)
With factory sights. **$525**
Without sights **445**

Remington Model 40X Centerfire Rifle **$375**
Specifications same as for Model 40X Rimfire (heavyweight). Calibers: 222 Rem., 222 Rem. Mag., 7.62mm NATO, 30-06 (others were available on special order). Made 1961–64. Value shown is for rifle w/o sights.

**Remington Model 40X Heavyweight Bolt Action
Target Rifle (Rimfire)**
Caliber: 22 LR. Single shot. Action similar to Model 722. Click adjustable trigger. 28-inch heavy barrel. Redfield Olympic sights. Scope bases. High-comb target stock, bedding device, adj. swivel, rubber buttplate. Weight: 12¾ pounds. Made 1955–1964.
With sights **$410**
Without sights **325**

Remington Model 40-X Sporter **$1175**
Same general specifications as Model 700 C Custom (*see* that listing), except in caliber 22 LR. Made 1972–77.

Remington Model 40X Standard Barrel
Same as Model 40X Heavyweight except has lighter barrel. Weight: 10¾ pounds.
With sights **$350**
Without sights **325**

**Remington Model 40-XB Centerfire
Match Rifle** **$695**
Bolt action, single shot. Calibers: 222 Rem., 222 Rem. Mag., 223 Rem., 22-250, 6×47mm, 6mm Rem., 243 Win.,

Remington Model 40-XB Rimfire

Remington Model 40-XB Varmint Special

Remington Model 40-XBBR

Remington Model 40-XC

Remington Model 40-XB Centerfire Match (cont.)

25-06, 7mm Rem. Mag., 30-06, 308 Win. (7.62mm NATO), 30-338, 300 Win. Mag. 27¼-inch standard or heavy barrel. Target stock w/adj. front swivel block on guide rail, rubber buttplate. Weight w/o sights: standard barrel, 9¼ lbs.; heavy barrel, 11¼ lbs. Value shown is for rifle without sights. Made 1964 to date.

Remington Model 40-XB Centerfire Repeater . . . $775

Same as Model 40-XB Centerfire except 5-shot repeater. Calibers: 222 Rem., 222 Rem. Mag., 223 Rem., 22-250, 6×47mm, 6mm Rem., 243 Win., 308 Win. (7.62mm NATO). Heavy barrel only. Discontinued.

Remington Model 40-XB Rangemaster Centerfire

Single-shot target rifle with same basic specifications as Model 40-XB Centerfire Match. Additional calibers in 220 Swift, 6mm BR Rem. and 7mm BR Rem., and stainless barrel only. American walnut or Kevlar (weighs 1 lb. less) target stock with forend stop. Discontinued 1994.

Model 40-XB Right-hand Model	$790
Model 40-XB Left-hand Model	835
For 2-oz. Trigger, **add**	100
Model 40-XB KS (Kevlar Stock, R.H.)	905
Model 40-XB KS (Kevlar Stock, L.H.)	950
For 2-oz. trigger, **add**	100
For Repeater Model, **add**	80

Remington Model 40-XB Rangemaster Rimfire Match Rifle $550

Bolt action, single shot. Caliber: 22 LR. 28-inch standard or heavy barrel. Target stock with adjustable front swivel

Remington 40-XB Rangemaster RF Match (cont.)

block on guide rail, rubber buttplate. Weight w/o sights: standard barrel, 10 lbs.; heavy barrel, 11¼ lbs. Value shown is for rifle without sights. Made 1964–1974.

Remington Model 40-XB Varmint Special Rifle . . $785

Same general specifications as Model 40-XB Repeater, except has synthetic stock of Kevlar. Made 1987–1994.

Remington Model 40-XBBR Bench Rest Rifle

Bolt action, single shot. Calibers: 222 Rem., 222 Rem. Mag., 223 Rem., 6×47mm, 308 Win. (7.62mm NATO). 20- or 26-inch unblued stainless-steel barrel. Supplied w/o sights. Weight: with 20-inch bbl., 9¼ lbs.; with 26-inch bbl., 12 lbs. (heavy Varmint class); 7¼ lbs. w/Kevlar stock (light Varmint class). Made 1969 to date.

Model 40-XBBR	$640
Model 40-XBBR KS (Kevlar Stock) (disc.)	960

Remington Model 40-XC National Match Course Rifle

Bolt-action repeater. Caliber: 308 Win. (7.62mm NATO). 5-shot magazine; clip slot in receiver. 24-inch barrel. Supplied w/o sights. Weight: 11 pounds. Thumb groove stock w/adj. hand stop and sling swivel, adj. buttplate. Made 1974 to date.

Model 40-XC	$795
Model 40-XC KS (Kevlar Stock) (disc. 1994)	960

Remington Model 40-XR Custom Sporter Rifle

Caliber: 22 RF. 24-inch contoured barrel. Supplied w/o sights. Made in four grades of checkering, engraving and

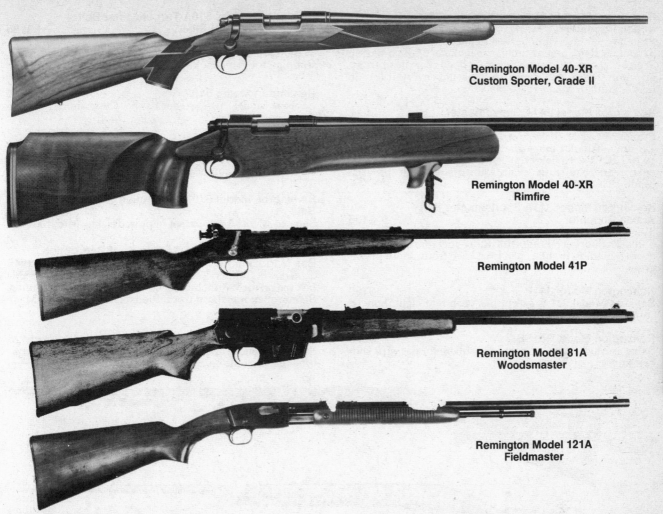

Remington Model 40-XR
Custom Sporter, Grade II

Remington Model 40-XR
Rimfire

Remington Model 41P

Remington Model 81A
Woodsmaster

Remington Model 121A
Fieldmaster

Remington Model 40-XR Custom Sporter (cont.)
other custom features. Made 1987 to date.
Grade I .... $ 850
Grade II 1540
Grade III 2450
Grade IV 3800

Remington Model 40-XR Rimfire Position Rifle
Bolt action, single shot. Caliber: 22 LR. 24-inch heavy barrel.
Supplied w/o sights. Weight: about 10 pounds. Position-
style stock w/thumb groove, adj. hand stop and sling swivel
on guide rail, adj. buttplate. Made 1974 to date.
Model 40-XR $895
Model 40-XR KS (Kevlar Stock) 950

**Remington Model 41A Targetmaster Bolt Action
Single Shot Rifle** $155
Takedown. Caliber: 22 Short, Long, LR. 27-inch barrel.
Weight: about 5½ pounds. Sights: open rear; bead front.
Plain pistol-grip stock. Made 1936–1940.

Remington Model 41AS $175
Same as Model 41A, except chambered for 22 Remington
Special (22 W.R.F.).

Remington Model 41P $100
Same as Model 41A, except has peep rear sight, hooded
front sight.

Remington Model 41SB $200
Same as Model 41A, except smoothbore for use with shot
cartridges.

**Remington Model 81A Woodsmaster Auto-
loader** $350
Standard Grade. Takedown. Calibers: 30, 32 and 35 Rem.,
300 Sav. 5-shot box magazine (not detachable). 22-inch
barrel. Weight: 8¼ pounds. Sights: open rear; bead front.
Plain walnut pistol-grip stock, forearm. Made 1936–1950.

**Remington Model 121A Fieldmaster Slide Action
Repeater** $265
Standard Grade. Hammerless. Takedown. Caliber: 22
Short, Long, LR. Tubular magazine holds 20 Short, 15
Long or 14 LR cartridges. 24-inch round barrel. Weight:
6 pounds. Plain, pistol-grip stock and grooved
semibeavertail slide handle. Made 1936–1954.

Remington Model 121S $325
Same as Model 121A, except chambered for 22 Remington
Special (22 W.R.F.). Magazine holds 12 rounds. Disc.

Remington Model 121SB $395
Same as Model 121A, except smoothbore. Discontinued.

Remington Model 141A Gamemaster Slide Action Repeater $295
Standard Grade. Hammerless. Takedown. Calibers: 30, 32 and 35 Rem. 5-shot tubular magazine. 24-inch barrel. Weight: about 7¾ pounds. Sights: open rear; bead front, on ramp. Plain, pistol-grip stock, semibeavertail forend (slide-handle). Made 1936–1950.

Remington Model 241A Speedmaster Autoloader $260
Standard Grade. Takedown. Calibers: 22 Short only, 22 LR only. Tubular magazine in buttstock, holds 15 Short or 10 LR. 24-inch barrel. Weight: about 6 pounds. Sights; open rear; bead front. Plain walnut stock and forearm. Made 1935–1951.

Remington Model 341A Sportsmaster Bolt Action Repeater $135
Takedown. Caliber: 22 Short, Long, LR. Tubular magazine holds 22 Short, 17 Long, 15 LR. 27-inch barrel. Weight: about 6 pounds. Sights; open rear; bead front. Plain pistol-grip stock. Made 1936–1940.

Remington Model 341P $160
Same as Model 341A, except has peep rear sight, hooded front sight.

Remington Model 341SB $275
Same as Model 341A, except smoothbore for use with shot cartridges.

Remington Model 510A Targetmaster Bolt Action Single Shot Rifle $195
Takedown. Caliber: 22 Short, Long, LR. 25-inch barrel. Weight: about 5½ pounds. Sights: open rear; bead front. Plain pistol-grip stock. Made 1939–1962.

Remington Model 510P $150
Same as Model 510A, except has peep rear sight, Patridge front, on ramp.

Remington Model 510SB $250
Same as Model 510A, except smoothbore for use with shot cartridges, shotgun bead front sight, no rear sight.

Remington Model 510X Bolt Action Single Shot Rifle $160
Same as Model 510A, except improved sights. Mfd. 1964–66.

Remington Model 511A Scoremaster Bolt Action Box Magazine Repeater $140
Takedown. Caliber: 22 Short, Long, LR. 6-shot detachable box magazine. 25-inch barrel. Weight: about 5½ pounds. Sights: open rear; bead front. Plain pistol-grip stock. Made 1939–1962.

Remington Model 511P $125
Same as Model 511A, except has peep rear sight, Patridge-type blade front, on ramp.

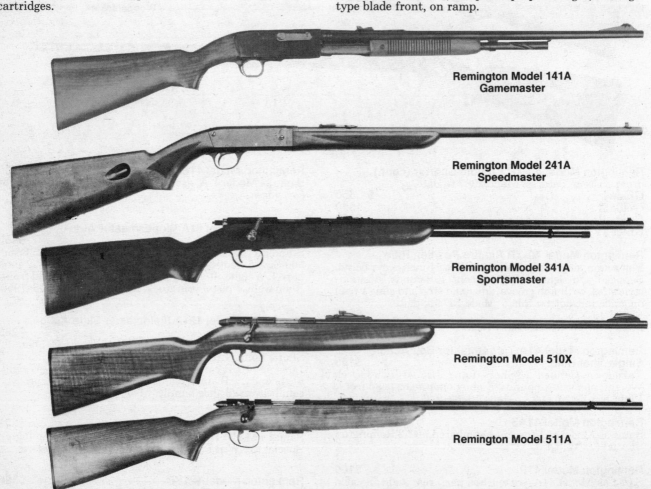

Remington Model 141A Gamemaster

Remington Model 241A Speedmaster

Remington Model 341A Sportsmaster

Remington Model 510X

Remington Model 511A

Remington Model 511X Bolt Action Repeater . . . **$150**
Clip type. Same as Model 511A, except improved sights. Made 1964–66.

Remington Model 512A Sportsmaster Bolt Action Repeater **$150**
Takedown. Caliber: 22 Short, Long, LR. Tubular magazine holds 22 Short, 17 Long, 15 LR. 25-inch barrel. Weight: about 5¾ pounds. Sights: open rear; bead front. Plain pistol-grip stock w/semibeavertail forend. Made 1940–1962.

Remington Model 512P **$195**
Same as Model 512A, except has peep rear sight, blade front, on ramp.

Remington Model 512X Bolt Action Repeater . . . **$210**
Tubular magazine type. Same as Model 512A, except has improved sights. Made 1964–66.

Remington Model 513S Bolt Action Sporting Rifle **$325**
Caliber: 22 LR. 6-shot detachable box magazine. 27-inch barrel. Weight: about 6¾ pounds. Marble open rear sight,

Remington Model 513S Sporter (cont.)
Patridge-type front. Checkered sporter stock. Made 1941–1956.

Remington Model 513TR Matchmaster Bolt Action Target Rifle **$250**
Caliber: 22 LR. 6-shot detachable box magazine. 27-inch barrel. Weight: about 9 pounds. Sights: Redfield No. 75 rear; globe front. Target stock. Sling and swivels. Made 1941–1969.

Remington Model 514 Bolt Action Single Shot . . **$135**
Takedown. Caliber: 22 Short, Long, LR. 24-inch barrel. Weight: 4¾ pounds. Sights: open rear; bead front. Plain pistol-grip stock. Made 1948–1971.

Remington Model 514BC Boy's Carbine **$175**
Same as Model 514, except has 21-inch barrel, 1-inch shorter stock. Made 1961–1971.

Remington Model 514P **$200**
Same as Model 514, except has receiver peep sight.

RIFLES

Remington Model 511X

Remington Model 512A Sportsmaster

Remington Model 513S

Remington Model 513TR Matchmaster

Remington Model 514BC

Remington Model 521TL

Remington Model 540-X

Remington Model 540-XR

Remington Model 541-S

Remington Model 541-T

Remington Model 521TL Junior Target Bolt Action Repeater **$225**
Takedown. Caliber: 22 LR. 6-shot detachable box magazine. 25-inch barrel. Weight: about 7 pounds. Sights: Lyman No. 57RS rear; blade front. Target stock. Sling and swivels. Made 1947–1969.

Remington Model 522 Viper **$125**
Calibers: 22 LR. 10-shot magazine. 20-inch barrel. 40 inches overall. Weight: 4⁵/₈ pounds. Checkered black PET resin stock with beavertail forend. Dupont high-tech synthetic receiver. Matte black finish on all exposed metal. Made 1993 to date.

Remington Model 540-X Rimfire Target Rifle . . . **$265**
Bolt action, single shot. Caliber: 22 LR. 26-inch heavy barrel. Supplied w/o sights. Weight: about 8 pounds. Target stock w/Monte Carlo cheekpiece and thumb groove, guide rail for hand stop and swivel, adj. buttplate. Made 1969–1974.

Remington Model 540-XR Position Rifle **$285**
Bolt action, single shot. Caliber: 22 LR. 26-inch medium-weight barrel. Supplied w/o sights. Weight: 8 lbs. 13 oz.

Remington Model 540-XR Position Rifle (cont.)
Position-style stock w/thumb groove, guide rail for hand stop and swivel, adj. buttplate. Made 1974–1984.

Remington Model 540-XRJR **$295**
Same as Model 540-XR, except 1³/₄-inch shorter stock. Made 1974–1984.

Remington Model 541-S Custom Sporter **$385**
Bolt-action repeater. Scroll engraving on receiver and trigger guard. Caliber: 22 Short, Long, LR. 5-shot clip magazine. 24-inch barrel. Weight: 5¹/₂ pounds. Supplied w/o sights. Checkered walnut stock w/rosewood-finished forend tip, pistol-grip cap and buttplate. Made 1972–1984.

Remington Model 541-T Bolt Action Rifle
Caliber: 22 RF. Clip-fed, 5-shot. 24-inch barrel. Weight: 5⁷/₈ pounds. Checkered walnut stock. Made 1986 to date; heavy barrel model introduced in 1993.
Model 541-T Standard **$250**
Model 541-T HB Heavy barrel **295**

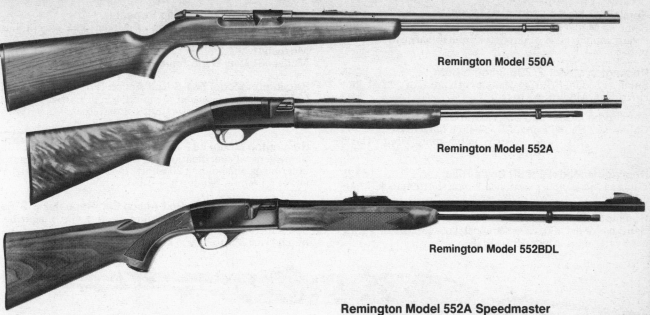

Remington Model 550A

Remington Model 552A

Remington Model 552BDL

Remington Model 550A Autoloader **$135**
Has "Power Piston" or floating chamber, which permits interchangeable use of 22 Short, Long or LR cartridges. Tubular magazine holds 22 Short, 17 Long, 15 LR. 24-inch barrel. Weight: about 6¼ pounds. Sights: open rear; bead front. Plain, one-piece pistol-grip stock. Made 1941–1971.

Remington Model 550P **$150**
Same as Model 550A, except has peep rear sight, blade front, on ramp.

Remington Model 550-2G **$195**
"Gallery Special." Same as Model 550A, except has 22-inch barrel, screweye for counter chain and fired shell deflector.

Remington Model 552A Speedmaster Autoloader **$150**
Caliber: 22 Short, Long, LR. Tubular magazine holds 20 Short, 17 Long, 15 LR. 25-inch barrel. Weight: about 5½ pounds. Sights: open rear; bead front. Pistol-grip stock, semibeavertail forearm. Made 1957–1988.

Remington Model 552BDL Deluxe **$175**
Same as Model 552A, except has checkered walnut stock and forearm. Made 1966 to date.

Remington Model 552C Carbine **$160**
Same as Model 552A, except has 21-inch barrel. Made 1961–1977.

Remington Model 552GS Gallery Special **$175**
Same as Model 552A, except chambered for 22 Short only. Made 1957–1977.

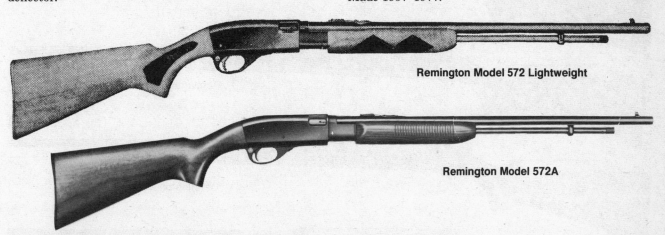

Remington Model 572 Lightweight

Remington Model 572A

Remington Model 572 Lightweight **$275**
Same as Model 572A, except has aluminum alloy receiver and outer barrel casing anodized in colors, chrome-plated magazine tube, trigger and trigger guard, checkered stock and forearm of light tan walnut. Weight: about 4 pounds. Colors: Buckskin Tan (Model 572BT), Teal Wing Blue (Model 572TWB), Crown Wing Black (Model 572CWB). Made 1958–1962.

Remington Model 572A Fieldmaster Slide Action Repeater **$150**
Hammerless. Caliber: 22 Short, Long, LR. Tubular magazine holds 20 Short, 17 Long, 15 LR. 23-inch barrel. Weight: about 5½ pounds. Sights: open rear; ramp front. Pistol-grip stock, grooved forearm. Made 1955–1988.

Remington Model 572BDL Deluxe **$185**
Same as Model 572A, except has blade ramp front sight, sliding ramp rear; checkered stock and forearm. Made 1966 to date.

Remington Model 572SB Smooth Bore **$245**
Same as Model 572A, except smooth bore for 22 LR shot cartridges. Made 1961 to date.

Remington Model 580 Bolt Action Single Shot . . **$115**
Caliber: 22 Short, Long, LR. 24-inch barrel. Weight: 4³/₄ pounds. Sights: bead front; U-notch rear. Monte Carlo stock. Made 1967–1978.

Remington Model 580BR Boy's Rifle **$125**
Same as Model 580, except has 1-inch shorter stock. Made 1971–78.

Remington Model 580SB Smooth Bore **$145**
Same as Model 580, except smooth bore for 22 Long Rifle shot cartridges. Made 1967–1978.

Remington Model 581 Clip Repeater
Same general specifications as Model 580, except has 5-shot clip magazine. Made 1967–1984.
Model 581 . . . . **$125**
Model 581 Left Hand (made 1969–1984) **150**

Remington Model 581-S Bolt Action Rifle **$150**
Caliber: 22 RF. Clip-fed, 5-shot. 24-inch barrel. Weight: about 4³/₄ pounds. Plain walnut-colored stock. Made 1987–1992.

Remington Model 582 Tubular Repeater **$135**
Same general specifications as Model 580, except has tubular magazine holding 20 Short, 15 Long, 14 LR. Weight: about 5 pounds. Made 1967–1984.

Remington Model 591 Bolt Action Clip Repeater . **$195**
Caliber: 5mm Rimfire Magnum. 4-shot clip magazine. 24-inch barrel. Weight: 5 pounds. Sights: bead front; U-notch rear. Monte Carlo stock. Made 1970–73.

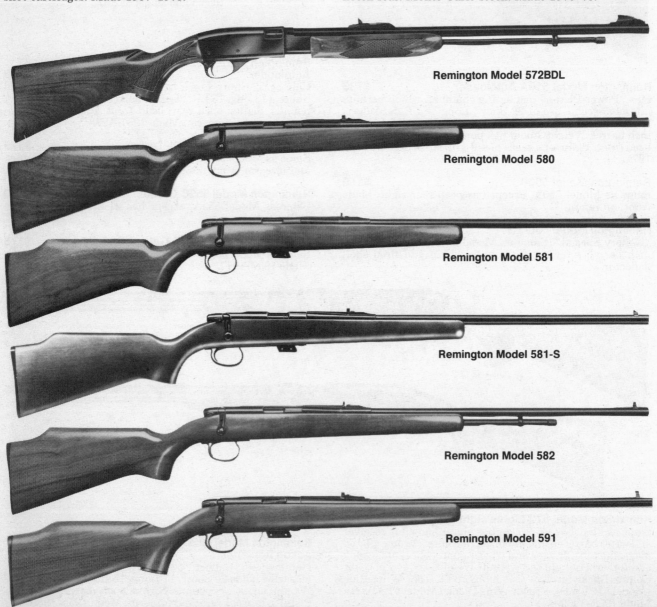

Remington Model 572BDL

Remington Model 580

Remington Model 581

Remington Model 581-S

Remington Model 582

Remington Model 591

Remington Model 592

Remington Model 600

Remington Model 600
Montana Territorial Centennial

Remington Model 660

Remington Model 660 Magnum

RIFLES

Remington Model 592 Tubular Repeater **$175**
Same as Model 591, except has tubular magazine holding
10 rounds, weighs 5½ pounds. Made 1970–73.

Remington Model 600 Bolt Action Carbine **$495**
Calibers: 222 Rem., 6mm Rem., 243 Win., 308 Win., 35
Rem. 5-shot box magazine (6-shot in 222 Rem.). 18½-
inch barrel with ventilated rib. Weight: 6 pounds. Sights:
open rear; blade ramp front. Monte Carlo stock w/pistol
grip. Made 1964–67.

Remington Model 600 Magnum **$595**
Same as Model 600, except calibers 6.5mm Rem. Mag.
and 350 Rem. Mag., 4-shot magazine, special Magnum-
type barrel with racket for scope back-up, laminated
walnut-and-beech stock w/recoil pad. QD swivels and
sling; weight: about 6½ pounds. Made 1965–67.

**Remington Model 600 Montana Territorial
Centennial** **$725**
Same as Model 600, except has commemorative medallion
embedded in buttstock. Made 1964. Value is for rifle in
new, unfired condition.

Remington Model 660 Bolt Action Carbine **$425**
Calibers: 222 Rem., 6mm Rem., 243 Win., 308 Win. 5-
shot box magazine (6-shot in 222). 20-inch barrel. Weight:
6½ pounds. Sights: open rear; bead front, on ramp. Monte
Carlo stock, checkered, black pistol-grip cap and forend
tip. Made 1968–1971.

Remington Model 660 Magnum **$575**
Same as Model 660, except calibers 6.5mm Rem. Mag.
and 350 Rem. Mag., 4-shot magazine, laminated walnut-
and-beech stock with recoil pad, QD swivels and sling.
Made 1968–1971.

Remington Model 700 ADL Centerfire Rifle **$285**
Calibers: 22-250, 222 Rem., 25-06, 6mm Rem., 243 Win.,
270 Win., 30-06, 308 Win., 7mm Rem. Mag. Magazine
capacity: 6-shot in 222 Rem.; 4-shot in 7mm Rem. Mag.;
5-shot in other calibers. Barrel lengths: 24-inch in 22-250,
222 Rem., 25-06, 7mm Rem. Mag.; 22-inch in other calibers. Weight: 7 lbs. standard; 7½ lbs. in 7mm Rem. Mag.
Sights: ramp front; sliding ramp open rear. Monte

Remington Model 700 ADL

Remington Model 700 BDL

Remington Model 700 BDL
Left Hand

Remington Model 700 BDL
Varmint Special

Remington Model 700 Classic

Remington Model 700 Classic
Magnum

Remington Model 700 ADL Centerfire Rifle (cont.)

Carlo stock w/cheekpiece, skip checkering, recoil pad on Magnum. Made 1962–1993.

Remington Model 700 BDL Custom Deluxe

Same as Model 700 ADL, except has hinged floorplate, hooded ramp front sight, stock w/black forend tip and pistol-grip cap, cut checkering, QD swivels and sling. Additional calibers: 17 Rem., 223 Rem., 264 Win. Mag., 7mm-08, 280, 300 Sav., 300 Win. Mag., 8mm Rem. Mag., 338 Win. Mag., 35 Whelen. All have 24-inch barrels. Magnums have 4-shot magazine, recoil pad, weigh 7½ pounds; 17 Rem. has 6-shot magazine, weighs 7 pounds. Made 1962 to date. Left-hand version available in calibers 270 Win., 30-06, 7mm Rem. Mag.; made 1973 to date.

Standard calibers except 17 Rem.	**$385**
Magnum calibers and 17 Rem.	**425**
Left-hand, 270 Win. and 30-06	**395**
Left-hand, 7mm Rem. Mag.	**400**

Remington Model 700 BDL European Rifle

Same general specifications as Model 700 BDL, except has oil-finished walnut stock. Calibers: 243, 270, 7mm-08,

Remington Model 700 BDL European Rifle (cont.)

7mm Mag., 280 Rem., 30-06. Made 1993 to date.

Standard Calibers	**$395**
Magnum Calibers	**415**

Remington Model 700 BDL SS Bolt Action Rifle

Same as Model 700 BDL, except has w/24-inch stainless barrel, receiver and bolt plus black synthetic stock. Calibers: 223 Rem., 243 Win., 6mm Rem., 25-06 Rem., 270 Win., 280 Rem., 7mm-08, 7mm Rem. Mag., 7mm Wby. Mag., 30-06, 300 Win., 308 Win., 338 Win. Mag. Made 1992 to date.

Standard Calibers	**$415**
Magnum Calibers, **add**	**25**
Detachable Box Magazine, **add**	**25**

Remington Model 700 BDL Varmint Special **$395**

Same as Model 700 BDL, except has 24-inch heavy barrel, no sights, weighs 9 lbs. (8¾ lbs. in 308 Win.). Calibers: 22-250, 222 Rem., 223 Rem., 25-06, 6mm Rem., 243 Win., 308 Win. Made 1967–1994.

Remington Model 700 Classic

Same general specifications as Model 700 BDL, except has "Classic" stock of high-quality walnut with full-

Remington Model 700 Custom Rifle, Grade I

Remington Model 700 Custom Rifle, Grade IV

Remington Model 700 KS Custom

Remington Model 700 RS

Remington Model 700 Safari

Remington Model 700 Classic (cont.)

pattern cut-checkering, special satin wood finish; schnabel forend. Brown rubber buttpad. Hinged floorplate. No sights. Weight: 7 pounds. Also chambered for "Classic" cartridges such as 257 Roberts and 250-3000. Intro. 1981.

Standard Calibers	**$345**
Magnum Calibers	385

Remington Model 700 Custom Bolt Action Rifle

Same general specifications as Model 700 BDL, except custom built, and available in choice of grades—each with higher quality wood, different checkering patterns, engraving, high-gloss blued finish. Introduced in 1965.

Model 700 C Grade I	**$ 850**
Model 700 C Grade II	1540
Model 700 C Grade III	2450
Model 700 C Grade IV	3800
Model 700 D Peerless	1350
Model 700 F Premier	2595

Remington Model 700 FS Bolt Action Rifle $425

Calibers: 243, 270 Win., 30-06, 308 and 7mm Rem. Mag. 22-inch barrel. Weight: 6¼ pounds. Straight-line fiberglass stock with solid black English-style buttpad and sling swivels. Made 1987–1990.

Remington Model 700 KS Custom Mountain Rifle

Calibers: 270 Win., 280 Rem., 30-06, 7mm Rem. Mag., 300 Win. Mag., 338 Win. Mag., 8mm Rem. Mag. and 375 H&H. 22-inch barrel. Weight: 6¾ pounds. Available in both right- and left-hand models. Synthetic stock with Kevlar aramid fiber. Made 1987–1993.

Standard Model	**$695**
Left-hand Model	725
Stainless Model	825

Remington Model 700 Mountain Rifle $375

Lightweight version (6¾ pounds) of Model 700, with 22-inch barrel, checkered straight-comb satin-finished stock in calibers 243 Win., 270 Win., 280 Rem., 7mm-08 Rem., 30-06 and 308 Win. Made 1986 to date.

Remington 700 MTRSS Bolt Action Rifle $400

Similar to the Model 700 Mountain Rifle, except in stainless steel with black textured synthetic stock. Calibers: 25-06, 270, 280 Rem., 30-06. Weights 6¼ pounds. Made 1993–94.

Remington Model 700 RS Bolt Action Rifle $370

Calibers: 270 Win., 280 Rem. and 30-06. 22-inch barrel. Weight: 7¼ pounds. Stock made of Du Pont Rynite. Made 1987–1990.

Remington Model 700 Safari Grade

Magnum version of Model 700 BDL, except in calibers 8mm Rem. Mag., 375 H&H Mag., 416 Rem. Mag. and 458

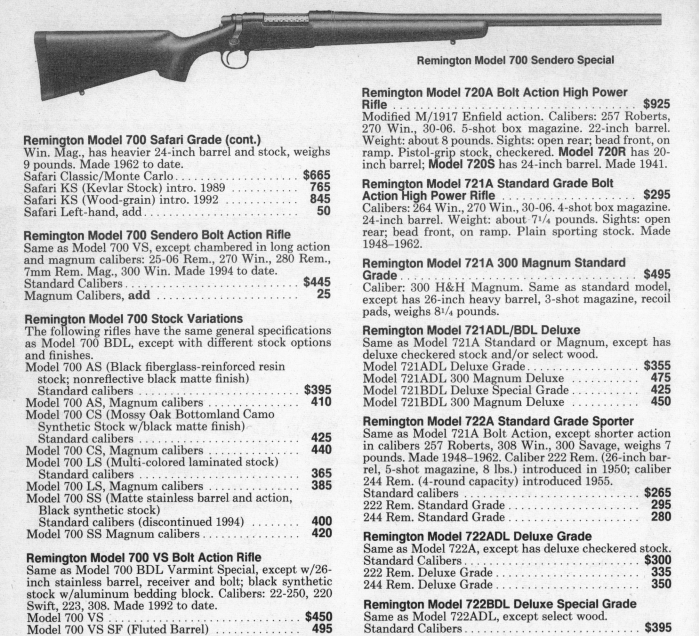

Remington Model 700 Sendero Special

Remington Model 700 Safari Grade (cont.)

Win. Mag., has heavier 24-inch barrel and stock, weighs 9 pounds. Made 1962 to date.

Safari Classic/Monte Carlo	$665
Safari KS (Kevlar Stock) intro. 1989	765
Safari KS (Wood-grain) intro. 1992	845
Safari Left-hand, add	50

Remington Model 700 Sendero Bolt Action Rifle

Same as Model 700 VS, except chambered in long action and magnum calibers: 25-06 Rem., 270 Win., 280 Rem., 7mm Rem. Mag., 300 Win. Made 1994 to date.

Standard Calibers	$445
Magnum Calibers, add	25

Remington Model 700 Stock Variations

The following rifles have the same general specifications as Model 700 BDL, except with different stock options and finishes.

Model 700 AS (Black fiberglass-reinforced resin stock; nonreflective black matte finish)	
Standard calibers	$395
Model 700 AS, Magnum calibers	410
Model 700 CS (Mossy Oak Bottomland Camo Synthetic Stock w/black matte finish)	
Standard calibers	425
Model 700 CS, Magnum calibers	440
Model 700 LS (Multi-colored laminated stock)	
Standard calibers	365
Model 700 LS, Magnum calibers	385
Model 700 SS (Matte stainless barrel and action, Black synthetic stock)	
Standard calibers (discontinued 1994)	400
Model 700 SS Magnum calibers	420

Remington Model 700 VS Bolt Action Rifle

Same as Model 700 BDL Varmint Special, except w/26-inch stainless barrel, receiver and bolt; black synthetic stock w/aluminum bedding block. Calibers: 22-250, 220 Swift, 223, 308. Made 1992 to date.

Model 700 VS	$450
Model 700 VS SF (Fluted Barrel)	495

Remington Model 720A Bolt Action High Power Rifle ... $925

Modified M/1917 Enfield action. Calibers: 257 Roberts, 270 Win., 30-06. 5-shot box magazine. 22-inch barrel. Weight: about 8 pounds. Sights: open rear; bead front, on ramp. Pistol-grip stock, checkered. **Model 720R** has 20-inch barrel; **Model 720S** has 24-inch barrel. Made 1941.

Remington Model 721A Standard Grade Bolt Action High Power Rifle ... $295

Calibers: 264 Win., 270 Win., 30-06. 4-shot box magazine. 24-inch barrel. Weight: about 7¼ pounds. Sights: open rear; bead front, on ramp. Plain sporting stock. Made 1948–1962.

Remington Model 721A 300 Magnum Standard Grade ... $495

Caliber: 300 H&H Magnum. Same as standard model, except has 26-inch heavy barrel, 3-shot magazine, recoil pads, weighs 8¼ pounds.

Remington Model 721ADL/BDL Deluxe

Same as Model 721A Standard or Magnum, except has deluxe checkered stock and/or select wood.

Model 721ADL Deluxe Grade	$355
Model 721ADL 300 Magnum Deluxe	475
Model 721BDL Deluxe Special Grade	425
Model 721BDL 300 Magnum Deluxe	450

Remington Model 722A Standard Grade Sporter

Same as Model 721A Bolt Action, except shorter action in calibers 257 Roberts, 308 Win., 300 Savage, weighs 7 pounds. Made 1948–1962. Caliber 222 Rem. (26-inch barrel, 5-shot magazine, 8 lbs.) introduced in 1950; caliber 244 Rem. (4-round capacity) introduced 1955.

Standard calibers	$265
222 Rem. Standard Grade	295
244 Rem. Standard Grade	280

Remington Model 722ADL Deluxe Grade

Same as Model 722A, except has deluxe checkered stock.

Standard Calibers	$300
222 Rem. Deluxe Grade	335
244 Rem. Deluxe Grade	350

Remington Model 722BDL Deluxe Special Grade

Same as Model 722ADL, except select wood.

Standard Calibers	$395

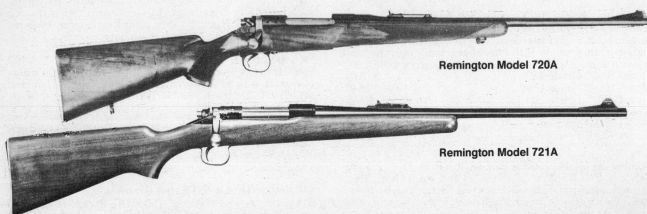

Remington Model 720A

Remington Model 721A

Remington Model 725 Kodiak

Remington Model 722BDL Deluxe Special (cont.)
222 Rem. Deluxe Special Grade **$425**
244 Rem. Deluxe Special Grade **445**

Remington Model 725 Kodiak Magnum Rifle . . **$2595**
Similar to Model 725ADL. Calibers: 375 H&H Mag., 458
Win. Mag. 3-shot magazine. 26-inch barrel with recoil
reducer built into muzzle. Weight: about 9 pounds. Deluxe,
reinforced Monte Carlo stock with recoil pad, black forend
tip, swivels, sling. Less than 100 made in 1961.

**Remington Model 725ADL Bolt Action
Repeating Rifle** **$600**
Calibers: 222, 243, 244, 270, 280, 30-06. 4-shot box
magazine (5-shot in 222). 22-inch barrel (24-inch in 222).
Weight: about 7 pounds. Sights: open rear; hooded ramp
front. Monte Carlo comb stock w/pistol grip, checkered,
swivels. Made 1958–1961.

**Remington Model 740A Woodsmaster
Autoloader Rifle** **$295**
Standard Grade. Gas-operated. Calibers: 30-06 or 308. 4-
shot detachable box magazine. 22-inch barrel. Weight:
about 7 1/2 pounds. Plain pistol-grip stock, semibeavertail
forend with finger grooves. Sights: open rear; ramp front.
Made 1955–1960.

Remington Model 740ADL/BDL Deluxe
Same as Model 740A, except has deluxe checkered stock,
standard or high comb, grip cap, sling swivels. Model
740BDL also has select wood. Made 1955–1960.

Remington Model 740ADL/BDL Deluxe (cont.)
Model 740ADL Deluxe Grade **$325**
Model 740BDL Deluxe Special Grade **350**

**Remington Model 742 Bicentennial
Commemorative** **$550**
Same as Model 742 rifle, except has commemorative
inscription on receiver. Made 1976.

Remington Model 742 Canadian Centennial **$565**
Same as Model 742 rifle, except has commemorative inscription on receiver. Made 1967. Value is for rifle in new,
unfired condition.

Remington Model 742 Carbine **$380**
Same as Model 742 Rifle, except made in calibers 30-06
and 308 only, has 18 1/2-inch barrel, weighs 6 3/4 pounds.
Made 1961–1980.

**Remington Model 742 Woodsmaster
Automatic Big Game Rifle** **$300**
Gas-operated semiautomatic. Calibers: 6mm Rem., 243
Win., 280 Rem., 30-06, 308 Win. 4-shot clip magazine.
22-inch barrel. Weight: 7 1/2 pounds. Sights: open rear; bead

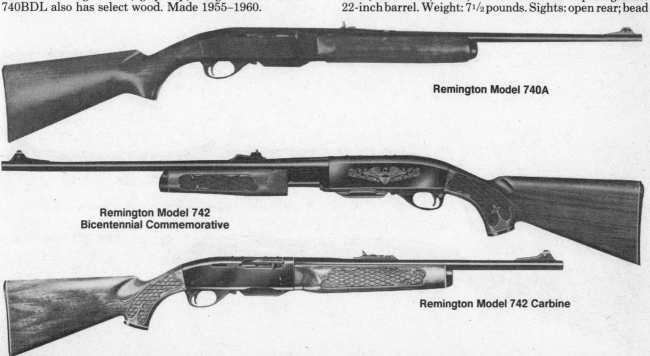

Remington Model 740A

**Remington Model 742
Bicentennial Commemorative**

Remington Model 742 Carbine

RIFLES

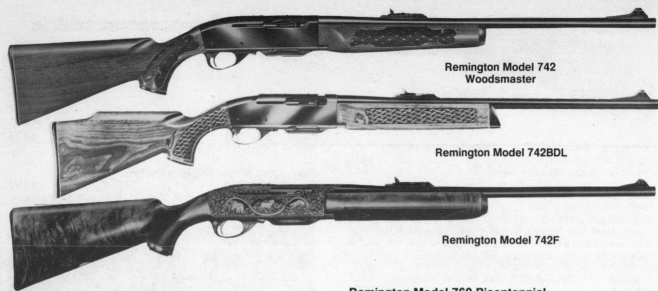

Remington Model 742
Woodsmaster

Remington Model 742BDL

Remington Model 742F

Remington Model 742 Woodsmaster (cont.)

front, on ramp. Checkered pistol-grip stock and forearm. Made 1960–1980.

Remington Model 742BDL Custom Deluxe $350

Same as Model 742 Rifle, except made in calibers 30-06 and 308 only, has Monte Carlo cheekpiece stock, forearm with black tip, basket-weave checkering. Available in left-hand model. Made 1966–1980.

Remington Model 742D Peerless Grade $1195

Same as Model 742 except scroll engraved, fancy wood. Made 1961–1980.

Remington Model 742F Premier Grade $2550

Same as Model 742 except extensively engraved with game scenes and scroll, finest grade wood. Also available with receiver inlaid with gold; adds 50 percent to value. Made 1961–1980.

Remington Model 760 Bicentennial Commemorative $550

Same as Model 760, except has commemorative inscription on receiver. Made 1976.

Remington Model 760 Carbine $355

Same as Model 760 Rifle, except made in calibers 270 Win., 280 Rem., 30-06 and 308 Win. only, has 18 1/2-inch barrel, weighs 7 1/4 pounds. Made 1961–1980.

Remington Model 760 Gamemaster Standard Grade Slide Action Repeating Rifle $300

Hammerless. Calibers: 223 Rem., 6mm Rem., 243 Win., 257 Roberts, 270 Win., 280 Rem., 30-06, 300 Sav., 308 Win., 35 Rem. 22-inch barrel. Weight: about 7 1/2 pounds. Sights: open rear; bead front, on ramp. Plain pistol-grip stock, grooved slide handle on early models; current production has checkered stock and slide handle. Made 1952–1980.

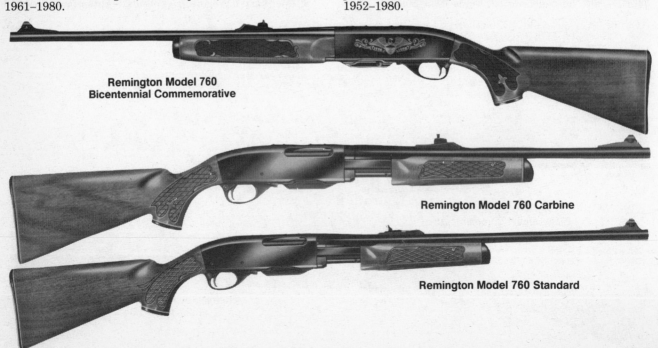

Remington Model 760
Bicentennial Commemorative

Remington Model 760 Carbine

Remington Model 760 Standard

Remington Model 760ADL

Remington Model 760BDL

Remington Model 788 Left Hand

RIFLES

Remington Model 760ADL Deluxe Grade **$395**
Same as Model 760, except has deluxe checkered stock, standard or high comb, grip cap, sling swivels. Made 1953–1963.

Remington Model 760BDL Custom Deluxe **$320**
Same as Model 760 Rifle, except made in calibers 270, 30-06 and 308 only, has Monte Carlo cheekpiece stock, forearm with black tip, basket-weave checkering. Available also in left-hand model. Made 1953–1980.

Remington Model 760D Peerless Grade **$1100**
Same as Model 760, except scroll engraved, fancy wood. Made 1953–1980.

Remington Model 760F Premier Grade **$2370**
Same as Model 760, except extensively engraved with game scenes and scroll, finest grade wood. Also available with receiver inlaid with gold; adds 50 percent to value. Made 1953–1980.

Remington Model 788 Centerfire Bolt Action
Calibers: 222 Rem., 22-250, 223 Rem., 6mm Rem., 243 Win., 308 Win., 30-30, 44 Rem. Mag. 3-shot clip magazine (4-shot in 222 and 223 Rem.). 24-inch barrel in 22s, 22-inch in other calibers. Weight: 7¹/₂ lbs. with 24-inch bbl.;

Remington Model 788 Centerfire Bolt Action (cont.)
7¹/₄ lbs. with 22-inch bbl. Sights: blade front, on ramp; U-notch rear. Plain Monte Carlo stock. Made 1967–1984.
Standard R.H. Model **$275**
Left Hand (6mm Rem. and 308 Win. only;
   made 1972–79) **295**

Remington Model 7400 Autoloader **$365**
Similar to Model Four, except has lower grade finishes. Made 1981 to date.

Remington Model 7400 Special Purpose **$375**
Same general specification as the Model 7400, except chambered only in 270 or 30-06. Special Purpose matte black finish on metal; American walnut stock with SP nonglare finish.

Remington Model 7600 Carbine **$335**
Same general specifications as Model 7600 Rifle, except has 18¹/₂-inch barrel and weighs 7¹/₄ pounds. Made 1987 to date.

Remington Model 7600 Rifle **$345**
Similar to Model Six, except has lower grade finishes. Made 1981 to date.

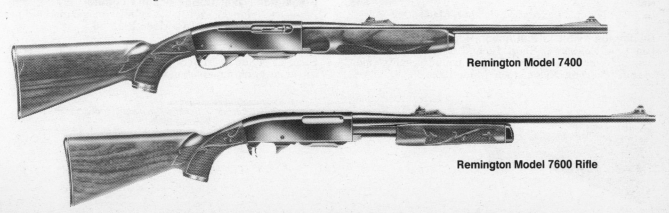

Remington Model 7400

Remington Model 7600 Rifle

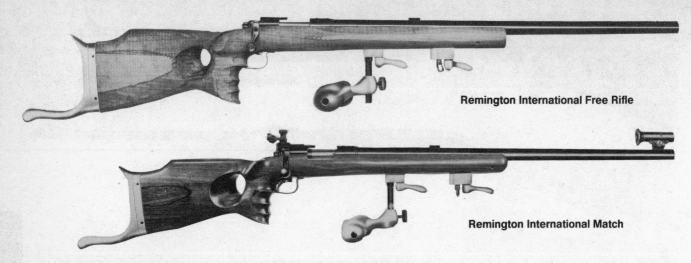

Remington International Free Rifle

Remington International Match

Remington Model 7600 Special Purpose $350
Same general specification as the Model 7600, except chambered only in 270 or 30-06. Special Purpose matte black finish on all exposed metal. American walnut stock with SP nonglare finish.

Remington International Free Rifle $695
Same as Model 40-XB rimfire and centerfire, except has "free rifle"-type stock with adj. buttplate and hook, adj. palmrest, movable front sling swivel, 2-oz. trigger. Weight: about 15 pounds. Made 1964–1974. Value shown is for rifle with professionally finished stock, no sights.

Remington International Match Free Rifle $810
Calibers: 22 LR, 222 Rem., 222 Rem. Mag., 7.62mm NATO, 30-06 (others were available on special order). Model 40X-type bolt action, single shot. 2-oz. adj. trigger. 28-inch heavy barrel. Weight: about 15½ pounds. "Free rifle"-style stock with thumbhole (furnished semifinished by mfr.); interchangeable and adj. rubber buttplate and hook buttplate, adj. palmrest, sling swivel. Made 1961–64. Value shown is for rifle with professionally finished stock, no sights.

Remington Nylon 11

Remington Nylon 12

Remington Nylon 10 Bolt Action Single Shot Rifle $85
Same as Nylon 11 except single shot. Made 1962–66.

Remington Nylon 11 Bolt Action Repeater $90
Clip type. Caliber: 22 Short, Long, LR. 6- or 10-shot clip mag. 19⅝-inch barrel. Weight: 4½ pounds. Sights: open rear; blade front. Nylon stock. Made 1962–66.

Remington Nylon 12 Bolt Action Repeater $90
Same as Nylon 11 except has tubular magazine holding 22 Short, 17 Long, 15 LR. Made 1962–66.

Remington Nylon 66 Apache Black $120
Same as Nylon 66 Mohawk Brown, except barrel and receiver cover chrome-plated, black stock. Made 1962–1984.

Remington Nylon 66 Apache Black

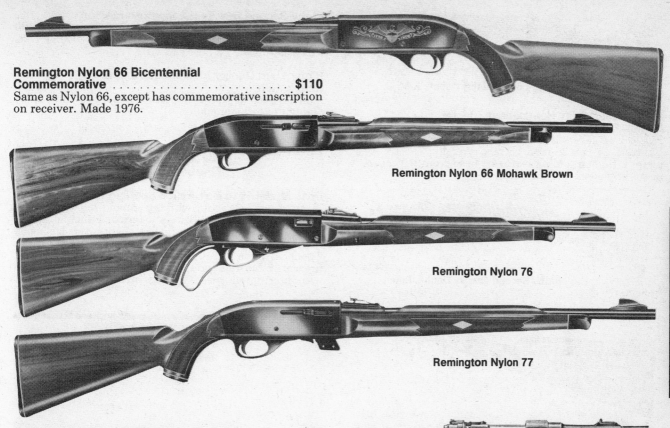

Remington Nylon 66 Bicentennial Commemorative **$110**
Same as Nylon 66, except has commemorative inscription on receiver. Made 1976.

Remington Nylon 66 Mohawk Brown

Remington Nylon 76

Remington Nylon 77

Remington Nylon 66 GS Gallery Special **$95**
Same as Nylon 66 Mohawk Brown except chambered for 22 Short only. Made 1959–1980.

Remington Nylon 66MB Autoloading Rifle **$125**
Similar to the early production Nylon 66 Black Apache, except with blued barrel and receiver cover. Made 1978 to date.

Remington Nylon 66 Mohawk Brown Autoloader . **$95**
Caliber: 22 LR. Tubular magazine in buttstock holds 14 rounds. 19$\frac{1}{2}$-inch barrel. Weight: about 4 pounds. Sights: open rear; blade front. Brown nylon stock and forearm. Made 1959 to date.

Remington Nylon 76 Lever Action Repeater **$250**
Short-throw lever action. Other specifications same as for Nylon 66. Made 1962–64.

Remington Nylon 77 Clip Repeater **$150**
Same as Nylon 66, except has 5-shot clip magazine. Made 1970–71.

Remington Sportsman 78 Bolt Action Rifle **$225**
Similar to Model 700 ADL, except with straight-comb walnut-finished hardwood stock in calibers 223 Rem., 243 Win., 270 Win., 30-06 Springfield and 308 Win. 22-inch barrel. Weight: 7 pounds. Adj. sights. Made 1984–1991.

JOHN RIGBY & CO.
London, England

Rigby 275 Lightweight Magazine Rifle . . . . . **$4000+**
Same as standard 275 rifle, except has 21-inch barrel and weighs only 6$\frac{3}{4}$ pounds.

Rigby 275 Magazine

Rigby 275 Magazine Sporting Rifle . . . . **$5000+**
Mauser action. Caliber: 275 High Velocity or 7×57mm. 5-shot box magazine. 25-inch barrel. Weight: about 7$\frac{1}{2}$ pounds. Sights: folding leaf rear; bead front. Sporting stock w/half-pistol grip, checkered. Specifications given are those of current model; however, in general, they apply also to prewar model.

Rigby 350 Magnum

Rigby 350 Magnum Magazine Sporting Rifle . . . **$3595**
Mauser action. Caliber: 350 Magnum. 5-shot box magazine. 24-inch barrel. Weight: about 7$\frac{3}{4}$ pounds. Sights: folding leaf rear; bead front. Sporting stock with full pistol grip, checkered. Currently mfd.

Rigby 416 Big Game Magazine Sporting Rifle . . **$6000+**
Mauser action. Caliber: 416 Big Game. 4-shot box magazine. 24-inch barrel. Weight: 9 to 9$\frac{1}{4}$ pounds. Sights: folding leaf rear; bead front. Sporting stock with full pistol grip, checkered. Currently manufactured.

RIFLES

Rigby Best Quality Double Rifle

Rigby Best Quality Hammerless Ejector
Double Rifle **$35,000**
Sidelocks. Calibers: 275 Magnum, 350 Magnum, 470 Nitro Express. 24- to 28-inch barrels. Weight: 7½ to 10½ pounds. Sights: folding leaf rear; bead front. Checkered pistol-grip stock and forearm.

Rigby Second Quality Double Rifle

Rigby Second Quality Hammerless Ejector
Double Rifle **$15,000**
Same general specifications as Best Quality double rifle, except boxlock.

Rigby Third Quality Hammerless Ejector
Double Rifle **$9500**
Same as Second Quality double rifle, except plainer finish and not of as high quality.

ROSS RIFLE CO.
Quebec, Canada

Ross Model 1910 Bolt Action Sporting Rifle **$225**
Straight-pull bolt action with interrupted-screw-type lugs. Calibers: 280 Ross, 303 British. 4-shot or 5-shot magazine. Barrel lengths: 22, 24, 26 inches. Sights: two-leaf open rear; bead front. Checkered sporting stock. Weight: about 7 pounds. Made c. 1910 to end of World War I. *Note:* Most firearm authorities agree that this and other Ross models with interrupted-screw-type lugs are unsafe to fire.

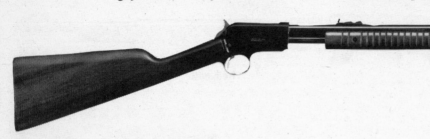
Rossi Gallery Model

ROSSI RIFLES
Sao Leopoldo, Brazil
Manufactured by Amadeo Rossi, S.A.

Rossi 62 Gallery Model SAC Carbine
Same as standard Gallery Model, except in 22 LR only with 16¼-inch barrel; weighs 5½ pounds. Made 1975 to date.
Blued Finish **$145**
Nickel Finish **165**

Rossi 62 Gallery Model Magnum **$145**
Same as standard Gallery Model, except chambered for 22 WMR, 10-shot magazine. Made 1975 to date.

Rossi 62 Gallery Model Slide Action Repeater
Similar to Winchester Model 62. Calibers: 22 LR, Long, Short or 22 WMR. Tubular magazine holds 13 LR, 16

Rossi 62 Gallery Model Slide Action (cont.)
Long, 20 Short. 23-inch barrel. 39¼ inches overall. Weight: 5¾ pounds. Sights: open rear; bead front. Straight-grip stock, grooved slide handle. Blued or nickel finish. Made 1970 to date.
Blued Finish **$150**
Nickel Finish **175**

Rossi Lever Action Carbine Engraved Model . . . **$250**
Same as standard model, except has engraved action. Made 1981 to date.

Rossi Lever Action Carbine **$225**
Similar to Winchester Model 92. Caliber: 357 Mag. Tubular magazine. 20-inch barrel. Weight: 5¾ pounds. Sights: open rear; bead front. Straight-grip walnut stock. Made 1978 to date.

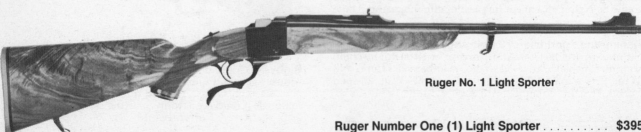
Ruger No. 1 Light Sporter

RUGER RIFLES
Southport, Connecticut
Manufactured by Sturm, Ruger & Co.

Ruger Number One (1) Light Sporter **$395**
Same as No. 1 Standard, except has 22-inch barrel, folding leaf rear sight on quarter-rib and ramp front sight, Henry pattern forearm, front swivel on barrel band. Weight: 7¼ pounds. Calibers: 243 Win., 270 Win., 7×57mm, 30-06. Made 1966–1983.

Ruger No. 1 Medium Sporter

Ruger No. 1 Special Varminter

Ruger No. 1 Standard Rifle

Ruger No. 3 Single Shot Carbine

Ruger Number One (1) Medium Sporter **$375**
Same as No. 1 Light Sporter, except has 26-inch barrel (22-inch in 45-70); weight is 8 pounds (7¼ pounds in 45-70). Calibers: 7mm Rem. Mag., 300 Win. Mag., 45-70. Made 1966 to date.

Ruger Number One (1) "North Americans"
Presentation Rifle **$50,000**
Same general specifications as the Ruger No. 1 Standard, except highly customized with elaborate engravings, carvings, fine-line checkering and gold inlays. A series of 21 is planned, each rifle depicting a North American big-game animal, chambered in the caliber appropriate to the game. Stock is of Northern California English walnut. Comes in trunk-style Huey case with Leupold scope and other accessories.

Ruger Number One (1) RSI International
Single Shot Rifle **$375**
Similar to the No. 1 Light Sporter, except with lightweight 20-inch barrel and full Mannlicher-style forend, in calibers 243 Win., 270 Win., 7×57mm, 30-06. Weight: 7¼ pounds.

Ruger Number One (1) Special Varminter **$395**
Same as No. 1 Standard, except has heavy 24-inch barrel with target scope bases, no quarter-rib. Weight: 9 pounds. Calibers: 22-250, 25-06, 7mm Rem. Mag., 300 Win. Mag. Made 1966 to date.

Ruger Number One (1) Standard Rifle **$375**
Falling-block single-shot action with Farquharson-type lever. Calibers: 22-250, 243 Win., 6mm Rem., 25-06, 270 Win., 30-06, 7mm Rem. Mag., 300 Win. Mag. 26-inch barrel. Weight: 8 pounds. No sights, has quarter-rib for scope mounting. Checkered pistol-grip buttstock and semibeavertail forearm, QD swivels, rubber buttplate. Made 1966 to date.

Ruger Number One (1) Tropical Rifle **$450**
Same as No. 1 Light Sporter, except has heavy 24-inch barrel; calibers are 375 H&H Mag. and 458 Win. Mag. Weight: 8¼ lbs. for 375; 9 lbs. for 458. Made 1966–1994.

Ruger Number Three (3) Single Shot Carbine . . . **$225**
Falling-block action with American-style lever. Calibers: 22 Hornet, 30-40, 45-70. 22-inch barrel. Weight, 6 pounds. Sights: folding leaf rear; gold bead front. Carbine-style stock w/curved buttplate, forearm with barrel band. Made 1972–1986.

Ruger 10/22 International

Ruger 10/22 Sporter

Ruger 10/22 Standard

Ruger Model 10/22 SP Deluxe Sporter

Ruger Model 10/22 Autoloading Carbine

Caliber: 22 LR. Detachable 10-shot rotary magazine. 18½-inch barrel. Weight: 5 pounds. Sights: folding leaf rear; bead front. Carbine-style stock with barrel band and curved buttplate (walnut stock discontinued 1980). Made 1964 to date. International and Sporter versions discontinued 1971.

10/22 Standard Carbine (Walnut stock) **$175**

Ruger Model 10/22 Autoloading Carbine (cont.)

10/22 Int'l (w/Mannlicher-style stock, swivels) Discontinued 1971 . . . . **$425**
10/22 RB (Birch stock, Blued) **125**
K10/22 RB (Birch stock, Stainless **150**
10/22 Sporter (Monte Carlo stock, flat buttplate Sling swivels) Discontinued 1971 . . . . **165**
10/22 SP Deluxe Sporter (w/Checkered stock, Flat buttplate, sling swivels; made since 1966) . . **185**
10/22 RBI Int'l (Blued); made since 1994 . . . . **175**

Ruger 44 Standard

Ruger 44 Sporter

Ruger Model 44 Autoloading Carbine

Gas-operated. Caliber: 44 Magnum. 4-shot tubular magazine (with magazine release button since 1967). 18½-inch barrel. Weight: 5¾ pounds. Sights: folding leaf rear; gold bead front. Carbine-style stock w/barrel band and curved buttplate. Made 1961–1986. International and Sporter versions discontinued 1971.

Ruger Model 44 Autoloading Carbine (cont.)

Model 44 Standard Autoloading Carbine **$365**
Model 44 Int'l (w/Mannlicher-style stock, swivels) **550**
Model 44 Sporter (w/Monte Carlo stock, flat buttplate, Sling swivels **360**
Model 44RS Carbine (w/Rear peep sight, Sling swivels; disc. 1978) **345**

Ruger Model 77 Magnum Action

Ruger Model 77 Round Top Receiver

Ruger Model 77 Short Action

Ruger Model 77RL Ultra Light

Ruger Model 77RSI International

Ruger Model 77 Bolt Action Rifle

Receiver with integral scope mount base or with round top. Short stroke or magnum length action (depending on caliber) in the former type receiver, magnum only in the latter. Calibers: 22-250, 220 Swift, 6mm Rem., 243 Win., 250-3000, 25-06, 257 Roberts, 270 Win., 7×57mm, 7mm Rem. Mag., 280 Rem., 308 Win., 30-06, 300 Win. Mag., 338 Win. Mag., 458 Win. Mag. 5-shot magazine standard, 4-shot in 220 Swift, 3-shot in magnum calibers. 22-, 24- or 26-inch barrel (depending on caliber). Weight: about 7 lbs.; 458 Mag. model, 8³/₄ lbs. Round-top model furnished w/folding leaf rear sight and ramp front; integral base model furnished w/scope rings, with or w/o open sights. Stock w/checkered pistol grip and forearm, pistol-grip cap, rubber recoil pad, QD swivel studs. Made 1968 to date.

Model 77, integral base, no sights	**$325**
Model 77, 338 Win. Mag.	375
Model 77RL Ultra Light, no sights, 20-inch ultralight bbl., 6 lbs. (1983 to date)	365
Model 77RS, integral base, open sights	355
Model 77RS, 338 Win. Mag., 458 Win. Mag. with standard stock	395
Model 77RS, 458 Win. Mag. with fancy Circassian walnut stock	550

Ruger Model 77 Bolt Action Rifle (cont.)

Model 77RSI International, Mannlicher stock, short action, 18¹/₂-inch bbl., 7 lbs.	**$395**
Model 77ST, round top, open sights	325
Model 77ST, 338 Win. Mag.	375

Ruger Model 77 (M-77) Ultra Light Carbine $340

Bolt action. Calibers: 270, 30-06, 243, 308. 18¹/₂-inch barrel. About 39 inches overall. Weight: 6 pounds. Hand-checkered American walnut stock with pistol grip. Open sights and equipped with Ruger Integral Scope bases with one-inch Ruger rings. Sling swivels. Made 1986 to date.

Ruger Model 77V/77NV Varmint Rifle

Same as standard Model 77 with integral base receiver, except has heavy 24-inch (26-inch in 220 Swift) barrel drilled and tapped for target scope bases. Weight: 9 pounds. Calibers: 22-250, 220 Swift, 243 Win., 6mm Rem., 25-06, 308. Made 1968–1992. Model M77NV with laminated American stock introduced in 1992.

Model 77V	**$375**
Model 77NV	465

Ruger Model 77 Mark II All-Weather Rifle $360

Revised Model 77 action. Same general specifications as Model M-77 Mark II, except with stainless barrel

Ruger Model 77 Mark II All-Weather Rifle (cont.)

and action. Zytel injection-molded stock. Calibers: 223, 243, 270, 308, 30-06, 7mm Mag., 300 Win. Mag., 338 Win. Mag. Made 1990 to date.

Ruger Model 77 Mark II Bolt Action Rifle

Revised Model 77 action. Same general specifications as Model M-77, except with new 3-position safety and fixed blade ejector system. Calibers 223 and 6.5×55 Swedish also available.

Model M77 MKIIR, SA, no sights $355
Model M77 MKIIRS, SA, sights 395
Model M77 MKIIRL, SA, 20-inch bbl. 380
Model M77 MKIILR, LA, left-hand 365

Ruger Model 77 Mark II (V2B) Target Rifle $435

Similar to the Model 77 Varmint Rifle, except with laminated American hardwood stock with flat forearm and no checkering. Calibers: 22 PPC, 22-250, 220 Swift, 223, 6mm PPC, 25-06, 308. 26-inch barrel. 44 inches overall. Weight: 9¼ pounds. Made 1992 to date.

Ruger Model 77 Mark II (EXP) Express Rifle $995

Calibers: 270, 30-06, 7mm Rem. Mag., 300 Win. Mag. 4-shot magazine. 22-inch barrel with integral rib. Weight: 7½ lbs. Ramp front sight, adjustable leaf rear. Checkered walnut stock with steel grip cap and black recoil pad. Blued finish. Made 1991 to date.

Ruger Model 77 Mark II (RSM) Magnum Rifle . . $1095

Calibers: 375 H&H, 404 Jeffery, (4-shot magazine); 416 Rigby, 458 Win. Mag.(3-shot magazine). 26-inch barrel with integral rib. Weight: 9¾ lbs. (375, 404); 10¼ lbs. (416, 458). Sights: ramp front; three-leaf Express rear. Checkered Circassian walnut stock with steel-grip cap and recoil pad. Blued finish. Made 1989 to date.

Ruger Model 77/22 Hornet Bolt Action Rifle

Mini-Sporter built on the 77/22 action in caliber 22 Hornet. 6-shot rotary magazine. 20-inch barrel. 40 inches overall. Weight: 6 pounds. Receiver machined for Ruger rings (included). Beaded front sight and open adj. rear, or no sights. Blued or stainless finish. Checkered American walnut stock. Made 1994 to date.

Model 77/22RH (Rings, No Sights) $300
Model 77/22RSH (Rings & Sights) 315
Model 77/22VH (S/S, Rings, No Sights) 370

Ruger Model 77/22 Rimfire Bolt Action Rifle

Calibers: 22 LR or 22 WMR. 10-shot (22 LR) or 9-shot (22 WMR) rotary magazine. 20-inch barrel. 39¾ inches overall. Weight: 5¾ pounds. Integral scope bases; with or w/o sights. Checkered American walnut or Zytel injection-molded stock. Stainless or blued finish. Made 1983 to date. (Blued); stainless introduced 1989.

77/22 R, rings, no sights, walnut stock $265
77/22 RS, rings, sights, walnut 275
77/22 RP, rings, no sights, synthetic stock 220
77/22 RSP, rings, sights, synthetic stock 235
K77/22 RP, s/s, rings, no sights, synthetic 275
K77/22 RSP, s/s, rings, sights, synthetic 285
77/22 RM, 22 WMR, rings, no sights, walnut 260
77/22 RSM, 22 WMR, rings, sights, walnut 275
K77/22 SMP, 22 WMR, s/s, rings, sights, syn. 290
K77/22 RMP, 22 WMR, s/s, no sights, syn. 315
K77/22 VBZ, 22 WMR, no sights, syn. (1993) 280

Ruger Mini-14 Semiautomatic Rifle

Gas-operated. Caliber: 223 Rem. (5.56mm). 5-, 10- or 20-shot box magazine. 18½-inch barrel. Weight: about 6½ pounds. Sights: peep rear; blade front. Pistol-grip stock w/curved buttplate, handguard. Made 1976 to date.

Mini-14/5 Blued $385
K-Mini-14/5 Stainless Steel 400

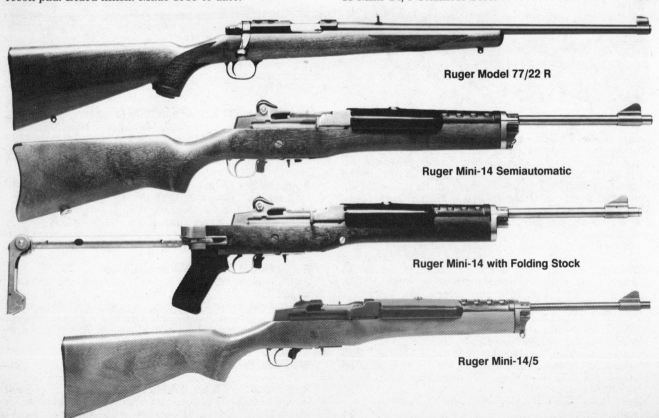

Ruger Model 77/22 R

Ruger Mini-14 Semiautomatic

Ruger Mini-14 with Folding Stock

Ruger Mini-14/5

Ruger Mini-Thirty Autoloader

Ruger Mini-14 Semiautomatic Rifle (cont.)
Mini-14/5F Blued, Folding Stock $550
K-Mini-14/5F Stainless, Folding Stock 600
Mini-14 Ranch Rifle, Scope Model, 6¼ lbs. 375
K-Mini-1H Ranch Rifle, Scope Model, Stainless . . . 495

Ruger Mini-Thirty (30) Autoloader
Caliber: 7.62 × 39mm. 5-shot detachable magazine. 18½-inch barrel. 37¼ inches overall. Weight: 7 lbs. 3 oz. Designed for use with telescopic sights. Walnut stained stock. Blued or stainless finish. Made 1986 to date.
Blued Finish $400
Stainless Finish 435

Russian Model 1891 Mosin

RUSSIAN MILITARY RIFLES
Principal U.S.S.R. Arms Plant is located at Tula

Russian Model 1891 Mosin Military Rifle $95
Nagant system bolt action. Caliber: 7.62mm Russian. 5-shot box magazine. 31½-inch barrel. Weight: about 9 pounds. Sights: open rear; blade front. Full stock w/ straight grip. Specifications given are for WWII version; earlier types differ slightly. *Note:* In 1916, Remington Arms Co. and New England Westinghouse Co. produced 250,000 of these rifles on a contract from the Imperial

Russian Model 1891 Mosin Military Rifle (cont.)
Russian Government. Few were delivered to Russia and the balance bought by the U.S. Government for training in 1918. Eventually, many of these rifles were sold to N.R.A. members for about $3 each by the director of Civilian Marksmanship.

Russian Tokarev Model 40 Semiautomatic
Military Rifle $495
Gas-operated. Caliber: 7.62mm Russian. 10-shot detachable box magazine. 24½-inch barrel. Muzzle brake. Weight: about 9 pounds. Sights: leaf rear; hooded post front. Full stock w/pistol grip. Differences among Models 1938, 1940 and 1941 are minor.

Sako Model 73

Sako Model 74 Carbine

SAKO RIFLES
Riihimaki, Finland
Manufactured by Oy Sako Ab

Sako Model 72 . . . . $645
Single model designation replacing Vixen Sporter, Vixen Carbine, Vixen Heavy Barrel, Forester Sporter, Forester Carbine, Forester Heavy Barrel, Finnbear Sporter, and Finnbear Carbine, with same specifications except all but heavy barrel models fitted with open rear sight. Values same as for corresponding earlier models. Made 1972–74.

Sako Model 73 Lever Action Rifle $725
Same as Finnwolf, except has 3-shot clip magazine, flush floorplate; stock has no cheekpiece. Made 1973–75.

Sako Model 74 Carbine $495
Long Mauser-type bolt action. Caliber: 30-06. 5-shot magazine. 20-inch barrel. Weight: about 7½ pounds. No sights. Checkered Mannlicher-type full stock of European walnut, Monte Carlo cheekpiece. Made 1974–78.

Sako Model 74 Heavy Barrel Rifle, Long Action . . $515
Same specifications as with short action, except has 24-inch heavy barrel, weighs about 8¾ pounds; magnum has 4-shot magazine. Calibers: 25-06, 7mm Rem. Mag. Made 1974–78.

Sako Model 74 Super Sporter

Sako Model 78 Super Rimfire

Sako Classic

Sako Deluxe Lightweight

Sako Model 74 Heavy Barrel Rifle, Medium Action **$525**
Same specifications as with short action, except has 23-inch heavy barrel, weighs about 8¹/₂ pounds. Calibers: 220 Swift, 22-250, 243 Win., 308 Win. Made 1974–78.

Sako Model 74 Heavy Barrel Rifle, Short Action **$550**
Mauser-type bolt action. Calibers: 222 Rem., 223 Rem. 5-shot magazine. 23¹/₂-inch heavy barrel. Weight: about 8¹/₄ pounds. No sights. Target-style checkered European walnut stock w/beavertail forearm. Made 1974–78.

Sako Model 74 Super Sporter, Long Action **$525**
Same specifications as with short action, except has 24-inch barrel, weighs about 8 pounds; magnums have 4-shot magazine, recoil pad. Calibers: 25-06, 270 Win. 7mm Rem. Mag., 30-06, 300 Win. Mag., 338 Win. Mag., 375 H&H Mag. Made 1974–78.

Sako Model 74 Super Sporter, Medium Action . . **$575**
Same specifications as with short action, except weight is 7¹/₄ pounds. Calibers: 220 Swift, 22-250, 243 Win. Made 1974–78.

Sako Model 74 Super Sporter, Short Action **$595**
Mauser-type bolt action. Calibers: 222 Rem., 223 Rem. 5-shot magazine. 23¹/₂-inch barrel. Weight: about 6¹/₂ pounds. No sights. Checkered European walnut stock with Monte Carlo cheekpiece, QD swivel studs. Made 1974, now discontinued.

Sako Model 78 Super Hornet Sporter **$395**
Same specifications as Model 78 Rimfire, except caliber 22 Hornet, 4-shot magazine. Intro. 1977; disc. 1987.

Sako Model 78 Super Rimfire Sporter **$325**
Bolt action. Caliber: 22 LR. 5-shot magazine. 22¹/₂-inch barrel. Weight, about 6³/₄ pounds. No sights. Checkered European walnut stock, Monte Carlo cheekpiece. Introduced 1977; discontinued.

Sako Classic Bolt Action Rifle
Medium Action (243. Win.) or Long Action (270 Win., 30-06, 7mm Rem. Mag.). American walnut stock. Made 1980–86. Reintroduced in 1993 with matte lacquer finish stock, 22- or 24-inch barrel, overall length of 42 to 44 inches, weight 6⁷/₈ to 7¹/₄ lbs.
Standard Calibers **$650**
Magnum Caliber **675**
Left-Hand Models **725**

Sako Deluxe Grade AI **$625**
Same specifications as Standard Grade, except with 22 lines to the inch French checkering, rosewood grip cap and forend tip, semibeavertail forend.

Sako Deluxe Grade AII **$650**
Same specifications as Standard Grade, except with 22 lines per inch French checkering, rosewood grip cap and forend tip, semibeavertail forend.

Sako Deluxe Grade AIII **$895**
Same specifications as with standard, except with French checkering, rosewood grip cap and forend tip, semibeavertail forend.

Sako Deluxe Lightweight Bolt Action Rifle **$845**
Same general specifications as Hunter Lightweight, except has beautifully grained French walnut stock, superb high-gloss finish, fine hand-cut checkering, rosewood forend tip and grip cap. Introduced 1985.

Sako Fiberclass

Sako Finnbear Sporter

Sako Finnfire 22 LR

Sako Finnwolf

Sako Forester Sporter

Sako Golden Anniversary Model

Sako Fiberclass Bolt Action Rifle **$795**
All-weather fiberglass stock version of Sako barreled long action. Calibers: 25-06, 270, 30-06, 7mm Rem. Mag., 300 Win. Mag., 338 Win. Mag., 375 H&H Mag. Barrel length: 22½ inches. Overall length: 44¼ inches. Weight: 7¼ pounds. Made 1984 to date.

Sako Finnbear Carbine **$720**
Same as Finnbear Sporter, except has 20-inch barrel, Mannlicher-type full stock. Made 1971.

Sako Finnbear Sporter **$695**
Long Mauser-type bolt action. Calibers: 25-06, 264 Mag., 270, 30-06, 300 Win. Mag., 338 Mag., 7mm Mag., 375 H&H Mag. Magazine holds 5 standard or 4 magnum cartridges. 24-inch barrel. Weight: about 7 pounds. Hooded ramp front sight. Sporter stock w/Monte Carlo cheekpiece, checkered pistol grip and forearm, recoil pad, swivels. Made 1961–1971.

Sako Finnfire Bolt Action Rifle **$495**
Mini-Sporter built for rimfires on a scaled-down Sako design. Caliber: 22 LR. 5- or 10-shot magazine. 22-inch barrel. 39½ inches overall. Weight: 5¼ pounds. Receiver machined for 11mm dovetail scope rings. Beaded blade front sight; open adj. rear. Blued finish. Checkered European walnut stock. Imported 1994 to date.

Sako Finnwolf Lever Action Rifle **$750**
Hammerless. Calibers: 243 Win., 308 Win. 4-shot clip magazine. 23-inch barrel. Weight: 6¾ pounds. Hooded ramp front sight. Sporter stock w/Monte Carlo cheekpiece, checkered pistol grip and forearm, swivels (available w/ right- or left-hand stock). Made 1963–1972.

Sako Finsport 2700 . . . . **$695**
Bolt-action centerfire rifle. Calibers: 270, 30-06, 7mm Rem. Mag., 300 Win. Mag. Barrel length: 24 inches. Weight: 8 pounds. Made 1984–86.

Sako Forester Carbine **$610**
Same as Forester Sporter, except has 20-inch barrel, Mannlicher-type full stock. Made 1958–1971.

Sako Forester Heavy Barrel **$595**
Same as Forester Sporter, except has 24-inch heavy barrel, weighs 7½ pounds. Made 1958–1971.

Sako Forester Sporter **$580**
Medium-length Mauser-type bolt action. Calibers: 22-250, 243 Win., 308 Win. 5-shot magazine. 23-inch barrel. Weight: 6½ pounds. Hooded ramp front sight. Sporter stock w/Monte Carlo cheekpiece, checkered pistol grip and forearm, swivels. Made 1957–1971.

Sako Golden Anniversary Model **$1800**
Special presentation-grade rifle issued in 1973 to commemorate Sako's 50th anniversary. 1,000 (numbered 1 to

Sako Hunter Lightweight

Sako Mannlicher-Style Carbine

Sako Sporter Deluxe

Sako Golden Anniversary Model (cont.)

1,000) made. Same specifications as Deluxe Sporter, long action, 7mm Rem. Mag. Receiver, trigger guard and floorplate decorated w/gold oak leaf and acorn motif. Stock of select European walnut, checkering bordered w/hand-carved oak leaf pattern.

Sako High-Power Mauser Sporting Rifle $525

FN Mauser action. Calibers: 270, 30-06. 5-shot magazine. 24-inch barrel. Sights: open rear leaf; Patridge front; hooded ramp. Checkered stock w/Monte Carlo comb and cheekpiece. Weight: about 7½ pounds. Made 1950–57.

Sako Hunter Lightweight Bolt Action Rifle

5- or 6-shot magazine. Barrel length: 21½ inches, AI; 22 inches, AII; 22½ inches, AIII. Overall length: 42¼-44½ inches. Weight: 5¾ lbs., AI; 6¾ lbs. AII; 7¼ lbs., AIII. Monte Carlo-style European walnut stock, oil finished. Hand-checkered pistol grip and forend. Introduced 1985. Left-hand version introduced 1987.

AI (Short Action) 17 Rem. . . . . $ 595
    222 Rem., 223 Rem. 600
AII (Medium Action)
    22-250 Rem., 243 Win., 308 Win. 520
AIII (Long Action)
    25-06 Rem., 270 Win., 30-06 580
    338 Win. Mag. 650
    375 H&H Mag. 700
Left-hand Model (Standard Cal.) 900
    Magnum Calibers 1050

Sako Laminated Stock Bolt Action Rifles

Similar in style and specifications to the Hunter Grade, except with stock of resin-bonded, hardwood veneers. Available 18 calibers in AI (Short), AII (Medium) or AV action; left-handed version in 10 calibers, AV only. Introduced in 1987.
Short or Medium Action $750
Long Action/Magnum 775

Sako Magnum Mauser $950

Same specifications as Standard Model, except has recoil pad. Calibers: 300 H&H Magnum, 375 H&H Magnum.

Sako Mannlicher-Style Carbine

Similar to the Hunter Model, except with full Mannlicher-style stock and 18½-inch barrel. Weights 7½ lbs. Chambered in 243, 25-06, 270, 308, 30-06, 7mm Rem. Mag., 300 Win. Mag., 338 Win. Mag., 375 H&H. Introduced in 1977.
Standard Calibers $850
Magnum Calibers (except 375) 875
375 H&H 900

Sako Safari Grade $1595

Classic bolt action. Calibers: 300 Win. Mag., 338 Win. Mag., 375 H&H. Oil-finished European walnut stock with hand-checkering. Barrel band swivel, express-type sight rib; satin or matte blue finish. Introduced in 1980.

Sako Sporter Deluxe $695

Same as Vixen, Forester, Finnbear and Model 74, except has fancy French walnut stock w/skip checkering, rosewood forend tip and pistol-grip cap, recoil pad, inlaid trigger guard and floorplate.

Sako Standard Grade AI $520

Short bolt action. Calibers: 17 Rem., 222 Rem., 223 Rem. 5-shot magazine. 23½-inch barrel. Weight: about 6½ pounds. No sights. Checkered European walnut stock w/ Monte Carlo cheekpiece, QD swivel studs. Made 1978 to date.

Sako Standard Grade AII $550

Medium bolt action. Calibers: 22-250 Rem., 243 Win., 308 Win. 23½-inch barrel in 22-250; 23-inch barrel in other calibers. 5-shot magazine. Weight: about 7¼ pounds. Checkered European walnut stock w/Monte Carlo cheekpiece, QD swivel studs. Made 1978–1985.

Sako Standard Grade AIII $595

Long bolt action. Calibers: 25-06 Rem., 270 Win., 30-06, 7mm Rem. Mag., 300 Win. Mag., 338 Win. Mag., 375 H&H. 24-inch barrel. 4-shot magazine. Weight: 8 pounds. Made 1978–1984.

Sako Super Deluxe Rifle $1550

Available in AI, AII, AIII action calibers. Select European walnut stock, hand-checkered, deep oak leaf hand-engraved design.

Sako TRG-21 Target Rifle $2800
Caliber: 308 Win. 10-shot magazine. 25³/₄-inch stainless heavy barrel. 46¹/₂ inches overall. Weight: 10¹/₂ lbs. No sights. Optional Q/D scope mount with 1-inch or 30mm rings. Reinforced polyurethane stock w/adj. cheekpiece and buttplate. Two-stage adj. trigger. Introduced in 1993.

Sako TRG-S Bolt Action Rifle
Calibers: 243, 7mm-08, 270, 30-06, 7mm Rem. Mag., 300 Win. Mag., 338 Win. Mag. 5-shot magazine (standard calibers), 4-shot (magnum), 22- or 24-inch barrel. 45¹/₂ inches overall. Weight: 7³/₄ lbs. No sights. Reinforced polyurethane stock w/Monte Carlo. Introduced in 1993.
Standard Calibers **$490**
Magnum Calibers **550**

Sako Vixen Carbine $695
Same as Vixen Sporter, except has 20-inch barrel, Mannlicher-type full stock. Made 1947–1971.

Sako Vixen Heavy Barrel $715
Same as Vixen Sporter, except calibers 222 Rem., 222 Rem. Mag., 223 Rem., heavy barrel, target-style stock w/ beavertail forearm. Weight: 7¹/₂ lbs. Made 1947–1971.

Sako Vixen Sporter $725
Short Mauser-type bolt action. Calibers: 218 Bee, 22 Hornet, 222 Rem., 222 Rem. Mag., 223 Rem. 5-shot magazine. 23¹/₂-inch barrel. Weight: 6¹/₂ pounds. Hooded ramp front sight. Sporter stock w/Monte Carlo cheekpiece, checkered pistol grip and forearm, swivels. Made 1946–1971.

RIFLES

Sako TRG 21

Sako TRG-S

Sako Vixen Carbine

Sako Vixen Heavy Barrel

Sako Vixen Sporter

J. P. SAUER & SOHN
Suhl, Germany
Imported by G.U., Inc. (Simmons Enterprises)

Sauer Mauser Bolt Action Sporting Rifle **$995**
Calibers: 7×57 and 8×57mm most common, but these rifles were produced in a variety of calibers, including most of the popular Continental numbers as well as our 30-06. 5-shot box magazine. 22- or 24-inch Krupp steel barrel, half-octagon with raised matted rib. Double-set trigger. Weight: about 7½ pounds. Sights: three-leaf open rear; ramp front. Sporting stock w/cheekpiece, checkered pistol grip, raised side-panels, schnabel tip, swivels. Also made w/20-inch barrel and full-length stock. Mfd before WWII.

Sauer Model S-90 Bolt Action Rifles
Calibers: 243 Win., 308 Win. (Short action); 25-06, 270 Win., 30-06 (Medium action); 7mm Rem. Mag., 300 Win. Mag., 300 Wby., 338 Win., 375 H&H (Magnum action). 4-shot (standard) or 3-shot magazine (magnum). Barrel length: 20-inch (Stutzen); 24-inch. Weight: 7 lbs. 6 oz. to 10 lbs. 12 oz. (Safari). Adj. open rear; ramp front. Checkered American or European walnut stock and pistol grip with matte (Safari—458 Win.), satin gloss (Lux—all actions, Stutzen—30-06, 270 Win.) or high-gloss finish (Supreme—all actions); Monte Carlo cheekpiece; sling swivels. Made 1986 to date.
S-90 Lux **$795**
S-90 Safari 895
S-90 Stutzen 850
S-90 Supreme 995

Sauer Model 200 Bolt Action Rifles
Calibers: 243 Win., 25-06, 270 Win., 30-06, 308 Win. Box magazine. 24-inch (American) or 26-inch (European) interchangeable barrel. Weight: 6¾ to 7¾ pounds. American Model has checkered European walnut straight stock w/ satin oil finish, no sights. European Model has Monte

Sauer Model 200 Bolt Action Rifles (cont.)
Carlo cheekpiece, contrasting forend and pistol grip cap w/high-gloss finish; with sights. Made late 1980s.
American/European Models **$695**
Left-hand Model **750**

SAVAGE INDUSTRIES
Westfield, Massachusetts
Formerly of Utica, New York

Savage Model 3 Bolt Action Single Shot Rifle . . . **$125**
Takedown. Caliber: 22 Short, Long, LR. 26-inch barrel on prewar rifles, postwar production has 24-inch barrel. Weight: about 5 pounds. Sights: open rear; bead front. Plain pistol-grip stock. Made 1933–1952.

Savage Model 3S **$165**
Same as Model 3, except has peep rear sight, hooded front. Made 1933–1942.

Savage Model 3ST **$175**
Same as Model 3S, except fitted with swivels and sling. Made 1933–1942.

Savage Model 4 Bolt Action Repeater **$105**
Takedown. Caliber: 22 Short, Long, LR. 5-shot detachable box magazine. 24-inch barrel. Weight: about 5½ pounds. Sights: open rear; bead front. Checkered pistol-grip stock on prewar models, early production had grooved forearm; postwar rifles have plain stocks. Made 1933–1965.

Savage Model 4M **$125**
Same as Model 4, except chambered for 22 Rimfire Magnum. Made 1961–65.

Savage Model 4S **$135**
Same as Model 4, except has peep rear sight, hooded front. Made 1933–1942.

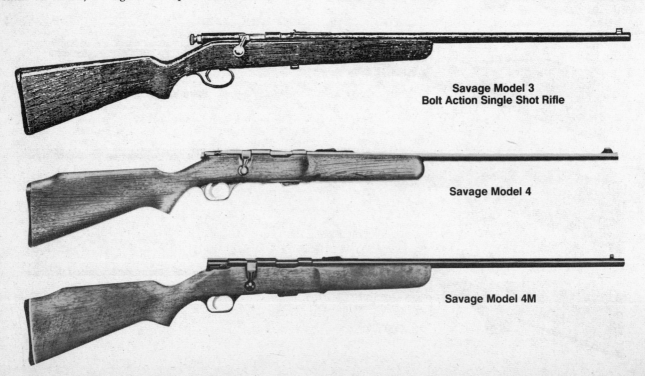

Savage Model 3
Bolt Action Single Shot Rifle

Savage Model 4

Savage Model 4M

Savage Model 5 Bolt Action Repeater **$125**
Same as Model 4, except has tubular magazine (holds 21 Short, 17 Long, 15 LR), weighs about 6 pounds. Made 1936–1961.

Savage Model 5S **$140**
Same as Model 5, except has peep rear sight, hooded front. Made 1936–1942.

Savage Model 6 Autoloading Rifle **$165**
Takedown. Caliber: 22 Short, Long, LR. Tubular magazine holds 21 Short, 17 Long, 15 LR. 24-inch barrel. Weight: about 6 pounds. Sights: open rear; bead front. Checkered pistol-grip stock on prewar models, postwar rifles have plain stocks. Made 1938–1968.

Savage Model 6S **$180**
Same as Model 6, except has peep rear sight, bead front. Made 1938–1942.

Savage Model 7 Autoloading Rifle **$150**
Same general specifications as Model 6, except has 5-shot detachable box magazine. Made 1939–1951.

Savage Model 7S **$175**
Same as Model 7, except has peep rear sight, hooded front. Made 1938–1942.

Savage Model 19 Bolt Action Target Rifle **$225**
Model of 1933. Speed lock. Caliber: 22 LR. 5-shot detachable box magazine. 25-inch barrel. Weight: about 8 pounds. Adj. rear peep sight, blade front on early models,

Savage Model 19 Bolt Action Target Rifle (cont.)
later production equipped w/extension rear sight, hooded front. Target stock w/full pistol grip and beavertail forearm. Made 1933–1946.

Savage Model 19 NRA Bolt Action Match Rifle . . **$295**
Model of 1919. Caliber: 22 LR. 5-shot detachable box magazine. 25-inch barrel. Weight: about 7 pounds. Sights: adj. rear peep; blade front. Full military stock w/pistol grip. Made 1919–1933.

Savage Model 19H **$395**
Same as standard Model 19 (1933), except chambered for 22 Hornet, has Model 23D-type bolt mechanism, loading port and magazine. Made 1933–1942.

Savage Model 19L **$250**
Same as standard Model 19 (1933), except equipped w/ Lyman 48Y receiver sight, 17A front sight. Made 1933–1942.

Savage Model 19M **$275**
Same as standard Model 19 (1933), except has heavy 28-inch barrel with scope bases, weighs about $9\frac{1}{4}$ pounds. Made 1933–1942.

Savage Model 20-1926 Hi-Power Bolt Action Rifle **$365**
Same as Model 1920, except has 24-inch medium weight barrel, improved stock, Lyman 54 rear peep sight, weighs about 7 pounds. Made 1926–29.

RIFLES

Savage Model 5

Savage Model 6

Savage Model 19 NRA (1933)

Savage Model 20 (1926)

Savage Model 23A

Savage Model 23AA

Savage Model 23B

Savage Model 29

Savage Model 23A Bolt Action Sporting Rifle . . . **$190**
Caliber: 22 LR. 5-shot detachable box magazine. 23-inch barrel. Weight: about 6 pounds. Sights: open rear; blade or bead front. Plain pistol-grip stock with slender forearm and schnabel tip. Made 1923–1933.

Savage Model 23AA **$250**
Model of 1933. Improved version of the Model 23A with same general specifications, except has speed lock, improved stock, weighs about 6¹/₂ pounds. Made 1933–1942.

Savage Model 23B **$215**
Same as Model 23A, except caliber 25/20, has 25-inch barrel. Model of 1933 has improved stock w/full forearm instead of the slender forearm w/schnabel found on earlier production. Weight: about 6¹/₂ pounds. Made 1923–1942.

Savage Model 23C **$225**
Same as Model 23B, except caliber 32/20. Made 1923–1942.

Savage Model 23D **$285**
Same as Model 23B, except caliber 22 Hornet. Made 1933–1947.

Savage Model 25 Slide Action Repeater **$325**
Takedown. Hammerless. Caliber: 22 Short, Long, LR. Tubular magazine holds 20 Short, 17 Long, 15 LR. 24-inch octagon barrel. Weight: about 5³/₄ pounds. Sights: open rear; blade front. Plain pistol-grip stock, grooved slide handle. Made 1925–29.

Savage Model 29 Slide Action Repeater **$300**
Takedown. Hammerless. Caliber: 22 Short, Long, LR. Tubular magazine holds 20 Short, 17 Long, 15 LR. 24-inch barrel, octagon on prewar, round on postwar production. Weight: about 5¹/₂ pounds. Sights: open rear; bead front. Stock w/checkered pistol grip and slide handle on prewar, plain stock and grooved forearm on postwar production. Made 1929–1967.

Savage Model 40 Bolt Action Sporting Rifle **$250**
Standard Grade. Calibers: 250/3000, 300 Sav., 30/30, 30/06. 4-shot detachable box magazine. 22-inch barrel in calibers 250/3000 and 30/30; 24-inch in 300 Sav. and 30/06. Weight: about 7¹/₂ pounds. Sights: open rear; bead front, on ramp. Plain pistol-grip stock w/tapered forearm and schnabel tip. Made 1928–1940.

Savage Model 40

Savage Model 45

Savage Model 60

Savage Model 63K

Savage Model 71 "Stevens Favorite"

Savage Model 45 Super Sporter **$350**
Special Grade. Same as Model 40, except has checkered pistol grip and forearm, Lyman No. 40 receiver sight. Made 1928–1940.

Savage Model 60 Autoloading Rifle **$115**
Caliber: 22 LR. 15-shot tubular magazine. 20-inch barrel. Weight: 6 pounds. Sights: open rear; ramp front. Monte Carlo stock of walnut w/checkered pistol grip and forearm. Made 1969–1972.

**Savage Model 63K Key Lock Bolt Action
Single Shot** **$75**
Trigger locked with key. Caliber: 22 Short, Long, LR. 18-inch barrel. Weight: 4 pounds. Sights: open rear; hooded ramp front. Full-length stock w/pistol grip, swivels. Made 1970–72.

Savage Model 63KM **$90**
Same as Model 63K, except chambered for 22 WMR. Made 1970–72.

**Savage Model 71 "Stevens Favorite" Single
Shot Lever Action Rifle** **$150**
Replica of the original Stevens Favorite issued as a tribute to Joshua Stevens, "Father of 22 Hunting." Caliber: 22 LR. 22-inch full-octagon barrel. Brass-plated hammer and lever. Sights: open rear; brass blade front. Weight: $4\frac{1}{2}$ pounds. Plain straight-grip buttstock and schnabel forend; brass commemorative medallion inlaid in buttstock, brass crescent-shaped buttplate. 10,000 produced. Made in 1971 only. Value is for new, unfired specimen.

Savage Model 90 Autoloading Carbine **$120**
Similar to Model 60, except has $16\frac{1}{2}$-inch barrel, 10-shot tubular magazine, folding leaf rear sight, bead front, carbine-style stock of uncheckered walnut with barrel band and sling swivels. Weight: $5\frac{3}{4}$ pounds. Made 1969–1972.

Savage Model 90

Savage Model 99 Lever Action Repeater

Introduced in 1899, this model has been produced in a variety of styles and calibers. Original designation "Model 1899" was changed to "Model 99" c.1920. Earlier rifles and carbines—similar to Models 99A, 99B and 99H—were supplied in calibers 25-35, 30-30, 303 Sav., 32-40 and 38-55. Post-WWII Models 99A, 99C, 99CD, 99DE, 99DL, 99F and 99PE have top tang safety; other 99s have slide safety on right side of trigger guard. Models 99C and 99CD have detachable box magazine instead of traditional Model 99 rotary magazine.

Savage Model 99A (I) $525

Hammerless. Solid frame. Calibers: 30/30, 300 Sav., 303 Sav. Five-shot rotary magazine. 24-inch barrel. Weight: about 7¼ pounds. Sights: open rear; bead front, on ramp. Plain straight-grip stock, tapered forearm. Made 1920–1936.

Savage Model 99A (II) $350

Current model. Similar to original Model 99A, except has top tang safety, 22-inch barrel, folding leaf rear sight, no crescent buttplate. Calibers: 243 Win., 250 Sav., 300 Sav., 308 Win. Made 1971–1982.

Savage Model 99B $650

Takedown. Otherwise same as Model 99A, except weight about 7½ pounds. Made 1920–1936.

Savage Model 99C $425

Current model. Same as Model 99F, except has clip magazine instead of rotary. Calibers: 243 Win., 284 Win., 308 Win. (4-shot detachable magazine holds one round less in 284). Weight: about 6¾ pounds. Made 1965 to date.

Savage Model 99CD $395

Deluxe version of Model 99C. Calibers: 243 Win., 250 Sav., 308 Win. Hooded ramp front sight. Weight: 8¼ pounds. Stock w/Monte Carlo comb and cheekpiece, checkered pistol grip, grooved forearm, swivels and sling. Made 1975 to 1981.

Savage Model 99DE Citation Grade $525

Same as Model 99PE, except has less elaborate engraving. Made 1968–1970.

Savage Model 99DL Deluxe $295

Postwar model. Calibers: 243 Win., 308 Win. Same as Model 99F, except has high comb Monte Carlo stock, sling swivels. Weight: about 6¾ pounds. Made 1960–1973.

Savage Model 99A

Savage Model 99A (current)

Savage Model 99C

Savage Model 99CD

Savage Model 99DE

Savage Model 99E Carbine (I) **$675**
Pre-WWII type. Solid frame. Calibers: 22 Hi-Power, 250/3000, 30/30, 300 Sav., 303 Sav. with 22-inch barrel; 300 Sav. 24-inch. Weight: about 7 pounds. Other specifications same as Model 99A. Made 1920–1936.

Savage Model 99E Carbine (II) **$275**
Current model. Solid frame. Calibers: 250 Sav., 243 Win., 300 Sav., 308 Win. 20- or 22-inch barrel. Checkered pistol-grip stock and forearm. Made 1960–1989.

Savage Model 99EG (I) **$535**
Pre-WWII type. Solid frame. Plain pistol-grip stock and forearm. Otherwise same as Model G. Made 1936–1941.

Savage Model 99EG (II) **$495**
Post-WWII type. Same as prewar model, except has checkered stock and forearm. Calibers: 250 Sav., 300 Sav.,

Savage Model 99EG (II) (cont.)
308 Win. (introduced 1955), 243 Win., and 358 Win. Made 1946–1960.

Savage Model 99F Featherweight (I) **$595**
Pre-WWII type. Takedown. Specifications same as Model 99E, except weight about 6½ pounds. Made 1920–1942.

Savage Model 99F Featherweight (II) **$325**
Postwar model. Solid frame. Calibers: 243 Win., 300 Sav., 308 Win. 22-inch barrel. Checkered pistol-grip stock and forearm. Weight: about 6½ pounds. Made 1955–1973.

Savage Model 99G **$595**
Takedown. Checkered pistol-grip stock and forearm. Weight: about 7¼ pounds. Other specifications same as Model 99E. Made 1920–1942.

Savage Model 99E (pre-WWII)

Savage Model 99E (current)

Savage Model 99EG (post-WWII)

Savage Model 99F (pre-WWII)

Savage Model 99G

RIFLES

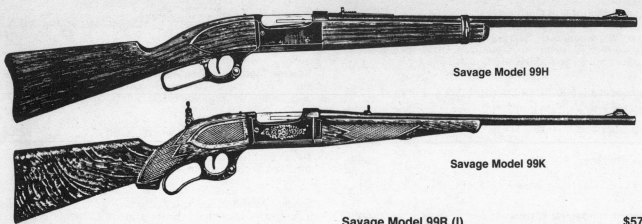

Savage Model 99H

Savage Model 99K

Savage Model 99H Carbine **$495**
Solid frame. Calibers: 250/3000, 30/30, 303 Sav. Carbine
stock and forearm. Weight: about 6½ pounds. Other
specifications same as Model 99A. Made 1931–1942.

Savage Model 99K **$1350**
Deluxe version of Model G with same specifications, ex-
cept has fancy stock and engraving on receiver and barrel,
Lyman peep rear sight, folding middle. Made 1931–1942.

Savage Model 99PE Presentation Grade **$1395**
Same as Model 99DL, except has engraved receiver (game
scenes on sides), tang and lever; fancy walnut Monte Carlo
stock and forearm with hand checkering, QD swivels.
Calibers: 243, 284, 308. Made 1968–1970.

Savage Model 99R (I) **$575**
Pre-WWII type. Solid frame. Calibers: 250/3000 with 22-
inch barrel; 300 Sav. with 24-inch barrel. Weight: about
7½ pounds. Special large pistol-grip stock and forearm,
checkered. General specifications same as other Model 99
rifles. Made 1936–1942.

Savage Model 99R (II) **$450**
Post-WWII type. Same as prewar model, except made
with 24-inch barrel only, has screw eyes for sling swivels.
Calibers: 250 Sav., 300 Sav., 308 Win., 243 Win. and 358
Win. Made 1946–1960.

Savage Model 99RS (I) **$550**
Pre-WWII type. Same as prewar Model 99r5, except
equipped w/Lyman rear peep sight and folding middle
sight, quick detachable swivels and sling. Made 1936–1942.

Savage Model 99PE

Savage Model 99R (pre-WWII)

Savage Model 99R (post-WWII)

Savage Model 99RS (pre-WWII)

Savage Model 99T

Savage Model 99-358

Savage Model 99RS (II) **$395**
Post-WWII type. Same as postwar Model 99r5, except equipped w/Redfield 70LH receiver sight, blank in middle sight slot. Made 1946–1958.

Savage Model 99T **$435**
Featherweight. Solid frame. Calibers: 22 Hi-Power, 30/30, 303 Sav. with 20-inch barrel; 300 Sav. with 22-inch barrel. Checkered pistol-grip stock and beavertail forearm. Weight: about 7 pounds. General specifications same as other Model 99 rifles. Made 1936–1942.

Savage Model 99-358 . . . . **$375**
Similar to current Model 99A, except caliber 358 Win., has grooved forearm, recoil pad, swivel studs. Made 1977–1980.

Savage Model 110 Sporter Bolt Action Repeater . . **$150**
Calibers: 243, 270, 308, 30-06. 4-shot box magazine. 22-inch barrel. Weight: about 6$\frac{3}{4}$ pounds. Sights: open rear; ramp front. Standard sporter stock with pistol grip, checkered. Made 1958–1963.

Savage Model 110B Bolt Action Rifle
Same as Model 110E, except with checkered select walnut Monte Carlo-style stock (early models) or brown laminated stock (late models). Calibers: 243 Win., 270 Win., 30-06, 7mm Rem. Mag., 338 Win. Mag. Made 1976 to date.
Early Model **$235**
Laminated Stock Model **275**

Savage Model 110BL **$285**
Same as Model 110B, except has left-hand action.

Savage Model 110

Savage Model 110B

Savage Model 110BL

Savage Model 110C

Calibers: 22-250, 243, 25-06, 270, 308, 30-06, 7mm Rem. Mag., 300 Win. Mag. 4-shot detachable clip magazine (3-shot in Magnum calibers). 22-inch barrel (24-inch in 22-250 Magnum calibers). Weight: 6¾ lbs.; Magnum, 7¾ to 8 lbs. Sights: open rear; ramp front. Checkered Monte Carlo-style walnut stock (Magnum has recoil pad). Made 1966–1988.

Standard Calibers............................ $275
Magnum Calibers **295**

Savage Model 110CL

Same as Model 110C, except has left-hand action. (Available only in 243 Win., 30-06, 270 and 7mm Mag.)

Standard Calibers............................ $275
Magnum Calibers **295**

Savage 110CY Youth/Ladies Rifle $255

Same as Model 110 G, except with walnut-finished hardwood stock with 12½-inch pull. Calibers: 243 and 300 Savage. Made 1991 to date.

Savage Model 110D

Similar to Model 110C, except has internal magazine with hinged floorplate. Calibers: 243 Win., 270 Win., 30-06, 7mm Rem. Mag., 300 Win. Mag. Made 1972–1988.

Standard Calibers............................ $250
Magnum Calibers **295**

Savage Model 110DL

Same as Model 110D, except has left-hand action. Discontinued.

Standard Calibers............................ $250
Magnum Calibers **295**

Savage Model 110E $215

Calibers: 22-250, 223 Rem., 243, 270 Win., 308, 7mm Rem. Mag., 30-06. 4-shot box magazine (3-shot in Magnum).

Savage Model 110E (cont.)

20- or 22-inch barrel (24-inch stainless steel in Magnum). Weight: 6¾ lbs.; Magnum, 7¾ lbs. Sights: open rear; ramp front. Plain Monte Carlo stock on early production; current models have checkered stocks of walnut-finished hardwood (Magnum has recoil pad). Made 1963 to date.

Savage Model 110EL $220

Same as Model 110E, except has left-hand action, made in 30-06 and 7mm Rem. Mag. only. Made 1969–1973.

Savage Model 110F/110K Bolt Action Rifle

Same as Model 110E, except **Model 110F** has black Rynite® synthetic stock, swivel studs; made 1988 to date. **Model 110K** has laminated camouflage stock; made 1986 to date.

Model 110F, Adj. Sights $270
Model 110FNS, No Sights **280**
Model 110K Standard Calibers **295**
Model 110K Magnum Calibers............... **325**

Savage Model 110FP Police Rifle $295

Calibers: 223, 308 Win. 4-shot magazine. 24-inch barrel. 45½ inches overall. Weight: 9 lbs. Black Rynite composition stock. Matte blue finish. Made 1990 to date.

Savage 110G Bolt Action Rifle

Calibers: 223, 22-250, 243, 270, 7mm Rem. Mag., 308 Win., 30-06, 300 Win. Mag. 5-shot (standard) or 4-shot magazine (magnum). 22- or 24-inch barrel. 42⅜ overall (standard). Weight: 6¾ to 7½ pounds. Ramp front sight, adj. rear. Checkered walnut-finished hardwood stock with rubber recoil pad. Made 1989 to date.

Model 110G Standard Calibers $255
Model 110G Magnum Calibers................. **270**
Model 110GLNS, Left-hand, No Sights **300**

Savage Model 110C

Savage Model 110DL

Savage Model 110E

Savage Model 110MCL

Savage Model 110P

Savage Model 110PE

Savage Model 110GV Varmint Rifle **$285**
Similar to the Model 110 G, except fitted with medium-weight varmint barrel with no sights. Receiver drilled and tapped for scope mount. Calibers 22-250 and 223 only. Made 1989 to date.

Savage Model 110M Magnum
Same as Model 110MC, except calibers: 7mm Rem. Mag., 264, 300 and 338 Win. 24-inch barrel. Stock with recoil pad. Weight: 7³/₄ to 8 pounds. Made 1963–69.
Model 110M Magnum **$225**
Model 110ML Magnum, Left-Hand Action **250**

Savage Model 110MC
Same as Model 110, except has Monte Carlo-style stock. Calibers: 22-250, 243, 270, 308, 30-06. 24-inch barrel in 22-250. Made 1959–1969.
Model 110MC **$150**
Model 110MCL w/Left-hand Action **160**

Savage Model 110P Premier Grade
Calibers: 243 Win., 7mm Rem. Mag., 30-06. 4-shot magazine (3-shot in Magnum). 22-inch barrel (24-inch stainless steel in Magnum). Weight: 7 lbs.; Magnum, 7³/₄ lbs. Sights: open rear folding leaf; ramp front. French walnut stock w/Monte Carlo comb and cheekpiece, rosewood forend tip and pistol-grip cap, skip checkering, sling swivels (Magnum has recoil pad). Made 1964–1970.
Calibers 243 Win. and 30-06 . . . . **$325**
Caliber 7mm Rem. Mag. **375**

Savage Model 110PE Presentation Grade
Same as Model 110P, except has engraved receiver, floorplate and trigger guard, stock of choice grade French walnut. Made 1968–1970.
Calibers 243 and 30-06 . . . . **$515**
Caliber 7mm Rem. Mag. **575**

Savage Model 110PEL Presentation Grade
Same as Model 110PE, except has left-hand action.
Calibers 243 and 30-06 . . . . **$670**
Caliber 7mm Rem. Mag. **695**

Savage Model 110PL Premier Grade
Same as Model 110P, except has left-hand action.
Calibers 243 Win. and 30-06 . . . . **$325**
Caliber 7mm Rem. Mag. **375**

Savage Model 110S/110V
Same as Model 110E, except **Model 110S** in 308 Win. only; **Model 110V** in 22-250 and 223 Rem. w/heavy 25-inch barrel, 47 inches overall, 9 pounds. Discont. 1989.
Model 110S **$265**
Model 110V **295**

Savage Model 111 Chieftain Bolt Action Rifle
Calibers: 243 Win., 270 Win., 7×57mm, 7mm Rem. Mag., 30-06. 4-shot clip magazine (3-shot in Magnum). 22-inch barrel (24-inch in Magnum). Weight: 7¹/₂ lbs.; 8¹/₄ lbs., Magnum. Sights: leaf rear; hooded ramp front. Select walnut stock w/Monte Carlo comb and cheekpiece, checkered, pistol-grip cap, QD swivels and sling. Made 1974–79.
Standard calibers **$295**
Caliber 7mm Rem. Mag. **325**

Savage Model 111 Chieftain

Savage Model 111F

Savage Model 112V

Savage Model 116FCSAK

Savage Models 111F, 111FC, 111FNS Classic Hunters
Similar to the Model 111G, except with graphite/fiberglass composition stock. Weight: 6¼ pounds. Made 1994 to date.
Model 111F (Box Mag., Right/Left Hand) **$260**
Model 111FC (Detachable Magazine) **280**
Model 111FNS (Box Mag., No Sights, R/L
Hand) **250**

Savage Models 111G, 111GC, 111GNS Classic Hunters
Calibers: 22-250 Rem., 223 Rem., 243 Win., 25-06 Rem., 250 Sav., 270 Win., 7mm-08 Rem., 7mm Rem. Mag., 30-06, 300 Sav., 300 Win. Mag., 308 Win., 338 Win. 22- or 24-inch barrel. Weight: 7 pounds. Ramp front sight; adj. open rear. Walnut-finished hardwood stock. Blued finish. Made 1994 to date.
Model 111G (Box Mag., Right/Left Hand) **$255**
Model 111GC (Detachable Mag., R/L Hand) **275**
Model 111GNS (Box Mag., No Sights) **245**

Savage Model 112BV, 112BVSS Heavy Varmint Rifles
Similar to the Model 110G, except fitted with 26-inch heavy barrel. Laminated wood stock with high comb. Calibers 22-250 and 223 only.
Model 112BV (Made 1993–94) **$375**
Model 112BVSS (Fluted stainless barrel; made since
1994) **395**

Savage Model 112FV, 112FVS, 112FVSS Varmint Rifles
Similar to the Model 110G, except fitted with 26-inch heavy barrel and Dupont Rynite stock. Calibers: 22-250, 223 and 220 Swift (112FVS only). Blued or stainless finish. Made 1991–94.
Model 112FV (blued) **$250**
Model 112FVS (blued, single shot) **275**
Model 112FVSS (stainless) **375**

Savage Model 112V Varmint Rifle **$305**
Bolt action, single shot. Caliber: 220 Swift, 222 Rem., 223 Rem., 22-250, 243 Win., 25-06. 26-inch heavy barrel with scope bases. Supplied w/o sights. Weight: 9¼ pounds. Select walnut stock in varmint style w/checkered pistol grip, high comb, QD sling swivels. Made 1975–79.

Savage Model 114CU Classic Ultra **$365**
Calibers: 270 Win., 7mm Rem. Mag., 30-06, 300 Win. Mag. 22- or 24-inch barrel. Weight: 7 pounds. Ramp front sight; adj. open rear. Checkered select walnut stock w/oil finish, red buttpad. High-luster blued finish. Made 1991 to date.

Savage Models 116FSAK, 116FCSAK Bolt Action Rifles
Similar to the Model 116FSK, except in calibers 270 Win., 30-06, 7mm Mag., 300 Win. Mag., 338 Win. Mag. Fluted 22-inch stainless barrel w/adj. muzzle brake. Weight: 6½ pounds. Made 1994 to date.
Model 116FSAK **$385**
Model 116FCSAK (Detachable Mag.) **445**

Savage Models 116FSC, 116FSS Bolt Action Rifles
Improved Model 110 with satin stainless action and barrel. Calibers: 223, 243, 270, 30-06, 7mm Rem. Mag., 300 Win. Mag., 338 Win. Mag. 22- or 24-inch barrel. 4- or 5-shot capacity. Weight: about 7½ pounds. Black Rynite® stock with recoil pad and swivel studs. Receiver drilled and tapped for scope mounts, no sights. Made 1991 to date.
Model 116FSS **$375**
Model 116FSC, Detachable Magazine **395**

Savage 116FSK Kodiak Rifle **$395**
Similar to the Model 116FSS, except with 22-inch barrel chambered for 338 Win. Mag. only. "Shock Suppressor" recoil reducer. Made 1993 to date.

Savage Model 116SE Safari Express **$695**
Calibers: 300 Win. Mag., 338 Win., 425 Express, 458 Win. Mag. 24-inch stainless barrel fitted w/adj. muzzle brake. 45½ inches overall. Weight: 8½ pounds. Ramp front sight; 3-leaf Express rear. Checkered select walnut stock. Stainless finish. Made 1994 to date.

Savage Model 170 Pump Action Centerfire Rifle . **$175**
Calibers: 30-30, 35 Rem. 3-shot tubular magazine. 22-inch barrel. Weight: 6¾ pounds. Sights: folding leaf rear; ramp front. Select walnut stock with checkered pistol grip, Monte Carlo comb, grooved slide handle. Made 1970–1981.

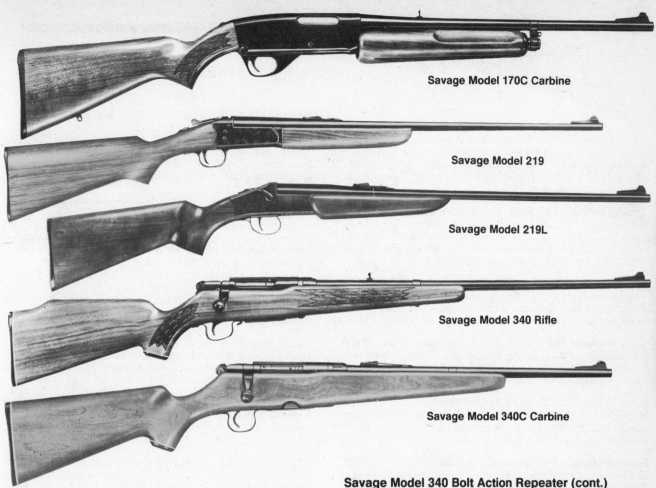

Savage Model 170C Carbine

Savage Model 219

Savage Model 219L

Savage Model 340 Rifle

Savage Model 340C Carbine

Savage Model 170C Carbine **$185**
Same as Model 170 Rifle, except has 18½-inch barrel, straight comb stock, weighs 6 pounds; caliber 30-30 only. Made 1974–1981.

Savage Model 219 Single Shot Rifle
Hammerless. Takedown. Shotgun-type action with top lever. Calibers: 22 Hornet, 25-20, 32-20, 30-30. 26-inch barrel. Weight: about 6 pounds. Sights: open rear; bead front. Plain pistol-grip stock and forearm. Made 1938–1965.
Model 219 . . . . **$175**
Model 219L (w/side lever, made 1965–67) 125

Savage Model 221-229 Utility Guns
Same as Model 219, except in various calibers, supplied in combination with an interchangeable shotgun barrel. All versions discontinued.
Model 221 (30-30, 12-ga. 30-inch bbl.) **$140**
Model 222 (30-30, 16-ga. 28-inch bbl.) 125
Model 223 (30-30, 20-ga. 28-inch bbl.) 110
Model 227 (22 Hornet, 12-ga. 30-inch bbl.) 150
Model 228 (22 Hornet, 16-ga. 28-inch bbl.) 145
Model 229 (22 Hornet, 20-ga. 28-inch bbl.) 140

Savage Model 340 Bolt Action Repeater
Calibers: 22 Hornet, 222 Rem., 223 Rem., 225 Win., 30-30. Clip magazine; 4-shot capacity (3-shot in 30-30). Barrel lengths: originally 20-inch in 30-30, 22-inch in 22 Hornet; later 22-inch in 30-30, 24-inch in other calibers.

Savage Model 340 Bolt Action Repeater (cont.)
Weight: 6½ to 7½ pounds depending on caliber and vintage. Sights: open rear (folding leaf on recent production); ramp front. Early models had plain pistol-grip stock; checkered since 1965. Made 1950–1985. (*Note:* 1947–1950 this was 22 Hornet Stevens Model 322 and 30-30 Model 325.)
Pre-1965 with plain stock **$175**
Current model **160**

Savage Model 340C Carbine **$185**
Same as Model 340, except caliber 30-30, 18½-inch barrel. Weight: about 6 pounds. Made 1962–64.

Savage Model 340S Deluxe **$225**
Same as Model 340, except has checkered stock, screw eyes for sling, peep rear sight, hooded front. Made 1955–1960.

Savage Model 342 . . . . **$250**
Designation, 1950 to 1955, of Model 340 22 Hornet.

Savage Model 342S Deluxe **$275**
Designation, 1950 to 1955, of Model 340S 22 Hornet.

Savage Anniversary Model 1895 Lever Action Rifle **$475**
Replica of Savage Model 1895 Hammerless Lever Action Rifle issued to commemorate the 75th anniversary (1895–1970) of Savage Arms. Caliber: 308 Win. 5-shot rotary magazine. 24-inch full-octagon barrel. Engraved receiver. Brass-plated lever. Sights: open rear; brass blade front.

Savage Anniversary Model 1895

Savage Anniversary Model 1895 (cont.)
Plain straight-grip buttstock, schnabel-type forend; brass medallion inlaid in buttstock, brass crescent-shaped buttplate. 9,999 produced. Made in 1970 only. Value is for new, unfired specimen.

Savage Model 1903 Slide Action Repeater $225
Hammerless. Takedown. Caliber: 22 Short, Long, LR. Detachable box magazine. 24-inch octagon barrel. Weight: about 5 pounds. Sights: open rear; bead front. Pistol-grip stock, grooved slide handle. Made 1903–1921.

Savage Model 1904 Bolt Action Single Shot Rifle . $100
Takedown. Caliber: 22 Short, Long, LR. 18-inch barrel. Weight: about 3 pounds. Sights: open rear; bead front. Plain, straight-grip, one-piece stock. Made 1904–1917.

Savage Model 1905 Bolt Action Single Shot Rifle . $100
Takedown. Caliber: 22 Short, Long, LR. 22-inch barrel. Weight: about 5 pounds. Sights: open rear; bead front. Plain, straight-grip one-piece stock. Made 1905–1919.

Savage Model 1909 Slide Action Repeater $195
Hammerless. Takedown. Similar to Model 1903, except has 20-inch round barrel, plain stock and forearm, weighs about 4³/₄ pounds. Made 1909–1915.

Savage Model 1912 Autoloading Rifle $325
Takedown. Caliber: 22 LR only. 7-shot detachable box magazine. 20-inch barrel. Weight: about 4¹/₂ pounds. Sights: open rear; bead front. Plain straight-grip stock and forearm. Made 1912–16.

Savage Model 1914 Slide Action Repeater $265
Hammerless. Takedown. Caliber: 22 Short, Long, LR. Tubular magazine holds 20 Short, 17 Long, 15 LR. 24-inch octagon barrel. Weight: about 5³/₄ pounds. Sights: open rear; bead front. Plain pistol-grip stock, grooved slide handle. Made 1914–1924.

Savage Model 1920 Hi-Power Bolt Action Rifle . $400
Short Mauser-type action. Calibers: 250/3000, 300 Sav. 5-shot box magazine. 22-inch barrel in 250 cal.; 24-inch in 300 cal. Weight: about 6 pounds. Sights: open rear; bead front. Checkered pistol-grip stock w/slender forearm and schnabel tip. Made 1920–26.

> **NOTE:** In 1965, Savage began the importation of rifles manufactured by J. G. Anschutz GmbH, Ulm, West Germany. Models designated "Savage/Anschutz" are listed in this section; those marketed in the U.S. under the "Anschutz" name are included in that firm's listings. Anschutz rifles are now distributed in the U.S. by Precision Sales Int'l., Westfield, Mass.

Savage/Anschutz Mark 10 Bolt Action Target
Rifle $295
Single shot. Caliber: 22 LR. 26-inch barrel. Weight: 8¹/₂ pounds. Sights: Anschutz micrometer rear; globe front. Target stock w/full pistol grip and cheekpiece, adj. hand stop and swivel. Made 1967–1972.

Savage/Anschutz Mark 10D $300
Same as Mark 10, except has redesigned stock with Monte Carlo comb, different rear sight. Weight: 7³/₄ pounds. Made 1972.

Savage/Anschutz Model 54 Custom Sporter . . . $515
Bolt action. Caliber: 22 LR. 5-shot clip magazine. 24-inch barrel. Weight: 6³/₄ pounds. Sights: folding leaf rear; hooded ramp front. Select walnut stock w/Monte Carlo comb and rollover cheekpiece, checkered pistol grip and schnabel-type forearm, QD swivel studs. Made 1969–1981. (*Note:* Same as Anschutz Model 1422D.)

Savage/Anschutz Model 54M $550
Same as Model 54, except chambered for 22 WMR, 4-shot clip magazine. Made 1972–1981. (*Note:* Same as Anschutz Model 1522D.)

Savage/Anschutz Mark 10D

Savage/Anschutz Model 54 Sporter

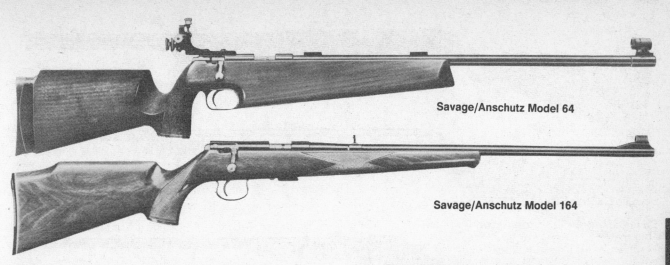

Savage/Anschutz Model 64

Savage/Anschutz Model 164

Savage/Anschutz Model 64 Bolt Action Target Rifle **$395**
Single shot. Caliber: 22 LR. 26-inch medium-heavy barrel. Weight: 7³/₄ pounds. Supplied w/o sights (add $40 for Anschutz match sight set). Target stock w/thumb groove, checkered pistol grip, high comb and cheekpiece, adj. buttplate, swivel rail. Model 64L has left-hand stock. Made 1965–1981. (*Note:* Same as Anschutz Model 1403.)

Savage/Anschutz Model 153 Bolt Action Sporter **$395**
Caliber: 222 Rem. 3-shot clip magazine. 24-inch barrel. Sights: folding leaf open rear; hooded ramp front. Weight: 6³/₄ pounds. French walnut stock w/cheekpiece, skip checkering, rosewood forend tip and grip cap, swivels. Made 1964–67.

Savage/Anschutz Model 153S **$495**
Same as Model 153, except has double-set trigger. Made 1965–67.

Savage/Anschutz Model 164 Custom Sporter . . **$250**
Bolt action. Caliber: 22 LR. 5-shot clip magazine. 23-inch barrel. Weight: 6 pounds. Sights: folding leaf rear; hooded ramp front. Select walnut stock w/Monte Carlo comb and cheekpiece, checkered pistol grip and schnabel-type forearm. Made 1969–1981 (*Note:* Same as Anschutz Model 1416.)

Savage/Anschutz Model 164M **$295**
Same as Model 164, except chambered for 22 WMR, 4-shot clip magazine. Made 1969 to date. (*Note:* Same as Anschutz Model 1516.)

Savage/Anschutz Model 184 Sporter **$315**
Bolt action. Caliber: 22 LR. 5-shot clip magazine. 21¹/₂-inch barrel. Weight: 4¹/₂ pounds. Sights: folding leaf rear; hooded ramp front. Monte Carlo stock w/checkered pistol grip and schnabel-type forearm. Made 1972–75. (*Note:* Same as Anschutz Model 1441.)

> **NOTE:** Since J. Stevens Arms (*see also* separate listing) is a division of Savage Industries, certain Savage models carry the "Stevens" name.

Savage-Stevens Model 34 Bolt Action Repeater . **$85**
Caliber: 22 Short, Long, LR. 5-shot clip magazine. 20-inch barrel. Weight: 5¹/₂ pounds. Sights: open rear; bead front. Checkered stock w/Monte Carlo comb. Made 1969–1981.

Savage-Stevens Model 34M **$90**
Same as Model 34, except chambered for 22 WMR. Made 1969–1973.

Savage-Stevens Model 35 . . . . **$80**
Bolt-action repeater. Caliber: 22 LR. 6-shot clip magazine. 22-inch barrel. Weight: about 5 pounds. Sights: open rear; ramp front. Monte Carlo stock w/checkered pistol grip and forearm. Made 1982 to date.

Savage-Stevens Model 35M **$90**
Same as Model 35, except chambered for 22 WMR. Made 1982 to date.

Savage-Stevens Model 34

Savage-Stevens Model 35

Savage-Stevens Model 46

Savage-Stevens Model 65

Savage-Stevens Model 72 Crackshot

Savage-Stevens Model 73

Savage-Stevens Model 80

Savage-Stevens Model 72 Crackshot (cont.)
This is a "Favorite"-type single-shot, unlike the smaller original "Crackshot" made by Stevens 1913–1939.)

Savage-Stevens Model 73 Bolt Action Single Shot **$75**
Caliber: 22 Short, Long, LR. 20-inch barrel. Weight: 4¾ pounds. Sights; open rear; bead front. Plain pistol-grip stock. Made 1965–1980.

Savage-Stevens 73Y Youth Model **$85**
Same as Model 73, except has 18-inch barrel, 1½-inch shorter buttstock, weighs 4½ pounds. Made 1965–1980.

Savage-Stevens Model 74 Little Favorite **$130**
Same as Model 72 Crackshot, except has black-finished frame, 22-inch round barrel, walnut-finished hardwood stock. Weight: 4¾ pounds. Made 1972–74.

Savage-Stevens Model 80 Autoloading Rifle . . . **$120**
Caliber: 22 LR. 15-shot tubular magazine. 20-inch barrel. Weight: 6 pounds. Sights: open rear; bead front. Monte Carlo stock of walnut with checkered pistol grip and forearm. Made 1976 to date. (*Note:* This rifle is essentially the same as Model 60 of 1969–72, except for a different style of checkering, side instead of top safety and plain bead instead of ramp front sight.)

Savage-Stevens Model 46 Bolt Action Tubular Repeater **$95**
Caliber: 22 Short, Long, LR. Tubular magazine holds 22 Short, 17 Long, 15 LR. 20-inch barrel. Weight: 5 pounds. Plain pistol-grip stock on early production; later models have Monte Carlo stock w/checkering. Made 1969–1973.

Savage-Stevens Model 65 Bolt Action Repeater . **$90**
Caliber: 22 Short, Long, LR. 5-shot clip magazine. 20-inch barrel. Weight: 5 pounds. Sights: open rear; ramp front. Monte Carlo stock w/checkered pistol grip and forearm. Made 1969–1973.

Savage-Stevens Model 65M **$105**
Same as Model 65, except chambered for 22 WMR, has 22-inch barrel, weighs 5¾ pounds. Made 1969–1981.

Savage-Stevens Model 72 Crackshot Single Shot Lever Action Rifle **$110**
Falling-block action. Casehardened frame. Caliber: 22 Short, Long, LR. 22-inch octagon barrel. Weight: 4½ pounds. Sights: open rear; bead front. Plain straight-grip stock and forearm of walnut. Made 1972 to date. (*Note:*

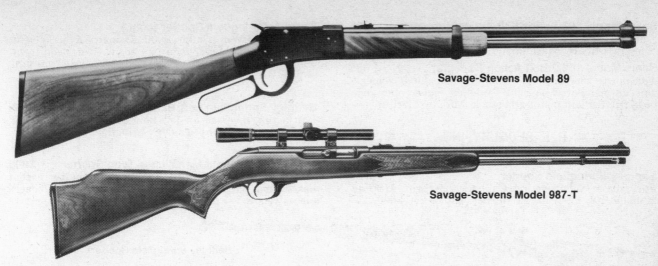

Savage-Stevens Model 89

Savage-Stevens Model 987-T

Savage-Stevens Model 88 Autoloading Rifle . . . **$125**
Similar to Model 60, except has walnut-finished hardwood stock, plain bead front sight; weight, 5³/₄ pounds. Made 1969–1972.

Savage-Stevens Model 89 Single Shot Lever Action Carbine **$100**
Martini-type action. Caliber: 22 Short, Long, LR. 18¹/₂-inch barrel. Weight: 5 pounds. Sights: open rear; bead front. Western-style carbine stock w/straight grip, forearm with barrel band. Made 1976–1989.

Savage-Stevens Model 987-T Autoloading Rifle . **$120**
Caliber: 22 LR. 15-shot tubular magazine. 20-inch barrel. Weight: 6 pounds. Sights: open rear; ramp front. Monte Carlo stock w/checkered pistol grip and forearm. Made 1981–89.

Savage "Stevens Favorite"
See **Savage Model 71.**

V. C. SCHILLING
Suhl, Germany

Schilling Mauser-Mannlicher Bolt Action
Sporting Rifle **$650**
Same general specifications as given for the Haenel Mauser-Mannlicher Sporter. *See* separate listing.

Schilling '88 Mauser Sporter **$505**
Same general specifications as Haenel '88 Mauser Sporter. *See* separate listing.

SCHULTZ & LARSEN GEVAERFABRIK
Otterup, Denmark

Schultz & Larsen Match Rifle No. 47 . . . . **$585**
Caliber: 22 LR. Bolt action, single shot, set trigger. 28¹/₂-inch heavy barrel. Weight: about 14 pounds. Sights: micrometer receiver; globe front. Free-rifle stock w/cheekpiece, thumbhole, adj. Schuetzen-type buttplate, swivels, palmrest.

Schultz & Larsen Free Rifle Model 54 . . . . **$750**
Calibers: 6.5×55mm or any standard American centerfire caliber. Schultz & Larsen M54 bolt action, single shot, set trigger. 27¹/₂-inch heavy barrel. Weight: about 15¹/₂ pounds. Sights: micrometer receiver; globe front. Free-

Schultz & Larsen Free Rifle Model 54 (cont.)
rifle stock w/cheekpiece, thumbhole, adj. Schuetzen-type buttplate, swivels, palmrest.

Schultz & Larsen Model 54J Sporting Rifle **$675**
Calibers: 270 Win., 30-06, 7×61 Sharpe & Hart. Schultz & Larsen bolt action. 3-shot magazine. 24-inch barrel in 270 and 30-06, 26-inch in 7×61 S&H. Checkered stock w/ Monte Carlo comb and cheekpiece. Value shown is for rifle less sights.

SEARS, ROEBUCK & COMPANY
Chicago, Illinois

The most encountered brands or model designations used by Sears are J. C. Higgins and Ted Williams. Firearms sold under these designations have been mfd. by various firms including Winchester, Marlin, Savage, Mossberg, etc.

Sears Model 2C Bolt Action Rifle **$85**
Caliber: 22RF. 7-shot clip magazine. 21-inch barrel. Weight: 5 pounds. Sights: open rear; ramp front. Plain Monte Carlo stock. Mfd. by Winchester.

Sears Model 42 Bolt Action Repeater **$80**
Takedown. Caliber: 22RF. 8-shot detachable box magazine. 24-inch barrel. Weight: 6 pounds. Sights: open rear; bead front. Plain pistol-grip stock. Mfd. by Marlin.

Sears Model 42DL Bolt Action Repeater **$85**
Same general specifications as Model 42 except fancier grade w/peep sight, hooded front sight and swivels.

Sears Model 44DL Lever Action Rifle **$140**
Caliber: 22RF. Tubular magazine holds 19 LR cartridges. 22-inch barrel. Weight: 6¹/₄ pounds. Sights: open rear; hooded ramp front. Monte Carlo-style stock w/pistol grip. Mfd. by Marlin.

Sears Model 53 Bolt Action Rifle **$195**
Calibers: 243, 270, 308, 30-06. 4-shot magazine. 22-inch barrel. Weight: 6³/₄ pounds. Sights: open rear; ramp front. Standard sporter stock w/pistol grip, checkered. Mfd. by Savage.

Sears Model 54 Lever Action Rifle **$145**
Similar general specifications as Winchester Model 94 carbine. Made in 30-30 caliber only. Mfd. by Winchester.

Sears Model 103 Series Bolt Action Repeater ... **$85**
Same general specifications as Model 103.2 with minor
changes. Mfd. by Marlin.

Sears Model 103.2 Bolt Action Repeater **$85**
Takedown. Caliber: 22RF. 8-shot detachable box magazine. 24-inch barrel. Weight: 6 pounds. Sights: open rear;
bead front. Plain pistol-grip stock. Mfd. by Marlin.

R. F. SEDGLEY, INC.
Philadelphia, Pennsylvania

Sedgley Springfield Sporter **$750**
Springfield '03 bolt action. Calibers: 220 Swift, 218 Bee,
22-3000, R2, 22-4000, 22 Hornet, 25-35, 250-3000, 257

Sedgley Springfield Sporter (cont.)
Roberts, 270 Win., 7mm, 30-06. 24-inch barrel. Weight:
7½ pounds. Sights: Lyman No. 48 receiver; bead front,
on matted ramp. Checkered walnut stock, grip cap, sling
swivels. Discontinued 1941.

Sedgley Springfield Left-Hand Sporter **$795**
Bolt action reversed for left-handed shooter; otherwise,
the same as standard Sedgley Springfield Sporter.

Sedgley Springfield Mannlicher-Type Sporter .. **$850**
Same as the standard Sedgley Springfield Sporter, except
has 20-inch barrel, Mannlicher-type full stock w/cheek-
piece, weighs 7¾ pounds.

Sedgley Springfield Sporter

Sedgley Springfield Left-Hand

Sedgley Springfield Mannlicher

SHILEN RIFLES, INC.
Ennis, Texas

Shilen DGA Benchrest Rifle **$895**
DGA single-shot bolt action. Calibers as listed for Sporter.
26-inch medium-heavy or heavy barrel. Weight: from 10½

Shilen DGA Benchrest Rifle (cont.)
pounds. No sights. Fiberglass or walnut stock, classic or
thumbhole pattern. Currently manufactured.

Shilen DGA Sporter **$750**
DGA bolt action. Calibers: 17 Rem., 222 Rem., 223 Rem.,
22-250, 220 Swift, 6mm Rem., 243 Win., 250 Sav., 257

Shilen DGA Benchrest Rifle

Shilen DGA Sporter

Shilen DGA Varminter

RIFLES

Shilen DGA Sporter (cont.)
Roberts, 284 Win., 308 Win., 358 Win. 3-shot blind magazine. 24-inch barrel. Average weight: 7¹/₂ pounds. No sights. Select Claro walnut stock w/cheekpiece, pistol grip, sling swivel studs. Currently manufactured.

Shilen DGA Varminter **$725**
Same as Sporter, except has 25-inch medium-heavy barrel. Weight: about 9 pounds.

SIG AMT Sporting Rifle

SIG SWISS INDUSTRIAL COMPANY
Neuhausen-Rhine Falls, Switzerland

SIG-AMT Semiautomatic Rifle **$4500**
Caliber: 308 Win.(7.62 NATO). 5, 10, or 20-shot magazine. 18¹/₂-inch barrel w/flash suppressor. Weight: 9¹/₂ pounds. Sights: adj. aperture rear; post front. Walnut buttstock and forend with synthetic pistol grip. Imported 1980s.

SIG-AMT Sporting Rifle **$2800**
Semiautomatic version of SG510-4 automatic assault rifle based on Swiss Army StGW57. Roller-delayed blowback action. Caliber: 7.62×51mm NATO (308 Win.). 5-, 10- and 20-round magazines. 19-inch barrel. Weight: about 10 pounds. Sights; aperture rear; post front. Wood buttstock and forearm, folding bipod. Made 1960–1974.

SIG-PE57 Semiautomatic Rifle **$3750**
Caliber: 7.65 Swiss. 24-shot magazine. 23³/₄-inch barrel. Weight: 12¹/₂ pounds. Sights: adj. aperture rear; post front. High-impact synthetic stock. Imported from Switzerland during the 1980s.

Smith & Wesson Model 1500DL

SMITH & WESSON
Springfield, Massachusetts
Mfd. by Husqvarna Vapenfabrik A.B., Huskvarna, Sweden

Smith & Wesson Model 1500 . . . . **$285**
Bolt action. Calibers: 243 Win., 270 Win., 30-06, 7mm Rem. Mag. 22-inch barrel (24-inch in 7mm Rem. Mag.). Weight: about 7¹/₂ pounds. American walnut stock w/ Monte Carlo comb and cheekpiece, cut checkering. Sights:

Smith & Wesson Model 1500 (cont.)
open rear; hooded ramp, gold bead front. Introduced in 1979, this model was also produced by Mossberg (*see* separate listings); now discontinued.

Smith & Wesson Model 1500DL Deluxe **$315**
Same as standard model, except w/o sights; has engine-turned bolt, decorative scroll on floorplate, French checkering.

Smith & Wesson Model A Bolt Action Sporting
Rifle **$350**
Similar to Husqvarna Model 9000 Crown Grade. Mauser-type bolt action. Calibers: 22-250, 243 Win., 270 Win., 308

Smith & Wesson Model A

Smith & Wesson Model B

Smith & Wesson Model C

Smith & Wesson Model D

Smith & Wesson Model E

Smith & Wesson Model A Bolt Action Sporter (cont.)
Win., 30-06, 7mm Rem. Mag., 300 Win. Mag. 5-shot magazine, except 3-round capacity in latter two calibers. 23³/₄-inch barrel. Weight: about 7 pounds. Sights: folding leaf rear; hooded ramp front. Checkered walnut stock w/Monte Carlo cheekpiece, rosewood forend tip and pistol-grip cap, swivels. Made 1969–1972.

Smith & Wesson Model B **$340**
Same as Model A, except has 20³/₄-inch extra-light barrel, Monte Carlo cheekpiece with schnabel-style forearm, weighs about 6 lbs. 10 oz. Calibers: 243 Win., 30-06.

Smith & Wesson Model C **$350**
Same as Model B, except has cheekpiece stock with straight comb.

Smith & Wesson Model D **$425**
Same as Model C, except has full-length Mannlicher-style forearm.

Smith & Wesson Model E **$475**
Same as Model B, except has full-length Mannlicher-style forearm.

SPRINGFIELD, INC.
Colona, Illinois
(formerly Springfield Armory of Geneseo, Ill.)

This is a private firm, not to be confused with the former U.S. Government facility in Springfield, Mass.

Springfield Armory BM-59 Semiautomatic Rifle
Gas-operated. Caliber: 308 Win. (7.62mm NATO). 20-shot detachable box magazine. 19.3-inch barrel with flash suppressor. About 43 inches overall. Weight: 9¹/₄ pounds. Adj. military aperture rear sight, square post front; direct and indirect grenade launcher sights. European walnut stock w/handguard or folding buttstock (Alpine Paratrooper).

Springfield Armory M1A

Springfield Armory BM-59 Semiauto Rifle (cont.)
Made 1981 to date.
Standard Model **$1795**
Paratrooper Model **1950**

Springfield Armory M-1 Garand Semiautomatic Rifle
Gas-operated. Calibers: 308 Win. (7.62 NATO), 30-06. 8-shot stripper clip. 24-inch barrel. 43½ inches overall. Weight: 9½ pounds. Adjustable aperture rear sight, military sqaure blade front. Standard "Issue-grade" walnut stock or folding buttstock. Made 1979 to date.
Standard Model .... **$ 775**
National Match **950**
Ultra Match **995**
Sniper Model **1095**
Paratrooper with folding stock **995**

Springfield Armory Match M1A
Same as Standard M1A, except has National Match grade barrel with modified flash suppressor, National Match sights, turned trigger pull, gas system assembly in one unit, modified mainspring guide, glass-bedded walnut stock. Super Match M1A has premium-grade heavy barrel (weighs 10 pounds).
Match M1A **$1095**
Super Match M1A **1250**

Springfield Armory Standard M1A Semiautomatic
Gas-operated. Similar to U.S. M14 service rifle, except has no provision for automatic firing. Caliber: 7.65mm NATO (308 Win.). 5-, 10- or 20-round detachable box

Springfield Armory Standard M1A Semiauto (cont.)
magazine. 25¹⁄₁₆-inch barrel with flash suppressor. Weight: about 9 pounds. Sights: adj. aperture rear; blade front. Fiberglass, birch or walnut stock, fiberglass handguard, sling swivels. Made 1974 to date.
W/fiberglass or birch stock **$695**
W/walnut stock **750**

SQUIRES BINGHAM CO., INC.
Makati, Rizal, Philippines

Squires Bingham Model 14D Deluxe Bolt Action Repeating Rifle **$125**
Caliber: 22 LR. 5-shot box magazine. 24-inch barrel. Sights: V-notch rear; hooded ramp front. Receiver grooved for scope mounting. Pulong Dalaga stock with contrasting forend tip and grip cap, checkered forearm and pistol grip. Weight: about 6 pounds. Currently mfd.

Squires Bingham Model 15 .... **$150**
Same as Model 14D, except chambered for 22 WMR. Currently manufactured.

Squires Bingham Model M16 Semiautomatic Rifle **$165**
Styled after U.S. M16 military rifle. Caliber: 22 LR. 15-shot box magazine. 19½-inch barrel with muzzle brake/flash hider. Rear sight in carrying handle, post front on high ramp. Black-painted mahogany buttstock and forearm. Weight: about 6½ pounds. Currently mfd.

Squires Bingham Model M20D Deluxe Semiautomatic Rifle **$175**
Caliber: 22 LR. 15-shot box magazine. 19½-inch barrel with muzzle brake/flash hider. Sights: V-notch rear; blade

RIFLES

Squires Bingham Model M16

Squires Bingham Model M20D

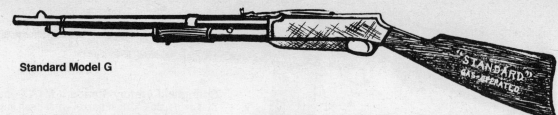

Standard Model G

Squires Bingham Model M20D Deluxe (cont.)
front. Receiver grooved for scope mounting. Pulong Dalaga stock w/contrasting forend tip and grip cap, checkered forearm/pistol grip. Weight: about 6 lbs. Currently mfd.

STANDARD ARMS COMPANY
Wilmington, Delaware

Standard Model G Automatic Rifle **$385**
Gas-operated. Autoloading. Hammerless. Takedown. Calibers: 25-35, 30-30, 25 Rem., 30 Rem., 35 Rem.

Standard Model G Automatic Rifle (cont.)
Magazine capacity: 4 rounds in 35 Rem., 5 rounds in other calibers. $22^3/_8$-inch barrel. Weight: about $7^3/_4$ pounds. Sights: open sporting rear; ivory bead front. Shotgun-type stock. Made c. 1910. *Note:* This was the first gas-operated rifle manufactured in the U.S. While essentially an autoloader, the gas port can be closed and the rifle operated as a slide-action repeater.

Standard Model M Hand-Operated Rifle **$295**
Slide-action repeater with same general specifications as Model G, except lacks autoloading feature. Weight: about 7 pounds.

Star Rolling Block

STAR
Eibar, Spain
Mfd. by Bonifacio Echeverria, S.A.

Star Rolling Block Carbine **$160**
Single-shot action similar to Remington Rolling Block. Calibers: 30-30, 357 Mag., 44 Mag. 20-inch barrel. Weight: about 6 pounds. Sights: folding leaf rear; ramp front. Walnut straight-grip stock w/crescent buttplate, forearm with barrel band. Made 1973–75.

STERLING
Imported by Lanchester U.S.A., Inc., Dallas, Texas

Sterling Mark 6 Semi-Automatic Carbine **$695**
Caliber: 9mm Para. 34-shot magazine. Barrel: 16.1 inches. Weight: about $7^1/_2$ lbs. Flip-type rear peep sight, ramp front. Folding metal skeleton stock. Made 1983–1994.

J. STEVENS ARMS CO.
Chicopee Falls, Massachusetts
Div. of Savage Industries, Westfield, Mass.

Since J. Stevens Arms is a division of Savage Industries, the "Stevens" brand name is used for some rifles by Savage; *see* separate Savage-Stevens listings under Savage.

Stevens No. 12 Marksman Single Shot Rifle **$145**
Lever action, tip-up. Takedown. Calibers: 22 LR, 25 R.F., 32 R.F. 22-inch barrel. Plain straight-grip stock, small tapered forearm.

Stevens No. 14½ Little Scout Single Shot Rifle **$150**
Rolling block. Takedown. Caliber: 22 LR. 18- or 20-inch barrel. Weight: about $2^3/_4$ pounds. Sights: open rear; blade front. Plain straight-grip stock, small tapered forearm.

Stevens No. 12 Marksman

Stevens No. 14½ Little Scout

Stevens Youth's Model 15Y

Stevens No. 44 Ideal

Stevens Ideal Schuetzen

Stevens No. 70 Visible Loading

Stevens Model 87

RIFLES

Stevens Model 15 . . . . **$130**
Same as Stevens-Springfield Model 15, except has 24-inch barrel, weighs about 5 pounds, has redesigned stock. Made 1948–1965.

Stevens Model 15Y Youth's Rifle **$125**
Same as Model 15, except has 21-inch barrel, short butt-stock, weighs about 4³/₄ pounds. Made 1958–1965.

Stevens No. 44 Ideal Single Shot Rifle **$650**
Rolling block. Lever action. Takedown. Calibers: 22 LR, 25 R.F., 32 R.F., 25-20 S.S., 32-20, 32-40, 38-40, 38-55, 44-40. Barrel lengths: 24-inch, 26-inch (round, half-octagon, full-octagon). Weight: about 7 pounds with 26-inch round bbl. Sights: open rear; Rocky Mountain front. Plain straight-grip stock and forearm. Made 1894–1932.

Stevens No. 44¹/₂ Ideal Single Shot Rifle **$725**
Falling-block lever action. Aside from the new design action introduced in 1903, the specifications of this model are the same as those of Model 44. Model 44¹/₂ discontinued about 1916.

Stevens Nos. 45 to 54 Ideal Single Shot Rifles
These are the higher grade models, differing from the standard No. 44 and No. 44¹/₂ chiefly in finish, engraving, set triggers, levers, barrels, stocks, etc. The Schuetzen types (including the "Stevens-Pope" models) are in this series. Model Nos. 45 to 54 were introduced about 1896

Stevens Nos. 45 to 54 Ideal Single Shot (cont.)
and originally had the No. 44-type rolling-block action, which was superseded in 1903 by the No. 44¹/₂-type falling-block action. These models were all discontinued about 1916. Generally speaking the 45-54 series rifles, particularly the "Stevens-Pope" and higher grade Schuetzen models, are collector's items, bringing much higher prices than the ordinary No. 44 and 44¹/₂.

Stevens No. 66 Bolt Action Repeating Rifle **$110**
Takedown. Caliber: 22 Short, Long, LR. Tubular magazine holds 13 LR, 15 Long, 19 Short. 24-inch barrel. Weight: about 5 pounds. Sights: open rear; bead front. Plain pistol-grip stock w/grooved forearm. Made 1931–35.

Stevens No. 70 Visible Loading Slide Action Repeating Rifle **$225**
Exposed hammer. Caliber: 22 LR, Long, Short. Tubular magazine holds 11 LR, 13 Long, 15 Short. 22-inch barrel. Weight: about 4¹/₂ pounds. Sights: open rear; bead front. Plain straight-grip stock, grooved slide handle. Made 1907–1934. *Note:* Nos. 70¹/₂, 71, 71¹/₂, 72, 72¹/₂ are essentially the same as No. 70, differing chiefly in barrel length or sight equipment.

Stevens Model 87 Autoloading Rifle **$150**
Takedown. Caliber: 22 LR. 15-shot tubular magazine. 24-inch barrel (20-inch on current model). Weight: about 6 pounds. Sights: open rear; bead front. Pistol-grip stock. Made 1938 to date. *Note:* This model originally bore the "Springfield" brand name, discontinued in 1948.

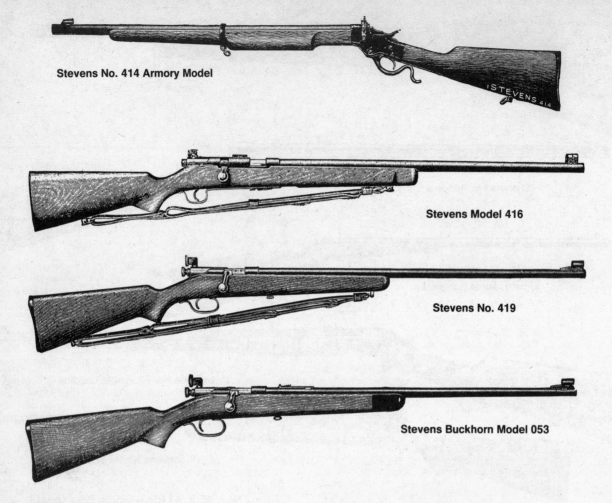

Stevens No. 414 Armory Model

Stevens Model 416

Stevens No. 419

Stevens Buckhorn Model 053

Stevens Model 322 Hi-Power Bolt Action Carbine **$225**
Caliber: 22 Hornet. 4-shot detachable box magazine. 21-inch barrel. Weight: about 6¾ pounds. Sights: open rear; ramp front. Pistol-grip stock. Made 1947–1950. (*See* Savage Models 340, 342.)

Stevens Model 322-S **$275**
Same as Model 325, except has peep rear sight. (*See* Savage Models 340S, 342S.)

Stevens Model 325 Hi-Power Bolt Action Carbine **$225**
Caliber: 30-30. 3-shot detachable box magazine. 21-inch barrel. Weight: about 6¾ pounds. Sights: open rear; bead front. Plain pistol-grip stock. Made 1947–1950. (*See* Savage Model 340.)

Stevens Model 325-S **$260**
Same as Model 325, except has peep rear sight. (*See* Savage Model 340S.)

Stevens No. 414 Armory Model Single Shot Rifle **$425**
No. 44-type lever action. Calibers: 22 LR only, 22 Short only. 26-inch barrel. Weight: about 8 pounds. Sights: Lyman receiver peep; blade front. Plain straight-grip stock, military-type forearm, swivels. Made 1912–1932.

Stevens Model 416 Bolt Action Target Rifle **$200**
Caliber: 22 LR. 5-shot detachable box magazine. 26-inch heavy barrel. Weight: about 9½ pounds. Sights: receiver peep; hooded front. Target stock, swivels, sling. Made 1937–1949.

Stevens No. 419 Junior Target Model Bolt Action Single Shot Rifle **$235**
Takedown. Caliber: 22 LR. 26-inch barrel. Weight: about 5½ pounds. Sights: Lyman No. 55 rear peep; blade front. Plain junior target stock w/pistol grip and grooved forearm, swivels, sling. Made 1932–36.

Stevens Buckhorn Model 053 Bolt Action Single Shot Rifle **$105**
Takedown. Calibers: 22 Short, Long, LR, 22 WMR. 25 Stevens R.F. 24-inch barrel. Weight: about 5½ pounds. Sights: receiver peep; open middle; hooded front. Sporting stock w/pistol grip and black forend tip. Made 1935–1948.

Stevens Buckhorn Model 53 . . . . **$125**
Same as Buckhorn Model 053, except has open rear sight and plain bead front sight.

Stevens Buckhorn Model 056 Bolt Action Repeating Rifle **$130**
Takedown. Caliber: 22 LR, Long, Short. 5-shot detachable box magazine. 24-inch barrel. Weight: about 6 pounds. Sights: receiver peep; open middle; hooded front. Sporting stock w/pistol grip and black forend tip. Made 1935–1948.

Stevens Buckhorn Model 56 . . . . $115
Same as Buckhorn Model 056, except has open rear sight
and plain bead front sight.

Stevens Buckhorn No. 057 . . . . $110
Same as Buckhorn Model 076, except has 5-shot detachable box magazine. Made 1939–1948.

Stevens Buckhorn No. 57 . . . . $120
Same as Buckhorn Model 76, except has 5-shot detachable
box magazine. Made 1939–1948.

**Stevens Buckhorn Model 066 Bolt Action
Repeating Rifle** $150
Takedown. Caliber: 22 LR, Long, Short. Tubular magazine
holds 21 Short, 17 Long, 15 LR. 24-inch barrel. Weight:
about 6 pounds. Sights: receiver peep; open middle; hooded
front. Sporting stock w/pistol grip and black forend tip.
Made 1935–1948.

Stevens Buckhorn Model 66 . . . . $110
Same as Buckhorn Model 066, except has open rear sight,
plain bead front sight.

Stevens Buckhorn No. 076 Autoloading Rifle . . . $150
Takedown. Caliber: 22 LR. 15-shot tubular magazine. 24-
inch barrel. Weight: about 6 pounds. Sights: receiver peep;
open middle; hooded front. Sporting stock w/pistol grip,
black forend tip. Made 1938–1948.

Stevens Buckhorn No. 76 . . . . $145
Same as Buckhorn No. 076, except has open rear sight,
plain bead front sight.

Stevens Crack Shot No. 26 Single Shot Rifle . . . $150
Lever action. Takedown. Calibers: 22 LR, 32 R.F. 18-inch
or 22-inch barrel. Weight: about $3\frac{1}{4}$ pounds. Sights: open
rear; blade front. Plain straight-grip stock, small tapered
forearm. Made 1913–1939.

Stevens Crack Shot No. 26½ $175
Same as Crack Shot No. 26, except has smoothbore barrel
for shot cartridges.

Stevens Favorite No. 17 Single Shot Rifle $165
Lever action. Takedown. Calibers: 22 LR, 25 R.F., 32 R.F.
24-inch round barrel, other lengths were available. Weight:
about $4\frac{1}{2}$ pounds. Sights: open rear; Rocky Mountain
front. Plain straight-grip stock, small tapered forearm.
Made 1894–1935.

Stevens Favorite No. 18 . . . . $245
Same as Favorite No. 17 except has Vernier peep rear
sight, leaf middle sight, Beach combination front sight.

Stevens Favorite No. 19 . . . . $265
Same as Favorite No. 17 except has Lyman combination
rear sight, leaf sight, Lyman front sight.

RIFLES

Stevens Buckhorn Model 066

Stevens Buckhorn Model 66

Stevens Buckhorn No. 076

Stevens Crack Shot No. 26

Stevens Favorite No. 17

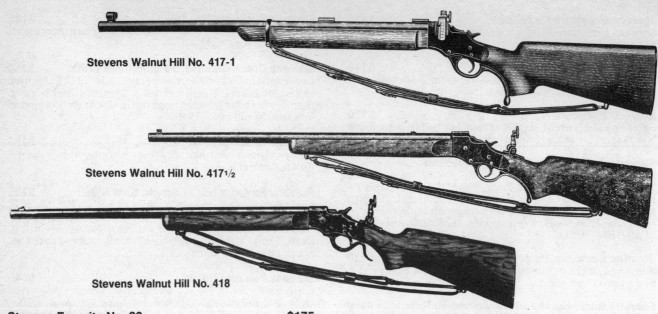

Stevens Walnut Hill No. 417-1

Stevens Walnut Hill No. 417½

Stevens Walnut Hill No. 418

Stevens Favorite No. 20 . . . . **$175**
Same as Favorite No. 17, except has smoothbore barrel
for 22 R.F. and 32 R.F. shot cartridges.

Stevens Favorite No. 27 . . . . **$195**
Same as Favorite No. 17, except has octagon barrel.

Stevens Favorite No. 28 . . . . **$240**
Same as Favorite No. 18, except has octagon barrel.

Stevens Favorite No. 29 . . . . **$250**
Same as Favorite No. 19, except has octagon barrel.

Stevens Walnut Hill No. 417-0 Single Shot
Target Rifle **$625**
Lever action. Calibers: 22 LR only, 22 Short only, 22
Hornet. 28-inch heavy barrel (extra heavy 29-inch barrel
also available). Weight: about 10½ pounds. Sights: Lyman
52L extension rear; 17A front, scope bases. Target stock
with full pistol grip, beavertail forearm, barrel band,
swivels, sling. Made 1932–1947.

Stevens Walnut Hill No. 417-1 . . . . **$650**
Same as No. 417-0, except has Lyman 48L receiver sight.

Stevens Walnut Hill No. 417-2 . . . . **$775**
Same as No. 417-0, except has Lyman No. 144 tang sight.

Stevens Walnut Hill No. 417-3 . . . . **$625**
Same as No. 417-0, except w/o sights.

Stevens Walnut Hill No. 417½ Single
Shot Rifle **$675**
Lever action. Calibers: 22 LR, 22 WMR, 25 R.F., 22
Hornet. 28-inch barrel. Weight: about 8½ pounds. Sights:
Lyman No. 144 tang peep; folding middle; bead front.
Sporting stock w/pistol grip, semibeavertail forearm,
swivels, sling. Made 1932–1940.

Stevens Walnut Hill No. 418 Single Shot Rifle . . . **$395**
Lever action. Takedown. Calibers: 22 LR only, 22 Short
only. 26-inch barrel. Weight: about 6½ pounds. Sights:
Lyman No. 144 tang peep; blade front. Pistol-grip stock,
semibeavertail forearm, swivels, sling. Made 1932–1940.

Stevens Walnut Hill No. 418½ **$475**
Same as No. 418, except also available in calibers 22 WMR
and 25 Stevens R.F., has Lyman No. 2A tang peep sight,
bead front sight.

Stevens-Springfield Model 15 Single Shot Bolt
Action Rifle **$115**
Takedown. Caliber: 22 LR, Long, Short. 22-inch barrel.
Weight: about 4 pounds. Sights: open rear; bead front.
Plain pistol-grip stock. Made 1937–1948.

Stevens-Springfield Model 82 Bolt Action
Single Shot Rifle **$110**
Takedown. Caliber: 22 LR, Long, Short. 22-inch barrel.
Weight: 4 pounds. Sights: open rear; gold bead front. Plain
pistol-grip stock w/grooved forearm. Made 1935–39.

Stevens-Springfield Model 15

Stevens-Springfield Model 82

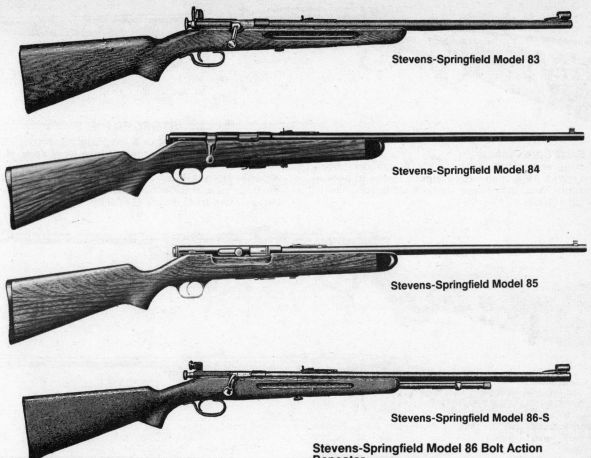

Stevens-Springfield Model 83

Stevens-Springfield Model 84

Stevens-Springfield Model 85

Stevens-Springfield Model 86-S

RIFLES

Stevens-Springfield Model 83 Bolt Action Single Shot Rifle **$110**
Takedown. Calibers: 22 LR, Long, Short; 22 WMR, 25 Stevens R.F. 24-inch barrel. Weight: about 4½ pounds. Sights: peep rear; open middle; hooded front. Plain pistol-grip stock with grooved forearm. Made 1935–39.

Stevens-Springfield Model 84 . . . . **$130**
Same as Model 86, except has 5-shot detachable box magazine. Pre-1948 rifles of this model were designated Springfield Model 84, later known as Stevens Model 84. Made 1940–1965.

Stevens-Springfield Model 84-S (084) **$135**
Same as Model 84, except has peep rear sight and hooded front sight. Pre-1948 rifles of this model were designated Springfield Model 084, later known as Stevens Model 84-S. Discontinued.

Stevens-Springfield Model 85 . . . . **$165**
Same as Stevens Model 87, except has 5-shot detachable box magazine. Made 1939 to date. Pre-1948 rifles of this model were designated Springfield Model 85, currently known as Stevens Model 85.

Stevens-Springfield Model 85-S (085) **$150**
Same as Model 85, except has peep rear sight and hooded front sight. Pre-1948 models were designated Springfield Model 085, now known as Stevens Model 85-S.

Stevens-Springfield Model 86 Bolt Action Repeater **$110**
Takedown. Caliber: 22 LR, Long, Short. Tubular magazine holds 15 LR, 17 Long, 21 Short. 24-inch barrel. Weight: about 6 pounds. Sights: open rear; gold bead front. Pistol-grip stock, black forend tip on later production. Made 1935–1965. *Note:* The "Springfield" brand name was discontinued in 1948.

Stevens-Springfield Model 86-S (086) **$125**
Same as Model 86, except has peep rear sight and hooded front sight. Pre-1948 rifles of this model were designated as Springfield Model 086, later known as Stevens Model 86-S. Discontinued.

Stevens-Springfield Model 87-S (087) **$145**
Same as Stevens Model 87, except has peep rear sight and hooded front sight. Pre-1948 rifles of this model were designated as Springfield Model 087, later known as Stevens Model 87-S. Discontinued.

STEYR-DAIMLER-PUCH A.-G.
Steyr, Austria
See also listings under Mannlicher.

Steyr AUG-SA Semiautomatic Rifle **$3500**
Gas-operated. Caliber: 223 Rem. (5.56mm). 30- or 40-shot magazine. 20-inch barrel standard; optional 16-inch or 24-inch heavy barrel w/folding bipod. 31 inches overall. Weight: 8½ pounds. Sights: Integral 1.5X scope and mount. Green high-impact synthetic stock with folding vertical grip.

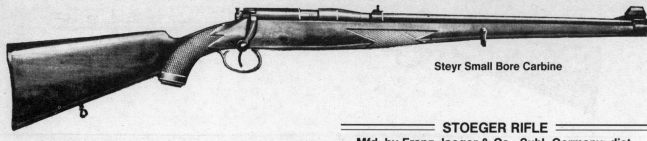

Steyr Small Bore Carbine

Steyr Small Bore Carbine **$425**
Bolt-action repeater. Caliber: 22 LR. 5-shot detachable
box magazine. 19½-inch barrel. Sights: leaf rear; hooded
bead front. Mannlicher-type stock, checkered, swivels.
Made 1953–1967.

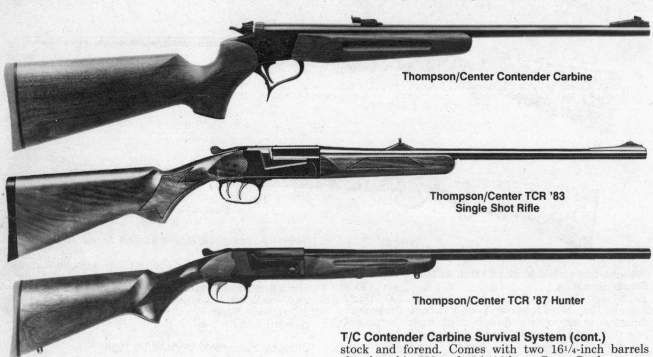

Thompson/Center Contender Carbine

Thompson/Center TCR '83
Single Shot Rifle

Thompson/Center TCR '87 Hunter

STOEGER RIFLE
**Mfd. by Franz Jaeger & Co., Suhl, Germany; dist.
in the U.S. by A. F. Stoeger, Inc., New York, N.Y.**

Stoeger Hornet Rifle **$1500**
Same as Herold Rifle. *See* listing of that rifle for specifications. Imported during the 1930s.

THOMPSON/CENTER ARMS
Rochester, New Hampshire

Thompson/Center Contender Carbine
Calibers: 22 LR, 22 Hornet, 222 Rem., 223 Rem., 7mm
T.C.U., 7×30 Waters, 30-30 Win., 35 Rem., 44 Mag., 357
Rem. Max. and .410 bore. 21-inch interchangeable barrels.
35 inches overall. Adjustable iron sights. Checkered
American walnut or Rynite stock and forend. Made 1985
to date.
Standard Model (rifle calibers) **$345**
Standard Model (.410 bore) **360**
Rynite Stock Model (rifle calibers) **295**
Rynite Stock Model (.410 bore) **335**
Extra Barrels (rifle calibers) **155**
Extra Barrels (.410 bore) **175**
Youth Model standard calibers, 16¼″ bbl. **275**
Youth Model 45/410 Bore **285**

**Thompson/Center Contender Carbine Survival
System** **$475**
Similar to the standard Contender Carbine with Rynite

T/C Contender Carbine Survival System (cont.)
stock and forend. Comes with two 16¼-inch barrels
chambered in 223 and 45/.410 bore. Camo Cordura case.

Thompson/Center Stainless Contender Carbine
Same as the standard Contender Carbine Model, except
stainless steel with blued sights. Calibers: 22 LR, 22 Hor-
net, 223 Rem., 7-30 Waters, 30-30 Win., .410 Ga. Walnut
or Rynite stock and forend. Made 1993 to date.
Walnut Stock Model **$395**
Rynite Stock Model **375**
Youth Stock Model **350**

Thompson/Center TCR '83 Single Shot Rifle
Break frame, overlever action. Calibers: 223 Rem., 22/250
Rem., 243 Win., 7mm Rem. Mag., 30-06 Springfield. Interchangeable barrels: 23 inches in length. Weight: 6
pounds, 14 oz. American walnut stock and forearm,
checkered, black rubber recoil pad, cheekpiece. Made
1983–87.
TCR '83 Standard Model **$295**
TCR '83 Aristocrat **365**

Thompson/Center TCR '87 Hunter Rifle
Similar to TCR '83, except in calibers 22 Hornet, 222
Rem., 223 Rem., 22-250 Rem., 243 Win., 270 Win., 7mm-

Tikka Model 412S Double Rifle

Tikka LSA55 Deluxe

Tikka LSA65 Deluxe

Tikka Model M 55 Deluxe

Tikka Model M 55 Standard

RIFLES

Thompson/Center TCR '87 Hunter Rifle (cont.)

08, 308 Win., 30-06, 32-40 Win. Also 12-ga. slug and 10- and 12-ga. field barrels. 23-inch standard or 25⅞-inch heavy barrel interchangeable. 39½ to 43⅜ inches overall. Weight: 6 lbs. 14 oz. to 7½ lbs. Iron sights optional. Checkered American black walnut buttstock w/fluted forend. Discontinued 1993.

Standard Model	**$375**
Extra Bbl. (rifle calibers and 10- or 12-ga. Field)	**190**
Extra Barrel (12-ga. slug)	**205**

TIKKA RIFLES
Produced in Italy by Armi Marocchi
Imported by Stoeger Industries, Inc.

Tikka Model 412S Double Rifle **$1025**
Formerly Valmet. Caliber: 9.3×74R. 24-inch barrel. 40 inches overall. Weight: 8½ pounds. European walnut stock. Automatic ejectors. Manufactured in Italy from 1990 to date.

Tikka LSA55 Deluxe **$365**
Same as LSA55 Standard, except has rollover cheekpiece, rosewood grip cap and forend tip, skip checkering, high-luster blue. Made 1965–1988.

Tikka LSA55 Sporter **$395**
Same as LSA55, except not available in 6mm Rem., has 22.8-inch heavy barrel, no sights, special stock with beavertail forearm, weighs about 9 pounds. Made 1965–1988.

Tikka LSA55 Standard Bolt Action Repeater . . . **$350**
Mauser-type action. Calibers: 222 Rem., 22-250, 6mm Rem. Mag., 243 Win., 308 Win. 3-shot clip magazine. 22.8-inch barrel. Weight: 6.8 pounds. Sights: folding leaf rear; hooded ramp front. Checkered walnut stock w/Monte Carlo cheekpiece, swivels. Made 1965–1988.

Tikka LSA65 Deluxe **$380**
Same as LSA65 Standard, except has special features of LSA55 Deluxe. Made 1970–1988.

Tikka LSA65 Standard **$330**
Same as LSA55 Standard, except calibers: 25-06, 6.5×55, 270 Win., 30-06. 5-shot magazine, 22-inch barrel, weighs 7½ pounds. Made 1970–1988.

Tikka Model M 55
Bolt action. Calibers: 222 Rem., 22-250 Rem., 223 Rem., 243 Win., 308 Win. (6mm Rem. and 17 Rem. available in Standard and Deluxe models only). 23.2-inch barrel (24.8-

Tikka Model M 65 Sporter

Tikka Continental/Varmint

Tikka New Generation

Tikka Premium Grade Rifle

Tikka Model M 55 (cont.)
inch in Sporter and Heavy Barrel models). 42.8 inches overall (44 inches in Sporter and Heavy Barrel models). Weight: 7¼ to 9 pounds. Monte Carlo-style stock with pistol grip. Sling swivels.

Continental	**$495**
Deluxe Model	500
Sporter	475
Sporter with sights	495
Standard	450
Super Sporter	540
Super Sporter with sights	575
Trapper	465

Tikka Model M 65
Bolt action. Calibers: 25-06, 270 Win., 308 Win., 30-06, 7mm Rem. Mag., 300 Win. Mag. (Sporter and Heavy Barrel models in 270 Win., 308 Win. and 30-06 only). 22.4-inch barrel (24.8-inch in Sporter and Heavy Barrel models). 43.2 inches overall (44 inches in Sporter, 44.8 inches in Heavy Barrel). Weight: 7½ to 9.9 pounds. Monte Carlo-style stock with pistol grip. Discontinued 1989.

Continental	**$530**
Deluxe Magnum	540
Deluxe Model	495
Magnum	490
Sporter	490
Sporter with sights	525

Tikka Model M 65 (cont.)

Standard	**$460**
Super Sporter	575
Super Sporter with sights	595
Super Sporter Master	730

Tikka Model M 65 Wildboar **$530**
Same general specifications as Model M 65, except 20.8-inch barrel, overall length of 41.6 inches and weight of 7½ pounds. Discontinued 1989.

Tikka Continental **$695**
Calibers: 223 Rem., 22-250 Rem., 243 Win., 308 Win. Overall length: 43¾ inches. Weight 8½ pounds. Prone-type stock and extra wide forend for varmint or target shooting. Made 1991 to date.

Tikka New Generation **$565**
Bolt action. Calibers: 223 Rem., 22-250 Rem., 243 Win., 270 Win., 308 Win., 30-06, 7mm Rem. Mag., 300 Win. Mag., and 338 Win. Mag. 3- and 5-round magazines. 22-inch barrel; 24 inches in Magnum. Weight: 7 lbs. 2 oz. Checkered walnut stock. Oversized trigger guard. Made 1989 to date.

Tikka Premium Grade **$625**
Bolt action. Calibers: 223 Rem., 22-250 Rem., 243 Win., 270 Win., 308 Win., 30-06, 7mm Rem. Mag., 300 Win. Mag. and 338 Win. Mag. 3- and 5-round magazine. Hand-checkered with matte lacquer stock and rollover cheek-piece. Rosewood pistol-grip cap and forend tip. Deep blued barrel. Made 1990 to date.

Tikka Whitetail/Battue

Tikka Whitetail Battue **$565**
Calibers: 308 Win., 270 Win., 30-06, 7mm Mag., 300 Win. Mag., 338 Win. Mag. 20 1/2-inch barrel. 40 1/2 inches overall. Weight: 7 pounds. Sights: wide V-shaped rear; hooded front. Optional 3-round detachable magazine. Matte lacquer stock. Made 1991 to date.

=========== **UBERTI USA, INC.** ===========
Lakeville, Connecticut

Uberti Model 1866 Sporting Rifle
Replica of Winchester Model 1866 lever-action repeater. Calibers: 22 LR, 22 WMR, 38 Spec., 44-40, 45 LC. 24 1/4-inch octagonal barrel. 43 1/4 inches overall. Weight: 8 1/4 pounds. Blade front sight; rear elevation leaf. Brass frame and buttplate. Barrel, magazine tube, other metal parts blued. Walnut buttstock and forearm.
Model 1866 Rifle. **$480**
Model 1866 Carbine (19-inch Round Bbl.) **465**
Model 1866 Trapper (16-inch Bbl.) **400**

Uberti Model 1873 Sporting Rifle
Replica of Winchester Model 1873 lever-action repeater. Calibers: 22 LR, 22 WMR, 38 Spec., 357 Mag., 44-40, 45 LC. 24 1/4- or 30-inch octagonal barrel. 43 1/4 inches overall. Weight: 8 pounds. Blade front sight; adj. open rear. Color casehardened frame. Barrel, magazine tube, hammer, lever and buttplate blued. Walnut buttstock and forearm.
Model 1873 Rifle. **$525**
Model 1873 Carbine (19-inch Round Bbl.) **495**
Model 1873 Trapper (16-inch Bbl.) **460**

Uberti Henry Rifle
Replica of Henry lever-action repeating rifle. Calibers: 44-40, 45 LC. 24 1/2-inch half-octagon barrel. 43 3/4 inches overall. Weight: 9 1/4 pounds. Blade front sight; rear sight adj. for elevation. Brass frame, buttplate and magazine follower. Barrel, magazine tube and remaining parts blued. Walnut buttstock.
Henry Rifle. **$550**
Henry Carbine (22 1/2-inch Bbl.) **525**
Henry Trapper (16- or 18-inch Bbl.) **560**

Ultra-Hi Model 2200

=========== **ULTRA-HI PRODUCTS COMPANY** ===========
Hawthorne, New Jersey

Ultra-Hi Model 2200 Single Shot Bolt Action Rifle **$100**
Caliber: 22 LR, Long, Short. 23-inch barrel. Weight: about 5 pounds. Sights: open rear; blade front. Monte Carlo stock w/pistol grip. Made in Japan. Introduced 1977; disc.

Ultra Light Arms Model 20 Series

=========== **ULTRA LIGHT ARMS COMPANY** ===========
Granville, West Virginia

Ultra Light Arms Model 20 Bolt Action Rifle
Calibers: 22-250 Rem., 243 Win., 6mm Rem., 250-3000 Savage, 257 Roberts, 257 Ack., 7mm Mauser, 7mm Ack., 7mm-08 Rem., 284 Win., 300 Savage, 308 Win., 358 Win. Box magazine. 22-inch ultra light barrel. Weight: 4 3/4 pounds. No sights. Synthetic stock of Kevlar or graphite finished seven different colors. Nonglare matte or bright metal finish. Medium-length action available L.H. models.

Ultra Light Arms Model 20 Rifle (cont.)
Standard Model **$1550**
Left-hand Model. **1625**

Ultra Light Arms Model 20S Bolt Action Rifle
Same general specifications as the Model 20, except w/ short action in calibers 17 Rem., 222 Rem., 223 Rem., 22 Hornet only.
Standard Model **$1595**
Left-hand Model. **1695**

RIFLES

Ultra Light Arms Model 24 Bolt Action Rifle

Same general specifications as the Model 20, except w/
long action in calibers 25-06, 270 Win., 30-06 and 7mm
Express only.

Standard Model **$1625**
Left-hand Model............................ **1700**

Ultra Light Arms Model 28 Bolt Action Rifle ... $1850

Same general specifications as the Model 20, except w/
long Magnum action in calibers 264 Win. Mag., 7mm Rem.

Ultra Light Arms Model 28 Rifle (cont.)

Mag., 300 Win. Mag., 338 Win. Mag. only. Offered w/
recoil arrestor. Left-hand model available.

Ultra Light Arms Model 40 Bolt Action Rifle

Similar to the Model 28, except in calibers 300 Wby. and
416 Rigby. Weight: 5 1/2 pounds. Made 1994 to date.

Standard Model **$1850**
Left Hand, **add**............................ **150**

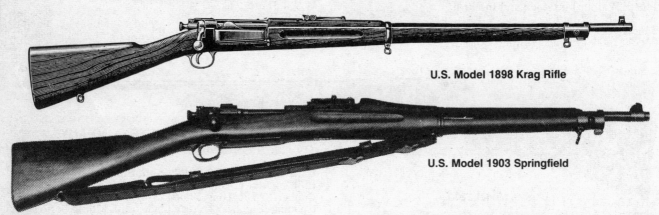

Unique T66 Match

UNIQUE RIFLE
Hendaye, France
Mfd. by Manufacture d'Armes des Pyrénées Francaises

Unique T66 Match Rifle $395

Single-shot bolt action. Caliber: 22 LR. 25 1/2-inch barrel.
Weight: about 10 1/2 pounds. Sights: micrometer aperture
rear; globe front. French walnut target stock w/Monte
Carlo comb, bull pistol grip, wide and deep forearm, stippled grip surfaces, adj. swivel on accessory track, adj. rubber buttplate. Made 1966 to date.

U.S. Model 1898 Krag Rifle

U.S. Model 1903 Springfield

U.S. MILITARY RIFLES
**Mfd. by Springfield Armory, Remington Arms Co.,
Winchester Repeating Arms Co., Inland Mfg. Div.
of G.M.C., and other contractors. See notes.**

Unless otherwise indicated, the following U.S. Military rifles
were mfd. at Springfield Armory, Springfield, Mass.

U.S. Model 1898 Krag-Jorgensen Carbine $495

Same general specifications as Model 1898 Rifle, except
has 22-inch barrel, weighs about 8 pounds, carbine-type
stock. *Note:* The foregoing specifications apply, in general,
to Carbine Models 1896 and 1899, which differed from
Model 1898 only in minor details.

U.S. Model 1898 Krag-Jorgensen Military Rifle .. $325

Bolt action. Caliber: 30-40 Krag. 5-shot hinged box magazine. 30-inch barrel. Weight: about 9 pounds. Sights: adj.
rear; blade front. Military-type stock, straight grip. *Note:*
The foregoing specifications apply, in general, to Rifle
Models 1892 and 1896, which differed from Model 1898
only in minor details. Made 1894–1904.

U.S. Model 1903 Mark I Springfield $345

Same as Standard Model 1903, except altered to permit
use of the Pedersen Device. This device, officially designated "U.S. Automatic Pistol Model 1918," converted the
M/1903 to a semiautomatic weapon firing a 30 caliber
cartridge similar to the 32 automatic pistol ammunition.
Mark I rifles have a slot milled in the left side of the
receiver to serve as an ejection port when the Pedersen
Device was in use; these rifles were also fitted with a special
sear and cut-off. Some 65,000 of these devices were manufactured and presumably a like number of M/1903 rifles
converted to handle them. During the early 1930s all Pedersen Devices were ordered destroyed and the Mark I rifles
were reconverted by replacement of the special sear and
cut-off with standard components. Some 20-odd specimens
are known to have escaped destruction and are in government museums and private collections. Probably more
are extant. Rarely is a Pedersen Device offered for sale,
so a current value cannot be assigned. However, many of
the altered rifles were bought by members of the National
Rifle Association through the Director of Civilian Marksmanship. Value shown is for the Mark I rifle without the
Pedersen Device.

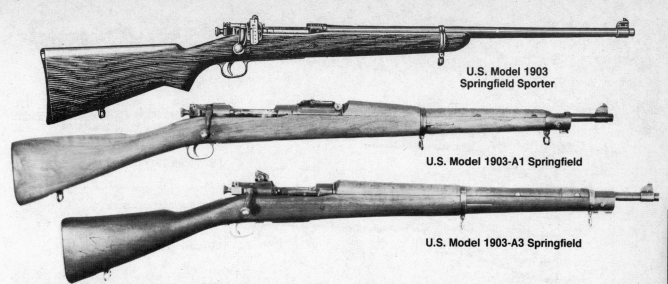

U.S. Model 1903 Springfield Sporter

U.S. Model 1903-A1 Springfield

U.S. Model 1903-A3 Springfield

U.S. Model 1903 National Match Springfield **$995**
Same general specifications as the Standard Model 1903, except specially selected with star-gauged barrel, Type C pistol-grip stock, polished bolt assembly; early types have headless firing pin assembly and reversed safety lock. Produced especially for target shooting.

U.S. Model 1903 Springfield Military Rifle
Modified Mauser-type bolt action. Caliber: 30-06. 5-shot box magazine. 23.79-inch barrel. Weight: about 8¾ pounds. Sights: adj. rear; blade front. Military-type stock, straight grip. *Note:* M/1903 rifles of Springfield manufacture with serial numbers under 800,000 (1903–1918) have casehardened receivers; those between 800,000 and 1,275,767 (1918–1927) were double-heat-treated; rifles numbered over 1,275,767 have nickel-steel bolts and receivers. Rock Island production from No. 1 to 285,507 have casehardened receivers. Improved heat treatment was adopted in May 1918 with No. 285,207; about three months later with No. 319,921 the use of nickel steel was begun, but the production of some double-heat-treated carbon-steel receivers and bolts continued. Made 1903–1930 at Springfield Armory; during WWI, M/1903 rifles were also made at Rock Island Arsenal, Rock Island, Ill.
W/casehardened receiver **$185**
W/double-heat-treated receiver **225**
W/nickel steel receiver **350**

U.S. Model 1903 Springfield Sporter **$975**
Same general specifications as the National Match, except has sporting design stock, Lyman No. 48 receiver sight.

U.S. Model 1903 Style T Springfield Match Rifle **$1095**
Same specifications as the Springfield Sporter, except has heavy barrel (26-, 28- or 30-inch), scope bases, globe front sight, weighs about 12½ pounds with 26-inch barrel.

U.S. Model 1903 Type A Springfield Free Rifle **$1350**
Same as Style T, except made with 28-inch barrel only, has Swiss buttplate, weighs about 13¼ pounds.

U.S. Model 1903 Type B Springfield Free Rifle **$1595**
Same as Type A, except has cheekpiece stock, palmrest, Woodie double-set triggers, Garand fast firing pin, weighs about 14¾ pounds.

U.S. Model 1903-A1 Springfield
Same general specifications as Model 1903, except may have Type C pistol-grip stock adopted in 1930. The last Springfields produced at the Springfield Armory were of this type, final serial number was 1,532,878 made in 1939. *Note:* Late in 1941, the Remington Arms Co., Ilion, N.Y., began production under government contract of Springfield rifles of this type with a few minor modifications. These rifles are numbered 3,000,001–3,348,085 and were manufactured before the adoption of Model 1903-A3.
Springfield manufacture **$325**
Remington manufacture **295**

U.S. Model 1903-A3 Springfield **$375**
Same general specifications as Model 1903-A1, except modified to permit increased production and lower cost; may have either straight-grip or pistol-grip stock, bolt is not interchangeable with earlier types, has receiver peep sight, many parts are stamped sheet steel, including the trigger guard and magazine assembly. Quality of these rifles, lower than that of other 1903 Springfields, reflects the emergency conditions under which they were produced. Mfd. during WWII by Remington Arms Co. and L. C. Smith Corona Typewriters, Inc.

U.S. Model 1922-M1 22 Springfield Target Rifle **$825**
Modified Model 1903. Caliber: 22 LR. 5-shot detachable box magazine. 24½-inch barrel. Weight: about 9 pounds. Sights: Lyman No. 48C receiver; blade front. Sporting-type stock similar to that of the Model 1903 Springfield Sporter. Issued 1927. *Note:* The earlier Model 1922, which is seldom encountered, differs from the foregoing chiefly in the bolt mechanism and magazine.

U.S. M2 22 Springfield Target Rifle **$850**
Same general specifications as Model 1922-MI, except has speedlock, improved bolt assembly adjustable for headspace. *Note:* These improvements were later incorporated in many rifles of the preceding models (M1922, M1922MI) and arms so converted were marked "M1922M2" or "M1922MII."

U.S. Rifle Cal. 30 M1 (Garand)

U.S. Model 1917 Enfield

U.S. Carbine Cal. 30 M1

U.S. Rifle, Caliber 30, M1 (Garand) Mil. Rifle **$695**
Clip-fed, gas-operated, air-cooled semiautomatic. Uses a clip containing 8 rounds. 24-inch barrel. Weight: without bayonet, 9½ pounds. Sights: adj. peep rear; blade front w/guards. Pistol-grip stock, handguards. Made 1937–1957. *Note:* Garand rifles have also been produced by Winchester Repeating Arms Co., Harrington & Richardson Arms Co., and International Harvester Co. Deduct 25% for arsenal-assembled mismatches.

U.S. Rifle, Caliber 30, M1, National Match **$1100**
Accurized target version of the Garand. Glass-bedded stock; match grade barrel, sights, gas cylinder. "NM" stamped on barrel forward of handguard.

NOTE: The U.S. Model 1917 Enfield was mfd. 1917–18 by Remington Arms Co. of Delaware (later Midvale Steel & Ordnance Co.), Eddystone, PA; Remington Arms Co., Ilion, NY; Winchester Repeating Arms Co., New Haven, CT.

U.S. Model 1917 Enfield Military Rifle **$275**
Modified Mauser-type bolt action. Caliber: 30-06. 5-shot box magazine. 26-inch barrel. Weight: about 9¼ pounds. Sights: adj. rear; blade front w/guards. Military-type stock w/semi-pistol grip. This design originated in Great Britain as their "Pattern '14" and was mfd. in caliber 303 for the British Government in three U.S. plants. In 1917, the U.S. Government contracted with these firms to produce the same rifle in caliber 30-06; over two million of these

U.S. Model 1917 Enfield Military Rifle (cont.)
Model 1917 Enfields were mfd. While no more were produced after WWI, the U.S. supplied over a million of them to Great Britain during WWII.

U.S. Carbine, Caliber 30, M1 .... **$495**
Gas-operated (short-stroke piston), semiautomatic. 15- or 30-round detachable box magazine. 18-inch barrel. Weight: about 5½ pounds. Sights: adj. rear; blade front sight w/guards. Pistol-grip stock w/handguard, side-mounted web sling. Made 1942–45. In 1963, 150,000 surplus M1 Carbines were sold at $20 each to members of the National Rifle Assn. by the Dept. of the Army. *Note:* For Winchester and Rock-Ola, add 30%; for Irwin Pedersen, add 80%. Quality Hardware did not complete its production run. Guns produced by other manufacturers were marked "Unquality" & command premium prices.

NOTE: The WWII-vintage 30-caliber U.S. Carbine was mfd. by Inland Mfg. Div. of G.M.C., Dayton, OH; Winchester Repeating Arms Co., New Haven, CT; and other contractors: International Business Machines Corp., Poughkeepsie, NY; National Postal Meter Co., Rochester, NY; Quality Hardware & Machine Co., and Rock-Ola Co., Chicago, IL; Saginaw Steering Gear Div. of G.M.C., Saginaw, MI; Standard Products Co., Port Clinton, OH; Underwood-Elliott-Fisher Co., Hartford, CT.

U.S. REPEATING ARMS CO.
See Winchester Rifle listings.

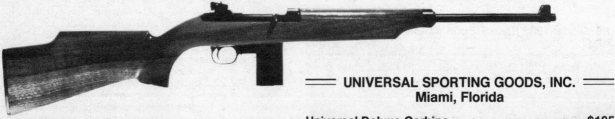

Universal Deluxe Carbine

UNIVERSAL SPORTING GOODS, INC.
Miami, Florida

Universal Deluxe Carbine **$195**
Same as standard model, except also available in caliber 256, has deluxe walnut Monte Carlo stock and handguard. Made 1965 to date.

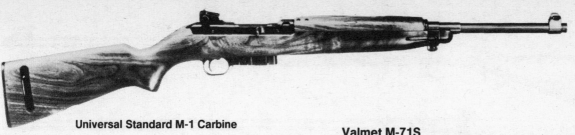

Universal Standard M-1 Carbine

Universal Standard M-1 Carbine **$180**
Same as U.S. Carbine, Cal. 30, M1, except may have either wood or metal handguard, barrel band with or w/o bayonet lug; 5-shot magazine standard. Made 1964 to date.

UZI CARBINE
Mfd. by Israel Military Industries, Israel

Uzi Semiautomatic Model B Carbine **$975**
Calibers: 9mm Parabellum, 41 Action Express, 45 ACP. 20- to 50-round magazine. 16.1-inch barrel. Weight: 8.4 pounds. Metal folding stock. Front post-type sight; open rear, both adjustable. Imported by Action Arms 1983–89.

VALMET OY
Jyväskylä, Finland

Valmet M-62S Semiautomatic Rifle **$995**
Semiautomatic version of Finnish M-62 automatic assault rifle based on Russian AK-47. Gas-operated rotating-bolt action. Caliber: 7.62mm × 39 Russian. 15- and 30-round magazines. 16⁵/₈-inch barrel. Weight: about 8 pounds w/ metal stock. Sights: tangent aperture rear; hooded blade front w/luminous flip-up post for low-light use. Tubular steel or wood stock. Introduced 1962, discontinued.

Valmet M-71S **$895**
Same specifications as M-62S, except caliber 5.56mm×45 (223 Rem.), has open rear sight, reinforced resin or wood stock, weighs 7³/₄ pounds with former. Made 1971 to date.

Valmet M-76 Semiautomatic Rifle
Semiautomatic assault rifle. Gas-operated, rotating bolt action. Caliber: 223 Rem. 15- and 30-shot magazines. Made 1984 to date.
Wooden stock . . . . **$ 895**
Folding stock **1025**

Valmet M-78 Semiautomatic Rifle **$1095**
Caliber: 7.62×51 (NATO). 24¹/₈-inch barrel. Overall length: 43¹/₈ inches. Weight: 10¹/₂ pounds.

Valmet M-82 Semiautomatic Carbine **$1550**
Caliber: 223 Rem. 15- or 30-shot magazine. 17-inch barrel. 27 inches overall. Weight: 7³/₄ pounds.

Valmet Model 412 S Double Rifle **$795**
Boxlock. Manual or automatic extraction. Calibers: 243, 308, 30-06, 375 Win., 9.3×74R. Barrels: 24-inch over/under. Weight: 8⁵/₈ pounds. American walnut checkered stock and forend.

Valmet Hunter Semiautomatic Rifle **$725**
Similar to the M-78, except in calibers 223 Rem. (5.56mm), 243 Win., 308 Win. (7.62 NATO) and 30-06. 5-, 9- or 15-shot magazine. 20¹/₂-inch plain barrel. 42 inches overall. Weight: 8 pounds. Sights: adj. 412 combination scope mount/rear; blade front, mounted on gas tube. Checkered European walnut buttstock and extended checkered forend and handguard. Imported since 1986.

RIFLES

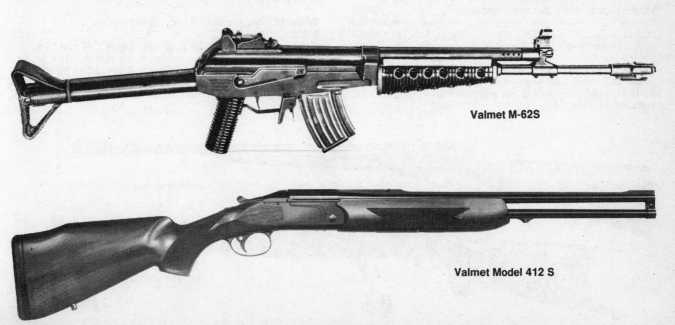

Valmet M-62S

Valmet Model 412 S

Vickers Empire Model

Vickers Jubilee Model

VICKERS LTD.
Crayford, Kent, England

Vickers Empire Model **$320**
Similar to Jubilee Model, except has 27- or 30-inch barrel, straight-grip stock, weighs about 9¼ pounds with 30-inch barrel. Made before WWII.

Vickers Jubilee Model Single Shot Target Rifle . **$395**
Round-receiver Martini-type action. Caliber: 22 LR. 28-inch heavy barrel. Weight: about 9½ pounds. Sights: Parker-Hale No. 2 front; Perfection rear peep. One-piece target stock w/full forearm and pistol grip. Made before WWII.

VOERE, VOELTER & COMPANY
Vaehrenbach, Germany

Mauser-Werke acquired Voere in 1987 and all models are now marketed under new designations.

Voere Model 1007 Biathlon Repeater **$245**
Caliber: 22 LR. 5-shot magazine. 19½-inch barrel. 39 inches overall. Weight: 5½ pounds. Sights: adj. rear; blade front. Plain beechwood stock. Imported 1984–86.

Voere Model 1013 Bolt Action Repeater **$425**
Same as Model 1007, except with military-style stock in 22 WMR caliber. Double-set triggers optional. Imported 1984–86 by KDF, Inc.

Voere Model 2107 Bolt Action Repeater
Caliber: 22 LR. 5 or 8-shot magazine. 19½-inch barrel. 41 inches overall. Weight: 6 pounds. Sights: adj. rear sight, hooded front. European hardwood Monte Carlo-style stock. Imported 1986 by KDF, Inc.
Standard Model **$175**
Deluxe Model **200**

WALTHER RIFLES
Mfd. by the German firms of Waffenfabrik Walther and Carl Walther Sportwaffenfabrik

The following Walther rifles were mfd. before WWII by Waffenfabrik Walther, Zella-Mehlis (Thür.), Germany.

Walther Model 1 Autoloading Rifle (Light) **$325**
Similar to Standard Model 2, but with 20-inch barrel, lighter stock, weighs about 4½ pounds.

Walther Model 2 Autoloading Rifle **$425**
Bolt action, may be used as autoloader, manually operated repeater or single shot. Caliber: 22 LR. 5- or 9-shot detachable box magazine. 24½-inch barrel. Weight: about 7 pounds. Sights: tangent-curve rear; ramp front. Sporting stock w/checkered pistol grip, grooved forearm, swivels. Discontinued.

Walther Olympic Bolt Action Single Shot Match Rifle **$925**
Caliber: 22 LR. 26-inch heavy barrel. Weight: about 13 pounds. Sights: micrometer extension rear; interchangeable front. Target stock w/checkered pistol grip, thumbhole, full beavertail forearm covered w/corrugated rubber, palmrest, adj. Swiss-type buttplate, swivels. Discontinued.

Walther Model 2

Walther Olympic

Walther Model V Meisterbüchse

Walther Model V Bolt Action Single Shot Rifle .. **$360**
Caliber: 22 LR. 26-inch barrel. Weight: about 7 pounds.
Sights: open rear; ramp front. Plain pistol-grip stock w/
grooved forearm. Discontinued.

Walther Model V Meisterbüchse (Champion) ... **$425**
Same as standard Model V, except has micrometer open
rear sight and checkered pistol grip. Discontinued.

> **NOTE:** The Walther rifles listed below have been manufactured since WWII by Carl Walther Sportwaffenfabrik, Ulm (Donau), Germany.

Walther Model GX-1 Free Rifle **$1295**
Bolt action, single shot. Caliber: 22 LR. 25½-inch heavy
barrel. Weight: 15.9 pounds. Sights: micrometer aperture
rear; globe front. Thumbhole stock w/adjustable cheekpiece and buttplate w/removable hook, accessory rail.
Left-hand stock available. Accessories furnished include
hand stop and sling swivel, palmrest, counterweight assembly.

Walther Model KKJ Sporter **$525**
Bolt action. Caliber: 22 LR. 5-shot box magazine. 22½-
inch barrel. Weight: 5½ pounds. Sights: open rear; hooded
ramp front. Stock w/cheekpiece, checkered pistol grip and
forearm, sling swivels. Discontinued.

Walther Model KKJ-Ho **$650**
Same as Model KKJ, except chambered for 22 Hornet.
Discontinued.

Walther Model KKJ-Ma **$495**
Same as Model KKJ, except chambered for 22 WMR.
Discontinued.

Walther Model KKM International Match Rifle ... **$795**
Bolt action, single shot. Caliber: 22 LR. 28-inch heavy
barrel. Weight: 15½ pounds. Sights: micrometer aperture
rear; globe front. Thumbhole stock w/high comb, adj. hook
buttplate, accessory rail. Left-hand stock available. Discontinued.

Walther Model KKM-S **$795**
Same specifications as Model KKM, except has adj.
cheekpiece. Discontinued.

RIFLES

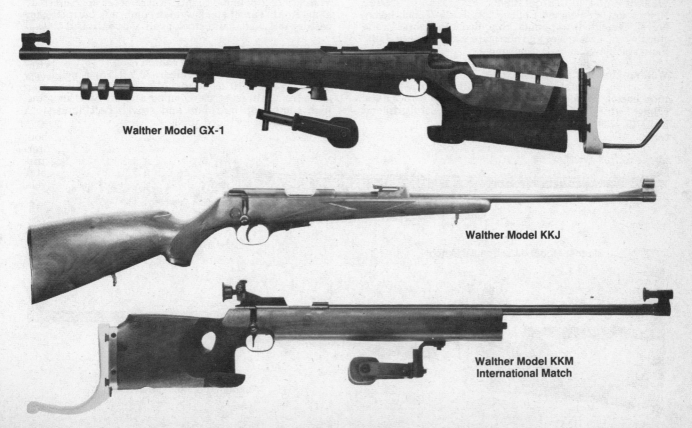

Walther Model GX-1

Walther Model KKJ

**Walther Model KKM
International Match**

Walther Moving Target Match

Walther Prone 400 Target

Walther Model SSV Varmint

Walther Moving Target Match Rifle **$625**
Bolt action, single shot. Caliber: 22 LR. 23.6-inch barrel
w/weight. Weight: 8.6 pounds. Supplied w/o sights.
Thumbhole stock w/adj. cheekpiece and buttplate. Left-
hand stock available.

Walther Prone 400 Target Rifle **$695**
Bolt action, single shot. Caliber: 22 LR. 25 1/2-inch heavy
barrel. Weight: 10 1/4 pounds. Supplied w/o sights. Prone
stock w/adj. cheekpiece and buttplate, accessory rail. Left-
hand stock available. Discontinued.

Walther Model SSV Varmint Rifle **$530**
Bolt action, single shot. Calibers: 22 LR, 22 Hornet. 25 1/2-
inch barrel. Weight: 6 3/4 pounds. Supplied w/o sights.
Monte Carlo stock w/high cheekpiece, full pistol grip and
forearm. Discontinued.

Walther Model U.I.T. Special Match Rifle **$840**
Bolt action, single shot. Caliber: 22 LR. 25 1/2-inch barrel.
Weight: 10.2 pounds. Sights: Micrometer aperture rear;
globe front. Target stock w/high comb, adj. buttplate, accessory rail. Left-hand stock avail. Discontinued 1993.

Walther Model U.I.T. Super Match Rifle **$895**
Bolt action, single shot. Caliber: 22 LR. 25 1/2-inch heavy
barrel. Weight: 10.2 pounds. Micrometer aperture rear;
globe front. Target stock w/support for off-hand shooting,
high comb, adj. buttplate and swivel. Left-hand stock
available. Discontinued 1993.

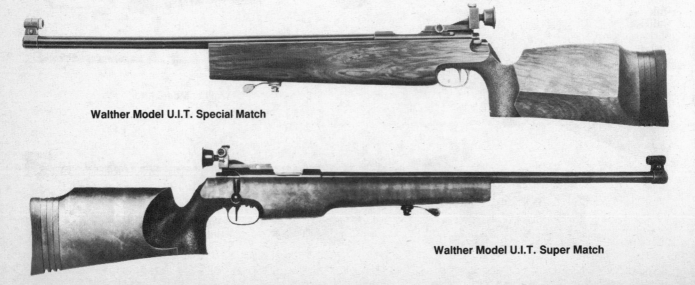

Walther Model U.I.T. Special Match

Walther Model U.I.T. Super Match

RIFLES

MONTGOMERY WARD
Chicago, Illinois
Western Field and Hercules Models

Firearms under the "private label" names of Western Field and Hercules are manufactured by such firms as Mossberg, Stevens, Marlin, and Savage for distribution and sale by Montgomery Ward.

Montgomery Ward Model 14M-497B Western Field Bolt Action Rifle **$80**
Caliber: 22 RF. 7-shot detachable box magazine. 24-inch barrel. Weight: about 5 pounds. Sights: receiver peep; open rear; hooded ramp front. Pistol-grip stock. Mfd. by Mossberg.

Montgomery Ward Model M771 Western Field Lever Action Rifle **$155**
Calibers: 30-30, 35 Rem. 6-shot tubular magazine. 20-inch barrel. Weight: 6¾ pounds. Sights: open rear; ramp front. Pistol-grip or straight stock, forearm w/barrel band. Mfd. by Mossberg.

Montgomery Ward Model M772 Western Field Lever Action Rifle **$165**
Calibers: 30-30, 35 Rem. 6-shot tubular magazine. 20-inch barrel. Weight: 6¾ pounds. Sights: open rear; ramp front. Pistol-grip or straight stock, forearm with barrel band. Mfd. by Mossberg.

Montgomery Ward Model M775 Bolt Action Rifle **$190**
Calibers: 222 Rem., 22-250, 243 Win., 308 Win. 4-shot magazine. Weight: about 7½ pounds. Sights: folding leaf rear; ramp front. Monte Carlo stock w/cheekpiece, pistol grip. Mfd by Mossberg.

Montgomery Ward Model M776 Bolt Action Rifle **$195**
Calibers: 222 Rem., 22-250, 243 Win., 308 Win. 4-shot magazine. Weight: about 7½ pounds. Sights: folding leaf rear; ramp front. Monte Carlo stock w/cheekpiece, pistol grip. Mfd. by Mossberg.

Montgomery Ward Model M778 Lever Action Rifle **$160**
Calibers: 30-30, 35 Rem. 6-shot tubular magazine. 20-inch barrel. Weight: 6¾ pounds. Sights: open rear; ramp front. Pistol-grip or straight stock, forearm w/barrel band. Mfd. by Mossberg.

Montgomery Ward Model M780 Bolt Action Rifle **$195**
Calibers: 222 Rem., 22-250, 243 Win., 308 Win. 4-shot magazine. Weight: about 7½ pounds. Sights: folding leaf rear; ramp front. Monte Carlo stock w/cheekpiece, pistol grip. Mfd. by Mossberg.

Montgomery Ward Model M782 Bolt Action Rifle **$195**
Same general specifications as Model M780.

Montgomery Ward Model M808 . . . . **$85**
Takedown. Caliber: 22RF. 15-shot tubular magazine. Barrels: 20- and 24-inch. Weight: about 6 pounds. Sights: open rear; bead front. Pistol-grip stock. Mfd. by Stevens.

Montgomery Ward Model M832 Bolt Action Rifle **$90**
Caliber: 22 RF. 7-shot clip magazine. 24-inch barrel. Weight: 6½ pounds. Sights: open rear; ramp front. Mfd. by Mossberg.

Montgomery Ward Model M836 . . . . **$95**
Takedown. Caliber: 22RF. 15-shot tubular magazine. Barrels: 20- and 24-inch. Weight: about 6 pounds. Sights: open rear; bead front. Pistol-grip stock. Mfd. by Stevens.

Montgomery Ward Model M865 Lever Action Carbine **$110**
Hammerless. Caliber: 22RF. Tubular magazine. Made with both 18½-inch and 20-inch barrel, forearm with barrel band, swivels. Weight: about 5 pounds. Mfd. by Mossberg.

Montgomery Ward Model M894 Autoloading Carbine **$105**
Caliber: 22 RF. 15-shot tubular magazine. 20-inch barrel. Weight: about 6 pounds. Sights: open rear; ramp front. Monte Carlo stock w/pistol grip. Mfd. by Mossberg.

Montgomery Ward Model M-SD57 . . . . **$90**
Takedown. Caliber: 22RF. 15-shot tubular magazine. Barrels: 20- and 24-inch. Weight: about 6 lbs. Sights: open rear; bead front. Pistol-grip stock. Mfd. by Stevens.

WEATHERBY, INC.
South Gate, California

Weatherby Classicmark I Rifle
Same general specifications as Mark V, except with checkered select American Claro walnut stock with oil finish and presentation recoil pad. Satin metal finish. Made 1992–93.
Calibers 240 to 300 Wby. . . . . $ 750
Caliber 340 Wby. 795
Caliber 378 Wby. 825
Caliber 416 Wby. 895
Caliber 460 Wby. 950

Weatherby Classicmark II Rifle
Same general specifications as Classicmark I, except with checkered select American walnut stock with oil finish, steel grip cap and Old English recoil pad. Satin metal finish. Right-hand only. Made 1992–93.
Calibers 240 to 340 Wby. (26-inch bbl.) $1150
Caliber 378 Wby. 1225
Caliber 416 Wby. 1350
Caliber 460 Wby. 1425

Weatherby Deluxe 378 Magnum Rifle **$1750**
Same general specifications as Deluxe Magnum in other calibers, except caliber 378 W. M. Schultz & Larsen action; 26-inch barrel. Discontinued 1958.

Weatherby Deluxe Magnum Rifle **$1200**
Calibers: 220 Rocket, 257 Weatherby Mag., 270 W.M., 7mm W.M., 300 W.M., 375 W.M. Specially processed FN Mauser action. 24-inch barrel (26-inch in 375 cal.). Monte Carlo-style stock with cheekpiece, black forend tip, grip cap, checkered pistol grip and forearm, quick-detachable

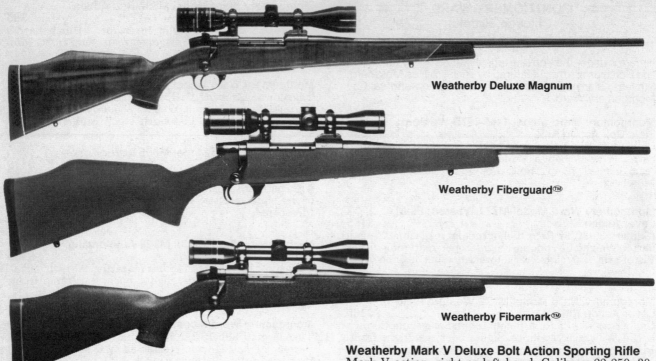

Weatherby Deluxe Magnum

Weatherby Fiberguard™

Weatherby Fibermark™

Weatherby Deluxe Magnum Rifle (cont.)
sling swivels. Value shown is for rifle without sights. Discontinued 1958.

Weatherby Deluxe Rifle **$995**
Same general specifications as Deluxe Magnum, except chambered for standard calibers such as 270, 30-06, etc. Discontinued 1958.

Weatherby Fiberguard™ Rifle **$415**
Same general specifications as Vanguard except for fiberglass stock and matte metal finish.

Weatherby Fibermark™ Rifle **$895**
Same general specifications as Mark V except with molded fiberglass stock, finished in a nonglare black wrinkle finish. The metal is finished in a non-glare matte finish. Discontinued 1993.

Weatherby Mark V Deluxe Bolt Action Sporting Rifle
Mark V action, right or left hand. Calibers: 22-250, 30-06; 224 Weatherby Varmintmaster; 240, 257, 270, 7mm, 300, 340, 378, 416, 460 Weatherby Magnums. Box magazine holds 2 to 5 cartridges depending on caliber. 24- or 26-inch barrel. Weight: 6½ to 10½ pounds. Monte Carlo-style stock with cheekpiece, skip checkering, forend tip, pistol-grip cap, recoil pad, QD swivels. Values shown are for rifles w/o sights. Made in Germany 1958–69; in Japan 1970–1994.

Calibers 22-250, 224 . . . . **$795**
Caliber 378 Weatherby Magnum **895**
Caliber 460 Weatherby Magnum **995**
Other calibers **650**
Add for left-hand action **100**
Deduct 30% if Japanese-made

Weatherby Mark V Euromark Bolt Action Rifle . . **$995**
Same general specifications as other Mark V rifles, except has hand-rubbed, satin oil finish Claro walnut stock and nonglare special process blue matte barreled action. Left-hand models available. Made 1986–1993; reintro. 1995.

Weatherby Mark V

Weatherby Mark V Euromark

RIFLES

Weatherby Mark V Lazermark

Weatherby Mark V Safari Grade

Weatherby Mark XXII Clip-fed

Weatherby Mark V Lazermark Rifle **$945**
Same general specifications as Mark V except with lazer-carved stock.

Weatherby Mark V Safari Grade Rifle **$1695**
Same general specifications as Mark V except extra capacity magazine, barrel sling swivel, and express rear sight, typical "Safari" style.

Weatherby Mark V Sporter Rifle
Sporter version of the Mark V, with low-luster metal finish. Stock without grip cap or forend tip. No sights. Made 1993 to date.
Calibers 257 to 300 Wby. **$550**
340 Weatherby 565
375 H&H 615
Other Non-Wby. Calibers 500

**Weatherby Mark XXII Deluxe 22 Automatic
Sporter Clip-fed Model** **$295**
Semiautomatic with single-shot selector. Caliber: 22 LR. 5- and 10-shot clip magazines. 24-inch barrel. Weight: 6 pounds. Sights: folding leaf open rear; ramp front. Monte Carlo-type stock w/cheekpiece, pistol grip, forend tip, grip cap, skip checkering, QD swivels. Introduced 1964. Made in Italy 1964–69; in Japan, 1970–1981; in the U.S., 1982–1990.

**Weatherby Mark XXII, Tubular Magazine
Model** **$275**
Same as Mark XXII, Clip-fed Model, except has 15-shot tubular magazine. Made in Japan 1973–1981; in the U.S., 1982–1990.

Weatherby Vanguard (I) Bolt Action Sporting Rifle
Mauser-type action. Calibers: 243 Win., 25-06, 270 Win., 7mm Rem. Mag., 30-06, 300 Win. Mag. 5-shot magazine; 3-shot in Magnum calibers). 24-inch barrel. Weight: 7 lbs. 14 oz. No sights. Monte Carlo-type stock w/cheekpiece, rosewood forend tip and pistol-grip cap, checkering, rubber buttpad, QD swivels. Made in Japan 1970–1984.
Vanguard Standard **$320**
Vanguard VGL (w/shorter 20-inch bbl., plain
   checkered stock, matte finish, 6½ lbs 325
Vanguard VGS (w/24-inch bbl., plain checkered
   stock, matte finish 345
Vanguard VGX (w/higher grade finish) 395

Weatherby Vanguard Classic I Rifle **$355**
Same general specifications as Vanguard VGX Deluxe, except with hand-checkered classic-style stock, black buttpad and satin finish. Calibers 223 Rem., 243 Win., 270 Win., 7mm-08, 7mm Rem. Mag., 30-06 and 308 Win. Made 1989–1994.

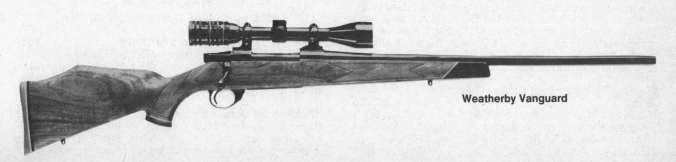

Weatherby Vanguard

Weatherby Vanguard VGX

Weatherby Vanguard Classic II Rifle **$495**
Same general specifications as Vanguard VGX Deluxe, except custom checkered classic-style American walnut stock with black forend tip, grip cap and solid black recoil pad, satin finish. Made 1989–1994.

Weatherby Vanguard VGX Deluxe **$495**
Calibers: 22-250 Rem., 243 Rem., 270 Wby. Mag., 270 Win., 7mm Rem. Mag., 30-06, 300 Win. Mag., 300 Wby. Mag., 338 Win. Mag. 3- or 5-round capacity. 24-inch barrel. About 44 inches overall. Weight: 7 to 8½ pounds. Custom checkered American walnut stock with Monte Carlo and recoil pad. Rosewood forend tip and pistol-grip cap. High-luster finish. Discontinued 1994.

Weatherby Weathermark Rifle
Same general specifications as Classicmark, except with checkered black Weathermark™ composite stock. Mark V bolt action. Calibers: 240, 257, 270, 300, 340, 378, 416 and 460 Weatherby Magnums; plus 270 Win., 7mm Rem.

Weatherby Weathermark Rifle (cont.)
Mag., 30-06 and 375 H&H Mag. Weight: 8 to 10 pounds. Right-hand only. Made 1992 to date.
Calibers 257 to 300 Wby.	**$475**
Caliber 340 Weatherby	**485**
375 H&H	**590**
Other non-Wby. calibers	**445**

Weatherby Weathermark Alaskan Rifle **$625**
Same general specifications as the Weathermark, except with nonglare electroless nickel finish. Right-hand only. Made 1992 to date.

WESTERN FIELD RIFLES
See listings under "W" for Montgomery Ward.

**Westley Richards Best Quality
Double Rifle**

**Westley Richards Best Quality
Magazine Rifle**

Westley Richards Best Quality Magazine Rifle (cont.)
Sights: leaf rear; hooded front. French walnut sporting stock w/cheekpiece, checkered pistol grip and forearm, horn forend tip, swivels.

WESTLEY RICHARDS & CO., LTD.
London, England

Westley Richards Best Quality Double Rifle . . **$29,500**
Boxlock, hammerless, ejector. Hand-detachable locks. Calibers: 30-06, 318 Accelerated Express, 375 Mag., 425 Mag. Express, 465 Nitro Express, 470 Nitro Express. 25-inch barrels. Weight: 8½ to 11 pounds. Sights: leaf rear; hooded front. French walnut stock w/cheekpiece, checkered pistol grip and forend.

**Westley Richards Best Quality Magazine
Rifle** **$6,750**
Mauser or Magnum Mauser action. Calibers: 7mm High Velocity, 30-06, 318 Accelerated Express, 375 Mag., 404 Nitro Express, 425 Mag. Barrel lengths: 24-inch; 7mm, 22-inch; 425 caliber, 25-inch. Weight: 7¼ to 9¼ pounds.

WICKLIFFE RIFLES
Wickliffe, Ohio
Mfd. by Triple S Development Co., Inc.

Wickliffe '76 Commemorative Model **$650**
Limited edition of 100. Same as Deluxe Model, except has filled etching on receiver sidewalls, U.S. silver dollar inlaid in stock, 26-inch barrel only, comes in presentation case. Made in 1976 only.

Wickliffe '76 Deluxe Model **$375**
Same as Standard Model, except 22-inch barrel in 30-06 only, has high-luster blued finish, fancy-grade figured American walnut stock with nickel silver grip cap.

**Wickliffe '76 Standard
Single Shot Rifle**

Wickliffe '76 Standard Model Single Shot Rifle . . **$325**
Falling-block action. Calibers: 22 Hornet, 223 Rem., 22-250, 243 Win., 25-06, 308 Win., 30-06, 45-70. 22-inch lightweight barrel (243 and 308 only) or 26-inch heavy sporter barrel. Weight: 6³/₄ or 8¹/₂ pounds, depending on barrel. No sights. Select American walnut Monte Carlo

Wickliffe '76 Standard Model Single Shot Rifle (cont.)
stock with right or left cheekpiece and pistol grip, semi-beavertail forearm. Introduced 1976; discontinued.

=== **TED WILLIAMS RIFLES** ===
See Sears, Roebuck and Company.

Winchester Model 02

Winchester Model 03

Winchester Model 04

=== **WINCHESTER RIFLES** ===
New Haven, Connecticut

Formerly Winchester Repeating Arms Co. Now mfd. by Winchester Western Div., Olin Corp., and by U.S. Repeating Arms Co. both of New Haven, CT.

NOTE: Thousands of Winchester rifles have been produced throughout the company's long, illustrious history. For ease in finding a particular model, the organization of Winchester rifles follows that of the other manufacturers (i.e., Model Numbers listed first, then Model Names in alphabetical order). The Model 70, however, which enjoyed a history all its own, is divided into Pre-1964, 1964-Type and 1972-Type variations. The Model 94 commemoratives are also grouped separately. In addition, please consult the Index.

**Winchester Model 02 Bolt Action Single Shot
Rifle** **$295**
Takedown. Basically the same as Model 1900 with minor improvements. Calibers: 22 Short and Long, 22 Extra Long, 22 LR. Weight: 3 pounds. Made 1902–1931.

**Winchester [Model 02] Thumb Trigger Bolt Action
Single Shot Rifle** **$550**
Takedown. Same as Model 02 except fired by pressing a button behind the cocking piece. Made 1904–1923.

Winchester Model 03 Self-Loading Rifle **$325**
Takedown. Caliber: 22 Win. Auto Rimfire. 10-shot tubular magazine in buttstock. 20-inch barrel. Weight: 5³/₄ pounds. Sights: open rear; bead front. Plain straight-grip stock and forearm (stock illustrated was extra-cost option). Made 1903–1936.

**Winchester Model 04 Bolt Action Single Shot
Rifle** **$225**
Similar to Model 02. Takedown. Caliber: 22 Short, Long, Extra Long, LR. 21-inch barrel. Weight: 4 pounds. Made 1904–1931.

RIFLES

Winchester Model 05

Winchester Model 06

Winchester Model 07

Winchester Model 10

Winchester Model 05 Self-Loading Rifle **$495**
Takedown. Calibers: 32 Win. S.L., 35 Win. S.L. 5- or 10-shot detachable box magazine. 22-inch barrel. Weight: 7½ pounds. Sights: open rear; bead front. Plain pistol-grip stock and forearm. Made 1905–1920.

Winchester Model 06 Slide Action Repeater **$475**
Takedown. Visible hammer. Caliber: 22 Short, Long, LR. Tubular magazine holds 20 Short, 16 Long or 14 LR. 20-inch barrel. Weight: 5 pounds. Sights: open rear; bead front. Straight-grip stock and grooved forearm. Made 1906–1932.

Winchester Model 07 Self-Loading Rifle **$550**
Takedown. Caliber: 351 Win. S.L. 5- or 10-shot detachable box magazine. 20-inch barrel. Weight: 7¾ pounds. Sights: open rear; bead front. Plain pistol-grip stock and forearm. Made 1907–1957.

Winchester Model 10 Self-Loading Rifle **$595**
Takedown. Caliber: 401 Win. S.L. 4-shot detachable box magazine. 20-inch barrel. Weight: 8½ pounds. Sights: open rear; bead front. Plain pistol-grip stock and forearm. Made 1910–1936.

Winchester Model 43 Bolt Action Sporting Rifle **$550**
Standard Grade. Calibers: 218 Bee, 22 Hornet, 25-20, 32-20 (latter two discontinued 1950). 3-shot detachable box magazine. 24-inch barrel. Weight: 6 pounds. Sights: open rear; bead front on hooded ramp. Plain pistol-grip stock with swivels. Made 1949–1957.

Winchester Model 43 Special Grade **$625**
Same as Standard Model 43, except has checkered pistol grip and forearm, grip cap.

Winchester Model 43 Special Grade

Winchester Model 47

Winchester Model 52 Standard Barrel

RIFLES

Winchester Model 47 Bolt Action Single Shot Rifle $235
Caliber: 22 Short, Long, LR. 25-inch barrel. Weight: 5½ pounds. Sights: peep or open rear; bead front. Plain pistol-grip stock. Made 1949–1954.

Winchester Model 52 Bolt Action Target Rifle
Standard Barrel. First type. Caliber: 22 LR. 5-shot box magazine. 28-inch barrel. Weight: 8¾ pounds. Sights: folding leaf peep rear; blade front sight; standard sights; various other combinations available. Scope bases. Semi-military type target stock w/pistol grip; original model has grasping grooves in forearm; higher comb and semi-beavertail forearm on later models. Numerous changes were made in this model, the most important was the adoption of the speed lock in 1929; Model 52 rifles produced before this change are generally referred to as "slow lock" models. Last arms of this type bore serial numbers followed by the letter "A." Made 1919–1937.
Slow Lock Model $525
Speed Lock Model 595

Winchester Model 52 Heavy Barrel $625
First type. Speed lock. Same general specifications as Standard Model 52 of this type, except has heavier barrel, Lyman 17G front sight, weighs 10 pounds.

Winchester Model 52 International Match Rifle
Similar to Model 52-D Heavy Barrel, except has special lead-lapped barrel, laminated "free rifle" style stock with high comb, thumbhole, hook buttplate, accessory rail, handstop/swivel assembly, palmrest. Weight: 13½ pounds. Made 1969–1978.
With standard trigger $660
With Kenyon or I.S.U. trigger 775

Winchester Model 52 International Prone Target Rifle $950
Similar to Model 52-D Heavy Barrel, except has special lead-lapped barrel, prone stock with fuller pistol grip, rollover cheekpiece removable for bore-cleaning. Weight: 11½ pounds. Made 1975 to date.

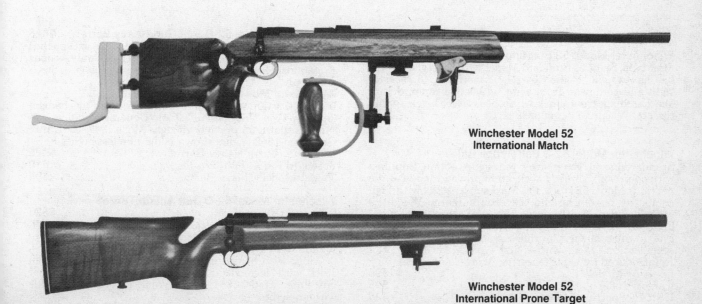

Winchester Model 52 International Match

Winchester Model 52 International Prone Target

Winchester Model 52-B Standard Barrel

Winchester Model 52-B Sporter

Winchester Model 52-C Heavy Barrel

Winchester Model 52-D Heavy Barrel

Winchester Model 52 Sporting Rifle $1725
First type. Same as Standard Model 52 of this type, except has lightweight 24-inch barrel, Lyman No. 48 receiver sight and gold bead front sight on hooded ramp, deluxe checkered sporting stock with cheekpiece, black forend tip, etc. Weight: 7³/₄ pounds.

Winchester Model 52-B Bolt Action Rifle
Standard barrel. Extensively redesigned action. Supplied with choice of "Target" stock, an improved version of the previous Model 52 stock, or "Marksman" stock with high comb, full pistol grip and beavertail forearm. Weight: 9 pounds. Offered with a wide choice of target sight combinations (Lyman, Marble-Goss, Redfield, Vaver, Winchester); value shown is for rifle less sight equipment. Other specifications as shown for first type. Made 1935–1947. Reintroduced by U.S. Repeating Arms Co. in 1993.
Sporting Model **$1595**
Target Model 595
USRAC Sporting Model 435

Winchester Model 52-B Bull Gun/Heavy Barrel . . $625
Same specifications as Standard Model 52-B, except Bull Gun has extra heavy barrel, Marksman stock only, weighs 12 pounds. Heavy Barrel model weighs 11 lbs.

Winchester Model 52-C Bolt Action Rifle
Improved action with "Micro-Motion" trigger mechanism and new-type "Marksman" stock. General specifications same as shown for previous models. Made 1947–1961; Bull Gun from 1952. Value shown is for rifle less sights.
Bull Gun (Extra Heavy Barrel, wt. 12 lbs.) **$625**
Standard Barrel (Wt. 9³/₄ lbs.) 610
Target Model (Heavy Barrel) 600

Winchester Model 52-D Bolt Action Target Rifle $625
Redesigned Model 52 action, single shot. Caliber: 22 LR. 28-inch standard or heavy barrel, free-floating, with blocks for standard target scopes. Weight: with standard barrel, 9³/₄ lbs.; with heavy barrel, 11 lbs. Restyled Marksman stock with accessory channel and forend stop, rubber buttplate. Made 1961–1978. Value shown is for rifle without sights.

Winchester Model 53

Winchester Model 54 National Match

Winchester Model 54 Standard Grade
Improved Type

Winchester Model 54 Super Grade

Winchester Model 53 Lever Action Repeater . . **$1550**
Modification of Model 92. Solid frame or takedown. Calibers: 25/20, 32/20, 44/40. 6-shot tubular half-magazine
in solid frame model. 7-shot in takedown. 22-inch nickel
steel barrel. Weight: 5¹/₂ to 6¹/₂ pounds. Sights: open rear;
bead front. Redesigned straight-grip stock and forearm.
Made 1924–1932.

**Winchester Model 54 Bolt Action High Power
Sporting Rifle (I)** **$550**
First type. Calibers: 270 Win., 7×57mm, 30-30, 30-06,
7.65×53mm, 9×57mm. 5-shot box magazine. 24-inch
barrel. Weight: 7³/₄ pounds. Sights: open rear; bead front.
Checkered stock w/pistol grip, tapered forearm w/
schnabel tip. This type has two-piece firing pin. Made
1925–1930.

**Winchester Model 54 Bolt Action High Power
Sporting Rifle (II)** **$675**
Standard Grade. Improved type with speed lock and one-
piece firing pin. Calibers: 22 Hornet, 220 Swift, 250/3000,
257 Roberts, 270 Win., 7×57mm, 30-06. 5-shot box
magazine. 24-inch barrel, 26-inch in cal. 220 Swift. Weight:
about 8 pounds. Sights: open rear; bead front on ramp.
NRA-type stock w/checkered pistol grip and forearm.
Made 1930–36.

Winchester Model 54 Carbine (I) **$650**
First type. Same as Model 54 rifle, except has 20-inch
barrel, plain lightweight stock with grasping grooves in
forearm. Weight: 7¹/₄ pounds.

Winchester Model 54 Carbine (II) **$695**
Improved type. Same as Model 54 Standard Grade Sport-
ing Rifle of this type, except has 20-inch barrel. Weight:
about 7¹/₂ pounds. This model may have either NRA-type
stock or the lightweight stock found on the first-type
Model 54 Carbine.

Winchester Model 54 National Match Rifle **$825**
Same as Standard Model 54, except has Lyman sights,
scope bases, Marksman-type target stock, weighs 9¹/₂
pounds. Same calibers as Standard Model.

Winchester Model 54 Sniper's Match Rifle **$895**
Similar to the earlier Model 54 Sniper's Rifle, except has
Marksman-type target stock, scope bases, weighs 12¹/₂
pounds. Available in same calibers as Model 54 Standard
Grade.

Winchester Model 54 Sniper's Rifle **$775**
Same as Standard Model 54, except has heavy 26-inch
barrel, Lyman #48 rear peep sight and blade front sight,
semi-military stock, weighs 11³/₄ pounds, cal. 30-06 only.

Winchester Model 54 Super Grade **$950**
Same as Standard Model 54 Sporter, except has deluxe
stock with cheekpiece, black forend tip, pistol-grip cap,
quick detachable swivels, 1-inch sling strap.

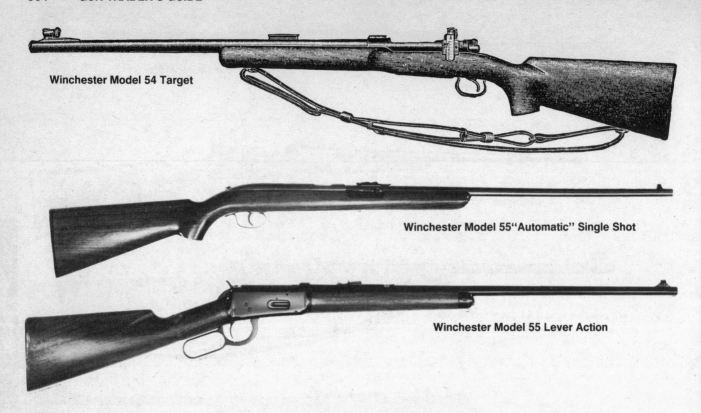

Winchester Model 54 Target

Winchester Model 55 "Automatic" Single Shot

Winchester Model 55 Lever Action

Winchester Model 54 Target Rifle **$825**
Same as Standard Model 54, except has 24-inch medium-weight barrel (26-inch in cal. 220 Swift), Lyman sights, scope bases, Marksman-type target stock, weighs 10¹/₂ pounds, same calibers as Standard Model.

Winchester Model 55 "Automatic" Single Shot **$225**
Caliber: 22 Short, Long, LR. 22-inch barrel. Sights: open rear; bead front. One-piece walnut stock. Weight: about 5¹/₂ pounds. Made 1958–1960.

Winchester Model 55 Lever Action Repeater
Modification of Model 94. Solid frame or takedown. Calibers: 25-35, 30-30, 32 Win. Special. 3-shot tubular half magazine. 24-inch nickel steel barrel. Weight: about 7 pounds. Sights: open rear; bead front. Made 1924–1932.

Winchester Model 55 Lever Action Repeater (cont)
Straight Grip . . . . **$ 950**
Pistol Grip **1700**

Winchester Model 56 Bolt Action Sporting Rifle **$495**
Solid frame. Caliber: 22 LR, 22 Short. 5- or 10-shot detachable box magazine. 22-inch barrel. Weight: 4³/₄ pounds. Sights: open rear; bead front. Plain pistol-grip stock with schnabel forend. Made 1926–29.

Winchester Model 57 Bolt Action Target Rifle . . **$525**
Solid frame. Same as Model 56, except available (until 1929) in 22 Short as well as LR, has semi-military style target stock, swivels and web sling, Lyman peep rear sight, blade front sight, weighs 5 lbs. Mfd. 1926–1936.

Winchester Model 56

Winchester Model 57 Target

Winchester Model 58

Winchester Model 60A Target

Winchester Model 61 Repeater

Winchester Model 62 Repeater

Winchester Model 63

RIFLES

Winchester Model 58 Bolt Action Single Shot . . . **$265**
Similar to Model 02. Takedown. Caliber: 22 Short, Long, LR. 18-inch barrel. Weight: 3 pounds. Sights; open rear; blade front. Plain, flat, straight-grip stock. Made 1928–1931.

Winchester Model 59 Bolt Action Single Shot . . . **$425**
Improved version of Model 58, has 23-inch barrel, redesigned stock w/pistol grip, weighs 4½ pounds. Made 1930.

Winchester Model 60 Bolt Action Single Shot . . . **$225**
Redesign of Model 59. Caliber: 22 Short, Long, LR. 23-inch barrel (27-inch after 1933). Weight: 4¼ pounds. Sights: open rear; blade front. Plain stock w/pistol grip. Made 1930–34.

Winchester Model 60A Target Rifle **$495**
Essentially the same as Model 60, except has Lyman peep rear sight and square top front sight, semi-military target stock and web sling, weighs 5½ pounds. Made 1932–39.

Winchester Model 61 Hammerless Slide Action Repeater **$495**
Takedown. Caliber: 22 Short, Long, LR. Tubular magazine holds 20 Short, 16 Long, 14 LR. 24-inch round barrel.

Winchester Model 61 Hammerless (cont.)
Weight: 5½ pounds. Sights: open rear; bead front. Plain pistol-grip stock, grooved semibeavertail slide handle. Also available with 24-inch full-octagon barrel and only calibers 22 LR, 22 Short or 22 WRF. Made 1932–1963. *Note:* Octagon barrel model commands higher prices (disc. 1943–44); assembled until 1948.

Winchester Model 61 Magnum **$625**
Same as Standard Model 61, except chambered for 22 WMR; magazine holds 12 rounds. Made 1960–63.

Winchester Model 62 Visible Hammer Slide Action Repeater **$450**
Modernized version of Model 1890. Caliber: 22 Short, Long, LR. 23-inch barrel. Weight: 5½ pounds. Plain straight-grip stock, grooved semibeavertail slide handle. Also available in Gallery Model chambered for 22 Short only. Made 1932–1959. *Note:* Pre-WWII model (small forearm) commands 25% higher price.

Winchester Model 63 Self-Loading Rifle **$495**
Takedown. Caliber: 22 LR High Speed only. 10-shot tubular magazine in buttstock. 23-inch barrel. Weight: 5½ pounds. Sights: open rear; bead front. Plain pistol-grip stock and forearm. Originally available with 20-inch barrel as well as 23-inch. Made 1933–1959.

Winchester Model 64 Deer Rifle

Winchester Model 64 (original)

Winchester Model 64, 1972-74 type

Winchester Model 64 Deer Rifle **$1695**
Same as Standard Model 64, calibers 30-30 and 32 Win.
Special, except has checkered pistol grip and semibeavertail forearm, swivels and sling, weighs 7¾ pounds. Made
1933–1956.

Winchester Model 64 Lever Action Repeater
Standard Grade. Improved version of Models 94 and 55.
Solid frame. Calibers: 25/35, 30-30, 32 Win. Special. 5-
shot tubular ⅔ magazine. 20- or 24-inch barrel. Weight:
about 7 pounds. Sights: open rear; bead front on ramp w/
sight cover. Plain pistol-grip stock and forearm. Made
1933–1956. Production resumed in 1972 (caliber 30-30,
24-inch barrel); discontinued 1974.
Original model **$595**
1972–74 model **395**

Winchester Model 64—219 Zipper **$1895**
Same as Standard Grade Model 64, except has 26-inch
barrel, peep rear sight. Made 1937–1947.

Winchester Model 65 Lever Action Repeater . . **$1595**
Improved version of Model 53. Solid frame. Calibers: 25-
20 and 32-20. Six-shot tubular half-magazine. 22-inch
barrel. Weight: 6½ pounds. Sights: open rear; bead front
on ramp base. Plain pistol-grip stock and forearm. Made
1933–1947.

Winchester Model 65—218 Bee **$1995**
Same as Standard Model 65, except has 24-inch barrel,
peep rear sight. Made 1938–1947.

**Winchester Model 67 Bolt Action Single Shot
Rifle** **$145**
Takedown. Calibers: 22 Short, Long, LR, 22 LR shot
(smoothbore), 22 WRF. 27-inch barrel. Weight: 5 pounds.
Sights: open rear; bead front. Plain pistol-grip stock
(original model had grasping grooves in forearm). Made
1934–1963.

Winchester Model 67 Boy's Rifle **$175**
Same as Standard Model 67, except has shorter stock, 20-
inch barrel, weighs 4¼ pounds.

Winchester Model 65

Winchester Model 67

Winchester Model 68

Winchester Model 69

Winchester Model 69 Match

RIFLES

PRE-1964 MODEL 70

Winchester Model 68 Bolt Action Single Shot . . . **$195**
Same as Model 67, except has rear peep sight. Made 1934–1946.

Winchester Model 69 Bolt Action Single Shot . . . **$215**
Takedown. Caliber: 22 S, L, LR. 5- or 10-shot box magazine. 25-inch barrel. Weight: 5½ pounds. Peep or open rear sight. Plain pistol-grip stock. Rifle cocks on closing motion of the bolt. Made 1935–1937.

Winchester Model 69A Bolt Action Single Shot
Same as the Model 69, except cocking mechanism was changed to cock the rifle by the opening motion of the bolt. Made 1937–1963. *Note:* Models with grooved receivers command 20% higher prices.
Model 69A Standard **$250**
Match Model w/Lyman #57EW receiver sight . . . **325**
Target Model w/Winchester peep rear sight,
  swivels, sling **350**

> **NOTE:** Introduced in 1937, the Model 70 Bolt Action Repeater was offered in several styles and calibers. Only minor design changes were made over 27 years, and more than one-half million of these rifles were sold. In 1964, the original Model 70 was superseded by a revised version with redesigned action, improved bolt, swaged barrel, restyled stock (barrel free-floating). This model again underwent major changes in 1972—most visible: new stock with contrasting forend tip and grip cap, cut checkering (instead of impressed as in predecessor), knurled bolt handle. Action (machined from a solid block of steel) and barrel are chrome molybdenum steel.

Winchester Model 70 African Rifle **$3295**
Same general specifications as Super Grade Model 70, except has 25-inch barrel, 3-shot magazine, Monte Carlo stock with recoil pad. Weight: about 9½ pounds. Caliber: 458 Winchester Magnum. Made 1956–1963.

Winchester Model 70 Alaskan **$1550**
Same as Standard Model 70, except calibers 338 Win. Mag., 375 H&H Mag.; 3-shot magazine in 338, 4-shot in 375 caliber; 25-inch barrel; stock with recoil pad. Weight: 8 lbs. in 338; 8¾ lbs. in 375 caliber. Made 1960–63.

Winchester Model 70 Bull Gun **$2750**
Same as Standard Model 70, except has heavy 28-inch barrel, scope bases, Marksman stock, weighs 13¼ pounds, caliber 300 H&H Magnum and 30-06 only. Disc. 1963.

Winchester Model 70 Featherweight Sporter . . . **$910**
Same as Standard Model 70, except has redesigned stock and 22-inch barrel, aluminum trigger guard, floorplate and buttplate. Calibers: 243 Win., 264 Win. Mag., 270 Win., 308 Win., 30-06, 358 Win. Weight: about 6½ pounds. Made 1952–1963.

Winchester Model 70 National Match Rifle **$1095**
Same as Standard Model 70, except has scope bases, Marksman-type target stock, weighs 9½ pounds, caliber 30-06 only. Discontinued 1960.

Winchester Model 70 Standard Grade **$895**
Calibers: 22 Hornet, 220 Swift, 243 Win., 250-3000, 257 Roberts, 270 Win., 7×57mm, 30-06, 308 Win., 300 H&H Mag., 375 H&H Mag. 5-shot box magazine (4-shot in Magnum calibers). 24-inch barrel standard; 26-inch in 220

Winchester Model 70 Standard
(Pre-1964)

Winchester Model 70 Standard Grade (cont.)

Swift and 300 Mag.; 25-inch in 375 Mag.; at one time a 20-inch barrel was available. Sights: open rear; hooded ramp front. Checkered walnut stock; Monte Carlo comb standard on later production. Weight: from 7¾ pounds depending on caliber and barrel length. Made 1937–1963.

Winchester Model 70 Super Grade $1995

Same as Standard Grade Model 70, except has deluxe stock w/cheekpiece, black forend tip, pistol-grip cap, quick detachable swivels, sling. Discontinued 1960.

Winchester Model 70 Super Grade
Featherweight $1695

Same as Standard Grade Featherweight except has deluxe stock w/cheekpiece, black forend tip, pistol-grip cap, quick detachable swivels, sling. Discontinued 1960. *Note:* SG-FWs are rare but, unless documented, will not command premium price of $2800–$3500; price here reflects "All" (incl. nondocumented transactions).

Winchester Model 70 Target Rifle $1395

Same as Standard Model 70, except has 24-inch medium-weight barrel, scope bases, Marksman stock, weight about 10½ pounds. Originally offered in all of the Model 70 calibers, this rifle was available later in calibers 243 Win. and 30-06. Discontinued 1963.

Winchester Model 70 Varmint Rifle $925

Same general specifications as Standard Model 70, except has 26-inch heavy barrel, scope bases, special varminter stock. Calibers: 220 Swift, 243 Win. Made 1956–1963.

Winchester Model 70 Westerner $950

Same as Standard Model 70, except calibers 264 Win. Mag., 300 Win. Mag.; 3-shot magazine; 26-inch barrel in former caliber, 24-inch in latter. Weight: about 8¼ pounds. Made 1960–63.

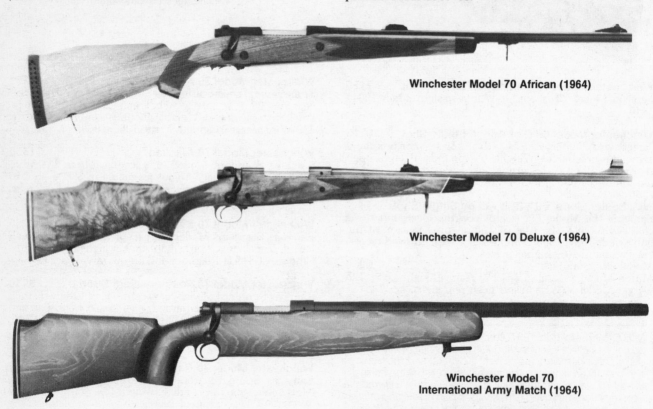

Winchester Model 70 African (1964)

Winchester Model 70 Deluxe (1964)

**Winchester Model 70
International Army Match (1964)**

1964-TYPE MODEL 70

Winchester Model 70 African $650

Caliber: 458 Win. Mag. 3-shot magazine. 22-inch barrel. Weight: 8½ pounds. Special "African" sights. Monte Carlo stock with ebony forend tip, hand-checkering, twin stock-reinforcing bolts, recoil pad, QD swivels. Made 1964–1971.

Winchester Model 70 Deluxe $595

Calibers: 243, 270 Win., 30-06, 300 Win. Mag. 5-shot box magazine (3-shot in Magnum). 22-inch barrel (24-inch in Magnum). Weight: 7½ pounds. Sights: open rear; hooded ramp front. Monte Carlo stock w/ebony forend tip, hand-checkering, QD swivels, recoil pad on Magnum. Made 1964–1971.

Winchester Model 70 International Army
Match Rifle $725

Caliber: 308 Win. (7.62 NATO). 5-shot box magazine. 24-inch heavy barrel. Externally adj. trigger. Weight: 11 pounds. ISU stock w/military oil finish, forearm rail for standard accessories, vertically adj. buttplate. Made in 1971. Value shown is for rifle w/o sights.

Winchester Model 70 Magnum

Calibers: 7mm Rem. Mag.; 264, 300, 338 Win. Mag.; 375 H&H Mag. 3-shot magazine. 24-inch barrel. Weight: 7¾ to 8½ pounds. Sights: open rear; hooded ramp front. Monte Carlo stock w/cheekpiece, checkering, twin stock-reinforcing bolts, recoil pad, swivels. Made 1964–1971.
Caliber 375 H&H Mag. $595
Other calibers 350

Winchester Model 70 Mannlicher (1964)

Winchester Model 70 Standard (1964)

Winchester Model 70 Target (1964)

Winchester Model 70 Mannlicher $495
Calibers: 243, 270, 308 Win., 30-06. 5-shot box magazine. 19-inch barrel. Sights: open rear; hooded ramp front. Weight: 7½ pounds. Mannlicher-style stock w/Monte Carlo comb and cheekpiece, checkering, steel forend cap, QD swivels. Made 1969–1971.

Winchester Model 70 Standard $425
Calibers: 22-250, 222 Rem., 225, 243, 270, 308 Win., 30-06. 5-shot box magazine. 22-inch barrel. Weight: 7½ pounds. Sights: open rear; hooded ramp front. Monte Carlo stock w/cheekpiece, checkering, swivels. Made 1964–1971.

Winchester Model 70 Target $595
Calibers: 308 Win. (7.62 NATO) and 30-06. 5-shot box magazine. 24-inch heavy barrel. Blocks for target scope, no sights. Weight: 10¼ pounds. High-comb Marksman-style stock, aluminum hand stop, swivels. Made 1964–1971.

Winchester Model 70 Varmint $575
Same as Model 70 Standard, except has 24-inch target weight barrel, blocks for target scope, no sights, available in calibers 22-250, 222 Rem., and 243 Win. only. Weight: 9¾ pounds. Made 1964–1971.

Winchester Model 70 African (1972)

Winchester Model 70 Classic Sporter
with BOSS

1972-TYPE MODEL 70

Winchester Model 70 African $625
Similar to Model 70 Magnum, except caliber 458 Win. Mag.; has 22-inch barrel, special African open rear sight, reinforced stock with ebony forend tip, detachable swivels and sling. Weight: about 8½ pounds. Made 1972 to date.

Winchester Model 70 Classic SM
Similar to the Model 70 Classic Sporter, except with checkered black composite stock and matte metal finish.

Winchester Model 70 Classic SM (cont.)
Made 1994 to date.
Standard Model **$335**
In caliber 375 H&H **375**
With BOSS, **add** **90**
With Open Sights, **add** **35**

Winchester Model 70 Classic Sporter
Similar to the Model 70 Sporter, except has pre-64-style action w/controlled round feeding, classic-style stock.

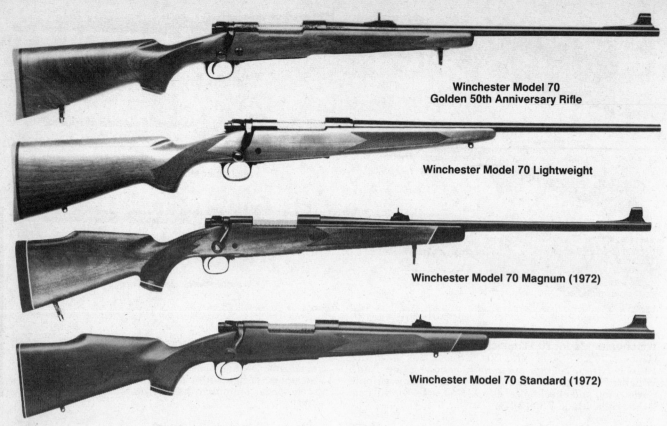

Winchester Model 70
Golden 50th Anniversary Rifle

Winchester Model 70 Lightweight

Winchester Model 70 Magnum (1972)

Winchester Model 70 Standard (1972)

Winchester Model 70 Classic Sporter (cont.)
Optional open sights. Made 1994 to date.
Standard Model $340
With BOSS, **add** 90
With Open Sights, **add** 35

Winchester Model 70 Classic Stainless
Similar to the Model 70 Classic Sporter, except with matte stainless steel finish. Weight: 8 pounds. No open sights, except 375 H&H. Made 1994 to date.
Standard Model $350
In caliber 375 H&H 395
With BOSS, **add** 90

Winchester Model 70 Custom Sharpshooter ... $1250
Calibers: 22-250, 223, 308 Win., 300 Win. Mag. 24- or 26-inch barrel. 44½ inches overall (24-inch bbl.). Weight: 11 pounds. Custom fitted, hand-honed action. McMillan A-2 target-style stock. Matte blue finish. Made 1992 to date.

Winchester Model 70 Custom Sporting
Sharpshooter $1195
Similar to the Custom Sharpshooter Model, except has McMillan sporter-style gray composite stock. Stainless 24- or 26-inch barrel with blued receiver. Calibers: 270, 7mm STW, 300 Win. Mag. Made 1993 to date.

Winchester Model 70 Golden 50th Anniversary
Edition Bolt Action Rifle $925
Caliber: 300 Win. 3-shot magazine. 24-inch barrel. 44½ inches overall. Weight: 7¾ pounds. Checkered American walnut stock. Hand-engraved American scroll pattern on barrel, receiver, magazine cover, trigger guard and pistol grip cap. Sights: adj. rear; hooded front ramp. Inscription

Winchester Model 70 Golden 50th Anniversary (cont.)
on barrel reads "The Rifleman's Rifle 1937–1987." Only 500 made 1986–87.

Winchester Model 70 Featherweight Classic ... $395
Similar to the Model 70 XTR Featherweight, except with controlled-round feeding system. Calibers: 270, 280 and 30-06. Made 1992 to date.

Winchester Model 70 International Army
Match $750
Caliber: 308 Win. (7.62mm NATO). 5-shot magazine, clip slot in receiver bridge. 24-inch heavy barrel. Weight: 11 pounds. No sights. ISU target stock. Intro. 1973; discont.

Winchester Model 70 Lightweight Bolt Action
Rifle $325
Calibers: 22-250 and 223 Rem.; 243, 270 and 308 Win.; 30-06 Springfld. 5-shot mag. capacity (6-shot 223 Rem.). 22-inch barrel. 42 to 42½ inches overall. Weight: 6 to 6¼ pounds. Checkered classic straight stock. Sling swivel studs. Made 1986 to date.

Winchester Model 70 Magnum
Same as Model 70, except has 3-shot magazine, 24-inch barrel, reinforced stock with recoil pad. Weight: about 7¾ pounds (except 8½ pounds in 375 H&H Mag.). Calibers: 264 Win. Mag., 7mm Rem. Mag., 300 Win. Mag., 338 Win. Mag., 375 H&H Mag. Made 1972 to date.
375 H&H Magnum $425
Other Magnum calibers 375

Winchester Model 70 Standard $345
Same as Model 70A, except has 5-shot magazine, Monte Carlo stock with cheekpiece, black forend tip and pistol-

Winchester Model 70 Target (1972)

Winchester Model 70 Varmint (1972)

Winchester Model 70 Win-Cam

Winchester Model 70 Win-Tuff

Winchester Model 70 Standard (cont.)

grip cap with white spacers, checkered pistol grip and forearm, detachable sling swivels. Same calibers plus 225 Win. Made 1972 to date.

Winchester Model 70 Sporter DBM

Same general specifications as Model 70 Sporter SSM, except with detachable box magazine. Calibers: 22-250 (discontinued 1994), 223 (discontinued 1994), 243 (discontinued 1994), 270, 7mm Rem. Mag., 308 (discontinued 1994), 30-06, 300 Win. Mag. Made 1992 to date.
Model 70 DBM **$365**
Model 70 DBM-S **385**

Winchester Model 70 Stainless Sporter SSM . . . $395

Same general specifications as Model 70 XTR Sporter, except with checkered black composite stock and matte finished receiver and barrel. Calibers: 270, 7mm Rem. Mag., 30-06, 300 Win. Mag., 338 Win. Mag. Weight: 7³/₄ pounds. Made 1992 to date.

Winchester Model 70 Super Grade $495

Calibers: 270, 7mm Rem. Mag., 30-06, 300 Win. Mag., 338 Win. Mag. 5-shot magazine (standard), 3-shot (magnum). 24-inch barrel. 44¹/₂ inches overall. Weight: 7³/₄ pounds. Checkered walnut stock with sculptured cheekpiece and tapered forend. Scope bases and rings, no sights. Controlled-round feeding system. Made 1990 to date.

Winchester Model 70 Target $495

Calibers: 30-06 and 308 Win. (7.62mm NATO). 5-shot magazine. 26-inch heavy barrel. Weight: 10¹/₂ pounds. No sights. High-comb Marksman-style target stock, aluminum hand stop, swivels. Made 1972 to date.

Winchester Model 70 Ultra Match $595

Similar to Model 70 Target, but custom grade; has 26-inch heavy barrel with deep counterbore, glass bedding, externally adj. trigger. Made 1972 to date.

Winchester Model 70 Varmint (Heavy Barrel)

Same as Model 70 Standard, except has medium-heavy, counter-bored 26-inch barrel, no sights, stock with less drop. Weight: 9 pounds. Calibers: 22-250 Rem., 223 Rem., 243 Win., 308 Win. Made 1972 to date. **Model 70 SHB**, in 308 Win. only with black synthetic stock and matte blue receiver/barrel, made 1992 to date.
Model 70 Varmint **$425**
Model 70 SHB (Synthetic Heavy Barrel) **465**

Winchester Model 70 Win-Cam Rifle $345

Caliber: 270 Win. and 30-06 Springfield. 24-inch barrel. Camouflage one-piece laminated stock. Recoil pad. Drilled and tapped for scope. Made 1986 to date.

Winchester Model 70 Winlite Bolt Action Rifle . . $475

Calibers: 270 Win., 280 Rem., 30-06 Springfield, 7mm Rem., 300 Win. Mag., and 338 Win. Mag. 5-shot magazine; 3-shot for Magnum calibers. 22-inch barrel; 24-inch for Magnum calibers. 42¹/₂ inches overall; 44¹/₂, Magnum calibers. Weight: 6¹/₄ to 7 pounds. Fiberglass stock with rubber recoil pad, sling swivel studs. Made 1986 to date.

Winchester Model 70 Win-Tuff Bolt Action Rifle

Calibers: 22-250, 223, 243, 270, 308 and 30-06 Springfield. 22-inch barrel. Weight: 6¹/₄–7 pounds. Laminated dye-shaded brown wood stock with recoil pad. Barrel drilled and tapped for scope. Swivel studs. FWT Model made 1986–1994. LW Model introduced in 1992.
Featherweight Model **$375**
Lightweight Model (Made 1992–93) **325**

Winchester Model 70 XTR
Featherweight (1972)

Winchester Model 70 XTR Sporter

Winchester Model 70 XTR Featherweight $365
Similar to Standard Win. Model 70, except lightweight American walnut stock with classic schnabel forend, checkered. 22-inch barrel, hooded blade front sight, folding leaf rear sight. Stainless-steel magazine follower. Weight: 6³/₄ pounds. Made 1984 to date.

Winchester Model 70 XTR 50th Anniversary $975
Same as XTR Sporter Magnum, except with checkered classic-style walnut stock with early-style Model 70 swivels. Hand-engraved receiver, floorplate, trigger guard and grip cap. "The Rifleman's Rifle 1937–1987" commemorative inscription engraved on barrel. Chambered in 300 Win. Mag. only. 500 produced in 1987.

Winchester Model 70 XTR Sporter Rifle $375
Calibers: 264 Win. Mag., 7mm Rem. Mag., 300 Win. Mag., 200 Weatherby Mag., and 338 Win. Mag. 3-shot magazine.

Winchester Model 70 XTR Sporter Rifle (cont.)
24-inch barrel. 44¹/₂ inches overall. Weight: 7³/₄ pounds. Walnut Monte Carlo stock. Rubber buttpad. Receiver tapped and drilled for scope mounting. Made 1986 to date.

Winchester Model 70 XTR Sporter Magnum $365
Calibers: 264 Win. Mag., 7mm Rem. Mag., 300 Win. Mag., 338 Win. Mag. 3-shot magazine. 24-inch barrel. 44¹/₂ inches overall. Weight: 7³/₄ pounds. No sights furnished, optional adjustable folding leaf rear; hooded ramp. Receiver drilled and tapped for scope. Checkered American walnut Monte Carlo-style stock with satin finish. Made 1986 to date.

Winchester Model 70 XTR Sporter Varmint $355
Same general specifications as Model 70 XTR Sporter, except in calibers 223, 22-250, 243 only. Checkered American walnut Monte Carlo-style stock w/cheekpiece.

Winchester Model 70A (1972)

Winchester Model 71 Special

Winchester Model 70A $275
Calibers: 222 Rem., 22-250, 243 Win., 25-06, 270 Win., 30-06, 308 Win. 4-shot magazine. 22-inch barrel (except 24- or 26-inch in 25-06). Weight: about 7¹/₂ pounds. Sights: open rear: hooded ramp front. Monte Carlo stock with checkered pistol grip and forearm, sling swivels. Made 1972 to date.

Winchester Model 70A Magnum $295
Same as Model 70A, except has 3-shot magazine, 24-inch barrel, recoil pad. Weight: about 7³/₄ pounds. Calibers:

Winchester Model 70A Magnum (cont.)
264 Win. Mag., 7mm Rem. Mag., 300 Win. Mag. Made 1972 to date.

Winchester Model 71 Special Lever Action
Repeater $1200
Solid frame. Caliber: 348 Win. 4-shot tubular magazine. 20- or 24-inch barrel. Weight: 8 pounds. Sights: open rear; bead front on ramp w/hood. Walnut stock, checkered pistol grip and forearm, grip cap, quick-detachable swivels and sling. Made 1935–1957.

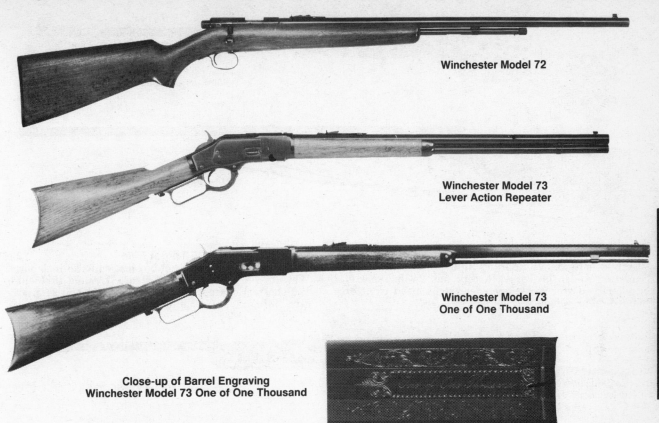

Winchester Model 72

Winchester Model 73
Lever Action Repeater

Winchester Model 73
One of One Thousand

Close-up of Barrel Engraving
Winchester Model 73 One of One Thousand

RIFLES

Winchester Model 71 Standard Grade $795
Plain Model. Same as Model 71 Special, except lacks checkering, grip car, sling and swivels.

Winchester Model 72 Bolt Action Repeater $195
Tubular magazine. Takedown. Caliber: 22 Short, Long, LR. Magazine holds 20 Short, 16 Long or 15 LR. 25-inch barrel. Weight: 5¾ pounds. Sights: peep or open rear; bead front. Plain pistol-grip stock. Made 1938–1959.

Winchester Model 73 Lever Action Carbine . . . $2795
Same as Standard Model 73 Rifle, except has 20-inch barrel, 12-shot magazine, weighs 7¼ pounds.

Winchester Model 73 Lever Action Repeater . . $2600
Calibers: 32-20, 38-40, 44-40; a few were chambered for 22 rimfire. 15-shot magazine, also made with 6-shot half magazine. 24-inch barrel (round, half-octagon, octagon). Weight: about 8½ pounds. Sights: open rear; bead or blade front. Plain straight-grip stock and forearm. Made 1873–1924. 720,610 rifles of this model were mfd.

Winchester Model 73 Rifle—One of One Thousand . . . . $50,000+
During the late 1870s Winchester offered Model 73 rifles of superior accuracy and extra finish, designated "One of One Thousand" grade, at $100. These rifles are marked "1 of 1000" or "One of One Thousand." Only 136 of this model are known to have been manufactured. This is one of the rarest of shoulder arms and, because so very few have been sold in recent years, it is extremely difficult to assign a value; however, in the author's opinion, an "excellent" specimen would probably bring a price upward of $35,000.

Winchester Model 73 Special Sporting Rifle . . . $2995
Same as Standard Model 73 Rifle, except this type has receiver casehardened in colors, pistol-grip stock of select walnut, octagon barrel only.

Winchester Model 74 Self-Loading Rifle $185
Takedown. Calibers: 22 Short only, 22 LR only. Tubular magazine in buttstock holds 20 Short, 14 LR. 24-inch barrel. Weight: 6¼ pounds. Sights: open rear; bead front. Plain pistol-grip stock, one-piece. Made 1939–1955.

Winchester Model 74

Winchester Model 75 Sporter

Winchester Model 75 Target

Winchester Model 75 Sporting Rifle **$695**
Same as Model 75 Target, except has 24-inch barrel, checkered sporter stock, open rear sight; bead front on hooded ramp, weighs 5½ pounds.

Winchester Model 75 Target Rifle **$325**
Caliber: 22 LR. 5- or 10-shot box magazine. 28-inch barrel. Weight: 8¾ pounds. Target sights (Lyman, Redfield or Winchester). Target stock w/pistol grip and semibeavertail forearm, swivels and sling. Made 1938–1959.

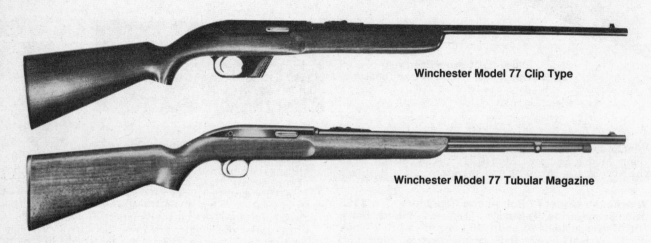

Winchester Model 77 Clip Type

Winchester Model 77 Tubular Magazine

Winchester Model 77 Semiautomatic Rifle, Clip Type **$195**
Solid frame. Caliber: 22 LR. 8-shot clip magazine. 22-inch barrel. Weight: about 5½ pounds. Sights: open rear; bead front. Plain, one-piece pistol-grip stock. Made 1955–1963.

Winchester Model 77, Tubular Magazine Type .. **$195**
Same as Model 77. Clip type, except has tubular magazine holding 15 rounds. Made 1955–1963.

Winchester Model 86
Lever Action Repeater

Winchester Model 86 Lever Action Carbine ... **$7950**
Same as standard Model 86 rifle, except with 22-inch barrel and weighs about 7¾ pounds.

Winchester Model 86 Lever Action Repeater .. **$2950**
Solid frame or takedown style. Calibers: 33 Win., 38-56-255, 38-70-255, 40-65-260, 40-70-330, 40-82-260, 45-70, 45-90-300, 50-100-450, 50-110-300. All but the 45-70

Winchester Model 86 Lever Action Repeater (cont.)
are now obsolete. The 33 Win. and 45-70 were the last calibers in which this model was supplied. 8-shot tubular magazine, also 4-shot half-magazine. 22- or 26-inch barrel (round, half-octagon, octagon). Weight: from 7½ pounds up. Sights: open rear; bead or blade front. Plain straight-grip stock and forearm. Made 1886–1935.

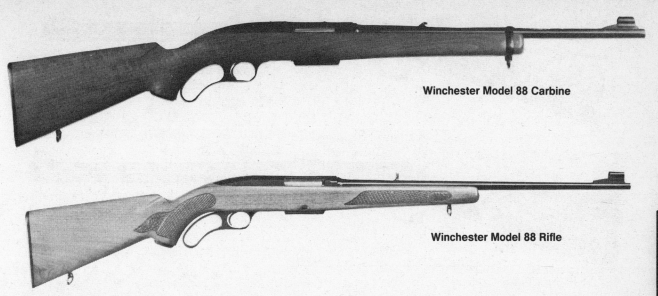

Winchester Model 88 Carbine

Winchester Model 88 Rifle

Winchester Model 88 Carbine **$495**
Same as Model 88 Rifle, except has 19-inch barrel, plain carbine-style stock and forearm with barrel band. Weight: 7 pounds. Made 1968–1973.

Winchester Model 88 Lever Action Rifle **$465**
Hammerless. Calibers: 243 Win., 284 Win., 308 Win., 358 Win. 4-shot box magazine. 3-shot in pre-1963 models and in current 284. 22-inch barrel. Weight: about 7¼ pounds. One-piece walnut stock with pistol grip, swivels (1965 and later models have basket-weave ornamentation instead of checkering). Made 1955–1973. *Note:* 243 and 358 introduced 1956, latter discontinued 1964; 284 introduced 1963.

Winchester Model 90 Slide Action Repeater **$995**
Visible hammer. Calibers: 22 Short, Long, LR; 22 WRF. (not interchangeable). Tubular magazine holds 15 Short, 12 Long, 11 LR; 12 WRF. 24-inch octagon barrel. Weight:

Winchester Model 90 Slide Action Repeater (cont.)
5¾ pounds. Sights: open rear; bead front. Plain straight-grip stock, grooved slide handle. Originally solid frame, after No. 15,499 all rifles of this model were takedown type. Fancy checkered pistol-grip stock, stainless-steel barrel supplied at extra cost. Made 1890–1932.

Winchester Model 92 Lever Action Carbine . . . **$1695**
Same as Model 92RR rifle, except has 20-inch barrel, 5-shot or 11-shot magazine, weighs about 5¾ pounds.

Winchester Model 92 Lever Action Repeater . . **$1595**
Solid frame or takedown. Calibers: 25/20, 32/20, 38/40, 44/40. 13-shot tubular magazine, also 7-shot half-magazine. 24-inch barrel (round, octagon, half-octagon). Weight: from 6¾ pounds up. Sights: open rear; bead front. Plain straight-grip stock and forearm (stock illustrated was extra cost option). Made 1892–1941.

Winchester Model 90

Winchester Model 92 Repeater

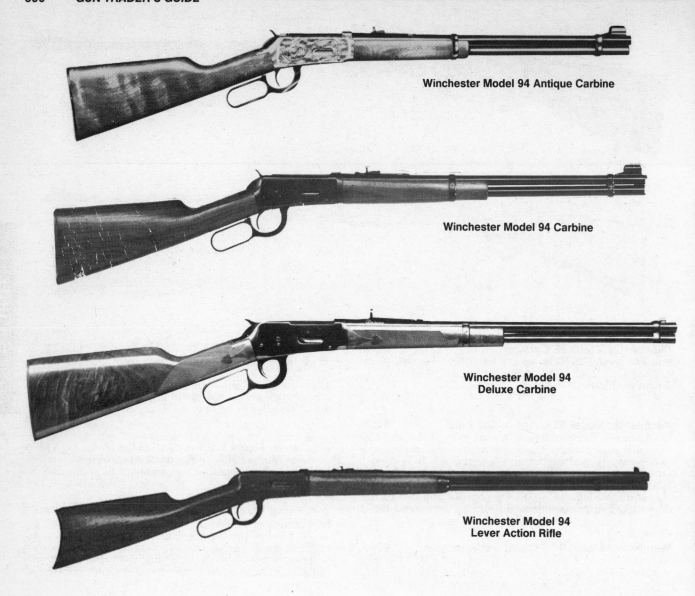

Winchester Model 94 Antique Carbine

Winchester Model 94 Carbine

Winchester Model 94 Deluxe Carbine

Winchester Model 94 Lever Action Rifle

Winchester Model 94 Antique Carbine **$295**
Same as standard Model 94 Carbine, except has receiver with decorative scrollwork and casehardened in colors, brass-plated loading gate, saddle ring; caliber 30-30 only. Made 1964–1984.

Winchester Model 94 Carbine
Same as Model 94 Rifle, except 20-inch round barrel, 6-shot full-length magazine. Weight: about 6½ pounds. Originally made in calibers 25-35, 30-30, 32 Special and 38-55. Currently mfd. in calibers 30-30 and 32 Special, solid frame only.
Pre-World War II (under No. 1,300,000) **$995**
Postwar, pre-1964 . . . . **550**

Winchester Model 94 Classic Carbine **$295**
Same as Model 67 Carbine, except without commemorative details; has scroll-engraved receiver, gold-plated loading gate. Made 1968–1970.

Winchester Model 94 Classic Rifle **$295**
Same as Model 67 Rifle, except without commemorative details; has scroll-engraved receiver, gold-plated loading gate. Made 1968–1970.

Winchester Model 94 Deluxe Carbine **$345**
Caliber: 30-30. 6-shot magazine. 20-inch barrel. 37¾ inches overall. Weight: 6½ pounds. Semi-fancy American walnut stock with rubber buttpad, long forearm and specially cut checkering. Engraved with "Deluxe" script. Made 1987 to date.

Winchester Model 94 Lever Action Rifle **$1295**
Solid frame or takedown. Calibers: 25-35, 30-30, 32-40, 32 Special, 38-55. 7-shot tubular magazine or 4-shot half-magazine. 26-inch barrel (octagon, half-octagon, round). Weight: about 7¾ pounds. Sights: open rear; bead front. Plain straight-grip stock and forearm; crescent-shaped or shotgun-style buttplate. Made 1894–1937.

RIFLES

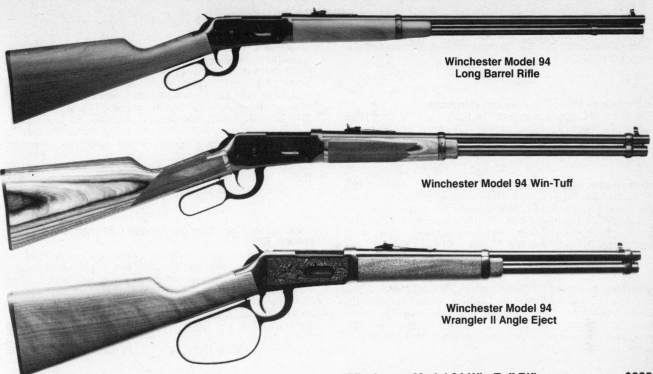

Winchester Model 94
Long Barrel Rifle

Winchester Model 94 Win-Tuff

Winchester Model 94
Wrangler II Angle Eject

Winchester Model 94 Long Barrel Rifle **$235**
Caliber: 30-30. 7-round magazine. 24-inch barrel. 41³/₄
inches overall. Weight: 7 pounds. American walnut stock.
Blade front sight. Made 1987 to date.

Winchester Model 94 Trapper **$195**
Same as Winchester Model 94 Carbine, except 16-inch
barrel and weighs 6 lbs. 2 oz. Made 1980 to date.

Winchester Model 94 Win-Tuff Rifle **$225**
Caliber: 30-30. 6-round magazine. 20-inch barrel. 37³/₄
inches overall. Weight: 6¹/₂ pounds. Brown laminated
wood stock. Made 1987 to date.

**Winchester Model 94 Wrangler II Angle Eject
Carbine** **$195**
Same as standard Model 94 Carbine, except has 16-inch
barrel, engraved receiver and chambered for 38-55 Win.
Introduced by U.S. Repeating Arms.

Winchester Model 94 XTR Big Bore

Winchester Model 94 XTR in 7-30 Waters

Winchester Model 94 XTR Big Bore
Modified Model 94 action for added strength. Caliber: 375
Win. 20-inch barrel. Rubber buttpad. Checkered stock and
forearm. Weight: 6¹/₂ pounds. Made 1978 to date.
Standard **$225**
Angle Eject **325**

**Winchester Model 94 XTR in 7-30 Waters
Lever Action Rifle** **$225**
Same general specifications as standard Angle Eject M94
except chambered for 7-30 Waters cartridge and has 24-
inch barrel. Weight: 7 pounds. Made 1985 to date by U.S.
Repeating Arms.

MODEL 94 COMMEMORATIVES

Values indicated are for commemorative Winchesters in new condition.

Winchester Model 94 Alaskan Purchase Centennial Commemorative Carbine $1695
Same as Wyoming issue, except different medallion and inscription. 1,501 made in 1967.

Winchester Model 94 Antlered Game $495
Standard Model 94 action. Gold-colored medallion inlaid in stock. Antique gold-plated receiver, lever tang and barrel bands. Medallion and receiver engraved with elk, moose, deer and caribou. 20½-inch barrel. Curved steel buttplate. In 30-30 caliber. 19,999 made in 1978.

Winchester Model 94 Bicentennial '76 Carbine . $595
Same as Standard Model 94 Carbine, except caliber 30-30 only; antique silver-finished, engraved receiver; stock and forearm of fancy walnut, checkered, Bicentennial medallion embedded in buttstock, curved buttplate. 20,000 made in 1976.

Winchester Model 94 Buffalo Bill Commemorative
Same as Centennial '66 Rifle, except receiver is black-chromed, scroll-engraved and bears name "Buffalo Bill"; hammer, trigger, loading gate, saddle ring, forearm cap, and buttplate are nickel-plated; Buffalo Bill Memorial Assn. commemorative medallion embedded in buttstock; "Buffalo Bill Commemorative" inscribed on barrel, facsimile signature "W.F. Cody, Chief of Scouts" on tang. Carbine has 20-inch barrel, 6-shot magazine, 7-pound weight. Made in 1968.

Carbine	**$375**
Rifle	395
Matched Carbine/Rifle Set (120,751 made)	895

Winchester Canadian Centennial Commemorative (Model 67)
Same as Centennial '66 Rifle, except receiver—engraved with maple leaves—and forearm cap are black-chromed, buttplate is blued, commemorative inscription in gold on barrel and top tang: "Canadian Centennial 1867–1967." Carbine has 20-inch barrel, 6-shot magazine, 7-pound weight. Made in 1967.

Carbine	**$350**
Rifle	375
Matched Carbine/Rifle Set (90,398 made)	795

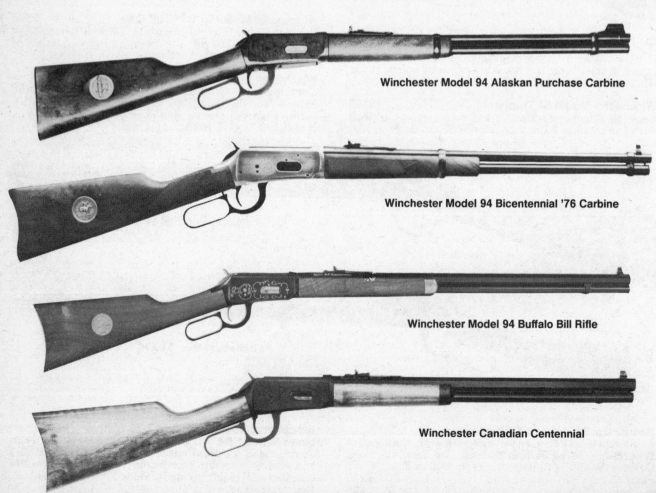

Winchester Model 94 Alaskan Purchase Carbine

Winchester Model 94 Bicentennial '76 Carbine

Winchester Model 94 Buffalo Bill Rifle

Winchester Canadian Centennial

MODEL 94 COMMEMORATIVES (cont.)

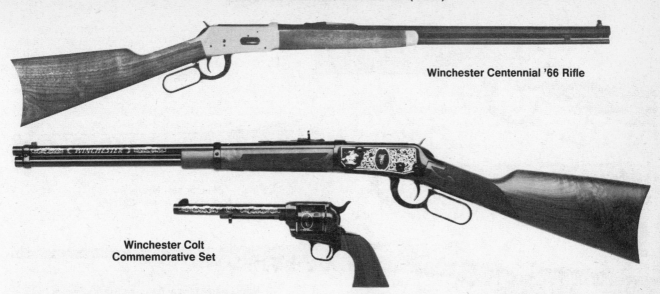

Winchester Centennial '66 Rifle

Winchester Colt
Commemorative Set

Winchester Centennial '66 Commemorative

Commemorates Winchester's 100th anniversary. Standard Model 94 action. Caliber: 30-30. Full-length magazine holds 8 rounds. 26-inch octagon barrel. Weight: 8 pounds. Gold-plated receiver and forearm cap. Sights: open rear; post front. Saddle ring. Walnut buttstock and forearm with high-gloss finish, solid brass buttplate. Commemorative inscription on barrel and top tang of receiver. Made in 1966.

Carbine	**$395**
Rifle	425
Matched Carbine/Rifle Set (100,478 made)	895

Winchester Model 94 Cheyenne Comm. **$750**

Available in Canada only. Same as Standard Model 94 Carbine, except chambered for 44-40. 11,225 made in 1977.

Winchester Model 94 Colt Commemorative
Carbine Set **$2595**

Standard Model 94 action. Caliber: 44-40 Win. 20-inch barrel. Weight: 6¼ pounds. Features a horse-and-rider trademark and distinctive WC monogram in gold etching on left side of receiver. Sold in set with Colt Single Action Revolver chambered for same caliber.

Winchester Model 94 Cowboy Carbine

Winchester Model 94 Golden Spike Carbine

Winchester Model 94 Cowboy Commemorative
Carbine **$475**

Same as Standard Model 94 Carbine, except caliber 30-30 only; nickel-plated receiver, tangs, lever, barrel bands; engraved receiver, "Cowboy Commemorative" on barrel, commemorative medallion embedded in buttstock; curved buttplate. 20,915 made in 1970.

Winchester Model 94 Golden Spike
Commemorative Carbine **$375**

Same as Standard Model 94 Carbine, except caliber 30-30 only; gold-plated receiver, tangs and barrel bands;

Winchester Model 94 Golden Spike (cont.)

engraved receiver, commemorative medallion embedded in stock. 64,758 made in 1969.

Winchester Model 94 Illinois Sesquicentennial
Commemorative Carbine **$395**

Same as Standard Model 94 Carbine, except caliber 30-30 only; gold-plated buttplate, trigger, loading gate, and saddle ring; receiver engraved with profile of Lincoln, commemorative inscriptions on receiver, barrel; souvenir medallion embedded in stock. 31,124 made in 1968.

MODEL 94 COMMEMORATIVES (cont.)

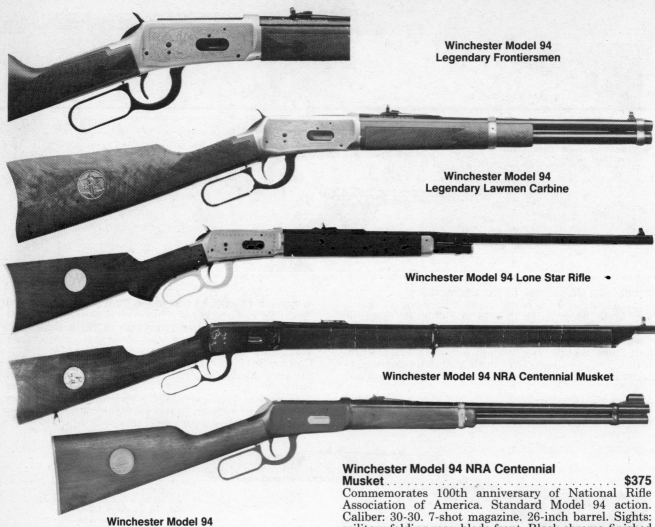

Winchester Model 94
Legendary Frontiersmen

Winchester Model 94
Legendary Lawmen Carbine

Winchester Model 94 Lone Star Rifle

Winchester Model 94 NRA Centennial Musket

Winchester Model 94
Nebraska Centennial Carbine

Winchester Model 94 Legendary Frontiersmen Commemorative $525
Standard Model 94 action. Caliber: 38-55. 24-inch round barrel. Nickel-silver medallion inlaid in stock. Antique silver-plated receiver engraved with scenes of the old frontier. Checkered walnut stock and forearm. 19,999 made in 1979.

Winchester Model 94 Legendary Lawmen Commemorative $525
Same as Standard Model 94 Carbine, except 30-30 only; antique silver-plated receiver engraved with action law-enforcement scenes. 16-inch Trapper barrel, antique silver-plated barrel bands. 19,999 made in 1978.

Winchester Model 94 Lone Star Commemorative
Same as Theodore Roosevelt Rifle, except yellow-gold plating; "Lone Star" engraving on receiver and barrel, commemorative medallion embedded in buttstock. Made in 1970.
Rifle $450
Matched Carbine/Rifle Set (30,669 made) 995

Winchester Model 94 NRA Centennial Musket $375
Commemorates 100th anniversary of National Rifle Association of America. Standard Model 94 action. Caliber: 30-30. 7-shot magazine. 26-inch barrel. Sights: military folding rear; blade front. Black chrome-finished receiver engraved "NRA 1871–1971" plus scrollwork. Barrel inscribed "NRA Centennial Musket." Musket-style buttstock and full-length forearm; commemorative medallion embedded in buttstock. Weight: 7 1/8 pounds. Made in 1971.

Winchester Model 94 NRA Centennial Rifle $375
Same as Model 94 Rifle, except has commemorative details as in NRA Centennial Musket (barrel inscribed "NRA Centennial Rifle"); caliber 30-30, 24-inch barrel, QD sling swivels. Made in 1971.

Winchester Model 94 NRA Centennial Matched Set $850
Rifle and musket were offered in sets with consecutive serial numbers. *Note:* Production figures not available. These rifles offered in Winchester's 1972 catalog.

Winchester Model 94 Nebraska Centennial Commemorative Carbine $1325
Same as Standard Model 94 Carbine, except caliber 30-30 only; gold-plated hammer, loading gate, barrel band, and buttplate; souvenir medallion embedded in stock, commemorative inscription on barrel. 2,500 made in 1966.

MODEL 94 COMMEMORATIVES (cont.)

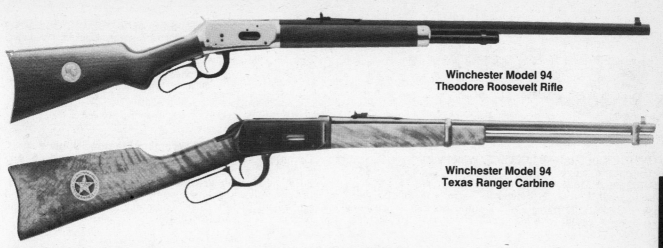

**Winchester Model 94
Theodore Roosevelt Rifle**

**Winchester Model 94
Texas Ranger Carbine**

Winchester Model 94 Theodore Roosevelt Commemorative Rifle/Carbine

Standard Model 94 action. Caliber: 30-30. Rifle has 6-shot half-magazine, 26-inch octagon barrel, 7½-pound weight. Carbine has 6-shot full magazine, 20-inch barrel, 7-pound weight. White gold-plated receiver, upper tang, and forend cap; receiver engraved with American Eagle, "26th President 1901–1909," and Roosevelt's signature. Commemorative medallion embedded in buttstock. Saddle ring. Half pistol grip, contoured lever. Made in 1969.

Carbine **$395**
Rifle **425**
Matched Set (49,505 made) **850**

Winchester Model 94 Texas Ranger Association Carbine **$2400**

Same as Texas Ranger Commemorative Model 94, except special edition of 150 carbines, numbered 1 through 150, with hand-checkered full-fancy walnut stock and forearm. Sold only through Texas Ranger Association. Made in 1973.

Winchester Model 94 Texas Ranger Commemorative Carbine **$725**

Same as Standard Model 94 Carbine, except caliber 30-30 only, stock and forearm of semi-fancy walnut, replica of Texas Ranger star embedded in buttstock, curved buttplate. 5,000 made in 1973.

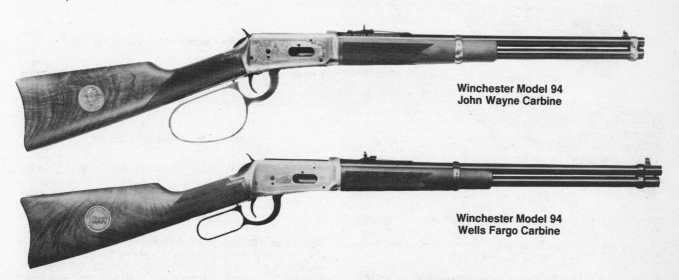

**Winchester Model 94
John Wayne Carbine**

**Winchester Model 94
Wells Fargo Carbine**

Winchester Model 94 John Wayne Comm. **$925**

Standard Model 94 action. Caliber: 32-40. 18½-inch barrel. Receiver is pewter-plated with engraving of Indian attack and cattle drive scenes. Oversized bow on lever. Nickel-silver medallion in buttstock bears a bas-relief portrait of Wayne. Selected American walnut stock with deep-cut checkering. Introduced by U.S. Repeating Arms.

Winchester Model 94 Wells Fargo & Co. Commemorative Carbine **$525**

Same as Standard Model 94 Carbine, except 30-30 only; antique silver-finished, engraved receiver; stock and forearm of fancy walnut, checkered, curved buttplate. Nickel-silver stagecoach medallion (inscribed "Wells Fargo & Co.—1852–1977—125 Years") embedded in buttstock. 20,000 made in 1977.

RIFLES

MODEL 94 COMMEMORATIVES (cont.)

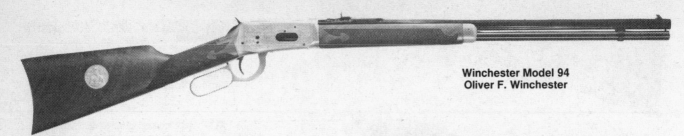

**Winchester Model 94
Oliver F. Winchester**

**Winchester Model 94 Oliver F. Winchester
Commemorative** **$595**
Standard Model 94 action. Caliber: 38-55. 24-inch
octagonal barrel. Receiver is satin gold-plated with
distinctive engravings. Stock and forearm semi-fancy
American walnut with high grade checkering. 19,999 made
in 1980.

**Winchester Model 94 Wyoming Diamond Jubilee
Commemorative Carbine** **$1495**
Same as Standard Model 94 Carbine, except caliber 30-
30 only, receiver engraved and casehardened in colors,
brass saddle ring and loading gate, souvenir medallion
embedded in buttstock, commemorative inscription on
barrel. 1,500 made in 1964.

Winchester Model 95 Carbine

Winchester Model 95 Rifle

Winchester Model 100 Autoloading Rifle

Winchester Model 100 Carbine

Winchester Model 95 Lever Action Carbine . . . **$1895**
Same as Model 95 Standard Rifle, except has 22-inch barrel, carbine-style stock, weighs about 8 pounds, calibers
30-40, 30-03, 30-06 and 303, solid frame only.

Winchester Model 95 Lever Action Repeater . . **$1400**
Calibers: 30-40 Krag, 30-03, 30-06, 303 British, 35 Win.,
405 Win.; original model supplied in the now obsolete
38-72 and 40-72 calibers. 4-shot box magazine, except 30-
40 and 303, which have 5-shot magazine. Barrel lengths:
24-, 26-, 28-inches (round, half-octagon, octagon). Weight:
about 8½ pounds. Sights: open rear; bead or blade front.
Plain straight-grip stock and forearm (standard). Both
solid frame and takedowns avail. Made 1895–1931.

Winchester Model 100 Autoloading Rifle **$425**
Gas-operated semiautomatic. Calibers: 243, 284, 308 Win.
4-shot clip magazine (3-shot in 284). 22-inch barrel.
Weight: 7¼ pounds. Sights: open rear; hooded ramp front.
One-piece stock w/pistol grip, basket-weave checkering,
grip cap, sling swivels. Made 1961–1973.

Winchester Model 100 Carbine **$450**
Same as Model 100 Rifle, except has 19-inch barrel, plain
carbine-style stock and forearm with barrel band. Weight:
7 pounds. Made 1967–1973.

Winchester Model 121 Deluxe

Winchester Model 131

Winchester Model 141

Winchester Model 135 . . . . **$125**
Same as Model 131, except chambered for 22 WMR cartridge. Magazine holds 5 rounds. Made in 1967.

Winchester Model 141 Bolt Action Tubular Repeater **$140**
Same as Model 131, except has tubular magazine in buttstock; holds 19 Short, 15 Long, 13 LR. Made 1967–1973.

Winchester Model 145 . . . . **$140**
Same as Model 141, except chambered for 22 WMR; magazine holds 9 rounds. Made in 1967.

Winchester Model 150 Lever Action Carbine . . . **$110**
Same as Model 250, except has straight loop lever, plain carbine-style straight-grip stock and forearm with barrel band. Made 1967–1973.

Winchester Model 190 Carbine **$120**
Same as Model 190 rifle, except has carbine-style forearm with barrel band. Made 1967–1973.

Winchester Model 121 Deluxe **$115**
Same as Model 121 Standard, except has ramp front sight, stock with fluted comb and sling swivels. Made 1967–1973.

Winchester Model 121 Standard Bolt Action Single Shot **$120**
Caliber: 22 Short, Long, LR. 20¾-inch barrel. Weight: 5 pounds. Sights: open rear; bead front. Monte Carlo-style stock. Made 1967–1973.

Winchester Model 121 Youth **$125**
Same as Model 121 Standard, except has 1¼-inch shorter stock. Made 1967–1973.

Winchester Model 131 Bolt Action Repeater . . . **$135**
Caliber: 22 Short, Long or LR. 7-shot clip magazine. 20¾-inch barrel. Weight: 5 pounds. Sights: open rear; ramp front. Plain Monte Carlo stock. Made 1967–1973.

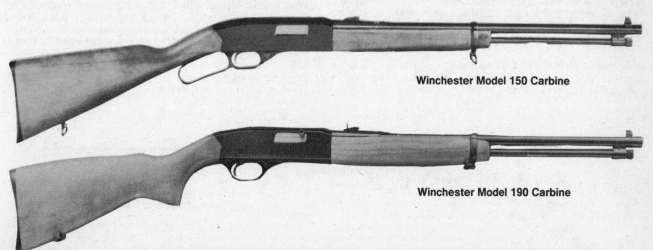

Winchester Model 150 Carbine

Winchester Model 190 Carbine

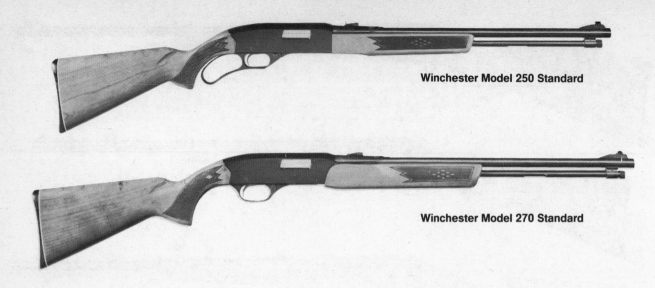

Winchester Model 250 Standard

Winchester Model 270 Standard

Winchester Model 190 Semiautomatic Rifle **$135**
Same as current Model 290, except has plain stock and
forearm. Made 1966–1978.

Winchester Model 250 Deluxe Rifle **$150**
Same as Model 250 Standard Rifle, except has fancy walnut Monte Carlo stock and forearm, sling swivels. Made
1965–1971.

**Winchester Model 250 Standard Lever Action
Rifle** **$150**
Hammerless. Caliber: 22 Short, Long or LR. Tubular
magazine holds 21 Short, 17 Long, 15 LR. 20½-inch barrel.
Sights: open rear; ramp front. Weight: about 5 pounds.
Plain stock and forearm on early production; later model
has checkering. Made 1963–1973.

Winchester Model 255 Deluxe Rifle **$170**
Same as Model 250 Deluxe Rifle, except chambered for
22 WMR cartridge. Magazine holds 11 rounds. Made
1965–1973.

Winchester Model 255 Standard Rifle **$150**
Same as Model 250 Standard Rifle, except chambered for
22 WMR cartridge. Magazine holds 11 rounds. Made
1964–1970.

Winchester Model 270 Deluxe Rifle **$195**
Same as Model 270 Standard Rifle, except has fancy walnut Monte Carlo stock and forearm. Maden 1965–1973.

**Winchester Model 270 Standard Slide Action
Rifle** **$125**
Hammerless. Caliber: 22 Short, Long or LR. Tubular
magazine holds 21 Short, 17 Long, 15 LR. 20½-inch barrel.
Sights: open rear; ramp front. Weight: about 5 pounds.
Early production had plain walnut stock and forearm
(slide handle); latter also furnished in plastic (Cycolac);
last model has checkering. Made 1963–1973.

Winchester Model 275 Deluxe Rifle **$165**
Same as Model 270 Deluxe Rifle, except chambered for
22 WMR cartridge. Magazine holds 11 rounds. Made
1965–1970.

Winchester Model 275 Standard Rifle **$125**
Same as Model 270 Standard Rifle, except chambered for
22 WMR cartridge. Magazine holds 11 rounds. Made
1964–1970.

Winchester Model 290 Deluxe Rifle **$175**
Same as Model 290 Standard Rifle, except has fancy walnut Monte Carlo stock and forearm. Made 1965–1973.

Winchester Model 290 Standard Semiautomatic Rifle
Caliber: 22 Long or LR. Tubular magazine holds 17 Long,
15 LR. 20½-inch barrel. Sights: open rear; ramp front.
Weight: about 5 pounds. Plain stock and forearm on early
production; current model has checkering. Made 1963–
1977.
W/plain stock/forearm **$185**
W/checkered stock/forearm **210**

Winchester Model 290 Standard

Winchester Model 310

Winchester Model 320

Winchester Model 490 Rifle

Winchester Model 310 Bolt Action Single Shot . . **$195**
Caliber: 22 Short, Long, LR. 22-inch barrel. Weight: 5⅝
pounds. Sights: open rear; ramp front. Monte Carlo stock
w/checkered pistol grip and forearm, sling swivels. Made
1972–75.

Winchester Model 320 Bolt Action Repeater . . . **$295**
Same as Model 310, except has 5-shot clip magazine. Made
1972–74.

Winchester Model 490 Semiautomatic Rifle **$240**
Caliber: 22 LR. 5-shot clip magazine. 22-inch barrel.
Weight: 6 pounds. Sights: folding leaf rear; hooded ramp
front. One-piece walnut stock w/checkered pistol grip and
forearm. Made 1975–77.

**Winchester Model 670 Bolt Action Sporting
Rifle** **$250**
Calibers: 225 Win., 243 Win., 270 Win., 30-06, 308 Win.
4-shot magazine. 22-inch barrel. Weight: 7 pounds. Sights:
open rear; ramp front. Monte Carlo stock w/checkered
pistol grip and forearm. Made 1967–1973.

Winchester Model 670 Carbine **$275**
Same as Model 670 Rifle, except has 19-inch barrel.
Weight: 6¾ pounds. Calibers: 243 Win., 270 Win., 30-06.
Made 1967–1970.

Winchester Model 670 Magnum **$295**
Same as Model 670 Rifle, except has 24-inch barrel, reinforced stock with recoil pad. Weight: 7¼ pounds. Calibers:
264 Win. Mag., 7mm Rem. Mag., 300 Win. Mag. Made
1967–1970.

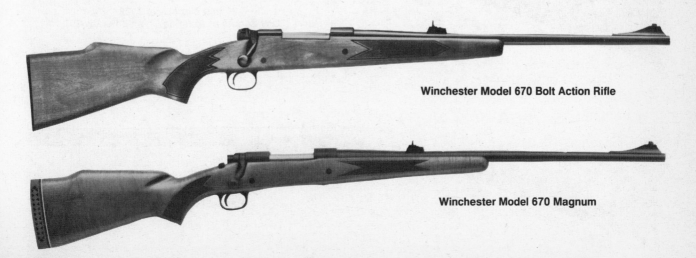

Winchester Model 670 Bolt Action Rifle

Winchester Model 670 Magnum

Winchester Model 770

Winchester Model 1900

Winchester Model 770 Bolt Action Sporting Rifle $295
Model 70-type action. Calibers: 22-250, 222 Rem., 243, 270 Win., 30-06. 4-shot box magazine. 22-inch barrel. Sights: open rear; hooded ramp front. Weight: 7 1/8 pounds. Monte Carlo stock, checkered, swivels. Made 1969–1971.

Winchester Model 770 Magnum $315
Same as Standard Model 770, except 24-inch barrel, weight 7 1/4 pounds, recoil pad. Calibers: 7mm Rem. Mag., 264 and 300 Win. Mag. Made 1969–1971.

Winchester Model 1900 Bolt Action Single Shot Rifle $360
Takedown. Caliber: 22 Short and Long. 18-inch barrel. Weight: 2 3/4 pounds. Sights: open rear; blade front. One-piece, straight-grip stock. Made 1899–1902.

Winchester Model 9422 Boy Scouts of America Commemorative $500
Standard Model 9422 action. Caliber: 22RF. 20 1/2-inch round barrel. Receiver roll-engraved and plated in antique pewter, illustrating the Boy Scout oath and law. Frame carries inscription, "1910–1985." "Boy Scouts of America" inscribed on right side of barrel. Checkered stock and forearm of American walnut with satin finish. A maximum of 15,000 were produced by U.S. Repeating Arms beginning with serial number BSA1.

Winchester Model 9422 Eagle Scout Commemorative $2195
Standard Model 9422 action. Caliber: 22 RF. Same general specifications as Boy Scout model except different engraving, jeweled bolt, antique gold-plated forearm cap and brass magazine tube. Only 1,000 were made by U.S. Repeating Arms bearing serial number Eagle 1 through Eagle 1,000.

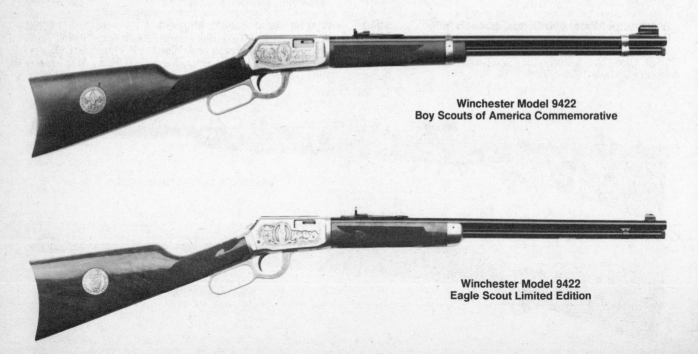

Winchester Model 9422
Boy Scouts of America Commemorative

Winchester Model 9422
Eagle Scout Limited Edition

Winchester Model 9422

Winchester Model 9422 XTR Classic

Winchester Model 9422 Lever Action Carbine .. **$245**
Styled after Model 94. Caliber: 22 Short, Long, LR. Tubular magazine holds 21 Short, 17 Long, 15 LR. 20½-inch barrel. Weight: 6¼ pounds. Sights: open rear; hooded ramp front. Carbine-style stock and forearm, barrel band. Made 1972 to date.

Winchester Model 9422M **$295**
Same as Model 9422, except chambered for 22 WMR; magazine holds 11 rounds. Stock options: Walnut, WinCam (laminated green), WinTuff (laminated brown). Made 1972 to date.

Winchester Model 9422 Win-Cam **$250**
Caliber: 22 RF. 11-shot magazine. 20½-inch barrel. 37⅛ inches overall. Weight: 6¼ pounds. Laminated non-glare green-shaded stock and forend. Made 1987 to date.

Winchester Model 9422 XTR Classic **$265**
Same general specifications as standard Model 9422, except has pistol-grip stock and weighs 6½ pounds.

Winchester Double Xpress Rifle **$2150**
Over/under double rifle. Caliber: 30-06. 23½-inch barrel. Weight: 8½ pounds. Made for Olin Corp. by Olin-Kodensha in Japan. Introduced 1982.

Winchester Lee Straight-Pull Bolt Action Repeating Rifle—Musket Model **$895**
Commercial version of U.S. Navy Model 1895 Rifle, caliber 6mm (1895–1897). Caliber: 236 U.S.N. 5-shot box magazine, clip-loaded. 28-inch barrel. Weight: 8½ pounds. Sights: folding leaf rear; post front. Military-type full stock w/semi-pistol grip. Made 1897–1902.

Winchester Lee Straight-Pull Sporting Rifle **$950**
Same as Musket Model except has 24-inch barrel, sporter-style stock, open sporting rear sight, bead front sight. Weight: about 7½ pounds. Made 1897–1902.

Winchester Ranger Angle Eject Lever Action Carbine **$180**
Caliber: 30-30. 5-shot tubular magazine. Barrel: 20-inch round. Weight: 6½ pounds. American hardwood stock. Economy version of Model 94. Made 1985 to date by U.S. Repeating Arms.

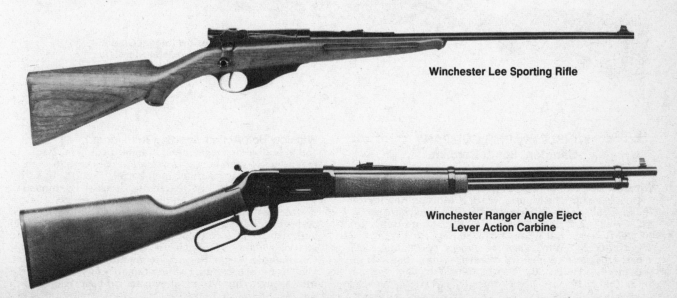

Winchester Lee Sporting Rifle

Winchester Ranger Angle Eject
Lever Action Carbine

Winchester Ranger Bolt Action Carbine

Winchester Ranger Youth Bolt Action Carbine

Winchester Ranger Bolt Action Carbine **$260**
Calibers: 223 Rem., 243 Win., 270, 30-06, 7mm Rem. (discontinued 1985), Mag. 3- and 4-shot magazine. Barrel: 24-inch in 7mm; 22-inch in 270 and 30-06. Open sights. American hardwood stock. Made 1985 to date by U.S. Repeating Arms.

Winchester Ranger Youth Bolt Action Carbine **$265**
Calibers: 223 (discontinued 1989), 243, and 308 Win. 4- and 5-shot magazine. Barrel: 20-inch. Weight: 5¾ pounds. American hardwood stock. Open rear sight. Made 1985 to date by U.S. Repeating Arms.

Winslow Crown Grade Plainsmaster Stock

Winslow Regent Grade Bushmaster Stock

WINSLOW ARMS COMPANY
Camden, South Carolina

Winslow Bolt Action Sporting Rifle
Action: FN Supreme Mauser, Mark X Mauser, Remington 700 and 788, Sako, Winchester 70. *Standard calibers:* 17-222, 17-223, 222 Rem., 22-250, 243 Win., 6mm Rem., 25-06, 257 Roberts, 270 Win., 7×57, 280 Rem., 284 Win., 308 Win., 30-06, 358 Win. *Magnum calibers:* 17-222 Mag., 257 Weatherby, 264 Win., 270 Weath., 7mm Rem., 7mm Weath., 300 H&H, 300 Weath., 300 Win., 308 Norma, 8mm Rem., 338 Win., 358 Norma, 375 H&H, 375 Weath.,

Winslow Bolt Action Sporting Rifle (cont.)
458 Win. 3-shot magazine in standard calibers, 2-shot in magnum. 24-inch barrel in standard calibers, 26-inch in magnum. Weight: with 24-inch barrel, 7 to 7½ lbs.; with 26-inch barrel, 8 to 9 lbs. No sights. Stocks: "Bushmaster" with slender pistol grip and beavertail forearm, "Plainsmaster" with full curl pistol grip and flat forearm; both styles have Monte Carlo cheekpiece; rosewood forend tip and pistol-grip cap, recoil pad, QD swivels; woods used include walnut, maple, myrtle. There are eight grades—Commander, Regal, Regent, Regimental, Royal, Imperial, Emperor—in ascending order of quality of wood, carving, inlays, engraving. Values shown are for basic rifle in each

Winslow Bolt Action Sporting Rifle (cont.)
grade; extras such as special fancy wood, more elaborate carving, inlays and engraving can increase these figures considerably. Made 1962–1989.

Commander Grade . . . . $ 495
Regal Grade 585
Regent Grade 695
Regimental Grade 895
Crown Grade 1200
Royal Grade 1400
Imperial Grade 3000
Emperor Grade 5500

ZEPHYR DOUBLE RIFLES
Manufactured by Victor Sarasqueta Company, Eibar, Spain

Zephyr Double Rifle $14,000
Boxlock. Calibers: Available in practically every caliber from .22 Hornet to .505 Gibbs. Barrels: 22 to 28 inches standard, but any lengths were available on special order. Weight: 7 pounds for the smaller caliber up to 12 or more pounds for the larger calibers. Checkered Spanish walnut stock and beavertail forearm. Receiver engraved with scroll patterns. Imported by Stoeger 1938–1951.

RIFLES

SHOTGUNS

Section III

ALDENS SHOTGUN
Chicago, Illinois

Aldens Model 670 Chieftain Slide Action **$155**
Hammerless. Gauges: 12, 20 and others. 3-shot tubular magazine. Barrel: 26- to 30-inch; various chokes. Weight: 6¼ to 7½ pounds depending on barrel length and gauge. Walnut-finished hardwood stock.

AMERICAN ARMS
N. Kansas City, Missouri

See also Franchi Shotguns.

American Arms Brittany Hammerless Double ... **$575**
Boxlock with engraved case-colored receiver. Single selective trigger. Selective automatic ejectors. Gauges: 12, 20. 3-inch chambers. Barrels: 25- or 27-inch with screw-in choke tubes (IC/M/F). Weight: 6½ pounds (20 ga.). Checkered English-style walnut stock with semibeavertail forearm or pistol-grip stock with high-gloss finish. Imported from 1989 to date.

American Arms Camper Special **$85**
Similar to the Single Barrel, except a takedown model with 21-inch barrel, Mod. choke and pistol-grip stock. Made in 1989 only.

American Arms Combo **$175**
Similar to the Single Barrel model, except available with interchangeable rifle and shotgun barrels. 22 LR/20-gauge shotgun or 22 Hornet/12-gauge shotgun. Rifle barrel has adj. rear sights; blade-type front sight. Made in 1989.

American Arms Derby Hammerless Double **$775**
Sidelock with engraved sideplates. Single non-selective trigger. Selective automatic ejectors. Gauges: 12, 20. 3-inch chambers. Barrels: 26-inch (IC/M) or 28-inch (M/F). Weight: 6 pounds (20 ga.). Checkered English-style walnut stock and splinter forearm with hand-rubbed oil finish. Engraved frame/sideplates w/antique silver finish.

American Arms Gentry Hammerless Double
Color casehardened boxlock receiver with scroll engraving. Double triggers. Extractors. Gauges: 12, 16, 20, 28, .410. 3-inch chambers (16 and 28 have 2¾-inch). Barrels: 26-inch (IC/M) or 28-inch (M/F, 12, 16 and 20). Weight: 6¾ pounds (12 ga.). Checkered walnut stock with pistol grip and beavertail forearm with semi-gloss finish. Imported from 1987 to date.
12, 16 or 20 Gauge **$450**
28 or .410 Gauge 495

American Arms Grulla #2 Hammerless Double
True sidelock with engraved detachable sideplates. Double triggers. Extractors and cocking indicators. Gauges: 12 and 20 w/2¾-inch chambers; 28 and .410 with 3-inch. Barrels: 26-inch (IC/M) or 28-inch (M/F, 12 and 28 ga. only). Weight: 6¼ pounds (12 gauge). English-style walnut stock and splinter forearm w/hand-rubbed oil finish and checkered grip, forearm and butt. Imported 1989 to date.
Standard Model **$2200**
Two-barrel Set 2995

American Arms Silver I Over/Under
Boxlock. Single selective trigger. Extractors. Gauges: 12, 20 and .410 with 3-inch chambers; 28 with 2¾. Barrels: 26-inch (IC/M), 28-inch (M/F, 12 and 20 ga. only). Weight: 6¾ pounds (12 ga.). Checkered walnut stock and forearm. Antique-silver receiver with scroll engraving.

American Arms Derby
Side-by-Side

American Arms Gentry

American Arms Grulla #2

American Arms Silver I
Over/Under

American Arms Silver Skeet/Trap

American Arms Silver I Over/Under (cont.)
Imported from 1987 to date.
12 or 20 Gauge **$395**
28 or .410 Gauge 450

American Arms Silver II Over/Under
Similar to Model Silver I, except with selective automatic ejectors and 26-inch barrels with screw-in tubes (12 and 20 ga.). Fixed chokes (28 and .410).
12 or 20 Gauge **$495**
28 or .410 550
Two-barrel Set 825

American Arms Silver Lite Over/Under
Similar to Model Silver II, except with blued, engraved alloy receiver. Available in 12 and 20 gauge only. Imported from 1990 to date.
Standard Model **$595**
Two-barrel Set 850

American Arms Silver Skeet/Trap **$695**
Similar to the Silver II Model, except has 28-inch (Skeet) or 30-inch (Trap) ported barrels with target-style rib and mid-bead sight. Imported from 1992 to date.

American Arms Silver Sporting Over/Under **$650**
Boxlock. Single selective trigger. Selective automatic ejectors. Gauges: 12; 2³/₄-inch chambers. Barrels: 28-inch with Franchoke tubes: SK, IC, M and F. Weight: 7¹/₂ pounds. Checkered walnut stock and forearm. Special broadway rib and vented side ribs. Engraved receiver with chrome-nickel finish. Imported from 1990 to date.

American Arms Single Barrel Shotgun **$85**
Break-open action. Gauges: 12, 20, .410; 3-inch chamber. Weight: about 6¹/₂ pounds. Bead front sight. Walnut-finished hardwood stock with checkered grip and forend. Made from 1988 to date.

American Arms Slugger Single Shot Shotgun **$95**
Similar to the Single Barrel model, except in 12 and 20 gauges only with 24-inch slug barrel. Rifle-type sights and recoil pad. Made from 1989 to date.

American Arms TS/OU 12 Shotgun **$540**
Turkey Special. Boxlock. Single selective trigger. Selective automatic ejectors. Gauge: 12; 3¹/₂-inch chambers. Barrels: 24-inch over/under with screw-in choke tubes (IC, M, F). Weight: 6 lbs. 15 oz. Checkered European walnut stock and beavertail forearm. Matte blue metal finish.

American Arms TS/SS 10 Hammerless Double . **$495**
Turkey Special. Same general specifications as Model WS/SS 10, except with 26-inch side-by-side barrels and screw-in choke tubes (F/F). Weight: 10 lbs. 13 oz.

American Arms TS/SS 12 Hammerless Double . **$475**
Same general specifications as Model WS/SS 10, except in 12 gauge with 26-inch side-by-side barrels and 3 screw-in choke tubes (IC/M/F). Weight: 7 lbs. 6 oz.

American Arms WS/OU 12 Shotgun **$450**
Waterfowl Special. Boxlock. Single selective trigger. Selective automatic ejectors. Gauge: 12; 3¹/₂-inch chambers. Barrels: 28-inch over/under with screw-in tubes (IC/M/F). Weight: 7 pounds. Checkered European walnut stock and beavertail forearm. Matte blue metal finish.

American Arms WS/SS 10 Hammerless Double .. **$495**
Waterfowl Special. Boxlock. Double triggers. Extractors. Gauge: 10; 3¹/₂-inch chambers. Barrels: 32-inch side/side choked F/F. Weight: about 11 pounds. Checkered walnut stock and beavertail forearm with satin finish. Parkerized metal finish. Imported from 1987 to date.

American Arms WT/OU 10 Shotgun **$725**
Same general specifications as Model WS/OU 12, except chambered for 10-gauge 3¹/₂-inch shells. Extractors. Satin wood finish and matte blue metal.

SHOTGUNS

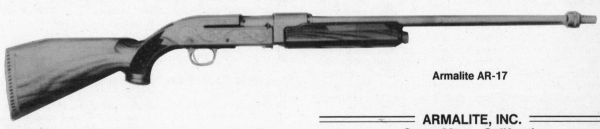

Armalite AR-17

ARMALITE, INC.
Costa Mesa, California

Armalite AR-17 Golden Gun **$525**
Recoil-operated semiautomatic. High-test aluminum barrel and receiver housing. 12 gauge only. 2-shot. 24-inch barrel with interchangeable choke tubes: IC/M/F. Weight: 5.6 pounds. Polycarbonate stock and forearm, recoil pad. Gold anodized finish standard; also made with black finish. Made 1964–65. Less than 2,000 produced.

NOTE: The following abbreviations are used throughout this section when referring to chokes: Cyl.=Cylinder; F=Full; IC=Improved Cylinder; IM=Improved Modified; M=Modified; SK=Skeet.

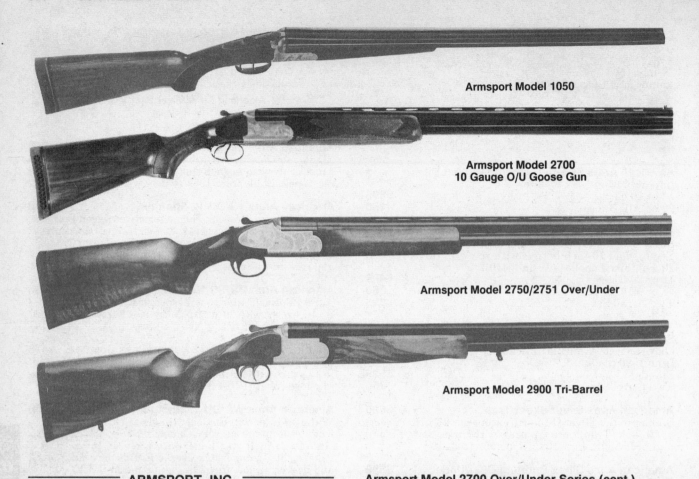

Armsport Model 1050

Armsport Model 2700
10 Gauge O/U Goose Gun

Armsport Model 2750/2751 Over/Under

Armsport Model 2900 Tri-Barrel

ARMSPORT, INC.
Miami, Florida

Armsport Models 1050, 1053, 1054 Hammerless Doubles
Side-by-side with engraved receiver, double triggers and extractors. Gauges: 12, 20, .410; 3-inch chambers. **Model 1050:** 12 ga., 28-inch bbl., M/F choke. **Model 1053:** 20 ga., 26-inch bbl., I/M choke. **Model 1054:** .410 ga., 26-inch bbl., I/M. Weight: 6 pounds (12 ga.). European walnut buttstock and forend. Made in Italy. Importation discontinued 1993.
Model 1050 . . . . **$595**
Model 1053 . . . . **625**
Model 1054 . . . . **675**

Armsport Model 2700 Goose Gun
Similar to the 2700 Standard Model, except 10 gauge with 3½-inch chambers. Double triggers with 28-inch barrel choked IC/M or 32-inch barrel, F/F. 12mm wide vent rib. Weight: 9½ pounds. Canada geese engraved on receiver. Antiqued silver-finished action. Checkered European walnut stock w/rubber recoil pad. Made in Italy. Importation discontinued 1993.
With Fixed Chokes **$795**
With Choke Tubes **850**

Armsport Model 2700 Over/Under Series
Hammerless, takedown shotgun with engraved receiver. Selective single or double triggers. Gauges: 10, 12, 20, 28 and .410. Barrel: 26- or 28-inch with fixed chokes or choke tubes. Weight: 8 pounds. Checkered European walnut buttstock and forend. Made in Italy. Importation discontinued 1993.

Armsport Model 2700 Over/Under Series (cont.)
Model 2705 (.410, DT, fixed chokes) **$515**
Model 2730, 2731 (Boss-style action, SST,
   Choke tubes) **625**
Model 2733, 2735 (Boss-style action, extractors) . . **675**
Model 2741 (Boss-style action, ejectors) **595**
Model 2742 Sporting Clays (12 ga./choke tubes) . . **615**
Model 2744 Sporting Clays (20 ga./choke tubes) . . **615**
Model 2750 Sporting Clays (12 ga./sideplates) . . . **695**
Model 2751 Sporting Clays (20 ga./sideplates) . . . **695**

Armsport Model 2755 Slide Action Shotgun
Pump action, hammerless shotgun. 12 gauge w/3-inch chamber. Tubular magazine. Barrels: 28- or 30-inch with fixed choke or choke tubes. Weight: 7 pounds; vent rib. European walnut stock. Made in Italy 1986–87.
Standard Model, Fixed Choke **$295**
Standard Model, Choke Tubes **325**
Police Model, 20-inch Barrel **250**

Armsport Model 2900 Tri-Barrel Shotgun **$2850**
Boxlock. Double triggers with top-tang barrel selector. Extractors. Gauge: 12; 3-inch chambers. Barrels: 28-inch (IC, M and F). Weight: 7¾ pounds. Checkered European walnut stock and forearm. Engraved silver receiver. Imported from Italy 1986–1993.

ASTRA SHOTGUNS
Guernica, Spain
Manufactured by Unceta y Compania

Astra Model 650 Over/Under Shotgun
Hammerless, takedown with double triggers. 12 gauge w/
2³/₄-inch chambers. Barrels: 28-inch (M/F or SK/SK);
30-inch (M/F). Weight: 6³/₄ pounds. Checkered European
walnut buttstock and forend.
With Extractors **$450**
With Ejectors **545**

Astra Model 750 Over/Under Shotgun
Similar to the Model 650, except with selective single trig-
ger and ejectors. Made in Field, Skeet and Trap config-
urations since 1980.
Field Model w/Extractors **$500**
Field Model w/Ejectors **595**
Trap or Skeet **710**

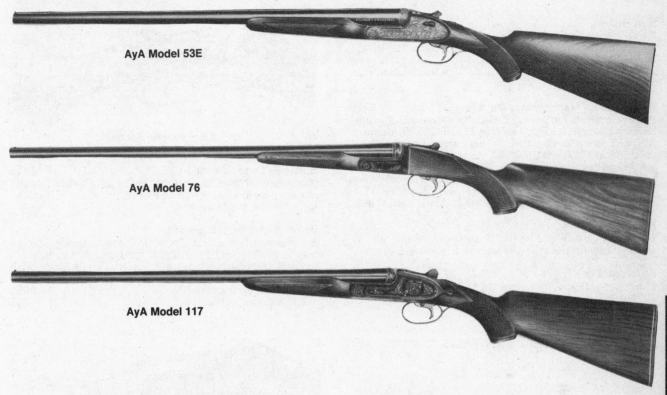

AyA Model 53E

AyA Model 76

AyA Model 117

=== **AYA (AGUIRRE Y ARANZABAL)** ===
Eibar, Spain

AyA Model 1 Hammerless Double
A Holland & Holland sidelock similar to the Model 2,
except in 12 and 20 gauge only, with special engraving
and exhibition-grade wood. Weight: 5–8 pounds, depend-
ing on gauge. Imported since 1992 by Armes de Chasse.
Model 1 w/Single Trigger (Early Importation) .. **$2795**
Model 1 w/Double Triggers **2395**
Two Barrel Set, **add** **2150**

AyA Model 2 Hammerless Double
Sidelock action with selective single or double triggers,
automatic ejectors and safety. Gauges: 12, 20, 28, (2³/₄-
inch chambers); .410 (3-inch chambers). Barrels: 26- or
28-inch with various fixed choke combinations. Weight:
7 pounds (12 ga.). English-style straight walnut buttstock
and splinter forend. Made in 1987.
12 or 20 ga. w/Double Triggers............... **$1450**
12 or 20 ga. w/Single Trigger **1525**
28 or .410 ga. w/Double Triggers **1600**
28 or .410 ga. w/Single Trigger............... **1750**
Two-barrel Set, **add**..................... **950**

AyA Model 37 Super Over/Under Shotgun **$2595**
Sidelock. Automatic ejectors. Selective single trigger.
Made in all gauges, barrel lengths and chokes. Vent-rib

AyA Model 37 Super Over/Under (cont.)
barrels. Elaborately engraved. Checkered stock (with
straight or pistol grip) and forend. Discontinued 1985.

AyA Model 53E **$1595**
Same general specifications as Model 117, except more
elaborate engraving and select figured wood. Disc. 1986.

AyA Model 76 Hammerless Double **$550**
Anson & Deeley boxlock. Auto ejectors. Selective single
trigger. Gauges: 12, 20 (3-inch). Barrels: 26-, 28-, 30-inch
(latter in 12 gauge only); any standard choke combination.
Checkered pistol-grip stock/beavertail forend. Disc.

AyA Model 76 — .410 Gauge **$610**
Same general specifications as 12 and 20 gauge Model 76,
except chambered for 3-inch shells in .410, has extractors,
double triggers, 26-inch barrels only, English-style stock
with straight grip and small forend. Discontinued.

AyA Model 117 Hammerless Double **$750**
Holland & Holland-type sidelocks, hand-detachable. Engraved action. Automatic ejectors. Selective single trigger.
Gauges: 12, 20 (3-inch). Barrels: 26-, 27-, 28-, 30-inch; 27-
and 30-inch in 12 gauge only; any standard choke combination. Checkered pistol-grip stock and beavertail forend
of select walnut. Manufactured in 1985.

AyA Matador II

AyA Bolero $450
Same general specifications as Matador except non-selective single trigger and extractors. Gauges: 12, 16, 20, 20 Magnum (3-inch), .410 (3-inch). *Note:* This model, prior to 1956, was designated F. I. Model 400 by the importer. Made 1955–1963.

AyA Matador Hammerless Double $425
Anson & Deeley boxlock. Selective automatic ejectors. Selective single trigger. Gauges: 12, 16, 20, 20 Magnum (3-inch). Barrels: 26-, 28-, 30-inch; any standard choke combination. Weight: 6½ to 7½ pounds, depending on gauge and barrel length. Checkered pistol-grip stock and beavertail forend. *Note:* This model, prior to 1956, was designated F. I. Model 400E by the U.S. importer, Firearms Int'l. Corp. of Washington, D.C. Made 1955–1963.

AyA Matador II $450
Improved version of Matador with same general specifications, except has vent-rib barrels. Made 1964–69.

AyA Matador III $675
Same general specifications as AyA Matador II. Made 1970–1985.

═══ BAIKAL SHOTGUNS ═══
See K.B.I., Inc.

═══ BAKER SHOTGUNS ═══
Batavia, New York
Made 1903–1933 by Baker Gun Company

Baker Batavia Ejector $770
Same general specifications as the Batavia Leader, except higher quality and finer finish throughout; has Damascus or homotensile steel barrels, checkered pistol-grip stock and forearm of select walnut; automatic ejectors standard; 12 and 16 gauge only.

Baker Batavia Leader

Baker Batavia Leader Hammerless Double
Sidelock. Plain extractors or automatic ejectors. Double triggers. Gauges: 12, 16, 20. Barrels: 26- to 32-inch; any standard boring. Weight: about 7¾ pounds (12 gauge with 30-inch barrels). Checkered pistol-grip stock and forearm.
With Plain Extractors $395
With Automatic Ejectors 450

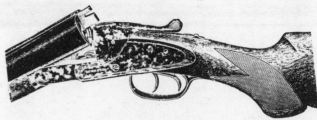

Baker Batavia Special

Baker Batavia Special $325
Same general specifications as the Batavia Leader, except plainer finish; 12 and 16 gauge only; has plain extractors, homotensile steel barrels.

Baker Black Beauty Special
Same general specifications as the Batavia Leader, except higher quality and finer finish throughout; has line engraving, special steel barrels, select walnut stock with straight, full or half-pistol grip.
With Plain Extractors $695
With Automatic Ejectors 795

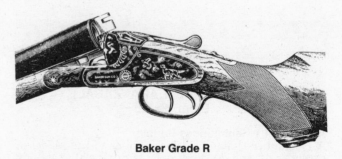

Baker Grade R

Baker Grade R
High-grade gun with same general specifications as the Batavia Leader, except has fine Damascus or Krupp fluid steel barrels, engraving in line, scroll and game scene designs, checkered stock and forearm of fancy European walnut; 12 and 16 gauges only.
Non-ejector $1000
With Automatic Ejectors 1200

Baker Grade S
Same general specifications as the Batavia Leader, except higher quality and finer finish throughout; has Flui-tempered steel barrels, line and scroll engraving, checkered stock with half-pistol grip and forearm of semifancy imported walnut; 10, 12 and 16 gauges.
Non-ejector $750
With Automatic Ejectors 975

Baker Paragon, Expert and Deluxe Grades
Made to order only, these are the higher grades of Baker hammerless sidelock double-barrel shotguns. After 1909,

Baker Paragon Grade

Baker Paragon, Expert and Deluxe Grades (cont.)

the Paragon Grade, as well as the Expert and Deluxe introduced that year, had a cross bolt in addition to the regular Baker system taper wedge fastening. There are early Paragon guns with Damascus barrels and some are non-ejector, but this grade was also produced with automatic ejectors and with the finest fluid steel barrels, in lengths to 34 inches, standard on Expert and Deluxe guns.

Differences among the three models are in overall quality, finish, elaborateness of engraving and grade of fancy figured walnut in the stock and forearm; Expert and Deluxe wood may be carved as well as checkered. Choice of straight, full or half-pistol grip was offered. A single trigger was available in the two higher grades. The Paragon was available in 10 gauge (Damascus barrels only); this and the other two models were regularly produced in 12, 16 and 20 gauges.

Paragon Grade, Non-ejector $1525
Paragon Grade, Automatic Ejectors 1600
Expert Grade. 2495
Deluxe Grade 3795
For Single Trigger, **add** 250

═══ BELKNAP SHOTGUNS ═══
Louisville, Kentucky

Belknap Model B-63 Single Shot Shotgun $75
Takedown. Visible hammer. Automatic ejector. Gauges: 12, 20 and .410. Barrels: 26- to 36-inch; F choke. Weight: average 6 pounds. Plain pistol-grip stock and forearm.

Belknap Model B-63E Single Shot Shotgun $75
Same general specifications as Model B-68, except has side lever opening instead of top lever.

Belknap Model B-64 Slide Action Shotgun $145
Hammerless. Gauges: 12, 16, 20 and .410. 3-shot tubular magazine. Various barrel lengths and chokes from 26-inch to 30-inch. Weight: 6¼ to 7½ pounds. Walnut-finished hardwood stock.

Belknap Model B-65C Autoloading Shotgun $265
Browning-type lightweight alloy receiver. 12 gauge only. 4-shot tubular magazine. Barrel: plain, 28-inch. Weight: about 8¼ pounds. Discontinued 1949.

Belknap Model B-68 Single Shot Shotgun $80
Takedown. Visible hammer. Automatic ejector. Gauges: 12, 16, 20 and .410. Barrels: 26-inch to 36-inch; F choke. Weight: 6 pounds. Plain pistol-grip stock and forearm.

═══ BENELLI SHOTGUNS ═══
Urbino, Italy

Benelli Model 121 M1 Military/Police
Autoloading Shotgun $350
Gauge: 12. 7-shot magazine. 19¾-inch barrel. 39¾ inches overall. Cylinder choke, 2¾-inch chamber. Weight: 7.4 pounds. Matte black finish and European hardwood stock. Post front sight, fixed buckhorn rear sight. Made in 1985.

Benelli Model Black Eagle Autoloading Shotgun
Two-piece aluminum and steel receiver. Gauge: 12; 3-inch chamber. 4-shot magazine. Screw-in choke tubes (SK, IC, M, IM, F). Barrels: ventilated rib; 21, 24, 26 or 28 inches w/bead front sight; 24-inch rifled slug. 42½ to 49½ inches overall. Weight: 7¼ pounds (28-inch bbl.). Matte black lower receiver with blued upper receiver and barrel. Checkered walnut stock with high-gloss finish and drop adjustment. Made from 1989 to date.
Competition Model $750
Slug Model (Discontinued 1992) 595
Standard Model (Discontinued 1992) 575

Benelli Model M1 Super 90 Defense Autoloader
Same general specifications as Model Super 90, except with pistol-grip stock. Available with Ghost Ring sight option. Made from 1986 to date.
Standard Defense Model $525
Defense Model w/Ghost Ring Sights. 575

SHOTGUNS

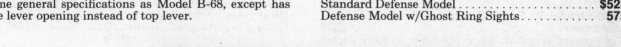

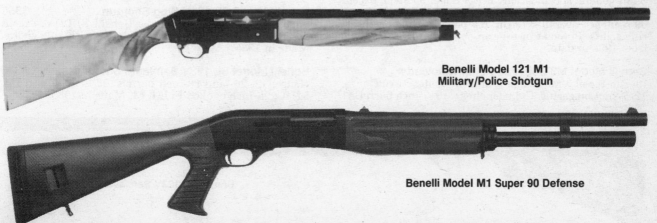

**Benelli Model 121 M1
Military/Police Shotgun**

Benelli Model M1 Super 90 Defense

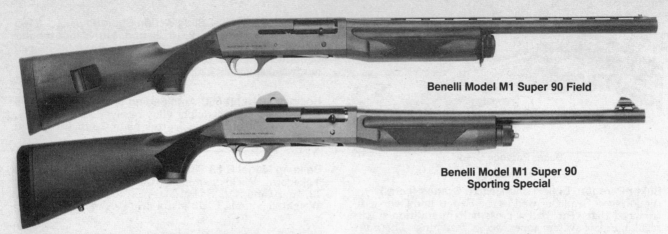

Benelli Model M1 Super 90 Field

Benelli Model M1 Super 90 Sporting Special

Benelli Model M1 Super 90 Entry Autoloader ... **$595**
Same gen. specifications as Model Super 90, except w/5-shot magazine, 14-inch barrel. 35½ inches overall. Weight: 6½ lbs. Standard or pistol-grip stock. Made 1992 to date. *Special permit required for under 18" barrel.*

Benelli Model M1 Super 90 Field
Inertia-recoil semiautomatic shotgun. Gauge: 12; 3-inch chamber. 3-shot magazine. Barrel: 21, 24, 26 or 28 inches. 42½ to 49½ inches overall. Choke: SK, IC, M, IM, F. Matte receiver. Standard polymer stock or satin walnut (26- or 28-inch bbl. only). Bead front sight. Made from 1990 to date.
With Polymer Stock **$450**
With Walnut Stock **475**

Benelli Model M1 Super 90 Slug Autoloader
Same general specifications as M1 Super 90 Field, except with 5-shot magazine. 18.5-inch barrel. Cylinder bore. 39¼ inches overall. Weight: 6.5 pounds. Polymer standard stock. Rifle or ghost-ring sights. Made from 1986 to date.
With Rifle Sights **$550**
With Ghost-ring Sights **595**

Benelli Model M1 Super 90 Sporting Special Autoloader **$575**
Same general specifications as M1 Super 90 Field, except with 18.5-inch barrel. 39¾ inches overall. Weight: 6.5 pounds. Ghost-ring sights. Polymer stock. Made from 1994 to date.

Benelli Model M1 Super 90 Tactical Autoloader **$595**
Same general specifications as M1 Super 90 Field, except with 18.5-inch barrel. 5-shot magazine. IC, M or F choke. 39¾ inches overall. Weight: 6.5 pounds. Rifle or ghost-ring sights. Polymer pistol-grip or standard stock. Made from 1994 to date.

Benelli Model M3 Super 90 Pump/Autoloader
Inertia-recoil semiautomatic and/or pump action. Gauge: 12. 7-shot magazine. Cylinder choke. 19¾-inch barrel. 41

Benelli Model M3 Super 90 Pump/Autoloader (cont.)
inches overall (31 inches folded). Weight: 7 to 7½ pounds. Matte black finish. Stock: standard synthetic, pistol-grip or folding tubular steel. Standard rifle or Ghost Ring sights. Made from 1989 to date. *Caution: Increasing the magazine capacity to more than 5 rounds in M3 shotguns w/pistol-grip stocks violates provisions of the 1994 Crime Bill. This model may be used legally only by the military and law-enforcement agencies.*
Standard Model **$675**
Pistol-grip Model **720**
With Folding Stock **750**
With Laser Sight **995**
For Ghost Ring Sights, **add** **50**

Benelli Montefeltro Super 90 Semiautomatic
Same general specifications as Model M1 Super 90, except has checkered walnut stock with high-gloss finish. Barrels: 21, 24, 26 or 28 inches, with screw-in choke tubes (IC, M, IM, F). Weight: 7½ pounds. Blued finish. Imported from 1987 to date.
Standard Model **$595**
Slug Model (Discontinued 1992) **625**
Turkey Model **615**
Uplander Model **625**
Left-hand Model **650**

Benelli Model SL 121V Semiauto Shotgun **$325**
Gauge: 12. 5-shot capacity. Barrels: 26-, 28- and 30-inch. 26-inch choked M, IM, IC; 28-inch, F, M, IM; 30-inch, F choke (Mag.). Straight walnut stock with hand-checkered pistol grip and forend. Ventilated rib. Made in 1985.

Benelli Model SL 121V Slug Shotgun **$350**
Same general specifications as Benelli SL121V, except designed for rifled slugs and equipped with rifle sights. Made in 1985.

Benelli Model SL 123V Semiauto Shotgun **$375**
Gauge: 12. 26- and 28-inch barrels. 26-inch choked IM, M, IC; 28-inch choked F, IM, M. Made in 1985.

Benelli SL 123V Semiautomatic

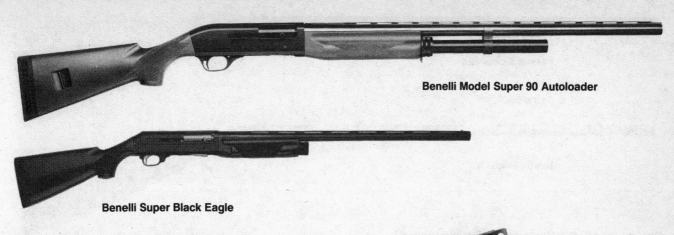

Benelli Model Super 90 Autoloader

Benelli Super Black Eagle

Benelli Model SL 201 Semiautomatic Shotgun .. $320
Gauge: 20. 26-inch barrel. Mod. choke. Weight: 5 lbs., 10 oz. Ventilated rib. Made in 1985.

Benelli Model Super 90 Autoloading Shotgun ... $515
Gauge: 12. 7-shot magazine. Cylinder choke. 19³/₄-inch barrel. 39³/₄ inches overall. Weight: 7 lbs. 4 oz. to 7 lbs. 10 oz. Matte black finish. Stock and forend made of fiberglass reinforced polymer. Sights: post front; fixed buckhorn rear, drift adjustable. Made from 1985 to date.

Benelli Super Black Eagle Autoloading Shotgun
Same general specifications as Model Black Eagle, except with 3¹/₂-inch chamber that accepts 2³/₄-, 3- and 3¹/₂-inch shells. 2-shot magazine (3¹/₂-inch), 3-shot magazine (2³/₄- or 3-inch). High-gloss or satin finish stock. Matte black or blued metal finish. Made from 1991 to date.
Custom Slug Model **$775**
Standard Model **795**

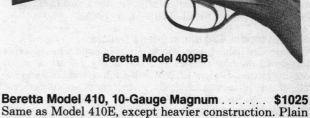

Beretta Model 409PB

Beretta Model 410, 10-Gauge Magnum $1025
Same as Model 410E, except heavier construction. Plain extractors. Double triggers. 10-gauge Magnum, 3¹/₂-inch chambers. 32-inch barrels, both F choke. Weight: about 10 pounds. Checkered pistol-grip stock and forearm, recoil pad. Made 1934–1984.

Beretta Model 410E

═══ BERETTA USA CORP. ═══
Accokeek, Maryland

Manufactured by Fabbrica D'Armi Pietro Beretta S.p.A. in the Gardone Valtrompia (Brescia), Italy

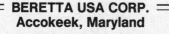

Beretta Model 57E

Beretta Model 57E Over-and-Under
Same general specifications as Golden Snipe, but higher quality throughout. Made 1955–1967.
With Non-selective Single Trigger **$755**
With Selective Single Trigger **825**

Beretta Model 409PB Hammerless Double $775
Boxlock. Double triggers. Plain extractors. Gauges: 12, 16, 20, 28. Barrels: 27¹/₂-, 28¹/₂- and 30-inch; IC/M choke or M/F choke. Weight: from 5¹/₂ to 7³/₄ pounds, depending on gauge and barrel length. Straight or pistol-grip stock and beavertail forearm, checkered. Made 1934–1964.

Beretta Model 410E $850
Same general specifications as Model 409PB, except has automatic ejectors and is of higher quality throughout. Made 1934–1964.

Beretta Model 411E $1295
Same general specifications as Model 409PB except has sideplates, automatic ejectors and is of higher quality throughout. Made 1934–1964.

Beretta Model 424 Hammerless Double $795
Boxlock. Light border engraving. Plain extractors. Gauges: 12, 20; chambers 2³/₄-inch in former, 3-inch in latter. Barrels: 28-inch M/F choke; 26-inch IC/M choke. Weight: 5 lbs. 14 oz. to 6 lbs. 10 oz., depending on gauge and barrel

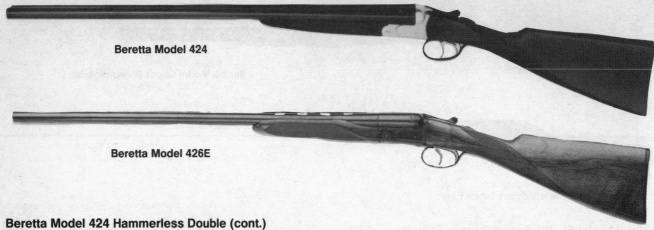

Beretta Model 424

Beretta Model 426E

Beretta Model 424 Hammerless Double (cont.)
length. English-style straight-grip stock and forearm, checkered. Made 1977–1984.

Beretta Model 426E $995
Same as Model 424, except action body is finely engraved, silver pigeon inlaid in top lever; has selective automatic ejectors and selective single trigger, stock and forearm of select European walnut. Made 1977–1984.

Beretta Model 452 Hammerless Double
Custom English-style sidelock. Single, single non-selective trigger or double triggers. Manual safety. Selective automatic ejectors. Gauge: 12; 2³/₄- or 3-inch chambers. Barrels: 26, 28 or 30 inches choked to customers specifications. Weight: 6³/₄ pounds. Checkered high-grade walnut stock. Receiver with coin-silver finish.
Model 452 Standard **$17,950**
Model 452 EELL **24,000**

Beretta Model 625 S/S Hammerless Double
Boxlock. Gauges: 12 or 20. Barrels: 26-, 28- or 30-inch w/ fixed choke combinations. Single selective or double triggers w/extractors. Checkered English-style buttstock and forend. Made 1984–87.
With Double Triggers **$695**
With Single Selective Trigger **795**

Beretta Model 626 S/S Hammerless Double
Field Grade side-by-side. Boxlock action with single selective trigger, extractors and automatic safety. Gauges: 12 (2³/₄-inch chambers); 20 (3-inch chambers). Barrels:

Beretta Model 626 S/S Hammerless Double (cont.)
26- or 28-inch with Mobilchoke® or various fixed-choke combinations. Weight: 6³/₄ pounds (12 ga.). Bright chrome finish. Checkered European walnut buttstock and forend in straight English style. Made 1985–1994.
Model 626 Field (Discontinued 1988) .... **$ 795**
Model 626 (3¹/₂-inch Magnum, Disc. 1993) **1250**
Model 626 Onyx **1195**

Beretta Model 627 S/S Hammerless Double
Same as Model 626 S/S, except with engraved sideplates and pistol-grip or straight English-style stock. Made 1985–1994.
Model 627 EL Field **$1995**
Model 627 EELL **3795**

Beretta Model 682 Over/Under Shotgun
Hammerless takedown with single selective trigger. Gauges: 12, 20, 28, .410. Barrels: 26- to 34-inch with fixed chokes or Mobilchoke® tubes. Checkered European walnut buttstock/forend in various grades and configurations.
Model 682 Comp Trap Standard **$1955**
Model 682 Comp Trap Top Single **2050**
Model 682 Comp Trap Pigeon **2290**
Model 682 Comp Trap Combo **2640**
Model 682 Comp Skeet **1450**
Model 682 Comp Skeet 2-Barrel Set **2900**
Model 682 Comp Skeet 4-Barrel Set **3000**

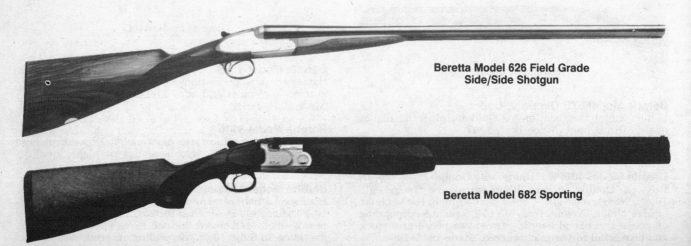

Beretta Model 626 Field Grade
Side/Side Shotgun

Beretta Model 682 Sporting

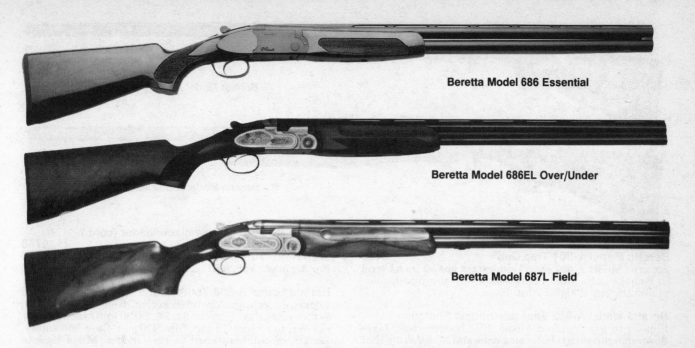

Beretta Model 686 Essential

Beretta Model 686EL Over/Under

Beretta Model 687L Field

Beretta Model 682 Over/Under (cont.)

Model 682 Continental Sport	**$1795**
Model 682 Sporting	**1800**
Model 682 Sporting Combo	**2300**
Model 682 Super Pigeon Trap	**1750**
Model 682 Super Sport	**1895**
Model 682 Super Trap	**2050**
Model 682 Super Trap Combo	**2650**
Model 682 Super Trap Top Single	**2195**
Model 682 Super Trap Unsingle	**1725**

Beretta Model 686 Essential O/U Shotgun $890
Boxlock. Gauge: 12; 3-inch chambers. 26- or 28-inch barrels. Chokes: F, M, IC or MC3 Mobilchoke®. 45.7 inches overall. Weight: 6.7 pounds. Checkered American walnut stock and forend. Matte black receiver. Made 1994 to date.

Beretta Model 686 Over/Under Shotgun
Low-profile improved boxlock. Single selective trigger. Selective automatic ejectors. Gauges: 12, 20, 28 with 3½-, 3- or 2¾-inch chambers. Barrels: 26-, 28-, 30-inch with fixed chokes or Mobilchoke® tubes. Weight: 5¾ to 7½ pounds. Checkered American walnut stock and forearm.

Model 686 Field, Onyx	**$ 925**
Model 686 (3½-inch Mag., Disc. 1993)	**1095**
Model 686 EL, English	**1495**
Model 686 EL Gold Perdiz	**1695**
Model 686 L Silver Perdiz	**1050**
Model 686 Skeet	**1095**
Model 686 Sporting (Disc. 1993)	**895**
Model 686 Sporting Onyx	**875**
Model 686 Sporting Onyx Gold (Disc. 1993)	**995**
Model 686 Sporting Combo	**1725**
Model 686 Two-barrel Set	**1495**
Model 686 Ultralight	**995**

Beretta Model 687 Over/Under Shotgun
Same as Model 686, except with decorative sideplates and varying grades of engraving and game-scene motifs.

Beretta Model 687 Over/Under (cont.)

Model 687L Field	**$1250**
Model 687 L Onyx (Disc. 1991)	**995**
Model 687 EL	**1895**
Model 687 EL Small Frame	**2250**
Model 687 EELL	**2850**
Model 687 EELL Combo	**3850**
Model 687 EELL Sporter, Trap, Skeet	**3470**
Model 687 EELL Skeet 4-barrel Set	**6030**
Model 687 Sporting	**1895**
Model 687 Sporting Combo	**2350**

Beretta Model 1200 Semiautoloading Shotgun
Short recoil action. Gauge: 12; 2¾- or 3-inch chamber. 6-shot magazine. 24-, 26- or 28-inch vent-rib barrel with fixed chokes or Mobilchoke® tubes. Weight: 7¼ pounds. Matte black finish. Adjustable technopolymer stock and forend. Made from 1988 to date.

Model 1200 w/Fixed Choke	**$425**
Model 1200 Riot	**475**
Model 1201 w/Mobilchoke®	**470**
Model 1201 Riot	**495**

Beretta Model A-301 Autoloading Shotgun $375
Field Gun. Gas-operated. Scroll-decorated receiver. Gauge: 12 or 20; 2¾-inch chamber in former, 3-inch in latter. 3-shot magazine. Barrel: ventilated rib; 28-inch F or M choke, 26-inch IC. Weight: 6 lbs. 5 oz.–6 lbs. 14 oz., depending on gauge and barrel length. Checkered pistol-grip stock/forearm. Made 1977–1982.

Beretta Model A-301 Magnum $395
Same as Model A-301 Field Gun, except chambered for 12 gauge 3-inch Magnum shells; 30-inch F choke barrel only, stock with recoil pad. Weight: 7¼ pounds.

Beretta Model A-301 Skeet Gun $400
Same as Model A-301 Field Gun, except 26-inch barrel SK choke only, skeet-style stock, gold-plated trigger.

Beretta Model A-301 Slug Gun $370
Same as Model A-301 Field Gun, except has plain 22-inch barrel, slug choke, with rifle sights. Weight: 6 lbs. 14 oz.

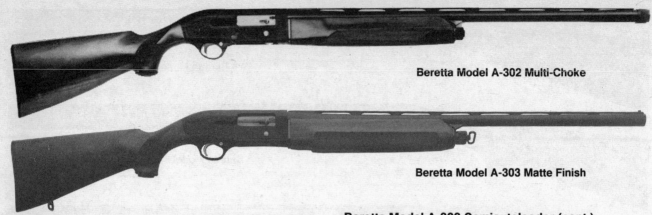

Beretta Model A-302 Multi-Choke

Beretta Model A-303 Matte Finish

Beretta Model A-301 Trap Gun **$405**
Same as Model A-301 Field Gun, except has 30-inch barrel
in F choke only, Monte Carlo stock with recoil pad, gold-
plated trigger. Weight: 7 lbs. 10 oz.

Beretta Model A-302 Semiautoloading Shotgun
Similar to gas-operated Model 301. Hammerless, takedown shotgun with tubular magazine and Mag-Action that
handles both 2³/₄- and 3-inch Magnum shells. Gauge: 12
or 20; 2³/₄- or 3-inch Mag. chambers. Barrel: vent or plain;
22-inch/Slug (12 ga.); 26-inch/IC (12 or 20); 28-inch/M
(20 ga.); 28-inch/Multi-choke (12 or 20 ga.); 30-inch/F
(12 ga.). Weight: 6¹/₂ lbs., 20 ga.; 7¹/₄ lbs., 12 ga. Blued/
black finish. Checkered European walnut, pistol-grip stock
and forend. Made 1983 to c. 1987.
Standard Model with Fixed Choke **$395**
Standard Model with Multi-choke **425**

Beretta Model A-302 Super Lusso **$1895**
A custom A-302 in presentation grade with hand-engraved
receiver and custom select walnut stock.

Beretta Model A-303 Semiautoloader
Similar to Model 302, except with target specifications in
Trap, Skeet and Youth configurations, and weighs 6¹/₂ to
8 pounds. Made from 1983 to date.
Field and Upland Models **$425**
Skeet and Trap (Discontinued 1994) **435**
Slug Model (Discontinued 1992) **455**
Sporting Clays **475**
Super Skeet **725**

Beretta Model A-303 Semiautoloader (cont.)
Super Trap **$750**
Waterfowl/Turkey (Discontinued 1992) **435**
For Mobilchoke®, **add** **50**

Beretta Model A-303 Youth Gun **$415**
Locked-breech, gas-operated action. Gauges: 12 and 20;
2-shot magazine. Barrels: 24, 26, 28, 30 or 32 inches; vent
rib. Weight: 7 lbs. (12 ga.); 6 lbs. (20 ga.). Crossbolt safety.
Length of pull shortened to 12¹/₂ inches. Made 1988 to
date.

Beretta Model A-390 Semiautoloading Shotgun
Gas-operated, self-regulating action designed to handle
any size load. Gauge: 12; 3-inch chamber. 3-shot magazine.
Barrel: 24, 26, 28 or 30 inches w/vent rib and Mobilchoke®
tubes. Weight: 7¹/₄ pounds. Select walnut stock w/adjust-
able comb. Blued or matte black finish. Made 1992 to
date.
Standard Model **$465**
Field Model **475**
Deluxe Model **495**
For Mobilchoke®, **add** **50**

Beretta Model A-390 Super Target
Similar to the Model 390 Field, except in 12 gauge only
with 2³/₄-inch chamber. Skeet: 28-inch ported barrel with
wide vent rib and fixed choke (SK). Trap: 30- or 32-inch
with Mobilchoke® tubes. Weight: 7¹/₂ pounds. Fully adjustable buttstock. Made from 1993 to date.
Super Trap Model **$875**
Super Skeet Model **850**
For Mobilchoke®, **add** **50**

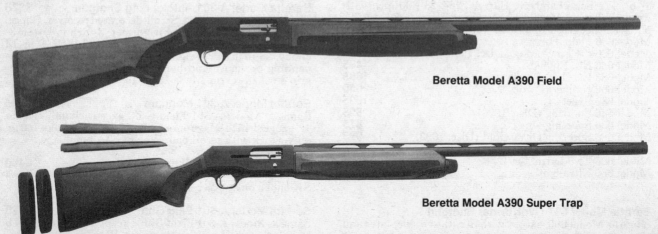

Beretta Model A390 Field

Beretta Model A390 Super Trap

Beretta Model AL-2 Field Gun

Beretta Model AL-1 Field Gun **$355**
Same as Model AL-2 Field Gun, except has barrel without
rib, no engraving on receiver. Made 1971–73.

Beretta Model AL-2 Autoloading Shotgun
Field Gun. Gas-operated. Engraved receiver (1968 version,
12 gauge only, had no engraving). Gauge: 12 or 20. 2³/₄-
inch chamber. 3-shot magazine. Barrels: vent rib; 30-inch
F choke; 28-inch F or M choke; 26-inch IC. Weight: 6¹/₂
to 7¹/₄ pounds, depending on gauge and barrel length.
Checkered pistol-grip stock and forearm. Made 1968–1975.
With Plain Receiver **$385**
With Engraved Receiver **440**

Beretta Model AL-2 Magnum **$415**
Same as Model AL-2 Field Gun, except chambered for 12
gauge 3-inch Magnum shells; 30-inch F or 28-inch M
choke barrel only. Weight: about 8 lbs. Made 1973–75.

Beretta Model AL-2 Skeet Gun **$395**
Same as Model AL-2 Field Gun, except has wide rib, 26-
inch barrel in SK choke only, beavertail forearm. Made
1969–1975.

Beretta Model AL-2 Trap Gun **$415**
Same as Model AL-2 Field Gun, except has wide rib, 30-
inch barrel in F choke only, beavertail forearm. Monte
Carlo stock with recoil pad. Weight: about 7³/₄ pounds.
Made 1969–1975.

Beretta Model AL-3
Similar to corresponding AL-2 models in design and gen-
eral specifications. Made 1975–76.
Field Model **$425**
Magnum Model **440**
Skeet Model **450**
Trap Model **495**

Beretta Model AL-3 Deluxe Trap Gun **$775**
Same as standard Model AL-3 Trap Gun, except has fully
engraved receiver, gold-plated trigger and safety, stock
and forearm of premium grade European walnut, gold
monogram escutcheon inlaid in buttstock. Made 1975–76.

Beretta Model ASE 90 Over-and-Under Shotgun
Competition-style receiver with coin-silver finish and gold
inlay featuring drop-out trigger group. Gauge: 12; 2³/₄-
inch chamber. Barrels: 28- or 30-inch w/fixed or Mobil-
choke® tubes; vent rib. Weight: 8¹/₂ pounds (30-inch bbl.).
Checkered high-grade walnut stock. Made 1992 to date.
Pigeon, Skeet, Trap Models **$5850**
Sporting Clays Model **5995**

Beretta Model Asel

Beretta Model Asel Over-and-Under Shotgun . . **$1110**
Boxlock. Single non-selective trigger. Selective automatic
ejectors. Gauges: 12, 20. Barrels: 26-, 28-, 30-inch; IC and
M choke or M and F choke. Weight: about 5³/₄ lbs., 20
ga.; about 7 lbs., 12 ga. Checkered pistol-grip stock and
forearm. Made 1947–1964.

Beretta Model BL-1/BL-2 Over/Under
Boxlock. Plain extractors. Double triggers. 12 gauge, 2³/₄-
inch chambers only. Barrels: 30- and 28-inch M/F choke;
26-inch IC/M choke. Weight: 6³/₄–7 pounds, depending
on barrel length. Checkered pistol-grip stock and forearm.
Made 1968–1973.
Model BL-1 . . . . **$325**
Model BL-2 (Single Selective Trigger) **375**

Beretta Model BL-2/S **$385**
Similar to Model BL-1, except has selective "Speed-Trig-
ger," vent-rib barrels, 2³/₄- or 3-inch chambers. Weight:
7–7¹/₂ pounds. Made 1974–76.

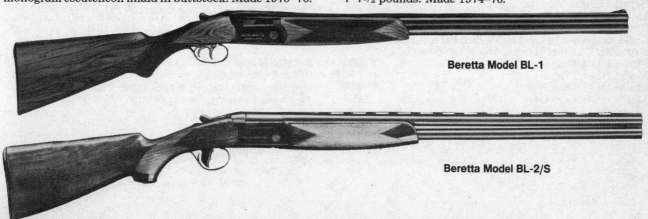

Beretta Model BL-1

Beretta Model BL-2/S

SHOTGUNS

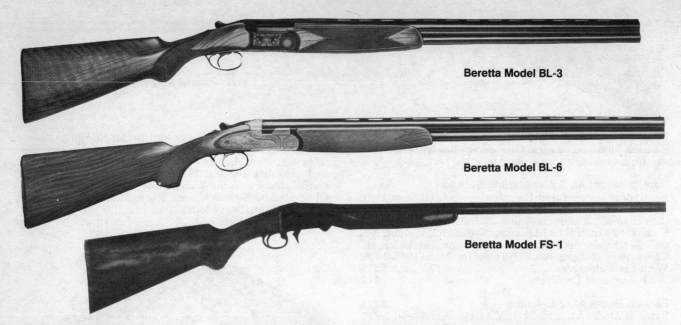

Beretta Model BL-3

Beretta Model BL-6

Beretta Model FS-1

Beretta Model BL-3 . . . . $555

Same as Model BL-1, except has deluxe engraved receiver, selective single trigger, vent-rib barrels; 12 or 20 gauge, 2³/₄-inch or 3-inch chambers in former, 3-inch in latter. Weight: 6–7¹/₂ pounds, depending on gauge and barrel length. Made 1968–1976.

Beretta Models BL-4, BL-5 and BL-6

Higher grade versions of Model BL-3 with more elaborate engraving and fancier wood; Model BL-6 has sideplates. Selective automatic ejectors standard. Made 1968–1976 (Model BL-6 introduced in 1973).

Model BL-4 . . . . $ 675
Model BL-5 875
Model BL-6 1095

Beretta Series BL Skeet Guns

Models BL-3, BL-4, BL-5 and BL-6 with standard features of their respective grades plus wider rib and skeet-style stock; 26-inch barrels SK choked. Weight: 6–7¹/₄ pounds, depending on gauge.

Model BL-3 Skeet Gun . . . . $ 600
Model BL-4 Skeet Gun 750
Model BL-5 Skeet Gun 925
Model BL-6 Skeet Gun 1295

Beretta Series BL Trap Guns

Models BL-3, BL-4, BL-5 and BL-6 with standard features of their respective grades plus wider rib and Monte Carlo stock with recoil pad; 30-inch barrels, improved M/F or both F choke. Weight: about 7¹/₂ pounds.

Model BL-3 Trap Gun . . . . $ 600
Model BL-4 Trap Gun 750
Model BL-5 Trap Gun 980
Model BL-6 Trap Gun 1295

Beretta Model FS-1 Folding Single $195

Formerly "Companion." Folds to length of barrel. Hammerless. Underlever. Gauge: 12, 16, 20, 28 or .410. Barrel: 30-inch in 12 ga.; 28-inch in 16 and 20 ga.; 26-inch in 28 and .410 ga.; all F choke. Checkered semipistol-grip stock/forearm. Weight: 4¹/₂–5¹/₂ pounds, depending on gauge. Discontinued 1971.

Beretta Golden Snipe Over-and-Under

Same as Silver Snipe, except has automatic ejectors, ventilated rib is standard feature. Made 1959–1967.

With Non-selective Single Trigger $625
Extra for Selective Single Trigger 100

Beretta Model GR-2 Hammerless Double $595

Boxlock. Plain extractors. Double triggers. Gauges: 12, 20; 2³/₄-inch chambers in former, 3-inch in latter. Barrels: vent rib; 30-inch M/F choke (12 ga. only); 28-inch M/F choke; 26-inch IC/M choke. Weight: 6¹/₂ to 7¹/₄ pounds, depending on gauge and barrel length. Checkered pistol-grip stock and forearm. Made 1968–1976.

Beretta Model GR-3 . . . . $695

Same as Model GR-2, except has selective single trigger; chambered for 12-gauge 3-inch or 2³/₄-inch shells. Magnum model has 30-inch M/F choke barrel, recoil pad. Weight: about 8 pounds. Made 1968–1976.

Beretta Model GR-4 . . . . $735

Same as Model GR-2, except has automatic ejectors and selective single trigger, higher grade engraving and wood. 12 gauge, 2³/₄-inch chambers only. Made 1968–1976.

Beretta Model GR-2

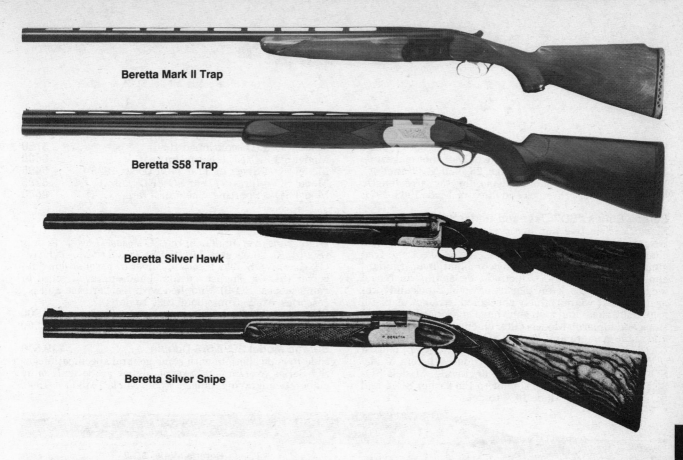

Beretta Mark II Trap

Beretta S58 Trap

Beretta Silver Hawk

Beretta Silver Snipe

Beretta Grade 100 Over-and-Under Shotgun . . **$1695**
Sidelock. Double triggers. Automatic ejectors. 12 gauge only. Barrels: 26-, 28-, 30-inch; any standard boring. Weight: about 7½ pounds. Checkered stock and forend, straight or pistol grip. Discontinued.

Beretta Grade 200 . . . . **$2095**
Same general specifications as Grade 100 except higher quality, bores and action parts hard chrome-plated. Discontinued.

Beretta Mark II Single Barrel Trap Gun **$550**
Boxlock action similar to that of Series "BL" Over-and-Unders. Engraved receiver. Automatic ejector. 12 gauge only. 32- or 34-inch barrel with wide vent rib. Weight: about 8½ pounds. Monte Carlo stock with pistol grip and recoil pad, beavertail forearm. Made 1972–76.

Beretta Model S55B Over-and-Under Shotgun . . **$475**
Boxlock. Plain extractors. Selective single trigger. Gauges: 12, 20; 2¾- or 3-inch chambers in former, 3-inch in latter. Barrels: vent rib; 30-inch M/F choke or both F choke in 12-gauge 3-inch Magnum only; 28-inch M/F choke; 26-inch IC/M choke. Weight: 6½ to 7½ pounds, depending on gauge and barrel length. Checkered pistol-grip stock and forearm. Introduced in 1977.

Beretta Model S56E **$550**
Same as Model S55B, except has scroll-engraved receiver, selective automatic ejectors. Introduced in 1977.

Beretta Model S58 Skeet Gun **$725**
Same as Model S56E, except has 26-inch barrels of Boehler Antinit Anticorro steel, SK choked, with wide vent rib; skeet-style stock and forearm. Weight: 7½ pounds. Introduced in 1977.

Beretta Model S58 Trap Gun **$695**
Same as Model S58 Skeet Gun, except has 30-inch barrels bored IM/Full Trap, Monte Carlo stock with recoil pad. Weight: 7 lbs. 10 oz. Introduced in 1977.

Beretta Silver Hawk Featherweight Hammerless Double Barrel Shotgun
Boxlock. Double triggers or non-selective single trigger. Plain extractor. Gauges: 12, 16, 20, 28, 12 Mag. Barrels: 26- to 32-inch with high matted rib; all standard choke combinations. Weight: 7 lbs. (12 ga. w/26-inch barrels). Checkered walnut stock with beavertail forearm. Discontinued 1967.
With Double Triggers **$475**
For Non-selective Single Trigger, **add** 65

Beretta Silver Snipe Over-and-Under Shotgun
Boxlock. Non-selective or selective single trigger. Plain extractor. Gauges: 12, 20, 12 Mag., 20 Mag. Barrels: 26-, 28-, 30-inch; plain or vent rib; chokes IC/M, M/F, SK #1 and #2, F/F. Weight: from about 6 pounds in 20 ga. to 8½ pounds in 12 ga. (Trap gun). Checkered walnut pistol-grip stock and forearm. Made 1955–1967.
With Plain Barrel, Non-selective Trigger **$425**
With Vent-rib Barrel, Non-sel. Single Trigger . . . 525
For Selective Single Trigger, **add** 65

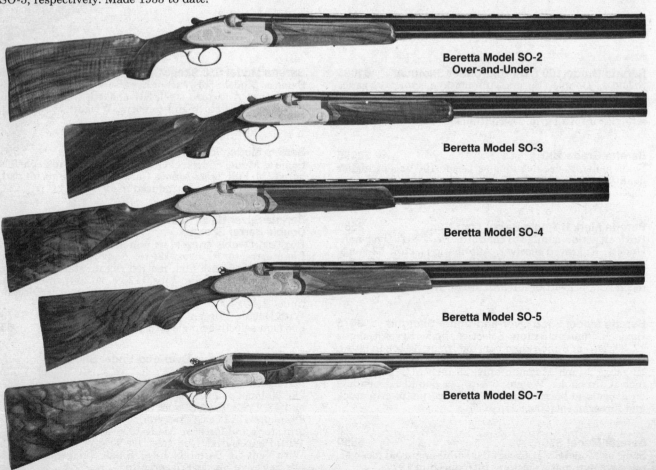

Beretta Model SL-2

Beretta Model SL-2 Pump Gun $285

Hammerless. Takedown. 12 gauge only. 3-shot magazine. Barrels: vent rib; 30-inch F choke, 28-inch M, 26-inch IC. Weight: about 7–7¼ pounds, depending on barrel length. Checkered pistol-grip stock and forearm. Made 1968–1971.

Beretta Series "SO" Over-and-Under Shotguns

Sidelock. Selective automatic ejectors. Selective single trigger or double triggers. 12 gauge only, 2¾- or 3-inch chambers. Barrels: vent rib (wide type on skeet and trap guns); 26-, 27-, 29-, 30-inch; any combination of standard chokes. Weight: 7 to 7¾ pounds, depending on barrel length, style of stock and density of wood. Stock and forearm of select walnut, finely checkered; straight or pistol grip; field, skeet and trap guns have appropriate styles of stock and forearm. Models differ chiefly in quality of wood and grade of engraving. Models SO-3EL, SO-3EELL, SO-4 and SO-5 have hand-detachable locks. "SO-4" is used to designate skeet and trap models derived from Model SO-3EL but with less elaborate engraving. Models SO-3EL and SO-3EELL are similar to the earlier SO-4 and SO-5, respectively. Made 1933 to date.

Beretta Series "SO" Over-Under Shotguns (cont.)

Model SO-2 (Discontinued 1986)	**$4025**
Model SO-3 (Discontinued 1986)	**5750**
Model SO-3EELL (Discontinued)	**9600**
Model SO-4 Skeet or Trap Gun (Disc. 1986)	**6495**
Model SO-4 (pre-1977) or SO-3EL (Disc.)	**6295**
Model SO-5 Sporting, Skeet or Trap	**9600**

Beretta Models SO-6 and SO-9 Premium Grade Shotguns

High-grade over/unders in the SO series. Gauges: 12 only (SO-6); 12, 20, 28 and .410 (SO-9). Fixed or Mobilchoke® (12 ga. only). Sidelock action. Silver or casehardened receiver (SO-6); English custom hand-engraved scroll or game scenes (SO-9). Supplied with leather case and accessories. Made from about 1990 to date.

SO-6 Over/Under	**$10,900**
SO-9 Over/Under	**19,500**

Beretta Model SO-7 S/S Double $19,500

Side-by-side shotgun with same general specifications as SO Series over/unders, except higher grade with more elaborate engraving, fancier wood. Made 1948 to c. 1990.

**Beretta Model SO-2
Over-and-Under**

Beretta Model SO-3

Beretta Model SO-4

Beretta Model SO-5

Beretta Model SO-7

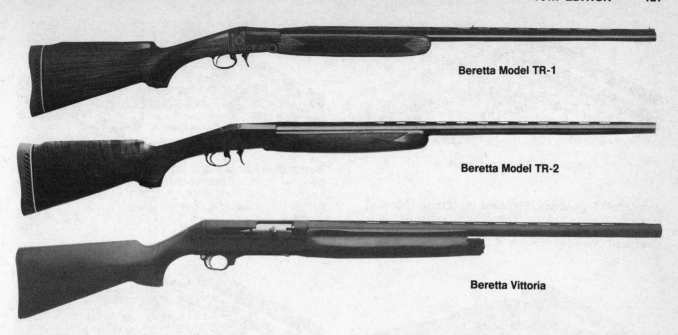

Beretta Model TR-1

Beretta Model TR-2

Beretta Vittoria

Beretta Model TR-1 Single Barrel Trap Gun $275
Hammerless. Underlever action. Engraved frame. 12 gauge only. 32-inch barrel with vent rib. Weight: about 8¼ pounds. Monte Carlo stock with pistol grip and recoil pad, beavertail forearm. Made 1968–1971.

Beretta Model TR-2 .... $295
Same as Model TR-1, except has extended ventilated rib. Made 1969–1973.

Beretta Vittoria Pintail Semiautoloader $450
Short Montefeltro-type recoil action. Gauge: 12; 3-inch chamber. Barrel: 24-inch slug; 24- or 26-inch vent rib w/ Mobilchoke® tubes. Weight: 7 pounds. Checkered walnut stock/forend. Matte finish on both metal and wood. Made 1993 to date.

Bernardelli Elio

Bernardelli Elio $1310
Lightweight game gun, 12 gauge only, with same general specifications as Standard Gamecock (S. Uberto 1), except weighs about 6 to 6¼ pounds, has automatic ejectors, fine English-pattern scroll engraving. No longer imported.

VINCENZO BERNARDELLI
Gardone V.T. (Brescia), Italy

Bernardelli Brescia

Bernardelli Brescia Hammer Double $1915
Back-action sidelock. Plain extractors. Double triggers. Gauges: 12, 20. Barrels: 27½ or 29½-inch M/F choke in 12 gauge, 25½-inch IC/M choke in 20 gauge. Weight: from 5¾ to 7 pounds, depending on gauge and barrel length. English-style stock and forearm, checkered. No longer imported.

Bernardelli Premier Gamecock

Bernardelli Gamecock, Premier (Roma 3) $1195
Same general specifications as Standard Gamecock (S. Uberto 1), except has sideplates, auto ejectors, single trigger. Currently manufactured.

Bernardelli Gamecock, Standard (S. Uberto 1)
Hammerless Double Barrel Shotgun $995
Boxlock. Plain extractors. Double triggers. Gauges: 12, 16, 20; 2¾-inch chambers in 12 and 16, 3-inch in 20 gauge. Barrels: 25½-inch IC/M choke; 27½-inch M/F choke.

SHOTGUNS

Bernardelli Standard Gamecock

Bernardelli Gamecock, Standard (S. Uberto 1) (cont.)
Weight: 5³/₄–6¹/₂ pounds, depending on gauge and barrel length. English-style straight-grip stock and forearm, checkered. No longer imported.

Bernardelli Gardone Hammer Double

Bernardelli Gardone Hammer Double $2065
Same general specifications as Brescia, except for higher grade engraving and wood, but not as high as the Italia. Half-cock safety. Discontinued 1956.

Bernardelli Hemingway Hammerless Double
Boxlock. Single or double triggers with hinged front. Selective automatic ejectors. Gauges: 12 and 20 w/2³/₄- or 3-inch chambers; 16 and 28 w/2³/₄-inch. Barrels: 23¹/₂- to 28-inch with fixed chokes. Weight: 6¹/₄ pounds. Checkered English-style European walnut stock. Silvered and engraved receiver.
Standard Model $1395
Deluxe Model w/Sideplates (Disc. 1993) 1595
For Single Trigger, **add** 75

Bernardelli Italia

Bernardelli Italia $2200
Same general specifications as Brescia, except higher grade engraving and wood. Discontinued 1986.

**Bernardelli
Roma 6**

Bernardelli Roma 4 and Roma 6
Same as Premier Gamecock (Roma 3), except higher grade engraving and wood, double triggers. Currently manufactured; Roma 6 discontinued 1993.
Roma 4 .... **$1295**
Roma 6 .... **1350**

**Bernardelli
S. Uberto 2**

Bernadelli S. Uberto 2 .... $1095
Same as Standard Gamecock (S. Uberto 1), except higher grade engraving and wood. Currently manufactured.

**Bernardelli
S. Uberto F.S.**

Bernardelli S. Uberto F.S. $1395
Same as Standard Gamecock, except with higher grade engraving, wood and has auto ejectors. Currently manufactured.

**Bernardelli
V.B. Holland Liscio**

Bernardelli V.B. Holland Liscio Deluxe Hammerless Double Barrel Shotgun $6950
Holland & Holland-type sidelock action. Auto ejectors. Double triggers. 12 gauge only. Any barrel length, chokes. Checkered stock (straight or pistol grip) and forearm. Currently manufactured.

BOSS & CO.
London, England

Boss Double Barrel

Boss Hammerless Double Barrel Shotgun

Sidelock. Automatic ejectors. Double triggers, non-selective or selective single trigger. Made in all gauges, barrel

Boss Hammerless Double Barrel Shotgun (cont.)

lengths and chokes. Checkered stock and forend, straight or pistol grip.

W/Double Triggers or Non-sel. Single Trigger . **$19,500**
W/Selective Single Trigger **23,000**

Boss Over-Under

Boss Hammerless Over/Under Shotgun **$33,500**

Sidelock. Automatic ejectors. Selective single trigger. Made in all gauges, barrel lengths and chokes. Checkered stock and forend, straight or pistol grip. Discontinued.

Breda Autoloading Shotgun

ERNESTO BREDA
Milan, Italy

Breda Autoloading Shotgun

Recoil-operated. 12 gauge, 2¾-inch chamber. 4-shell tubular magazine. Barrels: 25½- and 27½-inch; plain, matted or vent rib; IC, M or F choke; current model has 26-inch vent-rib barrel with interchangeable choke tubes. Weight: about 7¼ pounds. Checkered straight or pistol-grip stock and forearm. Discontinued 1988.

W/Plain Barrel **$325**
W/Raised Matted-rib Barrel **375**
W/Ventilated-rib Barrel **395**
W/Vent Rib, Interchangeable Choke Tubes **420**

Breda Magnum

Same general specifications as standard model, except chambered for 12-gauge 3-inch Magnum, 3-shot magazine; latest model has 29-inch vent-rib barrel. Disc. 1988.

W/Plain Barrel **$415**
W/Ventilated-rib Barrel **445**

BRNO SHOTGUNS
Manufactured in Czechoslovakia

Brno 500 Over/Under Shotgun **$595**

Hammerless boxlock with double triggers and ejectors. 12 gauge w/2¾-inch chambers. 27½-inch barrels choked M/F. Weight: 7 pounds. Checkered walnut stock with classic-style cheekpiece.

Brno 500 Series O/U Combination Guns

Similar to the 500 Series over/under shotgun, except lower barrel chambered in rifle calibers.

Model 571 12/6×65R (Disc. 1993) . . . . **$ 795**
Model 572 12/7×65R (Imported since 1992) **855**
Model 584 12/7×57R (Imported since 1992) **795**
Super Series, **add** **100**
Super Series 3-Bbl. Set (Disc. 1991) **1795**

Brno CZ 581 Over/Under Shotgun **$500**

Hammerless boxlock with double triggers, ejectors and automatic safety. 12 gauge w/2¾- or 3-inch chambers. 28-inch barrels choked M/F. Weight: 7½ pounds. Checkered walnut stock.

Brno Super Over/Under Shotgun **$795**

Hammerless sidelock with selective single or double triggers and ejectors. 12 gauge w/2¾- or 3-inch chambers. 27½-inch barrels choked M and F. Weight: 7¼ pounds. Checkered European walnut stock with classic-style cheekpiece.

Brno ZH 300 Series Over/Under Shotguns

Hammerless boxlock with double triggers. Gauge: 12 or 16 w/2¾- or 3-inch chambers. Barrels: 26, 27½ or 30 inches; choked M/F. Weight: 7 pounds. Skip-line checkered walnut stock with classic-style cheekpiece.

Model 300 (Discontinued 1993) **$415**
Model 301 Field (Discontinued 1991) **425**
Model 302 Skeet (Discontinued 1992) **475**
Model 303 Trap (Discontinued 1992) **495**

Brno ZH 300 Series O/U Combination Guns

Similar to the 300 Series over/under shotgun, except lower barrel chambered in rifle calibers.

Model 300 Combo 8-Bbl. Set (Disc. 1991) **$2995**
Model 304 12 Ga./7×57R (Disc. 1995) **525**
Model 305 12 Ga./5.6×52R (Disc. 1993) **595**
Model 306 12 Ga./5.6×50R (Disc. 1993) **625**
Model 307 12 Ga./22 Hornet (Imported since 1995) **550**
Model 324 16 Ga./7×57R (Disc. 1987) **500**

SHOTGUNS

Brno ZP 149 Hammerless Double

Sidelock action with double triggers, automatic ejectors and automatic safety. 12 gauge w/2³/₄- or 3-inch chambers. 28¹/₂-inch barrels choked M/F. Weight: 7¹/₄ pounds.

Brno ZP 149 Hammerless Double (cont.)

Checkered walnut buttstock with cheekpiece.
Standard Model **$465**
Engraved Model **490**

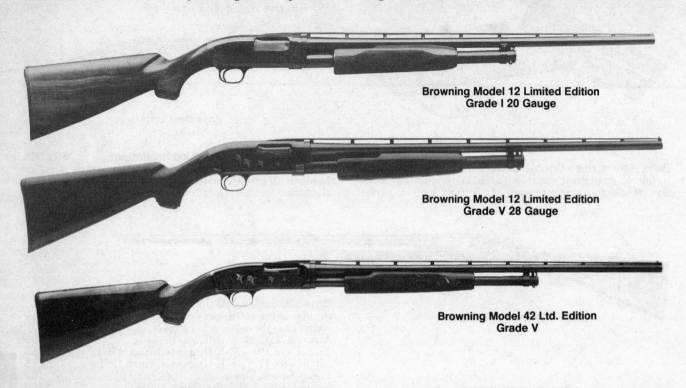

Browning Model 12 Limited Edition Grade I 20 Gauge

Browning Model 12 Limited Edition Grade V 28 Gauge

Browning Model 42 Ltd. Edition Grade V

BROWNING SHOTGUNS
Morgan (formerly Ogden), Utah

Designated "American" Browning because they were produced in Ilion, New York, the following Remington-made Brownings are almost identical to the Remington Model 11A and Sportsman and the Browning Auto-5. They are the only Browning shotguns manufactured in the U.S. during the 20th century and were made for Browning Arms when production was suspended in Belgium because of WW II (see **NOTE** below).

AMERICAN BROWNING SHOTGUNS

American Browning Grade I Autoloader **$450**
Recoil-operated. Gauges: 12, 16, 20. 2- or 4-shell tubular magazine. Plain barrel, 26- to 32-inch, any standard boring. Weight: about 6⁷/₈ (20 ga.) to 8 pounds (12 ga.). Checkered pistol-grip stock and forearm. Made 1940–49.

American Browning Special
Same general specifications as Grade I, except supplied with raised matted rib or vent rib. Discont. 1949.
With raised matted rib **$495**
With ventilated rib............................. **645**

American Browning Special Skeet Model **$595**
Same general specifications as Grade I, except has 26-inch barrel with vent rib and Cutts Compensator. Discontinued in 1949.

American Browning Utility Field Gun **$395**
Same general specifications as Grade I, except has 28-inch plain barrel with Poly Choke. Discontinued in 1949.

NOTE: Fabrique Nationale Herstal (formerly Fabrique Nationale d'Armes de Guerre) of Herstal, Belgium, is the long-time manufacturer of Browning shotguns, dating back to 1900. Miroku Firearms Mfg. Co. of Tokyo, Japan, bought into the Browning company and has, since the early 1970s, undertaken some of the production. The following shotguns were manufactured for Browning by these two firms.

Browning Model 12 Pump Shotgun
Special limited edition Winchester Model 12. Gauge: 20 or 28. Five-shot tubular magazine. 26-inch barrel, M choke. 45 inches overall. Weight: about 7 pounds. Grade I has blued receiver, checkered walnut stock with matte finish. Grade V has engraved receiver, checkered deluxe walnut stock with high-gloss finish. Made 1988–1992.
Grade I, 20 Gauge (8500)..................... **$ 715**
Grade I, 28 Gauge **725**
Grade V, 20 Gauge (4000) **1125**
Grade V, 28 Gauge **1200**

Browning Model 42 Limited Edition Shotgun
Special limited edition Winchester Model 42 pump shotgun. Same general specifications as Model 12, except with smaller frame in .410 gauge and 3-inch chamber. Made 1991–93.
Grade I (6000 produced) .... **$ 650**
Grade V (6000 produced) **1120**

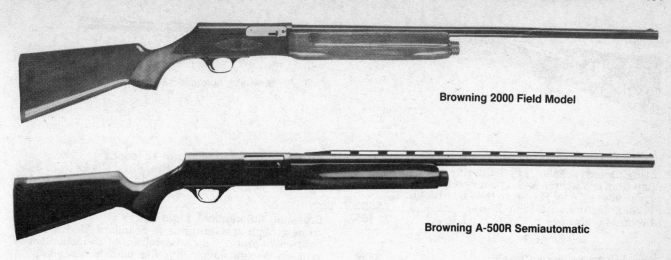

Browning 2000 Field Model

Browning A-500R Semiautomatic

SHOTGUNS

Browning 2000 Buck Special **$395**
Same as Field Model, except has 24-inch plain barrel bored
for rifled slug and buck shot, fitted with rifle sights (open
rear, ramp front). 12 gauge, 2³/₄-inch or 3-inch chamber;
20 gauge, 2³/₄-inch chamber. Weight: 12 ga., 7 lbs. 8 oz.;
20 ga., 6 lbs. 10 oz. Made 1974–1981 by FN.

Browning 2000 Gas Automatic Shotgun, Field Model
Gas-operated. Gauge: 12 or 20. 2³/₄-inch chamber. 4-shot
magazine. Barrel: 26-, 28-, 30-inch; any standard choke;
plain matted barrel (12 ga. only) or vent rib. Weight: 6
lbs. 11 oz.–7 lbs. 12 oz. depending on gauge and barrel
length. Checkered pistol-grip stock/forearm. Made 1974–
1981 by FN.
With Plain Matted Barrel **$425**
With Vent-rib Barrel **495**

Browning 2000 Magnum Model **$410**
Same as Field Model, except chambered for 3-inch shells,
3-shot magazine. Barrel: 26- (20 ga. only), 28-, 30- or 32-
inch (latter two 12 ga. only); any standard choke; vent
rib. Weight: 6 lbs. 11 oz.–7 lbs. 13 oz. depending on gauge
and barrel. Made 1974–1981 by FN.

Browning 2000 Skeet Model **$395**
Same as Field Model, except has skeet-style stock with
recoil pad, 26-inch vent-rib barrel, SK choke. 12 or 20
gauge, 2³/₄-inch chamber. Weight: 8 lbs. 1 oz. (12 ga.); 6
lbs. 12 oz.(20 ga.) Made 1974–1981 by FN.

Browning 2000 Trap Model **$395**
Same as Field Model, except has Monte Carlo stock with
recoil pad, 30- or 32-inch barrel w/high-post vent rib and
receiver extension; M/I/F chokes. 12 gauge, 2³/₄-inch
chamber. Weight: about 8 lbs. 5 oz. Made 1974–1981 by
FN.

Browning A-500G Gas-Operated Semiautomatic
Same general specifications as Browning Model A-500R,
except gas-operated. Made 1990 to date.
Buck Special **$495**
Hunting Model **475**

Browning A-500G Sporting Clays **$495**
Same general specifications as Model A-500G, except has
matte blued receiver with "Sporting Clays" logo. 28- or
30-inch barrel w/Invector choke tubes. Made 1992 to date.

Browning A-500R Semiautomatic
Recoil-operated. Gauge: 12. 26- to 30-inch vent-rib barrels;
24-inch Buck Special. Invector choke tube system. 2³/₄-
or 3-inch Magnum cartridges. Weight: 7 lbs. 3 oz.–8 lbs.
2 oz. Cross-bolt safety. Gold-plated trigger. Scroll-
engraved receiver. Gloss-finished walnut stock and forend.
Made by FN from 1987 to date.
Hunting Model **$455**
Buck Special **495**

Browning Autoloading Shotguns, Grade III and IV
These higher grade models differ from the Standard or
Grade I in general quality, grade of wood, checkering, en-
graving, etc., otherwise specifications are the same. Grade
IV guns, sometimes called Midas Grade, are inlaid with
yellow and green gold. Discontinued in 1940.
Grade III, Plain Barrel **$2300**
Grade IV, Plain Barrel **3700**
For Raised Matte-rib Barrel, **add** **225**
For Vent-rib Barrel, **add** **450**

Browning Automatic-5, Buck Special Models
Same as Light 12, Magnum 12, Light 20, Magnum 20, in
respective gauges, except 24-inch plain barrel bored for

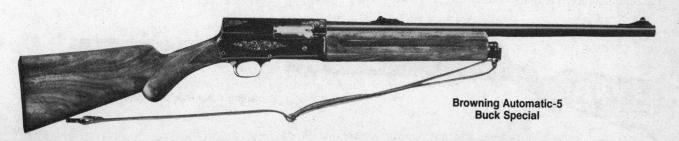

**Browning Automatic-5
Buck Special**

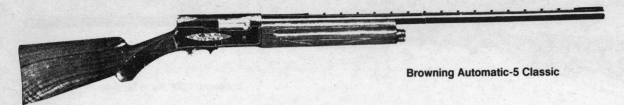

Browning Automatic-5 Classic

Browning Automatic-5, Buck Special Models (cont.)

rifled slug and buckshot, fitted with rifle sights (open rear, ramp front). Weight: 6 1/8–8 1/4 pounds depending on gauge. Made 1964–1976 by FN, since then by Miroku.

FN Manufacture, with Plain Barrel $590
Miroku Manufacture 455

Browning Automatic-5 Classic $850

Gauge: 12. 5-shot capacity. 28-inch vent-rib barrel/M choke. 2 3/4-inch chamber. Engraved silver grey receiver. Gold-plated trigger. Cross-bolt safety. High-grade, hand-checkered select American walnut stock w/rounded pistol grip. 5,000 issued; made in Japan in 1984, engraved in Belgium.

Browning Automatic-5 Gold Classic

Browning Automatic-5 Gold Classic $3495

Same general specifications as Automatic-5 Classic, except engraved receiver inlaid with gold. Pearl border on stock and forend plus fine-line hand-checkering. Each gun numbered "1 of Five Hundred," etc. 500 issued in 1984; made in Belgium.

Browning Automatic-5, Light 12

12 gauge only. Same general specifications as Standard Model, except lightweight (about 7 1/4 pounds), has gold-plated trigger. Guns without rib have striped matting on top of barrel. Fixed chokes or Invector tubes. Made 1948–1976 by FN, since then by Miroku.

FN Manufacture, Plain Barrel $550
FN Manufacture, Raised Matte Rib 625
FN Manufacture, Ventilated Rib 675

Browning Automatic-5, Light 12 (cont.)

Miroku Manufacture, Vent Rib, Fixed Choke $450
Miroku manufacture, Vent Rib, Invectors 495

Browning Automatic-5, Light 20

Same general specifications as Standard Model, except lightweight and 20 gauge. Barrel: 26- or 28-inch; plain or vent rib. Weight: about 6 1/4–6 1/2 pounds depending on barrel. Made 1958–1976 by FN, since then by Miroku.

FN Manufacture, Plain Barrel $545
FN Manufacture, Vent-rib Barrel 595
Miroku Manufacture, Vent Rib, Fixed Choke 415
Miroku Manufacture, Vent Rib, Invectors 475

Browning Automatic-5, Magnum 12 Gauge

Same general specifications as Standard Model. Chambered for 3-inch Magnum 12-gauge shells. Barrel: 28-inch M/F, 30- or 32-inch F/F; plain or vent rib. Weight: 8 1/2–9 pounds depending on barrel. Buttstock has recoil pad. Made 1958–1976 by FN, since then by Miroku. Fixed chokes or Invector tubes.

FN Manufacture, Plain Barrel $635
FN Manufacture, Vent-rib Barrel 680
Miroku Manufacture, Vent Rib, Fixed Chokes ... 435
Miroku Manufacture, Vent Rib, Invectors 495

Browning Automatic-5, Magnum 20 Gauge

Same general specifications as Standard Model, except chambered for 3-inch Magnum 20-gauge shell. Barrel: 26- or 28-inch, plain or vent rib. Weight: 7 lbs. 5 oz.–7 lbs. 7 oz. depending on barrel. Made 1967–1976 by FN, since then by Miroku.

FN Manufacture, Plain Barrel $645
FN Manufacture, Vent-rib Barrel 675
Miroku Manufacture, Vent Rib, Invectors 450

Browning Automatic-5, Skeet Model

12 gauge only. Same general specifications as Light 12. Barrel: 26- or 28-inch, plain or vent rib, SK choke. Weight: 7 lbs. 5 oz.–7 lbs. 10 oz. depending on barrel. Made by FN prior to 1976, since then by Miroku.

FN Manufacture, Plain Barrel $495
FN Manufacture, Vent-rib Barrel 525
Miroku Manufacture, Vent-rib Barrel 395

Browning Automatic-5 Magnum

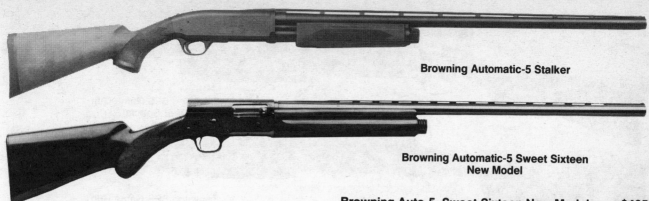

Browning Automatic-5 Stalker

**Browning Automatic-5 Sweet Sixteen
New Model**

Browning Automatic-5 Stalker
Same general specifications as Automatic-5 Light and
Magnum models, except with matte blue finish and black
graphite fiberglass stock and forearm. Made 1992 to date.
Light Model **$495**
Magnum Model **525**

Browning Automatic-5, Standard (Grade I)
Recoil-operated. Gauge: 12 or 16 (16-gauge guns made
prior to WW II were chambered for 2⁹/₁₆-inch shells;
standard 16 discontinued 1964). 4-shell magazine in five-
shot model; prewar guns were also available in three-shot
model. Barrels: 26- to 32-inch; plain, raised matted or vent
rib; choice of standard chokes. Weight: about 8 pounds,
12 ga.; 7¹/₄ pounds, 16 ga. Checkered pistol-grip stock and
forearm. (*Note:* Browning Special, discontinued about
1940, is Grade I gun with either vent or raised matted
rib.) Made 1900–1973 by FN.
Grade I, Plain Barrel **$575**
Grade I or Browning Special, Raised Matted
  Rib **605**
Grade I or Browning Special, Vent Rib **620**

Browning Automatic-5, Sweet 16
16 gauge only. Same general specifications as Standard
Model, except lightweight (about 6³/₄ pounds), has gold-
plated trigger. Guns without rib have striped matting on
top of barrel. Made 1937–1976 by FN.
With Plain Barrel **$650**
With Raised Matted Rib **675**
With Ventilated Rib **795**

Browning Auto-5, Sweet Sixteen New Model . . . $495
Reissue of popular 16-gauge Hunting Model with 5-shot
capacity, 2³/₄-inch chamber, scroll-engraved blued receiver, high-gloss French walnut stock with rounded pistol
grip. 26- or 28-inch vent-rib barrel. Full choke tube.
Weight: 7 lbs. 5 oz. Reintroduced 1987–1993.

Browning Automatic-5, Trap Model $550
12 gauge only. Same general specifications as Standard
Model, except has trap-style stock, 30-inch vent-rib barrel,
full choke. Weight: 8¹/₂ pounds. Discontinued 1971.

Browning Model B-80 Gas-Operated Automatic
Gauge: 12 or 20; 2³/₄-inch chamber. 4-shot magazine. Barrel:
26-, 28- or 30-inch; any standard choke; vent-rib barrel with
fixed chokes or Invector tubes. Weight: 6 lbs. 12 oz.–8 lbs.
1 oz. depending on gauge and barrel. Checkered pistol-grip
stock and forearm. Made 1981–87.
Model B-80 Standard **$395**
Model B-80 Magnum (3-inch Mag.) **425**

Browning Model B-80 Plus $425
Same general specifications as Browning Model B-80, except chambered for 3-inch shotshells. Made in 1988 only.

Browning Model B-80 Superlight $395
Same as Standard Model, except weighs 1 pound less.

Browning Model B-80 Upland Special $405
Gauge: 12 or 20. 22-inch vent-rib barrel. Invector choke
tube system. 2³/₄-inch chambers. 42 inches overall. Weight:
5 lbs. 7 oz. (20 ga.); 6 lbs. 10 oz. (12 ga.). German nickel-
silver sight bead. Cross-bolt safety. Checkered walnut
straight-grip stock and forend. Discontinued 1988.

SHOTGUNS

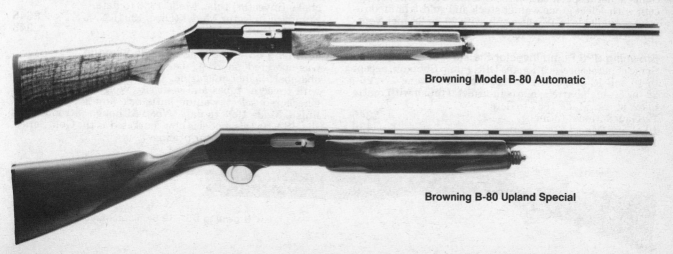

Browning Model B-80 Automatic

Browning B-80 Upland Special

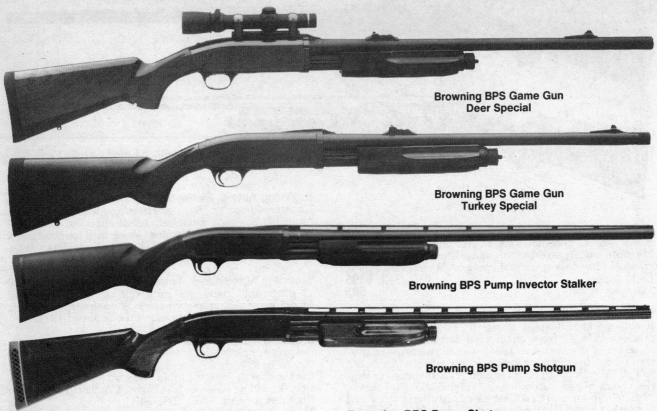

Browning BPS Game Gun Deer Special

Browning BPS Game Gun Turkey Special

Browning BPS Pump Invector Stalker

Browning BPS Pump Shotgun

Browning BPS Game Gun Deer Special **$375**
Same general specifications as Standard BPS Model, except has 20½-inch barrel with adjustable rifle-style sights, solid scope mounting system. Checkered walnut stock with sling swivel studs. Made from 1992 to date.

Browning BPS Game Gun Turkey Special **$360**
Same general specifications as Standard BPS Model, except with matte blue metal finish and satin-finished stock. Gauges: 10, 3½-inch chamber; 12, 3- or 3½-inch. Barrels: 22-, 28-, 30-inch with Extra-Full Invector choke system. Receiver drilled and tapped for scope. Made 1992 to date.

Browning BPS Pigeon Grade **$450**
Same general specifications as Standard BPS Model, except with select grade walnut stock and gold-trimmed receiver. Available in 12 gauge only with 26- or 28-inch vent-rib barrel. Made 1992 to date.

Browning BPS Pump Invector Stalker
Same general specifications as BPS Pump Shotgun, except in 10 and 12 gauge with Invector choke system; 22-, 26-, 28- or 30-inch barrels; matte blue metal finish with matte black stock. Made 1987 to date.
12-Gauge Model (3-inch) **$345**
12-Gauge Model (3½-inch) **435**
10-Gauge Model (3½-inch) **440**

Browning BPS Pump Shotgun
Takedown. Gauges: 10, 12 (3½-inch chamber); 12 or 20 (3-inch); 2¾-inch in 28 gauge and target models. Barrels: 22-, 24-, 26-, 28-, 30-, or 32-inch; fixed choke or Invector tubes. Weight: 7½ lbs. (with 28-inch barrel). Checkered select walnut pistol-grip stock and semibeavertail forearm, recoil pad. Introduced in 1977. Made by Miroku.
Hunting Model (10 or 12 ga., 3½″) **$450**
Hunting, Upland (12 or 20 ga.) **350**
Buck Special (10 or 12 ga., 3½″) **460**
Buck Special (12 or 20 ga.) **350**
With Fixed Choke, **deduct** **50**

Browning BPS Youth and Ladies' Model
Lightweight (6 lbs. 11 oz.) version of BPS Pump Shotgun in 20 gauge with 22-inch barrel and floating vent rib, full choke (invector) tube. Made 1986 to date.
Standard Invector Model (Disc. 1994) **$345**
Invector Plus Model **345**

Browning BSA 10 Semiautomatic Shotgun
Gas-operated short-stroke action. 10 gauge; 3½-inch chamber. 5-shot magazine. Barrels: 26-, 28- or 30-inch with Invector tubes and vent rib. Weight: 10½ pounds. Checkered select walnut buttstock and forend. Blued finish. Made 1993 to date. *Note:* Although introduced as the BSA 10, this model is now marketed as the Gold Series. *See* separate listing for pricing.

Browning BSA 10 Semiautomatic

Browning B-SS 20 Gauge Sporter

Browning BT-99

Browning B-SS Side-by-Side **$650**
Boxlock. Automatic ejectors. Non-selective single trigger. Gauges: 12, 20; 3-inch chambers. Barrels: 26-, 28-, or 30-inch (latter in 12 gauge only); IC/M, M/F, or F/F chokes; matte solid rib. Weight (w/28-inch barrels): 12 ga., 7 lbs. 5 oz.; 20 ga., 7 lbs. Checkered straight-grip stock and beavertail forearm. Made 1972–1987 by Miroku.

Browning B-SS Side-by-Side Sidelock **$1775**
Same general specifications as B-SS boxlock models, except sidelock version available in 26- or 28-inch barrel lengths. 26-inch choked IC/M; 28-inch, M/F. Double triggers. Satin greyed receiver engraved with rosettes and scrolls. German nickel-silver sight bead. Weight: 6 1/4 lbs. to 6 lbs. 11 oz. 12 ga. made in 1983; 20 ga. made in 1984.

Browning B-SS S/S 20 Gauge Sporter **$675**
Same as standard B-SS 20 gauge, except has selective single trigger, straight-grip stock. Introduced 1977. Discontinued 1987.

Browning BT-99 Competition Trap Special
Same as BT-99, except has super-high wide rib and standard, Monte Carlo or fully adjustable stock. Available with fixed choke or Invector Plus tubes with optional porting. Made 1976 to date.
Grade I w/Fixed Choke (Disc. 1992) . . . . **$ 695**
Grade I w/Invectors **850**
Grade I Stainless (Disc. 1994) **895**

Browning BT-99 Grade I Single Barrel Trap **$585**
Boxlock. Automatic ejector. 12 gauge only. 32- or 34-inch vent-rib barrel; M, IM or F choke. Weight: about 8 pounds. Checkered pistol-grip stock and beavertail forearm, recoil pad. Made 1971–76 by Miroku.

Browning BT-99 Plus
Similar to the BT-99 Competition, except with Browning Recoil Reduction System. Made 1989–1995.
Grade I . . . . **$ 995**
Pigeon Grade **1050**

Browning BT-99 Plus (cont.)
Signature Grade **$1025**
Stainless Model **1095**
Golden Clays **2195**

Browning BT-99 Plus Micro **$1095**
Same general specifications as BT-99 Plus, except scaled down for smaller shooters. 30-inch barrel with adjustable rib and Browning's recoil reducer system. Made 1991 to date.

Browning Citori Hunting Over/Under Models . . . **$795**
Boxlock. Gauges: 12, 16, 20, 28 and .410. Barrel lengths: 24-, 26-, 28-, or 30-inch with vent rib. Chokes: M/F or invector (30-inch bbl.); invector, M/F or IC/M (other bbl. lengths). Overall length ranges from 41–47 inches. 2 1/2-, 3- or 3-inch Mag. loads, depending on gauge. Weight: 5 3/4 lbs. to 7 lbs. 13 oz. Single selective, gold-plated trigger. Medium raised German nickel-silver sight bead. Checkered, rounded pistol-grip walnut stock with beavertail forend. Prices vary with the different grades. Made from 1973 to date by Miroku.

Browning Citori Lightning O/U Models
Same general specifications as the Citori Hunting Models, except with classic Browning rounded pistol-grip stock.
Grade I . . . . **$ 625**
Grade III **950**
Grade VI **1350**

Browning Citori Skeet Gun
Same as Hunting Model, except has skeet-style stock and forearm, 26- or 28-inch barrels, both bored SK choke. Available with either standard vent rib or special target-type, high-post, wide vent rib. Weight (with 26-inch barrels): 12 ga., 8 pounds; 20 ga., 7 pounds. Made 1974 to date by Miroku
Grade I . . . . **$ 795**
Grade III **950**
Grade VI **1495**
4-Barrel Set, Grade I **2795**
4-Barrel Set, Grade III **3190**
4-Barrel Set, Grade VI **3575**

SHOTGUNS

**Browning Citori O/U
Hunting Model**

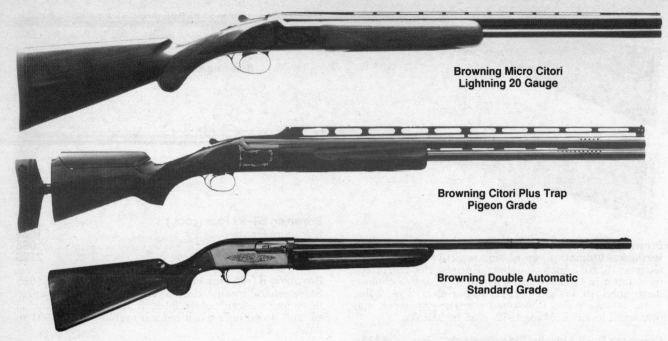

**Browning Micro Citori
Lightning 20 Gauge**

**Browning Citori Plus Trap
Pigeon Grade**

**Browning Double Automatic
Standard Grade**

Browning Citori Sporting Clays

Same general specifications as Hunting Model, except engraved, with gold-filled logos identifying each model.

Model 325 Grade II (Disc. 1994)	**$950**
Model 425 Grade I	975
GTI Model (Discontinued 1995)	825
Lightning Model	850
Micro Citori Lightning Model (w/Low Rib)	825
Special Model	850
Ultra Model (previously GTI)	925
For Golden Grade, **add**	900
For Pigeon Grade, **add**	100
For Two-barrel Set, **add**	850
For Adjustable Stock, **add**	200
For High Rib **add**	80
For Ported Barrels **add**	55

Browning Citori Superlight O/U Shotguns

Similar to the Citori Hunting Model, except with straight-grip stock and schnabel forend tip. Made by Miroku 1982 to date.

Grade I, Fixed Choke	**$ 695**
Grade I, Invector	725
Grade III, 12 and 20 ga.	995
Grade III, 28 and .410 ga.	1195
Grade VI, 12 and 20 ga.	1395
Grade VI, 28 and .410 ga.	1695

Browning Citori Trap Gun

Same as Hunting Model, except 12 gauge only, has Monte Carlo or fully adjustable stock and beavertail forearm, trap-style recoil pad; 30- or 32-inch barrels; M/F, IM/F,

Browning Citori Trap Gun (cont.)

or F/F. Available with either standard vent rib or special target-type, high-post, wide vent rib. Weight: 8 pounds. Made from 1974 to date by Miroku.

Citori Plus Trap	**$1025**
Citori Plus Trap w/ported barrel	1095
Grade I	975
Grade III	1095
Grade VI	1450

Browning Citori Upland Special O/U Shotgun $725

A shortened version of the Hunting Model, fitted with 24-inch barrels and straight-grip stock.

Browning Double Automatic, Standard Grade (Steel Receiver)

Short recoil system. Takedown. 12 gauge only. Two shots. Barrels: 26-, 28-, 30-inch; any standard choke. Checkered pistol-grip stock and forearm. Weight: about 7¾ pounds. Made 1955–1961.

With plain barrel	**$465**
With recessed-rib barrel	590

Browning Gold Series Autoloading Shotguns

Self-cleaning, gas-operated, short-stroke action. Gauges: 10 (3.5-inch chamber); 12 or 20 (3-inch). 26-, 28- or 30-inch barrel w/Invector or Invector Plus choke tubes. Checkered walnut or graphite/fiberglass composite stock. Polished or matte black metal finish. Made 1994 to date.

Gold Hunter Model w/Walnut Stock	**$425**
Gold Stalker Model w/Composite Stock	450
Gold 10 Hunter w/Walnut Stock	695
Gold 10 Stalker w/Composite Stock	725

Browning Gold Hunter (12 Ga.)

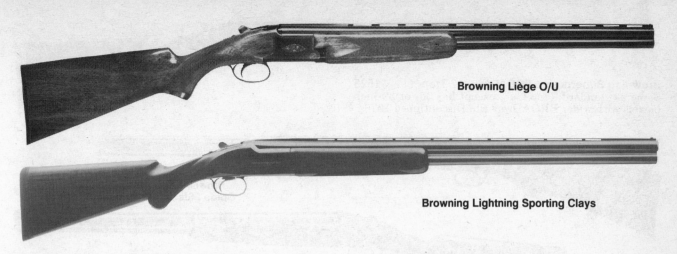

Browning Liège O/U

Browning Lightning Sporting Clays

Browning Liège Over/Under Shotgun $725
Boxlock. Automatic ejectors. Non-selective single trigger. 12 gauge only. Barrels: 26½-, 28-, or 30-inch; 2¾-inch chambers in 26½- and 28-inch, 3-inch in 30-inch; IC/M, M/F, or F/F chokes; vent rib. Weight: 7 lbs. 4 oz. to 7 lbs. 14 oz., depending on barrels. Checkered pistol-grip stock and forearm. Made 1973–75 by FN.

Browning Lightning Sporting Clays
Similar to the standard Citori Lightning Model, except Classic-style stock with rounded pistol grip. 30-inch back-bored barrels with Invector Plus tubes. Receiver with "Lightning Sporting Clays Edition" logo. Made 1989 to date.
Standard Model **$895**
Pigeon Grade **975**

Browning Over/Under Classic $1650
Gauge: 20, 2¾-inch chambers. 26-inch blued barrels choked IC/M. Gold-plated, single selective trigger. Manual, top-tang-mounted safety. Engraved receiver. High-grade, select American walnut straight-grip stock with schnabel forend. Fine-line checkering with pearl borders. High-gloss finish. 5,000 issued in 1986; made in Japan, engraved in Belgium.

Browning Over/Under
Gold Classic

Browning Over/Under Gold Classic $3995
Same general specifications as Over/Under Classic, except more elaborate engravings, enhanced in gold, including profile of John M. Browning. Fine oil finish. 500 issued; made in 1986 in Belgium.

Browning Recoilless Trap Shotgun
The action and barrel are driven forward when firing to achieve 70 percent less recoil. 12 gauge; 2¾-inch chamber. 30-inch barrel with Invector Plus tubes; adjustable vent rib. 51⅝ inches overall. Weight: 9 pounds. Adjustable checkered walnut buttstock and forend. Blued finish. Made from 1993 to date.
Standard Model **$1200**
Micro Model (27-inch bbl.) **1250**

Browning Superposed Bicentennial (Left Side)

Browning Superposed Bicentennial (Right Side)

Browning Superposed Bicentennial
Commemorative $12,950
Special limited edition issued to commemorate U.S. Bicentennial. 51 guns, one for each state in the Union plus one for Washington, D.C. Receiver with sideplates has engraved and gold-inlaid hunter and wild turkey on right side, U.S. flag and bald eagle on left side, together with state markings inlaid in gold, on blued background. Checkered straight-grip stock and schnabel-style forearm of highly figured American walnut. Velvet-lined wooden presentation case. Made in 1976 by FN. Value shown is for gun in new, unfired condition.

SHOTGUNS

Browning Superposed BROADway 12 Trap . . . **$1525**
Same as standard Trap Gun, except has 30- or 32-inch
barrels with wider BROADway rib. Discontinued 1976.

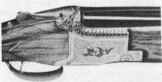

**Browning Superposed
Grade I Standard (Prewar)**

**Browning Superposed
Grade I Lightning (Prewar)**

**Pigeon Grade
(Prewar)**

**Diana Grade
(Prewar)**

**Midas Grade
(Prewar)**

Browning Superposed Hunting Models (cont.)

Pointer Grade discontinued in 1966, Grade I Standard in
1973, Pigeon Grade in 1974. Lightning Grade I, Diana
and Midas Grades were not offered after 1976.

Grade I Standard	**$1150**
Grade I Lightning.	1425
Grade I Lightning, prewar, matted bbl., no rib . .	2000
Grade II—Pigeon	2495
Grade III—Pointer	2950
Grade IV—Diana	3795
Grade V—Midas	4650
Grade VI	6295
Add for 28 or .410 gauge	995
Values shown are for models with ventilated rib, if gun has raised matted rib, *deduct*	200

Reissue

**Grade II Pigeon
(Postwar)**

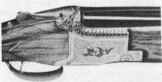

**Grade III Pointer
(Postwar)**

**Grade IV Diana
(Postwar)**

**Grade V Midas
(Postwar)**

Browning Superposed Shotguns, Hunting Models

Over/under boxlock. Selective automatic ejectors. Selective single trigger; earlier models (worth 25% less) supplied
with double triggers, twin selective triggers or non-selective single trigger. Gauges: 12, 20 (intro. 1949, 3-inch
chambers in later production), 28, .410 (latter two gauges
intro. 1960). Barrels: 26½-, 28-, 30-, 32-inch; raised matted
or vent rib; prewar Lightning Model made without ribbed
barrel, postwar version supplied only with vent rib; any
combination of standard chokes. Weight (w/26½-inch
vent-rib barrels): *Standard 12,* 7 lbs. 11 oz.; *Lightning 12,*
7 lbs. 6 oz.; *Standard 20,* 6 lbs. 8 oz.; *Lightning 20,* 6 lbs.
4 oz.; *Lightning 28,* 6 lbs. 7 oz.; *Lightning .410,* 6 lbs. 10
oz. Checkered pistol-grip stock/forearm.

Higher grades—Pigeon, Pointer, Diana, Midas, Grade
VI—differ from standard Grade I models in overall quality,
engraving, wood and checkering; otherwise, specifications
are the same. Midas Grade and Grade VI guns are richly
gold-inlaid. Made by FN 1928–1976. Prewar models may
be considered as discontinued in 1940 when Belgium was
occupied by Germany. Grade VI offered 1955–1960.

**Browning Superposed Ltd. Pintail
Duck Issue**

Browning Superposed Lightning and Superlight Models (Reissue)

Reissue of popular 12-and 20-gauge superposed shotguns. Lightning models available in 26¹/₂- and 28-inch barrel lengths with 2³/₄- or 3-inch chambering, full pistol grip. Superlight models available in 26¹/₂-inch barrel lengths with 2³/₄-inch chambering only, and straight-grip stock with schnabel forend. Both have hand-engraved receivers, fine-line checkering, gold-plated single selective trigger, automatic selective ejectors, manual safety. Weight: 6 to 7¹/₂ pounds. Reintroduced 1985–86.

Grade II, Pigeon	**$2595**
Grade III, Pointer	**2995**
Grade IV, Diana	**3195**
Grade V, Midas	**4195**

Browning Superposed Magnum **$1350**
Same as Grade I, except chambered for 12-gauge 3-inch shells, 30-inch vent-rib barrels, stock with recoil pad. Weight: about 8¹/₄ pounds. Discontinued 1976.

Browning Superposed Ltd. Black Duck Issue . . **$4600**
Gauge: 12. Superposed Lightning action. 28-inch vent-rib barrels. Choked M/F. 2³/₄-inch chambers. Weight: 7 lbs. 6 oz. Gold inlaid receiver and trigger guard engraved with Black Duck scenes. Gold-plated, single selective trigger. Top-tang mounted manual safety. Automatic, selective ejectors. Front and center ivory sights. High-grade, hand-checkered, hand-oiled select walnut stock and forend. 500 issued in 1983.

Browning Superposed Ltd. Mallard Duck Issue **$4650**
Same general specifications as Ltd. Black Duck Issue, except Mallard Duck scenes engraved on receiver and trigger guard; dark French walnut stock with rounded pistol grip. 500 issued in 1981.

Browning Superposed Ltd. Pintail Duck Issue . **$4650**
Same general specifications as Ltd. Black Duck Issue, except Pintail Duck scenes engraved on receiver and trigger guard; stock is of dark French walnut with rounded pistol grip. 500 issued in 1982.

Browning Superposed, Presentation Grades

Custom versions of Super-Light, Lightning Hunting, Trap and Skeet Models, with same general specifications as those of standard guns, but of higher overall quality. The four Presentation Grades differ in receiver finish (greyed or blued), engraving, gold inlays, wood and checkering; Presentation 4 has sideplates. Made by FN, these models were introduced in 1977.

Presentation 1	**$3200**
Presentation 1, gold-inlaid	**3600**
Presentation 2	**3800**
Presentation 2, gold-inlaid	**4600**
Presentation 3, gold-inlaid	**5520**
Presentation 4	**6500**
Presentation 4, gold-inlaid	**7500**

Browning Superposed Skeet Guns, Grade I
Same as standard Lightning 12, 20, 28 and .410 Hunting Models, except has skeet-style stock and forearm, 26¹/₂- or 28-inch vent-rib barrels with SK choke. Available also in All Gauge Skeet Set: Lightning 12 with one removable forearm and three extra sets of barrels in 20, 28 and .410 gauge in fitted luggage case. Discontinued 1976.

12 or 20 gauge	**$1495**
28 or .410 gauge	**1795**
All Gauge Skeet Set	**4250**

Browning Superposed Super-Light Model **$1425**
Ultralight field gun version of Standard Lightning Model has classic straight-grip stock and slimmer forearm. Available only in 12 and 20 gauges (2³/₄-inch chambers), with 26¹/₂-inch vent-rib barrels. Weight: 6¹/₂ pounds, 12 ga.; 6 pounds, 20 ga. Made 1967–1976.

Browning Superposed Trap Gun **$1475**
Same as Grade I, except has trap-style stock, beavertail forearm, 30-inch vent-rib barrels, 12 gauge only. Discont. 1976.

Browning Choke Marks. The following markings are used to indicate chokes on Browning shotguns:

Full *	Improved Cylinder **—
Improved Modified *—	Skeet **S
Modified **	Cylinder ***

SHOTGUNS

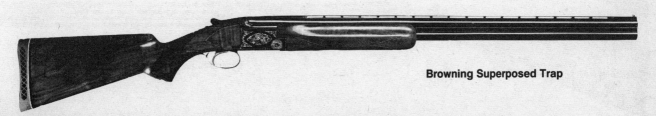

Browning Superposed Trap

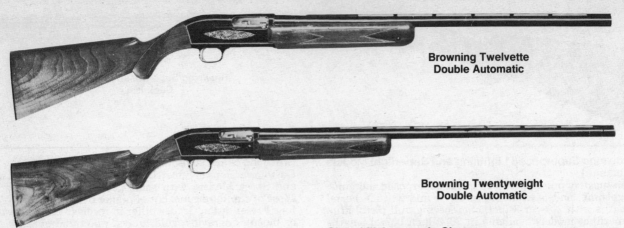

**Browning Twelvette
Double Automatic**

**Browning Twentyweight
Double Automatic**

Browning Twelvette Double Automatic
Lightweight version of Double Automatic with same general specifications except aluminum receiver. Barrel with plain matted top or vent rib. Weight: 6¾ to 7 pounds, depending on barrel. Receiver is finished in black w/gold engraving; 1956–1961 receivers were also anodized in grey, brown and green w/silver engraving. Made 1955–1971.
With Plain Barrel **$425**
With Vent-rib Barrel **525**

Browning Twentyweight Double Automatic
Same as Twelvette, but ¾ pound lighter. 26½-inch barrel only. Made 1956–1971.
With Plain Barrel **$450**
With Vent-rib Barrel **595**

=== **CHURCHILL SHOTGUNS** ===
Italy and Spain
**Imported by Ellett Brothers, Inc., Chapin, SC;
previously by Kassnar Imports, Inc., Harrisburg, PA**

Churchill Automatic Shotgun
Gas-operated. Gauge: 12, 2¾- or 3-inch. 5-shot magazine with cut-off. Barrel: 24-, 25-, 26-, 28-inch with ICT Choke tubes. Checkered walnut stock with satin finish. Made 1990–1994.
Standard Model **$425**
Turkey Model **450**

Churchill Monarch Over/Under Shotgun
Hammerless, takedown with engraved receiver. Selective single or double triggers. Gauges: 12, 20, 28, .410; 3-inch chambers. Barrels: 25- or 26-inch (IC/M); 28-inch (M/F). Weight: 6½–7½ pounds. Checkered European walnut buttstock and forend. Made in Italy 1986–1993.
With Double Triggers **$350**
With Single Trigger **425**

Churchill Regent Over/Under Shotguns
Gauges: 12 or 20; 2¾-inch chambers. 27-inch barrels w/ interchangeable choke tubes and wide vent rib. Single selective trigger, selective automatic ejectors. Checkered pistol-grip stock in fancy walnut. Imported from Italy 1984–88.
Regent V **$825**
Regent VII w/Sideplates **950**

Churchill Automatic Shotgun

Churchill Monarch O/U

Churchill Regent VII w/Sideplates

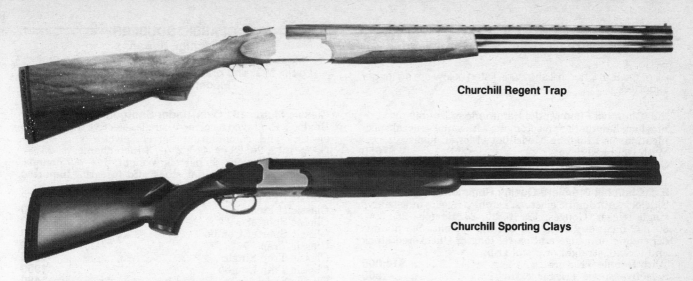

Churchill Regent Trap

Churchill Sporting Clays

Churchill Regent Side-by-Side Shotguns

12 gauge s/s. 25-, 27- or 28-inch barrels w/fixed choke or interchangeable choke tubes. Double triggers. Automatic top tang safety. Double safety sidelock, engraved antique silver receiver. Automatic selective ejectors. Oil-finished English-style stock of extra select European walnut. Imported from Spain 1984–1993.

Regent Standard	**$650**
Regent VI, Sidelock	**795**

Churchill Regent Skeet **$695**

12 or 20 gauge with 2³/₄-inch chambers. Selective automatic ejectors, single-selective trigger. 26-inch over/under barrels w/vent rib. Weight: 7 lbs. Made in Italy 1984–88.

Churchill Regent Trap **$685**

12-gauge competition shotgun w/2³/₄-inch chambers. 30-inch over/under barrels choked IM/F, vent side ribs. Weight: 8 pounds. Selective automatic ejectors, single-selective trigger. Checkered Monte Carlo stock with Supercushion recoil pad. Made in Italy 1984–88.

Churchill Sporting Clays Over/Under **$695**

Same general specifications as Windsor IV, except in 12 gauge only with 28-inch ported barrels and choke tubes. Selective automatic ejectors. Weight: 7¹/₂ pounds. Made from 1992–94.

Churchill Windsor Over/Under Shotguns

Hammerless, boxlock with engraved receiver, selective single trigger. Extractors or ejectors. Gauges: 12, 20, 28 or .410; 3-inch chambers. Barrels: 24 to 30 inches with fixed chokes or choke tubes. Weight: 6 lbs. 3 oz. (Flyweight) to 7 lbs. 10 oz. (12 ga.). Checkered straight (Flyweight) or pistol-grip stock and forend of European walnut. Imported from Italy 1984–1993.

Windsor III w/Fixed Chokes	**$500**
Windsor III w/Choke Tubes	**565**
Windsor IV w/Fixed Chokes (Disc. 1993)	**545**
Windsor IV w/Choke Tubes	**695**

Churchill Windsor Side-by-Side Shotguns

Boxlock action with double triggers, ejectors or extractors and automatic safety. Gauges: 10, (3¹/₂-inch chambers); 12, 20, 28, .410 (3-inch chambers); 16 (2³/₄-inch chambers). Barrels: 23 to 32 inches with various fixed choke or choke tube combinations. Weight: 5 lbs. 12 oz. (Flyweight) to 11¹/₂ lbs. (10 ga.). European walnut buttstock and forend. Imported from Spain 1984–1990.

Windsor I 10 ga.	**$550**
Windsor I 12 thru .410 ga.	**465**
Windsor II 12 or 20 ga.	**450**

SHOTGUNS

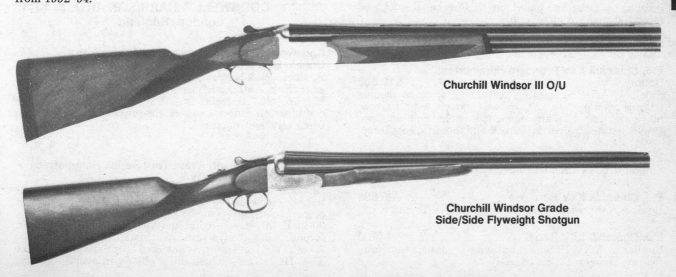

Churchill Windsor III O/U

**Churchill Windsor Grade
Side/Side Flyweight Shotgun**

E.J. CHURCHILL, LTD.
Surrey (previously London), England

All of the E.J. Churchill shotguns listed below are no longer imported.

E.J. Churchill Field Model Hammerless Double
Sidelock hammerless ejector gun with same general specifications as Premiere Model but of lower quality.
With Double Triggers **$7850**
Selective Single Trigger, **add** **400**

E.J. Churchill Premiere Quality Hammerless Double
Sidelock. Automatic ejectors. Double triggers or selective single trigger. Gauges: 12, 16, 20, 28. Barrels: 25-, 28-, 30-, 32-inch; any degree of boring. Weight: 5–8 pounds depending on gauge and barrel length. Checkered stock and forend, straight or pistol grip.
With Double Triggers **$14,000**
Selective Single Trigger, extra **900**

E.J. Churchill Premiere

E.J. Churchill Premiere Quality Under-and-Over Shotgun
Sidelock. Automatic ejectors. Double triggers or selective single trigger. Gauges: 12, 16, 20, 28. Barrels: 25-, 28-, 30-, 32-inch; any degree of boring. Weight: 5–8 pounds depending on gauge and barrel length. Checkered stock and forend, straight or pistol grip.
With Double Triggers **$14,995**
Selective Single Trigger, **add** **700**
Raised Vent Rib, **add** **400**

E.J. Churchill Utility Model Hammerless Double Barrel
Anson & Deeley boxlock action. Double triggers or single trigger. Gauges: 12, 16, 20, 28, .410. Barrels: 25-, 28-, 30-, 32-inch; any degree of boring. Weight: 4½–8 pounds depending on gauge and barrel length. Checkered stock and forend, straight or pistol grip.
With Double Triggers **$4125**
Selective Single Trigger, **add** **400**

E.J. Churchill XXV Premiere Hammerless
Double **$12,500**
Sidelock. Assisted opening. Automatic ejectors. Double triggers. Gauges: 12, 20. 25-inch barrels with narrow, quick-sighting rib; any standard choke combination. English-style straight-grip stock and forearm, checkered.

E.J. Churchill XXV Imperial **$9750**
Similar to XXV Premiere, but no assisted opening feature.

E.J. Churchill XXV Hercules **$7695**
Boxlock, otherwise specs same as for XXV Premiere.

E.J. Churchill XXV Regal **$4200**
Similar to XXV Hercules, but without assisted opening feature. Gauges: 12, 20, 28, .410.

CLASSIC DOUBLES
Tochigi, Japan
Imported by Classic Doubles International, St. Louis, MO, and previously by Olin as Winchester Models 101 and 23.

Classic Model 101 Over/Under Shotgun
Boxlock. Engraved receiver w/single selective trigger, auto ejectors and combination barrel selector and safety. Gauges: 12, 20, 28 or .410; 2¾-, 3-inch chambers. 25½-, 28- or 30-inch vent-rib barrels. Weight: 6¼–7¾ pounds. Checkered French walnut stock and forearm. Imported 1987–1990.
Classic I Field **$1295**
Classic II Field **1500**
Classic Sporter **1550**
Classic Sporter Combo **2450**
Classic Trap **1200**
Classic Trap Single **1295**
Classic Trap Combo **1950**
Classic Skeet **1450**
Classic Skeet 4-Bbl. Set **3795**
Classic Waterfowler **1095**
For Grade II (28 Ga.), **add** **750**
For Grade II (.410 Ga.), **add** **250**

Classic Model 201 Side-by-Side Shotgun
Boxlock. Single selective trigger, automatic safety and selective ejectors. Gauges: 12 or 20; 3-inch chambers. 26- or 28-inch vent-rib barrel; fixed chokes or internal tubes. Weight: 6 to 7 pounds. Checkered French walnut stock and forearm. Imported 1987–1990.
Field Model **$1295**
Skeet Model **1595**
For Internal Choke Tubes, **add** **100**

Classic Model 201 Small Bore Set **$3795**
Same general specifications as the Classic Model 201, except with smaller frame, in 28 gauge (IC/M) and .410 (F/M). Weight: 6–6½ lbs. Imported 1987–1990.

COGSWELL & HARRISON, LTD.
London, England

Cogswell & Harrison Ambassador Hammerless
Double Barrel Shotgun **$3195**
Boxlock. Sideplates with game scene or rose scroll engraving. Automatic ejectors. Double triggers. Gauges: 12, 16, 20. Barrels: 26-, 28-, 30-inch; any choke combination. Checkered straight-grip stock and forearm. Currently manufactured.

Cogswell & Harrison Avant Tout Series Hammerless Double Barrel Shotguns
Boxlock. Sideplates (except Avant Tout III Grade). Automatic ejectors. Double triggers or single trigger (selective or non-selective). Gauges: 12, 16, 20. Barrels: 25-, 27½-, 30-inch; any choke combination. Checkered stock and forend, straight grip standard. Made in three models— Avant Tout I or Konor, Avant Tout II or Sandhurst, Avant Tout III or Rex—which differ chiefly in overall quality,

Cogswell & Harrison Avant Tout Series (cont.)

engraving, grade of wood, checkering, etc.; general specifications are the same. Discontinued.

Avant Tout I	$2410
Avant Tout II	2325
Avant Tout III	1915
Single Trigger, Non-selective, **add**	225
Single Trigger, Selective, **add**	300

**Cogswell & Harrison Best Quality
Hammerless—Victor Model**

Cogswell & Harrison Best Quality Hammerless Sidelock Double Barrel Shotgun

Hand-detachable locks. Automatic ejectors. Double triggers or single trigger (selective or non-selective). Gauges: 12, 16, 20. Barrels: 25-, 26-, 28-, 30-inch; any choke combination. Checkered stock and forend, straight grip standard. Made in two models: Victor (currently manufactured) and Primic (with plainer finish, discontinued), otherwise the same.

Victor Model	$6795
Primic Model	4350
Single Trigger, Non-selective, **add**	225
Single Trigger, Selective, **add**	300

Cogswell & Harrison Huntic Model Hammerless Double

Sidelock. Automatic ejectors. Double triggers or single trigger (selective or non-selective). Gauges: 12, 16, 20. Barrels: 25-, 27$\frac{1}{2}$-, 30-inch; any choke combination. Checkered stock and forend, straight grip standard. Discontinued.

With Double Triggers	$3200
Single Trigger, Non-selective, **add**	225
Single Trigger, Selective, **add**	300

Cogswell & Harrison Markor Hammerless Double

Boxlock. Non-ejector or ejector. Double triggers. Gauges: 12, 16, 20. Barrels: 27$\frac{1}{2}$- or 30-inch; any choke combination. Checkered stock and forend, straight grip standard. Discontinued.

Non-ejector Model	$1295
Ejector Model	1695

Cogswell & Harrison Regency

Cogswell & Harrison Regency Hammerless Double $2550

Anson & Deeley boxlock action. Automatic ejectors. Double triggers. Gauges: 12, 16, 20. Barrels: 26-, 28-, 30-inch; any choke combination. Checkered straight-grip stock and forearm. Introduced in 1970 to commemorate the firm's bicentenary, this model has deep scroll engraving and the name "Regency" inlaid in gold on the rib. Currently manufactured.

**Colt Auto Shotgun—
Ultra Light Standard**

=== COLT INDUSTRIES ===
Hartford, Connecticut

Colt Auto Shotguns were made by Luigi Franchi S.p.A. and are similar to corresponding models of that manufacturer.

Colt Auto Shotgun—Magnum

Same as Standard Auto, except steel receiver, handles 3-inch Magnum shells, 30- and 32-inch barrels in 12 gauge, 28-inch in 20 gauge. Weight: 12 ga., about 8$\frac{1}{4}$ pounds. Made 1964–66.

With Plain Barrel	$345
With Solid-rib Barrel	375
With Ventilated-rib Barrel	395

Colt Auto Shotgun—Magnum Custom

Same as Magnum, except has engraved receiver, select walnut stock and forearm. Made 1964–66.

Colt Auto Shotgun—Magnum Custom (cont.)

With Solid-rib Barrel	$425
With Ventilated-rib Barrel	475

Colt Auto Shotgun—Ultra Light Custom

Same as Standard Auto, except has engraved receiver, select walnut stock and forearm. Made 1964–66.

With Solid-rib Barrel	$350
With Ventilated-rib Barrel	375

Colt Auto Shotgun—Ultra Light Standard

Recoil-operated. Takedown. Alloy receiver. Gauges: 12, 20. Magazine holds 4 shells. Barrels: plain, solid or vent rib; chrome-lined; 26-inch IC or M choke, 28-inch M or F choke, 30-inch F choke, 32-inch F choke. Weight: 12 ga., about 6$\frac{1}{4}$ pounds. Checkered pistol-grip stock and forearm. Made 1964–66.

With Plain Barrel	$245
With Solid-rib Barrel	275
With Vent-rib Barrel	295

SHOTGUNS

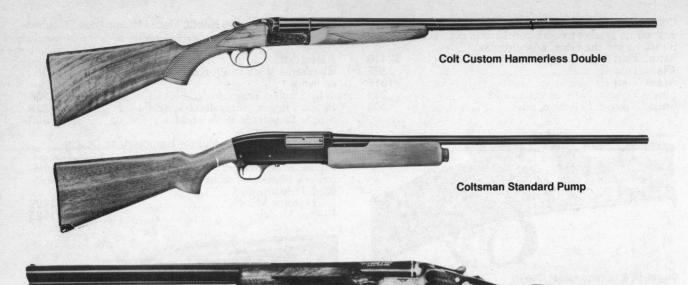

Colt Custom Hammerless Double

Coltsman Standard Pump

Colt-Sauer Drilling

Colt Custom Hammerless Double **$575**
Boxlock. Double triggers. Auto ejectors. Gauges: 12 Mag.,
16. Barrels: 26-inch IC/M; 28-inch M/F; 30-inch F/F.
Weight: 12 ga., about 7¹/₂ pounds. Checkered pistol-grip
stock and beavertail forearm. Made in 1961.

Coltsman Custom Pump **$320**
Same as Standard Pump except has checkered stock, vent-
rib barrel. Weight: about 6¹/₂ pounds. Made 1961–63.

Coltsman Standard Pump Shotgun **$295**
Takedown. Gauges: 12, 16, 20. Magazine holds 4 shells.
Barrels: 26-inch IC; 28-inch M or F choke; 30-inch F
choke. Weight: about 6 pounds. Plain pistol-grip stock
and forearm. Made 1961–65 by Manufrance.

Colt-Sauer Drilling **$3195**
Three-barrel combination gun. Boxlock. Set rifle trigger.
Tang barrel selector, automatic rear sight positioner. 12
gauge over 30-06 or 243 rifle barrel. 25-inch barrels, F and
M choke. Weight: about 8 pounds. Folding leaf rear sight,

Colt-Sauer Drilling (cont.)
blade front with brass bead. Checkered pistol-grip stock
and beavertail forearm, recoil pad. Made 1974 to date by
J. P. Sauer & Sohn, Eckernförde, Germany.

CONNECTICUT VALLEY CLASSICS
Westport, Connecticut

CVC Classic Field Waterfowler **$1495**
Similar to the standard Classic Sporter Model, except with
30-inch barrels only and non-reflective matte blued finish.
Made 1993 to date.

CVC Classic Sporter Over/Under
Gauge: 12; 3-inch chamber. Barrels: 28-, 30- or 32-inch
with screw-in tubes. Weight: 7³/₄ pounds. Engraved stain-

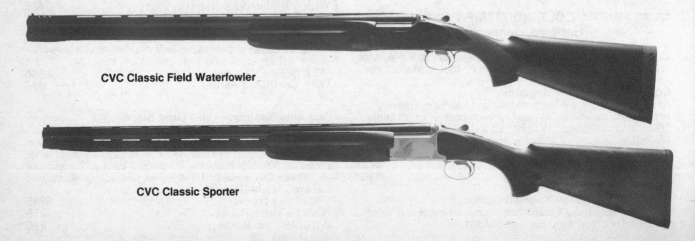

CVC Classic Field Waterfowler

CVC Classic Sporter

SHOTGUNS

CVC Classic Sporter Over/Under (cont.)

less or nitrided receiver; blued barrels. Checkered American black walnut buttstock and forend with low-luster satin finish. Made from 1993 to date.

Classic Sporter **$1595**
Stainless Classic Sporter **1895**

CHARLES DALY, INC.
New York, New York

The pre-WWII Charles Daly shotguns, with the exception of the Commander, were manufactured by various firms in Suhl, Germany. The postwar guns, except for the Novamatic series and the current models distributed by Outdoor Sports Headquarters, were produced by Miroku Firearms Mfg. Co., Tokyo.

Charles Daly Commander Over/Under Shotgun

Daly pattern Anson & Deeley system boxlock action. Automatic ejectors. Double triggers or Miller selective single trigger. Gauges: 12, 16, 20, 28, .410. Barrels: 26- to 30-inch, IC/M or M/F choke. Weight: 5¼ to 7¼ pounds depending on gauge and barrel length. Checkered stock and forend, straight or pistol grip. The two models, 100 and 200, differ in general quality, grade of wood, checkering, engraving, etc.; otherwise specs are the same. Made in Belgium c. 1939.

Model 100 . . . . **$420**
Model 200 . . . . **550**
Miller Single Trigger, **add** **100**

Daly Hammerless Double—
Diamond Quality

Daly Hammerless Double—
Regent Diamond

Daly Hammerless Double—
Superior Quality

Charles Daly Hammerless Double Barrel Shotgun

Daly pattern Anson & Deeley system boxlock action. Automatic ejectors—except "Superior Quality" is non-ejector. Double triggers. Gauges: 10, 12, 16, 20, 28, .410. Barrels: 26- to 32-inch, any combination of chokes. Weight: from 4 pounds to 8½ pounds depending on gauge and barrel length. Checkered pistol-grip stock and forend. The four grades—Regent Diamond, Diamond, Empire, Superior—differ in general quality, grade of wood, checkering, engraving, etc.; otherwise specifications are the same. Discontinued about 1933.

Diamond Quality **$7995**
Empire Quality **3595**
Regent Diamond Quality **9750**
Superior Quality **895**

Charles Daly Hammerless Drilling (Three Barrel Gun)

Daly pattern Anson & Deeley system boxlock action. Plain extractors. Double triggers, front single set for rifle barrel. Gauges: 12, 16, 20, 25-20, 25-35, 30-30 rifle barrel. Supplied in various barrel lengths and weights. Checkered pistol-grip stock and forend. Auto rear sight operated by rifle barrel selector. The three grades—Regent Diamond, Diamond, Superior—differ in general quality, grade of wood, checkering, engraving, etc.; otherwise, specs are the same. Discont. about 1933.

Diamond Quality **$4595**
Regent Diamond Quality **8550**
Superior Quality **2495**

Daly Hammerless—Empire Grade

Charles Daly Hammerless Double—
Empire Grade **$545**

Boxlock. Plain extractors. Non-selective single trigger. Gauges: 12, 16, 20; 3-inch chambers in 12 and 20, 2¾-

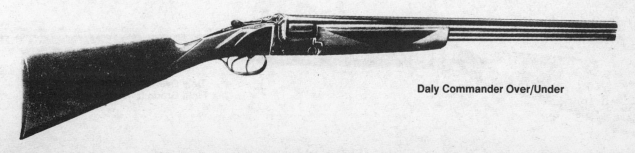

Daly Commander Over/Under

Daly Novamatic Autoloader

Charles Daly Hammerless Empire (cont.)

inch in 16 gauge. Barrels: vent rib; 26-, 28-, 30-inch (latter in 12 gauge only); IC/M, M/F, F/F. Weight: 6 to 7³/₄ pounds, depending on gauge and barrels. Checkered pistol-grip stock and beavertail forearm. Made 1968–1971.

Daly 1974 Wildlife Commemorative

Charles Daly 1974 Wildlife Commemorative . . . $1695

Limited issue of 500 guns. Similar to Diamond Grade over/under. 12-gauge trap and skeet models only. Duck scene engraved on right side of receiver, fine scroll on left side. Made in 1974.

> **NOTE:** The following Novamatic autoloaders were produced in 1968 by Ernesto Breda, Milan, Italy.

Charles Daly Novamatic Lightweight Autoloader

Same as Breda. Recoil-operated. Takedown. 12 gauge, 2³/₄-inch chamber. 4-shell tubular magazine. Barrels: plain, vent rib; 26-inch IC or Quick-Choke with three interchangeable tubes, 28-inch M or F choke. Weight (with 26-inch vent-rib barrel): 7 lbs. 6 oz. Checkered pistol-grip stock and forearm.

With Plain Barrel $350
With Vent-rib Barrel 395
For Quick-Choke, **add** 20

Charles Daly Novamatic Super Lightweight

Lighter version of Novamatic Lightweight. Gauges: 12, 20. Weight (with 26-inch vent-rib barrel): 12 ga., 6 lbs. 10 oz.; 20 ga., 6 lbs. SK choke available in 26-inch vent-rib barrel. 28-inch barrels in 12 gauge only. Quick-Choke in 20 gauge with plain barrel.

12 Gauge, Plain Barrel **$345**
12 Gauge, Vent-rib Barrel 375
20 Gauge, Plain Barrel 310
20 Gauge, Plain Barrel w/Quick-Choke 325
20 Gauge, Vent-rib Barrel 345

Charles Daly Novamatic Super Lightweight
20-Gauge Magnum $345

Same as Novamatic Super Lightweight 20, except 3-inch chamber, has 3-shell magazine, 28-inch vent-rib barrel, Full choke.

Charles Daly Novamatic 12-Gauge Magnum $350

Same as Novamatic Lightweight, except chambered for 12-gauge Magnum 3-inch shell, has 3-shell magazine, 30-inch vent-rib barrel, Full choke, and stock with recoil pad. Weight: 7³/₄ pounds.

Charles Daly Novamatic Trap Gun $375

Same as Novamatic Lightweight, except has 30-inch vent-rib barrel, Full choke and Monte Carlo stock with recoil pad. Weight: 7³/₄ pounds.

Charles Daly Over/Under Shotguns (Prewar)

Daly-pattern Anson & Deeley-system boxlock action. Sideplates. Auto ejectors. Double triggers. Gauges: 12, 16, 20. Supplied in various barrel lengths and weights. Checkered pistol-grip stock and forend. The two grades—Diamond and Empire—differ in general quality, grade of wood, checkering, engraving, etc.; otherwise specifications are the same. Discontinued about 1933.

Diamond Quality **$4295**
Empire Quality 2995

Charles Daly Over/Under Shotguns (Postwar)

Boxlock. Auto ejectors or selective auto/manual ejection. Selective single trigger. Gauges: 12, 12 Magnum (3-inch

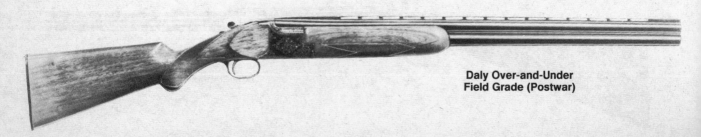

Daly Over-and-Under
Field Grade (Postwar)

Daly Over-and-Under
Venture (Postwar)

Charles Daly Over/Unders—Postwar (cont.)

chambers), 20 (3-inch chambers), 28, .410. Barrels: vent rib; 26-, 28-, 30-inch; standard choke combinations. Weight: 6 to 8 pounds depending on gauge and barrels. Select walnut stock with pistol grip, fluted forearm, checkered; Monte Carlo comb on trap guns; recoil pad on 12-ga. Mag. and trap models. The various grades differ in quality of engraving and wood. Made 1963–1976.

Diamond Grade $925
Field Grade 530
Superior Grade 625
Venture Grade 520

Daly Sextuple Trap

Charles Daly Sextuple Model Single Barrel Trap Gun

Daly pattern Anson & Deeley system boxlock action. Six locking bolts. Auto ejector. 12 gauge only. Barrels: 30-, 32-, 34-inch, vent rib. Weight: 7½ to 8¼ pounds. Checkered pistol-grip stock and forend. The two models made—Empire and Regent Diamond—differ in general quality, grade of wood, checkering, engraving, etc.; otherwise specs are the same. Discontinued about 1933.

Regent Diamond Quality $2650
Empire Quality 1995

Daly Single Barrel Trap

Charles Daly Single Barrel Trap Gun

Daly pattern Anson & Deeley system boxlock action. Auto ejector. 12 gauge only. Barrels: 30-, 32-, 34-inch, vent rib. Weight: 7½ to 8¼ pounds. Checkered pistol-grip stock and forend. This model was made in Empire Quality only.

Charles Daly Single Barrel Trap Gun (cont.)

Discontinued about 1933.

Diamond Grade $2750
Empire Grade 2095

Charles Daly Superior Grade Single
Barrel Trap $595

Boxlock. Automatic ejector. 12 gauge only. 32- or 34-inch vent-rib barrel, full choke. Weight: about 8 pounds. Monte Carlo stock with pistol grip and recoil pad, beavertail forearm, checkered. Made 1968–1976.

> **NOTE:** The following Charles Daly shotguns are distributed in the U.S. by Outdoor Sports Headquarters, Dayton, Ohio. The Daly semiauto guns are currently manufactured in Japan, while the o/u models are produced in Italy and Spain.

Charles Daly Diamond Grade Over/Under

Boxlock. Single selective trigger. Selective automatic ejectors. Gauges: 12 and 20; 3-inch chambers (2¾ target grade). Barrels: 26-, 27- or 30-inch with fixed chokes or screw-in tubes. Weight: 7 pounds. Checkered European walnut stock and forearm with oil finish. Engraved antique silver receiver and blued barrels. Made 1984–1990.

Standard Model $595
Skeet Model 650
Trap Model 695

Charles Daly DSS Hammerless Double $525

Boxlock. Single selective trigger. Selective automatic ejectors. Gauges: 12 and 20; 3-inch chambers. 26-inch barrels with screw-in choke tubes. Weight: 6¾ pounds. Checkered walnut pistol-grip stock and semibeavertail forearm with recoil pad. Engraved antique silver receiver and blued barrels. Made from 1990 to date.

Charles Daly Field Grade Over/Under $375

Boxlock. Single selective trigger. Extractors. Gauges: 12 and 20; 3-inch chambers. Barrels: 26-inch, IC/M; 28-inch, M/F. Weight: 6¾ pounds (12 ga.). Checkered walnut stock and forearm with semi-gloss finish and recoil pad. Engraved color-casehardened receiver and blued barrels. Made from 1989 to date.

SHOTGUNS

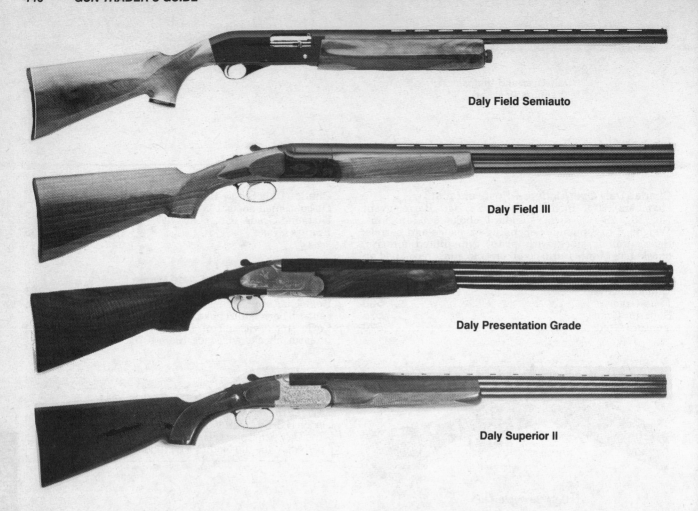

Daly Field Semiauto

Daly Field III

Daly Presentation Grade

Daly Superior II

Charles Daly Field Semiauto Shotgun **$300**
Recoil-operated. Takedown. 12-gauge and 12-gauge Magnum. Barrels: 27- and 30-inch; vent rib. Made 1982–88.

Charles Daly Field III Over/Under Shotgun **$410**
Boxlock. Plain extractors. Non-selective single trigger. Gauges: 12 or 20. Barrels: vent rib; 26- and 28-inch; IC/M, M/F. Weight: 6 to 7³/4 pounds depending on gauge and barrels. Chrome-molybdenum steel barrels. Checkered pistol-grip stock and forearm. Made from 1982 to date.

Charles Daly Lux Over/Under **$545**
Similar to the Field Grade, except with selective automatic ejectors and choke tubes. Gauges: 12, 20, 28 and .410. Receiver with antique silver finish and blued barrels. Made from 1989 to date.

Charles Daly Multi-XII Self-loading Shotgun **$395**
Similar to the gas-operated field semiauto, except with new Multi-Action gas system designed to shoot all loads without adjustment. 12 gauge w/3-inch chamber. 27-inch barrel with Invector choke tubes, vent rib. Made in Japan from 1987 to date.

Charles Daly Over/Under Presentation Grade . . **$795**
Purdey double cross-bolt locks. Single selective trigger. Gauges: 12 or 20. Barrels: chrome-molybdenum steel, rectified, honed and internally chromed; 27-inch vent rib. Hand-checkered deluxe European walnut stock. Made 1982–86.

Charles Daly Over/Under Superior II Shotgun . . . **$525**
Boxlock. Plain extractors. Non-selective single trigger. Gauges: 12 or 20. Barrels: chrome-molybdenum vent rib; 26-, 28-, 30-inch; latter in Magnum only; assorted chokes. Silver engraved receiver. Checkered pistol-grip stock and forearm. Made from 1982 to date.

Charles Daly Sporting Clays Over/Under **$695**
Similar to the Field Grade, exept in 12 gauge only w/ported barrels and internal choke tubes. Made from 1990 to date.

═══ **DARNE S.A.** ═══
Saint-Etienne, France

Darne Hammerless Double Barrel Shotguns
Sliding-breech action with fixed barrels. Auto ejectors. Double triggers. Gauges: 12, 16, 20, 28; also 12 and 20 Magnum with 3-inch chambers. Barrels: 27¹/2-inch standard, 25¹/2- to 31¹/2-inch lengths available; any standard choke combination. Weight: 5¹/2 to 7 pounds, depending on gauge and barrel length. Checkered straight-grip or pistol-grip stock and forearm. The various models differ in grade of engraving and wood. Currently manufactured.

Darne Model R11

Darne Model V
Hors Série No. 1

Darne Model V22

Darne Hammerless Double Barrel Shotguns (cont.)

Model R11 (Bird Hunter)	$ 795
Model R15 (Pheasant Hunter)	2000
Model R16 (Magnum)	1495
Model V19 (Quail Hunter)	2800
Model V22	3500
Model V Hors Série No. 1	6500

Davidson Model 63B

DAVIDSON GUNS

Mfd. by Fabrica de Armas ILJA, Eibar, Spain; distributed by Davidson Firearms Co., Greensboro, North Carolina

Davidson Model 63B Double Barrel Shotgun . . . **$250**
Anson & Deeley boxlock action. Frame-engraved and nickel plated. Plain extractors. Auto safety. Double triggers. Gauges: 12, 16, 20, 28, .410. Barrel lengths: 25 (.410 only), 26, 28, 30 inches (latter 12 ga. only). Chokes: IC/M, M/F, F/F. Weight: 5 lb. 11 oz. (.410) to 7 lbs. (12 ga.). Checkered pistol-grip stock and forearm of European walnut. Made from 1963 to date.

Davidson Model 63B Magnum
Similar to standard Model 63B, except chambered for 10 ga. 3½-inch, 12 and 20 ga. 3-inch Magnum shells; 10 gauge has 32-inch barrels, choked F/F. Weight: 10 lb. 10 oz. Made from 1963 to date.
12-and 20-gauge Magnum **$335**
10-gauge Magnum **395**

Davidson Model 69SL Double Barrel Shotgun . . **$415**
Sidelock action with detachable sideplates, engraved and nickel-plated. Plain extractors. Auto safety. Double triggers. 12 and 20 gauge. Barrels: 26-inch IC/M, 28-inch M/F. Weight: 12 ga., 7 pounds; 20 ga., 6½ pounds. Pistol-grip stock and forearm of European walnut, checkered. Made 1963–1976.

**Davidson Model 73 Stagecoach
Hammer Double** **$265**
Sidelock action with detachable sideplates and exposed hammers. Plain extractors. Double triggers. Gauges: 12, 20; 3-inch chambers. 20-inch barrels, M/F chokes. Weight: 7 lbs., 12 ga.; 6½ lbs., 20 ga. Checkered pistol-grip stock and forearm. Made from 1976 to date.

Exel Model 101 Shotgun

EXEL ARMS OF AMERICA
Gardner, Massachusetts

Exel Series 100 Over/Under Shotguns
Gauge: 12. Single selective trigger. Selective auto ejectors. Hand-checkered European walnut stock with full pistol grip, tulip forend. Black metal finish. Chambered for 2¾-inch shells (Model 103 for 3-inch). Weight: 6⅞ to 7⅞ pounds. Discontinued 1988.
Model 101, 26-inch bbl., IC/M **$360**

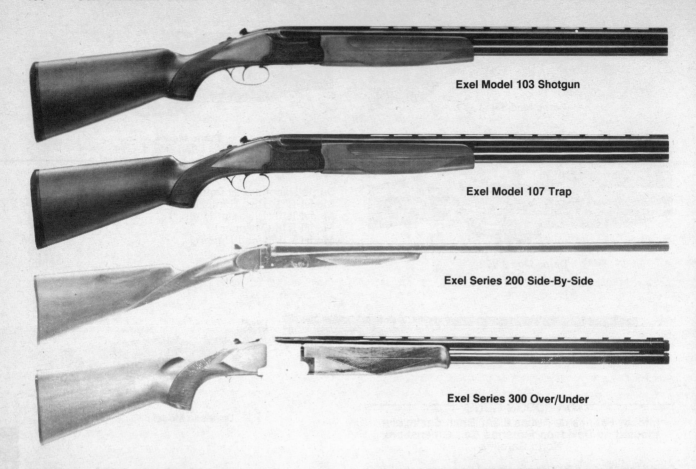

Exel Model 103 Shotgun

Exel Model 107 Trap

Exel Series 200 Side-By-Side

Exel Series 300 Over/Under

Exel Series 100 Over/Under Shotguns (cont.)
Model 102, 28-inch bbl., IC/IM $360
Model 103, 30-inch bbl., M/F 375
Model 104, 28-inch bbl., IC/IM 395
Model 105, 28-inch bbl., 5 choke tubes 495
Model 106, 28-inch bbl., 5 choke tubes 645
Model 107 Trap, 30-inch bbl., Full +5 tubes 675

Exel Series 200 Side-by-Side Shotgun $375
Gauges: 12, 20, 28 and .410. Barrels: 26-, 27- and 28-inch; various choke combinations. Weight: 7 pounds average. American or European-style stock and forend. Made 1985 to date.

Exel Series 300 Over/Under Shotgun $450
Gauge: 12. Barrels: 26-, 28- and 29-inch. Non-glare black-chrome matte finish. Weight: 7 pounds average. Selective auto ejectors, engraved receiver. Hand-checkered European walnut stock and forend. Made 1985–86.

═══ FOX SHOTGUNS ═══
Made by A. H. Fox Gun Co., Philadelphia, PA, 1903 to 1930, and since then by Savage Arms, originally of Utica, NY, now of Westfield, MA. In 1993 Connecticut Manufacturing Co. of New Britain, CT, reintroduced selected models.

Values shown are for 12 and 16 gauge doubles made by A. H. Fox. Twenty gauge guns often are valued up to 75% higher. Savage-made Fox models generally bring prices 25% lower. With the exception of Model B, production of Fox shotguns was discontinued about 1942.

Fox Model B Hammerless Double $235
Boxlock. Double triggers. Plain extractor. Gauges: 12, 16, 20, .410. 24- to 30-inch barrels; vent rib on current production; chokes: M/F, C/M, F/F (.410 only). Weight: about 7½ pounds, 12 ga. Checkered pistol-grip stock and forearm. Made about 1940–1985.

Fox Model B

Fox Model B-DE

Fox Model B-DL

Fox Model B-ST

Fox Grade CE

Fox Grade XE

Fox Model B-DE **$295**
Same as Model B-ST except frame finished in satin
chrome, select walnut buttstock with checkered pistol grip
and beavertail forearm. Made 1965–66.

Fox Model B-DL **$320**
Same as Model B-ST except frame finished in satin
chrome, select walnut buttstock with checkered pistol grip,
side panels, beavertail forearm. Made 1962–66.

Fox Model B-SE **$365**
Same as Model B except has selective ejectors and single
trigger. Made 1966–1989.

Fox Model B-ST **$255**
Same as Model B except has non-selective single trigger.
Made 1955–1966.

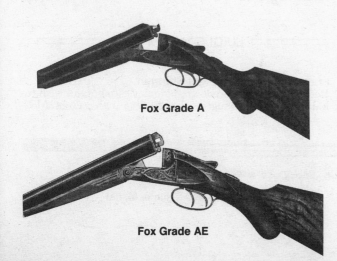

Fox Grade A

Fox Grade AE

Fox Hammerless Double Barrel Shotguns
The higher grades have the same general specifications
as the standard Sterlingworth model with differences
chiefly in workmanship and materials. Higher grade models are stocked in fine select walnut; quantity and quality
of engraving increases with price. Except for Grade A, all
have auto ejectors.

Grade A	$ 1,395
Grade AE	1,695
Grade BE	2,750
Grade CE	2,995
Grade DE	7,595
Grade FE	15,250
Grade XE	5,250
Fox-Kautzky selective single trigger, extra	300
Ventilated rib, extra	400
Beavertail forearm, extra	200

Fox Single Barrel Trap Guns
Boxlock. Auto ejector. 12 gauge only. 30- or 32-inch vent-
rib barrel. Weight: 7 1/2 to 8 pounds. Trap-style stock and
forearm of select walnut, checkered, recoil pad optional.

SHOTGUNS

Fox Single Barrel Trap Guns (cont.)

The four grades differ chiefly in quality of wood and engraving; Grade M guns, built to order, have finest Circassian walnut. Stock and receiver are elaborately engraved and inlaid with gold. Discontinued 1942. *Note:* In 1932 the Fox Trap Gun was redesigned and those manufactured after that date have a stock with full pistol grip and Monte Carlo comb; at the same time frame was changed to permit the rib line to extend across it to the rear.

Grade JE	$2595
Grade KE	2995
Grade LE	4850
Grade ME	9500

Fox "Skeeter" Double Barrel Shotgun $2595

Boxlock. Gauge: 12 or 20. Barrels: 28 inches w/full-length vent rib. Weight: approx. 7 pound. Buttstock and beavertail forend of select American walnut, finely checkered. Soft rubber recoil pad and ivory bead sights. Made in early 1930s.

Fox Sterlingworth Deluxe

Same general specifications as Sterlingworth, except 32-inch barrel also available; recoil pad, ivory bead sights.

With plain extractors	$1295
With automatic ejectors	1495

Fox Sterlingworth Hammerless Double

Boxlock. Double triggers (Fox-Kautzky selective single trigger extra). Plain extractors (auto ejectors extra). Gauges: 12, 16, 20. Barrel lengths: 26-, 28-, 30-inch; chokes F/F, M/F, C/M (any combination of C to F choke borings was available at no extra cost). Weight: 12 ga., $6\frac{7}{8}$ to $8\frac{1}{4}$ lbs.; 16 ga., 6 to 7 lbs.; 20 ga., $5\frac{3}{4}$ to $6\frac{3}{4}$ lbs. Checkered pistol-grip stock and forearm.

With plain extractors	$ 1095
With automatic ejectors	1450
Selective single trigger, extra	300

Fox Sterlingworth

Fox Sterlingworth Skeet and Upland Game Gun

Same general specifications as the standard Sterlingworth, except has 26- or 28-inch barrels with skeet boring only, straight-grip stock. Weight: 7 pounds, 12 ga.

With plain extractors	$1550
With automatic ejectors	1895

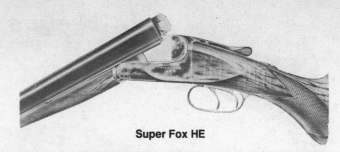

Super Fox HE

Super Fox HE Grade $2750

Long-range gun made in 12 gauge only (chambered for 3-inch shells on order), 30- or 32-inch Full choke barrels, auto ejectors standard. Weight: $8\frac{3}{4}$ to $9\frac{3}{4}$ pounds. General specifications same as standard Sterlingworth.

> **NOTE:** The following A.H. Fox Shotguns were reintroduced by the Connecticut Manufacturing Co. (New Britain, CT) in 1993.

**CMC Fox Hammerless Double
DE Grade**

CMC Fox Hammerless Double Barrel Shotguns

High-grade doubles similar to the original Fox models. 20 gauge only. 26-, 28- or 30-inch barrels. Double triggers, automatic safety and ejectors. Weight: $5\frac{1}{2}$ to 7 pounds. Custom Circassian walnut stock with hand-rubbed oil finish. Custom stock configuration: straight, semi- or full pistol-grip stock w/traditional pad, hard rubber plate, checkered or skeleton butt; schnabel, splinter or beavertail forend. Made 1993 to date.

CE Grade	$ 5,295
XE Grade	7,550
DE Grade	9,995
FE Grade	15,995
Exhibition Grade	20,950

LUIGI FRANCHI S.P.A.
Brescia, Italy

Franchi 48/AL Ultra Light Shotgun

Recoil-operated, takedown, hammerless shotgun with tubular magazine. Gauges: 12 or 20 ($2\frac{3}{4}$-inch); 12-ga. Mag-

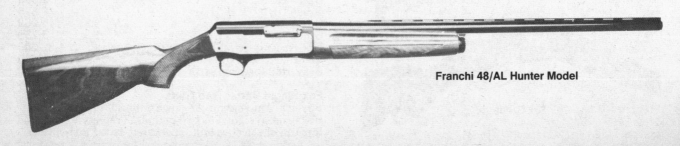

Franchi 48/AL Hunter Model

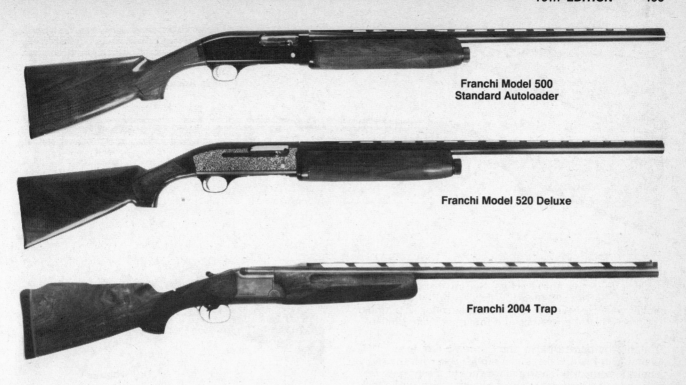

Franchi Model 500
Standard Autoloader

Franchi Model 520 Deluxe

Franchi 2004 Trap

Franchi 48/AL Ultra Light Shotgun (cont.)
num (3-inch chamber). Barrels: 24- to 32-inch w/various choke combinations. Weight: 5 lbs. 2 oz. (20 ga.) to $6^{1/4}$ lbs. (12 ga.). Checkered pistol-grip walnut stock and forend with high-gloss finish.
Standard Model **$365**
Hunter or Magnum Models **395**

Franchi Model 500 Standard Autoloader **$295**
Gas-operated. 12 gauge. 4-shot magazine. Barrels: 26-, 28-inch; vent rib; IC, M, IM, F chokes. Weight: about 7 pounds. Checkered pistol-grip stock and forearm. Made 1976–1980.

Franchi Model 520 Deluxe **$360**
Same as Model 500, except higher grade with engraved receiver. Made 1975–79.

Franchi Model 520 Eldorado Gold **$775**
Same as Model 520, except custom grade with engraved and gold-inlaid receiver, finer quality wood. Intro. 1977.

Franchi Model 2003 Trap Over/Under **$1050**
Boxlock. Auto ejectors. Selective single trigger. 12 gauge. Barrels: 30-, 32-inch; IM/F, F/F; high vent rib. Weight (with 30-inch barrel): $8^{1/4}$ pounds. Checkered walnut beavertail forearm and stock with straight or Monte Carlo comb, recoil pad. Luggage-type carrying case. Introduced 1976; discontinued.

Franchi Model 2004 Trap Single Barrel **$1095**
Same as Model 2003, except single barrel, 32- or 34-inch, Full choke. Weight (with 32-inch barrel): $8^{1/4}$ pounds. Introduced 1976; discontinued.

Franchi Model 2005 Combination Trap **$1550**
Model 2004/2005 type gun with two sets of barrels, single and over/under. Introduced 1976; discontinued.

Franchi Model 2005/3 Combination Trap **$1995**
Model 2004/2005 type gun with three sets of barrels, any combination of single and over/under. Introduced 1976; discontinued.

Franchi Model 3000/2 Combination Trap **$2500**
Boxlock. Automatic ejectors. Selective single trigger. 12 gauge. Barrels: 32-inch over/under choked F/IM; 34-inch underbarrel M choke; high vent rib. Weight (with 32-inch barrels): 8 lbs. 6 oz. Choice of six different castoff butt-stocks. Introduced 1979; discontinued.

Franchi Airone

Franchi Airone Hammerless Double **$950**
Boxlock. Anson & Deeley system action. Auto ejectors. Double triggers. 12 gauge. Various barrel lengths, chokes, weights. Checkered straight-grip stock and forearm. Made 1940–1950.

Franchi Alcione Over/Under Shotgun **$995**
Hammerless, takedown shotgun with engraved receiver. Selective single trigger and ejectors. 12 gauge w/3-inch chambers. Barrels: 26-inch (IC/M; 28-inch (M/F). Weight: $6^{3/4}$ pounds. Checkered French walnut buttstock and forend. Imported from Italy since 1982.

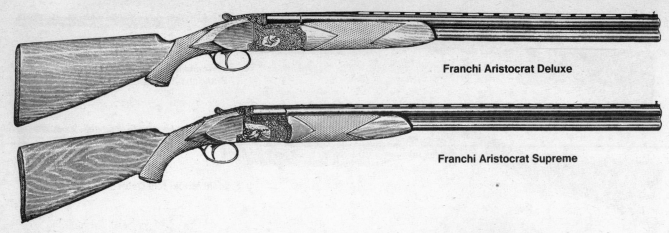

Franchi Aristocrat Deluxe

Franchi Aristocrat Supreme

Franchi Aristocrat Field Model Over/Under $525
Boxlock. Selective auto ejectors. Selective single trigger. 12 gauge. Barrels: 26-inch IC/M; 28- and 30-inch M/F choke; vent rib. Weight (w/26-inch barrels): 7 pounds. Checkered pistol-grip stock and forearm. Made 1960–69.

Franchi Aristocrat Deluxe and Supreme Grades
Available in Field, Skeet and Trap Models with the same general specifications as standard guns of these types. Deluxe and Supreme Grades are of higher quality with stock and forearm of select walnut, elaborate relief engraving on receiver, trigger guard, tang and top lever. Supreme game birds inlaid in gold. Made 1960–66.

Deluxe Grade . . . . $ 850
Supreme Grade 1195

Franchi Aristocrat Imperial and Monte Carlo Grades
Custom guns made in Field, Skeet and Trap Models with the same general specifications as standard for these types. Imperial and Monte Carlo Grades are of highest quality with stock and forearm of select walnut, fine engraving—elaborate on the latter grade. Made 1967–69.

Imperial Grade $2195
Monte Carlo Grade 3095

Franchi Aristocrat Magnum Model $465
Same as Field Model, except chambered for 3-inch shells, has 32-inch barrels choked F/F; stock has recoil pad. Weight: about 8 pounds. Made 1962–65.

Franchi Aristocrat Silver King $550
Available in Field, Magnum, Skeet and Trap models with the same general specifications as standard guns of these types. Silver King has stock and forearm of select walnut, more elaborately engraved silver-finished receiver. Made 1962–69.

Franchi Aristocrat Skeet Model $525
Same general specifications as Field Model, except made only with 26-inch vent-rib barrels with SK chokes #1 and #2; skeet-style stock and forearm. Weight: about 7½ pounds. Later production had wider (10mm) rib. Made 1960–69.

Franchi Aristocrat Trap Model $545
Same general specifications as Field Model, except made only with 30-inch vent-rib barrels, M/F choke; trap-style stock with recoil pad, beavertail forearm. Later production had Monte Carlo comb, 10mm rib. Made 1960–69.

Franchi Astore

Franchi Astore Hammerless Double $795
Boxlock. Anson & Deeley system action. Plain extractors. Double triggers. 12 gauge. Various barrel lengths, chokes, weights. Checkered straight-grip stock and forearm. Made 1937–1960.

Franchi Astore II $995
Similar to Astore S, but not as high grade. Furnished with either plain extractors or auto ejectors, double triggers, pistol-grip stock. Barrels: 27-inch IC/IM; 28-inch M/F chokes. Currently manufactured for Franchi in Spain.

Franchi Astore S

Franchi Astore S $1795
Same as Astore, except has higher grade wood, fine engraving. Automatic ejectors, single trigger, 28-inch barrel (M/F or IM/F choke) are standard on current production.

Franchi Crown, Diamond and Imperial Grade Autoloaders
Same general specifications as Standard Model, except these are custom guns of the highest quality. Crown Grade has hunting scene engraving; Diamond Grade has silver-inlaid scroll engraving; Imperial Grade has elaborately

Franchi Crown Grade

Franchi Diamond Grade

Franchi Crown, Diamond and Imperial Grades (cont.)
engraved hunting scenes with figures inlaid in gold. Stock and forearm of fancy walnut. Made 1954–1975.

Crown Grade	**$1295**
Diamond Grade	1695
Imperial Grade	1995

Franchi Dynamic-12
Same general specifications and appearance as Standard Model, except 12 gauge only, has heavier steel receiver. Weight: about 7 1/4 pounds. Made 1965–1972.

With plain barrel	**$310**
With ventilated rib	340

Franchi Dynamic-12 Slug Gun $320
Same as standard Slug Gun, except 12 gauge only, has heavier steel receiver. Made 1965–1972.

Franchi Dynamic-12 Skeet Gun $375
Same general specifications and appearance as Standard Model, except has heavier steel receiver; made only in 12 gauge with 26-inch vent-rib barrel, SK choke; stock and forearm of extra fancy walnut. Made 1965–1972.

Franchi Eldorado Model $450
Same general specifications as Standard Model except highest grade with gold-filled engraving, stock and forearm of select walnut; furnished with vent-rib barrel only. Made 1954–1975.

Franchi Falconet International Skeet Model $895
Similar to Standard Skeet Model, but higher grade. Made 1970–74.

Franchi Falconet International Trap Model $875
Similar to Standard Trap Model, but higher grade; with straight or Monte Carlo comb stock. Made 1970–74.

Franchi Falconet Over/Under Field Models
Boxlock. Auto ejectors. Selective single trigger. Gauges: 12, 16, 20, 28, .410. Barrels: 24-, 26-, 28-, 30-inch; vent rib. Chokes: C/IC, IC/M, M/F. Weight: from about 6 pounds. Engraved lightweight alloy receiver; light-colored in Buckskin Model, blued in Ebony Model, pickled silver in Silver Model. Checkered walnut stock and forearm. Made 1968–1975.

Buckskin or Ebony Model	**$495**
Silver Model	550

Franchi Falconet Standard Skeet Model $850
Same general specifications as Field Models, except made only with 26-inch barrels with SK chokes #1 and #2, wide vent rib, color-casehardened receiver, skeet-style stock and forearm. Weight: 12 ga., about 7 3/4 lbs. Made 1970–74.

Franchi Falconet Standard Trap Model $825
Same general specifications as Field Models, except made only in 12 gauge with 30-inch barrels, choked M/F; wide vent rib, color-casehardened receiver, Monte Carlo trap-style stock and forearm, recoil pad. Weight: about 8 pounds. Made 1970–74.

SHOTGUNS

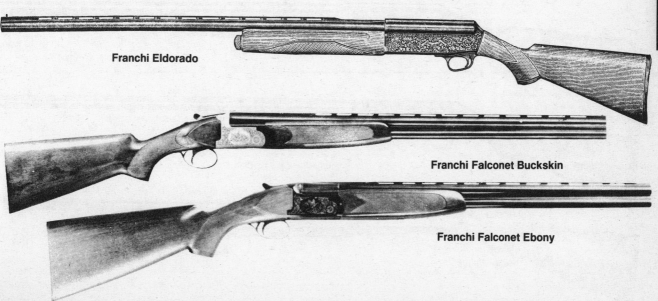

Franchi Eldorado

Franchi Falconet Buckskin

Franchi Falconet Ebony

Franchi Hammerless Condor Grade

Franchi Imperiale "S"

Franchi Hammerless Imperiale
Montecarlo Extra

Franchi Hammerless Sidelock Doubles
Hand-detachable locks. Self-opening action. Auto ejectors. Double triggers or single trigger. Gauges: 12, 16, 20. Barrel lengths, chokes, weights according to customer's specifications. Checkered stock and forend, straight or pistol grip. Made in six grades—Condor, Imperiale, Imperiale S, Imperiale Montecarlo No. 5, Imperiale Montecarlo No. 11, Imperiale Montecarlo Extra—which differ chiefly in overall quality, engraving, grade of wood, checkering, etc.; general specifications are the same. Only the Imperiale Montecarlo Extra Grade is currently manufactured.
Condor Grade .... $ 6,395
Imperiale, Imperiale S Grades 8,700
Imperiale Montecarlo Grades No. 5, 11 12,500
Imperiale Montecarlo Extra Grade 14,500

Franchi Hunter Model
Same general specifications as Standard Model except higher grade with engraved receiver; furnished with ribbed barrel only. Made 1950 to date.
With solid rib $325
With ventilated rib 340

Franchi Hunter Model Magnum $395
Same as Standard Model Magnum, except higher grade with engraved receiver, vent-rib barrel only. Formerly designated "Wildfowler Model." Made 1954–73.

Franchi Peregrine Model 400 .... $475
Same general specifications as Model 451, except has steel receiver. Weight (with 26½-inch barrel): 6 lbs. 15 oz. Made 1975–78.

Franchi Peregrine Model 451 Over-and-Under $530
Boxlock. Lightweight alloy receiver. Automatic ejectors. Selective single trigger. 12 gauge. Barrels: 26½-, 28-inch; choked C/IC, IC/M, M/F; vent rib. Weight (with 26½-inch barrels): 6 lbs. 1 oz. Checkered pistol-grip stock and forearm. Made 1975–78.

Franchi PG-80 Gas-Operated Semiautomatic Shotgun
Gas-operated, takedown, hammerless shotgun with tubular magazine. 12 gauge w/2¾-inch chamber. 5-shot magazine. Barrels: 24 to 30 inches w/vent rib. Weight: 7½ pounds. Gold-plated trigger. Checkered pistol-grip

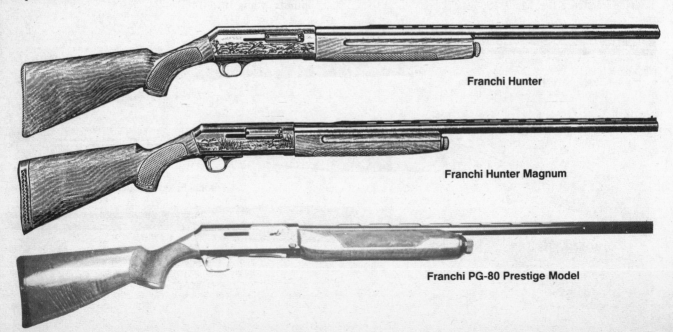

Franchi Hunter

Franchi Hunter Magnum

Franchi PG-80 Prestige Model

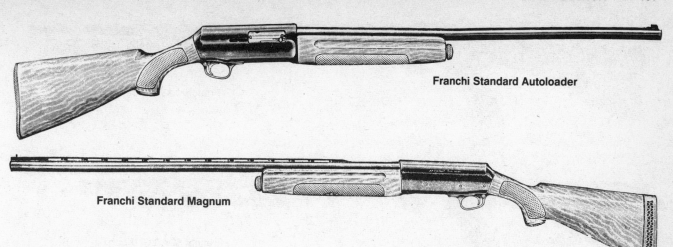

Franchi Standard Autoloader

Franchi Standard Magnum

Franchi PG-80 Semiautomatic Shotgun (cont.)
stock and forend of European walnut. Imported from Italy
1985–1990.
Prestige Model **$425**
Elite Model **475**

Franchi Skeet Gun **$395**
Same general specifications and appearance as Standard
Model, except made only with 26-inch vent-rib barrel, SK
choke. Stock and forearm of extra fancy walnut. Made
1972–74.

Franchi Slug Gun **$345**
Same as Standard Model, except has 22-inch plain barrel,
Cyl. bore, folding leaf open rear sight, gold bead front
sight. Made 1960 to date.

Franchi Standard Model Autoloader
Recoil operated. Light alloy receiver. Gauges: 12, 20. 4-
shot magazine. Barrels: 26-, 28-, 30-inch; plain, solid or
vent rib; IC, M, F chokes. Weight: 12 ga., about $6^1/4$ lbs.;
20 ga., $5^1/8$ lbs. Checkered pistol-grip stock and forearm.
Made 1950 to date.
With plain barrel **$300**
With solid rib **325**
With ventilated rib **340**

Franchi Standard Model Magnum
Same general specifications as Standard Model, except
has 3-inch chamber, 32-inch (12 ga.) or 28-inch (20 ga.)
F choke barrel, recoil pad. Weight: 12 ga., $8^1/4$ lbs.; 20 ga.,
6 lbs. Formerly designated "Superange Model." Made

Franchi Standard Model Magnum (cont.)
1954–1988.
With plain barrel **$345**
With ventilated rib **365**

Franchi Turkey Gun **$400**
Same as Standard Model Magnum, except higher grade
with turkey scene engraved receiver, 12 gauge only, 36-
inch matted-rib barrel, Extra Full choke. Made 1963–65.

> **NOTE:** The following Franchi shotguns are currently im-
> ported by American Arms, Inc.

Franchi Black Magic 48/AL Semiautomatic
Similar to the Franchi Model 48/AL, except with Franchoke screw-in tubes and matte black receiver with Black
Magic logo. Gauge: 12 or 20; $2^3/4$-inch chamber. Barrels:
24-, 26-, 28-inch with vent rib; 24-inch rifled slug with
sights. Weight: 5.2 pounds (20 ga.). Checkered walnut
buttstock and forend. Blued finish.
Standard Model **$425**
Slug Barrel Model **455**

Franchi Falconet 2000 Over/Under **$950**
Boxlock. Single selective trigger. Selective automatic
ejectors. Gauge: 12; $2^3/4$-inch chambers. Barrels: 26-inch
w/Franchoke tubes; IC/M/F. Weight: 6 pounds. Checkered walnut stock and forearm. Engraved silver receiver
w/gold-plated game scene. Imported from 1992 to date.

SHOTGUNS

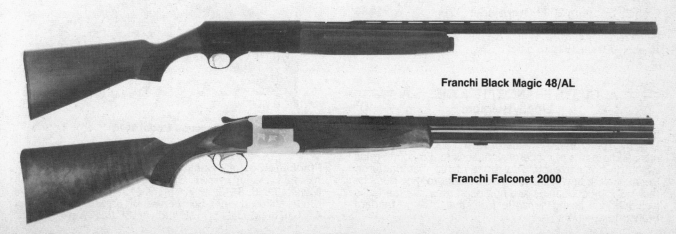

Franchi Black Magic 48/AL

Franchi Falconet 2000

Franchi LAW Shotgun

Franchi SPAS Shotgun

Franchi Sporting 2000 O/U

Franchi LAW-12 Shotgun **$455**
Similar to the SPAS-12 Model, except gas-operated semi-automatic action only, ambidextrous safety, decocking lever and adjustable sights. Made 1983–1994.

Franchi SPAS-12 Shotgun
Selective operating system functions as a gas-operated semiautomatic or pump action. Gauge: 12; 2³/₄-inch chamber. 7-shot magazine. Barrel: 21¹/₂ inches with cylinder bore and muzzle protector or optional screw-in choke tubes; matte finish. 41 inches overall with fixed stock. Weight: 8³/₄ pounds. Blade front sight, aperture rear sight. Folding or black nylon buttstock with pistol grip and forend; non-reflective anodized finish. Made 1983–1994.
Fixed Stock Model **$495**
Folding Stock Model **525**
Optional Choke Tubes, **add** **50**

Franchi Sporting 2000 Over/Under **$895**
Same general specifications as Falconet 2000, except with blued receiver, ported 28-inch barrels. Weight: 7³/₄ pounds. Imported from 1992 to date.

Francotte Model 6886

Francotte Model 8446

═══ **AUGUSTE FRANCOTTE & CIE., S.A.** ═══
Liège, Belgium

Francotte shotguns for many years were distributed in the U.S. by Abercrombie & Fitch of New York City. This firm has used a series of model designations for Francotte guns which do not correspond to those of the manufacturer. Because so many Francotte owners refer to their guns by the A & F model names and numbers, the A & F series is included in a listing separate from that of the standard Francotte numbers.

Francotte Boxlock Hammerless Doubles
Anson & Deeley system. Side clips. Greener crossbolt on Models 6886, 8446, 4996 and 9261; square crossbolt on Model 6930; Greener-Scott crossbolt on Model 8457; Purdey bolt on Models 11/18E and 10/18E/628. Auto ejectors.

Francotte Model 9261

Francotte No. 45 Eagle

Francotte Model 10/18E/628

Francotte Knockabout

Francotte Boxlock Hammerless Doubles (cont.)

Double triggers. Made in all standard gauges, barrel lengths, chokes, weights. Checkered stock and forend, straight or pistol grip. The eight models listed vary chiefly in fastening as described above, finish and engraving, etc.; general specifications are the same. All except Model 10/18E/628 are discontinued.

Model 6886	**$2500**
Model 8446 ("Francotte Special"), 6930, 4996	**2995**
Model 8457, 9261 ("Francotte Original"), 11/18E	**3650**
Model 10/18E/628	**4895**

Francotte Boxlock Hammerless Doubles—A & F Series

Boxlock, Anson & Deeley type. Crossbolt. Sideplate on all except Knockabout Model. Side clips. Auto ejectors. Double triggers. Gauges: 12, 16, 20, 28, .410. Barrels: 26- to 32-inch in 12 gauge, 26- and 28-inch in other gauges; any boring. Weight: $4^{3}/4$ to 8 pounds depending on gauge and barrel length. Checkered stock and forend; straight, half or full pistol grip. The seven grades—No. 45 Eagle Grade, No. 30, No. 25, No. 20, No. 14, Jubilee Model, Knockabout Model—differ chiefly in overall quality, engraving, grade of wood, checkering, etc.; general specifications are the same. Discontinued.

No. 14	**$1695**
No. 20	**2595**
No. 25	**2995**
No. 30	**4550**
No. 45 Eagle Grade	**5295**
Jubilee Model	**4100**
Knockabout Model	**1495**

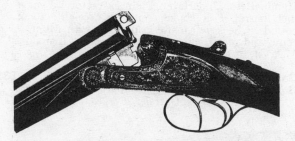

**Francotte Boxlock Hammerless
A&F Series—No. 20**

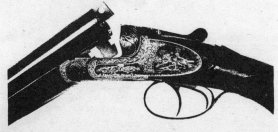

Francotte No. 30

**Francotte Boxlock Hammerless
Model 6982**

Francotte Boxlock Hammerless Doubles (Sideplates)

Anson & Deeley system. Reinforced frame with side clips. Purdey-type bolt except on Model 8455 which has Greener crossbolt. Auto ejectors. Double triggers. Made in all standard gauges, barrel lengths, chokes, weights. Checkered stock and forend, straight or pistol grip. Models 10594, 8455 and 6982 are of equal quality, differing chiefly

**Francotte Fine O/U
Model 9/40.SE**

Francotte Boxlock Hammerless—Sideplates (cont.)
in style of engraving; Model 9/40E/38321 is a higher grade gun in all details and has fine English-style engraving. Currently manufactured.
Models 10594, 8455, 6982 . . . . **$3895**
Model 9/40E/38321 . . . . **4750**

Francotte Fine Over/Under Shotgun **$9000**
Model 9/40.SE. Boxlock, Anson & Deeley system. Auto ejectors. Double triggers. Made in all standard gauges; barrel length, boring to order. Weight: about 6³/₄ pounds, 12 ga. Checkered stock and forend, straight or pistol grip. Currently manufactured.

**Francotte Fine Sidelock Hammerless
Double** **$18,250**
Model 120.HE/328. Automatic ejectors. Double triggers. Made in all standard gauges; barrel length, boring, weight to order. Checkered stock and forend, straight or pistol grip. Currently manufactured.

**Francotte Half-Fine O/U
Model SOB.E/11082**

Francotte Half-Fine Over/Under Shotgun **$7650**
Model SOB.E/11082. Boxlock, Anson & Deeley system. Auto ejectors. Double triggers. Made in all standard gauges; barrel length, boring to order. Checkered stock and forend, straight or pistol grip. *Note:* This model is similar to No. 9/40.SE, except gen. quality is not as high and frame is not fully engraved or scalloped. Discont.

GALEF SHOTGUNS

Manufactured for J. L. Galef & Son, Inc., New York, New York, by M.A.V.I., Gardone V.T., Italy, by Zabala Hermanos, Elquetta, Spain, and by Antonio Zoli, Gardone V.T., Italy

Galef Companion

Galef Companion Folding Single Barrel Shotgun
Hammerless. Underlever. Gauges: 12 Mag., 16, 20 Mag., 28, .410. Barrels: 26-inch (.410 only), 28-inch (12, 16, 20, 28), 30-inch (12 gauge only); Full choke; plain or vent rib. Weight: 4¹/₂ lbs. for .410 to 5 lbs. 9 oz. for 12 gauge. Checkered pistol-grip stock and forearm. Made by M.A.V.I. from 1968 to date.
With plain barrel . . . . **$ 95**
With ventilated rib **115**

Galef Golden Snipe **$445**
Same as Silver Snipe, except has selective automatic ejectors. Made by Antonio Zoli 1968 to date.

Galef Monte Carlo Trap Single Barrel Shotgun . . **$195**
Hammerless. Underlever. Plain extractor. 12 gauge. 32-inch barrel, Full choke, vent rib. Weight: about 8¹/₄ pounds. Checkered pistol-grip stock with Monte Carlo comb and recoil pad, beavertail forearm. Introduced by M.A.V.I. in 1968; discontinued.

Galef Silver Hawk Hammerless Double **$385**
Boxlock. Plain extractors. Double triggers. Gauges: 12, 20; 3-inch chambers. Barrels: 26-, 28-, 30-inch (latter in

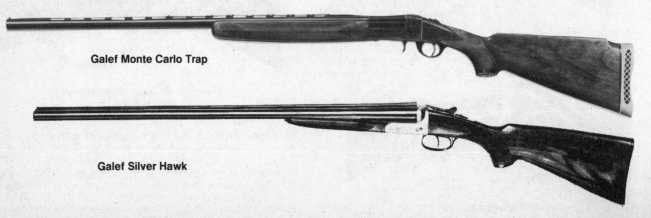

Galef Monte Carlo Trap

Galef Silver Hawk

Galef Silver Snipe

Galef Zabala

Galef Silver Hawk Hammerless Double (cont.)
12 gauge only); IC/M, M/F chokes. Weight: 12 ga. with 26-inch barrels, 6 lbs. 6 oz. Checkered walnut pistol-grip stock and beavertail forearm. Made by Antonio Zoli 1968–1972.

Galef Silver Snipe Over/Under Shotgun $415
Boxlock. Plain extractors. Single trigger. Gauges: 12, 20; 3-inch chambers. Barrels: 26-, 28-, 30-inch (latter in 12 gauge only); IC/M, M/F chokes; vent rib. Weight: 12 gauge with 28-inch barrels, 6½ pounds. Checkered walnut pistol-grip stock and forearm. Introduced by Antonio Zoli in 1968; discontinued.

Galef Zabala Hammerless Double Barrel Shotgun
Boxlock. Plain extractors. Double triggers. Gauges: 10 Mag., 12 Mag., 16, 20 Mag., 28, .410. Barrels: 22-, 26-, 28-, 30-, 32-inch; IC/IC, IC/M, M/F, F/F chokes. Weight: 12 gauge with 28-inch barrels, 7¾ pounds. Checkered walnut pistol-grip stock and beavertail forearm, recoil pad. Made by Zabala from 1972 to date.
10 gauge $235
Other gauges 180

GAMBA S.p.A.
Gardone V.T. (Brescia), Italy

Gamba Daytona Competition Over/Under
Boxlock with Boss-style locking system. Anatomical single trigger; optional adjustable, single-selective release trigger. Selective automatic ejectors. Gauge: 12 or 20; 2¾- or 3-inch chambers. Barrels: 26¾-, 28-, 30- or 32-inch choked SK/SK, IM/F or M/F. Weight: 7½ to 8½ pounds. Black or chrome receiver with blued barrels. Checkered select walnut stock and forearm with oil finish. Imported by Heckler & Koch until 1992.

Gamba Daytona Competition O/U (cont.)
American Trap Model	$ 4,045
Pigeon, Skeet, Trap Models	3,745
Sporting Model	3,595
Sideplate Model	8,625
Engraved Models . . . . 7500 to	10,000
Sidelock Model	18,750

GARBI SHOTGUNS
Eibar, Spain

Garbi Model 100 Sidelock Shotgun $2495
Gauges: 12, 16, 20 and 28. Barrels: 25-, 28-, 30-inch. Action: Holland & Holland pattern sidelock; automatic ejectors and double trigger. Weight: 5 lbs. 6 oz. to 7 lbs. 7 oz. English-style straight grip stock with fine-line hand-checkered butt; classic forend. Made 1985 to date.

Garbi Model 101 Sidelock Shotgun $3295
Same general specifications as Model 100, except the sidelocks are handcrafted with hand-engraved receiver; select walnut straight-grip stock.

Garbi Model 102 Sidelock Shotgun $3595
Similar to the Model 101, except with large scroll engraving. Made 1985–1993.

Garbi Model 103 Hammerless Double
Similar to Model 100, except with Purdey-type, higher grade engraving.
Model 103A	$3895
Model 103B	5750

Garbi Model 200 Hammerless Double $5895
Similar to Model 100, except with double heavy-duty locks. Continental-style floral and scroll engraving. Checkered deluxe walnut stock and forearm.

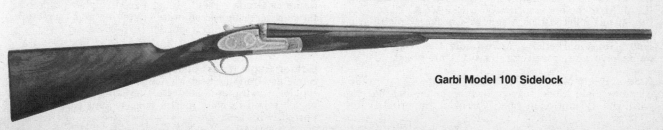

Garbi Model 100 Sidelock

SHOTGUNS

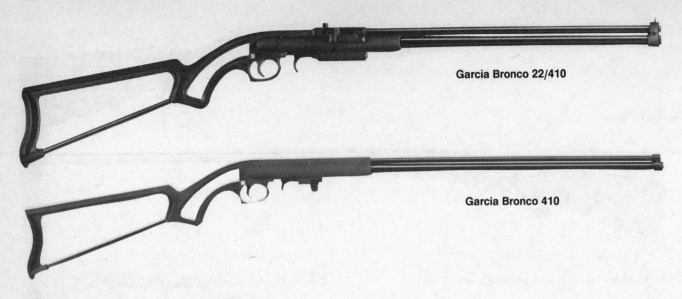

Garcia Bronco 22/410

Garcia Bronco 410

GARCIA CORPORATION
Teaneck, New Jersey

Garcia Bronco 22/.410 O/U Combination **$95**
Swing-out action. Takedown. 18½-inch barrels; 22 LR over, .410 gauge under. Weight: 4½ pounds. One-piece stock and receiver, crackle finish. Intro. 1976; disc.

Garcia Bronco .410 Single Shot **$70**
Swing-out action. Takedown. .410 gauge. 18½-inch barrel. Weight: 3½ pounds. One-piece stock and receiver, crackle finish. Introduced in 1967. Discontinued.

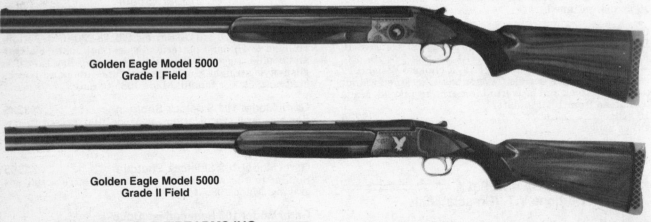

Golden Eagle Model 5000
Grade I Field

Golden Eagle Model 5000
Grade II Field

GOLDEN EAGLE FIREARMS INC.
Houston, Texas
Mfd. by Nikko Firearms Ltd., Tochigi, Japan

Golden Eagle Model 5000 Grade I Field O/U . . . **$725**
Receiver engraved and inlaid with gold eagle head. Box-lock. Auto ejectors. Selective single trigger. Gauges: 12, 20; 2¾- or 3-inch chambers, 12 ga., 3-inch, 20 ga. Barrels: 26-, 28-, 30-inch (latter only in 12-gauge 3-inch Magnum); IC/M, M/F chokes; vent rib. Weight: 6¼ lbs., 20 ga.; 7¼ lbs., 12 ga.; 8 lbs., 12-ga. Magnum. Checkered pistol-grip stock and semibeavertail forearm. Imported 1975–1982. *Note:* Guns marketed 1975-76 under the Nikko brand name have white receivers; since 1976 are blued.

Golden Eagle Model 5000 Grade I Skeet **$795**
Same as Field Model, except has 26- or 28-inch barrels with wide (11mm) vent rib, SK choked. Imported 1975–1982.

Golden Eagle Model 5000 Grade I Trap **$815**
Same as Field Model, except has 30- or 32-inch barrels with wide (11mm) vent rib (M/F, IM/F, F/F chokes), trap-style stock with recoil pad. Imported 1975–1982.

Golden Eagle Model 5000 Grade II Field **$795**
Same as Grade I Field Model, except higher grade with fancier wood, more elaborate engraving and "screaming eagle" inlaid in gold. Imported 1975–1982.

Golden Eagle Model 5000 Grade II Skeet **$825**
Same as Grade I Skeet Model, except higher grade with fancier wood, more elaborate engraving and "screaming eagle" inlaid in gold; inertia trigger, vent side ribs. Imported 1975–1982.

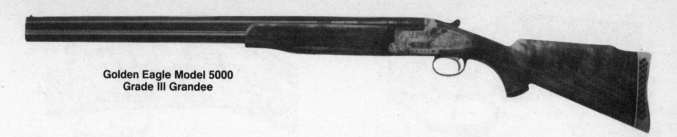

Golden Eagle Model 5000
Grade III Grandee

Golden Eagle Model 5000 Grade II Trap **$835**
Same as Grade I Trap Model, except higher grade with
fancier wood, more elaborate engraving and "screaming
eagle" inlaid in gold; inertia trigger, vent side ribs. Imported 1975–1982.

Golden Eagle Model 5000 Grade III Grandee . . **$1950**
Best grade, available in Field, Skeet and Trap Models
with same general specifications as lower grades. Has sideplates with game scene engraving, scroll on frame and
barrels, fancy wood (Monte Carlo comb, full pistol grip
and recoil pad on Trap Model). Made 1976 to date.

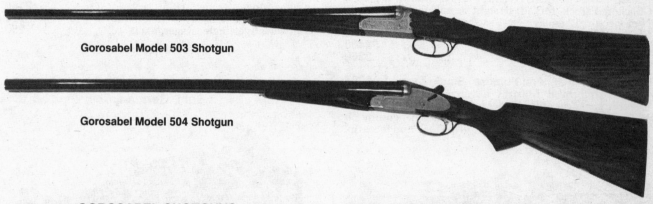

Gorosabel Model 503 Shotgun

Gorosabel Model 504 Shotgun

GOROSABEL SHOTGUNS
Spain

Gorosabel Model 503 Shotgun **$675**
Gauges: 12, 16, 20 and .410. Action: Anson & Deeley-style
boxlock. Barrels: 26-, 27- and 28-inch. Select European
walnut, English or pistol grip, silver or beavertail forend,
hand-checkering. Scalloped frame and scroll engraving.
Intro. 1985; discontinued.

Gorosabel Model 504 Shotgun **$710**
Gauge: 12 or 20. Action: Holland & Holland-style sidelock.
Barrel: 26-, 27- or 28-inch. Select European walnut, English or pistol grip, sliver or beavertail forend, hand-
checkering. Holland-style large scroll engraving. Intro.
1985; discontinued.

Gorosabel Model 505 Shotgun **$945**
Gauge: 12 or 20. Action: Holland & Holland-style sidelock.
Barrels: 26-, 27- or 28-inch. Select European walnut, En-
glish or pistol grip, sliver or beavertail forend, hand-
checkering. Purdey-style fine scroll and rose engraving.
Intro. 1985; discontinued.

STEPHEN GRANT
London, England

**Grant Best Quality Self-Opener Double Barrel
Shotgun** **$9995**
Sidelock, self-opener. Gauges: 12, 16 and 20. Barrels: 25
to 30 inches standard. Highest grade English or European
walnut straight-grip buttstock and forearm with Greener
type lever. Imported by Stoeger in the 1950s.

**Grant Best Quality Side-Lever Double Barrel
Shotgun** **$9995**
Sidelock, self-lever. Gauges: 12, 16 and 20. Barrels: 25 to
30 inches standard. Highest grade English or European
walnut straight-grip buttstock and forearm with Greener
type lever. Imported by Stoeger in the 1950s.

W. W. GREENER, LTD.
Birmingham, England

Greener Empire

Greener Empire Model Hammerless Doubles
Boxlock. Non-ejector or with automatic ejectors. Double
triggers. 12 gauge only (2¾-inch or 3-inch chamber). Barrels: 28- to 32-inch; any choke combination. Weight: from
7¼ to 7¾ pounds depending on barrel length. Checkered
stock and forend, straight- or half-pistol grip. Also furnished in "Empire Deluxe Grade," this model has same
general specs, but deluxe finish.

Empire Model, non-ejector	**$1550**
Empire Model, ejector	**1725**
Empire Deluxe Model, non-ejector	**1750**
Empire Deluxe Model, ejector	**1950**

SHOTGUNS

Greener Far-Killer

Greener Far-Killer Model Grade FH35 Hammerless Double Barrel Shotgun

Boxlock. Non-ejector or with automatic ejectors. Double triggers. Gauges: 12 (2¾-inch or 3-inch), 10, 8. Barrels: 28-, 30- or 32-inch. Weight: 7½–9 pounds in 12 gauge. Checkered stock, forend; straight or half-pistol grip.

Non-ejector, 12 gauge	**$2295**
Ejector, 12 gauge	**3150**
Non-ejector, 10 or 8 gauge	**2400**
Ejector, 10 or 8 gauge	**3200**

Greener G. P. (General Purpose) Single Barrel .. $395

Greener Improved Martini Lever Action. Takedown. Ejector. 12 gauge only. Barrel lengths: 26-, 30-, 32-inch. M or F choke. Weight: 6¼ to 6¾ pounds depending on barrel length. Checkered straight-grip stock and forearm.

Greener Jubilee

Greener Royal

Greener Hammerless Ejector Double Barrel Shotguns

Boxlock. Auto ejectors. Double triggers, non-selective or selective single trigger. Gauges: 12, 16, 20, 28, .410 (two latter gauges not supplied in Grades DH40 and DH35). Barrels: 26-, 28-, 30-inch; any choke combination. Weight: from 4¾ to 8 pounds depending on gauge and barrel length. Checkered stock and forend, straight- or half-pistol grip. The Royal, Crown, Sovereign and Jubilee Models differ in quality, engraving, grade of wood, checkering, etc. General specifications are the same.

Greener Sovereign

Greener Hammerless Ejector Doubles (cont.)

Royal Model Grade DH75	**$3995**
Crown Model Grade DH55	**2950**
Sovereign Model Grade DH40	**2595**
Jubilee Model Grade DH35	**2150**
Selective single trigger, extra	**330**
Non-selective single trigger, extra	**250**

GREIFELT & COMPANY
Suhl, Germany

Greifelt Grade No. 1 Over/Under

Greifelt Grade No. 1 Over-and-Under Shotgun

Anson & Deeley boxlock, Kersten fastening. Auto ejectors. Double triggers or single trigger. Elaborately engraved. Gauges: 12, 16, 20, 28, .410. Barrels: 26- to 32-inch, any combination of chokes, vent or solid matted rib. Weight: 4¼ to 8¼ pounds depending on gauge and barrel length. Straight- or pistol-grip stock, Purdey-type forend, both checkered. Manufactured prior to World War II.

With solid matted-rib barrel, except .410	**$2995**
With solid matted-rib barrel, .410 gauge	**3500**
Extra for ventilated rib	**380**
Extra for single trigger	**425**

Greifelt Grade No. 3 Over-and-Under Shotgun

Same general specifications as Grade No. 1 except not as fancy engraving. Manufactured prior to World War II.

With solid matted-rib barrel, except .410	**$2695**
With solid matted-rib barrel, .410 gauge	**2795**
Extra for ventilated rib	**380**
Extra for single trigger	**425**

Greifelt Model 22 Hammerless Double $1695

Anson & Deeley boxlock. Plain extractors. Double triggers. Gauges: 12 and 16. Barrels: 28- or 30-inch, M/F choke. Checkered stock and forend, pistol grip and cheekpiece standard, English-style stock also supplied. Manufactured since World War II.

Greifelt Model 22E Hammerless Double **$2050**
Same as Model 22, except has automatic ejectors.

Greifelt Model 103 Hammerless Double **$1595**
Anson & Deeley boxlock. Plain extractors. Double triggers. Gauges: 12 and 16. Barrels: 28- or 30-inch, M and F choke. Checkered stock and forend, pistol grip and cheekpiece standard, English-style stock also supplied. Manufactured since World War II.

Greifelt Model 103E Hammerless Double **$1750**
Same as Model 103, except has automatic ejectors.

Greifelt Model 143E Over-and-Under Shotgun
General specifications same as prewar Grade No. 1 Over-and-Under except this model is not supplied in 28 and .410 gauge or with 32-inch barrels. Model 143E is not as high quality as the Grade No. 1 gun. Mfd. since World War II.
With raised matted rib, double triggers......... **$1950**
With ventilated rib, selective single trigger **2795**

Greifelt Hammerless Drilling (Three Barrel Combination Gun) **$2950**
Boxlock. Plain extractors. Double triggers, front single set for rifle barrel. Gauges: 12, 16, 20; rifle barrel in any caliber adapted to this type of gun. 26-inch barrels. Weight: about 7½ pounds. Auto rear sight operated by rifle barrel selector. Checkered stock and forearm, pistol grip and cheekpiece standard. Manufactured prior to WW II. *Note:* Value shown is for guns chambered for cartridges readily obtainable; if rifle barrel is an odd foreign caliber, value will be considerably less.

Greifelt Over-and-Under Combination Gun
Similar in design to this maker's over-and-under shotguns. Gauges: 12, 16, 20, 28, .410; rifle barrel in any caliber adapted to this type of gun. Barrels: 24- or 26-inch, solid matted rib. Weight: from 4¾ to 7¼ pounds. Folding rear sight. Manufactured prior to WW II. *Note:* Values shown are for gauges other than .410, with rifle barrel chambered for a cartridge readily obtainable; if in an odd foreign caliber, value will be considerably less. .410 gauge increases in value by about 50%.
With nonautomatic ejector **$4800**
With automatic ejector **5200**

═ HARRINGTON & RICHARDSON ARMS CO. ═
Gardner, Massachusetts
Now H&R 1871, Inc.

In 1986, all H&R operations were discontinued. In 1992, the firm was purchased by New England Firearms of Gardner, Mass., and the H&R line was divided. Models are now manufactured under that banner as well as H&R 1871, Inc.

H&R No. 3 Hammerless

Harrington & Richardson No. 3 Hammerless Single Shot Shotgun **$90**
Takedown. Automatic ejector. Gauges: 12, 16, 20, .410. Barrels: plain, 26- to 32-inch, F choke. Weight: 6½ to 7¼

Harrington & Richardson No. 3 Hammerless (cont.)
pounds depending on gauge and barrel length. Plain pistol-grip stock and forend. Discontinued 1942.

H&R No. 5 Standard Lightweight

Harrington & Richardson No. 5 Standard Light Weight Hammer Single **$100**
Takedown. Auto ejector. Gauges: 24, 28, .410, 14mm. Barrels: 26- or 28-inch, F choke. Weight: about 4 to 4¾ pounds. Plain pistol-grip stock/forend. Discontinued 1942.

H&R No. 6 Heavy Breech

Harrington & Richardson No. 6 Heavy Breech Single Shot Hammer Shotgun **$100**
Takedown. Automatic ejector. Gauges: 10, 12, 16, 20. Barrels: plain, 28- to 36-inch, F choke. Weight: about 7 to 7¼ pounds. Plain stock and forend. Discontinued 1942.

H&R No. 7 Bay State

Harrington & Richardson No. 7 or 9 Bay State Single Shot Hammer Shotgun **$110**
Takedown. Automatic ejector. Gauges: 12, 16, 20, .410. Barrels: plain, 26- to 32-inch, Full choke. Weight: 5½ to 6½ pounds depending on gauge and barrel length. Plain pistol-grip stock and forend. Discontinued 1942.

H&R No. 8 Single Barrel

Harrington & Richardson No. 8 Standard Single Shot Hammer Shotgun **$135**
Takedown. Automatic ejector. Gauges: 12, 16, 20, 24, 28, .410. Barrels: plain, 26- to 32-inch, Full choke. Weight: 5½ to 6½ pounds depending on gauge and barrel length. Plain pistol-grip stock and forend. Made 1908–1942.

SHOTGUNS

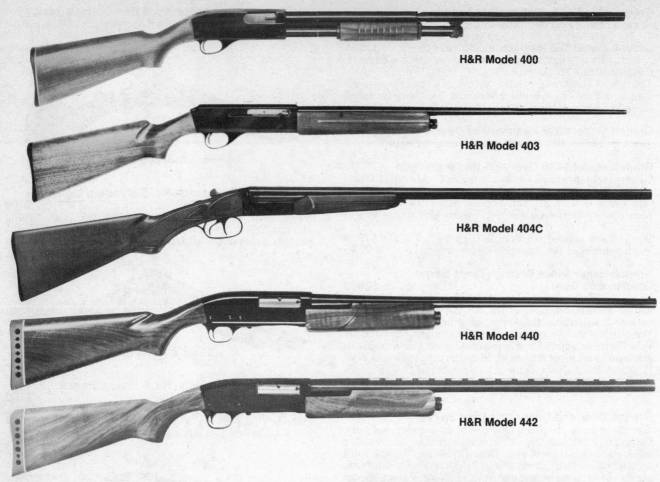

H&R Model 400

H&R Model 403

H&R Model 404C

H&R Model 440

H&R Model 442

**Harrington & Richardson Model 348 Gamester
Bolt Action Shotgun** **$95**
Takedown. 12 and 16 gauge. 2-shot tubular magazine, 28-
inch barrel, Full choke. Plain pistol-grip stock. Weight:
about 7¹/₂ pounds. Made 1949–1954.

**Harrington & Richardson Model 349
Gamester Deluxe** **$110**
Same as Model 348, except has 26-inch barrel with
adjustable choke device, recoil pad. Made 1953–55.

**Harrington & Richardson Model 351 Huntsman
Bolt Action Shotgun** **$125**
Takedown. 12 and 16 gauge. 2-shot tubular magazine.
Pushbutton safety. 26-inch barrel with H&R variable
choke. Weight: about 6³/₄ pounds. Monte Carlo stock with
recoil pad. Made 1956–58.

Harrington & Richardson Model 400 Pump **$175**
Hammerless. Gauges: 12, 16, 20. Tubular magazine holds
4 shells. 28-inch barrel, Full choke. Weight: about 7¹/₄
pounds. Plain pistol-grip stock (recoil pad in 12 and 16
ga.), grooved slide handle. Made 1955–1967.

Harrington & Richardson Model 401 . . . . **$175**
Same as Model 400, except has H&R variable choke. Made
1956–1963.

Harrington & Richardson Model 402 . . . . **$185**
Similar to Model 400, except .410 gauge, weighs about 5¹/₂
pounds. Made 1959–1967.

**Harrington & Richardson Model 403
Autoloading Rifle** **$200**
Takedown. .410 gauge. Tubular magazine holds four shells.
26-inch barrel, Full choke. Weight: about 5³/₄ pounds.
Plain pistol-grip stock and forearm. Made in 1964.

Harrington & Richardson Model 404 Double **$225**
Boxlock. Plain extractors. Double triggers. Gauges: 12,
20, .410. Barrels: 28-inch in 12 ga. (M/F choke), 26-inch
in 20 ga. (IC/M) and .410 (F/F). Weight: 5¹/₂ to 7¹/₄
pounds. Plain walnut-finished hardwood stock and forend.
Made in Brazil by Amadeo Rossi 1969–1972.

Harrington & Richardson Model 404C **$195**
Same as Model 404, except has checkered stock and forend. Made 1969–1972.

Harrington & Richardson Model 440 Pump **$145**
Hammerless. Gauges: 12, 16, 20. 2³/₄-inch chamber in 16
gauge, 3-inch in 12 and 20 gauges. 3-shot magazine. Barrels: 26-, 28-, 30-inch; IC, M, F choke. Weight: 6¹/₄ pounds.
Plain pistol-grip stock and slide handle, recoil pad. Made
1968–1973.

Harrington & Richardson Model 442 . . . . **$185**
Same as Model 440, except has vent-rib barrel, checkered
stock and forearm, weighs 6³/₄ pounds. Made 1969–1973.

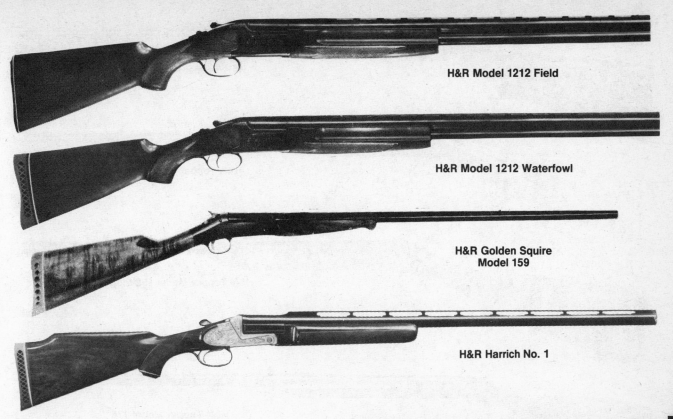

H&R Model 1212 Field

H&R Model 1212 Waterfowl

H&R Golden Squire Model 159

H&R Harrich No. 1

Harrington & Richardson Model 1212 Field **$295**
Boxlock. Plain extractors. Selective single trigger. 12 gauge, 2¾-inch chambers. 28-inch barrels, IC/IM, vent rib. Weight: 7 pounds. Checkered walnut pistol-grip stock and fluted forearm. Made 1976–1980 by Lanber Arms S.A., Zaldibar (Vizcaya), Spain.

Harrington & Richardson Model 1212 Waterfowl Gun **$350**
Same as Field Gun, except chambered for 12-gauge 3-inch Magnum shells, has 30-inch barrels, M/F chokes, stock and recoil pad, weighs 7½ pounds. Made 1976–1980.

Harrington & Richardson Model 1908 Single Shot Shotgun **$115**
Takedown. Automatic ejector. Gauges: 12, 16, 24 and 28. Barrels: 26- to 32-inch, Full choke. Weight: 5¼ to 6½ lbs., depending on gauge and barrel length. Casehardened receiver. Plain pistol-grip stock. Bead front sight. Made 1908–1934.

Harrington & Richardson Model 1908 .410 (12mm) Single Shot Shotgun **$125**
Same general specifications as standard Model 1908, except chambered for .410 or 12mm shot cartridge with barrel milled down at receiver to give a more pleasing contour.

Harrington & Richardson Model 1915 Single Shot Shotgun **$130**
Takedown. Both nonauto and auto ejectors available. Gauges: 24, 28, .410, 14mm and 12mm. Barrels: 26- or 28-inch, Full choke. Weight: 4 to 4¾ lbs., depending on gauge and barrel length. Plain black walnut stock with semi-pistol grip.

Harrington & Richardson Folding Gun **$135**
Single barrel hammer shotgun hinged at the front of the frame, the barrel folds down against the stock. *Light Frame Model:* gauges—28, 14mm, .410; 22-inch barrel; weighs about 4½ pounds. *Heavy Frame Model:* gauges—12, 16, 20, 28, .410; 26-inch barrel; weighs from 5¾ to 6½ pounds. Plain pistol-grip stock and forend. Discontinued 1942.

Harrington & Richardson Golden Squire Model 159 Single Barrel Hammer Shotgun **$100**
Hammerless. Side lever. Automatic ejection. Gauges: 12, 20. Barrels: 30-inch in 12 ga., 28-inch in 20 ga., both F choke. Weight: about 6½ pounds. Straight-grip stock with recoil pad, forearm with schnabel. Made 1964–66.

Harrington & Richardson Golden Squire Jr. Model 459 . . . . **$100**
Same as Model 159, except gauges 20 and .410, 26-inch barrel, youth-size stock. Made in 1964.

Harrington & Richardson Harrich No. 1 Single Barrel Trap Gun **$1750**
Anson & Deeley-type locking system with Kersten top locks and double underlocking lugs. Sideplates engraved with hunting scenes. 12 gauge. Barrels: 32-, 34-inch; Full choke; high vent rib. Weight: 8½ pounds. Checkered Monte Carlo stock with pistol grip and recoil pad, beavertail forearm, of select walnut. Made in Ferlach, Austria, 1971–75.

Harrington & Richardson "Top Rib" Single Barrel Shotgun **$165**
Takedown. Auto ejector. Gauges: 12, 16 and 20. Barrels: 28- to 30-inch, Full choke with full-length matted top rib. Weight: 6½ to 7 lbs. depending on gauge and barrel length. Black walnut pistol-grip stock (capped) and forend; both checkered. Flexible rubber buttplate. Made during 1930s.

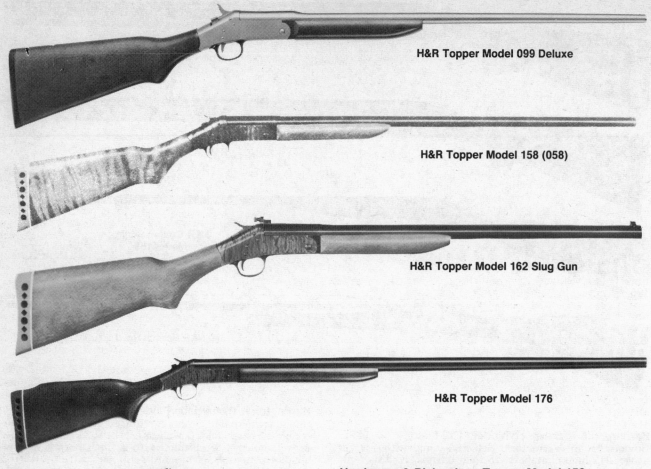

H&R Topper Model 099 Deluxe

H&R Topper Model 158 (058)

H&R Topper Model 162 Slug Gun

H&R Topper Model 176

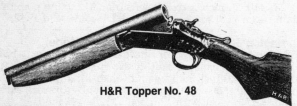

H&R Topper No. 48

Harrington & Richardson Topper No. 48 Single Barrel Hammer Shotgun $125

Similar to old Model 8 Standard. Takedown. Top lever. Auto ejector. Gauges: 12, 16, 20, .410. Barrels: plain; 26- to 30-inch; M or F choke. Weight: 5½ to 6½ pounds depending on gauge and barrel length. Plain pistol-grip stock and forend. Made 1946–1957.

Harrington & Richardson Topper Model 099 Deluxe $110

Same as Model 158, except has matte nickel finish, semi-pistol grip walnut-finished American hardwood stock; semibeavertail forearm; 12, 16, 20, and .410 gauges. Made 1982–86.

Harrington & Richardson Topper Model 148 Single Shot Hammer Shotgun $110

Takedown. Side lever. Auto ejection. Gauges: 12, 16, 20, .410. Barrels: 12 ga., 30-, 32- and 36-inch; 16 ga., 28- and 30-inch; 20 and .410 ga., 28-inch; F choke. Weight: 5 to 6½ pounds. Plain pistol-grip stock and forend, recoil pad. Made 1958–1961.

Harrington & Richardson Topper Model 158 (058) Single Shot Hammer Shotgun $110

Takedown. Side lever. Automatic ejection. Gauges: 12, 20, .410 (2³⁄₄-inch and 3-inch shells); 16 (2³⁄₄-inch). Barrel length and choke combinations: 12 ga., 36-inch/F, 32-inch/F, 30-inch/F, 28-inch/F or M; .410, 28-inch/F. Weight: about 5½ pounds. Plain pistol-grip stock and forend, recoil pad. Made 1962–1981. *Note:* Designation changed to 058 in 1974.

Harrington & Richardson Topper Model 162 Slug Gun $135

Same as Topper Model 158, except has 24-inch barrel, Cyl. bore, with rifle sights. Made 1968–1986.

Harrington & Richardson Topper Model 176 10 Gauge Magnum $145

Similar to Model 158, but has 36-inch heavy barrel chambered for 3½-inch 10-gauge Magnum shells, weighs 10 pounds; stock with Monte Carlo comb and recoil pad, longer and fuller forearm. Made 1977–1986.

Harrington & Richardson Topper Model 188 Deluxe $125

Same as standard Topper Model 148, except has chromed frame, stock and forend in black, red, yellow, blue, green, pink, or purple colored finish. .410 gauge only. Made 1958–1961.

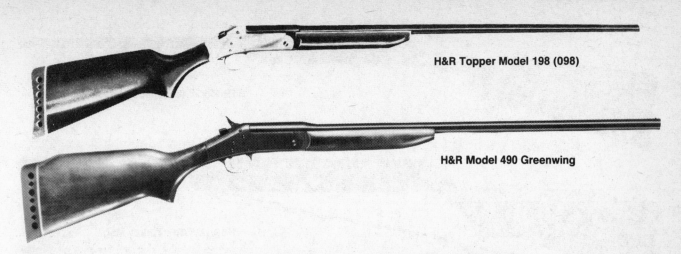

H&R Topper Model 198 (098)

H&R Model 490 Greenwing

Harrington & Richardson Topper Model 198 (098) Deluxe **$130**
Same as Model 158, except has chrome-plated frame, black finished stock and forend; 12, 20 and .410 gauges. Made 1962–1981. *Note:* Designation changed to 098 in 1974.

Harrington & Richardson Topper Jr. Model 480 . **$115**
Similar to No. 48 Topper, except has youth-size stock, 26-inch barrel, .410 gauge only. Made 1958–1961.

Harrington & Richardson Topper No. 488 Deluxe **$110**
Same as standard No. 48 Topper, except chrome-plated frame, black lacquered stock and forend, recoil pad. Discontinued 1957.

Harrington & Richardson Topper Model 490 . . . . **$115**
Same as Model 158, except has youth-size stock (3 inches shorter), 26-inch barrel; 20 and 28 gauge (M choke), .410 (F). Made 1962–1986.

Harrington & Richardson Topper Model 490 Greenwing **$130**
Same as the Model 490, except has a special high-polished finish. Made 1981–86.

Harrington & Richardson Topper Jr. Model 580 . **$100**
Same as Model 480, except has colored stocks as on Model 188. Made 1958–1961.

Harrington & Richardson Topper Model 590 . . . . **$105**
Same as Model 490, except has chrome-plated frame, black finished stock and forend. Made 1962–63.

> **NOTE:** The following models are manufactured and distributed by the reorganized company of H&R 1871, Inc.

H&R Model 098 Topper Classic Youth **$95**
Same as Topper Junior, except also available in 28 gauge and has checkered American black walnut stock/forend w/satin finish and recoil pad. Made 1991 to date.

H&R Model 098 Topper Deluxe **$95**
Same as Model 098 Single Shot Hammer, except in 12 gauge, 3-inch chamber only. 28-inch barrel; Mod. choke tube. Made 1992 to date.

H&R Model 098 Topper Hammer Single Shot Shotgun **$80**
Side lever. Automatic ejector. Gauges: 12, 20 and .410; 3-inch chamber. Barrels: 28-inch, (12 ga./M); 26-inch, (20 ga./M); 26-inch (.410/F). Weight: 5 to 6 pounds. Satin nickel receiver, blued barrel. Plain pistol-grip stock and semibeavertail forend w/black finish. Reintroduced 1992.

SHOTGUNS

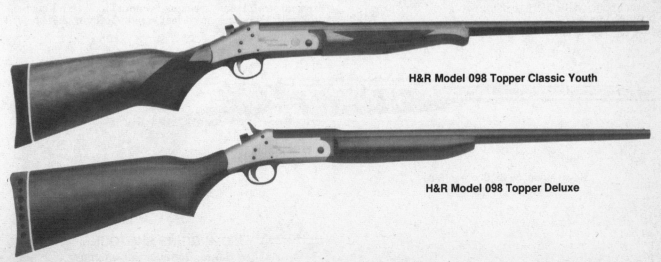

H&R Model 098 Topper Classic Youth

H&R Model 098 Topper Deluxe

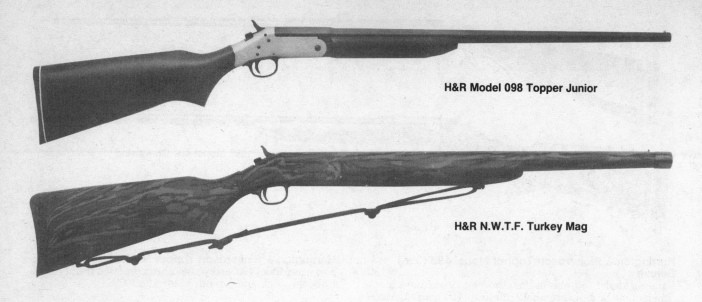

H&R Model 098 Topper Junior

H&R N.W.T.F. Turkey Mag

H&R Model 098 Topper Junior **$85**
Same as Model 098, except has youth-size stock and 22-inch barrel. 20 or .410 gauge only. Made 1991 to date.

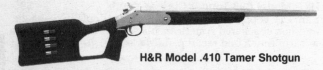

H&R Model .410 Tamer Shotgun

H&R Model .410 Tamer Shotgun **$90**
Takedown. Topper-style single-shot, side lever action w/auto ejector. Gauge: .410; 3-inch chamber. 19.5-inch barrel. 33 inches overall. Weight: 5.75 pounds. Black polymer thumbhole stock designed to hold 4 extra shotshells. Matte electroless nickel finish. Made 1994 to date.

H&R Model N.W.T.F. Turkey Mag
Same as Model 098 Single Shot Hammer, except w/24-inch barrel, 3.5-inch chamber w/screw-in choke tube. Weight: 6 pounds. American hardwood stock, Mossy Oak camo finish. Made 1991 to date.
NWTF Turkey Mag. **$120**
NWTF Youth Turkey Mag. **115**

HERCULES SHOTGUNS
See listings under "W" for Montgomery Ward.

HEYM SHOTGUNS
Münnerstadt, Germany

Heym Model 22S "Safety" Shotgun/Rifle Combination **$2495**
Gauges: 16 and 20. Calibers: 22 Mag., 22 Hornet, 222 Rem., 222 Rem. Mag., 5.6 × 50 R Mag., 6.5 × 57 R, 7 × 57 R, 243 Win. 24-inch barrels. 40 inches overall. Weight: about 5½ pounds. Single-set trigger. Left-side barrel selector. Integral dovetail base for scope mounting. Arabesque engraving. Walnut stock. Discontinued 1993.

Heym Model 55 BF Shotgun/Rifle Combo **$4995**
Gauges: 12, 16 and 20. Calibers: 5.6 × 50 R Mag., 6.5 × 57 R, 7 × 57 R, 7 × 65 R, 243 Win., 308 Win., 30-06. 25-inch barrels. 42 inches overall. Weight: about 6¾ pounds. Black satin-finished, corrosion-resistant barrels of Krupps special steel. Hand-checkered walnut stock with long pistol grip. Hand-engraved leaf scroll. German cheekpiece. Discontinued 1988.

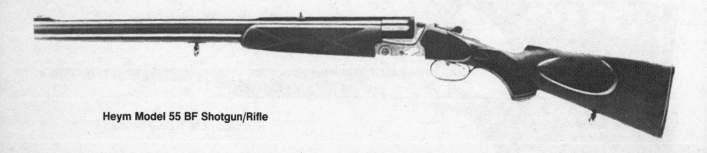

Heym Model 55 BF Shotgun/Rifle

J. C. HIGGINS SHOTGUNS
See Sears, Roebuck & Company.

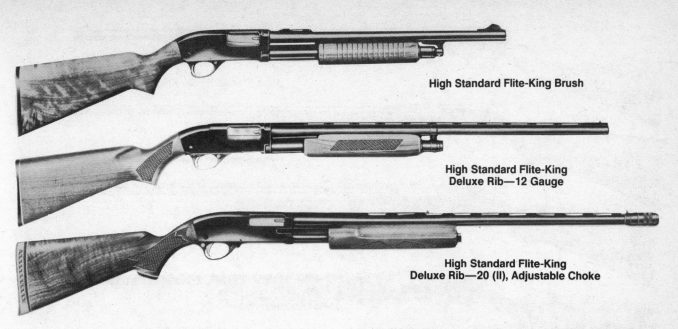

High Standard Flite-King Brush

High Standard Flite-King Deluxe Rib—12 Gauge

High Standard Flite-King Deluxe Rib—20 (II), Adjustable Choke

HIGH STANDARD SPORTING ARMS
East Hartford, Connecticut
Formerly High Standard Mfg. Corp. of Hamden, Conn.

In 1966, High Standard introduced new series of Flite-King pumps and Supermatic autoloaders, both readily identifiable by the damascened bolt and restyled checkering. To avoid confusion, these models are designated "Series II" in this text. This is *not* an official factory designation. Operation of this firm was discontinued in 1984.

High Standard Flite-King Brush—12 Gauge **$200**
Same as Flite-King Field 12, except has 18- or 20-inch barrel (cylinder bore) with rifle sights. Made 1962–64.

High Standard Flite-King Brush Deluxe **$255**
Same as Flite-King Brush, except has adjustable peep rear sight, checkered pistol grip, recoil pad, fluted slide handle, swivels and sling. Not available with 18-inch barrel. Made 1964–66.

High Standard Flite-King Brush (Series II) **$235**
Same as Flite-King Deluxe 12 (II), except has 20-inch barrel, cylinder bore, with rifle sights. Weight: 7 pounds. Made 1966–1975.

High Standard Flite-King Brush Deluxe (II) **$260**
Same as Flite-King Brush (II), except has adjustable peep rear sight, swivels and sling. Made 1966–1975.

High Standard Flite-King Deluxe—12 Ga. (Series II)
Hammerless. 5-shot magazine. Barrels: plain; 27-inch with adjustable choke. 26-inch IC, 28-inch M or F, 30-inch Full choke. Weight: about 7 1/4 pounds. Checkered pistol-grip stock and forearm, recoil pad. Made 1966–1975.
With adjustable choke **$275**
Without adjustable choke **250**

High Standard Flite-King Deluxe—20, 28, .410 Gauge (Series II) **$235**
Same as Flite-King Deluxe 12 (II), except chambered for 20 and .410 gauge 3-inch shell, 28 gauge 2 3/4-inch shell;

High Standard Flite-King Deluxe—20, 28, .410 (cont.)
plain barrel in IC (20), M (20, 28), F choke (20, 28, .410). Weight: about 6 pounds. Made 1966–1975.

High Standard Flite-King Deluxe Rib—12 Ga. . . . **$295**
Same as Flite-King Field 12, except vent-rib barrel (28-inch M or F, 30-inch F), checkered stock and forearm. Made 1961–66.

High Standard Flite-King Deluxe Rib—12 Gauge (II)
Same as Flite-King Deluxe 12 (II), except has vent-rib barrel; available in 27-inch with adjustable choke, 28-inch M or F, 30-inch F choke. Made 1966–1975.
With adjustable choke **$300**
Without adjustable choke **295**

High Standard Flite-King Deluxe Rib—20 Ga. . . . **$275**
Same as Flite-King Field 20, except vent-rib barrel (28-inch M or F), checkered stock and slide handle. Made 1962–66.

High Standard Flite-King Deluxe Rib—20, 28, .410 Ga. (Series II)
Same as Flite-King Deluxe 20, 28, .410 (II), except 20 gauge available with 27-inch adjustable choke, 28-inch M or F choke. Weight: about 6 1/4 pounds. Made 1966–1975.
With adjustable choke **$300**
Without adjustable choke **295**

High Standard Flite-King Deluxe Skeet Gun— 12 Gauge (Series II) **$275**
Same as Flite-King Deluxe Rib 12 (II), except available only with 26-inch vent-rib barrel, skeet choke; recoil pad optional. Made 1966–1975.

High Standard Flite-King Deluxe Skeet Gun— 20, 28, 410 Gauge (Series II) **$305**
Same as Flite-King Deluxe Rib 20, 28, .410 (II) except available only with 26-inch vent-rib barrel, skeet choke. Made 1966–1975.

High Standard Flite-King Deluxe Trap Gun (II) . . **$275**
Same as Flite-King Deluxe Rib 12 (II), except available only with 30-inch vent-rib barrel, Full choke; trap-style stock. Made 1966–1975.

SHOTGUNS

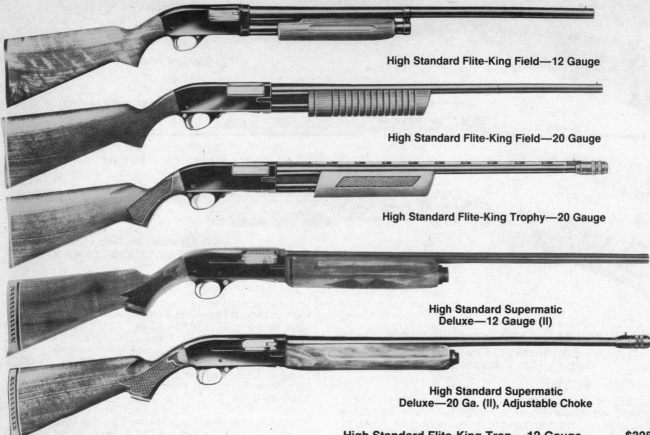

High Standard Flite-King Field—12 Gauge

High Standard Flite-King Field—20 Gauge

High Standard Flite-King Trophy—20 Gauge

High Standard Supermatic
Deluxe—12 Gauge (II)

High Standard Supermatic
Deluxe—20 Ga. (II), Adjustable Choke

High Standard Flite-King Field Pump—12 Ga. . . . **$225**
Hammerless. Magazine holds 5 shells. Barrels: 26-inch
IC, 28-inch M or F, 30-inch F choke. Weight: 7¼ pounds.
Plain pistol-grip stock and slide handle. Made 1960–66.

High Standard Flite-King Field Pump—20 Ga. . . . **$205**
Hammerless. Chambered for 3-inch Magnum shells, also
handles 2¾-inch. Magazine holds four shells. Barrels: 26-
inch IC, 28-inch M or F choke. Weight: about 6 pounds.
Plain pistol-grip stock and slide handle. Made 1961–66.

High Standard Flite-King Pump Shotguns—16 Gauge
Same general specifications as Flite-King 12, except not
available in Brush, Skeet and Trap Models, or 30-inch
barrel. Values same as for 12-gauge guns. Made 1961–65.

High Standard Flite-King Pump Shotguns—.410 Ga.
Same general specifications as Flite-King 20, except not
available in Special and Trophy Models, or with other
than 26-inch Full choke barrel. Values same as for 20-
gauge guns. Made 1962–66.

High Standard Flite-King Skeet—12 Gauge **$310**
Same as Flite-King Deluxe Rib, except 26-inch vent-rib
barrel, with SK choke. Made 1962–66.

High Standard Flite-King Special—12 Gauge . . . **$225**
Same as Flite-King Field 12, except has 27-inch barrel
with adjustable choke. Made 1960–66.

High Standard Flite-King Special—20 Gauge . . . **$230**
Same as Flite-King Field 20, except has 27-inch barrel
with adjustable choke. Made 1961–66.

High Standard Flite-King Trap—12 Gauge **$325**
Same as Flite-King Deluxe Rib 12, except 30-inch vent-
rib barrel, Full choke; special trap stock with recoil pad.
Made 1962–66.

High Standard Flite-King Trophy—12 Gauge . . . **$310**
Same as Flite-King Deluxe Rib 12, except has 27-inch
vent-rib barrel with adjustable choke. Made 1960–66.

High Standard Flite-King Trophy—20 Gauge . . . **$325**
Same as Flite-King Deluxe Rib 20, except has 27-inch
vent-rib barrel with adjustable choke. Made 1962–66.

High Standard Supermatic Deer Gun **$300**
Same as Supermatic Field 12, except has 22-inch barrel
(cylinder bore) with rifle sights, checkered stock and forearm, recoil pad. Weight: 7¾ pounds. Made in 1965.

High Standard Supermatic Deluxe—12 Ga. (Series II)
Gas-operated autoloader. 4-shot magazine. Barrels: plain;
27-inch with adjustable choke (discontinued about 1970);
26-inch IC, 28-inch M or F, 30-inch F choke. Weight:
about 7½ pounds. Checkered pistol-grip stock and forearm, recoil pad. Made 1966–1975.
With adjustable choke **$310**
Without adjustable choke **275**

High Standard Supermatic Deluxe—20 Ga. (Series II)
Same as Supermatic Deluxe 12 (II), except chambered for
20 gauge 3-inch shell; barrels available in 27-inch with
adjustable choke (discontinued about 1970), 26-inch IC,
28-inch M or F choke. Weight: about 7 pounds. Made
1966–1975.
With adjustable choke **$295**
Without adjustable choke **275**

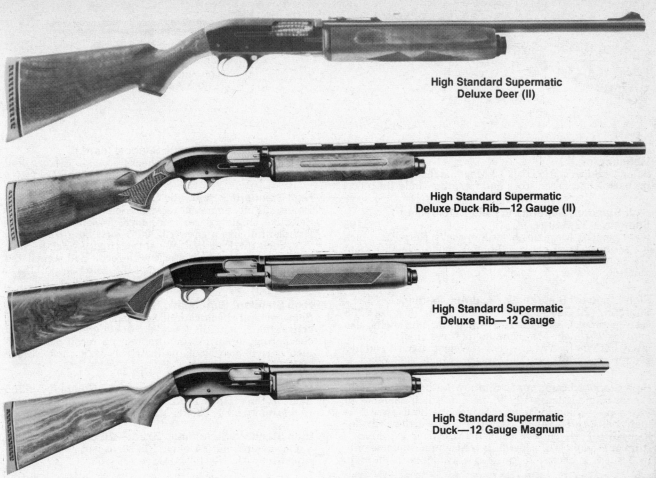

High Standard Supermatic
Deluxe Deer (II)

High Standard Supermatic
Deluxe Duck Rib—12 Gauge (II)

High Standard Supermatic
Deluxe Rib—12 Gauge

High Standard Supermatic
Duck—12 Gauge Magnum

High Standard Supermatic Deluxe Deer Gun (II) . . . **$310**
Same as Supermatic Deluxe 12 (II), except has 22-inch barrel, cylinder bore, with rifle sights. Weight: 7¾ pounds. Made 1966–1974.

**High Standard Supermatic Deluxe Duck—
12 Gauge Magnum (Series II)** **$225**
Same as Supermatic Deluxe 12 (II), except chambered for 3-inch Magnum shell, 3-shot magazine; 30-inch plain barrel, Full choke. Weight: 8 pounds. Made 1966–1974.

**High Standard Supermatic Deluxe Duck Rib—
12 Gauge Magnum (Series II)** **$245**
Same as Supermatic Deluxe Rib 12 (II), except chambered for 3-inch Magnum shell, 3-shot magazine; 30-inch vent-rib barrel, Full choke. Weight: 8 pounds. Made 1966–1975.

High Standard Supermatic Deluxe Rib—12 Ga. **$215**
Same as Supermatic Field 12, except vent-rib barrel (28-inch M or F, 30-inch F), checkered stock and forearm. Made 1961–66.

High Standard Supermatic Deluxe Rib—12 Gauge (II)
Same as Supermatic Deluxe 12 (II), except has vent-rib barrel; available in 27-inch with adjustable choke, 28-inch M or F, 30-inch F choke. Made 1966–1975.
With adjustable choke **$275**
Without adjustable choke **250**

High Standard Supermatic Deluxe Rib—20 Ga. **$275**
Same as Supermatic Field 20, except vent-rib barrel (28-inch M or F), checkered stock and forearm. Made 1963–66.

High Standard Supermatic Deluxe Rib—20 Ga. (II)
Same as Supermatic Deluxe 20 (II), except has vent-rib barrel. Made 1966–1975.
With adjustable choke **$275**
Without adjustable choke **245**

**High Standard Supermatic Deluxe Skeet Gun—
12 Gauge (Series II)** **$265**
Same as Supermatic Deluxe Rib 12 (II), except available only with 26-inch vent-rib barrel, SK choke. Made 1966–1975.

**High Standard Supermatic Deluxe Skeet Gun—
20 Gauge (Series II)** **$275**
Same as Supermatic Deluxe Rib 20 (II), except available only with 26-inch vent-rib barrel, SK choke. Made 1966–1975.

**High Standard Supermatic Deluxe Trap Gun
(Series II)** **$280**
Same as Supermatic Deluxe Rib 12 (II), except available only with 30-inch vent-rib barrel, Full choke; trap-style stock. Made 1966–1975.

High Standard Supermatic Duck—12 Ga. Mag. . . **$245**
Same as Supermatic Field 12, except chambered for 3-inch Magnum shell, 30-inch Full choke barrel, recoil pad. Made 1961–66.

**High Standard Supermatic
Duck Rib—12 Gauge**

**High Standard Supermatic Duck Rib—12 Gauge
Magnum** **$265**
Same as Supermatic Duck 12 Magnum, except has vent-rib barrel, checkered stock and forearm. Made 1961–66.

**High Standard Supermatic Field Autoloading
Shotgun—12 Gauge** **$195**
Gas-operated. Magazine holds four shells. Barrels: 26-inch IC, 28-inch M or F choke, 30-inch F choke. Weight: about 7 1/2 pounds. Plain pistol-grip stock and forearm. Made 1960–66.

**High Standard Supermatic Field Autoloading
Shotgun—20 Gauge** **$205**
Gas-operated. Chambered for 3-inch Magnum shells, also handles 2 3/4-inch. Magazine holds three shells. Barrels: 26-inch IC, 28-inch M or F choke. Weight: about 7 pounds. Plain pistol-grip stock and forearm. Made 1963–66.

High Standard Supermatic Shadow Automatic . . **$290**
Gas-operated. Gauge: 12, 20, 2 3/4- or 3-inch chamber in 12 gauges, 3-inch in 20 gauge. Magazine holds four 2 3/4-inch shells, three 3-inch. Barrels: full-size airflow rib; 26-inch (IC or SK choke); 28-inch (M, IM or F); 30-inch (trap or F choke); 12-gauge 3-inch Magnum available only in 30-inch F choke; 20 gauge not available in 30-inch.

High Standard Supermatic Shadow (cont.)
Weight: 12 ga., 7 pounds. Checkered walnut stock and forearm. Made 1974–75 by Caspoll Int'l., Inc., Tokyo.

High Standard Supermatic Shadow Indy O/U . . . **$795**
Boxlock. Fully engraved receiver. Selective auto ejectors. Selective single trigger. 12 gauge. 2 3/4-inch chambers. Barrels: full-size airflow rib; 27 1/2-inch both SK choke, 29 3/4-inch IM/F or F/F. Weight: with 29 3/4-inch barrels, 8 lbs. 2 oz. Pistol-grip stock with recoil pad, ventilated forearm, skip checkering. Made 1974–75 by Caspoll Int'l., Inc., Tokyo.

High Standard Supermatic Shadow Seven **$625**
Same general specifications as Shadow Indy, except has conventional vent rib, less elaborate engraving, standard checkering; forearm is not vented, no recoil pad. 27 1/2-inch barrels also available in IC/M, M/F choke. Made 1974–75.

High Standard Supermatic Skeet—12 Gauge . . . **$205**
Same as Supermatic Deluxe Rib 12, except 26-inch vent-rib barrel with SK choke. Made 1962–66.

High Standard Supermatic Skeet—20 Gauge . . . **$230**
Same as Supermatic Deluxe Rib 20, except 26-inch vent-rib barrel with SK choke. Made 1964–66.

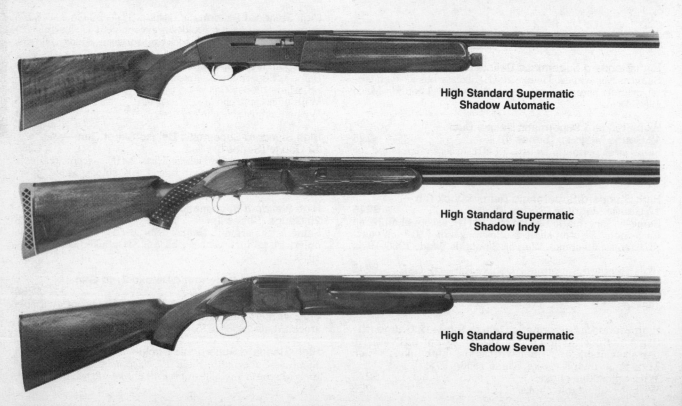

**High Standard Supermatic
Shadow Automatic**

**High Standard Supermatic
Shadow Indy**

**High Standard Supermatic
Shadow Seven**

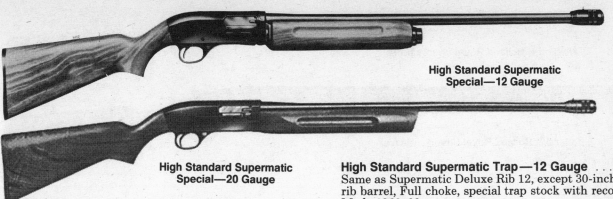

**High Standard Supermatic
Special—12 Gauge**

**High Standard Supermatic
Special—20 Gauge**

High Standard Supermatic Trap—12 Gauge . . . **$225**
Same as Supermatic Deluxe Rib 12, except 30-inch vent-rib barrel, Full choke, special trap stock with recoil pad. Made 1962–66.

High Standard Supermatic Special—12 Gauge . **$210**
Same as Supermatic Field 12, except has 27-inch barrel with adjustable choke. Made 1960–66.

High Standard Supermatic Trophy—12 Gauge . . **$225**
Same as Supermatic Deluxe Rib 12, except has 27-inch vent-rib barrel with adjustable choke. Made 1961–66.

High Standard Supermatic Special—20 Gauge . **$220**
Same as Supermatic Field 20, except has 27-inch barrel with adjustable choke. Made 1963–66.

High Standard Supermatic Trophy—20 Gauge . . **$230**
Same as Supermatic Deluxe Rib 20, except has 27-inch vent-rib barrel with adjustable choke. Made 1963–66.

**High Standard Supermatic
Trophy—12 Gauge**

**High Standard Supermatic
Trophy—20 Gauge**

**Holland & Holland Centenary Model Hammerless
Double Barrel Shotgun**
Lightweight (5½ lbs.). 12 gauge game gun designed for 2-inch shell. Made in four grades—Model Deluxe, Royal, Badminton, Dominion—values same as shown for standard guns in those grades. Discontinued 1962.

HOLLAND & HOLLAND, LTD.
London, England

Holland & Holland Badminton Model Hammerless Double Barrel Shotgun. Originally No. 2 Grade
General specifications same as Royal Model except without self-opening action. Made as a Game Gun or Pigeon and Wildfowl Gun. Made from 1902 to date.
With double triggers **$8250**
With single trigger **8950**

**Holland & Holland Dominion Model Hammerless
Double Barrel Shotgun** **$4695**
Game Gun. Sidelock. Auto ejectors. Double triggers. Gauges: 12, 16, 20. Barrels: 25- to 30-inch, any standard boring. Checkered stock and forend, straight grip standard. Discontinued 1967.

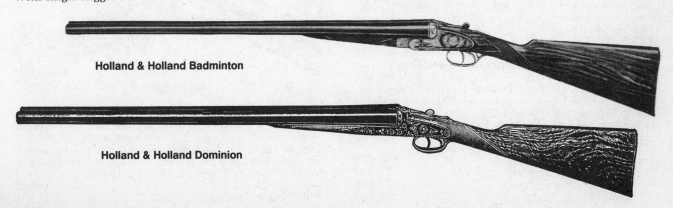

Holland & Holland Badminton

Holland & Holland Dominion

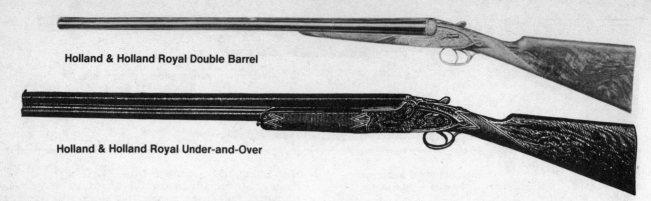

Holland & Holland Royal Double Barrel

Holland & Holland Royal Under-and-Over

Holland & Holland Model Deluxe Hammerless Double
Same as Royal Model, except has special engraving and exhibition grade stock and forearm. Currently mfd.
With Double Triggers **$25,950**
With Single Trigger **27,950**

Holland & Holland Northwood

Holland & Holland Northwood Model Hammerless
Double Barrel Shotgun **$5295**
Anson & Deeley system boxlock. Auto ejectors. Double triggers. Gauges: 12, 16, 20, 28 in Game Model; 28 gauge not offered in Pigeon Model; Wildfowl Model in 12 gauge only (3-inch chambers available). Barrels: 28-inch standard in Game and Pigeon Models, 30-inch in Wildfowl Model; other lengths, any standard choke combination available. Weight: from 5 to 7³/₄ pounds depending on gauge and barrels. Checkered straight-grip or pistol-grip stock and forearm. Discontinued.

Holland & Holland Riviera Model Pigeon Gun . . . $10,500
Same as Badminton Model but supplied with two sets of barrels, double triggers. Discontinued 1967.

Holland & Holland Royal Model Hammerless Double
Self-opening. Sidelocks, hand-detachable. Auto ejectors. Double triggers or single trigger. Gauges: 12, 16, 20, 28, .410. Built to customer's specifications as to barrel length, chokes, etc. Made as a Game Gun or Pigeon and Wildfowl Gun, the latter having treble-grip action and side clips. Checkered stock and forend, straight grip standard. Made from 1885 to date.
With Double Triggers **$23,950**
With Single Trigger **25,250**

Holland & Holland Royal Model Under-and-Over
Sidelocks, hand-detachable. Auto ejectors. Double triggers or single trigger. 12 gauge. Built to customer's specifications as to barrel length, chokes, etc. Made as a Game Gun or Pigeon and Wildfowl Gun. Checkered stock and forend, straight grip standard. *Note:* In 1951 Holland & Holland introduced its New Model Under/Over with an improved, narrower action body. Discont. 1960.
New Model (Double Triggers) **$25,000**
New Model (Single Trigger) **27,500**
Old Model (Double Triggers) **17,500**
Old Model (Single Trigger) **19,500**

Holland & Holland Single Shot Super Trap Gun
Anson & Deeley system boxlock. Auto ejector. No safety. 12 gauge. Barrels: wide vent rib, 30- or 32-inch, with Extra Full choke. Weight: about 8³/₄ pounds. Monte Carlo stock with pistol grip and recoil pad, full beavertail forearm. Models differ in grade of engraving and wood. Discontinued.
Standard Grade **$4750**
Deluxe Grade **6850**
Exhibition Grade **8950**

HUNTER ARMS COMPANY
Fulton, New York

Hunter Fulton

Hunter Fulton Hammerless Double Barrel Shotgun
Boxlock. Plain extractors. Double triggers or non-selective single trigger. Gauges: 12, 16, 20. Barrels: 26- to 32-inch, various choke combinations. Weight: about 7 pounds. Checkered pistol-grip stock and forearm. Discont. 1948.
With Double Triggers **$325**
With Single Trigger **550**

Hunter Special

Hunter Special Hammerless Double Barrel Shotgun
Boxlock. Plain extractors. Double triggers or non-selective single trigger. Gauges: 12, 16, 20. Barrels: 26- to 30-inch, various choke combinations. Weight: 6¹/₂ to 7¹/₄ pounds depending on barrel length and gauge. Checkered full pistol-grip stock and forearm. Discont. 1948.
With Double Triggers **$525**
With Single Trigger **610**

IGA SHOTGUNS
South Hackensack, New Jersey
Distributed by Stoeger Industries, Inc.

IGA Coach Gun **$195**
Gauges: 12, 20 and .410. 20-inch side-by-side barrels of chrome-molybdenum steel. Chokes: IC/M, 3-inch chambers. Weight: 6½ pounds. Double triggers. Automatic safety. Hand-rubbed, oil-finish pistol grip hardwood stock and forend with hand-checkering. Made from 1983 to date.

IGA Condor I O/U Single Trigger Shotgun
Gauge: 12 or 20. 26- or 28-inch barrels of chrome-molybdenum steel. Chokes: Fixed—M/F or IC/M; screw-in choke tubes (12 ga. only). 3-inch chambers. Weight: 6¾ to 7 pounds. Sighting rib with anti-glare surface. Hand-checkered, hardwood pistol grip stock and forend. Made from 1983 to date.
With Fixed Chokes **$395**
With Screw-in Tubes 425

IGA Condor II O/U Double Trigger Shotgun **$295**
Same general specifications as the Condor I Over/Under, except with double triggers and fixed chokes only.

IGA Era 2000 O/U Shotgun **$425**
Gauge: 12 with 3-inch chambers. 26- or 28-inch barrels of chrome-molybdenum steel with screw-in choke tubes. Extractors. Manual safety. (Mechanical triggers.) Weight: 7 pounds. Checkered Brazilian hardwood stock with oil finish. Made 1992–95.

IGA Reuna Single Shot Shotgun **$80**
Visible hammer. Under-lever release. Gauges: 12, 20 and .410; 3-inch chambers. 26- or 28-inch barrels with fixed chokes or screw-in choke tubes (12 gauge only). Extractors. Weight: 5¼ to 6½ pounds. Plain Brazilian hardwood stock and semibeavertail forend. Made from 1992 to date.

IGA Uplander Side-by-Side Shotgun
Gauges: 12, 20, 28 and .410. 26- or 28-inch barrels of chrome-molybdenum steel. Various fixed-choke combinations; screw-in choke tubes (12 ga. only). 3-inch chambers (2¾-inch in 28 ga.). Weight: 6¼ to 7 pounds. Double triggers. Automatic safety. Matte-finished solid sighting rib. Hand-rubbed, oil-finish pistol grip stock and forend with hand-checkering. Made from 1983 to date.
With Fixed Chokes **$240**
With Screw-in Tubes 265

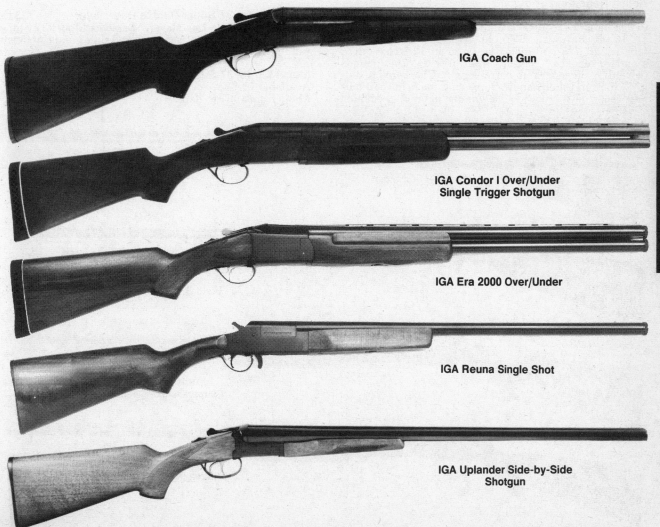

IGA Coach Gun

IGA Condor I Over/Under
Single Trigger Shotgun

IGA Era 2000 Over/Under

IGA Reuna Single Shot

IGA Uplander Side-by-Side
Shotgun

SHOTGUNS

ITHACA GUN COMPANY
King Ferry (formerly Ithaca), New York
Now Ithaca Acquisition Corp./Ithaca Gun Co.

In 1988 Ithaca Gun Company was reorganized as Ithaca Acquisition Corporation. While some models were discontinued, others have been reintroduced and updated.

Ithaca Model 37 Bicentennial Commemorative . . **$395**
Limited to issue of 1976. Similar to Model 37 Supreme, except has special Bicentennial design etched on receiver, full-fancy walnut stock and slide handle. Serial numbers U.S.A. 0001 to U.S.A. 1976. Comes in presentation case with cast pewter belt buckle. Made in 1976. Value is for gun in new, unfired condition.

Ithaca Model 37 English Ultra **$345**
Same general specifications as Model 37 Ultralite, except straight buttstock, 25-inch Rot-Forged vent-rib barrel. Made 1984–87.

Ithaca Model 37 Featherlight Standard Grade Slide Action Repeating Shotgun
Adaptation of the earlier Remington Model 17, a Browning design patented in 1915. Hammerless. Takedown. Gauges: 12, 16 (discontinued 1973), 20. 4-shell magazine. Barrel lengths: 26-, 28-, 30-inch (the latter in 12 gauge only); standard chokes. Weight: from 5¾ to 7½ pounds depending on gauge and barrel length. Checkered pistol-grip stock and slide handle. Some guns made in the 1950s and 1960s have grooved slide handle; plain or checkered

Ithaca Model 37 Featherlight Standard (cont.)
pistol grip. Made 1937–1984.
Standard w/checkered pistol grip **$230**
Standard w/plain stock **205**
Model 37D Deluxe (1954–1977) **285**
Model 37DV Deluxe Vent Rib (1962–1984) **315**
Model 37R Deluxe Solid Rib (1955–1961) **305**
Model 37V Standard Vent Rib (1962–1984) **265**

Ithaca Model 37 Field Grade Mag. w/Tubes **$295**
Same general specifications as Model 37 Featherlight, except 32-inch barrel and detachable choke tubes. Vent-rib barrel. Made 1984–87.

Ithaca Model 37 $5000 Grade **$5795**
Custom built, elaborately engraved and inlaid with gold, hand-finished working parts, stock and forend of select figured walnut. General specifications same as standard Model 37. *Note:* The same gun was designated the $1000 Grade prior to World War II. Made 1937–1967.

Ithaca Model 37 Standard Deerslayer **$285**
Same as Model 37 Standard, except has 20- or 26-inch barrel bored for rifled slugs, rifle-type open rear sight and ramp front sight. Weight: 5¾ to 6½ pounds depending on gauge and barrel length. Made 1959 to date.

Ithaca Model 37 Super Deluxe Deerslayer **$315**
Formerly "Deluxe Deerslayer." Same as Model 37 Standard Deerslayer, except has stock and slide handle of fancy walnut. Made from 1962 to date.

Ithaca Model 37 Supreme Grade **$425**
Available in Skeet or Trap Gun, similar to Model 37T. Made from 1967 to date.

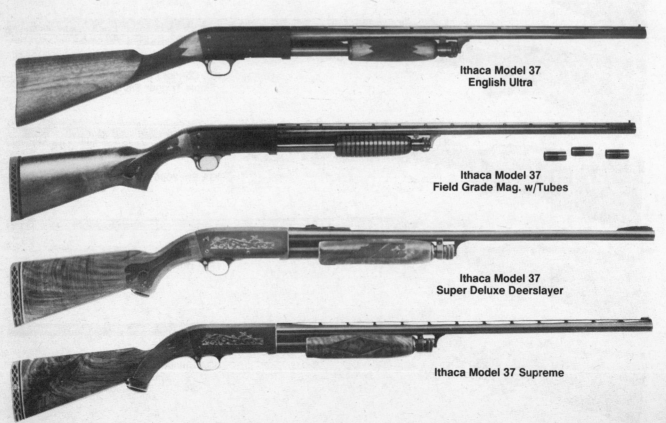

Ithaca Model 37
English Ultra

Ithaca Model 37
Field Grade Mag. w/Tubes

Ithaca Model 37
Super Deluxe Deerslayer

Ithaca Model 37 Supreme

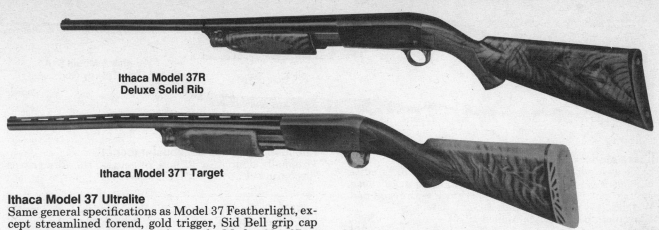

**Ithaca Model 37R
Deluxe Solid Rib**

Ithaca Model 37T Target

Ithaca Model 37 Ultralite
Same general specifications as Model 37 Featherlight, except streamlined forend, gold trigger, Sid Bell grip cap and vent rib. Weight: 5 to 5³/₄ pounds. Made 1984–87.
Standard **$315**
With Choke Tubes **355**

Ithaca Model 37R Solid Rib Grade
Same general specifications as the Model 37 Featherlight, except has a raised solid rib, adding about ¹/₄ pound of weight. Made 1937–1967.
With checkered grip and slide handle **$300**
With plain stock **295**

Ithaca Model 37S Skeet Grade **$465**
Same general specifications as the Model 37 Featherlight, except has vent rib and large extension-type forend; weighs about ¹/₂ pound more. Made 1937–1955.

Ithaca Model 37T Target Grade **$450**
Same general specifications as Model 37 Featherlight, except has vent-rib barrel, checkered stock and slide handle of fancy walnut (choice of skeet- or trap-style stock). *Note:* This model replaced Model 37S Skeet and Model 37T Trap. Made 1955–1961.

Ithaca Model 37T Trap Grade **$465**
Same general specifications as the Model 37S, except has straighter trap-style stock of select walnut, recoil pad; weighs about ¹/₂ pound more. Made 1937–1955.

Ithaca Model 51 Deerslayer **$295**
Same as Model 51 Standard, except has 24-inch plain barrel with slug boring, rifle sights, recoil pad. Weight: about 7¹/₄ pounds. Made 1972–1984.

Ithaca Model 51 Deluxe Skeet Grade **$385**
Same as Model 51 Standard, except 26-inch vent-rib barrel only, SK choke, skeet-style stock, semi-fancy wood. Weight: about 8 pounds. Made 1970–1987.

Ithaca Model 51 Deluxe Trap Grade
Same as Model 51 Standard, except 12 gauge only, 30-inch barrel with broad floating rib, F choke, trap-style stock w/straight or Monte Carlo comb, semifancy wood, recoil pad. Weight: about 8 lbs. Made 1970–1987.
With straight stock **$315**
With Monte Carlo stock **345**

Ithaca Model 51 Standard Automatic Shotgun
Gas-operated. Gauges: 12, 20. 3-shot. Barrels: plain or vent rib; 30-inch F choke (12 gauge only), 28-inch F or M, 26-inch IC. Weight: 7¹/₄–7³/₄ pounds depending on gauge and barrel. Checkered pistol-grip stock, forearm. Made 1970–1980. Still avail. in 12 and 20 ga., 28-inch M choke only.
With plain barrel **$230**
With ventilated rib **275**

SHOTGUNS

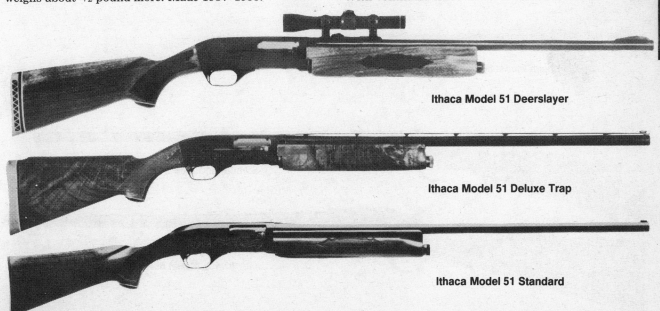

Ithaca Model 51 Deerslayer

Ithaca Model 51 Deluxe Trap

Ithaca Model 51 Standard

**Ithaca Model 51A
Turkey Gun**

Ithaca Model 51 Standard Magnum

Same as Model 51 Standard, except has 3-inch chamber, handles Magnum shells only; 30-inch barrel in 12 gauge, 28-inch in 20 gauge, F or M choke, stock with recoil pad. Weight: 7¾–8 pounds. Made 1972 to date.

With plain barrel (discontinued 1976). **$250**
With ventilated rib. **295**

Ithaca Model 51A Turkey Gun **$325**

Same general specifications as standard Model 51 Magnum, except 26-inch barrel and matte finish. Disc. 1986.

Ithaca Model 66 Long Tom **$100**

Same as Model 66 Standard, except has 36-inch Full choke barrel, 12 gauge only, checkered stock and recoil pad standard. Made 1969–1974.

Ithaca Model 66 Standard Supersingle Lever

Single shot. Hand-cocked hammer. Gauges: 12 (discont. 1974), 20, .410; 3-inch chambers. Barrels: 12 ga., 30-inch Full choke, 28-inch F or M; 20 ga., 28-inch F or M; .410, 26-inch F. Weight: about 7 pounds. Plain or checkered straight-grip stock, plain forend. Made 1963–1978.

Standard Model **$125**
Vent Rib Model (20 ga., checkered stock, recoil
  pad, 1969–1974) **145**
Youth Model (20 & .410 ga., 26-inch bbl., shorter
  stock, recoil pad, 1965–1978) **105**

Ithaca Model 66RS Buckbuster **$150**

Same as Model 66 Standard, except has 22-inch barrel, cylinder bore with rifle sights; later version has recoil pad.

Ithaca Model 66RS Buckbuster (cont.)

Originally offered in 12 and 20 gauges; the former was discontinued in 1970. Made 1967–1978.

> **NOTE:** Previously issued as the Ithaca Model 37, the Model 87 listed below is now made available through the Ithaca Acquisition Corp.

Ithaca Model 87 Deerslayer Shotgun

Gauges: 12 or 20, 3-inch chamber. Barrels: 18½-, 20- or 25-inch (w/special or rifled bore). Weight: 6 to 6¾ pounds. Ramp blade front sight, adjustable rear. Receiver grooved for scope. Checkered American walnut pistol-grip stock and forearm. Made from 1988 to date.

Basic Model **$285**
Basic Field Combo (w/extra 28-inch bbl.) **345**
Deluxe Model **320**
Deluxe Combo (w/extra 28-inch bbl.) **410**
DSPS Model (8-shot) **280**
Field Model **240**
Monte Carlo Model **255**
Ultra Model (discontinued 1991) **295**

Ithaca Model 87 Deerslayer II Rifled Shotgun $360

Similar to the Standard Deerslayer Model, except with solid frame construction and 25-inch rifled barrel. Monte Carlo stock. Made from 1988 to date.

Ithaca Model 87 Ultralite Field Pump Shotgun . . . $295

Gauges: 12 and 20; 2¾-inch chambers. 25-inch barrel with choke tube. Weight: 5 to 6 pounds. Made 1988–1990.

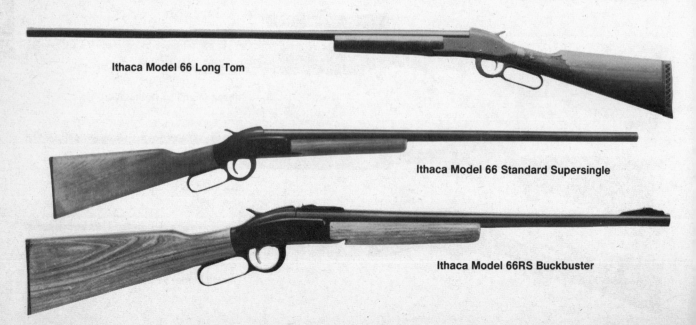

Ithaca Model 66 Long Tom

Ithaca Model 66 Standard Supersingle

Ithaca Model 66RS Buckbuster

Ithaca Model 87 Field Grade
Gauge: 12 or 20; 3-inch chamber. 5-shot magazine. Fixed chokes or screw-in choke tubes (IC, M, F). Barrels: 18½-inch (M&P); 20- and 25-inch (Combo); 26-, 28-, 30-inch vent rib. Weight: 5 to 7 pounds. Made from 1988 to date.

Basic Field Model	**$290**
Camo Model	365
Deluxe Model	340
Deluxe Combo Model	375
English Model	295
Hand Grip Model (w/polymer pistol-grip)	305
M&P Model	280
Supreme Model	595
Turkey Model	295
Ultra Deluxe Model (discontinued 1992)	365
Ultra Field Model (discontinued 1992)	335

Ithaca Field Grade

Ithaca No. 1

Ithaca No. 2

Ithaca No. 3

Ithaca No. 4E

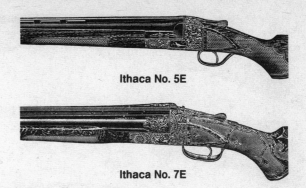

Ithaca No. 5E

Ithaca No. 7E

Ithaca Hammerless Double Barrel Shotguns
Boxlock. Plain extractors, auto ejectors standard on the "E" grades. Double triggers, non-selective or selective single trigger extra. Gauges: Magnum 10, 12; 12, 16, 20, 28, .410. Barrels: 26- to 32-inch, any standard boring. Weight: 5¾ (.410) to 10½ pounds (Magnum 10). Checkered pistol-grip stock and forearm standard. Higher grades differ from Field Grade in quality of workmanship, grade of wood, checkering, engraving, etc.; general specifications are the same. Ithaca doubles made before 1925 had underbolts and a bolt thru the rib extension. In 1925 (serial number 425,000) the rotary bolt and a stronger frame were adopted. Values shown are for this latter type; earlier models valued about 50% lower. Smaller gauge guns may command up to 75% higher. Discontinued 1948.

Field Grade	$ 650
No. 1 Grade	595
No. 2 Grade	950
No. 3 Grade	1,200
No. 4E Grade (ejector)	2,495
No. 5E Grade (ejector)	3,295
No. 7E Grade (ejector)	8,595
$2000 (prewar $1000) Grade (ejector and selective single trigger standard)	12,000

Extras:

Magnum 10 or 12 gauge (in other than the four highest grades), **add**	$200
Automatic ejectors (Grades No. 1, 2, 3, w/ejectors are designated No. 1E, 2E, 3E), **add**	200
Selective single trigger, **add**	150
Non-selective single trigger, **add**	100
Beavertail forend (Field No. 1 or 2), **add**	150
Beavertail forend (No. 3 or 4), **add**	175
Beavertail forend (No. 5, 7 or $2000 Grade), **add**	250
Ventilated rib (No. 4, 5, 7 or $2000 Grade), **add**	250
Ventilated rib (lower grades), **add**	175

Ithaca LSA-55 Turkey Gun $525
Over/under shotgun/rifle combination. Boxlock. Exposed hammer. Plain extractor. Single trigger. 12 gauge/222 Rem. 24½-inch ribbed barrels (rifle barrel has muzzle brake). Weight: about 7 pounds. Folding leaf rear sight, bead front sight. Checkered Monte Carlo stock and forearm. Made 1970–77 by Oy Tikkakoski AB, Finland.

SHOTGUNS

Ithaca LSA-55 Turkey Gun

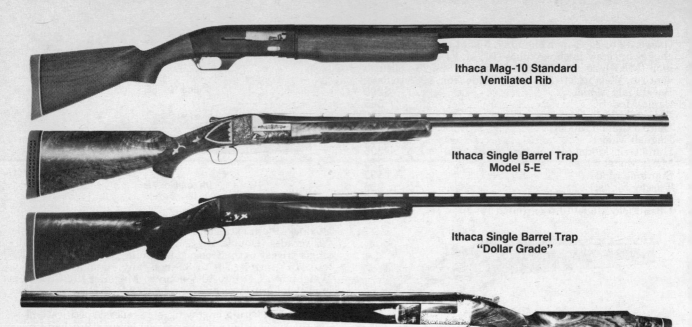

Ithaca Mag-10 Standard Ventilated Rib

Ithaca Single Barrel Trap Model 5-E

Ithaca Single Barrel Trap "Dollar Grade"

Ithaca Single Barrel Super Trap

Ithaca Mag-10 Automatic Shotgun
Gas-operated. 10 gauge. 3½-inch Magnum. 3-shot. 32-inch plain (Standard Grade only) or vent-rib barrel. Full choke. Weight: 11 lbs., plain barrel; 11½ lbs., vent rib. Standard Grade has plain stock and forearm. Deluxe and Supreme Grades have checkering, semi-fancy and fancy wood respectively, and stud swivel. All have recoil pad. Deluxe and Supreme Grades made 1974–1982. Standard Grade introduced in 1977. All grades discontinued 1986.

Camo Model	**$650**
Deluxe Grade	**695**
Roadblocker	**595**
Standard Grade, plain barrel	**550**
Standard Grade, ventilated rib	**650**
Standard Grade, with tubes	**695**
Supreme Grade	**840**

Ithaca Single Shot Trap, Flues and Knick Models
Boxlock. Hammerless. Ejector. 12 gauge only. Barrel lengths: 30-, 32-, 34-inch (32-inch only in Victory Grade). Vent rib. Weight: about 8 pounds. Checkered pistol-grip stock and forend. Grades differ only in quality of workmanship, engraving, checkering, wood, etc. Flues Model, serial numbers under 400,000, made 1908–1921. Triple-bolted Knick Model, serial numbers above 400,000, made since 1921. Victory Model discontinued in 1938, No. 7-E in 1964, No. 4-E in 1976, No. 5-E in 1986. $5000 Grade currently manufactured. Values shown are for Knick Model; Flues Model guns bring prices about 50% lower.

Ithaca Single Shot Trap Victory Grade

Ithaca Single Shot Trap, Flues and Knick (cont.)

Victory Grade	$ **895**
No. 4-E	**1,295**
No. 5-E	**2,650**
No. 7-E	**4,595**
$5000 Grade (prewar $1000 Grade)	**8,700**
Sousa Grade	**10,000**

NOTE: The following Ithaca-Perazzi shotguns were manufactured by Manifattura Armi Perazzi, Brescia, Italy. *See also* separate Perazzi listings.

Ithaca-Perazzi Competition I Skeet $2595
Same as Competition I Trap, except has 26¾-inch barrels with integral muzzle brakes, skeet choke, skeet-style stock and forearm. Weight: 7¾ pounds. Made 1969–1974.

Ithaca-Perazzi Competition I Skeet

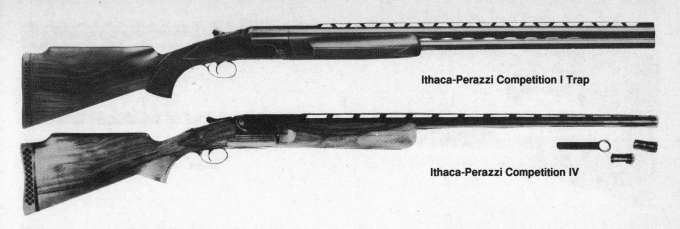

Ithaca-Perazzi Competition I Trap

Ithaca-Perazzi Competition IV

Ithaca-Perazzi Competition I Trap O/U **$2650**
Boxlock. Auto ejectors. Single trigger. 12 gauge. 30- or 32-inch vent-rib barrels, IM/F choke. Weight: about 8½ pounds. Checkered pistol-grip stock, forearm; recoil pad. Made 1969–1974.

Ithaca-Perazzi Competition I Trap Single Barrel **$1850**
Boxlock. Auto ejection. 12 gauge. 32- or 34-inch barrel, vent rib, Full choke. Weight: 8½ pounds. Checkered Monte Carlo stock and beavertail forearm, recoil pad. Made 1973–78.

Ithaca-Perazzi Competition IV Trap Gun **$2350**
Boxlock. Auto ejection. 12 gauge. 32- or 34-inch barrel with high, wide vent rib, four interchangeable choke tubes (Extra Full, F, IM, M). Weight: about 8¾ pounds. Checkered Monte Carlo stock and beavertail forearm, recoil pad. Fitted case. Made 1977–78.

Ithaca-Perazzi Light Game O/U Field **$2895**
Boxlock. Auto ejectors. Single trigger. 12 gauge. 27½-inch vent-rib barrels, M/F or IC/M choke. Weight: 6¾ pounds. Checkered field-style stock and forearm. Made 1972–74.

Ithaca-Perazzi Mirage Live Bird **$3250**
Same as Mirage Trap, except has 28-inch barrels, Mod. and Extra Full choke, special stock and forearm for live bird shooting. Weight: about 8 pounds. Made 1973–78.

Ithaca-Perazzi Mirage Skeet **$2750**
Same as Mirage Trap, except has 28-inch barrels with integral muzzle brakes, SK choke, skeet-style stock and forearm. Weight: about 8 pounds. Made 1973–78.

Ithaca-Perazzi Mirage Trap **$2850**
Same general specifications as MX-8 Trap, except has tapered rib. Made 1973–78.

Ithaca-Perazzi MT-6 Skeet **$2795**
Same as MT-6 Trap, except has 28-inch barrels with two skeet choke tubes instead of Extra Full and Full, skeet-style stock and forearm. Weight: about 8 pounds. Made 1976–78.

Ithaca-Perazzi MT-6 Trap Combo **$3595**
MT-6 with extra single under barrel with high-rise aluminum vent rib, 32- or 34-inch; seven interchangeable choke tubes (IC through Extra Full). Fitted case. Made 1977–78.

SHOTGUNS

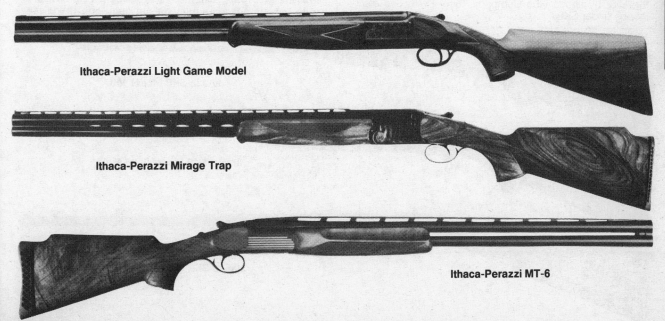

Ithaca-Perazzi Light Game Model

Ithaca-Perazzi Mirage Trap

Ithaca-Perazzi MT-6

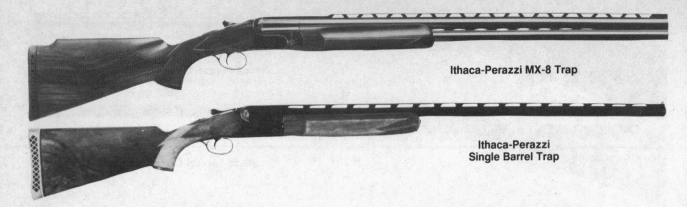

Ithaca-Perazzi MX-8 Trap

Ithaca-Perazzi Single Barrel Trap

Ithaca-Perazzi MT-6 Trap Over/Under **$2495**
Boxlock. Auto selective ejectors. Non-selective single trigger. 12 gauge. Barrels separated, wide vent rib, 30- or 32-inch, five interchangeable choke tubes (Extra Full, F, IM, M, IC). Weight: about 8½ lbs. Checkered pistol-grip stock/forearm, recoil pad. Fitted case. Made 1976–78.

Ithaca-Perazzi MX-8 Trap Combo **$3950**
MX-8 with extra single barrel, vent rib, 32- or 34-inch, Full choke, forearm; two trigger groups included. Made 1973–78.

Ithaca-Perazzi MX-8 Trap Over/Under **$2895**
Boxlock. Auto selective ejectors. Non-selective single trigger. 12 gauge. Barrels: high vent rib; 30- or 32-inch, IM/F choke. Weight: 8¼–8½ pounds. Checkered Monte Carlo stock and forearm, recoil pad. Made 1969–1978.

Ithaca-Perazzi Single Barrel Trap Gun **$1925**
Boxlock. Auto ejection. 12 gauge. 34-inch vent-rib barrel, Full choke. Weight: about 8½ pounds. Checkered pistol-grip stock, forearm; recoil pad. Made 1971–72.

> **NOTE:** The following Ithaca-SKB shotguns, manufactured by SKB Arms Company, Tokyo, Japan, were distributed in the U.S. by Ithaca Gun Company 1966–1976. *See also* listings under SKB.

Ithaca-SKB Model 100 Side-by-Side **$435**
Boxlock. Plain extractors. Selective single trigger. Auto safety. Gauges: 12 and 20; 2¾-inch and 3-inch chambers respectively. Barrels: 30-inch, F/F (12 ga. only); 28-inch, F/M; 26-inch, IC/M (12 ga. only); 25-inch, IC/M (20 ga. only). Weight: 12 ga., about 7 lbs.; 20 ga., about 6 lbs. Checkered stock and forend. Made 1966–1976.

Ithaca-SKB Model 150 Field Grade **$450**
Same as Model 100, except has fancier scroll engraving, beavertail forearm. Made 1972–74.

Ithaca-SKB Model 200E Field Grade S/S **$550**
Same as Model 100, except auto selective ejectors, engraved and silver-plated frame, gold-plated nameplate and trigger, beavertail forearm. Made 1966–1976.

Ithaca-SKB Model 200E Skeet Gun **$595**
Same as Model 200E Field Grade, except 26-inch (12 ga.) and 25-inch (20 ga./2¾-inch chambers) barrels, SK choke; nonautomatic safety and recoil pad. Made 1966–1976.

Ithaca-SKB Model 280 English **$675**
Same as Model 200E, except has scrolled game scene engraving on frame, English-style straight-grip stock; 30-inch barrels not available; special quail gun in 20 gauge has 25-inch barrels, both bored IC. Made 1971–76.

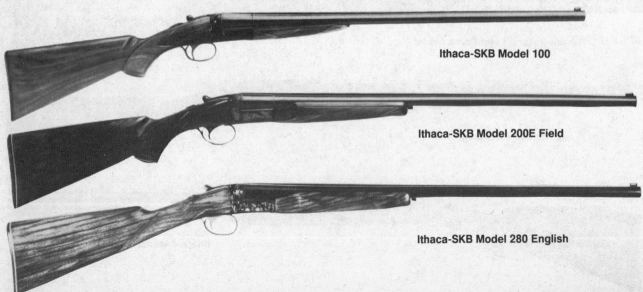

Ithaca-SKB Model 100

Ithaca-SKB Model 200E Field

Ithaca-SKB Model 280 English

Ithaca-SKB Model 300

Ithaca-SKB Model 500 Field

Ithaca-SKB Model 300 Standard Automatic Shotgun
Recoil-operated. Gauges: 12, 20 (3-inch). 5-shot. Barrels: plain or vent rib; 30-inch Full choke (12 gauge only), 28-inch F or M, 26-inch IC. Weight: about 7 pounds. Checkered pistol-grip stock and forearm. Made 1968–1972.
With plain barrel **$235**
With ventilated rib **265**

Ithaca-SKB Model 500 Field Grade O/U **$450**
Boxlock. Auto selective ejectors. Selective single trigger. Nonautomatic safety. Gauges: 12 and 20; 2¾-inch and 3-inch chambers respectively. Vent-rib barrels: 30-inch M/F (12 ga. only); 28-inch M/F; 26-inch IC/M. Weight: 12 ga., about 7½ lbs.; 20 ga., about 6½ lbs. Checkered stock and forearm. Made 1966–1976.

Ithaca-SKB Model 500 Magnum **$485**
Same as Model 500 Field Grade, except chambered for 3-inch 12 gauge shells, has 30-inch barrels, IM/F choke. Weight: about 8 pounds. Made 1973-76.

Ithaca-SKB Model 600 Doubles Gun **$585**
Same as Model 600 Trap Grade, except specially choked for 21-yard first target, 30-yard second. Made 1973–75.

Ithaca-SKB Model 600 Field Grade **$525**
Same as Model 500, except has silver-plated frame, higher grade wood. Made 1969–1976.

Ithaca-SKB Model 600 Magnum **$545**
Same as Model 600 Field Grade, except chambered for 3-inch 12 gauge shells; has 30-inch barrels, IM/F choke. Weight: 8½ pounds. Made 1969-72.

Ithaca-SKB Model 600 Skeet Grade
Same as Model 500, except also available in 28 and .410 gauge, has silver-plated frame, higher grade wood, recoil pad, 26- or 28-inch barrels (28-inch only in 28 and .410), skeet choke. Weight: 7 to 7¾ pounds depending on gauge and barrel length. Made 1966–1976.
12 or 20 gauge **$550**
28 or .410 gauge **625**

Ithaca-SKB Model 600 Skeet Combo Set **$1495**
Model 600 Skeet Grade with matched set of 20, 28 and .410 gauge barrels, 28-inch, fitted case. Made 1970–76.

Ithaca-SKB Model 600 Trap Grade O/U **$565**
Same as Model 500, except 12 gauge only, has silver-plated frame, 30- or 32-inch barrels choked F/F or F/IM, choice of Monte Carlo or straight stock of higher grade wood, recoil pad. Weight: about 8 pounds. Made 1966–1976.

Ithaca-SKB Model 680 English **$595**
Same as Model 600 Field Grade, except has intricate scroll engraving, English-style straight-grip stock and forearm of extra-fine walnut; 30-inch barrels not available. Made 1973–76.

SHOTGUNS

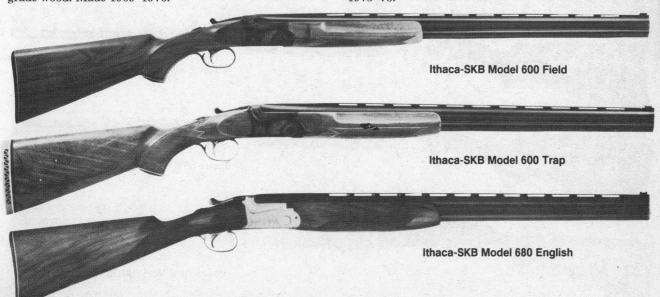

Ithaca-SKB Model 600 Field

Ithaca-SKB Model 600 Trap

Ithaca-SKB Model 680 English

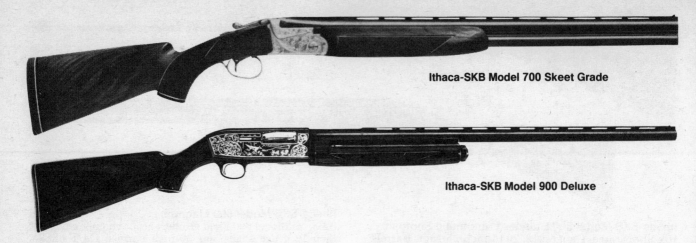

Ithaca-SKB Model 700 Skeet Grade

Ithaca-SKB Model 900 Deluxe

Ithaca-SKB Model 700 Doubles Gun **$775**
Same as Model 700 Trap Grade, except choked for 21-yard first target, 30-yard second target. Made 1973–75.

Ithaca-SKB Model 700 Skeet Combo Set **$1895**
Model 700 Skeet Grade with matched set of 20, 28 and .410 gauge barrels, 28-inch, fitted case. Made 1970–71.

Ithaca-SKB Model 700 Skeet Grade **$750**
Same as Model 600 Skeet Grade, except not available in 28 and .410 gauge, has more elaborate scroll engraving, extra-wide rib, higher grade wood. Made 1969–1975.

Ithaca-SKB Model 700 Trap Grade **$765**
Same as Model 600 Trap Grade, except has more elaborate scroll engraving, extra-wide rib, higher grade wood. Made 1969–1975.

Ithaca-SKB Model 900 Deluxe Automatic **$315**
Same as Model 300, except has game scene etched and gold-filled on receiver, vent rib standard. Made 1968–1972.

Ithaca-SKB Model 900 Slug Gun **$275**
Same as Model 900 Deluxe, except has 24-inch plain barrel with slug boring, rifle sights. Weight: about $6\frac{1}{2}$ pounds. Made 1970–72.

Ithaca-SKB Century Single Shot Trap Gun **$515**
Boxlock. Auto ejector. 12 gauge. Barrels: 32- or 34-inch, vent rib, Full choke. Weight: about 8 pounds. Checkered walnut stock with pistol grip, straight or Monte Carlo comb, recoil pad, beavertail forearm. Made 1973–74. *Note:* Current SKB Century is same as Ithaca-SKB Century II.

Ithaca-SKB Century II **$575**
Improved version of Century. Same general specifications, except has higher stock, reverse-taper beavertail forearm with redesigned locking iron. Made 1975–76.

Ithaca-SKB Model XL300 Standard Automatic
Gas-operated. Gauges: 12, 20 (3-inch). 5-shot. Barrels: plain or vent rib; 30-inch Full choke (12 gauge only), 28-inch F or M, 26-inch IC. Weight: 6 to $7\frac{1}{2}$ pounds depending on gauge and barrel. Checkered pistol-grip stock, forearm. Made 1972–76.
With plain barrel **$215**
With ventilated rib **235**

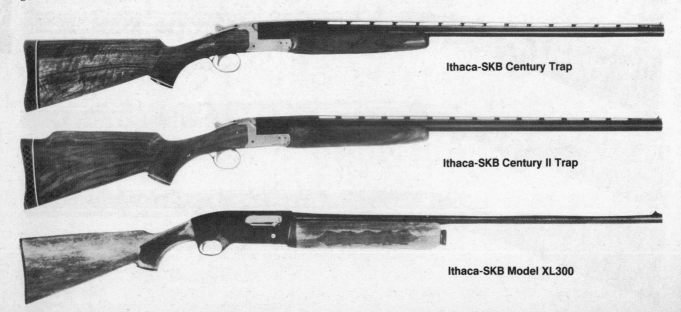

Ithaca-SKB Century Trap

Ithaca-SKB Century II Trap

Ithaca-SKB Model XL300

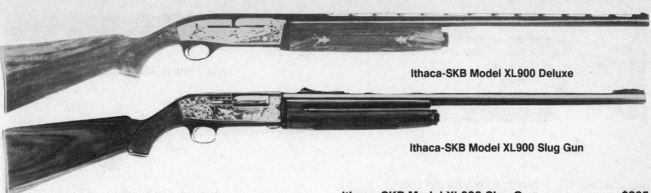

Ithaca-SKB Model XL900 Deluxe

Ithaca-SKB Model XL900 Slug Gun

Ithaca-SKB Model XL900 Slug Gun **$295**
Same as Model XL900 Deluxe, except has 24-inch plain barrel with slug boring, rifle sights. Weight: 6½ or 7 pounds depending on gauge. Made 1972–76.

Ithaca-SKB Model XL900 Deluxe Automatic **$275**
Same as Model XL300, except has game scene finished in silver on receiver, vent rib standard. Made 1972–76.

Ithaca-SKB Model XL900 Trap Grade **$335**
Same as Model XL900 Deluxe, except 12 gauge only, has scrolled receiver finished in black chrome, 30-inch barrel only, IM or F choke, trap style with straight or Monte Carlo comb, recoil pad. Weight: about 7¾ pounds. Made 1972–76.

Ithaca-SKB Model XL900 Skeet Grade **$325**
Same as Model XL900 Deluxe, except has scrolled receiver finished in black chrome, 26-inch barrel only, skeet choke, skeet-style stock. Weight: 7 or 7½ pounds depending on gauge. Made 1972–76.

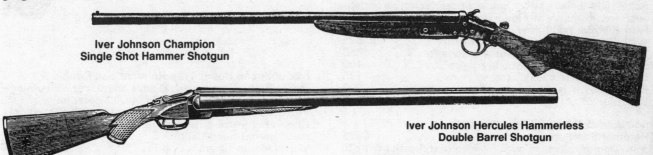

**Iver Johnson Champion
Single Shot Hammer Shotgun**

**Iver Johnson Hercules Hammerless
Double Barrel Shotgun**

Iver Johnson Hercules Hammerless Double (cont.)
with both 2½ and 3-inch chambers. Extras include Miller Single Trigger, Jostam Anti-Flinch Recoil Pad and Lyman Ivory Sights at extra cost. Discont. 1946.
With double triggers, extractors **$475**
With double triggers, automatic ejectors 575
Extra for non-selective single trigger 100
Extra for selective single trigger 135
Extra for .410 gauge 185

IVER JOHNSON'S ARMS
Jacksonville, Arkansas

Formerly Iver Johnson's Arms & Cycle Works of Fitchburg, Mass., and Middlesex, N.J. Now a division of the American Military Arms Corporation.

Iver Johnson Champion Grade Single Shot Hammer Shotgun **$150**
Auto ejector. Gauges: 12, 16, 20, 28 and .410. Barrels: 26- to 36-inch, Full choke. Weight: 5¾ to 6½ pounds depending on gauge and barrel length. Plain pistol-grip stock and forend. Extras include checkered stock and forend, pistol-grip cap and knob forend. Known as Model 36. Also made in a Semi-Octagon Breech, Top Matted and Jacketed Breech (extra heavy) model. Made in Champion Lightweight as Model 39 in gauges 24, 28, 32 and .410; 44 and 45 caliber; 12 and 14mm with same extras—$200; add $100 in the smaller and obsolete gauges. Made 1909–1973.

Iver Johnson Hercules Grade Hammerless Double
Boxlock. (Some made with false sideplates.) Plain extractors and auto ejectors. Double or Miller Single triggers (both selective or non-selective). Gauges: 12, 16, 20 and .410. Barrel lengths: 26- to 32-inch, all chokes. Weight: 5¾ to 7¾ pounds depending on gauge and barrel length. Checkered stock and forend. Straight grip in .410 gauge

Iver Johnson Matted Rib

Iver Johnson Matted Rib Single Shot Hammer Shotgun in smaller gauges **$220**
Same general specifications as Champion Grade except has solid matted top rib, checkered stock and forend. Weight: 6 to 6¾ pounds. Discont. 1948.

Iver Johnson Silver Shadow Over/Under Shotgun
Boxlock. Plain extractors. Double triggers or non-selective single trigger. 12 gauge, 3-inch chambers. Barrels: 26-inch IC/M; 28-inch IC/M; 28-inch M/F; 30-inch both F choke; vent rib. Weight: w/28-inch barrels, 7½ pounds. Checkered pistol-grip stock/forearm. Made by F. Marocchi,

SHOTGUNS

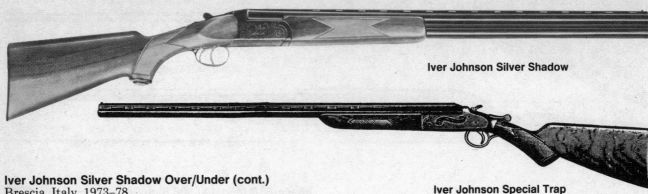

Iver Johnson Silver Shadow

Iver Johnson Special Trap

Iver Johnson Silver Shadow Over/Under (cont.)
Brescia, Italy, 1973–78.
Model 412 w/Double Triggers **$400**
Model 422 w/Single Trigger **440**

Iver Johnson Skeeter Model Hammerless Double
Boxlock. Plain extractors or selective auto ejectors. Double triggers or Miller Single Trigger (selective or non-selective). Gauges: 12, 16, 20, 28 and .410. 26- or 28-inch barrels, skeet boring standard. Weight: about 7¹/₂ pounds; less in smaller gauges. Pistol- or straight-grip stock and beavertail forend, both checkered, of select fancy figured black walnut. Extras include Miller Single Trigger, selective or non-selective, Jostam Anti-Flinch Recoil Pad and Lyman Ivory Rear Sight at additional cost. Discont. 1942.
With Double Triggers, plain extractors.......... **$ 895**
With Double Triggers, automatic ejectors **1050**
Extra for non-selective single trigger........... **100**
Extra for selective single trigger.............. **135**
Extra for .410 gauge **200**
Extra for 28 gauge **300**

Iver Johnson Special Trap Single Shot
Hammer Shotgun **$295**
Auto ejector. 12 gauge only. 32-inch barrel with vent rib, Full choke. Checkered pistol-grip stock and forend. Weight: about 7¹/₂ pounds. Discontinued 1942.

Iver Johnson Super Trap

Iver Johnson Super Trap Hammerless Double
Boxlock. Plain extractors. Double triggers or Miller Single Trigger (selective or non-selective), 12 gauge only, 32-inch Full choke barrels, vent rib. Weight: about 8¹/₂ pounds. Checkered pistol-grip stock and beavertail forend, recoil pad. Discontinued 1942.
With Double Triggers **$850**
Extra for Non-selective Single Trigger **200**
Extra for Selective Single Trigger **200**

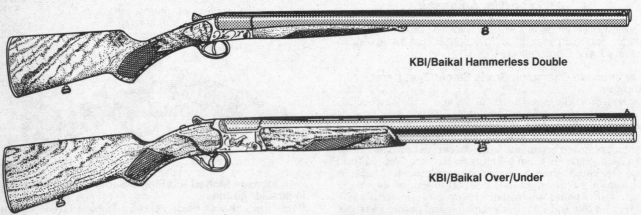

KBI/Baikal Hammerless Double

KBI/Baikal Over/Under

═══ KBI INC. SHOTGUNS ═══
Harrisburg, Pennsylvania

KBI/Baikal Hammerless Double **$275**
Boxlock. Double triggers with extractors. 12 gauge; 2³/₄-inch chambers. Barrels: 26-inch, IC/M; 28-inch, M/F with fixed chokes. Weight: 6³/₄ pounds. Made in Russia.

KBI/Baikal Over/Under
Boxlock. Single selective trigger with automatic ejectors or double triggers with extractors. Gauge: 12 or 20; 2³/₄-inch chambers. Barrels: 26-inch, IC/M; 28-inch, M/F; fixed chokes or screw-in choke tubes. Weight: 7 pounds. Checkered European walnut stock and forearm. Made in Russia.
12 Gauge **$325**
20 Gauge **350**

KBI/Baikal Single Shot $265
Hammerless. Automatic ejector. Manual safety. Gauges: 12 (2³/₄-inch chamber), 20 or .410 with 3-inch. Barrels: 26-, 28-inch with fixed chokes (IC, M, F). Weight: 5¹/₂ to 6 pounds. Made in Russia.

KBI/Fias Grade I Over/Under
Boxlock. Single selective trigger. Gauges: 12, 20, 28, .410; 3-inch chambers. Barrels: 26-inch IC/M; 28-inch M/F; screw-in choke tubes. Weight: 6¹/₂ to 7¹/₂ pounds. Checkered European walnut stock and forearm. Engraved receiver and blued finish.

12 Gauge Model	$375
20 Gauge Model	450
28 and .410 Models........................	560

KBI/Kassnar Grade II Side-by-Side Shotgun $415
Gauges: 10, 12, 20, 28 and .410. 26- to 32-inch chromed barrels. Weight: 5 pounds (.410 ga.) to 9 pounds (10 ga.). Double-hinged triggers. Automatic top tang safety. Extractors. Casehardened antique silver receiver with fine scroll engraving. Checkered European walnut stock. Discontinued 1990.

KBI/Omega Over-Under
Boxlock. Single selective trigger. Gauges: 12, 20, 28, .410; 3-inch chambers. Barrels: 26- or 28-inch vent-rib with fixed chokes (IC/M or M/F). Automatic safety. Weight: 6 to 7¹/₂ pounds. Checkered European walnut stock and forearm. Discontinued 1992.

Deluxe Model (12 gauge only)	$350
Standard Model	305

KESSLER ARMS CORP.
Silver Creek, New York

Kessler Lever-Matic Repeating Shotgun $135
Lever action. Takedown. Gauges: 12, 16, 20; three-shot magazine. Barrels: 26-, 28-, 30-inch; F choke. Plain pistol-grip stock, recoil pad. Weight: 7 to 7³/₄ pounds. Discont. 1953.

Kessler Three Shot Bolt Action Repeater $75
Takedown. Gauges: 12, 16, 20. Two-shell detachable box magazine. Barrels: 28-inch in 12 and 16 gauge; 26-inch in 20 gauge; Full choke. Weight: 6¹/₄ to 7¹/₄ pounds depending on gauge and barrel length. Plain one-piece pistol-grip stock, recoil pad. Made 1951–53.

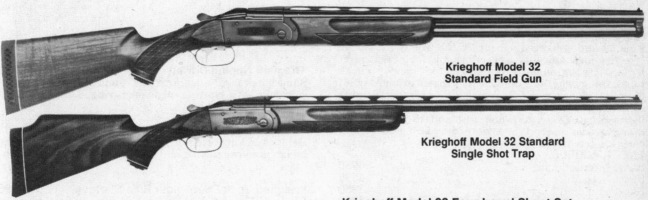

Krieghoff Model 32
Standard Field Gun

Krieghoff Model 32 Standard
Single Shot Trap

Krieghoff Model 32 Four-barrel Skeet Set
Over/under w/four sets of matched barrels in 12, 20, 28 and .410 gauge, in fitted case. Available in six grades that differ in quality of engraving and wood. Discontinued 1979.

Standard Grade	$ 6,850
München Grade	8,595
San Remo Grade	9,725
Monte Carlo Grade	15,950
Crown Grade	17,250
Super Crown Grade	18,595
Exhibition Grade	29,950

Krieghoff Model 32 Standard Grade Over/Under
Similar to prewar Remington Model 23. Boxlock. Auto ejector. Single trigger. Gauges: 12, 20, 28, .410. Barrels: vent rib, 26¹/₂- to 32-inch, any chokes. Weight: 12 gauge field gun with 28-inch barrels, about 7¹/₂ pounds. Checkered pistol-grip stock and forearm of select walnut; available in field, skeet and trap styles. Made 1958–1981.

With one set of barrels	$1995
Low-rib Two-barrel Trap Combo.............	2995
Vandalia (high-rib) Two-barrel Trap Combo....	3995

Krieghoff Model 32 Standard Grade Single Shot Trap Gun $1495
Same action as over/under. 12 gauge. 32- or 34-inch barrel with high vent rib; M, IM, or F choke. Monte Carlo stock with recoil pad, beavertail forearm. Disc. 1979.

H. KRIEGHOFF JAGD UND SPORTWAFFENFABRIK
Ulm (Donau), West Germany

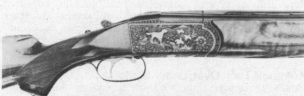

Krieghoff Model 32 Monte Carlo

Krieghoff Model 32 San Remo

SHOTGUNS

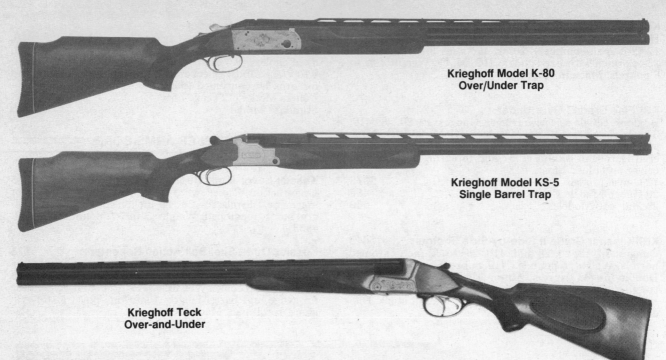

**Krieghoff Model K-80
Over/Under Trap**

**Krieghoff Model KS-5
Single Barrel Trap**

**Krieghoff Teck
Over-and-Under**

Krieghoff Model K-80

Refined and enhanced version of the Model 32. Single selective mechanical trigger, adjustable for position; release trigger optional. Fixed chokes or screw-in choke tubes. Interchangeable front barrel hangers to adjust point of impact. Quick-removable stock. Color casehardened or satin grey finished receiver; aluminum alloy receiver on lightweight models. Available in standard plus five engraved grades. Made 1980 to date. Standard grade shown except where noted.

SKEET MODELS

Skeet International	**$4950**
Skeet Special	4595
Skeet Standard Model	3950
Skeet w/Tubla Chokes	4750

SKEET SETS

Standard Grade 2-Barrel Set	**$ 6,550**
Standard Grade 4-Barrel Set	8,595
Bavaria Grade 4-Barrel Set	12,250
Danube Grade 4-Barrel Set	15,950
Gold Target Grade 4-Barrel Set	18,750

SPORTING MODELS

Pigeon	**$4595**
Sporting Clays	4950

TRAP MODELS

Trap Combo	**$6995**
Trap Single	4950
Trap Standard	4595
Trap Unsingle	5145
RT Models (Removable Trigger) **Add**	1385

Krieghoff Model KS-5 Single Barrel Trap

Boxlock with no sliding top-latch. Adjustable or optional release trigger. Gauge: 12; 2³/₄-inch chamber. Barrel: 32-, 34-inch with fixed choke or screw-in tubes. Weight: 8¹/₂ pounds. Adjustable or Monte Carlo European walnut stock. Blued or nickel receiver. Made from 1980 to date. Redesigned and streamlined in 1993.

Standard Model w/Fixed Chokes	**$1950**
Standard Model w/Tubes	2595
Special Model w/Adjustable Rib & Stock	2750
Special Model w/Adj. Rib & Stock, Tubes	3295

Krieghoff Neptun Drilling $9250

Same general specifications as Trumpf model, except has sidelocks with hunting scene engraving. Currently manufactured.

Krieghoff Neptun-Primus Drilling $10,595

Deluxe version of Neptun model; has detachable sidelocks, higher grade engraving and fancier wood. Currently manufactured.

Krieghoff Teck Over/Under Rifle-Shotgun $4995

Boxlock. Kersten double crossbolt system. Steel or dural receiver. Split extractor or ejector for shotgun barrel. Single or double triggers. Gauges: 12, 16, 20; latter with either 2³/₄- or 3-inch chamber. Calibers: 22 Hornet, 222 Rem., 222 Rem. Mag., 7×57r5, 7×64, 7×65r5, 30-30, 300 Win. Mag., 30-06, 308, 9.3×74R. 25-inch barrels with solid rib, folding leaf rear sight, post or bead front sight; over barrel is shotgun, under barrel rifle (later fixed or interchangeable; extra rifle barrel, $175). Weight: 7.9 to 9.5 pounds depending on type of receiver and caliber. Checkered pistol-grip stock with cheekpiece and semibeavertail forearm of figured walnut, sling swivels. Made 1967 to date. *Note:* This combination gun is similar in appearance to the same model shotgun.

Krieghoff Teck Over/Under Shotgun $3750

Boxlock. Kersten double crossbolt system. Auto ejector. Single or double triggers. Gauges: 12, 16, 20; latter with either 2³/₄- or 3-inch chambers. 28-inch vent-rib barrel, M/F choke. Weight: about 7 pounds. Checkered walnut pistol-grip stock and forearm. Made 1967–1989.

Krieghoff Trumpf Drilling $5595

Boxlock. Steel or dural receiver. Split extractor or ejector for shotgun barrels. Double triggers. Gauges: 12, 16, 20; latter with either 2³/₄- or 3-inch chambers. Calibers: 243, 6.5×57r5, 7×57r5, 7×65r5, 30-06; other calibers available. 25-inch barrels with solid rib, folding leaf rear sight, post

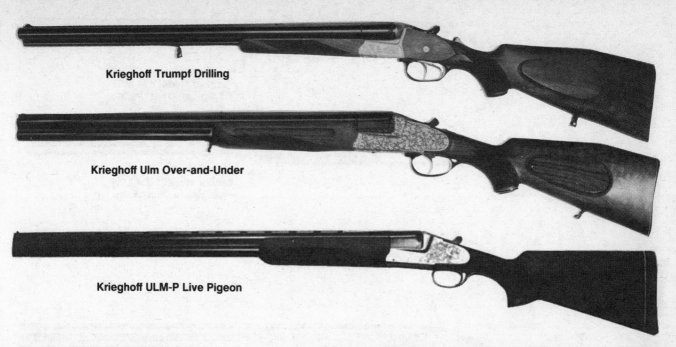

Krieghoff Trumpf Drilling

Krieghoff Ulm Over-and-Under

Krieghoff ULM-P Live Pigeon

Krieghoff Trumpf Drilling (cont.)

or bead front sight; rifle barrel soldered or free floating. Weight: 6.6 to 7.5 pounds depending on type of receiver, gauge and caliber. Checkered pistol-grip stock with cheekpiece and forearm of figured walnut, sling swivels. Made 1953 to date.

Krieghoff Ulm Over/Under Rifle-Shotgun **$8595**

Same general specifications as Teck model, except has sidelocks with leaf arabesque engraving. Made from 1963 to date. *Note:* This combination gun is similar in appearance to the same model shotgun.

Krieghoff Ulm Over/Under Shotgun **$7395**

Same general specifications as Teck model, except has sidelocks with leaf arabesque engraving. Made 1958 to date.

Krieghoff ULM-P Live Pigeon Gun

Sidelock. Gauge: 12. 28- and 30-inch barrels. Chokes: F/IM Weight: 8 pounds. Oil-finished, fancy English walnut stock with semibeavertail forearm. Light scrollwork engraving. Tapered, vent rib. Made from 1983 to date.
Bavaria **$10,250**
Standard 8950

Krieghoff Ulm-Primus Over/Under **$7995**

Deluxe version of Ulm model; detachable sidelocks, higher grade engraving and fancier wood. Made 1958 to date.

Krieghoff Ulm-Primus O/U Rifle-Shotgun **$8895**

Deluxe version of Ulm model; has detachable sidelocks, higher grade engraving and fancier wood. Made 1963 to date. *Note:* This combination gun is similar in appearance to the same model shotgun.

Krieghoff ULM-S Skeet Gun

Sidelock. Gauge: 12. Barrel: 28-inch. Chokes: skeet/skeet. Other specifications similar to the Model ULM-P. Made 1983–86.
Bavaria **$7250**
Standard 5995

Krieghoff ULM-T O/U Live Trap Gun

Over/under sidelock. Gauge: 12. 30-inch barrel. Tapered vent rib. Chokes: IM/F.; optional screw-in choke. Custom grade versions command a higher price. Discontinued 1986.
Bavaria **$7150**
Standard 5895

Krieghoff Ultra O/U Rifle-Shotgun

Deluxe Over/Under combination with 25-inch vent-rib barrels chambered 12 gauge only and various rifle calibers for lower barrel. Kickspanner design permits cocking with thumb safety. Satin receiver. Weight: 6 lbs. Made from 1985 to date.
Ultra O/U Combination **$2595**
Ultra B w/Selective Front Trigger 2795

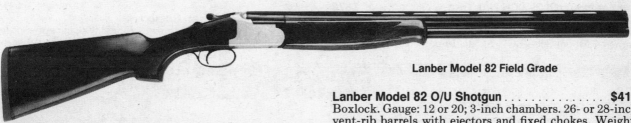

Lanber Model 82 Field Grade

LANBER SHOTGUNS
Spain

Lanber Model 82 O/U Shotgun **$415**

Boxlock. Gauge: 12 or 20; 3-inch chambers. 26- or 28-inch vent-rib barrels with ejectors and fixed chokes. Weight: 7 lbs. 2 oz. Double or single-selective trigger. Engraved silvered receiver. Checkered European walnut stock and forearm. Imported 1994.

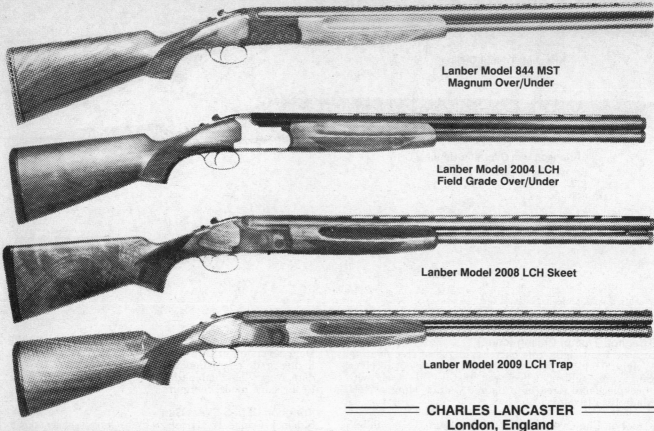

Lanber Model 844 MST
Magnum Over/Under

Lanber Model 2004 LCH
Field Grade Over/Under

Lanber Model 2008 LCH Skeet

Lanber Model 2009 LCH Trap

Lanber Model 844 MST Magnum O/U **$350**
Field grade. Gauge: 12. 3-inch Mag. chambers. 30-inch
flat vent-rib barrels. Chokes: M/F. Weight: 7 lbs. 7 oz.
Single selective trigger. Blued barrels and engraved receiver. European walnut stock with hand-checkered pistol
grip and forend. Made 1984⅓6.

Lanber Model 2004 LCH O/U **$550**
Field grade. Gauge: 12. 2³/₄-inch chambers. 28-inch flat
vent-rib barrels. 5 interchangeable choke tubes: cyl., IC,
M, IM, F. Weight: about 7 pounds. Single selective trigger.
Engraved silver receiver with fine-line scroll. Walnut stock
with checkered pistol grip and forend. Rubber recoil pad.
Imported 1984–86.

Lanber Model 2008 LCH O/U Skeet **$630**
Gauge: 12. 28-inch vent-rib barrels. 5 interchangeable
choke tubes: same as Model 2004 LCH. Single selective
trigger. Auto safety. Blued barrels and engraved receiver.
Hand-checkered European walnut stock with pistol grip.
Imported 1984–86.

Lanber Model 2009 LCH O/U Trap **$675**
Gauge: 12. 30-inch vent-rib barrels. 3 interchangeable
choke tubes: M, IM, F. Manual safety. Other specifications
same as Model 2008 LCH Skeet. Imported 1984–86.

CHARLES LANCASTER
London, England

**Lancaster "Twelve-Twenty" Double Barrel
Shotgun** **$12,250**
Sidelock, self-opener. Gauge: 12. Barrels: 24 to 30 inches
standard. Weight: about 5³/₄ pounds. Elaborate metal
engraving. Highest quality English or French walnut buttstock and forearm. Imported by Stoeger in the 1950s.

JOSEPH LANG & SONS
London, England

Highest Quality Over/Under Shotgun **$14,600**
Sidelock. Gauges: 12, 16, 20, 28 and .410. Barrels: 25 to
30 inches standard. Highest grade English or French walnut buttstock and forearm. Selective single trigger. Imported by Stoeger in 1950s.

LAURONA SHOTGUNS
Spain

Laurona Grand Trap Combo
Same general specifications as Model 300, except supplied
with 29-inch over/under barrels, screw-in choke tubes and

Laurona Grand Trap-GTO

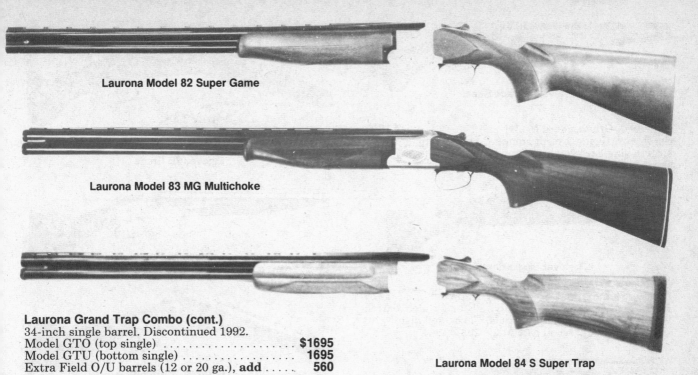

Laurona Model 82 Super Game

Laurona Model 83 MG Multichoke

Laurona Model 84 S Super Trap

Laurona Grand Trap Combo (cont.)
34-inch single barrel. Discontinued 1992.
Model GTO (top single) **$1695**
Model GTU (bottom single) **1695**
Extra Field O/U barrels (12 or 20 ga.), **add** **560**

Laurona Silhouette 300 Over/Under
Boxlock. Single selective trigger. Selective automatic ejectors. Gauge: 12; 2³/₄-, 3- or 3¹/₂-inch chambers. 28- or 29-inch vent-rib barrels with flush or knurled choke tubes. Weight: 7³/₄ to 8 pounds. Checkered pistol-grip European walnut stock and beavertail forend. Engraved receiver with silvered finish and black chrome barrels. Made 1988–1992.
Model 300 Sporting Clays .... **$ 995**
Model 300 Trap **1015**
Model 300 Trap, Single **1095**
Model 300 Ultra-Magnum.................. **975**

Laurona Super Model Over/Under Shotguns
Boxlock. Single selective or twin single triggers. Selective automatic ejectors. Gauges: 12 or 20; 2³/₄- or 3-inch chambers. 26-, 28- or 29-inch vent-rib barrels with fixed chokes or screw-in choke tubes. Weight: 7 to 7¹/₄ pounds. Checkered pistol-grip European walnut stock. Engraved receiver with silvered finish and black chrome barrels. Made from 1985 to date.
Model 82 Super Game (discontinued) .... **$ 795**
Model 83 MG Super Game **925**
Model 84 S Super Trap **1025**
Model 85 MG Super Game **935**
Model 85 MG 2-Barrel Set **1325**
Model 85 MS Special Sporting (discontinued) ... **995**
Model 85 MS Super Trap **1025**
Model 85 MS Pigeon **995**
Model 85 S Super Skeet **995**

LEBEAU-COURALLY SHOTGUNS
Belgium

Lebeau-Courally Boxlock Side-by-Side Shotguns **$8950**
Gauges: 12, 16, 20 and 28. 26- to 30-inch barrels. Weight: 6¹/₂ pounds average. Checkered, hand-rubbed, oil-finished, straight-grip stock of French walnut. Classic forend. Made from 1986 to date.

LEFEVER ARMS COMPANY
Syracuse and Ithaca, N.Y.

Lefever sidelock hammerless double-barrel shotguns were made by Lefever Arms Company of Syracuse, New York, from about 1885–1915 (serial numbers 1 to 70,000) when the firm was sold to Ithaca Gun Company of Ithaca, New York. Production of these models was continued at the Ithaca plant until 1919 (serial numbers 70,001 to 72,000). Grades listed are those that appear in the last catalog of the Lefever Gun Company, Syracuse. In 1921, Ithaca introduced the boxlock Lefever Nitro Special double, followed in 1934 by the Lefever Grade A; there also were two single barrel Lefevers made from 1927–1942. Manufacture of Lefever brand shotguns was discontinued in 1948. *Note:* "New Lefever" boxlock shotguns made circa 1904–1906 by D. M. Lefever Company, Bowling Green, Ohio, are included in a separate listing.

Lefever A Grade

Lefever A Grade Hammerless Double Barrel Shotgun
Boxlock. Plain extractors or auto ejector. Single or double triggers. Gauges: 12, 16, 20, .410. Barrels: 26–32 inches, standard chokes. Weight: about 7 pounds in 12 gauge. Checkered pistol-grip stock and forearm. Made 1934–1942.
With Plain Extractors, Double Triggers **$750**
Extra for Automatic Ejector **100**
Extra for Single Trigger **100**
Extra for Beavertail Forearm **75**

SHOTGUNS

Lefever A Grade Skeet

Lefever A Grade Skeet Model $1095
Same as A Grade, except standard features include auto ejector, single trigger, beavertail forearm; 26-inch barrels, skeet boring. Discontinued 1942.

Lefever Single Shot Trap

Lefever Hammerless Single Shot Trap Gun $425
Boxlock. Ejector. 12 gauge only. 30- or 32-inch barrel; vent rib. Weight: about 8 pounds. Checkered pistol-grip stock and forend, recoil pad. Made 1927–1942.

Lefever Long Range

Lefever Long Range Hammerless Single Barrel Field Gun $275
Boxlock. Plain extractor. Gauges: 12, 16, 20, .410. Barrel lengths: 26–32-inches. Weight: 5½ to 7 pounds depending on gauge and barrel length. Checkered pistol-grip stock and forend. Made 1927–1942.

Lefever Nitro Special

Lefever Nitro Special Hammerless Double
Boxlock. Plain extractors. Single or double triggers. Gauges: 12, 16, 20, .410. Barrels: 26- to 32-inch, standard chokes. Weight: about 7 pounds in 12 gauge. Checkered pistol-grip stock and forend. Made 1921–1948.
With Double Triggers **$475**
With Single Trigger **595**

Lefever F Grade

Lefever EE Grade

Lefever DS Grade

Lefever DE Grade

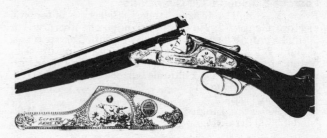

Lefever CE Grade

Lefever Sidelock Hammerless Doubles
Plain extractors or auto ejectors. Double triggers or selective single trigger. Gauges: 10, 12, 16, 20. Barrels: 26–32 inches; standard choke combinations. Weight: 5¾ to 10½ pounds depending on gauge and barrel length. Checkered walnut straight-grip or pistol-grip stock and forearm. Grades differ chiefly in quality of workmanship, engraving, wood, checkering, etc.; general specifications are the same. DS and DSE Grade guns lack the cocking indicators found on all other models. Suffix "E" means model has auto ejector; also standard on A, AA, Optimus, and Thousand Dollar Grade guns.

H Grade	$ 1250
HE Grade	1695
G Grade	1450
GE Grade	1795
F Grade	1550
FE Grade	1925
E Grade	1950
EE Grade	2725
D Grade	2050
DE Grade	2995
DS Grade	995
DSE Grade	1295
C Grade	3795
CE Grade	5995

Lefever BE Grade

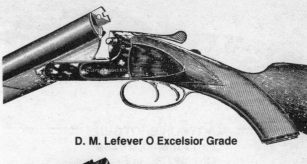

D. M. Lefever O Excelsior Grade

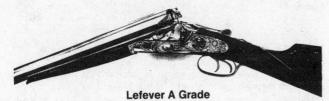

Lefever A Grade

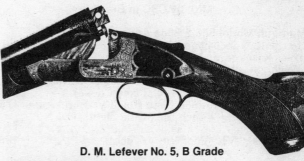

D. M. Lefever No. 5, B Grade

Lefever Optimus Grade

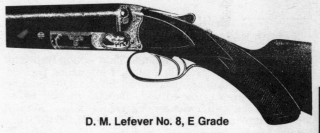

D. M. Lefever No. 8, E Grade

Lefever Sidelock Hammerless Doubles (cont.)

B Grade	$ 4,950
BE Grade	8,395
A Grade	15,000
AA Grade	20,000
Optimus Grade	27,500
Thousand Dollar Grade	38,500
Extra for single trigger	500

D. M. LEFEVER COMPANY
Bowling Green, Ohio

In 1901, D. M. "Uncle Dan" Lefever, founder of the Lefever Arms Company, withdrew from that firm to organize D. M. Lefever, Sons & Company (later D. M. Lefever Company) to manufacture the "New Lefever" boxlock double and single barrel shotguns. These were produced at Bowling Green, Ohio, from about 1904–1906, when Dan Lefever died and the factory closed permanently. Grades listed are those that appear in the last catalog of D. M. Lefever Co.

D. M. Lefever Hammerless Double Barrel Shotguns

"New Lefever." Boxlock. Auto ejector standard on all grades except O Excelsior, which was regularly supplied with plain extractors (auto ejector offered as an extra). Double triggers or selective single trigger (latter standard on Uncle Dan Grade, extra on all others). Gauges: 12, 16, 20. Barrels: any length and choke combination. Weight: 5½ to 8 pounds depending on gauge and barrel length. Checkered walnut straight-grip or pistol-grip stock and forearm. Grades differ chiefly in quality of workmanship, engraving, wood, checkering, etc.; general specifications are the same.

O Excelsior Grade with plain extractors	$ 2,550
O Excelsior Grade with automatic ejectors	2,895
No. 9, F Grade	3,595
No. 8, E Grade	4,375
No. 6, C Grade	5,195
No. 5, B Grade	6,895
No. 4, AA Grade	10,000
Uncle Dan Grade	15,000
Extra for single trigger	400

D. M. Lefever Single Trap

D. M. Lefever Single Barrel Trap Gun $4995
Boxlock. Auto ejector. 12 gauge only. Barrels: 26- to 32-inches, Full choke. Weight: 6½ to 8 pounds, depending on barrel length. Checkered walnut pistol-grip stock and forearm.

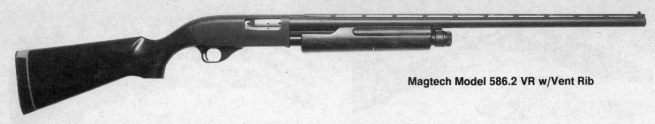

Magtech Model 586.2 VR w/Vent Rib

MAGTECH SHOTGUNS
San Antonio, Texas
Mfd. by CBC in Brazil

Magtech Model 586.2 Slide Action Shotgun
Gauge: 12; 3-inch chamber. 19-, 24-, 26- or 28-inch barrel; fixed chokes or internal tubes. 46½ or 48½ inches overall. Weight: 8½ lbs. Double-action slide bars. Brazilian hardwood stock. Polished blued finish. Imported 1992 to date.
Model 586.2 F (28-inch Bbl., Fixed Choke) **$165**
Model 586.2 P (19-inch Plain Bbl., Cyl. Bore) **175**
Model 586.2 S (24-inch Bbl., Rifle Sights, Cyl. Bore) **170**
Model 586.2 VR (Vent Rib w/Tubes) **185**

MARLIN FIREARMS CO.
North Haven (formerly New Haven), Conn.

Marlin Model 16 Visible Hammer Slide Action Repeater
Takedown. 16 gauge. 5-shell tubular magazine. Barrels: 26- or 28-inc2, standard chokes. Weight: about 6¼ pounds. Pistol-grip stock, grooved slide handle; checkering on higher grades. Difference among grades is in quality of wood, engraving on Grades C and D. Made 1904–1910.
Grade A .... **$ 325**
Grade B **425**
Grade C **525**
Grade D **1095**

Marlin Model 17 Brush Gun **$325**
Same as Model 17 Standard, except has 26-inch barrel, cylinder bore. Weight: about 7 pounds. Made 1906–1908.

Marlin Model 17 Riot Gun **$300**
Same as Model 17 Standard, except has 20-inch barrel, cylinder bore. Weight: about 6⅞ pounds. Made 1906–1908.

Marlin Model 17 Standard Visible Hammer Slide Action Repeater **$295**
Solid frame. 12 gauge. 5-shot tubular magazine. Barrels: 30- or 32-inch, Full choke. Weight: about 7½ pounds. Straight-grip stock, grooved slide handle. Made 1906–1908.

Marlin Model 19 Visible Hammer Slide Action Repeater
Similar to Model 1898, but improved, lighter weight, with two extractors, matted sighting groove on receiver top. Weight: about 7 pounds. Made 1906–1907.

Marlin Model 19 Visible Hammer Repeater (cont.)
Grade A .... **$ 295**
Grade B **395**
Grade C **525**
Grade D **1095**

Marlin Model 21 Trap Visible Hammer Slide Action Repeater
Similar to Model 19 with same general specifications, except has straight-grip stock. Made 1907–1909.
Grade A .... **$ 325**
Grade B **435**
Grade C **550**
Grade D **1125**

Marlin Model 24 Visible Hammer Slide Action Repeater
Similar to Model 19, but has improved takedown system and auto recoil safety lock, solid matted rib on frame. Weight: about 7½ pounds. Made 1908–1915.
Grade A .... **$ 315**
Grade B **415**
Grade C **575**
Grade D **1150**

Marlin Model 26 Brush Gun **$235**
Same as Model 26 Standard, except has 26-inch barrel, cylinder bore. Weight: about 7 pounds. Made 1909–1915.

Marlin Model 26 Riot Gun **$200**
Same as Model 26 Standard, except has 20-inch barrel, cylinder bore. Weight: about 6⅞ pounds. Made 1909–1915.

Marlin Model 26 Standard Visible Hammer Slide Action Repeater **$230**
Similar to Model 24 Grade A, except solid frame and straight-grip stock. 30- or 32-inch Full choke barrel. Weight: about 7⅛ pounds. Made from 1909–1915.

Marlin Model 28 Hammerless Slide Action Repeater
Takedown. 12 gauge. 5-shot tubular magazine. Barrels: 26-, 28-, 30-, 32-inch, standard chokes; matted-top barrel except on Model 28D which has solid matted rib. Weight: about 8 pounds. Pistol-grip stock, grooved slide handle; checkering on higher grades. Grades differ in quality of wood, engraving on Models 28C and 28D. Made 1913–1922; all but Model 28A discontinued in 1915.

Marlin Model 17 Standard

Marlin Model 28B

Marlin Model 30 Grade D

Marlin Model 28 Hammerless Repeater (cont.)
Model 28A	$ 300
Model 28B	400
Model 28C	500
Model 28D	1195

Marlin Model 28T Trap Gun $515
Same as Model 28, except has 30-inch matted-rib barrel, Full choke, straight-grip stock with high-fluted comb of fancy walnut, checkered. Made in 1915.

Marlin Model 28TS Trap Gun $295
Same as Model 28T, except has matted-top barrel, plainer stock. Made in 1915.

Marlin Model 30 Field Gun $285
Same as Model 30 Grade B, except has 25-inch barrel, Mod. choke, straight-grip stock. Made 1913–1914.

Marlin Model 30 Visible Hammer Slide Action Repeater
Similar to Model 16, but with Model 24 improvements. Made 1910–1914.
Grade A	$ 275
Grade B	425
Grade C	545
Grade D	1150

Marlin Models 30A, 30B, 30C, 30D
Same as Model 30; designations were changed in 1915. Also available in 20 gauge with 25- or 28-inch barrel; matted-top barrel on all grades. Suffixes "A," "B," "C" and "D" correspond to former grades. Made in 1915.

Marlin Models 30A, 30B, 30C, 30D (cont.)
Model 30A	$ 320
Model 30B	400
Model 30C	595
Model 30D	1075

Marlin Model 31 Hammerless Slide Action Repeater
Similar to Model 28, except scaled down for 16 and 20 gauges. Barrels: 25-inch (20 gauge only), 26-inch (16 gauge only), 28-inch; all with matted top; standard chokes. Weight: 16 ga., about $6\frac{3}{4}$ pounds; 20 ga., about 6 pounds. Pistol-grip stock, grooved slide handle; checkering on higher grades; straight-grip stock optional on Model 31D. Made 1915–1917; Model 31A until 1922.
Model 31A	$ 295
Model 31B	445
Model 31C	545
Model 31D	1215

Marlin Model 31F Field Gun $425
Same as Model 31B, except has 25-inch barrel, Modified choke, straight- or pistol-grip stock. Made 1915–1917.

Marlin Model 42A Visible Hammer Slide Action Repeater $245
Similar to pre-World War I Model 24 Grade A with same general specifications, but not of as high quality. Made from 1922–1934.

Marlin Model 43 Hammerless Slide Action Repeater
Similar to pre-World War I Models 28A, 28T and 28TS, with same general specifications, but not of as high quality. Made 1923–1930.

SHOTGUNS

Marlin Model 42A

Marlin Model 43A

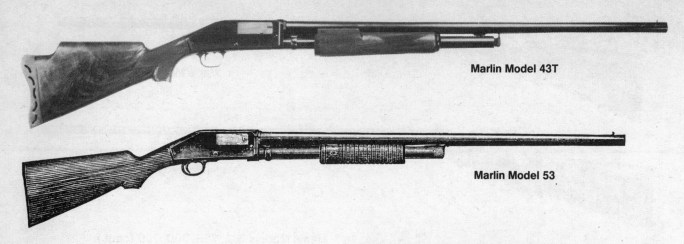

Marlin Model 43T

Marlin Model 53

Marlin Model 43 Hammerless Repeater (cont.)
Model 43A **$250**
Model 43T **500**
Model 43TS **525**

Marlin Model 44 Hammerless Slide Action Repeater
Similar to pre-World War I Model 31A, with same general specifications, but not of as high quality. 20 gauge only. Model 44A is a standard grade field gun. Model 44S Special Grade has checkered stock and slide handle of fancy walnut. Made 1923–1935.
Model 44A **$300**
Model 44S **395**

Marlin Model 49 Visible Hammer Slide Action Repeating Shotgun **$375**
Economy version of Model 42A, offered as a bonus on the purchase of four shares of Marlin stock. About 3000 were made 1925–28.

Marlin Model 53 Hammerless Slide Action Repeater **$305**
Similar to Model 43A, with same general specifications. Made 1929–1930.

Marlin Model 55 Goose Gun **$175**
Same as Model 55 Hunter, except chambered for 12-gauge 3-inch magnum shell, has 36-inch barrel, Full choke, swivels and sling. Weight: about 8 pounds. Made 1962 to date.

Marlin Model 55 Hunter Bolt Action Repeater
Takedown. Gauges: 12, 16, 20. 2-shot clip magazine. 28-inch barrel (26-inch in 20 ga.), Full or adjustable choke. Plain pistol-grip stock; 12 ga. has recoil pad. Weight: about 7$1/4$ pounds; 20 ga., 6$1/2$ pounds. Made 1954–1965.
With plain barrel .... **$ 95**
With adjustable choke **115**

Marlin Model 55 Swamp Gun **$125**
Same as Model 55 Hunter except chambered for 12-gauge 3-inch magnum shell, has 20$1/2$-inch barrel with adjustable

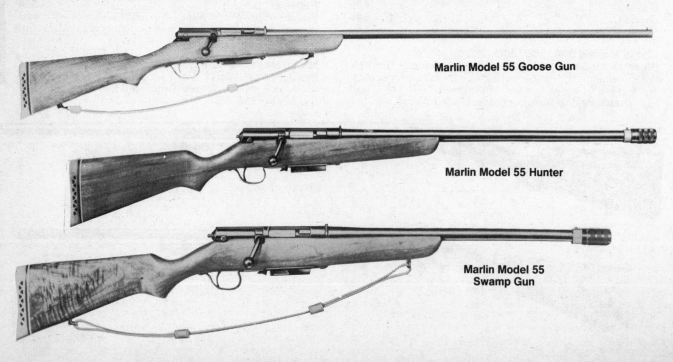

Marlin Model 55 Goose Gun

Marlin Model 55 Hunter

Marlin Model 55 Swamp Gun

**Marlin Model 59
Bolt Action Single**

**Marlin Model 60
Single Shot**

Marlin Model 55 Swamp Gun (cont.)
choke, sling swivels. Weight: about 6¹/₂ pounds. Made 1963–65.

Marlin Model 55S Slug Gun **$140**
Same as Model 55 Goose Gun, except has 24-inch barrel, cylinder bore, rifle sights. Weight: about 7¹/₂ pounds. Made 1974–79.

Marlin Model 59 Auto-Safe Bolt Action Single . . . **$85**
Takedown. Auto thumb safety. 410 gauge. 24-inch barrel, Full choke. Weight: about 5 pounds. Plain pistol-grip stock. Made 1959–1961.

Marlin Model 60 Single Shot Shotgun **$220**
Visible hammer. Takedown. Boxlock. Automatic ejector. 12 gauge. 30- or 32-inch barrel, Full choke. Weight: about 6¹/₂ pounds. Pistol-grip stock, beavertail forearm. *Note:* About 600 were produced in 1923.

Marlin Model 63 Hammerless Slide Action Repeater
Similar to Models 43A and 43T with same general specifications. Model 63TS Trap Special is same as Model 63T Trap Gun except stock style and dimensions to order. Made 1931–35.
Model 63A **$245**
Model 63T or 63TS **350**

Marlin Model 90 Standard Over-and-Under Shotgun
Hammerless. Boxlock. Double triggers; non-selective single trigger was available as an extra on prewar guns except .410. Gauges: 12, 16, 20, .410. Barrels: plain; 26-, 28- or 30-inch; chokes IC/M or M/F; barrel design changed in 1949, eliminating full-length rib between barrels. Weight: 12 ga., about 7¹/₂ lbs.; 16 and 20 ga., about 6¹/₄ lbs. Checkered pistol-grip stock and forearm, recoil pad standard on prewar guns. Postwar production: Model 90-DT (double trigger), Model 90-ST (single trigger). Made 1937–1958.
With double triggers **$395**
With single trigger **495**

**Marlin Model 120 Magnum Slide Action
Repeater** **$225**
Hammerless. Takedown. 12 gauge (3-inch). 4-shot tubular magazine. Barrels: 26-inch vent rib, IC; 28-inch vent rib, M choke; 30-inch vent rib, Full choke; 38-inch plain, Full choke; 40-inch plain, Full choke; 26-inch slug barrel with rifle sights, IC. Weight: about 7³/₄ pounds. Checkered pistol-grip stock and forearm, recoil pad. Made 1971–1985.

Marlin Model 120 Slug Gun **$200**
Same general specifications as Model 120 Magnum, except with 20-inch barrel and about ¹/₂ pound lighter in weight. No vent rib. Adjustable rear rifle sights; hooded front sight. Discontinued 1990.

SHOTGUNS

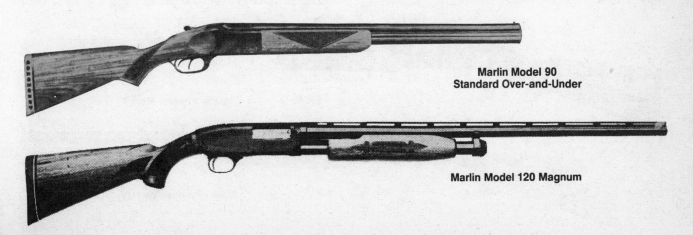

**Marlin Model 90
Standard Over-and-Under**

Marlin Model 120 Magnum

Marlin Model 410

Marlin Model 512 Slugmaster

Marlin Model 5510 Super Goose 10

Marlin Model 410 Lever Action Repeater **$650**
Action similar to that of Marlin Model 93 rifle. Visible hammer. Solid frame. .410 gauge (2½-inch shell). 5-shot tubular magazine. 22- or 26-inch barrel, Full choke. Weight: about 6 pounds. Plain pistol-grip stock and grooved beavertail forearm. Made 1929–1932.

Marlin Model 512 Slugmaster Shotgun **$220**
Bolt-action repeater. Gauge: 12; 3-inch chamber. 2-shot magazine. 21-inch rifled barrel w/adj. open sights. Weight: 8 pounds. Walnut-finished birch stock. Made 1994 to date.

Marlin Model 1898 Visible Hammer Slide Action Repeater
Takedown. 12 gauge. 5-shell tubular magazine. Barrels: 26-, 28-, 30-, 32-inch; standard chokes. Weight: about 7¼ pounds. Pistol-grip stock, grooved slide handle; checkering on higher grades. Difference among grades is in quality of wood, engraving on Grades C and D. Made 1898–1905. *Note:* This was the first Marlin shotgun.

Marlin Model 1898 Visible Hammer Repeater (cont.)
Grade A (Field) .... $ 325
Grade B 495
Grade C 695
Grade D 1595

Marlin Model 5510 Super Goose 10 .... **$175**
Similar to Model 55 Goose Gun, except chambered for 10 gauge 3½-inch magnum shell, has 34-inch heavy barrel, Full choke. Weight: about 10½ pounds. Made 1976–1985.

Marlin Premier Mark I Slide Action Repeater ... **$175**
Hammerless. Takedown. 12 gauge. Magazine holds 3 shells. Barrels: 30-inch Full choke, 28-inch M, 26-inch IC or SK choke. Weight: about 6 pounds. Plain pistol-grip stock and forearm. Made in France 1960–63.

Marlin Premier Mark II and IV
Same as Premier Mark I, except engraved receiver (Mark IV is more elaborate), checkered stock and forearm, fancier wood. Made 1960–63.
Premier Mark II **$205**
Premier Mark IV (plain barrel) 275
Premier Mark IV (vent-rib barrel) 325

Marlin Premier Mark I

Marlin Premier Mark IV

Marlin-Glenfield Model 50

Marlin-Glenfield Model 50 Bolt Action Repeater . . **$65**
Similar to Model 55 Hunter, except chambered for 12-or
20-gauge, 3-inch magnum shell; has 28-inch barrel in 12
gauge, 26-inch in 20 gauge, Full choke. Made 1966–1974.

Marlin-Glenfield 778 Slide Action Repeater
Hammerless. 12 gauge 2³/₄-inch or 3-inch. 4-shot tubular
magazine. Barrels: 26-inch IC, 28-inch M, 30-inch Full,

Marlin-Glenfield 778 Slide Action Repeater (cont.)
38-inch MXR, 20-inch slug barrel. Weight: 7³/₄ pounds.
Checkered pistol grip. Made from 1979–1984.
With plain barrel **$140**
With vent-rib barrel **175**

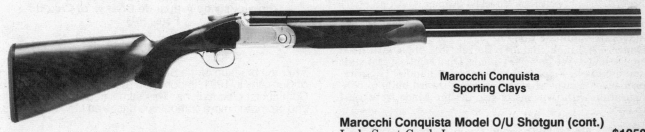

**Marocchi Conquista
Sporting Clays**

MAROCCHI SHOTGUNS
Brescia, Italy
Imported by Precision Sales International of
Westfield, MA.

Marocchi Conquista Model O/U Shotgun
Boxlock. Gauge: 12; 2³/₄-inch chamber. 28-, 30- or 32-inch
vent-rib barrel. Fixed choke or internal tubes. 44³/₈ to 48
inches overall. Weight: 7¹/₂ to 8¹/₄ lbs. Adjustable single-
selective trigger. Checkered American walnut stock w/
recoil pad. Imported since 1994.

Marocchi Conquista Model O/U Shotgun (cont.)

Lady Sport Grade I	**$1250**
Lady Sport Grade II	1495
Lady Sport Grade III	2295
Skeet Model Grade I	1295
Skeet Model Grade II	1550
Skeet Model Grade III	2350
Sporting Clays Grade I	1235
Sporting Clays Grade II	1475
Sporting Clays Grade III	2250
Trap Model Grade I	1295
Trap Model Grade II	1560
Trap Model Grade III	2375
Left-Handed Action, **add**	100

SHOTGUNS

**Maverick Model 60
Turkey/Deer Combo**

MAVERICK ARMS, INC.
Eagle Pass, Texas

Maverick Model 60 Autoloading Shotgun
Gauge: 12; 2³/₄- or 3-inch chamber. 5-round capacity. Barrels: magnum or non-magnum; 24- or 28-inch with fixed
choke or screw-in tubes; plain or vent rib; blued. Weight:

Maverick Model 60 Autoloading Shotgun (cont.)
7¹/₄ pounds. Black synthetic buttstock and forend. Made
from 1993 to date.
Standard Model **$210**
Combo Model w/extra 18¹/₂" bbl. 235
Turkey/Deer Model (w/Ghost Ring sights) 245

Maverick Model 88 Pump Vent Rib

Maverick Model 88 Bullpup

Maverick Model 88 Bullpup $295
Gauge: 12; 3-inch chamber. Barrel: 18¹/₂-inch with fixed choke; blued. Weight: 9¹/₂ pounds. Dual safeties: grip style and crossbolt. Fixed sights in carrying handle. High-impact black synthetic stock; trigger-forward bullpup configuration with twin pistol-grip design. Made from 1991 to date.

Maverick Model 88 Pump Shotgun
Gauge: 12; 2³/₄- or 3-inch chamber. Barrel: 28 inches/M or 30 inches/F with fixed choke or screw-in tubes; plain or vent rib; blued. Weight: 7¹/₄ pounds. Bead front sight. Black synthetic or wood buttstock and forend. Made from 1989 to date.

Synthetic stock w/plain bbl.	$150
Synthetic stock w/vent-rib bbl.	$160
Synthetic Combo w/18¹/₂" bbl.	180
Wood stock w/vent-rib bbl./tubes	175
Wood Combo w/vent-rib bbl./tubes	200

Maverick Model 91 Pump Shotgun
Same as Model 88, except with 2³/₄-, 3- or 3¹/₂-inch chamber, 28-inch barrel with ACCU-full choke, crossbolt safety and synthetic stock only.

Synthetic stock w/plain bbl.	$180
Synthetic stock w/vent-rib bbl.	210

Maverick Model HS410 Pump Shotgun
Similar to the Model 88, except in .410 bore with 3-inch chamber. Blued 18¹/₂-inch barrel with muzzle brake. Weight: 6¹/₄ pounds. Optional laser sight. Synthetic stock. Made from 1993 to date. A similar gun is marketed by Mossberg under the same model designation.

Standard Model	$170
Laser Model	275

GEBRÜDER MERKEL
Suhl, Germany
Imported by GSI, Inc., of Tussville, AL (previously by Armes de Chasse of Chadds Ford, PA)

After the breakup of the Soviet Union and the reunification of Germany in 1991, importation restrictions were lifted on Communist bloc nations. This stimulated increased trade and promoted more competitive prices on Merkel firearms.

Merkel Model 8 Hammerless Double $895
Anson & Deeley boxlock action with Greener double-barrel hook lock. Double triggers. Extractors. Automatic safety. Gauges: 12, 16, 20; 2³/₄- or 3-inch chambers. 26- or 28-inch barrels with fixed standard chokes. Checkered European walnut stock, pistol-grip or English-style with or without cheek-piece. Scroll engraved receiver with tinted marble finish. Importation discontinued 1994.

Merkel Model 47LSC Sporting Clays S/S $2195
Anson & Deeley boxlock w/single-selective adj. trigger, cocking indicators and manual safety. Gauge: 12; 3-inch chambers. 28-inch barrels w/Briley choke tubes and H&H-style ejectors. Weight: 7¹/₄ pounds. Color casehardened receiver w/Arabesque engraving. Checkered select-grade walnut stock, beavertail forearm. Imported since 1993.

Merkel Models 47S, 147S, 247S, 347S, 447S Hammerless Sidelocks
Same general specifications as Model 147E, except has sidelocks engraved with arabesques, borders, scrolls or game scenes in varying degrees of elaborateness.
Model 47S **$2995**

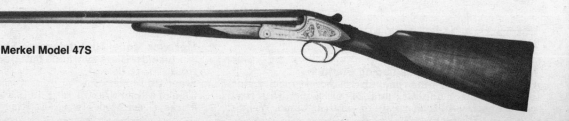

Merkel Model 47S

Merkel Model 147S

Merkel Models 47S, 147S, 247S, 347S, 447S (cont.)
Model 147S **$3795**
Model 247S **3995**
Model 347S **4550**
Model 447S **4895**

Merkel Model 100

Merkel Model 100 Over/Under Shotgun
Hammerless. Boxlock. Greener crossbolt. Plain extractor.
Double triggers. Gauges: 12, 16, 20. Made with plain or
ribbed barrels in various lengths and chokes. Plain finish,
no engraving. Checkered forend and stock with pistol grip
and cheekpiece or English style. Made prior to WWII.
With plain barrel **$1095**
With ribbed barrel **1150**

Merkel Model 101

Merkel Models 101 and 101E Over/Unders
Same as Model 100, except ribbed barrel standard, has
separate extractors (ejectors on Model 101E), English en-
graving. Made prior to World War II.
Model 101 . . . . **$1250**
Model 101E **1350**

Merkel Model 122 Hammerless Double **$2195**
Similar to the Model 147S, except with nonremovable
sidelocks, in gauges 12, 16 or 20. Imported since 1993.

Merkel Model 122E Hammerless Sidelock **$2395**
Similar to the Model 122, except w/removable sidelocks
and cocking indicators. Importation discontinued 1992.

Merkel Model 127

Merkel Model 127 Hammerless Sidelock
Double **$15,750**
Holland & Holland system, hand-detachable locks. Auto
ejectors. Double triggers. Made in all standard gauges,
barrel lengths and chokes. Checkered forend and stock
with pistol grip and cheekpiece or English style. This is
a highest quality deluxe gun, elaborately engraved in arabesque or hunting scene pattern. Made prior to WW II.

Merkel Model 130

Merkel Model 130 Hammerless Boxlock
Double **$8250**
Anson & Deeley system. Sideplates. Auto ejectors. Double
triggers. Elaborate hunting scene or arabesque engraving.
Made in all standard gauges, various barrel lengths and
chokes. Checkered forend and stock with pistol grip and
cheekpiece or English style. Made prior to WW II.

Merkel Model 147E Hammerless Boxlock
Double Barrel Shotgun **$1595**
Anson & Deeley system. Auto ejectors. Double triggers.
Gauges: 12, 16, 20 (3-inch chambers available in 12 and
20 gauge). Barrels: 26-inch standard, other lengths
available; any standard choke combination. Weight: about
6¹/₂ pounds. Checkered straight-grip stock and forearm.
Discontinued 1989.

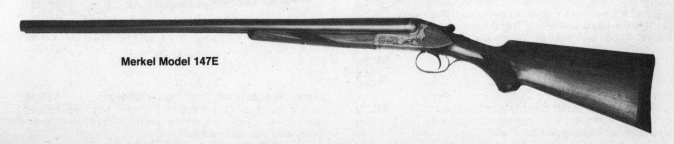

Merkel Model 147E

Merkel Model 201

Merkel Model 300E

Merkel Models 200, 201, and 202 Series Over/Under Shotguns

Hammerless. Boxlock. Kersten double crossbolt. Scalloped frame. Sideplates on Models 202 and 202E. Arabesque or hunting engraving supplied on all except Models 200 and 200E. "E" models have ejectors, others have separate extractors. Signal pins. Double triggers. Gauges: 12, 16, 20, 24, 28, 32 (last three not available in postwar guns). Ribbed barrels in various lengths and chokes. Weight: 5³/₄ to 7¹/₂ pounds depending on barrel length and gauge. Checkered forend and stock with pistol grip and cheekpiece or English style. The 200, 201, and 202 differ in overall quality, engraving, wood, checkering, etc.; aside from the faux sideplates on Models 202 and 202E, general specifications are the same. Models 200, 201 and 202, all made before WW II, are discontinued. Model 202E still in production.

Model 200 (Discontinued)	**$1295**
Model 200E	**1595**
Model 200ES Skeet	**3595**
Model 200ET Trap	**3550**
Model 200SC Sporting Clays	**3795**
Model 201 (Discontinued)	**1625**
Model 201E (Pre-WW II)	**1895**
Model 201E (Post-WW II)	**2595**
Model 201ES Skeet	**4295**
Model 201ET Trap	**4250**
Model 202 (Discontinued)	**2495**
Model 202E (Pre-WW II)	**2795**
Model 202E (Post-WW II)	**4995**

Merkel Model 302

Merkel Models 300, 300E, 301, 301E and 302 O/U

Merkel-Anson system boxlock. Kersten double crossbolt, two underlugs, scalloped frame, sideplates on Model 302. Arabesque or hunting engraving. "E" models and Model 302 have auto ejectors, others have separate extractors. Signal pins. Double triggers. Gauges: 12, 16, 20, 24, 28, 32. Ribbed barrels in various lengths and chokes. Checkered forend and stock with pistol grip and cheekpiece or English style. Grades 300, 301 and 302 differ in overall quality, engraving, wood, checkering, etc.; aside from the dummy sideplates on Model 302, general specifications are the same. Manufactured prior to World War II.

Model 300	**$1850**
Model 300E	**1995**
Model 301	**3995**
Model 301E	**4875**
Model 302	**6495**

Merkel Model 303E Over/Under Shotgun $10,995

Similar to Model 203E. Has Kersten crossbolt, double underlugs, Holland & Holland-type hand-detachable sidelocks, auto ejectors. This is a finer gun than Model 203E. Currently manufactured.

Merkel Model 203E

Merkel Model 203E Over/Under Shotgun

Hammerless. Hand-detachable sidelocks, Kersten fastening, auto ejectors, double triggers. Arabesque engraving standard, hunting engraving optional. Gauges: 12, 16, 20. Ribbed barrels in various lengths and chokes. Checkered forend and stock with pistol grip and cheekpiece or English style. Currently manufactured.

Model 203E	**$4795**
Model 203ES Skeet	**7150**
Model 203ET Trap	**7095**

Merkel Model 204E Over/Under Shotgun $4500

Similar to Model 203E; has Merkel sidelocks, fine English engraving. Made prior to World War II.

Merkel Model 304E

Merkel Model 304E Over/Under Shotgun $15,500

Special version of the Model 303E-type, but higher quality throughout. This is the top grade Merkel over/under. Currently manufactured.

Merkel Model 400

Merkel Models 400, 400E, 401, 401E Over/Unders

Similar to Model 101 except have Kersten double cross-bolt, arabesque engraving on Models 400 and 400E, hunting engraving on Models 401 and 401E, finer general quality. "E" models have Merkel ejectors, others have separate extractors. Made prior to World War II.

Model 400	**$1250**
Model 400E	**1395**
Model 401	**1450**
Model 401E	**1725**

Merkel O/U Combination Model 210

Merkel Over-and-Under Combination Guns ("Bock-Büchsflinten")

Shotgun barrel over, rifle barrel under. Gauges: 12, 16, 20; calibers: 5.6×35 Vierling, 7×57r5, 8×57JR, 8×60R Magnum, 9.3×53r5, 9.3×72r5, 9.3×74R and others. Various barrel lengths, chokes and weights. Other specifications and values correspond to those of Merkel over/under shotguns listed below. Currently manufactured. Model 210 & 211 series discontinued 1992.

Models 410, 410E, 411E .... **see shotgun Models 400, 400E, 401, 401E respectively**
Models 210, 210E, 211, 211E, 212, 212E .. **see shotgun Models 200, 200E, 201, 201E, 202, 202E**

Merkel Anson Drilling Model 144

Merkel Anson Drillings

Three-barrel combination guns; usually made with double shotgun barrels, over rifle barrel, although "Doppel-büchsdrillingen" were made with two rifle barrels over and shotgun barrel under. Hammerless. Boxlock. Anson & Deeley system. Side clips. Plain extractors. Double triggers. Gauges: 12, 16, 20; rifle calibers: 7×57r5, 8×57JR and 9.3×74R are most common, but other calibers from 5.6mm to 10.75mm available. Barrels: standard drilling, 25.6 inches; short drilling, 21.6 inches. Checkered pistol-grip stock and forend. The three models listed differ chiefly in overall quality, grade of wood, etc.; general specifications are the same. Made prior to WW II.

Model 144	**$7000**
Model 142	**4500**
Model 145	**3500**

MIIDA SHOTGUNS

Manufactured for Marubeni America Corp., New York, N.Y., by Olin-Kodensha Co., Tochigi, Japan

Miida Model 612 Field Grade Over-and-Under .. **$750**
Boxlock. Auto ejectors. Selective single trigger. 12 gauge. Barrels: vent rib; 26-inch, IC/M; 28-inch, M/F choke. Weight: with 26-inch barrel, 6 lbs. 11 oz. Checkered pistol-grip stock and forearm. Made 1972–74.

SHOTGUNS

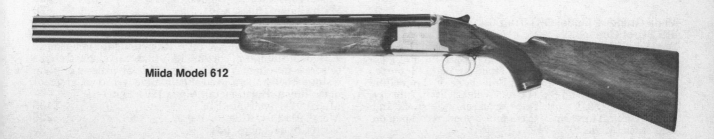

Miida Model 612

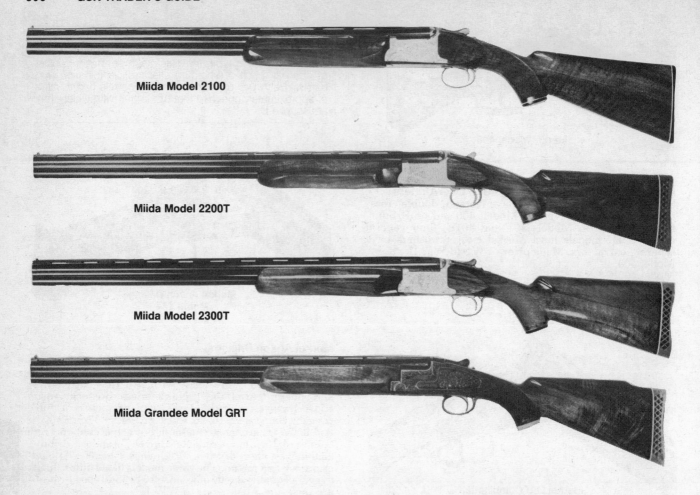

Miida Model 2100

Miida Model 2200T

Miida Model 2300T

Miida Grandee Model GRT

Miida Model 2100 Skeet Gun **$795**
Similar to Model 612, except has more elaborate engraving on frame (50 percent coverage), skeet-style stock and forearm of select grade wood; 27-inch vent-rib barrels, SK choke. Weight: 7 lbs. 11 oz. Made 1972–74.

**Miida Model 2200T Trap Gun, Model 2200S
Skeet Gun** **$850**
Similar to Model 612, except more elaborate engraving on frame (60 percent coverage), trap- or skeet-style stock and semibeavertail forearm of fancy walnut, recoil pad on trap stock. Barrels: wide vent rib; 29¾-inch, IM/F choke on Trap Gun; 27-inch, SK choke on Skeet Gun. Weight: Trap, 7 lbs. 14 oz.; Skeet, 7 lbs. 11 oz. Made 1972–74.

**Miida Model 2300T Trap Gun, Model 2300S
Skeet Gun** **$895**
Same as Models 2200T and 2200S, except more elaborate engraving on frame (70% coverage). Made 1972–74.

**Miida Grandee Model GRT Trap Gun, Model
IRS Skeet Gun** **$2195**
Boxlock with sideplates. Frame, breech ends of barrels, trigger guard and locking lever fully engraved and gold inlaid. Auto ejectors. Selective single trigger. 12 gauge. Barrels: wide vent rib; 29-inch, Full choke on Trap Gun; 27-inch, SK choke on Skeet Gun. Weight: Trap, 7 lbs. 14 oz.; Skeet, 7 lbs. 11 oz. Trap- or skeet-style stock and semibeavertail forearm of extra fancy wood, recoil pad on trap stock. Made 1972–74.

MITCHELL ARMS
Santa Ana, California

Mitchell Model 9104/9105 Pump Shotguns
Slide action in Field/Riot configuration. Gauge: 12; 5-shot tubular magazine. 20-inch barrel; fixed choke or screw-in tubes. Weight: 6.5 pounds. Plain walnut stock. Made 1994 to date.
Model 9104 (w/Plain Bbl.) **$175**
Model 9105 (w/Rifle Sights) **195**
With Choke Tubes, **add** **20**

Mitchell Model 9108/9109 Pump Shotguns
Slide action in Military/Police/Riot configuration. Gauge: 12; 7-shot tubular magazine. 20-inch barrel; fixed choke or screw-in tubes. Weight: 6.5 pounds. Plain walnut stock and grooved slide handle w/brown, green or black finish. Blued metal. Made 1994 to date.
Model 9108 (w/Plain Bbl.) **$180**
Model 9109 (w/Rifle Sights) **200**
With Choke Tubes, **add** **20**

Mitchell Model 9111/9113 Pump Shotguns
Slide action in Military/Police/Riot configuration. Gauge: 12; 6-shot tubular magazine. 18.5-inch barrel; fixed choke or screw-in tubes. Weight: 6.5 pounds. Synthetic or plain walnut stock and grooved slide handle w/brown, green or black finish. Blued metal. Made 1994 to date.
Model 9111 (w/Plain Bbl.) **$185**
Model 9113 (w/Rifle Sights) **205**
With Choke Tubes, **add** **20**

Mitchell Model 9114/9114FS Pump Shotguns
Slide action in Military/Police/Riot configuration. Gauge: 12; 7-shot tubular magazine. 20-inch barrel; fixed choke. Weight: 6.5–7 pounds. Rifle sights. Synthetic pistol-grip or folding stock. Blued metal. Made 1994 to date.

Model 9114 (w/Fixed Stock) **$225**
Model 9114FS (w/Folding Stock) **240**

Mitchell Model 9115/9115FS Pump Shotguns . . . **$250**
Slide action in Military/Riot configuration. Gauge: 12; 6-shot tubular magazine. 18.5-inch barrel w/heat-shield hand guard. Weight: 7 pounds. Gray synthetic stock and slide handle. Parkerized metal. Made 1994 to date.

MONTGOMERY WARD
See shotgun listings under "W."

MORRONE SHOTGUN
Manufactured by Rhode Island Arms Company, Hope Valley, RI

Morrone Standard Model 46 Over-and-Under . . . **$725**
Boxlock. Plain extractors. Non-selective single trigger. Gauges: 12, 20. Barrels: plain, vent rib; 26-inch IC/M; 28-inch M/F choke. Weight: about 7 lbs., 12 ga.; 6 lbs., 20 ga. Checkered straight- or pistol-grip stock and forearm. Made 1949–1953. *Note:* Less than 500 of these guns were produced, about 50 in 20 gauge; a few had vent-rib barrels. Value shown is for 12 gauge with plain barrels; the rare 20 ga. and vent-rib types should bring considerably more.

O. F. MOSSBERG & SONS, INC.
North Haven (Formerly New Haven), CT

Mossberg Model 83D or 183D **$100**
3-shot. Takedown. .410-bore only. 2-shell fixed, top-loading magazine. 23-inch barrel with two interchangeable choke tubes (M/F). Later production had 24-inch barrel. Plain one-piece, pistol-grip stock. Weight: about 5½ pounds. Originally designated Model 83D, changed in 1947 to Model 183D. Made 1940–1971.

Mossberg Model 85D or 185D Bolt Action Repeating Shotgun **$90**
Takedown. 3-shot. 20 gauge only. 2-shell detachable box magazine. 25-inch barrel, three interchangeable choke tubes (F, M, IC). Later production had 26-inch barrel with F/IC choke tubes. Weight: about 6¼ pounds. Plain one-piece, pistol-grip stock. Originally designated Model 85D, changed in 1947 to Model 185D. Made 1940–1971.

Mossberg Model 183K **$95**
Same as Model 183D, except has 25-inch barrel with variable C-Lect-Choke instead of interchangeable choke tubes. Made 1953–1986.

Mossberg Model 185K **$100**
Same as Model 185D, except has variable C-Lect-Choke instead of interchangeable choke tubes. Made 1950–1963.

SHOTGUNS

Mossberg Model 83D

Mossberg Model 85D

Mossberg Model 183K

Mossberg Model 185K

Mossberg Model 190D

Mossberg Model 195D

Mossberg Model 200K

Mossberg Model 395K

Mossberg Model 500 Accu-Steel Pump Shotgun

Mossberg Model 190D **$95**
Same as Model 185D, except in 16 gauge. Weight: about 6 pounds. Made 1955–1971.

Mossberg Model 190K **$100**
Same as Model 185K, except in 16 gauge. Weight: about 6³/₄ pounds. Made 1956–1963.

Mossberg Model 195D **$110**
Same as Model 185D, except in 12 gauge. Weight: about 6³/₄ pounds. Made 1955–1971.

Mossberg Model 195K **$100**
Same as Model 185K, except in 12 gauge. Weight: about 7¹/₂ pounds. Made 1956–1963.

Mossberg Model 200D **$115**
Same as Model 200K, except with two interchangeable choke tubes instead of C-Lect-Choke. Made 1955–59.

Mossberg Model 200K Slide Action Repeater . . . **$115**
12 gauge. 3-shot detachable box magazine. 28-inch barrel. C-Lect-Choke. Plain pistol-grip stock. Black nylon slide handle. Weight: about 7¹/₂ pounds. Made 1955–59.

Mossberg Model 385K **$100**
Same as Model 395K, except 20 gauge (3-inch), 26-inch barrel with C-Lect-Choke. Weight: about 6¹/₄ pounds. Made 1963–1983.

Mossberg Model 390K **$115**
Same as Model 395K, except 16 gauge (2³/₄-inch). Made 1963–1974.

Mossberg Model 395K Bolt Action Repeater . . . **$100**
Takedown. 3-shot (detachable-clip magazine holds two shells). 12 gauge (3-inch chamber). 28-inch barrel with C-Lect-Choke. Weight: about 7¹/₂ pounds. Monte Carlo stock with recoil pad. Made 1963–1983.

Mossberg Model 395S Slugster **$130**
Same as Model 395K, except has 24-inch barrel, cylinder bore, rifle sights, swivels and web sling. Weight: about 7 pounds. Made 1968–1981.

Mossberg Model 500 Accu-Steel Shotgun
Pump. Gauge: 12. 24- or 28-inch barrel. Weight: 7¹/₄ pounds. Checkered walnut-finished woodstock with ventilated recoil pad. Available with synthetic field or Speed-feed stocks. Drilled and tapped receivers, swivels and camo sling on camo models. Made 1987–1990.
Accu-Steel Model **$265**
With Camo, Synthetic or Speedfeed Stocks,
   add **30**

Mossberg Model 500 Bantam Shotgun **$185**
Same as Model 500 Sporting Pump, except 20 or .410 gauge only. 22-inch w/ACCU-Choke tubes or 24-inch w/ F choke; vent rib. Scaled-down checkered hardwood stock. Made from 1992 to date.

Mossberg Model 500 Bullpup Shotgun **$375**
Pump. Gauge: 12. 6- or 8-shot capacity. Barrel: 18¹/₂ to 20 inches. 26¹/₂ and 28¹/₂ inches overall. Weight: about 9¹/₂ pounds. Multiple independent safety systems. Dual pistol grips, rubber recoil pad. Fully enclosed rifle-type sights. Synthetic stock. Ventilated barrel heat shield. Made 1987–1990.

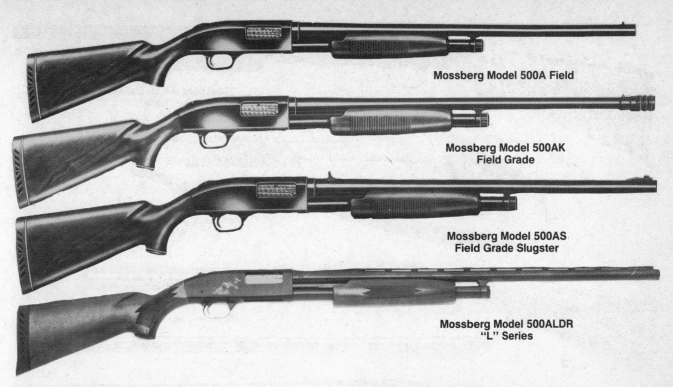

Mossberg Model 500A Field

Mossberg Model 500AK Field Grade

Mossberg Model 500AS Field Grade Slugster

Mossberg Model 500ALDR "L" Series

Mossberg Model 500 Camo Pump

Same as Model 500 Sporting Pump, except 12 gauge only. Receiver drilled and tapped. QD swivels and camo sling. Special camouflage finish. Made from 1987 to date.

Standard Model	**$195**
Combo Model (w/extra Slugster bbl.)	**250**
With Ghost Ring Sight, **add**	**35**

Mossberg Model 500 Field Grade Hammerless Slide Action Repeater (Pre-1977)

Pre-1977 type. Takedown. Gauges: 12, 16, 20, .410. 3-inch chamber (2³/₄-inch in 16 gauge). Tubular magazine holds five 2³/₄-inch shells or four three-inch. Barrels: plain; 30-inch regular or heavy magnum, Full choke (12 ga. only); 28-inch, M or F; 26-inch, IC or adj. C-Lect-Choke; 24-inch Slugster, cylinder bore, with rifle sights. Weight: 5³/₄ to 8 pounds. Plain pistol-grip stock with recoil pad, grooved slide handle. After 1973, these guns have checkered stock and slide handle, Models 500AM and 500AS have receivers etched with game scenes. The latter has swivels and sling. Made 1962–1976.

Model 500A, 12 gauge	**$200**
Model 500AM, 12 gauge, heavy Magnum barrel	**200**
Model 500AK, 12 gauge, C-Lect-Choke	**225**
Model 500AS, 12 gauge, Slugster	**220**
Model 500B, 16 gauge	**200**
Model 500BK, 16 gauge, C-Lect-Choke	**235**
Model 500BS, 16 gauge, Slugster	**225**
Model 500C, 20 gauge	**200**
Model 500CK, 20 gauge, C-Lect-Choke	**240**
Model 500CS, 20 gauge, Slugster	**225**
Model 500E, .410 gauge	**240**
Model 500EK, .410 gauge, C-Lect-Choke	**275**

Mossberg Model 500 Field Grade (Post-1977)

Gauges: 12, 20 and .410; 3-inch chambers. 5-shot tubular magazine. 20- to 28-inch barrel; fixed choke or Accu-Choke (intro. 1984, standardized 1994). Synthetic or checkered hardwood stock w/walnut or camo finish. Made from 1977 to date.

Mossberg Model 500 Field Grade—Post-1977 (cont.)

Standard Field Model	**$150**
With Camo Finish, **add**	**25**
With Rifled Barrel, **add**	**30**
With .410 Barrel, **add**	**15**
With Accu-Choke, **add**	**15**
With Additional Options	**See Specific Models**

Mossberg Model 500 "L" Series

"L" in model designation. Same as pre-1977 Model 500 Field Grade, except not available in 16 gauge, has receiver etched with different game scenes; Accu-Choke with three interchangeable tubes (IC, M, F) standard, restyled stock and slide handle. Barrels: plain or vent rib; 30- or 32-inch, heavy, F choke (12 ga. Magnum and vent rib only); 28-inch, Accu-Choke (12 and 20 ga.); 26-inch F choke (.410 bore only); 18¹/₂-inch (12 ga. only), 24-inch (12 and 20 ga.) Slugster with rifle sights, cylinder bore. Weight: 6 to 8¹/₂ pounds. Intro. 1977.

Model 500ALD, 12 gauge, plain barrel (Disc. 1980)	**$210**
Model 500ALDR, 12 gauge, vent rib	**250**
Model 500ALMR, 12 ga., Heavy Duck Gun (Disc. 1980)	**250**
Model 500ALS, 12 gauge, Slugster (Disc. 1981)	**200**
Model 500CLD, 20 gauge, plain barrel (Disc. 1980)	**200**
Model 500CLDR, 20 gauge, vent rib	**250**
Model 500CLS, 20 gauge, Slugster (Disc. 1980)	**250**
Model 500EL, .410 gauge, plain barrel (Disc. 1980)	**200**
Model 500ELR, .410 gauge, vent rib	**250**

Mossberg Model 500 Mariner Shotgun

Slide action. Gauge: 12. 18¹/₂ or 20-inch barrel. 6-shot and 9-shot respectively. Weight: 7¹/₄ pounds. High-strength synthetic stock/forend. Available in extra round-carrying speedfeed synthetic stock. All metal treated for protection against saltwater corrosion. Made 1987 to date.

SHOTGUNS

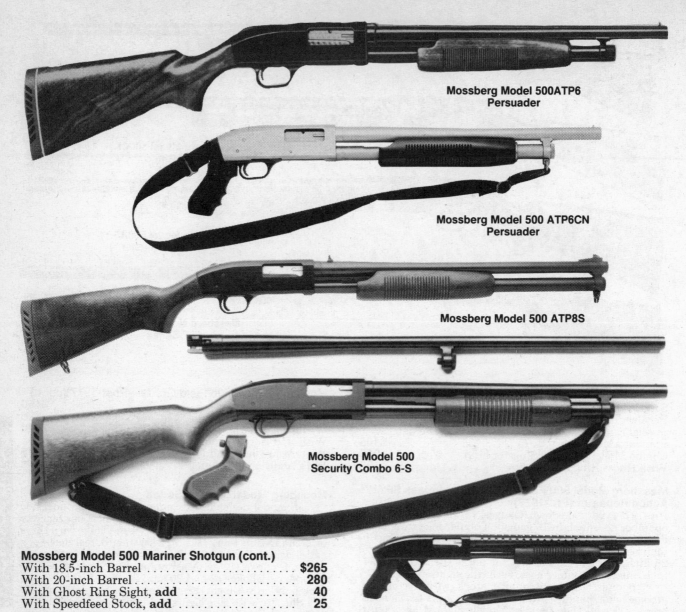

Mossberg Model 500ATP6 Persuader

Mossberg Model 500 ATP6CN Persuader

Mossberg Model 500 ATP8S

Mossberg Model 500 Security Combo 6-S

Mossberg Model 500 Cruiser

Mossberg Model 500 Mariner Shotgun (cont.)
With 18.5-inch Barrel **$265**
With 20-inch Barrel **280**
With Ghost Ring Sight, **add** **40**
With Speedfeed Stock, **add** **25**

Mossberg Model 500 Muzzleloader Combo **$270**
Same asModel 500 Sporting Pump, except with extra 24-inch rifled 50-caliber muzzleloading barrel and ramrod. Made from 1992 to date.

Mossberg Model 500 Persuader Law Enforcement Shotgun
Similar to pre-1977 Model 500 Field Grade, except 12 gauge only, 6- or 8-shot, has 18½- or 20-inch plain barrel, cylinder bore, either shotgun or rifle sights, plain pistol-grip stock and grooved slide handle, sling swivels. Special Model 500ATP8-SP has bayonet lug, Parkerized finish. Currently manufactured.
Model 500ATP6, 6-shot, 18½-inch barrel,
 shotgun sights **$185**
Model 500ATP6CN, 6-shot, nickel finish,
 "Cruiser" pistol grip **190**
Model 500ATP6N, 6-shot, nickel finish,
 2¾- or 3-inch Mag. shells **190**
Model 500ATP6S, 6-shot, 18½" barrel, rifle
 sights **185**

Mossberg Model 500 Persuader (cont.)
Model 500ATP8, 8-shot, 20-inch bbl., shotgun
 sights **$200**
Model 500ATP8S, 8-shot, 20-inch barrel, rifle
 sights **200**
Model 500ATP8-SP Special Enforcement **250**
Model 500 Bullpup **350**
Model 500 Cruiser w/Pistol Grip **155**
Model 500 Cruiser w/Camper Case **185**
Model 500 Cruiser w/.410 Bbl. **195**
Model 500 Cruiser w/14-inch Bbl.* **275**
Model 500 Intimidator w/Laser Sight **375**
Model 500 Night Persuader w/Night Sight **225**
Model 500 Security Combo Pack **150**
Caution: 14-inch shotgun barrels are illegal except for use by military and law-enforcement agencies. A special permit from the BATF is required for all civilians. Shotgun barrels must be 18 inches or longer.

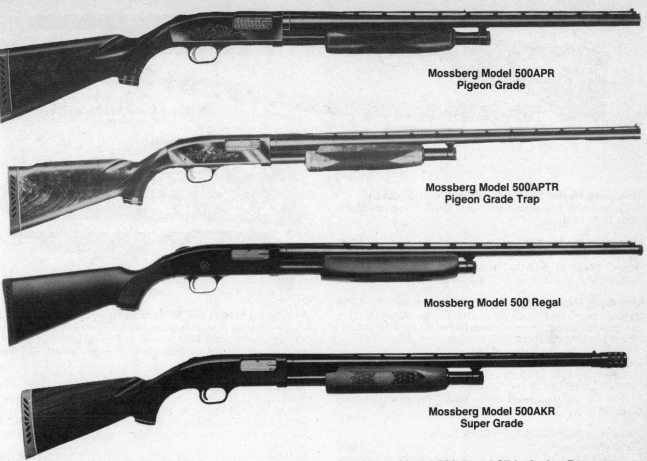

Mossberg Model 500APR Pigeon Grade

Mossberg Model 500APTR Pigeon Grade Trap

Mossberg Model 500 Regal

Mossberg Model 500AKR Super Grade

Mossberg Model 500 Pigeon Grade

Same as Model 500 Super Grade, except higher quality with fancy wood, floating vent rib; field gun hunting dog etching, trap and skeet guns have scroll etching. Barrels: 30-inch, F choke (12 gauge only); 28-inch, M choke; 26-inch, SK choke or C-Lect-Choke. Made 1971–75.

Model 500APR, 12 gauge, Field, Trap or Skeet . . . **$350**
Model 500APKR, 12 gauge, Field Gun, C-Lect-
   Choke **360**
Model 500 APTR, 12 gauge, Trap Gun, Monte
   Carlo stock **425**
Model 500CPR, 20 gauge, Field or Skeet Gun **375**
Model 500EPR, .410 gauge, Field or Skeet Gun . . **375**

Mossberg Model 500 Pump Combo Shotgun

Gauges: 12 and 20. 24-, 26- or 28-inch barrel w/additional 18.5-inch barrel; adjustable rifle sights. Weight: 7–7¼ pounds. Blued or camo finish. Drilled and tapped receiver w/sling swivels and camo web sling. Made from 1987 to date.

Standard Combo Model. **$210**
With Accu-Choke, **add** **15**
With .410 Barrel, **add** **20**

Mossberg Model 500 Pump Slugster Shotgun

Gauge: 12 or 20. 24-inch barrel w/adjustable rifle sights. Weight: 7 pounds. Synthetic or hardwood stock w/camo or walnut finish. Drilled and tapped receiver w/camo sling and swivels. Made 1987 to date.

Standard Barrel Model **$195**
Rifled Barrel Model **220**
Rifled Barrel w/Integral Scope Mount **240**

Mossberg Model 500 Regal Slide Action Repeater

Similar to regular Model 500 except higher quality workmanship throughout. Gauges: 12 and 20. Barrels: 26- and 28-inch with various chokes, or Accu-Choke. Weight: 6¾ to 7½ pounds. Checkered walnut stock and forearm. Made 1985 to date.

Model 500 with Accu-Choke **$185**
Model 500 with fixed choke **170**

Mossberg Model 500 Sporting Pump

Gauges: 12, 20 or .410; 2¾- or 3-inch chamber. Barrels: 22 to 28 inches with fixed choke or screw-in tubes; plain or vent rib. Weight: 6¼ to 7¼ pounds. White bead front sight, brass mid-bead. Checkered hardwood buttstock and forend with walnut finish.

Standard Model **$190**
Field Combo (w/extra Slugster bbl.) **240**

Mossberg Model 500 Super Grade

Same as pre-1977 Model 500 Field Grade, except not made in 16 gauge, has vent-rib barrel, checkered pistol grip and slide handle. Made 1965–1976.

Model 500AR, 12 gauge **$195**
Model 500AMR, 12 gauge, heavy Magnum bbl. **220**
Model 500AKR, 12 gauge, C-Lect-Choke **225**
Model 500CR, 20 gauge **210**
Model 500CKR, 20 gauge, C-Lect-Choke **295**
Model 500ER, .410 gauge **190**
Model 500EKR, .410 gauge, C-Lect-Choke **240**

Mossberg Model 500 Turkey/Deer Combo **$255**

Pump. Gauge: 12. 20- and 24-inch barrels. Weight: 7¼ pounds. Drilled and tapped receiver, camo sling and swiv-

Mossberg Model 500 Turkey/Deer Combination

Mossberg Model 500/410 Camper

Mossberg Model 500 Turkey/Deer Combo (cont.)
els. Adjustable rifle sights and camo finish. Vent rib. Made from 1987 to date.

Mossberg Model 500 Turkey Gun $260
Same as Model 500 Camo Pump, except with 24-inch ACCU-Choke barrel with Extra Full choke tube and Ghost Ring sights. Made from 1992 to date.

Mossberg Model 500 Waterfowl/Deer Combo . . $265
Same general specifications as the Turkey/Deer Combo, except with either 28- or 30-inch barrel along with the 24-inch barrel. Made from 1987 to date.

Mossberg Model 500ATR Super Grade Trap . . . $290
Same as pre-1977 Model 500 Field Grade, except 12 gauge only with vent-rib barrel; 30-inch Full choke, checkered Monte Carlo stock with recoil pad, beavertail forearm (slide handle). Made 1968–1971.

Mossberg Model 500DSPR Duck Stamp Commemorative $645
Limited edition of 1000 to commemorate the Migratory Bird Hunting Stamp Program. Same as Model 500DSPR Pigeon Grade 12-Gauge Magnum Heavy Duck Gun with heavy 30-inch vent-rib barrel, Full choke; receiver has special Wood Duck etching. Gun accompanied by a special wall plaque. Made in 1975. *Note:* Value is for gun in new, unfired condition.

Mossberg Model 500/410 Camper $180
Similar to regular Model 500 action, except in .410 only. Barrel: 18½-inch; IC choke. Synthetic pistol-grip stock, ribbed forearm. Made from 1985 to date.

Mossberg Model 590 Military Security Shotgun . $275
Same general specifications as the Model 590 Military, except there is no heat shield and gun has short pistol-grip style instead of buttstock. Weight: about 6¾ lbs. Made from 1987 to date.

Mossberg Model 590 Military Shotgun
Slide-action. Gauge: 12. 9-shot capacity. 20-inch barrel. Weight: about 7 pounds. Synthetic or hardwood buttstock and forend. Ventilated barrel heat shields. Equipped with bayonet lug. Blue or Parkerized finish. Made from 1987 to date.
Synthetic Model, blued $265
Synthetic Model, Parkerized 285
Speedfeed Model, blued 280
Speedfeed Model, Parkerized 285
Intimidator Model w/Laser Sight, blued 365
Intimidator Model w/Laser Sight, Parkerized 375
For Ghost Ring Sight, **add** 50

Mossberg Model 595 Bolt Action Repeater $135
12 gauge only. 4-shot detachable magazine. 18½-inch barrel. Weight: about 7 pounds. Walnut finished stock with recoil pad and sling swivels. Made 1985–86.

Mossberg Model 590 Military Shotgun

Mossberg Model 595 Bolt Action

Mossberg Model 712 Slugster

Mossberg Model 835 "NWTF" Ulti-Mag™

Mossberg Model 712 Autoloading Shotgun **$265**
Gas-operated, takedown, hammerless shotgun with 5-shot (4-shot w/3-inch chamber) tubular magazine. 12 gauge. Barrels: 28-inch vent rib or 24-inch plain barrel Slugster with rifle sights; ACCU-Choke tube system. Weight: 7¹/₂ pounds. Plain alloy receiver, top-mounted ambidextrous safety. Checkered walnut stained hardwood stock with recoil pad. Imported from Japan 1988–1990

Mossberg Model 835 Field Pump Shotgun
Similar to the Model 9600 Regal, except has walnut-stained hardwood stock and one ACCU-Choke tube only.
Standard Model **$210**
Turkey Model **205**
Combo Model (24- & 28-inch bbls.) **240**

Mossberg Model 835 "NWTF" Ulti-Mag™
Shotgun **$375**
National Wild Turkey Federation pump-action. Gauge: 12; 3¹/₂-inch chamber. 24-inch vent-rib barrel with four **ACCU-MAG** chokes. Realtree® Camo finish. QD swivel and post. Made 1989–1993.

Mossberg Model 835 Regal Ulti-Mag Pump
Gauge: 12; 3¹/₂-inch chamber. Barrels: 24- or 28-inch vent-rib with ACCU-Choke screw-in tubes. Weight: 7³/₄ pounds. White bead front, brass mid-bead. Checkered hardwood or synthetic stock with camo finish.
Special Model **$210**
Standard Model **280**
Camo Synthetic Model **300**
Combo Model **325**

Mossberg Model 1000 Autoloading Shotgun
Gas-operated, takedown, hammerless shotgun with tubular magazine. Gauges: 12, 20; 2³/₄- or 3-inch chamber. Barrels: 22- to 30-inch vent rib w/fixed choke or ACCU-Choke tubes; or 22-inch plain barrel Slugster with rifle sights. Weight: 6¹/₂ to 7¹/₂ pounds. Scroll-engraved alloy receiver, crossbolt-type safety. Checkered American walnut buttstock and forend. Imported from Japan.
Junior Model, 20 ga., 22-inch bbl. **$340**
Standard Model with Fixed Choke **325**
Standard Model with Choke Tubes **375**

Mossberg Model 1000 Super Autoloading Shotgun
Similar to Model 1000, but in 12 gauge only with 3-inch chamber and new gas metering system. Barrels: 26-, 28- or 30-inch vent rib with ACCU-Choke tubes.
Standard Model w/Choke Tubes **$395**
Waterfowler Model (Parkerized) **425**

Mossberg Model 1000S Super Skeet **$495**
Similar to Model 1000 in 12 or 20 gauge, except with all-steel receiver and vented jug-type choke for reduced muzzle jump. Bright-point front sight and brass mid-bead. 1 and 2 oz. forend cap weights.

Mossberg Model 5500 Autoloading Shotgun
Gas-operated. Takedown. 12 gauge only. 4-shot magazine (3-shot with 3-inch shells). Barrels: 18¹/₂- to 30-inch; various chokes. Checkered walnut finished hardwood. Made 1985–86.
Model 5500 w/ACCU-Choke **$250**
Model 5500 Modified Junior **255**
Model 5500 Slugster **265**
Model 5500 12 gauge **225**
Model 5500 Guardian **215**

Mossberg Model 5500 MKII Autoloading Shotgun
Same as Model 5500, except equipped with two Accu-Choke barrels: 26-inch ported for non-magnum 2³/₄-inch shells; 28-inch for magnum loads. Made 1988–1993.
Standard Model **$270**
Camo Model **285**
NTWF Mossy Oak Model **295**

Mossberg Model 6000 Auto Shotgun **$240**
Similar to the Model 9200 Regal, except has 28-inch vent-rib barrel w/Mod. ACCU-Choke tube only. Made 1993–94.

Mossberg Model 9200 Camo Shotgun
Similar to the Model 9200 Regal, except has synthetic stock and forend and is completely finished in camouflage pattern (incl. barrel). Made from 1993 to date.
Standard Model (OFM Camo) **$295**
Turkey Model (Mossy Oak® camo) **325**
Combo Model (24- & 28-inch bbls. w/OFM
 Camo) **375**

SHOTGUNS

**Mossberg Model 5500
Accu-Choke**

Mossberg Model 9200 Regal

Mossberg Model HS410 Home Security Shotgun

Mossberg Model 9200 Regal Autoloader
Gauge: 12; 3-inch chamber. Barrels: 24- to 28-inch w/ ACCU-Choke tubes; plain or vent rib. Weight: 7¼ to 7½ pounds. Checkered hardwood buttstock and forend with walnut finish. Made from 1992 to date.
Model 9200 w/ACCU-Choke **$280**
Model 9200 w/rifled barrel **295**
Model 9200 Combo (w/extra Slugster bbl.) **330**

Mossberg Model 9200 USST Autoloader **$280**
Similar to the Model 9200 Regal, except has 26-inch vent-rib barrel w/ACCU-Choke tubes. "United States Shooting Team" engraved on receiver. Made from 1993 to date.

Mossberg Model HS410 Home Security Pump Shotgun
Gauge: .410; 3-inch chamber. Barrel: 18½-inch with muzzle brake; blued. Weight: 6¼ pounds. Synthetic stock and pistol-grip slide. Optional laser sight. Made from 1990 to date. A similar version of this gun is marketed by Maverick Arms under the same model designation.
Standard Model **$190**
Laser Model **340**

Mossberg "New Haven Brand" Shotguns
Promotional models, similar to their standard guns but plainer in finish, are marketed by Mossberg under the "New Haven" brand name. Values generally are about 20 percent lower than for corresponding standard models.

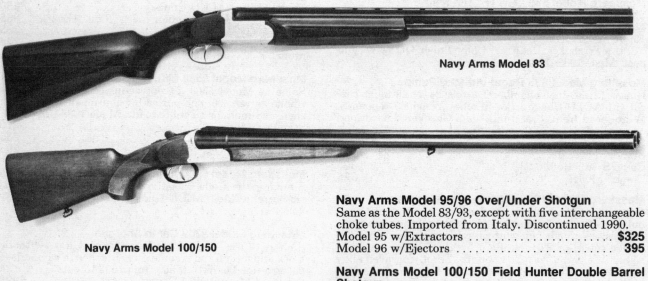

Navy Arms Model 83

Navy Arms Model 100/150

NAVY ARMS SHOTGUNS
Ridgefield, New Jersey

Navy Arms Model 83/93 Bird Hunter Over/Under
Hammerless. Boxlock, engraved receiver. Gauges: 12 and 20; 3-inch chambers. Barrels: 28-inch chrome lined with double vent-rib construction. Checkered European walnut stock and forearm. Gold plated triggers. Made 1984–1990.
Model 83 w/Extractors **$235**
Model 93 w/Ejectors **275**

Navy Arms Model 95/96 Over/Under Shotgun
Same as the Model 83/93, except with five interchangeable choke tubes. Imported from Italy. Discontinued 1990.
Model 95 w/Extractors **$325**
Model 96 w/Ejectors **395**

Navy Arms Model 100/150 Field Hunter Double Barrel Shotgun
Boxlock. Gauges: 12 and 20. Barrels: 28-inch chrome lined. Checkered European walnut stock and forearm. Made 1984–1990.
Model 100 . . . . **$275**
Model 150 (auto ejectors) **375**

Navy Arms Model 410 Over/Under Shotgun **$240**
Hammerless, takedown shotgun with engraved chrome receiver. Single trigger. .410 gauge w/3-inch chambers. Barrels: 26-inch (F/F or SK/SK); vent rib. Weight: 6¼ pounds. Checkered European walnut buttstock and forend. Imported from Italy since 1986.

**New England Firearms
NWTF Turkey Special**

**New England Firearms
Tracker II Rifled Slug Gun**

**New England Firearms
Turkey/Goose Shotgun**

NEW ENGLAND FIREARMS
Gardner, Massachusetts

New England Firearms NWTF Turkey Special .. **$150**
Similar to Turkey and Goose Model, except has 24-inch plain barrel with screw-in Turkey Full choke tube. Mossy Oak Camo finish on entire gun. Made from 1992 to date.

New England Firearms Pardner Shotgun
Takedown. Side lever. Single barrel. Gauges: 12, 20 and .410 w/3-inch chamber; 16 and 28 w/2¾-inch chamber. Barrel: 26- or 28-inch, plain; fixed choke. Weight: 5–6 pounds. Bead front sight. Pistol grip-style hardwood stock with walnut finish. Made from 1988 to date.
Standard Model **$75**
Youth Model **80**

New England Firearms Tracker Slug Gun
Similar to Pardner Model, except in 12 or 20 gauge only. Barrel: 24-inch with cylinder choke or rifled slug (Tracker II). Weight: 6 pounds. American hardwood stock with walnut or camo finish, schnabel forend, sling swivel studs. Made from 1992 to date.
Tracker Slug . . . . **$ 95**
Tracker II (rifled bore) **100**

New England Firearms Turkey and Goose Gun
Similar to Pardner Model, except chambered in 10 gauge w/3½-inch chamber. 28-inch plain barrel w/F choke. Weight: 9½ pounds. American hardwood stock with walnut or camo finish. Made from 1992 to date.
Standard Model **$110**
Camo Model **120**

NIKKO FIREARMS LTD.
Tochigi, Japan
See listings under Golden Eagle Firearms, Inc.

SHOTGUNS

Noble Model 65

NOBLE MANUFACTURING CO.
Haydenville, Massachusetts

Noble Series 602 and 70 are similar in appearance to the corresponding Model 66 guns.

**Noble Model 40 Hammerless Slide Action
Repeating Shotgun** **$110**
Solid frame. 12 gauge only. 5-shell tubular magazine. 28-inch barrel with ventilated Multi-Choke. Weight: about 7½ pounds. Plain pistol-grip stock, grooved slide handle. Made 1950–55.

Noble Model 50 . . . . **$100**
Same as Model 40, except without Multi-Choke. M or F choke barrel. Made 1953–55.

**Noble Model 60 Hammerless Slide Action
Repeating Shotgun** **$155**
Solid frame. 12 and 16 gauge. 5-shot tubular magazine. 28-inch barrel with adjustable choke. Plain pistol-grip stock with recoil pad, grooved slide handle. Weight: about 7½ pounds. Made 1955–1966.

Noble Model 65 . . . . **$135**
Same as Model 60, except without adjustable choke and recoil pad. M or F choke barrel. Made 1955–1966.

Noble Model 66RCLP

Noble Model 66XL

Noble Model 80

Noble Model 66CLP $125
Same as Model 66RCLP, except has plain barrel. Introduced in 1967. Discontinued.

Noble Model 66RCLP Hammerless Slide Action Repeating Shotgun $165
Solid frame. Key lock fire control mechanism. Gauges: 12, 16. 3-inch chamber in 12 gauge. 5-shot tubular magazine. 28-inch barrel, vent rib, adjustable choke. Weight: about 7$\frac{1}{2}$ pounds. Checkered pistol-grip stock and slide handle, recoil pad. Made 1967–1970.

Noble Model 66RLP $145
Same as Model 66RCLP, except with F or M choke. Made 1967–1970.

Noble Model 66XL $125
Same as Model 66RCLP, except has plain barrel, F or M choke, slide handle only checkered, no recoil pad. Made 1967–1970.

Noble Model 70CLP Hammerless Slide Action Repeating Shotgun $150
Solid frame. .410 gauge. Magazine holds 5 shells. 26-inch barrel with adjustable choke. Weight: about 6 pounds. Checkered buttstock and forearm, recoil pad. Made 1958–1970.

Noble Model 70RCLP $165
Same as Model 70CLP, except has vent rib. Made 1967–1970.

Noble Model 70RLP $150
Same as Model 70CLP, except has vent rib and no adjustable choke. Made 1967–1970.

Noble Model 70XL $105
Same as Model 70CLP, except without adjustable choke and checkering on buttstock. Made 1958–1970.

Noble Model 80 Autoloading Shotgun $225
Recoil-operated. .410 gauge. Magazine holds three 3-inch shells, four 2$\frac{1}{2}$-inch shells. 26-inch barrel, Full choke. Weight: about 6 pounds. Plain pistol-grip stock and fluted forearm. Made 1964–1966.

Noble Key Lock Fire Control Mechanism Model 166L Deergun

Noble Model 166L Deergun $230
Solid frame. Key lock fire control mechanism. 12 gauge. 2$\frac{3}{4}$-inch chamber. 5-shot tubular magazine. 24-inch plain barrel, specially bored for rifled slug. Lyman peep rear sight, post ramp front sight. Receiver dovetailed for scope mounting. Weight: about 7$\frac{1}{4}$ pounds. Checkered pistol-grip stock and slide handle, swivels and carrying strap. Made 1967–1970.

Noble Model 166L Deergun

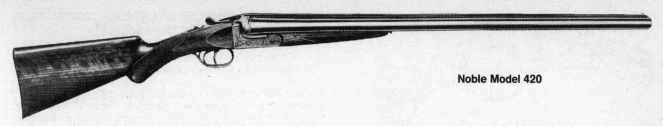

Noble Model 420

Noble Model 450E

Noble Model 420 Hammerless Double **$310**
Boxlock. Plain extractors. Double triggers. Gauges: 12 ga. 3-inch mag.; 16 ga.; 20 ga. 3-inch mag.; .410 ga. Barrels: 28-inch, except 26-inch in .410; M/F choke. Weight: about 6³/₄ pounds. Engraved frame. Checkered walnut stock and forearm. Made 1958–1970.

Noble Model 450E Hammerless Double **$395**
Boxlock. Engraved frame. Selective auto ejectors. Double triggers. Gauges: 12, 16, 20. 3-inch chambers in 12 and 20 gauge. 28-inch barrels, M/F choke. Weight: about 6 lbs. 14 oz., 12 ga. Checkered pistol-grip stock and beavertail forearm, recoil pad. Made 1967–1970.

Noble Model 602CLP **$155**
Same as Model 602RCLP, except has plain barrel. Made 1958–1970.

Noble Model 602RCLP Hammerless Slide Action Repeating Shotgun **$185**
Solid frame. Key lock fire control mechanism. 20 gauge. 3-inch chamber. 5-shot tubular magazine. 28-inch barrel, vent rib, adjustable choke. Weight: about 6¹/₂ pounds. Checkered pistol-grip stock/slide handle, recoil pad. Made 1967–1970.

Noble Model 602RLP **$165**
Same as Model 602RCLP, except without adjustable choke, bored F or M choke. Made 1967–1970.

Noble Model 602XL **$125**
Same as Model 602RCLP, except has plain barrel, F or M choke, slide handle only checkered, no recoil pad. Made 1958–1970.

Noble Model 662 . . . . **$175**
Same as Model 602CLP, except has aluminum receiver and barrel. Weight: about 4¹/₂ pounds. Made 1966–1970.

Omega Single Shot Shotgun

═══ OMEGA SHOTGUNS ═══
Brescia, Italy, and Korea
Formerly imported by K.B.I., Inc., Harrisburg, PA

Omega Folding Over/Under Shotgun **$295**
Hammerless. Single trigger with automatic safety. Gauges: 12, 20, 28 and .410; 3-inch chambers. Barrels: 26- or 28-inch with various fixed choke combinations. Weight: 5¹/₂–6 pounds. Checkered European walnut buttstock and forend. Imported from Italy 1986–1994.

Omega Over/Under Shotgun, Deluxe **$320**
Gauges: 20, 28 and .410. 26- or 28-inch vent-rib barrels. 40¹/₂ inches overall (42¹/₂ inches, 20 ga., 28-inch bbl.). Chokes: IC/M, M/F or F/F (.410). Weight: about 5¹/₂–6 pounds. Single trigger. Automatic safety. European walnut stock with checkered pistol grip and tulip forend. Made in Italy from 1984–1991.

Omega Side-by-Side Shotgun, Deluxe **$190**
Same general specifications as the Standard Side-by-Side, except has checkered European walnut stock and low barrel rib. Made in Italy from 1984–1990.

Omega Side-by-Side Shotgun, Standard **$165**
Gauge: .410. 26-inch barrel. 40¹/₂ inches overall. Choked F/F. Weight: 5¹/₂ pounds. Double trigger. Manual safety. Checkered beechwood stock and semi-pistol grip. Made in Italy from 1984–1990.

Omega Single Shot Shotgun, Deluxe **$105**
Same general specifications as the Standard Single Barrel, except has checkered walnut stock, top lever break, fully blued receiver, vent rib. Made in Korea from 1984 to date.

Omega Single Shot Shotgun, Standard
Gauges: 12, 16, 20, 28 and .410. Barrel lengths: 26-, 28- or 30-inch. Weight: 5 lbs. 4 oz.–5 lbs. 11 oz. Indonesian walnut stock. Matte-chromed receiver and top lever break. Made in Korea from 1984–88.
Standard Fixed . . . . **$ 80**
Standard Folding **125**
Deluxe Folding **175**

SHOTGUNS

Parker G.H.E.

Parker D.H.E.

Parker C.H.E.

Parker B.H.E.

Parker A.H.E.

PARKER BROTHERS
Meriden, Connecticut
This firm was taken over by Remington Arms Company in 1934 and its production facilities removed to Remington's Ilion, New York, plant.

Parker Hammerless Double Barrel Shotguns
Grades V.H.E. through A-1 Special. Boxlock. Auto ejectors. Double triggers or selective single trigger. Gauges: 10, 12, 16, 20, 28, .410. Barrels: 26- to 32-inch, any standard boring. Weight: 6⅞–8½ pounds, 12 ga. Stock and forearm of select walnut, checkered; straight, half or full pistol grip. Grades differ only in quality of workmanship, grade of wood, engraving, checkering, etc.; general specifications are the same for all. Discontinued about 1940.

V.H.E. Grade, 12 or 16 gauge	$ 2,495
V.H.E. Grade, 20 gauge	3,650
V.H.E. Grade, 28 gauge	5,950
V.H.E. Grade, .410 gauge	14,500
G.H.E. Grade, 12 or 16 gauge	3,295
G.H.E. Grade, 20 gauge	3,850
G.H.E. Grade, 28 gauge	6,200
G.H.E. Grade, .410 gauge	15,500
D.H.E. Grade, 12 or 16 gauge	4,995
D.H.E. Grade, 20 gauge	5,850
D.H.E. Grade, 28 gauge	12,500
D.H.E. Grade, .410 gauge	19,500
C.H.E. Grade, 12 or 16 gauge	7,250
C.H.E. Grade, 20 gauge	8,450
C.H.E. Grade, 28 gauge	17,500
C.H.E. Grade, .410 gauge	35,250
B.H.E. Grade, 12 or 16 gauge	7,995
B.H.E. Grade, 20 gauge	12,950
B.H.E. Grade, 28 gauge	19,500
B.H.E. Grade, .410 gauge	32,500
A.H.E. Grade, 12 or 16 gauge	16,500
A.H.E. Grade, 20 gauge	22,750
A.H.E. Grade, 28 gauge	32,500
A.A.H.E. Grade, 12 or 16 gauge	29,950
A.A.H.E. Grade, 20 gauge	55,000
A.A.H.E. Grade, 28 gauge	75,500
A-1 Special Grade, 12 or 16 gauge	68,000
A-1 Special Grade, 20 gauge	90,000
A-1 Special Grade, 28 gauge	130,000

For non-ejector guns, **deduct** 30% from values shown. For vent-rib barrels, **add** 20% to values shown.

Parker Single Shot Trap Guns
Hammerless. Boxlock. Ejector. 12 gauge only. Barrel lengths: 30-, 32-, 34-inch; any boring. vent rib. Weight: 7½–8½ pounds. Stock and forearm of select walnut, checkered; straight, half or full pistol grip. The five grades differ only in quality of workmanship, grade of wood, checkering, engraving, etc.; general specifications same for all. Discontinued about 1940.

S.C. Grade	$ 2,595
S.B. Grade	3,550
S.A. Grade	4,500
S.A.A. Grade	5,750
S.A.1 Special	19,000

Parker Single Shot Trap

Parker Skeet Gun

Same as other Parker doubles from Grade V.H.E. up, except selective single trigger and beavertail forearm are standard on this model, as are 26-inch barrels, SK choke. Discontinued about 1940. Values are 20 percent higher.

Parker Trojan

Parker Trojan Hammerless Double Barrel Shotgun

Boxlock. Plain extractors. Double trigger or single trigger. Gauges: 12, 16, 20. Barrels: 30-inch both F choke (12 ga. only), 26- or 28-inch M and F choke. Weight: 6¼–7¾ pounds. Checkered pistol-grip stock and forearm. Discont. 1939.

12 or 16 gauge	**$1595**
20 gauge	**2800**

PARKER REPRODUCTIONS
Middlesex, New Jersey

Parker Hammerless Double Barrel Shotguns

Reproduction of the original Parker boxlock. Single selective trigger or double triggers. Selective automatic ejectors. Automatic safety. Gauges: 12, 16, 20 or 28; 2¾- or 3-inch chambers. Barrels: 26- or 28-inch choked SK/SK, IC/M, M/F. Weight: 5½–7 pounds. Checkered English-style or pistol-grip American walnut stock with beavertail or splinter forend and checkered skeleton buttplate. Color casehardened receiver with game scenes and scroll engraving. Imported from Japan 1984–89. *Note:* Distribution continues from a limited inventory.

D Grade	**$ 2,295**
D Grade 2-barrel set	**3,795**
B Grade Bank Note Limited Edition	**3,550**
B Grade 2-barrel set	**4,750**
B Grade 3-barrel set	**5,595**
A-1 Special Grade	**6,995**
A-1 Special Grade 2-barrel set	**7,950**
A-1 Special Grade Custom Engraved	**8,995**
A-1 Special Grade 3-barrel set	**10,500**

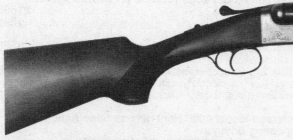

Parker-Hale Model 645A

Parker-Hale Model 645A American S/S (cont.)

beavertail forend. English scroll-design engraved receiver. Discontinued 1990.

Parker-Hale Model 645E (English) Side-by-Side Shotgun

Same general specifications as the Model 645A, except double triggers, straight grip, splinter forend, checkered butt and concave rib. Discontinued 1990.

Model 645E

12, 16, 20 ga. with 26- or 28-inch bbl.	**$750**
28, .410 ga. with 27-inch bbl.	**795**

Model 645E-XXV

12, 16, 20 ga. with 25-inch bbl.	**715**
28, .410 ga. with 25-inch bbl.	**795**

PARKER-HALE SHOTGUNS
Mfd. by Ignacio Ugartechea, Spain

Parker-Hale Model 645A (American) Side-by-Side

Shotgun **$695**
Boxlock action. Gauges: 12, 16 and 20. 26- and 28-inch barrels; raised matted rib.. Chokes: IC/M, M/F. Weight: 6 pounds avg. Single non-selective trigger. Automatic safety. Hand-checkered pistol-grip walnut stock with

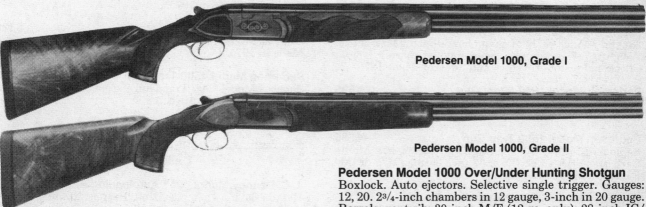

Pedersen Model 1000, Grade I

Pedersen Model 1000, Grade II

Pedersen Model 1000 Over/Under Hunting Shotgun

Boxlock. Auto ejectors. Selective single trigger. Gauges: 12, 20. 2¾-inch chambers in 12 gauge, 3-inch in 20 gauge. Barrels: vent rib; 30-inch M/F (12 ga. only); 28-inch IC/M (12 ga. only), M/F; 26-inch IC/M. Checkered pistol-grip stock and forearm. Grade I is the higher quality gun with custom stock dimensions, fancier wood, more elaborate engraving, silver inlays. Made 1973–75.

Grade I	**$1850**
Grade II	**1525**

PEDERSEN CUSTOM GUNS
North Haven, Connecticut
Division of O. F. Mossberg & Sons, Inc.

SHOTGUNS

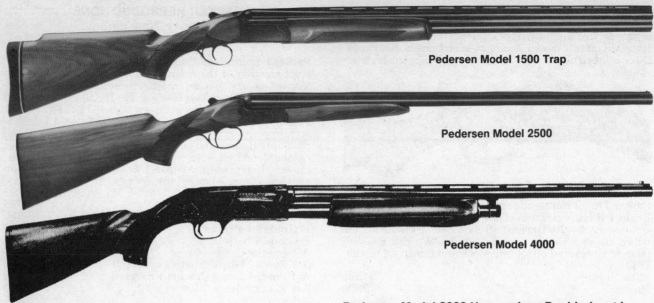

Pedersen Model 1500 Trap

Pedersen Model 2500

Pedersen Model 4000

Pedersen Model 1000 Magnum
Same as Model 1000 Hunting Gun, except chambered for 12-gauge Magnum 3-inch shells, 30-inch barrels, IM/F choke. Made 1973–75.
Grade I **$1950**
Grade II **1595**

Pedersen Model 1000 Skeet Gun
Same as Model 1000 Hunting Gun, except has skeet-style stock; 26- and 28-inch barrels (12 gauge only), SK choke. Made 1973–75.
Grade I **$1995**
Grade II **1550**

Pedersen Model 1000 Trap Gun
Same as Model 1000 Hunting Gun, except 12 gauge only, has Monte Carlo trap-style stock, 30- or 32-inch barrels, M/F or IM/F choke. Made 1973–75.
Grade I **$1995**
Grade II **1550**

Pedersen Model 1500 O/U Hunting Shotgun **$550**
Boxlock. Auto ejectors. Selective single trigger. 12 gauge. 2³/₄- or 3-inch chambers. Barrels: vent rib; 26-inch IC/M; 28- and 30-inch M/F; Magnum has 30-inch, IM/F choke. Weight: 7–7¹/₂ pounds, depending on barrel length. Checkered pistol-grip stock and forearm. Made 1973–75.

Pedersen Model 1500 Skeet Gun **$595**
Same as Model 1500 Hunting Gun, except has skeet-style stock, 27-inch barrels, SK choke. Made 1973–75.

Pedersen Model 1500 Trap Gun **$595**
Same as Model 1500 Hunting Gun, except has Monte Carlo trap-style stock, 30- or 32-inch barrels, M/F or IM/F chokes. Made 1973–75.

Pedersen Model 2000 Hammerless Double
Boxlock. Auto ejectors. Selective single trigger. Gauges: 12, 20. 2³/₄-inch chambers in 12 gauge, 3-inch in 20 gauge. Barrels: vent rib; 30-inch M/F (12 gauge only); 28-inch M/F; 26-inch IC/M choke. Checkered pistol-grip stock and forearm. Grade I is the higher quality gun with custom dimensions, fancier wood, more elaborate engraving, silver inlays. Made 1973–74.

Pedersen Model 2000 Hammerless Double (cont.)
Grade I **$1595**
Grade II **1295**

Pedersen Model 2500 Hammerless Double **$380**
Boxlock. Auto ejectors. Selective single trigger. Gauges: 12, 20. 2³/₄-inch chambers in 12 gauge, 3-inch in 20 gauge. Barrels: vent rib; 28-inch M/F; 26-inch IC/M choke. Checkered pistol-grip stock and forearm. Made 1973–74.

Pedersen Model 4000 Hammerless Slide Action
Repeating Shotgun **$380**
Custom version of Mossberg Model 500. Full-coverage floral engraving on receiver. Gauges: 12, 20, .410. 3-inch chamber. Barrels: vent rib; 26-inch IC or SK choke; 28-inch F or M; 30-inch F. Weight: 6–8 pounds depending on gauge and barrel. Checkered stock and slide handle of select wood. Made in 1975.

Pedersen Model 4000 Trap Gun **$395**
Same as standard Model 4000, except 12 gauge only, has 30-inch F choke barrel, Monte Carlo trap-style stock with recoil pad. Made in 1975.

Pedersen Model 4500 . . . . **$325**
Same as Model 4000, except has simpler scroll engraving. Made in 1975.

Pedersen Model 4500 Trap Gun **$350**
Same as Model 4000 Trap Gun, except has simpler scroll engraving. Made in 1975.

J. C. PENNEY CO., INC.
Dallas, Texas

J. C. Penney Model 4011 Autoloading Shotgun . **$175**
Hammerless. 5-shot magazine. Barrels: 26-inch IC; 28-inch M or F; 30-inch F choke. Weight: 7¹/₄ lbs. Plain pistol-grip stock and slide handle.

J. C. Penney Model 6610 Single Shot Shotgun . . . **$80**
Hammerless. Takedown. Auto ejector. Gauges: 12, 16, 20 and .410. Barrel length: 28–36 inches. Weight: about 6 pounds. Plain pistol-grip stock and forearm.

J. C. Penney Model 6630 Bolt Action Shotgun . . $110

Takedown. Gauges: 12, 16, 20. 2-shot clip magazine. 26- and 28-inch barrel lengths; with or without adjustable choke. Plain pistol-grip stock. Weight: about 7 1/4 pounds.

J. C. Penney Model 6670 Slide Action Shotgun . $130

Hammerless. Gauges: 12, 16, 20, and .410. 3-shot tubular magazine. Barrels: 26- to 30-inch; various chokes. Weight: 6 1/4–7 1/2 pounds. Walnut finished hardwood stock.

J. C. Penney Model 6870 Slide Action Shotgun . $195

Hammerless. Gauges: 12, 16, 20, .410. 4-shot magazine. Barrels: vent rib; 26- to 30-inch, various chokes. Weight: average 6 1/2 pounds. Plain pistol-grip stock.

═══ PERAZZI SHOTGUNS ═══

Manufactured by Manifattura Armi Perazzi, Brescia, Italy. See *also* listings under Ithaca-Perazzi.

Perazzi DB81 Over/Under Trap $4650

Gauge: 12; 2 3/4-inch chambers. 29 1/2- or 31 1/2-inch barrels with wide vent rib; M/F chokes. Weight: 8 lbs. 6 oz. Detachable and interchangeable trigger with flat V-springs. Bead front sight. Interchangeable and custom-made checkered stock; beavertail forend. Made from 1988 to date.

Perazzi DB81 Single Shot Trap $3850

Same general specifications as the DB81 Over/Under, except in single barrel version with 32- or 34-inch wide vent-rib barrel, Full choke. Made from 1988 to date.

> **NOTE:** Prices shown reflect Standard Grade values, except where noted. For SC3 Grade add 70%, for SCO Grade add 190% and for SHO Grade add 500%.

Perazzi Grand American 88 Special Single Trap

Same general specifications as MX8 Special Single Trap, except with high ramped rib. Fixed choke or screw-in choke tubes.

Perazzi Grand American 88 Special Trap (cont.)

Model 88 Standard	**$4125**
Model 88 w/Interchangeable Choke Tubes	**4425**

Perazzi Mirage Over/Under Shotgun

Gauge: 12; 2 3/4-inch chambers. Barrels: 27 5/8-, 29 1/2 or 31 1/2-inch vent-rib w/fixed chokes or screw-in choke tubes. Single selective trigger. Weight: 7 to 7 3/4 pounds. Interchangeable and custom-made checkered stock/forend.

Competition Trap, Skeet, Pigeon, Sporting . . .	**$ 4,700**
Skeet 4-Barrel Sets	**12,400**
Competition Special (w/adjustable 4-position trigger), **add**	**400**

Perazzi MX1 Over/Under Shotgun

Similar to Model MX8, except with a ramp-style, tapered rib and modified stock configuration.

Competition Trap, Skeet, Pigeon & Sporting. . . .	**$3600**
MX1C (w/Choke Tubes)	**3750**
MX1B (w/Flat Low-Rib)	**3560**

Perazzi MX2 Over/Under Shotgun

Similar to Model MX8, except with broad high-ramped competition rib.

Competition-Trap, Skeet, Pigeon & Sporting . . .	**$3750**
MX2C (w/choke tubes)	**3750**

Perazzi MX3 Over/Under Shotgun

Similar to Model MX8, except with a ramp-style, tapered rib and modified stock configuration.

Competition Trap, Skeet, Pigeon & Sporting. . . .	**$3295**
Competition Special (w/adj. 4-pos. trigger) **add** .	**300**
Game Models	**3195**
Combo O/U plus SB	**3950**
SB Trap 32- or 34-inch	**2695**
Skeet 4-barrel sets	**8950**
Skeet Special 4-barrel sets	**9395**

Perazzi MX3 Special Pigeon Shotgun $5100

Gauge: 12; 2 3/4-inch chambers. 29 1/2- or 31 1/2-inch vent-rib barrel; IC/M and Extra Full chokes. Weight: 8 lbs. 6 oz. Detachable and interchangeable trigger group with flat V-springs. Bead front sight. Interchangeable and custom-made checkered stock for live pigeon shoots; splinter forend. Made from 1991 to date.

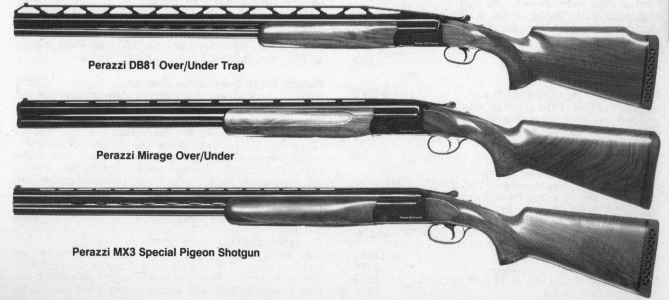

Perazzi DB81 Over/Under Trap

Perazzi Mirage Over/Under

Perazzi MX3 Special Pigeon Shotgun

SHOTGUNS

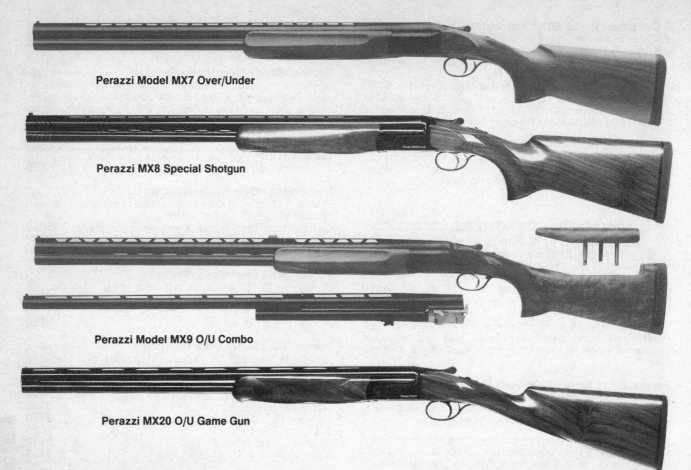

Perazzi Model MX7 Over/Under

Perazzi MX8 Special Shotgun

Perazzi Model MX9 O/U Combo

Perazzi MX20 O/U Game Gun

Perazzi MX4 Over/Under Shotgun
Similar to Model MX3 in appearance and shares the MX8 locking system. Detachable, adjustable 4-position trigger standard. Interchangeable choke tubes optional.
Competition Trap, Skeet, Pigeon & Sporting.... **$3650**
MX4C (w/Choke Tubes) 3895

Perazzi MX5 Over/Under Game Gun
Similar to Model MX8, except in hunting configuration chambered in 12 or 20 gauge. Non-detachable single selective trigger.
MX5 Standard **$2495**
MX5C (w/Choke Tubes) 2750

Perazzi MX7 Over/Under Shotgun **$4575**
Similar to Model MX12, except with MX3-style receiver and top-mounted trigger selector. Barrels: 28³/4-, 29¹/2-, 31¹/2-inch w/vent rib; screw-in choke tubes. Made from 1992 to date.

Perazzi MX8 Over/Under Shotgun
Gauge: 12; 2³/4-inch chambers. Barrels: 27⁵/8-, 29¹/2- or 31¹/2-inch vent-rib w/fixed chokes or screw-in choke tubes. Weight: 7 to 8¹/2 pounds. Interchangeable and custom-made checkered stock; beavertail forend. Special models have detachable and interchangeable 4-position trigger group with flat V-springs. Made from 1988 to date.
MX8 Standard **$3695**
MX8 Special (adj. 4-pos. trigger) 3795
MX8 Special Single (32- or 34-inch bbl.) 3595
MX8 Special Combo 7390

Perazzi MX8/20 Over/Under Shotgun **$3750**
Similar to the Model MX8, except with smaller frame and custom stock. Available in sporting or game configurations with fixed chokes or screw-in tubes. Made from 1993 to date.

Perazzi MX9 Over/Under Shotgun **$5995**
Gauge: 12; 2³/4-inch chambers. Barrels: 29¹/2- or 30¹/2-inch with choke tubes and vent side rib. Selective trigger. Checkered walnut stock with adjustable cheekpiece. Available in single barrel, combo, O/U trap, skeet, pigeon and sporting models. Made from 1993 to date.

Perazzi MX10 Over/Under Shotgun **$7495**
Similar to the Model MX9, except with fixed chokes and different rib configuration. Made from 1993 to date.

Perazzi MX12 Over/Under Game Gun
Gauge: 12; 2³/4-inch chambers. Barrels: 26-, 27⁵/8-, 28³/8- or 29¹/2-inch, vent-rib, fixed chokes or screw-in choke tubes. Non-detachable single selective trigger group with coil springs. Weight: 7¹/4 pounds. Interchangeable and custom-made checkered stock; schnabel forend.
MX12 Standard **$3850**
MX12C (w/Choke Tubes) 4250

Perazzi MX20 O/U Game Gun
Gauges: 20, 28 and .410; 2³/4- or 3-inch chambers. 26-inch vent-rib barrels; M/F chokes or screw-in chokes. Auto selective ejectors. Selective single trigger. Weight: 6 lbs. 6 oz. Non-detachable coil-spring trigger. Bead front sight.

SHOTGUNS

Perazzi MX20 O/U Game Gun (cont.)
Interchangeable and custom-made checkered stock with schnabel forend. Made from 1988 to date.

Standard Grade	$ 3,995
Standard Grade w/Gold Outline	6,950
MX20C w/Choke Tubes	4,295
SC3 Grade	7,500
SCO Grade	10,350

Perazzi MX28 Over/Under Game Gun $10,950
Similar to the Model MX12, except chambered in 28 gauge with 26-inch barrels fitted to smaller frame. Made from 1993 to date.

Perazzi MX410 Over/Under Game Gun $10,950
Similar to the Model MX12, except in .410 bore w/3-inch chambers, 26-inch barrels fitted to smaller frame. Made from 1993 to date.

Perazzi TM1 Special Single Shot Trap $3295
Gauge: 12; 2³/₄-inch chambers. 32- or 34-inch barrel with wide vent rib; Full choke. Weight: 8 lbs. 6 oz. Detachable and interchangeable trigger group with coil springs. Bead front sight. Interchangeable and custom-made stock with checkered pistol grip and beavertail forend. Made from 1988 to date.

Perazzi TMX Single Barrel Trap

Perazzi TMX Special Single Shot Trap $3350
Same general specifications as Model TM1 Special, except with ultra-high rib. Interchangeable choke tubes optional.

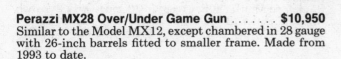

Piotti Piuma Boxlock

PIOTTI SHOTGUNS
Italy

Piotti King No. 1 Sidelock $12,995
Gauges: 10, 12, 16, 20, 28 and .410. 25- to 30-inch barrels (12 ga.); 25- to 28-inch (other gauges). Weight: about 5 lbs. (.410) to 8 lbs. (12 ga.) Holland & Holland pattern sidelock. Double triggers standard. Coin finish or color casehardened. Level file-cut rib. Full-coverage scroll engraving, gold inlays. Hand-rubbed, oil-finished, straight-grip stock with checkered butt, splinter forend.

Piotti King Extra Side-by-Side Shotgun $17,500
Same general specifications as the Piotti King No. 1, except has choice of engraving, gold inlays plus stock is of exhibition grade wood.

Piotti Lunik Sidelock Shotgun $12,500
Same general specifications as the Monte Carlo model, except has level, file-cut rib. Renaissance-style, large scroll engraving in relief, gold crown in top lever, gold name, and gold crest in forearm, finely figured wood.

Piotti Monte Carlo Sidelock Shotgun $8350
Gauges: 10, 12, 16, 20, 28 or .410. Barrels: 25- to 30-inch. Holland & Holland pattern sidelock. Weight: 5–8 pounds. Automatic ejectors. Double triggers. Hand-rubbed oil-finished straight-grip stock with checkered butt. Choice of Purdey-style scroll and rosette or Holland & Holland-style large scroll engraving.

Piotti Piuma Boxlock Side-by-Side Shotgun ... $7995
Same general specifications as the Monte Carlo model, except has Anson & Deeley boxlock action with demi-bloc barrels, scalloped frame. Standard scroll and rosette engraving. Hand-rubbed, oil-finished straight-grip stock.

WILLIAM POWELL & SON LTD.
Birmingham, England

Powell No. 1 Best Grade Double-Barrel Shotgun $25,000
Sidelock. Gauges: Made to order, with 12, 16 and 20 the most common. Barrels: Made to order in any length, but 28 inches was recommended. Highest grade French walnut buttstock and forearm with fine checkering. Metal elaborately engraved. Imported by Stoeger about 1938–1951.

Powell No. 2 Best Grade Double $20,000
Same general specifications as the Powell No. 1, except plain finish without engraving. Imported by Stoeger about 1938–1951.

Powell No. 6 Crown Grade Double $8000
Boxlock. Gauges: Made to order, with 12, 16 and 20 the most common. Barrels: Made to order, but 28 inches was recommended. Highest grade French walnut buttstock and forearm with fine checkering. Metal elaborately engraved. Uses Anson & Deeley locks. Imported by Stoeger about 1938–1951.

Powell No. 7 Aristocrat Grade Double $2500
Same general specifications as the Powell No. 6, except with lower quality wood and metal engraving.

PRECISION SPORTS SHOTGUNS
Cortland, New York
Mfd. by Ignacio Ugartechea, Spain; previously imported by Parker-Hale Ltd.

Precision Sports 600 Series American Hammerless Doubles
Boxlock. Single selective trigger. Selective automatic ejectors. Automatic safety. Gauges: 12, 16, 20, 28, .410; 2³/₄- or 3-inch chambers. Barrels: 26-, 27- or 28-inch with raised matte rib; choked IC/M or M/F. Weight: 5³/₄–7

Precision Sports 600 Series American Doubles (cont.)

pounds. Checkered pistol-grip walnut buttstock with beavertail forend. Engraved silvered receiver with blued barrels. Imported from Spain 1986–1993.

640A (12, 16, 20 ga. w/extractors)	**$625**
640A (28, .410 ga. w/extractors)	**750**
640 Slug Gun (12 ga. w/extractors)	**735**
645A (12, 16, 20 ga. w/ejectors)	**695**
645A (28, .410 ga. w/ejectors)	**850**
645A (20/28 ga. two-bbl. set)	**995**
650A (12 ga. w/extractors, choke tubes)	**655**
655A (12 ga. w/ejectors, choke tubes)	**725**

Precision Sports 600 Series English Hammerless Doubles

Same general specifications as American 600 Series, except with double triggers and concave rib. Checkered English-style walnut stock with splinter forend, straight grip and oil finish.

640E (12, 16, 20 ga. w/extractors)	**$535**
640E (28, .410 ga. w/extractors)	**625**

Precision Sports 600 Series English Doubles (cont.)

640 Slug Gun (12 ga. w/extractors)	**$735**
645E (12, 16, 20 ga. w/ejectors)	**750**
645E (28, .410 ga. w/ejectors)	**715**
645E (20/28 ga. two-bbl. set)	**945**
650E (12 ga. w/extractors, choke tubes)	**650**
655E (12 ga. w/ejectors, choke tubes)	**695**

Precision Sports Model 640M Magnum 10 Hammerless Double

Similar to Model 640E, except in 10 gauge with 3½-inch Mag. chambers. Barrels: 26-, 30-, 32-inch choked F/F.
Model 640M Big Ten, Turkey or Goose Gun **$655**

Precision Sports Model 645E-XXV Hammerless Double

Similar to Model 645E, except with 25-inch barrel and Churchill-style rib.

645E-XXV (12, 16, 20 ga. w/ejectors)	**$715**
645E-XXV (28, .410 ga. w/ejectors)	**795**

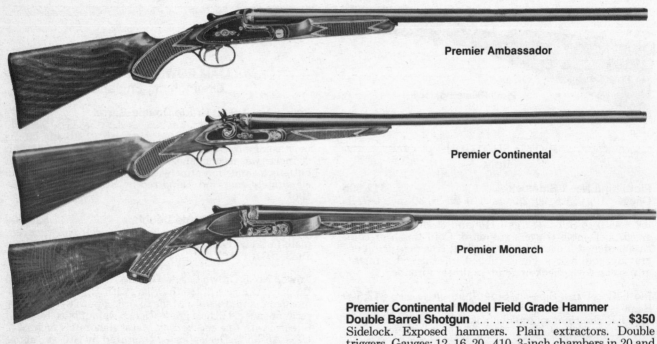

Premier Ambassador

Premier Continental

Premier Monarch

PREMIER SHOTGUNS

Premier shotguns have been produced by various gun-makers in Europe.

Premier Ambassador Model Field Grade Hammerless Double Barrel Shotgun **$350**

Sidelock. Plain extractors. Double triggers. Gauges: 12, 16, 20, .410. 3-inch chambers in 20 and .410 gauge, 2¾-inch in 12 and 16 gauge. Barrels: 26-inch in .410 gauge, 28 inch in other gauges; choked M/F. Weight: 6 lbs. 3 oz.–7 lbs. 3 oz. depending on gauge. Checkered pistol-grip stock and beavertail forearm. Intro. in 1957; discontinued.

Premier Brush King **$250**

Same as standard Regent Model, except chambered for 12 (2¾-inch) and 20 gauge (3-inch) only; has 22-inch barrels, IC/M choke, straight-grip stock. Weight: 6 lbs. 3 oz. in 12 ga.; 5 lbs. 12 oz. in 20 ga. Intro. 1959; discont.

Premier Continental Model Field Grade Hammer Double Barrel Shotgun **$350**

Sidelock. Exposed hammers. Plain extractors. Double triggers. Gauges: 12, 16, 20, .410. 3-inch chambers in 20 and .410 gauge, 2¾-inch in 12 and 16 gauge. Barrels: 26-inch in .410 gauge; 28-inch in other gauges; choked M/F. Weight: 6 lbs. 3 oz.–7 lbs. 3 oz. depending on gauge. Checkered pistol-grip stock and English-style forearm. Introduced in 1957; discontinued.

Premier Monarch Supreme Grade Hammerless Double Barrel Shotgun **$375**

Boxlock. Auto ejectors. Double triggers. Gauges: 12, 20. 2¾-inch chambers in 12 gauge, 3-inch in 20 gauge. Barrels: 28-inch M/F; 26-inch IC/M choke. Weight: 6 lbs. 6 oz.–7 lbs. 2 oz. depending on gauge and barrel. Checkered pistol-grip stock and beavertail forearm of fancy walnut. Introduced in 1959; discontinued.

Premier Presentation Custom Grade **$895**

Similar to Monarch model, but made to order; of higher quality with hunting scene engraving gold and silver inlaid, fancier wood. Introduced in 1959; discontinued.

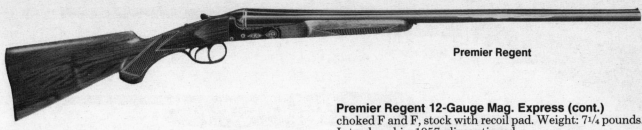

Premier Regent

Premier Regent 10-Gauge Magnum Express . . . **$295**
Same as standard Regent Model, except chambered for
10-gauge Magnum 3½-inch shells, has heavier construction, 32-inch barrels choked F/F, stock with recoil pad.
Weight: 11¼ pounds. Introduced in 1957; discontinued.

Premier Regent 12-Gauge Magnum Express . . . **$265**
Same as standard Regent Model, except chambered for
12-gauge Magnum 3-inch shells, has 30-inch barrels

Premier Regent 12-Gauge Mag. Express (cont.)
choked F and F, stock with recoil pad. Weight: 7¼ pounds.
Introduced in 1957; discontinued.

Premier Regent Model Field Grade Hammerless
Double Barrel Shotgun **$225**
Boxlock. Plain extractors. Double triggers. Gauges: 12, 16,
20, 28, .410. 3-inch chambers in 20 and .410 gauge, 2¾-inch
in other gauges. Barrels: 26-inch IC/M, M/F (28 and .410
gauge only); 28-inch M/F; 30-inch M/F (12 ga. only). Weight:
6 lbs. 2 oz.–7 lbs. 4 oz. depending on gauge and barrel.
Checkered pistol-grip stock and beavertail forearm.
Introduced in 1955; discontinued.

Purdey Over-and-Under

Purdey Single Barrel Trap

JAMES PURDEY & SONS, LTD.
London, England

Purdey Hammerless Double Barrel

Purdey Hammerless Double Barrel Shotgun
Sidelock. Auto ejectors. Single or double triggers. Gauges:
12, 16, 20. Barrels: 26-, 27-, 28-, 30-inch (latter in 12 gauge
only); any boring, any shape or style of rib. Weight: 5¼–
6½ pounds depending on model, gauge and barrel length.

Purdey Hammerless Double Barrel Shotgun (cont.)
Checkered stock and forearm, straight grip standard, pistol-grip also available. Purdey guns of this type have been
made from about 1880 to date. Models include: Game Gun,
Featherweight Game Gun, Two-Inch Gun (chambered for
12 gauge 2-inch shells), Pigeon Gun (with 3rd fastening
and side clips); values of all models are the same.
With Double Triggers **$31,500**
With Single Trigger **34,550**

Purdey Over/Under Gun
Sidelock. Auto ejectors. Single or double triggers. Gauges:
12, 16, 20. Barrels: 26-, 27-, 28-, 30-inch (latter in 12 gauge
only); any boring, any style rib. Weight: 6–7½ pounds
depending on gauge and barrel length. Checkered stock
and forend, straight or pistol grip. Prior to WW II, the
Purdey Over/Under Gun was made with a Purdey action;
since the war James Purdey & Sons have acquired the
business of James Woodward & Sons and all Purdey over/
under guns are now built on the Woodward principle.
General specifications of both types are the same.
With Purdey action, double triggers **$45,000**
With Woodward action, double triggers **48,000**
Single trigger, extra **1,000**

Purdey Single Barrel Trap Gun **$9,000**
Sidelock. Mechanical features similar to those of the over/
under model with Purdey action. 12 gauge only. Built to
customer's specifications. Made prior to World War II.

SHOTGUNS

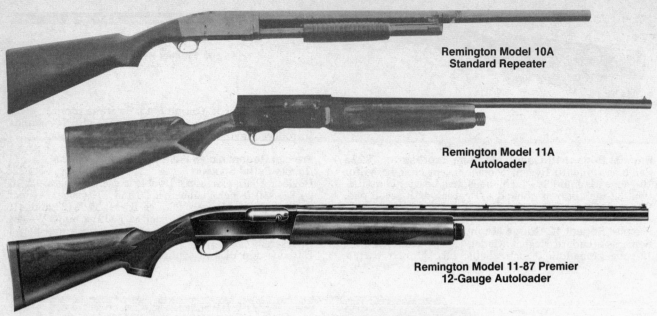

Remington Model 10A
Standard Repeater

Remington Model 11A
Autoloader

Remington Model 11-87 Premier
12-Gauge Autoloader

REMINGTON ARMS CO.
Ilion, New York

Eliphalet Remington Jr. began making long arms with his father in 1816. In 1828 they moved their facility to Ilion, N.Y., where it remained a family-run business for decades. As the family died, other people bought controlling interests and today, still a successful gunmaking company, it is a subsidiary of the du Pont Corporation.

Remington Model 10A Standard Grade Slide Action Repeating Shotgun $275
Hammerless. Takedown. 6-shot. 12 gauge only. 5-shell tubular magazine. Barrels: plain; 26- to 32-inch; choked F, M or Cyl. Weight: about 7 1/2 pounds. Plain pistol-grip stock, grooved slide handle. Made 1907–1929.

Remington Model 11 Special, Tournament, Expert and Premier Grade Guns
These higher grade models differ from the Model 11A in general quality, grade of wood, checkering, engraving, etc. General specifications are the same.
Model 11B Special Grade .... $ 425
Model 11D Tournament Grade 850
Model 11E Expert Grade.................... 1125
Model 11F Premier Grade................... 1950

Remington Model 11A Standard Grade Autoloader
Hammerless Browning type. 5-shot. Takedown. Gauges: 12, 16, 20. Tubular magazine holds four shells. Barrels: plain, solid or vent rib; lengths from 26–32 inches; F, M, IC, Cyl., SK chokes. Weight: about 8 pounds, 12 ga.; 7 1/2 pounds, 16 ga.; 7 1/4 pounds, 20 ga. Checkered pistol grip and forend. Made 1905–1949.
With plain barrel $255
With solid-rib barrel 345
With ventilated-rib barrel 365

Remington Model 11R Riot Gun $265
Same as Model 11A Standard Grade, except has 20-inch plain barrel, 12 gauge only.

Remington Model 11-48.
See Remington Sportsman-48 Series.

Remington Model 11-87 Premier Autoloader
Gas-operated. Hammerless. Gauge: 12; 3-inch chamber. Barrel: 26-, 28- or 30-inch with REM choke. Weight: 8 1/8–8 3/8 pounds, depending on barrel length. Checkered walnut stock and forend in satin finish. Made 1987 to date.
Premier Deer Gun $415
Premier Deer Gun w/Cantilever scope mount 470
Premier Skeet 395
Premier Sporting Clays 520
Premier Standard Autoloader................. 425
For Left-Hand Models, **add** 50

Remington Model 11-87 Premier Trap Gun
Similar to Model 11-87 Premier, except with deluxe walnut stock in trap configuration. 30-inch vent-rib trap barrel; fixed or REM-choke. Weight: 8.25 pounds. Made 1987 to date.
With Fixed Choke Barrel $375
With REM-Choke Barrel 395
Left-handed Action 415

Remington Model 11-87 Special Purpose Magnum
Same general specifications Model 11-87 Premier, except with non-reflective wood finish and Parkerized metal. 21-, 26- or 28-inch vent-rib barrel with REM Choke tubes. Made 1987–1993.
Model 11-87 SP Field Magnum $450
Model 11-87 SP Deer Gun (w/21-inch bbl.) 425
Model 11-87 SP Deer Gun w/cantilever
 scope mount 475

Remington 11-87 SPS Magnum
Same general specifications Model 11-87 Special Purpose Magnum, except with synthetic stock and forend. 21-, 26- or 28-inch vent-rib barrel with REM Choke tubes. Matte black or Mossy Oak Camo finish (except NWTF Turkey Gun). Made 1990 to date.
Model 11-87 SPS Magnum (Matte black) $425
Model 11-87 SPS Camo (Mossy Oak Camo) 475
Model 11-87 NWTF Turkey Gun (Brown
 Trebark) Discontinued 1993 495
Model 11-87 SPST Turkey Gun (Matte black) ... 450

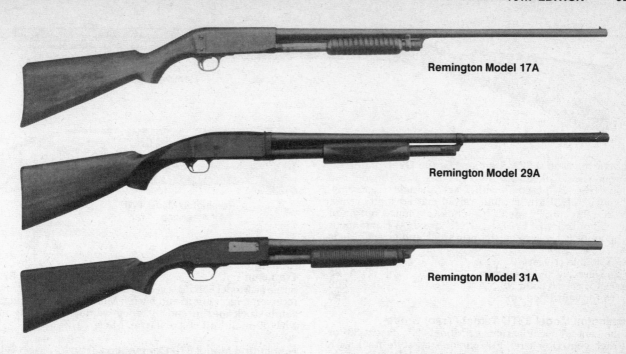

Remington Model 17A

Remington Model 29A

Remington Model 31A

Remington Model 17A Standard Grade Slide Action Repeating Shotgun $365

Hammerless. Takedown. 5-shot. 20 gauge only. 4-shell tubular magazine. Barrels: plain; 26- to 32-inch; choked F, M or Cyl.. Weight: about 5¾ pounds. Plain pistol-grip stock, grooved slide handle. Made 1921–1933. *Note:* The present Ithaca Model 37 is an adaptation of this Browning design.

Remington Model 29A Standard Grade Slide Action Repeating Shotgun $350

Hammerless. Takedown. 6-shot. 12 gauge only. 5-shell tubular magazine. Barrels: plain; 26- to 32-inch; choked F, M or Cyl. Weight: about 7½ pounds. Checkered pistol-grip stock and slide handle. Made 1929–1933.

Remington Model 29T Target Grade $360

Same general specifications as Model 29A, except has trap-style stock with straight grip, extension slide handle, vent-rib barrel. Discontinued 1933.

Remington Model 31 Skeet Grade

Same general specifications as Model 31A, except has 26-inch barrel with raised solid or vent rib, SK choke, checkered pistol-grip stock and beavertail forend. Weight: about 8 pounds, 12 ga.
With raised solid rib **$395**
With ventilated rib........................... **495**

Remington Model 31 Special, Tournament, Expert and Premier Grade Guns

These higher grade models differ from the Model 31A in general quality, grade of wood, checkering, engraving, etc. General specifications are the same.
Model 31B Special Grade .... **$ 475**
Model 31D Tournament Grade **775**
Model 31E Expert Grade..................... **1095**
Model 31F Premier Grade.................... **1500**

Remington Model 31A Standard Grade Slide Action Repeater

Hammerless. Takedown. 3- or 5-shot. Gauges: 12, 16, 20. Tubular magazine holds two or four shells. Barrels: plain,

Remington Model 31A Standard Grade (cont.)

solid or vent rib; lengths from 26–32 inches; F, M, IC, C or SK choke. Weight: about 7½ lbs., 12 ga.; 6¾ lbs., 16 ga.; 6½ lbs., 20 ga. Earlier models have checkered pistol-grip stock and slide handle; later models have plain stock and grooved slide handle. Made 1931–1949.
Model 31A with plain barrel **$315**
Model 31A with solid-rib barrel **395**
Model 31A with vent-rib barrel **425**
Model 31H Hunters' Special w/sporting-style stock **375**
Model 31R Riot Gun w/20-inch plain bbl., 12 ga... **225**

Remington Model 31S Trap Special/31TC Trap Grade

Same general specifications as Model 31A, except 12 gauge only, has 30- or 32-inch vent-rib barrel, Full choke, checkered trap stock with full pistol grip and recoil pad, checkered extension beavertail forend. Weight: about 8 pounds. (Trap Special has solid-rib barrel, half-pistol grip stock with standard walnut forend).
Model 31S Trap Special **$425**
Model 31TC Trap Grade **595**

Remington Model 32 Skeet Grade

Same general specifications as Model 32A, except 26- or 28-inch barrel, SK choke, beavertail forend, selective single trigger only. Weight: about 7½ pounds. Made 1932–1942.
With plain barrels **$1495**
With raised solid rib **1650**
With ventilated rib.......................... **1750**

Remington Model 32 Tournament, Expert and Premier Grade Guns

These higher grade models differ from the Model 32A in general quality, grade of wood, checkering, engraving, etc. General specifications are the same. Made 1932–1942.
Model 32D Tournament Grade .... **$ 2,995**
Model 32E Expert Grade.................... **3,795**
Model 32F Premier Grade................... **8,750**

Remington Model 32A

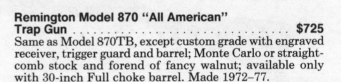

Remington Model 870
"All American" Trap

Remington Model 32A Standard Grade Over/Under

Hammerless. Takedown. Auto ejectors. Early model had double triggers, later built with selective single trigger only. 12 gauge only. Barrels: plain, raised matted solid or vent rib; 26-, 28-, 30-, 32-inch; F/M choke standard, option of any combination of F, M, IC, C, SK choke. Weight: about 7³/₄ pounds. Checkered pistol-grip stock and forend. Made 1932–1942.

With double triggers $1595
With selective single trigger 1795
Extra for raised solid rib $200
Extra for ventilated rib 250

Remington Model 32TC Target (Trap) Grade

Same general specifications as Model 32A, except 30- or 32-inch vent-rib barrel, Full choke, trap-style stock with checkered pistol-grip and beavertail forend. Weight: about 8 pounds. Made 1932–1942.

With double triggers $2395
With selective single trigger 3595

Remington Model 90-T Single Shot Trap $2200

Gauge: 12; 2³/₄-inch chambers. 30-, 32- or 34-inch vent-rib barrel with fixed chokes or screw-in REM Chokes; ported or non-ported. Weight: 8¹/₄ pounds. Checkered American walnut standard or Monte Carlo stock with low-luster finish. Engraved sideplates and drop-out trigger group optional. Made 1990 to date.

NOTE: In 1980 Remington changed the stock styling for all Model 870 shotguns.

Remington Model 870 "All American" Trap Gun $725

Same as Model 870TB, except custom grade with engraved receiver, trigger guard and barrel; Monte Carlo or straight-comb stock and forend of fancy walnut; available only with 30-inch Full choke barrel. Made 1972–77.

Remington Model 870 Competition Trap $495

Based on standard Model 870 receiver, except is single-shot with gas-assisted recoil-reducing system, new choke design, a high step-up vent rib and redesigned stock and forend with cut checkering and a satin finish. Weight: 8¹/₂ pounds. Made 1981 to date.

Remington Model 870 Deer Gun Brushmaster Deluxe

Same as Model 870 Standard Deer Gun, except available in 20 gauge as well as 12, has cut-checkered, satin-finished American walnut stock and forend, recoil pad.

Right-Hand Model $285
Left-Hand Model 335

Remington Model 870 Deer Gun Standard $275

Same as Model 870 Wingmaster Riot Gun, except has rifle-type sights.

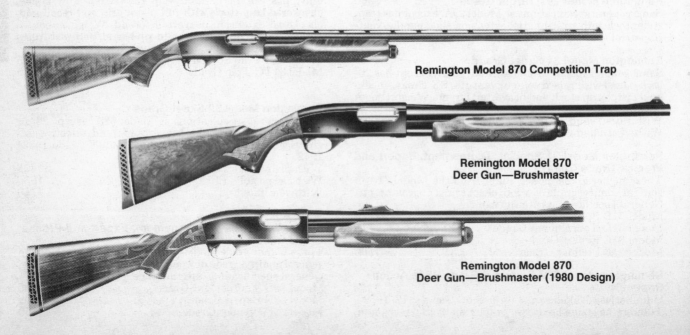

Remington Model 870 Competition Trap

Remington Model 870
Deer Gun—Brushmaster

Remington Model 870
Deer Gun—Brushmaster (1980 Design)

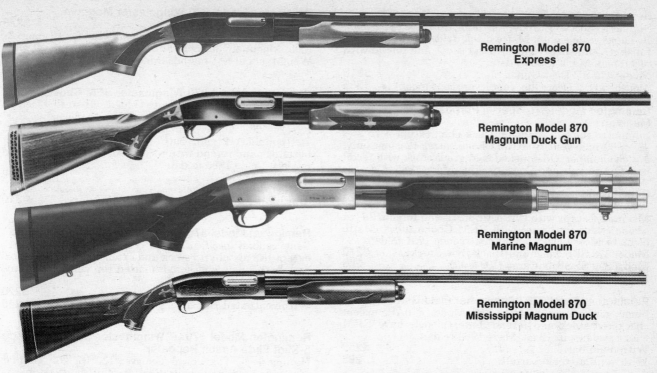

**Remington Model 870
Express**

**Remington Model 870
Magnum Duck Gun**

**Remington Model 870
Marine Magnum**

**Remington Model 870
Mississippi Magnum Duck**

SHOTGUNS

Remington Model 870 Express

Same general specifications Model 870 Wingmaster, except has low-luster walnut-finished hardwood stock with pressed checkering and black recoil pad. Gauges: 12, 20 or .410; 3-inch chambers. Barrels: 26- or 28-inch vent-rib with REM Choke; 25-inch vent-rib with fixed Full choke (.410 only). Black oxide metal finish. Made 1987 to date.

Model 870 Express (12 or 20 ga., REM Choke) . . . **$195**
Model 870 Express (.410 w/fixed choke) **215**
Express Combo (w/extra 20-inch Deer Barrel) . . . **270**

Remington Model 870 Express Deer Gun

Same general specifications as Model 870 Express, except in 12 gauge only, 20-inch barrel with fixed IC choke, adj. rifle sights and Monte Carlo stock. Made 1991 to date.

Express Deer Gun w/standard barrel **$190**
Express Deer Gun w/fully rifled barrel **225**

Remington Model 870 Express Turkey Gun **$215**

Same general specifications as Model 870 Express, except has 21-inch vent-rib barrel and Turkey Extra-Full REM choke. Made 1991 to date.

Remington Model 870 Express Youth Gun **$245**

Same general specifications as Model 870 Express, except has scaled-down stock with 12½-inch pull and 21-inch vent-rib barrel with REM choke. Made 1991 to date.

Remington Model 870 Lightweight

Same as standard Model 870, but with scaled-down receiver and lightweight mahogany stock; 20 gauge only. 2¾-inch chamber. Barrels: plain or vent rib; 26-inch, IC; 28-inch, M or F choke. REM choke available from 1987. Weight: 5¾ pounds w/26-inch plain barrel. American walnut stock and forend with satin or Hi-gloss finish. Made 1972 to date.

With plain barrel **$235**
With ventilated-rib barrel **260**
With REM choke barrel **325**

Remington Model 870 Lightweight Magnum

Same as Model 870 Lightweight, but chambered for 20 gauge Magnum 3-inch shell; 28-inch barrel, plain or vent rib, Full choke. Weight: 6 pounds with plain barrel. Made 1972 to date.

With plain barrel **$295**
With ventilated-rib barrel **325**

Remington Model 870 Magnum Duck Gun

Same as Model 870 Field Gun, except has 3-inch chamber, 12 and 20 gauge Magnum only. 28- or 30-inch barrel, plain or vent rib, M or F choke; recoil pad. Weight: about 7½ or 6¾ pounds. Made 1964 to date.

With plain barrel **$275**
With ventilated-rib barrel **305**

Remington Model 870 Marine Magnum **$295**

Same general specifications as Model 870 Wingmaster, except with 7-shot magazine, 18-inch plain barrel with fixed IC choke, bead front sight and electroless nickel finish. Made 1992 to date.

Remington Model 870 Mississippi Magnum
Duck Gun **$320**

Same as Remington Model 870 Magnum Duck Gun except has 32-inch barrel. Engraved receiver, "Ducks Unlimited." Made in 1983.

Remington Model 870 SA Skeet Gun, Small
Bore **$295**

Similar to Wingmaster Model 870SA, except chambered for 28 and .410 gauge (2½-inch chamber for latter); 25-inch vent-rib barrel, SK choke. Weight: 6 lbs., 28 ga.; 6½ lbs., .410. Made 1969–1982.

Remington Model 870 Special Field Shotgun . . . **$325**

Pump action. Hammerless. Gauge: 12 or 20. 21-inch vent-rib barrel with REM choke. 41½ inches overall. Weight: 6–7 pounds. Straight-grip checkered walnut stock and forend. Made 1987 to date.

Remington Model 870 Special Purpose Deer Gun
Similar to Special Purpose Magnum, except with 20-inch, IC choke, rifle sights. Matte black oxide and Parkerized finish. Oil-finished, checkered buttstock and forend with recoil pad. Made 1986 to date.
Model 870 SP Deer Gun **$315**
Model 870 SP Deer Gun, cantilever scope mount ... **355**

Remington Model 870 Special Purpose Magnum **$290**
Similar to the 870 Magnum Duck Gun, except with 26-, 28- or 30-inch vent-rib REM Choke barrel. 12 gauge only; 3-inch chamber. Oil-finished field-grade stock with recoil pad, QD swivels and Cordura sling. Made 1985 to date.

Remington Model 870 SPS Magnum
Same general specifications Model 870 Special Purpose Magnum, except with synthetic stock and forend. 26- or 28-inch vent-rib barrel with REM Choke tubes. Matte black or Mossy Oak Camo finish. Made 1991 to date.
Model 870 SPS Magnum (Black Syn. Stock) **$270**
Model 870 SPS BG-Camo (1994–95) **285**
Model 870 SPS-T Camo (Mossy Oak Camo) **280**

Remington Model 870 Wingmaster Field Gun
Same general specifications as Model 870AP, except checkered stock and forend. Later models have REM choke systems in 12 ga. Made 1964 to date.
With plain barrel **$250**
With ventilated-rib barrel **295**

Remington Model 870 Wingmaster Field Gun, Small Bore
Same as standard Model 870, but scaled down. Gauges: 20, 28, .410. 25-inch barrel, plain or vent rib; IC, M or F choke; 26-, 28-inch (20 ga.) vent rib with REM Choke tubes. Weight: 5$\frac{1}{2}$–6$\frac{1}{4}$ pounds depending on gauge and barrel. Made 1969 to date.
With plain barrel **$325**
With ventilated-rib barrel **340**
With REM Choke **350**

Remington Model 870 Wingmaster Magnum Deluxe Grade **$310**
Same as Model 870 Magnum Standard Grade, except has checkered stock and extension beavertail forearm, barrel with matted top surface. Discontinued in 1963.

Remington Model 870 Wingmaster Magnum Standard Grade **$275**
Same as Model 870AP, except chambered for 12 gauge 3-inch Magnum, 30-inch Full choke barrel, recoil pad. Weight: about 8$\frac{1}{4}$ pounds. Made 1955–1963.

Remington Model 870 Wingmaster REM Choke Series
Hammerless, takedown with blued all-steel receiver. Gauges: 12, 20; 3-inch chamber. Tubular magazine. Barrels: 21-, 26-, 28-inch vent-rib with REM Choke. Weight: 7$\frac{1}{2}$ pounds (12 ga.). Satin-finished, checkered walnut buttstock and forend with recoil pad. Right- or left-hand models. Made 1986 to date.
Standard Model, 12 ga. **$305**
Standard Model, 20 ga. **315**
Youth Model, 21-inch barrel **310**

Remington Model 870ADL Wingmaster Deluxe Grade
Same general specifications as Wingmaster Model 870AP, except has pistol-grip stock and extension beavertail forend, both finely checkered; matted top surface or vent-rib barrel. Made 1950–1963.
With matted top-surface barrel **$220**
With ventilated-rib barrel **245**

Remington Model 870AP Wingmaster Standard Grade 5-Shot Slide Action Repeater
Hammerless. Takedown. Gauges: 12, 16, 20. Tubular magazine holds four shells. Barrels: plain, matted top surface or vent rib; 26-inch IC, 28-inch M or F choke, 30-inch F choke (12 ga. only). Weight: about 7 pounds, 12 ga.; 6$\frac{3}{4}$ pounds, 16 ga.; 6$\frac{1}{2}$ pounds, 20 ga. Plain pistol-grip stock, grooved forend. Made 1950–1963.
With plain barrel **$200**
With matted top-surface barrel **210**
With ventilated-rib barrel **230**
Left-hand model **240**

Remington Model 870BDL Wingmaster Deluxe Special
Same as Model 870ADL, except select American walnut stock and forend. Made 1950–1963.
With matted top-surface barrel **$270**
With ventilated-rib barrel **305**

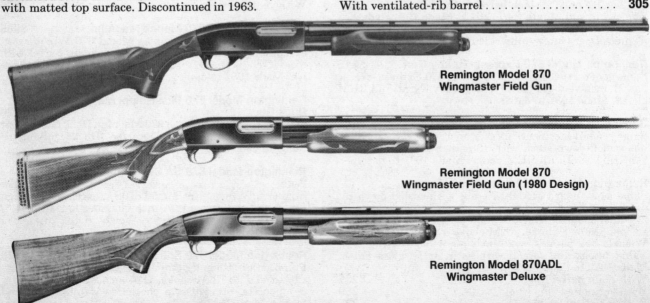

**Remington Model 870
Wingmaster Field Gun**

**Remington Model 870
Wingmaster Field Gun (1980 Design)**

**Remington Model 870ADL
Wingmaster Deluxe**

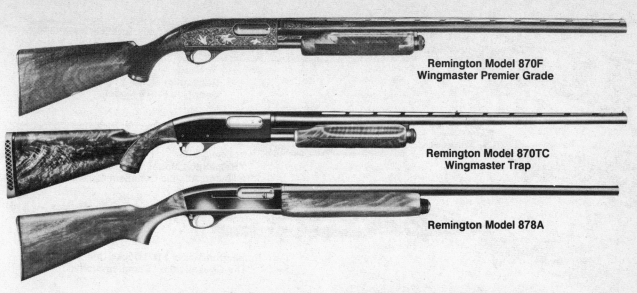

**Remington Model 870F
Wingmaster Premier Grade**

**Remington Model 870TC
Wingmaster Trap**

Remington Model 878A

Remington Model 870D, 870F Wingmaster Tournament and Premier Grade Guns

These higher grade models differ from the Model 870AP in general quality, grade of wood, checkering, engraving, etc. Gen. specifications are the same. Made 1950 to date.

Model 870D Tournament Grade	**$1895**
Model 870F Premier Grade	4250
Model 870F Premier Grade with gold inlay	6295

Remington Model 870R Wingmaster Riot Gun .. $275

Same as Model 870AP, except 20-inch barrel, IC, 12 gauge only.

Remington Model 870SA Wingmaster Skeet Gun

Same general specifications as Model 870AP, except has 26-inch vent-rib barrel, SK choke, ivory bead front sight, metal bead rear sight, pistol-grip stock and extension beavertail forend. Weight: 6³/₄ to 7¹/₂ pounds depending on gauge. Made 1950–1982.

Model 870SA Skeet Grade (Disc. 1982)	**$ 275**
Model 870SC Skeet Target Grade (Disc 1980)	425
Model 870SD Skeet Tournament Grade	1250
Model 870SF Skeet Premier Grade	2495

Remington Model 870TB Wingmaster
Trap Special $335

Same general specifications as Model 870AP Wingmaster, except has 28- or 30-inch vent-rib barrel, Full choke, metal bead front sight, no rear sight. "Special" grade trap-style stock and forend, both checkered, recoil pad. Weight: about 8 pounds. Made 1950–1981.

Remington Model 870TC Trap

Same general specifications Model 870TC Wingmaster, except with REM Choke high-rib vent barrel. Redesigned satin finished stock and forend with cut-checkering. Made

Remington Model 870TC Trap (cont.)

1987 to date.

Model 870 TC Trap (Standard)	**$460**
Model 870 TC Trap (Monte Carlo)	475

Remington Model 870TC Wingmaster Trap Grade

Same as Model 870TB, except higher grade walnut in stock and forend, has both front and rear sights. Made 1950–1979. Model 870 TC reissued in 1987. See separate listing.

Model 870TC Trap Grade	**$ 425**
Model 870TD Trap Tournament Grade	1295
Model 870TF Trap Premier Grade	2550

Remington Model 878A Automaster $225

Gas-operated Autoloader. 12 gauge, 3-shot magazine. Barrels: 26-inch IC, 28-inch M choke, 30-inch F choke. Weight: about 7 pounds. Plain pistol-grip stock and forearm. Made 1959–1962.

> **NOTE:** New stock checkering patterns and receiver scroll markings were incorporated on all standard Model 1100 field, magnum, skeet and trap models in 1979.

Remington Model 1100 Automatic Field Gun

Gas-operated. Hammerless. Takedown. Gauges: 12, 16, 20. Barrels: plain or vent. rib; 30-inch F, 28-inch M or F, 26-inch IC; or REM choke tubes. Weight: average 7¹/₄–7¹/₂ pounds depending on gauge and barrel length. Checkered walnut pistol-grip stock and forearm in high-gloss finish. Made 1963–1988.

With Plain Barrel	**$285**
With Vent-rib Barrel	325
REM Choke Model	365
REM Chokes, Left-hand Action	385

**Remington Model 1100 Field
Left-hand Action**

SHOTGUNS

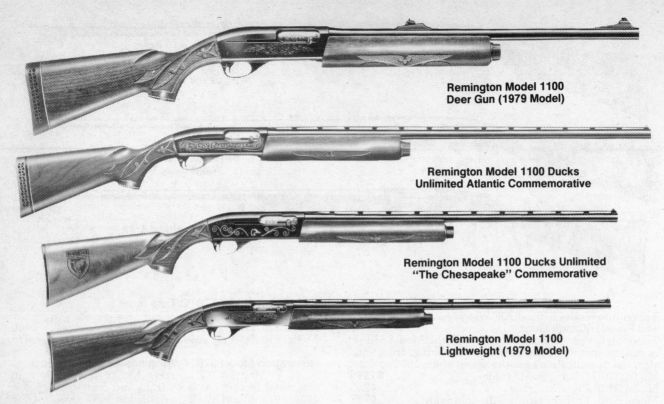

**Remington Model 1100
Deer Gun (1979 Model)**

**Remington Model 1100 Ducks
Unlimited Atlantic Commemorative**

**Remington Model 1100 Ducks Unlimited
"The Chesapeake" Commemorative**

**Remington Model 1100
Lightweight (1979 Model)**

Remington Model 1100 Deer Gun $395
Same as Model 1100 Field Gun, except has 22-inch barrel, IC, with rifle-type sights; 12 and 20 gauge only; recoil pad. Weight: about 7¼ pounds. Made 1963–1987.

Remington Model 1100 Ducks Unlimited
Atlantic Commemorative $660
Limited production for one year. Similar specifications to Model 1100 Field, except with 32-inch Full choke, vent-rib barrel. 12-gauge Magnum only. Made in 1982.

Remington Model 1100 Ducks Unlimited
"The Chesapeake" Commemorative $495
Limited edition 1 to 2400. Same general specifications as Model 1100 Field, except sequentially serial numbered with markings "The Chesapeake." 12-gauge Magnum with 30-inch Full choke, vent-rib barrel. Made in 1981.

Remington Model 1100 Field Grade, Small Bore
Same as standard Model 1100, but scaled down. Gauges: 28, .410. 25-inch barrel, plain or vent rib; IC, M or F choke. Weight: 6¼–7 pounds depending on gauge and barrel. Made 1969–1994.
With Plain Barrel $380
With Ventilated Rib 425

Remington Model 1100 Lightweight
Same as standard Model 1100, but scaled-down receiver and lightweight mahogany stock; 20 gauge only, 2¾-inch chamber. Barrels: plain or vent rib; 26-inch IC; 28-inch M and F choke. Weight: 6¼ pounds. Made 1971 to date.
With Plain Barrel $375
With Ventilated Rib 395

Remington Model 1100 Lightweight Magnum
Same as Model 1100 Lightweight, but chambered for 20 gauge Magnum 3-inch shell; 28-inch barrel, plain or vent rib, Full choke. Weight: 6½ pounds. Made 1971 to date.
With Plain Barrel $385
With Ventilated Rib 415
With Choke Tubes 445

Remington Model 1100 LT-20 Ducks Unlimited
Special Commemorative $495
Limited edition 1 to 2400. Same general specifications as Model 1100 Field, except sequentially serial numbered with markings "The Chesapeake." 20-gauge only. 26-inch IC, vent-rib barrel. Made in 1981.

Remington Model 1100 LT-20 Series
Same as Model 1100 Field Gun, except in 20 gauge with shorter 23-inch vent-rib barrel, straight-grip stock. REM choke series has 21-inch vent-rib barrel, choke tubes. Weight: 6¼ pounds. Checkered grip and forearm. Made 1983 to date.

**Remington Model 1100 LT-20
Ducks Unlimited Special**

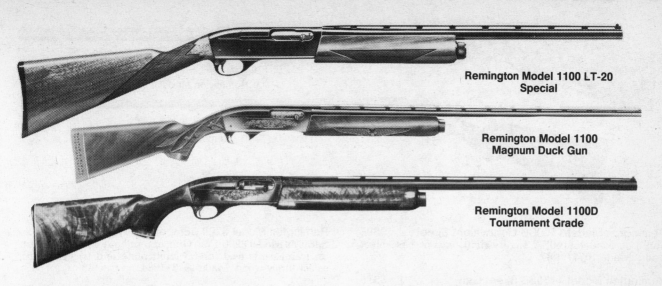

Remington Model 1100 LT-20 Special

Remington Model 1100 Magnum Duck Gun

Remington Model 1100D Tournament Grade

Remington Model 1100 LT-20 Series (cont.)
Model 1100 LT-20 Special **$425**
Model 1100 LT-20 Deer Gun **385**
Model 1100 LT-20 Youth **415**

Remington Model 1100 Magnum **$345**
Limited production. Similar to the Model 1100 Field, except with 26-inch Full choke, vent-rib barrel and 3-inch chamber. Made in 1981.

Remington Model 1100 Magnum Duck Gun
Same as Model 1100 Field Gun, except has 3-inch chamber, 12 and 20 gauge magnum only. 30-inch plain or vent-rib barrel in 12 gauge, 28-inch in 20 gauge; M or F choke. Recoil pad. Weight: about 7³/₄ pounds. Made 1963–1988.
With Plain Barrel **$295**
With Vent-rib Barrel **335**

Remington Model 1100 One of 3000 Field **$895**
Limited edition, numbered 1 to 3000. Similar to Model 1100 Field, except with fancy wood and gold-trimmed etched hunting scenes on receiver. 12 gauge with 28-inch Mod., vent-rib barrel. Made in 1980.

Remington Model 1100 Special Field Shotgun . . **$395**
Gas-operated. 5-shot. Hammerless. Gauges: 12 and 20. 21-inch vent-rib barrel with REM choke. Weight: 6¹/₂–7¹/₄ pounds. Straight-grip checkered walnut stock and forend. Made 1987 to date.

Remington Model 1100 SP Magnum
Same as Model 1100 Field, except 12 gauge only with 3-inch chambers. Barrels: 26- or 30-inch F choke; or 26-inch with REM Choke tubes; vent rib. Non-reflective, matte black, Parkerized barrel and receiver. Satin-finished stock and forend. Made 1981–1987.
With Fixed Choke **$375**
With REM Choke **395**

Remington Model 1100 Tournament Skeet **$415**
Similar to Model 1100 Field, except with 26-inch barrel, SK choke. Gauges: 12, LT-20, 28, and .410. Features select walnut stocks and new cut-checkering patterns. Made 1979–1989.

Remington Model 1100 Tournament Trap **$425**
Similar to Model 1100 Field Gun, except with 30-inch Full or mod. trap barrels. 12-gauge. Features select walnut stocks with cut-checkering patterns. Made 1979–1987.

Remington Model 1100D Tournament/1100F Premier
These higher grade guns differ from standard models in overall quality, grade of wood, checkering, engraving, gold inlays, etc. General specifications are the same. Made 1963 to date.
Model 1100D Tournament **$1695**
Model 1100F Premier **3250**
Model 1100F Premier w/Gold Inlay **4295**

Remington Model 1100SA Skeet Gun
Same as Model 1100 Field Gun, 12 and 20 gauge, except has 26-inch vent-rib barrel, SK choke or with Cutts Compensator. Weight: 7¹/₄–7¹/₂ pounds. Made 1963–1987.
With Skeet-choke Barrel **$375**
With Cutts Comp **395**
Left-hand Action **415**

Remington Model 1100SA Lightweight Skeet . . . **$375**
Same as Model 1100 Lightweight, except has skeet-style stock and forearm, 26-inch vent-rib barrel, SK choke. Made 1971–1987.

Remington Model 1100SA Skeet Small Bore . . . **$415**
Similar to standard Model 1100SA, except chambered for 28 and .410 gauge (2¹/₂-inch chamber for latter); 25-inch vent-rib barrel, SK choke. Weight: 6³/₄ pounds, 28 ga.; 7¹/₄ pounds, .410. Made 1969–1994.

**Remington Model 1100SA Skeet Gun
Left-hand Action**

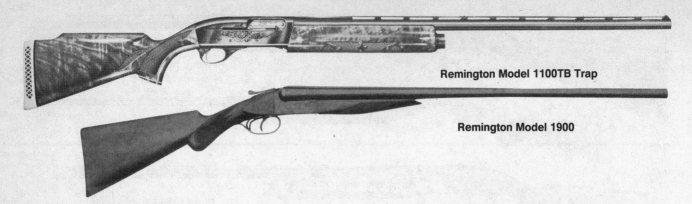

Remington Model 1100TB Trap

Remington Model 1900

Remington Model 1100SB Lightweight Skeet ... **$395**
Same as Model 1100SA Lightweight, except has select wood. Made 1977–1987.

Remington Model 1100SB Skeet Gun **$375**
Same as Model 1100SA, except has select wood. Made 1963–1987.

Remington Model 1100TA Trap Gun **$360**
Similar to Model 1100TB Trap Gun, except with regular-grade stocks. Available in both left- and right-hand versions. Made 1979–1987.

Remington Model 1100TB Trap Gun
Same as Model 1100 Field Gun, except has special trap stock, straight or Monte Carlo comb, recoil pad; 30-inch vent-rib barrel, F or mod. trap choke; 12 gauge only. Weight: 8¼ pounds. Made 1963–1979.
With straight stock **$395**
With Monte Carlo stock **415**

Remington Model 1900 Hammerless Double ... **$595**
Improved version of Model 1894. Boxlock. Auto ejector. Double triggers. Gauges: 10, 12, 16. Barrels: 28 to 32 inches. Value shown is for standard grade with ordnance steel barrels. Made 1900–1910.

Remington Model 3200 Competition Skeet Gun .. **$1400**
Same as Model 3200 Skeet Gun, except has gilded scrollwork on frame, engraved forend latch plate and trigger guard, select fancy wood. Made 1973–1984.

Remington Model 3200 Competition Skeet Set .. **$4995**
Similar specifications to Model 3200 Field. 12-gauge over-and-under with additional, interchangeable barrels in 20, 28, and .410 gauges. Cased. Made 1980–84.

Remington Model 3200 Competition Trap Gun ... **$1595**
Same as Model 3200 Trap Gun, except has gilded scrollwork on frame, engraved forend latch plate and trigger guard, select fancy wood. Made 1973–1984.

Remington Model 3200 Field Grade Magnum ... **$1395**
Same as Model 3200 Field Grade, except chambered for 12 gauge magnum 3-inch shell; 30-inch barrels, M and F or both F choke. Made 1975–1984.

Remington Model 3200 Field Grade O/U **$995**
Boxlock. Auto ejectors. Selective single trigger. 12 gauge. 2¾-inch chambers. Barrels: vent rib; 26- and 28-inch M/F; 30-inch IC/M. Weight: about 7¾ pounds with 26-inch barrels. Checkered pistol-grip stock/forearm. Made 1973–78.

Remington Model 3200 "One of 1000" Skeet ... **$2150**
Same as Model 3200 "One of 1000" Trap Gun, except has 26- or 28-inch barrels, SK choke, skeet-style stock and forearm. Made in 1974.

Remington Model 3200 "One of 1000" Trap **$2195**
Limited edition numbered 1 to 1000. Same general specifications as Model 3200 Trap Gun, but has frame, trigger guard and forend latch elaborately engraved (designation "One of 1,000" on frame side), stock and forearm of high grade walnut. Supplied in carrying case. Made in 1973.

Remington Model 3200 Skeet Gun **$1150**
Same as Model 3200 Field Grade, except skeet-style stock and full beavertail forearm; 26- or 28-inch barrels, SK choke. Made 1973–1980.

Remington Model 3200 Special Trap Gun **$1195**
Same as Model 3200 Trap Gun, except has select wood. Made 1973–1984.

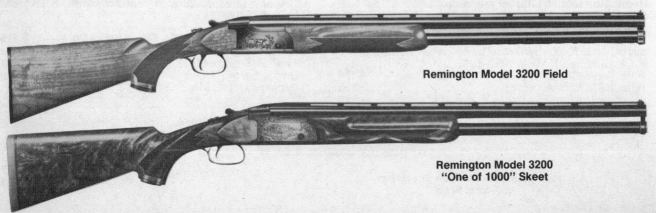

Remington Model 3200 Field

Remington Model 3200 "One of 1000" Skeet

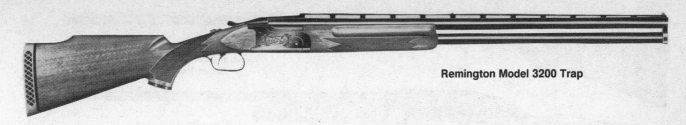

Remington Model 3200 Trap

Remington Model 3200 Trap Gun **$1095**
Same as Model 3200 Field Grade, except trap-style stock
w/Monte Carlo or straight comb, beavertail forearm; 30- or
32-inch barrels, IM/F or F/F chokes. Made 1973–77.

Remington Peerless O/U Field Grade **$895**
Similar in appearance to the Model 3200 Field boxlock action
w/sideplates, except without top locking latch. 26-, 28- or
30-inch vent-rib barrels w/side ribs. Weight: about 7.5
pounds. Made 1993 to date.

Remington Rider No. 9 Single Shot Shotgun **$295**
Improved version of No. 3 Single Barrel Shotgun made in
the late 1800s. Semihammerless. Gauges 10, 12, 16, 20, 24,
28. 30- to 32-inch plain barrel. Weight: about 6 pounds. Plain
pistol-grip stock and forearm. Auto ejector. Made 1902–1910.

Remington SP-10 Magnum **$695**
Takedown. Gas-operated with stainless steel piston. 10
gauge; 3$\frac{1}{2}$-inch chamber. Barrels: 26- or 30-inch vent-rib
with REM Choke screw-in tubes. Weight: 11 to 11$\frac{1}{4}$ pounds.
Metal bead front. Checkered walnut stock with satin finish.
Made 1989 to date.

Remington SP-10 Magnum Turkey Combo **$775**
Same general specifications as Model SP-10 Magnum, except
has extra 22-inch REM Choke barrel with M, F and Turkey
Extra-Full tubes. Rifle sights. QD swivels and camo sling.
Made 1991–95.

Remington Sportsman A Standard Grade Autoloader
Same general specifications as Model 11A, except magazine
holds two shells. Also available in "B" Special Grade, "D"
Tournament Grade, "E" Expert Grade, "F" Premier Grade.
Made 1931–1948. Same values as for Model 11A.

Remington Sportsman Skeet Gun
Same general specifications as the Sportsman A, except has
26-inch barrel (plain, solid or vent rib), SK choke, beavertail
forend. Discontinued 1949.

Remington Sportsman Skeet Gun (cont.)
With plain barrel **$350**
With solid-rib barrel **435**
With ventilated-rib barrel **465**

**Remington Sportsman-48A Standard Grade 3-Shot
Autoloader**
Streamlined receiver. Hammerless. Takedown. Gauges:
12, 16, 20. Tubular magazine holds two shells. Barrels:
plain, matted top surface or vent rib; 26-inch IC, 28-inch
M or F choke, 30-inch F choke (12 ga. only). Weight:
about 7$\frac{1}{2}$ pounds, 12 ga.; 6$\frac{3}{4}$ pounds, 16 ga.; 6$\frac{1}{2}$ pounds,
20 ga. Pistol-grip stock, grooved forend, both checkered.
Made 1949–1959.
With plain barrel **$295**
With matted top-surface barrel **310**
With ventilated-rib barrel **325**

**Remington Sportsman 48D
Tournament Grade**

**Remington Sportsman-48B Special, 48D Tournament
and 48F Premier Grade Guns**
These higher grade models differ from the Sportsman-
48A in general quality, grade of wood, checkering, engraving, etc. General specifications are the same. Made
1949–1959.
Sportsman-48B Special Grade . . . . **$ 355**
Sportsman-48D Tournament Grade **725**
Sportsman-48F Premier Grade **1695**

Remington Sportsman-48SA, SC, SD, SF Skeet Gun
Same general specifications as Sportsman-48A, except has
26-inch barrel with matted top surface or vent rib, SK
choke, ivory bead front sight, metal bead rear sight. Made
1949–1960.

SHOTGUNS

Remington Rider No. 9

Remington Sportsman Autoloader

Remington Sportsman-48SC
Skeet Target Grade

Remington Model 11-48A
Standard

Remington Model 11-48A, .410 & 28

Remington Sportsman-58ADL

Remington Sportsman-48SA, SC, SD, SF Skeet (cont.)

With matted top-surface barrel . . . . $ 265
With ventilated-rib barrel 325
Sportsman-48SC Skeet Target Grade 405
Sportsman-48SD Skeet Tournament Grade 595
Sportsman-48SF Skeet Premier Grade 1695

Remington Model 11-48A Riot Gun $245

Same as Model 11-48A, except 20-inch plain barrel and
12 gauge only. Discontinued in 1969.

Remington Model 11-48A Standard Grade 4-Shot Autoloader. 410 & 28 Gauge

Same general specifications as Sportsman-48A, except
gauge, 3-shell magazine, 25-inch barrel. Weight: about 6¼
pounds. 28 gauge introduced 1952, .410 in 1954. Discontinued in 1969. Prices same as shown for Sportsman-48A.

Remington Model 11-48A Standard Grade 5-Shot Autoloader

Same general specifications as Sportsman-48A, except
magazine holds four shells, forend not grooved. Also
available in Special Grade (11-48B), Tournament Grade
(11-48D) and Premier Grade (11-48F). Made 1949–1969.
Prices same as shown for Sportsman-48A.

Remington Model 11-48SA 28 Gauge Skeet $320

Same general specifications as Model 11-48A 28 Gauge,
except has 25-inch vent-rib barrel, SK choke. 28 gauge
introduced 1952, .410 in 1954.

Remington Sportsman-58 Skeet Target, Tournament and Premier Grades

These higher grade models differ from the Sportsman-
58SA in general quality, grade of wood, checkering, en-
graving, etc. General specifications are the same.
Sportsman-58C Skeet Target Grade . . . . $ 495
Sportsman-58D Skeet Tournament Grade 695
Sportsman-58SF Skeet Premier Grade 1250

Remington Sportsman-58 Tournament and Premier

These higher grade models differ from the Sportsman-
58ADL with vent-rib barrel in general quality, grade of
wood, checkering, engraving, etc. General specifications
are the same.
Sportsman-58D Tournament Grade . . . . $ 800
Sportsman-58F Premier Grade. 1400

Remington Sportsman-58ADL Autoloader

Deluxe Grade. Gas-operated. 12 gauge. 3-shot magazine.
Barrels: plain or vent rib; 26-, 28- or 30-inch; IC, M or F
choke, or Remington Special Skeet choke. Weight: about
7 pounds. Checkered pistol-grip stock and forearm. Made
1956–1964.
With plain barrel $275
With ventilated-rib barrel 315

Remington Sportsman-58BDL Deluxe Special Grade

Same as Model 58ADL, except select grade wood.
With plain barrel $295
With ventilated-rib barrel 335

Remington Sportsman-58SA Skeet Grade $330

Same general specifications as Model 58ADL with vent-
rib barrel, except special skeet stock and forearm.

REVELATION SHOTGUNS
See Western Auto listings.

RICHLAND ARMS COMPANY
Blissfield, Michigan
Manufactured in Italy and Spain

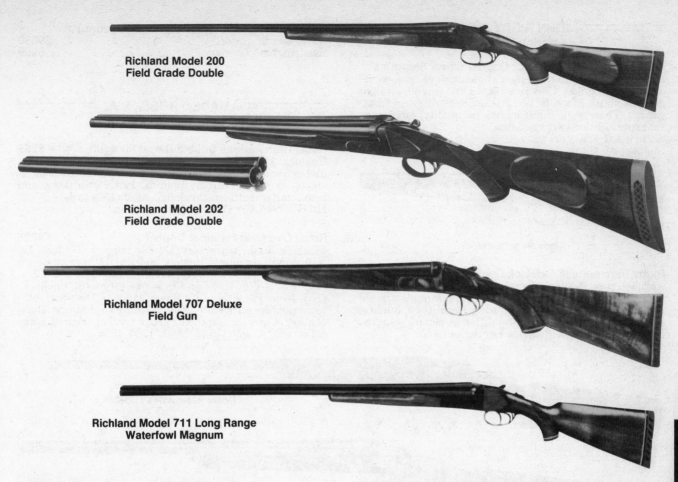

Richland Model 200
Field Grade Double

Richland Model 202
Field Grade Double

Richland Model 707 Deluxe
Field Gun

Richland Model 711 Long Range
Waterfowl Magnum

SHOTGUNS

Richland Model 200 Field Grade Double **$295**
Hammerless, boxlock, Anson & Deeley-type. Plain extractors. Double triggers. Gauges: 12, 16, 20, 28, .410 (3-inch chambers in 20 and .410; others have 2¾-inch). Barrels: 28-inch M/F choke; 26-inch IC/M; .410 with 26-inch M/F only; 22-inch IC/M in 20 ga. only. Weight: 6 lbs. 2 oz. to 7 lbs. 4 oz. Checkered walnut stock with cheekpiece, pistol grip, recoil pad; beavertail forend. Made in Spain 1963 to date.

Richland Model 202 All-Purpose Field Gun **$325**
Same as Model 200, except has two sets of barrels same gauge. 12 gauge: 30-inch barrels F/F, 3-inch chambers; 26-inch barrels IC/M, 2¾-inch chambers. 20 gauge: 28-inch barrels M/F; 22-inch barrels IC/M, 3-inch chambers. Made 1963 to date.

Richland Model 707 Deluxe Field Gun **$310**
Hammerless, boxlock, triple bolting system. Plain extractors. Double triggers. Gauges: 12, 2¾-inch chambers; 20, 3-inch chambers. Barrels: 12 gauge, 28-inch M/F, 26-

Richland Model 707 Deluxe Field Gun (cont.)
inch IC/M; 20 gauge, 30-inch F/F, 28-inch M/F, 26-inch IC/M. Weight: 6 lbs. 4 oz. to 6 lbs. 15 oz. Checkered walnut stock and forend, recoil pad. Made 1963–1972.

Richland Model 711 Long Range Waterfowl Magnum Double Barrel Shotgun
Hammerless, boxlock, Anson & Deeley-type, Purdey triple lock. Plain extractors. Double triggers. Auto safety. Gauges: 10, 3½-inch chambers; 12, 3-inch chambers. Barrels: 10 ga., 32-inch; 12 ga., 30-inch; F/F. Weight: 10 ga., 11 pounds; 12 ga., 7¾ pounds. Checkered walnut stock and beavertail forend; recoil pad. Made in Spain 1963 to date.
10 Gauge Magnum **$345**
12 Gauge Magnum **275**

Richland Model 808 Over-and-Under Gun **$375**
Boxlock. Plain extractors. Non-selective single trigger. 12 gauge only. Barrels (Vickers steel): 30-inch F/F; 28-inch M/F; 26-inch IC/M. Weight: 6 lbs. 12 oz. to 7 lbs. 3 oz. Checkered walnut stock/forend. Made in Italy 1963–68.

Richland Model 808
Over-and-Under

JOHN RIGBY & CO.
London, England

Rigby Hammerless Boxlock Double Barrel Shotguns
Auto ejectors. Double triggers. Made in all gauges, barrel
lengths and chokes. Checkered stock and forend, straight
grip standard. Made in two grades: Sackville and Chatsworth. These guns differ in general quality, engraving,
etc.; specifications are the same.
Sackville Grade **$5125**
Chatsworth Grade **3750**

Rigby Regal Sidelock

Rigby Hammerless Sidelock Double Barrel Shotguns
Auto ejectors. Double triggers. Made in all gauges, barrel
lengths and chokes. Checkered stock and forend, straight
grip standard. Made in two grades: Regal (best quality)
and Sandringham; these guns differ in general quality,
engraving, etc.; specifications are the same.

Rigby Hammerless Sidelock Doubles (cont.)
Regal Grade **$9050**
Sandringham Grade **6950**

AMADEO ROSSI, S.A.
Sao Leopoldo, Brazil

Rossi Hammerless Double Barrel Shotgun **$255**
Boxlock. Plain extractors. Double triggers. 12 gauge. 3-
inch chambers. Barrels: 26-inch IC/M; 28-inch M/F
choke. Weight: 7 to 7½ pounds. Pistol-grip stock and
beavertail forearm, uncheckered. Made 1974 to date. *Note:*
H&R Model 404 (1969-72) is same gun.

Rossi Overland Hammer Double **$225**
Sidelock. Plain extractors. Double triggers. Gauges: 12,
.410; 3-inch chambers. Barrels: 20-inch, IC/M in 12 gauge;
26-inch, F/F choke in .410. Weight: 7 lbs., 12 ga.; 6 lbs.,
.410. Pistol-grip stock and beavertail forearm, uncheckered. *Note:* Because of its resemblance to the short-barreled doubles carried by guards riding shotgun on 19th-
century stagecoaches, the 12 gauge version originally was
called the "Coach Gun." Made 1968–1989.

Rossi Hammerless Double

Rossi Overland

ROTTWEIL SHOTGUNS
West Germany

Rottweil Model 72 Over/Under Shotgun **$1595**
Hammerless, takedown with engraved receiver. 12 gauge;
2¾-inch chambers. 26¾-inch barrels with SK/SK chokes.
Weight: 7½ pounds. Interchangeable trigger groups and
buttstocks. Checkered French walnut buttstock and forend. Imported from West Germany.

Rottweil Model 650 Field O/U Shotgun **$650**
Breech action. Gauge: 12. 28-inch barrels. Six screw-in
choke tubes. Automatic ejectors. Engraved receiver.
Checkered pistol grip stock. Made 1984–86.

Rottweil American Skeet **$1575**
Boxlock action. Gauge: 12. 27-inch vent-rib barrels. 44½
inches overall. SK chokes. Weight: 7½ pounds. Designed
for tube sets. Hand-checkered European walnut stock with
modified forend. Made 1984–87.

Rottweil International Trap Shotgun **$1595**
Boxlock action. Gauge: 12. 30-inch barrels. 48½ inches
overall. Weight: 8 pounds. Choked IM/F. Selective single
trigger. Metal bead front sight. Checkered European walnut stock w/pistol grip. Engraved action. Made 1984–87.

Rottweil American Skeet

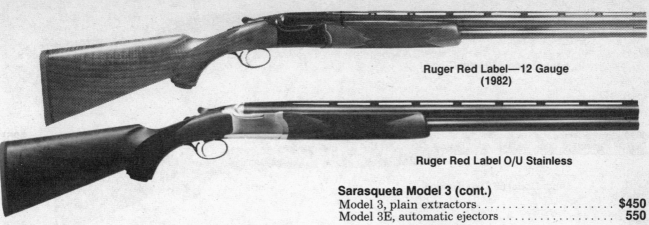

Ruger Red Label—12 Gauge
(1982)

Ruger Red Label O/U Stainless

RUGER SHOTGUN
Southport, Connecticut
Manufactured by Sturm, Ruger & Company

Ruger Plain Grade Red Label Over/Under **$725**
Boxlock. Auto ejectors. Selective single trigger. 20 gauge. 3-inch chambers. 26-inch vent-rib barrel, IC/M or SK choke. Weight: about 7 pounds. Checkered pistol-grip stock and forearm. Introduced in 1977; 12 gauge version, 1982. Chambers: 2³/₄- and 3-inch. Barrels: 26-, 28- and 30-inch. Weight: about 7¹/₂ pounds.

Ruger Red Label Over/Under Stainless
Gauges: 12, 20 and 28; 3-inch chambers. Barrels: 26- or 28-inch. Various chokes, fixed or screw-in tubes. Weight: 7–7¹/₂ pounds. Single selective trigger. Selective automatic ejectors. Automatic top safety. Standard gold bead front sight. Pistol-grip or English-style American walnut stock w/hand-cut checkering. Made 1985 to date.
With Fixed Chokes **$795**
With Screw-in Tubes 850

Ruger Sporting Clays Over/Under Stainless **$880**
Similar to the Red Label O/U Stainless, except in 12 and 20 gauge w/30-inch vent-rib barrels, no side ribs; back-bored with screw-in choke tubes (not interchangeable w/ other Red Label O/U models). Brass front and mid-rib beads. Made 1992 to date.

VICTOR SARASQUETA, S. A.
Eibar, Spain

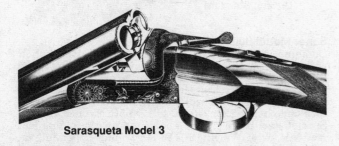

Sarasqueta Model 3

Sarasqueta Model 3 Hammerless Boxlock Double Barrel Shotgun
Plain extractors or auto ejectors. Double triggers. Gauges: 12, 16, 20. Made in various barrel lengths, chokes and weights. Checkered stock and forend, straight grip standard. Currently manufactured.

Sarasqueta Model 3 (cont.)
Model 3, plain extractors **$450**
Model 3E, automatic ejectors 550

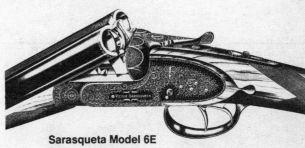

Sarasqueta Model 6E

Sarasqueta Model 11E

Sarasqueta Model 12E

Sarasqueta Hammerless Sidelock Doubles
Automatic ejectors (except on Models 4 and 203 which have plain extractors). Double triggers. Gauges: 12, 16, 20. Barrel lengths, chokes and weights made to order. Checkered stock and forend, straight grip standard. Models differ chiefly in overall quality, engraving, grade of wood, checkering, etc.; general specifications are the same. Currently manufactured.

Model 4	$ 575
Model 4E	625
Model 203	575
Model 203E	615
Model 6E	705
Model 7E	750
Model 10E	1525
Model 11E	1650
Model 12E	1895

SHOTGUNS

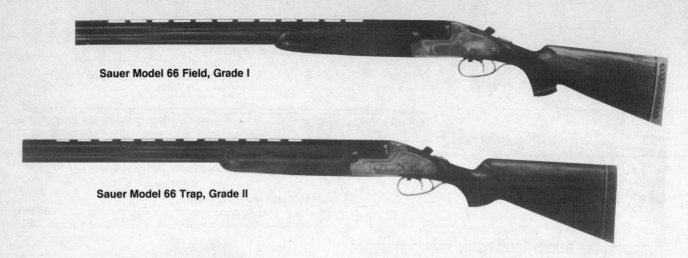

Sauer Model 66 Field, Grade I

Sauer Model 66 Trap, Grade II

J. P. SAUER & SOHN
Eckernförde, Germany
Formerly located in Suhl, Germany

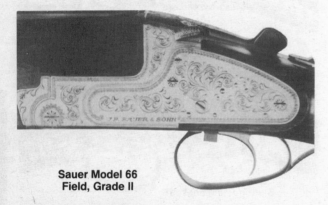

Sauer Model 66
Field, Grade II

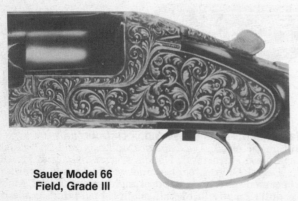

Sauer Model 66
Field, Grade III

Sauer Model 66 Over/Under Field Gun
Purdey-system action with Holland & Holland-type sidelocks. Selective single trigger. Selective auto ejectors. Automatic safety. Available in three grades of engraving. 12 gauge only. Krupp-Special steel barrels with vent rib, 28-inch, M/F choke. Weight: about 7¼ pounds. Checkered walnut stock and forend; recoil pad. Made 1966–1975.

Grade I	$1600
Grade II	2100
Grade III	2900

Sauer Model 66 Over-and-Under Skeet Gun
Same as Model 66 Field Gun, except 26-inch barrels with wide vent rib, SK choked; skeet-style stock and ventilated beavertail forearm; nonautomatic safety. Made 1966–1975.

Grade I	$1595
Grade II	2000
Grade III	2895

Sauer Model 66 Over/Under Trap Gun
Same as Model 66 Skeet Gun, except has 30-inch barrels choked F/F or M/F; trap-style stock. Values same as for Skeet Model. Made 1966–1975.

Sauer Model 3000E
Drilling, Standard

Sauer Model 3000E Drilling
Combination rifle and double-barrel shotgun. Blitz action with Greener crossbolt, double underlugs, separate rifle cartridge extractor, front set trigger, firing pin indicators, Greener side safety, sear slide selector locks right shotgun barrel for firing rifle barrel. Gauge/calibers: 12 gauge (2¾-inch chambers); 222, 243, 30-06, 7×65R. 25-inch Krupp-Special steel barrels; M/F choke, automatic folding leaf rear rifle sight. Weight: 6½ to 7¼ pounds depending on rifle caliber. Checkered walnut stock and forend; pistol grip, M Monte Carlo comb and cheekpiece, sling swivels. Standard Model with arabesque engraving; Deluxe Model with hunting scenes engraved on action. Currently manufactured. *Note:* Also see listing under Colt.

Standard Model	$2495
Deluxe Model	3250

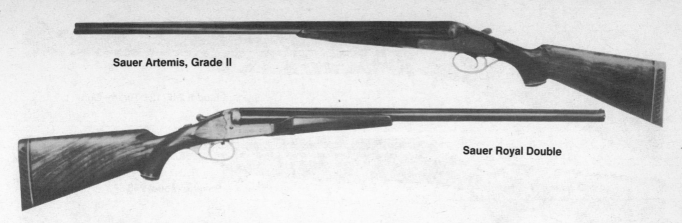

Sauer Artemis, Grade II

Sauer Royal Double

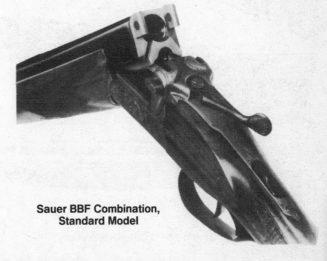

Sauer BBF Combination, Standard Model

SHOTGUNS

Sauer Artemis Double Barrel Shotgun

Holland & Holland-type sidelock with Greener crossbolt, double underlugs, double sear safeties, selective single trigger, selective auto ejectors. Grade I with fine-line engraving; Grade II with full English arabesque engraving. 12 gauge (2³/₄-inch chambers). Krupp-Special steel barrels, 28-inch, M/F choke. Weight: about 6¹/₂ pounds. Checkered walnut pistol-grip stock and beavertail forend; recoil pad. Made 1966–1977.

Grade I **$3995**
Grade II **4950**

Sauer BBF Over/Under Combination Rifle/Shotgun

Blitz action with Kersten lock, front set trigger fires rifle barrel, slide-operated sear safety. Gauge/calibers: 16 gauge; 30-30, 30-06, 7×65R. 25-inch Krupp-Special steel barrels; shotgun barrel Full choke, folding-leaf rear sight. Weight: about 6 pounds. Checkered walnut stock and forend; pistol grip, mod. Monte Carlo comb and cheekpiece, sling swivels. Standard Model with arabesque engraving; Deluxe Model with hunting scenes engraved on action. Currently manufactured.

Standard Model **$1850**
Deluxe Model **2295**

Sauer Royal Double Barrel Shotguns

Anson & Deeley action (boxlock) with Greener crossbolt, double underlugs, signal pins, selective single trigger, selective auto ejectors, auto safety. Scalloped frame with arabesque engraving. Krupp-Special steel barrels. Gauges:

Sauer Royal Double Barrel Shotguns (cont.)

12, 2³/₄-inch chambers; 20, 3-inch chambers. Barrels: 30-inch (12 ga. only) and 28-inch, M/F; 26-inch (20 ga. only), IC/M. Weight: 12 ga., about 6¹/₂ pounds; 20 ga., 6 pounds. Checkered walnut pistol-grip stock and beavertail forend; recoil pad. Made 1955–1977.

Standard Model **$1295**
20 Gauge **1740**

Savage Model 24D

SAVAGE ARMS
Westfield, Massachusetts
Formerly located in Utica, New York

Savage Model 24 22-.410 O/U Combination **$130**

Same as Stevens No. 22-.410, has walnut stock and forearm. Made 1950–1965.

Savage Model 24C Camper's Companion **$145**

Same as Model 24FG, except made in 22 Magnum/20 gauge only; has 20-inch barrels, shotgun tube Cyl. bore.

Savage Model 24C Camper's Companion (cont.)

Weight: 5³/₄ pounds. Trap in butt provides ammunition storage; comes with carrying case. Made 1972–1989.

Savage Model 24D **$185**

Same as Models 24DL and 24MDL, except frame has black or casehardened finish. Game scene decoration of frame eliminated in 1974; forearm uncheckered after 1976. Made 1970–1988.

Savage Model 24DL **$190**

Same general specifications as Model 24S, except top lever opening; satin-chrome-finished frame decorated with game scenes, checkered Monte Carlo stock and forearm. Made 1965–69.

Savage Model 24F-12T Turkey Gun

Savage Model 24S

Savage Model 24V

Savage Model 24-VS Camper/Survival

Savage Model 28A

Savage Model 24F-12T Turkey Gun **$255**
12- or 20-gauge shotgun barrel/22 Hornet, 223 or 30-30 caliber rifle. 24-inch blued barrels; 3-inch chambers; extra removable Full choke tube. Hammer block safety. Color casehardened frame. du Pont Rynite® camo stock. Swivel studs. Made 1989 to date.

Savage Model 24FG Field Grade **$125**
Same general specifications as Model 24S, except top lever opening. Made 1972 to date.

Savage Model 24MDL **$135**
Same as Model 24DL, except rifle barrel chambered for 22 WMR. Made 1965–69.

Savage Model 24MS **$125**
Same as Model 24S, except rifle barrel chambered for 22 WMR. Made 1965–1971.

Savage Model 24S Over/Under Combination . . . **$140**
Boxlock. Visible hammer. Side lever opening. Plain extractors. Single trigger. 20 ga. or .410 bore shotgun barrel under 22 LR barrel; 24-inch. Open rear sight, ramp front, dovetail for scope mounting. Weight: about 6¾ pounds. Plain pistol-grip stock and forearm. Made 1965–1971.

Savage Model 24V **$235**
Similar to Model 24D, except 20 gauge under 222 Rem., 22 Rem., 357 Mag., 22 Hornet or 30-30 rifle barrel. Made 1971–1989.

**Savage Model 24-VS Camper/Survival/
Centerfire Rifle/Shotgun** **$175**
Similar to Model 24V except 357 Rem. Mag. over 20 gauge. Nickel finish, full-length stock and accessory pistol-grip stock. Overall length: 36 inches with full stock; 26 inches w/pistol grip. Weight: about 6½ pounds. Made 1983–88.

**Savage Model 28A Standard Grade Slide Action
Repeating Shotgun** **$225**
Hammerless. Takedown. 12 gauge. 5-shell tubular magazine. Plain barrel; lengths: 26-, 28-, 30-, 32-inches; choked C/M/F. Weight: about 7½ pounds with 30-inch barrel. Plain pistol-grip stock, grooved slide handle. Made 1928–1931.

Savage Model 28B **$235**
Raised matted rib; otherwise the same as Model 28A.

Savage Model 28D Trap Grade **$300**
Same general specifications as Model 28A, except has 30-inch Full choke barrel with matted rib, trap-style stock with checkered pistol grip, checkered slide handle of select walnut.

**Savage Model 30 Solid Frame Hammerless
Slide Action Shotgun** **$180**
Gauges: 12, 16, 20, .410. 2¾-inch chamber in 16 gauge, 3-inch in other gauges. Magazine holds four 2¾-inch shells or three 3-inch shells. Barrels: vent rib; 26-, 28-, 30-inch;

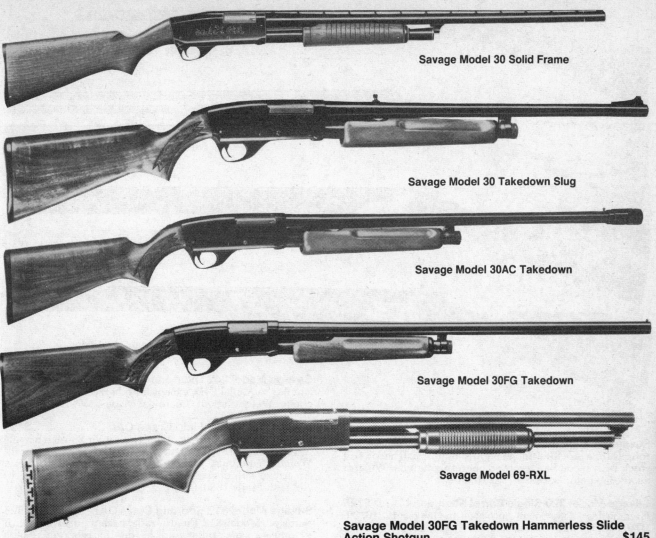

Savage Model 30 Solid Frame

Savage Model 30 Takedown Slug

Savage Model 30AC Takedown

Savage Model 30FG Takedown

Savage Model 69-RXL

SHOTGUNS

Savage Model 30 Solid Frame Hammerless (cont.)
IC, M, F choke. Weight: average 6¼ to 6¾ pounds depending on gauge. Plain pistol-grip stock (checkered on later production), grooved slide handle. Made 1958–1970.

Savage Model 30 Takedown Slug Gun **$175**
Same as Model 30FG, except 21-inch Cyl. bore barrel with rifle sights. Made 1971–79.

Savage Model 30AC Solid Frame **$190**
Same as Model 30 Solid Frame, except has 26-inch barrel with adjustable choke; 12 gauge only. Made 1959–1970.

Savage Model 30AC Takedown **$170**
Same as Model 30FG, except has 26-inch barrel with adjustable choke; 12 and 20 gauge only. Made 1971–72.

Savage Model 30ACL Solid Frame **$195**
Same as Model 30AC Solid Frame, except left-hand model with ejection port and safety on left side; 12 gauge only. Made 1960–64.

Savage Model 30D Takedown **$175**
Deluxe Grade. Same as Model 30FG, except has receiver engraved with game scene, vent-rib barrel, recoil pad. Made 1971 to date.

Savage Model 30FG Takedown Hammerless Slide Action Shotgun **$145**
Field Grade. Gauges: 12, 20, .410. 3-inch chamber. Magazine holds four 2¾-inch shells or three 3-inch shells. Barrels: plain; 26-inch Full choke (.410 ga. only); 28-inch M/F choke; 30-inch Full choke (12 ga. only). Weight: average 7 to 7¾ pounds depending on gauge. Checkered pistol-grip stock, fluted slide handle. Made 1970–79.

Savage Model 30L Solid Frame **$170**
Same as Model 30 Solid Frame, except left-handed model with ejection port and safety on left side; 12 gauge only. Made 1959–1970.

Savage Model 30T Solid Frame Trap and Duck . **$195**
Same as Model 30 Solid Frame, except only in 12 gauge with 30-inch Full choke barrel; has Monte Carlo stock with recoil pad, weighs about 8 pounds. Made 1963–1970.

Savage Model 30T Takedown Trap Gun **$175**
Same as Model 30D, except only in 12 gauge with 30-inch Full choke barrel. Monte Carlo stock with recoil pad. Made 1970–73.

Savage Model 69-RXL Slide Action Shotgun . . . **$160**
Hammerless, side ejection, top tang safe for left- or right-hand use. 12 gauge, chambered for 2¾- and 3-inch magnum shells. 18¼-inch barrel. Tubular magazine holds 6

Savage Model 220

Savage Model 242

Savage Model 312 Field Grade O/U

Savage Model 312 Trap Over/Under

Savage Model 69-RXL Slide Action (cont.)
rounds (one less for 3-inch mag). Walnut finish hardwood stock with recoil pad, grooved operating handle. Weight: about 6½ pounds. Made 1982 to date.

Savage Model 220 Single Barrel Shotgun $125
Hammerless. Takedown. Auto ejector. Gauges: 12, 16, 20, .410. Single shot. Barrel lengths: 12 ga., 28- to 36-inch; 16 ga., 28- to 32-inch; 20 ga., 26- to 32-inch; .410 bore, 26- and 28-inch. Full choke. Weight: about 6 pounds. Plain pistol-grip stock and wide forearm. Made 1938–1965.

Savage Model 220AC $150
Same as Model 220, except has Savage adjustable choke.

Savage Model 220L $120
Same general specifications as Model 220, except has side lever opening instead of top lever. Made 1965–1972.

Savage Model 220P $135
Same as Model 220, except has Poly Choke built integrally with barrel; made in 12 gauge with 30-inch barrel, 16 and 20 gauge with 28-inch barrel, not made in .410 bore; has recoil pad.

Savage Model 242 Over-and-Under Shotgun ... $285
Similar to Model 24D, except both barrels .410 bore, Full choke. Weight: about 7 pounds. Made 1977–1980.

Savage Model 312 Field Grade O/U $495
Gauge: 12; 2¾- or 3-inch chambers. 26- or 28-inch barrels w/vent rib; F/M/IC chokes. 43 or 45 inches overall. Weight: 7 pounds. Internal hammers. Top tang safety. American walnut stock with checkered pistol grip and recoil pad. Made 1990–93.

Savage Model 312 Sporting Clays O/U $525
Same as Model 312 Field Grade, except furnished with #1 and #2 skeet tubes and 28-inch barrels only. Made 1990–93.

Savage Model 312 Trap Over/Under $530
Same as Model 312 Field Grade, except with 30-inch barrels only, Monte Carlo buttstock and weight of 7½ pounds. Made 1990–93.

> **NOTE:** Savage Models 330, 333T, 333, and 2400 were manufactured by Valmet Oy, Helsinki, Finland.

Savage Model 330 Over-and-Under Shotgun ... $425
Boxlock. Plain extractors. Selective single trigger. Gauges: 12, 20. 2¾-inch chambers in 12 gauge, 3-inch in 20 gauge. Barrels: 26-inch IC/M; 28-inch M/F; 30-inch M/F choke

Savage Model 330

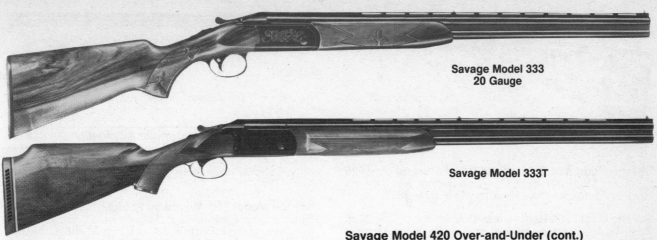

**Savage Model 333
20 Gauge**

Savage Model 333T

Savage Model 330 Over-and-Under (cont.)
(12 ga. only). Weight: 6¼ to 7¼ pounds, depending on gauge. Checkered pistol-grip stock and forearm. Made 1969–1978.

Savage Model 333 Over-and-Under Shotgun ... $525
Boxlock. Auto ejectors. Selective single trigger. Gauges: 12, 20. 2¾-inch chambers in 12 gauge, 3-inch in 20 gauge. Barrels: vent rib; 26-inch SK choke, IC/M; 28-inch M/F; 30-inch M/F choke (12 ga. only). Weight: average 6¼ to 7¼ pounds. Checkered pistol-grip stock and forearm. Made 1973–79.

Savage Model 333T Trap Gun $495
Similar to Model 330, except only in 12 gauge with 30-inch vent-rib barrels, IM/F choke; Monte Carlo stock with recoil pad. Weight: 7¾ pounds. Made 1972–79.

Savage Model 420 Over-and-Under Shotgun
Boxlock. Hammerless. Takedown. Automatic safety. Double triggers or non-selective single trigger. Gauges: 12, 16, 20. Barrels: plain; 26- to 30-inch (the latter in 12 gauge only); choked M/F, C/IC. Weight with 28-inch bar-

Savage Model 420 Over-and-Under (cont.)
rels: 12 ga., 7¾ lbs.; 16 ga., 7½ lbs.; 20 ga., 6¾ lbs. Plain pistol-grip stock and forearm. Made 1938–1942.
With double triggers **$495**
With single trigger **575**

Savage Model 430
Same as Model 420, except has matted top barrel, checkered stock of select walnut with recoil pad, checkered forearm. Made 1938–1942.
With double triggers **$550**
With single trigger **600**

Savage Model 440 Over-and-Under Shotgun ... $475
Boxlock. Plain extractors. Selective single trigger. Gauges: 12, 20. 2¾-inch chambers in 12 gauge, 3-inch in 20 gauge. Barrels: vent rib; 26-inch SK choke, IC/M; 28-inch M/F; 30-inch M/F choke (12 ga. only). Weight: average 6 to 6½ pounds depending on gauge. Made 1968–1972.

Savage Model 440T Trap Gun $465
Similar to Model 440, except only in 12 gauge with 30-inch barrels, extra-wide vent rib, IM/F choke. Trap-style Monte Carlo stock and semibeavertail forearm of select walnut, recoil pad. Weight: 7½ pounds. Made 1969–1972.

SHOTGUNS

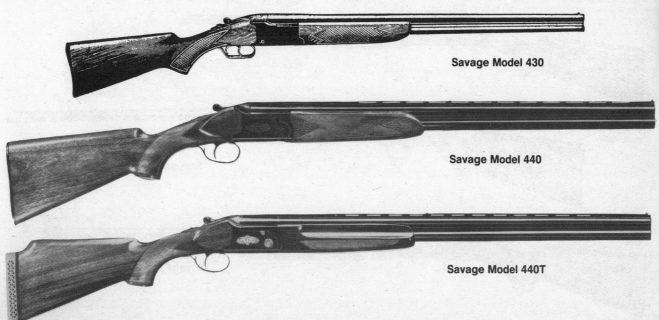

Savage Model 430

Savage Model 440

Savage Model 440T

Savage Model 550

Savage Model 444 Deluxe Over/Under Shotgun .. **$525**
Similar to Model 440, except has auto ejectors, select walnut stock and semibeavertail forearm. Made 1969–1972.

Savage Model 550 Hammerless Double **$225**
Boxlock. Auto ejectors. Non-selective single trigger. Gauges: 12, 20. 2³/₄-inch chamber in 12 gauge, 3-inch in 20 gauge. Barrels: vent rib; 26-inch IC/M; 28-inch M/F; 30-inch M/F choke (12 ga. only). Weight: 7 to 8 lbs. Checkered pistol-grip stock and semibeavertail forearm. Made 1971–73.

**Savage Model 720 Standard Grade 5-Shot
Autoloading Shotgun** **$250**
Browning type. Takedown. 12 and 16 gauge. 4-shell tubular magazine. Barrel: plain; 26- to 32-inch (the latter in 12 gauge only); choked C, M, F. Weight: about 8¹/₄ pounds, 12 ga. with 30-inch barrel; 16 ga., about ¹/₂ pound lighter. Checkered pistol-grip stock and forearm. Made 1930–1949.

**Savage Model 726 Upland Sporter Grade 3-Shot
Autoloading Shotgun** **$240**
Same as Model 720, except has 2-shell magazine capacity. Made 1931–1949.

Savage Model 740C Skeet Gun **$295**
Same as Model 726, except has special skeet stock and full beavertail forearm, equipped with Cutts Compensator, barrel length overall with spreader tube is about 24¹/₂ inches. Made 1936–1949.

Savage Model 745 Lightweight Autoloader **$210**
Three- or five-shot model. Same general specifications as Model 720, except has lightweight alloy receiver, 12 gauge only, 28-inch plain barrel. Weight: about 6³/₄ pounds. Made 1940–49.

Savage Model 750 Automatic Shotgun **$210**
Browning-type autoloader. Takedown. 12 gauge. 4-shot tubular magazine. Barrels: 28-inch F or M choke; 26-inch IC. Weight: about 7¹/₄ pounds. Checkered walnut pistol-grip stock and grooved forearm. Made 1960–67.

Savage Model 750-AC **$275**
Same as Model 750, except has 26-inch barrel with adjustable choke. Made 1964–67.

Savage Model 750-SC **$250**
Same as Model 750, except has 26-inch barrel with Savage Super Choke. Made 1962–63.

**Savage Model 755 Standard Grade
Autoloader** **$210**
Streamlined receiver. Takedown. 12 and 16 gauge. 4-shell tubular magazine (a three-shot model with magazine capacity of two shells was also produced until 1951). Barrel: plain; 30-inch F choke (12 ga. only), 28-inch F or M, 26-inch IC. Weight: about 8¹/₄ pounds, 12 ga. Checkered pistol-grip stock and forearm. Made 1949–1958.

Savage Model 755-SC **$200**
Same as Model 755, except has 26-inch barrel with recoil-reducing, adjustable Savage Super Choke.

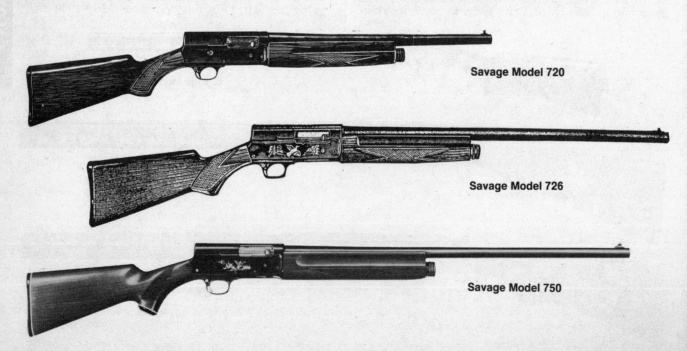

Savage Model 720

Savage Model 726

Savage Model 750

Savage Model 775

Savage Model 775-SC

Savage Model 2400
Over/Under Combination

Savage Model 775 Lightweight **$210**
Same general specifications as Model 755, except has lightweight alloy receiver and weighs about 6¾ pounds. Made 1950–1965.

Savage Model 775-SC **$215**
Same as Model 775, except has 26-inch barrel with Savage Super Choke.

Savage Model 2400 Over/Under Combination . . **$595**
Boxlock action similar to that of Model 330. Plain extractors. Selective single trigger. 12-gauge (2¾-inch chamber) shotgun barrel, Full choke, over 308 Win. or 222 Rem. rifle barrel; 23½-inch; solid matted rib with blade front sight and folding leaf rear, dovetail for scope mounting. Weight: about 7½ pounds. Monte Carlo stock with pistol grip and recoil pad, semibeavertail forearm, checkered. Made 1975–79 by Valmet.

=== **SEARS, ROEBUCK & COMPANY** ===
Chicago, Illinois
J. C. Higgins and Ted Williams Models

Although they do not correspond to specific models below, the names Ted Williams and J. C. Higgins have been used to designate various Sears shotguns at various times.

Sears Model 18 Bolt Action Repeater **$80**
Takedown. 3-shot top-loading magazine. Gauge: .410 only. Barrel: 25-inch with variable choke. Weight: about 5¾ pounds.

Sears Model 20 Slide Action Repeater **$160**
Hammerless. 5-shot magazine. Barrels: 26- to 30-inch with various chokes. Weight: 7¼ pounds. Plain pistol-grip stock and slide handle.

Sears Model 21 Slide Action Repeater **$185**
Same general specifications as the Model 20 except vent rib and adjustable choke.

Sears Model 30 Slide Action Repeater **$175**
Hammerless. Gauges: 12, 16, 20 and .410. 4-shot magazine. Barrels: 26- to 30-inch, various chokes. Weight: 6½ pounds. Plain pistol-grip stock, grooved slide handle.

Sears Model 97 Single Shot Shotgun **$65**
Takedown. Visible hammer. Automatic ejector. Gauges: 12, 16, 20 and .410. Barrels: 26- to 36-inch, Full choke. Weight: average 6 pounds. Plain pistol-grip stock and forearm.

Sears Model 97-AC Single Shot Shotgun **$80**
Same general specifications as Model 97 except fancier stock and forearm.

Sears Model 101.7 Double Barrel Shotgun **$160**
Boxlock. Double triggers. Gauges: 12, 16, 20, .410. Barrels: 26- to 32-inch, choked M and F. Weight: from 6 to 7½ pounds. Plain stock and forend.

Sears Model 101.7C Double Barrel Shotgun **$175**
Same general specifications as Model 101.7, except checkered stock and forearm.

Sears Model 101.25 Bolt Action Shotgun **$80**
Takedown. .410 gauge. 5-shell tubular magazine. 24-inch barrel, Full choke. Weight: about 6 pounds. Plain, one-piece pistol-grip stock.

Sears Model 101.40 Single Shot Shotgun **$65**
Takedown. Visible hammer. Automatic ejector. Gauges: 12, 16, 20 and .410. Barrels: 26- to 36-inch, Full choke. Weight: average 6 pounds. Plain pistol-grip stock and forearm.

Sears Model 101.1120 Bolt Action Repeater **$80**
Takedown. .410 gauge. 24-inch barrel, Full choke. Weight: about 5 pounds. Plain one-piece pistol-grip stock.

Sears Model 101.1380 Bolt Action Repeater **$90**
Takedown. Gauges: 12, 16, 20. 2-shell detachable box magazine. 26-inch barrel, Full choke. Weight: about 7 pounds. Plain one-piece pistol-grip stock.

Sears Model 101.1610 Double Barrel Shotgun . . **$235**
Boxlock. Double triggers. Plain extractors. Gauges: 12, 16, 20 and .410. Barrels: 24- to 30-inch. Various chokes,

SHOTGUNS

Sears Model 101.1610 Double Barrel (cont.)
but mostly M and F. Weight: about 7¹/₂ pounds, 12 ga.
Checkered pistol-grip stock and forearm.

Sears Model 101.1701 Double Barrel Shotgun . . **$245**
Same general specifications as Model 101.1610 except
satin chrome frame and select walnut stock and forearm.

Sears Model 101.5350-D Bolt Action Repeater . . . **$80**
Takedown. Gauges: 12, 16, 20. 2-shell detachable box
magazine. 26-inch barrel, Full choke. Weight: about 7¹/₄
pounds. Plain one-piece pistol-grip stock.

Sears Model 101.5410 Bolt Action Repeater **$80**
Same general specifications as Model 101.5350-D.

Sears Model 103.720 Bolt Action Repeater **$75**
Takedown. Automatic thumb safety. .410 gauge. 24-inch
barrel, Full choke. Weight: about 5 pounds. Plain pistol-
grip stock.

Sears Model 103.740 Bolt Action Repeater **$75**
Same general specifications as Model 103.720.

Sears Model 200 Slide Action Repeater **$165**
Front-locking rotary bolt. Takedown. 4-shot magazine.
Gauges: 12, 16 and 20. Barrel: plain or vent rib. Weight:
6¹/₂ to 7¹/₄ pounds. Checkered pistol grip and forearm.

Sears Model 300 Autoloading Shotgun **$195**
Gas-operated. Front-locking rotary bolt. Takedown. 2-
shot magazine. Gauges: 12, 16, 20. Barrel: plain or vent
rib. Various chokes. Weight: 6¹/₂ to 7¹/₂ pounds. Checkered
pistol-grip stock and forearm, recoil pad.

Sears Model 5100 Double Barrel Shotgun **$150**
Boxlock. Double triggers. Gauges: 12, 16, 20, .410. Barrels:
26- to 32-inch, various chokes. Weight: 6 to 7¹/₂ pounds.

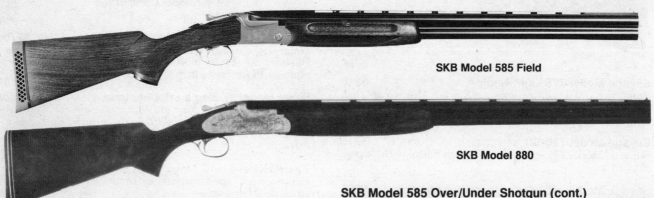

SKB Model 585 Field

SKB Model 880

SKB ARMS COMPANY
Tokyo, Japan
**Imported since 1987 by G.U. Inc., Omaha, NE;
formerly by Ithaca Gun Co., Ithaca, NY**

SKB Models 300 and 400 Side-by-Side Doubles
Similar to Model 200E, except higher grade. Models 300
and 400 differ in that the latter has more elaborate en-
graving and fancier wood.
Model 300 . . . . **$595**
Model 400 . . . . **795**

SKB Model 400 Skeet **$825**
Similar to Model 200E Skeet, except higher grade with
more elaborate engraving and full fancy wood.

SKB Model 480 English **$850**
Similar to Model 280 English, except higher grade with
more elaborate engraving and full fancy wood.

SKB Model 500 Small Gauge O/U Shotgun **$565**
Similar to Model 500, except gauges 28 and .410; has 28-
inch vent-rib barrels, M/F chokes. Weight: about 6¹/₂
pounds.

SKB Model 585 Over/Under Shotgun
Boxlock. Gauges: 12, 20, 28 and .410; 2³/₄-or 3-inch chambers. Barrels: 26-, 28-, 30-, 32- or 34-inch with vent rib;
fixed chokes or Inter-choke tubes. Weight: 6¹/₂ to 8¹/₂
pounds. Single selective trigger. Selective automatic ejec-

SKB Model 585 Over/Under Shotgun (cont.)
tors. Manual safety. Checkered walnut stock in standard
or Monte Carlo style. Silver nitride finish with engraved
game scenes. Made 1987 to date.
Field, Skeet, Trap Grade . . . . **$ 750**
Field Grade, Two-barrel Set **1395**
Skeet Set (20, 28, .410 ga.) **1895**
Sporting Clays **825**
Trap Combo, Two-barrel Set **1350**

SKB Model 600 Small Gauge **$650**
Same as Model 500 Small Gauge, except higher grade with
more elaborate engraving and fancier wood.

SKB Model 685 Over/Under
Similar to the 585 Deluxe, except with semi-fancy Amer-
ican walnut stock. Gold trigger and jeweled barrel block.
Silvered receiver with fine engraving.
Field, Skeet, Trap Grade . . . . **$ 850**
Field Grade, Two-barrel Set **1495**
Skeet Set **1995**
Sporting Clays **895**
Trap Combo, Two-barrel Set **1450**

SKB Model 800 Skeet/Trap Over/Under
Similar to Model 700 Skeet and Trap, except higher grade
with more elaborate engraving and fancier wood.
Model 800 Skeet **$825**
Model 800 Trap **850**

SKB Model 880 Skeet/Trap
Similar to Model 800 Skeet, except has sideplates.
Model 880 Skeet **$1095**
Model 880 Trap **1125**

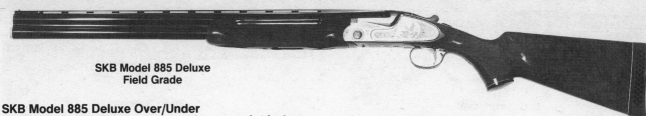

**SKB Model 885 Deluxe
Field Grade**

SKB Model 885 Deluxe Over/Under

Similar to the 685 Deluxe, except with engraved sideplates.

Field, Skeet, Trap Grade	$ 995
Field Grade, Two-barrel Set	1550
Skeet Set	2595
Sporting Clays	1025
Trap Combo, Two-barrel Set	1495

NOTE: The following SKB shotguns were distributed by Ithaca Gun Co. 1966–1976. For specific data, please see corresponding listings under Ithaca.

SKB Century Single Barrel Trap Gun

The SKB catalog does not differentiate between Century and Century II; however, specifications of current Century are those of Ithaca-SKB Century II.

Century	$495
Century II	595

SKB Gas-operated Automatic Shotguns

Model XL300 with plain barrel	$250
Model XL300 with vent rib	275
Model XL900	295
Model XL900 Trap	350
Model XL900 Skeet	345
Model XL900 Slug	290
Model 1300 Upland, Slug	365
Model 1900 Field, Trap, Slug	415

SKB Over/Under Shotguns

Model 500 Field	$ 505
Model 500 Magnum	525
Model 600 Field	575
Model 600 Magnum	585
Model 600 Trap	595
Model 600 Doubles	595
Model 600 Skeet—12 or 20 gauge	590
Model 600 Skeet—28 or .410	595
Model 600 Skeet Combo	1795
Model 600 English	595
Model 700 Trap	775
Model 700 Doubles	775
Model 700 Skeet	775
Model 700 Skeet Combo	1895

SKB Recoil-operated Automatic Shotguns

Model 300—with plain barrel	$215
Model 300—with vent rib	235
Model 900	275
Model 900 Slug	255

SKB Side-by-Side Double Barrel Shotguns

Model 100	$385
Model 150	395
Model 200E	525
Model 200E Skeet	550
Model 280 English	630

SHOTGUNS

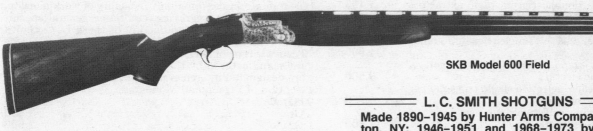

SKB Model 600 Field

L. C. Smith Crown

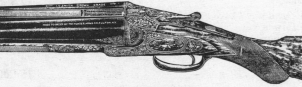

L. C. Smith Field

L. C. SMITH SHOTGUNS

Made 1890–1945 by Hunter Arms Company, Fulton, NY; 1946–1951 and 1968–1973 by Marlin Firearms Company, New Haven, CT

L. C. Smith Double Barrel Shotguns

Values shown are for L. C. Smith doubles made by Hunter. Those of 1946–1951 Marlin manufacture generally bring prices about 1/3 lower. Smaller gauge models, especially in the higher grades, command premium prices: up to 50 percent more for 20 gauge, up to 200 percent for .410 gauge.

Crown Grade, double triggers, automatic ejectors	$ 4,500
Crown Grade, selective single trigger, automatic ejectors	4,800
Deluxe Grade, selective single trigger, automatic ejectors	14,995
Field Grade, double triggers, plain extractors	995
Field Grade, double triggers, auto ejectors	1,100
Field Grade, non-selective single trigger, plain extractors	1,025
Field Grade, selective single trigger, automatic ejectors	1,495

L. C. Smith Ideal

L. C. Smith Monogram

L. C. Smith Olympic

L. C. Smith Premier

L. C. Smith Double Barrel Shotguns (cont.)

Ideal Grade, double triggers, plain extractors .. **1,195**

Ideal Grade, double triggers, automatic
ejectors.................................. **1,650**

Ideal Grade, selective single trigger, automatic
ejectors................................. **1,900**

Monogram Grade, selective single trigger,
automatic ejectors **9,500**

Olympic Grade, selective single trigger,
automatic ejectors **1,750**

Premier Grade, selective single trigger,
automatic ejectors **11,500**

L. C. Smith Skeet

L. C. Smith Specialty

L. C. Smith Trap

L. C. Smith Double Barrel Shotguns (cont.)

Skeet Special, non-selective single trigger,
automatic ejectors .... **$ 1,695**

Skeet Special, sel. single trigger, auto
ejectors.................................. **1,950**

.410 Gauge **12,000**

Specialty Grade, double triggers, auto ejectors . **2,495**

Specialty Grade, selective single trigger,
automatic ejectors **2,695**

Trap Grade, sel. single trigger, auto ejectors .. **1,295**

L. C. Smith Hammerless Double Barrel Shotguns

Sidelock. Auto ejectors standard on higher grades, extra on Field and Ideal Grades. Double triggers or Hunter single trigger (non-selective or selective). Gauges: 12, 16, 20, .410. Barrels: 26- to 32-inch, any standard boring. Weight: $6^1/_2$ to $8^1/_4$ pounds, 12 ga. Checkered stock and forend; choice of straight, half or full pistol grip, beavertail or standard-type forend. Grades differ only in quality of workmanship, wood, checkering, engraving, etc. Same general specifications apply to all. Manufacture of these L. C. Smith guns was discontinued in 1951. Production of Field Grade 12 gauge was resumed 1968–1973. *Note:* L. C. Smith Shotguns manufactured by the Hunter Arms Co. 1890–1913 were designated by numerals to indicate grade, with the exception of Pigeon and Monogram.

00 Grade	**$ 995**
0 Grade	**1,350**
1 Grade	**1,500**
2 Grade	**1,750**
3 Grade	**2,550**
Pigeon	**2,850**
4 Grade	**5,850**
5 Grade	**5,750**
Monogram	**8,500**
A1	**3,500**
A2	**8,400**
A3	**+15,000**

L. C. Smith Model 1968
Field Grade

L. C. Smith Hammerless Double Model 1968

Field Grade **$595**

"Re-creation" of the original L. C. Smith double. Sidelock. Plain extractors. Double triggers. 12 gauge. 28-inch vent-

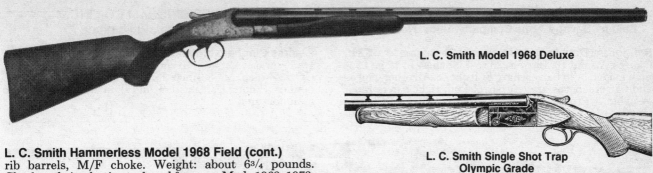

L. C. Smith Model 1968 Deluxe

L. C. Smith Single Shot Trap Olympic Grade

L. C. Smith Hammerless Model 1968 Field (cont.)
rib barrels, M/F choke. Weight: about 6³/₄ pounds. Checkered pistol-grip stock and forearm. Made 1968–1973.

L. C. Smith Hammerless Double Model 1968 Deluxe **$625**
Same as 1968 Field Grade, except has Simmons floating vent rib, beavertail forearm. Made 1971–73.

L. C. Smith Single Shot Trap Guns
Boxlock. Hammerless. Auto ejector. 12 gauge only. Barrel lengths: 32- or 34-inch. Vent rib. Weight: 8 to 8¹/₄ pounds. Checkered pistol-grip stock and forend, recoil pad. Grades vary in quality of workmanship, wood, engraving, etc.; general specifications are the same. Discont. 1951. *Note:*

L. C. Smith Single Shot Trap Guns (cont.)
Values shown are for L. C. Smith single barrel trap guns made by Hunter. Those of Marlin manufacture generally bring prices about one-third lower.

Olympic Grade	$ 1275
Specialty Grade	1595
Crown Grade	2995
Monogram Grade	4350
Premier Grade	7000
Deluxe Grade	11,995

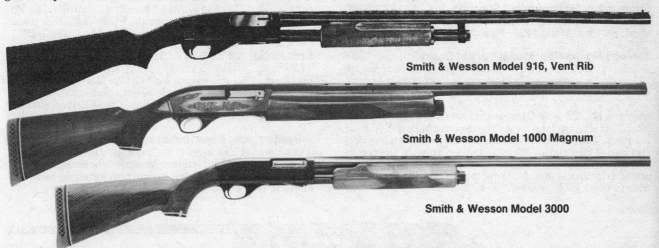

Smith & Wesson Model 916, Vent Rib

Smith & Wesson Model 1000 Magnum

Smith & Wesson Model 3000

SMITH & WESSON SHOTGUNS
Springfield, Massachusetts
Mfd. by Howa Machinery, Ltd., Nagoya, Japan

In 1985 Smith and Wesson sold its shotgun operation to O. F. Mossberg & Sons, Inc.

Smith & Wesson Model 916 Slide Action Repeater
Hammerless. Solid frame. Gauges: 12, 16, 20. 3-inch chamber in 12 and 20 gauge. 5-shot tubular magazine. Barrels: plain or vent rib; 20-inch C (12 ga., plain only); 26-inch IC; 28-inch M or F; 30-inch F choke (12 ga. only). Weight: with 28-inch plain barrel, 7¹/₄ pounds. Plain pistol-grip stock, fluted slide handle. Made 1972–1981.

With plain barrel	**$145**
With ventilated-rib barrel	**175**

Smith & Wesson Model 916T
Same as Model 916, except takedown, 12 gauge only. Not available with 20-inch barrel. Made 1976–1981.

With plain barrel	**$165**
With ventilated-rib barrel	**195**

Smith & Wesson Model 1000 Autoloader **$315**
Gas-operated. Takedown. Gauges: 12, 20. 2³/₄-inch chamber in 12 ga., 3-inch in 20 ga. 4-shot magazine. Barrels: vent rib; 26-inch SK choke, IC; 28-inch M or F; 30-inch F choke (12 ga. only). Weight: with 28-inch barrel, 6¹/₂ lbs. in 20 ga., 7¹/₂ lbs. in 12 ga. Checkered pistol-grip stock and forearm. Made 1972 to date.

Smith & Wesson Model 1000 Magnum **$375**
Same as standard Model 1000, except chambered for 12 gauge magnum, 3-inch shell; 30-inch barrel only, M or F choke; stock with recoil pad. Weight: about 8 pounds. Introduced in 1977.

Smith & Wesson Model 1000P **$295**
Same general specifications as Model C 3000 Slide Action, but an earlier version.

Smith & Wesson Model 3000 Slide Action **$275**
Hammerless. 20-gauge. Barrels: 26-inch IC; 28-inch M or F. Chambered for 3-inch magnum and 2³/₄-inch loads. American walnut stock and forearm. Checkered pistol grip and forearm. Intro. 1982.

SHOTGUNS

SPRINGFIELD ARMS
Built by Savage Arms Company, Utica, New York

Springfield Double-Barrel Hammer Shotgun **$295**
Gauges: 12 and 16. Barrels: 28 to 32 inches. In 12 ga., 32-inch model, both barrels have Full choke. All other gauges and barrel lengths are left barrel Full, right barrel Mod. Weight: 7¼ to 8¼ lbs., depending on gauge and barrel length. Black walnut checkered buttstock and forend. Discontinued 1934.

J. STEVENS ARMS COMPANY
Chicopee Falls, Massachusetts
Division of Savage Arms Corporation

Stevens No. 20 "Favorite" Shotgun **$350**
Calibers: 22 and 32 Shot. Smoothbore barrel. Blade front sight; no rear. Made 1893–1939.

Stevens No. 39 New Model Pocket Shotgun **$525**
Gauge: .410. Calibers: 38-40 Shot, 44-40 Shot. Barrels: 10, 12, 15 or 18 inches, half-octagonal smoothbore. Shotgun sights. Made 1895–1906.

Stevens No. 22-.410 Over-and-Under Combination Gun
22 caliber rifle barrel over .410 bore shotgun barrel. Visible hammer. Takedown. Single trigger. 24-inch barrels, shotgun barrel Full choke. Weight: about 6 pounds. Open rear sight and ramp front sight of sporting rifle type. Plain pistol-grip stock and forearm; originally supplied with walnut stock and forearm. "Tenite" (plastic) was used in

SQUIRES BINGHAM CO., INC.
Makati, Rizal, Philippines

Squires Bingham Model 30 Pump Shotgun **$150**
Hammerless. 12 gauge. 5-shot magazine. Barrels: 20-inch Cyl.; 28-inch M; 30-inch Full choke. Weight: about 7 pounds. Pulong Dalaga stock and slide handle. Currently manufactured.

**Squires Bingham Model 30
Pump Shotgun**

Stevens No. 22-.410 Over/Under Combo (cont.)
later production. Made 1938–1950. *Note:* This gun is now manufactured as the Savage Model 24.
With wood stock and forearm **$175**
With Tenite stock and forearm **140**

Stevens Model 51 Bolt Action Shotgun **$80**
Single shot. Takedown. .410 gauge. 24-inch barrel, Full choke. Weight: about 4¾ pounds. Plain one-piece pistol-grip stock, checkered on later models. Made 1962–1971.

Stevens Model 58 Bolt Action Repeater **$95**
Takedown. Gauges: 12, 16, 20. 2-shell detachable box magazine. 26-inch barrel, Full choke. Weight: about 7¼ pounds. Plain one-piece pistol-grip stock. Made 1933–1981. *Note:* Later production models have 3-inch chamber in 20 gauge, checkered stock with recoil pad.

Stevens Model 58-.410 Bolt Action Repeater **$85**
Takedown. .410 gauge. 3-shell detachable box magazine. 24-inch barrel, Full choke. Weight: about 5½ pounds. Plain one-piece pistol-grip stock, checkered on later production. Made 1937–1981.

Stevens Model 51

Stevens Model 58

Stevens Model 58-410

Stevens Model 59

Stevens Model 59 Bolt Action Repeater **$125**
Takedown. .410 gauge. 5-shell tubular magazine. 24-inch
barrel, Full choke. Weight: about 6 pounds. Plain, one-
piece pistol-grip stock, checkered on later production.
Made 1934–1973.

Stevens Model 67 Pump Shotgun
Hammerless, side-ejection solid steel receiver. Gauges: 12,
20 and .410; 2³/₄- or 3-inch shells. Barrels: 21-, 26-, 28-,
30-inch with fixed chokes or interchangeable choke tubes;
plain or vent rib. Weight: 6¹/₄ to 7¹/₂ pounds. Optional
rifle sights. Walnut-finished hardwood stock with corn
cob-style forend.

Standard Model, Plain Barrel	**$180**
Standard Model, Vent Rib	215
Standard Model, w/Choke Tubes	225
Slug Model, w/Rifle Sights	195
Lobo Model, Matte Finish	205
Youth Model, 20 ga.	175
Camo Model, w/Choke Tubes	250

Stevens Model 67 Waterfowl Shotgun **$225**
Hammerless. Gauge: 12. 3-shot tubular magazine. Walnut
finished hardwood stock. Weight: about 7¹/₂ pounds. Made
1972–1989.

Stevens Model 77 Slide Action Repeater **$210**
Solid frame. Gauges: 12, 16, 20. 5-shot tubular magazine.
Barrels: 26-inch IC; 28-inch M or F choke. Weight: about
7¹/₂ pounds. Plain pistol-grip stock with recoil pad, grooved
slide handle. Made 1954–1971.

Stevens Model 77-AC **$225**
Same as Model 77, except has Savage Super Choke.

Stevens Model 79-VR Super Value **$215**
Hammerless, side ejection. Barrel: chambered for 2³/₄-inch
and 3-inch mag. shells. 12, 20, and .410 gauge. vent rib.
Walnut finished hardwood stock with checkering on grip.
Weight: 6³/₄-7 pounds. Made 1979 to date.

Stevens Model 94 Single Shot Shotgun **$100**
Takedown. Visible hammer. Auto ejector. Gauges: 12, 16,
20, 28, .410. Barrels: 26-, 28-, 30-, 32-, 36-inch; Full choke.
Weight: about 6 pounds depending on gauge and barrel.
Plain pistol-grip stock and forearm. Made 1939–1961.

Stevens Model 94C **$125**
Same as Model 94, except has checkered stock, fluted
forearm on late production. Made 1965 to date.

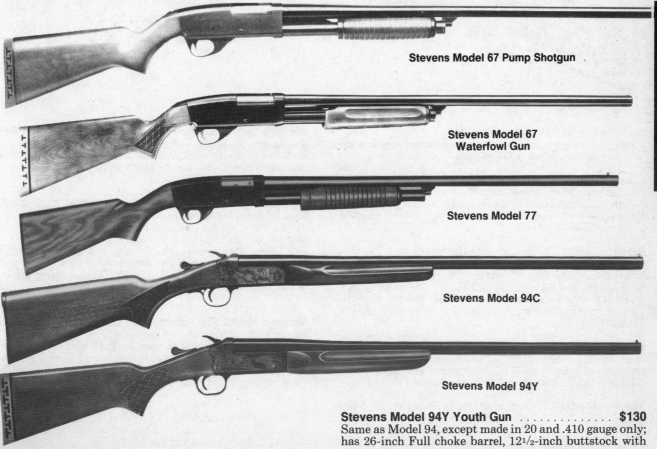

Stevens Model 67 Pump Shotgun

Stevens Model 67 Waterfowl Gun

Stevens Model 77

Stevens Model 94C

Stevens Model 94Y

SHOTGUNS

Stevens Model 94Y Youth Gun **$130**
Same as Model 94, except made in 20 and .410 gauge only;
has 26-inch Full choke barrel, 12¹/₂-inch buttstock with

Stevens Model 95

Stevens Model 107

Stevens Model 124

Stevens Model 258

Stevens Model 311-R

Stevens Model 94Y Youth Gun (cont.)
recoil pad; checkered pistol grip and fluted forearm on late production. Made 1959 to date.

Stevens Model 95 Single Shot Shotgun **$90**
Solid frame. Visible hammer. Plain extractor. 12 gauge. 3-inch chamber. Barrels: 28-inch M; 30-inch Full choke. Weight: about 7¼ pounds. Plain pistol-grip stock, grooved forearm. Made 1965–69.

Stevens Model 107 Single Shot Hammer Shotgun **$85**
Takedown. Auto ejector. Gauges: 12, 16, 20, .410. Barrel lengths: 28- and 30-inch (12 and 16 ga.), 28-inch (20 ga.), 26-inch (.410); Full choke only. Weight: about 6 pounds, 12 bore ga. Plain pistol-grip stock and forearm. Made about 1937–1953.

Stevens Model 124 Cross Bolt Repeater **$140**
Hammerless. Solid frame. 12 gauge only. 2-shot tubular magazine. 28-inch barrel; IC, M or F choke. Weight: about 7 pounds. Tenite stock and forearm. Made 1947–1952.

Stevens Model 240 Over-and-Under Shotgun . . . **$495**
Visible hammer. Takedown. Double triggers. .410 gauge. 26-inch barrels, Full choke. Weight: 6 lbs. Tenite (plastic) pistol-grip stock and forearm. Made 1940–49.

Stevens Model 258 Bolt Action Repeater **$95**
Takedown. 20-gauge. 2-shell detachable box magazine. 26-inch barrel, Full choke. Weight: about 6¼ pounds. Plain one-piece pistol-grip stock. Made 1937–1965.

Stevens Model 311-R Hammerless Double **$245**
Same general specifications as Stevens-Springfield Model 311 except compact design for law enforcement use. Barrels: 18¼-inch 12 gauge with solid rib, chambered for 2¾- and 3-inch Mag. shells. Double triggers and auto top tang safety. Walnut finished hardwood stock with recoil pad and semibeavertail forend. Weight: about 6¾ pounds. Made 1982–89.

Stevens Model 530 Hammerless Double **$265**
Boxlock. Double triggers. Gauges: 12, 16, 20, .410. Barrel lengths: 26- to 32-inch; choked M/F, C/M, F/F. Weight: 6 to 7½ pounds depending on gauge and barrel length. Checkered pistol-grip stock and forearm; some early models with recoil pad. Made 1936–1954.

Stevens Model 530M **$230**
Same as Model 530, except has Tenite (plastic) stock and forearm. Discontinued about 1947.

Stevens Model 530ST

Stevens Model 620

Stevens Model 530ST Double Gun $250
Same as Model 530, except has non-selective single trigger.
Discontinued.

Stevens Model 620 Hammerless Slide Action
Repeating Shotgun $215
Takedown. Gauges: 12, 16, 20. 5-shell tubular magazine.
Barrel lengths: 26-, 28-, 30-, 32-inch; choked F, M, IC, C.
Weight: about 7^{3}/$_{4}$ lbs., 12 ga.; 7^{1}/$_{4}$ lbs., 16 ga.; 6 lbs., 20
ga. Checkered pistol-grip stock and slide handle. Made
1927–1953.

Stevens Model 621 .... $265
Same as Model 620, except has raised solid matted-rib
barrel. Discontinued.

Stevens Model 820 Hammerless Slide Action
Repeating Shotgun $200
Solid frame. 12 gauge only. 5-shell tubular magazine. 28-
inch barrel; IC, M or F choke. Weight: about 7^{1}/$_{2}$ pounds.
Plain pistol-grip stock, grooved slide handle. Made 1949–
1954.

Stevens Model 820-SC $225
Same as Model 820, except has Savage Super Choke.

Stevens Model 940 Single Barrel Shotgun $85
Same general specifications as Model 94, except has side
lever opening instead of top lever. Made 1961–1970.

Stevens Model 940Y Youth Gun $90
Same general specifications as Model 94Y, except has side
lever opening instead of top lever. Made 1961–1970.

Stevens Model 9478 .... $95
Takedown. Visible hammer. Automatic ejector. Gauges:
12, 20, .410. Barrels: 26-, 28-, 30-, 36-inch; Full choke.
Weight: average 6 pounds depending on gauge and barrel.
Plain pistol-grip stock and forearm. Made 1978–1985.

Stevens-Springfield Model 311 Hammerless Double
Same general specifications as Stevens Model 530, except
earlier production has plain stock and forearm; checkered
on current guns. Originally produced as a "Springfield"
gun, this model became a part of the "Stevens" line in
1948 when the "Springfield" brand name was discontinued. Made 1931–1989.
Pre-WW II $325
Post-WW II 295

SHOTGUNS

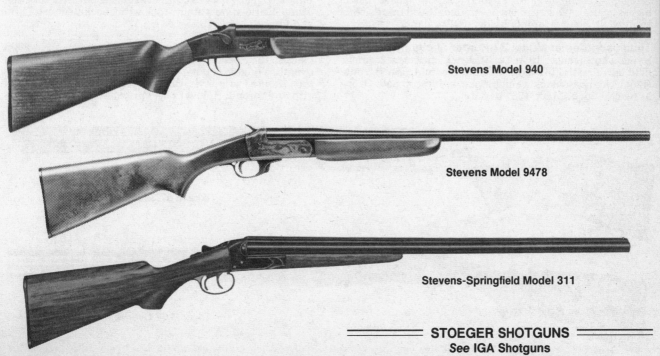

Stevens Model 940

Stevens Model 9478

Stevens-Springfield Model 311

STOEGER SHOTGUNS
See IGA Shotguns

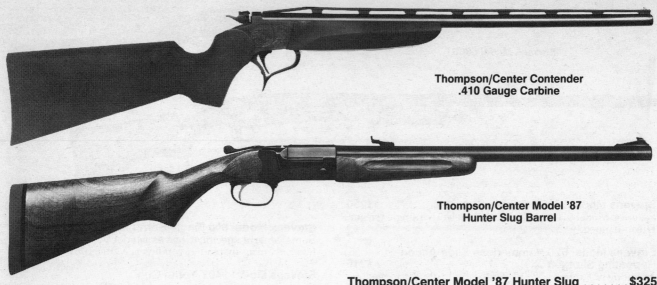

Thompson/Center Contender
.410 Gauge Carbine

Thompson/Center Model '87
Hunter Slug Barrel

TECNI-MEC SHOTGUNS
Italy

Tecni-Mec Model SPL 640 Folding Shotgun **$345**
Gauges: 12, 16, 20, 24, 28, 32 and .410 bore. 26-inch barrel.
Chokes: IC/IM Weight: 6½ pounds. Checkered walnut
pistol grip stock and forend. Engraved receiver. Available
with double triggers. Made 1988 to date.

THOMPSON/CENTER ARMS
Rochester, New Hampshire

Thompson/Center Contender .410 Ga. Carbine . . **$315**
Gauge: .410 smoothbore. 21-inch vent-rib barrel. 34³/₄
inches overall. Weight: about 5¼ pounds. Bead front sight.
Rynite® stock and forend. Made 1991 to date.

Thompson/Center Model '87 Hunter Shotgun **$355**
Single shot. Gauge: 10 or 12; 3½-inch chamber. 25-inch
field barrel with Full choke. Weight 8 pounds. Bead front
sight. American black walnut stock with recoil pad. Drop
at heel ⁷/₈ inch. Made 1987 to date.

Thompson/Center Model '87 Hunter Slug **$325**
Gauge: 10 (3½-inch chamber) or 12 (3-inch chamber).
Same general specifications as Model '87 Hunter Shotgun,
except with 22-inch slug (rifled) barrel and rifle sights.
Made 1987 to date.

TIKKA SHOTGUNS
Manufactured by Armi Marocchi of Italy; formerly by Valmet. Imported by Stoeger Industries, Inc., Wayne, New Jersey

Tikka M 07 Shotgun/Rifle Combination **$795**
Gauge/caliber: 12/222 Rem. Shotgun barrel: about 25
inches; rifle barrel: about 22³/₄ inches. 40²/₃ inches overall.
Weight: about 7 pounds. Dovetailed for telescopic sight.
Single trigger with selector between the barrels. Vent rib.
Monte Carlo-style walnut stock with checkered pistol grip
and forend. Made 1965–1987.

Tikka M 77 Over/Under Shotgun **$995**
Gauge: 12. 27-inch vent-rib barrels. Approx. 44 inches
overall. Weight: about 7¼ pounds. Barrel selector. Ejectors. Monte Carlo-style walnut stock with checkered pistol
grip and forend; rollover cheekpiece. Made 1977–1987.

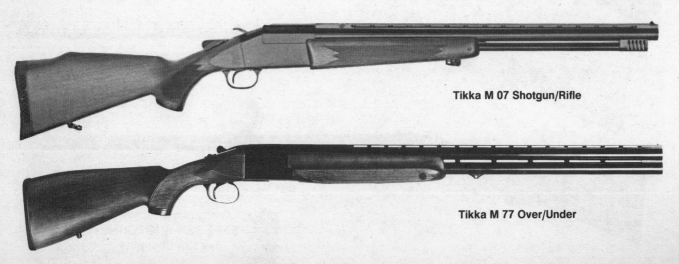

Tikka M 07 Shotgun/Rifle

Tikka M 77 Over/Under

Tikka Model 412S Over/Under
Field Grade

Tikka M 77K Shotgun/Rifle Combination **$1050**
Gauge: 12/70. Calibers: 222 Rem., 5.6×52r5, 6.5×55, 7×57r5, 7×65r5, 308 Win. Vent-rib barrels: about 25 inches (shotgun); almost 23 inches (rifle). 42.3 inches overall. Weight: about 7½ pounds. Double triggers. Monte Carlo-style walnut stock with checkered pistol grip and forend; rollover cheekpiece. Made 1977–1986.

Tikka Model 412S Over/Under
Gauge: 12; 3-inch chambers. 24-, 26-, 28- or 30-inch blued chrome-lined barrels with five integral stainless steel choke tubes. Weight: 7¼ to 7½ pounds. Matte nickel receiver. Select American walnut stock with checkered pistol grip and forend. (Same as the former Valmet Model 412.) Manufactured in Italy by arrangement with Marocchi from 1990 to date.
Field Model **$850**
Sporting Clays Model 925

SHOTGUNS OF ULM
Ulm, West Germany
See listings under Krieghoff.

U.S. REPEATING ARMS CO.
New Haven, Connecticut
See Winchester Shotgun listings.

VALMET OY
Jyväskylä, Finland

See also Savage Models 330, 333T, 333 and 2400, which are Valmet guns.

Valmet Lion Over-and-Under Shotgun **$385**
Boxlock. Selective single trigger. Plain extractors. 12 gauge only. Barrels: 26-inch IC/M; 28-inch M/F; 30-inch M/F, F/F. Weight: about 7 pounds. Checkered pistol-grip stock and forearm. Made 1947–1968.

Valmet Model 412 K Over/Under Field Shotgun . . . **$615**
Hammerless. 12-gauge, 3-inch chamber. 36-inch barrel, F/F chokes. Amer. walnut Monte Carlo stock. Made 1982–87.

Valmet Model 412 K Shotgun/Rifle Combination . . **$795**
Similar to Model 412 K, except bottom barrel chambered for either 222 Rem., 223 Rem., 243 Win., 308 Win. or 30-06. 12-gauge shotgun barrel with IM choke. Monte Carlo American walnut stock, recoil pad.

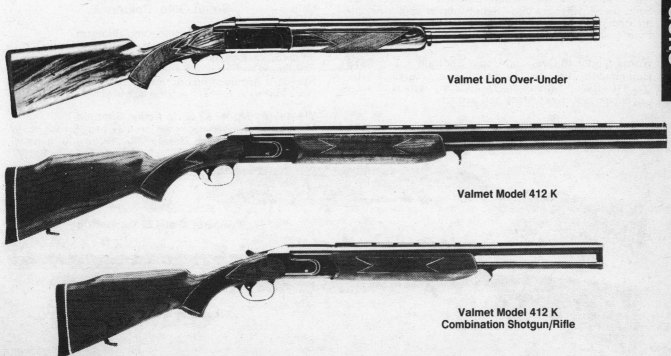

Valmet Lion Over-Under

Valmet Model 412 K

Valmet Model 412 K
Combination Shotgun/Rifle

SHOTGUNS

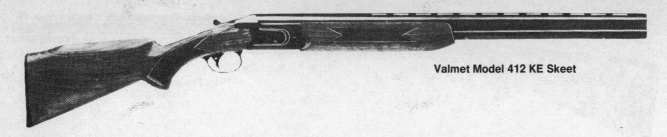

Valmet Model 412 KE Skeet

Valmet Model 412 KE Over/Under Field Shotgun . . **$625**
12-gauge chambered for 2³/₄-inch shells; 26-inch barrel, IC/
M chokes; 28-inch barrel, M/F chokes; 12-gauge chambered
for 3-inch shells, 30-inch barrel, M/F chokes. 20-gauge (3-
inch shells); 26-inch barrel IC/M chokes; 28-inch barrel, M/
F chokes. American walnut Monte Carlo stock.

Valmet Model 412 KE Skeet **$685**
Similar to Model 412 K, except Skeet stock and chokes. 12
and 20 gauges. Discontinued 1989.

Valmet Model 412 KE Trap **$695**
Similar to Model 412 K Field, except trap stock, recoil pad.
30-inch barrels, IM/F chokes. Discontinued 1989.

Valmet 3-Barrel Set **$1795**

MONTGOMERY WARD
Chicago, Illinois
Western Field and Hercules Models

Although they do not correspond to specific models below,
the names Western Field and Hercules have been used to
designate various Montgomery Ward shotguns at various
times.

Wards Model 25 Slide Action Repeater **$150**
Solid frame. 12 gauge only. 5-shot tubular magazine. 28-
inch barrel, various chokes. Weight: about 7¹/₂ pounds.
Plain pistol-grip stock, grooved slide handle.

Wards Model 40 Over-and-Under Shotgun **$575**
Hammerless. Boxlock. Double triggers. Gauges: 12, 16,
20, .410. Barrels: plain; 26- to 30-inch, various chokes.
Checkered pistol-grip stock and forearm.

Wards Model 40N Slide Action Repeater **$165**
Same general specifications as Model 25.

Wards Model 172 Bolt Action Shotgun **$85**
Takedown. 2-shot detachable clip magazine. 12 gauge. 28-
inch barrel with variable choke. Weight: about 7¹/₂ pounds.
Monte Carlo stock with recoil pad.

Wards Model 550A Slide Action Repeater **$215**
Takedown. Gauges: 12, 16, 20, .410. 5-shot tubular magazine. Barrels: plain, 26- to 30-inch, various chokes.
Weight: 6 to 8 pounds. Plain pistol-grip stock and grooved
slide handle.

Wards Model SB300 Double Barrel Shotgun **$230**
Same general specifications as Model SD52A.

Wards Model SB312 Double Barrel Shotgun **$250**
Boxlock. Double triggers. Plain extractors. Gauges: 12,
16, 20, .410. Barrels: 24- to 30-inch. Various chokes.
Weight, about 7¹/₂ pounds in 12 gauge. Checkered pistol-
grip stock and forearm.

Wards Model SD52A Double Barrel Shotgun . . . **$195**
Boxlock. Double triggers. Gauges: 12, 16, 20, .410. Barrels:
26- to 32-inch, various chokes. Weight: 6 to 7¹/₂ pounds.

WEATHERBY, INC.
South Gate, California

Weatherby Model 82 Autoloading Shotgun
Hammerless, gas-operated. 12 gauge only. Barrels: 22- to
30-inch, various integral chokes. Weight: 7¹/₂ pounds.
Checkered walnut stock and forearm. Made 1982–89.
Standard Autoloading Shotgun **$355**
BuckMaster Auto Slug w/rifle sights (1986–90) . . **375**

Weatherby Model 92 Slide Action Shotgun
Hammerless, short-stroke action. 12 gauge; 3-inch chamber. Tubular magazine. Barrels: 22-, 26-, 28-, 30-inch with

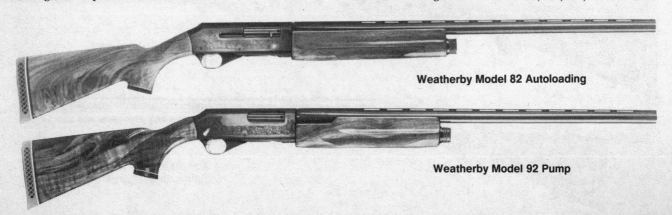

Weatherby Model 82 Autoloading

Weatherby Model 92 Pump

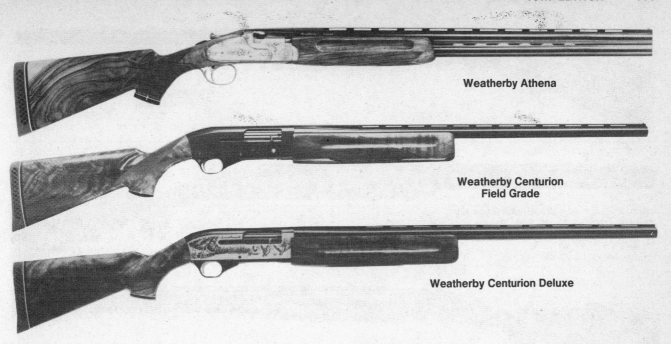

Weatherby Athena

Weatherby Centurion Field Grade

Weatherby Centurion Deluxe

Weatherby Model 92 Slide Action Shotgun (cont.)
fixed choke or IMC choke tubes; plain or vent rib with rifle sights. Weight: 7½ pounds. Engraved, matte black receiver and blued barrel. Checkered high-gloss buttstock and forend. Imported from Japan since 1982.

Standard Model 92	**$275**
BuckMaster Pump Slug w/rifle sights (intro. 1986)	295

Weatherby Athena Over/Under Shotgun
Engraved boxlock action with Greener crossbolt and sideplates. Gauges: 12, 20, 28 and .410; 2¾- or 3½-inch chambers. Barrels: 26-, 28-, 30- or 32-inch with fixed or IMC Multi-choke tubes. Weight: 6¾ to 7⅜ pounds. Single selective trigger. Selective auto ejectors. Top tang safety. Checkered Claro walnut stock and forearm with high-luster finish. Made 1982 to date.

Field Model w/IMC Multi-choke (12 or 20 ga.)	**$1150**
Field Model w/Fixed Chokes (28 or .410 ga.)	1295
Skeet Model w/Fixed Chokes (12 or 20 ga.)	1275
Skeet Model w/Fixed Chokes (28 or .410 ga.)	1425
Master Skeet Tube Set	2195
Trap Model w/IMC Tubes	1250
Grade V	1595

Weatherby Centurion Automatic Shotgun
Gas-operated. Takedown. 12 gauge. 2¾-inch chamber. 3-shot magazine. Barrels: vent ribs; 26-inch SK, IC or M; 28-inch M or F; 30-inch Full choke. Weight: with 28-inch barrel, 7 lbs. 10½ oz. Checkered pistol-grip stock and forearm, recoil pad. Made in Japan 1972–1981.

Weatherby Centurion Automatic Shotgun (cont.)

Centurion Field Grade	**$295**
Centurion Trap Gun (30-inch Full choke bbl.)	320
Centurion Deluxe (etched receiver, fancy grade wood, made 1972 to date)	360

Weatherby Ducks Unlimited Shotgun $525

Weatherby Orion Over/Under Shotgun
Boxlock with Greener crossbolt. Gauges: 12, 20, 28 and .410; 2¾- or 3-inch chambers. Barrels: 26-, 28, 30-, 32- or 34-inch with fixed or IMC Multi-choke tubes. Weight: 6½ to 9 pounds. Single selective trigger. Selective auto ejectors. Top tang safety. Checkered, high-gloss pistol-grip Claro walnut stock and forearm. Finish: Grade I, plain blued receiver; Grade II, engraved blued receiver; Grade III, silver gray receiver. Made 1982 to date.

Orion I Field w/IMC (12 or 20 ga.)	**$750**
Orion II Field w/IMC (12 or 20 ga.)	825
Orion III Field w/IMC (12 or 20 ga.)	850
Skeet II w/Fixed Chokes	895
Sporting Clays II	925
Trap II	900

Weatherby Patrician Slide Action Shotgun
Hammerless. Takedown. 12 gauge. 2¾-inch chamber. 4 shot tubular magazine. Barrels: vent rib; 26-inch, SK, IC, M; 28-inch, M, F; 30-inch, Full choke. Weight: with 28-

Weatherby Orion

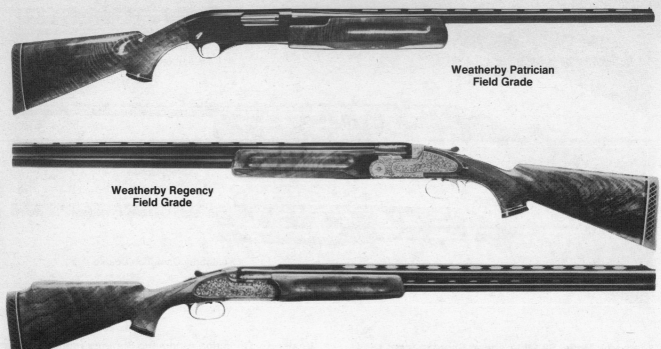

Weatherby Patrician Field Grade

Weatherby Regency Field Grade

Weatherby Regency Trap

Weatherby Patrician Slide Action Shotgun (cont.)
inch barrel, 7 lbs. 7 oz. Checkered pistol-grip stock and slide handle, recoil pad. Made in Japan 1972–1982.
Patrician Field Grade **$235**
Patrician Deluxe (etched receiver, fancy grade
   wood) **275**
Patrician Trap Gun (30-inch Full choke bbl.) **250**

Weatherby Regency Field Grade O/U Shotgun . . . **$750**
Boxlock with sideplates, elaborately engraved. Auto ejectors. Selective single trigger. Gauges: 12, 20. 2¾-inch chamber in 12 gauge, 3-inch in 20 gauge. Barrels: vent rib; 26-inch SK, IC/M, M/F (20 ga. only); 28-inch SK, IC/M, M/F; 30-inch M/F (12 ga. only). Weight with 28-inch barrels: 7 lbs. 6 oz., 12 ga.; 6 lbs. 14 oz., 20 ga. Checkered pistol-grip stock and forearm of fancy walnut. Made in Italy 1965–1982.

Weatherby Regency Trap Gun **$775**
Similar to Regency Field Grade, except has trap-style stock with straight or Monte Carlo comb. Barrels have vent side ribs and high, wide vent top rib; 30- or 32-inch, M/F, IM/ F or F/F chokes. Weight: with 32-inch barrels, 8 pounds. Made in Italy 1965–1982.

WESTERN ARMS CORP.
Ithaca, New York
Division of Ithaca Gun Company

Western Long Range

Western Long Range Hammerless Double
Boxlock. Plain extractors. Single or double triggers. Gauges: 12, 16, 20, .410. Barrels: 26- to 32-inch, M/F choke standard. Weight: 7½ pounds, 12 ga. Plain pistol-grip stock and forend. Made 1929–1946.
With double triggers **$250**
With single trigger **325**

WESTERN AUTO SHOTGUNS
Kansas City, Missouri

Revelation Model 300H Slide Action Repeater . . **$195**
Gauges: 12, 16, 20, .410. 4-shot tubular magazine. Barrels: 26- to 30-inch, various chokes. Weight: about 7 pounds. Plain pistol-grip stock, grooved slide handle.

Revelation Model 310A Slide Action Repeater . . **$195**
Takedown. 12 gauge. 5-shot tubular magazine. Barrels: 28- and 30-inch. Weight: about 7½ pounds. Plain pistol-grip stock.

Revelation Model 310B Slide Action Repeater . . **$165**
Same general specifications as Model 310A except chambered for 16 gauge.

Revelation Model 310C Slide Action Repeater . . **$200**
Same general specifications as Model 310A except chambered for 20 gauge.

Revelation Model 310E Slide Action Repeater . . **$200**
Same general specifications as Model 310A except chambered for .410 bore.

Revelation Model 325BK Bolt Action Repeater . . . **$80**
Takedown. 2-shot detachable clip magazine. 20 gauge. 26-inch barrel with variable choke. Weight: 6¼ pounds.

WESTERN FIELD SHOTGUNS
See "W" for listings under Montgomery Ward.

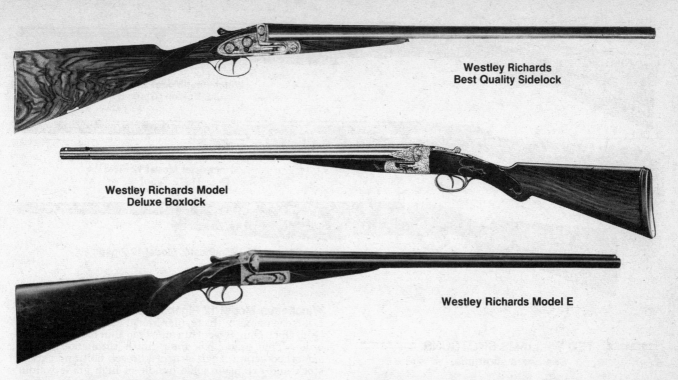

**Westley Richards
Best Quality Sidelock**

**Westley Richards Model
Deluxe Boxlock**

Westley Richards Model E

WESTLEY RICHARDS & CO., LTD.
Birmingham, England

The Pigeon and Wildfowl Gun, available in all of the Westley Richards models except the Ovundo, has the same general specifications as the corresponding standard field gun, except has magnum action of extra strength and treble bolting; chambered for 12 gauge only (2³/₄- or 3-inch); 30-inch Full choke barrels standard. Weight: about 8 pounds. The manufacturer warns that 12-gauge magnum shells should not be used in their standard weight double barrel shotguns.

Westley Richards Best Quality Boxlock Hammerless Double Barrel Shotgun
Boxlock. Hand-detachable locks and hinged cover plate. Selective ejectors. Double triggers or selective single trigger. Gauges: 12, 16, 20. Barrel lengths and boring to order. Weight: 5¹/₂ to 6¹/₄ pounds depending on gauge and barrel length. Checkered stock and forend, straight or half-pistol grip. Also supplied in Pigeon and Wildfowl Model with same values. Made from 1899 to date.
With double triggers **$10,500**
With selective single trigger **11,595**

Westley Richards Best Quality Sidelock Hammerless Double Barrel Shotgun
Hand-detachable sidelocks. Selective ejectors. Double triggers or selective single trigger. Gauges: 12, 16, 20, 28, .410. Barrel lengths and boring to order. Weight: 4³/₄ to 6³/₄ pounds depending on gauge and barrel length. Checkered stock and forend, straight or half-pistol grip. Also supplied in Pigeon and Wildfowl Model with same values. Currently manufactured.
With Double Triggers **$18,995**
With Selective Single Trigger. **20,000**

Westley Richards Model Deluxe Boxlock Hammerless Double Barrel Shotgun
Same general specifications as standard Best Quality gun, except higher quality throughout. Has Westley Richards

Westley Richards Deluxe Boxlock Hammerless (cont.)
top-projection and treble-bite lever-work, hand-detachable locks. Also supplied in Pigeon and Wildfowl Model with same values. Currently manufactured.
With double triggers . . . . **$ 8,950**
With selective single trigger **10,000**

**Westley Richards Model
Deluxe Sidelock**

Westley Richards Model Deluxe Sidelock
Same as Best Quality Sidelock, except higher grade engraving and wood. Currently manufactured.
With Double Triggers **$20,000**
With Single Trigger **24,000**

Westley Richards Model E Hammerless Double
Anson & Deeley-type boxlock action. Selective ejector or non-ejector. Double triggers. Gauges: 12, 16, 20. Barrel lengths and boring to order. Weight: 5¹/₂ to 7¹/₄ pounds depending on type, gauge and barrel length. Checkered stock and forend, straight or half-pistol grip. Also supplied in Pigeon and Wildfowl Model with same values. Currently manufactured.
Ejector model **$3795**
Non-ejector model **3300**

Westley Richards Ovundo (Over/Under) **$14,995**
Hammerless. Boxlock. Hand-detachable locks. Dummy sideplates. Selective ejectors. Selective single trigger. 12 gauge. Barrel lengths and boring to order. Checkered stock/forend, straight or half-pistol grip. Mfd. before WW II.

SHOTGUNS

Winchester Model 12 Classic
Ltd. Edition (Grade I)

Winchester Model 12 Field
(1972 Type)

Winchester Model 12 Pigeon

TED WILLIAMS SHOTGUNS
See Sears shotguns.

WINCHESTER SHOTGUNS
New Haven, Connecticut

Formerly Winchester Repeating Arms Co. Now mfd. by Winchester-Western Div., Olin Corp., and by U.S. Repeating Arms Co.

Winchester Model 12 Classic Limited Edition
Gauge: 20; 2³/₄-inch chamber. Barrel: 26-inch vent rib; IC. Weight: 7 pounds. Checkered walnut buttstock and forend. Polished blue finish (Grade I) or engraved with gold inlays (Grade IV). Made 1993 to date.
Grade I (4000) .... $ 660
Grade IV (1000) 950

Winchester Model 12 Featherweight $450
Same as Plain Barrel Model 12 Standard, except has alloy guard, modified takedown. 12 gauge only. Barrels: 26-inch IC; 28-inch M or F; 30-inch F choke. Weight: about 6³/₄ pounds. Made 1959–1962.

Winchester Model 12 Field Gun, 1972 Type $575
Same general specifications as Standard Model 12. 12 gauge only. 26-, 28- or 30-inch vent-rib barrel, standard chokes. Engine-turned bolt and carrier. Hand-checkered stock/slide handle of semi-fancy walnut. Made 1972–75.

Winchester Model 12 Heavy Duck Gun $695
12 gauge only, chambered for 3-inch shells. Same general specifications as Standard Grade, except 30- or 32-inch plain Full choke barrel only, 3-shot magazine, recoil pad. Weight: about 8³/₄ pounds. Discont. 1964.

Winchester Model 12 Heavy Duck Gun, Matte Rib ... $850
Same as Plain Barrel Model 12 Heavy Duck Gun, except has solid raised matted rib. Discont. 1959.

Winchester Model 12 Pigeon Grade
Deluxe versions of the regular Model 12 Standard or Field Gun, Duck Gun, Skeet Gun and Trap Gun made on special order. This grade has finer finish throughout, hand-smoothed action, engine-turned breech bolt and carrier, stock and extension slide handle of high grade walnut, fancy checkering, stock dimensions to individual specifications. Engraving and carving available at extra cost ranging from about $35 to over $200. Discont. 1965.
Field Gun, plain barrel **$1150**
Field Gun, vent rib **1395**
Skeet Gun, matted rib **1450**
Skeet Gun, vent rib **1595**
Skeet Gun, Cutts Compensator **995**
Trap Gun, matted rib **1350**
Trap Gun, vent rib **1425**

Winchester Model 12 Riot Gun $595
Same general specifications as Plain Barrel Model 12 Standard, except has 20-inch cylinder bore barrel, 12 gauge only. Made 1918–1963.

Winchester Model 12 Skeet Gun $850
Gauges: 12, 16, 20, 28. 5-shot tubular magazine. 26-inch matted rib barrel, SK choke. Weight: about 7³/₄ lbs., 12 ga.; 6³/₄ lbs., other gauges. Bradley red or ivory bead front sight. Winchester 94B middle sight. Checkered pistol-grip stock and extension slide handle. Discont. after WWII.

Winchester Model 12 Skeet Gun, Cutts Compensator ... $750
Same general specifications as standard Model 12 Skeet Gun, except has plain barrel fitted with Cutts Compensator, 26 inches overall. Discont. 1954.

Winchester Model 12 Skeet Gun, Plain Barrel .. $745
Same general specifications as standard Model 12 Skeet Gun, except has plain barrel. Made 1937–1947.

Winchester Model 12 Skeet Gun, Vent Rib $1095
Same general specifications as standard Model 12 Skeet Gun, except has 26-inch barrel with vent rib, 12 and 20 gauge. Discontinued in 1965.

Winchester Model 12 Skeet Gun, 1972 Type ... $725
Same gen. specifications as Standard Model 12. 12 ga. only. 26-inch vent-rib barrel, SK choke. Engine-turned

Winchester Model 12 Skeet Gun, 1972 Type (cont.)

bolt and carrier. Hand-checkered skeet-style stock and slide handle of choice walnut, recoil pad. Made 1972–75.

Winchester Model 12 Standard Gr., Matted Rib . $750

Same general specifications as Plain Barrel Model 12 Standard, except has solid raised matted rib. Discontinued after World War II.

Winchester Model 12 Standard Gr., Vent Rib ... $825

Same general specifications as Plain Barrel Model 12 Standard, except has vent rib. 26³/₄- or 30-inch barrel, 12 gauge only. Discont. after World War II.

Winchester Model 12 Standard Slide Action Repeater

Hammerless. Takedown. Gauges: 12, 16, 20, 28. 6-shell tubular magazine. Plain barrel. Lengths: 26- to 32-inches; choked F to Cyl. Weight: about 7¹/₂ lbs., 12 ga. 30-inch; 6¹/₂ lbs. in other gauges with 28-inch barrel. Plain pistol-grip stock, grooved slide handle. Made 1912–1964.

28 gauge	$2995
12-ga., 28-inch barrel (Full)	595
Other gauges, etc.	575

Winchester Model 12 Super Pigeon Grade $1995

Custom version of Model 12 with same general specifications as standard models. 12 gauge only. 26-, 28- or 30-inch vent-rib barrel, any standard choke. Engraved receiver. Hand-smoothed and fitted action. Full fancy walnut stock and forearm made to individual order. Made 1965–1972.

Winchester Model 12 Trap Gun

Same general specifications as standard Model 12, except has straighter stock, checkered pistol grip and extension slide handle, recoil pad, 30-inch matted-rib barrel, F choke, 12 gauge only. Discont. after World War II; vent-rib model discontinued 1965.

Matted-rib barrel	$850
With straight stock, vent rib	950
With Monte Carlo stock, vent rib	995

Winchester Model 12 Trap Gun, 1972 Type $695

Same general specifications as Standard Model 12. 12 gauge only. 30-inch vent-rib barrel, Full choke. Engine-turned bolt and carrier. Hand-checkered trap-style stock (straight or Monte Carlo comb) and slide handle of select walnut, recoil pad. Intro. in 1972. Discont.

Winchester Model 20 Single Shot Hammer Gun .. $395

Takedown. .410 bore. 2¹/₂-inch chamber. 26-inch barrel, Full choke. Checkered pistol-grip stock and forearm. Weight: about 6 pounds. Made 1919–1924.

Winchester Model 21 Custom, Pigeon, Grand American

Since 1959, the Model 21 has been offered only in deluxe models: Custom, Pigeon, Grand American—on special order. General specifications same as for Model 21 standard models, except these custom guns have full fancy American walnut stock and forearm with fancy checker-

Winchester Model 12 Skeet
(1972 Type)

Winchester Model 12
Standard

Winchester Model 12
Super Pigeon Trap

Winchester Model 12 Trap
(1972 Type)

Winchester Model 20

Winchester Model 21 Grand American

Winchester Model 21 Pigeon

Winchester Model 21 Field

Winchester Model 24

Winchester Model 25 Repeater

Winchester Model 21 Custom, Pigeon, Gr. Amer. (cont.)

ing, finely polished and hand-smoothed working parts, etc.; engraving inlays, carved stocks and other extras are available at additional cost. Made 1960 to date.

Custom Grade	$ 5,500
Pigeon Grade	7,500
Grand American	16,500

Winchester Model 21 Double Barrel Field Gun

Hammerless. Boxlock. Automatic safety. Double triggers or selective single trigger, selective or non-selective ejection (all postwar Model 21 shotguns have selective single trigger and selective ejection). Gauges: 12, 16, 20. Barrels: raised matted rib or vent rib; 26-, 28-, 30-, 32-inch, the latter in 12 gauge only; F, IM, M, IC, SK chokes. Weight: 7½ pounds, 12 ga. w/30-inch barrel; about 6½ pounds, 16 or 20 ga. w/28-inch barrel. Checkered pistol- or straight-grip stock, regular or beavertail forend. Made 1930–1958.

With double trigger, non-selective ejection	$2795
With double trigger, selective ejection	2995
With selective single trigger, non-selective ejection	3250
With selective single trigger, selective ejection	3400
Extra for vent rib	500

Winchester Model 21 Duck Gun

Same general specifications as Model 21 Field Gun, except chambered for 12 gauge 3-inch shells, 30- or 32-inch barrels only, Full choke, selective single trigger, selective ejection, pistol-grip stock with recoil pad, beavertail forearm, both checkered. Discont. 1958.

With matted-rib barrels	$2995
With vent-rib barrels	3250

Winchester Model 21 Skeet Gun

Same general specifications as Model 21 Standard, except has 26- or 28-inch barrels only, SK chokes No. 1 and 2, Bradley red bead front sight, selective single trigger, selective ejection, nonauto safety, checkered pistol- or straight-grip stock without buttplate or pad (wood butt

Winchester Model 21 Skeet Gun (cont.)

checkered), checkered beavertail forearm. Discont. 1958.

With matted-rib barrels	$3600
With vent-rib barrels	4200

Winchester Model 21 Trap Gun

Same general specifications as Model 21 Standard, except has 30- or 32-inch barrels only, Full choke, selective single trigger, selective ejection, nonauto safety, checkered pistol- or straight-grip stock with recoil pad, checkered beavertail forearm. Discont. 1958.

With matted-rib barrels	$3575
With vent-rib barrels	4200

Winchester Model 23 Side-by-Side Shotgun

Boxlock. Single trigger. Automatic safety. Gauges: 12, 20, 28, .410. Barrels: 25½-, 26-, 28-inch with fixed chokes or Winchoke tubes. Weight: 5⅞ to 7 pounds. Checkered American walnut buttstock and forend. Made 1979 to date for Olin at its Olin-Kodensha facility, Japan.

Classic 23—Gold inlay, Engraved	$1450
Custom 23—Plain receiver, Winchoke system	850
Heavy Duck 23—Standard	1225
Lightweight 23—Classic Style	1215
Light Duck 23—Standard	1150
Light Duck 23—12 ga. Golden Quail	1350
Light Duck 23—.410 Golden Quail	2195
Custom Set 23—20 & 28 gauge	3560

Winchester Model 24 Hammerless Double $495

Boxlock. Double triggers. Plain extractors. Auto safety. Gauges: 12, 16, 20. Barrels: 26-inch IC/M; 28-inch M/F (also IC/M in 12 ga. only); 30-inch M and F in 12 ga. only. Weight: about 7½ pounds, 12 ga. Metal bead front sight. Plain pistol-grip stock, semibeavertail forearm. Made 1939–1957.

Winchester Model 25 Riot Gun $350

Same as Model 25 Standard, except has 20-inch cylinder bore barrel, 12 gauge only. Made 1949–1955.

Winchester Model 25 Slide Action Repeater $395

Hammerless. Solid frame. 12 gauge only. 4-shell tubular magazine. 28-inch plain barrel; IC, M or F choke. Weight:

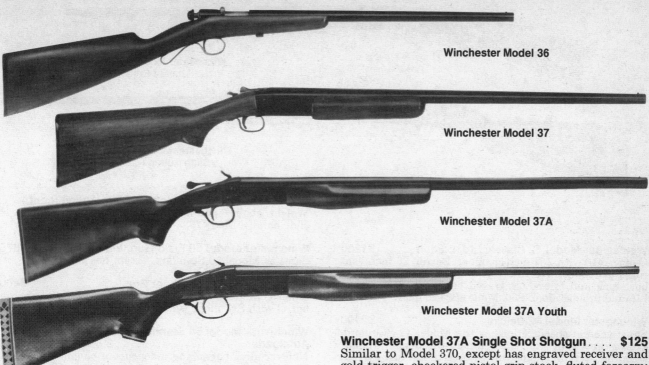

Winchester Model 36

Winchester Model 37

Winchester Model 37A

Winchester Model 37A Youth

Winchester Model 25 Slide Action Repeater (cont.)
about 7½ pounds. Metal bead front sight. Plain pistol-grip stock, grooved slide handle. Made 1949–1955.

Winchester Model 36 Single Shot Bolt Action . . . $295
Takedown. Uses 9mm Short or Long shot or ball cartridges interchangeably. 18-inch barrel. Plain stock. Weight: about 3 pounds. Made 1920–27.

Winchester Model 37 Single Shot Shotgun
Semi-hammerless. Auto ejection. Takedown. Gauges: 12, 16, 20, 28, .410. Barrel lengths: 28-, 30-, 32-inch in all gauges except .410; 26- or 28-inch in .410; all barrels plain with Full choke. Weight: about 6½ pounds, 12 ga. Made 1937–1963.

12 Gauge	$225
28 Gauge	825
Other Gauges	150

Winchester Model 37A Single Shot Shotgun $125
Similar to Model 370, except has engraved receiver and gold trigger, checkered pistol-grip stock, fluted forearm; 16 gauge available with 30-inch barrel only. Made 1973–1980.

Winchester Model 37A Youth $135
Similar to Model 370 Youth, except has engraved receiver and gold trigger, checkered pistol-grip stock, fluted forearm. Made 1973–1980.

Winchester Model 40 Skeet Gun $795
Same general specifications as Model 40 Standard, except has 24-inch plain barrel with Cutts Compensator, checkered forearm and pistol grip, grip cap. Made 1940–41.

Winchester Model 40 Standard Autoloader $545
Streamlined receiver. Hammerless. Takedown. 12 gauge only. 4-shell tubular magazine. 28- or 30-inch barrel; M or F choke. Weight: about 8 pounds. Bead sight on ramp. Plain pistol-grip stock, semibeavertail forearm. Made 1940–41.

Winchester Model 41 Single Shot Bolt Action . . . $525
Takedown. .410 bore. 2½-inch chamber (chambered for 3-inch shells after 1932). 24-inch barrel, Full choke. Plain straight stock standard. Made 1920–1934.

SHOTGUNS

Winchester Model 40 Skeet

Winchester Model 41

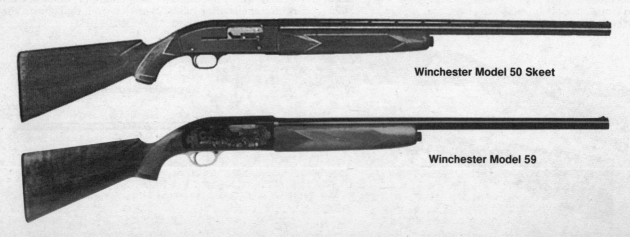

**Winchester Model 42 Classic
Limited Edition**

**Winchester Model 42 Standard
Slide Action Repeater**

Winchester Model 42 Standard Slide Action (cont.)
Weight: about 6 pounds. Plain pistol-grip stock; grooved slide handle. Made 1933–1963.

Winchester Model 42 Classic Ltd. Edition **$1250**
Gauge: .410 with 2³/₄-inch chamber. Barrel: 26-inch vent rib; Full choke. Weight: 7 pounds. Checkered walnut buttstock and forend. Engraved blue with gold inlays. Limited production of 850. Made 1993 to date.

Winchester Model 42 Deluxe **$2100**
Same general specifications as the Model 42 Standard, except has vent rib, finer finish throughout, hand-smoothed action, engine-turned breech bolt and carrier, stock and extension slide handle of high grade walnut, fancy checkering, stock dimensions to individual specifications. Engraving and carving were offered at extra cost. Made 1933–1963.

Winchester Model 42 Skeet Gun **$1750**
Same general specifications as Model 42 Standard, except has checkered straight or pistol-grip stock and extension slide handle, 26- or 28-inch matted-rib barrel, SK choke. *Note:* Some Model 42 Skeet Guns are chambered for 2¹/₂-inch shells only. Discont. 1963.

Winchester Model 42 Standard Grade, Matt Rib **$1495**
Same general specifications as Plain Barrel Model 42, except has solid raised matted rib. Discont. 1963.

Winchester Model 42 Standard Slide Action Repeating Shotgun **$995**
Hammerless. Takedown. .410 bore (3- or 2¹/₂-inch shell). Tubular magazine holds five 3-inch or six 2¹/₂-inch shells. 26- or 28-inch plain barrel; cylinder bore, M or F choke.

Winchester Model 50 Field Gun, Vent Rib **$375**
Same as Model 50 Standard, except has vent rib.

Winchester Model 50 Skeet Gun **$460**
Same as Model 50 Standard, except has 26-inch vent-rib barrel with SK choke, skeet-style stock of select walnut.

Winchester Model 50 Standard Grade Autoloader **$350**
Non-recoiling barrel and independent chamber. Gauges: 12 and 20. 2-shot tubular magazine. Barrels: 12 ga.—26-, 28-, 30-inch; 20 ga.—26-, 28-inch; IC, SK, M, F choke. Checkered pistol-grip stock and forearm. Weight: about 7³/₄ pounds. Made 1954–1961.

Winchester Model 50 Trap Gun **$475**
Same as Model 50 Standard, except 12 gauge only, has 30-inch vent-rib barrel with F choke, Monte Carlo stock of select walnut.

Winchester Model 59 Autoloading Shotgun **$435**
12 gauge. Magazine holds two shells. Alloy receiver. Win-Lite steel and fiberglass barrel: 26-inch IC, 28-inch M or F choke, 30-inch F choke; also furnished with 26-inch barrel with Versalite choke (interchangeable F, M, IC tubes; one supplied with gun). Weight: about 6¹/₂ pounds. Checkered pistol-grip stock and forearm. Made 1959–1965.

Winchester Model 97 Riot Gun **$595**
Takedown or solid frame. Same general specifications as standard Model 97, except 12 gauge only, 20-inch cylinder bore barrel. Made 1897–1957.

Winchester Model 50 Skeet

Winchester Model 59

**Winchester Model 97
Visible Hammer**

Winchester Model 97 Trap, Tournament and Pigeon

These higher grade models offer higher overall quality than the standard grade. Discont. 1939.

Trap Gun **$695**
Tournament Grade 995
Pigeon Grade 995

Winchester Model 97 Trench Gun **$1495**

Solid frame. Same as Model 97 Riot Gun, except has handguard and is equipped with a bayonet. World War I government issue, 1917–1918.

Winchester Model 97 Visible Hammer Slide Action Repeating Shotgun **$425**

Standard Grade. Takedown or solid frame. Gauges: 12 and 16. 5-shell tubular magazine. Barrel: plain; 26 to 32 inches, the latter in 12 ga. only; choked F to Cyl. Weight: about 7¾ pounds (12 ga./28-inch barrel). Plain pistol-grip stock, grooved slide handle. Made 1897–1957.

> **NOTE:** All Winchester Model 101s were mfd. for Olin Corp. at its Olin-Kodensha facility in Tochigi, Japan. Production for Olin Corp. stopped in Nov. 1987. Importation of Model 101s was continued by Classic Doubles under that logo until 1990. *See* separate heading for additional data.

Winchester Model 101 Diamond Grade Target . . **$1350**

Similar to Model 101 Standard except silvered frame and Winchoke interchangeable choke tubes. Made 1981–1990.

Winchester Model 101 Field Gun Over/Under

Boxlock. Engraved receiver. Auto ejectors. Single selective trigger. Combination barrel selector and safety. Gauges: 12

Winchester Model 101 Field Gun Over/Under (cont.)

and 28, 2¾-inch chambers; 20 and .410, 3-inch chambers. Vent-rib barrels: 30- (12 ga. only) and 26½-inch, IC/M. Weight: 6¼ to 7¾ pounds depending on gauge and barrel length. Hand-checkered French walnut stock and forearm. Made 1963–1981; gauges other than 12 intro. 1966.

12 and 20 gauge **$695**
28 and .410 gauge 875

Winchester Model 101 Grand European **$1295**

Similar to Model 101 Pigeon Grade except silvered frame and Winchoke interchangeable choke tubes. Made 1981–1987.

Winchester Model 101 Magnum Field Gun **$710**

Same as Model 101 Field Gun, except chambered for 12 or 20 ga. 3-inch magnum shells only, 30-inch barrels (F/F or M/F), recoil pad. Made 1966–1981.

Winchester Model 101 Pigeon Grade

Same general specifications as standard Model 101 Field and Skeet, except higher grade with more elaborately engraved satin gray steel receiver, fancier wood and finer checkering. 12 and 20 gauge only. Made 1974–1981.

Field Gun . . . . **$ 995**
Skeet Gun 1125
Trap Gun with straight stock 1140
Trap Gun with Monte Carlo stock 1175

Winchester Model 101 Quail Special— Small Frame **$1595**

Same specifications as Model 101 in small-frame. Calibers: 28 and .410 ga.; 3-inch chambers. 25½-inch barrels with choke tubes (28 ga.) or M/F chokes (.410). Imported from Japan in 1987.

SHOTGUNS

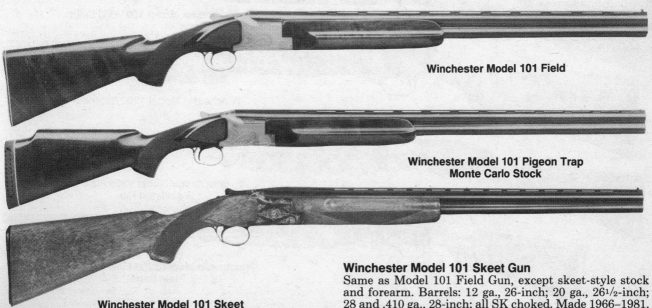

Winchester Model 101 Field

**Winchester Model 101 Pigeon Trap
Monte Carlo Stock**

Winchester Model 101 Skeet

Winchester Model 101 Skeet Gun

Same as Model 101 Field Gun, except skeet-style stock and forearm. Barrels: 12 ga., 26-inch; 20 ga., 26½-inch; 28 and .410 ga., 28-inch; all SK choked. Made 1966–1981.

Winchester Model 370

Winchester Model 101 Skeet Gun (cont.)
12 and 20 gauge **$795**
28 and .410 gauge . . . . , . . . 810

Winchester Model 101 Waterfowl **$1025**
Similar to Model 101 Magnum Field, except silvered frame and Winchoke interchangeable choke tubes. Made 1981 to date.

Winchester Model 370 Single Shot Shotgun **$95**
Visible hammer. Auto ejector. Takedown. Gauges: 12, 16, 20, 28, .410. 2³/₄-inch chambers in 16 and 28 gauge, 3-inch in other gauges. Barrels: 12 ga., 30-, 32- or 36-inch; 16 ga., 30- or 32-inch; 20 and 28 ga., 28-inch; .410 bore, 26-inch; all Full choke. Weight: 5¹/₂ to 6¹/₄ pounds depending on gauge and barrel. Plain pistol-grip stock and forearm. Made 1968–1973.

Winchester Model 370 Youth **$105**
Same as standard Model 370, except has 26-inch barrel and 12¹/₂-inch stock with recoil pad; 20 gauge with IM choke, .410 bore with Full choke. Made 1968–1973.

Winchester Model 1001 O/U Shotgun
Boxlock. 12 gauge; 2³/₄- or 3-inch chambers. Barrels: 28- or 30-inch vent rib; WinPlus choke tubes. Weight: 7–7³/₄ pounds. Checkered walnut buttstock and forend. Blued finish with scroll engraved receiver. Made 1993 to date.
Field Model (28″ bbl., 3″) **$795**
Sporting Clays I (28″ bbl.) 895
Sporting Clays II (30″ bbl.) 895

Winchester Model 1200 Deer Gun **$200**
Same as standard Model 1200, except has special 22-inch barrel with rifle-type sights, for rifled slug or buckshot; 12 gauge only. Weight: 6¹/₂ pounds. Made 1965–1974.

Winchester Model 1200 Defender Slide Action Security Shotgun **$195**
Hammerless. 12 and 20 gauge (3-inch chambers). 18-inch barrel. 8-shot capacity. Low-glare blued finish. Weight: 6³/₄ pounds. Made 1984 to date by U. S. Repeating Arms.

Winchester Model 1200 Field Gun
Front-locking rotary bolt. Takedown. 4-shot magazine. Gauges: 12, 16, 20 (2³/₄-inch chamber). Barrel: plain or vent rib; 26-, 28-, 30-inch; IC, M, F choke or with Winchoke (interchangeable tubes IC-M-F). Weight: 6¹/₂ to 7¹/₄ pounds. Checkered pistol-grip stock and forearm (slide handle), recoil pad; also avail. 1966–70 w/Winchester Recoil Reduction System (Cycolac stock). Made 1964–1983.
With Plain Barrel **$185**
With Vent-rib Barrel 205
For Winchester Recoil Reduction System, **add** . . . 50
For Winchoke, **add** 25

Winchester Model 1200 Field Gun—Magnum
Same as standard Model 1200, except chambered for 3-inch 12 and 20 gauge magnum shells; plain or vent-rib barrel, 28- or 30-inch, Full choke. Weight: 7³/₈ to 7⁷/₈ pounds. Made 1964–1983.
With Plain Barrel **$185**
With Vent-rib Barrel 210
For Winchester Recoil Reduction System, **add** . . . 50

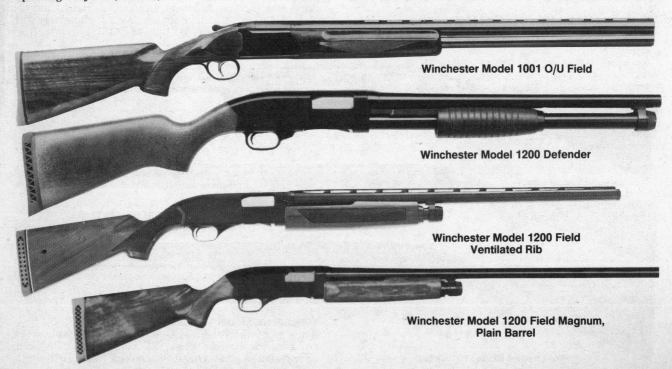

Winchester Model 1001 O/U Field

Winchester Model 1200 Defender

**Winchester Model 1200 Field
Ventilated Rib**

**Winchester Model 1200 Field Magnum,
Plain Barrel**

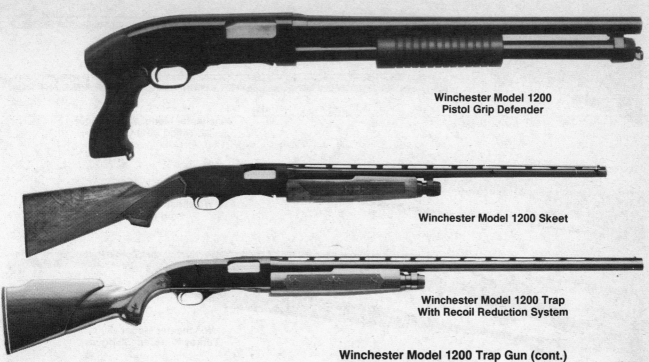

**Winchester Model 1200
Pistol Grip Defender**

Winchester Model 1200 Skeet

**Winchester Model 1200 Trap
With Recoil Reduction System**

Winchester Model 1200 Pistol Grip Defender . . . **$195**
Same general specifications as standard Model 1200, except has 18-inch barrel, 7-shot magazine and pistol grip. Mfd. by U. S. Repeating Arms.

Winchester Model 1200 Police **$195**
Same general specifications as 1200 Defender, except has rifle-type front and rear sights. Stainless-steel barrel and satin chrome finish on all external metal parts.

Winchester Model 1200 Skeet Gun **$195**
Same as standard Model 1200, except 12 and 20 gauge only; has 2-shot magazine, specially tuned trigger, 26-inch vent-rib barrel SK choke, semi-fancy walnut stock and forearm. Weight: 7$1/4$ to 7$1/2$ pounds. Made 1965–1973. Also avail. 1966–70 with Winchester Recoil Reduction System (add $50 to value).

Winchester Model 1200 Stainless **$260**
Same as standard Model 1200 Defender, except has stainless-steel barrel and special bright chrome finish on external metal parts.

Winchester Model 1200 Trap Gun
Same as standard Model 1200, except 12 gauge only. Has 2-shot magazine, 30-inch vent-rib barrel, Full choke or 28-inch with Winchoke. Semi-fancy walnut stock, straight or Monte Carlo trap style. Weight: about 8$1/4$ pounds. Made 1965–1973. Also available 1966–70 with Winchester Recoil Reduction System.

Winchester Model 1200 Trap Gun (cont.)
With Straight-trap Stock **$275**
With Monte Carlo Stock **325**
For Winchester Recoil Reduction System, **add** . . . **50**
For Winchoke, **add** **25**

Winchester Model 1300 CamoPack **$315**
Gauge: 12. 3-inch Magnum. 5-shot magazine. Barrels: 30- and 22-inch with Winchoke system. Weight: 7 pounds. Laminated stock with Win-Cam camouflage green, cut checkering, recoil pad, swivels and sling. Made 1987.

Winchester Model 1300 Deer Gun **$285**
Same as standard Model 1300, except has special 24$1/8$-inch barrel with rifle-type sights, for rifled slug or buckshot; 12 gauge only. Weight: 6$1/2$ pounds.

Winchester Model 1300 Deluxe Slide Action Pump
Gauges: 12 and 20; 3-inch chamber. 5-shot magazine. Barrel: 22, 26 or 28 inches with vent rib; Winchoke tubes. Weight: 6$1/2$ pounds. Checkered walnut buttstock and forend. Polished blued finish with roll-engraved receiver. Made 1984 to date.
Model 1300 Deluxe . . . . **$ 280**
Model 1300 Ladies/Youth (22-inch bbl.) **235**

**Winchester Model 1300 Featherweight Slide
Action Shotgun** **$265**
Hammerless. Takedown. 4-shot magazine. Gauges: 12 and 20 (3-inch chambers). Barrel: 22-inch vent rib. Weight: 6$3/8$ pounds. Checkered walnut buttstock, rib slide handled. Made 1985 to date.

SHOTGUNS

**Winchester Model 1300
Featherweight w/Winchoke**

Winchester Model 1300 Ranger
22" Rifled Deer Combo

Winchester Model 1300
Slug Hunter

Winchester Model 1300
Turkey Win-Cam Shotgun

Winchester Model 1300 XTR
w/Winchoke

Winchester Model 1300 Ranger Series
Gauges: 12 and 20; 3-inch chamber. 5-shot magazine. Barrel: 22 (Rifled), 26 or 28 inches with vent rib; Winchoke tubes. Weight: 7¼ pounds. Walnut-finished hardwood buttstock and forend. Blued finish. Made 1984 to date.
Standard Model **$220**
Combo Model **275**
Rifled Deer Combo (D&T w/rings & bases) **290**

Winchester Model 1300 Slug Hunter
Similar to the Model 1300, except has 22-inch rifled barrel with rifle sights and walnut stock.
Hunter Model **$315**
Whitetails Unlimited Model **320**

Winchester Model 1300 Turkey Slide Action ... $250
Same general specifications as Model 1300 Featherweight, except low-luster finish on walnut stock and forearm; non-glare matte finish on receiver, barrel and exterior metal surfaces.

Winchester Model 1300 Turkey Win-Cam $295
Same as Model 1300 CamoPack, except has only one 22-inch barrel. Made 1987 to date.

Winchester Model 1300 Waterfowl Slide Action Shotgun $275
Same general specifications as Model 1300 Featherweight, except 30-inch barrel. Weight: 7 pounds. Made 1985–1992.

Winchester Model 1300 XTR Slide Action $305
Hammerless. Takedown. 4-shot magazine. Gauges: 12 and 20 (3-inch chambers). Barrel: plain or vent rib; 28-inch barrels; Winchoke (interchangeable tubes IC-M-F). Weight: about 7 pounds.

NOTE: Model 1400 shotguns were available in left-hand versions (ejection port and safety on left side), with values the same as for right-hand models. In 1968, Model 1400 was replaced by Model 1400 Mark II, which is the same gun with an improved action release and restyled checkering on stock and forearm. Winchester dropped the "Mark II" designation in 1972; however, to distinguish between the two types, it has been retained in the following listings. Until 1973, the Mark II shotguns were available in left-hand versions (ejection port and safety on left side), with values the same as for right-hand models.

Winchester Model 1400 Automatic Field Gun
Gas-operated. Front-locking rotary bolt. Takedown. 2-shot magazine. Gauges: 12, 16, 20 (2¾-inch chamber). Barrel: plain or vent rib; 26-, 28-, 30-inch; IC, M, F choke, or with Winchoke (interchangeable tubes IC-M-F). Weight: 6½ to 7¼ pounds. Checkered pistol-grip stock and forearm, recoil pad; also available with Winchester Recoil Reduction System (Cycolac stock). Made 1964–68.

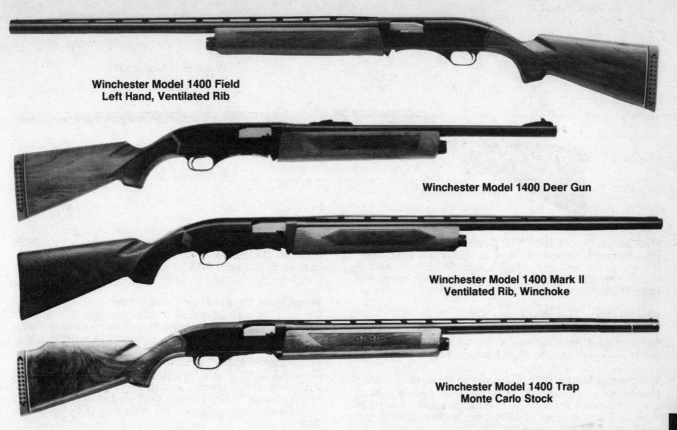

Winchester Model 1400 Field
Left Hand, Ventilated Rib

Winchester Model 1400 Deer Gun

Winchester Model 1400 Mark II
Ventilated Rib, Winchoke

Winchester Model 1400 Trap
Monte Carlo Stock

Winchester Model 1400 Automatic Field Gun (cont.)
With Plain Barrel **$235**
With Vent-rib Barrel 265
For Winchester Recoil Reduction System, **add** . . . 75
For Winchoke, **add** 25

Winchester Model 1400 Deer Gun **$225**
Same as standard Model 1400, except has special 22-inch barrel with rifle-type sights, for rifle slug or buckshot; 12 gauge only. Weight: 6½ pounds. Made 1965–68.

Winchester Model 1400 Mark II Deer Gun **$275**
Same general specifications as Model 1400 Deer Gun. Made 1968–1973.

Winchester Model 1400 Mark II Field Gun
Same general specifications as Model 1400 Field Gun, except not chambered for 16 gauge; Winchester Recoil Reduction System not available after 1970; only 28-inch barrels w/Winchoke offered after 1973. Made 1968–1978.
With Plain Barrel **$240**
With Plain Barrel and Winchoke 260
With Vent-rib Barrel 275
With Vent-rib Barrel and Winchoke 295
For Winchester Recoil Reduction System, **add** . . . 75

Winchester Model 1400 Mark II Skeet Gun **$340**
Same general specifications as Model 1400 Skeet Gun. Made 1968–1973.

Winchester Model 1400 Mark II Trap Gun
Same general specifications as Model 1400 Trap Gun, except also furnished with 28-inch barrel and Winchoke. Winchester Recoil Reduction System not available after 1970. Made 1968–1973.

Winchester Model 1400 Mark II Trap Gun (cont.)
With Straight Stock **$340**
With Monte Carlo Stock 375
For Winchester Recoil Reduction System, **add** . . . 75
For Winchoke, **add** 25

Winchester Model 1400 Mark II Utility Skeet **$245**
Same general specifications as Model 1400 Mark II Skeet Gun, except has stock and forearm of field grade walnut. Made 1970–73.

Winchester Model 1400 Mark II Utility Trap **$265**
Same as Model 1400 Mark II Trap Gun, except has Monte Carlo stock/forearm of field grade walnut. Made 1970–73.

Winchester Model 1400 Skeet Gun **$275**
Same as standard Model 1400, except 12 and 20 gauge only, 26-inch vent-rib barrel, SK choke, semi-fancy walnut stock and forearm. Weight: 7¼ to 7½ pounds. Made 1965–1968. Also available with Winchester Recoil Reduction System (add $50 to value).

Winchester Model 1400 Trap Gun
Same as standard Model 1400, except 12 gauge only with 30-inch vent-rib barrel, Full choke. Semi-fancy walnut stock, straight or Monte Carlo trap style. Also available with Winchester Recoil Reduction System. Weight: about 8¼ pounds. Made 1965–68.
With straight stock **$325**
With Monte Carlo stock 360
Add for Winchester Recoil Reduction System 75

Winchester Model 1901

Winchester Model 1911

Winchester Model 1500 XTR Semiautomatic ... **$305**
Gas-operated. Gauges: 12 and 20 (2³/₄-inch chambers). Barrel: plain or vent rib; 28-inch; Winchoke (interchangeable tubes IC-M-F). American walnut stock and forend; checkered grip and forend. Weight: 7¹/₄ pounds.

Winchester Model 1901 Lever Action Repeater **$1195**
Same general specifications as Model 1887 of which this is a redesigned version. 10 gauge only. Made 1901–1920.

Winchester Model 1911 Autoloading Shotgun .. **$425**
Hammerless. Takedown. 12 gauge only. 4-shell tubular magazine. Barrels: plain, 26- to 32-inch, standard borings. Weight: about 8¹/₂ pounds. Plain or checkered pistol-grip stock and forearm. Made 1911–1925.

Winchester Pistol Grip Stainless Marine **$225**
Same general specifications as standard Model 1200, except has 18-inch barrel, 6-shot magazine and pistol grip. Mfd. by U. S. Repeating Arms.

Winchester Pistol Grip Stainless Police **$225**
Same general specifications as standard Model 1200, except has 18-inch barrel, 6-shot magazine and pistol grip. Mfd. by U. S. Repeating Arms.

Winchester Ranger Combination Shotgun **$225**
Same as Ranger Deer Combination, except has one 28-inch vent-rib barrel with M choke and one 18-inch Police Cyl. bore. Made 1987 to date.

Winchester Ranger Deer Combination **$240**
Gauge: 12; 3-inch Magnum. 3-shot magazine. Barrels: 24-inch Cyl. bore deer barrel and 28-inch vent-rib barrel with Winchoke system. Weight: 7¹/₄ pounds. Made 1987 to date.

Winchester Ranger Semiautomatic **$195**
Gauges: 12, 20. 2-shot magazine. 28-inch vent-rib barrel with Full choke. Overall length: 48⁵/₈ inches. Weight: 7 to 7¹/₄ pounds. Walnut finish, hardwood stock and forearm with cut checkering. Made 1984 to date by U. S. Repeating Arms.

Winchester Ranger Semiauto Deer Shotgun **$210**
Same general specifications as Ranger Semiautomatic, except 24¹/₈-inch plain barrel with rifle sights. Mfd. by U.S. Repeating Arms.

Winchester Ranger Slide Action Shotgun **$180**
Hammerless. 12 and 20 gauge; 3-inch chambers. Walnut finished hardwood stock, ribbed forearm. 28-inch vent-rib barrel; Winchoke system. Weight: 7¹/₄ pounds. Made 1982 to date by U. S. Repeating Arms.

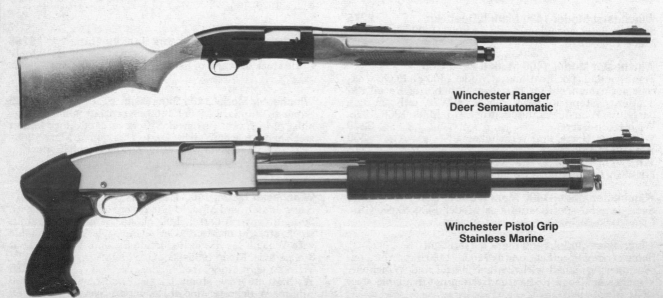

Winchester Ranger Deer Semiautomatic

Winchester Pistol Grip Stainless Marine

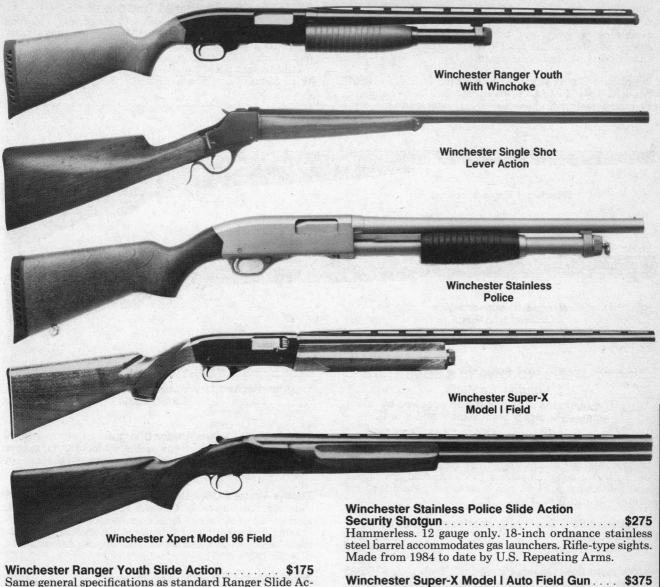

**Winchester Ranger Youth
With Winchoke**

**Winchester Single Shot
Lever Action**

**Winchester Stainless
Police**

**Winchester Super-X
Model I Field**

Winchester Xpert Model 96 Field

Winchester Ranger Youth Slide Action **$175**
Same general specifications as standard Ranger Slide Action except chambered for 20 gauge only, has 4-shot magazine, recoil pad on buttstock and weighs 6½ pounds. Mfd. by U. S. Repeating Arms.

Winchester Shotgun/Rifle (Model 101) **$1995**
12-gauge Winchoke barrel on top and rifle barrel chambered for 30-06 on bottom (over/under). 25-inch barrels. Engraved receiver. Hand-checkered walnut stock and forend. Weight: 8½ pounds. Mfd. for Olin Corp. in Japan.

Winchester Single Shot Lever Action Shotgun . . . **$1295**
Falling-block action, same as in Single Shot Rifle. High-wall receiver. Solid frame or takedown. 20 gauge. 3-inch chamber. 26-inch barrel; plain, matted or matted rib; Cyl. bore, M or Full choke. Weight: about 5½ pounds. Straight-grip stock and forearm. Made 1914–1916.

**Winchester Stainless Marine Slide Action
Security Shotgun** **$275**
Hammerless. 12 gauge only. 18-inch barrel of ordnance stainless steel. 7-shot capacity. Weight: 7 pounds. Made 1984 to date by U. S. Repeating Arms.

**Winchester Stainless Police Slide Action
Security Shotgun** **$275**
Hammerless. 12 gauge only. 18-inch ordnance stainless steel barrel accommodates gas launchers. Rifle-type sights. Made from 1984 to date by U.S. Repeating Arms.

Winchester Super-X Model I Auto Field Gun **$375**
Gas-operated. Takedown. 12 gauge. 2³/₄-inch chamber. 4-shot magazine. Barrels: vent rib; 26-inch IC; 28-inch M or F; 30-inch Full choke. Weight: about 7 pounds. Checkered pistol-grip stock and forearm. Made 1974–1984.

Winchester Super-X Model I Skeet Gun **$495**
Same as Super-X Field Gun, except has 26-inch barrel, SK choke, skeet-style stock and forearm of select walnut. Made 1974–1984.

Winchester Super-X Model I Trap Gun
Same as Super-X Field Gun, except has 30-inch barrel, IM or F choke, trap-style stock (straight or Monte Carlo comb) and forearm of select walnut, recoil pad. Made 1974–1984.
With Straight Stock **$425**
With Monte Carlo Stock **475**

Winchester Xpert Model 96 O/U Field Gun **$575**
Boxlock action similar to Model 101. Plain receiver. Auto ejectors. Selective single trigger. Gauges: 12, 20. 3-inch chambers. Barrels: vent rib; 26-inch IC/M; 28-inch M/F;

Winchester Xpert Model 96 O/U Field Gun (cont.)

30-inch F/F choke (12 ga. only). Weight: 6¼ to 8¼ pounds depending on gauge and barrels. Checkered pistol-grip stock and forearm. Made 1976–1981 for Olin Corp. at its Olin-Kodensha facility in Japan.

Winchester Xpert Model 96 Skeet Gun $600

Same as Xpert Field Gun, except has 2³⁄₄-inch chambers, 27-inch barrels, SK choke, skeet-style stock and forearm. Made 1976–1981.

Winchester Xpert Model 96 Trap Gun

Same as Xpert Field Gun, except 12 gauge only, 2³⁄₄-inch chambers, has 30-inch barrels, IM/F or F/F choke, trap-style stock (straight or Monte Carlo comb) with recoil pad. Made 1976–1981.

With Straight Stock	**$580**
With Monte Carlo Stock	**595**

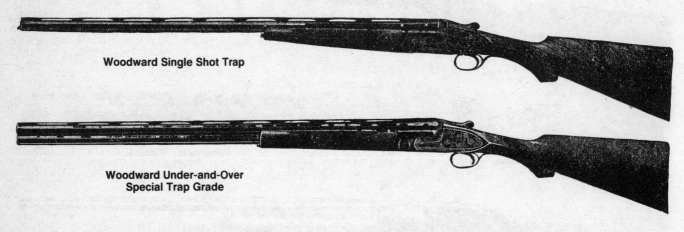

Woodward Single Shot Trap

Woodward Under-and-Over Special Trap Grade

JAMES WOODWARD & SONS
London, England
The business of this firm was acquired by James Purdey & Sons after World War II.

Woodward Best Quality Hammerless Double

Sidelock. Automatic ejectors. Double triggers or single trigger. Built to order in all standard gauges, barrel lengths, boring and other specifications; made as a field gun, pigeon and wildfowl gun, skeet gun or trap gun. Manufactured prior to World War II.

Woodward Best Quality Hammerless Double (cont.)

With double triggers	**$20,500**
With single trigger	**21,950**

Woodward Best Quality Single Shot Trap $10,925

Sidelock. Mechanical features of the Under and Over Gun. vent-rib barrel. 12 gauge only. Built to customers' specifications. Made prior to World War II.

Woodward Best Quality Under-and-Over

Woodward Best Quality Under-and-Over Shotgun

Sidelock. Automatic ejectors. Double triggers or single trigger. Built to order in all standard gauges, barrel lengths, boring and other specifications, including Special Trap Grade with vent rib. Woodward introduced this type of gun in 1908. Made until World War II. *See* listing of Purdey Over/Under Gun.

With double triggers	**$24,500**
Single trigger, extra	**1,000**

ZEPHYR SHOTGUNS
Manufactured by Victor Sarasqueta Company, Eibar, Spain

Zephyr Model 1 Over/Under Shotgun $895

Same general specifications as Field Model O/U, except with more elaborate engraving, finer wood and checkering. Imported by Stoeger 1930s–1951.

Zephyr Model 2 Over/Under Shotgun $1145

Sidelock. Auto ejectors. Gauges: 12, 16, 20, 28 and .410. Barrels: 25 to 30 inches most common. Modest scroll engraving on receiver and sideplates. Checkered, straight-grain select walnut buttstock and forend. Imported by Stoeger 1930s–1951.

Zephyr Model 3 Over/Under Shotgun $1595

Same general specifications as Zephyr Model 2 O/U, except with more elaborate engraving, finer wood and checkering. Imported by Stoeger 1930s–1951.

Zephyr Model 400E Field Grade Double Barrel Shotgun

Anson & Deeley boxlock system. Gauges: 12, 16, 20, 28 and .410. Barrels: 25 to 30 inches. Weight: 4¹⁄₂ lbs. (.410) to 6¹⁄₄ lbs. (12 ga.). Checkered French walnut buttstock and forearm. Modest scroll engraving on barrels, receiver and trigger guard. Imported by Stoeger 1930s–1950s.

12, 16 or 20 gauge	**$1100**
28 or .410 gauge	**1250**
Add for selective single trigger	**200**

Zephyr Model 401E Skeet Grade Double Barrel Shotgun

Same general specifications as Field Grade (above), except with beavertail forearm. Barrels: 25 to 28 inches. Imported by Stoeger 1930s–1950s.

12, 16 or 20 gauge	**$1400**
28 or .410 gauge	**1500**
Extra for selective single trigger	**350**
Extra for nonselective single trigger	**250**

Zephyr Model 402E Deluxe Double Barrel Shotgun **$1700**
Same general specifications as Model 400E Field Grade, except for custom refinements. The action was carefully hand-honed for smoother operation; finer, elaborate engraving throughout plus higher quality wood in stock and forearm. Imported by Stoeger 1930s–1950s.

Zephyr Crown Grade

Zephyr Crown Grade **$1200**
Boxlock. Gauges: 12, 16, 20, 28 and .410. Barrels: 25 to 30 inches standard, but any lengths could be ordered. Weight: 6 lbs. 4 oz. (.410) to 7 lbs. 4 oz. (12 ga.). Checkered Spanish walnut stock and beavertail forearm. Receiver engraved with scroll patterns. Imported by Stoeger 1938–1951.

Zephyr Field Model Over/Under Shotgun **$625**
Anson & Deeley boxlock. Auto ejectors. Gauges: 12, 16 and 20. Barrels: 25 to 30 inches standard; full-length matt rib. Double triggers. Checkered buttstock and forend. Light scroll engraving on receiver. Imported by Stoeger 1930s–1951.

Zephyr Honker Single-Shot Shotgun **$895**
Sidelock. Gauge: 10; 3¹/₂-inch magnum. 36-inch vent-rib barrel w/Full choke. Weight: 10¹/₂ pounds. Checkered select Spanish walnut buttstock and beavertail forend; recoil pad. Imported by Stoeger 1950s–1972.

Zephyr Pinehurst Double Barrel Shotgun **$895**
Boxlock. Gauges: 12, 16, 20, 28 and .410. Barrels: 25 to 28 inches most common. Checkered, select walnut buttstock and forend. Selective single trigger and auto ejectors. Imported by Stoeger 1950s–1972.

Zephyr Premier Grade

Zephyr Premier Grade Double Barrel Shotgun . **$2000**
Sidelock. Gauges: 12, 16, 20, 28 and .410. Barrels: any length, but 25 to 30 inches most popular. Weight: 4¹/₂ lbs. (.410) to 7 lbs. (12 ga.). Checkered high-grade French walnut buttstock and forend. Imported by Stoeger 1930s–1951.

Zephyr Royal Grade

Zephyr Royal Grade Double Barrel Shotgun . . . **$3000**
Same general specifications as the Premier Grade, except with more elaborate engraving, finer checkering and wood. Imported by Stoeger 1930s–1951.

Zephyr Sterlingworth II Double Barrel Shotgun . . **$995**
Action: genuine sidelocks with color-casehardened sideplates. Gauges: 12, 20, 20 and .410. Barrels: 25 to 30 inches. Weight: 6 lbs. 4 oz. (.410) to 7 lbs. 4 oz. (12 ga.). Select Spanish walnut buttstock and beavertail forearm. Light scroll engraving on receiver and sideplates. Automatic, sliding-tang safety. Imported by Stoeger 1950s–1972.

Zephyr Thunderbird Double Barrel Shotgun . . . **$1150**
Sidelock. Gauges: 12 and 10 Magnum. Barrels: 32-inch, both Full choke. Weight: 8 lbs. 8 oz. (12 ga.); 12 lbs. (10 ga.). Receiver elaborately engraved with waterfowl scenes. Checkered select Spanish walnut buttstock and beavertail forend. Plain extractors, double triggers. Imported by Stoeger 1950–1972.

Zephyr Upland King Double Barrel Shotgun . . . **$1125**
Sidelock. Gauges: 12, 16, 20, 28 and .410. Barrels: 25 to 28 inches most popular. Checkered buttstock and forend of select walnut. Selective single trigger and auto ejectors. Imported by Stoeger 1950–1972.

Zephyr Uplander Double Barrel Shotgun **$1050**
Same general specifications as the Zephyr Sterlingworth II, except with selective auto ejectors and highly polished sideplates. Imported by Stoeger 1951–1972.

Zephyr Woodlander II Double Barrel Shotgun . . . **$545**
Boxlock. Gauges: 12, 20 and .410. Barrels: 25 to 30 inches. Weight: 6 lbs. 4 oz. (.410) to 7 lbs. 4 oz. (12 ga.). Checkered Spanish walnut stock and beavertail forearm. Receiver engraved with Moorish patterns and game scenes. Imported by Stoeger 1950–1972.

ANGELO ZOLI
Mississauga, Ontario, Canada

Angelo Zoli Alley Cleaner S/S Shotgun **$595**
Gauges: 12 and 20. 20-inch barrel. 26¹/₂ inches overall. Weight: 7 pounds average. Chokes: F/M, F, IM, M, IC, SK. Chrome-lined barrels. Walnut stock and engraved action. Made 1986–87.

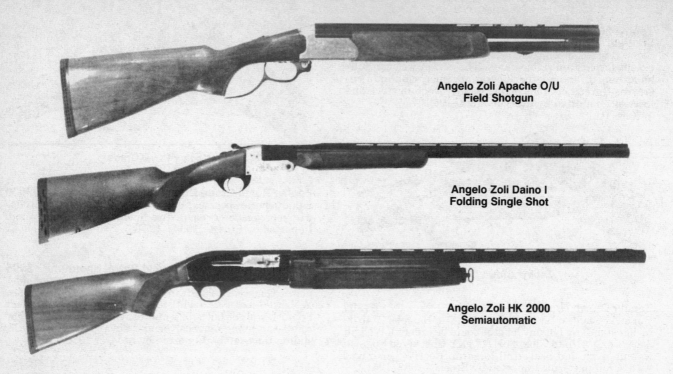

**Angelo Zoli Apache O/U
Field Shotgun**

**Angelo Zoli Daino I
Folding Single Shot**

**Angelo Zoli HK 2000
Semiautomatic**

Angelo Zoli Apache O/U Field Shotgun **$425**
Gauge: 12. Chokes: F/M, F, IM, M, IC, SK. 20-inch barrel.
Short vent rib. Weight: 7¹/₂ pounds. Checkered walnut stock
and forearm. Lever action. Pistol grip. Made 1986–88.

Angelo Zoli Daino I Folding Single Shot **$135**
Gauges: 12, 20 and .410. 28- or 30-inch barrel. Weight: 6
pounds average. Choke: Full. Chrome-lined barrel, vent rib.
Pistol-grip walnut stock. Engraved action. Made 1986–88.

Angelo Zoli HK 2000 Semiautomatic Shotgun **$525**
Gauge: 12. 5-shot capacity. Barrels: 24-, 26-, 28- and 30-
inch; vent rib. Weight: 6¹/₂ to 7¹/₂ pounds. Checkered walnut
stock and forearm. Glossy finish. Pistol grip. Engraved receiver. Made 1988.

Angelo Zoli Patricia Side-by-Side Shotguns **$1295**
Gauge: .410 only. 28-inch barrel. Choke: F/M. Weight: 5¹/₂
lbs. Automatic ejectors; Zoli single selective trigger, boxlock.
Hand-checkered walnut stock with English straight grip,
splinter forearm. Made 1986–88.

**Angelo Zoli Saint George O/U Competition Trap
Combo** **$1050**
Gauge: 12. 30- and 32-inch vent rib barrels. Weight: 8 pounds.
Single selective trigger. Oil-finished, pistol-grip walnut stock.
Made 1986–88.

Angelo Zoli Silver Snipe Over/Under Shotgun . . **$695**
Purdey-type boxlock with crossbolt. Selective single trigger. Gauges: 12, 20; 3-inch chambers. Barrels: 26-, 28- or
30-inch with a variety of choke combinations. Weight:
5³/₄ to 6³/₄ pounds. Checkered European walnut buttstock
and forend. Made in Italy.

Angelo Zoli Z43 Standard O/U Shotgun **$410**
Gauge: 12 or 20. 26-, 28- or 30-inch barrels. Chokes: F/
M, M/IC Weight: 6³/₄ to 8 pounds. vent lateral ribs, standard extractors,, single non-selective trigger. Glossy-fin-
ished walnut stock and forearm. Automatic safety. Made
1986–88.

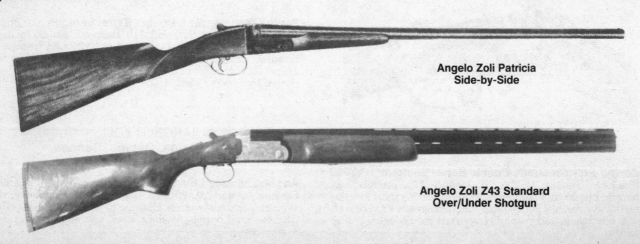

**Angelo Zoli Patricia
Side-by-Side**

**Angelo Zoli Z43 Standard
Over/Under Shotgun**

ANTONIO ZOLI, U.S.A., INC.
Fort Wayne, Indiana
Manufactured in Italy

Antonio Zoli Silver Falcon O/U **$775**
Gauges: 12 and 20; 3-inch chambers. 26- or 28-inch blued barrels. Weight: 6¼ to 7¼ pounds. Antiqued silver finish

Antonio Zoli Silver Falcon O/U (cont.)
on receiver. Pistol-grip stock of Turkish Circassian walnut with polyurethane-type finish. Imported 1989–1990.

Antonio Zoli Uplander Side/Side Shotgun **$725**
Gauges: 12 and 20. Casehardened receiver. Checkered oil-finished, hand-rubbed stock of Turkish Circassian walnut; splinter forend. Imported 1989–1990.

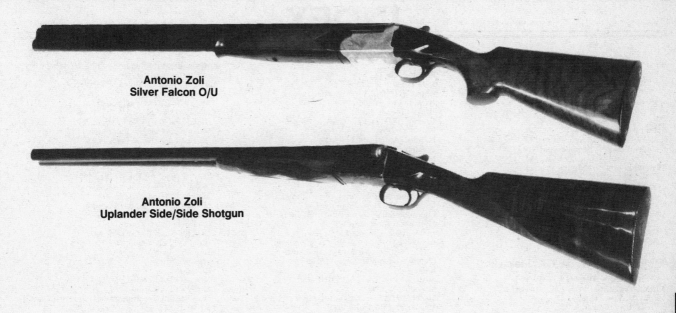

**Antonio Zoli
Silver Falcon O/U**

**Antonio Zoli
Uplander Side/Side Shotgun**

SHOTGUNS

NOTE: The following abbreviations are used throughout this section when referring to chokes: Cyl.=Cylinder; F=Full; IC=Improved Cylinder; IM=Improved Modified; M=Modified; SK=Skeet.

INDEX